1000
LOW

FAT

SALT

SUGAR

CHOLESTEROL

HEALTHY

RECIPES

1000

LOW

FAT

SALT

SUGAR

CHOLESTEROL

HEALTHY

RECIPES

p

This is a Parragon Book
This edition published in 2003

Parragon
Queen Street House
4 Queen Street
Bath BA1 1HE, UK

Copyright © Parragon 2001

ISBN: 1-40541-589-4

Printed in China

NOTE

This book uses metric and imperial measurements. Follow the same units
of measurement throughout; do not mix metric and imperial.
All spoon measurements are level: teaspoons are assumed to be 5 ml, and
tablespoons are assumed to be 15 ml. Unless otherwise stated,
milk is assumed to be full fat, eggs and individual vegetables such as potatoes
are medium, and pepper is freshly ground black pepper.

The nutritional information provided for each recipe is per serving or per person.
Optional ingredients, variations or serving suggestions have
not been included in the calculations. The times given for each recipe are an approximate
guide only because the preparation times may differ according to the techniques used by
different people and the cooking times may vary as a result of the type of oven used.

Recipes using raw or very lightly cooked eggs should be
avoided by infants, the elderly, pregnant women, convalescents,
and anyone suffering from an illness.

contents

INTRODUCTION

This book contains 1,000 recipes selected to help you improve your health by reducing your intake of saturated fats, salt and sugar. Each recipe contains the following information: nutritional calculations, preparation and cooking times, and level of difficulty (one chef's hat for an easy recipe, rising to five chef's hats for a difficult recipe).

basic recipes

Many recipes can be adapted by choosing low-fat alternatives to the basic ingredients.

Cornflour Paste

Cornflour paste is made by mixing 1 part cornflour with about 1½ parts of cold water. Stir the mixture until smooth. This paste can be used to thicken sauces.

Basic Pasta Dough

450g/1 lb durum wheat flour

4 eggs, lightly beaten

1 tbsp olive oil

pinch of low-sodium salt

1 Lightly flour a work surface. Sift the flour with a pinch of salt into a mound. Make a well in the centre and add the eggs and olive oil. Bring the mixture together using a fork or your fingertips, until the ingredients are well combined. Knead the dough vigorously for 10–15 minutes.

2 Set the dough aside to rest for about 25 minutes, before rolling it out as thinly and evenly as possible.

Bechamel Sauce

275 ml/9½ fl oz skimmed milk

4 cloves

1 bay leaf

pinch of freshly grated nutmeg

2 tbsp polyunsaturated margarine

2 tbsp plain flour

pepper and low-sodium salt

1 Put the milk in a saucepan and add the cloves, bay leaf and nutmeg. Gradually bring to the boil. Remove from the heat and leave for 15 minutes.

2 Melt the margarine in another saucepan and stir in the flour to make a roux. Cook gently, stirring, for 1 minute. Remove the pan from the heat.

3 Strain the milk and gradually blend into the roux. Return the pan to the heat and gently bring to the boil, stirring, until the sauce thickens. Season with pepper and a pinch of salt.

Variations

All sorts of ingredients can be added to the basic Béchamel recipe to make interesting, low-fat sauces which go particularly well with vegetables and fish.

Watercress Sauce

Add 1 small bunch of watercress, finely chopped, to the basic sauce.

Green Herb Sauce

Add 1–2 tablespoon chopped fresh mixed herbs to the sauce just before serving.

Parsley Sauce

Add 2 tablespoons finely chopped fresh parsley to the basic sauce.

Mushroom Sauce

Wash and finely slice 125 g/4 oz button mushrooms, and add them to the basic sauce with 1 tablespoon of finely chopped fresh tarragon.

Lemon Sauce

Add some finely grated lemon rind and juice to the basic sauce.

Mustard Sauce

Add 1 tablespoon French mustard and a squeeze of lemon juice to the basic sauce.

Basic Tomato Sauce

1 tbsp olive oil

1 small onion, chopped

1 garlic clove, chopped

400 g/14 oz canned chopped tomatoes

2 tbsp chopped fresh parsley

1 tsp dried oregano

2 bay leaves

2 tbsp tomato purée

1 tsp sugar

pepper and low-sodium salt

1 Heat the oil in a pan over a medium heat and fry the onion for 2–3 minutes or until translucent. Add the garlic and fry for 1 minute. Stir in the chopped tomatoes, parsley, oregano, bay leaves, tomato purée, and sugar, and season with pepper and a pinch of salt.

2 Bring the sauce to the boil, then lower the heat and simmer, uncovered, for 15–20 minutes, or until the sauce has reduced by half. Discard the bay leaves just before serving.

Red Wine Sauce

425 ml/15 fl oz Vegetable Stock (see page 8)

425 ml/15 fl oz red wine

small piece of onion, peeled

1 garlic clove, peeled and sliced

1 bay leaf

1 sprig fresh thyme

2–3 sprigs fresh parsley

½ tsp black peppercorns

1 tbsp redcurrant jelly

3 tbsp polyunsaturated margarine

1½ tbsp plain flour

pepper and low-sodium salt

1 Put the stock and red wine in a pan with the onion, garlic, bay leaf, thyme and parsley sprigs, and peppercorns. Bring to the boil and boil for 10–15 minutes to reduce the liquid by half.

2 Strain the liquid into a clean pan and mix in the redcurrant jelly, some pepper and a pinch of salt.

3 Mix half the margarine with the flour to make a paste and add to the warm sauce in small pieces. Mix well after each addition.

4 Return the sauce to the heat and stir gently until it thickens slightly. Simmer gently for a few minutes to cook the flour. Beat in the remaining margarine just before serving.

Cheese Sauce

2 tbsp polyunsaturated margarine

25 g/1 oz plain flour

1 bay leaf

425 ml/15 fl oz skimmed milk

60 g/2¼ oz grated mature half-fat Cheddar cheese

1 tsp English mustard powder

pinch of cayenne pepper

black pepper

1 Melt the margarine in a pan and stir in the flour. Cook, stirring, over a low heat until the roux is light in colour and crumbly in texture. Add the bay leaf. Stir in one-third of the milk, beat until the sauce is thick, then repeat twice to use all the milk.

2 Remove the sauce from the heat, remove the bay leaf, and beat in the grated cheese, mustard, a tiny pinch of cayenne pepper, and the black pepper. There is no need to add extra salt because the cheese will be salty.

Sweet and Sour Sauce

1 onion

1 tbsp oil

2 tsp cornflour

425 ml/15 fl oz water

¼ tsp mustard powder

1 tbsp wine vinegar

1 tsp sugar

1 tsp soy sauce

225 g/8 oz pineapple, canned in its own juice

½ very small green pepper

1 tomato, skinned

black pepper and salt

1 Finely chop the onion and fry it gently in the oil until tender, then add the cornflour. Remove from the heat and add the water, stirring constantly.

2 Simmer gently for 5 minutes. Add the mustard, vinegar, sugar and soy sauce. Drain and chop the pineapple, then add it to the mixture with the chopped green pepper and tomato. Season with pepper and a pinch of salt and simmer for another 2–3 minutes.

Yogurt and Cucumber Sauce

Mix together 300 ml/10 fl oz low-fat natural yogurt with 3–4 tablespoons finely chopped cucumber and 1 tablespoon chopped fresh herbs such as fennel, dill and mint.

Yogurt and Fresh Herb Sauce

Mix 300 ml/10 fl oz low-fat natural yogurt with 2 tablespoons chopped fresh herbs – parsley, chives, thyme or mint – and season with pepper and a little low-sodium salt.

Lemon Lentil Sauce

Use this sauce to add low-fat protein to vegetables.

Soak 125 g/4½ oz lentils overnight in water, then simmer until tender. Chop 1 onion and fry it gently in 1 tablespoon of oil with 2 teaspoons of curry power for 10 minutes. Add the juice and grated rind of one lemon, then liquidize the sauce. Season with pepper and a pinch of salt.

Fresh Fish Stock

450 g/1 lb fish trimmings

600 ml/1 pint water

1 onion, quartered

2 celery sticks, chopped

3–4 sprigs fresh parsley

1 bay leaf

pinch of dried thyme

150 ml/5 fl oz white wine

pepper and low-sodium salt

1 Place the fish trimmings in a large pan, add the rest of the ingredients, and season with pepper and a pinch of salt.

2 Bring the stock to simmering point, and simmer, uncovered, for about 20 minutes.

3 Strain the stock and cool. Store in the refrigerator and use within 2 days.

Chinese Stock

Use this tasty stock to add an authentic flavour to Chinese soups and other recipes where cooking liquid is required. Makes 2.5 litres/4½ pints.

750 g/1 lb 10 oz chicken pieces

750 g/1 lb 10 oz pork spare ribs

3.75 litres/6½ pints cold water

3–4 pieces ginger root, crushed

3–4 spring onions, each tied into a knot

3–4 tbsp Chinese rice wine or dry sherry

1 Trim off any excess fat from the chicken and spare ribs; chop them into large pieces.

2 Place the chicken and pork in a large pan with the water, and add the ginger and spring onion knots.

3 Bring to the boil, and skim off any scum. Reduce the heat and simmer, uncovered, for at least 2–3 hours.

4 Strain the stock, discarding the chicken, pork, ginger and spring onions. Add the wine and return to the boil. Simmer for 2–3 minutes.

5 Cool the stock and store in the refrigerator – it will keep for up to 4–5 days. Alternatively, freeze in small containers and use as required.

Fresh Vegetable Stock

Keep this stock refrigerated for up to 3 days, or frozen for up to 3 months. Makes 1.5 litres/2¾ pints.

250 g/9 oz shallots

1 large carrot, diced

1 celery stick, chopped

½ fennel bulb

1 garlic clove

1 bay leaf

4–6 sprigs of fresh parsley and tarragon

2 litres/3½ pints water

pepper

1 Put all the ingredients in a large saucepan and bring to the boil.

2 Skim off the surface scum with a flat spoon and reduce to a gentle simmer. Partially cover and cook for 45 minutes. Leave to cool.

3 Line a sieve with clean muslin and put it over a large jug or bowl. Pour

the stock through the sieve. Discard the herbs and vegetables.

4 Cover with clingfilm and store in the refrigerator or freezer until ready to use.

Fresh Beef Stock

Makes 1.75 litres/3 pints.

1 kg/2 lb 4 oz bones from a cooked joint or raw chopped beef

2 onions, studded with 6 cloves, or sliced or roughly chopped

2 carrots, sliced

1 leek, sliced

1–2 celery sticks, sliced

1 bouquet garni

about 2.25 litres/4 pints water

1 Use chopped marrow bones with a few strips of shin of beef if possible. If uncooked, roast in a preheated oven at 230°C/450°F/Gas Mark 8 for 30–50 minutes, until browned.

2 Transfer to a large saucepan with the other ingredients. Bring to the boil and remove any scum from the surface with a perforated spoon.

3 Cover and simmer gently for 3–4 hours. Strain the stock and leave to cool. Remove any fat from the surface, cover with clingfilm, and chill in the refrigerator. Use within 24 hours.

4 The stock may be frozen for up to 2 months. Place in a large plastic bag and seal, leaving at least 2.5 cm/1 inch of headspace to allow for expansion.

Fresh Chicken Stock

Makes 1.75 litres/3 pints.

1 kg/2 lb 4 oz chicken, skinned

2 celery sticks, roughly chopped

1 onion, sliced

2 carrots, sliced

1 garlic clove

3 sprigs of fresh parsley

2 litres/3½ pints water

pepper and low-sodium salt

1 Put all the ingredients into a large saucepan.

2 Bring to the boil. Skim away surface scum using a large flat spoon. Reduce the heat to a gentle simmer, partially cover, and cook for 2 hours. Allow to cool.

3 Line a sieve with clean muslin and place over a large jug or bowl. Pour the stock through the sieve. Use the cooked in another recipe. Discard the other solids. Cover the stock with clingfilm and chill.

4 Skim away any fat that forms before using the stock. Store in the refrigerator for 3–4 days, until required, or freeze in small batches.

Salads and Starters

Salads are among the most versatile of dishes, and can serve a multitude of purposes. Some, such as Spicy Chicken Salad and Lentil & Shiitake Salad, are substantial enough for a main course. Others, such as Mozzarella & Tomato Salad, make superb accompaniments — especially to  grilled meat and fish. Still others, such as Lobster & Avocado Salad, are perfect appetisers for a dinner party.

This chapter also includes a wide range of hot and cold appetisers, from familiar favourites, such as Taramasalata and Guacamole, to more exotic dishes, such as Asian Lettuce Cups and Salpicon of Crab. There is something special here for everyone and for every occasion.

Spicy Chicken Salad

This is an excellent recipe for leftover roast chicken. Add the dressing just before serving, so that the spinach retains its crispness.

NUTRITIONAL INFORMATION

Calories	225	Sugars	.........4g
Protein	........25g	Fat	..........12g
Carbohydrate	....4g	Saturates	......2g

 10 mins   0 mins

SERVES 4

INGREDIENTS

225 g/8 oz young spinach leaves

3 celery sticks, thinly sliced

½ cucumber, thinly sliced

2 spring onions, thinly sliced

3 tbsp chopped fresh parsley

350g/12 oz boneless, lean roast chicken, thinly sliced

smoked almonds, to garnish (optional)

DRESSING

2.5 cm/1 inch piece fresh root ginger, finely grated

3 tbsp olive oil

1 tbsp white wine vinegar

1 tbsp clear honey

½ tsp ground cinnamon

salt and pepper

1 Thoroughly wash and dry the spinach leaves on kitchen paper.

2 Toss the celery, cucumber and spring onions with the spinach and parsley in a large bowl.

3 Transfer the salad ingredients to serving plates and arrange the chicken on top.

4 To make the dressing, combine the grated ginger, olive oil, wine vinegar, honey and cinnamon in a screw-topped jar and shake well to mix. Season with salt and pepper to taste.

5 Pour the dressing over the salad. Scatter a few smoked almonds over the salad to garnish, if using.

COOK'S TIP

For extra colour, add some cherry tomatoes and some thin strips of red and yellow peppers and garnish with a little grated carrot.

Oriental Chicken Salad

Mirin – Japanese sweet rice wine – soy sauce and sesame oil give an oriental flavour to this delicious salad.

NUTRITIONAL INFORMATION

Calories	.361	Sugars	.2g
Protein	.34g	Fat	.16g
Carbohydrate	.17g	Saturates	.3g

5 mins   35 mins

SERVES 4

INGREDIENTS

4 skinless, boneless chicken breasts

5 tbsp mirin or sweet sherry

5 tbsp light soy sauce

1 tbsp sesame oil

3 tbsp olive oil

1 tbsp red wine vinegar

1 tbsp Dijon mustard

250 g/9 oz egg noodles

250 g/9 oz beansprouts

250 g/9 oz Chinese leaves, shredded

2 spring onions, sliced

115 g/4 oz mushrooms, sliced

1 fresh red chilli, finely sliced, to garnish

1 Pound the chicken breasts out to an even thickness between two sheets of clingfilm with a rolling pin or cleaver.

2 Put the chicken breasts in a roasting tin. Combine the mirin and soy sauce and brush over the chicken.

3 Cook the chicken in a preheated oven, 200°C/400°F/Gas Mark 6, for 20–30 minutes, basting often.

4 Remove the chicken from the oven and allow to cool slightly.

5 Combine the sesame oil, olive oil and red wine vinegar with the mustard in a small bowl.

6 Cook the noodles according to the instructions on the packet. Rinse under cold running water to prevent any further cooking, then drain.

7 Toss the noodles in the dressing until the noodles are completely coated.

8 Toss the beansprouts, Chinese leaves, spring onions and mushrooms with the noodles.

9 Slice the cooked chicken very thinly and stir it into the noodles. Garnish the salad with the chilli slices and serve.

Chicken & Papaya Salad

Try this recipe with a selection of different tropical fruits for an equally tasty and refreshing salad.

NUTRITIONAL INFORMATION

Calories .... .408	Sugars 8g
Protein .... .30g	Fat .... .28g
Carbohydrate ...10g	Saturates 5g

 5 mins   15 mins

SERVES 4

INGREDIENTS

4 skinless, boneless chicken breasts

1 red chilli, deseeded and chopped

2 tbsp red wine vinegar

5 tbsp olive oil

1 papaya, peeled

1 avocado, peeled

125 g/4½ oz alfalfa sprouts

125 g/4½ oz beansprouts

salt and pepper

TO GARNISH

diced red pepper

diced cucumber

1 Poach the chicken breasts in boiling water for about 15 minutes or until cooked through.

2 Remove the chicken with a draining spoon and set aside to cool.

3 To make the dressing, combine the chilli, red wine vinegar and olive oil, season well with salt and pepper and set aside.

4 Place the chicken breasts on a chopping board. Using a very sharp knife, cut the chicken breasts across the grain into thin diagonal slices. Set aside.

5 Slice the papaya and avocado to the same thickness as the chicken.

6 Arrange the slices of papaya and avocado, together with the chicken, in an alternating pattern on four serving plates.

7 Arrange the alfalfa sprouts and beansprouts on the serving plates and garnish with the diced red pepper and cucumber. Serve the salad with the dressing.

VARIATION

Try this recipe with peaches or nectarines instead of sliced papaya.

Mango Salad

This is an unusual combination but works well as long as the mango is very unripe. Papaya can be used instead, if you prefer.

NUTRITIONAL INFORMATION

Calories	26	Sugars	........3g
Protein	.........1g	Fat	..........0.2g
Carbohydrate	....6g	Saturates	.......0g

  10 mins   0 mins

SERVES 4

INGREDIENTS

1 large unripe mango, peeled and cut into long thin shreds

1 small fresh red chilli, deseeded and finely chopped

2 shallots, finely chopped

2 tbsp lemon juice

1 tbsp light soy sauce

6 roasted canned chestnuts, quartered

1 watermelon, to serve

1 lollo biondo lettuce, or any crunchy lettuce

15 g/½ oz coriander leaves

1 Soak the mango briefly in cold water, in order to remove any syrup. Meanwhile, combine the chilli, shallots, lemon juice and soy sauce. Drain the mango and combine with the chestnuts.

2 To make the melon basket, stand the watermelon on one end on a level surface. Holding a knife level and in one place, turn the watermelon on its axis so that the knife marks an even line all around the middle. Mark a 2.5 cm/1 inch wide handle across the top and through the centre stem, joining the middle line at either end. (If you prefer a zigzag finish, mark the shape to be cut at this point

before any cuts are made, to ensure an even zigzag line.)

3 Take a sharp knife and, following the marks made for the handle, make the first vertical cut. Then cut down the other side of the handle. Now follow the middle line and make your straight or zigzag cut, taking care that the knife is always pointing towards the centre of the

watermelon and is level with the work surface, as this ensures that when you reach the handle cuts, the cut out piece of melon will pull away cleanly.

4 Hollow out the flesh with a spoon, leaving a clean edge. Line the melon basket with the lettuce and coriander. Fill with the salad, pour over the dressing and serve immediately.

Grapefruit & Cheese Salad

Fresh pink grapefruit segments, ripe avocados and sliced Italian dolcelatte cheese make a deliciously different salad combination.

NUTRITIONAL INFORMATION

Calories	390	Sugars	. . . . .3g
Protein	. . . . .13g	Fat	. . . . .36g
Carbohydrate	. . . .4g	Saturates	. . . . . .13g

 25 mins   0 mins

SERVES 4

INGREDIENTS

½ cos lettuce

½ oak leaf lettuce

2 pink grapefruit

2 ripe avocados

175 g/6 oz dolcelatte cheese, thinly sliced

fresh basil sprigs, to garnish

DRESSING

4 tbsp olive oil

1 tbsp white wine vinegar

salt and pepper

1 Arrange the lettuce leaves on 4 serving plates or in a salad bowl.

2 Remove the peel and pith from the grapefruit with a sharp serrated knife, catching the grapefruit juice in a bowl.

3 Segment the grapefruit by cutting down each side of the membrane. Remove all the membrane. Arrange the segments on the serving plates.

4 Peel, stone and slice the avocados, dipping them in the grapefruit juice to prevent them from going brown. Arrange the slices on the salad with the dolcelatte cheese.

5 To make the dressing, combine any remaining grapefruit juice with the olive oil and wine vinegar. Season with salt and pepper to taste, mixing thoroughly to combine.

6 Drizzle the dressing over the salads. Garnish with fresh basil leaves and serve immediately.

COOK'S TIP

Pink grapefruit segments make a very attractive colour combination with the avocados, but ordinary grapefruit will work just as well. To help avocados to ripen, keep them at room temperature in a brown paper bag.

Tomato & Pasta Salad

Pasta tastes perfect in this lively salad, combined with onion and cherry tomatoes and dressed with wine vinegar, lemon juice, basil and olive oil.

NUTRITIONAL INFORMATION

Calories ....228 Sugars 4g
Protein ....5g Fat 12g
Carbohydrate ...27g Saturates 2g

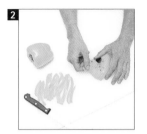

50 mins   20 mins

SERVES 4

INGREDIENTS

175 g/6 oz dried pasta shapes

1 yellow pepper, halved, and deseeded

2 small courgettes, sliced

1 red onion, thinly sliced

125 g/4½ oz cherry tomatoes, halved

salt

fresh basil sprigs, to garnish

DRESSING

4 tbsp olive oil

2 tbsp red wine vinegar

2 tsp lemon juice

1 tsp mustard

½ tsp caster sugar

a handful of fresh basil leaves, torn into small pieces

salt and pepper

1 Cook the pasta shapes in a large pan of lightly salted boiling water for 8–10 minutes or until tender, but still firm to the bite.

2 Meanwhile, place the pepper halves, skin side up, under a preheated grill until they just begin to char. Remove with tongs, place in a plastic bag and tie the top. When cool enough to handle, peel off the skins and slice the flesh into strips.

3 Cook the courgettes in a small amount of lightly salted boiling water for 3–4 minutes until cooked, yet still crunchy. Drain and refresh under cold running water to cool quickly and prevent any further cooking.

4 To make the dressing, mix together the olive oil, red wine vinegar, lemon juice, mustard and sugar. Season well with salt and pepper. Add the basil leaves.

5 Drain the pasta well and tip it into a large serving bowl. Add the dressing and toss thoroughly to combine. Add the pepper strips, courgettes, onion and cherry tomatoes, stirring to combine. Cover and set aside at room temperature for about 30 minutes to allow the flavours to develop.

6 Serve the salad, garnished with a few sprigs of fresh basil.

Peppers & Rosemary

The flavour of grilled or roasted peppers is very different
from when they are eaten raw, so do try them cooked in this way.

NUTRITIONAL INFORMATION

Calories 201	Sugars 6g	
Protein 2g	Fat 19g	
Carbohydrate 6g	Saturates 2g	

   20 mins   10 mins

SERVES 4

I N G R E D I E N T S

4 tbsp olive oil

finely grated rind of 1 lemon

4 tbsp lemon juice

1 tbsp balsamic vinegar

1 tbsp crushed fresh rosemary, or 1 tsp
    dried rosemary

2 garlic cloves, crushed

2 red peppers, halved and deseeded

2 yellow peppers, halved and deseeded

2 tbsp pine kernels

salt and pepper

fresh rosemary sprigs, to garnish

1 Mix together the olive oil, lemon rind,
lemon juice, balsamic vinegar,
rosemary and garlic. Season with salt and
pepper to taste.

2 Place the red and yellow peppers, skin
side up, on the rack of a grill pan,
lined with foil. Brush the olive oil mixture
over them.

3 Grill the peppers for 3–4 minutes or
until the skin begins to char, basting
frequently with the olive oil mixture.
Remove from the heat, cover with foil to
trap the steam and leave for 5 minutes.

4 Meanwhile, scatter the pine kernels
on to the grill rack and toast them
lightly for 2–3 minutes. Keep a close eye
on them, as they tend to burn very quickly.

5 Peel the peppers, slice into strips and
place in a warmed serving dish.
Sprinkle with the pine kernels and drizzle
over any remaining olive oil mixture.
Garnish with rosemary sprigs and serve.

COOK'S TIP

A combination of red and
yellow peppers looks attractive,
but you could use all one colour
or substitute an orange pepper.
However, do not use green
peppers, which are not really
sweet enough for this dish.

Lentil & Tuna Salad

In this recipe, lentils, combined with spices, lemon juice and tuna, make a wonderfully tasty and filling salad.

NUTRITIONAL INFORMATION

Calories 227   Sugars 2g
Protein ....19g   Fat 9g
Carbohydrate ...19g   Saturates 1g

 25 mins   0 mins

SERVES 4

INGREDIENTS

2 ripe tomatoes

1 small red onion

3 tbsp virgin olive oil

1 tbsp lemon juice

1 tsp wholegrain mustard

1 garlic clove, crushed

½ tsp ground cumin

½ tsp ground coriander

400 g/14 oz can lentils, drained

185 g/6½ oz can tuna, drained

2 tbsp chopped fresh coriander

pepper

1 Using a sharp knife, deseed the tomatoes and then chop them into fine dice. Finely chop the red onion.

2 To make the dressing, whisk together the virgin olive oil, lemon juice, mustard, garlic, cumin and ground coriander in a small bowl until thoroughly combined. Set aside until required.

3 Mix together the chopped onion, diced tomatoes and drained lentils in a large bowl.

4 Flake the tuna with a fork and stir it into the onion, tomato and lentil mixture. Stir in the chopped fresh coriander and mix well.

5 Pour the dressing over the lentil and tuna salad and season with pepper to taste. Serve immediately.

COOK'S TIP

Lentils are an excellent source of protein and contain several important vitamins and minerals. Buy them dried for soaking and cooking yourself, or buy canned varieties for speed and convenience.

Mixed Bean & Apple Salad

Use any mixture of beans you have to hand in this recipe, but the wider the variety, the more colourful the salad.

NUTRITIONAL INFORMATION

Calories 183	Sugars 8g
Protein 6g	Fat 7g
Carbohydrate ...26g	Saturates 1g

  20 mins 20 mins

SERVES 4

INGREDIENTS

225 g/8 oz new potatoes, scrubbed and quartered

225 g/8 oz mixed canned beans, such as red kidney beans, flageolet and borlotti beans, drained and rinsed

1 red eating apple, diced and tossed in 1 tbsp lemon juice

1 yellow pepper, deseeded and diced

1 shallot, sliced

½ fennel bulb, sliced

oakleaf lettuce leaves

DRESSING

1 tbsp red wine vinegar

2 tbsp olive oil

1½ tsp American mustard

1 garlic clove, crushed

2 tsp chopped fresh thyme

1 Cook the quartered potatoes in a saucepan of boiling water for 15 minutes until tender. Drain and transfer to a large bowl.

2 Add the mixed beans to the potatoes, with the apple, yellow pepper, shallot and fennel. Mix well, taking care not to break up the cooked potatoes.

3 To make the dressing, whisk all the dressing ingredients together until thoroughly combined, then pour it over the potato salad.

4 Line a serving plate or salad bowl with the oakleaf lettuce leaves and spoon the potato mixture into the centre. Serve the salad immediately.

VARIATION

Use Dijon or wholegrain mustard in place of American mustard for a different flavour.

Radish & Cucumber Salad

The radishes and the herb and mustard dressing give this colourful salad a mildly pungent flavour that complements the potatoes perfectly.

NUTRITIONAL INFORMATION

Calories	140	Sugars	.........3g
Protein	.........3g	Fat	...........6g
Carbohydrate	...20g	Saturates	.......1g

50 mins   20 mins

SERVES 4

INGREDIENTS

500 g/1 lb 2 oz new potatoes, scrubbed and halved

½ cucumber, thinly sliced

2 tsp salt

1 bunch of radishes, thinly sliced

DRESSING

1 tbsp Dijon mustard

2 tbsp olive oil

1 tbsp white wine vinegar

2 tbsp chopped fresh mixed herbs

1 Cook the potatoes in a large saucepan of boiling water for 10–15 minutes or until tender. Drain and set aside to cool.

2 Meanwhile, spread out the cucumber slices on a plate and sprinkle with the salt. Set aside for 30 minutes, then rinse under cold running water and pat dry with kitchen paper.

3 Arrange the cucumber and radish slices on a serving plate in a decorative pattern and pile the cooked potatoes in the centre.

4 To make the dressing, put the mustard, olive oil, vinegar and mixed herbs into a small bowl and whisk until thoroughly combined. Alternatively, place the ingredients in a screw-top jar and shake vigorously until combined. Pour the dressing over the salad. Chill in the refrigerator before serving.

COOK'S TIP

Cucumber adds not only colour but also a real freshness to the salad. It is salted and left to stand to remove the excess water, which would make the salad soggy. Wash the cucumber well to remove all of the salt before adding to the salad.

Potato, Rocket & Apple Salad

This green and white salad is made with creamy, salty-flavoured goat's cheese – its distinctive flavour is perfect with salad leaves.

NUTRITIONAL INFORMATION

Calories	104	Sugars	. . . . . . .3.1g
Protein	. . . . .3.1g	Fat	. . . . .5.3g
Carbohydrate	. .11.8g	Saturates	. . . . .1.5g

20 mins   15 mins

SERVES 4

I N G R E D I E N T S

600 g/1 lb 5 oz potatoes, unpeeled
  and sliced

2 green dessert apples, diced

1 tsp lemon juice

25 g/1 oz walnut pieces

115 g/4 oz goat's cheese, cubed

150 g/5½ oz rocket leaves

salt and pepper

D R E S S I N G

2 tbsp olive oil

1 tbsp red wine vinegar

1 tsp clear honey

1 tsp fennel seeds

1 Cook the potatoes in a pan of boiling water for 15 minutes until tender. Drain and leave to cool. Transfer the cooled potatoes to a serving bowl.

2 Toss the diced apples in the lemon juice, then drain and stir them into the cold potatoes.

3 Add the walnut pieces, cheese cubes and rocket leaves, then toss the ingredients together to mix.

4 In a small bowl, whisk all of the dressing ingredients together and then pour the dressing over the salad. Season to taste and serve immediately.

COOK'S TIP

Serve this salad immediately to prevent the apple from discolouring. Alternatively, prepare all of the other ingredients in advance and add the apple at the last minute.

Root Vegetable Salad

This salad of grated vegetables is perfect for a light starter.
The peppery flavours of the mooli and radishes are refreshingly pungent.

NUTRITIONAL INFORMATION

Calories 132	Sugars 9g
Protein 4g	Fat 8g
Carbohydrate ...12g	Saturates 1g

20 mins　　　0 mins

SERVES 4

INGREDIENTS

350 g/12 oz carrots

225 g/8 oz mooli

115 g/4 oz radishes

350 g/12 oz celeriac

1 tbsp orange juice

2 celery sticks with leaves, washed
　and trimmed

100 g/3½ oz assorted salad leaves

25 g/1 oz walnuts, chopped

DRESSING

1 tbsp walnut oil

1 tbsp white wine vinegar

1 tsp wholegrain mustard

½ tsp finely grated orange rind

1 tsp celery seeds

salt and pepper

1 Peel and coarsely grate or very finely shred the carrots, mooli and radishes. Set them aside in separate bowls.

2 Peel and coarsely grate or finely shred the celeriac and mix it immediately with the orange juice to prevent it from turning brown.

3 Remove the celery leaves and reserve. Finely chop the celery sticks.

4 Divide the salad leaves among 4 serving plates and arrange the vegetables in small piles on top.

5 Mix all of the dressing ingredients together and season well. Drizzle a little over each salad.

6 Shred the reserved celery leaves and sprinkle over the salad with the chopped walnuts.

COOK'S TIP

Also known as Chinese white radish and daikon, mooli resembles a large white parsnip. It has crisp, slightly pungent flesh, which can be eaten raw or cooked. It is a useful ingredient in stir-fries.

Beetroot & Orange Salad

Use freshly cooked beetroot in this unusual combination of colours and flavours, as beetroot soaked in vinegar will spoil the delicate balance.

NUTRITIONAL INFORMATION

Calories	240	Sugars	.......29g
Protein	........10g	Fat	..........2g
Carbohydrate	...49g	Saturates	.....0.3g

2¼ hrs   1 hr

SERVES 4

INGREDIENTS

225 g/8 oz mixed long grain and wild rice

4 large oranges

450 g/1 lb cooked beetroot, peeled and drained (if necessary)

2 heads of chicory

salt and pepper

snipped fresh chives, to garnish

DRESSING

4 tbsp low-fat natural fromage frais

1 garlic clove, crushed

1 tbsp wholegrain mustard

½ tsp finely grated orange rind

2 tsp clear honey

1 Cook the mixed rice according to the packet instructions. Drain and set aside to cool.

2 Meanwhile, slice the top and bottom off each orange. Using a sharp knife, remove the skin and pith. Holding the orange over a bowl to catch the juice, carefully slice between each segment. Place the segments in a separate bowl. Cover with clingfilm and chill.

3 Dice the beetroot into small cubes. Mix with the orange segments, cover the bowl again and chill.

4 When the rice has cooled completely, mix in the reserved orange juice until thoroughly incorporated and season with salt and pepper to taste.

5 Line 4 individual bowls or plates with the chicory leaves. Spoon the rice over them and top with the beetroot and orange mixture.

6 Mix all the dressing ingredients together and spoon the dressing over the salad or serve separately in a bowl, if preferred. Garnish with snipped fresh chives and serve.

Red Hot Slaw

As well as being an exciting side dish, this colourful salad makes an unusual filling for jacket potatoes.

NUTRITIONAL INFORMATION

Calories	169	Sugars	. . . . .16g
Protein	. . . . .11g	Fat	. . . . .7g
Carbohydrate	. . .17g	Saturates	. . . . . .3g

 1 hr   🕐 0 mins

SERVES 4

INGREDIENTS

½ small red cabbage

1 large carrot

2 red-skinned apples

1 tbsp lemon juice

1 medium red onion

100 g/3½ oz reduced-fat Cheddar cheese, grated

TO GARNISH

fresh red chilli strips

carrot strips

DRESSING

3 tbsp reduced-calorie mayonnaise

3 tbsp low-fat natural yogurt

1 garlic clove, crushed

1 tsp paprika

1–2 tsp chilli powder

pinch of cayenne pepper (optional)

salt and pepper

1 Cut the red cabbage in half and remove the central core. Finely shred the leaves and place in a large bowl. Peel and coarsely grate or finely shred the carrot and mix it into the cabbage.

2 Core the apples and finely dice, leaving on the skins. Place in another bowl and toss in the lemon juice to help prevent the apple from browning. Mix the apple into the cabbage and carrot.

3 Peel and finely shred or grate the onion. Stir into the other vegetables with the cheese and mix together.

4 To make the dressing, mix together the mayonnaise, yogurt, garlic and paprika in a small bowl. Add chilli powder according to taste and the cayenne pepper (if using) – remember this will add more spice to the dressing. Season to taste with salt and pepper.

5 Add the dressing to the vegetables and toss well to mix. Cover and leave to chill in the refrigerator for 1 hour to allow the flavours to develop.

6 Serve garnished with strips of fresh red chilli and carrot.

Chicken & Spinach Salad

Slices of lean chicken with fresh young spinach leaves and a few fresh raspberries are served with a refreshing yogurt and honey dressing.

NUTRITIONAL INFORMATION

Calories 235	Sugars 9g
Protein 37g	Fat 6g
Carbohydrate 9g	Saturates 2g

3½ hrs   25 mins

SERVES 4

INGREDIENTS

4 boneless, skinless chicken breasts,
  150 g/5½ oz each

450 ml/16 fl oz chicken stock

1 bay leaf

225 g/8 oz fresh young spinach leaves

1 small red onion, shredded

115 g/4 oz fresh raspberries

salt and freshly ground pink peppercorns

fresh toasted croûtons, to garnish

DRESSING

4 tbsp low-fat natural yogurt

1 tbsp raspberry vinegar

2 tsp clear honey

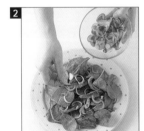

1 Place the chicken breasts in a frying pan. Pour over the stock and add the bay leaf. Bring to the boil, cover and simmer for 15–20 minutes, turning halfway through, until the chicken is cooked through. Leave to cool in the liquid.

2 Arrange the spinach on 4 serving plates and top with the onion. Cover and leave to chill.

3 Drain the cooked chicken and pat dry on absorbent kitchen paper. Slice the chicken breasts thinly and arrange, fanned out, on top of the spinach and onion. Sprinkle the salad with the raspberries.

4 To make the dressing, mix all the ingredients together in a small bowl. Drizzle a spoonful of dressing over each chicken breast and season with salt and ground pink peppercorns to taste. Serve the salad with freshly toasted croûtons.

VARIATION

This recipe is delicious with smoked chicken, but it will be more expensive and richer, so use slightly less. It would make an impressive starter for a dinner party.

Turkey & Rice Salad

Rice salads are perfect at any time of year and are both economical and very easy to prepare.

NUTRITIONAL INFORMATION

Calories ....373 Sugars 2g
Protein ....22g Fat 14g
Carbohydrate ...40g Saturates 1g

🧊 25 mins   🕐 30 mins

SERVES 4

I N G R E D I E N T S

1 litre/1¾ pints chicken stock

175 g/6 oz mixed long-grain and wild rice

2 tbsp sunflower or corn oil

225 g/8 oz skinless, boneless turkey breast, trimmed of all fat and cut into thin strips

225 g/8 oz mangetout

115 g/4 oz oyster mushrooms, torn into pieces

55 g/2 oz shelled pistachio nuts, finely chopped

2 tbsp chopped fresh coriander

1 tbsp snipped fresh garlic chives

salt and pepper

1 tbsp balsamic vinegar

fresh garlic chives, to garnish

1 Reserve 3 tablespoons of the chicken stock and bring the remainder to the boil in a large saucepan. Add the rice and cook for 30 minutes, or until tender. Drain and leave to cool slightly.

2 Meanwhile, heat 1 tablespoon of the oil in a preheated wok or frying pan. Add the turkey and stir-fry over a medium heat for 3–4 minutes, or until cooked through. Using a slotted spoon, transfer the turkey to a dish. Add the mangetout and mushroom pieces to the wok and stir-fry for 1 minute. Add the reserved stock, bring to the boil, then reduce the heat, cover and simmer for 3–4 minutes. Transfer the vegetables to the dish and leave to cool slightly.

3 Thoroughly mix the rice, turkey, mangetout, mushrooms, nuts, coriander and garlic chives together, then season to taste with salt and pepper. Drizzle with the remaining sunflower oil and the vinegar and garnish with fresh garlic chives. Serve warm.

COOK'S TIP
Before adding any of the ingredients to the preheated hot wok, swirl the sunflower oil gently so that it coats the sides as well as the base of the wok.

Tuna Niçoise Salad

This is a classic version of the French Salade Niçoise. It is a substantial salad, suitable for a lunch or light summer supper.

NUTRITIONAL INFORMATION

Calories 109   Sugars 1.1g
Protein . . . . .7.2g   Fat 7.0g
Carbohydrate . . .4.8g   Saturates 1.2g

 10 mins   20 mins

SERVES 4

I N G R E D I E N T S

4 eggs

450 g/1 lb new potatoes

115 g/4 oz dwarf green beans, trimmed and halved

2 x 175 g/6 oz tuna steaks

6 tbsp olive oil, plus extra for brushing

1 garlic clove, crushed

1½ tsp Dijon mustard

2 tsp lemon juice

2 tbsp chopped fresh basil

2 Little Gem lettuces

200 g/7 oz cherry tomatoes, halved

175 g/6 oz cucumber, peeled, cut in half and sliced

55 g/2 oz stoned black olives

55 g/2 oz canned anchovies in olive oil, drained

salt and pepper

1 Bring a small saucepan of water to the boil. Add the eggs and cook for 7–9 minutes from when the water returns to a boil – 7 minutes for a slightly soft centre or 9 minutes for a firm centre. Drain and refresh under cold running water. Set aside.

2 Cook the potatoes in lightly salted boiling water for 10–12 minutes until tender. Add the beans 3 minutes before the end of the cooking time. Drain both vegetables well and refresh under cold water. Drain well.

3 Wash and dry the tuna steaks. Brush with a little olive oil and season to taste. Cook on a preheated ridged griddle for 2–3 minutes each side, until just tender but still slightly pink in the centre. Set aside to rest.

4 Whisk together the garlic, mustard, lemon juice, basil and seasoning. Whisk in the olive oil.

5 To assemble the salad, break apart the lettuces and tear into large pieces. Divide among individual serving plates. Next, add the potatoes and beans, tomatoes, cucumber and olives. Toss lightly together. Shell the eggs and cut into quarters lengthways. Arrange these on top of the salad. Scatter the anchovies over the top.

6 Flake the tuna steaks and arrange on the salad. Pour over the dressing and serve.

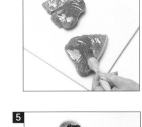

Moroccan Couscous Salad

Couscous is a type of fine semolina made from wheat. You can buy couscous pre-cooked so that it needs only the addition of boiling water.

NUTRITIONAL INFORMATION

Calories 329   Sugars 12g
Protein ....19g   Fat 11g
Carbohydrate ...42g   Saturates 2g

 40 mins   🕐 20 mins

SERVES 4

INGREDIENTS

225 g/8 oz couscous

1 cinnamon stick, about 5 cm/2 inches

2 tsp coriander seeds

1 tsp cumin seeds

2 tbsp olive oil

1 small onion, finely chopped

2 garlic cloves, finely chopped

½ tsp ground turmeric

pinch of cayenne pepper

1 tbsp lemon juice

50 g/1¾ oz sultanas

3 ripe plum tomatoes, chopped

85 g/3 oz cucumber, chopped

4 spring onions, sliced

200 g/7 oz can tuna in olive oil, drained and flaked

3 tbsp chopped fresh coriander

salt and pepper

1 Cook the couscous according to the packet instructions, omitting any butter recommended. Transfer to a large bowl and set aside.

2 Heat a small frying pan and add the cinnamon stick, coriander seeds and cumin seeds. Cook over a high heat until the seeds begin to pop and smell fragrant.

Remove from the heat and grind to a fine powder with a pestle and mortar or in a spice grinder. Set aside.

3 Heat the oil in a clean frying pan and add the onion. Cook over a low heat for 7–8 minutes until softened and lightly browned. Add the garlic and cook for a further minute. Stir in the roasted and ground spices, turmeric and cayenne and cook for a further minute. Remove from

the heat and stir in the lemon juice. Add this mixture to the couscous and mix well together, ensuring that all of the grains are well coated.

4 Add the sultanas, tomatoes, cucumber, spring onions, tuna and chopped coriander. Season with salt and pepper to taste and mix together well. Allow the salad to cool completely and serve at room temperature.

Tuna Bean Salad

Tuna is rich in omega-3 fatty acids which help to reduce cholesterol levels – and it tastes wonderful in this classic salad.

NUTRITIONAL INFORMATION

Calories	529	Sugars	.........3g
Protein	........54g	Fat	..........23g
Carbohydrate	...29g	Saturates	.......4g

 8¼ hrs   1½ hrs

SERVES 4

INGREDIENTS

225 g/8 oz dried haricot beans

1 tbsp lemon juice

5 tbsp extra virgin olive oil, plus extra for brushing

1 garlic clove, finely chopped

1 small red onion, very thinly sliced (optional)

1 tbsp chopped fresh parsley

4 x 175 g/6 oz tuna steaks

salt and pepper

TO GARNISH

fresh parsley sprigs

lemon wedges

1 Soak the haricot beans for 8 hours or overnight in at least twice their volume of cold water.

2 Drain the beans and place in a saucepan with twice their volume of fresh water. Bring to the boil over a low heat, skimming off any scum that rises to the surface. Boil the beans rapidly for 10 minutes, then reduce the heat and simmer for a further 1¼–1½ hours until the beans are tender.

3 Meanwhile, mix together the lemon juice, olive oil, garlic and seasoning. Drain the beans thoroughly and mix together with the olive oil mixture, onion and parsley. Season to taste and set aside.

4 Brush the tuna steaks lightly with olive oil and season. Cook on a preheated ridged griddle for 2 minutes on each side until just pink in the centre.

5 Divide the bean salad between 4 serving plates. Top each with a tuna steak. Garnish with parsley sprigs and lemon wedges and serve immediately.

COOK'S TIP

You could use canned haricot beans instead of dried. Reheat according to the instructions on the can, drain and toss with the dressing as above.

Thai Seafood Salad

This colourful mixture of vegetables, topped with succulent seafood and tossed in a piquant dressing, is best served chilled.

NUTRITIONAL INFORMATION

Calories	310	Sugars	.........4g
Protein	........30g	Fat	..........18g
Carbohydrate	....7g	Saturates	.......3g

1¼ hrs   10 mins

SERVES 4

INGREDIENTS

450 g/1 lb live mussels, scrubbed

8 raw tiger prawns

350 g/12 oz prepared squid sliced into rings

115 g/4 oz peeled cooked prawns

½ red onion, thinly sliced

115 g/4 oz beansprouts

½ red pepper, deseeded and thinly sliced

115 g/4 oz pak choi, shredded

DRESSING

1 garlic clove, crushed

1 tsp grated fresh root ginger

1 red chilli, deseeded and finely chopped

2 tbsp chopped fresh coriander

1 tbsp lime juice

1 tsp finely grated lime rind

1 tbsp light soy sauce

5 tbsp sunflower or groundnut oil

2 tsp sesame oil

salt and pepper

1 Place the mussels in a large pan with just the water that clings to the shells. Cook over a high heat for 3–4 minutes, shaking the pan occasionally, until they have opened. Discard any that remain closed. Strain, reserving the liquid, and refresh under cold water. Drain again.

2 Bring the reserved liquid to the boil and simmer the tiger prawns for 5 minutes. Add the squid and cook for a further 2 minutes. Remove them with a draining spoon and plunge into a large bowl of cold water. Reserve the poaching liquid. Drain the prawns and squid again.

3 Remove the mussels from their shells and mix with the tiger prawns, squid and peeled prawns. Chill for 1 hour.

4 Put all the dressing ingredients, except the oils, into a blender and blend to a smooth paste. Add the oils, reserved poaching liquid, seasoning and 4 tbsp cold water. Blend again to combine.

5 Combine all the vegetables and toss with 2–3 tbsp of the dressing. Transfer to a large serving plate. Toss the seafood with the remaining dressing and add to the vegetables. Serve immediately.

Skate & Spinach Salad

Packed with flavour and contrasting textures, this salad makes
a filling main course for four people or would serve six as a starter.

NUTRITIONAL INFORMATION

Calories	316	Sugars	........18g
Protein	........32g	Fat	..........13g
Carbohydrate	...18g	Saturates	.......1g

30 mins | 15 mins

SERVES 4

INGREDIENTS

700 g/1 lb 9 oz skate wings, trimmed

2 fresh rosemary sprigs

1 fresh bay leaf

1 tbsp black peppercorns

1 lemon, quartered

450 g/1 lb baby spinach leaves

1 tbsp olive oil

1 small red onion, thinly sliced

2 garlic cloves, crushed

½ tsp chilli flakes

50 g/1¾ oz pine kernels, lightly toasted

50 g/1¾ oz raisins

1 tbsp light muscovado sugar

2 tbsp chopped fresh parsley

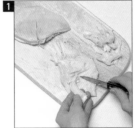

1 Put the skate into a large saucepan with the herbs, peppercorns and lemon. Cover with water and bring to the boil. Cover and simmer for 4–5 minutes until the flesh begins to come away from the cartilage. Remove from the heat and set aside for 15 minutes. Lift the fish from the water and remove the flesh in shreds.

2 Meanwhile, put the spinach into a pan with just the water that clings to the leaves. Cook over a high heat for 30 seconds until wilted. Drain, refresh under cold water and drain again. Squeeze out any excess water and set aside.

3 Heat the oil in a large frying pan. Fry the onion for 3–4 minutes until softened, but not browned. Add the garlic, chilli flakes, pine kernels, raisins and sugar. Cook for 1–2 minutes, then add the spinach and toss for 1 minute until heated through. Gently fold in the skate and cook for a further minute. Season well.

4 Divide the salad between 4 serving plates and sprinkle with the parsley.

Lobster & Avocado Salad

This isn't really a main course dish but would serve very well as a light lunch with some bread or as part of a buffet.

NUTRITIONAL INFORMATION

Calories	.313	Sugars	.3g
Protein	.19g	Fat	.25g
Carbohydrate	.4g	Saturates	.4g

25 mins   3 mins

SERVES 4

INGREDIENTS

2 x 400 g/14 oz cooked lobsters

1 large avocado

1 tbsp lemon juice

225 g/8 oz green beans

4 spring onions, thinly sliced

2 tbsp chopped fresh chervil

1 tbsp chopped fresh chives

DRESSING

1 garlic clove, crushed

1 tsp Dijon mustard

pinch of sugar

1 tbsp balsamic vinegar

5 tbsp olive oil

salt and pepper

1 To prepare the lobsters, cut them in half lengthways. Remove the intestinal vein which runs down the tail, the stomach sac and any grey beards from the body cavity at the head end of the lobster. Crack the claws and remove the meat – in one piece if possible. Remove the meat from the tail of the lobster. Roughly chop all the meat and set aside.

2 Split the avocado lengthways and remove the stone. Cut each half in half again and peel away the skin. Cut the avocado flesh into chunks and toss with the lemon juice to prevent it from discolouring. Add to the lobster meat.

3 Bring a large pan of lightly salted water to the boil and add the green beans. Cook for 3 minutes, then drain and immediately refresh under cold water. Drain again and set aside to cool completely. Cut the beans in half, then add them to the avocado and lobster.

4 Meanwhile, make the dressing by whisking together the garlic, mustard, sugar, vinegar and seasoning. Gradually add the oil, whisking, until thickened.

5 Add the spring onions, chervil and chives to the lobster and avocado mixture and toss gently together. Drizzle over the dressing and serve immediately.

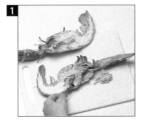  

Spicy Tropical Salad

This colourful salad, with its sweet and spicy flavours, is the perfect foil to a meaty main dish, and is wonderful with barbecued food.

NUTRITIONAL INFORMATION

Calories	194	Sugars	.........7g
Protein	.........4g	Fat	..........16g
Carbohydrate	....9g	Saturates	.......3g

 20 mins   🕐 0 mins

SERVES 4–6

INGREDIENTS

200 g/7 oz mixed green salad leaves

2–3 spring onions, chopped

3–4 tbsp chopped fresh coriander

1 small papaya

2 red peppers

1 avocado

1 tbsp lime juice

3–4 tbsp pumpkin seeds, toasted (optional)

DRESSING

juice of 1 lime

pinch of paprika

pinch of ground cumin

pinch of sugar

1 garlic clove, finely chopped

4 tbsp extra virgin olive oil

dash of white wine vinegar (optional)

salt

1 Combine the mixed salad leaves with the spring onions and coriander. Mix well, then transfer the salad to a large serving dish.

2 Cut the papaya in half, scoop out the seeds with a spoon and discard. Cut the papaya into quarters, remove the peel and slice the flesh. Arrange the slices on top of the salad leaves.

3 Cut the red peppers in half lengthways, remove the cores and seeds, then slice thinly. Add the peppers to the salad leaves.

4 Cut the avocado in half around the stone. Twist apart, then remove the stone with a knife. Carefully peel off the skin, dice the flesh and toss in lime juice to prevent it from discolouring. Add to the other salad ingredients.

5 To make the dressing, whisk together the lime juice, paprika, ground cumin, sugar, garlic and olive oil. Season with salt to taste.

6 Pour the dressing over the salad and toss lightly to coat, adding a dash of wine vinegar if a flavour with a little more 'bite' is preferred. Sprinkle the toasted pumpkin seeds, if using, over the salad and serve immediately.

Green Bean Salad with Feta

This fresh-tasting salad is flavoured with fresh coriander, a herb that resembles flat leaf parsley in appearance, but tastes quite different.

NUTRITIONAL INFORMATION

Calories 275	Sugars 7g	
Protein 6g	Fat 25g	
Carbohydrate 8g	Saturates 6g	

 10 mins   5 mins

SERVES 4

I N G R E D I E N T S

350 g/12 oz green beans, trimmed

1 red onion, chopped

3–4 tbsp chopped fresh coriander

2 radishes, thinly sliced

75 g/2¾ oz feta cheese, crumbled

1 tsp chopped fresh oregano or ½ tsp dried oregano

2 tbsp red wine or fruit vinegar

5 tbsp extra virgin olive oil

3 ripe tomatoes, cut into wedges

pepper

1 Bring about 5 cm/2 inches water to the boil in the base of a steamer or in a medium saucepan. Add the green beans to the top of the steamer or place them in a metal colander set over the pan of water. Cover and steam for about 5 minutes until just tender.

2 Transfer the beans to a bowl and add the onion, coriander, radishes and feta cheese.

3 Sprinkle the oregano over the salad, then grind pepper over to taste. Whisk the vinegar and olive oil together and then pour over the salad. Toss gently to mix well.

4 Transfer to a serving platter, surround with the tomato wedges and serve at once or chill until ready to serve.

VARIATION

This recipe is also delicious made with nopales, or edible cactus, which is available in specialist stores in cans or jars. Drain, then slice and use instead of the green beans, missing out Step 1. Replace the feta with 1–2 chopped hard-boiled eggs.

Mexican Citrus Salad

A salad like this reminds one of how much Mexico and the Mediterranean share in terms of sunny flavours and ingredients.

NUTRITIONAL INFORMATION

Calories 267   Sugars 15g
Protein ....3g   Fat 21g
Carbohydrate ...16g   Saturates 4g

20 mins   0 mins

SERVES 4

INGREDIENTS

1 large pomegranate

1 grapefruit

2 sweet oranges

finely grated rind of ½ lime

1–2 garlic cloves, finely chopped

3 tbsp red wine vinegar

juice of 2 limes

½ tsp sugar

¼ tsp mustard powder

4–5 tbsp extra virgin olive oil

1 head red leafy lettuce, such as oakleaf, washed and dried

1 avocado, stoned, peeled, diced and tossed with a little lime juice

salt and pepper

½ red onion, thinly sliced, to garnish

1 Cut the pomegranate into quarters, then press back the outer skin to push out the seeds into a bowl.

2 Using a sharp knife, cut a slice off the top and bottom of the grapefruit, then remove the peel and pith, cutting downwards. Cut out the segments from between the membranes, then add to the pomegranate seeds.

3 Finely grate the rind of half an orange and set aside. Using a sharp knife, cut a slice off the top and bottom of both oranges, then remove the peel and pith, cutting downwards and taking care to retain the shape of the oranges. Slice horizontally into slices, then cut into quarters. Add the oranges to the pomegranate and grapefruit and stir to mix well.

4 Combine the reserved orange rind with the lime rind, garlic, vinegar, lime juice, sugar and mustard. Season with salt and pepper, then whisk in the olive oil.

5 Place the lettuce leaves in a serving bowl, then top with the citrus mixture and the avocado. Pour over the dressing and toss gently. Garnish with the onion rings and serve immediately.

Crab & Celeriac Remoulade

Finely shredded celeriac in a mustard-flavoured mayonnaise is a popular dish throughout France and here it is given a distinctly Provençal touch.

NUTRITIONAL INFORMATION

Calories 492	Sugars 2g
Protein 20g	Fat 45g
Carbohydrate 3g	Saturates 6g

 45 mins   0 mins

SERVES 4

I N G R E D I E N T S

1½ tsp lemon juice

1 tsp salt

450 g/1 lb celeriac

4½ tsp Dijon mustard

1 large egg yolk

150 ml/5 fl oz extra virgin olive oil

2 tsp white wine vinegar

2 tbsp capers in brine, rinsed

300 g/10½ oz fresh crab meat

radicchio leaves, rinsed and dried

fresh dill or parsley sprigs, to garnish

1 Put the lemon juice and salt into a large bowl of cold water. Using the shredding disc of a food processor or a hand grater, shred the celeriac. Put the celeriac into the bowl of acidulated water as it is grated, to prevent discoloration.

2 To make the sauce, beat the mustard and egg yolk together in a bowl. Gradually whisk in the olive oil, drop by drop, until a mayonnaise forms (see Cook's Tip). Stir in the vinegar.

3 Drain the celeriac and pat dry with kitchen paper. Add to the mayonnaise, stirring to coat well. Cover with clingfilm and chill.

4 About 20 minutes before serving, remove the remoulade from the refrigerator to allow it to come to room temperature. Gently stir in the capers and crab meat.

5 Line a platter or serving bowl with radicchio leaves and spoon the celeriac remoulade mixture on top. Garnish with fresh dill or parsley sprigs and serve immediately.

COOK'S TIP

If the sauce begins to curdle, beat another egg yolk in a bowl, then slowly beat into the sauce to rectify. Continue to add the remaining oil.

Greek Salad

The combination of juicy, ripe tomatoes and black olives is a classic partnership, but Greek cooks also add feta cheese for a salty flavour.

NUTRITIONAL INFORMATION

Calories	347	Sugars	.........6g
Protein	........12g	Fat	..........31g
Carbohydrate	....6g	Saturates	......11g

 15 mins   0 mins

SERVES 4

INGREDIENTS

250 g/9 oz feta cheese

250 g/9 oz cucumber

250 g/9 oz Greek kalamata olives

1 red onion or 4 spring onions

2 large juicy tomatoes

1 tsp clear honey

4 tbsp extra virgin olive oil

½ lemon

salt and pepper

fresh or dried oregano, to garnish

pitta bread, to serve

1 Drain the feta cheese if it is packed in brine. Place it on a chopping board and cut into 1 cm/½ inch dice. Transfer to a salad bowl.

2 Cut the cucumber in half lengthways and use a teaspoon to scoop out the seeds. Cut the flesh into 1 cm/½ inch slices and add to the bowl.

3 Stone the olives, if liked, and add them to the salad bowl. Slice the red onion or finely chop the the spring onions and add to the salad bowl. Cut each tomato into quarters and scoop out the seeds with a teaspoon. Cut the flesh into bite-size pieces and add to the bowl.

4 Using your hands, gently toss all the ingredients together. Stir the honey into the olive oil (see Cook's Tip), add to the salad and squeeze in lemon juice to taste. Season with pepper and a little salt, if wished. Cover with clingfilm and chill until required.

5 Garnish the salad with the oregano and serve with pitta bread.

COOK'S TIP

The small amount of honey helps to bring out the full flavour of the tomatoes.

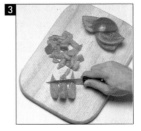

Baked Goat's Cheese Salad

Scrumptious hot goat's cheese and herb croûtes are served with a tossed leafy salad to make an excellent light snack, capturing Provençal flavours.

NUTRITIONAL INFORMATION

Calories 509	Sugars 3g
Protein 18g	Fat 33g
Carbohydrate . . .35g	Saturates 10g

10 mins   10 mins

SERVES 4

I N G R E D I E N T S

250 g/9 oz mixed salad leaves, such as rocket, lamb's lettuce and chicory

12 slices French bread, plus extra to serve

extra virgin olive oil, for brushing

12 thin slices of Provençal goat's cheese, such as Picodon

fresh herbs, such as rosemary, thyme or oregano, finely chopped

DRESSING

6 tbsp extra virgin olive oil

3 tbsp red wine vinegar

½ tsp sugar

½ tsp Dijon mustard

salt and pepper

1 To prepare the salad, rinse the leaves under cold water and pat dry with a tea towel. Wrap in kitchen paper and put in a plastic bag. Seal tightly and store in the refrigerator until required.

2 To make the dressing, place all the ingredients in a screw-top jar and shake until well blended. Season with salt and pepper to taste and shake again. Set aside while preparing the croûtes.

3 Toast the slices of bread on both sides until they are crisp. Brush a little olive oil on one side of each slice while still hot, so the oil is absorbed.

4 Place the croûtes on a baking sheet and top each with a slice of cheese. Sprinkle the herbs over the cheese and drizzle with olive oil. Bake in a preheated oven, 180°C/350°F/Gas Mark 4, for 5 minutes.

5 While the croûtes are in the oven, place the salad leaves in a bowl. Shake the dressing again, pour it over the leaves and toss together. Divide the salad between 4 plates.

6 Transfer the hot croûtes to the salads. Serve at once with extra slices of French bread.

Orange & Fennel Salad

Fresh, juicy oranges and the sharp aniseed flavour of fennel combine to make this refreshing Spanish salad.

NUTRITIONAL INFORMATION

Calories	136	Sugars	........19g
Protein	.........3g	Fat	...........6g
Carbohydrate	...19g	Saturates	.......1g

 30 mins   0 mins

SERVES 4

INGREDIENTS

4 large oranges

1 large bulb fennel

2 tsp fennel seeds

2 tbsp extra virgin olive oil

freshly squeezed orange juice, to taste

finely chopped fresh parsley, to garnish

1 Using a small serrated knife, remove the rind and pith from 1 orange, cutting carefully from the top to the bottom of the orange so it retains its shape. Work over a small bowl to catch the juices.

2 Peel the remaining oranges the same way, reserving all the juices. Cut the oranges horizontally into 5 mm/¼ inch slices and arrange in an attractive serving bowl; reserve the juices.

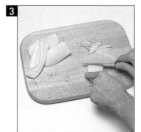

VARIATION

Replace the fennel with a finely sliced onion or a large bunch of spring onions, finely chopped. This version is from Spain, where orange-coloured oranges would be used, but in Sicily the dish is made with blood-red oranges.

3 Cut the fronds from the fennel bulb, cut the bulb in half lengthways and then into quarters. Cut crossways into the very thin slices. Immediately place in the bowl of oranges and toss with a little of the reserved juice to prevent browning.

4 Sprinkle the fennel seeds over the oranges and fennel.

5 Whisk the olive oil with the remaining reserved orange juice, plus extra fresh orange juice to taste. Pour over the oranges and fennel and toss gently. Cover with clingfilm and chill until ready to serve.

6 Just before serving, remove from the refrigerator and sprinkle with parsley. Serve chilled.

Salade Niçoise

This classic salad from Nice is often made with canned tuna, but using seared fresh tuna steaks instead gives it a sophisticated twist.

NUTRITIONAL INFORMATION

Calories	356	Sugars	.........3g
Protein	........22g	Fat	..........26g
Carbohydrate	...10g	Saturates	.......4g

  45 mins   20 mins

SERVES 4

INGREDIENTS

250 g/9 oz French beans, trimmed

250 g/9 oz small waxy potatoes, scrubbed and halved

1 large tomato, cut into 8 wedges

1 large tuna steak, about 350 g/12 oz and 2 cm/¾ inch thick, seared (see page 30)

3 large eggs, hard-boiled

55 g/2 oz black olives

50 g/1¾ oz can anchovy fillets in oil, drained

1 tbsp chopped fresh flat leaf parsley

GARLIC VINAIGRETTE

100 ml/3½ fl oz extra virgin olive oil

3 tbsp red or white wine vinegar

½ tsp sugar

½ tsp Dijon mustard

2 garlic cloves, crushed

salt and pepper

1 Put all the vinaigrette ingredients in a screw-top jar and shake well. Season with salt and pepper to taste. Set aside.

2 Blanch the beans in boiling water for 3 minutes, then drain and place in a large bowl. Pour over the vinaigrette.

3 Cook the potatoes in boiling water for about 15 minutes until tender, then

drain and add to the beans and dressing while still hot. Toss gently and set the vegetables aside to cool.

4 Add the tomato pieces to the vegetables and toss together. Break the seared tuna into large chunks, add to the vegetables and toss gently.

5 Shell the hard-boiled eggs and cut each into quarters lengthways.

6 Mound the tuna and vegetables on a large serving platter. Arrange the hard-boiled egg quarters around the side. Scatter the olives over the salad, then arrange the anchovies in a lattice on top. Cover and chill.

7 About 15 minutes before serving, remove the salad from the refrigerator and leave to come to room temperature. Sprinkle with parsley and serve.

Lobster Salad

Lobsters are best prepared simply to ensure that none of the rich, sweet flavour is lost amid a mass of other ingredients.

NUTRITIONAL INFORMATION

Calories 487   Sugars 2g
Protein . . . . .24g   Fat 42g
Carbohydrate . . . .2g   Saturates 6g

 15 mins   6 mins

SERVES 2

INGREDIENTS

2 raw lobster tails

salt and pepper

LEMON-DILL MAYONNAISE

1 large lemon

1 large egg yolk

½ tsp Dijon mustard

150 ml/5 fl oz olive oil

1 tbsp chopped fresh dill

TO GARNISH

radicchio leaves

lemon wedges

fresh dill sprigs

1 To make the lemon-dill mayonnaise, finely grate the lemon rind and squeeze the juice. Beat the egg yolk in a small bowl and beat in the mustard and 1 teaspoon of the lemon juice.

2 Using a balloon whisk or electric mixer, beat in the olive oil, drop by drop, until a thick mayonnaise forms. Stir in half the lemon rind and 1 tablespoon of the juice.

3 Season with salt and pepper, and add more lemon juice if desired. Stir in the dill and cover with clingfilm. Chill in the refrigerator until required.

4 Bring a large saucepan of lightly salted water to the boil. Add the lobster tails, bring back to the boil and cook for 6 minutes until the flesh is opaque and the shells are red. Drain immediately and set aside to cool.

5 Remove the lobster flesh from the shells and cut into bite-size pieces. Arrange the radicchio leaves on individual plates and top with the lobster flesh. Place a spoonful of the lemon-dill mayonnaise on the side. Garnish with lemon wedges and fresh dill sprigs and serve.

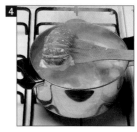

Mozzarella & Tomato Salad

Take advantage of the delicious varieties of cherry tomatoes that are available to make a refreshing Italian-style salad with lots of eye-appeal!

NUTRITIONAL INFORMATION

Calories	295	Sugars	.........3g
Protein	.........9g	Fat	..........27g
Carbohydrate	....3g	Saturates	.......7g

  4¼ hrs   0 mins

SERVES 4-6

INGREDIENTS

450 g/1 lb cherry tomatoes

4 spring onions

120 ml/4 fl oz extra virgin olive oil

2 tbsp balsamic vinegar

200 g/7 oz buffalo mozzarella (see Cook's Tip), cut into cubes

15 g/½ oz fresh flat leaf parsley

25 g/1 oz fresh basil leaves

salt and pepper

1 Using a sharp knife, cut the tomatoes in half and place them in a large bowl. Trim the spring onions and finely chop both the green and white parts, then add to the bowl.

2 Pour in the olive oil and balsamic vinegar and use your hands to toss together. Season with salt and pepper to taste, add the mozzarella and toss again. Cover with clingfilm and chill in the refrigerator for 4 hours.

3 Remove the salad from the refrigerator 10 minutes before serving. Finely chop the parsley and add to the salad. Tear the basil leaves and scatter them over the salad. Toss all the ingredients together again. Adjust the seasoning and serve.

COOK'S TIP
For the best flavour, buy buffalo mozzarella – mozzarella di bufala – rather than the factory-made cow's milk version. This salad would also look good made with bocconcini which are small balls of mozzarella. Look out for these in Italian delicatessens.

Roasted Pepper Salad

This is a classic way of serving the large, intensely flavoured sweet peppers that are so abundant throughout the summer months.

NUTRITIONAL INFORMATION

Calories	144	Sugars	.........9g
Protein	.........2g	Fat	...........11g
Carbohydrate	....9g	Saturates	.......2g

 30 mins   10 mins

SERVES 4–6

INGREDIENTS

4–6 large red, yellow and/or
  orange peppers

2 spring onions, trimmed

crusty bread, to serve

LEMON-PARSLEY VINAIGRETTE

6 tbsp extra virgin olive oil

4½ tsp freshly squeezed lemon juice

2 tbsp finely chopped fresh flat leaf parsley

salt and pepper

1 To make the dressing, put the oil, lemon juice and parsley in a screw-top jar and shake until well blended. Add salt and pepper to taste. Set aside.

2 Slice the tops off the peppers, then cut each into quarters or thirds, depending on the size. Remove the cores and seeds – the flatter the pieces are, the easier they are to cook.

3 Thinly slice the spring onions on the diagonal and set aside.

4 Place the pepper pieces on a grill rack under a preheated hot grill and grill for about 10 minutes or until the skins are charred and the flesh is softened.

5 Using tongs, remove each piece as it is ready. Immediately place in a bowl and cover with clingfilm. Set aside for about 20 minutes to cool.

6 When cool enough to handle, peel the skins from the peppers, then slice the flesh into long, thin strips.

7 Arrange the pepper strips on a serving platter. Shake the dressing again, then pour it over the salad. Scatter the spring onions over the top. Serve with crusty bread, or cover with clingfilm and chill until required.

VARIATIONS

For a party, marinate small, cooked prawns in the dressing and scatter them over the salad. Other Mediterranean ingredients you can add to the salad include capers, anchovies, stoned and sliced green or black olives and finely grated lemon rind.

Green Tabbouleh

Tomatoes are sometimes included in this refreshing bulgur wheat salad from Turkey, but this version relies on herbs and vegetables for its flavour.

NUTRITIONAL INFORMATION

Calories	333	Sugars	.........2g
Protein	.........9g	Fat	...........7g
Carbohydrate	...59g	Saturates	.......1g

30 mins   0 mins

SERVES 4

INGREDIENTS

300 g/10½ oz bulgur wheat

200 g/7 oz cucumber

6 spring onions

15 g/½ oz fresh flat leaf parsley

1 lemon

about 2 tbsp garlic-flavoured olive oil

salt and pepper

1 Place the bulgur wheat in a heatproof bowl, pour over 600 ml/1 pint boiling water and cover with an upturned plate. Set aside for at least 20 minutes until the wheat has absorbed the water and become tender.

2 Meanwhile, cut the cucumber in half lengthways and then cut each half into 3 strips lengthways. Using a teaspoon, scoop out and discard the seeds. Chop the cucumber strips into bite-size pieces. Put the cucumber pieces in a serving bowl.

3 Trim the top of the green parts of each of the spring onions, then cut each in half lengthways. Finely chop and add to the cucumber.

4 Place the parsley on a chopping board and sprinkle with a little salt. Using a cook's knife or a mezzaluna, very finely chop both the leaves and stalks. Add to the bowl with the cucumber and spring onions. Finely grate the lemon rind into the bowl.

5 When the bulgur wheat is cool enough to handle, either squeeze out any excess water with your hands or press out the water through a sieve, then add the wheat to the bowl and mix with the other ingredients.

6 Cut the lemon in half and squeeze the juice of 1 half over the salad. Add 2 tablespoons of the garlic-flavoured oil and stir all the ingredients together. Adjust the seasoning with salt and pepper to taste and extra lemon juice or oil if needed. Cover the bowl with clingfilm and chill until required.

Warm Rice Salad

This easy-to-make rice salad has all the flavours of the Aegean – olive oil, lemon, feta cheese, capers and tomatoes.

NUTRITIONAL INFORMATION

Calories 374   Sugars 4g
Protein ....9g   Fat 24g
Carbohydrate ...33g   Saturates 8g

 10 mins   20 mins

SERVES 4–6

INGREDIENTS

200 g/7 oz long grain white rice

5 tbsp extra virgin olive oil

2–3 tbsp lemon juice

1 tbsp chopped fresh oregano or 1 tsp
  dried oregano

½ tsp Dijon mustard

2 large ripe tomatoes, deseeded and chopped

1 red or green pepper, deseeded
  and chopped

75 g/2¾ oz Kalamata or other brine-cured
  black olives, stoned and halved

225 g/8 oz feta cheese, crumbled, plus
  extra cubes, to garnish

1 tbsp capers, rinsed and drained

2–4 tbsp chopped fresh flat leaf parsley
  or coriander

salt and pepper

diced cucumber, to garnish

VARIATION

This salad is also delicious made
with brown rice – just increase the
cooking time to 25–30 minutes.

1 Bring a pan of lightly salted water to the boil. Add the rice, return to the boil, stirring once or twice, and simmer for 15–20 minutes until tender. Drain, rinse with hot water and drain again.

2 Meanwhile, whisk the olive oil with the lemon juice, oregano, mustard and salt and pepper in a bowl. Add the tomatoes, pepper, olives, feta, capers and parsley and stir to coat in the dressing. Set aside to marinate.

3 Turn the rice into a large bowl, then add to the vegetable mixture and toss to mix well. Season the salad with salt and pepper to taste, then divide between 4–6 individual dishes and garnish with extra feta cheese cubes and diced cucumber. Serve just warm.

Wild Rice & Bacon Salad

Wild rice has a nutty texture, which is great in salads, and bacon and scallops make a perfect combination.

NUTRITIONAL INFORMATION

Calories	580	Sugars	.........1g
Protein	........19g	Fat	..........41g
Carbohydrate	...35g	Saturates	.......6g

 15 mins   ⏱ 1 hr

SERVES 4

INGREDIENTS

150 g/5½ oz wild rice

600 ml/1 pint water or more, if necessary

55 g/2 oz pecans or walnuts

2 tbsp vegetable oil

4 slices smoked bacon, diced or sliced

3–4 shallots, finely chopped

5 tbsp walnut oil

2–3 tbsp sherry or cider vinegar

2 tbsp chopped fresh dill

8–12 large scallops, cut in half lengthways

salt and pepper

lemon and lime slices, to serve

1 Put the wild rice in a saucepan with the water and bring to the boil, stirring once or twice. Reduce the heat, cover, and simmer gently for 30–50 minutes, depending on whether you prefer a chewy or tender texture. Using a fork, fluff the rice into a large bowl and set aside to cool slightly.

2 Meanwhile, dry-fry the nuts in a frying pan, stirring frequently, for 2–3 minutes until just beginning to colour. Cool and chop coarsely, then set aside.

3 Heat 1 tablespoon of the vegetable oil in the pan. Stir in the bacon and cook, stirring occasionally, until crisp and brown. Transfer to kitchen paper to drain. Remove some of the oil from the pan and stir in the shallots. Cook, stirring occasionally, for 3–4 minutes, until soft.

4 Stir the toasted nuts, bacon and shallots into the rice. Add the walnut oil, vinegar, half the chopped dill and salt and pepper to taste. Toss well to combine the ingredients, then set aside.

5 Brush a large non-stick frying pan with the remaining oil. Heat until very hot, add the scallops and cook for 1 minute on each side until golden (do not overcook). Remove them from the pan.

6 Divide the wild rice salad among 4 plates. Top with the scallops and sprinkle with the remaining dill. Garnish with a sprig of dill, if desired, and serve immediately with the lemon and lime slices.

Rice, Bean & Corn Salad

This hearty rice salad was inspired by the famous American dish called succotash. It is incredibly easy to put together and tastes wonderful.

NUTRITIONAL INFORMATION

Calories	218	Sugars	.........3g
Protein	........11g	Fat	...........5g
Carbohydrate	...34g	Saturates	.......1g

20 mins   30 mins

SERVES 4–6

INGREDIENTS

100 g/3½ oz long grain white or brown rice

3 corn cobs

3–4 tbsp groundnut oil

1 small red onion, finely chopped

1 fresh red or green chilli, deseeded and · finely chopped

1 tbsp lemon juice

1 tbsp lime juice

½ tsp cayenne pepper

2 tbsp chopped fresh coriander

400 g/14 oz can butter beans, drained

115 g/4 oz cooked ham, diced

salt and pepper

1 Bring a a large saucepan of lightly salted water to the boil. Add the rice and return to the boil, stirring once or twice. Reduce the heat and simmer for 15–20 minutes until the rice is tender. (Brown rice will take 25–30 minutes.) Drain and rinse under cold running water; drain again and set aside.

2 Scrape down each corn cob with a knife to remove the kernels. Place in a bowl and set aside. Scrape along each cob to remove the milky residue and transfer to another small bowl.

3 Heat 1 tablespoon of the oil in a saucepan. Add the corn kernels and cook gently, stirring frequently, for about 5 minutes until tender. Add the red onion and chilli and stir over a low heat for about 1 minute until blended. Transfer to a plate and set aside to cool slightly.

4 Place the lemon and lime juices in a large bowl and whisk in the cayenne pepper, 2–3 tablespoons of the remaining oil and the milky corn liquid. Whisk in the chopped coriander until well combined.

5 Using a fork, fluff in the cooked rice and corn and onion mixture. Add the beans and ham and season with salt and pepper to taste. Transfer to a serving bowl and serve immediately.

Gazpacho Rice Salad

All the flavours of a zesty Spanish gazpacho – garlic, tomatoes,
peppers and cucumber combined with rice – make a great summer salad.

NUTRITIONAL INFORMATION

Calories	253	Sugars	........15g
Protein	.........7g	Fat	...........5g
Carbohydrate	...46g	Saturates	.......1g

   30 mins   35 mins

SERVES 4

INGREDIENTS

7 tbsp extra virgin olive oil

1 onion, finely chopped

4 garlic cloves, finely chopped

200 g/7 oz long grain white rice

350 ml/12 fl oz vegetable stock or water

1½ tsp dried thyme

3 tbsp sherry vinegar

1 tsp Dijon mustard

1 tsp clear honey

1 red pepper, deseeded and chopped

½ yellow pepper, deseeded and chopped

½ green pepper, deseeded and chopped

1 red onion, finely chopped

½ cucumber, peeled, deseeded and
  chopped (optional)

3 tomatoes, deseeded and chopped

2–3 tbsp chopped flat leaf parsley

salt and pepper

TO SERVE

12 cherry tomatoes, halved

12 black olives, stoned and
  coarsely chopped

1 tbsp flaked almonds, toasted

1 Heat 2 tablespoons of the oil in a large saucepan. Add the onion and cook, stirring frequently, for 2 minutes until beginning to soften. Stir in half the garlic and cook for a further minute.

2 Add the rice, stir to coat and cook for about 2 minutes until translucent. Stir in the stock and half the thyme and bring to the boil. Season to taste. Cover and simmer gently for about 20 minutes until tender. Stand, still covered, for about 15 minutes; uncover and cool completely.

3 Whisk the vinegar with the remaining garlic and thyme, the mustard, honey and salt and pepper in a large bowl. Gradually whisk in the remaining olive oil. Using a fork, gently fluff the rice into the vinaigrette.

4 Add the peppers, red onion, cucumber, tomatoes and parsley; toss and adjust the seasoning. Transfer the salad to a serving bowl and garnish with the tomatoes, black olives and toasted almonds. Serve warm.

Lentil & Shiitake Salad

Fresh shiitakes, which are now widely available, give this substantial salad a good mushroomy flavour.

NUTRITIONAL INFORMATION

Calories	469	Sugars	.........3g
Protein	........14g	Fat	..........30g
Carbohydrate	...37g	Saturates	.......4g

15 mins   1¼ hrs

SERVES 6–8

INGREDIENTS

225 g/8 oz Puy lentils, rinsed

4 tbsp olive oil

1 onion, finely chopped

200 g/7 oz long grain brown rice

½ tsp dried thyme

450 ml/16 fl oz chicken stock

350 g/12 oz shiitake mushrooms, sliced

2 garlic cloves, finely chopped

115 g/4 oz diced smoked bacon, fried crisp

2 small courgettes, diced

1–2 celery sticks, thinly sliced

6 spring onions, thinly sliced

2–3 tbsp chopped fresh flat leaf parsley

2 tbsp walnut halves, toasted and chopped

salt and pepper

DRESSING

2 tbsp red or white wine vinegar

1 tbsp balsamic vinegar

1 tsp Dijon mustard

1 tsp sugar

5 tbsp extra virgin olive oil

2–3 tbsp walnut oil

1 Bring a pan of water to the boil. Add the lentils and simmer for 30 minutes. Drain and rinse under cold running water.

2 Heat 2 tablespoons of the oil in a large saucepan. Fry the onion until softened. Stir in the rice and add the thyme, stock and salt and pepper. Bring to the boil, cover and simmer gently for 40 minutes until the rice is tender.

3 Heat the remaining oil in a frying pan and stir-fry the mushrooms for about 5 minutes until golden. Stir in the garlic and cook for a further 30 seconds. Season.

4 To make the dressing, whisk together the wine and balsamic vinegars, mustard and sugar in a large bowl. Gradually whisk in the oils. Season with salt and pepper. Add the lentils and toss gently. Fork in the rice and toss again.

5 Stir in the bacon and mushrooms, then the courgettes, celery, spring onions and parsley and season to taste. Serve sprinkled with walnuts.

Moroccan Mixed Rice Salad

The combination of spices gives this rice salad a slightly exotic scent.
Toasting the spices mellows the harshness and brings out their flavours.

NUTRITIONAL INFORMATION

Calories ....469 Sugars 24g
Protein ....11g Fat 22g
Carbohydrate ...60g Saturates 3g

 15 mins   1½ hrs

SERVES 4–6

I N G R E D I E N T S

1 tbsp soy sauce

1 tbsp molasses

75 g/2¾ oz wild rice

2 tbsp olive oil

100 g/3½ oz long grain rice

425 g/15 oz can chickpeas, drained

½ red onion, finely chopped

1 small red pepper, deseeded and diced

80 g/3 oz ready-soaked dried
 apricots, sliced

75 g/2¾ oz raisins

2 tbsp chopped fresh mint or coriander

55 g/2 oz flaked almonds, toasted

lettuce leaves, to garnish

lemon wedges, to serve

S P I C E D   D R E S S I N G

1 tsp hot curry powder

1 tsp ground coriander

1 tsp ground turmeric

1 tsp freshly ground nutmeg

½ tsp cayenne pepper

50 ml/2 fl oz rice vinegar

2 tbsp clear honey

1 tbsp lemon juice

5 tbsp extra virgin olive oil

1 Bring 350 ml/12 fl oz water, the soy sauce and molasses to the boil in a large pan. Add the wild rice and bring back to the boil. Cover and simmer gently for 30–50 minutes. Remove from the heat.

2 Heat the oil in a pan, add the brown rice and stir for 2 minutes to coat. Add 450 ml/16 fl oz water and bring to the boil. Cover and simmer for 40 minutes until tender. Remove from the heat.

3 Meanwhile, make the dressing. Dry-fry the spices in a small frying pan, stirring, for 4–5 minutes. Cool on a plate. Whisk the vinegar with the honey and lemon juice in a large bowl, then whisk in the oil. Whisk in the cooled spice mixture.

4 Fork the rices into the dressing and mix well. Stir in the chickpeas, onion, pepper, apricots, raisins and mint. Sprinkle with the almonds, garnish and serve.

Pesto Risotto-rice Salad

This is a cross between a risotto and a rice salad – using Italian arborio rice produces a slightly heavier, stickier result.

NUTRITIONAL INFORMATION

Calories 406	Sugars 5g	
Protein 7g	Fat 28g	
Carbohydrate ...34g	Saturates 5g	

 45 mins   30 mins

SERVES 4–6

INGREDIENTS

3 tbsp extra virgin olive oil, plus extra for drizzling

1 onion, finely chopped

200 g/7 oz arborio rice

450 ml/16 fl oz boiling water

6 sun-dried tomatoes in oil, drained and cut into thin slivers

½ small red onion, very thinly sliced

3 tbsp lemon juice

PESTO

55 g/2 oz fresh basil leaves

2 garlic cloves, finely chopped

2 tbsp pine kernels, lightly toasted

125 ml/4 fl oz extra virgin olive oil

55 g/2 oz freshly grated Parmesan cheese

salt and pepper

TO GARNISH

fresh basil leaves

Parmesan shavings

2 Heat 1 tablespoon of the oil in a saucepan and fry the chopped onion until softened. Stir in the rice and cook, stirring occasionally, for 2 minutes. Stir in the water and season. Cover and simmer for 20 minutes until the rice is tender and the water absorbed. Cool slightly.

3 Put the sun-dried tomatoes and sliced onion in a bowl, add the lemon juice and 2 tablespoons of oil. Fork in the hot rice and stir in the pesto. Toss to combine. Adjust the seasoning if necessary. Cover and cool to room temperature.

4 Fork the rice mixture into a shallow serving bowl. Drizzle with some olive oil and garnish with basil leaves and Parmesan shavings. Serve the salad at room temperature, not chilled.

1 To make the pesto, put the basil, garlic and pine kernels in a food processor and process for 30 seconds. With the motor running, gradually add the olive oil through the feeder tube until a smooth paste forms. Add the cheese and pulse until blended, but still with texture. Scrape into a small bowl and season to taste.

Red Rice Salad

This hearty salad is made with red rice from the French Camargue. It has an earthy flavour, which goes well with the other robust ingredients.

NUTRITIONAL INFORMATION

Calories ....192 Sugars 5g
Protein ....6g Fat 5g
Carbohydrate ...33g Saturates 1g

1½ hrs   30 mins

SERVES 6–8

INGREDIENTS

1 tbsp olive oil

200 g/7 oz red rice

600 ml/1 pint water

400 g/14 oz can red kidney beans, drained and rinsed

1 small red pepper, deseeded and diced

1 small red onion, finely chopped

2 small cooked beetroots (not in vinegar), peeled and diced

6–8 red radishes, thinly sliced

2–3 tbsp chopped fresh chives

salt and pepper

fresh chives, to garnish

HOT DRESSING

2 tbsp creamed horseradish

1 tbsp Dijon mustard

1 tsp sugar

50 ml/2 fl oz red wine vinegar

125 ml/4 fl oz extra virgin olive oil

1 Put the olive oil and red rice in a heavy-based saucepan and place over a medium heat. Add the water and 1 teaspoon of salt. Bring to the boil, reduce the heat, cover and simmer gently until the rice is tender and all the water has been absorbed. (There are several varieties, which differ in cooking times, so follow the packet instructions.) Remove the pan from the heat and set aside to cool to room temperature.

2 To make the dressing, put the creamed horseradish, Dijon mustard and sugar into a small bowl and whisk thoroughly to combine. Whisk in the red wine vinegar, then gradually whisk in the oil to form a smooth dressing.

3 In a large bowl, combine the kidney beans, red pepper, onion, beetroot, radishes and chives and toss together. Season with salt and pepper to taste.

4 Using a fork, fluff the rice into the bowl with the vegetables. Pour over the dressing and toss well. Cover and leave the salad to stand for about 1 hour. Spoon into a large shallow serving bowl, garnish with fresh chives and serve immediately.

Fruity Wild Rice Salsa

Wild rice has a nutty flavour and a good texture, ideal for salsas and salads, and goes well with the black beans in this dish.

NUTRITIONAL INFORMATION

Calories	467	Sugars	........15g
Protein	........10g	Fat	..........20g
Carbohydrate	...49g	Saturates	.......4g

2¼ hrs   1 hr

SERVES 4–6

INGREDIENTS

150 g/5½ oz small black beans, soaked overnight in cold water

1 onion, studded with 4 cloves

150 g/5½ oz wild rice

2 garlic cloves

450 ml/16 fl oz boiling water

1 red onion, finely chopped

2 fresh red chillies, deseeded and thinly sliced

1 large red pepper, deseeded and chopped

1 small mango or papaw, peeled and diced

2 oranges, segments removed and juice reserved

4 passion fruits, pulp and juice

juice of 3–4 limes

½ tsp ground cumin

1 tbsp maple syrup or light brown sugar

150 ml/5 fl oz extra virgin olive oil

1 small bunch of fresh coriander, leaves stripped from stems and chopped

lime slices, to garnish

1 Drain the beans and put in a large pan with the clove-studded onion. Cover with cold water by at least 5 cm/2 in. Bring to the boil, lower the heat and simmer for 1 hour until the beans are tender. Discard the onion, rinse the beans under cold running water and drain.

2 Meanwhile, put the wild rice and garlic in a pan and pour in the boiling water. Cover and simmer over a low heat for 30–50 minutes. Cool slightly and discard the garlic cloves.

3 Put the beans in a large bowl and fork in the wild rice. Add the onion, chillies, pepper, mango, orange segments and their juice and the passion fruit pulp and juice. Toss well together.

4 Combine the lime juice, cumin and maple syrup or sugar. Whisk in the olive oil and half the coriander, then pour over the rice mixture and toss well. Cover and set aside for up to 2 hours.

5 Spoon into a serving bowl, sprinkle with the remaining coriander and serve garnished with lime slices.

Prawn Salad & Toasted Rice

This simple salad is tossed with an unusual Vietnamese-style dressing and sprinkled with dry toasted rice, which gives interesting texture.

NUTRITIONAL INFORMATION

Calories	156	Sugars	.........4g
Protein	........12g	Fat	...........7g
Carbohydrate	....11g	Saturates	.......1g

 45 mins   5 mins

SERVES 4

INGREDIENTS

225 g/8 oz peeled cooked prawns, with tail shells left on

cayenne pepper

1 tbsp long grain white rice

2 tbsp sunflower oil

1 large head cos lettuce with outer leaves removed or 2 hearts

½ small cucumber, peeled, deseeded and thinly sliced

1 small bunch of fresh chives, sliced into 2.5 cm/1 inch pieces

handful of fresh mint leaves

salt and pepper

DRESSING

50 ml/2 fl oz rice vinegar

1 fresh red chilli, deseeded and thinly sliced

7.5 cm/3 inch piece of lemon grass stalk, crushed

juice of 1 lime

2 tbsp Thai fish sauce

1 tsp sugar

1 Split each prawn in half lengthways, leaving the tail attached to one half. Remove the dark intestinal veins and pat dry on kitchen paper. Sprinkle with a little salt and cayenne pepper.

2 To make the dressing, combine the vinegar with the chilli and lemon grass. Set aside to marinate.

3 Heat a wok or heavy-based frying pan over a high heat. Add the rice and stir until brown and fragrant. Turn into a mortar and cool completely. Crush gently with a pestle until coarse crumbs form.

4 Heat the oil in a clean pan and stir-fry the prawns for 1 minute. Transfer to a plate and season with pepper.

5 Tear or shred the lettuce into bite-size pieces and transfer to a shallow salad bowl. Add the cucumber, chives and mint leaves and toss to combine.

6 Remove the lemon grass and most of the chilli slices from the rice vinegar and whisk in the lime juice, fish sauce and sugar. Pour most of the dressing over the salad and toss well to mix. Top with the prawns and drizzle with the remaining dressing. Sprinkle with the toasted rice and serve immediately.

Prawn & Noodle Salad

This delicious combination of rice noodles and prawns, lightly dressed with typical Thai flavours, makes an impressive first course or light lunch.

NUTRITIONAL INFORMATION

Calories 204	Sugars 8g	
Protein 15g	Fat 3g	
Carbohydrate ...29g	Saturates 1g	

 15 mins   2 mins

SERVES 4

INGREDIENTS

85 g/3 oz rice vermicelli or rice sticks

175 g/6 oz mangetouts, cut crossways in half, if large

5 tbsp lime juice

4 tbsp Thai fish sauce

1 tbsp sugar

2.5 cm/1 inch piece of fresh root ginger, finely chopped

1 fresh red chilli, deseeded and thinly sliced on the diagonal

4 tbsp chopped fresh coriander or mint, plus extra to garnish

10 cm/4 inch piece of cucumber, peeled, deseeded and diced

2 spring onions, thinly sliced on the diagonal

16–20 large peeled cooked prawns

2 tbsp chopped unsalted peanuts or cashews (optional)

4 whole cooked prawns and lemon slices, to garnish

1 Put the rice noodles in a large bowl and pour over enough hot water to cover. Set aside for about 4 minutes until soft. Drain and rinse under cold running water; drain again and set aside.

2 Bring a saucepan of water to the boil. Add the mangetouts and return to the boil. Lower the heat and simmer for 1 minute. Drain, rinse under cold running water until cold, then drain and set aside.

3 Whisk together the lime juice, fish sauce, sugar, ginger, chilli and coriander in a large bowl. Stir in the cucumber and spring onions. Add the drained noodles, mangetouts and the prawns. Toss the salad gently together.

4 Divide the noodle salad between 4 large plates. Sprinkle with chopped coriander and the peanuts, if using, then garnish each plate with a whole prawn and a lemon slice. Serve immediately.

Sweet & Sour Fruit

This mixture of fresh and canned fruit, which has a sweet and sour flavour, is very cooling, especially in the summer.

NUTRITIONAL INFORMATION

Calories 240   Sugars 58g
Protein . . . . .2g   Fat 0.4g
Carbohydrate . . .60g   Saturates 0g

5 mins   0 mins

SERVES 4

I N G R E D I E N T S

400 g/14 oz can mixed fruit cocktail

400 g/14 oz can guavas

2 large bananas

3 apples (optional)

1 tsp ground black pepper

1 tsp salt

½ tsp ground ginger

2 tbsp lemon juice

fresh mint leaves, to garnish

1 Drain the can of mixed fruit cocktail and place the fruit in a large, deep mixing bowl.

2 Mix the the drained fruit cocktail with the guavas and their syrup so that the fruit is well coated.

3 Peel the bananas and cut them into thick slices.

4 Peel and core the apples, if using, and cut them into dice.

5 Add the fresh fruit to the bowl containing the canned fruit and mix thoroughly together.

6 Add the ground black pepper, salt and ginger and stir to mix. Add the lemon juice to prevent the banana and apple from turning brown and mix again.

7 Serve the sweet and sour fruit as a snack, garnished with a few fresh mint leaves.

COOK'S TIP
Guavas are tropical fruits with a powerful, exotic smell. You may find fresh guavas in specialist shops and large supermarkets, but the canned variety is more widely available. Surprisingly, they have a higher vitamin C content than many citrus fruits.

Mussel Salad

A colourful combination of cooked mussels tossed together with chargrilled red peppers and salad leaves in a lemon dressing.

NUTRITIONAL INFORMATION

Calories	124	Sugars	.........5g
Protein	........16g	Fat	...........5g
Carbohydrate	....5g	Saturates	......1g

40 mins   10 mins

SERVES 4

INGREDIENTS

2 large red peppers, halved and deseeded

350 g/12 oz cooked shelled mussels, thawed if frozen

1 head of radicchio

25 g/1 oz rocket leaves

8 cooked green-lipped mussels in their shells

TO SERVE

lemon wedges

crusty bread

DRESSING

1 tbsp olive oil

1 tbsp lemon juice

1 tsp finely grated lemon rind

2 tsp clear honey

1 tsp French mustard

1 tbsp snipped fresh chives

salt and pepper

1 Preheat the grill to hot. Place the peppers, skin side up, on the rack. Grill for 8–10 minutes until the skin is charred and blistered and the flesh is soft. Remove from the grill with tongs, place in a bowl and cover with clingfilm. Set aside for 10 minutes until cool enough to handle, then peel off the skins.

2 Slice the pepper flesh into thin strips and place in a bowl. Gently stir in the shelled mussels.

3 To make the dressing, whisk together the oil, lemon juice and rind, honey, mustard and chives. until well blended. Season to taste with salt and pepper. Add the pepper and mussel mixture and toss gently until coated.

4 Remove the central core of the radicchio and shred the leaves. Place in a serving bowl with the rocket leaves and toss together.

5 Pile the mussel mixture into the centre of the leaves and arrange the green-lipped mussels in their shells around the edge of the bowl. Serve with lemon wedges and crusty bread.

Hot & Spicy Rice Salad

Serve this spicy Indian-style dish with a low-fat natural yogurt raita for a delightfully refreshing contrast.

NUTRITIONAL INFORMATION

Calories 329	Sugars 27g	
Protein 8g	Fat 8g	
Carbohydrate ...59g	Saturates 1g	

30 mins | 25 mins

SERVES 4

I N G R E D I E N T S

2 tsp vegetable oil

1 onion, finely chopped

1 fresh red chilli, deseeded and
   finely chopped

8 cardamom pods

1 tsp ground turmeric

1 tsp garam masala

350 g/12 oz basmati rice, rinsed

700 ml/1¼ pints boiling water

1 orange pepper, chopped

225 g/8 oz cauliflower florets, divided into
   small sprigs

4 ripe tomatoes, peeled, deseeded and
   chopped

125 g/4½ oz seedless raisins

25 g/1 oz toasted flaked almonds

salt and pepper

raita of low-fat natural yogurt, onion,
   cucumber and mint, to serve

1 Heat the oil in a large non-stick saucepan. Add the onion, chilli, cardamom pods, turmeric and garam masala and fry over a low heat for 2–3 minutes until the vegetables are just softened.

2 Stir in the rice, boiling water, orange pepper and cauliflower. Season to taste with salt and pepper.

3 Cover with a tight-fitting lid and bring to the boil. Lower the heat and simmer for 15 minutes without lifting the lid.

4 Uncover the pan and fork through the rice. Stir in the tomatoes and raisins.

5 Cover the pan again, turn off the heat and leave for 15 minutes. Discard the cardamom pods.

6 Pile on to a warmed serving platter and sprinkle over the toasted flaked almonds.

7 Serve the rice salad with the yogurt raita.

Layered Chicken Salad

This layered main course salad has lively tastes and textures.
For an interesting variation, substitute canned tuna for the chicken.

NUTRITIONAL INFORMATION

Calories	352	Sugars	.........9g
Protein	.......29g	Fat	..........9g
Carbohydrate	...43g	Saturates	......2g

 1 hr   40 mins

SERVES 4

INGREDIENTS

750 g/1 lb 10 oz new potatoes, scrubbed

1 red pepper, halved and deseeded

1 green pepper, halved and deseeded

2 small courgettes, sliced

1 small onion, thinly sliced

3 tomatoes, sliced

350 g/12 oz cooked chicken, sliced

snipped fresh chives, to garnish

YOGURT DRESSING

150 ml/5 fl oz low-fat natural yogurt

3 tbsp low-fat mayonnaise

1 tbsp snipped fresh chives

salt and pepper

1   Put the potatoes into a large saucepan, add just enough cold water to cover and bring to the boil. Lower the heat, cover and simmer for 15–20 minutes until tender.

2   Meanwhile, place the pepper halves, skin side up, under a preheated hot grill and grill until the skins blacken and begin to char.

3   Remove the peppers with tongs, place in a bowl and cover with clingfilm. Set aside until cool enough to handle, then peel off the skins and slice the flesh.

4   Bring a small pan of lightly salted water to the boil. Add the courgettes, bring back to the boil and simmer for 3 minutes. Drain, rinse under cold running water to prevent any further cooking and drain again. Set aside.

5   To make the dressing, whisk the yogurt, low-fat mayonnaise and snipped chives together in a small bowl until well blended. Season to taste with salt and pepper.

6   When the potatoes are tender, drain, cool and slice them. Add them to the dressing and mix gently to coat evenly. Spoon the potatoes on to 4 serving plates, dividing them equally.

7   Top each plate with one quarter of the pepper slices and courgettes. Layer one quarter of the onion and tomato slices, then the sliced chicken, on top of each serving. Garnish with snipped chives and serve immediately.

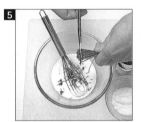

Melon and Mango Salad

A little freshly grated root ginger mixed with creamy yogurt and clear honey makes a perfect dressing for this refreshing salad.

NUTRITIONAL INFORMATION

Calories 189   Sugars 30g
Protein ....5g   Fat 7g
Carbohydrate ...30g   Saturates 1g

15 mins   0 mins

SERVES 4

INGREDIENTS

1 cantaloupe melon

55 g/2 oz black grapes, halved and seeded

55 g/2 oz green grapes

1 large mango

1 bunch of watercress, trimmed

iceberg lettuce leaves, shredded

2 tbsp olive oil

1 tbsp cider vinegar

1 passion fruit

salt and pepper

DRESSING

150 ml/5 fl oz low-fat natural yogurt

1 tbsp clear honey

1 tsp grated fresh root ginger

1 To make the dressing, for the melon, whisk together the yogurt, honey and ginger in a small bowl.

2 Halve the melon, scoop out the seeds with a spoon and discard. Slice, peel and dice the flesh. Place in a bowl with the grapes.

3 Slice the mango on each side of its large flat stone. On each mango half, slash the flesh into a criss-cross pattern down to, but not through the skin. Push the skin from underneath to turn the mango halves inside out. Now remove the flesh and add to the melon mixture.

4 Arrange the watercress and lettuce leaves on 4 serving plates.

5 Make the dressing for the salad leaves by whisking together the olive oil and vinegar with a little salt and pepper. Drizzle over the salad leaves.

6 Divide the melon mixture between the 4 plates and spoon over the yogurt dressing.

7 Scoop the seeds out of the passion fruit and sprinkle them over the salads. Serve immediately or chill in the refrigerator until required.

Mango & Wild Rice Salad

The very slight edge that counteracts the sweetness of the fruit makes a juicy ripe mango the perfect choice for a summery salad.

NUTRITIONAL INFORMATION

Calories	320	Sugars	........10g
Protein	.........6g	Fat	..........20g
Carbohydrate	...30g	Saturates	......2g

 15 mins　 1¼ hrs

SERVES 4

INGREDIENTS

85 g/3 oz wild rice

150 g/5½ oz basmati rice

3 tbsp hazelnut oil

1 tbsp sherry vinegar

1 ripe mango

3 celery sticks

85 g/3 oz ready-to-eat dried apricots, chopped

55 g/2 oz flaked almonds, toasted

2 tbsp chopped, fresh coriander or mint

salt and pepper

fresh coriander or mint sprigs, to garnish

1 Cook the wild rice and basmati rice in separate saucepans of lightly salted boiling water. Cook the wild rice for 45–50 minutes and the basmati rice for 10–12 minutes. Drain, rinse well and drain again. Place both rices in a large bowl.

2 Whisk together the oil and vinegar and season to taste with salt and pepper. Pour over the rice and toss well.

3 Cut the mango in half lengthways, as close to the stone as possible. Remove and discard the stone.

4 Peel the skin from the mango and cut the flesh into slices.

5 Thinly slice the celery and add to the cooled rice with the mango, apricots, almonds and chopped herbs. Toss together and transfer to a serving dish.

6 Garnish the salad with coriander or mint sprigs and serve.

COOK'S TIP

To toast almonds, place them on a baking sheet in a preheated oven, 180°C/350°F/Gas Mark 4, for 5–10 minutes. Alternatively, toast them under the grill, turning frequently and keeping a close eye on them because they will quickly burn.

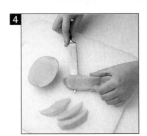

Parsley, Chicken & Ham Pâté

Pâté is easy to make at home, and this combination of lean chicken and ham mixed with herbs is especially straightforward.

NUTRITIONAL INFORMATION

Calories	119	Sugars	........2g
Protein	........20g	Fat	..........3g
Carbohydrate	....2g	Saturates	......1g

40 mins   0 mins

SERVES 4

INGREDIENTS

225 g/8 oz skinless, boneless lean chicken, cooked

100 g/3½ oz lean ham

small bunch of fresh parsley

1 tsp grated lime rind, plus extra to garnish

2 tbsp lime juice

1 garlic clove, peeled

125 ml/4 fl oz low-fat natural fromage frais

salt and pepper

TO SERVE

lime wedges

crispbread or Melba toast

green salad

1 Roughly dice the chicken. Trim off and discard any fat from the ham and dice the meat. Place the chicken and ham in a blender or food processor.

2 Add the parsley, lime rind and juice, and garlic and process until finely minced. Alternatively, finely chop the chicken, ham, parsley and garlic and place in a bowl. Gently stir in the lime rind and lime juice.

3 Transfer the mixture to a bowl and stir in the fromage frais. Season with salt and pepper to taste, cover with clingfilm and chill in the refrigerator for about 30 minutes.

4 Spoon the pâté into individual serving dishes and garnish with extra grated lime rind. Serve the pâté with lime wedges, crispbread or Melba toast and a fresh green salad.

VARIATION

This pâté can be made successfully with other kinds of minced, lean, cooked meat, such as turkey, beef and pork. Alternatively, replace the meat with peeled prawns and/or white crab meat, or with canned tuna in brine, drained.

Fragrant Asparagus Risotto

Soft, creamy rice combines with the flavours of citrus and light aniseed to make this a substantial starter for six hungry people.

NUTRITIONAL INFORMATION

Calories 223	Sugars 9g
Protein 6g	Fat 6g
Carbohydrate . . .40g	Saturates 1g

 10 mins   45 mins

SERVES 6

INGREDIENTS

115 g/4 oz fine asparagus spears, trimmed

1.2 litres/2 pints vegetable stock

2 fennel bulbs

25 g/1 oz low-fat spread

1 tsp olive oil

2 celery sticks, chopped

2 medium leeks, shredded

350 g/12 oz arborio rice

3 medium oranges

salt and pepper

1 Bring a small saucepan of water to the boil and cook the asparagus for 1 minute. Drain and set aside.

2 Pour the stock into a saucepan and bring to the boil. Reduce the heat to maintain a gentle simmer.

3 Meanwhile, trim the fennel, reserving the fronds. Use a sharp knife to cut into thin slices.

4 Carefully melt the low-fat spread with the oil in a large saucepan, taking care that the water in the low-fat spread does not evaporate, and gently fry the fennel, celery and leeks for 3–4 minutes until just softened. Add the rice and cook, stirring, for a further 2 minutes until mixed.

5 Add a ladleful of stock to the pan and cook gently, stirring, until absorbed.

6 Continue adding the stock to the rice, a ladleful at a time, until the rice becomes creamy, thick and tender. This process will take about 25 minutes and should not be hurried.

7 Finely grate the rind and extract the juice from 1 orange and mix into the rice. Carefully remove the peel and pith from the remaining oranges. Holding the fruit over the saucepan, cut out the orange segments and add to the rice, along with any juice that falls.

8 Stir the orange into the rice along with the asparagus spears. Season to taste with salt and pepper and garnish with the fennel fronds. Serve immediately.

Chargrilled Chicken Salad

This is a quick starter to serve at a barbecue – if the bread is bent in half, the chicken salad can be put in the middle and eaten as finger food.

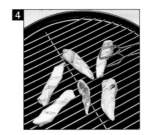

NUTRITIONAL INFORMATION

Calories ....225 Sugars 5g
Protein ....16g Fat 12g
Carbohydrate ...15g Saturates 2g

10 mins   15 mins

SERVES 4

INGREDIENTS

2 skinless, boneless chicken breasts

1 red onion

sunflower oil for brushing

1 avocado, peeled and stoned

1 tbsp lemon juice

125 ml/4 fl oz low-fat mayonnaise

¼ tsp chilli powder

¼ tsp salt

½ tsp pepper

4 tomatoes, quartered

½ loaf sun-dried tomato focaccia bread

green salad, to serve

1 Using a sharp knife, cut the chicken breasts into 1 cm/½ inch strips.

2 Cut the onion into 8 pieces, held together at the root. Rinse under cold running water and then brush with oil.

3 Purée or mash the avocado and lemon juice together. Whisk in the mayonnaise. Add the chilli powder and season with the salt and pepper.

4 Put the chicken and onion over a hot barbecue and grill for 3–4 minutes on each side. Combine the chicken, onion, tomatoes and avocado mixture.

5 Cut the bread in half twice, so that you have quarter-circle-shaped pieces, then in half horizontally. Toast on the hot barbecue for about 2 minutes on each side.

6 Spoon the chicken mixture on to the focaccia toasts and serve immediately with a green salad.

VARIATION
Instead of focaccia, serve the salad in pitta breads which have been warmed through on the side of the barbecue.

Kachumbers

Kachumbers can be made with fruit as well as vegetables. They are served at Indian tables as an appetiser or a garnish for the main meal.

NUTRITIONAL INFORMATION

Calories 55	Sugars 4g
Protein 1g	Fat 4g
Carbohydrate 4g	Saturates 0.5g

🧀

🍲 15 mins   🕐 0 mins

EACH SERVES 6

I N G R E D I E N T S

TOMATO, ONION & CUCUMBER KACHUMBER

3 ripe tomatoes

¼ cucumber, peeled

1 small onion, quartered

1 tsp lime juice

2 green chillies, deseeded and chopped (optional)

MANGO KACHUMBER

½ mango, peeled and chopped

1 small onion, chopped

1 tbsp chopped fresh coriander

2 tomatoes, chopped

RADISH KACHUMBER

8 large radishes, sliced

½ cucumber, peeled and chopped

1 small onion, chopped

1 tbsp chopped fresh coriander

1 tbsp oil

1 tbsp vinegar

1 To make the tomato, onion and cucumber kachumber, peel the tomatoes. Make a small cross in the top of each one with a pointed knife, place in a bowl and cover with boiling water. Leave for 1 minute before draining. The skins will slip off easily. Cut the tomatoes into quarters and cut each quarter in half. The seeds can be removed at this stage, if you prefer. Cut the cucumber lengthways into quarters. Remove the seeds and cut the flesh into cubes. Cut each onion quarter into slices. Combine all the ingredients in a bowl and sprinkle with the lime juice. Add the chillies, if using, and serve.

2 To make the mango kachumber, mix all the ingredients together and serve.

3 To make the radish kachumber, combine all the ingredients in a bowl and serve.

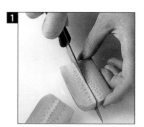

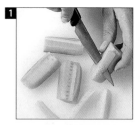

Figs & Parma Ham

This colourful fresh salad is delicious at any time of the year. Prosciutto di Parma is thought to be the best ham in the world.

NUTRITIONAL INFORMATION

Calories	121	Sugars	6g
Protein	1g	Fat	11g
Carbohydrate	6g	Saturates	2g

15 mins   5 mins

SERVES 4

INGREDIENTS

40 g/1½ oz rocket

4 fresh figs

4 slices Parma ham

4 tbsp olive oil

1 tbsp fresh orange juice

1 tbsp clear honey

1 small fresh red chilli

1 Tear the rocket into manageable pieces and arrange on 4 individual serving plates.

2 Using a sharp knife, cut each of the figs into quarters and place them on top of the rocket leaves.

3 Using a sharp knife, cut the Parma ham into strips and scatter over the rocket and figs.

4 Place the oil, orange juice and honey in a screw-top jar. Shake the jar vigorously until the mixture emulsifies and forms a thick dressing. Transfer the dressing to a bowl.

5 Using a sharp knife, dice the chilli. (You can remove the seeds first if you prefer a milder flavour.) Add the chopped chilli to the dressing and mix well.

6 Drizzle the dressing over the Parma ham, rocket and figs, tossing to mix well. Serve immediately.

COOK'S TIP
Chillies can burn the skin for several hours after chopping, so it is advisable to wear gloves when you are handling any very hot varieties and to wash your hands.

Capri Salad

This tomato, olive and mozzarella salad, dressed with balsamic vinegar and extra virgin olive oil, makes a delicious starter on its own.

NUTRITIONAL INFORMATION

Calories	95	Sugars	.........3g
Protein	.........3g	Fat	...........8g
Carbohydrate	....3g	Saturates	.......3g

 20 mins 3–5 mins

SERVES 4

INGREDIENTS

2 beef tomatoes

125 g/4½ oz mozzarella cheese

12 black olives

8 fresh basil leaves

1 tbsp balsamic vinegar

1 tbsp extra virgin olive oil

salt and pepper

fresh basil leaves, to garnish

1 Using a sharp knife, cut the tomatoes into thin slices.

2 Drain the mozzarella, if necessary, and cut into slices.

3 Stone the black olives and slice them into rings.

4 Layer the tomatoes, mozzarella slices, olives and basil leaves in a stack, finishing with a layer of cheese on top.

5 Place each stack under a preheated hot grill for 2–3 minutes or just long enough to melt the mozzarella.

6 Drizzle over the balsamic vinegar and olive oil, and season to taste with a little salt and pepper.

7 Transfer to individual serving plates and garnish with fresh basil leaves. Serve immediately.

COOK'S TIP

Buffalo mozzarella cheese, although it is usually more expensive because of the comparative rarity of buffalo, does have a better flavour than the cow's milk variety. It is popular in salads, but also provides a tangy layer in baked dishes.

Mushroom Salad

In Italy, raw mushrooms are a great favourite in salad dishes – they have a fresh, almost creamy flavour.

NUTRITIONAL INFORMATION

Calories 121   Sugars 0.1g
Protein . . . . .2g   Fat 13g
Carbohydrate . . .0.1g   Saturates 2g

 20 mins   0 mins

SERVES 4

I N G R E D I E N T S

150 g/5½ oz firm white mushrooms

4 tbsp virgin olive oil

1 tbsp lemon juice

5 canned anchovy fillets, drained
  and chopped

1 tbsp fresh marjoram

salt and pepper

1 Gently wipe each mushroom with a damp cloth or damp kitchen paper in order to remove any dirt.

2 Slice the mushrooms thinly, using a sharp knife and place in a bowl.

3 To make the dressing, whisk together the olive oil and lemon juice.

4 Pour the dressing mixture over the mushrooms. Toss together so that the mushrooms are completely coated with the lemon juice and oil.

5 Stir the chopped anchovy fillets into the mushrooms. Season the mixture with pepper to taste and garnish with the fresh marjoram.

6 Set the mushroom salad aside at room temperature for about 5 minutes before serving to allow all the flavours to be absorbed.

7 Season the mushroom salad with a little salt (see Cook's Tip) and then serve immediately.

COOK'S TIP

Do not season the mushroom salad with salt until the very last minute as it will cause the mushrooms to blacken and the juices to leak. The result will not be so tasty, as the full flavours won't be absorbed and it will also look very unattractive.

Spinach Salad

Fresh baby spinach is tasty and light, and it makes an excellent
and nutritious salad to go with the chicken and creamy dressing.

NUTRITIONAL INFORMATION

Calories	145	Sugars	.........3g
Protein	........10g	Fat	..........10g
Carbohydrate	....4g	Saturates	.......1g

 30 mins   0 mins

SERVES 4

INGREDIENTS

55 g/2 oz mushrooms

100 g/3½ oz baby spinach, washed

85 g/3 oz radicchio leaves, shredded

100 g/3½ oz cooked skinless chicken
  breast fillet

55 g/2 oz Parma ham

2 tbsp olive oil

finely grated rind of ½ orange and juice of
  1 orange

1 tbsp natural yogurt

salt and pepper

1 Wipe the mushrooms with a damp
cloth or damp kitchen paper to
remove any dirt.

2 Mix together the spinach and
radicchio in a large salad bowl.

3 Using a sharp knife, thinly slice the
mushrooms and add them to the
salad bowl.

4 Shred the cooked chicken breast with
your fingers and tear the Parma ham
into strips. Mix them into the salad.

5 To make the dressing, place the olive
oil, grated orange rind, orange juice
and yogurt into a screw-top jar. Shake the
jar vigorously until the mixture is
thoroughly combined. Season to taste
with salt and pepper.

6 Drizzle the dressing over the spinach
salad and toss to mix well. Serve.

VARIATION
Spinach is delicious when served
raw. Try raw spinach in a salad
garnished with bacon or garlicky
croûtons. The young leaves have
a wonderfully sharp flavour.

Tortelloni

These tasty little squares of pasta stuffed with mushrooms and cheese are surprisingly filling. This recipe makes 36 tortelloni.

NUTRITIONAL INFORMATION

Calories 360	Sugars 1g
Protein 9g	Fat 21g
Carbohydrate ...36g	Saturates 12g

1¼ hrs   25 mins

SERVES 4

INGREDIENTS

about 300 g/10½ oz Pasta Dough (see page 6), rolled out to thin sheets

5 tbsp butter

55 g/2 oz shallots, finely chopped

3 garlic cloves, crushed

55 g/2 oz mushrooms, wiped and finely chopped

½ celery stick, finely chopped

5 tbsp grated pecorino cheese, plus extra to garnish

1 tbsp vegetable oil

salt and pepper

1 Using a serrated pasta cutter, cut 5 cm/2 inch squares from the sheets of fresh pasta. To make 36 tortelloni you will need 72 squares. Once the pasta is cut, cover the squares with clingfilm to prevent them from drying out.

2 Heat 3 tbsp of the butter in a frying pan. Add the shallots, 1 crushed garlic clove, the mushrooms and celery and cook for 4–5 minutes.

3 Remove the pan from the heat, stir in the cheese and season with salt and pepper to taste.

4 Spoon ½ teaspoon of the mixture on to the middle of 36 pasta squares. Brush the edges of the squares with water and top with the remaining 36 squares. Press the edges together to seal. Set aside to rest for 5 minutes.

5 Bring a large pan of water to the boil, add the oil and cook the tortelloni, in batches, for 2–3 minutes. The tortelloni will rise to the surface when cooked and the pasta should be tender, but still firm to the bite. Remove from the pan with a draining spoon and drain thoroughly.

6 Meanwhile, melt the remaining butter in a pan over a low heat. Add the remaining garlic and plenty of pepper and cook for 1–2 minutes. Transfer the tortelloni to serving plates and pour the garlic butter over them. Garnish with grated pecorino and serve immediately.

Aubergine & Linguine

Prepare the marinated aubergines well in advance so – when you are ready to eat – all you have to do is cook the pasta.

NUTRITIONAL INFORMATION

Calories	378	Sugars	.........3g
Protein	........12g	Fat	..........30g
Carbohydrate	...16g	Saturates	.......3g

12¼ hrs   15 mins

SERVES 4

INGREDIENTS

150 ml/5 fl oz vegetable stock

150 ml/5 fl oz white wine vinegar

2 tsp balsamic vinegar

3 tbsp olive oil

fresh oregano sprig

450 g/1 lb aubergines, peeled and thinly sliced

400 g/14 oz dried linguine

MARINADE

2 tbsp extra virgin olive oil

2 garlic cloves, crushed

2 tbsp chopped fresh oregano

2 tbsp finely chopped roasted almonds

2 tbsp diced red pepper

2 tbsp lime juice

grated rind and juice of 1 orange

salt and pepper

1 Put the vegetable stock, wine vinegar and balsamic vinegar into a saucepan and bring to the boil over a low heat. Add 2 teaspoons of the olive oil and the sprig of oregano and simmer gently for about 1 minute.

2 Add the aubergine slices to the pan, remove from the heat and set aside for 10 minutes.

3 Meanwhile, make the marinade. Combine the oil, garlic, fresh oregano, almonds, red pepper, lime juice, orange rind and juice in a large bowl and season to taste with salt and pepper.

4 Carefully remove the aubergine from the saucepan with a draining spoon, and drain well. Add the aubergine slices to the marinade, mixing well to coat. Cover with clingfilm and set aside in the refrigerator for about 12 hours.

5 Bring a large pan of lightly salted water to the boil. Add half of the remaining oil and the linguine. Bring back to the boil and cook for 8–10 minutes until just tender, but still firm to the bite.

6 Drain the pasta thoroughly and toss with the remaining oil while it is still warm. Arrange the pasta on a serving plate with the aubergine slices and the marinade and serve immediately.

Tricolour Timballini

An unusual way of serving pasta, these cheese moulds make a charming starter and are excellent with a crunchy salad for a light lunch.

NUTRITIONAL INFORMATION

Calories 529   Sugars 7g
Protein . . . . .18g   Fat 29g
Carbohydrate . . .46g   Saturates 12g

30 mins · 1 hr

SERVES 4

INGREDIENTS

1 tbsp butter, softened

60 g/2 oz dry white breadcrumbs

175 g/6 oz dried tricolour spaghetti, broken into 5 cm/2 inch lengths

3 tbsp olive oil

1 egg yolk

115 g/4 oz Gruyère cheese, grated

300 ml/10 fl oz Béchamel Sauce (see page 6)

1 onion, finely chopped

1 bay leaf

150 ml/5 fl oz dry white wine

150 ml/5 fl oz passata

1 tbsp tomato purée

salt and pepper

fresh basil leaves, to garnish

1 Grease four 175 ml/6 fl oz moulds or ramekins with the butter. Evenly coat the insides with half of the breadcrumbs.

2 Bring a pan of lightly salted water to the boil. Add the spaghetti and 1 tablespoon of the oil. Bring back to the boil and cook for 8–10 minutes until just tender, but still firm to the bite. Drain and transfer to a mixing bowl. Add the egg yolk and cheese to the pasta and season.

3 Stir the Béchamel sauce into the pasta and mix well. Spoon the pasta mixture into the prepared moulds or ramekins and sprinkle the remaining breadcrumbs over the top.

4 Stand the ramekins on a baking sheet and bake in a preheated oven, 220°C/425°F/Gas Mark 7, for 20 minutes. Remove the baking sheet from the oven and set the moulds aside for 10 minutes.

5 Meanwhile, make the sauce. Heat the remaining oil in a pan and gently fry the onion and bay leaf for 2–3 minutes. Stir in the wine, passata and tomato purée and season with salt and pepper to taste. Simmer for 20 minutes until thickened. Remove and discard the bay leaf.

6 Turn the timballini out on to serving plates, garnish with the basil leaves and serve with the tomato sauce.

Pasta with Pesto Vinaigrette

Sun-dried tomatoes and olives enhance this delicious pesto-inspired salad, which tastes superb served warm or cold.

NUTRITIONAL INFORMATION

Calories	275	Sugars	.........2g
Protein	.........9g	Fat	..........19g
Carbohydrate	...17g	Saturates	.......4g

 35–40 mins 15 mins

SERVES 6

INGREDIENTS

225 g/8 oz dried pasta spirals

4 tomatoes, peeled

55 g/2 oz black olives

25 g/1 oz sun-dried tomatoes in oil, drained

2 tbsp pine kernels, toasted

2 tbsp Parmesan shavings

fresh basil sprig, to garnish

PESTO VINAIGRETTE

4 tbsp chopped fresh basil

1 garlic clove, crushed

2 tbsp freshly grated Parmesan cheese

4 tbsp olive oil

2 tbsp lemon juice

pepper

1 Bring a large pan of lightly salted water to the boil. Add the pasta, return to the boil and cook for 8–10 minutes until tender, but still firm to the bite. Drain the pasta, rinse well in hot water, then drain again.

2 To make the vinaigrette, whisk together the basil, garlic, Parmesan, olive oil and lemon juice until well blended. Season to taste with pepper.

3 Put the pasta into a bowl, pour the pesto vinaigrette over it and toss thoroughly.

4 Cut the tomatoes into wedges. Halve and stone the olives and slice the sun-dried tomatoes. Add the tomatoes, olives and sun-dried tomatoes to the pasta and toss well to mix.

5 Transfer the pasta mixture to a salad bowl and scatter the pine kernels and Parmesan shavings over the top. Serve warm, garnished with a sprig of basil.

Pasta-stuffed Tomatoes

This unusual and inexpensive dish would make a good starter
for eight people or a delicious light and summery lunch for four.

NUTRITIONAL INFORMATION

Calories . . . . . . .298 Sugars 4g
Protein . . . . .10g Fat 20g
Carbohydrate . . .20g Saturates 5g

15 mins   35 mins

SERVES 4

I N G R E D I E N T S

4 tbsp extra virgin olive oil, plus extra
for greasing

8 beef tomatoes or large round tomatoes

115 g/4 oz dried ditalini or other very
small pasta shapes

8 black olives, stoned and finely chopped

2 tbsp finely chopped fresh basil

1 tbsp finely chopped fresh parsley

55 g/2 oz Parmesan cheese, freshly grated

salt and pepper

fresh basil sprigs, to garnish

1 Brush a baking sheet with olive oil.
Slice the tops off the tomatoes and
reserve to use as lids. If the tomatoes will
not stand up, cut a thin slice off the
bottom of each tomato.

2 Using a teaspoon, scoop out the
tomato pulp into a sieve, but do not
pierce the tomato shells. Invert the
tomato shells on to kitchen paper, pat dry
and then set aside to drain.

3 Bring a large saucepan of lightly
salted water to the boil. Add the
pasta, bring back to the boil and cook for
8–10 minutes or until the pasta is tender,
but still firm to the bite. Drain the pasta
and set aside.

4 Put the olives, basil, parsley and
Parmesan cheese into a large mixing
bowl and stir in the drained tomato pulp.
Add the pasta to the bowl. Stir in the olive
oil, mix together well and season to taste
with salt and pepper.

5 Spoon the pasta mixture into the
tomato shells and replace the lids.
Arrange the stuffed tomatoes on the
prepared baking sheet and bake in a

preheated oven, 190°C/375°F/Gas Mark 5,
for 15–20 minutes.

6 Remove the tomatoes from the oven
and set aside to cool until they are
just warm.

7 Arrange the pasta-stuffed tomatoes
on a serving dish, garnish with the
basil sprigs and serve.

Beetroot Cannolicchi

Quick and simple, this colourful, warm salad works equally well as a tasty starter or as a main dish for a light lunch.

NUTRITIONAL INFORMATION

Calories	449	Sugars	........13g
Protein	........13g	Fat	..........16g
Carbohydrate	...70g	Saturates	.......2g

🍲 10 mins   🕐 25 mins

SERVES 4

I N G R E D I E N T S

300 g/11 oz dried ditalini rigati

5 tbsp olive oil

2 garlic cloves chopped

400 g/14 oz can chopped tomatoes

400 g/14 oz cooked beetroot, diced

2 tbsp chopped fresh basil leaves

1 tsp mustard seeds

salt and pepper

TO SERVE

mixed salad leaves, tossed in olive oil

4 Italian plum tomatoes, sliced

1 Bring a large saucepan of lightly salted water to the boil. Add the pasta and 1 tbsp of the oil. Bring back to the boil and cook for 8–10 minutes until tender, but still firm to the bite. Drain and set aside.

2 Heat the remaining olive oil in a large saucepan. Add the garlic and fry over a low heat for 3 minutes. Add the chopped tomatoes and cook for 10 minutes.

3 Remove the pan from the heat and carefully add the beetroot, basil, mustard seeds and pasta and season to taste with salt and pepper.

4 Serve while still warm on a bed of mixed salad leaves, tossed in olive oil, and sliced plum tomatoes.

COOK'S TIP

To cook raw beetroot, trim off the leaves about 5 cm/2 inches above the root and ensure that the skin is not broken. Boil in very lightly salted water for 30–40 minutes, until tender. Set aside to cool and then rub off the skin.

 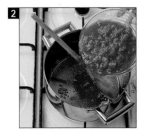 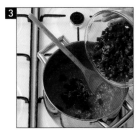

Salmon Pancakes

These pancakes are based on the latke, which is a thin, crisp pancake, and are served with smoked salmon and soured cream for a taste of luxury.

NUTRITIONAL INFORMATION

Calories	142	Sugars	.........1g
Protein	........6.8g	Fat	..........7.8g
Carbohydrate	..11.9g	Saturates	.....2.8g

5 mins   25 mins

SERVES 4

INGREDIENTS

450 g/1 lb floury potatoes, grated

2 spring onions, chopped

2 tbsp self-raising flour

2 eggs, beaten

2 tbsp vegetable oil

salt and pepper

fresh chives, to garnish

TOPPING

150 ml/5 fl oz soured cream

125 g/4½ oz smoked salmon

1 Rinse the grated potatoes under cold running water, drain and pat dry on kitchen paper. Transfer to a mixing bowl.

2 Mix the spring onions, flour and eggs into the potatoes and season well with salt and pepper.

3 Heat 1 tablespoon of the vegetable oil in a frying pan. Drop about 4 tablespoons of the mixture into the pan and spread each one with the back of a spoon to form a round (the mixture should make 16 pancakes). Cook for 5–7 minutes, turning once, until golden. Drain well.

4 Heat the remaining oil and cook the remaining mixture in batches.

5 Top the pancakes with the soured cream and smoked salmon, garnish with fresh chives and serve hot.

VARIATION

These pancakes are equally delicious topped with Parma ham or any other dry-cured ham instead of the smoked salmon.

Carrot & Potato Soufflé

Hot soufflés have a reputation for being difficult to make, but this one is both simple and impressive. Make sure you serve it as soon as it is ready.

NUTRITIONAL INFORMATION

Calories	294	Sugars	.........6g
Protein	........10g	Fat	...........9g
Carbohydrate	...46g	Saturates	.......4g

15 mins   40 mins

SERVES 4

INGREDIENTS

2 tbsp butter, melted

4 tbsp fresh wholemeal breadcrumbs

3 floury potatoes, baked in their skins

2 carrots, grated

2 eggs, separated

2 tbsp orange juice

¼ tsp grated nutmeg

salt and pepper

carrot curls, to garnish

1 Brush the inside of an 850 ml/ 1½ pint soufflé dish with the butter. Sprinkle about three-quarters of the breadcrumbs over the base and sides.

2 Cut the baked potatoes in half and scoop the flesh into a mixing bowl.

3 Add the carrots, egg yolks, orange juice and nutmeg to the potato flesh. Season to taste with salt and pepper.

4 In a separate bowl, whisk the egg whites until soft peaks form, then gently fold into the potato mixture with a metal spoon until well incorporated.

5 Gently spoon the potato and carrot mixture into the prepared soufflé dish. Sprinkle the remaining breadcrumbs over the top of the mixture.

6 Cook in a preheated oven, 200°C/ 400°F/Gas Mark 6, for 40 minutes, until risen and golden. Do not open the oven door during the cooking time, otherwise the soufflé will sink. Serve at once, garnished with carrot curls.

COOK'S TIP

To bake the potatoes, prick the skins and cook in a preheated oven, 190°C/375°F/Gas Mark 5, for about 1 hour.

Chicory Salad

The contrast of the pink grapefruit, creamy chicory and bright green lamb's lettuce makes this dish look simply stunning.

NUTRITIONAL INFORMATION

Calories 137	Sugars 4g
Protein 1g	Fat 13g
Carbohydrate 4g	Saturates 2g

 10 mins 🕐 0 mins

SERVES 4

INGREDIENTS

1 pink grapefruit

1 avocado

55 g/2 oz lamb's lettuce

2 heads chicory, sliced diagonally

1 tbsp chopped fresh mint

FRENCH DRESSING

3 tbsp olive oil

1 tbsp wine vinegar

1 small garlic clove, crushed

½ tsp Dijon or Meaux mustard

1 tsp clear honey

salt and pepper

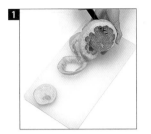  

1 Peel the grapefruit with a serrated knife. Cut the grapefruit into segments by cutting between the membranes. Set aside.

2 To make the French dressing, put the oil, vinegar, garlic, mustard and honey into a screw-top jar and shake vigorously. Season to taste with salt and pepper. Pour the dressing into a bowl.

3 Halve and stone the avocado and cut it into thin slices. Peel off the skin, put the sliced flesh into the bowl of French dressing and toss gently to coat.

4 Remove any stalks from the lamb's lettuce and put into a bowl with the grapefruit, chicory and chopped mint.

5 Add the avocado slices and 2 tablespoons of the French dressing. Toss well and transfer to individual serving plates. Serve immediately.

COOK'S TIP

Lamb's lettuce is so called because the shape of its dark green leaves resembles a lamb's tongue. It is also known as corn salad and the French call it mâche. It is easy to grow in the garden and will withstand the frost.

Aubergine & Rice Rolls

Slices of aubergine are blanched and stuffed with a savoury rice
and nut mixture, then baked in a piquant tomato and wine sauce.

NUTRITIONAL INFORMATION

Calories 142   Sugars 3g
Protein ....6g   Fat 9g
Carbohydrate ....9g   Saturates 3g

🍲 30 mins   🕐 1hr 5 mins

SERVES 8

INGREDIENTS

3 aubergines (total weight about 750 g /
  1 lb 10 oz)

55 g/2 oz mixed long grain and wild rice

4 spring onions, thinly sliced

3 tbsp chopped cashew nuts or toasted
  chopped hazelnuts

2 tbsp capers, rinsed

1 garlic clove, crushed

2 tbsp grated Parmesan cheese

1 egg, beaten

1 tbsp olive oil

1 tbsp balsamic vinegar

2 tbsp tomato purée

150 ml/5 fl oz water

150 ml/5 fl oz white wine

salt and pepper

fresh coriander sprigs, to garnish

3 Cook the rice in lightly salted boiling water for about 12 minutes or until just tender. Drain and place in a bowl. Add the spring onions, nuts, capers, garlic, cheese and egg, season with salt and pepper to taste and mix well.

4 Spread a thin layer of the savoury rice mixture over each slice of aubergine and then roll up the aubergine carefully, securing with a wooden cocktail stick. Place the rolls in a single layer in a lightly greased ovenproof dish and brush them with the olive oil.

5 Combine the vinegar, tomato purée and water and pour over the aubergine rolls. Cook in a preheated oven, 180°C/350°F/Gas Mark 4, for about 40 minutes or until tender and most of the liquid has been absorbed. Transfer the rolls to a serving dish.

6 Add the wine to the pan juices and heat, stirring, until the sediment loosens. Simmer for 2–3 minutes. Adjust the seasoning and strain the sauce over the aubergine rolls. Cool and chill well. Garnish with sprigs of coriander and serve.

1 Using a sharp knife, cut off the stem end of each aubergine, then cut off and discard a strip of skin from alternate sides of each one. Cut each aubergine into thin slices to give a total of 16 slices.

2 Blanch the aubergine slices in boiling water for 5 minutes, then drain on kitchen paper.

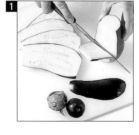

Garden Salad

This chunky salad includes tiny new potatoes tossed in a minty dressing, and is served with a wonderfully piquant mustard dip.

NUTRITIONAL INFORMATION

Calories 227	Sugars 6g	
Protein 4g	Fat 17g	
Carbohydrate ...16g	Saturates 4g	

  15-20 mins   20 mins

SERVES 8

INGREDIENTS

500 g/1 lb 2 oz tiny new or salad potatoes

225 g/8 oz broccoli florets

125 g/4½ oz sugar snap peas

2 large carrots

4 celery sticks

1 yellow or orange pepper, deseeded

1 bunch spring onions

1 head chicory

DRESSING

3 tbsp olive oil

1 tbsp white wine vinegar

1 tsp Dijon mustard

2 tbsp chopped fresh mint

MUSTARD DIP

6 tbsp soured cream

3 tbsp thick mayonnaise

2 tsp balsamic vinegar

1½ tsp coarse-grain mustard

½ tsp creamed horseradish

pinch of brown sugar

salt and pepper

1 Cook the potatoes in lightly salted boiling water for about 10 minutes until just tender. Meanwhile, whisk together the dressing ingredients.

2 Drain the potatoes, add to the dressing while still hot, toss well and set aside until cold, stirring occasionally.

3 To make the dip, combine the soured cream, mayonnaise, vinegar, mustard, horseradish and sugar and season to taste with salt and pepper. Transfer to a small bowl, cover and chill until required.

4 Cut the broccoli into bite-size sprigs and blanch for 2 minutes in boiling water. Drain and plunge immediately into cold water. When cold, drain thoroughly.

5 Blanch the sugar snap peas in boiling water for 1 minute. Drain, rinse in cold water and drain again.

6 Cut the carrots and celery into matchsticks. Slice the pepper or cut it into small cubes. Cut off some of the green parts of the spring onions and separate the chicory leaves.

7 Arrange the vegetables attractively in a fairly shallow bowl with the potatoes piled up in the centre. Serve with the mustard dip.

Mini Kebabs

Cubes of smoked tofu are speared on bamboo satay sticks with crisp vegetables and marinated with lemon juice and olive oil.

NUTRITIONAL INFORMATION

Calories ....322 Sugars 9g
Protein ....13g Fat 24g
Carbohydrate ...13g Saturates 7g

25 mins   15–20 mins

SERVES 6

I N G R E D I E N T S

300 g/10½ oz smoked tofu, cut into cubes

1 large red pepper, deseeded and diced

1 large yellow pepper, deseeded and diced

175 g/6 oz button mushrooms

1 small courgette, sliced

finely grated rind and juice of 1 lemon

3 tbsp olive oil

1 tbsp chopped parsley

1 tsp caster sugar

salt and pepper

fresh parsley sprigs, to garnish

S A U C E

115 g/4 oz cashew nuts

1 tbsp butter

1 garlic clove, crushed

1 shallot, finely chopped

1 tsp ground coriander

1 tsp ground cumin

1 tbsp caster sugar

1 tbsp desiccated coconut

150 ml/5 fl oz natural yogurt

1 Thread the tofu cubes, red and yellow peppers, mushrooms and courgettes on to bamboo satay sticks. Arrange them in a shallow dish.

2 Mix together the lemon rind and juice, olive oil, parsley and sugar. Season to taste with salt and pepper. Pour over the kebabs and brush them with the mixture. Set aside for 10 minutes.

3 To make the sauce, scatter the cashew nuts on to a baking sheet and toast them under a hot grill until lightly browned.

4 Melt the butter in a saucepan and sauté the garlic and shallot over a low heat until softened. Transfer to a blender or food processor and add the nuts, coriander, cumin, sugar, coconut and yogurt. Process for about 15 seconds or until combined. Alternatively, chop the nuts very finely and mix with the remaining ingredients.

5 Place the kebabs under a preheated grill and cook, turning and basting with the lemon juice mixture, until lightly browned. Garnish with sprigs of parsley and serve with the cashew nut sauce.

Avocado Cream Terrine

The smooth, rich taste of ripe avocados combines well with thick, creamy yogurt and single cream to make this impressive terrine.

NUTRITIONAL INFORMATION

Calories	327	Sugars	........3g
Protein	.........6g	Fat	..........32g
Carbohydrate	....4g	Saturates	.......8g

2¼ hrs   0 mins

SERVES 6

INGREDIENTS

2 ripe avocados

4 tbsp cold water

2 tsp gelatine

1 tbsp lemon juice

4 tbsp low-fat mayonnaise

150 ml5 fl oz natural yogurt

150 ml5 fl oz single cream

salt and pepper

mixed salad leaves, to serve

TO GARNISH

cucumber slices

nasturtium flowers

1 Peel the avocados and remove and discard the stones. Put the flesh in a blender or food processor or a large bowl with the water, gelatine, lemon juice, mayonnaise, yogurt and cream. Season to taste with salt and pepper.

2 Process for about 10–15 seconds or beat by hand, using a fork or whisk, until smooth.

3 Transfer the mixture to a small, heavy-based pan and heat very gently, stirring constantly, until just beginning to boil.

4 Pour the mixture into a 900 ml/ 1½ pint terrine, non-stick loaf tin or plastic food storage box and smooth the surface. Allow the mixture to cool and set and then chill in the refrigerator for about 1½–2 hours.

5 Turn the terrine out of its container and cut into neat slices. Arrange a bed of salad leaves on 6 serving plates. Place a slice of avocado terrine on top and garnish with cucumber slices and nasturtium flowers.

Stuffed Chinese Leaves

Mushrooms, spring onions, celery and rice are flavoured with five-spice powder and wrapped in Chinese leaves.

NUTRITIONAL INFORMATION

Calories 166   Sugars 3g
Protein ....3g   Fat 13g
Carbohydrate ...10g   Saturates 8g

25 mins   45 mins

SERVES 4

INGREDIENTS

8 large Chinese leaves

½ vegetable stock cube

55 g/2 oz long grain rice

4 tbsp butter

1 bunch spring onions, trimmed and finely chopped

1 celery stick, finely chopped

125 g/4½ oz button mushrooms, sliced

1 tsp Chinese five-spice powder

300 ml/10 fl oz passata

salt and pepper

fresh chives, to garnish

1 Blanch the Chinese leaves in boiling water for 1 minute. Refresh under cold running water and drain well. Be careful not to tear them.

2 Bring a large pan of water to the boil and stir in the stock cube. Add the rice, bring back to the boil and simmer for 10–12 minutes until just tender. Drain well and set aside until required.

3 Meanwhile, melt the butter in a frying pan and fry the spring onions and celery over a low heat for 3–4 minutes until softened, but not browned.

4 Add the mushrooms to the frying pan and cook for a further 3–4 minutes, stirring frequently.

5 Add the cooked rice to the pan with the five-spice powder. Season to taste with salt and pepper and stir well.

6 Spread out the Chinese leaves on a work surface and divide the rice mixture between them. Roll each leaf into a neat parcel, tucking in the sides to enclose the stuffing. Place the stuffed leaves, seam side down, in a greased ovenproof dish. Pour the passata over them and cover with foil. Bake in a preheated oven, 190°C/375°F/Gas Mark 5, for 25–30 minutes.

7 Garnish the stuffed Chinese leaves with fresh chives and serve immediately straight from the dish.

Marinated Vegetable Salad

Lightly steamed vegetables taste superb served slightly warm in a marinade of olive oil, white wine, vinegar and fresh herbs.

NUTRITIONAL INFORMATION

Calories 114	Sugars 4g
Protein 3g	Fat 9g
Carbohydrate 5g	Saturates 1g

🍲 10 mins   🕐 10 mins

SERVES 6

I N G R E D I E N T S

175 g/6 oz baby carrots

2 celery hearts, cut into 4 pieces

115g/4 oz sugar snap peas or mangetouts

1 fennel bulb, sliced

175 g/6 oz small asparagus spears

4½ tsp sunflower seeds

fresh dill sprigs, to garnish

D R E S S I N G

4 tbsp extra virgin olive oil

4 tbsp dry white wine

2 tbsp white wine vinegar

1 tbsp chopped fresh dill

1 tbsp chopped fresh parsley

salt and pepper

1 Put the carrots, celery, sugar snap peas or mangetouts, fennel and asparagus into a steamer and cook over gently simmering water for 3–5 minutes until just tender. It is important that they retain a little bite.

2 Meanwhile, make the dressing. Mix together the olive oil, wine, vinegar and chopped herbs, whisking until thoroughly combined. Season to taste with salt and pepper.

3 When the vegetables are cooked, transfer them to a serving dish and immediately pour the dressing over them. The hot vegetables will absorb the flavour of the dressing as they cool.

4 Spread out the sunflower seeds on a baking sheet and toast them under a preheated grill for 3-4 minutes or until lightly browned and are beginning to smell fragrant. Sprinkle the toasted sunflower seeds over the vegetables.

5 Serve the salad while the vegetables are still slightly warm, garnished with sprigs of fresh dill.

Mozzarella with Radicchio

Sliced mozzarella is served with tomatoes and radicchio, which is singed over hot coals and drizzled with pesto dressing.

NUTRITIONAL INFORMATION

Calories	.413	Sugars	.6g
Protein	.12g	Fat	.38g
Carbohydrate	.6g	Saturates	.14g

 15 mins   2–3 mins

SERVES 4

I N G R E D I E N T S

500 g/1 lb 2 oz mozzarella cheese

4 large tomatoes, sliced

2 heads of radicchio

fresh basil leaves, to garnish

D R E S S I N G

1 tbsp red or green pesto

6 tbsp extra virgin olive oil

3 tbsp red wine vinegar

handful of fresh basil leaves

salt and pepper

1 First make the dressing. Whisk together the pesto, olive oil and red wine vinegar in a small bowl until thoroughly combined.

2 Tear the basil leaves into tiny pieces and add them to the dressing. Season to taste with salt and pepper.

3 Thinly slice the mozzarella and arrange it on 4 serving plates with the tomatoes, overlapping the slices.

4 Leaving the root end on the heads of radicchio, slice each one into quarters. Grill them quickly on the barbecue, so that the leaves just singe on the outside. Place 2 quarters on each serving plate.

5 Drizzle the dressing over the radicchio, cheese and tomatoes. Garnish with fresh basil leaves and serve immediately.

Warm Goat's Cheese Salad

This delicious salad combines soft goat's cheese with walnut halves, served on a bed of mixed salad leaves.

NUTRITIONAL INFORMATION

Calories	408	Sugars	.........8g
Protein	.........9g	Fat	..........38g
Carbohydrate	....8g	Saturates	.......8g

 5 mins   5 mins

SERVES 4

INGREDIENTS

85 g/3 oz walnut halves

mixed salad leaves

125 g/4½ oz soft goat's cheese

snipped fresh chives, to garnish

DRESSING

6 tbsp walnut oil

3 tbsp white wine vinegar

1 tbsp clear honey

1 tsp Dijon mustard

pinch of ground ginger

salt and pepper

1 To make the dressing, whisk together the walnut oil, wine vinegar, honey, mustard and ginger in a small saucepan. Season to taste with salt and pepper.

2 Heat the dressing gently, stirring occasionally, until warm. Add the walnut halves and continue to heat for 3–4 minutes.

3 Arrange the salad leaves on 4 serving plates and place spoonfuls of goat's cheese on top. Lift the walnut halves from the dressing with a draining spoon and scatter them over the salads.

4 Transfer the warm dressing to a small jug. Sprinkle chives over the salads and serve with the dressing.

VARIATION

You could also use a ewe's milk cheese, such as feta, in this recipe for a sharper flavour.

Potato Skins & Two Fillings

Potato skins are always a favourite. Prepare the skins in advance and warm them through before serving with the salad fillings.

NUTRITIONAL INFORMATION

Calories 279	Sugars 2g	
Protein 5g	Fats 11g	
Carbohydrate ...44g	Saturates 7g	

30 mins   1¼ hrs

SERVES 4

INGREDIENTS

4 large baking potatoes

2 tbsp vegetable oil

4 tsp salt

snipped fresh chives, to garnish

TO SERVE

150 ml/5 fl oz soured cream

2 tbsp chopped fresh chives

BEANSPROUT SALAD

55 g/2 oz beansprouts

1 celery stick, sliced

1 orange, peeled and segmented

1 red eating apple, chopped

½ red pepper, deseeded and chopped

1 tbsp chopped fresh parsley

1 tbsp light soy sauce

1 tbsp clear honey

1 small garlic clove, crushed

BEAN FILLING

100 g/3½ oz canned, mixed beans, drained

1 onion, halved and sliced

1 tomato, chopped

2 spring onions, chopped

2 tsp lemon juice

salt and pepper

1 Scrub the potatoes and put on a baking sheet. Prick the potatoes all over with a fork and rub the oil and salt into the skin.

2 Cook in a preheated oven, 200°C/400°F/Gas Mark 6, for 1 hour or until soft.

3 Cut the potatoes in half lengthways and scoop out the flesh, leaving a 1 cm/½ inch thick shell. Reserve the flesh for another dish, if liked. Return the shells, skin side uppermost, to the oven for 10 minutes until crisp.

4 Mix the ingredients for the beansprout salad in a bowl, tossing well in the soy sauce, honey and garlic to coat.

5 Mix all the ingredients for the bean filling together in a separate bowl.

6 In another bowl, mix together the soured cream and chopped chives until well combined.

7 Serve the potato skins hot, with the two salad fillings, garnished with snipped chives, and the soured cream and chive sauce.

Tomato & Cheese Bruschetta

These simple toasts are filled with colour and flavour. They are great as a speedy starter and delicious as a light meal or snack.

NUTRITIONAL INFORMATION

Calories 232	Sugars 4g
Protein 4g	Fat 15g
Carbohydrate . . .20g	Saturates 8g

5–10 mins   10 mins

SERVES 4

INGREDIENTS

4 muffins

4 garlic cloves, crushed

2 tbsp butter

1 tbsp chopped basil

4 large, ripe tomatoes

1 tbsp tomato purée

8 stoned black olives, halved

55 g/2 oz mozzarella cheese, sliced

salt and pepper

fresh basil leaves, to garnish

DRESSING

1 tbsp extra virgin olive oil

2 tsp lemon juice

1 tsp clear honey

1 Cut the muffins in half to give 8 thick pieces. Toast the muffin halves under a hot grill for 2–3 minutes until golden.

2 Beat the garlic, butter and basil together and spread on to each muffin half.

3 Cut a cross shape at the top of each tomato. Plunge the tomatoes into a bowl of boiling water – this will make the skin easier to peel. After a few minutes, pick each tomato up with a fork and peel away the skin. Chop the tomato flesh and mix with the tomato purée and olives. Divide the mixture between the muffins.

4 Mix the dressing ingredients and drizzle over each muffin. Arrange the mozzarella cheese on top and season to taste with salt and pepper.

5 Return the muffins to the grill for 1–2 minutes until the cheese has melted. Serve, garnished with basil leaves.

VARIATION
Use balsamic vinegar instead of the lemon juice for an authentic Italian flavour.

Vegetable-topped Muffins

Roasted vegetables are delicious and attractive. Served on warm muffins with a herb sauce, they are unbeatable.

NUTRITIONAL INFORMATION

Calories	740	Sugars	........27g
Protein	........20g	Fat	.........45g
Carbohydrate	...67g	Saturates	......17g

1¼ hrs   35 mins

SERVES 4

1 red onion, cut into 8 wedges

1 aubergine, halved and sliced

1 yellow pepper, deseeded and sliced

1 courgette, sliced

4 tbsp olive oil

1 tbsp garlic vinegar

2 tbsp vermouth

2 garlic cloves, crushed

1 tbsp chopped fresh thyme

2 tsp light brown sugar

4 muffins, halved

SAUCE

2 tbsp butter

1 tbsp plain flour

150 ml/5 fl oz milk

5 tbsp vegetable stock

85 g/3 oz Cheddar cheese, grated

1 tsp wholegrain mustard

3 tbsp chopped fresh mixed herbs

salt and pepper

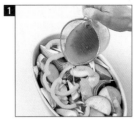

1 Arrange the onion, aubergine, yellow pepper and courgette in a shallow non-metallic dish. Mix together the olive oil, garlic vinegar, vermouth, garlic, thyme and sugar and pour over the vegetables, turning to coat well. Set aside to marinate for 1 hour.

2 Transfer the vegetables to a baking sheet. Roast in a preheated oven, 200°C/400°F/Gas Mark 6, for about 20–25 minutes or until the vegetables have softened.

3 Meanwhile, make the sauce. Melt the butter in a small pan and stir in the flour. Cook for 1 minute, stirring constantly, then remove from the heat. Gradually stir in the milk and stock and

return the pan to the heat. Bring to the boil, stirring constantly until thickened. Stir in the cheese, mustard and mixed herbs and season well.

4 Cut the muffins in half and toast under a preheated grill for 2–3 minutes until golden brown, then transfer to a serving plate. Spoon the roasted vegetables on to the muffins and pour the sauce over the top. Serve immediately.

Carrot & Potato Medley

This is a colourful dish of shredded vegetables in a fresh garlic and honey dressing. It is delicious served with crusty bread to mop up the dressing.

NUTRITIONAL INFORMATION

Calories	81	Sugars	.......4.1g
Protein	.........1g	Fat	..........5.6g
Carbohydrate	....7g	Saturates	.....0.8g

5 mins   5 mins

SERVES 4

I N G R E D I E N T S

2 tbsp olive oil

225 g/8 oz potatoes, cut into thin strips

1 fennel bulb, cut into thin strips

2 carrots, grated

1 red onion, cut into thin strips

chopped chives and fennel fronds
   to garnish

crusty bread, to serve

D R E S S I N G

3 tbsp olive oil

1 tbsp garlic wine vinegar

1 garlic clove, crushed

1 tsp Dijon mustard

2 tsp clear honey

salt and pepper

1 Heat the olive oil in a large, heavy-based frying pan, add the potato and fennel slices and cook over a low heat, stirring occasionally, for 2–3 minutes until beginning to brown. Remove from the pan with a draining spoon and drain on kitchen paper.

2 Arrange the grated carrots, red onion strips and potato and fennel mixture in separate piles on a serving plate.

3 To make the dressing, whisk together the oil, vinegar, garlic, mustard and honey and season to taste with salt and pepper. Pour the dressing over the vegetables. Toss well and sprinkle with chopped chives and fennel fronds. Serve immediately or cool and store in the refrigerator until required. Serve with crusty bread.

VARIATION
Use mixed, grilled peppers or shredded leeks in this dish for variety, or add beansprouts and a segmented orange, if you prefer.

Aubergine Timbale

This is a great way to serve pasta as a starter, wrapped in an aubergine mould. It looks really impressive, yet it is so easy to make.

NUTRITIONAL INFORMATION

Calories	.291	Sugars	.11g
Protein	.8g	Fat	.18g
Carbohydrate	...25g	Saturates	.4g

25 mins   40 mins

SERVES 4

1 large aubergine

55 g/2 oz dried macaroni

1 tbsp vegetable oil

1 onion, chopped

2 garlic cloves, crushed

2 tbsp drained canned sweetcorn

2 tbsp frozen peas, thawed

100 g/3½ oz spinach

4 tbsp grated Cheddar cheese

1 egg, beaten

225 g/8 oz canned, chopped tomatoes

1 tbsp chopped fresh basil

salt and pepper

SAUCE

4 tbsp olive oil

2 tbsp white wine vinegar

2 garlic cloves, crushed

3 tbsp chopped basil

1 tbsp caster sugar

1 Cut the aubergine lengthways into thin strips, using a potato peeler. Place in a bowl of salted boiling water and leave to stand for 3–4 minutes. Drain well.

2 Grease 4 x 150 ml/5 fl oz ramekin dishes and line with the aubergine strips, leaving 2.5 cm/1 inch overlapping.

3 Bring a pan of lightly salted water to the boil. Add the pasta, bring back to the boil and cook for 8–10 minutes until tender, but still firm to the bite. Drain.

4 Heat the oil in a pan and sauté the onion and garlic for 2–3 minutes. Stir in the sweetcorn and peas and remove the pan from the heat.

5 Blanch the spinach, drain well, chop and reserve. Add the pasta to the onion mixture with the cheese, egg,

tomatoes and basil. Season and mix. Half-fill each ramekin with some of the pasta. Place the spinach on top and then the remaining pasta mixture. Fold the aubergine over the pasta filling to cover. Put the ramekins in a roasting tin half-filled with boiling water, cover and cook in a preheated oven, 180°C/350°F/Gas Mark 4, for 20–25 minutes or until set.

6 Meanwhile, heat all the sauce ingredients in a pan. Turn out the ramekins and serve with the sauce.

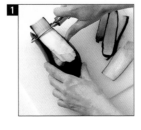

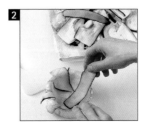

Walnut, Egg & Cheese Pâté

This unusual pâté, flavoured with parsley and dill, can be served with crackers, crusty bread or toast. The pâté requires chilling until set.

NUTRITIONAL INFORMATION

Calories	438	Sugars	.........2g
Protein	........21g	Fat	..........38g
Carbohydrate	....2g	Saturates	......18g

 20 mins   2 mins

SERVES 2

INGREDIENTS

1 celery stick

1–2 spring onions

25 g/1 oz shelled walnuts

1 tbsp chopped fresh parsley

1 tsp chopped fresh dill or ½ tsp dried dill

1 garlic clove, crushed

dash of Worcestershire sauce

115 g/4 oz cottage cheese

55 g/2 oz blue cheese, such as
    Stilton or Danish Blue

1 hard-boiled egg

2 tbsp butter

salt and pepper

fresh herbs, to garnish

crackers, toast or crusty bread and
    crudités, to serve

1 Finely chop the celery, slice the spring onions very thinly and chop the walnuts evenly. Place in a bowl.

2 Add the chopped herbs and garlic and Worcestershire sauce to taste and mix well, then stir the cottage cheese evenly through the mixture.

3 Grate the blue cheese finely into the pâté mixture. Finely chop the hard-boiled egg and stir it into the mixture. Season to taste with salt and pepper.

4 Melt the butter and stir it into the pâté, then spoon into 1 serving dish or 2 individual dishes. Smooth the top, but do not press down firmly. Chill until set.

5 Garnish with fresh herbs and serve with crackers, toast or fresh, crusty bread and a few crudités, if liked.

COOK'S TIP

You can also use this as a stuffing for vegetables. Cut the tops off extra-large tomatoes, scoop out the seeds and fill with the pâté, piling it well up, or spoon into the hollows of celery sticks cut into 5 cm/2 inch pieces.

Thai Fish Cakes

These little fish cakes are very popular as street food in Thailand and also make a perfect starter with a spicy peanut dip.

NUTRITIONAL INFORMATION

Calories	205	Sugars	.........6g
Protein	........17g	Fat	..........12g
Carbohydrate	....7g	Saturates	.......2g

 15 mins   15 mins

SERVES 4–5

350 g/12 oz white fish fillet, such as cod or haddock, skinned

1 tbsp Thai fish sauce

2 tsp Thai red curry paste

1 tbsp lime juice

1 garlic clove, crushed

4 dried kaffir lime leaves, crumbled

1 egg white

3 tbsp chopped fresh coriander

vegetable oil, for frying

green salad leaves, to serve

PEANUT DIP

1 small fresh red chilli

1 tbsp light soy sauce

1 tbsp lime juice

1 tbsp soft light brown sugar

3 tbsp chunky peanut butter

4 tbsp coconut milk

salt and pepper

1 Put the fish fillet in a food processor with the fish sauce, curry paste, lime juice, garlic, lime leaves and egg white, and process until a smooth paste forms.

2 Add the chopped coriander and quickly process again until mixed. Divide the mixture into 8–10 pieces and roll into balls between the palms of your hands, then flatten to make small round patties and set aside.

3 For the dip, halve and deseed the chilli, then chop finely. Place in a small pan with the soy sauce, lime juice, sugar, peanut butter and coconut milk and heat gently, stirring constantly, until thoroughly blended. Adjust the seasoning, adding more lime juice or sugar to taste.

4 Heat the oil in a frying pan and fry the fish cakes in batches for 3–4 minutes on each side until golden brown. Drain on kitchen paper and serve them hot on a bed of green salad leaves with the chilli-flavoured peanut dip.

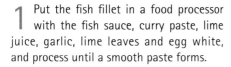

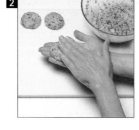

Steamed Crab Cakes

These pretty little steamed and fried crab cakes are usually served as a snack, but you can serve them as a starter instead.

NUTRITIONAL INFORMATION

Calories 156   Sugars 1g
Protein ....13g   Fat 11g
Carbohydrate ....2g   Saturates 4g

25 mins   20 mins

SERVES 4

INGREDIENTS

1–2 banana leaves

2 garlic cloves, crushed

1 tsp finely chopped lemon grass

½ tsp ground black pepper

2 tbsp chopped fresh coriander

3 tbsp creamed coconut

1 tbsp lime juice

200 g/7 oz cooked crab meat, flaked

1 tbsp Thai fish sauce

2 egg whites

1 egg yolk, lightly beaten

8 fresh coriander leaves

sunflower oil, for deep-frying

chilli sauce, to serve

1 Line 8 x 100 ml/3½ fl oz ramekins or foil containers with the banana leaves, cutting them to shape.

2 Mix together the garlic, lemon grass, pepper and coriander. Mash the creamed coconut with the lime juice until smooth. Stir it into the other ingredients with the crab meat and fish sauce.

3 In a clean, dry bowl, whisk the egg whites until stiff, then lightly and evenly fold them into the crab mixture.

4 Spoon the mixture into the ramekins or foil containers lined with banana leaves and press down lightly. Brush the tops with egg yolk and top each with a coriander leaf.

5 Place in a steamer half-filled with boiling water, then cover with a close-fitting lid and steam for 15 minutes,

or until firm to the touch. Pour off the excess liquid and remove from the ramekins or foil containers.

6 Heat the oil to 180°C/350°F or until a cube of bread browns in 30 seconds. Add the crab cakes and deep-fry for about 1 minute, turning them over once, until golden brown. Serve hot with chilli sauce.

Crispy Pork & Peanut Baskets

These tasty little appetite-teasers are an adaptation of a traditional recipe made with a light batter, but filo pastry is just as good.

NUTRITIONAL INFORMATION

Calories 243	Sugars 1g	
Protein 12g	Fat 16g	
Carbohydrate ...12g	Saturates 3g	

 10 mins   15 mins

SERVES 4

INGREDIENTS

2 sheets filo pastry, each about
42 x 28 cm/16½ x 11 inches

2 tbsp vegetable oil

1 garlic clove, crushed

125 g/4½ oz minced pork

1 tsp Thai red curry paste

2 spring onions, finely chopped

3 tbsp crunchy peanut butter

1 tbsp light soy sauce

1 tbsp chopped fresh coriander

salt and pepper

fresh coriander sprigs, to garnish

1 Cut each sheet of filo pastry into 24 squares, 7 cm/ 2¾ inches across, to make a total of 48 squares. Brush each square lightly with oil, and arrange the squares in stacks of 4 in 12 small patty tins, pointing outwards. Press the pastry down into the patty tins.

2 Bake the pastry cases in a preheated oven, 200°C/ 400°F/Gas Mark 6, for 6–8 minutes until golden brown.

3 Meanwhile, heat 1 tablespoon of the oil in a wok. Add the garlic and fry for 30 seconds, then stir in the pork and stir-fry over a high heat for 4–5 minutes until the meat is golden brown.

4 Add the curry paste and spring onions and continue to stir-fry for a further minute, then stir in the peanut butter, soy sauce and chopped coriander. Season to taste with salt and pepper.

5 Spoon the pork mixture into the filo baskets and serve hot, garnished with coriander sprigs.

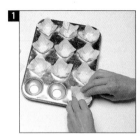

COOK'S TIP

When using filo pastry, remember that it dries out very quickly and becomes brittle and difficult to handle. Work quickly and keep any sheets of pastry you're not using covered with clingfilm and a dampened cloth.

Chicken Balls with Sauce

Serve these bite-size chicken starters warm as a snack,
with drinks or packed cold for a picnic or lunch-box treat.

NUTRITIONAL INFORMATION

Calories	214	Sugars	........29g
Protein	........20g	Fat	..........13g
Carbohydrate	....5g	Saturates	.......2g

10 mins   25 mins

SERVES 4

I N G R E D I E N T S

2 large skinless, boneless chicken breasts

3 tbsp vegetable oil

2 shallots, finely chopped

½ celery stick, finely chopped

1 garlic clove, crushed

2 tbsp light soy sauce

1 small egg

1 bunch of spring onions

salt and pepper

spring onion tassels, to garnish

D I P P I N G   S A U C E

3 tbsp dark soy sauce

1 tbsp rice wine

1 tsp sesame seeds

1 Cut the chicken into 2 cm/³/₄ inch pieces. Heat half of the oil in a frying pan or wok and stir-fry the chicken over a high heat for 2–3 minutes until golden. Remove from the pan or wok with a draining spoon and set aside.

2 Add the shallots, celery and garlic to the pan or wok and stir-fry for 1–2 minutes until softened.

3 Place the chicken, shallots, celery and garlic in a food processor and process until finely minced. Add 1 tablespoon of the light soy sauce and just enough egg to make a fairly firm mixture. Season to taste with salt and pepper.

4 Trim the spring onions and cut into 5 cm/2 inch lengths. Make the dipping sauce by mixing together the dark soy sauce, rice wine and sesame seeds in a small serving bowl and set aside.

5 Shape the chicken mixture into 16–18 walnut-size balls. Heat the remaining oil in the frying pan or wok and stir-fry the chicken balls in small batches for 4–5 minutes until golden brown. As each batch is cooked drain on kitchen paper and keep hot.

6 Add the spring onions to the pan or wok and stir-fry for 1–2 minutes until they begin to soften, then stir in the remaining light soy sauce. Serve with the chicken balls and the bowl of dipping sauce on a platter, garnished with the spring onion tassels.

Warm Tuna Salad

This colourful, refreshing first course is perfect for a special occasion.
The dressing can be made in advance and spooned over just before serving.

NUTRITIONAL INFORMATION

Calories 127   Sugars 4g
Protein ....13g   Fat 5g
Carbohydrate ....6g   Saturates 1g

 15 mins   8 mins

SERVES 4

INGREDIENTS

55 g/2 oz Chinese leaves, shredded

3 tbsp rice wine

2 tbsp Thai fish sauce

1 tbsp finely shredded fresh root ginger

1 garlic clove, finely chopped

½ small fresh red bird-eye chilli,
   finely chopped

2 tsp soft light brown sugar

2 tbsp lime juice

400 g/14 oz fresh tuna steak

sunflower oil, for brushing

125 g/4½ oz cherry tomatoes

chopped fresh mint leaves and fresh mint
   sprigs, to garnish

1 Place a small pile of shredded Chinese leaves on a serving plate. Place the rice wine, fish sauce, ginger, garlic, chilli, brown sugar and 1 tablespoon of the lime juice in a screw-top jar and shake well to combine evenly.

2 Cut the tuna into strips of an even thickness. Sprinkle with the remaining lime juice.

3 Brush a wide frying pan or ridged griddle with the oil and heat until very hot. Arrange the tuna strips in the pan and cook until just firm and light golden, turning them over once. Remove and set aside.

4 Add the tomatoes to the pan and cook over a high heat until lightly browned. Spoon the tuna and tomatoes over the Chinese leaves and spoon over the dressing. Garnish with chopped fresh mint and mint sprigs and serve warm.

COOK'S TIP

You can make a quick version of this dish using canned tuna. Just drain and flake the tuna, omit steps 2 and 3 and continue as in the recipe.

Thai-style Sweetcorn Fritters

These quick, little fritters make a really appetizing first course, served with a spoonful of spicy chilli relish and a squeeze of lime juice.

NUTRITIONAL INFORMATION

Calories 203	Sugars 3g	
Protein 7g	Fat 7g	
Carbohydrate ...29g	Saturates 1g	

15 mins | 30 mins

SERVES 4

INGREDIENTS

55 g/2 oz plain flour

1 large egg

2 tsp Thai green curry paste

5 tbsp coconut milk

400 g/14 oz canned or frozen sweetcorn kernels

4 spring onions

1 tbsp chopped fresh coriander

1 tbsp chopped fresh basil

salt and pepper

vegetable oil, for frying

TO SERVE

lime wedges

chilli relish

1 Place the flour, egg, curry paste, coconut milk and about half the sweetcorn kernels in a food processor and process until a smooth, thick batter forms. Pour into a bowl.

2 Finely chop the spring onions and stir into the batter with the remaining sweetcorn, chopped coriander and basil. Season to taste with salt and pepper.

3 Heat a small amount of oil in a wide, heavy-based frying pan. Drop in tablespoonfuls of the batter and cook for 2–3 minutes until golden brown.

4 Turn them over and cook for a further 2–3 minutes until golden. Fry in batches, making about 12–16 fritters, keeping the cooked fritters hot while you cook the remaining batter.

5 Serve the fritters hot with lime wedges and a chilli relish.

COOK'S TIP

If you prefer to use fresh sweetcorn, strip the kernels from the cobs with a sharp knife, then cook in boiling water for about 4–5 minutes until just tender. Drain well before using as instructed.

Steamed Chicken Parcels

A healthy recipe with a delicate oriental flavour. Use large spinach leaves to wrap around the chicken, but make sure they are young leaves.

NUTRITIONAL INFORMATION

Calories	216	Sugars	.........7g
Protein	........31g	Fat	..........7g
Carbohydrate	....7g	Saturates	......2g

🍲 20 mins   🕐 30 mins

SERVES 4

INGREDIENTS

4 lean skinless boneless chicken breasts

1 tsp ground lemon grass

2 spring onions, finely chopped

250 g/9 oz young carrots

250 g/9 oz young courgettes

2 celery sticks

1 tsp light soy sauce

250 g/9 oz spinach leaves

2 tsp sesame oil

salt and pepper

1 With a sharp knife, make a slit through 1 side of each chicken breast to open out a large pocket.

2 Sprinkle the inside of the pocket with lemon grass and season with salt and pepper to taste. Tuck the spring onions into the chicken pockets.

3 Trim the carrots, courgettes and celery, then cut into small batons. Plunge them into a pan of boiling water for 1 minute, then drain and toss in the soy sauce.

4 Pack the pockets in each chicken breast with the vegetable mixture,

but do not overfill. Fold over firmly to enclose. Reserve the remaining vegetables. Wash and dry the spinach leaves, then wrap the chicken breasts firmly in the leaves to enclose completely. If the leaves are too firm, steam them gently for a few seconds until they are softened and become flexible.

5 Place the wrapped chicken in a steamer and steam over rapidly boiling water for 20–25 minutes until tender and cooked through.

6 Stir-fry any leftover vegetable batons and spinach for 1–2 minutes in the sesame oil and serve with the chicken.

Toasted Nibbles

These tiny cheese balls are rolled in fresh herbs, toasted nuts or paprika to make tasty nibbles for parties, buffets or pre-dinner drinks.

NUTRITIONAL INFORMATION

Calories	310	Sugars	.........1g
Protein	........15g	Fat	..........27g
Carbohydrate	....1g	Saturates	......12g

 40 mins   5 mins

SERVES 4

I N G R E D I E N T S

115 g/4 oz ricotta cheese

115 g/4 oz finely grated Double
   Gloucester cheese

2 tsp chopped fresh parsley

55 g/2 oz chopped mixed nuts

3 tbsp chopped mixed fresh herbs, such as
   parsley, chives, marjoram, lovage
   and chervil

2 tbsp mild paprika

pepper

fresh herb sprigs, to garnish

4 Place the nuts, mixed herbs and paprika into 3 separate small bowls. Remove the cheese balls from the refrigerator and divide into 3 equal piles. Roll 1 quantity of the cheese balls in the nuts, 1 quantity in the herbs and 1 quantity in the paprika.

5 Arrange the coated cheese balls alternately on a large serving platter. Cover and chill in the refrigerator until ready to serve and then garnish with sprigs of fresh herbs.

1 Combine the ricotta and Double Gloucester cheeses. Add the parsley and pepper and work together until thoroughly combined.

2 Form the mixture into small balls and place on a plate. Cover and chill in the refrigerator for about 20 minutes until they are firm.

3 Scatter the chopped nuts on to a baking sheet and place them under a preheated grill until lightly browned. Take care as they can easily burn. Remove from the grill and set aside to cool.

Fiery Salsa

Make this Mexican-style salsa to perk up jaded palates. Its lively flavours really get the taste-buds going. Serve with hot tortilla chips.

NUTRITIONAL INFORMATION

Calories 328	Sugars 2g
Protein 4g	Fat 26g
Carbohydrate ...21g	Saturates 5g

30 mins   0 mins

SERVES 4

INGREDIENTS

2 small fresh red chillies

1 tbsp lime or lemon juice

2 large ripe avocados

5 cm/2 inch piece of cucumber

2 tomatoes, peeled

1 small garlic clove, crushed

dash of Tabasco sauce

salt and pepper

lime or lemon slices, to garnish

tortilla chips, to serve

avocados. Add the flesh to the mixing bowl and mash thoroughly with a fork. The salsa should be slightly chunky. (The lime or lemon juice prevents the avocado from turning brown.)

4 Chop the cucumber and tomatoes finely and add to the avocado mixture with the crushed garlic.

5 Stir in the Tabasco sauce and season with salt and pepper. Transfer the salsa to a serving bowl. Garnish with slices of lime or lemon and the chilli flower.

6 Put the bowl on a large plate, surround with tortilla chips and serve. Do not keep this dip standing for long or it will discolour.

1 Remove and discard the stem and seeds from 1 fresh red chilli. Chop the flesh very finely and place in a large mixing bowl.

2 Use the other red chilli make a 'flower' for the garnish. Using a small, sharp knife, slice the remaining chilli from the stem to the tip several times without removing the stem, so the slices remain attached. Place in a bowl of iced water so that the 'petals' open out.

3 Add the lime or lemon juice to the mixing bowl. Halve, stone and peel the

Mint & Cannellini Bean Dip

This dip is ideal for pre-dinner drinks or for handing around at a party. The cannellini beans require soaking overnight, so prepare in advance.

NUTRITIONAL INFORMATION

Calories 208	Sugars 1g
Protein 10g	Fat 12g
Carbohydrate . . .16g	Saturates 2g

40 mins   30 mins

SERVES 6

INGREDIENTS

175 g/6 oz dried cannellini beans

1 small garlic clove, crushed

1 bunch of spring onions,
    roughly chopped

handful of fresh mint leaves

2 tbsp tahini

2 tbsp olive oil

1 tsp ground cumin

1 tsp ground coriander

lemon juice

salt and pepper

fresh mint sprigs, to garnish

TO SERVE

fresh vegetable crudités, such as
    cauliflower florets, carrots, cucumber,
    radishes and peppers

1 Put the cannellini beans into a bowl and add sufficient cold water to cover. Set aside to soak for at least 4 hours or overnight .

2 Rinse and drain the beans, put them into a large saucepan and cover them with cold water. Bring to the boil and boil rapidly for 10 minutes. Reduce the heat, cover and simmer until tender.

3 Drain the beans thoroughly and transfer them to a bowl or food processor. Add the garlic, spring onions, mint, tahini and olive oil.Process the mixture for about 15 seconds or mash well by hand until smooth.

4 Scrape the mixture into a bowl, if necessary and stir in the cumin, coriander and lemon juice. Season to taste

with salt and pepper. Mix thoroughly, cover with clingfilm and set aside in a cool place, but not the refrigerator, for 30 minutes to allow the flavours to develop fully.

5 Spoon the dip into individual serving bowls and garnish with sprigs of fresh mint. Place the bowls on plates and surround them with vegetable crudités. Serve at room temperature.

Fat Horses

A mixture of meats is flavoured with coconut milk,
fish sauce and coriander in this curious sounding dish.

NUTRITIONAL INFORMATION

Calories 195	Sugars 1g	
Protein 23g	Fat 11g	
Carbohydrate 1g	Saturates 6g	

 10 mins   30 mins

SERVES 4

INGREDIENTS

2 tbsp creamed coconut

115 g/4 oz lean pork

115 g/4 oz skinless, boneless
chicken breast

115 g/4 oz canned crab meat, drained

2 eggs

2 garlic cloves, crushed

4 spring onions, chopped

1 tbsp Thai fish sauce

1 tbsp chopped fresh coriander leaves
and stems

1 tbsp dark muscovado sugar

salt and pepper

TO GARNISH

finely sliced mooli or turnip

fresh chives

fresh red chilli

fresh coriander sprigs

3 Add the coconut mixture to the food
processor or blender with the eggs,
garlic, spring onions, fish sauce, coriander
and sugar. Season to taste and process for
a few more seconds. Alternatively, mix
these ingredients into the chopped pork,
chicken and crab meat.

4 Grease 6 ramekin dishes with a little
butter. Spoon in the minced mixture,
levelling the surface. Place them in a
steamer, then set the steamer over a pan
of gently simmering water. Cook for about
30 minutes until set.

5 Lift out the dishes and set aside to
cool for a few minutes. Run a knife
around the edge of each dish, then invert
on to warmed plates. Serve immediately
garnished with finely sliced mooli or
turnip, fresh chives, red chilli and sprigs of
fresh coriander.

1 Mix the coconut with 3 tablespoons
hot water. Stir to dissolve the coconut.

2 Put the pork, chicken and crab meat
into a food processor or blender and
process for 10–15 seconds until minced or
chop them finely by hand and put in a
mixing bowl.

Aubergine Dipping Platter

Dipping platters are very sociable dishes, bringing together all the diners at the table. They are easy to prepare, too.

NUTRITIONAL INFORMATION

Calories	81	Sugars	.........4g
Protein	.........4g	Fat	...........5g
Carbohydrate	....5g	Saturates	.......1g

 15 mins   10 mins

SERVES 4

I N G R E D I E N T S

1 aubergine, peeled and cut into 2.5 cm/ 1 inch cubes

3 tbsp sesame seeds, roasted in a dry pan over a low heat

1 tsp sesame oil

grated rind and juice of ½ lime

1 small shallot, diced

1 tsp sugar

1 fresh red chilli, deseeded and sliced

115 g/4 oz broccoli florets

2 carrots, cut into batons

8 baby corn cobs, cut in half lengthways

2 celery sticks, cut into batons

1 baby red cabbage, cut into 8 wedges, the leaves of each wedge held together by the core

salt and pepper

1 Cook the diced aubergine in a pan of boiling water for 7–8 minutes. Drain well and set aside to cool slightly.

2 Meanwhile, grind the sesame seeds with the oil in a food processor or in a mortar with a pestle.

3 Add the aubergine, lime rind and juice, shallot, sugar and chilli to the sesame seeds. Season to taste with salt and pepper, then process or chop and mash by hand, until smooth.

4 Adjust the seasoning to taste, then spoon the dip into a bowl.

5 Serve the aubergine dipping platter surrounded by the broccoli, carrots, baby corn, celery and red cabbage.

VARIATION
You can vary the selection of vegetables depending on your preference or whatever you have at hand. Other vegetables you could use are cauliflower florets and cucumber batons.

Chickpeas & Parma Ham

Prosciutto is a cured ham, which is air- and salt-dried for up to 1 year. Parma ham is said to be the best of the many different varieties available.

NUTRITIONAL INFORMATION

Calories 180	Sugars 2g	
Protein 12g	Fat 7g	
Carbohydrate ...18g	Saturates 1g	

 10 mins   15 mins

SERVES 4

INGREDIENTS

1 tbsp olive oil

1 medium onion, thinly sliced

1 garlic clove, chopped

1 small red pepper, deseeded and cut into thin strips

200 g/7 oz Parma ham, diced

400g/14 oz can chickpeas, drained and rinsed

1 tbsp chopped fresh parsley, to garnish

crusty bread, to serve

COOK'S TIP

Whenever possible, use fresh herbs. They are becoming more readily available, especially since the introduction of 'growing' herbs, small pots of herbs which you can buy from the supermarket or greengrocer and grow at home. This ensures the herbs are fresh and also provides a continuous supply.

1 Heat the oil in a frying pan. Add the onion, garlic and pepper and cook over a medium heat, stirring occasionally, for 3–4 minutes or until the vegetables have softened. Add the Parma ham and fry for 5 minutes or until the ham is just beginning to brown.

2 Add the chickpeas to the pan and cook, stirring constantly, for about 2–3 minutes until warmed through.

3 Sprinkle with chopped parsley and transfer to warm serving plates. Serve with lots of fresh crusty bread.

Mixed Bean Pâté

This is a really quick starter to prepare if canned beans are used.
Choose a wide variety of beans for colour and flavour.

NUTRITIONAL INFORMATION

Calories 126   Sugars 3g
Protein ....5g   Fat 6g
Carbohydrate ...13g   Saturates 1g

 45 mins   🕐 0 mins

SERVES 4

INGREDIENTS

400 g/14 oz can mixed beans, drained

2 tbsp olive oil

juice of 1 lemon

2 garlic cloves, crushed

1 tbsp chopped fresh coriander

2 spring onions, chopped

salt and pepper

shredded spring onions, to garnish

1 Rinse the beans thoroughly under cold running water and drain well.

2 Transfer the beans to a food processor or blender and process until smooth. Alternatively, place the beans in a bowl and mash thoroughly by hand with a fork or potato masher.

3 Add the olive oil, lemon juice, garlic, coriander and spring onions and blend until fairly smooth. Season with salt and pepper to taste.

4 Transfer the pâté to a serving bowl, cover and chill in the refrigerator for at least 30 minutes.

5 Garnish with shredded spring onions and serve.

Giant Garlic Prawns

In Spain, giant garlic prawns are cooked in small half-glazed earthenware dishes called cazuelas. The prawns arrive at your table sizzling.

NUTRITIONAL INFORMATION

Calories	385	Sugars	.........0g
Protein	........26g	Fat	..........31g
Carbohydrate	....1g	Saturates	.......5g

 5 mins   5–8 mins

SERVES 4

INGREDIENTS

125 ml/4 fl oz olive oil

4 garlic cloves, finely chopped

2 hot fresh red chillies, deseeded and finely chopped

450 g/1 lb cooked king prawns

2 tbsp chopped fresh flat leaf parsley

salt and pepper

lemon wedges, to garnish

crusty bread, to serve

1 Heat the olive oil in a large, heavy-based frying pan over a low heat. Add the garlic and chillies and cook, stirring occasionally, for 1–2 minutes until softened but not coloured.

2 Add the prawns and stir-fry for 2–3 minutes until heated through and coated in the oil and garlic mixture.

3 Turn off the heat and add the chopped parsley, stirring well to mix. Season to taste with salt and pepper.

4 Divide the prawns and garlic-flavoured oil between warmed serving dishes and serve with lots of crusty bread. Garnish with lemon wedges.

COOK'S TIP

If you can get hold of raw prawns, cook them as above but increase the cooking time to 5–6 minutes until the prawns are cooked through and turn bright pink. If using frozen prawns, make sure they are thoroughly thawed before cooking.

Mussels with Pesto

These delicious morsels make an impressive, yet quick appetiser.
Serve them with some crusty bread to mop up any juices.

NUTRITIONAL INFORMATION

Calories 399	Sugars 1g	
Protein 14g	Fat 31g	
Carbohydrate ...17g	Saturates 5g	

20 mins   12 mins

SERVES 4

INGREDIENTS

900g/2 lb live mussels

6 tbsp chopped fresh basil

2 garlic cloves, crushed

1 tbsp pine kernels, toasted

2 tbsp freshly grated Parmesan cheese

100 ml/3½ fl oz olive oil

115 g/4 oz fresh white breadcrumbs

salt and pepper

TO GARNISH

tomato slices

fresh basil leaves

1 Clean the mussels by scrubbing or scraping the shells and pulling out any beards that are attached to them. Discard any with broken shells or any that refuse to close when tapped. Put the mussels into a large pan with just the water on their shells, cover and cook over a high heat for 3–4 minutes, shaking the pan occasionally, until all the mussels have opened. Discard any mussels that remain closed. Drain, reserving the cooking liquid, and set aside until cool enough to handle.

2 Strain the cooking liquid into a clean pan and simmer until reduced to about 1 tablespoon. Put the liquid into a food processor with the basil, garlic, pine kernels and Parmesan and process until finely chopped. Add the olive oil and breadcrumbs and process until well mixed.

3 Open the mussels and loosen from their shells, discarding the empty half of the shell. Divide the pesto breadcrumbs between the mussels.

4 Cook under a preheated grill until the breadcrumbs are crisp and golden and the mussels are heated through. Serve immediately, garnished with slices of tomato and basil leaves.

VARIATION

If you want an alternative to pine kernels, add 85 g/3 oz roughly chopped, drained sun-dried tomatoes in oil to the pesto instead.

Stuffed Squid

This is a very typical Greek recipe for stuffing squid. Most large supermarkets with fish counters sell baby squid already cleaned.

NUTRITIONAL INFORMATION

Calories	300	Sugars	.........9g
Protein	........12g	Fat	..........18g
Carbohydrate	...19g	Saturates	.......2g

25 mins   1 hr

SERVES 4

INGREDIENTS

12 baby squid, cleaned

4 tbsp olive oil

1 small onion, finely chopped

1 garlic clove, finely chopped

40g /1½ oz basmati rice

1 tbsp seedless raisins

1 tbsp pine kernels, toasted

1 tbsp chopped fresh flat leaf parsley

400 g/14 oz can chopped tomatoes

25 g/1 oz sun-dried tomatoes in oil, drained and finely chopped

125 ml/4 fl oz dry white wine

salt and pepper

crusty bread, to serve

1 Chop off the tentacles from the squid. Chop the tentacles and set aside. Rub the squid tubes inside and out with 1 teaspoon salt and set aside.

2 Heat 1 tablespoon of the olive oil in a frying pan and add the onion and garlic. Cook, stirring occasionally, for 4–5 minutes until softened and lightly browned. Add the tentacles and fry for 2–3 minutes. Add the rice, raisins, pine kernels and parsley and season to taste. Remove the pan from the heat.

3 Allow the rice mixture to cool slightly, then spoon it into the squid tubes, so they are about three-quarters full. Secure each filled squid with a cocktail stick.

4 Heat the remaining oil in a large flameproof casserole. Add the squid and fry for a few minutes on all sides until lightly browned. Add the tomatoes, sun-dried tomatoes, wine and seasoning. Bake in a preheated oven, 180°C/350°F/Gas Mark 4, for 45 minutes. Serve hot or cold with plenty of crusty bread.

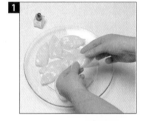  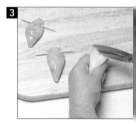

COOK'S TIP

You may need to open the squid tubes a little when stuffing them. Make a small cut with a sharp knife or kitchen scissors. Do not fill the tubes more than three-quarters full to allow the rice to expand.

Smoked Mackerel Pâté

This is a quick and easy pâté with plenty of flavour. It originates from Goa, on the west coast of India, an area famous for its seafood.

NUTRITIONAL INFORMATION

Calories	316	Sugars	3g
Protein	13g	Fat	23g
Carbohydrate	14g	Saturates	8g

4 hrs   5 mins

SERVES 4

INGREDIENTS

200g /7 oz smoked mackerel fillet

1 small, hot fresh green chilli, deseeded and chopped

1 garlic clove, chopped

3 tbsp fresh coriander leaves

150 ml/5 fl oz pint soured cream

1 small red onion, chopped

2 tbsp lime juice

salt and pepper

4 slices white bread, crusts removed

1 Skin and flake the mackerel fillet, removing any small bones. Put the flesh in the bowl of a food processor with the chilli, garlic, coriander and soured cream. Process until smooth.

2 Transfer the mixture to a bowl and mix in the onion and lime juice. Season to taste with salt and pepper. The pâté will seem very soft at this stage, but will firm up in the refrigerator. Cover with clingfilm and chill for several hours or overnight if possible.

3 To make the Melba toasts, place the trimmed bread slices under a preheated medium grill and toast lightly on both sides. Using a long, sharp knife, split the toasts in half horizontally, then

cut each across diagonally to form 4 triangles per slice.

4 Put the triangles, untoasted side up, under the grill and toast until golden and curled at the edges. Serve warm or cold with the smoked mackerel pâté.

COOK'S TIP
This pâté is also very good served with crudités.

Smoked Haddock Salad

Smoked haddock has an affinity with eggs. Here it is teamed with hard-boiled quail's eggs and topped with a creamy chive dressing.

NUTRITIONAL INFORMATION

Calories 366	Sugars 3g	
Protein 26g	Fat 20g	
Carbohydrate ...21g	Saturates 5g	

 40 mins   15 mins

SERVES 4

INGREDIENTS

350 g/12 oz smoked haddock fillet

4 tbsp olive oil

1 tbsp lemon juice

2 tbsp soured cream

1 tbsp hot water

2 tbsp chopped fresh chives, plus extra
  to garnish

1 plum tomato, peeled, deseeded and diced

8 quail's eggs

4 thick slices Granary or multigrain bread

115 g/4 oz mixed salad leaves

salt and pepper

1 Fill a large frying pan with water and bring to the boil. Add the smoked haddock fillet, cover and remove from the heat. Set aside for 10 minutes until the fish is tender. Lift from the poaching water, drain and set aside until cool enough to handle. Flake the flesh, removing any small bones. Discard the poaching water.

2 Whisk together the olive oil, lemon juice, soured cream, hot water and chives and season to taste with salt and pepper. Stir in the tomato. Set aside.

3 Bring a small pan of water to the boil. Carefully lower the quail's eggs into the water. Bring back to the boil and cook the eggs for 3–4 minutes (3 minutes for a slightly soft centre, 4 minutes for a firm centre). Drain immediately and refresh under cold running water until cold. Carefully shell the eggs, cut in half lengthways and set aside.

4 Toast the bread and cut each slice diagonally to form 4 triangles. Arrange 2 halves on each of 4 serving plates. Top with the salad leaves, then the flaked fish and finally the quail's eggs. Spoon over the dressing and garnish with a few extra chives.

COOK'S TIP

When buying smoked haddock, and smoked fish in general, look for undyed fish, which is always superior in quality.

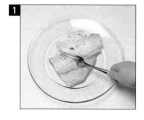

Fish Cakes with Chilli Sauce

If you can find them, use small chillies, called bird-eye, for the dipping sauce. They are very hot, however, so remove the seeds if you prefer.

NUTRITIONAL INFORMATION

Calories	223	Sugars	........23g
Protein	........21g	Fat	...........4g
Carbohydrate	...25g	Saturates	.......1g

 15 mins   10 mins

SERVES 4

I N G R E D I E N T S

450 g/1 lb firm white fish, such as hake, haddock or cod, skinned and roughly chopped

1 tbsp Thai fish sauce

1 tbsp red curry paste

1 kaffir lime leaf, finely shredded

2 tbsp chopped fresh coriander

1 egg

1 tsp brown sugar

40 g/1½ oz green beans, thinly sliced crossways

vegetable oil, for frying

salt

SWEET AND SOUR DIPPING SAUCE

4 tbsp sugar

1 tbsp cold water

3 tbsp white rice vinegar

2 small, hot fresh red chillies, finely chopped

1 tbsp Thai fish sauce

1 For the fish cakes, put the fish, fish sauce, curry paste, lime leaf, coriander, egg, sugar and salt into the bowl of a food processor. Process until smooth. Scrape into a bowl and stir in the green beans. Set aside.

2 To make the sauce, put the sugar, water and vinegar into a small pan and heat gently until the sugar has dissolved. Bring to the boil and simmer for 2 minutes. Remove from the heat, stir in the chillies and fish sauce and set aside.

3 Heat a frying pan with enough oil to cover the bottom generously. Divide the fish mixture into 16 little balls. Flatten the balls into little patties and fry in the hot oil for 1–2 minutes on each side until golden. Drain on kitchen paper. Serve hot with the dipping sauce.

COOK'S TIP

It isn't necessary to use the most expensive cut of white fish in this recipe as the other flavours are very strong. Use whatever is cheapest.

Lime & Basil Cured Salmon

It is very important to use fresh salmon for this dish. The salt and sugar draw the moisture from the fish, leaving it raw but cured.

NUTRITIONAL INFORMATION

Calories 382	Sugars 27g	
Protein 31g	Fat 17g	
Carbohydrate ...27g	Saturates 3g	

24–48 hrs   8 mins

SERVES 4

INGREDIENTS

900 g/2 lb very fresh salmon fillet, from the
head end, skinned

55 g/2 oz sugar

55 g/2 oz sea salt

5 tbsp chopped fresh basil

finely grated rind of 2 limes

1 tsp white peppercorns, lightly crushed

DRESSING

200 ml/7 fl oz rice vinegar

5 tbsp sugar

finely grated rind of 1 lime

½ tsp English mustard

3 tbsp chopped fresh basil

1 tbsp Japanese pickled ginger,
finely shredded

150 g/5½ oz mixed salad leaves, to serve

TO GARNISH

lime wedges

fresh basil leaves

1 Remove any small pin bones that remain in the salmon fillet with tweezers. Wash and pat the fish dry with kitchen paper. Place the salmon in a large non-metallic dish and sprinkle evenly with the sugar, sea salt, basil, lime rind and peppercorns. Cover and chill for 24–48 hours, turning the fish occasionally.

2 For the dressing, put the rice vinegar and sugar in a small pan and stir gently over a low heat until the sugar has dissolved. Bring to the boil and simmer for 5–6 minutes until the liquid is reduced by about one-third. Turn off the heat and stir in the lime rind and mustard. Set aside.

3 Remove the salmon fillet from the marinade, wiping off any excess with kitchen paper. Using a long, sharp knife, slice very thinly.

4 To serve, stir the chopped basil and ginger into the dressing. Toss the salad leaves with a little of the dressing and arrange on 6 serving plates. Divide the salmon slices between the plates and drizzle a little dressing over each. Garnish with lime wedges and basil leaves.

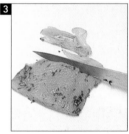

Griddled Smoked Salmon

It is best to buy packets of smoked salmon strips for this recipe because they lend themselves to folding more easily than freshly sliced salmon.

NUTRITIONAL INFORMATION

Calories 232	Sugars 1g	
Protein 23g	Fat 15g	
Carbohydrate 1g	Saturates 2g	

10 mins   6–9 mins

SERVES 4

INGREDIENTS

350 g/12 oz sliced smoked salmon

115 g/4 oz mixed salad leaves

fresh dill sprigs, to garnish

VINAIGRETTE

1 tsp Dijon mustard

1 garlic clove, crushed

2 tsp chopped fresh dill

2 tsp sherry vinegar

4 tbsp olive oil

salt and pepper

1 Take the slices of smoked salmon, 1 at a time, and carefully fold them, making 2 folds accordion style, so that they form little parcels.

2 To make the vinaigrette, whisk the mustard, garlic, dill and sherry vinegar together. Season to taste with salt and pepper. Gradually whisk in the olive oil until thoroughly combined.

3 Heat a ridged griddle pan until smoking. Cook the salmon parcels on 1 side only for 2–3 minutes until heated through and marked from the pan. Cook in batches, if necessary.

4 Meanwhile, toss the salad leaves with some of the vinaigrette and divide them equally between 4 serving plates.

Top with the cooked smoked salmon, cooked side up. Drizzle with the remaining dressing, garnish with fresh dill sprigs and serve immediately.

COOK'S TIP
Smoked salmon is very expensive. This recipe would also work well with smoked trout.

Salmon Tartare

This would make a stunning appetiser for a dinner party, yet it is incredibly easy and speedy to prepare.

NUTRITIONAL INFORMATION

Calories 315	Sugars 2g	
Protein 31g	Fat 20g	
Carbohydrate 2g	Saturates 3g	

 30 mins   🕐 0 mins

SERVES 4

I N G R E D I E N T S

900 g/2 lb very fresh salmon fillet, skinned

3 tbsp lemon juice

3 tbsp lime juice

2 tsp sugar

1 tsp Dijon mustard

1 tbsp chopped fresh dill

1 tbsp chopped fresh basil

2 tbsp olive oil

55 g/2 oz rocket

handful of fresh basil leaves

55 g/2 oz mixed salad leaves

salt and pepper

T O   G A R N I S H

fresh dill sprigs

fresh basil leaves

1 Cut the salmon into very tiny dice and season to taste with salt and pepper. Put into a large bowl.

2 Combine the lemon juice, lime juice, sugar, mustard, dill, chopped basil and olive oil. Pour the mixture over the salmon and mix well. Set aside for 15–20 minutes until the fish becomes opaque.

3 Meanwhile, mix together the rocket, basil leaves and salad leaves. Divide between 4 serving plates.

4 To serve the salmon, fill a small ramekin or mini pudding basin with the mixture and turn out on to the centre of the salad leaves. Garnish with dill sprigs and basil leaves.

VARIATION

Haddock also responds very well to this treatment. Use half the quantity of salmon and an equal weight of very fresh haddock.

Gravadlax

You need two salmon fillets for this dish, approximately the same size. Ask your fishmonger to remove all the bones and scale the fish.

NUTRITIONAL INFORMATION

Calories 608   Sugars 11g
Protein ....37g   Fat 34g
Carbohydrate ...41g   Saturates 14g

48 hrs   0 mins

SERVES 6

I N G R E D I E N T S

2 x 450 g/1 lb salmon fillets,
   with skin on

6 tbsp roughly chopped fresh dill

115 g/4 oz sea salt

55 g/2 oz sugar

1 tbsp white peppercorns, roughly crushed

12 slices brown bread, buttered,
   to serve

G A R N I S H

lemon slices

fresh dill sprigs

1   Wash the salmon fillets and dry with kitchen paper. Put 1 fillet, skin side down, in a non-metallic dish.

2   Combine the dill, sea salt, sugar and peppercorns. Spread this mixture over the first fillet of fish and place the second fillet, skin side up, on top. Put a plate, the same size as the fish, on top and put a weight on the plate (3 or 4 cans of tomatoes or similar will do).

3   Chill in the refrigerator for 2 days, turning the fish about every 12 hours and basting with any juices which have come out of the fish.

4   Remove the salmon from the brine and slice thinly, without slicing the skin, as you would smoked salmon. Cut the brown bread into triangles and serve with the salmon. Garnish with lemon wedges and sprigs of fresh dill.

COOK'S TIP

You can brush the marinade off the salmon before slicing, but the line of green along the edge of the salmon is quite attractive and, of course, full of flavour.

Thai Crab Omelette

Don't be put off by the long list of ingredients. The omelette
is served cold and so can be made entirely ahead of time.

NUTRITIONAL INFORMATION

Calories 262	Sugars 5g
Protein 18g	Fat 19g
Carbohydrate 5g	Saturates 7g

2½ hrs   10 mins

SERVES 4

INGREDIENTS

225 g/8 oz white crab meat, thawed
   if frozen

3 spring onions, finely chopped

1 tbsp chopped fresh coriander

1 tbsp chopped fresh chives

pinch of cayenne pepper

2 tbsp vegetable oil

2 garlic cloves, crushed

1 tsp freshly grated fresh root ginger

1 fresh red chilli, deseeded and
   finely chopped

2 tbsp lime juice

2 lime leaves, shredded

2 tsp sugar

2 tsp Thai fish sauce

3 eggs

4 tbsp coconut cream

1 tsp salt

finely chopped spring onion, to garnish

1 Put the crab meat into a bowl and
   check for any small pieces of shell.
Add the spring onions, coriander, chives
and cayenne and set aside.

2 Heat 1 tablespoon of the vegetable oil
   in a small pan and stir-fry the garlic,

ginger and chilli for 30 seconds. Add the
lime juice, lime leaves, sugar and fish
sauce. Simmer for 3–4 minutes until
reduced. Remove from the heat and set
aside to cool, then add to the crab mixture.

3 Lightly beat the eggs with the
   coconut cream and salt. Heat the
remaining oil n a frying pan over a
medium heat. Add the egg mixture and as
it sets on the bottom, carefully pull the

edges in towards the centre, allowing
unset egg to run underneath.

4 When the egg is nearly set, spoon the
   crab mixture down the centre. Cook
for a further 1–2 minutes to finish cooking
the egg, then turn the omelette out of the
pan on to a serving dish. Set aside to cool,
then chill in the refrigerator for 2–3 hours
or overnight. Cut into 4 pieces and garnish
with spring onion.

A Modern Kedgeree

This is a modern version of the classic dish, using smoked salmon as well as fresh salmon and lots of fresh herbs – perfect for a dinner party.

NUTRITIONAL INFORMATION

Calories . . . . .370 Sugars 3g
Protein . . . . .10g Fat 19g
Carbohydrate . . .39g Saturates 9g

10 mins   35 mins

SERVES 6

INGREDIENTS

2 tbsp butter

1 tbsp olive oil

1 onion, finely chopped

1 garlic clove, finely chopped

175 g/6 oz long grain rice

400 ml/14 fl oz fish stock

175 g/6 oz salmon fillet, skinned
    and chopped

85 g/3 oz smoked salmon, chopped

2 tbsp double cream

2 tbsp chopped fresh dill

3 spring onions, finely chopped

salt and pepper

fresh dill sprigs and lemon slices, to garnish

1 Melt the butter with the oil in a large saucepan. Add the onion and cook over a low heat for 10 minutes until softened, but not coloured. Add the garlic and cook for a further 30 seconds.

2 Add the rice and cook for 2–3 minutes, stirring constantly, until transparent. Add the fish stock and stir well. Bring to the boil, cover and simmer very gently for 10 minutes.

3 Add the salmon fillet and the smoked salmon and stir well, adding a little more stock or water if the mixture seems dry. Cook for a further 6–8 minutes until the fish and rice are tender and all the stock is absorbed.

4 Turn off the heat and stir in the cream, chopped dill and spring onions. Season to taste with salt and pepper and serve immediately, garnished with sprigs of fresh dill and slices of lemon.

COOK'S TIP
Use smoked salmon
trimmings for a budget dish.

Taramasalata with Pitta

Forget the artificially dyed, bright pink taramasalata sold in supermarkets. This is the version you will find in Greek homes.

NUTRITIONAL INFORMATION

Calories	279	Sugars	.........4g
Protein	.........9g	Fat	..........21g
Carbohydrate	...14g	Saturates	.......3g

 20 mins   20 mins

SERVES 6

INGREDIENTS

225 g/8 oz smoked cod's roe

1 small onion, finely chopped

1 garlic clove

55 g/2 oz fresh white bread, rusts removed

finely grated rind of 1 lemon

4 tbsp lemon juice

150 ml/5 fl oz extra virgin olive oil

6 tbsp hot water

salt and pepper

hollowed-out tomatoes, to serve

fresh flat leaf parsley sprigs, to garnish

PITTA WEDGES

2 pitta breads

olive oil, for brushing

1 Remove the skin from the smoked cod's roe. Put the roe and onion in a food processor and process until well blended and smooth. Add the garlic and process again.

2 Break the bread into the food processor, then add the lemon rind and the lemon juice. Process again until the bread is well incorporated.

3 With the motor running, gradually add the olive oil through the feeder tube, as if making a mayonnaise. When all the oil is incorporated, add the hot water and process again. Add salt and pepper to taste, plus extra lemon juice if wished. Spoon into a bowl, cover with clingfilm and chill until ready to serve.

4 To make the pitta wedges, using a serrated knife, cut the pitta breads in half through the centre. Cut each half into 6–8 wedges, depending on the size. Place on a baking sheet and brush the inside surfaces of the wedges with olive oil.

5 Bake in a preheated oven, 180°C/350°F/Gas Mark 4, for 20 minutes. Place on wire racks to cool.

6 Spoon the taramasalata into the tomato shells, garnish with parsley and serve with the pitta wedges for dipping.

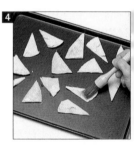

COOK'S TIP

If you see smoked grey mullet roe, buy it for this dish. It is more authentic – and finer tasting – than smoked cod's roe.

Hummus

Quick and easy to make, this dip features regularly on Mediterranean menus. Serve it with fingers of pitta bread or vegetable sticks for dipping.

NUTRITIONAL INFORMATION

Calories	204	Sugars	.........1g
Protein	.........7g	Fat	..........14g
Carbohydrate	...13g	Saturates	.......2g

 13 hrs   1–2 hrs

SERVES 8

INGREDIENTS

200 g/7 oz dried chickpeas

2 large garlic cloves

7 tbsp extra virgin olive oil

2½ tbsp tahini

1 tbsp lemon juice

salt and pepper

fresh coriander

TO SERVE

extra virgin olive oil

paprika

1 Place the chickpeas in a large bowl. Pour in at least twice their volume of cold water and set aside to soak for at least 12 hours until they double in size.

2 Drain the chickpeas. Put them in a large flameproof casserole or saucepan and add twice their volume of water. Bring to the boil and boil vigorously for 10 minutes, skimming the surface.

3 Lower the heat and simmer, skimming the surface from time to time if necessary, for 1–2 hours or until the chickpeas are tender.

4 Meanwhile, cut the garlic cloves in half, remove and discard the pale

green or white cores and coarsely chop the cloves. Set aside.

5 Drain the chickpeas, reserving 4 tablespoons of the cooking liquid. Put the olive oil, garlic, tahini and lemon juice in a food processor and blend to a smooth paste.

6 Add the chickpeas and pulse until they are finely ground, but the

hummus is still lightly textured. Add a little of the reserved cooking liquid if the mixture is too thick. Season with salt and pepper to taste.

7 Scrape the hummus into a bowl, cover with clingfilm and chill in the refrigerator until ready to serve. To serve, drizzle with some extra virgin olive oil, sprinkle a little paprika over and garnish with fresh coriander.

Tzatziki

Simple to make, this creamy Greek dip is very refreshing on a hot day and is particularly good for parties.

NUTRITIONAL INFORMATION

Calories ....75 Sugars 2g
Protein ....4g Fat 6g
Carbohydrate ....2g Saturates 3g

 3½ hrs   3–5 mins

SERVES 12

INGREDIENTS

2 large cucumbers

600 ml/1 pint Greek Strained Yogurt (see page 432) or natural thick yogurt

3 garlic cloves, crushed

1 tbsp finely chopped fresh dill

1 tbsp extra virgin olive oil

salt and pepper

TO GARNISH

1 tbsp sesame seeds

cayenne pepper

fresh dill sprigs (optional)

1 Using the coarse side of a grater, grate the cucumbers into a bowl lined with an absorbent, perforated kitchen cloth. Pull up the corners of the cloth to make a tight bundle and squeeze very hard to extract all the moisture (see Cook's Tip).

2 Put the cucumbers in a bowl and stir in the yogurt, garlic, dill and olive oil and season with salt and pepper to taste. Cover with clingfilm and chill for at least 3 hours for the flavours to blend.

3 When ready to serve, remove the dip from the refrigerator and stir. Taste and adjust the seasoning if necessary.

4 Put the sesame seeds in a small, ungreased frying pan and dry-fry them over a medium heat until they turn golden and start to give off their aroma. Immediately pour them out of the pan on to the tzatziki – they will sizzle.

5 Sprinkle some cayenne pepper on to a plate. Lightly dip the tip of a dry pastry brush into the cayenne, then tap a light sprinkling of cayenne all over the tzatziki. Garnish with fresh dill, if wished, and serve. (Ungarnished tzatziki will keep for up to 3 days in the refrigerator.)

COOK'S TIP

It is essential to squeeze all the moisture out of the cucumbers in Step 1, or the dip will be unpleasantly watery and will separate.

Aubergine Spread

This simple, quick dip is so good that it is often called 'poor man's caviar'. Originally Middle Eastern, it is found throughout the Mediterranean.

NUTRITIONAL INFORMATION

Calories	90	Sugars 2g
Protein	.........1g	Fat 8g
Carbohydrate	....2g	Saturates 1g

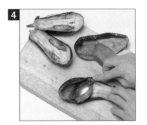

1¼ hrs   20–25 mins

SERVES 6–8

I N G R E D I E N T S

2 large aubergines

1 tomato

1 garlic clove, chopped

4 tbsp extra virgin olive oil

2 tbsp lemon juice

2 tbsp pine kernels, lightly toasted

2 spring onions, finely chopped

salt and pepper

TO GARNISH

ground cumin

2 tbsp finely chopped fresh flat
    leaf parsley

1 Using a fork or metal skewer, pierce the aubergines all over. Place them on a baking sheet in a preheated oven, 230°C/450°F/Gas Mark 8, and roast for 20–25 minutes until they are very soft.

2 Use a folded tea towel to remove the aubergines from the baking sheet and set them aside to cool.

3 Place the tomato in a heatproof bowl, pour boiling water over to cover and leave for 30 seconds. Drain, then plunge into cold water to prevent it from cooking. Peel the tomato, then cut in half and scoop out the seeds with a teaspoon. Finely dice the flesh and set aside.

4 Cut the cooled aubergines in half lengthways. Scoop out the flesh with a spoon and transfer to a food processor. Add the garlic, olive oil, lemon juice and pine kernels and season with salt and pepper to taste. Process until smooth. Alternatively, mash by hand.

5 Scrape the mixture into a bowl and stir in the spring onions and diced tomato. Cover with clingfilm and chill for 30 minutes before serving.

6 Garnish the dip with a pinch of ground cumin and the finely chopped parsley, then serve.

Tapenade

These robust olive and anchovy spreads can be as thick or as thin as you like. They make flavourful appetisers spread on toast.

NUTRITIONAL INFORMATION

Calories	227	Sugars	.........0g
Protein	.........5g	Fat	..........23g
Carbohydrate	....0g	Saturates	.......3g

 10–15 mins   5 mins

SERVES 6

INGREDIENTS

thin slices of day-old baguette (optional)

olive oil (optional)

finely chopped fresh flat leaf parsley sprigs, to garnish

BLACK OLIVE TAPENADE

250 g/9 oz black Niçoise olives in brine, rinsed and stoned

1 large garlic clove

2 tbsp walnut pieces

4 canned anchovy fillets, drained

about 125 ml/4 fl oz extra virgin olive oil

lemon juice, to taste

pepper

GREEN OLIVE TAPENADE

250 g/9 oz green olives in brine, rinsed and stoned

4 canned anchovy fillets, rinsed

4 tbsp blanched almonds

1 tbsp capers in brine or vinegar, rinsed

about 125 ml/4 fl oz extra virgin olive oil

1½–3 tsp finely grated orange rind

pepper

1 To make the black olive tapenade, put the olives, garlic, walnut pieces and anchovies in a food processor and process until blended.

2 With the motor running, slowly add the olive oil through the feeder tube, as if making mayonnaise. Add lemon juice and pepper to taste. Transfer to a bowl, cover with clingfilm and chill until required.

3 To make the green olive tapenade, put the olives, anchovies, almonds and capers in a food processor and process until blended. With the motor running, slowly add the olive oil through the feeder tube, as if making mayonnaise. Add orange rind and pepper to taste. Transfer to a bowl, cover with clingfilm and chill until required.

4 To serve on croûtes, if wished, toast the slices of bread on both sides until crisp. Brush 1 side of each slice with a little olive oil while they are still hot, so the oil is absorbed by the toast.

5 Spread the croûtes with the tapenade of your choice and garnish with parsley.

Ceviche

This no-cook seafood salad is popular throughout the Mediterranean where freshly caught fish and shellfish are plentiful.

NUTRITIONAL INFORMATION

Calories	.201	Sugars	.3g
Protein	.23g	Fat	.11g
Carbohydrate	.4g	Saturates	.2g

2½ hrs   0 mins

SERVES 4

INGREDIENTS

8 fresh scallops

16 large prawns in shells

2 sea bass fillets, about 150 g/5½ oz each, skinned

1 large lemon

1 lime

1 red onion, thinly sliced

½ fresh red chilli, deseeded and finely chopped

2–4 tbsp extra virgin olive oil

TO SERVE

salad leaves

lemon or lime wedges

pepper

1 If the scallops are in shells, use an oyster knife or small knife to prise the shells open, then rinse under running cold water. Cut the scallops and coral free from the shells. Slice the scallop flesh into 2–3 horizontal slices each. Place in a non-metallic bowl with the corals.

2 Remove the heads and peel the prawns. Using a small sharp knife, devein them. Add to the scallops.

3 Cut the sea bass fillet into thin slices across the grain and add to the bowl of seafood.

4 Firmly roll the lemon and lime backwards and forwards on a work surface to help release the juice. Cut the lemon in half and squeeze the juice over the fish. Repeat with the lime.

5 Gently stir to coat the seafood well in the citrus juices, then cover with clingfilm and chill in the refrigerator for 2 hours or until the seafood becomes opaque, but do not leave for longer otherwise the seafood will be too soft.

6 Using a draining spoon, transfer the seafood to another bowl. Add the onion, chilli and olive oil and stir gently. Set aside at room temperature for about 5 minutes.

7 Spoon the seafood on to individual serving plates and serve immediately with salad leaves, lemon or lime wedges and black pepper.

Lemon Risotto

This is a stylish first course, with an aroma and fresh taste that stimulate the taste buds for the meal to follow.

NUTRITIONAL INFORMATION

Calories	442	Sugars	........3g
Protein	.........6g	Fat	..........15g
Carbohydrate	...68g	Saturates	.......6g

 10 mins 35 mins

SERVES 4

INGREDIENTS

2–3 lemons

2 tbsp olive oil

2 shallots, finely chopped

300 g/10½ oz arborio rice

125 ml/4 fl oz dry white vermouth

1 litre/1¾ pints vegetable or chicken stock, simmering

1 tbsp very finely chopped fresh flat leaf parsley

2 tbsp butter

TO GARNISH

thin strips of pared lemon rind

fresh parsley sprigs

TO SERVE

Parmesan cheese shavings, to serve

avocado slices

1 Finely grate the rind from 2 lemons. Roll the rindless lemons backwards and forwards on a board, then squeeze 100 ml/3½ fl oz juice. If you don't have enough, squeeze another lemon. Set the rind and juice aside.

2 Heat the olive oil in a heavy-based pan. Add the shallots and fry, stirring , for about 3 minutes until soft. Add the rice and stir until all the grains are well coated.

3 Stir in the vermouth and cook until it evaporates. Lower the heat to medium–low. Add the lemon juice and a ladleful of simmering stock. Stir, then simmer, stirring occasionally, until all the liquid is absorbed.

4 Add another ladleful of stock and stir, then simmer until absorbed. Continue adding stock in this way, allowing it to be absorbed after each addition, until all the stock has been incorporated and the risotto is creamy.

5 Stir in the lemon rind and parsley. Add the butter, cover, remove from the heat and set aside for 5 minutes. Stir well and then garnish with lemon strips and parsley. Serve with Parmesan cheese and avocado slices.

Broad Beans with Feta

This simple dish captures the heady flavours of the Greek islands and can be served as a salad or as a hot or cold appetizer.

NUTRITIONAL INFORMATION

Calories 140	Sugars 1g
Protein 6g	Fat 10g
Carbohydrate 6g	Saturates 3g

15–90 mins · 5 mins

SERVES 4–6

INGREDIENTS

500 g/1 lb 2 oz shelled broad beans

4 tbsp extra virgin olive oil

1 tbsp lemon juice

1 tbsp finely chopped fresh dill, plus extra to garnish

55 g/2 oz feta cheese, drained and diced

salt and pepper

lemon wedges, to serve

1 Bring a pan of water to the boil. Add the broad beans and cook for about 2 minutes until tender. Drain thoroughly and set aside.

2 When the beans are cool enough to handle, remove and discard the outer skins to reveal the bright green beans underneath. (See Cook's Tip). Put the peeled beans in a serving bowl.

3 Combine the olive oil and lemon juice, then season to taste with salt and pepper. Pour the dressing over the warm beans, add the dill and stir gently. Adjust the seasoning, if necessary.

4 If serving hot, add the feta cheese, toss gently and sprinkle with extra

dill, then serve immediately. Alternatively, set aside the beans in their dressing to cool and then chill until required.

5 To serve cold, remove from the refrigerator 10 minutes before serving to bring to room temperature. Taste and adjust the seasoning, if necessary, then sprinkle with the feta and extra dill. Serve with lemon wedges.

COOK'S TIP

If you are lucky enough to have very young broad beans at the start of the season, it isn't necessary to remove the outer skin.

Aïoli

This garlic mayonnaise features in many traditional Provençal recipes, but also makes a delicious dip, surrounded by a selection of vegetables.

NUTRITIONAL INFORMATION

Calories	239	Sugars	.........0g
Protein	.........1g	Fat	..........26g
Carbohydrate	....1g	Saturates	.......4g

 15 mins   0 mins

SERVES 6

I N G R E D I E N T S

4 large garlic cloves or to taste

2 large egg yolks

300 ml/10 fl oz extra virgin olive oil

1–2 tbsp lemon juice

1 tbsp fresh white breadcrumbs

sea salt and pepper

TO SERVE (OPTIONAL)

a selection of raw vegetables, such as sliced red peppers, courgette slices, whole spring onions and tomato wedges

a selection of blanched and cooled vegetables, such as baby artichoke hearts, cauliflower or broccoli florets or French beans

COOK'S TIP

The amount of garlic in a traditional Provençal aïoli is a matter of personal taste. Local cooks use 2 cloves per person as a rule of thumb, but this version is slightly milder, although still bursting with flavour.

1 Finely chop the garlic on a chopping board. Add a pinch of sea salt to the garlic and use the tip and broad side of a knife to work the garlic and salt into a smooth paste.

2 Transfer the garlic paste to a food processor. Add the egg yolks and process until well blended, scraping down the side of the bowl with a rubber spatula, if necessary.

3 With the motor running, slowly pour in the olive oil in a steady stream

through the feeder tube, processing until a thick mayonnaise forms.

4 Add 1 tablespoon of the lemon juice and the breadcrumbs and process again. Taste and add more lemon juice if necessary. Season to taste with sea salt and pepper.

5 Place the aïoli in a bowl, cover and chill until ready to serve. To serve, place the bowl of aïoli on a large platter and surround with a selection of raw and lightly blanched vegetables.

Skordalia

This thick Greek almond and garlic sauce makes an ideal dip to serve with crudités, grissini or Sesame Breadsticks, as here.

NUTRITIONAL INFORMATION

Calories 304	Sugars 1g	
Protein 5g	Fat 29g	
Carbohydrate 5g	Saturates 4g	

30 mins | 0 mins

SERVES 6

INGREDIENTS

5 g/2 oz day-old bread

50 g/5½ oz almonds

4–6 large garlic cloves, coarsely chopped

50 ml/5 fl oz extra virgin olive oil

2 tbsp white wine vinegar

salt and pepper

fresh coriander or flat leaf parsley sprigs, to garnish

Sesame Breadsticks (see page 473), to serve

1 Cut the crusts off the bread and tear the bread into small pieces. Put in a bowl, pour over enough water to cover and set aside to soak for 10–15 minutes. Squeeze the bread dry, then set aside.

2 To blanch the almonds, put them in a heatproof bowl and pour over just enough boiling water to cover. Leave for 30 seconds, then drain. The skins should slide off easily.

3 Transfer the almonds and garlic to a food processor and process until finely chopped. Add the squeezed bread and process again until well blended.

4 With the motor running, gradually add the olive oil through the feeder

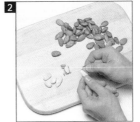

tube in a thin, steady stream until a thick paste forms. Add the vinegar and process again. Season with salt and pepper to taste.

5 Scrape the mixture into a bowl, cover and chill until required. It will keep in the refrigerator for up to 4 days. To serve, garnish with herbs sprigs. Serve with sesame breadsticks.

VARIATIONS

Many versions of this rustic sauce exist. For variety, replace the bread with 4 tablespoons well-drained canned cannellini or broad beans. You can replace the white wine vinegar with freshly squeezed lemon juice.

Wild Rice Blinis

Blinis are small Russian pancakes made with white and buckwheat flours. Wild rice adds more texture and a nutty flavour to a real classic.

NUTRITIONAL INFORMATION

Calories	37	Sugars	.........1g
Protein	.........1g	Fat	...........2g
Carbohydrate	....4g	Saturates	.......1g

 40 mins 🕐 30 mins

SERVES 4–6

I N G R E D I E N T S

butter or vegetable oil, for frying

4 spring onions, thinly sliced diagonally

115 g/4 oz smoked salmon, thinly sliced into strips or shredded

125 ml /4 fl oz soured cream

chopped fresh chives, to garnish

B L I N I S

75 ml/3 fl oz lukewarm water

1½ tsp dried yeast

55 g/2 oz plain flour

70 g/2½ oz buckwheat flour

2 tbsp sugar

½ tsp salt

225 ml/8 fl oz milk

2 eggs, separated

2 tbsp butter, melted

55 g/2 oz cooked wild rice

1 To make the blinis, pour the water into a small bowl and sprinkle the yeast over it. Set aside until the yeast has dissolved and the mixture is beginning to froth.

2 Sift the flours into a large bowl and stir in the sugar and salt. Make a well in the centre. Warm 175 ml/ 6 fl oz of the milk and add to the well with the yeast mixture. Gradually whisk the flour into the liquid to form a smooth batter. Cover the bowl with clingfilm and set aside in a warm place until light and bubbly.

3 Beat the remaining milk with the egg yolks and the melted butter and then beat into the batter.

4 Using an electric mixer, whisk the egg whites until soft peaks form. Fold a spoonful into the batter, then fold in the remaining egg whites and the wild rice alternately. Be careful not to overmix.

5 Heat just enough butter or oil in a large, heavy-based frying pan to coat lightly. Drop tablespoonfuls of the batter into the pan and cook for 1–2 minutes until tiny bubbles form on the surface. Turn and cook for 30 seconds. Remove and keep warm in a low oven while cooking the remaining batter. Add a little more butter or oil if necessary.

6 To serve, top with the spring onions, smoked salmon strips, a spoon of soured cream and a sprinkling of chopped chives.

Vietnamese Rice Paper Wraps

A great idea for a party – just lay out the fillings, with the two dipping sauces, and let guests assemble their own 'wraps'.

NUTRITIONAL INFORMATION

Calories	78	Sugars	.........4g
Protein	.........6g	Fat	..........3g
Carbohydrate	....6g	Saturates	.......1g

30 mins   0 mins

MAKES 20–30 WRAPS

INGREDIENTS

25 g/8 oz salmon fillet, seared

25 g/8 oz tuna steak, seared

25 g/8 oz cooked peeled prawns

avocados, stoned, peeled, sliced and sprinkled with lime juice

–8 asparagus tips, blanched

small red onion, thinly sliced

6 spring onions, sliced

2 black Niçoise olives, sliced

4 cherry tomatoes, halved

5–55 g/1–2 oz fresh coriander leaves

0–30 18 cm/7 inch rice paper wrappers

me wedges

VINEGAR SAUCE

tbsp rice vinegar

tbsp Thai fish sauce

tbsp caster sugar

garlic clove, finely chopped

fresh red chillies, deseeded and sliced

tbsp chopped fresh coriander

SOY DIPPING SAUCE

25 ml/4 fl oz Thai fish sauce

–6 tbsp lime juice

tbsp Japanese soy sauce

–3 tbsp light brown sugar

tbsp finely chopped fresh root ginger

–4 garlic cloves, minced

1. To make the dipping sauces, put the ingredients for each into separate bowls and stir together to blend.

2. Cut the salmon and tuna into 5mm/¼ inch pieces. Arrange them with the prawns, avocados, asparagus, onion, spring onions, olives, tomatoes and coriander leaves on a large serving platter in groups, ready to use as different fillings for the wrappers. Cover loosely with clingfilm and chill until ready to serve.

3. Dip each wrapper very briefly into a bowl of warm water to soften. Lay on clean tea towels to absorb any excess water, then pile on to a serving plate and cover with a damp tea towel.

4. To serve, allow each guest to fill their own wrappers. Offer lime wedges for squeezing over the fillings and pass the dipping sauces separately.

Orange-scented Risotto

This fragrant risotto makes a delicate first course for a special meal.
Serve with a sprinkling of grated Parmesan, if wished.

NUTRITIONAL INFORMATION

Calories	599	Sugars	.........9g
Protein	........10g	Fat	..........22g
Carbohydrate	...95g	Saturates	.......9g

 10 mins   35 mins

SERVES 4

INGREDIENTS

2 tbsp pine kernels

4 tbsp unsalted butter

2 shallots, finely chopped

1 leek, finely shredded

400 g/14 oz arborio or carnaroli rice

2 tbsp orange-flavoured liqueur or dry white vermouth

1.5 litres/2¾ pints chicken or vegetable stock, simmering

grated rind of 1 orange

juice of 2 oranges, strained

3 tbsp snipped fresh chives

salt and pepper

1 Toast the pine kernels in a frying pan over a medium heat for about 3 minutes, stirring and shaking frequently, until golden brown. Set aside.

2 Heat half the butter in a large heavy-based pan over a medium heat. Add the shallots and leek and cook for about 2 minutes until they begin to soften. Add the rice and cook, stirring frequently, for about 2 minutes until the rice is translucent and well coated.

3 Pour in the liqueur or vermouth; it will evaporate almost immediately.

Add a ladleful (about 225 ml/8 fl oz) of the stock and cook, stirring, until absorbed. Continue adding the stock, about half a ladleful at a time, allowing each addition to be absorbed before adding the next – never allow the rice to cook 'dry'.

4 After about 15 minutes, add the orange rind and juice and continue to

cook, adding more stock, until the rice tender, but firm to the bite. The risot should have a creamy consistency.

5 Remove from the heat and stir in th remaining butter and 2 tablespoons the chives. Season to taste with salt a pepper. Spoon into serving dishes ar sprinkle with the toasted pine kernels a the remaining chives.

Black Risotto

This classic recipe gets its name from the squid ink which turns the risotto 'black'. A sophisticated dish, sure to impress.

NUTRITIONAL INFORMATION

Calories	377	Sugars	.........0g
Protein	........16g	Fat	..........12g
Carbohydrate	...52g	Saturates	.......4g

🕐 10 mins   🕐 35 mins

SERVES 6

INGREDIENTS

2–3 tbsp olive oil

450 g/1 lb cleaned squid or cuttlefish, cut crossways into thin strips, rinsed and patted dry

2 tbsp lemon juice

2 tbsp unsalted butter

3–4 garlic cloves, finely chopped

1 tsp crushed dried chilli, or to taste

350 g/12 oz arborio or carnaroli rice

125 ml/4 fl oz dry white wine

1 litre/1¾ pints fish stock, simmering

2 sachets squid or cuttlefish ink

2 tbsp chopped fresh flat leaf parsley

salt and pepper

1 Heat half the olive oil in a large heavy-based frying pan over a medium-high heat. When the oil is very hot, add the squid strips and stir-fry for 2–3 minutes until just cooked. Transfer to a plate and sprinkle with the lemon juice.

2 Heat the remaining olive oil and butter in a large heavy-based pan over a medium heat. Add the garlic and chilli and cook gently for 1 minute. Add the rice and cook, stirring frequently, for 2 minutes until translucent and well coated.

3 Pour in the white wine; it will bubble and steam rapidly. Cook, stirring frequently, until the wine is completely absorbed by the rice. Add a ladleful (about 225 ml/8 fl oz) of the simmering fish stock and cook, stirring constantly, until it is completely absorbed.

4 Continue adding the stock, about half a ladleful at a time, allowing each addition to be absorbed before adding the next – never allow the rice to cook 'dry'.

This should take 20–25 minutes. The risotto should have a creamy consistency and the rice should be tender, but still firm to the bite.

5 Just before adding the last ladleful of stock, add the squid ink to the stock and stir to blend completely. Stir into the risotto with the reserved squid pieces and the chopped flat leaf parsley. Season the risotto with salt and pepper to taste and serve immediately.

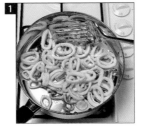

Dolmades

These stuffed vine leaves are popular all over the Middle East, where they are served as part of a meze – a selection of appetisers.

NUTRITIONAL INFORMATION

Calories 111	Sugars 2g
Protein 2g	Fat 4g
Carbohydrate . . .17g	Saturates 2g

1 hr   1hr 20 mins

SERVES 10–12

INGREDIENTS

115 g/4 oz (about 24) large vine leaves, packed in brine, drained

5 tbsp olive oil

1 onion, finely chopped

2 garlic cloves, finely chopped

¾ tsp dried thyme

¾ tsp dried oregano

½ tsp ground cinnamon

200 g/7 oz long grain white rice

350 ml/12 fl oz water

2 tsp raisins

2 tbsp pine kernels, lightly toasted

2 tbsp chopped fresh mint

1 tbsp chopped fresh flat leaf parsley

4 tbsp lemon juice

350 ml/12 fl oz chicken stock

salt and pepper

1 Put the vine leaves in a dish, cover with boiling water and set aside for 2 minutes. Drain, rinse and pat dry. Cut off any thick stems. Place the leaves shiny side down on kitchen paper.

2 Heat 2 tablespoons of the olive oil in a heavy-based pan. Cook the onion for about 3 minutes until soft. Stir in the garlic, dried herbs and cinnamon, then add the rice and cook for about 2 minutes, stirring, until translucent and well coated.

3 Stir in the water and raisins and bring to the boil, stirring twice. Cover and simmer for 15 minutes until the liquid is absorbed and the rice just tender.

4 Fork the rice into a bowl and add the pine kernels, mint, parsley and half the lemon juice. Stir and season with salt and pepper and 1 tablespoon olive oil.

5 Place about 1 tablespoon of the rice mixture on a vine leaf near the stem end and roll the leaf once over the filling.

Fold in each side of the leaf, then finish rolling. Repeat with the remaining leaves.

6 Brush a large casserole with 2 tablespoons oil. Arrange the dolmades in rows, making a second layer if necessary. Sprinkle with the remaining oil and lemon juice. Add the stock to cover the rolls; add extra water if necessary.

7 Weight down the rolls with a heatproof plate, cover tightly and cook over a very low heat for 1 hour. Remove from the heat and allow to cool to room temperature. Drain and serve with a little of the cooking juices, if wished.

Mujadarah

This delicious combination of rice, lentils and caramelised onions is often served as part of a Lebanese meze.

NUTRITIONAL INFORMATION

Calories	458	Sugars	.........7g
Protein	........13g	Fat	..........21g
Carbohydrate	...54g	Saturates	.......3g

10 mins   45 mins

SERVES 6

I N G R E D I E N T S

225 g/8 oz green or brown
  lentils, rinsed

125 ml/4 fl oz olive oil

3 large onions, thinly sliced

200 g/7 oz basmati or long grain white rice

700 ml/1¼ pints chicken or vegetable stock

1 tsp ground allspice

salt and pepper

T O   S E R V E

lemon wedges

spring onions, thinly sliced diagonally

natural yogurt

1 Bring a large saucepan of water to the boil. Gradually pour in the lentils (so the water remains boiling). Reduce the heat to medium-low and simmer, skimming off any foam that rises to the surface, for about 25 minutes until just tender. Drain the lentils and set aside.

2 Meanwhile, heat the oil in a large, deep frying pan over a medium heat until very hot. Add the onions and cook for 4–5 minutes until soft. Using a draining spoon, transfer about two-thirds of the onions to a bowl. Continue cooking the remaining onions until brown and crisp, then drain on kitchen paper.

3 Add the rice to the pan and cook, stirring frequently, for 2 minutes until translucent and well coated. Add the less-cooked onions with the lentils and stock and stir gently, scraping the base of the pan to release any crispy bits. Add the allspice and season with salt and pepper.

4 Tightly cover the pan and cook over a very low heat for about 20 minutes until the rice is tender and all the stock has been absorbed.

5 Fork the rice mixture into a warmed serving bowl. Top with the crispy onions. Serve immediately with the lemon wedges, thinly sliced spring onions and natural yogurt.

Mediterranean Peppers

Serve the peppers with their tops for an attractive finish – blanch the tops with the peppers, then bake separately for the last 10 minutes.

NUTRITIONAL INFORMATION

Calories	366	Sugars	.......24g
Protein	........12g	Fat	..........12g
Carbohydrate	...54g	Saturates	.......4g

 20 mins   1¼ hrs

SERVES 6

6 large peppers, red, yellow and orange

200 g/7 oz long grain white rice

2–3 tbsp olive oil, plus extra for greasing and drizzling

1 large onion

2 celery sticks, chopped

2 garlic cloves, finely chopped

½ tsp ground cinnamon or allspice

85 g/3 oz raisins

4 tbsp pine kernels, lightly toasted

4 ripe plum tomatoes, deseeded and chopped

50 ml/2 fl oz white wine

4 anchovy fillets, chopped

½ bunch of chopped fresh parsley

½ bunch of chopped fresh mint

6 tbsp freshly grated Parmesan cheese

salt and pepper

fresh tomato sauce (see page 7), to serve (optional)

1 Slice off the tops of the peppers, then remove the cores and seeds. Blanch the peppers in boiling water for 2–3 minutes. Carefully remove and drain upside down.

2 Bring a pan of lightly salted water to the boil. Gradually pour in the rice and return to the boil. Simmer for 15–20 minutes until tender, but firm to the bite. Drain and rinse under cold running water. Set aside.

3 Heat the oil in a large frying pan. Add the onion and celery and cook for 2 minutes. Stir in the garlic, cinnamon and raisins and cook for 1 minute. Fork in the rice, then stir in the pine kernels, tomatoes, wine, anchovies, parsley and mint and cook for 4 minutes. Remove from the heat, season with salt and pepper and stir in half the Parmesan.

4 Brush the bottom of an ovenproof dish with a little oil. Arrange the peppers in the dish. Divide the rice mixture equally among them and sprinkle with the remaining Parmesan. Drizzle with a little more oil and pour in enough water to come 1 cm/½ inch up the sides of the peppers. Loosely cover the dish with kitchen foil. Bake in a preheated oven,180°C/350°F/Gas Mark 4, for about 40 minutes. Uncover and cook for a further 10 minutes. Serve hot with tomato sauce, if liked.

Japanese Sushi

These little snacks are made with special seasoned rice and a variety of toppings. Sushi rice is available from Japanese food stores.

NUTRITIONAL INFORMATION

Calories	403	Sugars	6g
Protein	24g	Fat	8g
Carbohydrate	56g	Saturates	1g

1 hr   30 mins

SERVES 4–6

I N G R E D I E N T S

400 g/14 oz sushi rice

480 ml/17 fl oz water

4 tbsp Japanese rice vinegar

1½ tbsp caster sugar

1½ tsp salt

1½ tbsp mirin (Japanese rice wine)

N O R I M A K I   S U S H I

2 eggs

pinch of ground turmeric

1–2 tbsp vegetable oil

4 sheets dried nori seaweed

115 g/4 oz smoked salmon slices, cut into 7.5 cm/3 inch pieces

½ cucumber, lightly peeled, quartered, deseeded, then thinly sliced lengthways

fresh chives

N I G I R I   S U S H I

16 cooked peeled prawns

wasabi paste (Japanese horseradish)

85 g/3 oz smoked salmon fillet, cut into 5 mm/¼ inch slices

sesame seeds, lightly toasted

T O   S E R V E

pickled ginger

Japanese soy sauce

1 Put the rice and water in a pan and bring to the boil. Cover and simmer, for 20 minutes. Set aside for 10 minutes. Bring the vinegar, sugar, salt and mirin to the boil. Pour the mixture evenly over the surface of the rice and blend in, fanning the rice at the same time.

2 For the norimaki sushi, beat the eggs with the turmeric and 1 teaspoon of the oil, then make 2 omelettes, cooking in the remaining oil. Cut in half. Pass the sheets of nori over a flame for a few minutes to toast. Lay a piece of nori, toasted side down, on a sushi mat. Lay an omelette half on top, leaving a border. Spread a thin layer of sushi rice over. Place a piece of smoked salmon on the bottom third of the rice, trimming to fit, and top with cucumber and chives. Moisten the border of the nori with water and roll up. Repeat with the rest and leave to set.. Cut into 2.5 cm/1 inch slices, cover and chill.

3 For the nigiri sushi, using wet hands, shape 2 tablespoons of the rice at a time into ovals. Top with 2 prawns or a dab of wasabi and some smoked salmon. Sprinkle with the sesame seeds. Serve the sushi with the ginger and soy sauce.

Authentic Guacamole

Guacamole is at its best when freshly made, with enough texture to really taste the avocado. Serve with vegetable sticks or tortilla chips.

NUTRITIONAL INFORMATION

Calories 212	Sugars 1g	
Protein 2g	Fat 21g	
Carbohydrate 3g	Saturates 4g	

 15 mins   0 mins

SERVES 4

INGREDIENTS

1 ripe tomato

2 limes

2–3 ripe small to medium avocados, or 1–2 large ones

¼–½ onion, finely chopped

pinch of ground cumin

pinch of mild chilli powder

½–1 fresh green chilli, such as jalapeño or serrano, deseeded and finely chopped

1 tbsp finely chopped fresh coriander leaves, plus extra for garnishing

salt (optional)

tortilla chips, to serve (optional)

1 Place the tomatoes in a heatproof bowl, pour boiling water over to cover and leave for 30 seconds. Drain and plunge into cold water. Peel off the skins. Cut the tomatoes in half, deseed and chop the flesh.

COOK'S TIP

Try spooning guacamole into soups, especially chicken or seafood, or spreading it into sandwiches on thick crusty rolls (tortas). Spoon guacamole over refried beans and melted cheese, then dig into it with salsa and crisp tortilla chips.

2 Squeeze the juice from the limes into a small bowl. Cut 1 avocado in half around the stone. Twist the 2 halves apart in opposite directions, then remove the stone with a knife. Carefully peel off the skin, dice the flesh and toss in the bowl of lime juice to prevent the flesh from discolouring. Repeat with the remaining avocados. Mash the avocados coarsely with a fork.

3 Add the onion, tomato, cumin, chilli powder, chillies and fresh coriander to the avocados. If using as a dip for tortilla chips, do not add salt. If using as a dip for vegetable sticks, add salt to taste.

4 To serve the guacamole, transfer to a serving dish, garnish with finely chopped fresh coriander and serve with tortilla chips.

Veracruz Cocktail

This is a typically colourful Mexican salad dish,
full of spicy flavours and wonderfully succulent seafood.

NUTRITIONAL INFORMATION

Calories 183   Sugars 10g
Protein . . . . .18g   Fat 7g
Carbohydrate . . .13g   Saturates 1g

 50 mins   15 mins

SERVES 6

I N G R E D I E N T S

1 litre/1¾ pints fish stock or water mixed
with 1 fish stock cube

2 bay leaves

1 onion, chopped

3–5 garlic cloves, cut into large chunks

650 g/1 lb 7 oz mixed seafood, such as
prawns in their shells, scallops, squid
rings, pieces of squid tentacles, etc

175 ml/6 fl oz tomato ketchup

50 ml/2 fl oz Mexican hot sauce

generous pinch of ground cumin

6–8 tbsp chopped fresh coriander

4 tbsp lime juice, plus extra for tossing

salt

1 avocado, to garnish

1 Pour the stock in a pan and add the
bay leaves, half the onion and all of
the garlic. Bring to the boil, then simmer
gently for about 10 minutes or until the
onion and garlic are soft and the stock
tastes flavourful.

2 Add the seafood in the order of the
amount of cooking time required.
Most small pieces of shellfish take a very
short time to cook and can be added
together. Cook for 1 minute, then remove

the pan from the heat and set aside so
that the seafood finishes cooking by
standing in the cooling stock.

3 When the stock has cooled, remove
the seafood from it with a draining
spoon. Shell the prawns and any other
shellfish. Reserve the stock.

4 Combine the ketchup, hot sauce and
cumin in a bowl, reserve a quarter of
the sauce mixture for serving. Add the
seafood to the bowl with the remaining
onion, fresh coriander, lime juice and

about 225 ml/8 fl oz of the reserved
cooled fish stock. Stir carefully to mix and
season with salt to taste.

5 Peel and stone the avocado, then dice
or slice the flesh. Toss gently in lime
juice to prevent discoloration.

6 Serve the seafood cocktail in
individual bowls, garnished with the
avocado and topped with a spoonful of
the reserved sauce.

Citrus-marinated Fish

This is one of Mexico's classic dishes: raw fish, cured in a bath of citrus juices, chillies and aromatics. It must be made with the freshest fish.

NUTRITIONAL INFORMATION

Calories	292	Sugars	.........4g
Protein	.........2g	Fat	..........21g
Carbohydrate	....4g	Saturates	.......3g

🧊 5½ hrs   🕐 0 mins

SERVES 4

I N G R E D I E N T S

450 g/1 lb white fish fillets, cut into bite-size chunks

juice of 6–8 limes

2–3 tomatoes, diced

3 fresh green chillies, such as jalapeño or serrano, deseeded and thinly sliced

½ tsp dried oregano

5 tbsp extra virgin olive oil

1 small onion, finely chopped

salt and pepper

2 tbsp chopped fresh coriander

1 Place the fish in a non-metallic dish, add the lime juice and mix well. Marinate in the refrigerator for 5 hours or until the mixture looks opaque. Turn from time to time so that the lime juice permeates the fish.

2 An hour before serving, add the tomatoes, chillies, oregano, olive oil and onion and then season with salt and pepper to taste.

3 About 15 minutes before serving, remove the dish from the refrigerator so that the olive oil comes to room temperature. Serve the dish sprinkled with fresh coriander.

COOK'S TIP

This dish makes an elegant starter served layered with rounds of crisp tortillas, like a stacked tostada.

Salpicon of Crab

This lightly spiced crab salad is a cooling treat for a hot day. Eat it with crisp tortilla chips or wrapped in a tender warm corn tortilla.

NUTRITIONAL INFORMATION

Calories	186	Sugars	.........2g
Protein	........13g	Fat	..........13g
Carbohydrate	....3g	Saturates	.......2g

 15 mins   0 mins

SERVES 4

I N G R E D I E N T S

¼ red onion, chopped

½–1 fresh green chilli, deseeded and chopped

juice of ½ lime

1 tbsp cider or other fruit vinegar, such as raspberry

1 tbsp chopped fresh coriander

1 tbsp extra virgin olive oil

225–350 g/8–12 oz fresh crab meat

lettuce leaves, to serve

TO GARNISH

1 avocado

lime juice, for tossing

1–2 ripe tomatoes

3–5 radishes

1 Combine the onion, chilli, lime juice, vinegar, fresh coriander and olive oil. Add the crab meat and toss the ingredients lightly together.

2 To make the garnish, cut each avocado in half around the stone . Twist the halves apart in opposite directions, then remove the stone with a knife. Carefully peel off the skin and slice the flesh. Toss the avocado gently in lime juice to prevent discoloration.

3 Halve the tomatoes, then remove the cores and seeds. Dice the flesh. Slice the radishes thinly.

4 Arrange the crab salad on a bed of lettuce leaves, garnish with the avocado, tomatoes and radishes and serve the salpicon immediately.

VARIATION

For a toasted crab salad sandwich, split open a baguette and heap on crab salad. Top generously with cheese. Place the open roll under the grill to melt the cheese. Spread the toasted plain side with mayonnaise and close the sandwich. Cut and serve with salsa.

Mexican Pickles

In Mexican cantinas, these pickled vegetables are munched alongside a stack of warm buttered tortillas and washed down with glasses of beer.

NUTRITIONAL INFORMATION

Calories 101	Sugars 7g	
Protein 3g	Fat 6g	
Carbohydrate 8g	Saturates 1g	

 30 mins   8–12 mins

SERVES 6

INGREDIENTS

3 tbsp vegetable oil

1 onion, thinly sliced

5 garlic cloves, cut into slivers

3 carrots, thinly sliced

2 fresh green chillies, such as jalapeño or serrano, deseeded and cut into strips

1 small cauliflower, broken into florets or cut into bite-size chunks

½ red pepper, cored, deseeded and diced or cut into strips

1 celery stick, cut into bite-size pieces

½ tsp oregano leaves

1 bay leaf

¼ tsp ground cumin

5 tbsp cider vinegar

salt and pepper

COOK'S TIP

Wear rubber gloves when slicing and deseeding fresh chillies and do not touch your eyes during preparation.

1 Heat the oil in a heavy-based frying pan and add the onion, garlic, carrots, chillies, cauliflower, red pepper and celery. Cook over a low heat, stirring occasionally, for about 1 minute until just softened, but not browned.

2 Add the oregano, bay leaf, cumin and cider vinegar and season with salt and pepper to taste. Add just enough water to cover the vegetables. Cook for a further 5–10 minutes or just long enough for the vegetables to be tender, but still firm to the bite.

3 Adjust the seasoning, adding more vinegar if needed. Set aside to cool and serve as a relish or with buttered tortillas Mexican style. The Mexican pickles will keep for up to 2 weeks, if stored in a sealed container the refrigerator.

Cheese & Bean Quesadillas

These bite-size rolls are made from flour tortillas filled with a scrumptious mixture of refried beans, melted cheese, coriander and salsa.

NUTRITIONAL INFORMATION

Calories 452	Sugars 11g
Protein 18g	Fat 16g
Carbohydrate ...62g	Saturates 7g

10 mins 10 mins

SERVES 4–6

INGREDIENTS

400g/14 oz can refried beans

8 flour tortillas

200 g/7 oz Cheddar cheese, grated

1 onion, chopped

½ bunch of fresh coriander leaves, chopped

1 quantity Salsa Cruda (see page 447)

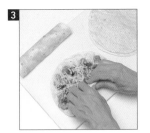

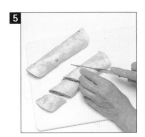

1 Place the beans in a small pan and set over a low heat to warm through.

2 Meanwhile, make the tortillas pliable, by warming them gently in a lightly greased non-stick frying pan.

3 Remove the tortillas from the pan and quickly spread with a layer of warm beans. Top each tortilla with grated cheese, onion, fresh coriander and a spoonful of salsa. Roll up tightly.

4 Just before serving, heat the non-stick frying pan over a medium heat, sprinkling lightly with a couple of drops of water. Add the tortilla rolls, cover the pan and heat through until the cheese melts. Allow to brown lightly, if wished.

5 Remove the tortilla rolls from the pan and slice each roll, on the diagonal, into about 4 bite-size pieces. Serve the quesadillas at once.

COOK'S TIP
Flour tortillas can also be warmed in the microwave, but take care not to heat them for too long as they can become leathery.

Spicy Prawn Wedges

A winning combination of textures and flavours, spiced prawns and creamy avocado are served on crisply fried tortilla wedges.

NUTRITIONAL INFORMATION

Calories	255	Sugars	.........2g
Protein	........15g	Fat	..........13g
Carbohydrate	...22g	Saturates	.......4g

 4¼ hrs   ⏱ 12–15 mins

SERVES 8–10

I N G R E D I E N T S

500 g /1 2 oz lb cooked prawns

4 garlic cloves, finely chopped

½ tsp mild chilli powder

½ tsp ground cumin

juice of 1 lime

1 ripe tomato, diced

salt

6 corn tortillas

vegetable oil, for frying

2 avocados

200 ml/7 fl oz soured cream

mild chilli powder, to garnish

1 Place the prawns in a bowl with the garlic, chilli powder, cumin, lime juice and tomato. Add salt to taste and stir gently to mix. Chill for at least 4 hours or overnight to allow the flavours to mingle.

2 Cut the tortillas into wedges. Heat a little oil in a non-stick frying pan, add a batch of tortilla wedges and fry over a medium heat until crisp. Repeat with the remaining wedges and transfer to a serving platter.

3 Cut each avocado in half around the stone. Twist the halves apart in opposite directions, then remove the stone with a knife. Carefully peel off the skin and dice the flesh. Gently stir the avocado into the prawn mixture.

4 Top each tortilla wedge with a small mound of the prawn and avocado mixture. Finish with a dab of soured cream, garnish with a light sprinkling of chilli powder and serve immediately while hot and crisp.

COOK'S TIP

For speed, you can use crisp corn tortillas or nacho chips (not too salty) instead of the corn tortillas.

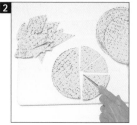

Black Bean Nachos

Packed with authentic Mexican flavours, this tasty black bean and cheese dip is fun to eat and will get any meal off to a good start!

NUTRITIONAL INFORMATION

Calories 429	Sugars 2g	
Protein 28g	Fat 24g	
Carbohydrate ...25g	Saturates 15g	

8¼ hrs   1¾ hrs

SERVES 4

INGREDIENTS

225 g/8 oz dried black beans, or canned black beans, drained and rinsed

175–225 g/6–8 oz grated cheese, such as Cheddar, Fontina, pecorino, asiago or a combination

about ¼ tsp cumin seeds or ground cumin

about 4 tbsp soured cream

thinly sliced pickled jalapeños (optional)

1 tbsp chopped fresh coriander

handful of shredded lettuce

tortilla chips, to serve

1 If using dried black beans, place them in a bowl and add water to cover. Set aside to soak overnight, then drain. Put in a pan, cover with water and bring to the boil. Boil for 10 minutes, then reduce the heat and simmer for about 1½ hours until tender. Drain well.

2 Spread the cooked or canned beans in the base of a shallow ovenproof dish, then sprinkle the cheese over the top. Sprinkle with cumin to taste.

3 Bake in a preheated oven, 190°C/ 375°F/Gas Mark 5, for 10–15 minutes or until the beans are cooked through and the cheese is bubbling and melted.

4 Remove the beans and cheese from the oven and spoon the soured cream on top. Add the jalapeños, if using, and sprinkle with fresh coriander and lettuce.

5 Arrange the tortilla chips around the beans, sticking them into the mixture. Serve the nachos at once.

VARIATION

To add a meaty flavour, spoon chopped and browned chorizo on top of the beans, before sprinkling over the cheese, and cook as in Step 3 – the combination is excellent. Finely chopped leftover cooked meat can also be added in this way.

Refried Bean Nachos

A Mexican classic, refried beans and tortilla crisps are
topped with luscious melted cheese, salsa and assorted toppings.

NUTRITIONAL INFORMATION

Calories	287	Sugars	.........2g
Protein	........15g	Fat	..........15g
Carbohydrate	...22g	Saturates	.......7g

 15 mins   15 mins

SERVES 6–8

I N G R E D I E N T S

400 g/14 oz can refried beans

400 g/14 oz can pinto beans, drained

large pinch of ground cumin

large pinch of mild chilli powder

175 g/6 oz tortilla chips

225 g/8 oz grated cheese, such as Cheddar

salsa of your choice

1 avocado, stoned, diced and tossed with
   lime juice

½ small onion or 3–5 spring
   onions, chopped

2 ripe tomatoes, diced

handful of shredded lettuce

3–4 tbsp chopped fresh coriander

soured cream, to serve

VARIATION
Replace the soured cream with
Greek-style yogurt as an alternative.

1 Place the refried beans in a pan with the pinto beans, cumin and chilli powder. Add enough water to make a thick soup-like consistency, stirring gently so that the beans do not lose their texture.

2 Heat the bean mixture over a medium heat until hot, then reduce the heat and keep the mixture warm while you prepare the rest of the dish.

3 Arrange half the tortilla chips in the bottom of a flameproof casserole or gratin dish and cover with the bean mixture. Sprinkle with the cheese and bake in a preheated oven, 200°C/400°F/Gas Mark 6, until the cheese melts.

4 Alternatively, place the casserole under a preheated grill and grill for 5–7 minutes or until the cheese melts and lightly sizzles in places.

5 Arrange the salsa, avocado, onion, tomato, lettuce and fresh coriander on top of the melted cheese. Surround with the remaining tortilla chips and serve immediately with with soured cream.

Masa Tartlets

Packed with Mexican flavours, these little golden tartlets make a colourful start to a meal.

NUTRITIONAL INFORMATION

Calories	474	Sugars	.........4g
Protein	........11g	Fat	..........23g
Carbohydrate	...58g	Saturates	.......8g

 35 mins 30 mins

SERVES 4

INGREDIENTS

-10 tbsp masa harina

tbsp plain flour

nch of baking powder

bout 225 ml/8 fl oz warm water

egetable oil, for frying

25 g/8 oz pinto beans or refried beans, heated through

avocado, stoned, sliced and tossed with lime juice

5 g/3 oz queso fresco or fresh cream cheese or crumbled feta

alsa of your choice

spring onions, thinly sliced

TO GARNISH

esh flat leaf parsley sprigs

mon wedges

1 Mix the masa harina with the plain flour and baking powder in a bowl, then mix in enough warm water to make a firm yet moist dough.

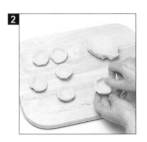

2 Pinch off about a walnut-size piece of dough and, using your fingers, shape into a tiny tartlet shape, pressing and pinching to make it as thin as possible without falling apart. Repeat with the remaining dough.

3 Heat a layer of oil in a deep frying pan until it is smoking. Add a batch of tartlets to the hot oil and fry, spooning the hot fat into the centre of the tartlets and turning once, until golden on all sides.

4 Using a draining spoon, remove the tartlets from the hot oil and drain on kitchen paper towels. Place on a baking sheet and keep warm in the oven on a low temperature, while cooking the remaining tartlets.

5 To serve, fill each tartlet shell with the warmed beans, avocado, cheese, salsa and spring onions. Garnish with parsley and lemon wedges and serve immediately.

Garlic Chive & Coriander Dip

Creamy dips can undo all the benefits of eating raw vegetables. This is the perfect solution – all the richness and flavour, but none of the fat.

NUTRITIONAL INFORMATION

Calories	67	Sugars 8g
Protein	........7g	Fat 1g
Carbohydrate	....9g	Saturates 0g

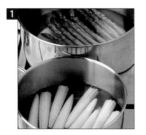

10 mins 2 mins

SERVES 4

INGREDIENTS

CRUDITES

115 g/4 oz baby corn cobs

115 g/4 oz young asparagus spears or sprue, trimmed

1 head of chicory, leaves separated

1 red pepper, deseeded and sliced

1 orange pepper, deseeded and sliced

8 radishes, trimmed

DIP

1 tbsp hot water

1 tsp saffron threads

225 g/8 oz fat-free fromage frais

3 tbsp chopped fresh coriander

1 tbsp snipped fresh garlic chives

salt and pepper

fresh coriander sprigs, to garnish

COOK'S TIP

The fat content of fromage frais ranges between 0 and 8 per cent. This is reflected in the consistency. Fat-free fromage frais is great for dips because it is soft and easily mixed with other ingredients.

1 Blanch the corn and asparagus in separate saucepans of boiling water for 2 minutes. Drain, plunge into iced water and drain again. Arrange all the vegetables on a serving platter and cover with a damp tea towel.

2 For the dip, put the water in a small bowl. Lightly crush the saffron threads between your fingers and add to the bowl, then leave to stand for 3–4 minutes, or until the water is a ri golden colour.

3 Put the fromage frais into a separa bowl and beat until smooth, then be in the infused saffron water. Stir in th chopped coriander and snipped chives a season to taste with salt and peppe Transfer to a serving bowl and garnish wi a few sprigs of fresh coriander. Ser immediately with the prepared vegetable

Tuna & Anchovy Pâté

An excellent tangy combination which can be used for a sandwich filling or as a dip. The pâté will keep well in the refrigerator for up to a week.

NUTRITIONAL INFORMATION

Calories	183	Sugars	.........3g
Protein	........25g	Fat	...........6g
Carbohydrate	....9g	Saturates	......2g

🍰 1¼ hrs   🕐 25 mins

SERVES 6

I N G R E D I E N T S

P A T E

50 g/1¾ oz can anchovy fillets, drained

about 400 g/14 oz canned tuna fish in brine, drained

175 g/6 oz low-fat cottage cheese

125 g/4½ oz skimmed milk soft cheese

1 tbsp horseradish relish

½ tsp grated orange rind

white pepper

M E L B A   C R O U T O N S

4 slices, thick sliced wholemeal bread

T O   G A R N I S H

orange slices

fresh dill sprigs

1 To make the pâté, separate the anchovy fillets and pat well with kitchen paper to remove all traces of oil.

2 Place the anchovy fillets and all the remaining pâté ingredients into a blender or food processor. Process for a few seconds until smooth. Alternatively, finely chop the anchovy fillets and flake the tuna, then beat together with the remaining ingredients; this will make a more textured pâté.

3 Transfer to a mixing bowl, cover and chill for 1 hour.

4 To make the melba croûtons, place the bread slices under a preheated medium grill for 2–3 minutes on each side until lightly browned.

5 Using a serrated knife, slice off the crusts and slide the knife between the toasted edges of the bread.

6 Stamp out circles using a 5 cm/2 inch round cutter and place on a baking sheet. Alternatively, cut each piece of toast in half diagonally. Bake in a preheated oven,150°C/300°F/Gas Mark 2, for 15–20 minutes until curled and dry.

7 Spoon the pâté on to serving plates and garnish with orange slices and fresh dill sprigs. Serve with the freshly baked melba croûtons.

Spinach Cheese Moulds

These flavour-packed little moulds are a perfect starter or a tasty light lunch. Serve them with warm pitta bread.

NUTRITIONAL INFORMATION

Calories	119	Sugars	.........2g
Protein	.........6g	Fat	...........9g
Carbohydrate	....2g	Saturates	.......6g

1¼ hrs   50 mins

SERVES 4

INGREDIENTS

100 g/3½ oz fresh spinach leaves

300 g/10½ oz skimmed milk soft cheese

2 garlic cloves, crushed

fresh parsley, tarragon and chive sprigs, finely chopped

salt and pepper

TO SERVE

mixed salad leaves and fresh herbs

warm pitta bread

1 Trim the stalks from the spinach leaves and rinse the leaves under cold running water. Pack the leaves into a saucepan while they are still wet, cover and cook over a medium heat for about 3–4 minutes until wilted – they will cook in the steam from the wet leaves (do not overcook). Drain well and pat dry with absorbent kitchen paper.

2 Line the bases of 4 small pudding basins or individual ramekin dishes with baking paper. Line the basins or ramekins with the spinach leaves so that the leaves overhang the edges.

3 Place the cheese in a bowl and add the garlic and herbs. Mix together thoroughly and season to taste.

4 Spoon the cheese and herb mixture into the basins or ramekins and pull over the overlapping spinach to cover the cheese or lay extra leaves to cover the top. Place a greaseproof paper disc on top of each dish and weigh down with a 100 g/ 3½ oz weight. Chill in the refrigerator for 1 hour.

5 Remove the weights and peel off the greaseproof paper. Loosen the moulds gently by running a small palette knife around the edges of each dish and turn them out on to individual serving plates. Serve the moulds immediately with a mixture of salad leaves and fresh herbs and warm pitta bread.

Aubergine Salad

This tasty Middle Eastern-style salad, with tomatoes and chickpeas, is perfect to serve with lamb or chicken dishes.

NUTRITIONAL INFORMATION

Calories 206	Sugars 11g
Protein 10g	Fat 7g
Carbohydrate ... 28g	Saturates 1g

2½ hrs   25 mins

SERVES 4

INGREDIENTS

500 g/1 lb 2 oz aubergines

4 tbsp salt

1 tbsp olive oil

1 large onion, chopped

1 garlic clove, crushed

150 ml/5 fl oz vegetable stock

400 g/14 oz can chopped tomatoes

2 tbsp tomato purée

1 tsp ground cinnamon

2 tsp caster sugar

1 tbsp chopped fresh coriander

1 tbsp lemon juice

425 g/15 oz can chickpeas, drained

pepper

fresh coriander sprigs to garnish

TO SERVE

warm pitta bread

lemon wedges

1 Cut the aubergines into 1 cm/½ inch thick slices and then dice. Layer them in a bowl, sprinkling well with salt as you go. Set aside for 30 minutes for the bitter juices to drain out.

2 Transfer to a colander and rinse well under cold running water to remove the salt. Drain thoroughly and pat dry with kitchen paper.

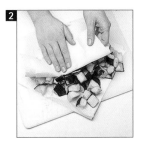

3 Heat the oil in a large non-stick frying pan, add the onion and garlic and fry over a low heat, stirring occasionally, for 2–3 minutes until slightly softened.

4 Pour in the stock and bring to the boil. Add the aubergines, canned tomatoes, tomato purée, cinnamon, sugar and pepper. Mix well and simmer gently, uncovered, for 20 minutes until softened. Remove from the heat and set aside to cool completely.

5 Stir in the fresh coriander, lemon juice and chickpeas, cover and chill for 1 hour.

6 Garnish with coriander sprigs and serve with warmed pitta bread and lemon wedges.

Green Bean & Carrot Salad

This colourful, summery salad of crisp vegetables is tossed in a delicious sun-dried tomato dressing.

NUTRITIONAL INFORMATION

Calories 104   Sugars 9g
Protein . . . . .2g   Fat 6g
Carbohydrate . . .10g   Saturates 1g

 10 mins   5 mins

SERVES 4

INGREDIENTS

350 g/12 oz green beans

225 g/8 oz carrots

1 red onion

1 red pepper

DRESSING

2 tbsp extra virgin olive oil

1 tbsp red wine vinegar

2 tsp sun-dried tomato paste

¼ tsp caster sugar

salt and pepper

1 Trim the green beans and blanch them in boiling water for 4 minutes until just tender. Drain the beans and rinse them under cold water until they are cool. Drain again thoroughly.

2 Transfer the drained beans to a large salad bowl.

3 Peel the carrots and cut them into thin matchsticks, using a mandoline if you have one.

4 Peel the red onion and cut it into thin slices.

5 Halve and deseed the red pepper and cut the flesh into thin strips.

6 Add the carrot, pepper and onion to the beans and toss to mix.

7 To make the dressing, place the oil, wine vinegar, sun-dried tomato paste and sugar in a small screw-top jar and season to taste with salt and pepper. Shake vigorously to mix.

8 Pour the dressing over the vegetables and serve immediately or chill in the refrigerator until required.

COOK'S TIP

Use canned beans if fresh ones are unavailable. Rinse off the salty canning liquid and drain well. There is no need to blanch canned beans.

Mixed Leaf Salad

Make this green leafy salad with as many varieties of salad leaves and edible flowers as you can find to give an unusual effect.

NUTRITIONAL INFORMATION

Calories 51	Sugars 0.1g
Protein 0.1g	Fat 6g
Carbohydrate 1g	Saturates 1g

  5 mins   0 mins

SERVES 4

I N G R E D I E N T S

½ head frisée

½ head oakleaf lettuce or quattro stagione

few leaves of radicchio

1 head chicory)

25 g/1 oz rocket leaves

few fresh basil or flat leaf parsley sprigs

edible flowers, to garnish (optional)

F R E N C H   D R E S S I N G

1 tbsp white wine vinegar

pinch of sugar

½ tsp Dijon mustard

3 tbsp extra virgin olive oil

salt and pepper

1 Tear the frisée, oakleaf lettuce and radicchio into pieces. Place the salad leaves in a large serving bowl or individual bowls if you prefer.

2 Cut the chicory into diagonal slices and add to the bowl with the rocket leaves, basil or parsley.

3 To make the dressing, beat the vinegar, sugar and mustard in a small bowl until the sugar has dissolved. Gradually beat in the olive oil until creamy and thoroughly mixed. Season to taste with salt and pepper.

4 Pour the dressing over the salad and toss thoroughly. Sprinkle a mixture of edible flowers over the top and serve.

COOK'S TIP

Violas, rock geraniums, nasturtiums, chive flowers and pot marigolds add vibrant colours and a sweet flavour to any salad. Use it as a centrepiece at a dinner party, or to liven up a simple everyday meal.

Spinach & Orange Salad

This is a refreshing and very nutritious salad. Add the dressing just before serving so that the leaves do not become soggy.

NUTRITIONAL INFORMATION

Calories 126	Sugars 10g	
Protein 3g	Fat 9g	
Carbohydrate ...10g	Saturates 1g	

 10 mins   🕐 0 mins

SERVES 4

INGREDIENTS

225 g/8 oz baby spinach leaves

2 large oranges

½ red onion, chopped

DRESSING

3 tbsp extra virgin olive oil

2 tbsp freshly squeezed orange juice

2 tsp lemon juice

1 tsp clear honey

½ tsp wholegrain mustard

salt and pepper

1 Wash the spinach leaves under cold running water and then dry them thoroughly on absorbent kitchen paper. Remove any tough stalks and tear the larger leaves into smaller pieces.

2 Slice the top and bottom off each orange with a sharp knife, then remove the peel and pith. Carefully slice between the membranes of the orange to remove the segments. Reserve any juices for the salad dressing. (Working over a small bowl may be the easiest way of doing this.)

3 Mix together the spinach leaves and orange segments and arrange them in a serving dish. Scatter the chopped onion over the salad.

4 To make the dressing, whisk together the olive oil, orange juice, lemon juice, honey, mustard in a small bowl. Season to taste with salt and pepper.

5 Pour the dressing over the salad just before serving. Toss the salad well to coat the leaves with the dressing.

VARIATION

Use a mixture of spinach and watercress leaves, if you prefer a slightly more peppery flavour.

Three-bean Salad

Fresh thin green beans are combined with soya beans and red kidney beans in a chive and tomato dressing to make a tasty salad.

NUTRITIONAL INFORMATION

Calories	276	Sugars 7g
Protein	........18g	Fat 15g
Carbohydrate	...18g	Saturates 4g

10 mins   5 mins

SERVES 6

I N G R E D I E N T S

3 tbsp olive oil

1 tbsp lemon juice

1 tbsp tomato purée

1 tbsp light malt vinegar

1 tbsp snipped fresh chives, plus extra
to garnish

175g/6 oz thin green beans

400 g/14 oz can soya beans, rinsed
and drained

400 g/14 oz can red kidney beans, rinsed
and drained

2 tomatoes, chopped

4 spring onions, trimmed and chopped

125 g/4½ oz feta cheese, cut into cubes

salt and pepper

mixed salad leaves, to serve

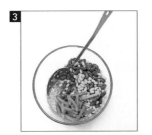

1 Put the olive oil, lemon juice, tomato purée, light malt vinegar and snipped fresh chives into a large bowl and mix thoroughly. Set aside until required.

2 Cook the thin green beans in a small pan of , lightly salted boiling water for 4–5 minutes. Drain, refresh under cold water to prevent any further cooking and drain well again. Pat dry with absorbent kitchen paper.

3 Add all the beans to the dressing, stirring well to mix.

4 Add the tomatoes, spring onions and feta cheese to the bean mixture, tossing gently to coat in the dressing. Season to taste with salt and pepper.

5 Arrange the salad leaves on serving plates. Pile the bean salad on top, garnish with extra chives and serve.

COOK'S TIP
For a more substantial light meal, top the salad with 2–3 sliced hard-boiled eggs and serve with crusty bread to mop up the juices.

Smoked Trout & Apple Salad

Smoked trout and horseradish are natural partners, but with apple and watercress this makes a wonderful first course.

NUTRITIONAL INFORMATION

Calories 133	Sugars 11g
Protein 12g	Fat 5g
Carbohydrate 11g	Saturates 1g

 10 mins　　🕐 0 mins

SERVES 4

INGREDIENTS

2 orange-red eating apples

2 tbsp French Dressing (see page 309)

½ bunch watercress

1 smoked trout, about 175 g/6 oz

melba toast, to serve

HORSERADISH DRESSING

125 ml/4 fl oz low-fat natural yogurt

½–1 tsp lemon juice

1 tbsp horseradish sauce

milk (optional)

salt and pepper

TO GARNISH

1 tbsp snipped chives

chive flowers (optional)

1 Leaving the skin on, cut the apples into quarters and remove the cores. Slice the apples into a bowl and toss in the French dressing to prevent them from turning brown.

2 Break the watercress into sprigs and arrange on 4 serving plates.

3 Skin the trout and take out the bone. Carefully remove any fine bones that remain, with your fingers or using tweezers. Flake the trout into fairly large pieces and arrange between the watercress with the apple.

4 To make the horseradish dressing whisk all the ingredients together adding a little milk if too thick, then drizzle over the trout. Sprinkle the chopped chives and flowers (if using) over the trout and serve with melba toast.

COOK'S TIP

To make Melba toast, toast thinly sliced bread, then cut off the crusts and carefully slice in half horizontally using a sharp knife. Cut in half diagonally and place toasted side down in a warm oven for 15–20 minutes until the edges start to curl and the toast is crisp.

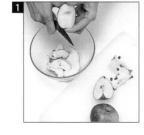

Potato Salad

You can use left-over cold potatoes, cut into bite-size pieces, for this salad, but tiny new potatoes are best for maximum flavour.

NUTRITIONAL INFORMATION

Calories	275	Sugars 8g
Protein	.........5g	Fat 13g
Carbohydrate	...38g	Saturates 2g

 20 mins 20 mins

SERVES 4

INGREDIENTS

700 g/1 lb 9 oz tiny new potatoes

3 spring onions

1 hard-boiled egg (optional)

250 ml/9 fl oz low-fat mayonnaise

1 tsp paprika

salt and pepper

TO GARNISH

2 tbsp snipped chives

pinch of paprika

1 Bring a large pan of lightly salted water to the boil. Add the potatoes and cook for 10–15 minutes or until they are just tender.

2 Drain the potatoes in a colander and rinse them under cold running water until they are completely cold. Drain them again thoroughly. Transfer to a mixing bowl and set aside until required.

3 Trim and slice the spring onions thinly on the diagonal.

4 Shell and chop the hard-boiled egg (if using).

5 Mix together the mayonnaise, paprika and salt and pepper to taste in a bowl until well blended. Pour the mixture over the potatoes.

6 Add the sliced spring onions and chopped egg, if using, and toss together gently.

7 Transfer the potato salad to a serving bowl, sprinkle with snipped chives and a pinch of paprika. Cover and chill in the refrigerator until required.

COOK'S TIP

To make a lighter dressing, use a mixture of half mayonnaise and half natural yogurt.

Hot Potato & Ham Salad

With potatoes as a base you can vary the other ingredients, using egg, pickled herring or beetroot in place of the smoked ham.

NUTRITIONAL INFORMATION

Calories	224	Sugars	.........6g
Protein	........14g	Fat	..........7g
Carbohydrate	...28g	Saturates	......2g

10 mins   10 mins

SERVES 4

INGREDIENTS

175 g/6 oz lean smoked ham

500 g/1 lb 2 oz salad potatoes

6 spring onions, white and green parts, sliced

3 pickled dill cucumbers, halved and sliced

4 tbsp low-fat mayonnaise

4 tbsp low-fat thick natural yogurt

2 tbsp chopped fresh dill

salt and pepper

1 Cut the ham into 3.5 cm/1½ inch long strips. Cut the potatoes into 1 cm/ ½ inch pieces. Cook the potatoes in lightly salted boiling water for about 8 minutes until tender.

2 Drain the potatoes well and return to the pan. Add the spring onions, ham and cucumber.

3 To make the dressing, combine the mayonnaise, yogurt and chopped fresh dill in a small bowl, beating well until thoroughly mixed. Season to taste with salt and pepper.

4 Add the dressing to the pan and sti gently until the potatoes are coate with the dressing.

5 Transfer the salad into a warm dis and serve.

COOK'S TIP

The feathery green leaves of fresh dill are used to flavour many dishes – salads, soups, sauces and vegetables. The distinctive flavour of fresh dill is far superior to the dried form which should, therefore, not be substituted.

Chicken & Grape Salad

Tender chicken breast, sweet grapes and crisp celery coated
in a mild curry mayonnaise make a wonderful al fresco lunch.

NUTRITIONAL INFORMATION

Calories 413	Sugars 20g
Protein 39g	Fat 20g
Carbohydrate . . .20g	Saturates 3g

15 mins   0 mins

SERVES 4

I N G R E D I E N T S

500 g/1 lb 2 oz cooked skinless, boneless
  chicken breasts

2 celery sticks, thinly sliced

250 g/9 oz black grapes

55 g/2 oz flaked almonds, toasted

pinch of paprika

fresh coriander or flat leaf parsley sprigs,
  to garnish

C U R R Y   S A U C E

150 ml/¼ pint low-fat mayonnaise

125 g/4½ oz low-fat fromage frais

1 tbsp clear honey

1 tbsp curry paste

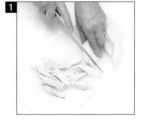

1 Cut the chicken into fairly large
pieces and transfer to a bowl with the
sliced celery.

2 Halve the grapes, remove the seeds
and add the fruit to the bowl.

3 To make the curry sauce, mix the
mayonnaise with the fromage frais,
honey and curry paste until blended.

4 Pour the curry sauce over the salad
and mix together carefully until
thoroughly coated.

5 Transfer to a shallow serving dish and
sprinkle with the toasted almonds
and paprika.

6 Garnish the salad with the coriander (
or parsley and serve.

COOK'S TIP
To save time, use seedless grapes,
now widely available in supermarkets,
and add them whole to the salad.

Carrot & Orange Salad

A crunchy and colourful, sweet and savoury dish which makes a refreshing accompaniment or an excellent appetiser.

NUTRITIONAL INFORMATION

Calories	194	Sugars	.......25g
Protein	.........6g	Fat	..........8g
Carbohydrate	...26g	Saturates	......1g

 20 mins | 0 mins

SERVES 4

INGREDIENTS

500 g/1 lb 2 oz celeriac

2 tbsp orange juice

350 g/12 oz carrots, thinly sliced

2 celery sticks, finely chopped

25 g/1 oz celery leaves

4 oranges

4 tbsp walnut pieces

DRESSING

1 tbsp walnut oil

½ tsp grated orange rind

3 tbsp orange juice

1 tbsp white wine vinegar

1 tsp clear honey

salt and pepper

1 Trim and peel the celeriac and slice or grate finely into a bowl. Add the orange juice and toss together to prevent it from turning brown.

2 Stir in the carrots, celery and celery leaves. Cover with clingfilm and chill in the refrigerator while you are preparing the oranges.

3 Slice off the tops and bottoms from the oranges. Using a sharp knife, slice off the skin, removing the pith at the same time. Cut out the orange flesh by slicing along the side of the membranes dividing the segments. reserve any juice for the dressing. Gently mix the orange segments into the celeriac mixture.

4 To make the dressing, place all the ingredients in a small screw-top jar. Shake well to mix.

5 Pile the vegetable mixture on to a plate. Sprinkle over the walnut pieces and serve with the dressing.

COOK'S TIP

Celeriac is a variety of celery with a bulbous, knobbly root. It has a rough, light brown skin and creamy white flesh and is delicious raw or cooked.

Sweet & Sour Tuna Salad

Flageolet beans, courgettes and tomatoes are briefly cooked in a sweet and sour sauce, before being mixed with tuna.

NUTRITIONAL INFORMATION

Calories	245	Sugars	.........5g
Protein	........22g	Fat	...........8g
Carbohydrate	...24g	Saturates	......1g

15 mins   10 mins

SERVES 4

INGREDIENTS

tbsp olive oil

onion, chopped

garlic cloves, chopped

courgettes, sliced

tomatoes, peeled

00 g/14 oz can flageolet beans, drained and rinsed

0 black olives, halved and stoned

tbsp capers

tsp caster sugar

tbsp wholegrain mustard

tbsp white wine vinegar

00 g/7 oz can tuna fish, drained

tbsp chopped fresh parsley, plus extra to garnish

rusty bread, to serve

1 Heat the olive oil in a large, heavy-based frying pan. Add the onion and garlic and fry over a low heat, stirring occasionally, for 5 minutes until softened, but not browned.

2 Add the courgette slices and cook, stirring occasionally, for a further minutes.

3 Cut the tomatoes in half, then into thin wedges.

4 Add the tomatoes to the pan with the beans, olives, capers, sugar, mustard and vinegar.

5 Simmer for 2 minutes, stirring gently, then set aside to cool slightly.

6 Flake the tuna and stir it into the bean mixture with the parsley. Transfer to a serving dish, garnish with the extra chopped parsley and serve lukewarm with crusty bread.

COOK'S TIP
Capers are the flower buds of the caper bush, which is native to the Mediterranean region. Capers are preserved in vinegar and salt and give a distinctive flavour to this salad. They are much used in Italian and Provençal cooking.

Cool Bean Salad

This is ideal for serving at a barbecue, for accompanying one of the hotter Indian curries, or for serving as part of a salad buffet at parties.

NUTRITIONAL INFORMATION

Calories	98	Sugars	.........5g
Protein	.........9g	Fat	...........1g
Carbohydrate	...14g	Saturates	.....0.3g

15 mins   15 mins

SERVES 4

INGREDIENTS

1 red onion, thinly sliced

350 g/12 oz broad beans, fresh or frozen

150 ml/5 fl oz natural yogurt

1 tbsp chopped fresh mint

1½ tsp lemon juice

1 garlic clove, halved

½ cucumber, peeled, halved and sliced

salt and ground white pepper

1 Rinse the red onion slices briefly under cold running water and drain well.

2 Cook the broad beans in a small pan of boiling water and until tender: 8–10 minutes for fresh beans, 5–6 minutes for frozen.

3 Drain, rinse under cold running water and drain again.

4 If you wish, shell the beans from their white outer shells to leave the sweet green bean.

5 Combine the yogurt, mint, lemon juice, garlic and seasoning in a bowl.

6 Combine the onion, cucumber and broad beans. Toss them in the yogurt dressing until well coated. Remove and discard the garlic halves.

7 Spoon the salad on to a serving plate and serve immediately.

COOK'S TIP

Rinsing the onion under the cold running water takes the edge off the raw taste, as it washes away some of the juices. The same technique can be used on other pungent vegetables and salads, such as spring onions, bitter cucumbers and chillies.

Chilli & Pepper Pasta

This roasted pepper and chilli sauce is sweet and spicy – the perfect combination for those who like to add just a little spice to life!

NUTRITIONAL INFORMATION

Calories . . . . . . .423 Sugars 5g
Protein . . . . .9g Fat 27g
Carbohydrate . . .38g Saturates 4g

🥗 25 mins ⏰ 30 mins

SERVES 4

INGREDIENTS

red peppers, halved and deseeded

small fresh red chilli

tomatoes, halved

garlic cloves

5 g/2 oz ground almonds

tbsp olive oil

75 g/1½ lb fresh pasta or 350 g/12 oz
dried pasta

fresh oregano leaves, to garnish

1 Place the peppers, skin side up, on a baking sheet with the chilli and tomatoes. Cook under a preheated grill for 5 minutes or until charred. After 0 minutes turn the tomatoes skin side up. Place the peppers and chillies in a plastic bag and set aside for 10 minutes.

2 Peel the skins from the peppers and chillies and slice the flesh into strips. Peel the garlic, and peel and deseed the tomato halves.

3 Place the ground almonds on a baking sheet and place under the grill for 2-3 minutes until golden.

4 In a food processor, process the peppers, chilli, garlic and tomatoes to make a purée. With the motor still running

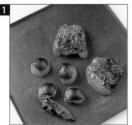

slowly add the olive oil through the feeder tube to form a thick sauce. Alternatively, mash the mixture with a fork and beat in the olive oil, drop by drop.

5 Stir the toasted ground almonds into the mixture. Warm the sauce in a saucepan until it is heated through.

6 Bring a large pan of lightly salted water to the boil. Add the pasta, bring back to the boil and cook for 3-5 minutes if using fresh, o r 8-10 minutes if using dried. Drain the pasta thoroughly and transfer to a serving dish. Pour over the

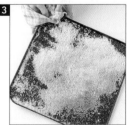

sauce and toss to mix. Garnish with the fresh oregano leaves and serve.

VARIATION

Add 2 tablespoons of red wine vinegar to the sauce and use as a dressing for a cold pasta salad, if you wish.

Pasta & Herring Salad

This salad, which many countries claim as their own, is generally considered to be a typically Dutch dish.

NUTRITIONAL INFORMATION

Calories	774	Sugars	........21g
Protein	........33g	Fat	..........31g
Carbohydrate	...97g	Saturates	.......4g

 15 mins   🕐 12 mins

SERVES 4

INGREDIENTS

250 g/9 oz dried pasta shells

400 g/14 oz rollmop herrings in brine

6 small potatoes, boiled and cooled

2 large tart apples

2 baby frisée lettuces

2 baby beetroots

4 hard-boiled eggs

6 pickled onions

6 pickled gherkins

2 tbsp capers, rinsed

4 tbsp olive oil

3 tbsp tarragon vinegar

salt and pepper

1 Bring a large saucepan of lightly salted water to the boil. Add the pasta, bring back to the boil and cook for 8–10 minutes until tender, but still firm to the bite. Drain the pasta thoroughly and then refresh in cold water. Drain well again and set aside.

2 Cut the rollmop herrings, cooled potatoes, apples, frisée lettuces and baby beetroots into small pieces. Put all of these ingredients into a large salad bowl. Add the pasta and toss lightly to mix.

3 Carefully shell and slice the eggs. Garnish the salad with the slices of egg, pickled onions gherkins and capers, sprinkle with the olive oil and the tarragon vinegar and serve immediately.

COOK'S TIP

Tarragon vinegar is available from most supermarkets, but you can easily make your own. Add a bunch of fresh tarragon to a bottle of white or red wine vinegar and set aside to infuse for 48 hours.

Cantaloupe & Crab Salad

This colourful salad combines delicious fresh crab meat with flavoursome raw fruit and vegetables and a low-fat dressing.

NUTRITIONAL INFORMATION

Calories . . . . . . .252 Sugars 9g
Protein . . . . .20g Fat 15g
Carbohydrate . . .10g Saturates 1g

 15 mins   0 mins

SERVES 4

INGREDIENTS

350 g/12 oz fresh crab meat

5 tbsp low-fat mayonnaise

50 ml/2 fl oz low-fat natural yogurt

4 tsp extra virgin olive oil

4 tsp lime juice

1 spring onion, finely chopped

4 tsp finely chopped fresh parsley

pinch of cayenne pepper

1 cantaloupe melon

2 radicchio heads, separated into leaves

fresh parsley sprigs, to garnish

1 Place the crab meat in a large bowl and pick over it very carefully to remove any remaining shell or cartilage, but try not to break the meat up.

2 Put the low-fat mayonnaise, yogurt, olive oil, lime juice, spring onion, chopped fresh parsley and cayenne pepper into a separate bowl and mix until thoroughly blended. Fold in the crab meat.

3 Cut the melon in half and remove and discard the seeds. Thinly slice, then cut off the rind with a sharp knife.

4 Arrange the melon slices and radicchio leaves on 4 large serving plates, then arrange the crabmeat mixture on top. Garnish with a few sprigs of fresh parsley and serve.

COOK'S TIP
If fresh crab meat is not available, you can use frozen crab meat. Allow the crab to thaw thoroughly before making the salad.

Italian Pasta Salad

Tomatoes and mozzarella cheese are a classic Italian combination.
Here they are joined with pasta and avocado for an extra touch of luxury.

NUTRITIONAL INFORMATION

Calories 541	Sugars 5g
Protein 12g	Fat 43g
Carbohydrate . . .29g	Saturates 10g

 15 mins   15 mins

SERVES 4

INGREDIENTS

2 tbsp pine kernels

175 g/6 oz dried fusilli

1 tbsp olive oil

6 tomatoes

225 g/8 oz mozzarella cheese

1 large avocado

2 tbsp lemon juice

3 tbsp chopped fresh basil

salt and pepper

fresh basil sprigs, to garnish

DRESSING

6 tbsp extra virgin olive oil

2 tbsp white wine vinegar

1 tsp wholegrain mustard

pinch of sugar

1 Spread the pine kernels out on a baking sheet and toast them under a preheated grill for 1–2 minutes. Remove and set aside to cool.

2 Bring a large pan of lightly salted water to the boil. Add the pasta, bring back to the boil and cook for 8–10 minutes or until tender, but still firm to the bite. Drain the pasta and refresh in cold water. Drain again and set aside to cool.

3 Thinly slice the tomatoes and the mozzarella cheese.

4 Cut the avocado in half lengthways, carefully remove the stone, then peel. Cut the flesh into thin slices lengthways and sprinkle with lemon juice to prevent it from turning brown.

5 To make the dressing, whisk together the oil, vinegar, mustard and sugar in a small bowl and season to taste with salt and pepper.

6 Arrange the tomatoes, mozzarella cheese and avocado pear alternately in overlapping slices on a large serving platter leaving room in the centre.

7 Toss the pasta with half of the dressing and the chopped basil and season to taste with salt and pepper. Spoon the pasta into the centre of the platter and pour over the remaining dressing. Sprinkle over the pine kernels, garnish with fresh sprigs of basil and serve immediately.

Rare Beef Pasta Salad

This mouth-watering salad is a meal in itself and would be perfect for an al fresco lunch, perhaps with a bottle of red wine.

NUTRITIONAL INFORMATION

Calories 575   Sugars 4g
Protein ....31g   Fat 33g
Carbohydrate ...44g   Saturates 9g

15 mins   30 mins

SERVES 4

INGREDIENTS

450 g/1 lb rump or sirloin steak in a
  single piece

450 g/1 lb dried fusilli

4 tbsp olive oil

2 tbsp lime juice

2 tbsp Thai fish sauce (see Cook's Tip)

2 tsp clear honey

4 spring onions, sliced

1 cucumber, peeled and cut into 2.5 cm/
  1 inch chunks

3 tomatoes, cut into wedges

1 tbsp finely chopped fresh mint

salt and pepper

1 Season the steak with salt and pepper. Grill or pan-fry it for 4 minutes on each side. Allow to rest for 5 minutes, then slice thinly across the grain.

2 Meanwhile, bring a large saucepan of lightly salted water to the boil. Add the pasta, bring back to the boil and cook for 8–10 minutes or until tender, but still firm to the bite. Drain the fusilli, refresh in cold water and drain again thoroughly. Toss the fusilli in the olive oil and set aside until required.

3 Combine the lime juice, fish sauce and honey in a small saucepan and cook over a medium heat for 2 minutes.

4 Add the spring onions, cucumber, tomatoes and mint to the pan, then add the steak and mix well. Season to taste with salt.

5 Transfer the fusilli to a large, warm serving dish and top with the steak and salad mixture. Serve just warm or allow to cool completely.

COOK'S TIP

Thai fish sauce, also known as *nam pla*, is made from salted anchovies and has quite a strong flavour, so it should be used with discretion. It is available from some supermarkets and from Oriental food stores.

Tuna, Bean & Anchovy Salad

Serve as part of a selection of antipasti, or for a summer lunch with hot garlic bread. Tuna and beans make a classic combination.

NUTRITIONAL INFORMATION

Calories 397	Sugars 8g
Protein 23g	Fat 30g
Carbohydrate ...10g	Saturates 4g

  20 mins 0 mins

SERVES 4

INGREDIENTS

500 g/1 lb 2 oz tomatoes

200 g/7 oz canned tuna fish, drained

2 tbsp chopped fresh parsley

½ cucumber

1 small red onion, sliced

225 g/8 oz cooked green beans

1 small red pepper, deseeded

1 small crisp lettuce

6 tbsp Italian-style dressing

3 hard-boiled eggs

55 g/2 oz canned anchovies, drained

12 black olives, stoned

1 Cut the tomatoes into wedges, flake the tuna and put both into a bowl with the parsley.

2 Cut the cucumber into slices. Slice the onion. Add the cucumber and onion to the bowl.

3 Cut the beans in half, chop the pepper and add both to the bowl with the lettuce leaves. Pour over the dressing and toss to mix, then spoon into a salad bowl. Shell the eggs and cut into quarters, arrange over the top with the anchovies and scatter with the olives.

Vegetable & Pasta Salad

Roasted vegetables and pasta make a delicious, colourful salad, ideal as a starter or to serve with a platter of cold meats.

NUTRITIONAL INFORMATION

Calories	462	Sugars	.........9g
Protein	........11g	Fat	..........32g
Carbohydrate	...33g	Saturates	.......7g

1½ hrs   1 hr

SERVES 4

INGREDIENTS

2 small aubergines , thinly sliced

1 large onion, sliced

2 large beef tomatoes, peeled and cut into wedges

1 red pepper, deseeded and sliced

1 fennel bulb, thinly sliced

2 garlic cloves, sliced

3 tbsp olive oil

175 g/6 oz small pasta shapes

85 g/3 oz feta cheese, crumbled

a few fresh basil leaves, torn

salt and pepper

salad leaves, to serve

DRESSING

5 tbsp olive oil

juice of 1 orange

1 tsp grated orange rind

¼ tsp paprika

4 canned anchovies, finely chopped

1 Place the sliced aubergines in a colander, sprinkle with salt and set them aside for about 1 hour to draw out some of the bitter juices. Rinse under cold, running water to remove the salt, then drain. Toss on kitchen paper to dry.

2 Arrange the aubergines, onion, tomatoes, pepper, fennel and garlic in a single layer in an ovenproof dish, sprinkle with the oil and season. Bake in a preheated oven, 220°C/450°F/Gas Mark 7, for 45 minutes until the vegetables begin to turn brown. Remove from the oven and set aside to cool.

3 Bring a large pan of lightly salted water to the boil. Add the pasta, bring back to the boil and cook for 10 minutes until tender, but still firm to the bite. Drain and turn into a bowl.

4 To make the dressing, mix together the olive oil, orange juice, orange rind and paprika. Stir in the finely chopped anchovies and season with pepper to taste. Pour the dressing over the pasta while it is still hot and toss well. Set the pasta aside to cool.

5 To assemble the salad, line a shallow serving dish with the salad leaves and arrange the cold roasted vegetables in the centre. Spoon the pasta in a ring around the vegetables and scatter over the feta cheese and basil leaves.

Sweet Potato & Bean Salad

This piquant vegetarian salad is a meal in itself or can be served as an accompaniment to chicken or fish.

NUTRITIONAL INFORMATION

Calories	143	Sugars	........22g
Protein	.........6g	Fat	...........1g
Carbohydrate	...29g	Saturates	.......1g

10 mins   10 mins

SERVES 4

I N G R E D I E N T S

1 sweet potato

4 baby carrots, halved

4 tomatoes

4 celery sticks, chopped

225 g/8 oz canned borlotti beans, drained and rinsed

115 g/4 oz mixed salad leaves, such as frisée, rocket, radicchio and oakleaf lettuce

1 tbsp sultanas

4 spring onions, finely chopped

125 ml/4 fl oz Honey and Yogurt Dressing (see Cook's Tip)

1 Peel and dice the sweet potato. Bring a saucepan of water to the boil over a medium heat. Add the sweet potato and cook for 10 minutes, until tender. Drain the potato, transfer to a bowl and set aside.

2 Cook the carrots in a separate saucepan of boiling water for 1 minute. Drain thoroughly and add to the sweet potato. Cut the tops off the tomatoes and scoop out the seeds. Cho... the flesh and add to the bowl with th... celery and beans. Mix well.

3 Line a large serving bowl with th... mixed salad leaves. Spoon the swee... potato and bean mixture on top, the... sprinkle with the sultanas and sprin... onions. Spoon over the dressing and serv... immediately.

COOK'S TIP

For a quick and easy low-fat dressing, put 1 tablespoon of clear honey in a bowl, add 6 tablespoons of low-fat natural yogurt and beat until blended. Season to taste.

Pasta Niçoise Salad

Based on the classic French salad niçoise, this recipe has a light olive oil dressing with the tang of capers and the fragrance of fresh basil.

NUTRITIONAL INFORMATION

Calories	214	Sugars	.........2g
Protein	........26g	Fat	...........7g
Carbohydrate	...14g	Saturates	......1g

15 mins   35 mins

SERVES 4

I N G R E D I E N T S

225 g/8 oz dried farfalle

175 g/6 oz French beans

350 g/12 oz fresh tuna steaks

115 g/4 oz baby plum tomatoes, halved

8 anchovy fillets, drained

2 tbsp capers in brine, rinsed and drained

25 g/1 oz stoned black olives in brine, drained

fresh basil leaves, to garnish

salt and pepper

DRESSING

1 tbsp olive oil

1 garlic clove, crushed

1 tbsp lemon juice

½ tsp finely grated lemon rind

1 tbsp shredded fresh basil leaves

1 Bring a pan of lightly salted water to the boil. Add the pasta, bring back top the boil and cook for 8–10 minutes until tender, but still firm to the bite. Drain well, set aside and keep warm.

2 Bring a small pan of lightly salted water to the boil and cook the beans for 5–6 minutes until tender. Drain well and toss into the pasta.

3 Rinse and pat the tuna steaks dry on absorbent kitchen paper. Place the tuna steaks on the grill rack and then season on both sides with pepper. Cook under a preheated grill for 4-5 minutes on each side until cooked through.

4 Drain the tuna on absorbent kitchen paper and flake into bite-size pieces. Toss the tuna into the pasta with the tomatoes, anchovies, capers and olives. Set aside and keep warm.

5 Meanwhile, prepare the dressing. Mix all the ingredients together and season well. Pour the dressing over the pasta mixture and mix carefully. Transfer to a warmed serving bowl and serve sprinkled with fresh basil leaves.

VARIATION

Any pasta shape is suitable for this salad – to make it even more colourful, use tricolour pasta.

Italian Mozzarella Salad

This colourful and nutritious salad is packed full of delicious flavours, but is simplicity itself to make.

NUTRITIONAL INFORMATION

Calories	79	Sugars	.........2g
Protein	.........4g	Fat	...........6g
Carbohydrate	....2g	Saturates	.......2g

  20 mins 0 mins

SERVES 6

INGREDIENTS

200 g/7 oz baby spinach

125 g/4½ oz watercress

125 g/4½ oz mozzarella cheese

225 g/8 oz cherry tomatoes

2 tsp balsamic vinegar

4½ tsp extra virgin olive oil

salt and pepper

1 Wash the spinach and watercress and drain thoroughly on absorbent kitchen paper. Remove any tough stalks. Place the spinach and watercress leaves in a large serving dish.

2 Cut the mozzarella into small pieces and sprinkle them over the spinach and watercress leaves.

3 Cut the cherry tomatoes in half and scatter them over the salad.

4 Sprinkle over the balsamic vinegar and olive oil and season with salt and pepper to taste. Toss the mixture together to coat the leaves. Serve at once or chill in the refrigerator until required.

Sesame Seed Salad

This salad uses tahini paste – sesame seed paste – as a flavouring for the dressing, which complements the aubergine.

NUTRITIONAL INFORMATION

Calories ....89 Sugars 1g
Protein ....3g Fat 8g
Carbohydrate ....1g Saturates 1g

45 mins   15 mins

SERVES 4

INGREDIENTS

1 large aubergine

3 tbsp tahini paste

juice and rind of 1 lemon

1 garlic clove, crushed

pinch of paprika

1 tbsp chopped fresh coriander

Little Gem lettuce leaves

salt and pepper

GARNISH

strips of pimiento

lemon wedges

toasted sesame seeds

1 Cut the aubergine in half, place in a colander and sprinkle with salt. Set aside for 30 minutes to allow the juices to drain. Rinse thoroughly under cold running water and drain well. Pat dry with kitchen paper.

2 Place the aubergine halves, skin side uppermost, on an oiled baking sheet. Cook in a preheated oven, 230°C/450°F/Gas Mark 8, for 10–15 minutes. Remove from the oven and set aside to cool.

3 When the aubergine is cool enough to handle, cut it into cubes and set aside until required.

4 Combine the tahini paste, lemon juice, lemon rind, garlic, paprika and chopped coriander in a medium-size bowl. Season with salt and pepper to taste and stir in the aubergine cubes.

5 Line a serving dish with lettuce leaves and spoon the aubergine cubes into the centre. Garnish the salad with pimiento slices, lemon wedges and toasted sesame seeds and serve immediately.

Lobster Salad & Lime Dressing

The lobster makes this a special-occasion salad, both in cost and flavour.
The richness of the lobster meat is offset by the tangy lime dressing.

NUTRITIONAL INFORMATION

Calories 181   Sugars 0.8g
Protein . . . . .6.8g   Fat 13.9g
Carbohydrate . . .7.6g   Saturates 2.2g

5 mins

10–15 mins

SERVES 4

INGREDIENTS

450 g/1 lb waxy potatoes, scrubbed
   and sliced

225 g/8 oz cooked lobster meat

150 ml/5 fl oz mayonnaise

2 tbsp lime juice

finely grated rind of 1 lime

1 tbsp chopped fresh parsley

2 tbsp olive oil

2 tomatoes, deseeded and diced

2 hard-boiled eggs, quartered

1 tbsp quartered stoned green olives

salt and pepper

COOK'S TIP

As seafood is used in this
salad, serve it immediately
or keep covered and chilled
for up to 1 hour before serving.

1 Cook the potatoes in a saucepan of boiling water for 10–15 minutes or until cooked through. Drain and reserve.

2 Remove the lobster meat from the shell and then separate it into large pieces.

3 In a bowl, mix together the mayonnaise, 1 tablespoon of the lime juice, half the grated lime rind and half the chopped parsley, then set aside.

4 In a separate bowl, whisk the remaining lime juice with the olive oil and pour the dressing over the potatoes. Arrange the potatoes on a serving plate.

5 Top with the lobster meat, tomatoes, eggs and olives. Season to taste and sprinkle with the reserved parsley.

6 Spoon the mayonnaise on to the centre of the salad, top with the reserved rind and serve.

Mexican Potato Salad

The flavours of Mexico are echoed in this dish where potato slices are topped with tomatoes and chillies and served with guacamole.

NUTRITIONAL INFORMATION

Calories ....260 Sugars 6g
Protein ....6g Fat 9g
Carbohydrate ...41g Saturates 2g

20 mins   20 mins

SERVES 4

INGREDIENTS

4 large waxy potatoes, sliced

1 ripe avocado

1 tsp olive oil

1 tsp lemon juice

1 garlic clove, crushed

1 onion, chopped

2 large tomatoes, sliced

1 fresh green chilli, deseeded and chopped

1 yellow pepper, deseeded and sliced

2 tbsp chopped fresh coriander

salt and pepper

lemon or lime wedges, to garnish

1 Bring a large pan of water to the boil. Add the potato slices, bring back to the boil and cook for 10–15 minutes or until tender. Drain and set aside to cool.

2 Meanwhile, cut the avocado in half and remove the stone. Scoop the flesh into a bowl and mash with a fork. Guacamole is best with a slightly chunky, rather than completely smooth texture.

3 Add the olive oil, lemon juice, garlic and chopped onion to the avocado flesh and stir to mix. Cover the bowl tightly with clingfilm to minimize discoloration and set aside.

4 Mix the tomatoes, chopped chilli and yellow pepper together and transfer to a salad bowl or serving platter. Add the potato slices and mix gently.

5 Arrange the avocado mixture on top of the salad and sprinkle with the chopped coriander. Season to taste with salt and pepper and serve immediately garnished with lemon or lime wedges.

VARIATION

You can omit the green chilli from this salad if you do not like hot dishes.

Pear & Roquefort Salad

The sweetness of the pear is a perfect partner to the peppery 'bite' of the radicchio and the piquancy of the cheese.

NUTRITIONAL INFORMATION

Calories	94	Sugars	........10g
Protein	.........5g	Fat	...........4g
Carbohydrate	...10g	Saturates	......3g

 10 mins   0 mins

SERVES 4

I N G R E D I E N T S

55 g/2 oz Roquefort cheese

150 ml/5 fl oz low-fat natural yogurt

2 tbsp snipped fresh chives

few leaves of lollo rosso

few leaves of radicchio

few leaves of lamb's lettuce

2 ripe pears

pepper

whole fresh chives, to garnish

1 Place the cheese in a bowl and mash with a fork. Gradually blend the yogurt into the cheese to make a smooth dressing. Add the chives and season with pepper to taste.

2 Tear the lollo rosso, radicchio and lamb's lettuce leaves into manageable pieces. Arrange the salad leaves on a large serving platter or divide them between individual serving plates.

3 Cut the pears into quarters and remove the cores. Cut the quarters into slices. Arrange the pear slices over the salad leaves.

4 Drizzle the Roquefort dressing over the pears and garnish with a few whole chives.

COOK'S TIP

Look out for bags of mixed salad leaves as these are generally more economical than buying lots of different leaves separately.

Carrot & Nut Coleslaw

This simple salad has a dressing made from poppy seeds pan-fried in sesame oil to bring out their flavour and aroma.

NUTRITIONAL INFORMATION

Calories 220	Sugars 7g	
Protein 4g	Fat 19g	
Carbohydrate ...10g	Saturates 3g	

 15 mins   5–10 mins

SERVES 4

INGREDIENTS

1 large carrot, grated

1 small onion, finely chopped

2 celery sticks, chopped

¼ small hard white cabbage, shredded

1 tbsp chopped fresh parsley

4 tbsp sesame oil

½ tsp poppy seeds

55 g/2 oz cashew nuts

2 tbsp white wine vinegar or cider vinegar

salt and pepper

fresh parsley sprigs, to garnish

1 In a large salad bowl, combine the carrot, onion, celery and cabbage. Stir in the chopped parsley and season to taste with salt and pepper.

2 Heat the sesame oil in a saucepan with a lid. Add the poppy seeds and cover the pan. Cook over a medium-high heat until the seeds start to make a popping sound. Remove from the heat and set aside to cool.

3 Spread out the cashew nuts on a baking sheet. Place them under a preheated medium-hot grill and toast until

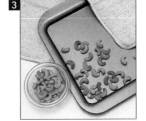

lightly browned, being careful not to burn them. Remove from the heat and set aside to cool.

4 Add the vinegar to the oil and poppy seed mixture, then pour the poppy seed dressing over the vegetable mixture.

Add the cooled cashew nuts. Toss together to coat well.

5 Garnish the salad with sprigs of fresh parsley and serve immediately.

Melon & Strawberry Salad

This refreshing fruit-based salad is perfect for a hot summer's day and would be perfect served with barbecued chicken or fish.

NUTRITIONAL INFORMATION

Calories	112	Sugars	........22g
Protein	.........5g	Fat	...........1g
Carbohydrate	...22g	Saturates	.....0.3g

 15 mins   🕐 0 mins

SERVES 4

INGREDIENTS

½ iceberg lettuce, shredded

1 small honeydew melon

225 g/8 oz strawberries, sliced

5 cm/2 inch piece of cucumber, thinly sliced

fresh mint sprigs to garnish

DRESSING

200 g/7 fl oz natural yogurt

5 cm/2 inch piece of cucumber, peeled

a few fresh mint leaves

½ tsp finely grated lime or lemon rind

pinch of caster sugar

3–4 ice cubes

1 Arrange the shredded lettuce on 4 serving plates.

2 Cut the melon lengthways into quarters. Scoop out the seeds and cut through the flesh down to the skin at 2.5 cm/1 inch intervals. Cut the melon close to the skin and detach the flesh.

3 Place the chunks of melon on the beds of lettuce with the strawberries and cucumber slices.

4 To make the dressing, put the yogurt, cucumber, mint leaves, lime or lemon rind, caster sugar and ice cubes into a blender or food processor. Blend together for about 15 seconds until smooth. Alternatively, chop the cucumber and mint finely, crush the ice cubes and combine with the other ingredients.

5 Serve the salad with a little dressing poured over it. Garnish with sprigs of fresh mint.

VARIATION

Omit the ice cubes from the dressing if you prefer, but make sure that the ingredients are well-chilled. This will ensure that the finished dressing is really cool.

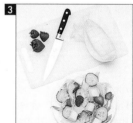

Salad with Garlic Dressing

This is a very quick and refreshing salad using a whole range of colourful ingredients which make it look as good as it tastes.

NUTRITIONAL INFORMATION

Calories ....82 Sugars 5g
Protein ....2g Fat 6g
Carbohydrate ....5g Saturates 1g

10 mins   0 mins

SERVES 4

INGREDIENTS

85 g/3 oz cucumber, cut into batons

6 spring onions, halved

2 tomatoes, deseeded and cut into 8 wedges

1 yellow pepper, deseeded and cut into strips

2 celery sticks, cut into strips

4 radishes, quartered

85 g/3 oz rocket

1 tbsp chopped fresh mint, to garnish

DRESSING

2 tbsp lemon juice

1 garlic clove, crushed

150 ml/5 fl oz low-fat natural yogurt

2 tbsp olive oil

salt and pepper

1 To make the salad, gently mix the cucumber batons, spring onions, tomato wedges, yellow pepper strips, celery, radishes and rocket in a large serving bowl.

2 To make the dressing, stir the lemon juice, garlic, natural yogurt and olive oil together in a small bowl until thoroughly combined. Season with salt and pepper to taste.

3 Spoon the dressing over the salad and toss to mix. Sprinkle the salad with chopped mint and serve.

COOK'S TIP

Rocket has a distinctive warm, peppery flavour which is ideal in green salads. If rocket is unavailable, lamb's lettuce makes a good substitute.

Courgette & Mint Salad

This salad uses lots of green-coloured ingredients which look and taste wonderful with the minty yogurt dressing.

NUTRITIONAL INFORMATION

Calories	49	Sugars	.........5g
Protein	.........4g	Fat	...........1g
Carbohydrate	....6g	Saturates	.......0g

30 mins   7–8 mins

SERVES 4

I N G R E D I E N T S

2 courgettes, cut into batons

100 g/3½ oz French beans, cut into thirds

1 green pepper, deseeded and cut into strips

2 celery sticks, sliced

1 bunch of watercress

D R E S S I N G

200 ml/7 fl oz natural yogurt

1 garlic clove, crushed

2 tbsp chopped fresh mint

pepper

1 Cook the courgette batons and beans in a saucepan of lightly salted boiling water for 7–8 minutes. Drain, rinse under cold running water and drain again. Set aside to cool completely.

2 Mix the courgettes and beans with the green pepper strips, celery and watercress in a large serving bowl.

3 To make the dressing, combine the natural yogurt, garlic and chopped mint in a small bowl. Season with pepper to taste.

4 Spoon the dressing on to the salad and serve immediately.

COOK'S TIP

The salad must be served as soon as the yogurt dressing has been added – the dressing will start to separate if it is kept for any length of time.

Bean & Tomato Salad

This is a colourful salad with a Mexican theme, using beans, tomatoes and avocado. The chilli dressing adds a little kick.

NUTRITIONAL INFORMATION

Calories .... 347 Sugars 7g
Protein .... 9g Fat 26g
Carbohydrate ... 21g Saturates 5g

10 mins   0 mins

SERVES 4

INGREDIENTS

ollo rosso lettuce

2 ripe avocados

2 tsp lemon juice

4 medium tomatoes

1 onion

175 g/6 oz canned mixed beans, rinsed
  and drained

DRESSING

4 tbsp olive oil

dash of chilli oil

2 tbsp garlic wine vinegar

pinch of caster sugar

pinch of chilli powder

1 tbsp chopped fresh parsley

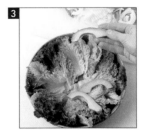

1 Line a serving bowl with the lollo rosso lettuce leaves.

2 Cut the avocados in half and remove and discard the stones. Peel and thinly slice the flesh. Sprinkle with the lemon juice to prevent the flesh from turning brown.

3 Thinly slice the tomatoes and onion. Arrange the avocado, tomato and onion slices around the salad bowl, leaving a space in the centre. Spoon the beans into the centre of the salad.

4 Whisk all the dressing ingredients together in a small bowl until thoroughly combined. Pour the dressing over the salad and serve immediately.

COOK'S TIP

Instead of whisking the dressing, place all the ingredients in a screw-top jar and shake vigorously. Any leftover dressing can then be kept and stored in the same jar.

Grilled Vegetable Salad

The vegetables for this dish are best prepared well in advance and chilled for at least an hour before serving.

NUTRITIONAL INFORMATION

Calories	230	Sugars	........10g
Protein	.........2g	Fat	..........20g
Carbohydrate	....11g	Saturates	.......3g

 1¼ hrs 🕐 10 mins

SERVES 4

INGREDIENTS

1 courgette, sliced

1 yellow pepper, deseeded and sliced

1 aubergine, sliced

1 fennel bulb, cut into 8 wedges

1 red onion, cut into 8 wedges

16 cherry tomatoes

3 tbsp olive oil

1 garlic clove, crushed

fresh rosemary sprigs, to garnish

DRESSING

4 tbsp olive oil

2 tbsp balsamic vinegar

2 tsp chopped fresh rosemary

1 tsp Dijon mustard

1 tsp clear honey

2 tsp lemon juice

1 Spread out all of the vegetables, except for the cherry tomatoes, on a baking sheet.

2 Mix the oil and garlic and brush over the vegetables. Cook under a medium-hot grill for 10 minutes until tender and beginning to char. Set aside to cool. Spoon the vegetables into a serving bowl with the cherry tomatoes.

3 Mix the dressing ingredients and pour over the vegetables. Cover and chill for 1 hour. Garnish and serve.

VARIATION

This salad can also be served warm. Prepare the vegetables as above, but do not allow to cool completely. Heat the dressing in a small pan over a low heat, then pour it over the vegetables and toss to mix.

Red Cabbage & Pear Salad

Red cabbage is much underused – it is a colourful and tasty ingredient which is perfect with fruits, such as pears or apples.

NUTRITIONAL INFORMATION

Calories	143	Sugars	........14g
Protein	.........2g	Fat	..........9g
Carbohydrate	...15g	Saturates	.......1g

15 mins 0 mins

SERVES 4

INGREDIENTS

350 g/12 oz red cabbage, finely shredded

2 Conference pears, cored and thinly sliced

4 spring onions, sliced

lollo biondo leaves

1 carrot, grated

fresh chives, to garnish

DRESSING

4 tbsp pear juice

1 tsp wholegrain mustard

3 tbsp olive oil

1 tbsp garlic wine vinegar

1 tbsp chopped chives

1 Put the red cabbage, pears and spring onions into a bowl and toss gently together to mix.

2 Line a serving dish with lollo biondo lettuce leaves and spoon the cabbage and pear mixture into the centre.

3 Sprinkle the grated carrot into the centre of the cabbage to form a domed pile.

4 To make the dressing, combine the pear juice, wholegrain mustard, olive oil, garlic wine vinegar and chives, stirring until well mixed.

5 Pour the dressing over the salad, garnish and serve immediately. (Do not make the salad much in advance of serving because the colour from the red cabbage will bleed into the other ingredients, spoiling the appearance.)

VARIATION
Experiment with different types of salad leaves. The slightly bitter flavour of chicory or radicchio would work well with the sweetness of the pears.

Alfalfa & Beetroot Salad

This refreshing salad must be assembled just before serving to prevent all of the ingredients being coloured pink by the beetroot.

NUTRITIONAL INFORMATION

Calories	139	Sugars	.........7g
Protein	.........2g	Fat	...........11g
Carbohydrate	....8g	Saturates	.......2g

 10 mins   0 mins

SERVES 4

INGREDIENTS

100 g/3½ oz baby spinach

85 g/3 oz alfalfa sprouts

2 celery sticks, sliced

4 cooked beetroot, cut into 8 wedges

DRESSING

4 tbsp olive oil

4½ tsp garlic wine vinegar

1 garlic clove, crushed

2 tsp clear honey

1 tbsp chopped fresh chives

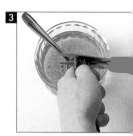

VARIATION

Add the segments of 1 large orange to the salad to make it even more colourful and refreshing. Replace the garlic wine vinegar with plain and use a different flavoured oil such as chilli or herb, if you prefer.

1 If the spinach leaves are large, tear them into smaller pieces. (Cutting them would bruise them.) Place the spinach and alfalfa sprouts in a large bowl and mix together.

2 Add the celery and mix well. Toss in the beetroot and mix again.

3 To make the dressing, mix the oil, wine vinegar, garlic, honey and chopped chives in a small bowl.

4 Pour the dressing over the salad, toss well and serve immediately.

Egg Noodle Salad

A good dish for summer eating, this is light and refreshing in flavour and easy to cook. The turkey can be replaced with cooked chicken.

NUTRITIONAL INFORMATION

Calories 355	Sugars 6g	
Protein 22g	Fat 10g	
Carbohydrate . . .46g	Saturates 2g	

20 mins   4–5 mins

SERVES 4

INGREDIENTS

225 g/8 oz dried egg noodles

2 tsp sesame oil

1 carrot

115 g/4 oz beansprouts

½ cucumber

2 spring onions, finely shredded

150 g/5½ oz cooked turkey breast meat, shredded into thin slivers

DRESSING

5 tbsp coconut milk

3 tbsp lime juice

1 tbsp light soy sauce

2 tsp Thai fish sauce

1 tsp chilli oil

1 tsp sugar

2 tbsp chopped fresh coriander

2 tbsp chopped fresh sweet basil

TO GARNISH

peanuts

chopped fresh basil

1 Cook the noodles in boiling water for 4 minutes, or according to the package instructions. Plunge them into a bowl of cold water to prevent any further cooking, then drain and toss in sesame oil.

2 Use a vegetable peeler to shave off thin ribbons from the carrot. Blanch the ribbons and beansprouts in boiling water for 30 seconds, then plunge into cold water for 30 seconds. Drain well. Shave thin ribbons of cucumber with the vegetable peeler.

3 Place the carrots, beansprouts, cucumber, spring onions and turkey in a large bowl. Add the noodles and toss thoroughly to mix.

4 Place all the dressing ingredients in a screw-top jar and shake vigorously to mix evenly.

5 Add the dressing to the noodle mixture and toss. Pile the salad on to a serving dish. Sprinkle with peanuts and basil. Serve cold.

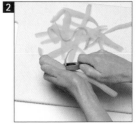
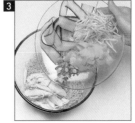

Cucumber Salad

This refreshing spicy salad makes an excellent accompaniment for spicy grilled fish, meat and poultry dishes.

NUTRITIONAL INFORMATION

Calories	32	Sugars	.........3g
Protein	.........1g	Fat	...........1g
Carbohydrate	....5g	Saturates	.......0g

1 hr   0 mins

SERVES 4

INGREDIENTS

1 cucumber

1 tsp salt

1 small red onion

1 garlic clove, crushed

½ tsp chilli paste

2 tsp Thai fish sauce

1 tbsp lime juice

1 tsp sesame oil

1 Trim the cucumber and coarsely grate the flesh. Place it in a sieve over a bowl, sprinkle with the salt and set aside to drain for about 20 minutes. Discard the liquid and rinse the cucumber.

2 Peel the onion and chop finely, then add it to the cucumber. Toss to mix. Spoon the mixture into 4 individual bowls or a large serving bowl.

3 Mix together the garlic, chilli paste, fish sauce, lime juice and sesame oil, then spoon the dressing over the salad. Cover the salad tightly with clingfilm and chill in the refrigerator before serving.

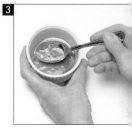

COOK'S TIP

Once the salad is made, it can be chilled with the dressing for about 1–2 hours, but is best eaten on the day of making.

Thai Green Salad

An unusual side salad that is a good accompaniment to any simple Thai main dish, especially grilled meats and fish.

NUTRITIONAL INFORMATION

Calories 42   Sugars 3g
Protein ....2g   Fat 2g
Carbohydrate ....4g   Saturates 2g

12 mins   0 mins

SERVES 4–6

I N G R E D I E N T S

small head cos lettuce

bunch of spring onions

½ cucumber

4 tbsp fresh coconut, coarsely shredded and toasted

D R E S S I N G

4 tbsp lime juice

2 tbsp Thai fish sauce

small fresh red bird-eye chilli, seeded and finely chopped

tsp sugar

garlic clove, crushed

tbsp chopped fresh coriander

tbsp chopped fresh mint

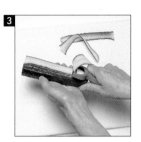

1 Tear or roughly shred the lettuce leaves and place them in a large salad bowl. (Do not cut or you will bruise them.)

2 Trim and thinly slice the spring onions diagonally, then add them to the salad bowl.

3 Use a vegetable peeler to shave thin slices along the length of the cucumber and add to the salad bowl.

4 Place all the ingredients for the dressing in a screw-top jar, close the lid tightly and shake vigorously until thoroughly mixed.

5 Pour the dressing over the salad and toss well to coat the leaves evenly.

6 Sprinkle the coconut over the salad and toss in lightly just before serving.

COOK'S TIP
This salad is good for picnics. Pack the leaves into a plastic container and nestle the jar of dressing in the centre. Cover with clingfilm. Packed this way, the salad stays crisp and if the dressing leaks during transit, there's no mess.

Aubergine & Sesame Salad

Aubergines are a popular vegetable in Thailand and grow easily throughout the Far East. This dish works very well as a first course.

NUTRITIONAL INFORMATION

Calories 106   Sugars 6g
Protein . . . . .3g   Fat 8g
Carbohydrate . . . .7g   Saturates 1g

1¼ hrs   10 mins

SERVES 4

I N G R E D I E N T S

8 baby aubergines

2 tsp chilli oil

1 tbsp soy sauce

1 tbsp Thai fish sauce

1 garlic clove, thinly sliced

1 fresh red bird-eye chilli, deseeded and sliced

1 tbsp sunflower oil

1 tsp sesame oil

1 tbsp lime juice

1 tsp soft light brown sugar

1 tbsp chopped fresh mint

1 tbsp sesame seeds, toasted

salt

fresh mint leaves, to garnish

1 Cut the aubergines lengthways into thin slices to within 2.5 cm/1 inch of the stem end. Place in a colander, sprinkling with salt between the slices and set aside to drain for about 30 minutes. Rinse under cold running water and pat dry with kitchen paper.

2 Mix the chilli oil, soy sauce and fish sauce and then brush over the aubergines. Cook under a preheated hot grill or barbecue over hot coals, turning them over occasionally and brushing with more chilli oil glaze, for 6–8 minutes until golden brown and softened. Arrange them on a serving platter.

3 Fry the garlic and chilli in the sunflower oil for 1–2 minutes until just beginning to brown. Remove from the heat and add the sesame oil, lime juice, brown sugar and any spare chilli oil glaze.

4 Add the chopped mint and spoon th warm dressing over the aubergines.

5 Set aside to marinate for abou 20 minutes, then sprinkle with toaste sesame seeds. Serve garnished with fres mint leaves.

Oriental Lettuce Cups

A crisp and tasty salad with a rich and warmly spiced
coconut and peanut dressing is served in pretty lettuce cups.

NUTRITIONAL INFORMATION

Calories . . . . . . .136 Sugars 7g
Protein . . . . .5g Fat 9g
Carbohydrate . . . .9g Saturates 2g

15 mins   0 mins

SERVES 4

INGREDIENTS

leaves cos lettuce or other firm
lettuce leaves

carrots

celery sticks

15 g/4 oz oz baby sweetcorn

spring onions

15 g/4 oz beansprouts

tbsp chopped roasted peanuts

DRESSING

tbsp smooth peanut butter

tbsp lime juice

tbsp coconut milk

tsp Thai fish sauce

tsp caster sugar

tsp fresh ginger root, grated

tsp Thai red curry paste

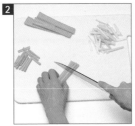

1 Wash and trim the lettuce leaves, leaving them whole. Arrange on a serving plate or on individual plates.

2 Trim the carrots and celery and cut into fine batons. Trim the baby sweetcorn and onions and slice both diagonally into thick slices.

3 Toss together all the prepared vegetables with the beansprouts.

Divide the salad mixture equally between the individual lettuce cups.

4 To make the dressing, place all the ingredients in a screw-top jar and shake vigorously until thoroughly mixed.

5 Divide the dressing equally between the salad cups, spooning it over the vegetables, then sprinkle with chopped peanuts. Serve immediately.

COOK'S TIP

Choose leaves with a deep cup shape to hold the salad neatly. If you prefer, Chinese leaves may be used in place of lettuce. To remove the leaves from the head without tearing them, cut a thick slice from the base, then gently ease away the leafy parts.

Carrot & Mango Salad

A wonderfully refreshing, simple salad to serve as a side dish with hot and spicy meat or fish dishes. It can be prepared in advance and chilled.

NUTRITIONAL INFORMATION

Calories 109   Sugars 14g
Protein . . . . .5g   Fat 4g
Carbohydrate 14   Saturates 1g

 10 mins   0 mins

SERVES 4

INGREDIENTS

4 carrots

1 small, ripe mango

200 g/7 oz firm tofu

1 tbsp chopped fresh chives

DRESSING

2 tbsp orange juice

1 tbsp lime juice

1 tsp clear honey

½ tsp orange-flower water

1 tsp sesame oil

1 tsp sesame seeds, toasted

1 Peel and coarsely grate the carrots. Peel, stone and thinly slice the mango.

2 Cut the tofu into 1 cm/½ inch dice and toss together with the carrots and mango in a wide salad bowl.

3 For the dressing, place all the ingredients in a screw-top jar and shake vigorously to mix evenly.

4 Pour the dressing over the salad and toss well to coat the salad evenly.

5 Chill the salad for 1–2 hours, wished. Just before serving, toss th salad lightly and sprinkle with chive Serve immediately.

COOK'S TIP

A food processor will grate the carrots in seconds, and is especially useful for time-saving if you're catering for a crowd.

Bamboo Shoot Salad

In Thailand, fresh bamboo would always be used for this salad, but canned bamboo shoots make a very good alternative.

NUTRITIONAL INFORMATION

Calories	54	Sugars	3g
Protein	3g	Fat	2g
Carbohydrate	7g	Saturates	0g

15 mins   8–10 mins

SERVES 4

INGREDIENTS

shallots

garlic cloves

tbsp Thai fish sauce

tbsp lime juice

tsp dried chilli flakes

tsp granulated sugar

tbsp round grain rice

tsp sesame seeds

50 g/12 oz can bamboo shoots, rinsed and drained

spring onions, chopped

fresh mint leaves, to garnish

Chinese leaves or lettuce, shredded, to serve

1 Place the whole shallots and garlic under a preheated medium-hot grill and grill until charred on the outside and tender inside. Remove the skins and place the flesh in a mortar. Grind to a smooth paste with a pestle.

2 Mix the paste with the fish sauce, lime juice, chilli flakes and sugar.

3 Place the rice and sesame seeds in a heavy-based frying pan over a low heat and cook to a rich golden brown, shaking the pan to brown evenly. Remove from the heat and crush lightly in a mortar with a pestle.

4 Use a sharp knife to slice the bamboo shoots into fine shreds. Stir in the shallot and garlic dressing, tossing well to coat the mixture evenly.

Stir in the toasted rice and sesame seeds, then the spring onions.

5 Pile the salad on to a serving dish and surround it with shredded Chinese leaves. Garnish with fresh mint leaves and serve immediately.

Hot & Sour Beef Salad

Thais are primarily fish-eaters, so beef usually appears on the menu only on feast days, but, as in this dish, a little can go a long way.

NUTRITIONAL INFORMATION

Calories	207	Sugars	.........7g
Protein	........15g	Fat	..........13g
Carbohydrate	....9g	Saturates	.......3g

40 mins   8 mins

SERVES 4

I N G R E D I E N T S

1 tsp black peppercorns

1 tsp coriander seeds

1 dried red bird-eye chilli

¼ tsp Chinese five-spice powder

250 g/9 oz beef fillet

1 tbsp dark soy sauce

6 spring onions

1 carrot

¼ cucumber

8 radishes

1 red onion

¼ head Chinese leaves

2 tbsp groundnut oil

1 garlic clove, crushed

1 tsp finely chopped lemon grass

1 tbsp chopped fresh mint

1 tbsp chopped fresh coriander

D R E S S I N G

3 tbsp lime juice

1 tbsp light soy sauce

2 tsp soft light brown sugar

1 tsp sesame oil

1 Crush the peppercorns, coriander seeds and chilli in a mortar with a pestle, then mix with the five-spice powder and sprinkle on a plate. Brush the beef all over with soy sauce, then roll it in the spices to coat evenly.

2 Cut the spring onions into 6 cm/ 2½ inch lengths, then shred finely lengthways. Place in iced water until curled. Drain well.

3 Trim the carrot and cut into very thin diagonal slices. Halve the cucumber, scoop out and discard the seeds, then slice the flesh thinly. Trim the radishes and cut into flower shapes.

4 Slice the onion thinly. Roughly shred the Chinese leaves. Toss all the vegetables together in a large salad bowl.

5 Heat the oil in a frying pan and fry the garlic and lemon grass until golden. Add the steak and cook for 3–4 minutes, turning once. Remove from the heat.

6 Slice the steak thinly and toss into the salad with the mint and coriander. Mix together the dressing ingredients and stir into the pan, then spoon over the salad. Serve immediately.

Chinese Chicken Salad

This is a refreshing dish, full of contrasting flavours and textures, that is ideal for a light lunch or an al fresco supper on a hot summer's evening.

NUTRITIONAL INFORMATION

Calories 162	Sugars 3g	
Protein 15g	Fat 10g	
Carbohydrate 5g	Saturates 2g	

25 mins   25 mins

SERVES 4

INGREDIENTS

225 g/8 oz skinless, boneless
chicken breasts

1 tsp light soy sauce

1 tsp sesame oil

1 tsp sesame seeds

1 tbsp vegetable oil

125 g/4½ oz beansprouts

1 red pepper, deseeded and thinly sliced

1 carrot, cut into matchsticks

6 baby corn cobs, sliced

SAUCE

1 tsp rice wine vinegar

1 tbsp light soy sauce

dash of chilli oil

TO GARNISH

snipped chives

carrot matchsticks

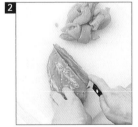

1 Place the chicken breasts in a shallow glass dish. Mix together the soy sauce and sesame oil and pour over the chicken. Sprinkle with the sesame seeds and set aside for 20 minutes, turning the chicken over occasionally.

2 Remove the chicken from the marinade and cut the meat into thin slices.

3 Heat the vegetable oil in a preheated wok or large frying pan. Add the chicken and fry for 4–5 minutes until cooked through and golden brown on both sides. Remove the chicken from the wok with a draining spoon, set aside and leave to cool.

4 Add the beansprouts, pepper, carrot and baby corn cobs to the wok and stir-fry for 2–3 minutes. Remove from the wok with a draining spoon, set aside and leave to cool.

5 To make the sauce, mix together the rice wine vinegar, light soy sauce and chilli oil.

6 Arrange the chicken and vegetables together on a serving plate. Spoon the sauce over the salad, garnish with chives and carrot matchsticks and serve.

Soups and Light Meals

There is nothing to compare with home-made soup – even the aroma as it is cooking is appetizing. Light, delicately flavoured soups, served hot or chilled, are a wonderful way to start a meal and stimulate the appetite, while hearty soups, brimming with vegetables, chicken or seafood, are warming and satisfying. Serve them with some fresh crusty bread and you have a meal in a bowl. This chapter also features other good ideas for light lunches and suppers, from Mexican tacos to Italian risottos. Recipes for all tastes include new variations on stir-fries, omelettes, hash, crêpes and even the humble baked potato.

Spinach Soup

This soup has a rich brilliant colour and an intense pure flavour.
Ready-washed spinach makes it especially quick to make.

NUTRITIONAL INFORMATION

Calories 98	Sugars 4g
Protein 4g	Fat 4g
Carbohydrate . . .12g	Saturates 1g

10 mins   40 mins

SERVES 4

I N G R E D I E N T S

1 tbsp olive oil

1 onion, halved and thinly sliced

1 leek, split lengthways and thinly sliced

1 potato, finely diced

1 litre/1¾ pints water

2 sprigs fresh marjoram sprigs or ¼ tsp dried marjoram

2 fresh thyme sprigs of ¼ tsp dried thyme

1 bay leaf

400 g/14 oz young spinach

freshly grated nutmeg

salt and pepper

4 tbsp single cream, to serve

1 Heat the oil in a heavy-based pan over a medium heat. Add the onion and leek and cook, stirring occasionally, for about 3 minutes until they are just beginning to soften.

2 Add the potato, water, marjoram, thyme and bay leaf and season with a pinch of salt. Bring to the boil, reduce the heat, cover and cook gently for about 25 minutes until the vegetables are tender. Remove the bay leaf and the herb stems.

3 Add the spinach and continue cooking for 3–4 minutes, stirring frequently, just until it is completely wilted. Remove the pan from the heat and set aside to cool slightly.

4 Transfer the soup to a blender or food processor and process to a smooth smooth purée, working in batches if necessary. (If using a food processor, strain off the cooking liquid and reserve. Process the soup solids with enough cooking liquid to moisten them, then combine with the remaining liquid.)

5 Return the soup to the pan and thin with a little more water, if wished. Season to taste with salt, pepper and nutmeg. Place over a low heat and simmer until reheated. Ladle the soup into warmed bowls and swirl a tablespoonful of cream into each serving.

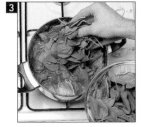

Green Vegetable Soup

This soup takes advantage of summer vegetables bursting with flavour.
If you find fresh flageolets or other fresh beans, be sure to include them.

NUTRITIONAL INFORMATION

Calories	260	Sugars	.........7g
Protein	........12g	Fat	..........15g
Carbohydrate	...21g	Saturates	.......4g

15 mins | 45 mins

SERVES 6

INGREDIENTS

1 tbsp olive oil

1 onion, finely chopped

1 large leek, split and thinly sliced

1 celery stick, thinly sliced

1 carrot, quartered and thinly sliced

1 garlic clove, finely chopped

1.4 litres/2½ pints water

1 potato, diced

1 parsnip, finely diced

1 small kohlrabi or turnip, diced

150 g/5½ oz green beans, cut in
  small pieces

150 g/5½ oz fresh or frozen peas

2 small courgettes, quartered lengthways
  and sliced

400 g/14 oz can flageolet beans, drained
  and rinsed

100 g/3½ oz spinach leaves, cut into
  thin ribbons

salt and pepper

PESTO

1 large garlic clove, very finely chopped

15 g/½ oz basil leaves

85 g/3 oz Parmesan cheese, grated

4 tbsp extra virgin olive oil

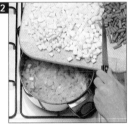

1 Heat the oil in a large pan. Cook the onion and leek over a low heat, stirring occasionally, for 5 minutes. Add the celery, carrot and garlic, cover and cook for a further 5 minutes.

2 Add the water, potato, parsnip, kohlrabi or turnip and green beans. Bring to the boil, reduce the heat, cover and simmer for 5 minutes.

3 Add the peas, courgettes and flageolet beans and season to taste.

Cover and simmer for about 25 minutes until all the vegetables are tender.

4 Meanwhile, make the pesto. Put all the ingredients in a food processor and process until smooth, scraping down the sides as necessary. Alternatively, pound together using a pestle and mortar.

5 Add the spinach to the soup and simmer for 5 minutes. Stir a spoon of the pesto into the soup. Ladle into bowls and pass the remaining pesto separately.

Celeriac, Leek & Potato Soup

It is hard to imagine that celeriac, a coarse, knobbly vegetable, can taste so sweet. It makes a wonderfully flavourful soup.

NUTRITIONAL INFORMATION

Calories	20	Sugars	1.3g
Protein	0.8g	Fat	0.7g
Carbohydrate	2.7g	Saturates	0.4g

 10 mins   35 mins

SERVES 4

INGREDIENTS

1 tbsp butter

1 onion, chopped

2 large leeks, halved lengthways and sliced

1 large celeriac (about 750 g/1 lb 10 oz), peeled and cubed

1 potato, cubed

1 carrot, quartered and thinly sliced

1.2 litres/2 pints water

⅛ tsp dried marjoram

1 bay leaf

freshly grated nutmeg

salt and pepper

celery leaves, to garnish

3 Allow the soup to cool slightly. Transfer to a blender or food processor and purée until smooth. (If using food processor, strain off cooking liquid and reserve. Purée the soup solids with enough cooking liquid to moisten them, then combine with remaining liquid.)

4 Return the puréed soup to the saucepan and stir to blend. Season with salt, pepper and nutmeg. Simmer over a medium-low heat until reheated.

5 Ladle the soup into warm bowls, garnish with celery leaves and serve.

1 Melt the butter in a large saucepan over a medium-low heat. Add the onion and leeks and cook for about 4 minutes, stirring frequently, until just softened; do not allow to colour.

2 Add the celeriac, potato, carrot, water, marjoram and bay leaf, with a large pinch of salt. Bring to the boil, reduce the heat, cover and simmer for about 25 minutes until the vegetables are tender. Remove the bay leaf.

Tarragon Pea Soup

This soup is simple and quick to make using frozen peas and stock made from a cube, ingredients you are likely to have on hand.

NUTRITIONAL INFORMATION

Calories	....	129
Protein	....	9g
Carbohydrate	...	16g

Sugars	....	6g
Fat	....	4g
Saturates	....	2g

  10 mins   55 mins

SERVES 4

I N G R E D I E N T S

2 tsp butter

1 onion, finely chopped

2 leeks, finely chopped

1½ tbsp white rice

500 g/1 lb 2 oz frozen peas

1 litre/1¾ pints water

1 chicken or vegetable stock cube

½ tsp dried tarragon

salt and pepper

chopped hard-boiled egg or croûtons,
    to garnish

1 Melt the butter in a large pan over a medium-low heat. Add the onion, leeks and rice. Cover and cook, stirring occasionally, for about 10 minutes until the vegetables are softened.

2 Add the peas, water, stock cube and tarragon and bring just to the boil. Season with a little pepper. Cover and simmer gently, stirring occasionally, for about 35 minutes until the vegetables are very tender.

3 Allow the soup to cool slightly, then transfer to a blender or food processor and process to a smooth purée, in batches if necessary. (If using a food processor, strain off the cooking liquid and reserve.

Purée the soup solids with enough cooking liquid to moisten them, then combine with the remaining liquid.)

4 Return the soup to the pan. Taste and adjust the seasoning. Gently reheat the soup over a low heat for about 10 minutes until hot.

5 Ladle into warm bowls and garnish with hard-boiled egg or croûtons.

VARIATION

Substitute frozen green beans for the peas and omit the tarragon, replacing it with a little dried thyme and/or marjoram.

Sweet & Sour Cabbage Soup

This healthy soup is made with an unusual combination of fruits and vegetables, creating a tantalising flavour that will keep people guessing.

NUTRITIONAL INFORMATION

Calories 103	Sugars 24g	
Protein 2g	Fat 0g	
Carbohydrate . . .25g	Saturates 0g	

🍲 25 mins   🕐 1½ hrs

SERVES 4–6

I N G R E D I E N T S

70 g/2½ oz sultanas

125 ml/4 fl oz orange juice

1 tbsp olive oil

1 large onion, chopped

250 g/9 oz cabbage, shredded

2 apples, peeled and diced

125 ml/4 fl oz apple juice

400 g/14 oz can peeled tomatoes

225 ml/8 fl oz tomato or vegetable juice

100 g/3½ oz pineapple flesh, finely chopped

1.2 litres/2 pints water

2 tsp wine vinegar

salt and pepper

fresh mint leaves, to garnish

1 Put the sultanas in a bowl, pour the orange juice over them and set aside to soak for 15 minutes.

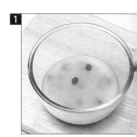

2 Heat the oil in a large pan over a medium heat. Add the onion and cook, stirring occasionally, for 3–4 minutes until it starts to soften. Add the cabbage and cook for a further 2 minutes, but do not allow it to brown.

3 Add the apples and apple juice, cover and cook for 5 minutes. Stir in the tomatoes, tomato juice, pineapple and water. Season to taste with salt and pepper and add the vinegar. Add the sultanas with the orange juice. Bring to the boil, lower the heat, partially cover and simmer for 1 hour until the fruit and vegetables are tender.

4 Remove the pan from the heat and set aside to cool slightly. Transfer the soup to a blender or food processor and process to a smooth purée, working in batches if necessary. (If using a food processor, strain off the cooking liquid and reserve. Purée the soup solids with enough cooking liquid to moisten them, then combine with the remaining liquid.)

5 Return the soup to the pan and simmer gently for about 10 minutes to reheat. Ladle into warm bowls. Garnish with mint leaves and serve immediately.

COOK'S TIP

You can use green or white cabbage to make this soup, but red cabbage would require a much longer cooking. Savoy cabbage has too powerful a flavour.

Parsnip Soup with Ginger

The exotic flavours give this simple soup a lift. If you wish, use bought ginger purée instead of grating it; add to taste as the strength varies.

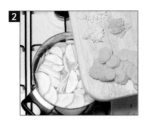

NUTRITIONAL INFORMATION

Calories	151	Sugars	19g
Protein	4g	Fat	3g
Carbohydrate	29g	Saturates	0g

10 mins   55 mins

SERVES 6

I N G R E D I E N T S

2 tsp olive oil

1 large onion, chopped

1 large leek, sliced

800 g/1 lb 12 oz parsnips, sliced

2 carrots, thinly sliced

4 tbsp grated fresh root ginger

2–3 garlic cloves, finely chopped

grated rind of ½ orange

1.4 litres/2½ pints water

225 ml/8 fl oz orange juice

salt and pepper

snipped chives or slivers of spring onion,
   to garnish

1 Heat the olive oil in a large pan over a medium heat. Add the onion and leek and cook, stirring occasionally, for about 5 minutes until softened.

2 Add the parsnips, carrots, ginger, garlic, grated orange rind, water and a pinch of salt. Reduce the heat, cover and simmer, stirring occasionally, for about 40 minutes until the vegetables are soft.

3 Remove from the heat and set aside to cool slightly, then transfer to a blender or food processor and process to a smooth purée, in batches if necessary.

4 Return the soup to the pan and stir in the orange juice. Add a little water or more orange juice, if you prefer a thinner consistency. Taste and adjust the seasoning with salt and pepper.

5 Simmer for about 10 minutes to heat through. Ladle into warmed bowls, garnish with chives or slivers of spring onion and serve immediately.

VARIATION

You could make the soup using equal amounts (450 g/1 lb each) of carrots and parsnips.

Wild Mushroom Soup

This soup has an intense, earthy flavour that brings to mind woodland aromas. It makes a memorable, rich-tasting starter.

NUTRITIONAL INFORMATION

Calories	130	Sugars	.........5g
Protein	.........3g	Fat	...........9g
Carbohydrate	....6g	Saturates	.......5g

  20 mins   1 hr

SERVES 4

INGREDIENTS

25 g/1 oz dried porcini mushrooms

350 ml/12 fl oz boiling water

125 g/4½ oz fresh porcini mushrooms

2 tsp olive oil

1 celery stick, chopped

1 carrot, chopped

1 onion, chopped

3 garlic cloves, crushed

1.2 litres/2 pints vegetable stock or water

leaves from 2 fresh thyme sprigs

1 tbsp butter

3 tbsp dry or medium sherry

2–3 tbsp soured cream

salt and pepper

chopped fresh parsley, to garnish

1 Put the dried mushrooms in a bowl and pour the boiling water over them. Set aside to soak for 10–15 minutes.

2 Brush or wash the fresh mushrooms. Trim and reserve the stems. Slice any large mushroom caps.

3 Heat the oil in a large saucepan over a medium heat. Add the celery, carrot, onion and mushroom stems. Cook, stirring frequently, for about 8 minutes until the onion begins to colour. Stir in the garlic and continue cooking for 1 minute.

4 Add the vegetable stock or water and thyme leaves with a pinch of salt. Using a draining spoon, transfer the soaked dried mushrooms to the pan. Strain the soaking liquid through a muslin-lined strainer into the pan. Bring to the boil, reduce the heat, partially cover and simmer gently for 30–40 minutes or until the carrots are tender.

5 Remove the pan from the heat and set aside to cool slightly, then transfer the soup solids with enough of the cooking liquid to moisten to a blender or food processor and purée until smooth. Return it to the pan, combine with the remaining cooking liquid, cover and simmer gently.

6 Meanwhile, melt the butter in a frying pan over a medium heat. Add the fresh mushroom caps and season to taste with salt and pepper. Cook, stirring occasionally, for about 8 minutes until they start to colour. Stirring more frequently as the liquid evaporates. When the pan becomes dry, add the sherry and cook briefly.

7 Add the mushrooms and sherry to the soup. Taste and adjust the seasoning if necessary. Ladle into warmed soup bowls, put a spoon of soured cream in each and garnish with parsley. Serve the soup immediately.

Provençal Fish Soup

For the best results, you need to use flavourful fish, such as cod or haddock, for this recipe. Frozen fish fillets are also suitable.

NUTRITIONAL INFORMATION

Calories	122	Sugars	.........6g
Protein	........12g	Fat	...........3g
Carbohydrate	....7g	Saturates	.......0g

10 mins   1½ hrs

SERVES 4–6

INGREDIENTS

1 tbsp olive oil

2 onions, finely chopped

1 small leek, thinly sliced

1 small carrot, finely chopped

1 celery stick, finely chopped

1 small fennel bulb, finely chopped (optional)

3 garlic cloves, finely chopped

225 ml/8 fl oz dry white wine

400 g/14 oz can tomatoes

1 bay leaf

pinch of fennel seeds

2 strips of orange rind

¼ tsp saffron threads

1.2 litres/2 pints water

350 g/12 oz white fish fillets, skinned

salt and pepper

croûtons, to serve (optional)

2 Add the wine and simmer for 1 minute. Add the tomatoes, bay leaf, fennel seeds, orange rind, saffron and water. Bring just to the boil, reduce the heat, cover and simmer gently, stirring occasionally, for 30 minutes.

3 Add the fish and cook for a further 20–30 minutes until it flakes easily. Remove the bay leaf and orange rind.

4 Remove the pan from the heat and set aside to cool slightly, then transfer to a blender or food processor and process to a smooth purée, working in batches if necessary. (If using a food processor, strain off the cooking liquid and reserve. Purée the soup solids with enough cooking liquid to moisten them, then combine with the remaining liquid.)

5 Return the soup to the pan. Taste and adjust the seasoning, if necessary, and simmer for 5–10 minutes until heated through. Ladle the soup into warmed bowls and sprinkle with croûtons, if using. Serve the soup immediately.

1 Heat the oil in a large pan over a medium heat. Add the onions and cook, stirring occasionally, for about 5 minutes until softened. Add the leek, carrot, celery, fennel, if using, and garlic and continue cooking for 4–5 minutes until the leek is wilted.

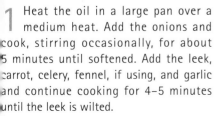

Fennel & Tomato Soup

This light and refreshing soup is also good served cold. It is an ideal starter for a summer meal, served with crunchy Melba toast.

NUTRITIONAL INFORMATION

Calories 110	Sugars 8g	
Protein 10g	Fat 2g	
Carbohydrate . . .13g	Saturates 0g	

 30 mins   40 mins

SERVES 4

INGREDIENTS

2 tsp olive oil

1 large onion, halved and sliced

2 large fennel bulbs, halved and sliced

1 small potato, diced

850 ml/1½ pints water

400 ml/14 fl oz tomato juice

1 bay leaf

115 g/4 oz peeled cooked prawns

2 tomatoes, peeled, deseeded and chopped

½ tsp snipped fresh dill

salt and pepper

fresh dill sprigs or fennel fronds, to garnish

1 Heat the olive oil in a large saucepan over a medium heat. Add the sliced onion and fennel and cook, stirring occasionally, for 3–4 minutes until the onion is just softened.

2 Add the potato, water, tomato juice and bay leaf with a pinch of salt. Reduce the heat, cover and simmer for about 25 minutes, stirring once or twice, until the vegetables are soft.

3 Remove the pan from the heat and set the soup aside to cool slightly, then transfer to a blender or food processor and process until smooth, working in batches if necessary. (If using a food processor, strain off the cooking liquid and reserve. Purée the soup solids with enough cooking liquid to moisten them, then combine with the remaining liquid.)

4 Return the soup to the saucepan and add the prawns. Simmer gently for about 10 minutes to reheat the soup and allow it to absorb the prawn flavour.

5 Stir in the tomatoes and dill. Taste and adjust the seasoning, adding more salt, if needed, and pepper. Thin the soup with a little more tomato juice, if wished. Ladle into warm bowls, garnish with dill sprigs or fennel fronds and serve.

Thai-style Seafood Soup

As taste and tolerance for chillies varies, using chilli purée, instead of fresh chillies, offers more control of the heat.

NUTRITIONAL INFORMATION

Calories 132	Sugars 7g
Protein 20g	Fat 2g
Carbohydrate 9g	Saturates 0g

 10 mins   🕐 20 mins

SERVES 4

INGREDIENTS

1.2 litres/2 pints fish stock

1 lemon grass stalk, split lengthways

pared rind of ½ lime or 1 lime leaf

2.5 cm/1 inch piece of fresh root ginger, sliced

¼ tsp chilli purée

4–6 spring onions, sliced

200 g/7 oz large of medium raw prawns, peeled and deveined

250 g/9 oz scallops (about 16–20)

2 tbsp fresh coriander leaves

salt

finely chopped red pepper or fresh red chilli rings, to garnish

1 Put the stock in a pan with the lemon grass, lime rind or lime leaf, ginger and chilli purée. Bring just to the boil, reduce the heat, cover and simmer for 10–15 minutes.

2 Cut the spring onions in half lengthways, then slice crossways very thinly. Cut the prawns almost in half lengthways, keeping the tails intact.

3 Strain the stock, return to the pan and bring to a simmer, with bubbles rising at the edges and the surface trembling. Add the spring onions and cook for 2–3 minutes. Taste and season with salt, if needed, and stir in a little more chilli purée if wished.

4 Add the scallops and prawns and poach for about 1 minute until they turn opaque and the prawns curl.

5 Add the coriander leaves, ladle the soup into warmed bowls and garnish with red pepper or chillies.

VARIATION
Substitute very small baby leeks, slivered or thinly sliced diagonally, for the spring onions. Include the green parts.

Caribbean Seafood Soup

This pretty soup is packed with exotic flavours. It is traditionally made with local vegetables, but potato and spinach are practical alternatives.

NUTRITIONAL INFORMATION

Calories	106	Sugars	. . . . .4g
Protein	. . . . .14g	Fat	. . . . .1g
Carbohydrate	. . . .11g	Saturates	. . . . . . .0g

10 mins   45 mins

SERVES 4–6

INGREDIENTS

150 g/5½ oz peeled medium prawns

200 g/7 oz firm white fish fillets, skinned and cubed

¾ tsp ground coriander

¼ tsp ground cumin

1 tsp chilli purée

3 tbsp fresh lemon juice

1 tbsp butter

1 onion, halved and thinly sliced

2 large leeks, thinly sliced

3 garlic cloves, finely chopped

1 large potato, diced

1.2 litres/2 pints chicken or vegetable stock

250 g/9 oz spinach leaves

125 ml/4 fl oz coconut milk

salt and pepper

1 Put the prawns and fish in a bowl with the coriander, cumin, chilli purée and lemon juice and set aside to marinate.

2 Melt the butter in a large pan over a medium heat. Add the onion and leeks, cover and cook, stirring occasionally, for about 10 minutes until they are softened. Add the garlic and cook for a further 3–4 minutes.

3 Add the diced potato and stock and season to taste with salt. Bring to the boil, reduce the heat, then cover and simmer gently for 15–20 minutes until the potato is tender.

4 Stir in the spinach and continue cooking, uncovered, for about 3 minutes until it is just wilted.

5 Remove the pan from the heat and set aside to cool slightly, then transfer to a blender or food processor, in batches if necessary. Purée the soup until smooth. (If using a food processor, strain off the cooking liquid and reserve. Purée the soup solids with enough cooking liquid to moisten them, then combine with the remaining liquid.)

6 Return the soup to the pan and stir in the coconut milk. Add the fish and prawns with their marinade. Simmer over a medium-low heat, stirring gently, but frequently, for about 8 minutes until the soup is heated through and the fish is cooked and flakes easily.

7 Taste and adjust the seasoning, if necessary, adding more chilli purée and/or lemon juice if wished. Ladle into warmed bowls and serve immediately.

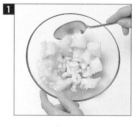

Beef Broth

This light, lean soup is studded with small diced vegetables and fragrant herbs. The stock may be used as a basis for other soups.

NUTRITIONAL INFORMATION

Calories	21	Sugars	. . . . .3g
Protein	. . . . .1g	Fat	. . . . .1g
Carbohydrate	. . . .4g	Saturates	. . . . . . .0g

  15 mins   5¼ hrs

SERVES 4–6

I N G R E D I E N T S

200 g/7 oz celeriac, finely diced

2 large carrots, finely diced

2 tsp chopped fresh marjoram

2 tsp chopped fresh parsley

2 plum tomatoes, peeled, deseeded
  and diced

salt and pepper

B E E F S T O C K

550 g/1 lb 4 oz boneless beef shin or
  stewing steak, cut into large cubes

750 g/1 lb 10 oz veal, beef or pork bones

2 onions, quartered

2.5 litres/4½ pints water

4 garlic cloves, sliced

2 carrots, sliced

1 large leek, sliced

1 celery stick, cut into 5 cm/2 inch pieces

1 bay leaf

4–5 fresh thyme sprigs or ¼ tsp dried thyme

salt

1 To make the stock, trim the fat from the beef and put the beef and the fat into a large roasting tin with the bones and onions. Roast in a preheated oven, 190°C/375°F/Gas Mark 5, for 30–40 minutes until browned, turning once or twice. Transfer the ingredients to a large flameproof casserole and discard the beef fat.

2 Add the water (it should cover by at least 5 cm/2 inches) and bring to the boil. Skim off any foam, reduce the heat and add the garlic, carrots, leek, celery, bay leaf, thyme and a pinch of salt. Simmer very gently for 4 hours, skimming occasionally. If the ingredients emerge from the liquid, top up with water.

3 Strain the stock through a muslin-lined sieve into a large container and remove as much fat as possible. Save the meat for another purpose, if wished, and discard the bones and vegetables.

4 Boil the stock very gently until it is reduced to 1.5 litres/2¾ pints. Taste and adjust the seasoning if necessary.

5 Bring a pan of salted water to the boil and add the celeriac and carrots. Reduce the heat, cover and simmer for about 15 minutes until tender. Drain.

6 Add the herbs to the boiling beef stock. Divide the cooked vegetables and tomatoes among warmed bowls, ladle over the stock and serve.

Chicken Soup with Stars

How delicious a simple, fresh soup can be. Chicken wings are good to use for making the stock, as the meat is very sweet and doesn't dry out.

NUTRITIONAL INFORMATION

Calories	119	Sugars	.........2g
Protein	........14g	Fat	..........2g
Carbohydrate	...13g	Saturates	.......0g

20 mins   2¾ hrs

SERVES 5–6

I N G R E D I E N T S

85 g/3 oz small pasta stars, or other very small shapes

chopped fresh parsley

C H I C K E N   S T O C K

1.25 kg/2 lb 12 oz chicken pieces, such as wings or legs

2.5 litres/4½ pints water

1 celery stick, sliced

1 large carrot, sliced

1 onion, sliced

1 leek, sliced

2 garlic cloves, crushed

8 peppercorns

4 allspice berries

3–4 parsley stems

2–3 fresh thyme sprigs

1 bay leaf

salt and pepper

2 Remove the chicken from the stock and set aside to cool. Continue simmering the stock, uncovered, for about 30 minutes. When the chicken is cool enough to handle, remove the meat from the bones and, if necessary, cut into bite-size pieces.

3 Strain the stock and remove as much fat as possible. Discard the vegetables and flavourings. (There should be about 1.8 litres/3 pints chicken stock.)

4 Bring the stock to the boil in a clean span. Add the pasta and lower the heat so that the stock boils very gently. Cook for about 10 minutes or until the pasta is tender, but still firm to the bite.

5 Stir in the chicken meat. Taste the soup and adjust the seasoning if necessary. Ladle into warmed bowls and serve sprinkled with parsley.

1 Put the chicken in a large flameproof casserole with the water, celery, carrot, onion, leek, garlic, peppercorns, allspice, herbs and ½ teaspoon salt. Bring just to the boil and skim off the foam that rises to the surface. Reduce the heat, partially cover and simmer, for 2 hours.

Chicken & Rice Soup

Any kind of rice is suitable for this soup – white or brown long grain rice, or even wild rice. Leftover cooked rice is a handy addition for soups.

NUTRITIONAL INFORMATION

Calories	165	Sugars	.........2g
Protein	........14g	Fat	..........4g
Carbohydrate	...19g	Saturates	.......1g

5 mins   25 mins

SERVES 4

INGREDIENTS

1.5 litres/2¾ pints chicken stock (see Cook's Tip)

2 small carrots, very thinly sliced

1 celery stick, finely diced

1 baby leek, halved lengthways and thinly sliced

115 g/4 oz petit pois, thawed if frozen

175 g/6 oz cooked rice

150 g/5½ oz cooked chicken meat, sliced

2 tsp chopped fresh tarragon

1 tbsp chopped fresh parsley

salt and pepper

fresh parsley sprigs, to garnish

crusty bread, to serve

1 Put the chicken stock in a large pan and add the carrots, celery and leek. Bring to the boil, reduce the heat to low, partially cover and simmer gently for 10 minutes until the vegetables are tender.

2 Stir in the peas, rice and chicken meat and continue cooking for a further 10–15 minutes or until the vegetables are tender.

3 Add the chopped tarragon and parsley and season to taste with salt and pepper as needed.

4 Ladle the soup into warmed bowls, garnish with fresh parsley sprigs and serve immediately with crusty bread.

COOK'S TIP

If the stock you are using is a little weak or if you have used a stock cube, add the herbs at the beginning, so that they can flavour the stock for a longer time.

Provençal Turkey Soup

No need to wait for Christmas leftovers – pre-packed turkey, such as boneless breast or stir-fry meat, makes this a year-round favourite.

NUTRITIONAL INFORMATION

Calories 216   Sugars 8g
Protein . . . . .25g   Fat 6g
Carbohydrate . . .10g   Saturates 1g

  10 mins   50 mins

SERVES 4–5

I N G R E D I E N T S

1 tbsp olive oil

2 red, yellow or green peppers, deseeded and finely chopped

1 celery stick, thinly sliced

1 large onion, finely chopped

125 ml/4 fl oz dry white wine

400 g/14 oz can plum tomatoes

3–4 garlic cloves, finely chopped

1 litre/1¾ pints turkey or chicken stock

¼ tsp dried thyme

1 bay leaf

2 courgettes, finely diced

350 g/12 oz cooked diced turkey

salt and pepper

fresh basil leaves, to garnish

1 Heat the oil in a large pan over a medium heat. Add the peppers, celery and onion and cook for about 8 minutes until softened and just beginning to colour.

2 Add the wine and simmer for 1 minute. Add the tomatoes and garlic.

3 Stir in the stock. Add the thyme and bay leaf, season to taste with salt and pepper and bring to the boil. Reduce the heat, cover and simmer for about 25 minutes until the vegetables are tender.

4 Add the courgettes and turkey. Continue cooking for a further 10–15 minutes until the courgettes are completely tender.

5 Taste the soup and adjust the seasoning if necessary. Ladle into warmed bowls, garnish with basil leaves and serve immediately.

COOK'S TIP

A large turkey leg can be used to make this soup. Put in a pan, add water to cover generously and add 1 each carrot, celery stick, leek and onion, coarsely chopped, and a little salt. Poach for 3 hours. Remove the fat from the stock before making the soup.

Oriental Duck Broth

This soup combines delicate flavours with a satisfying meaty taste. Although duck is notoriously fatty, the legs are leaner than the breast.

NUTRITIONAL INFORMATION

Calories 98	Sugars 4g
Protein 9g	Fat 3g
Carbohydrate 9g	Saturates 1g

🍲 10 mins   🕐 1¾ hrs

SERVES 4–6

I N G R E D I E N T S

2 duck leg quarters, skinned

1 litre/1¾ pints water

600 ml/1 pint chicken stock

2.5 cm/1 inch piece of fresh root ginger, sliced

1 large carrot, sliced

1 onion, sliced

1 leek, sliced

3 garlic cloves, crushed

1 tsp black peppercorns

2 tbsp soy sauce

1 small carrot, cut into thin strips or slivers

1 small leek, cut into thin strips or slivers

100 g/3½ oz shiitake mushrooms, thinly sliced

25 g/1 oz watercress leaves

salt and pepper

1 Put the duck in a large pan with the water. Bring just to the boil and skim off the foam that rises to the surface. Add the stock, ginger, carrot, onion, leek, garlic, peppercorns and soy sauce. Reduce the heat, partially cover and simmer gently for 1½ hours.

2 Remove the duck from the stock and set aside. When the duck is cool enough to handle, remove the meat from the bones and slice thinly or shred into bite-size pieces, discarding any fat.

3 Strain the stock and press with the back of a spoon to extract all the liquid. Remove as much fat as possible. Discard the vegetables and flavourings.

4 Bring the stock just to the boil in a clean saucepan and add the strips of carrot and leek and the mushrooms with the duck meat. Reduce the heat and simmer gently for 5 minutes or until the carrot is just tender.

5 Stir in the watercress and continue simmering for 1–2 minutes until it is wilted. Taste the soup and adjust the seasoning if necessary, adding a little more soy sauce if wished. Ladle the soup into warmed soup bowls and serve immediately.

White Bean Soup

In this elegant soup, the pungent green olive purée provides
a pleasant counterpoint to the natural sweetness of the beans.

NUTRITIONAL INFORMATION

Calories	286	Sugars	........3g
Protein	........11g	Fat	..........14g
Carbohydrate	...30g	Saturates	.......2g

6¼ hrs   2 hrs

SERVES 8

INGREDIENTS

350 g/12 oz dried haricot beans

1 tbsp olive oil

1 large onion, finely chopped

1 large leek (white part only), thinly sliced

3 garlic cloves, finely chopped

2 celery sticks finely chopped

2 small carrots, finely chopped

1 small fennel bulb, finely chopped

2 litres/3½ pints water

¼ tsp dried thyme

¼ tsp dried marjoram

salt and pepper

TAPENADE

1 garlic clove

1 small bunch of fresh flat leaf parsley,
 stems removed

250 g/9 oz almond-stuffed green
 olives, drained

5 tbsp olive oil

1 Pick over the beans, cover generously with cold water and set aside to soak for 6 hours or overnight. Drain the beans, put in a pan and add cold water to cover by 5 cm/2 inches. Bring to the boil and boil for 10 minutes. Drain and rinse well.

2 Heat the oil in a large heavy-based pan over a medium heat. Add the onion and leek, cover and cook for about 3–4 minutes, stirring occasionally, until just softened. Add the garlic, celery, carrots and fennel and continue cooking for 2 minutes.

3 Add the water, beans, thyme and marjoram. When the mixture begins to simmer, reduce the heat to low. Cover and simmer gently, stirring occasionally, for about 1½ hours until the beans are very tender.

4 Meanwhile make the tapenade. Put the garlic, parsley and olives into a blender or food processor with the olive oil. Process to a purée and scrape into a small serving bowl.

5 Remove the pan from the heat and set aside to cool slightly, then transfer to a blender or food processor and process to a smooth purée, in batches if necessary. (If using a food processor, strain off the cooking liquid and reserve. Purée the soup solids with enough cooking liquid to moisten them, then combine with the remaining liquid.)

6 Return the soup to the pan. Season with salt and pepper to taste and simmer until heated through. Ladle into bowls and serve, stirring a teaspoon of the tapenade into each serving.

Beans & Greens Soup

Include some pungent greens in this soup, if you can. They add a wonderful gutsy flavour and, of course, are very good for you!

NUTRITIONAL INFORMATION

Calories	282	Sugars	.........8g
Protein	........16g	Fat	...........4g
Carbohydrate	...46g	Saturates	.......1g

6¼ hrs   2 hrs

SERVES 4

INGREDIENTS

250 g/9 oz dried haricot or cannellini beans

1 tbsp olive oil

2 onions, finely chopped

4 garlic cloves, finely chopped

1 celery stick, thinly sliced

2 carrots, halved and thinly sliced

1.2 litres/2 pints water

¼ tsp dried thyme

¼ tsp dried marjoram

1 bay leaf

115 g/4 oz leafy greens, such as chard, mustard, spinach and kale, washed

salt and pepper

1 Cover the beans with cold water and soak for 6 hours or overnight. Drain, put in a pan and add water to cover by 5 cm/2 inches. Bring to the boil and boil for 10 minutes. Drain and rinse.

2 Heat the olive oil in a large pan over a medium heat. Add the onion and cook, stirring occasionally, for about 3–4 minutes until just softened. Add the garlic, celery and carrots and continue cooking for 2 minutes.

3 Add the water, beans, thyme, marjoram and bay leaf. When the mixture begins to simmer, reduce the heat to low. Cover and simmer gently, stirring occasionally, for about 1¼ hours until the beans are tender. The cooking time will vary depending on the type of bean. Season to taste with salt and pepper.

4 Remove the pan from the heat and set aside to cool slightly, then transfer 450 ml/16 fl oz to a blender or food processor. Process to a smooth purée and recombine with the soup.

5 Cut the greens crossways into thin ribbons, keeping tender leaves, such as spinach, separate. Add the thicker leaves and cook gently for 10 minutes. Stir in any remaining greens and cook for a further 5–10 minutes until all the greens are tender. Taste and adjust the seasoning if necessary. Ladle the soup into warmed bowls and serve immediately.

Greek Bean Soup

This is based on a simple soup typical of Greek home cooking.
The artichoke hearts make it fancier, but they are not essential.

NUTRITIONAL INFORMATION

Calories 109	Sugars 7g
Protein 6g	Fat 3g
Carbohydrate . . .16g	Saturates 0g

  10 mins   1¼ hrs

SERVES 6

INGREDIENTS

1 tbsp olive oil

1 large onion, finely chopped

1 large carrot, finely diced

2 celery sticks, finely chopped

4 tomatoes, peeled, deseeded and chopped, or 250 g/9 oz drained canned tomatoes

2 garlic cloves, finely chopped

2 x 400 g/14 oz cans cannellini or haricot beans, drained and rinsed

1.2 litres/2 pints water

1 courgette, finely diced

grated rind of ½ lemon

1 tbsp chopped fresh mint or ¼ tsp dried mint

1 tsp chopped fresh thyme or ⅛ tsp dried thyme

1 bay leaf

400 g/14 oz can artichoke hearts, drained

salt and pepper

1 Heat 1 teaspoon of the olive oil in a large pan over a medium heat. Add the onion and cook, stirring occasionally, for 3–4 minutes until softened. Add the carrot, celery, tomatoes and garlic and continue cooking for a further 5 minutes, stirring frequently.

2 Add the beans and water. Bring to the boil, reduce the heat, cover and cook gently for about 10 minutes.

3 Add the courgette, lemon rind, mint, thyme and bay leaf and season to taste with salt and pepper. Cover and simmer for about 40 minutes until all the vegetables are tender. Remove the pan from the heat and set aside to cool slightly. Remove the bay leaf and transfer 450 ml/16 fl oz of the soup to a blender or food processor, process to a smooth purée and recombine.

4 Meanwhile, heat the remaining oil in a frying pan over a medium heat. Fry the artichokes, cut side down, until lightly browned. Turn over and fry long enough to heat through. Ladle the soup into warmed bowls and top each with an artichoke heart. Serve immediately.

Bean & Pumpkin Soup

Pumpkin, a greatly underrated vegetable, balances the spicy heat in this soup and gives it a splash of colour, too.

NUTRITIONAL INFORMATION

Calories 170	Sugars 8g
Protein 11g	Fat 3g
Carbohydrate ...27g	Saturates 0g

    6¼ hrs   2½ hrs

SERVES 4–6

INGREDIENTS

250 g/9 oz dried kidney beans

1 tbsp olive oil

2 onions, finely chopped

4 garlic cloves, finely chopped

1 celery stick, thinly sliced

1 carrot, halved and thinly sliced

2 tsp tomato purée

pinch of dried thyme

pinch of dried oregano

pinch of ground cumin

1.2 litres/2 pints water

1 bay leaf

400 g/14 oz can chopped tomatoes

250 g/9 oz peeled pumpkin flesh, diced

¼ tsp chilli purée

salt and pepper

fresh coriander leaves, to garnish

1 Pick over the beans, cover generously with cold water and set aside to soak for 6 hours or overnight. Drain the beans, put in a pan and add enough cold water to cover by 5 cm/2 inches. Bring to the boil and boil for 10 minutes. Drain and rinse.

2 Heat the olive oil in a large pan over a medium heat. Add the onions and cook, stirring occasionally, for 3–4 minutes until they are just softened. Add the garlic, celery and carrot and continue cooking for 2 minutes.

3 Add the kidney beans, tomato purée, thyme, oregano, cumin, water and bay leaf. When the mixture is just beginning to simmer, reduce the heat to low. Cover and simmer gently, stirring occasionally, for 1 hour.

4 Stir in the tomatoes, pumpkin and chilli purée. Continue simmering, stirring occasionally, for about 1 hour more or until the beans and pumpkin are tender.

5 Season the soup to taste with salt and pepper and stir in a little more chilli purée if liked. Ladle the soup into warmed bowls, garnish with coriander leaves and serve immediately.

Split Pea & Ham Soup

A hearty and heart-warming soup, this is perfect for weekend lunches – or make it ahead for a nourishing mid-week supper, all ready to reheat.

NUTRITIONAL INFORMATION

Calories	300	Sugars	.........5g
Protein	........23g	Fat	...........9g
Carbohydrate	...35g	Saturates	.......2g

10 mins   1¼–1½ hrs

SERVES 6–8

INGREDIENTS

500 g/1 lb 2 oz split green peas

1 tbsp olive oil

1 large onion, finely chopped

1 large carrot, finely chopped

1 celery stick, finely chopped

1 litre/1¾ pints chicken or vegetable stock

1 litre/1¾ pints water

225 g/8 oz lean smoked ham, finely diced

¼ tsp dried thyme

¼ tsp dried marjoram

1 bay leaf

salt and pepper

1 Rinse the peas under cold running water. Put in a pan and cover generously with water. Bring to the boil and boil for 3 minutes, skimming off the foam from the surface. Drain the peas.

2 Heat the oil in a large pan over a medium heat. Add the onion and cook, stirring occasionally, for about 3–4 minutes, until just softened.

3 Add the carrot and celery and continue cooking for 2 minutes. Add the peas, pour in the stock and water and stir to combine.

4 Bring just to the boil and stir the ham into the soup. Add the thyme, marjoram and bay leaf. Reduce the heat, cover and cook gently for 1–1½ hours until the ingredients are very soft. Remove and discard the bay leaf.

5 Taste and adjust the seasoning if necessary. Ladle into warm soup bowls and serve immediately.

VARIATION
You could add sliced, cooked sausages instead of or in addition to the ham.

Split Pea & Parsnip Soup

This soup is surprisingly delicate. The yellow peas give it an appealing light colour, while the parsnips add an aromatic flavour.

NUTRITIONAL INFORMATION

Calories	270	Sugars	5g
Protein	16g	Fat	7g
Carbohydrate	39g	Saturates	1g

🧊 10 mins   🕐 1 hr

SERVES 4

INGREDIENTS

250 g/9 oz split yellow peas

1 tbsp olive oil

1 onion, finely chopped

1 small leek, finely chopped

3 garlic cloves, finely chopped

2 parsnips, sliced (about 225 g/8 oz)

2 litres/3½ pints water

10 fresh sage leaves or ¼ tsp dried sage

pinch of dried thyme

¼ tsp ground coriander

1 bay leaf

salt and pepper

freshly grated nutmeg

chopped fresh coriander leaves or parsley, to garnish

1 Rinse the peas well under cold running water. Put in a pan and cover generously with water. Bring to the boil and boil for 3 minutes, skimming off the foam from the surface. Drain the peas.

2 Heat the oil in a large pan over a medium heat. Add the onion and leek and cook, stirring occasionally, for about 3 minutes until just softened. Add the garlic and parsnips and continue cooking, stirring occasionally, for 2 minutes.

3 Add the peas, water, sage, thyme, coriander and bay leaf. Bring almost to the boil, reduce the heat, cover and simmer gently for about 40 minutes until the vegetables are very soft. Remove the bay leaf.

4 Remove the pan from the heat and set aside to cool slightly, then transfer to a blender or food processor and process to a smooth purée, in batches if necessary. (If using a food processor, strain off the cooking liquid and reserve. Purée the soup solids with enough cooking liquid to moisten them, then combine with the remaining liquid.)

5 Return the soup to the pan and thin with a little more water, if wished. Season generously with salt, pepper and nutmeg. Place over a low heat and simmer until reheated. Ladle into warmed soup plates and garnish with fresh coriander leaves or parsley.

Chickpea Soup with Chorizo

This soup is satisfying and colourful, with an appealing piquancy from the chorizo. Try to find the Iberico style, which is very meaty and lean.

NUTRITIONAL INFORMATION

Calories ....394 Sugars 11g
Protein ....24g Fat 12g
Carbohydrate ...52g Saturates 3g

 10 mins   1¾ hrs

SERVES 4

INGREDIENTS

250 g/9 oz dried chickpeas, soaked overnight in cold water to cover

115 g/4 oz lean chorizo, skinned and finely diced

1 onion, finely chopped

1 shallot, finely chopped

1 carrot, thinly sliced

2 garlic cloves, finely chopped

400 g/14 oz can chopped tomatoes

1.2 litres/2 pints water

1 bay leaf

¼ tsp dried thyme

¼ tsp dried oregano

225 g/8 oz pumpkin, diced

225 g/8 oz potato, diced

115 g/4 oz curly kale leaves, finely chopped

salt and pepper

1 Drain the chickpeas and put in a pan with enough cold water to cover generously. Bring to the boil over a high heat and cook for 10 minutes. Drain.

2 Put the chorizo in a large, dry pan over a medium-low heat. Cook, stirring frequently, for 5–10 minutes to render as much fat as possible. Remove with a draining spoon and drain on absorbent kitchen paper.

3 Pour off the excess fat from the pan and return to the heat. Add the onion, shallot, carrot and garlic and cook, stirring occasionally, for 3–4 minutes.

4 Transfer to a larger pan if necessary. Add the chickpeas, tomatoes, water, herbs and chorizo. Bring almost to the boil, reduce the heat, cover and simmer gently for 30 minutes.

5 Stir in the pumpkin and potato, cover and continue cooking for about 30 minutes until the chickpeas are tender. Season to taste with salt and pepper.

6 Stir in the kale and continue to cook, uncovered, for 15–20 minutes or until it is tender. Taste and adjust the seasoning if necessary. Ladle the soup into warmed bowls and serve immediately.

COOK'S TIP

You can easily chop the kale in a food processor; it should be like chopped parsley. Alternatively, slice crossways into very thin ribbons.

Hummus & Courgette Soup

This light and elegant soup couldn't be easier. Its subtle flavour makes it a great starter for entertaining, especially when feeding vegetarians.

NUTRITIONAL INFORMATION

Calories	135	Sugars	.........3g
Protein	.........5g	Fat	...........9g
Carbohydrate	....8g	Saturates	.......0g

🍲 10 mins 🕐 30 mins

SERVES 4

INGREDIENTS

tsp olive oil

small onion, sliced

courgettes, sliced (about 450 g/1 lb)

50 ml/16 fl oz vegetable or chicken stock

75 g/6 oz ready-made hummus

fresh lemon juice, to taste

salt and pepper

finely chopped fresh parsley, to garnish

1 Heat the olive oil in a pan over a medium heat. Add the onion and courgette slices, cover and cook, stirring occasionally, for about 3 minutes until they begin to soften.

2 Add the stock and season lightly with salt and pepper. Bring to the boil, reduce the heat, cover and simmer gently for about 20 minutes until the vegetables are tender.

3 Remove the pan from the heat and set aside to cool slightly, then transfer to a blender or food processor and process to a smooth purée. (If using a food processor, strain off the cooking liquid and reserve. Purée the soup solids with enough cooking liquid to moisten them, then combine with the remaining liquid.)

4 Add the hummus to the puréed soup in the blender or processor and process to combine.

5 Return the soup to the pan and reheat gently over a medium-low heat. Taste and adjust the seasoning, if necessary, adding a little lemon juice if wished. Ladle into warmed bowls, sprinkle with parsley and serve immediately.

COOK'S TIP
If you wish, peel the courgettes. It gives the soup a nice pale colour.

Tomato & Lentil Soup

This soup is simple and satisfying, with subtle flavours. It uses ingredients you are likely to have on hand, so it's ideal for a last-minute meal.

NUTRITIONAL INFORMATION

Calories	197	Sugars	.........9g
Protein	.......12g	Fat	..........3g
Carbohydrate	...33g	Saturates	.......0g

10 mins   🕐 1 hr

SERVES 6

I N G R E D I E N T S

1 tbsp olive oil

1 leek, thinly sliced

1 large carrot, quartered and thinly sliced

1 large onion, finely chopped

2 garlic cloves, finely chopped

250 g/9 oz split red lentils

1.2 litres/2 pints water

350 ml/12 fl oz tomato juice

400 g/14 oz can chopped tomatoes

¼ tsp ground cumin

¼ tsp ground coriander

1 bay leaf

salt and pepper

chopped fresh dill or parsley, to garnish

1 Heat the oil in a large pan over a medium heat. Add the leek, carrot, onion and garlic. Cover and cook, stirring occasionally, for 4–5 minutes until the vegetables are slightly softened.

2 Rinse and drain the lentils (check for any small stones). Add the lentils to the pan and stir in the water, tomato juice and tomatoes. Add the cumin, coriander and bay leaf with a pinch of salt. Bring to the boil, reduce the heat and simmer gently for about 45 minutes or until the vegetables are tender. Remove the bay leaf.

3 Remove the pan from the heat and set aside to cool slightly. If you prefer a smooth soup, transfer the mixture to a blender or food processor and process to a smooth purée, working in batches if necessary. (If using a food processor, strain off the cooking liquid and reserve. Purée the soup solids with enough cooking liquid to moisten them, then combine with the remaining liquid.) Process only about half of the mixture if you prefer a soup with a chunkier texture.

4 Return the puréed soup to the pan and stir to blend. Season with salt and pepper to taste. Simmer over a medium-low heat until reheated.

5 Ladle the soup into warm bowls, garnish with dill or parsley and serve.

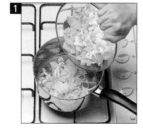  

Golden Vegetable Soup

In this simple-to-make soup, the flavours meld after blending to create a delicious taste. It is also very healthy and looks appealing.

NUTRITIONAL INFORMATION

Calories	155	Sugars	.........5g
Protein	........10g	Fat	...........3g
Carbohydrate	...22g	Saturates	.......0g

10 mins   1½ hrs

SERVES 6

INGREDIENTS

1 tbsp olive oil

1 onion, finely chopped

1 garlic clove, finely chopped

1 carrot, halved and thinly sliced

450 g/1 lb green cabbage, shredded

400 g/14 oz can chopped tomatoes

½ tsp dried thyme

2 bay leaves

1.5 litres/2¾ pints vegetable stock

200 g/7 oz Puy lentils

450 ml/16 fl oz water

salt and pepper

fresh coriander leaves or parsley, to garnish

1 Heat the oil in a large pan over a medium heat. Add the onion, garlic and carrot and cook, stirring occasionally, for 3–4 minutes. Add the cabbage and cook for a further 2 minutes.

2 Add the tomatoes, thyme and 1 bay leaf, then pour in the stock. Bring to the boil, reduce the heat, partially cover and simmer for about 45 minutes until the vegetables are tender.

3 Meanwhile, put the lentils in another pan with the remaining bay leaf and the water. Bring just to the boil, reduce

the heat and simmer for about 25 minutes until tender. Drain off any remaining water and set aside.

4 Remove the soup pan from the heat and set aside to cool slightly, then transfer to a blender or food processor and process to a smooth purée, working in batches, if necessary. (If using a food processor, strain off the cooking liquid and

reserve. Purée the soup solids with enough cooking liquid to moisten them, then combine with the remaining liquid.)

5 Return the soup to the pan and add the cooked lentils. Taste and adjust the seasoning, if necessary, and cook for about 10 minutes to heat through. Ladle into warm bowls and garnish with coriander leaves or parsley.

Mushroom & Barley Soup

This old-fashioned soup is nourishing and warming, with distinctive flavours and a nice chewy texture.

NUTRITIONAL INFORMATION

Calories	204	Sugars	.........7g
Protein	.........5g	Fat	...........8g
Carbohydrate	...31g	Saturates	.......3g

 5 mins 1¼ hrs

SERVES 4

INGREDIENTS

60 g/2 oz pearl barley

1.5 litres/2¾ pints chicken or vegetable stock

1 bay leaf

1 tbsp butter

350 g/12 oz mushrooms, thinly sliced

1 tsp olive oil

1 onion, finely chopped

2 carrots, thinly sliced

1 tbsp chopped fresh tarragon

1 tbsp chopped fresh parsley

salt and pepper

1 tbsp chopped fresh parsley or tarragon, to garnish

1 Rinse and drain the barley. Bring 450 ml/16 fl oz of the stock to the boil in a small pan. Add the bay leaf and a pinch of salt. Stir in the barley, reduce the heat, cover and simmer for 40 minutes.

2 Melt the butter in a large frying pan over a medium heat. Add the mushrooms and season to taste with salt and pepper. Cook, stirring occasionally, for about 8 minutes until they are golden brown. Stir more often after the mushrooms start to colour. Remove the mushrooms from the heat.

3 Heat the oil in a large pan over a medium heat and add the onion and carrots. Cook, stirring occasionally, for about 3 minutes until the onion is softened and translucent.

4 Add the remaining stock and bring to the boil. Stir in the barley with its cooking liquid and add the mushrooms. Reduce the heat, cover and simmer gently, stirring occasionally, for about 20 minutes or until the carrots are tender.

5 Stir in the tarragon and parsley. Ladle into warmed bowls, garnish with fresh parsley or tarragon and serve.

COOK'S TIP

The barley will continue to absorb liquid if the soup is stored, so if you are making ahead, you may need to add a little more stock or water when reheating the soup.

Rice & Bean Soup

This soup is satisfying and very healthy. Brown rice gives a pleasing chewy texture, but white rice could be used instead.

NUTRITIONAL INFORMATION

Calories	285	Sugars	.........7g
Protein	........18g	Fat	...........5g
Carbohydrate	...43g	Saturates	.......1g

6¼ hrs   2 hrs

SERVES 4

I N G R E D I E N T S

250 g/9 oz dried black-eye beans

1 tbsp olive oil

1 large onion, finely chopped

2 garlic cloves, finely chopped or crushed

2 carrots, finely chopped

2 celery sticks, finely chopped

1 small red pepper, deseeded and
  finely chopped

85 g/3 oz lean smoked ham, finely diced

½ tsp fresh thyme leaves

1 bay leaf

1.2 litres/2 pints chicken or vegetable stock

600 ml/1 pint water

100 g/3½ oz brown rice

salt and pepper

chopped fresh parsley or chives, to garnish

1 Put the beans in a bowl, cover generously with cold water and set aside to soak for at least 6 hours or overnight. Drain the beans, put in a pan and add enough cold water to cover by 5 cm/2 inches. Bring to the boil and boil for 10 minutes. Drain and rinse well.

2 Heat the oil in a large heavy-based pan over a medium heat. Add the onion, cover and cook, stirring frequently, for 3–4 minutes until just softened. Add the garlic, carrots, celery and pepper, stir well and cook for a further 2 minutes.

3 Transfer to a larger pan if necessary. Add the beans, ham, thyme, bay leaf, stock and water. Bring to the boil, reduce the heat, cover and simmer gently, stirring occasionally, for 1 hour or until the beans are just tender.

4 Stir in the rice and season the soup with salt, if needed, and pepper. Continue cooking for 30 minutes or until the rice and beans are tender.

5 Remove and discard the bay leaf. Taste the soup and adjust the seasoning if necessary. Ladle into warmed bowls and serve garnished with parsley or chives.

Piquant Oatmeal Soup

This unusual soup, of Mexican origin, is simple and comforting.
It has a hint of chilli heat, but its character is more sweet than spicy.

NUTRITIONAL INFORMATION

Calories	172	Sugars	.........4g
Protein	.........4g	Fat	...........9g
Carbohydrate	...21g	Saturates	.......4g

15 mins   40 mins

SERVES 6

INGREDIENTS

85 g/3 oz rolled oats

3 tbsp butter

1 large sweet onion

2–3 garlic cloves

350 g/12 oz tomatoes, peeled, deseeded and chopped

1.4 litres/2½ pints chicken stock

¼ tsp ground cumin

1 tsp harissa or ½ tsp chilli purée

1–2 tbsp lime juice

salt and pepper

chopped spring onions, to garnish

1 Place a heavy-based frying pan over a medium heat. Add the oats and toast, stirring frequently for about 25 minutes until lightly and evenly browned. Remove the oats from the pan and set aside to cool completely.

2 Melt the butter in a large pan over a medium heat. Add the onion and garlic and cook, stirring occasionally, until the onion is softened.

3 Add the tomatoes, stock, cumin, harissa or chilli purée and season to taste with salt.

4 Stir in the oats and bring to the boil. Lower the heat so that the soup simmers gently and cook for 6 minutes.

5 Stir in 1 tablespoon of the lime juice. Taste and adjust the seasoning. Add more lime juice if desired. Ladle the soup into warmed bowls and sprinkle with spring onions to garnish.

COOK'S TIP

This soup is very quick to prepare once the oats are toasted. The oats could be prepared in advance at a convenient time.

Melon Gazpacho

Glass bowls are pretty for serving this soup, which makes a very light and refreshing starter for warm days.

NUTRITIONAL INFORMATION

Calories	98	Sugars	.......20g
Protein	.........3g	Fat	...........1g
Carbohydrate	...21g	Saturates	.......0g

45 mins   6–7 mins

SERVES 4

I N G R E D I E N T S

tsp oil	
onion, finely chopped	
large garlic clove, finely chopped	
tsp chopped fresh chilli	
00 g/1 lb 9 oz seedless Cantaloupe melon flesh, cubed	
tsp raspberry vinegar or 1 tsp lemon juice	
ripe green melon, such as Galia (about 500 g/1 lb 2 oz)	
alt	
nipped chives, to garnish	

1 Heat the oil in a small pan over a low heat. Add the onion, garlic and chilli and cook, stirring occasionally, for about 6–7 minutes until the onion is softened, but not browned.

2 Put the Cantaloupe melon flesh in a blender or food processor, add the onion, garlic and chilli and process to a smooth purée, stopping to scrape down the sides as needed. You may need to work in batches. Add the vinegar or lemon juice with a pinch of salt and process briefly to combine.

3 Cover with clingfilm and chill in the refrigerator for about 30 minutes or until the mixture is cold.

4 Remove the seeds from the green melon, then cut into balls with a melon baller. Alternatively, cut into cubes with a sharp knife.

5 Divide the soup among 4 shallow bowls and top with the green melon balls. Sprinkle lightly with chives to garnish and serve.

COOK'S TIP

If you are wary of using fresh chilli, omit it and add a few drops of hot pepper sauce to taste at the end of Step 2 to liven up the soup.

Cold Tomato & Orange Soup

This soup is made from raw vegetables and fruit, so it is full of goodness as well as flavour and is wonderfully refreshing on a warm day.

NUTRITIONAL INFORMATION

Calories 98	Sugars 22g	
Protein 3g	Fat 0g	
Carbohydrate ...22g	Saturates 0g	

🍞 45 mins 🕐 0 mins

SERVES 4

I N G R E D I E N T S

3 large seedless oranges

4 ripe tomatoes

2 celery sticks, chopped

3 carrots, grated

350 ml/12 fl oz tomato juice

salt

Tabasco sauce (optional)

1 tbsp chopped fresh mint

fresh mint sprigs, to garnish

1 Working over a bowl to catch the juices, peel the oranges. Cut down between the membranes and drop the orange segments into the bowl.

2 Put the tomatoes in a small bowl and pour over boiling water to cover. Stand for 10 seconds, then drain. Peel off the skins and cut the tomatoes in half crossways. Scoop out the seeds into a strainer set over a bowl; reserve the tomato juices.

3 Put the tomatoes, celery and carrots in a blender or food processor. Add the orange segments and their juice and the juice saved from the tomatoes. Process to a smooth purée.

4 Scrape into a bowl and stir in th[e] tomato juice. Cover with clingfil[m] and chill until cold.

5 Taste the soup and add salt, [if] needed, and a few drops of Tabasc[o] sauce, if wished. Stir in the chopped min[t,] ladle into cold bowls and garnish wit[h] fresh mint sprigs.

COOK'S TIP

This soup really needs to be made in a blender for the best texture. A food processor can be used, but the soup will not be completely smooth.

Avocado & Almond Soup

This rich-tasting chilled soup has an inviting colour and would make an appetising start to a dinner party.

NUTRITIONAL INFORMATION

Calories	392	Sugars	.........5g
Protein	.........8g	Fat	..........36g
Carbohydrate	....9g	Saturates	.......6g

50 mins | 30 mins

SERVES 4

I N G R E D I E N T S

600 ml/1 pint water

onion, finely chopped

celery stick, finely chopped

carrot, grated

garlic cloves, chopped or crushed

bay leaf

100 g/3½ oz ground almonds

2 ripe avocados (about 450 g/1 lb)

3–4 tbsp fresh lemon juice

salt

snipped fresh chives, to garnish

1 Combine the water, onion, celery, carrot, garlic, bay leaf and ½ teaspoon salt in a pan. Bring to the boil, reduce the heat, cover and simmer for about 30 minutes or until the vegetables are very tender.

2 Strain the mixture, reserving the liquid and the vegetables separately. Remove and discard the bay leaf.

3 Put the vegetables into a blender or food processor. Add the almonds and a small amount of the liquid and process to a very smooth purée, scraping down the sides as necessary. Add as much of the remaining liquid as the capacity of the blender or processor permits and process to combine. Scrape into a bowl, stir in any remaining liquid, cover and chill until cold.

4 Cut the avocados in half, discard the stones and scoop the flesh into the blender or food processor. Add the cold soup base and process to a smooth purée, scraping down the sides as necessary. For a thinner consistency, add a few spoonfuls of cold water.

5 Add the lemon juice and season with salt to taste. Ladle into chilled small bowls and sprinkle each serving lightly with chives.

Chilled Borscht

There are innumerable versions of this soup of Eastern European origin. This refreshing vegetarian version is light and flavourful.

NUTRITIONAL INFORMATION

Calories	93	Sugars	........12g
Protein	.........4g	Fat	...........3g
Carbohydrate	...15g	Saturates	.......0g

 45 mins   1½ hrs

SERVES 4–6

INGREDIENTS

¼ medium cabbage, cored and coarsely chopped

1 tbsp vegetable oil

1 onion, finely chopped

1 leek, halved lengthways and sliced

400 g/14 oz can peeled tomatoes

1.2 litres/2 pints water, plus extra if needed

1 carrot, thinly sliced

1 small parsnip, finely chopped

3 beetroot (raw or cooked), peeled and cubed

1 bay leaf

350 ml/12 fl oz tomato juice

2–3 tbsp chopped fresh dill

fresh lemon juice (optional)

salt and pepper

soured cream or natural yogurt, to garnish

1 Cover the cabbage generously with cold water in a pan. Bring to the boil, boil for 3 minutes, then drain.

2 Heat the oil in a large pan over a medium-low heat. Add the onion and leek, cover and cook, stirring occasionally, for about 5 minutes until the vegetables begin to soften.

3 Add the tomatoes, water, carrot, parsnip, beetroot and bay leaf. Stir in the blanched cabbage and add a pinch of salt. Bring to the boil, reduce the heat and simmer for about 1¼ hours until all the vegetables are tender. Remove and discard the bay leaf.

4 Remove the pan from the heat and set aside to cool slightly, then transfer to a blender or food processor and process to a smooth purée, working in batches if necessary. (If using a food processor, strain off the cooking liquid and reserve. Purée the soup solids with enough cooking liquid to moisten them, then combine with the remaining liquid.)

5 Scrape the soup into a large container and stir in the tomato juice. Set aside to cooe, then chill in the refrigerator.

6 Stir in the dill. Thin the soup with more tomato juice or water, if wished. Season to taste with salt and pepper and lemon juice, if wished. Ladle into chilled soup bowls, top each with a spiral of soured cream or a spoon of yogurt.

Iced Salsa Soup

A chunky mix of colourful vegetables, highlighted with Mexican flavours, this cold soup makes a lively starter to any meal.

NUTRITIONAL INFORMATION

Calories ....138 Sugars 12g

Protein ....5g Fat 4g

Carbohydrate ...22g Saturates 1g

45 mins   12–15 mins

SERVES 4

INGREDIENTS

2 large corn cobs or 225 g/8 oz frozen
sweetcorn kernels

1 tbsp olive oil

1 orange or red pepper, deseeded and
finely chopped

1 green pepper, deseeded and
finely chopped

1 sweet onion, such as Vidalia,
finely chopped

3 ripe tomatoes, peeled, deseeded
and chopped

½ tsp chilli powder

125 ml/4 fl oz water

450 ml/16 fl oz tomato juice

chilli purée (optional)

salt and pepper

TO GARNISH

3–4 spring onions, finely chopped

fresh coriander leaves

1 Cut the corn kernels from the cobs, or if using frozen sweetcorn, thaw and drain.

2 Heat the oil in a pan over a medium-high heat. Add the peppers and cook, stirring briskly, for 3 minutes. Add the onion and continue cooking for about 2 minutes or until it starts to colour slightly.

3 Add the tomatoes, corn and chilli powder. Continue cooking, stirring frequently, for 1 minute. Pour in the water and when it begins to boil, reduce the heat, cover and cook for a further 4–5 minutes or until the peppers are just barely tender.

4 Transfer the mixture to a large container and stir in the tomato juice. Season with salt and pepper to taste and add more chilli powder if wished. Cover with clingfilm and chill in the refrigerator until cold.

5 Taste and adjust the seasoning. For a spicier soup, stir in a little chilli purée to taste. For a thinner soup, add a small amount of iced water. Ladle into chilled bowls and garnish with spring onions and fresh coriander leaves.

Spicy Red Pepper Soup

This brilliantly coloured soup makes a great summer starter, especially when peppers are abundant in farm markets – or in your garden.

NUTRITIONAL INFORMATION

Calories	90	Sugars	........13g
Protein	.........3g	Fat	...........3g
Carbohydrate	...15g	Saturates	.......0g

 45 mins   45 mins

SERVES 6

INGREDIENTS

1 tbsp olive oil

450 g/1 lb leeks, thinly sliced

1 large onion, halved and thinly sliced

2 garlic cloves, finely chopped or crushed

6 red peppers, deseeded and sliced

1 litre/1¾ pints water

½ tsp ground cumin

½ tsp ground coriander

1 tsp chilli purée

1–2 tsp fresh lemon juice

salt and pepper

finely chopped spring onion greens or fresh chives, to garnish

1 Heat the oil in a large pan over a medium heat. Add the leeks, onion and garlic and cook, stirring occasionally, for about 5 minutes until the onion is softened.

2 Stir in the peppers and cook for a further 2–3 minutes. Add the water, cumin, ground coriander and chilli purée with a pinch of salt. Bring to the boil, reduce the heat, cover and simmer gently for about 35 minutes until all the vegetables are tender.

3 Set aside to cool slightly, then transfer to a blender or food processor and process to a smooth purée, in batches if necessary. (If using a food processor, strain off the cooking liquid and reserve. Purée the soup solids with enough cooking liquid to moisten them, then combine with the remaining liquid.)

4 Put the soup in a large bowl, then season with salt and pepper and add lemon juice to taste. Allow to coo completely, cover with clingfilm and chil in the refrigerator until cold.

5 Before serving, taste and adjust the seasoning, if necessary. Add a little more chilli purée if a spicy taste is preferred. Ladle into chilled bowls and garnish with spring onion greens or chives.

Cucumber Soup

Parsley tames the pungent garlic flavour of this traditional Balkan soup.
The cucumber and yogurt make it a refreshing summer starter.

NUTRITIONAL INFORMATION

Calories	208	Sugars	........10g
Protein	.........8g	Fat	..........15g
Carbohydrate	...10g	Saturates	.......2g

45 mins · 0 mins

SERVES 4

INGREDIENTS

large cucumber

50 g/2 oz walnut pieces, toasted
(see Cook's Tip)

15 g/½ oz fresh parsley leaves

small garlic clove, very finely chopped

2 tbsp olive oil

4 tbsp water

tbsp fresh lemon juice

300 ml/½ pint Greek-style yogurt

salt and pepper

fresh mint leaves, to garnish

1 Peel the cucumber, slice lengthways and scoop out the seeds with a small pointed spoon. Cut the flesh into 2.5 cm/1 inch pieces.

2 Put the walnuts, parsley leaves, garlic, oil and water in a blender or food processor with half of the cucumber and process to a smooth purée, stopping to scrape down the sides as necessary.

3 Add the remaining cucumber to the blender or processor with a pinch of salt and the lemon juice. Process briefly until smooth.

4 Scrape the purée into a large bowl and stir in the yogurt. Season to taste with salt and pepper and add a little more lemon juice, if wished.

5 Cover with clingfilm and chill in the refrigerator for about 30 minutes or until cold. Taste and adjust the seasoning if necessary. Ladle into chilled bowls and garnish with mint leaves.

COOK'S TIP
Toasting the walnuts gives them extra flavour. Just heat them in a dry frying pan over a medium-low heat until they begin to colour and smell aromatic.

Cold Coriander Soup

This soup brings together Thai flavours for a cool, refreshing starter.
It highlights fresh coriander, now much more widely available.

NUTRITIONAL INFORMATION

Calories	79	Sugars	.........5g
Protein	........3g	Fat	..........3g
Carbohydrate	...13g	Saturates	.......0g

45 mins   30 mins

SERVES 4

I N G R E D I E N T S

2 tsp olive oil

1 large onion, finely chopped

1 leek, thinly sliced

1 garlic clove, thinly sliced

1 litre/1¾ pints water

1 courgette, about 200 g/7 oz, peeled
   and chopped

4 tbsp long grain white rice

5 cm/2 inch piece of lemon grass

2 lime leaves

55 g/2 oz fresh coriander leaves and
   soft stems

chilli purée, (optional)

salt and pepper

finely chopped red pepper and/or fresh red
   chillies, to garnish

1 Heat the oil in a large pan over a
   medium heat. Add the onion, leek and
garlic and cook, stirring occasionally, for
4–5 minutes until the onion is softened,
but not browned.

2 Add the water, courgette and rice with
   a pinch of salt and some pepper. Stir
in the lemon grass and lime leaves. Bring
just to the boil and reduce the heat to low.
Cover and simmer for 15–20 minutes until
the rice is soft and tender.

3 Add the fresh coriander leaves and
   stems, pushing them down into the
liquid. Continue cooking over a low heat
for 2–3 minutes until the leaves are
wilted. Remove and discard the lemon
grass and lime leaves.

4 Remove from the heat and set aside
   to cool slightly, then transfer to a
blender or food processor and process to a
smooth purée, working in batches if
necessary. (If using a food processor, strain
off the cooking liquid and reserve. Purée
the soup solids with enough cooking liquid
to moisten them, then combine with the
remaining liquid.)

5 Scrape the soup into a large
   container. Season to taste with salt
and pepper. Cover with clingfilm and chill
in the refrigerator until cold.

6 Taste and adjust the seasoning. For a
   spicier soup, stir in a little chilli purée
to taste. For a thinner soup, add a small
amount of iced water. Ladle into chilled
bowls and garnish with finely chopped red
pepper and/or chillies.

Cock-a-Leekie Soup

A traditional Scottish soup in which a whole chicken is cooked with the vegetables to add extra flavour to the stock.

NUTRITIONAL INFORMATION

Calories ....45 Sugars 4g
Protein ....5g Fat 1g
Carbohydrate ....5g Saturates 0.2g

2½ hrs   2 hrs

SERVES 4–6

INGREDIENTS

—1.5 kg/2lb 4 oz–3 lb 5 oz oven-ready
  chicken plus giblets, if available

.75–2 litres/3–3½ pints chicken stock

1 onion, sliced

4 leeks, thinly sliced

pinch of ground allspice or
  ground coriander

1 bouquet garni

12 no-need-to-soak prunes, halved
  and stoned

salt and pepper

warm crusty bread, to serve

1 Put the chicken, giblets, if using, stock and onion in a large pan. Bring to the boil and skim off any scum that rises to the surface.

2 Add the leeks, allspice or coriander and bouquet garni to the pan, season with salt and pepper, cover and simmer gently for about 1½ hours until the chicken flesh is falling off the bones.

3 Remove the chicken and bouquet garni from the pan and skim any fat from the surface of the soup.

4 Chop some of the chicken flesh and return to the pan. Add the prunes, bring back to the boil and simmer, uncovered, for about 20 minutes. Taste and adjust the seasoning, if necessary, and serve with warm crusty bread.

VARIATION

You can replace the chicken stock with 3 chicken stock cubes dissolved in the same amount of water, if you prefer.

Hot & Sour Soup

Hot-and-sour mixtures are popular throughout the East, especially in Thailand. This soup typically has either prawns or chicken added.

NUTRITIONAL INFORMATION

Calories	71	Sugars	.........0g
Protein	.........8g	Fat	...........4g
Carbohydrate	....1g	Saturates	.......0g

15 mins   30 mins

SERVES 4

INGREDIENTS

350 g/12 oz raw or cooked prawns in shells

1 tbsp vegetable oil

1 lemon grass stalk, roughly chopped

2 kaffir lime leaves, shredded

1 fresh green chilli, deseeded and chopped

1.2 litres/2 pints chicken or fish stock

1 lime

1 tbsp Thai fish sauce

1 fresh red bird-eye chilli, deseeded and thinly sliced

1 spring onion, thinly sliced

salt and pepper

1 tbsp finely chopped fresh coriander, to garnish

1 Peel the prawns and reserve the shells. Devein the prawns, cover with clingfilm and chill.

2 Heat the oil in a large pan. Add the prawn shells and stir-fry for 3–4 minutes until they turn pink. Add the lemon grass, lime leaves, chilli and stock. Pare a thin strip of rind from the lime and grate the rest. Add the pared rind to the pan.

3 Bring to the boil, then lower the heat, cover and simmer for about 20 minutes.

4 Strain the liquid and pour it back into the pan. Squeeze the juice from the lime and add to the pan with the fish sauce and season with salt and pepper to taste.

5 Bring the mixture to the boil. Lower the heat, add the prawns and simmer for 2–3 minutes.

6 Add the thinly sliced chilli and spring onion. Sprinkle with the chopped coriander and grated lime rind and serve immediately.

COOK'S TIP

To devein the prawns, remove the shells. Cut a slit along the back of each prawn and remove the fine black vein that runs along the length of the back. Wipe with kitchen paper.

Creamy Sweetcorn Soup

This filling combination of tender sweetcorn kernels and a creamy stock is extra delicious with lean diced ham sprinkled on top.

NUTRITIONAL INFORMATION

Calories 307   Sugars 15g
Protein . . . . .19g   Fat 14g
Carbohydrate . . .28g   Saturates 5g

15 mins   25 mins

SERVES 4

INGREDIENTS

1 large onion, chopped

300 g/10½ oz potatoes, diced

1 litre/1¾ pints skimmed milk

1 bay leaf

½ tsp freshly grated nutmeg

450 g/1 lb sweetcorn kernels, canned or frozen, drained or thawed

1 tbsp cornflour

3 tbsp cold water

4 tbsp low-fat natural yogurt

salt and pepper

TO GARNISH

100 g/3½ oz lean ham, diced

2 tbsp snipped fresh chives

1 Place the onion and potato in a large saucepan and pour over the milk.

2 Add the bay leaf, nutmeg and half the sweetcorn to the saucepan. Bring to the boil, cover and simmer over a low heat for 15 minutes until the potato is softened. Stir the soup occasionally and keep the heat low so that the milk does not burn on the base of the pan.

3 Remove and discard the bay leaf and set the liquid aside to cool for about 10 minutes. Transfer to a blender and process for a few seconds. Alternatively, rub the soup through a sieve.

4 Pour the smooth liquid into a saucepan. Blend the cornflour with the cold water to make a paste and stir it into the soup.

5 Bring the soup back to the boil, stirring until it thickens, and add the remaining sweetcorn. Heat through for 2–3 minutes until piping hot.

6 Remove the soup from the heat and season with salt and pepper to taste. Add the yogurt and stir until it is thoroughly blended.

7 Ladle the creamy sweetcorn soup into warm bowls and serve sprinkled with the diced ham and snipped chives.

Pumpkin & Coconut Soup

This substantial soup is filling and, if served with crusty bread, is all you need for a satisfying lunch. For a first course, serve in small bowls.

NUTRITIONAL INFORMATION

Calories	105	Sugars	6g
Protein	3g	Fat	7g
Carbohydrate	8g	Saturates	4g

 15 mins   40 mins

SERVES 6

INGREDIENTS

1 kg/2 lb 4 oz pumpkin

1 tbsp groundnut oil

1 tsp yellow mustard seeds

1 garlic clove, crushed

1 large onion, chopped

1 celery stick, chopped

1 small fresh red chilli, chopped

850 ml/1½ pints stock

1 tsp shrimp paste

5 tbsp coconut cream, plus extra
   to garnish

salt and pepper

1 Cut the pumpkin in half and remove the seeds. Cut away the skin and dice the flesh.

2 Heat the oil in a large flameproof casserole and fry the mustard seeds until they begin to pop. Stir in the garlic, onion, celery and chilli and stir-fry for 1–2 minutes.

3 Add the pumpkin with the stock and shrimp paste and bring to the boil. Lower the heat, cover and simmer gently for about 30 minutes until the ingredients are very tender.

4 Remove from the heat and set aside to cool slightly, then transfer the mixture to a food processor or blender, and process to a smooth purée. Return the mixture to the pan and stir in the coconut cream. Re-heat gently.

5 Adjust the seasoning to taste with salt and pepper, ladle into bowls and serve hot, with a little extra coconut cream swirled in each bowl.

COOK'S TIP

Made from ground shrimps that have been fermented in brine, shrimp paste is widely used throughout South-east Asia to add a savoury flavour.

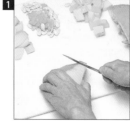

Mushroom & Tofu Broth

Dried black mushrooms are sold in Oriental stores. Although they are expensive, they are worth buying as they have a distinctive flavour.

NUTRITIONAL INFORMATION

Calories 65   Sugars 1g
Protein ....4g   Fat 5g
Carbohydrate ....2g   Saturates 1g

35 mins   15 mins

SERVES 4

INGREDIENTS

4 dried black mushrooms

1 tbsp sunflower oil

1 tsp sesame oil

1 garlic clove, crushed

1 fresh green chilli, deseeded and
   finely chopped

6 spring onions

85 g/3 oz fresh oyster mushrooms, sliced

2 kaffir lime leaves, finely shredded

1 litre/1¾ pints Fresh Beef Stock (see
   page 9)

2 tbsp lime juice

1 tbsp rice vinegar

1 tbsp Thai fish sauce

85 g/3 oz firm tofu, diced

salt and pepper

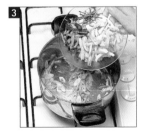

1 Pour 150 ml/5 fl oz boiling water over the dried black mushrooms in a heatproof bowl and set aside to soak for about 30 minutes. Drain, reserving the soaking liquid, then chop the black mushrooms roughly.

2 Heat the sunflower and sesame oils in a large pan or wok over a high heat. Add the garlic, chilli and spring onions and stir-fry for 1 minute until softened, but not browned.

3 Add all of the mushrooms, the kaffir lime leaves, stock and reserved mushroom liquid. Bring to the boil.

4 Stir in the lime juice, rice vinegar and fish sauce, lower the heat and simmer gently for 3–4 minutes.

5 Add the tofu and season to taste with salt and pepper. Heat gently until boiling, then serve immediately.

COOK'S TIP

To make a vegetarian version of the broth, use a well-flavoured vegetable stock and replace the fish sauce with light soy sauce.

Rice Soup with Eggs

This version of a classic Thai soup, sometimes eaten for breakfast, is a good way of using up any leftover cooked rice.

NUTRITIONAL INFORMATION

Calories 197   Sugars 1g
Protein ....11g   Fat 10g
Carbohydrate ...17g   Saturates 2g

 5 mins    10 mins

SERVES 4

I N G R E D I E N T S

1 tsp sunflower oil

1 garlic clove, crushed

55 g/2 oz minced pork

3 spring onions, sliced

1 tbsp grated fresh root ginger

1 fresh red bird-eye chilli, deseeded
   and chopped

1 litre/1¾ pints chicken stock

200 g/7 oz cooked long grain rice

1 tbsp Thai fish sauce

4 small eggs

salt and pepper

2 tbsp shredded fresh coriander, to garnish

1 Heat the oil in a large pan or wok. Add the garlic and pork and cook gently, stirring constantly, for about 1 minute until the meat is broken up, but not browned.

2 Stir in the spring onions, ginger, chilli and stock and bring to the boil, stirring constantly. Add the rice, lower the heat and simmer for 2 minutes.

3 Add the fish sauce and season to taste with salt and pepper. Carefully break the eggs into the soup and simmer over a very low heat for 3–4 minutes until set.

4 Ladle the soup into large, warmed bowls, allowing 1 egg per portion. Garnish with shredded fresh coriander and serve immediately.

COOK'S TIP

If you prefer, beat the eggs together and cook like an omelette until set, then cut into ribbon-like strips and added to the soup just before serving.

Spinach & Ginger Soup

This mildly spiced, rich green soup is delicately scented with ginger
and lemon grass. It makes a good light starter or summer lunch dish.

NUTRITIONAL INFORMATION

Calories	38	Sugars	.......0.8g
Protein	.......3.2g	Fat	..........1.8g
Carbohydrate	...2.4g	Saturates	.....0.2g

5-10 mins   25 mins

SERVES 4

I N G R E D I E N T S

2 tbsp sunflower oil

1 onion, chopped

2 garlic cloves, finely chopped

2 tsp finely chopped fresh root ginger

250 g/9 oz young spinach leaves

1 small lemon grass stalk, finely chopped

1 litre/1¾ pints chicken or vegetable stock

225 g/8 oz potatoes, chopped

1 tbsp rice wine or dry sherry

1 tsp sesame oil

salt and pepper

1 Heat the oil in a large saucepan. Add
the onion, garlic and ginger and fry
over a low heat, stirring occasionally, for
3–4 minutes until softened.

2 Reserve 2–3 small spinach leaves. Add
the remaining leaves and lemon grass
to the saucepan, stirring until the spinach
is wilted. Add the stock and potatoes to
the pan and bring to the boil. Lower the heat,
cover and simmer for about 10 minutes.

3 Remove the pan from the heat and set
aside to cool slightly. Then tip the
soup into a blender or food processor and
process until completely smooth.

4 Return the soup to the pan and add
the rice wine, then adjust the
seasoning to taste with salt and pepper.
Heat until just about to boil.

5 Finely shred the reserved spinach
leaves and sprinkle some over the top.
Drizzle a few drops of sesame oil into the
soup. Ladle into warmed soup bowls,
sprinkle the remaining shredded spinach
on each and serve the soup immediately.

COOK'S TIP

To make a creamy-textured
spinach and coconut soup,
stir in about 4 tablespoons
creamed coconut or replace
about 300 ml/10 fl oz of the stock
with coconut milk. Serve the soup
with shavings of fresh coconut
scattered over the surface.

Avocado & Lime Soup

A delightfully simple soup with a blend of typical Thai flavours, which needs no cooking and can be served at any time of day.

NUTRITIONAL INFORMATION

Calories 188	Sugars 2g	
Protein 3g	Fat 18g	
Carbohydrate 4g	Saturates 5g	

15 mins   0 mins

SERVES 4

I N G R E D I E N T S

2 ripe avocados

1 small mild onion, chopped

1 garlic clove, crushed

2 tbsp chopped fresh coriander

1 tbsp chopped fresh mint

2 tbsp lime juice

700 ml/1¼ pints vegetable stock

1 tbsp rice vinegar

1 tbsp light soy sauce

salt and pepper

GARNISH

2 tbsp soured cream or crème fraîche

1 tbsp finely chopped fresh coriander

2 tsp lime juice

finely shredded lime rind

1 Halve, stone the avocados and scoop out the flesh. Place in a blender or food processor with the onion, garlic, coriander, mint, lime juice and about half the vegetable stock, and process until completely smooth.

2 Add the remaining stock, rice vinegar and soy sauce and process again to mix well. Taste and season, if necessary, with salt and pepper or with a little extra lime juice if required. Cover and chill in the refrigerator until needed.

3 To make the lime and coriander cream garnish, combine the soured cream, coriander and lime juice in a bowl. Ladle the soup into chilled bowl, spoon the lime and coriander cream into them and sprinkle with lime rind.

COOK'S TIP

The top surface of the soup may darken slightly if the soup is stored for longer than about an hour, but don't worry – just give it a quick stir before serving. If you plan to keep the soup for several hours, lay a piece of clingfilm over the surface to seal it from the air.

Spinach & Tofu Soup

This is a very colourful and delicious soup. If spinach is
not in season, watercress or lettuce can be used instead.

NUTRITIONAL INFORMATION

Calories	33	Sugar	.........1g
Protein	.........4g	Fat	...........2g
Carbohydrate	....1g	Saturates	.....0.2g

 15 mins   10 mins

SERVES 4

INGREDIENTS

1 cake of firm tofu

125 g/4½ oz spinach leaves without stems

700 ml/1¼ pints Chinese Stock (see page 8)
  or water

1 tbsp light soy sauce

salt and pepper

1 Using a sharp knife to avoid
squashing it, cut the tofu into small
pieces about 5 mm/¼ inch thick.

2 Wash the spinach leaves under cold,
running water and drain well.

3 Cut the spinach leaves into small
pieces or shreds, discarding any
discoloured leaves and tough stalks. (If
possible, use fresh young spinach leaves,
which have not yet developed tough ribs.
Otherwise, it is important to cut out all
the ribs and stems for this soup.) Set the
spinach aside until required.

4 In a preheated wok or large frying
pan, bring the Chinese stock or water
to a rolling boil.

5 Add the tofu cubes and light soy
sauce, bring back to the boil and
simmer for about 2 minutes over a
medium heat.

6 Add the spinach and simmer for
1 more minute, stirring gently. Skim
the surface of the soup to make it clear
and season to taste.

7 Transfer the soup to a warm soup
tureen or individual serving bowls and
serve with chopsticks to pick up the pieces
of food and a broad, shallow spoon for
drinking the soup.

COOK'S TIP

Soup is an integral part
of a Chinese meal; it is usually
presented in a large bowl placed
in the centre of the table, and
consumed as the meal progresses.
It serves as a refresher between
different dishes and as a beverage
throughout the meal.

Green Soup

This fresh-tasting soup with green beans, cucumber and watercress can be served warm, or chilled on a hot summer day.

NUTRITIONAL INFORMATION

Calories 121	Sugars 2g	
Protein 2g	Fat 8g	
Carbohydrate . . .10g	Saturates 1g	

15–45 mins   25 mins

SERVES 4

INGREDIENTS

1 tbsp olive oil

1 onion, chopped

1 garlic clove, chopped

200 g/7 oz potato, cut into 2.5 cm/ 1 inch cubes

700 ml/1¼ pints vegetable or chicken stock

1 small cucumber or ½ large cucumber, cut into chunks

85 g/3 oz watercress

125 g/4½ oz green beans, trimmed and halved lengthways

salt and pepper

1 Heat the oil in a large pan and cook the onion and garlic over a medium heat for 3–4 minutes or until softened.

2 Add the cubed potato and cook for a further 2–3 minutes. Stir in the stock and bring to the boil. Lower the heat and simmer for 5 minutes.

3 Add the cucumber to the pan and cook for a further 3 minutes or until the potatoes are tender. Test by inserting the tip of a knife into the potato cubes – it should pass through easily.

4 Add the watercress and cook until just wilted. Remove from heat and set aside to cool slightly, then transfer to a food processor and process to a smooth purée. Alternatively, before adding the watercress, mash the vegetables with a potato masher and push through a sieve, then chop the watercress finely and stir into the soup.

5 Bring a small pan of water to the boil and steam the beans for 3–4 minutes or until tender. Add the beans to the soup, season to taste with salt and pepper and warm through. Ladle into warmed soup bowls and serve immediately or set aside to cool and then chill.

VARIATION

Try using 125 g/4½ oz mangetouts instead of the beans.

Pumpkin Soup

This thick, creamy soup has a wonderful, warming golden colour. It is flavoured with orange and thyme.

NUTRITIONAL INFORMATION

Calories	111	Sugars	4g
Protein	2g	Fat	6g
Carbohydrate	5g	Saturates	2g

 10 mins   35–40 mins

SERVES 4

INGREDIENTS

2 tbsp olive oil

2 medium onions, chopped

2 garlic cloves, chopped

900 g/2 lb pumpkin, peeled and cut into 2.5 cm/1 inch chunks

1.5 litres /2¾ pints boiling vegetable or chicken stock

finely grated rind and juice of 1 orange

3 tbsp fresh thyme leaves

150 ml/5 fl oz milk

salt and pepper

crusty bread, to serve

1 Heat the olive oil in a large pan. Add the onions and cook over a medium heat, stirring occasionally, for 3–4 minutes or until softened. Add the garlic and pumpkin and cook, stirring frequently, for a further 2 minutes.

2 Add the boiling vegetable or chicken stock, orange rind and juice and 2 tablespoons of the thyme to the pan. Cover and simmer for 20 minutes or until the pumpkin is tender.

3 Transfer to a food processor and process until smooth. Alternatively, mash the mixture with a potato masher until smooth. Season to taste.

4 Return the soup to the pan and add the milk. Reheat for 3–4 minutes or until it is piping hot, but not boiling.

5 Sprinkle with the remaining fresh thyme just before serving.

6 Divide the soup among 4 warmed soup bowls and serve with lots of fresh crusty bread.

COOK'S TIP

Pumpkins are usually large vegetables. To make things a little easier, ask the greengrocer to cut a chunk off for you. Alternatively, make double the quantity and freeze the soup for up to 3 months.

Curried Chicken Soup

Tender cooked chicken strips and baby corn cobs are the main flavours in this delicious clear soup, with just a hint of ginger.

NUTRITIONAL INFORMATION

Calories	206	Sugars	.........5g
Protein	........29g	Fat	..........5g
Carbohydrate	...13g	Saturates	.......1g

5 mins   30 mins

SERVES 4

INGREDIENTS

175 g/6 oz can sweetcorn, drained

850 ml/1½ pints chicken stock

350 g/12 oz cooked, lean chicken, cut into strips

16 baby corn cobs

1 tsp Chinese curry powder

1 cm/½ inch piece of fresh root ginger, grated

3 tbsp light soy sauce

2 tbsp chopped fresh chives

1 Place the canned sweetcorn in a food processor, with 150 ml/¼ pint of the chicken stock and process until the mixture forms a smooth purée.

2 Pass the sweetcorn purée through a fine sieve, pressing with the back of a spoon to remove any husks.

3 Pour the remaining chicken stock into a large pan and add the strips of cooked chicken. Stir in the sweetcorn purée to combine.

4 Add the baby corn cobs and bring the soup to the boil. Boil over a medium heat for 10 minutes.

5 Add the Chinese curry powder, grated fresh root ginger and light soy sauce and stir well to combine. Cook for a further 10–15 minutes.

6 Stir in the chopped chives. Transfer the soup to warmed soup bowls and serve immediately.

COOK'S TIP

Prepare the soup up to 24 hours in advance without adding the chicken. Cool, cover and store in the refrigerator. Add the chicken and heat the soup through thoroughly before serving.

Beef Noodle Soup

Thin strips of beef are marinated in soy sauce and garlic to form the basis of this delicious soup. Served with noodles, it is both filling and delicious.

NUTRITIONAL INFORMATION

Calories 186	Sugars 1g
Protein 17g	Fat 5g
Carbohydrate ...20g	Saturates 1g

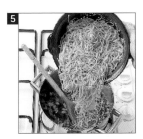

35 mins   20 mins

SERVES 4

INGREDIENTS

225 g/8 oz lean beef

1 garlic clove, crushed

2 spring onions, chopped

3 tbsp soy sauce

1 tsp sesame oil

225 g/8 oz egg noodles

850 ml/1½ pints beef stock

3 baby corn cobs, sliced

½ leek, shredded

125 g/4½ oz broccoli, cut into florets

pinch of chilli powder

1 Using a sharp knife, cut the beef into thin strips and place in a bowl with the garlic, spring onions, soy sauce and sesame oil.

2 Combine the ingredients in the bowl, turning the beef to coat. Cover and set aside to marinate in the refrigerator for 30 minutes.

3 Cook the noodles in a pan of boiling water for 3–4 minutes. Drain thoroughly and set aside.

4 Put the beef stock in a large pan and bring to the boil. Add the beef, with the marinade, the baby corn, shredded leek and broccoli florets. Cover and simmer over a low heat for 7–10 minutes or until the beef and vegetables are tender and cooked through.

5 Stir in the noodles and chilli powder and cook for a further 2–3 minutes.

6 Transfer the soup to warmed bowls and serve immediately.

VARIATION

Vary the vegetables used or use those to hand. If preferred, use a few drops of chilli sauce instead of chilli powder, but remember it is very hot!

Sweet Potato & Onion Soup

This simple recipe uses the sweet potato with its distinctive flavour and colour, combined with a hint of orange and coriander.

NUTRITIONAL INFORMATION

Calories	320	Sugars	........26g
Protein	.........7g	Fat	...........7g
Carbohydrate	...62g	Saturates	......1g

  15 mins   30 mins

SERVES 4

INGREDIENTS

2 tbsp vegetable oil

900 g/2 lb sweet potatoes, diced

1 carrot, diced

2 onions, sliced

2 garlic cloves, crushed

600 ml/1 pint vegetable stock

300 ml/10 fl oz unsweetened orange juice

225 ml/8 fl oz low-fat natural yogurt

2 tbsp chopped fresh coriander

salt and pepper

TO GARNISH

fresh coriander sprigs

orange rind

1 Heat the vegetable oil in a large, heavy-based saucepan and add the sweet potatoes, carrot, onions and garlic. Sauté the vegetables over a low heat, stirring constantly for 5 minutes until softened.

2 Pour in the vegetable stock and orange juice and bring to the boil.

3 Reduce the heat to a simmer, cover the saucepan and cook the vegetables for 20 minutes or until the sweet potatoes and carrot are tender.

4 Transfer the mixture to a food processor or blender in batches and process for 1 minute until puréed. Return the purée to the rinsed-out saucepan.

5 Stir in the yogurt and chopped coriander and season to taste with salt and pepper.

6 Serve the soup in warm bowls and garnish with coriander sprigs and orange rind.

VARIATION

This soup can be chilled before serving, if preferred. If chilling, stir the yogurt into the dish just before serving. Serve in chilled bowls.

Red Pepper Soup

This soup has a real Mediterranean flavour, using sweet red peppers, tomato, chilli and basil. It is great served with a warm olive bread.

NUTRITIONAL INFORMATION

Calories	55	Sugar	.........10g
Protein	.........2g	Fats	.........0.5g
Carbohydrates	...11g	Saturates	.....0.1g

5 mins

25 mins

SERVES 4

I N G R E D I E N T S

225 g/8 oz red peppers, deseeded and sliced

1 onion, sliced

2 garlic cloves, crushed

1 fresh green chilli, chopped

300 m/10 fl oz passata

600 ml/1 pint vegetable stock

2 tbsp chopped fresh basil

fresh basil sprigs, to garnish

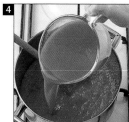

1 Put the red peppers in a large, heavy-based pan with the onion, garlic and chilli. Add the passata and vegetable stock and bring to the boil over a medium heat, stirring constantly.

2 Reduce the heat to low and simmer for 20 minutes or until the peppers have softened. Drain, reserving the liquid and vegetables separately.

3 Sieve the vegetables by pressing through a strainer with the back of a spoon. Alternatively, process in a food processor to a smooth purée.

4 Return the vegetable purée to a clean pan and add the reserved cooking liquid. Add the basil and heat through until hot. Garnish the soup with fresh basil sprigs and serve.

VARIATION
This soup is also delicious served cold with 150 ml/¼ pint natural yogurt swirled into it.

Avgolemono

The hallmarks of this traditional Greek lemon and egg soup are its fresh flavour and its lightness. Serve with Olive Rolls (see page 474).

NUTRITIONAL INFORMATION

Calories 138   Sugars 1g
Protein ....8g   Fat 6g
Carbohydrate ...15g   Saturates 1g

10 mins

12 mins

SERVES 4–6

INGREDIENTS

1.2 litres/2 pints chicken stock

100 g/3½ oz dried orzo, or other small pasta shapes

2 large eggs

4 tbsp lemon juice

salt and pepper

TO GARNISH

finely chopped fresh flat leaf parsley

1 Pour the stock into a flameproof casserole or heavy-based pan and bring to the boil. Sprinkle in the orzo, return to the boil and cook for 8–10 minutes until the pasta is tender, but still firm to the bite.

2 Whisk the eggs in a bowl for at least 30 seconds. Add the lemon juice and continue whisking for a further 30 seconds.

3 Reduce the heat under the pan of stock and orzo until the stock is not boiling.

4 Very gradually add 4–5 tablespoons of the hot (not boiling) stock to the lemon and egg mixture, whisking constantly. Gradually add another 225 ml/8 fl oz of the stock, whisking to prevent the eggs from curdling.

5 Gradually pour the lemon and egg mixture into the pan, whisking until the soup thickens slightly. Do not allow it to boil. Season to taste with salt and pepper.

6 Spoon the soup into warmed soup bowls and sprinkle with chopped flat leaf parsley. Serve immediately.

VARIATION

To make a more substantial soup, add 300 g/10½ oz finely chopped cooked, skinless chicken meat. This version uses orzo, a small pasta shape that looks like barley grains, but you can substitute long grain rice.

Red Pepper & Tomato Soup

Juicy tomatoes and sweet red peppers are roasted and then combined with fresh dill and orange to make a fantastic soup.

NUTRITIONAL INFORMATION

Calories 54	Sugars 9g	
Protein 2g	Fat 1g	
Carbohydrate . . .10g	Saturates 0g	

10 mins | 1 hr

SERVES 6–8

INGREDIENTS

1 kg/2 lb 4 oz plum tomatoes, halved

2 large red peppers, deseeded and halved

1 onion, quartered

3 fresh dill sprigs, tied together, plus extra to garnish

1 thin piece of orange rind

juice of 1 orange

600 ml/1 pint vegetable stock

1–1½ tbsp red wine vinegar

salt and pepper

Mediterranean Bread (see page 472), to serve

1 Place the tomatoes and peppers on a baking sheet, cut sides up to catch the juices. Add the onion quarters. Place in a preheated oven, 230°C/450°F/Gas Mark 8, and roast for 20–25 minutes until the vegetables just start to blacken and char on the edges.

2 As the vegetables become charred, transfer them to a large flameproof casserole or stockpot. Add the dill, orange rind and juice, stock and salt and pepper to taste. Bring to the boil.

3 Lower the heat, partially cover and simmer for 25 minutes. Remove the bundle of dill and transfer the rest of the ingredients to a food mill (see Cook's Tip) and purée. Alternatively, process in a food processor and press though a fine sieve.

4 Return the soup to the rinsed casserole or stockpot and reheat. Stir in the vinegar and adjust the seasoning with salt and pepper, if necessary. Ladle into warmed bowls and garnish with extra dill sprigs. Serve hot with slices of Mediterranean bread.

COOK'S TIP

A food mill, or mouli-legume as it is called in France, is ideal for puréeing vegetable soups and sauces because it removes the skin and seeds in the process.

Pistou

This hearty soup of beans and vegetables is from Nice and gets its name from the fresh basil sauce stirred in at the last minute.

NUTRITIONAL INFORMATION

Calories	55	Sugars	.......1.2g
Protein	........3.8g	Fat	.........2.6g
Carbohydrate	...4.2g	Saturates	.....0.6g

10 mins   25 mins

SERVES 6

INGREDIENTS

2 young carrots

450 g/1 lb potatoes

200 g/7 oz fresh peas in their pods

200 g/7 oz thin green beans

150 g/5½ oz young courgettes

2 tbsp olive oil

1 garlic clove, crushed

1 large onion, finely chopped

2.5 litres/4½ pints vegetable stock or water

1 bouquet garni of 2 fresh parsley sprigs and 1 bay leaf tied in a 7.5 cm/3 inch piece of celery

85 g/3 oz dried small soup pasta

1 large tomato, peeled, deseeded and chopped or diced

Parmesan cheese shavings, to serve

PISTOU SAUCE

85 g/3 oz fresh basil leaves

1 garlic clove

5 tbsp extra virgin olive oil

salt and pepper

1 To make the pistou sauce, put the basil leaves, garlic and olive oil in a food processor and process until thoroughly blended. Season with salt and pepper to taste. Scrape the sauce into a bowl, cover with clingfilm and store in the refrigerator until required.

2 Cut the carrots in half lengthways, then slice. Cut the potatoes into quarters lengthways, then slice. Set aside in a bowl of water until ready to use to prevent them from discolouring.

3 Shell the peas. Trim the beans and cut them into 2.5 cm/1 inch pieces. Cut the courgettes in half lengthways, then slice.

4 Heat the oil in a large saucepan or flameproof casserole. Add the garlic and fry for 2 minutes, stirring constantly. Add the onion and fry for for a further 2 minutes until soft. Add the carrots and potatoes and stir for about 30 seconds.

5 Pour in the stock and bring to the boil. Lower the heat, partially cover and simmer for 8 minutes until the vegetables are starting to become tender.

6 Stir in the peas, beans, courgettes, bouquet garni and pasta. Season and cook for 4 minutes or until the vegetables and pasta are tender. Stir in the pistou sauce and serve with Parmesan shavings.

Tomato & Red Rice Soup

The firm texture and nutty flavour of red rice is particularly good in this soup, but if you have difficulty in finding it, use long grain brown rice.

NUTRITIONAL INFORMATION

Calories	150	Sugars	.........8g
Protein	.........3g	Fat	...........5g
Carbohydrate	...24g	Saturates	.......1g

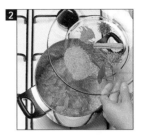

10 mins   50 mins

SERVES 4–6

INGREDIENTS

2 tbsp olive oil

1 onion, finely chopped

1 carrot, finely chopped

1 celery stick, finely chopped

3–4 garlic cloves, finely chopped

900 g/2 lb fresh ripe tomatoes, peeled, deseeded and finely chopped

1 bay leaf

½ cinnamon stick (optional)

1 tsp fresh thyme leaves or ½ tsp dried thyme

1 tsp dried oregano

1 tbsp brown sugar

½ tsp cayenne pepper

1.5 litres/2¾ pints chicken stock or water

100 g/3½ oz red rice or long grain brown rice

1 tbsp chopped fresh oregano leaves

salt and pepper

freshly grated Parmesan cheese, to serve

1 Heat the oil in a large pan over a medium heat. Add the onion, carrot and celery and cook, stirring occasionally, for about 10 minutes until very soft and beginning to colour. Stir in the garlic and cook for a further minute.

2 Add the tomatoes, bay leaf, cinnamon stick, if using, thyme, dried oregano, sugar and cayenne and cook, stirring occasionally, for about 5 minutes until the tomatoes begin to disintegrate.

3 Add the stock and the rice and bring to the boil, skimming off any foam that rises to the surface. Reduce the heat, cover and simmer for about 30 minutes until the rice is tender, adding more stock if necessary.

4 Stir in the fresh oregano leaves and season to taste with salt and pepper. Remove and discard the bay leaf and cinnamon stick. Serve immediately with Parmesan cheese for sprinkling.

Barley & Rice Soup

This hearty winter soup makes a warming lunch or supper when served with a crusty loaf of ciabatta.

NUTRITIONAL INFORMATION

Calories	260	Sugars	.........8g
Protein	.........9g	Fat	...........6g
Carbohydrate	...46g	Saturates	.......1g

15 mins   1½ hrs

SERVES 4–6

I N G R E D I E N T S

100 g/3½ oz pearl barley

100 g/3½ oz long grain brown rice

450 g/1 lb Swiss chard, trimmed and soaked for 10 minutes

2 tbsp olive oil

1 large onion, finely chopped

2 carrots, finely chopped

2 celery sticks, finely chopped

2 garlic cloves, finely chopped

400 g/14 oz can chopped Italian plum tomatoes

1 bay leaf

1 tsp dried thyme

1 tsp herbes de Provence or dried oregano

1 litre/1¾ pints chicken or vegetable stock

450 g/1 lb can cannellini beans, drained

2 tbsp chopped fresh parsley

salt and pepper

freshly grated Parmesan cheese, to serve

1 Bring a large pan of water to the boil. Add the barley and the brown rice and return to the boil. Reduce the heat and simmer gently for 30–35 minutes until just tender. Drain and set aside.

2 Drain the Swiss chard. Cut out the hard white stems. Slice the stems crossways into very thin strips and set aside. Roll the leaves into a long cigar shape, shred thinly and set aside.

3 Heat the oil in a large, heavy-based pan. Add the onion, carrots and celery and cook, stirring frequently, for about 5 minutes until soft and beginning to colour. Add the garlic and cook for a minute longer. Add the tomatoes with their juice, the bay leaf, thyme and herbes de Provence. Reduce the heat, partially cover and simmer for about 7 minutes until all the vegetables are soft.

4 Stir in the sliced white chard stems and the stock. Simmer gently for about 20 minutes. Add the shredded green chard and simmer for a further 15 minutes.

5 Stir in the beans and parsley with the cooked barley and brown rice. Season with salt and pepper. Bring back to the boil and simmer for a further 8–10 minutes. Remove the bay leaf and serve with Parmesan.

Italian Chicory & Rice Soup

This is a simple Italian soup made with the slightly bitter green scarola, or escarole, a member of the chicory family.

NUTRITIONAL INFORMATION

Calories	183	Sugars	.........2g
Protein	.........4g	Fat	...........11g
Carbohydrate	...19g	Saturates	.......7g

15 mins   1¼ hrs

SERVES 4–6

I N G R E D I E N T S

450 g/1 lb chicory

4 tbsp butter

1 onion, finely chopped

1 litre/1¾ pints chicken stock

100 g/3½ oz arborio or carnaroli rice

freshly grated nutmeg

2–4 tbsp freshly grated Parmesan cheese

salt and pepper

fresh herbs, to garnish

1 Separate the leaves from the chicory. Wash under cold running water and drain. Stack several leaves in a pile and roll tightly, then shred the leaves into 1 cm/½ inch ribbons. Continue with the remaining leaves.

2 Melt the butter in a large heavy-based pan over a medium heat. Add the onion and cook, stirring occasionally, for about 4 minutes until soft and just beginning to colour. Stir in the shredded chicory and cook, stirring frequently, for 2 minutes until the leaves wilt.

3 Add half the stock and season to taste with salt and pepper. Reduce the heat, cover the pan and simmer gently over a very low heat for 25–35 minutes until tender.

4 Add the remaining stock, and bring to the boil. Sprinkle in the rice, partially cover and simmer over a medium heat, stirring occasionally, for 15–20 minutes until the rice is just tender, but still slightly firm to the bite.

5 Remove from the heat and season with more salt and pepper, if necessary, and nutmeg. Ladle into bowls and sprinkle with a little Parmesan. Serve immediately, garnished with herbs.

COOK'S TIP

Long grain white rice can be substituted for arborio or carnaroli, but the round, risotto rice is slightly more starchy.

Turkey & Rice Soup

You can always use the leftover turkey from Christmas or Thanksgiving to make the stock for this rich and satisfying soup.

NUTRITIONAL INFORMATION

Calories 189	Sugars 4g
Protein 18g	Fat 3g
Carbohydrate ...23g	Saturates 1g

20 mins

2¾–3¾ hrs

SERVES 8–10

INGREDIENTS

1 onion, finely chopped

2 carrots, diced

200 g/7 oz long grain white rice

2 leeks, thinly sliced

225 g/8 oz frozen peas

115 g/4 oz fresh or thawed frozen mangetouts, thinly sliced

115 g/4 oz fresh spinach or watercress, washed and shredded

450 g/1 lb cooked turkey meat, diced

1 tbsp finely chopped fresh parsley

salt and pepper

STOCK

1 bunch of fresh parsley

2 turkey legs

1 bay leaf

1 tsp dried thyme

2 onions, unpeeled, cut into quarters

2 carrots, cut into chunks

2 celery sticks, cut into chunks

1 parsnip, cut into chunks (optional)

1 eating apple or pear (optional)

1 tbsp black peppercorns

1 To make the stock, first tie the parsley sprigs into a bundle, then put in a large pan with the remaining stock ingredients and enough cold water to cover by 2.5 cm/1 inch.

2 Bring to the boil, skimming off any foam. Boil for 2 minutes, then reduce the heat to low and simmer very gently for 2–3 hours. Cool the stock slightly, then strain into a large bowl. Skim off any fat from the surface, then wipe kitchen paper across the surface.

3 Measure 3 litres/5¼ pints of the turkey stock into a large pan. Add the onion and carrots and bring to the boil.

4 Add the rice, reduce the heat and simmer, stirring once or twice for 15–20 minutes until the rice is tender.

5 Stir the remaining vegetables into the soup and simmer for 10 minutes. Add the cooked turkey meat, heat through and season to taste with salt and pepper. Stir in the parsley and serve.

Yucatecan Citrus Soup

Roasted onion and garlic are combined with tangy citrus flavours to create a soup full of tantalising tastes.

NUTRITIONAL INFORMATION

Calories 119	Sugars 14g
Protein 4g	Fat 4g
Carbohydrate . . .17g	Saturates 0g

10 mins   45 mins

SERVES 4

I N G R E D I E N T S

onions

5 large garlic cloves, unpeeled

tbsp extra virgin olive oil

.3 litres/2¼ pints vegetable, chicken or
   fish stock

25 ml/8 fl oz water

ripe tomatoes, diced

inch of dried oregano

fresh green chilli, such as jalapeño or
   serrano, deseeded and chopped

inch of ground cumin

tsp finely grated grapefruit rind

tsp finely grated lime rind

tsp finely grated orange rind

ice and diced flesh of 2 limes

ice of 1 orange

ice of 1 grapefruit

alt and pepper

TO GARNISH

ortilla chips, or sliced tortilla strips fried
   until crisp

tbsp chopped fresh coriander

1 Cut 1 unpeeled onion in half. Peel and finely chop the other onion.

2 Heat a large heavy-based frying pan, add the unpeeled onion halves and garlic and cook over a medium-high heat until the skins char and the onions are caramelised on their cut sides; the garlic should be soft on the inside. Remove from the pan and set aside to cool slightly.

3 Meanwhile, heat the oil in a pan and lightly cook the remaining onion until softened. Add the stock and water and bring to the boil. Reduce the heat and simmer for a few minutes.

4 Peel the charred onion and garlic, then chop coarsely and add to the simmering soup, with the tomatoes, oregano, chilli and cumin. Cook, stirring occasionally, for about 15 minutes.

5 Add the citrus rind, season to taste with salt and pepper, then simmer for a further 2 minutes. Remove from the heat and stir in the lime flesh and citrus juices.

6 Ladle into warmed soup bowls, garnish with tortilla chips and fresh coriander and serve immediately.

Spicy Gazpacho

This classic Spanish cold soup is given a Mexican twist by adding chillies and fresh coriander. Serve with chunks of crusty bread.

NUTRITIONAL INFORMATION

Calories 125   Sugars 10g
Protein ....3g   Fat 8g
Carbohydrate ....11g   Saturates 1g

3–4 hrs   0 mins

SERVES 4–6

I N G R E D I E N T S

1 cucumber

2 green peppers

6 ripe tomatoes

½ fresh hot chilli

½–1 onion, finely chopped

3–4 garlic cloves, chopped

4 tbsp extra virgin olive oil

¼ –½ tsp ground cumin

2–4 tsp sherry vinegar or a combination of balsamic vinegar and wine vinegar

4 tbsp chopped fresh coriander

2 tbsp chopped fresh parsley

300 ml/10 fl oz vegetable or chicken stock

600 ml/1 pint tomato juice or canned crushed tomatoes

salt and pepper

ice cubes, to serve

1 Cut the cucumber in half lengthways, then cut into quarters. Remove the seeds with a teaspoon and dice the flesh. Cut the peppers in half, remove the cores and seeds, then dice the flesh.

2 If you prefer to peel the tomatoes, place in a heatproof bowl, pour boiling water over to cover and stand for 30 seconds. Drain and plunge into cold water. The skins will then slide off easily. Cut the tomatoes in half, deseed if wished, then chop the flesh. Deseed and chop the fresh chilli.

3 Combine half the cucumber, green pepper, tomatoes and onion in a

blender or food processor with all the chilli, garlic, olive oil, cumin, vinegar coriander and parsley. Process with enough stock for a smooth purée.

4 Pour the puréed soup into a bowl and stir in the remaining stock and tomato juice or crushed tomatoes. Add the remaining green pepper, cucumber tomatoes and onion, stirring well. Season with salt and pepper to taste, then cover with clingfilm and chill in the refrigerator for a few hours.

5 Ladle the chilled soup into bowls and serve with ice cubes in each bowl.

VARIATION

Freeze tomato juice ice cubes as a delicious alternative.

Spicy Courgette Soup

Mild red chilli powder and pan-browned garlic give flavour to this simple, homely soup. Quick to make, it's ideal for a light lunch.

NUTRITIONAL INFORMATION

Calories	98	Sugars	.........1g
Protein	.........2g	Fat	...........7g
Carbohydrate	....8g	Saturates	.......1g

5 mins   15 mins

SERVES 4

INGREDIENTS

tbsp vegetable oil

garlic cloves, thinly sliced

—2 tbsp mild red chilli powder

¼–½ tsp ground cumin

.5 litres/2¾ pints chicken, vegetable or beef stock

courgettes, cut into bite-size chunks

tbsp long grain rice

alt and pepper

esh oregano sprigs, to garnish

me wedges, to serve (optional)

1 Heat the oil in a heavy-based pan, add the garlic and cook, stirring frequently, for about 2 minutes until softened and just beginning to change colour. Stir in the chilli powder and cumin and cook over a medium-low heat, stirring constantly, for a minute.

2 Stir in the stock, courgettes and rice, then cook over a medium-high heat for about 10 minutes until the courgettes are just tender and the rice is cooked through. Season the soup to taste with salt and pepper.

3 Ladle into warmed soup bowls, garnish with oregano and serve with lime wedges.

VARIATION

Instead of rice, use rice-shaped pasta, such as orzo or semone de melone, or very thin pasta known as fideo. Use yellow summer squash instead of the courgettes and add cooked pinto beans in place of the rice. Diced tomatoes also make a tasty addition.

Mexican Vegetable Soup

Crisp tortilla chips act as croûtons in this hearty vegetable soup which is found throughout Mexico. Add cheese to melt in, if you wish.

NUTRITIONAL INFORMATION

Calories	201	Sugars	9g
Protein	6g	Fat	9g
Carbohydrate	27g	Saturates	1g

    10 mins   40 mins

SERVES 4

INGREDIENTS

2 tbsp vegetable or extra virgin olive oil

1 onion, finely chopped

4 garlic cloves, finely chopped

¼–½ tsp ground cumin

2–3 tsp mild chilli powder

1 carrot, sliced

1 waxy potato, diced

350 g/12 oz diced fresh or
   canned tomatoes

1 courgette, diced

¼ small cabbage, shredded

1 litre/1¾ pints vegetable or chicken
   stock or water

1 corn cob, the kernels cut off the cob or
   canned sweetcorn

about 10 green beans, cut into bite-size
   lengths

salt and pepper

TO SERVE

4–6 tbsp chopped fresh coriander

salsa of your choice or chopped fresh chilli,
   to taste

tortilla chips

1 Heat the oil in a heavy-based pan. Add the onion and garlic and cook for a few minutes until softened, then sprinkle in the cumin and chilli powder. Stir in the carrot, potato, tomatoes, courgettes and cabbage and cook, stirring occasionally, for 2 minutes.

2 Pour in the stock. Cover and cook over a medium heat for about 20 minutes until the vegetables are tender.

3 Add extra water if necessary, then st in the sweetcorn and green beans an cook for a further 5–10 minutes or unt the beans are tender. Season with salt an pepper to taste, bearing in mind that th tortilla chips may be salty.

4 Ladle the soup into soup bowls an sprinkle each portion with fres coriander. Top with a spoon of salsa, the add a handful of tortilla chips.

Crab & Cabbage Soup

From the Vera Cruz region of Mexico, this delicious soup uses fresh crab meat to add a rich flavour to a mildly spicy vegetable and fish broth.

NUTRITIONAL INFORMATION

Calories	131	Sugars	10g
Protein	13g	Fat	4g
Carbohydrate	12g	Saturates	0g

🦀 🦀 🦀

🧊 25 mins   🕐 35 mins

SERVES 4

INGREDIENTS

cabbage

50 g/1 lb ripe tomatoes

litre/1¾ pints fish stock or water mixed with 1–2 fish stock cubes

onion, thinly sliced

small carrot, diced

garlic cloves, finely chopped

tbsp chopped fresh coriander

tsp mild chilli powder

whole cooked crab or 175–225 g/6–8 oz crab meat

tbsp torn fresh oregano leaves

salt and pepper

TO SERVE

–2 limes, cut into wedges

salsa of your choice

1 Cut out and discard any thick stalk from the cabbage, then shred the leaves finely using a large knife.

2 To peel the tomatoes, place in a heatproof bowl, pour boiling water over to cover and stand for 30 seconds. Drain and plunge into cold water. The skins will then slide off easily. Chop the skinned tomatoes.

3 Place the tomatoes and stock in a pan with the onion, carrot, cabbage, garlic, fresh coriander and chilli powder. Bring to the boil, then reduce the heat and simmer for about 20 minutes until the vegetables are just tender.

4 Remove the crab meat from the whole crab, if using. Twist off the legs and claws and crack with a heavy knife. Remove the flesh from the legs with a skewer; leave the cracked claws intact, if wished. Remove the body section from the main crab shell and remove the meat, discarding the stomach sac and feathery gills that lie along each side of the body.

5 Add the oregano leaves and crab meat to the pan and simmer for 10–15 minutes to combine the flavours. Season to taste with salt and pepper.

6 Ladle into deep soup bowls and serve immediately with 1–2 wedges of lime, per serving. Hand round a bowl of your chosen salsa separately.

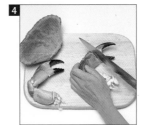

Fish & Roasted Tomato Soup

Mexico's long shoreline yields an abundance of fish and shellfish, which are often turned into spicy, satisfying soups – just like this one.

NUTRITIONAL INFORMATION

Calories	220	Sugars	.........6g
Protein	........27g	Fat	..........10g
Carbohydrate	....7g	Saturates	.......1g

 20 mins   30–60 mins

SERVES 4

INGREDIENTS

5 ripe tomatoes

5 garlic cloves, unpeeled

500 g/1 lb 2 oz red snapper, cut into chunks

1 litre/1¾ pints fish stock, or water plus 1–2 fish stock cubes

2–3 tbsp olive oil

1 onion, chopped

2 fresh chillies, such as serrano, deseeded and thinly sliced

lime wedges, to serve

3 Poach the snapper in the stock over a medium heat for about 5 minutes just until it is opaque and firm. Remove the pan from the heat and set aside.

4 Heat the oil in another pan and cook the chopped onion until softened. Strain in the cooking liquid from the fish, then add the coarsely chopped tomatoes and garlic and stir.

5 Bring to the boil, then reduce the hea and simmer gently for abou 5 minutes to combine the flavours. Add th sliced chillies.

6 Divide chunks of the poached re snapper between warmed soup bowl ladle over the hot soup and serv immediately with lime wedges fo squeezing over the top.

1 Heat an ungreased heavy-based frying pan, add the whole tomatoes and garlic and cook over a high heat until charred. Alternatively, place under a preheated grill until the skins of the vegetables blacken and char and the flesh inside is tender. As another alternative, place the tomatoes and garlic cloves in a roasting tin and bake in a preheated oven, 190–200°C/375–400°F/Gas Mark 5–6 for about 40 minutes.

2 Set the tomatoes and garlic aside to cool, then remove the skins and chop coarsely, combining them with any juices from the pan or roasting tin. Set aside.

Chicken & Chipotle Soup

This soup evolved from the foodstalls that line the streets of Tlalpan, a suburb of Mexico City: avocado, chicken and chillies make it special.

NUTRITIONAL INFORMATION

Calories	216	Sugars	1g
Protein	28g	Fat	11g
Carbohydrate	2g	Saturates	2g

10 mins   5 mins

SERVES 4

INGREDIENTS

1.5 litres/2¾ pints chicken stock

2–3 garlic cloves, finely chopped

1–2 chipotle chillies, cut into very thin strips (see Cook's Tip)

1 avocado

lime or lemon juice, for tossing

3–5 spring onions, thinly sliced

350–400 g/12–14 oz skinless boneless cooked chicken breast, torn or cut into shreds or thin strips

2 tbsp chopped fresh coriander

TO SERVE

1 lime, cut into wedges

handful of tortilla chips (optional)

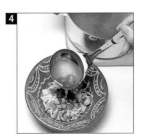

1 Place the stock in a pan with the garlic and chipotle chillies and bring to the boil.

2 Meanwhile, cut the avocado in half around the stone. Twist apart, then remove the stone with a knife. Carefully peel off the skin, dice the flesh and toss in lime or lemon juice to prevent the flesh from turning brown.

3 Arrange the spring onions, chicken, avocado and fresh coriander in the base of 4 individual soup bowls or in a large tureen.

4 Ladle the hot stock into the bowls and serve with lime wedges and a handful of tortilla chips if using.

COOK'S TIP

Chipotle chillies are smoked and dried jalapeño chillies and are available canned or dried. They add a distinctive smoky flavour to dishes and are very hot. Drain canned chipotles before using. Dried chipotles need to be reconstituted before using.

Chicken & Asparagus Soup

This light, clear soup has a delicate flavour of asparagus and herbs. Use a good quality stock for best results.

NUTRITIONAL INFORMATION

Calories	224	Sugars	.........2g
Protein	........27g	Fat	...........5g
Carbohydrate	...12g	Saturates	......1g

 10 mins   🕐 15 mins

SERVES 4

INGREDIENTS

225 g/8 oz fresh asparagus

850 ml/1½ pints chicken stock

150 ml/5 fl oz dry white wine

fresh parsley sprig

fresh dill sprig

fresh tarragon sprig

1 garlic clove

55 g/2 oz vermicelli rice noodles

350 g/12 oz lean cooked chicken,
   finely shredded

1 small leek

salt and white pepper

1 Wash the asparagus and trim away the woody ends. Cut each spear into pieces 4 cm/1½ inches long.

2 Pour the stock and wine into a large pan and bring to the boil over a medium heat.

3 Wash the herbs and tie them together with clean string. Peel the garlic clove and add, with the herbs, to the pan. Add the asparagus and noodles. Lower the heat, cover and simmer for 5 minutes.

4 Stir in the chicken and season to taste with salt and pepper. Simmer gently for a further 3-4 minutes until heated through.

5 Trim the leek, slice it down the centre and wash under running water to remove any dirt. Shake dry and shred very finely.

6 Remove the herbs and garlic from the pan and discard. Ladle the soup into warmed bowls, sprinkle with shredded leek and serve immediately.

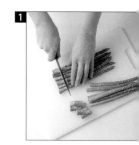

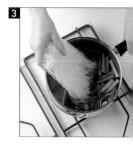

VARIATION

You can use any of your favourite herbs in this recipe, but choose those with a subtle flavour so that they do not overpower the asparagus. Small, tender asparagus spears give the best results and flavour.

Beetroot & Potato Soup

A deep red soup makes a stunning first course – and it's easy in the microwave. A swirl of soured cream gives a very pretty effect.

NUTRITIONAL INFORMATION

Calories ....120 Sugars 11g
Protein ....4g Fat 2g
Carbohydrate ...22g Saturates 1g

20 mins   30 mins

SERVES 6

INGREDIENTS

onion, chopped

350 g/12 oz potatoes, diced

small cooking apple, peeled, cored and grated

3 tbsp water

tsp cumin seeds

500 g/1 lb 2 oz cooked beetroot, peeled and diced

bay leaf

pinch of dried thyme

tsp lemon juice

600 ml/1 pint hot vegetable stock

tbsp soured cream

salt and pepper

fresh dill sprigs, to garnish

1 Place the onion, potatoes, apple and water in a large bowl. Cover and cook on HIGH power for 10 minutes.

2 Stir in the cumin seeds and cook on HIGH power for 1 minute.

3 Stir in the beetroot, bay leaf, thyme, lemon juice and stock. Cover and cook on HIGH power for 12 minutes, stirring halfway through. Set aside, uncovered, for 5 minutes.

4 Remove and discard the bay leaf. Strain the vegetables and reserve the liquid in a jug.

5 Place the vegetables with a little of the reserved liquid in a food processor or blender and process to a smooth and creamy purée. Alternatively, either mash the vegetable with a potato masher or press through a sieve.

6 Pour the vegetable purée into a clean bowl with the reserved liquid and mix well. Season with salt and pepper to taste. Cover and cook on HIGH power for 4–5 minutes until piping hot.

7 Serve the soup in warmed bowls. Swirl 1 tablespoon of soured cream into each serving and garnish with a few sprigs of fresh dill.

Spiced Fruit Soup

This delicately flavoured apple and apricot soup is gently spiced with ginger and allspice and finished with a swirl of soured cream.

NUTRITIONAL INFORMATION

Calories	147	Sugar	........28g
Protein	.........3g	Fats	.........0.4g
Carbohydrates	...29g	Saturates	......0g

7¾ hours   25 mins

SERVES 4–6

INGREDIENTS

125 g/4½oz dried apricots, soaked overnight or no-need-to-soak dried apricots

500 g/1 lb 2 oz eating apples, peeled, cored and chopped

1 small onion, chopped

1 tbsp lemon or lime juice

700 ml/1¼ pints chicken stock

150 ml/5 fl oz dry white wine

¼ tsp ground ginger

pinch of ground allspice

salt and pepper

TO GARNISH

4–6 tbsp soured cream

ground ginger or ground allspice

1 Drain the apricots, if necessary and chop coarsely.

2 Put the apricots in a pan and add the apples, onion, lemon or lime juice and stock. Bring to the boil, cover and simmer gently for about 20 minutes.

3 Set the soup aside to cool a little, then press through a sieve or process in a food processor or blender until a smooth purée. Pour the fruit soup into clean pan.

4 Add the wine and spices and seaso to taste. Bring back to the boil, the set aside to cool. If it is too thick, add little more stock or water and then chill i the refrigerator for several hours.

5 Garnish with soured cream and dus lightly with ginger or allspice.

VARIATION

Other fruits can be combined with apples to make fruit soups — try raspberries, blackberries, blackcurrants or cherries. If the fruits have a lot of pips or stones, the soup should be sieved after puréeing.

Beef Soup with Rice

Strips of tender lean beef are combined with crisp water chestnuts and cooked rice in a tasty beef broth with a tang of orange.

NUTRITIONAL INFORMATION

Calories	210	Sugar	. . . . .4g
Protein	. . . . .20g	Fats	. . . . .5g
Carbohydrates	. . .21g	Saturates	. . . . . .2g

25 mins   25 mins

SERVES 4

I N G R E D I E N T S

350 g/12 oz lean beef, such as rump or sirloin)

litre/1¾ pints beef stock

cinnamon stick, broken

star anise

tbsp dark soy sauce

tbsp dry sherry

tbsp tomato purée

15 g/4 oz can water chestnuts, drained and sliced

75 g/6 oz cooked white rice

tsp finely grated orange rind

tbsp orange juice

salt and pepper

TO GARNISH

strips of orange rind

tbsp snipped fresh chives

1 Carefully trim away any fat from the beef. Cut the beef into thin strips and then place in a large pan.

2 Pour in the beef stock and add the cinnamon, star anise, soy sauce, sherry, tomato purée and water chestnuts. Bring to the boil over a medium heat, skimming off any scum that rises to the surface with a flat ladle or skimmer. Cover

the pan, lower the heat and simmer gently for about 20 minutes or until the beef strips are tender.

3 Skim the soup with a flat ladle again to remove any more scum. Remove and discard the 2 pieces of cinnamon stick and the star anise and blot the surface of the soup with absorbent kitchen paper to remove as much fat as possible.

4 Stir in the rice, grated orange rind and orange juice. Season to taste with salt and pepper. Heat through for 2–3 minutes before ladling into warmed bowls. Serve garnished with strips of orange rind and snipped chives.

Mixed Bean Soup

This is a really hearty soup, filled with colour, flavour and goodness, which may be adapted to any vegetables that you have at hand.

NUTRITIONAL INFORMATION

Calories	190	Sugars	.........9g
Protein	........10g	Fat	...........4g
Carbohydrate	...30g	Saturates	.....0.5g

 5 mins   40 mins

SERVES 4

I N G R E D I E N T S

1 tbsp vegetable oil

1 red onion, halved and sliced

100 g/3½ oz potato, diced

1 carrot, diced

1 leek, sliced

1 fresh green chilli, sliced

3 garlic cloves, crushed

1 tsp ground coriander

1 tsp chilli powder

1 litre/1¾ pints vegetable stock

450 g/1 lb mixed canned beans, such as red kidney, borlotti, black eye or flageolet, drained and rinsed

salt and pepper

2 tbsp chopped fresh coriander, to garnish

COOK'S TIP

Serve this soup with slices of warm corn bread or a cheese loaf.

1 Heat the oil in a large pan and add the onion, potato, carrot and leek. Cook, stirring occasionally, for 2 minutes until the vegetables are slightly softened.

2 Add the chilli and garlic and cook for 1 further minute.

3 Stir in the ground coriander, chilli powder and the vegetable stock.

4 Bring the soup to the boil, reduce the heat and cook for 20 minutes or until the vegetables are tender.

5 Stir in the beans, season to taste and cook, stirring occasionally, for a further 10 minutes.

6 Ladle the soup into bowls, garnish with chopped coriander and serve.

Yogurt & Spinach Soup

Whole young spinach leaves add vibrant colour to this unusual soup.
Serve with hot, crusty bread for a nutritious light meal.

NUTRITIONAL INFORMATION

Calories ....227 Sugars 13g
Protein ....14g Fat 7g
Carbohydrate ...29g Saturates 2g

15 mins   30 mins

SERVES 4

I N G R E D I E N T S

600 ml/1 pint chicken stock

4 tbsp long grain rice, rinsed and drained

4 tbsp water

1 tbsp cornflour

600 ml/1 pint low-fat natural yogurt

3 egg yolks, lightly beaten

juice of 1 lemon

350 g/12 oz young spinach leaves, washed
   and drained

salt and pepper

1 Pour the stock into a large pan, season and bring to the boil. Add the rice and simmer for 10 minutes until barely cooked. Remove from the heat.

2 Combine the water and cornflour to a smooth paste. Pour the yogurt into a second pan and stir in the cornflour mixture. Set the pan over a low heat and bring the yogurt to the boil, stirring with a wooden spoon in one direction only. This will stabilise the yogurt and prevent it from separating or curdling on contact with the hot stock. When the yogurt has reached boiling point, stand the pan on a heat diffuser and simmer gently for 10 minutes. Remove the pan from the heat and set the mixture aside to cool slightly before stirring in the beaten egg yolks.

3 Pour the yogurt mixture into the stock, stir in the lemon juice and stir to blend thoroughly. Keep the soup warm, but do not allow it to boil.

4 Blanch the washed and drained spinach leaves in a large pan of boiling, salted water for 2–3 minutes until they begin to soften but have not wilted. Tip the spinach into a colander, drain well and stir it into the soup. Warm through. Taste the soup and adjust the seasoning if necessary. Serve immediately in wide shallow soup plates, with hot, fresh crusty bread.

Coconut & Crab Soup

Thai red curry paste is quite fiery, but adds a superb flavour to this dish. It is available in jars or packets from supermarkets.

NUTRITIONAL INFORMATION

Calories ....122 Sugar 9g
Protein ....11g Fats 4g
Carbohydrates ...11g Saturates 1g

5 mins   8–10 mins

SERVES 4

INGREDIENTS

1 tbsp groundnut oil

2 tbsp Thai red curry paste

1 red pepper, deseeded and sliced

600 ml/1 pint coconut milk

600 ml/1 pint fish stock

2 tbsp Thai fish sauce

225 g/8 oz canned or fresh white crab meat

225 g/8 oz fresh or frozen crab claws

2 tbsp chopped fresh coriander

3 spring onions, sliced

1 Heat the oil in a large preheated wok, swirling it around to coat. Add the red curry paste and red pepper and stir-fry over a medium heat for 1 minute.

2 Add the coconut milk, fish stock and fish sauce and bring to the boil.

3 Add the crab meat, crab claws, coriander and spring onions.

4 Stir the mixture well and heat thoroughly for 2–3 minutes or until all the ingredients are warmed through.

5 Transfer the soup to 4 warmed bowls and serve hot.

COOK'S TIP

Clean the wok after use by washing it with water, using a mild detergent if necessary, and a soft cloth or brush. Do not scrub or use any abrasive cleaner as this will scratch the surface. Dry thoroughly then wipe the surface all over with a little oil to protect it.

Red Lentil Soup with Yogurt

Tasty red lentil soup flavoured with chopped coriander is an easy microwave dish. The yogurt adds a light piquancy to the soup.

NUTRITIONAL INFORMATION

Calories 280	Sugars 6g	
Protein 17g	Fat 7g	
Carbohydrate ...40g	Saturates 4g	

5 mins   30 mins

SERVES 4

I N G R E D I E N T S

2 tbsp butter

1 onion, finely chopped

1 celery stick, finely chopped

1 large carrot, grated

1 bay leaf

225 g/8 oz red lentils

1.2 litres/2 pints hot vegetable or
   chicken stock

2 tbsp chopped fresh coriander

4 tbsp low-fat natural yogurt

salt and pepper

fresh coriander sprigs, to garnish

1 Place the butter, onion and celery in a large bowl. Cover and cook on HIGH power for 3 minutes.

2 Add the carrot, bay leaf and lentils. Pour in the stock. Cover and cook on HIGH power for 15 minutes, stirring halfway through.

3 Remove the bowl from the microwave oven, cover and stand for 5 minutes.

4 Remove and discard the bay leaf, then process in batches in a food processor, until smooth. Alternatively, press the soup through a sieve.

5 Pour the soup into a clean bowl. Season with salt and pepper to taste and stir in the coriander. Cover and cook on HIGH power for 4–5 minutes until piping hot.

6 Serve in warmed soup bowls. Stir 1 tablespoon of yogurt into each serving and garnish with small sprigs of fresh coriander.

COOK'S TIP

For an extra creamy soup try adding low-fat crème fraîche or soured cream instead of yogurt.

Spicy Lentil Soup

For a warming, satisfying meal on a cold day,
this lentil dish is packed full of flavour and goodness.

NUTRITIONAL INFORMATION

Calories	155	Sugars	.........4g
Protein	........11g	Fat	...........3g
Carbohydrate	...22g	Saturates	.....0.4g

1 hour   1¼ hours

SERVES 4

I N G R E D I E N T S

115 g/4 oz red lentils

2 tsp vegetable oil

1 large onion, finely chopped

2 garlic cloves, crushed

1 tsp ground cumin

1 tsp ground coriander

1 tsp garam masala

2 tbsp tomato purée

1 litre/1¾ pints vegetable stock

350 g/12 oz can sweetcorn, drained

salt and pepper

TO SERVE

low-fat natural yogurt

chopped fresh parsley

warmed pitta bread

1 Rinse the red lentils thoroughly under cold running water. Drain well and set side.

2 Heat the oil in a large non-stick pan and fry the onion and garlic gently until softened but not browned.

3 Stir in the cumin, coriander, garam masala, tomato purée and 4 tablespoons of the stock. Mix well and simmer gently for 2 minutes.

4 Add the lentils and pour in the remaining stock. Bring to the boil, reduce the heat, cover and simmer for 1 hour until the lentils are tender and the soup thickened. Stir in the sweetcorn and heat through for 5 minutes. Season to taste with salt and pepper.

5 Ladle into warmed soup bowls and top each with a spoonful of yogurt and a sprinkling of parsley. Serve with warmed pitta bread.

COOK'S TIP

Many of the ready-prepared ethnic breads available today either contain fat or are brushed with oil before baking. Always check the ingredients list for fat content.

Lentil & Ham Soup

This is a good hearty soup, based on a stock made from a ham knuckle, with plenty of vegetables and red lentils to thicken it and add flavour.

NUTRITIONAL INFORMATION

Calories 219   Sugars 4g
Protein . . . . .17g   Fat 3g
Carbohydrate . . .33g   Saturates 1g

2¼ hours   1¾ hours

SERVES 4–6

I N G R E D I E N T S

225 g/8 oz red lentils

1.5 litres/2¾ pints stock or water

2 onions, chopped

1 garlic clove, crushed

2 large carrots, chopped

1 lean ham knuckle or 175 g/6 oz lean
    bacon, chopped

4 large tomatoes, peeled and chopped

2 bay leaves

250 g/9 oz potatoes, chopped

1 tbsp white wine vinegar

¼ tsp ground allspice

salt and pepper

chopped spring onions or chopped fresh
    parsley, to garnish

1 Put the lentils and stock or water in a pan and set aside to soak for 1–2 hours.

2 Add the onions, garlic, carrots, ham knuckle or chopped bacon, tomatoes and bay leaves. Season to taste with salt and pepper.

3 Bring the mixture to the boil over a medium heat, then lower the heat, cover and simmer for about 1 hour until the lentils are tender, stirring occasionally to prevent the lentils from sticking to the bottom of the pan.

4 Add the potatoes and continue to simmer for about 20 minutes until the potatoes and the meat on the ham knuckle are tender.

5 Remove and discard the bay leaves. Remove the knuckle and chop 125 g/4½ oz of the meat and reserve. If liked, press half the soup through a sieve or process in a food processor or blender until smooth. Return to the pan with the rest of the soup.

6 Adjust the seasoning, add the vinegar and allspice and the reserved chopped ham. Simmer gently for a further 5–10 minutes. Serve sprinkled liberally with spring onions or chopped parsley.

Smoked Haddock Soup

Smoked haddock gives this soup a wonderfully rich flavour, while the mashed potatoes and cream thicken and enrich the stock.

NUTRITIONAL INFORMATION

Calories	169	Sugars	.........8g
Protein	........16g	Fat	...........5g
Carbohydrate	...16g	Saturates	......3g

 25 mins   40 mins

SERVES 4–6

INGREDIENTS

225 g/8 oz smoked haddock fillet

1 onion, finely chopped

1 garlic clove, crushed

600 ml/1 pint water

600 ml/1 pint skimmed milk

225–350 g/8–12 oz hot mashed potatoes

2 tbsp butter

about 1 tbsp lemon juice

6 tbsp low-fat natural fromage frais

4 tbsp fresh parsley, chopped

salt and pepper

1 Put the fish, onion, garlic and water into a pan. Bring to the boil, cover and simmer over a low heat for 15–20 minutes.

2 Remove the fish from the pan. Strip off the skin and remove all the bones and reserve both. Flake the flesh finely with a fork.

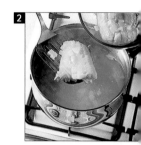

3 Return the skin and bones to the cooking liquid and simmer for 10 minutes. Strain, discarding the skin and bones. Pour the cooking liquid into a clean pan.

4 Add the milk and flaked fish and season to taste with salt and pepper. Bring to the boil and simmer for about 3 minutes.

5 Gradually whisk in sufficient mashed potato to give a fairly thick soup, then stir in the butter and sharpen to taste with lemon juice.

6 Add the fromage frais and 3 tablespoons of the chopped parsley. Reheat gently and adjust the seasoning if necessary. Sprinkle with the remaining parsley and serve immediately.

COOK'S TIP

Undyed smoked haddock may be used in place of the bright yellow fish; it will give a paler colour but just as much flavour. Alternatively, use smoked cod or smoked whiting.

Carrot & Cumin Soup

Carrot soups are very popular and and here cumin, tomato, potato and celery give the soup both richness and depth.

NUTRITIONAL INFORMATION

Calories 114	Sugars 8g	
Protein 3g	Fat 6g	
Carbohydrate ...12g	Saturates 4g	

15 mins   45 mins

SERVES 4–6

INGREDIENTS

3 tbsp butter or margarine

1 large onion, chopped

1–2 garlic cloves, crushed

350 g/12 oz carrots, sliced

900 ml/1½ pints chicken or vegetable stock

¾ tsp ground cumin

2 celery sticks, thinly sliced

115 g/4 oz potato, diced

2 tsp tomato purée

2 tsp lemon juice

2 fresh or dried bay leaves

about 300 ml/ 10 fl oz skimmed milk

salt and pepper

celery leaves to garnish

1 Melt the butter or margarine in a large pan. Add the onion and garlic and cook very gently until softened.

2 Add the carrots and cook gently for a further 5 minutes, stirring frequently and taking care they do not brown.

3 Add the stock, cumin, seasoning, celery, potato, tomato purée, lemon juice and bay leaves and bring to the boil. Cover and simmer for about 30 minutes until the vegetables are tender.

4 Remove and discard the bay leaves, cool the soup a little and then press it through a sieve or process in a food processor or blender until smooth.

5 Pour the soup into a clean pan, add the milk and bring to the boil over a low heat. Taste and adjust the seasoning if necessary.

6 Ladle into warmed bowls, garnish each serving with a small celery leaf and serve.

COOK'S TIP
This soup can be frozen for up to 3 months. Add the milk when reheating.

Spiced Cauliflower Soup

This thick puréed soup flavoured with Indian spices and yogurt is a good choice for the microwave. Serve with hot naan bread.

NUTRITIONAL INFORMATION

Calories ....123 Sugars 13g
Protein ....8g Fat 4g
Carbohydrate ...14g Saturates 1g

10 mins   25 mins

SERVES 4

I N G R E D I E N T S

350 g/12 oz cauliflower, divided into small florets

350 g/12 oz swede, diced

1 onion, chopped

1 tbsp vegetable oil

3 tbsp water

1 garlic clove, crushed

2 tsp grated fresh root ginger

1 tsp cumin seeds

1 tsp black mustard seeds

2 tsp ground coriander

2 tsp ground turmeric

850 ml/1½ pints hot vegetable stock

300 ml/10 fl oz low-fat yogurt

salt and pepper

chopped fresh coriander, to garnish

1 Place the cauliflower, swede, onion, oil and water in a large bowl. Cover and cook on HIGH power for 10 minutes, stirring halfway through.

2 Add the garlic, ginger, cumin, mustard seeds, ground coriander and turmeric. Stir well, cover and cook on HIGH power for 2 minutes.

3 Pour in the stock, cover and cook on HIGH power for 10 minutes. Stand, covered, for 5 minutes.

4 Strain the vegetables and reserve the liquid. Process the vegetables with a little of the reserved liquid in a food processor or blender until smooth and creamy. Alternatively, either mash the soup or press it through a sieve.

5 Pour the vegetable purée and remaining reserved liquid into a clean bowl and mix well. Season to taste with salt and pepper.

6 Stir in the yogurt and cook on HIGH power for 3-4 minutes until hot but not boiling, otherwise the yogurt will curdle. Ladle into warmed bowls and serve garnished with chopped fresh coriander.

Cucumber & Tomato Soup

Although this chilled soup is not an authentic Indian dish, it is wonderful served as a 'cooler' between hot, spicy courses.

NUTRITIONAL INFORMATION

Calories	73	Sugar	........16g
Protein	.........2g	Fats	...........1g
Carbohydrates	...16g	Saturates	.....0.2g

12 hours   0 mins

SERVES 6

I N G R E D I E N T S

tomatoes, peeled and deseeded

.5 kg/3 lb 5 oz watermelon, seedless if available

0 cm/4 inch piece cucumber, peeled and deseeded

2 spring onions, green part only, chopped

tbsp chopped fresh mint

salt and pepper

fresh mint sprigs, to garnish

1 Using a sharp knife, cut 1 tomato into 1 cm/½ inch dice.

2 Remove the rind from the melon, and remove the seeds if it is not seedless.

3 Put the 3 remaining tomatoes into a blender or food processor and, with the motor running, add the deseeded cucumber, chopped spring onions and watermelon. Blend until smooth.

4 If not using a food processor, push the deseeded watermelon through a sieve. Stir the diced tomatoes and mint into the melon mixture. Adjust the seasoning to taste. Chop the cucumber, spring onions and the 3 remaining tomatoes finely and add to the melon.

5 Chill the cucumber and tomato soup overnight in the refrigerator. Check the seasoning and transfer to a serving dish. Garnish with mint sprigs.

COOK'S TIP

Although this soup does improve if chilled overnight, it is also delicious as a quick appetiser if whipped up just before a meal, and served immediately.

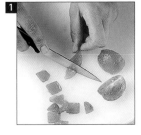

Chunky Potato & Beef Soup

This is a real winter warmer – pieces of tender beef and chunky mixed vegetables are cooked in a stock flavoured with sherry.

NUTRITIONAL INFORMATION

Calories 187   Sugars 3g
Protein ....14g   Fat 9g
Carbohydrate ...12g   Saturates 2g

5 mins   35 mins

SERVES 4

I N G R E D I E N T S

2 tbsp vegetable oil

225 g/8 oz lean braising or frying steak, cut into strips

225 g/8 oz new potatoes, halved

1 carrot, diced

2 celery sticks, sliced

2 leeks, sliced

850 ml/1½ pints beef stock

8 baby corn cobs, sliced

1 bouquet garni

2 tbsp dry sherry

salt and pepper

chopped fresh parsley, to garnish

crusty bread, to serve

COOK'S TIP

Make double the quantity of soup and freeze the remainder in a rigid container for later use. When ready to use, leave in the refrigerator to thaw thoroughly, then heat until piping hot.

1 Heat the vegetable oil in a large pan. Add the strips of steak to the pan and cook for 3 minutes, turning constantly.

2 Add the halved potatoes, diced carrot and sliced celery and leeks. Cook, stirring constantly, for a further 5 minutes.

3 Pour in the beef stock and bring to the boil over a medium heat. Reduce the heat until the liquid is simmering gently, then add the sliced baby corn cobs and the bouquet garni.

4 Cook the soup for a further 20 minutes or until the meat and all the vegetables are tender.

5 Remove the bouquet garni from the pan and discard. Stir the dry sherry into the soup and then season to taste with salt and pepper.

6 Pour the soup into warmed soup bowls and garnish with the chopped fresh parsley. Serve immediately with crusty bread.

Carrot, Apple & Celery Soup

For this fresh-tasting soup, use your favourite variety of eating apple rather than a cooking variety, which will give too tart a flavour.

NUTRITIONAL INFORMATION

Calories . . . . 153g   Sugars 34g
Protein . . . . .2g   Fat 1g
Carbohydrate . . .36g   Saturates 0.2g

1¼ hours   40 mins

SERVES 4

INGREDIENTS

1.00 g/2 lb carrots, finely diced

1 medium onion, chopped

3 celery sticks, diced

1 litre/1¾ pints vegetable stock

3 medium-sized eating apples

2 tbsp tomato purée

1 bay leaf

2 tsp caster sugar

¼ large lemon

salt and pepper

celery leaves, shredded, to garnish

3 Meanwhile, wash, core and cut the remaining apple into thin slices, without peeling.

4 Place the apple slices in a small pan and squeeze over the lemon juice. Heat the apple slices gently and simmer for 1–2 minutes until tender.

5 Drain the apple slices and set aside until required.

6 Place the carrot and apple mixture in a blender or food processor and process until smooth. Alternatively, press the mixture through a sieve with the back of a wooden spoon.

7 Gently re-heat the soup if necessary and season with salt and pepper to taste. ladle the soup into warmed bowls and serve topped with the reserved apple slices and shredded celery leaves.

1 Place the carrots, onion and celery in a large, heavy-based pan and add the stock. Bring to the boil, lower the heat, cover and simmer for 10 minutes.

2 Meanwhile, peel, core and dice 2 of the apples. Add the pieces of apple, the tomato purée, bay leaf and caster sugar to the pan and bring to the boil over a medium heat. Reduce the heat, half-cover and simmer for 20 minutes. Remove and discard the bay leaf.

Peking Duck Soup

This is a hearty and robustly flavoured soup, containing pieces of duck and vegetables cooked in a rich stock.

NUTRITIONAL INFORMATION

Calories 92   Sugars 3g
Protein ....8g   Fat 5g
Carbohydrate ....3g   Saturates 1g

5 mins   35 mins

SERVES 4

INGREDIENTS

115 g/4 oz lean duck breast meat

225 g/8 oz Chinese leaves

850 ml/1½ pints chicken or duck stock

1 tbsp dry sherry or Chinese rice wine

1 tbsp light soy sauce

2 garlic cloves, crushed

pinch of ground star anise

1 tbsp sesame seeds

1 tsp sesame oil

1 tbsp chopped fresh parsley

1 Remove the skin from the duck breast and finely dice the flesh. Using a sharp knife, shred the Chinese leaves.

2 Put the stock in a large pan and bring to the boil over a medium heat. Add the sherry or rice wine, soy sauce, diced duck meat and shredded Chinese leaves and stir thoroughly. Reduce the heat and simmer gently for 15 minutes.

3 Stir in the garlic and star anise and cook over a low heat for a further 10–15 minutes or until the duck is tender.

4 Meanwhile, dry-fry the sesame seeds in a preheated, heavy-based frying pan or wok, stirring constantly until they give off their fragrance.

5 Remove the sesame seeds from the pan and stir them into the soup, with the sesame oil and the chopped fresh parsley.

6 Ladle the Peking duck soup into warmed bowls and serve immediately.

VARIATION

If Chinese leaves are unavailable, use leafy green cabbage instead. You may wish to adjust the quantity to taste, as Western cabbage has a stronger flavour and odour than Chinese leaves.

Prawn Gumbo

This soup is packed with onions, red peppers, rice, prawns and okra,
a vegetable which both adds flavour and acts as a thickening agent.

NUTRITIONAL INFORMATION

Calories	177	Sugar	.........5g
Protein	........12g	Fats	...........8g
Carbohydrates	...15g	Saturates	......1g

🍲 1 hour   🕐 45 mins

SERVES 4–6

INGREDIENTS

2 tbsp olive oil

1 large onion, finely chopped

2 slices lean bacon, finely
  chopped (optional)

1–2 garlic cloves, crushed

1 large or 2 small red peppers, finely
  chopped or coarsely minced

850 ml/1½ pints fish or vegetable Stock

1 bay leaf

1 mace blade

pinch of ground allspice

3 tbsp long grain rice

1 tbsp white wine vinegar

125–175 g/4½–6 oz okra, trimmed and very
  thinly sliced

90–125 g/3–4½ oz peeled prawns

1 tbsp anchovy essence

2 tsp tomato purée

1–2 tbsp chopped fresh parsley

salt and pepper

TO GARNISH

whole prawns

fresh parsley sprigs

1 Heat the oil in a large pan and cook the onion, bacon, if using, and garlic over a low heat for 4–5 minutes until soft. Add the peppers and cook gently for a further 2 minutes.

2 Add the stock, bay leaf, mace, allspice, rice, vinegar and seasoning and bring to the boil. Cover and simmer gently for about 20 minutes, stirring occasionally, until the rice is just tender.

3 Add the okra, prawns, anchovy essence and tomato purée, cover and simmer gently for about 15 minutes until the okra is tender and the mixture has thickened slightly.

4 Remove and discard the bay leaf and mace and adjust the seasoning if necessary. Stir in the parsley, ladle into warmed bowls and serve garnished with a whole prawn and parsley sprigs.

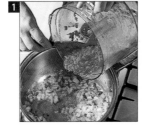

Pork Chilli Soup

This meaty chilli tastes lighter than one made with beef.
Good for informal entertaining, the recipe is easily doubled.

NUTRITIONAL INFORMATION

Calories	308	Sugars	........13g
Protein	........40g	Fat	..........10g
Carbohydrate	...15g	Saturates	.......3g

 10 mins   50–60 mins

SERVES 3

INGREDIENTS

2 tsp olive oil

500 g/1 lb 2 oz lean minced pork

1 onion, finely chopped

1 celery stick, finely chopped

1 pepper, deseeded and finely chopped

2–3 garlic cloves, finely chopped

400 g/14 oz can chopped tomatoes in juice

3 tbsp tomato purée

450 ml/16 fl oz chicken or meat stock

¼ tsp ground coriander

¼ tsp ground cumin

¼ tsp dried oregano

1 tsp mild chilli powder

salt and pepper

chopped fresh coriander leaves or parsley,
  to garnish

soured cream, to serve

1 Heat the oil in a large pan over a medium-high heat. Add the pork, season with salt and pepper, and cook, stirring frequently, until no longer pink. Reduce the heat to medium and add the onion, celery, pepper and garlic. Cover and cook, stirring occasionally, for a further 5 minutes until the onion is softened.

2 Add the tomatoes, tomato purée and the stock. Stir in the coriander, cumin, oregano and chilli powder. Season with salt and pepper to taste.

3 Bring just to the boil, then reduce the heat to low, cover and simmer for about 30–40 minutes until all the vegetables are very tender. Taste and adjust the seasoning, adding more chilli powder if you like it hotter.

4 Ladle the chilli into warm bowls and sprinkle with chopped coriander or parsley. You can either hand the soured cream separately or top each serving with a spoonful.

Oriental Pork Balls in Broth

Steaming the meatballs over the soup gives added flavour to the broth.
A bamboo steamer that rests on the top of a pan is useful for this recipe.

NUTRITIONAL INFORMATION

Calories	67	Sugars	.........1g
Protein	.........9g	Fat	..........2g
Carbohydrate	....3g	Saturates	.......1g

15 mins   18 mins

SERVES 6

INGREDIENTS

2 litres/3½ pints chicken stock

85 g/3 oz shiitake mushrooms, thinly sliced

175 g/6 oz pak choi or other Chinese
   greens, sliced into thin ribbons

6 spring onions, finely sliced

salt and pepper

PORK BALLS

225 g/8 oz lean minced pork

25 g/1 oz fresh spinach leaves,
   finely chopped

2 spring onions, finely chopped

1 garlic clove, very finely chopped

pinch of Chinese five-spice powder

1 tsp soy sauce

1 To make the pork balls, put the pork, spinach, spring
onions and garlic in a bowl. Add the five-spice powder
and soy sauce and mix until thoroughly combined.

2 Shape the pork mixture into 24 balls. Place them in a
single layer in a steamer that will fit over the top of a
pan or in a wok.

3 Bring the stock just to the boil in a pan or wok that
will accommodate the steamer. Lower the heat so that
the liquid just bubbles gently. Add the mushrooms to the
stock and place the steamer, covered, on top of the pan or
wok. Steam for 10 minutes. Remove the steamer and set
aside on a plate.

4 Add the pak choi and spring onions to the pan or wok
and cook gently in the stock for 3-4 minutes or until
the leaves are wilted. Season the broth to taste with salt
and pepper.

5 Divide the pork balls evenly among 6 warmed bowls
and ladle the soup over them. Serve immediately.

Spicy Lamb Soup

Packed with tomatoes, chickpeas and vegetables, this thick and hearty main course soup is bursting with exotic flavours and aromas.

NUTRITIONAL INFORMATION

Calories	323	Sugars	.........6g
Protein	........27g	Fat	..........13g
Carbohydrate	...25g	Saturates	.......4g

10 mins   1¾ hrs

SERVES 4–5

INGREDIENTS

1–2 tbsp olive oil

450 g/1 lb lean boneless lamb, such as shoulder or neck fillet, trimmed of fat and cut into 1 cm/½ inch cubes

1 onion, finely chopped

2–3 garlic cloves, crushed

1.2 litres/2 pints water

400 g/14 oz can chopped tomatoes in juice

1 bay leaf

½ tsp dried thyme

½ tsp dried oregano

pinch of ground cinnamon

¼ tsp ground cumin

¼ tsp ground turmeric

1 tsp harissa

400 g/14 oz can chickpeas, rinsed and drained

1 carrot, diced

1 potato, diced

1 courgette, quartered lengthways and sliced

100 g/3½ oz fresh or thawed frozen green peas

salt and pepper

chopped fresh mint or coriander leaves, to garnish

1 Heat the oil in a large pan or flameproof casserole over a medium-high heat. Add the lamb, in batches if necessary, and cook, stirring occasionally, until evenly browned on all sides, adding a little more oil if needed. Remove the meat, with a draining spoon.

2 Reduce the heat and add the onion and garlic to the pan. Cook, stirring frequently, for 1–2 minutes.

3 Add the water and return all the meat to the pan. Bring just to the boil and skim off any foam that rises to the surface. Reduce the heat and stir in the tomatoes, bay leaf, thyme, oregano, cinnamon, cumin, turmeric and harissa. Simmer for about 1 hour or until the meat is very tender. Discard the bay leaf.

4 Stir in the chickpeas, carrot and potato and simmer for 15 minutes. Add the courgette and peas and simmer for a further 15–20 minutes or until all the vegetables are tender.

5 Season to taste with salt and pepper and add more harissa if desired. Ladle the soup into warmed bowls, garnish with chopped fresh mint or coriander and serve immediately.

Scotch Broth

This traditional winter soup is full of goodness, with lots of tasty golden vegetables along with tender barley and lamb.

NUTRITIONAL INFORMATION

Calories 186	Sugars 6g
Protein 13g	Fat 5g
Carbohydrate ...23g	Saturates 2g

10–15 mins   1½ hrs

SERVES 4–6

INGREDIENTS

55 g/2 oz pearl barley

300 g/10½ oz lean boneless lamb, such as shoulder or neck fillet, trimmed of fat and cut into 1 cm/½ inch cubes

700 ml/1¼ pints water

2 garlic cloves, finely chopped or crushed

1 litre/1¾ pints chicken or meat stock

1 onion, finely chopped

1 bay leaf

1 large leek, quartered lengthways and sliced

2 large carrots, finely diced

1 parsnip, finely diced

125 g/4½ oz swede, diced

2 tbsp chopped fresh parsley

salt and pepper

1 Rinse the barley under cold running water. Put in a pan and add water to cover generously. Bring to the boil over a medium heat and boil for 3 minutes, skimming off the foam from the surface. Remove the pan from the heat, cover and set aside.

2 Put the lamb in another large pan with the measured water and bring to the boil. Skim off the foam that rises to the surface.

3 Stir in the garlic, stock, onion and bay leaf. Reduce the heat, partially cover and simmer for 15 minutes.

4 Drain the barley and add to the soup. Add the leek, carrots, parsnip and swede. Simmer, stirring occasionally, for about 1 hour or until the lamb and vegetables are tender.

5 Season to taste with salt and pepper, stir in the parsley and serve.

COOK'S TIP

This soup is lean when the lamb is trimmed. By making it beforehand, you can remove any hardened fat before reheating.

Hunter's Soup

This soup is perfect for the sweet meat of rabbit, which is traditionally paired with tomatoes and mushrooms.

NUTRITIONAL INFORMATION

Calories	377	Sugars	........13g
Protein	........36g	Fat	..........17g
Carbohydrate	...16g	Saturates	.......6g

20 mins   2½ hours

SERVES 4

INGREDIENTS

1–2 tbsp olive oil

900 g/2 lb rabbit, jointed

1 onion, finely chopped

2–3 garlic cloves, finely chopped or crushed

100 g/3½ oz lean smoked back bacon, finely chopped

125 ml/4 fl oz white wine

1.2 litres/2 pints chicken stock

450 ml/16 fl oz tomato juice

2 tbsp tomato purée

2 carrots, halved lengthways and sliced

1 bay leaf

¼ tsp dried thyme

¼ tsp dried oregano

1 tbsp butter

300 g/10½ oz mushrooms, sliced or quartered if small

salt and pepper

chopped fresh parsley, to garnish

1 Heat the oil in a large pan over a medium heat. Add the rabbit, in batches if necessary, and cook until lightly browned on all sides, adding a little more oil if needed. Remove from the pan.

2 Reduce the heat slightly and add the onion, garlic and bacon to the pan.

Cook, stirring frequently, for a further 2 minutes until the onion has softened.

3 Add the wine and simmer for 1 minute. Add the stock and return the rabbit to the pan with any juices. Bring to the boil and skim off any foam that rises to the surface.

4 Reduce the heat and stir in the tomato juice, tomato purée, carrots, bay leaf, thyme and oregano. Season with salt and pepper. Cover and simmer gently for 1 hour or until very tender.

5 Remove the rabbit pieces with draining spoon and, when coo enough to handle, remove the meat from the bones. Discard any fat or gristle, along with the bones. Cut the meat into bite size pieces and return to the soup.

6 Melt the butter in a frying pan over medium-high heat. Add th mushrooms and season with salt and pepper. Fry gently until lightly golden then add to the soup. Simmer fo 10-15 minutes to blend. Season to tast and serve sprinkled with parsley.

 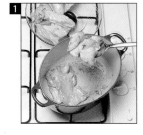 

Potato & Chickpea Soup

This spicy and substantial soup uses ingredients you are likely to have on hand and makes a delicious meal-in-a-bowl.

NUTRITIONAL INFORMATION

Calories	40	Sugars	.......1.6g
Protein	........1.8g	Fat	...........1g
Carbohydrate	...6.5g	Saturates	.....0.1g

5 mins   50 mins

SERVES 4

I N G R E D I E N T S

1 tbsp olive oil

1 large onion, finely chopped

2–3 garlic cloves, finely chopped or crushed

1 carrot, quartered and thinly sliced

350 g/12 oz potatoes, diced

¼ tsp ground turmeric

¼ tsp garam masala

¼ tsp mild curry powder

400 g/14 oz canned chopped tomatoes

850 ml/1½ pints water

¼ tsp chilli purée, or to taste

400 g/14 oz canned chickpeas, rinsed and drained

85 g/3 oz fresh or frozen peas

salt and pepper

chopped fresh coriander, to garnish

1 Heat the olive oil in a large saucepan over a medium heat. Add the onion and garlic and cook for 3–4 minutes, stirring occasionally, until the onion is beginning to soften.

2 Add the carrot, potatoes, turmeric, garam masala and curry powder and continue cooking for 1–2 minutes.

3 Add the tomatoes, water and chilli purée with a pinch of salt. Reduce the heat, cover and simmer for 30 minutes, stirring occasionally.

4 Add the chickpeas and peas to the pan, then simmer for a further 15 minutes or until all the vegetables are tender.

5 Taste the soup and adjust the seasoning, if necessary, adding a little more chilli if desired. Ladle into warm soup bowls and sprinkle with coriander.

Lentil, Potato & Ham Soup

A comforting and satisfying cold-weather soup, this is good served with bread as a main course, but it is not too filling to serve as a starter.

NUTRITIONAL INFORMATION

Calories 61   Sugars 1.4g
Protein . . . . .5.4g   Fat 0.8g
Carbohydrate . . .8.6g   Saturates 0.3g

 5 mins   45 mins

SERVES 5

INGREDIENTS

300 g/10½ oz Puy lentils

2 tsp butter

1 large onion, finely chopped

2 carrots, finely chopped

1 garlic clove, finely chopped

450 ml/16 fl oz water

1 bay leaf

¼ tsp dried sage or rosemary

1 litre/1¾ pints chicken stock

225 g/8 oz potatoes, diced (see Cook's Tip)

1 tbsp tomato purée

115 g/4 oz smoked ham, finely diced

salt and pepper

chopped fresh parsley, to garnish

1 Rinse and drain the lentils and remove any small stones if necessary.

2 Melt the butter in a large saucepan or flameproof casserole over a medium heat. Add the onion, carrots and garlic, cover and fry, stirring occasionally, for about 4–5 minutes until the onion is slightly softened.

3 Add the lentils with the water, bay leaf and sage or rosemary. Bring to the boil, reduce the heat, cover and simmer for 10 minutes.

4 Add the stock, potatoes, tomato purée and ham. Bring back to a simmer. Cover and continue simmering for 25–30 minutes or until the vegetables are tender.

5 Season to taste with salt and pepper and remove and discard the bay leaf. Ladle into warm bowls, garnish with parsley and serve immediately.

COOK'S TIP

Cut the potatoes into small cubes, about 5 mm/¼ inch, so that they will be in proportion with the lentils.

Fennel & Broccoli Soup

This rustic vegetable soup is appealing in its simplicity. Served with ciabatta, focaccia or garlic bread, it makes a good light lunch.

NUTRITIONAL INFORMATION

Calories	108	Sugars	3g
Protein	6g	Fat	3g
Carbohydrate	15g	Saturates	0g

15 mins   1¼ hrs

SERVES 4

INGREDIENTS

5 g/2 oz pearl barley

.5 litres/2¾ pints chicken or vegetable stock

bay leaf

tsp chopped fresh thyme leaves, or ⅛ tsp dried thyme

50 g/9 oz broccoli

tsp olive oil

large leek, halved lengthways and finely chopped

garlic cloves, finely chopped

celery stick, thinly sliced

large fennel bulb, thinly sliced

tbsp chopped fresh basil

alt and pepper

eshly grated Parmesan cheese, to serve

1 Rinse the barley and drain. Bring 450 ml/16 fl oz of the stock to the boil in a small pan. Add the bay leaf and thyme. Add a pinch of salt. Stir in the barley, reduce the heat, partially cover and simmer for 30–40 minutes until tender.

2 Cut the broccoli into florets and peel the stems. Cut the stems into very thin batons, about 2.5 cm/1 inch long. Cut the florets into small slivers and reserve them separately.

3 Heat the oil in a large pan over a medium-low heat and add the leek and garlic. Cook, stirring frequently, for about 5 minutes until softened. Add the celery, fennel and broccoli stems and cook for 2 minutes.

4 Stir in the remaining stock and bring to the boil. Add the barley with its cooking liquid. Season to taste with salt and pepper. Reduce the heat, cover the pan and simmer gently, stirring occasionally, for 10 minutes.

5 Uncover the pan and adjust the heat so the soup bubbles gently. Stir in the broccoli florets and cook for a further 10–12 minutes or until the broccoli is tender. Stir in the basil. Taste and adjust the seasoning if necessary. Ladle into warmed bowls and serve with plenty of Parmesan cheese to sprinkle over.

Vegetable Soup with Bulgur

This healthy and colourful soup makes good use of your herb garden. The fresh herbs give it a vibrant flavour.

NUTRITIONAL INFORMATION

Calories 93   Sugars 8g
Protein . . . . .5g   Fat 3g
Carbohydrate . . .13g   Saturates 0g

 10 mins   1 hr

SERVES 5–6

INGREDIENTS

1 tbsp olive oil

2 onions, chopped

3 garlic cloves, finely chopped or crushed

55 g/2 oz bulgur wheat

5 tomatoes, peeled and sliced or 400 g/
   14 oz can plum tomatoes in juice

225 g/8 oz peeled pumpkin or acorn
   squash, diced

1 large courgette, quartered lengthways
   and sliced

1 litre/1¾ pints boiling water

2 tbsp tomato purée

¼ tsp chilli purée

40 g/1½ oz chopped mixed fresh oregano,
   basil and flat leaf parsley

25 g/1 oz rocket leaves, coarsely chopped

175 g/6 oz shelled fresh or frozen peas

salt and pepper

freshly grated Parmesan cheese, to serve

1 Heat the oil in a large pan over a medium-low heat and add the onions and garlic. Cook for 5–8 minutes, stirring occasionally, until the onions soften.

2 Stir in the bulgur wheat and continue cooking, stirring constantly, for 1 minute.

3 Layer the tomatoes, pumpkin or squash and courgette in the pan.

4 Combine half the water with the tomato purée, chilli purée and a pinch of salt. Pour over the vegetables. Cover and simmer for 15 minutes.

5 Uncover the pan and stir. Put all the herbs and the rocket on top of the soup and layer the peas over them. Pour in the remaining water and gradually bring to the boil. Reduce the heat and simmer for about 20–25 minutes or until all the vegetables are tender.

6 Stir the soup. Taste and adjust the seasoning, adding salt and pepper, if necessary, and a little more chilli purée if you wish. Ladle into warmed bowls and serve with Parmesan cheese.

Bouillabaisse

This world-famous French soup makes a festive seafood extravaganza worthy of any special occasion or celebration.

NUTRITIONAL INFORMATION

Calories	55	Sugars	.......1.1g
Protein	........7.2g	Fat	..........1.8g
Carbohydrate	...2.6g	Saturates	.....0.3g

10 mins   1 hr

SERVES 6

INGREDIENTS

50 g/1 lb Mediterranean prawns

50 g/1 lb 10 oz firm white fish fillets, such as sea bass, snapper and monkfish

tbsp olive oil

rated rind of 1 orange

large garlic clove, finely chopped

tsp chilli paste or harissa

large leek, sliced

onion, halved and sliced

red pepper, deseeded and sliced

–4 tomatoes, cored and cut into 8 wedges

garlic cloves, sliced

bay leaf

inch of saffron threads

tsp fennel seeds

00 ml/1 pint water

.2 litres/2 pints fish stock

fennel bulb, finely chopped

large onion, finely chopped

25 g/8 oz potatoes, halved and thinly sliced

50 g/9 oz scallops

alt and pepper

oasted French bread slices, to serve

eady-prepared aïoli, to serve

1 Peel the prawns and reserve the shells. Cut the fish fillets into serving pieces about 5 cm/2 inches square. Trim off any ragged edges and reserve. Put the fish in a bowl with 2 tablespoons of the olive oil, the orange rind, garlic and chilli paste or harissa. Turn to coat well, cover and chill the prawns and fish separately.

2 Heat 1 tablespoon of the olive oil in a large saucepan over a medium heat. Add the leek, sliced onion and red pepper. Cover and cook for 5 minutes, stirring, until the onion softens. Stir in the tomatoes, sliced garlic, bay leaf, saffron, fennel seeds, prawn shells, fish trimmings, water and fish stock. Bring to the boil, then simmer, covered, for 30 minutes. Strain the stock.

3 Heat the remaining oil in a large pan. Add the fennel and chopped onion and cook for 5 minutes, stirring, until softened.

Add the stock and potatoes and bring to the boil. Reduce the heat slightly, cover and cook for 12–15 minutes until just tender.

4 Lower the heat and add the fish, thick pieces first and thinner ones after 2–3 minutes. Add the prawns and scallops and simmer until all the seafood is cooked and opaque throughout.

5 Taste the soup and adjust the seasoning. Ladle into warm bowls. Spread the aïoli sauce on the toasted bread slices and arrange on top of the soup.

Beef & Spring Vegetable Soup

This lean, pretty soup makes an elegant light main course for 4 or it will serve 6 as a starter. Last-minute assembly is needed, but it's worth it.

NUTRITIONAL INFORMATION

Calories	166	Sugars	.........3g
Protein	........16g	Fat	..........4g
Carbohydrate	...17g	Saturates	.......1g

15–20 mins

35 mins

SERVES 4–6

I N G R E D I E N T S

12 small new potatoes, quartered

4 slim carrots, quartered lengthways and cut into 4 cm/1½ inch lengths

150 g/5½ oz tiny French beans, cut into 4 cm/1½ inch lengths

1.5 litres/2¾ pints rich beef or meat stock

2 tbsp soy sauce

3 tbsp dry sherry

350 g/12 oz beef fillet, about 5 cm/ 2 inches thick

150 g/5½ oz shiitake mushrooms, sliced

1 tbsp chopped fresh parsley

1 tbsp chopped fresh chives

salt and pepper

1 Bring a pan of lightly salted water to the boil and add the potatoes and carrots. Reduce the heat, cover and boil gently for about 15 minutes until tender. Bring another pan of lightly salted water to the boil, add the beans and boil for about 5 minutes until just tender. Drain the vegetables and reserve.

2 Bring the stock to the boil in a pan and add the soy sauce and sherry. Season with salt and pepper. Reduce the heat, add the beef and simmer gently for 10 minutes. (The beef should be very rare, as it will continue cooking in the bowls.)

3 Add the mushrooms and simmer for a further 3 minutes. Warm the bowls in a low oven.

4 Remove the meat and set aside to rest on a carving board. Taste the stock and adjust the seasoning, if necessary. Bring the stock back to the boil.

5 Cut the meat in half lengthways and slice each half into pieces about 3 mm/⅛ inch thick. Season the meat lightly with salt and pepper and divide among the warm bowls.

6 Drop the reserved vegetables into the stock and heat through for about 1 minute. Ladle the stock over the meat, dividing the vegetables as evenly as possible. Sprinkle over the parsley and chives and serve immediately.

Chicken & Chickpea Soup

This main-course soup is Mexican in origin. Its appeal comes from an unusual combination of fruits and vegetables.

NUTRITIONAL INFORMATION

Calories	304	Sugars	........17g
Protein	........18g	Fat	...........7g
Carbohydrate	...45g	Saturates	.......1g

45 mins   1½ hrs

SERVES 8

INGREDIENTS

00 g/1 lb 12 oz skinless chicken legs or thighs

celery stick, sliced

large carrot, halved and sliced

large onion, finely chopped

garlic cloves, finely chopped

5 litres/4½ pints chicken stock

–5 fresh parsley stems

bay leaf

15 g/4 oz lean smoked ham, diced

00 g/14 oz can chickpeas, drained and rinsed

large turnip, diced

courgettes, halved and sliced

large potato, diced

sweet potato, diced

75 g/6 oz sweetcorn kernels

large pears, peeled, cored and cut into bite-size pieces

tbsp fresh lime juice

tbsp olive oil

very green, unripe bananas, cut into 5 mm/¼ inch slices

lt and pepper

hopped fresh parsley, to garnish

1 Put the chicken into a large pan or flameproof casserole with the celery, carrot, onion, garlic, stock, parsley stems and bay leaf. Bring just to the boil over a medium-high heat and skim off any foam that rises to the surface. Reduce the heat, partially cover and simmer for about 45 minutes or until the chicken is tender.

2 Remove the chicken from the stock and set aside to cool. Reserve the stock, but discard the parsley stems and bay leaf. Remove the chicken meat from the bones and cut into bite-size pieces. Skim the fat from the stock.

3 Bring the stock just to the boil. Add the ham, chickpeas, turnip, courgettes, potato, sweet potato and sweetcorn. Return the meat to the stock. Lower the heat, partially cover and simmer for about 30 minutes or until all the vegetables are tender.

4 Add the pears and lime juice to the soup and cook for about 5 minutes until they are just poached. Season to taste and add more lime juice if wished.

5 Heat the oil in a frying pan over a medium-high heat. Fry the bananas until golden. Drain on kitchen paper and keep warm. Ladle the soup into bowls and top with fried banana slices. Garnish with parsley and serve.

Beef & Vegetable Soup

A wonderful meal-in-a-bowl, this soup is ideal for a winter supper or lunch. The beefy flavour, enhanced with spices, is very warming.

NUTRITIONAL INFORMATION

Calories 167	Sugars 7g	
Protein 16g	Fat 5g	
Carbohydrate ...17g	Saturates 2g	

15 mins   20 mins

SERVES 4–6

INGREDIENTS

225 g/8 oz tomatoes

2 corn cobs

1 litre/1¾ pints beef soup

1 carrot, thinly sliced

1 onion, chopped

1–2 small waxy potatoes, diced

¼ cabbage, thinly sliced

¼ tsp ground cumin

¼ tsp mild chilli powder

¼ tsp paprika

225 g/8 oz cooked beef, cut into bite-size pieces

3–4 tbsp chopped fresh coriander (optional)

hot salsa of your choice, to serve

1 To peel the tomatoes, place them in a heatproof bowl, pour in enough boiling water to cover and stand for 30 seconds. Drain and plunge into cold water. The skins will then slide off easily. Chop the tomatoes.

2 Using a large knife, cut the corn cobs into 2.5 cm/1 inch pieces.

3 Place the stock in a pan with the tomatoes, carrot, onion, potatoes and cabbage. Bring to the boil, then reduce the heat and simmer for 10–15 minutes o until the vegetables are tender.

4 Add the corn cob pieces, the cumin chilli powder, paprika and beef pieces Bring back to the boil over a medium hea and cook until heated through.

5 Ladle into warmed soup bowls and serve sprinkled with fresh coriander, i using, with a salsa of your choice handed round separately.

COOK'S TIP

To thicken the soup and give it a flavour of the popular Mexican steamed dumplings, known as a tamale, add a few tablespoons of masa harina, mixed into a thinnish paste with a little water, at Step 4. Stir well, then continue cooking until thickened.

Pozole

The dish of hulled maize kernels – hominy – simmered in rich stock
is eaten all over Mexico, and is served with lots of fresh garnishes.

NUTRITIONAL INFORMATION

Calories	300	Sugars	.........3g
Protein	........39g	Fat	..........8g
Carbohydrate	...19g	Saturates	.......2g

45 mins 1 hr

SERVES 4

I N G R E D I E N T S

450 g/1 lb stewing pork, such as lean belly

½ small chicken

about 2 litres/3½ pints water

1 chicken stock cube

1 garlic bulb, divided into cloves but
   not peeled

1 onion, chopped

2 bay leaves

450 g/1 lb canned or cooked
   hominy or chickpeas

¼–½ tsp ground cumin

salt and pepper

TO SERVE

½ small cabbage, thinly shredded

fried pork skin

dried oregano leaves

dried chilli flakes

tortilla chips

lime wedges

1 Place the pork and chicken in a large pan. Add enough water to fill the pan. (Do not worry about having too much stock – it is wonderful for the rest of the week and freezes well.)

2 Bring to the boil, then skim off the scum that rises to the surface. Reduce the heat and add the stock cube, garlic, onion and bay leaves. Cover and simmer over a medium-low heat until the pork and chicken are both tender and cooked through.

3 Using a draining spoon, remove the pork and chicken from the soup and set aside to cool. When cool enough to handle, remove the chicken flesh from the bones and cut into small pieces. Then, cut the pork into bite-size pieces. Set aside.

4 Skim the fat off the soup and discard the bay leaves. Add the hominy or chickpeas and cumin. Season with salt and pepper to taste. Bring to the boil.

5 To serve, place a little pork and chicken in soup bowls. Top with cabbage, fried pork skin, oregano and chilli flakes, then ladle in the hot soup. Serve with tortilla chips and lime wedges.

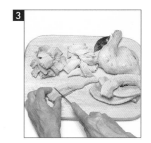

Crab & Avocado Soft Tacos

Crab and avocado make an elegant yet authentic filling for tacos. Taste and you will be transported to a beach somewhere south of Acapulco!

NUTRITIONAL INFORMATION

Calories	522	Sugars	.........4g
Protein	........22g	Fat	..........19g
Carbohydrate	...69g	Saturates	.......7g

  10–15 mins 10 mins

SERVES 4

I N G R E D I E N T S

8 corn tortillas

1 avocado

lime or lemon juice, for tossing

4–6 tbsp soured cream

250–275 g/9–10 oz cooked crab meat

½ lime

½ fresh green chilli, such as jalapeño or serrano, deseeded and chopped or thinly sliced

1 ripe tomato, deseeded and diced

½ small onion, finely chopped

2 tbsp chopped fresh coriander

salsa of your choice, to serve (optional)

VARIATION

For tostadas, fry the tortillas in a little oil in a non-stick pan until crisp. Top one crisp tortilla with the filling. Prepare a second tortilla with the filling and place on top of the first. Repeat once more, to make a small tower, top with shredded lettuce and serve.

1 Heat the tortillas in an ungreased non-stick frying pan, sprinkling them with a few drops of water as they heat; wrap in a clean tea towel as you work to keep them warm.

2 Cut the avocado in half around the stone. Twist apart, then remove the stone with a knife. Carefully peel off the skin from the avocado, slice the flesh and toss in lime or lemon juice to prevent it from turning brown.

3 Spread 1 tortilla with soured cream. Top with crab meat, a squeeze of lime juice and a sprinkling of chilli, tomato, onion, coriander and avocado, adding a splash of salsa if desired. Repeat the procedure with the remaining tortillas and serve immediately.

Fish Tacos Ensenada Style

These tacos of fried fish chunks and red cabbage salad are served up in the cantinas and fondas of the coastal town of Ensenada in Mexico.

NUTRITIONAL INFORMATION

Calories ....491 Sugars 5g
Protein ....32g Fat 5g
Carbohydrate ...84g Saturates 0g

10–15 mins   25 mins

SERVES 4

INGREDIENTS

about 450 g/1 lb firm-fleshed white fish filets, such as red snapper or cod

¼ tsp dried oregano

¼ tsp ground cumin

1 tsp mild chilli powder

2 garlic cloves, finely chopped

3 tbsp plain flour

vegetable oil, for frying

¼ red cabbage, thinly sliced or shredded

juice of 2 limes

hot pepper sauce or salsa to taste

8 corn tortillas

1 tbsp chopped fresh coriander

½ onion, chopped (optional)

salt and pepper

salsa of your choice

1 Place the fish on a plate and sprinkle with half the oregano, cumin, chilli powder and garlic. Season with salt and pepper, then dust with the flour.

2 Heat the oil in a heavy-based frying pan until it is smoking, then fry the fish in several batches until it is golden on the outside, and just tender in the middle. Remove from the pan and place on kitchen paper to drain.

3 Combine the cabbage with the remaining oregano, cumin, chilli and garlic, then stir in the lime juice, salt and hot pepper sauce to taste. Set aside.

4 Heat the tortillas in an ungreased non-stick frying pan, sprinkling with a few drops of water as they heat. Wrap the tortillas in a clean tea towel as you work to keep them warm. Alternatively, heat through in a stack in the pan, alternating the tortillas from the top to the bottom so that they warm evenly.

5 Place some of the warm fried fish in each tortilla, along with a large spoonful of the hot cabbage salad. Sprinkle with chopped fresh coriander and onion, if desired. Add the salsa to taste and serve immediately.

Fish & Bean Tostadas

Crisp tostadas are topped with spiced fish, refried beans and crunchy lettuce – perfect for a well-balanced lunch.

NUTRITIONAL INFORMATION

Calories 519	Sugars 2g
Protein 35g	Fat 6g
Carbohydrate . . .82g	Saturates 0g

45 mins 10–15 mins

SERVES 4

INGREDIENTS

about 450 g/1 lb firm-fleshed white fish, such as red snapper or cod

125 ml/4 fl oz fish stock, or water mixed with a fish stock cube

¼ tsp ground cumin

¼ tsp mild chilli powder

pinch of dried oregano

4 garlic cloves, finely chopped

juice of ½ lemon or lime

8 soft corn tortillas

vegetable oil, for frying

400 g/14 oz can refried beans, warmed with 2 tbsp water

salsa of your choice

2–3 leaves cos lettuce, shredded

3 tbsp chopped fresh coriander

2 tbsp chopped onion

salt and pepper

TO GARNISH

soured cream

chopped fresh herbs

1 Put the fish in a pan with the fish stock, cumin, chilli, oregano and garlic. Season with salt and pepper to taste. Bring to the boil over a low heat, then immediately remove the pan from the heat and set the fish aside to cool in the cooking liquid.

2 When cool enough to handle, remove the fish from the liquid with a draining spoon; reserve the cooking liquid. Break the fish up into bite-size pieces, put in a bowl, sprinkle with the lemon or lime juice and set aside.

3 To make tostadas, fry the tortillas in a small amount of oil in a non-stick frying pan until crisp. Spread the tostadas evenly with the warm refried beans.

4 Gently reheat the fish with a little of the reserved cooking liquid, then spoon the fish on top of the beans. Top each tostada with some of the salsa, lettuce, chopped fresh coriander and onion. Garnish each one with a spoon of soured cream and a sprinkling of chopped fresh herbs. Serve immediately.

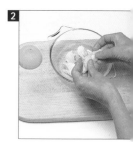

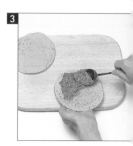

Fish Burritos

You can use any fish you like in this tasty Mexican snack.
Tacos are eaten in the hand, rather like sandwiches.

NUTRITIONAL INFORMATION

Calories	269	Sugars	.........3g
Protein	........20g	Fat	...........2g
Carbohydrate	...46g	Saturates	.......0g

  45 mins 10–15 mins

SERVES 4–6

I N G R E D I E N T S

about 450 g/1 lb firm-fleshed white fish, such as red snapper or cod

¼ tsp ground cumin

pinch of dried oregano

4 garlic finely cloves, chopped

125 ml/4 fl oz fish stock, or water mixed with a fish stock cube

juice of ½ lemon or lime

8 flour tortillas

2–3 leaves cos lettuce, shredded

2 ripe tomatoes, diced

Salsa Cruda (see page 447)

salt and pepper

lemon slices, to garnish

1 Season the fish to taste with salt and pepper, then put in a pan with the cumin, oregano, garlic and enough fish stock to cover.

2 Bring to the boil and cook for about a minute. Remove the pan from the heat and set the fish aside to cool in the cooking liquid for about 30 minutes.

3 Remove the fish from the stock and break up into bite-size pieces. Sprinkle with the lemon or lime juice and set aside.

4 Heat the tortillas in an ungreased non-stick frying pan, sprinkling them with a few drops of water as they heat. Wrap in a clean tea towel as you work to keep them warm.

5 Arrange shredded lettuce in the middle of a tortilla, spoon on a few chunks of the fish, then sprinkle with the tomato. Add a little salsa cruda. Repeat with the other tortillas and serve immediately garnished with lemon slices.

VARIATION

Cook several peeled waxy potatoes in the fish stock, then dice and serve wrapped up in the warm tortillas with the lettuce, fish, tomato and salsa. Alternatively, add sliced lime-dressed avocado with the filling.

Chicken Tacos from Puebla

Seasoned chicken fills these soft tacos, along with creamy refried beans, avocado, smoky chipotle and soured cream. A feast of tastes!

NUTRITIONAL INFORMATION

Calories	674	Sugars	.........6g
Protein	........34g	Fat	..........25g
Carbohydrate	...80g	Saturates	.......9g

10 mins   15 mins

SERVES 4

INGREDIENTS

8 corn tortillas

2 tsp vegetable oil

225–350 g/8–12 oz cooked chicken, diced or shredded

225 g/8 oz can refried beans, warmed with 2 tbsp water

¼ tsp ground cumin

¼ tsp dried oregano

1 avocado, stoned, peeled, sliced and tossed with lime juice

Salsa Verde (see page 448)

1 canned chipotle chilli in adobo marinade, chopped, or bottled chipotle salsa

175 ml/6 fl oz soured cream

½ onion, chopped

handful of lettuce leaves

5 radishes, diced

salt and pepper

1 Heat the tortillas in an ungreased non-stick frying pan in a stack, alternating the top and bottom tortillas so that they all heat evenly. Wrap in kitchen foil or a clean tea towel to keep warm.

2 Heat the oil in a frying pan, add the chicken and heat through. Season with salt and pepper to taste.

3 Combine the refried beans with the cumin and oregano.

4 Spread a tortilla with warm refried beans, then top with a spoonful of the chicken, 1–2 slices of avocado, a dab of salsa, chipotle to taste, a spoon of soured cream and a sprinkling of onion, lettuce and radishes. Season with salt and pepper to taste, then roll up as tightly as you can. Repeat with the remaining tortillas and serve immediately.

VARIATION

Replace the chicken with 450 g/1 lb minced beef browned with a seasoning of chopped onion, mild chilli powder and ground cumin to taste.

Chicken Tostadas

Chicken makes a delicate, yet satisfying topping for crisp tostadas. Leftover cooked chicken can also be used and tastes delicious.

NUTRITIONAL INFORMATION

Calories	663	Sugars	.........3g
Protein	........45g	Fat	.........32g
Carbohydrate	...49g	Saturates	......11g

20 mins   10–15 mins

SERVES 4–6

INGREDIENTS

6 corn tortillas

vegetable oil, for frying

450 g/1 lb skinless, boneless chicken breast or thigh, cut into strips or diced

225 ml/8 fl oz chicken stock

2 garlic cloves, finely chopped

400 g/14 oz can refried beans

2 tbsp water

large pinch of ground cumin

225 g/8 oz grated cheese

1 tbsp chopped fresh coriander

2 ripe tomatoes, diced

crisp lettuce leaves, such as cos or iceberg, shredded

4–6 radishes, diced

3 spring onions, thinly sliced

1 ripe avocado, stoned, peeled, diced or sliced and tossed with lime juice

soured cream to taste

1–2 canned chipotle chillies in adobo marinade, cut into thin strips

1 To make tostadas, heat a small amount of oil in a heavy-based, non-stick frying pan and fry the tortillas, in batches, until crisp.

2 Put the chicken in a pan with the stock and garlic. Bring to the boil, then reduce the heat and simmer for 1–2 minutes until the chicken begins to turn opaque.

3 Remove the chicken from the heat and set aside to steep in the hot liquid to cook through.

4 Gently heat the beans with the water. Stir in the cumin and keep warm.

5 Reheat the tostadas under a preheated grill, if necessary. Spread the hot beans on the tostadas, then sprinkle with the grated cheese. Lift the cooked chicken from the cooking liquid with a draining spoon and divide between the tostadas. Top with the chopped coriander, diced tomatoes, lettuce, radishes, spring onions, avocado, soured cream and a few strips of chipotle chilli. Serve immediately.

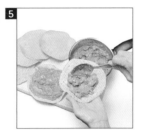

Santa Fe Enchiladas

These enchiladas are served stacked, in the traditional New Mexican style, but you can always roll them up with the filling if you prefer.

NUTRITIONAL INFORMATION

Calories 645   Sugars 2g
Protein ....47g   Fat 22g
Carbohydrate ...75g   Saturates 7g

 15 mins   🕐 30–35 mins

SERVES 4

INGREDIENTS

2–3 tbsp masa harina or 1 corn tortilla, crushed or crumbled

4 tbsp mild chilli powder

2 tbsp paprika

2 garlic cloves, finely chopped

¼ tsp ground cumin

pinch of ground cinnamon

pinch of ground allspice

pinch of dried oregano

1 litre/1¾ pints vegetable, chicken or beef stock, simmering

1 tbsp lime juice

8 flour tortillas

about 450 g/1 lb cooked chicken or pork, cut into pieces

85 g/3 oz grated cheese

1 tbsp extra virgin olive oil

4–6 eggs

TO SERVE

½ onion, finely chopped

1 tbsp finely chopped fresh coriander

salsa of your choice

1 Mix the masa harina or crushed tortilla with the chilli powder, paprika, garlic, cumin, cinnamon, allspice, oregano and enough water to make a thin paste. Process in a blender or food processor until smooth.

2 Stir the paste into the simmering stock, reduce the heat and cook until it thickens slightly, then remove the sauce from the heat and stir in the lime juice.

3 Dip the tortillas into the warm sauce. Cover 1 tortilla with some of the cooked meat. Top with a second dipped tortilla and more meat filling. Make 3 more towers in this way.

4 Transfer the tortilla towers to an ovenproof dish, pour the remaining sauce over them, then sprinkle with the grated cheese. Bake the enchiladas in a preheated oven, 180°C/350°F/Gas Mark 4, for 15-20 minutes or until the cheese has melted and is bubbling.

5 Meanwhile, heat the olive oil in a non-stick frying pan and cook the eggs until the whites are set and the yolks are still soft.

6 To serve the enchiladas, top each with a fried egg. Serve with the chopped onion mixed with fresh coriander and a salsa of your choice.

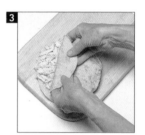

Chicken Tortilla Flutes

These crisply fried, rolled tortillas are known as 'flautas', meaning 'flutes' in Spanish, because of their delicate, long shape.

NUTRITIONAL INFORMATION

Calories 551	Sugars 5g	
Protein 37g	Fat 17g	
Carbohydrate 71g	Saturates 4g	

 15 mins   10–15 mins

SERVES 4

I N G R E D I E N T S

8 corn tortillas

350 g/12 oz cooked chicken, diced

1 tsp mild chilli powder

1 onion, chopped

2 tbsp finely chopped fresh coriander

1–2 tbsp crème fraîche

vegetable oil, for frying

1 quantity of Guacamole (see page 138)

salsa of your choice

salt

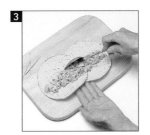

1 Heat the tortillas in an ungreased, heavy-based, non-stick frying pan in a stack, alternating the top and bottom tortillas so that all of them warm evenly. Wrap in kitchen foil or a clean tea towel to keep warm.

2 Place the chicken in a bowl with the chilli powder, half the onion and half the coriander. Season to taste with salt. Stir in enough crème fraîche to hold the mixture together.

3 Arrange 2 corn tortillas on a work surface so that they are overlapping, then spoon some of the filling along the centre. Roll up very tightly and secure in place with 1–2 cocktail sticks. Repeat with the remaining tortillas and filling.

4 Heat the oil in a deep frying pan and fry the rolls until golden and crisp. Carefully remove from the oil with a draining spoon and drain on kitchen paper.

5 Place the rolls on warmed individual plates and garnish with the guacamole, salsa, diced tomato and the remaining onion and remaining fresh coriander. Serve immediately.

VARIATION

Replace the chicken with seafood, such as cooked prawns or crab meat, and serve the rolls with lemon wedges.

Tortilla & Chorizo Casserole

Called 'chilaquiles' in Mexico, this dish turns everyday leftovers into something quite special! Excellent served for brunch, topped with an egg.

NUTRITIONAL INFORMATION

Calories	402	Sugars	.........4g
Protein	........17g	Fat	..........15g
Carbohydrate	...53g	Saturates	.......8g

 10 mins 1¼ hrs

SERVES 6–8

INGREDIENTS

12 stale tortillas, cut into strips

1 tbsp vegetable oil

2–3 chorizo sausages, thinly sliced or diced

2 garlic cloves, finely chopped

225 g/8 oz chopped canned tomatoes

3 tbsp chopped fresh coriander

450 ml/16 fl oz chicken or vegetable stock

225 g/8 oz grated cheese

1 onion, finely chopped

salt and pepper

1 Place the tortilla strips in a roasting tin, toss with the oil and bake in a preheated oven, 190°C/375°F/Gas Mark 5, for about 30 minutes until they are crisp and golden.

2 Brown the chorizo sausages with the garlic in a heavy-based frying pan until the meat is cooked. Pour away any excess fat. Add the tomatoes and chopped coriander and season with salt and pepper to taste.

3 In an ovenproof dish, about 30 cm/ 12 inches square, layer the tortilla strips and chorizo mixture, finishing with the tortilla strips.

4 Pour the stock over the top of the dish, then sprinkle with the grated cheese. Bake in a preheated oven, 190°C/ 375°F/Gas Mark 5, for about 40 minutes until the tortilla strips are fairly soft.

5 Serve immediately, sprinkled with the chopped onion.

VARIATION

Serve with a fried egg or two alongside. The soft yolk tastes wonderful with the spicy casserole – offer a bowl of spicy salsa for those who want it hotter.

Tamales

Traditional Mexican fare, tamales are large dumplings of cornmeal, stuffed with a moist filling. They make attractive party food.

NUTRITIONAL INFORMATION

Calories	264	Sugars 2g
Protein	.........5g	Fat 13g
Carbohydrate	...34g	Saturates 6g

3½ hrs ⏱ 40–60 mins

SERVES 4–6

INGREDIENTS

8–10 corn husks or several banana leaves, cut into 30 cm/12 inch squares

6 tbsp lard or vegetable shortening

½ tsp salt

pinch of sugar

pinch of ground cumin

225 g/8 oz masa harina

½ tsp baking powder

about 225 ml/8 fl oz beef, chicken or vegetable stock

TO SERVE

shredded lettuce

salsa of your choice

FILLING

115 g/4 oz cooked sweetcorn, mixed with a little grated cheese and chopped fresh green chilli, or simmered pork in a mild chilli sauce

1 If using corn husks, soak in hot water to cover for at least 3 hours or overnight. If using banana leaves, warm them by placing over an open flame for just a few seconds to make them pliable.

2 To make the tamale dough, beat the lard or shortening until it is fluffy, then beat in the salt, sugar, cumin, masa harina and baking powder until the mixture resembles tiny crumbs.

3 Add the stock very gradually, in several batches, beating until the mixture becomes fluffy and resembles whipped cream.

4 Spread 1–2 tablespoons of the tamale mixture on either a soaked and drained corn husk or a piece of pliable heated banana leaf.

5 Spoon in the filling. Fold the sides of the husks or leaves over the filling to enclose. Wrap each parcel in a square of kitchen foil, and arrange in a steamer.

6 Pour hot water in the base of the steamer, cover, and steam. Cook for 40–60 minutes, topping up the water in the base of the steamer when needed. Remove the tamales and serve with lettuce and salsa.

Jalisco-style Eggs

This hearty breakfast dish from Jalisco is a classic Mexican way of serving eggs – a feast of flavours!

NUTRITIONAL INFORMATION

Calories	410	Sugars	.........3g
Protein	........19g	Fat	..........32g
Carbohydrate	...12g	Saturates	......13g

15 mins   20 mins

SERVES 4

INGREDIENTS

4 corn tortillas

1 avocado

lime or lemon juice, for tossing

175 g/6 oz chorizo sausage, sliced or diced

2 tbsp butter or water, for cooking

4 eggs

4 tbsp feta or Wensleydale
cheese, crumbled

salsa of your choice

1 tbsp chopped fresh coriander

1 tbsp finely chopped spring onions

1 Heat the tortillas in an ungreased, heavy-based, non-stick frying pan, sprinkling them with a few drops of water as they heat. Wrap the tortillas in a clean tea towel or kitchen foil as you work to keep them warm. Alternatively, heat through in a stack in the pan, alternating the top and bottom tortillas so that they warm evenly. Wrap in a tea towel or kitchen foil to keep warm.

2 Cut the avocado in half around the stone. Twist the halves apart, then remove the stone with a knife. Carefully peel off the skin, dice the flesh and toss in lime or lemon juice to prevent it from turning brown.

3 Brown the chorizo sausage in a pan, then arrange on each warmed tortilla. Keep warm.

4 Meanwhile, heat the butter or water in a non-stick frying pan, break in an egg and cook until the white is just set but the yolk still soft. Remove from the pan and place on top of one tortilla. Keep warm while you cook the remaining eggs.

5 Arrange the avocado, cheese and a spoonful of salsa on each tortilla. Add the fresh coriander and spring onions and serve immediately.

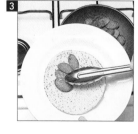

Fish & Crab Chowder

Packed full of flavour, this delicious fish dish is really a
meal in itself, but it is ideal accompanied by a crisp side salad.

NUTRITIONAL INFORMATION

Calories	440	Sugars	........10g
Protein	........49g	Fat	...........7g
Carbohydrate	...43g	Saturates	......1g

40 mins   25 mins

SERVES 4

I N G R E D I E N T S

1 large onion, finely chopped

2 celery sticks, finely chopped

150 ml/5 fl oz dry white wine

600 ml/1 pint fish stock

600 ml/1 pint skimmed milk

1 bay leaf

225 g/8 oz smoked cod fillet, skinned and
cut into 2.5 cm/1 inch cubes

225 g/8 oz smoked haddock fillets, skinned
and cut into 2.5 cm/1 inch cubes

2 x 175 g/6 oz cans crab meat, drained

225 g/8 oz blanched French beans, sliced
into 2.5 cm/1 inch pieces

225 g/8 oz cooked brown rice

4 tsp cornflour mixed with 4 tbsp water

salt and pepper

chopped fresh parsley to garnish

mixed green salad, to serve

1 Place the onion, celery and wine in a
large non-stick saucepan. Bring to the
boil, cover and cook over a low heat for
5 minutes.

2 Uncover the pan and cook for a
further 5 minutes until almost all the
liquid has evaporated.

3 Pour in the stock and milk and add
the bay leaf. Bring to a simmer and
stir in the cod and haddock. Simmer over a
low heat, uncovered, for 5 minutes.

4 Add the crab meat, beans and cooked
brown rice and simmer gently for
2–3 minutes until just heated through.

Remove the bay leaf with a draining spoon
and discard.

5 Stir in the cornflour mixture until
thickened slightly. Season to taste
with salt and pepper and ladle into
warmed soup bowls. Garnish with chopped
parsley and serve with a mixed salad.

Pad Thai

All over Thailand and South-east Asia, street stalls (even floating ones) sell these simple delicious rice noodles, stir-fried to order.

NUTRITIONAL INFORMATION

Calories	527	Sugars	.........8g
Protein	........34g	Fat	..........17g
Carbohydrate	...58g	Saturates	.......3g

30 mins   10 mins

SERVES 4

INGREDIENTS

225 g/8 oz flat rice noodles

2 tbsp groundnut or vegetable oil

225 g/8 oz skinless, boneless chicken breasts, thinly sliced

4 shallots, finely chopped

2 garlic cloves, finely chopped

4 spring onions, cut on the diagonal into 5 cm/2 inch pieces

350 g/12 oz fresh white crab meat

75 g/2¾ oz fresh beansprouts, rinsed

1 tbsp preserved radish or fresh radish, finely diced

2–4 tbsp roasted peanuts, chopped

fresh coriander sprigs, to garnish

SAUCE

3 tbsp Thai fish sauce

2–3 tbsp rice vinegar or cider vinegar

1 tbsp chilli bean sauce or oyster sauce

1 tbsp toasted sesame oil

1 tbsp palm sugar or light brown sugar

½ tsp cayenne pepper or fresh red chilli, thinly sliced

1 To make the sauce, whisk together all the sauce ingredients in a small bowl and set aside.

2 Put the rice noodles in a large bowl and pour over enough hot water to cover; set aside for 15 minutes until softened. Drain, rinse and drain again.

3 Heat the oil in a heavy-based wok over a high heat until very hot, but not smoking. Add the chicken strips and stir-fry for 1–2 minutes until they just begin to colour. Using a draining spoon, transfer to a plate. Reduce the heat to medium-high.

4 Stir the shallots, garlic and spring onions into the wok and stir-fry for about 1 minute. Stir in the drained noodles, then the prepared sauce.

5 Return the reserved chicken to the pan with the crab meat, beansprouts and radish. Toss well and cook for about 5 minutes until heated through, tossing frequently. If the noodles begin to stick, add a little water.

6 Turn into a warmed serving dish and sprinkle with the chopped peanuts. Garnish with coriander sprigs and serve immediately.

Chicken & Cheese Jackets

Use the breasts from a roasted chicken to make these delicious potatoes and serve as a light lunch or supper dish.

NUTRITIONAL INFORMATION

Calories 417   Sugars 4g
Protein . . . . .28g   Fat 10g
Carbohydrate . . .57g   Saturates 5g

10 mins   50 mins

SERVES 4

INGREDIENTS

4 large baking potatoes

225 g/8 oz cooked, skinless, boneless chicken breasts

4 spring onions

250 g/9 oz low-fat soft cheese or Quark

pepper

coleslaw, green salad or mixed salad, to serve

1 Scrub the potatoes and pat dry with absorbent kitchen paper.

2 Prick the potatoes all over with a fork. Bake in a preheated oven, 200°C/400°F/Gas Mark 6, for about 50 minutes until tender.

3 Meanwhile, using a sharp knife, dice the chicken breasts and trim and thickly slice the spring onions. Place the chicken and spring onions in a bowl.

4 Add the low-fat soft cheese or Quark to the bowl and stir well to combine and coat the chicken.

5 Cut a cross through the top of each potato and pull slightly apart. Spoon the chicken filling into the potatoes and sprinkle with pepper.

6 Serve the chicken and cheese jackets immediately with coleslaw, green salad or a mixed salad.

COOK'S TIP

Look for Quark in the chilled section of the supermarket. It is a low-fat, white, fresh curd cheese made from cow's milk and has a delicate, slightly sour flavour.

Teppanyaki

This simple, Japanese style of cooking is ideal for thinly sliced breast of chicken. You can use thin turkey escalopes, if you prefer.

NUTRITIONAL INFORMATION

Calories	206	Sugars	.........4g
Protein	........30g	Fat	..........7g
Carbohydrate	....6g	Saturates	......2g

    5 mins   10 mins

SERVES 4

INGREDIENTS

4 boneless chicken breasts

1 red pepper

1 green pepper

4 spring onions

8 baby corn cobs

100 g/3½ oz beansprouts

1 tbsp sesame or sunflower oil

4 tbsp shoyu or soy sauce

4 tbsp mirin

1 tbsp grated fresh root ginger

COOK'S TIP

Mirin is a rich, sweet rice wine from Japan. You can buy it in Asian supermarkets, but if it is not available, add 1 tablespoon soft light brown sugar to the sauce instead.

1 Remove the skin from the chicken and slice at a slight angle, to a thickness of about 5 mm/¼ inch.

2 Deseed and thinly slice the red and green peppers and trim and slice the spring onions and corn cobs.

3 Arrange the peppers, spring onions, corn cobs and beansprouts on a plate with the sliced chicken.

4 Heat a large griddle or heavy-based frying pan, then lightly brush with sesame or sunflower oil. Add the vegetables and chicken slices, in small batches, allowing space between them so that they cook thoroughly.

5 Combine the shoyu or soy sauce, mirin and ginger in a small serving bowl and serve as a dip with the chicken and vegetables.

Pasta & Chicken Medley

Strips of cooked chicken are tossed with coloured pasta, grapes and carrot sticks in a pesto-flavoured dressing.

NUTRITIONAL INFORMATION

Calories	609	Sugars	........11g
Protein	........26g	Fat	..........38g
Carbohydrate	...45g	Saturates	.......6g

30 mins   10 mins

SERVES 2

INGREDIENTS

125–150 g/4½–5½ oz dried pasta shapes, such as twists or bows

2 tbsp mayonnaise

2 tsp bottled pesto sauce

1 tbsp soured cream or fromage frais

175 g/6 oz cooked skinless, boneless chicken meat

1–2 celery sticks

125 g/4½ oz black grapes (preferably seedless)

1 large carrot

salt and pepper

celery leaves, to garnish

FRENCH DRESSING

1 tsp wine vinegar

1 tbsp extra virgin olive oil

salt and pepper

1 To make the French dressing, whisk all the ingredients together until smooth.

2 Bring a large pan of lightly salted water to the boil. Add the pasta, bring back to the boil and cook for 8–10 minutes until tender, but still firm to the bite. Drain thoroughly, rinse and drain again. Transfer to a bowl and mix in the French dressing while still hot, then set aside until cold.

3 Combine the mayonnaise, pesto sauce and soured cream or fromage frais in a bowl and season to taste with salt and pepper.

4 Cut the chicken into thin strips. Cut the celery diagonally into thin slices. Reserve a few grapes for garnish, halve the rest and remove any seeds. Cut the carrot into narrow julienne strips.

5 Add the chicken, celery, halved grapes, carrot and mayonnaise mixture to the pasta and toss thoroughly. Taste and adjust the seasoning, adding more salt and pepper if necessary.

6 Arrange the pasta mixture on 2 plates and garnish with the reserved black grapes and the celery leaves.

Vegetable Frittata

A frittata is a type of Italian omelette – you can add almost anything to the eggs. It is also delicious eaten cold and makes an ideal picnic dish.

NUTRITIONAL INFORMATION

Calories 310	Sugars 4g	
Protein 18g	Fat 17g	
Carbohydrate . . .24g	Saturates 4g	

 15 mins   20 mins

SERVES 4

I N G R E D I E N T S

3 tbsp olive oil

1 onion, chopped

2 garlic cloves, chopped

225 g/8 oz courgettes, thinly sliced

4 eggs

400 g/14 oz can borlotti beans, rinsed
   and drained

3 tomatoes, peeled and chopped

2 tbsp chopped fresh parsley

1 tbsp chopped fresh basil

55 g/2 oz grated Gruyère cheese

salt and pepper

1 Heat 2 tablespoons of the oil in a frying pan. Add the onion and garlic and cook over a medium heat, stirring occasionally, for 2–3 minutes or until softened. Add the courgettes and cook, stirring occasionally, for 3–4 minutes or until softened.

2 Break the eggs into a bowl and season with salt and pepper to taste. Beat lightly and stir in the onion and courgette mixture, the beans, tomatoes, parsley and basil.

3 Heat the remaining oil in a 24 cm/9½ inch omelette pan, add the egg mixture and cook over a low heat for about 5 minutes until the eggs have almost set and the underside of the frittata is golden brown.

4 Sprinkle the cheese over the top and place the pan under a preheated moderate grill for 3–4 minutes or until set on the top, but still moist in the middle. Cut into wedges and serve warm or at room temperature.

COOK'S TIP

Gruyère cheese is made from unpasteurised cow's milk and has a sweet, nutty flavour, which enhances the taste of this frittata. It is firm and close textured and has small holes interspersed throughout.

Mediterranean Chicken

This recipe uses ingredients found in the Languedoc area of France, where cooking over hot embers is a way of life.

NUTRITIONAL INFORMATION

Calories	143	Sugars	.........4g
Protein	........13g	Fat	...........8g
Carbohydrate	....4g	Saturates	......2g

2¾ hours   40 mins

SERVES 4

INGREDIENTS

4 chicken quarters

green salad, to serve

MARINADE

4 tbsp low-fat natural yogurt

3 tbsp sun-dried tomato paste

1 tbsp olive oil

15 g/½ oz fresh basil leaves, lightly crushed

2 garlic cloves, coarsely chopped

1 First, make the marinade. Combine the yogurt, sun-dried tomato paste, olive oil, crushed basil leaves and garlic in a small bowl and stir well to mix.

2 Transfer the marinade to a dish large enough to hold the chicken quarters in a single layer. Add the chicken quarters and turn them to ensure that all the chicken pieces are thoroughly coated in the marinade.

3 Cover with clingfilm and set aside to marinate in the refrigerator for at least 2 hours. Remove the dish from the refrigerator and set aside, still covered, at room temperature for 30 minutes.

4 Place the chicken over a medium barbecue and cook for about 30–40 minutes, turning frequently. Test for readiness by piercing the flesh at the thickest part – usually at the top of the drumstick – with the point of a sharp knife. If the juices that run out are clear, it is cooked through. If there is any sign of pink, cook for a further 5–10 minutes, then test again.

5 Serve immediately with a green salad. This dish is also delicious eaten cold.

VARIATION

For a marinade with an extra zingy flavour combine 2 coarsely grated garlic cloves, the juice of lemons and 3 tbsp olive oil. Prepare and cook the chicken in the same way.

Pasta & Prawn Parcels

This is the ideal dish when you have unexpected guests because the parcels can be prepared in advance, then put in the oven when you are ready to eat.

NUTRITIONAL INFORMATION

Calories . . . . . . .640 Sugars 1g
Protein . . . . .50g Fat 29g
Carbohydrate . . .42g Saturates 4g

 15 mins ⏱ 30 mins

SERVES 4

INGREDIENTS

450 g/1 lb dried fettuccine

150 ml/5 fl oz ready-made pesto sauce

4 tsp extra virgin olive oil

750 g/1 lb 10 oz large raw prawns, peeled and deveined

2 garlic cloves, crushed

125 ml/4 fl oz dry white wine

salt and pepper

1 Cut out 4 x 30 cm/12 inch squares of greaseproof paper.

2 Bring a pan of lightly salted water to the boil. Add the pasta, bring back to the boil and cook for 2–3 minutes until just softened. Drain and set aside.

3 Mix together the fettuccine and half of the pesto sauce. Spread out the paper squares and put 1 teaspoon of the olive oil in the middle of each. Divide the fettuccine between the the squares, then divide the prawns and place on top of the fettuccine.

4 Mix together the remaining pesto sauce and the garlic and spoon it over the prawns. Season each parcel with salt and pepper to taste and sprinkle with the white wine.

5 Dampen the edges of the greaseproof paper and wrap the parcels loosely twisting the edges to seal.

6 Place the parcels on a baking sheet and bake in a preheated oven, 200°C, 400°F/Gas Mark 6, for 10–15 minutes until piping hot and the prawns have changed colour. Transfer the parcels to 4 individual serving plates and serve.

COOK'S TIP

Traditionally, these parcels are designed to look like money bags. The resemblance is more effective with greaseproof paper than with foil.

Citrus Fish Kebabs

Use your favourite fish for this dish as long as it is firm enough to thread on to skewers. The tang of orange makes this a refreshing meal.

NUTRITIONAL INFORMATION

Calories	333	Sugar	.........0g
Protein	........18g	Fats	...........3g
Carbohydrates	...18g	Saturates	......4g

2½ hours   10 mins

SERVES 4

INGREDIENTS

450 g/1 lb firm white fish fillet, such as cod or monkfish

450 g/1 lb thick salmon fillet

2 large oranges

1 pink grapefruit

1 bunch of fresh bay leaves

1 tsp finely grated lemon rind

3 tbsp lemon juice

2 tsp clear honey

2 garlic cloves, crushed

salt and pepper

TO SERVE

crusty bread

mixed salad

1 Skin the white fish fillet and the salmon, then rinse and pat dry on kitchen paper. Cut each fillet into 6 pieces.

2 Using a sharp knife, remove the skin and pith from the oranges and grapefruit. Cut out the segments of flesh, removing all remaining traces of the pith and dividing membranes.

3 Thread the pieces of fish alternately with the orange and grapefruit segments and the bay leaves on to

8 skewers. Place the fish kebabs in a shallow dish.

4 In a small bowl, mix together the lemon rind, lemon juice, honey and crushed garlic. Pour the mixture over the fish kebabs and season to taste with salt and pepper. Cover with clingfilm and set aside in the refrigerator to marinate for 2 hours, turning occasionally.

5 Remove the fish kebabs from the marinade and place on a grill rack. Cook under a preheated medium grill, turning once, for 7–8 minutes until cooked through and the fish is opaque.

6 Transfer the kebabs to warmed individual serving plates and serve immediately with crusty bread and a fresh mixed salad.

Crab with Chinese Leaves

The delicate flavours of Chinese leaves and crab meat
are enhanced by the coconut milk in this recipe.

NUTRITIONAL INFORMATION

Calories 109	Sugars 1g
Protein 11g	Fat 6g
Carbohydrate 2g	Saturates 1g

5 mins   10 mins

SERVES 4

I N G R E D I E N T S

225 g/8 oz shiitake mushrooms

2 tbsp vegetable oil

2 garlic cloves, crushed

6 spring onions, sliced

1 head Chinese leaves, shredded

1 tbsp mild curry paste

6 tbsp coconut milk

200 g/7 oz canned white crab
meat, drained

1 tsp chilli flakes

1 Using a sharp knife, cut the
mushrooms into slices.

2 Heat the vegetable oil in a large
preheated wok or a frying pan with a
heavy base.

COOK'S TIP

Shiitake mushrooms are
now readily available in the
fresh vegetable section of
most large supermarkets.

3 Add the mushrooms and garlic to the
wok or frying pan and stir-fry over a
medium heat for 3 minutes or until the
mushrooms have softened.

4 Add the spring onions and shredded
Chinese leaves to the wok and stir-fry
for about 10 minutes until the leaves have
just wilted.

5 Mix together the mild curry paste
and coconut milk in a small bowl.

6 Add the curry paste and coconut milk
mixture to the wok, together with the
crab meat and chilli flakes. Mix together
until thoroughly combined. Continue to
heat the mixture in the wok until the
juices start to bubble.

7 Transfer the crab and vegetable stir
fry to warm individual serving bowls
and serve immediately.

Basque Tuna Stew

Although versions of this stew are eaten throughout Spain, it originated in the Basque region to satisfy the hearty appetites of local fishermen.

NUTRITIONAL INFORMATION

Calories 718   Sugars 9g
Protein . . . . .63g   Fat 26g
Carbohydrate . . .62g   Saturates 5g

10 mins   1 hr

SERVES 4

INGREDIENTS

tbsp olive oil

large onion, chopped

garlic cloves, chopped

200 g/7 oz can chopped tomatoes

700 g/1 lb 9 oz potatoes, cut into 5 cm/
2 inch chunks

3 green peppers, deseeded and
roughly chopped

300 ml/10 fl oz cold water

900 g/2 lb tuna fillet, cut into chunks

slices crusty white bread

salt and pepper

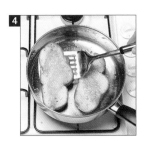

1 Heat 2 tablespoons of the oil in a saucepan and add the onion. Cook over a low heat, stirring occasionally for 8–10 minutes until softened and brown. Add the garlic and cook a further minute. Add the tomatoes, cover and simmer for 30 minutes until thickened.

2 Meanwhile, place the potatoes and green peppers in another saucepan. Add the water, which should just cover the vegetables. If necessary, add a little more or pour a little away. Bring to the boil, cover and simmer over a medium heat for about 15 minutes until the potatoes are almost tender.

3 Add the tuna and the tomato mixture to the potatoes and peppers and season to taste with salt and pepper. Cover and simmer for 6–8 minutes until the tuna is tender.

4 Meanwhile, heat the remaining oil in a large frying pan over a medium heat and add the bread slices. Fry on both sides until golden. Drain on kitchen paper. Serve the fried bread with the stew.

VARIATION

Substitute any very firm-fleshed fish, such as shark or swordfish, for the tuna used in this recipe.

Crab Cakes with Salsa Verde

These spicy fish cakes are popular throughout Thailand, where they are eaten as between-meal snacks.

NUTRITIONAL INFORMATION

Calories	318	Sugars	.........1g
Protein	........26g	Fat	..........23g
Carbohydrate	....2g	Saturates	.......3g

45–75 mins   15 mins

SERVES 4

INGREDIENTS

250 g/9 oz crab meat, thawed if frozen

250 g/9 oz white fish fillet, such as cod, skinned and roughly chopped

1 fresh red chilli, deseeded and roughly chopped

1 garlic clove, roughly chopped

2.5 cm/1 inch piece of fresh root ginger, roughly chopped

1 lemon grass stalk, roughly chopped

3 tbsp chopped fresh coriander

1 egg white

groundnut or sunflower oil, for frying

SALSA VERDE

2 fresh green chillies, deseeded and roughly chopped

8 spring onions, roughly chopped

2 garlic cloves, roughly chopped

1 bunch of fresh parsley

grated rind and juice of 1 lime

juice of 1 lemon

4 tbsp olive oil

1 tbsp green Tabasco sauce

salt and pepper

1 Place the crab meat, fish, red chilli, garlic, ginger, lemon grass, coriander and egg white in a food processor and process until thoroughly blended, then transfer to a bowl, cover with clingfilm and chill in the refrigerator for 30–60 minutes.

2 Meanwhile, make the salsa verde. Put the green chillies, spring onions, garlic and parsley in a food processor and process until finely chopped.

3 Transfer to a small bowl and stir in the lime rind, lime and lemon juice, olive oil and green Tabasco sauce. Season to taste with salt and pepper, cover with clingfilm and leave to chill in the refrigerator until ready to serve.

4 Heat 2 tablespoons of the groundnut oil in a non-stick frying pan. Add spoonfuls of the crab mixture, flattening them gently with a spatula and keeping them spaced well apart. Cook for 4 minutes, then turn with a spatula and cook the other side for 3 minutes, or until golden brown.

5 Remove from the frying pan and keep warm while you cook the remaining batches, adding more oil if necessary. Transfer the crab cakes to a large serving plate, garnish and serve with the salsa verde.

Prawn Rostis

These crisp little vegetable and prawn cakes make an
ideal light lunch or supper, accompanied by a mixed leaf salad.

NUTRITIONAL INFORMATION

Calories	445	Sugars	.........9g
Protein	........19g	Fat	..........29g
Carbohydrate	...29g	Saturates	.......4g

10 mins · 1 hr

SERVES 4

I N G R E D I E N T S

350 g/12 oz potatoes

350 g/12 oz celeriac

1 carrot

½ small onion

225 g/8 oz peeled cooked prawns,
    thawed if frozen and well-drained on
    kitchen paper

2½ tbsp plain flour

1 egg, lightly beaten

vegetable oil, for frying

salt and pepper

C H E R R Y   T O M A T O   S A L S A

225 g/8 oz mixed cherry
    tomatoes, quartered

½ small mango, finely diced

1 fresh red chilli, deseeded and
    finely chopped

½ small red onion, finely chopped

1 tbsp chopped fresh coriander

1 tbsp chopped fresh chives

2 tbsp olive oil

2 tsp lemon juice

salt and pepper

1 For the salsa, mix the tomatoes,
  mango, chilli, onion, coriander, chives,
olive oil, lemon juice and seasoning. Set
aside for the flavours to infuse.

2 Using a food processor or the fine
  blade of a box grater, finely grate the
potatoes, celeriac, carrot and onion. Mix
together with the prawns, flour and egg.
Season well and set aside.

3 Divide the prawn mixture into 8 equal
  pieces. Press each into a greased
10 cm/4 inch metal pastry cutter (if you
have only 1 cutter, you can simply shape
the rostis individually).

4 Heat a shallow layer of oil in a large
  frying pan. When hot, transfer the
rostis, still in the cutters, to the frying
pan, in 4 batches if necessary. When the
oil sizzles underneath, remove the cutter.
Fry gently, pressing down with a spatula,
for 6–8 minutes on each side, until crisp
and browned and the vegetables are
tender. Drain on kitchen paper and keep
warm. Serve hot with the tomato salsa.

Provençal Mussels

This recipe conjures up southern France – tomatoes, wine, herbs and garlic combine to make a flavourful mussel stew.

NUTRITIONAL INFORMATION

Calories	194	Sugars	.........5g
Protein	........12g	Fat	..........10g
Carbohydrate	....9g	Saturates	.......2g

10 mins   1¼ hrs

SERVES 4

INGREDIENTS

900 g/2 lb live mussels

3 tbsp olive oil

1 onion, finely chopped

3 garlic cloves, finely chopped

2 tsp fresh thyme leaves

150 ml/ 5 fl oz red wine

2 x 400 g/14 oz cans chopped tomatoes

2 tbsp chopped fresh parsley

salt and pepper

crusty bread, to serve

1 Clean the mussels by scrubbing or scraping the shells and pulling out any beards. Discard any mussels with broken shells or that do not close when tapped sharply. Put the mussels in a large saucepan with just the water that clings to their shells. Cover and cook over a high heat, vigorously shaking the pan occasionally, for 3–4 minutes until all the mussels have opened. Discard any mussels that remain closed. Drain, reserving the cooking liquid. Set aside.

2 Heat the oil in a large saucepan and add the onion. Cook over a low heat for 8–10 minutes until softened, but not coloured. Add the garlic and thyme and cook for a further minute. Add the wine and simmer rapidly until reduced an syrupy. Add the tomatoes and strain in th mussel cooking liquid. Bring to the boi cover and simmer for 30 minutes. Uncove the pan and cook for a further 15 minutes

3 Add the mussels and cook for further 5 minutes until heate through. Stir in the parsley, season to tast with salt and pepper and serve with plent of fresh crusty bread.

VARIATION
Replace the mussels with an equal quantity of clams.

Sicilian Pasta

This is based on a traditional dish combining broccoli and anchovies, but here lemon and garlic have been added for more flavour.

NUTRITIONAL INFORMATION

Calories	529	Sugars	.........4g
Protein	........17g	Fat	..........20g
Carbohydrate	...75g	Saturates	.......3g

10 mins   30 mins

SERVES 4

INGREDIENTS

6 tbsp olive oil

55 g/2 oz fresh white breadcrumbs

450g/1 lb broccoli, cut into small florets

350 g/12 oz dried tagliatelle

4 canned anchovy fillets, drained and chopped

2 garlic cloves, sliced

grated rind 1 lemon

large pinch of chilli flakes

salt and pepper

freshly grated Parmesan cheese, to serve

1 Heat 2 tablespoons of the olive oil in a frying pan and add the breadcrumbs. Stir-fry over a medium heat for 4–5 minutes until golden and crisp. Drain on kitchen paper.

2 Bring a large pan of lightly salted water to the boil and add the broccoli. Blanch for 3 minutes, then drain, reserving the water. Refresh the broccoli under cold water and drain again. Pat dry on kitchen paper and set aside.

3 Bring the water back to the boil and add the tagliatelle. Bring back to the boil and cook for 8–10 minutes until tender, but still firm to the bite.

4 Meanwhile, heat 2 tablespoons of the remaining oil in a large, heavy-based frying pan or wok and add the anchovies. Cook over a low heat for 1 minute, then mash with a wooden spoon to a paste. Add the garlic, lemon rind and chilli flakes and cook gently for 2 minutes. Add the broccoli and cook for a further 3–4 minutes until heated through.

5 Drain the cooked pasta and combine with the broccoli mixture and the remaining olive oil. Season to taste with salt and pepper. Toss together well.

6 Divide the tagliatelle between warmed serving plates. Top with the fried breadcrumbs and Parmesan cheese and serve immediately.

Pasta Puttanesca

The story goes that this was a sauce made and eaten by Italian prostitutes who needed a quick and simple meal to keep them going.

NUTRITIONAL INFORMATION

Calories	359	Sugars	........10g
Protein	........10g	Fat	..........14g
Carbohydrate	...51g	Saturates	.......2g

 5 mins   25 mins

SERVES 4

INGREDIENTS

3 tbsp extra virgin olive oil

1 large red onion, finely chopped

4 canned anchovy fillets, drained

pinch of chilli flakes

2 garlic cloves, finely chopped

400 g/14 oz can chopped tomatoes

2 tbsp tomato purée

225 g/8 oz dried spaghetti

25 g/1 oz stoned black olives, roughly chopped

25 g/1 oz stoned green olives, roughly chopped

1 tbsp capers, rinsed and drained

4 sun-dried tomatoes in oil, drained and roughly chopped

salt and pepper

1 Heat the oil in a saucepan and cook the onion, anchovies and chilli flakes. for 10 minutes until softened. Add the garlic and cook for 30 seconds. Stir in the tomatoes and tomato purée and bring to the boil. Simmer gently for 10 minutes.

2 Meanwhile, bring a pan of lightly salted water to the boil. Add the pasta, bring back to the boil and cook for 8–10 minutes until tender, but still firm to the bite.

3 Add the olives, capers and sun-dried tomatoes to the sauce. Simmer for a further 2–3 minutes. Season to taste.

4 Drain the pasta well and stir in the sauce. Toss thoroughly to mix Transfer to a serving dish and serve hot.

Linguine with Sardines

This is a very quick dish that is ideal for midweek suppers as it is so simple to prepare but is packed full of flavour.

NUTRITIONAL INFORMATION

Calories	547	Sugars	.........5g
Protein	........23g	Fat	..........23g
Carbohydrate	...68g	Saturates	.......3g

10 mins 12 mins

SERVES 4

INGREDIENTS

sardines, filleted

fennel bulb

tbsp olive oil

garlic cloves, sliced

tsp chilli flakes

50 g/12 oz dried linguine

tsp finely grated lemon rind

tbsp lemon juice

tbsp pine kernels, toasted

tbsp chopped fresh parsley

salt and pepper

1 Wash the sardine fillets and pat dry on kitchen paper. Roughly chop them into large pieces and set aside. Trim the fennel bulb and slice very thinly.

2 Heat 2 tablespoons of the olive oil in a large, heavy-based frying pan and add the garlic and chilli flakes. Cook for minute, then add the fennel slices. Cook over a medium-high heat, stirring occasionally, for 4–5 minutes until softened. Lower the heat, add the sardine pieces and cook for a further 3–4 minutes until just cooked.

3 Meanwhile, bring a pan of lightly salted water to the boil. Add the pasta, bring back to the boil and cook for 8–10 until tender, but still firm to the bite. Drain well and return to the pan.

4 Add the lemon rind, lemon juice, pine kernels and parsley to the sardines and toss together. Season to taste with salt and pepper. Add to the pasta with the remaining olive oil and toss together gently. Transfer to a warmed serving dish and serve immediately.

COOK'S TIP

Reserve a couple of tablespoons of the pasta cooking water and add to the pasta with the sauce if the mixture seems a little dry.

Crab Ravioli

These small parcels are made from wonton wrappers, filled with mixed vegetables and crab meat for a melt-in-the-mouth starter.

NUTRITIONAL INFORMATION

Calories 292   Sugars 1g
Protein ....25g   Fat 17g
Carbohydrate ....11g   Saturates 5g

20 mins   25 mins

SERVES 4

INGREDIENTS

450 g/1 lb fresh or canned crab meat, drained

½ red pepper, deseeded and finely diced

115 g/4 oz Chinese leaves, shredded

25 g/1 oz beansprouts, roughly chopped

1 tbsp light soy sauce

1 tsp lime juice

16 wonton wrappers

1 small egg, beaten

2 tbsp groundnut oil

1 tsp sesame oil

salt and pepper

1 Mix together the crab meat, red pepper, Chinese leaves, beansprouts, soy sauce and lime juice. Season and set aside for 15 minutes.

2 Spread out the wonton wrappers on a work surface. Spoon a little of the crab meat mixture into the centre of each wrapper. Brush the edges with egg and fold in half, pushing out any air. Press the edges together to seal.

3 Heat the groundnut oil in a preheate wok or frying pan. Fry the ravioli, batches for 3–4 minutes, turnir frequently, until browned. Remove with slotted spoon and drain on kitchen paper.

4 Heat any remaining filling in the wo or frying pan over a gentle heat un' hot. Sprinkle the ravioli with the sesam oil, transfer to a warmed platter and serv immediately.

COOK'S TIP

Make sure that the edges of the ravioli are sealed well and that all of the air is pressed out to prevent them from opening during cooking.

Spaghettini with Crab

This dish is probably one of the simplest in the book, yet the flavour is as impressive as a recipe over which you have slaved for hours.

NUTRITIONAL INFORMATION

Calories	488	Sugars 3g
Protein	........13g	Fat 19g
Carbohydrate	...65g	Saturates 3g

 10 mins   🕙 10 mins

SERVES 4

I N G R E D I E N T S

dressed crab, about 450 g/1 lb including the shell

350 g/12 oz dried spaghettini

5 tbsp extra virgin olive oil

1 fresh red chilli, deseeded and finely chopped

2 garlic cloves, finely chopped

3 tbsp chopped fresh parsley

2 tbsp lemon juice

1 tsp finely grated lemon rind

salt and pepper

lemon wedges, to garnish

1 Scoop the meat from the crab shell into a bowl. Mix the white and brown meat lightly together and set aside.

2 Bring a large saucepan of lightly salted water to the boil. Add the pasta, bring back to the boil and cook for 8–10 minutes until tender, but still firm to the bite. Drain well and return to the pan.

3 Meanwhile, heat 2 tablespoons of the olive oil in a frying pan. Add the chilli and garlic. Cook for 30 seconds, then add the crab meat, parsley, lemon juice and lemon rind. Stir-fry over a low heat for a further minute until the crab is just heated through.

4 Add the crab mixture to the pasta with the remaining olive oil and season to taste with salt and pepper. Toss together thoroughly, transfer to a warmed serving dish and serve immediately, garnished with lemon wedges.

COOK'S TIP
If you prefer to buy your own fresh crab you will need a large crab weighing about 1 kg/2 lb 4 oz.

Spicy Crab Soup

Use only white crab meat for this Chinese-style soup, as the brown meat will disintegrate. You can use fresh, frozen or canned crab.

NUTRITIONAL INFORMATION

Calories	95	Sugars	........2g
Protein	........9g	Fat	..........3g
Carbohydrate	....9g	Saturates	.......0g

 10 mins   🕐 15 mins

SERVES 4

INGREDIENTS

1 litre/1¾ pints chicken stock

2 tomatoes, peeled and finely chopped

2.5 cm/1 inch piece of fresh root ginger, finely chopped

1 small fresh red chilli, deseeded and finely chopped

2 tbsp Chinese rice wine

1 tbsp rice vinegar

¾ tsp sugar

1 tbsp cornflour

2 tbsp water

175 g/6 oz white crab meat, thawed if frozen or drained if canned

salt and pepper

2 spring onions, shredded, to garnish

COOK'S TIP

Chinese rice wine and rice vinegar are usually available from some large supermarkets as well as from Chinese food shops.

1 Pour the chicken stock into a large, heavy-based saucepan and add the tomatoes, ginger, chilli, rice wine, vinegar and sugar. Bring to the boil, then reduce the heat, cover and simmer for 10 minutes.

2 Mix the cornflour and water together in a small bowl until a smooth paste forms, then stir into the soup. Simmer,

stirring constantly, for 2 minutes, or unt slightly thickened.

3 Gently stir in the crab meat and hea through for 2 minutes. Season t taste with salt and pepper, then ladl into warmed soup bowls and serv immediately, garnished with the shredde spring onions.

Salt Cod Hash

As well as being a simple supper dish, this would make a delicious addition to a brunch menu.

NUTRITIONAL INFORMATION

Calories	857	Sugars	.........5g
Protein	........58g	Fat	..........36g
Carbohydrate	...82g	Saturates	......10g

5 mins, plus 50 hrs soaking/salting

30 mins

SERVES 4

INGREDIENTS

25 g/1 oz sea salt

750 g/1 lb 10 oz fresh boneless cod fillet

4 eggs

3 tbsp olive oil, plus extra for drizzling

8 rashers rindless smoked streaky
   bacon, chopped

700 g/1 lb 9 oz old potatoes, diced

8 garlic cloves

8 thick slices white bread

2 plum tomatoes, peeled and chopped

2 tsp red wine vinegar

2 tbsp chopped fresh parsley, plus extra
   to garnish

salt and pepper

lemon wedges, to garnish

1 Sprinkle the salt over both sides of the cod fillet. Place in a shallow dish, cover and chill for 48 hours. When ready to cook, remove the cod from the refrigerator and rinse under cold water. Set aside to soak in cold water for 2 hours, then drain well.

2 Bring a large saucepan of water to the boil and add the fish. Remove from the heat and set aside for 10 minutes. Drain the fish on kitchen paper and flake the flesh. Discard the soaking water.

3 Bring a saucepan of water to the boil. Add the eggs and simmer for 7–9 minutes from when the water returns to the boil – 7 minutes for a slightly soft centre, 9 for a firm centre. Drain, then plunge the eggs into cold water. Shell the eggs and roughly chop. Set aside.

4 Heat the oil in a large frying pan and add the bacon. Cook over a medium heat for 4–5 minutes until crisp and brown. Remove with a draining spoon and drain on kitchen paper. Put the potatoes and garlic in the pan and cook over a medium heat for 8–10 minutes until crisp and golden. Meanwhile, toast the bread on both sides. Drizzle the bread with olive oil and set aside.

5 Add the tomatoes, bacon, fish, vinegar and chopped egg to the potatoes and garlic. Cook for 2 minutes. Stir in the parsley and season. Put the toast on to serving plates, top with the hash and garnish with parsley and lemon wedges.

Onion & Tuna Tart

This is a variation of Pissaladière, the classic French tart of slow-cooked onions on a bread base, very like a pizza.

NUTRITIONAL INFORMATION

Calories	541	Sugars	.......14g
Protein	........22g	Fat	..........25g
Carbohydrate	...61g	Saturates	.......9g

🍚 1½ hrs   🕐 1¾ hrs

SERVES 4

I N G R E D I E N T S

225 g/8 oz strong white bread flour, plus extra for dusting

1 tsp salt

7 g sachet easy-blend yeast

2 tbsp olive oil, plus extra for greasing

150 ml/5 fl oz lukewarm water

T O P P I N G

55 g/2 oz butter

2 tbsp olive oil

900 g/2 lb onions, thinly sliced

1 tsp sugar

1 tsp salt

1 tsp fresh thyme leaves

200 g/7 oz can tuna, drained

85 g/3 oz stoned black olives

pepper

green salad, to serve

1 To make the topping, heat the butter and oil in a large saucepan and add the onions. Stir well, cover and cook over a very low heat for 20 minutes. Add the sugar and salt. Cook over the lowest heat for a further 30–40 minutes, stirring until collapsed and beginning to brown. Cook for a further 15–20 minutes until evenly golden. Remove from the heat, stir in the thyme and season to taste.

2 Meanwhile, make the base. Combine the flour, salt and yeast in a large bowl. Add the oil and enough water to make a soft dough that leaves the sides of the bowl clean. Tip the dough on to a lightly floured surface and knead for 5 minutes until smooth and elastic. Alternatively, use a food mixer with a dough hook and knead for 5 minutes.

3 Form the dough into a neat ball and place in a lightly oiled bowl. Lightly oil the top of the dough, cover with a clean tea towel and set aside to rise in a warm place for about 1 hour or until doubled in bulk.

4 Preheat the oven to 220°C/450°F/Gas Mark 7 with a baking sheet on the top shelf. Knock back the risen dough by punching down the centre with your fist. Tip out the dough on to the work surface and knead briefly. Roll out the dough, using a rolling pin, to fit a lightly oiled Swiss roll tin measuring 32.5 x 23 cm/13 x 9 inches, leaving a rim. You may have to stretch the dough to fit the tin as it is very springy.

5 Spread the onions in an even layer over the dough. Flake the tuna with a fork and sprinkle it evenly over the top of the onions. Arrange the olives over the tuna and season to taste with pepper. Transfer the tin to the preheated baking sheet and bake for about 20 minutes until the dough is golden. Serve immediately with a green salad.

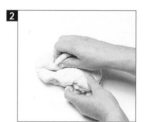

Smoked Salmon Pancakes

Buckwheat flour is traditionally used for the pancakes in this Breton recipe. It is available from large supermarkets and health food stores.

NUTRITIONAL INFORMATION

Calories	385	Sugars	........4g
Protein	........24g	Fat	..........21g
Carbohydrate	...27g	Saturates	.......9g

25 mins   25 mins

SERVES 4

I N G R E D I E N T S

55 g/2 oz plain flour

55 g/2 oz buckwheat flour

pinch of salt

2 large eggs

200 ml/7 fl oz milk

85 ml/3 fl oz water

1 tbsp butter, melted

vegetable oil, for frying

FILLING

125 ml/4 fl oz crème fraîche

1 tbsp capers, rinsed, drained and
roughly chopped

3 spring onions, finely chopped

1 fresh red chilli, deseeded and
finely chopped

1 tbsp chopped fresh dill

1 tbsp chopped fresh chives

1 tsp lemon rind

225 g /8 oz sliced smoked salmon

salt and pepper

1 For the filling, combine the crème fraîche, capers, spring onions, chilli, dill, chives, lemon rind and seasoning.

2 To make the buckwheat pancakes, sift together the flours and salt into a large bowl. Make a well in the centre and add the eggs. Combine the milk and water and add half this mixture to the flour and eggs. Mix together until smooth. Gradually add the remaining milk mixture to make a smooth batter. Stir in the melted butter.

3 Heat a 20 cm/8 inch pancake pan or frying pan over a medium heat. Dip a piece of wadded kitchen paper into a little vegetable oil and rub this over the surface of the pan to give a thin coating. Ladle about 2 tablespoons of the pancake mixture into the pan, tilting and shaking the pan to coat the base evenly. Cook for 1 minute until the edges start to lift away from the pan. Using a large palette knife, carefully lift the pancake and turn it over. It should be pale golden. Cook for 30 seconds on the second side. Remove from the pan and place on a warmed plate. Re-grease and reheat the pan and repeat with the remaining mixture to make 12–14 pancakes, depending on their thickness. Stack the cooked pancakes, interleaved with greaseproof paper.

4 Place a slice of smoked salmon on each pancake and top with about 2 teaspoons of the crème fraîche mixture. Fold the pancake in half, then in half again to form a triangle and serve.

Crab Soufflé

Soufflés are always impressive and this one is no exception. Serve straight from the oven but don't worry if it sinks en route to the table.

NUTRITIONAL INFORMATION

Calories	.214	Sugars	.1g
Protein	.15g	Fat	.14g
Carbohydrate	.8g	Saturates	.7g

15 mins   35 mins

SERVES 4–6

INGREDIENTS

3 tbsp butter, plus extra for greasing

25 g/1 oz dried breadcrumbs

1 small onion, finely chopped

1 garlic clove, crushed

2 tsp mustard powder

25 g/1 oz plain flour

225 ml/8 fl oz milk

55 g/2 oz Gruyère cheese, grated

3 eggs, separated

225 g/8 oz crab meat, thawed if frozen

2 tbsp chopped fresh chives

pinch of cayenne pepper

salt and pepper

1 Generously butter a 1.15 litre/2½ pint soufflé dish. Add the breadcrumbs, then shake and turn the dish to coat the base and sides completely. Shake out any excess. Set aside on a baking sheet.

2 Melt the butter in a large saucepan. Add onion and cook over a low heat, stirring occasionally, for 5 minutes until softened, but not coloured. Add the garlic and cook for a further minute. Stir in the mustard powder and flour and cook, stirring constantly, for 1 minute. Gradually add the milk, stirring constantly, until smooth. Increase the heat slightly and gradually bring to the boil, stirring constantly. Simmer gently for 2 minutes. Remove from the heat and stir in the cheese. Set aside to cool slightly.

3 Lightly beat in the egg yolks, then gently fold in the crab meat, chives and cayenne and season to taste with salt and pepper.

4 In a clean bowl, whisk the egg whites until they form stiff peaks. Add a large spoonful of the egg whites to the crab mixture and fold together to slacken. Add the remaining egg whites and fold together carefully, but thoroughly. Spoon into the prepared dish.

5 Cook in a preheated oven, 200°C/ 400°F/Gas Mark 6, for 25 minutes until risen and golden. Serve immediately.

Chorizo & Chickpea Tapas

A glass of chilled sherry and a selection of Spanish tapas is a great way to unwind at the end of the day.

NUTRITIONAL INFORMATION

Calories 462   Sugars 3g
Protein ....18g   Fat 36g
Carbohydrate ...17g   Saturates 9g

 10 mins   8 mins

SERVES 4

INGREDIENTS

00 ml/3½ fl oz olive oil

bout 2 tbsp sherry vinegar

50 g/9 oz fresh chorizo sausage, in 1 piece

small Spanish onion, finely chopped

00 g/14 oz can chickpeas

alt and pepper

nely chopped fresh oregano or flat leaf parsley, to garnish

hunks of fresh bread, to serve

1. Place 6 tablespoons of the olive oil and 2 tablespoons of the vinegar in a bowl and whisk together. Taste and add a little more sherry vinegar, if desired. Season with salt and pepper to taste and set aside.

2. Using a small, sharp knife, remove the casing from the chorizo sausage. Cut the meat into 5 mm/¼ inch thick slices, then cut each slice into half-moon shapes.

3. Heat the remaining olive oil in a small, heavy-based frying pan over a medium-high heat. Add the onion and cook, stirring occasionally, for 2–3 minutes. Add the chorizo sausage and cook for about 3 minutes or until the sausage is cooked through.

4. Using a draining spoon, remove the sausage and onion and drain on crumpled kitchen paper. Transfer to the bowl with the dressing while they are still hot and stir together.

5. Empty the chick-peas into a sieve and rinse well under cold running water; shake off the excess water. Add to the bowl with the other ingredients and stir together. Set aside to cool.

6. Just before serving, adjust the seasoning, then spoon the salad into a serving bowl and sprinkle with chopped herbs. Serve with chunks of fresh bread.

Grilled Sardines

If you drive along the Mediterranean coast, you'll come across small harbour-side restaurants grilling the day's catch of sardines.

NUTRITIONAL INFORMATION

Calories	399	Sugars	.........1g
Protein	........21g	Fat	..........34g
Carbohydrate	....2g	Saturates	.......6g

  2½ hrs 3 mins

SERVES 4–6

I N G R E D I E N T S

12 sardines

olive oil

fresh flat-leaf parsley sprigs, to garnish

lemon wedges, to serve

D R E S S I N G

150 ml/5 fl oz extra virgin olive oil

finely grated rind of 1 large lemon

4 tbsp lemon juice

4 shallots, thinly sliced

1 small fresh red chilli, deseeded and finely chopped

1 large garlic clove, finely chopped

salt and pepper

1 To make the dressing, place all the ingredients in a screw-top jar, season with salt and pepper, then shake until blended. Pour into a non-metallic dish that is large enough to hold the sardines in a single layer. Set aside.

2 To prepare the sardines, chop off the heads and make a slit all along the length of each belly. Pull out the insides, rinse the fish inside and out with cold water and pat dry with kitchen paper.

3 Line the grill pan with foil, shiny side up. Brush the foil with a little olive oil to prevent the sardines from sticking. Arrange the sardines on the foil in a single layer and brush with a little of the dressing. Grill under a preheated grill for about 90 seconds.

4 Turn the fish over, brush with a little more dressing and continue grilling for a further 90 seconds or until they are cooked through and flake easily.

5 Transfer the fish to the dish with the dressing. Spoon the dressing over the fish and set aside to cool completely. Cover with clingfilm and chill in the refrigerator for at least 2 hours to allow the flavours to blend.

6 Transfer the sardines to a serving platter and garnish with parsley sprigs. Serve with lemon wedges for squeezing over the fish.

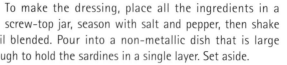

Spanish Tortilla

This classic Spanish dish is often served as part of a tapas selection.
A variety of cooked vegetables can be added to this recipe.

NUTRITIONAL INFORMATION

Calories	430	Sugars 6g
Protein	........16g	Fat 20g
Carbohydrate	...50g	Saturates 4g

10 mins   35 mins

SERVES 4

I N G R E D I E N T S

1 kg/2 lb 4 oz waxy potatoes, thinly sliced

4 tbsp vegetable oil

1 onion, sliced

2 garlic cloves, crushed

1 green pepper, deseeded and diced

2 tomatoes, deseeded and chopped

25 g/1 oz canned sweetcorn, drained

6 large eggs, beaten

2 tbsp chopped fresh parsley

salt and pepper

1 Parboil the potatoes in a saucepan of lightly salted boiling water for 5 minutes. Drain well.

2 Heat the oil in a large frying pan, add the potatoes and onion and

then sauté over a low heat, stirring constantly, for 5 minutes until the potatoes have browned.

3 Add the garlic, green pepper, tomatoes and sweetcorn, mixing well.

4 Pour in the eggs and add the parsley. Season to taste with salt and pepper. Cook for 10–12 minutes until the underside is cooked through.

5 Remove the frying pan from the heat and continue to cook the tortilla under a preheated medium grill for 5–7 minutes or until the tortilla is set and the top is golden brown.

6 Cut the tortilla into wedges or cubes, depending on your preference, and transfer to serving dishes. Serve with salad. In Spain tortillas are served hot, cold or warm.

COOK'S TIP

Ensure that the handle of your pan is heatproof before placing it under the grill and be sure to use an oven glove when removing it because it will be very hot.

Piperade

Serve this rustic egg and pepper dish to add a Mediterranean flavour to a light lunch. It's particularly good with Parma ham.

NUTRITIONAL INFORMATION

Calories 316   Sugars 8g
Protein . . . . .17g   Fat 15g
Carbohydrate . . .31g   Saturates 4g

 10 mins   25 mins

SERVES 4–6

INGREDIENTS

2 tbsp olive oil

1 large onion, finely chopped

1 large red pepper, deseeded and sliced

1 large yellow pepper, deseeded and sliced

1 large green pepper, deseeded and sliced

8 large eggs

2 tomatoes, deseeded and chopped

2 tbsp finely chopped fresh flat leaf parsley

salt and pepper

fresh flat leaf parsley sprigs, to garnish

4–6 slices thick country-style bread, toasted, to serve

1 Heat the olive oil in a heavy-based frying pan over a medium–high heat. Add the onion and peppers, reduce the heat and cook, stirring occasionally, for 15–20 minutes until softened.

2 Place the eggs in a mixing bowl and whisk until well blended. Season with salt and pepper to taste. Set aside.

3 When the peppers are soft, pour the eggs into the pan and cook, stirring constantly, over a very low heat until they are almost set, but still creamy. Remove the pan from the heat.

4 Stir in the chopped tomatoes and chopped parsley. Taste and adjust the seasoning, if necessary. Place the slices of toast on individual serving plates and spoon the eggs and vegetables on top. Garnish with sprigs of flat leaf parsley and serve immediately.

COOK'S TIP

To make this dish more substantial, serve with thickly cut slices of Serrano ham from Spain or Parma ham from Italy. The salty taste of both contrasts well with the sweetness of the peppers.

Corsican Clam Spaghetti

Fresh mussels can also be used to make this simple but delicious pasta sauce. Serve with a glass of chilled white wine.

NUTRITIONAL INFORMATION

Calories 550	Sugars 10g	
Protein 25g	Fat 16g	
Carbohydrate ...82g	Saturates 2g	

 50 mins   25 mins

SERVES 4

INGREDIENTS

400 g/14 oz dried or fresh spaghetti

salt and pepper

CORSICAN CLAM SAUCE

900 g/2 lb live clams

4 tbsp olive oil

3 large garlic cloves, crushed

pinch of dried chilli flakes (optional)

900 g/2 lb tomatoes, peeled and chopped, with juice reserved

60 g/2 oz green or black olives, stoned and chopped

1 tbsp chopped fresh oregano or
½ tsp dried oregano

1 Place the clams in a bowl of lightly salted water and set aside to soak for 30 minutes. Rinse them under cold, running water and scrub lightly to remove any sand from the shells.

2 Discard any broken clams or open clams that do not shut when firmly tapped with the back of a knife. This indicates they are dead and could cause food poisoning if eaten. Set the clams aside to soak in a large bowl of water. Meanwhile, bring a large pan of lightly salted water to the boil.

3 Heat the oil in a large frying pan over a medium heat. Add the garlic and chilli flakes, if using, and fry, stirring constantly, for about 2 minutes.

4 Stir in the tomatoes, olives and oregano. Lower the heat and simmer, stirring frequently, until the tomatoes soften and start to break up. Cover and simmer for 10 minutes.

5 Meanwhile, add the spaghetti to the pan of boiling water, bring back to the boil and cook until tender, but still

firm to the bite – 8–10 minutes for dried spaghetti and 2–3 minutes for fresh. Drain well, reserving about 125 ml/4 fl oz of the cooking water. Keep the pasta warm.

6 Add the clams and reserved cooking liquid to the sauce and stir. Bring to the boil, stirring constantly. Discard any clams that have not opened and transfer the sauce to a larger pan.

7 Add the pasta to the sauce and toss until well coated. Transfer the pasta to individual dishes. Serve immediately.

Pasta with Broccoli

Orecchiette, the cup-shaped pasta from southern Italy, is excellent for this filling dish because it scoops up the robust, chunky sauce.

NUTRITIONAL INFORMATION

Calories 685   Sugars 4g
Protein ....33g   Fat 29g
Carbohydrate ...78g   Saturates 9g

 10 mins   15 mins

SERVES 4

INGREDIENTS

500 g/1 lb 2 oz broccoli

400 g/14 oz dried orecchiette

5 tbsp olive oil

2 large garlic cloves, crushed

50 g/1¾ oz can anchovy fillets in oil, drained and finely chopped

55 g/2 oz Parmesan cheese, grated

55 g/2 oz pecorino cheese, grated

salt and pepper

1 Bring 2 pans of lightly salted water to the boil. Chop the broccoli florets and stems into bite-size pieces. Add them to 1 pan and cook for 10 minutes. Drain well.

2 Add the pasta to the other pan of boiling water, bring back to the boil and cook for 8–10 minutes until tender, but still firm to the bite.

VARIATIONS

You could add dried chilli flakes to taste with the garlic in Step 3, if you wish to. If you have difficulty in finding orecchiette, try using pasta bows instead.

3 Meanwhile, heat the oil in a large pan over a medium heat. Add the garlic and fry, stirring constantly, for 3 minutes. Add the chopped anchovies to the pan and cook for 3 minutes, stirring and mashing with a wooden spoon to break them up.

4 Drain the pasta, add it to the anchovy mixture and stir. Add the broccoli and stir gently to mix.

5 Add the grated cheeses to the pasta and stir constantly over medium–high heat until the cheeses melt and the pasta and broccoli are coated.

6 Adjust the seasoning to taste – the anchovies and cheeses are salty, so you will need to add pepper, if anything. Spoon into bowls or on to warmed plates and serve immediately.

Panzanella

This traditional, refreshing Italian salad of day-old bread is ideal to serve for lunch or as a simple supper on a hot day.

NUTRITIONAL INFORMATION

Calories 213	Sugars 11g	
Protein 7g	Fat 6g	
Carbohydrate . . .33g	Saturates 1g	

45 mins   10 mins

SERVES 4–6

INGREDIENTS

250 g/9 oz day-old Herb Focaccia (see page 476) or ciabatta bread or French bread

large, vine-ripened tomatoes

extra virgin olive oil

red, yellow and/or orange peppers

100 g/3½ oz cucumber

large red onion, finely chopped

canned anchovy fillets, drained and chopped

tbsp capers in brine, rinsed and patted dry

about 4 tbsp red wine vinegar

about 2 tbsp balsamic vinegar

salt and pepper

fresh basil leaves, to garnish

1 Cut the bread into 2.5 cm/1 inch cubes and place in a large bowl. Working over a plate to catch any juices, quarter the tomatoes, reserving the juices. Using a teaspoon, scoop out the cores and seeds, then finely chop the flesh. Add to the bread cubes.

2 Drizzle 5 tablespoons olive oil over the mixture and toss with your hands until well coated. Pour in the reserved tomato juice and toss again. Set aside for about 30 minutes.

3 Meanwhile, halve and deseed the peppers. Place on a grill rack, skin side up, and cook under a preheated grill for 10 minutes or until the skins are charred and the flesh softened. Place in a plastic bag, seal and set aside for 20 minutes. Peel off the skins and finely chop the flesh.

4 Cut the cucumber in half lengthways, then cut each half into 3 strips lengthways. Using a teaspoon, scoop out and discard the seeds. Dice the cucumber.

5 Add the onion, peppers, cucumber, anchovy fillets and capers to the bread and toss together. Sprinkle with the red wine and balsamic vinegars and season to taste with salt and pepper.

6 Drizzle with extra olive oil or vinegar if necessary, but be careful not to let the salad become too oily or soggy. Sprinkle the fresh basil leaves over the salad to garnish and serve immediately.

Rice & Chicken Chowder

Wild rice gives soups a wonderful texture as well as flavour – and it looks good too. Smoked chicken complements the nuttiness of the rice.

NUTRITIONAL INFORMATION

Calories	322	Sugars	4g
Protein	14g	Fat	19g
Carbohydrate	25g	Saturates	9g

 15 mins   1¾ hrs

SERVES 6–8

INGREDIENTS

85 g/3 oz wild rice

3 fresh corn cobs, husks and silks removed

2 tbsp vegetable oil

1 large onion, finely chopped

1 celery stick, thinly sliced

1 leek, trimmed and thinly sliced

½ tsp dried thyme

2 tbsp plain flour

1 litre/1¾ pints chicken stock

250 g/9 oz skinless, boneless smoked chicken, diced or shredded

225 ml/8 fl oz double or whipping cream

1 tbsp chopped fresh dill

salt and pepper

fresh dill sprigs, to garnish

1 Bring a large saucepan of water to the boil. Add a tablespoon of salt and sprinkle in the wild rice. Return to the boil, then reduce the heat, cover and simmer for about 40 minutes until just tender, but still firm to the bite. Do not overcook the rice, as it will continue to cook in the soup. Drain and rinse; then set aside.

2 Hold the corn cobs vertical to a chopping board and, using a sharp, heavy knife, cut down along the cobs to remove the kernels. Set aside the kernels. Scrape the cob to remove the milky juices and reserve for the soup.

3 Heat the vegetable oil in a large pan over a medium heat. Add the onion, celery, leek and dried thyme. Cook, stirring frequently, for about 8 minutes until the vegetables are very soft.

4 Sprinkle over the flour and stir until blended. Gradually whisk in the stock, add the corn with any juices and bring to the boil. Skim off any foam. Reduce the heat and simmer for about 25 minutes until the vegetables are very soft and tender.

5 Stir in the smoked chicken, wild rice, cream and dill. Season with salt and pepper to taste. Simmer for about 10 minutes until the chicken and rice are heated through. Garnish with dill sprigs and serve immediately.

Baked Tomato Rice

A great quick supper for the family, this dish is incredibly simple to put together, yet is truly scrumptious!

NUTRITIONAL INFORMATION

Calories 708   Sugars 7g
Protein . . . . .27g   Fat 35g
Carbohydrate . . .76g   Saturates 16g

5 mins   45 mins

SERVES 4

INGREDIENTS

2 tbsp vegetable oil

1 onion, coarsely chopped

1 red pepper, deseeded and chopped

2 garlic cloves, finely chopped

½ tsp dried thyme

300 g/10½ oz long grain rice

1 litre/1¾ pints chicken or vegetable stock

225 g/8 oz can chopped tomatoes

1 bay leaf

2 tbsp shredded fresh basil

175 g/6 oz mature Cheddar cheese, grated

2 tbsp chopped fresh chives

4 herbed pork sausages, cooked and cut into 1 cm/½ inch pieces

2–3 tbsp freshly grated Parmesan cheese

1 Heat the vegetable oil in a large flameproof casserole over a medium heat. Add the onion and red pepper and cook, stirring frequently, for about 5 minutes until soft and lightly coloured. Stir in the garlic and thyme and cook for 1 further minute.

2 Add the rice and cook, stirring frequently, for about 2 minutes until the rice is well coated and translucent. Stir in the stock, tomatoes and bay leaf.

Bring to the boil and simmer vigorously for 5 minutes until the stock is almost completely absorbed.

3 Stir in the basil, Cheddar cheese, chives and pork sausages and bake, covered, in a preheated oven, 180°C/350°F/Gas Mark 4, for about 25 minutes.

4 Sprinkle with the Parmesan cheese and return to the oven, uncovered, for 5 minutes until the top is golden. Serve hot straight from the casserole.

VARIATION

For a vegetarian version, replace the pork sausages with a 400 g/14 oz can of drained butter beans, kidney beans or sweetcorn. Alternatively, try a mixture of sautéed mushrooms and courgettes.

Mexican Tomato Rice

The tomatoes in this recipe give the rice its distinctive pinkish colour. The texture of the rice will be slightly 'wet'.

NUTRITIONAL INFORMATION

Calories	.311	Sugars	.4g
Protein	.7g	Fat	.11g
Carbohydrate	.50g	Saturates	.2g

30 mins   40 mins

SERVES 6–8

INGREDIENTS

400 g/14 oz long grain rice

1 large onion, chopped

2–3 garlic cloves, crushed

350 g/12 oz canned Italian plum tomatoes

3–4 tbsp olive oil

1 litre/1¾ pints chicken stock

1 tbsp tomato purée

1 habañero or other hot chilli

175 g/6 oz frozen peas, thawed

4 tbsp chopped fresh coriander

salt and pepper

TO SERVE

1 large avocado, peeled, stoned, sliced and sprinkled with lime juice

lime wedges

4 spring onions , chopped

1 tbsp chopped fresh coriander

1 Cover the rice with hot water and set aside to stand for 15 minutes. Drain, then rinse under cold running water.

2 Place the onion and garlic in a food processor and process until a smooth purée forms. Scrape the purée into a small bowl and set aside. Put the tomatoes in the food processor and process until smooth, then strain into another bowl, pushing through any solids with the back of a wooden spoon.

3 Heat the oil in a flameproof casserole over a medium heat. Add the rice and cook, stirring frequently, for 4 minutes until golden and translucent. Add the onion purée and cook, stirring frequently, for a further 2 minutes. Add the stock, processed canned tomatoes and tomato purée and bring to the boil.

4 Using a pin or long needle, carefully pierce the chilli in 2–3 places. Add to the rice, season to taste with salt and pepper and reduce the heat to low. Cover and simmer for about 25 minutes until the rice is tender and the liquid just absorbed. Discard the chilli, stir in the peas and coriander and cook for about 5 minutes to heat through.

5 To serve, gently fork the rice mixture into a warmed, large, shallow serving bowl. Arrange the avocado slices and lime wedges on top. Sprinkle the chopped spring onions and chopped coriander over and serve immediately.

Curried Rice Patties

Substantial and flavourful, these patties are a delicious alternative to beef burgers. Leave the rice with a little bite to give extra texture.

NUTRITIONAL INFORMATION

Calories 311	Sugars 4g	
Protein 7g	Fat 11g	
Carbohydrate . . .50g	Saturates 2g	

1¼ hrs   55 mins

SERVES 4–6

INGREDIENTS

0 g/2½ oz basmati rice

tbsp olive oil, plus extra for drizzling

red onion, finely chopped

garlic cloves

tsp curry powder

tsp crushed dried chilli flakes

small red pepper, deseeded and diced

15 g/4 oz frozen peas, thawed

small leek, finely chopped

tomato, peeled, deseeded and chopped

10 g/11 oz can chickpeas, rinsed
  and drained

5 g/3 oz fresh white breadcrumbs

–2 tbsp chopped fresh coriander or mint

egg, lightly beaten

egetable oil, for frying

alt and pepper

ucumber slices, to garnish

me wedges, to serve

DRESSING

20 ml/4 fl oz tahini

garlic cloves, crushed

tsp ground cumin

inch of cayenne pepper

tbsp lemon juice

1 To make the dressing, process the tahini, garlic, cumin, cayenne and lemon juice in a food processor until creamy. Slowly pour in the oil, then gradually add enough water to make a creamy dressing (about 125 ml/4 fl oz).

2 Bring a saucepan of water to the boil. Add ½ teaspoon of the salt and sprinkle in the rice; simmer for 15–20 minutes until the rice is just tender. Drain, rinse and set aside.

3 Heat the olive oil in a large pan. Add the onion and garlic and cook until beginning to soften. Stir in the curry powder and chilli flakes and cook for 2 minutes. Add the red pepper, peas, leek and tomato and cook gently for about 7 minutes until tender. Set aside.

4 Process the chickpeas in a food processor until smooth. Add half the vegetables and process again. Transfer to a large bowl and add the remaining vegetable mixture, breadcrumbs, coriander and egg. Mix well. Stir in the rice and season to taste with salt and pepper. Chill for 1 hour in the refrigerator, then shape into 4–6 patties.

5 Fry the patties in oil for 6–8 minutes until golden. Garnish with cucumber slices and serve with the dressing and lime wedges.

Easy Cheese Risotto

Although this is the easiest, most basic risotto, it is one of the most delicious. Because there are few ingredients, use the best of each.

NUTRITIONAL INFORMATION

Calories 353	Sugars 2g	
Protein 10g	Fat 15g	
Carbohydrate . . .40g	Saturates 9g	

5 mins   30 mins

SERVES 4–6

I N G R E D I E N T S

4–6 tbsp unsalted butter

1 onion, finely chopped

300 g/10½ oz arborio or carnaroli rice

125 ml/4 fl oz dry white vermouth or white wine

1.2 litres/2 pints chicken or vegetable stock, simmering

85 g/3 oz freshly grated Parmesan cheese, plus extra for sprinkling

salt and pepper

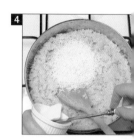

1 Heat about 2 tablespoons of the butter in a large heavy-based saucepan over a medium heat. Add the onion and cook for about 2 minutes until just beginning to soften. Add the rice and cook, stirring frequently, for about 2 minutes until translucent and well coated with the butter.

COOK'S TIP

If you prefer not to use butter, soften the onion in 2 tablespoons olive oil and stir in about 2 tablespoons extra virgin olive oil with the Parmesan at the end.

2 Pour in the vermouth: it will bubble and steam rapidly and evaporate almost immediately. Add a ladleful (about 225 ml/8 fl oz) of the simmering stock and cook, stirring constantly, until the stock is completely absorbed.

3 Continue adding the stock, about half a ladleful at a time, allowing each addition to be absorbed before adding the next – never allow the rice to cook 'dry'.

This should take 20–25 minutes. The risotto should have a creamy consistency and the rice grains should be tender, but still firm to the bite.

4 Switch off the heat and stir in the remaining butter and Parmesan. Season with salt and pepper to taste. Cover, leave to stand for about 1 minute, then serve with extra Parmesan for sprinkling.

Minted Green Risotto

This tasty risotto gets its vibrant green colour from the spinach and mint. Serve with Italian-style rustic bread and salad for an informal supper.

NUTRITIONAL INFORMATION

Calories 512	Sugars 7g
Protein 20g	Fat 24g
Carbohydrate ...51g	Saturates 12g

10 mins   35 mins

SERVES 6

I N G R E D I E N T S

2 tbsp unsalted butter

450 g/1 lb fresh shelled peas or thawed frozen peas

1 kg/2 lb 4 oz young spinach leaves, washed and drained

1 bunch of fresh mint, leaves stripped from stalks

2 tbsp chopped fresh basil

2 tbsp chopped fresh oregano

pinch of freshly grated nutmeg

4 tbsp mascarpone cheese or double cream

2 tbsp vegetable oil

1 onion, finely chopped

4 celery sticks, including leaves, finely chopped

2 garlic cloves, finely chopped

½ tsp dried thyme

300 g/10½ oz arborio or carnaroli rice

50 ml/2 fl oz dry white vermouth

1 litre/1¾ pints chicken or vegetable stock, simmering

85 g/3 oz freshly grated Parmesan cheese

1 Heat half the butter in a deep frying pan over a medium-high heat until sizzling. Add the peas, spinach, mint leaves, basil and oregano and season with the nutmeg. Cook, stirring frequently, for about 3 minutes until the spinach and mint leaves are wilted. Cool slightly.

2 Pour the spinach mixture into a food processor and process for 15 seconds. Add the mascarpone or cream and process again for about 1 minute. Transfer to a bowl and set aside.

3 Heat the oil and remaining butter in a large, heavy-based saucepan over a medium heat. Add the onion, celery, garlic and thyme and cook for about 2 minutes until the vegetables are softened. Add the rice and cook, stirring frequently, for about 2 minutes until the rice is translucent and well coated.

4 Add the vermouth to the rice; it will bubble and steam rapidly. When it is almost absorbed, add a ladleful (about 225 ml/8 fl oz) of the simmering stock. Cook, stirring constantly, until the stock is completely absorbed.

5 Continue adding the stock, about half a ladleful at a time, allowing each addition to be absorbed before adding the next. This should take 20–25 minutes. The risotto should have a creamy consistency and the rice should be just tender. Stir in the spinach-cream mixture and the Parmesan. Serve immediately.

Cannellini Bean Risotto

The Italians, particularly the Tuscans, love dishes made with beans.
This recipe combines beans and rice to make a rich and creamy risotto.

NUTRITIONAL INFORMATION

Calories .... .424 Sugars 2g
Protein ....15g Fat 19g
Carbohydrate ...50g Saturates 9g

🥘 10 mins   🕐 35 mins

SERVES 6–8

INGREDIENTS

300 g/10½ oz cannellini or white kidney beans, soaked and cooked according to packet instructions

2–3 tbsp olive oil

1 large red or sweet white onion, finely chopped

3–4 celery sticks, finely chopped

115 g/4 oz pancetta or thick-cut smoked bacon

2–3 garlic cloves, minced

¾ tsp dried oregano or 1 tbsp chopped fresh oregano

400 g/14 oz arborio or carnaroli rice

1 litre/1¾ pints chicken stock, simmering

4 tbsp unsalted butter at room temperature

115 g/4 oz freshly grated Parmesan cheese

salt and pepper

1 Mash half of the cannellini beans and set aside. Alternatively, press them through a food mill.

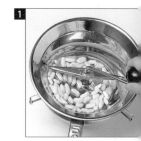

2 Heat the olive oil in a large heavy-based saucepan over a medium heat. Add the onion and celery and cook, stirring occasionally, for about 2 minutes until softened. Add the pancetta or bacon, garlic and oregano and cook, stirring occasionally, for a further 1–2 minutes. Add the rice and cook, stirring frequently, for about 2 minutes until it is translucent and well coated with the oil.

3 Add a ladleful (about 225 ml/8 fl oz) of the simmering stock; it will bubble and steam rapidly. Cook, stirring constantly, until the stock is absorbed.

4 Continue adding the stock, about half a ladleful at a time, allowing each addition to be absorbed before adding the next. This should take 20–25 minutes. The risotto should have a creamy consistency and the rice should be tender, but still firm to the bite.

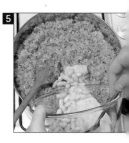

5 Stir in the beans and the bean purée, season with salt and pepper to taste and heat through. Add a little more stock if necessary.

6 Remove from the heat and stir in the butter and half the Parmesan. Cover and leave to stand for about 1 minute. Serve sprinkled with the remaining Parmesan.

Wild Mushroom Risotto

Distinctive-tasting wild mushrooms, so popular in Italy, give this aromatic risotto a wonderful, robust flavour.

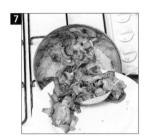

NUTRITIONAL INFORMATION

Calories ....425 Sugars 2g
Protein ....16g Fat 17g
Carbohydrate ...54g Saturates 6g

35 mins   35 mins

SERVES 6

INGREDIENTS

55 g/2 oz dried porcini or morel mushrooms

about 500 g/1 lb 2 oz mixed fresh wild mushrooms, such as porcini, girolles, horse mushrooms and chanterelles, halved if large

4 tbsp olive oil

3–4 garlic cloves, finely chopped

4 tbsp unsalted butter

1 onion, finely chopped

350 g/12 oz arborio or carnaroli rice

50 ml/2 fl oz dry white vermouth

1.2 litres/2 pints chicken stock, simmering

115 g/4 oz freshly grated Parmesan cheese

4 tbsp chopped fresh flat leaf parsley

salt and pepper

1 Place the dried mushrooms in a bowl and add boiling water to cover. Set aside to soak for 30 minutes, then carefully lift out and pat dry. Strain the soaking liquid through a sieve lined with kitchen paper and set aside.

2 Trim the wild mushrooms and gently brush clean.

3 Heat 3 tablespoons of the oil in a large frying pan. Add the fresh mushrooms and stir-fry for 1–2 minutes.

Add the garlic and the soaked mushrooms and cook, stirring frequently, for 2 minutes. Transfer to a plate.

4 Heat the remaining oil and half the butter in a large heavy-based saucepan. Add the onion and cook, stirring occasionally, for about 2 minutes until softened. Add the rice and cook, stirring frequently, for about 2 minutes until translucent and well coated.

5 Add the vermouth. When almost absorbed, add a ladleful (about 225 ml/8 fl oz) of the stock. Cook, stirring constantly, until the liquid is absorbed.

6 Continue adding the stock, about half a ladleful at a time, allowing each addition to be completely absorbed before adding the next. This should take 20–25 minutes. The risotto should have a creamy consistency and the rice should be tender, but firm to the bite.

7 Add half the reserved mushroom soaking liquid to the risotto and stir in the mushrooms. Season with salt and pepper to taste and add more mushroom liquid if necessary. Remove the pan from the heat and stir in the remaining butter, the grated Parmesan and chopped parsley. Serve immediately.

Roasted Pumpkin Risotto

The combination of sweet creamy pumpkin with the slight saltiness of dolcelatte cheese and the pungency of sage is delicious.

NUTRITIONAL INFORMATION

Calories	615	Sugars	.........2g
Protein	........19g	Fat	..........37g
Carbohydrate	...53g	Saturates	......18g

 10 mins   40 mins

SERVES 6

INGREDIENTS

4 tbsp olive oil

4 tbsp unsalted butter, diced

450 g/1 lb pumpkin flesh, cut into 1 cm/ ½ inch dice

¾ tsp dried sage

2 garlic cloves, finely chopped

2 tbsp lemon juice

2 large shallots, finely chopped

350 g/12 oz arborio or carnaroli rice

50 ml/2 fl oz dry white vermouth

1.2 litres/2 pints chicken stock, simmering

55 g/2 oz freshly grated Parmesan cheese

300 g/10½ oz dolcelatte cheese, diced

salt and pepper

celery leaves, to garnish

1 Put half the olive oil and about 1 tablespoon of the butter in a roasting tin and heat in a preheated oven, 200°C/ 400°F/Gas Mark 6.

2 When the butter has melted, arrange the pumpkin in the tin and sprinkle with the sage, half the garlic and salt and pepper to taste. Toss together and roast for about 10 minutes until just softened and beginning to caramelise. Transfer the pumpkin to a plate.

3 Roughly mash about half the cooked pumpkin with the lemon juice and reserve with the remaining diced pumpkin.

4 Heat the remaining oil and 1 tablespoon of the remaining butter in a large, heavy-based saucepan over a medium heat. Add the shallots and remaining garlic and cook, stirring occasionally, for about 1 minute. Add the rice and cook, stirring constantly, for about 2 minutes until well coated.

5 Pour in the vermouth; it will bubble and steam rapidly. Add a ladleful (about 225 ml/8 fl oz) of the simmering stock and cook, stirring constantly, until the stock is absorbed.

6 Continue adding the stock, about half a ladleful at a time, allowing each addition to be absorbed before adding the next – never allow the rice to cook 'dry'. This should take 20–25 minutes. The risotto should have a creamy consistency and the rice should be tender, but still firm to the bite.

7 Stir all the pumpkin – mashed and diced – into the risotto with the remaining butter and the grated Parmesan. Remove from the heat and fold in the diced dolcelatte. Serve immediately, garnished with celery leaves.

Hot Pink Risotto

The beetroot and red wine give this risotto its stunning colour and also impart a rich sweet flavour, which is unusual but surprisingly delicious.

NUTRITIONAL INFORMATION

Calories	397	Sugars	.........9g
Protein	........11g	Fat	...........11g
Carbohydrate	...61g	Saturates	.......3g

10 mins | 40 mins

SERVES 4–6

INGREDIENTS

75 g/6 oz dried sour cherries or dried cranberries

225 ml/8 fl oz fruity red wine, such as Valpolicella

3 tbsp olive oil

1 large red onion, finely chopped

2 celery sticks, finely chopped

½ tsp dried thyme

1 garlic clove, finely chopped

350 g/12 oz arborio or carnaroli rice

1.2 litres/2 pints chicken or vegetable stock, simmering

4 cooked beetroot (not in vinegar), diced

2 tbsp chopped fresh dill

2 tbsp snipped fresh chives

salt and pepper

55 g/2 oz freshly grated Parmesan cheese, to serve (optional)

1 Put the cherries or cranberries in a saucepan with the wine and bring to the boil. Simmer for 2–3 minutes until slightly reduced. Remove from the heat and set aside.

2 Heat the oil in a large heavy-based saucepan over a medium heat. Add the onion, celery and thyme and cook, stirring occasionally, for about 2 minutes until just beginning to soften. Add the garlic and rice and cook, stirring constantly, until the rice is well coated.

3 Add a ladleful (about 225 ml/8 fl oz) of the simmering stock; it will bubble and steam rapidly. Cook, stirring constantly, until the stock is absorbed.

4 Continue adding the stock, about half a ladleful at a time, allowing each addition to be absorbed before adding the next. This should take 20–25 minutes. The risotto should have a creamy consistency and the rice should be tender, but firm to the bite. Half way through the cooking time, remove the cherries or cranberries from the wine with a draining spoon and add to the risotto with the beetroot and half the wine. Continue adding the stock or remaining wine.

5 Stir in the dill and chives and season to taste with salt and pepper. Serve with the Parmesan, if wished.

Rocket & Tomato Risotto

It's worth searching around for wild rocket as its robust peppery flavour makes all the difference to this dish.

NUTRITIONAL INFORMATION

Calories	546	Sugars	.........6g
Protein	........23g	Fat	..........24g
Carbohydrate	...57g	Saturates	......12g

10 mins   30 mins

SERVES 4–6

INGREDIENTS

2 tbsp olive oil

2 tbsp unsalted butter

1 large onion, finely chopped

2 garlic cloves, finely chopped

350 g/12 oz arborio rice

125 ml/4 fl oz dry white vermouth

1.5 litres/2¾ pints chicken or vegetable stock, simmering

6 vine-ripened or Italian plum tomatoes, deseeded and chopped

125 g/4½ oz wild rocket

handful of fresh basil leaves

115 g/4 oz freshly grated Parmesan cheese

225 g/8 oz fresh Italian buffalo mozzarella, coarsely grated or diced

salt and pepper

1 Heat the oil and half the butter in a large frying pan. Add the onion and cook for about 2 minutes until just beginning to soften. Stir in the garlic and rice and cook, stirring frequently, until the rice is translucent and well coated.

2 Pour in the vermouth; it will evaporate almost immediately. Add a ladleful (about 225 ml/8 fl oz) of the stock and cook, stirring, until it is absorbed.

3 Continue adding the stock, about half a ladleful at a time, allowing each addition to be absorbed before adding the next. Just before the rice is tender, stir in the chopped tomatoes and rocket. Shred the basil leaves and immediately stir into the risotto. Continue to cook, adding more stock, until the risotto is creamy and the rice is tender, but firm to the bite.

4 Remove from the heat and stir in the remaining butter, the grated Parmesan and mozzarella. Season to taste with salt and pepper. Remove the pan from the heat, cover and leave to stand for about 1 minute. Serve immediately, before the mozzarella melts completely.

Sunshine Risotto

Pecorino is an Italian cheese made from ewe's milk. Although it is made all over Italy, the aged pecorino from Sardinia is particularly fine.

NUTRITIONAL INFORMATION

Calories	436	Sugars	.........8g
Protein	........15g	Fat	..........14g
Carbohydrate	...66g	Saturates	.......5g

35 mins 35 mins

SERVES 6

INGREDIENTS

bout 12 sun-dried tomatoes

tbsp olive oil

large onion, finely chopped

–6 garlic cloves, finely chopped

00 g/14 oz arborio or carnaroli rice

.5 litres/2¾ pints chicken or vegetable
  stock, simmering

tbsp chopped fresh flat-leaf parsley

15 g/4 oz grated aged pecorino cheese

xtra virgin olive oil, for drizzling

1. Place the sun-dried tomatoes in a bowl and pour over enough boiling ater to cover. Set aside to soak for about 0 minutes until soft and supple. Drain and at dry, then shred thinly and set aside.

2. Heat the oil in a heavy-based saucepan over a medium heat. Add he onion and cook for about 2 minutes ntil beginning to soften. Add the garlic nd cook for 15 seconds. Add the rice and ook, stirring frequently, for 2 minutes ntil the rice is translucent and well oated with oil.

3. Add a ladleful (about 225 ml/8 fl oz) of the simmering stock; the stock will ubble and steam rapidly. Cook, stirring onstantly, until the liquid is absorbed.

4. Continue adding the stock, about half a ladleful at a time, allowing each addition to be absorbed before adding the next – never allow the rice to cook 'dry'.

5. After about 15 minutes, stir in the sun-dried tomatoes. Continue to cook, adding the stock, until the rice is tender, but firm to the bite. The risotto should have a creamy consistency.

6. Remove the pan from the heat and stir in the chopped parsley and half the pecorino. Remove the pan from the heat, cover, leave to stand for about 1 minute, then spoon into serving dishes. Drizzle with extra virgin olive oil and sprinkle the remaining pecorino over the top. Serve immediately.

Radicchio Risotto

The slightly bitter flavour of radicchio is balanced by the addition of sweet double cream, while pancetta provides a smoky contrast.

NUTRITIONAL INFORMATION

Calories	358	Sugars	.........2g
Protein	........11g	Fat	..........16g
Carbohydrate	...46g	Saturates	.......7g

 10 mins 30 mins

SERVES 6–8

INGREDIENTS

1 large head radicchio, outer damaged leaves removed

2 tbsp sunflower or other vegetable oil

2 tbsp unsalted butter

115 g/4 oz pancetta or thick-cut smoked bacon, diced

1 large onion, finely chopped

1 garlic clove, finely chopped

400 g/14 oz arborio or carnaroli rice

1 .5 litres/2¾ pints chicken or vegetable stock, simmering

50 ml/2 fl oz double cream

55 g/2 oz freshly grated Parmesan cheese

3–4 tbsp chopped fresh flat leaf parsley

salt and pepper

fresh flat leaf parsley sprigs, to garnish

1 Cut the radicchio head in half lengthways; remove the triangular core. Place the halves cut side down and shred finely. Set aside.

2 Heat the oil and butter in a heavy-based pan over a medium heat. Add the pancetta or bacon and cook for 3–4 minutes, stirring occasionally, until it begins to colour. Add the onion and garlic and cook for 1 minute.

3 Add the rice and cook, stirring frequently, for 2 minutes until translucent and well coated. Stir in the radicchio for 1 minute until just beginning to wilt. Reduce the heat to medium.

4 Add a ladleful (about 225 ml/8 fl oz) of the simmering stock; the stock will bubble and steam rapidly. Cook, stirring constantly, until all the stock has been completely absorbed.

5 Continue adding the stock, about ha a ladleful at a time, allowing eac addition to be absorbed before adding th next. This should take 20–25 minutes. Th risotto should have a creamy consistenc and the rice should be tender.

6 Stir in the cream, Parmesan an parsley. Season with salt and peppe Remove from the heat. Cover and stand fo 1 minute. Garnish with parsley and serve.

Frittata Risotto

An excellent way of using up leftover risotto, this fried risotto 'cake' makes a great light lunch or evening snack.

NUTRITIONAL INFORMATION

Calories	567	Sugars	.......14g
Protein	........14g	Fat	.........34g
Carbohydrate	...50g	Saturates	......14g

10 mins   15 mins

SERVES 4-6

INGREDIENTS

about 80 ml/3 fl oz olive oil

1 large red onion, finely chopped

1 red pepper, deseeded and chopped

1 garlic clove, finely chopped

3-4 sun-dried tomatoes, finely shredded

2 tbsp chopped fresh flat leaf parsley or basil

1 quantity Easy Cheese Risotto with Parmesan (see page 340) or other risotto, cooled

about 55 g/2 oz freshly grated Parmesan cheese

1 Heat 2 tablespoons of the oil in a large, heavy-based frying pan over a medium-high heat. Add the onion and red pepper and cook for 3-4 minutes until the vegetables are soft.

2 Add the garlic and sun-dried tomatoes and cook for 2 minutes. Remove from the heat. Stir in the parsley and set aside to cool slightly.

3 Put the risotto in a bowl and break it up with a fork. Stir in the vegetable mixture with half the Parmesan.

4 Reserve 1 tablespoon of the remaining oil and heat the rest in the cleaned frying pan over a medium heat. Remove from the heat and spoon in the risotto mixture, pressing it into an even cake-like layer, about 2-2.5 cm/^{3}/$_4$-1 inch thick. Return the pan to the heat and cook for about 4 minutes until crisp and brown on the underside.

5 With a palette knife, loosen the edges and give the pan a shake. Slide the frittata on to a large plate. Protecting your hands, invert the frying pan over the frittata and, holding both firmly together, flip them over. Return to the heat and drizzle the remaining oil around the edge of the frittata, gently pulling the edges towards the centre with the palette knife. Cook for 1-2 minutes to seal the bottom, then slide on to a serving plate.

6 Sprinkle the top with some of the remaining Parmesan. Cut into wedges and serve with the rest of the Parmesan.

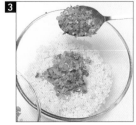

Oven-baked Risotto

This easy-to-make risotto is a good choice for entertaining because it eliminates the need for constant stirring.

NUTRITIONAL INFORMATION

Calories 428	Sugars 2g	
Protein 15g	Fat 18g	
Carbohydrate ...14g	Saturates 6g	

 10 mins   50 mins

SERVES 4

INGREDIENTS

4 tbsp olive oil

400 g/14 oz portobello or large field mushrooms, thickly sliced

115 g/4 oz pancetta or thick-cut smoked bacon, diced

1 large onion, finely chopped

2 garlic cloves, finely chopped

350 g/12 oz arborio or carnaroli rice

1.2 litres/2 pints chicken stock, simmering

2 tbsp chopped fresh tarragon or flat leaf parsley

85 g/3 oz freshly grated Parmesan cheese, plus extra for sprinkling

salt and pepper

1 Heat 2 tablespoons of the oil in a large, heavy-based frying pan over a high heat. Add the mushrooms and stir-fry for 2–3 minutes until golden and tender-crisp. Transfer to a plate.

2 Add the pancetta or bacon to the pan and cook for about 2 minutes, stirring frequently, until crisp and golden. Remove with a draining spoon and add to the mushrooms on the plate.

3 Heat the remaining oil in a heavy-based saucepan over a medium heat. Add the onion and cook for about 2 minutes. Add the garlic and rice and cook, stirring, for about 2 minutes until the rice is well coated with the oil.

4 Gradually stir the stock into the rice, then add the mushroom and pancetta or bacon mixture and the tarragon. Season with salt and pepper. Bring to the boil.

5 Remove from the heat and transfer a casserole.

6 Cover and bake in a preheated ove 180°C/350°F/Gas Mark 4, for abou 20 minutes until the rice is almost tend and most of the liquid is absorbed. Uncov and stir in the Parmesan. Continue to bak for about 15 minutes longer until the ri is tender, but still firm to the bite. Serve once with extra Parmesan for sprinkling.

Jamaican Rice and Peas

A favourite Caribbean dish, this was probably originally made with pigeon peas, but you can use any dried bean you like.

NUTRITIONAL INFORMATION

Calories	482	Sugars	........11g
Protein	........19g	Fat	...........8g
Carbohydrate	...89g	Saturates	.......2g

🍲 8 hrs   🕐 2–3 hrs

SERVES 6–8

I N G R E D I E N T S

450 g/1 lb dried beans, such as black-eyed beans, black beans or small red kidney beans, soaked in cold water overnight

2 tbsp vegetable oil

1 large onion, chopped

2–3 garlic cloves, finely chopped

2 fresh red chillies, deseeded and chopped

450 g/1 lb long grain white rice

400 ml/14 fl oz canned coconut milk

½ tsp dried thyme

salt

TOMATO SALSA

4 ripe tomatoes, deseeded and cut into 5 mm/¼ inch dice

1 red onion, finely chopped

4 tbsp chopped fresh coriander

2 garlic cloves, finely chopped

1–2 jalapeño chillies, deseeded and thinly sliced

1–2 tbsp extra virgin olive oil

1 tbsp fresh lime juice

1 tsp light brown sugar

salt and pepper

1 Drain the beans, rinse and put in a large pan. Cover with cold water by about 5 cm/2 inches and bring to the boil over a high heat, skimming off any foam.

2 Boil the beans vigorously for about 10 minutes, then drain and rinse. Return to the pan, cover with cold water and bring to the boil over a high heat.

3 Reduce the heat, partially cover and simmer for 1¼–1½ hours for black-eyed beans, 1½–2 hours for black beans or 50–60 minutes for kidney beans, until tender. Drain, reserving the cooking liquid.

4 Heat the oil in another pan. Cook the onion for about 2 minutes. Stir in the garlic and chillies and cook for a further minute. Add the rice and stir until coated.

5 Stir in the coconut milk, thyme and 1 teaspoon salt. Add the cooked beans and 450 ml/16 fl oz of the reserved bean cooking liquid to cover. Bring the mixture to the boil, then reduce the heat to low, cover tightly and cook for 20–25 minutes.

6 Meanwhile, make the tomato salsa. Combine all the ingredients in a bowl, cover and set aside at room temperature.

7 Remove the rice from the heat and stand, covered, for 5 minutes, then fork into a warmed serving bowl. Serve hot with the tomato salsa.

Creole Jambalaya

This rich, rice-based stew combines a fabulous mix of meat and seafood with exciting peppery flavourings of Creole cuisine.

NUTRITIONAL INFORMATION

Calories 424   Sugars 8g
Protein ....31g   Fat 11g
Carbohydrate ...54g   Saturates 2g

15 mins   45 mins

SERVES 6–8

INGREDIENTS

2 tbsp vegetable oil

85 g/3 oz smoked ham, cut into bite-size pieces

85 g/3 oz andouille or other smoked pork sausage, cut into chunks

2 large onions, finely chopped

3–4 celery sticks, finely chopped

2 green peppers, deseeded and diced

2 garlic cloves, finely chopped

225 g/8 oz skinless boneless chicken breast or thighs, cut into pieces

4 ripe tomatoes, peeled and chopped

175 ml/6 fl oz passata

450 ml/16 fl oz fish stock

400 g/14 oz long grain white rice

4 spring onions, thickly sliced

250 g/9 oz peeled raw prawns

250 g/9 oz cooked white crab meat

12 oysters, shelled , with their liquor

SEASONING MIX

2 dried bay leaves

1 tsp salt

1½–2 tsp cayenne pepper

1½ tsp dried oregano

1 tsp ground white pepper

1 tsp black pepper

1 To make the seasoning mix, combine all the ingredients in a bowl.

2 Heat the oil in a flameproof casserole over a medium heat. Add the ham and sausage and cook for 8 minutes, stirring frequently, until golden. Using a draining spoon, transfer to a large plate.

3 Add the onions, celery and peppers to the casserole and cook for about 4 minutes until just softened. Stir in the garlic, then remove and set aside.

4 Add the chicken to the casserole and cook for 3–4 minutes until beginning to colour. Stir in the seasoning mix to coa Return the ham, sausage and vegetables t the casserole and stir to combine. Add th tomatoes and passata, then pour in th stock. Bring to the boil.

5 Stir in the rice, reduce the heat an simmer for about 12 minutes. Stir i the spring onions and prawns, cover agai and cook for 4 minutes.

6 Gently stir in the crab meat an oysters with their liquor. Cook unt the rice is just tender. Remove from th heat and leave to stand, covered, for abou 3 minutes before serving.

Murgh Pullau

In India, the meat and rice are cooked together for ease of preparation, but here they are cooked separately to ensure perfect timing.

NUTRITIONAL INFORMATION

Calories 850	Sugars 14g	
Protein 44g	Fat 47g	
Carbohydrate . . .63g	Saturates 20g	

 15 mins   ⏱ 50 mins

SERVES 4–6

INGREDIENTS

50 g/12 oz basmati rice

tbsp ghee or butter

15 g/4 oz flaked almonds

5 g/3 oz unsalted, shelled pistachio nuts

–6 skinless boneless chicken breasts, each cut into 4 pieces

onions, thinly sliced

garlic cloves, finely chopped

bay leaves

.5 cm/1 inch piece fresh root ginger, chopped

green cardamom pods, lightly crushed

–6 cloves

tsp ground coriander

tsp cayenne pepper

25 ml/8 fl oz natural yogurt

25 ml/8 fl oz double cream

–4 tbsp chopped fresh coriander or mint

25 g/8 oz seedless green grapes, halved if large

alt and pepper

1 Bring a pan of salted water to the boil. Gradually pour in the rice, return to the boil, then simmer until the rice is just tender. Drain and rinse under cold running water. Set aside.

2 Meanwhile, heat the ghee in a deep frying pan over a medium heat. Add the nuts and cook, stirring constantly, for 3 minutes until golden. Remove from the pan and set aside.

3 Add the chicken to the pan and cook for about 5 minutes, turning, until golden. Remove from the pan. Add the onions to the pan. Cook for 10 minutes until golden. Stir in the garlic, bay leaf and spices and cook for 3 minutes.

4 Add 2–3 tablespoons of the yogurt and cook, stirring constantly, until all the moisture evaporates. Continue adding the remaining yogurt in the same way until it is all incorporated.

5 Return the chicken and nuts to the pan and stir to coat. Stir in 125 ml/ 4 fl oz boiling water. Season with salt and pepper, cover and cook over a low heat for about 10 minutes until the chicken is cooked through. Stir in the cream, coriander and grapes and remove the pan from the heat.

6 Fork the rice into a bowl, then gently fold in the chicken and sauce. Stand for 5 minutes before serving.

Singapore Noodles

This is a special and well-known dish, which is a delicious meal in itself, packed with chicken, prawns and vegetables.

NUTRITIONAL INFORMATION

Calories	627	Sugars	.........3g
Protein	........44g	Fat	..........32g
Carbohydrate	...44g	Saturates	.......4g

 5 mins   🕐 20 mins

SERVES 4

I N G R E D I E N T S

225 g/8 oz dried egg noodles

6 tbsp vegetable oil

4 eggs, beaten

3 garlic cloves, crushed

1½ tsp chilli powder

225 g/8 oz skinless, boneless chicken, cut into thin strips

3 celery sticks, sliced

1 green pepper, deseeded and sliced

4 spring onions, sliced

25 g/1 oz water chestnuts, quartered

2 fresh red chillies, sliced

300 g/10 oz peeled, cooked prawns

175 g/6 oz beansprouts

2 tsp sesame oil

1 Soak the noodles in boiling water for 4 minutes or until soft. Set aside to drain on kitchen paper.

2 Heat 2 tablespoons of the oil in a preheated wok. Add the eggs and stir until set. Remove the cooked eggs from the wok, set aside and keep warm.

3 Add the remaining oil to the wok. Add the garlic and chilli powder and stir-fry for 30 seconds.

4 Add the chicken and stir-fry for 4–5 minutes until beginning to brown.

5 Stir in the celery, green pepper, spring onions, water chestnuts and chillies and cook for a further 8 minutes or until the chicken is cooked through.

6 Add the prawns and the reserved noodles to the wok, together with the beansprouts, and toss to mix well.

7 Break the cooked egg with a fork and sprinkle it over the noodles, then sprinkle the sesame oil over the noodles. Serve immediately.

COOK'S TIP

When mixing pre-cooked ingredients into the dish, such as the egg and noodles, ensure that they are heated right through and are hot when ready to serve.

Steak & Bean Salad

The Californian influence on Mexican food is evident in this big, hearty salad. Packed with delicious ingredients, it is a meal in itself.

NUTRITIONAL INFORMATION

Calories . . . . . . .498 Sugars 12g
Protein . . . . .29g Fat 27g
Carbohydrate . . .38g Saturates 6g

  25 mins   4–6 mins

SERVES 4

INGREDIENTS

350 g/12 oz tender steak, such as sirloin or filet

4 garlic cloves, chopped

juice of 1 lime

4 tbsp extra virgin olive oil

1 tbsp white or red wine vinegar

¼ tsp mild chilli powder

¼ tsp ground cumin

½ tsp paprika

pinch of sugar (optional)

6 spring onions, thinly sliced

about 200 g/7 oz crisp lettuce leaves, such as cos, or mixed herb leaves

225 g/8 oz can sweetcorn, drained

400 g/14 oz can pinto, black or red kidney beans, rinsed and drained

1 avocado, stoned, sliced and tossed with a little lime juice

2 ripe tomatoes, diced

¼ fresh green or red chilli, chopped

3 tbsp chopped fresh coriander

generous handful of crisp tortilla chips, broken into pieces

salt and pepper

1 Place the steak in a non-metallic dish with the garlic, half the lime juice and half the olive oil. Season with salt and pepper, cover with clingfilm, then set aside to marinate for at least 15 minutes, preferably longer.

2 To make the dressing, combine the remaining lime juice with the rest of the olive oil, the vinegar, chilli powder, cumin and paprika. Add sugar to taste, if wished. Set aside.

3 Pan fry the steak or cook under a preheated grill until browned on the outside and cooked to your liking in the middle. Remove from the pan, cut into strips and set aside. Keep warm or allow to cool, according to taste.

4 Toss the spring onions with the lettuce and arrange on a serving platter. Pour about half the dressing over the leaves, then arrange the sweetcorn, beans, avocado and tomatoes over the top. Sprinkle with the chilli and chopped fresh coriander.

5 Arrange the steak and the tortilla chips on top, pour over the rest of the dressing, and serve immediately.

Thai Potato Crab Cakes

These small crab cakes are based on a traditional Thai recipe. They make a delicious snack when served with this sweet and sour cucumber sauce.

NUTRITIONAL INFORMATION

Calories	254	Sugars	........9g
Protein	........12g	Fat	..........6g
Carbohydrate	...40g	Saturates	......1g

10 mins   30 mins

SERVES 4

INGREDIENTS

450 g/1 lb floury potatoes, diced

175 g/6 oz white crab meat, drained if canned

4 spring onions, chopped

1 tsp light soy sauce

½ tsp sesame oil

1 tsp chopped lemon grass

1 tsp lime juice

3 tbsp plain flour

2 tbsp vegetable oil

salt and pepper

SAUCE

4 tbsp finely chopped cucumber

2 tbsp clear honey

1 tbsp garlic wine vinegar

½ tsp light soy sauce

1 chopped fresh red chilli

TO GARNISH

1 fresh red chilli, sliced

cucumber slices

1 Cook the diced potatoes in a saucepan of boiling water for 10 minutes until cooked through. Drain well and mash.

2 Mix the crab meat into the potato with the spring onions, soy sauce, sesame oil, lemon grass, lime juice and flour. Season with salt and pepper.

3 Divide the crab and potato mixture into 8 equal portions and shape them into small rounds, using floured hands.

4 Heat the oil in a wok or frying pan and cook the cakes, in batches of 4 at a time, for 5–7 minutes, turning once.

Remove from the pan with a fish slice and keep warm.

5 Meanwhile, make the sauce. In a small serving bowl, mix the cucumber, honey, vinegar, soy sauce and chilli.

6 Garnish the cakes with the sliced red chilli and cucumber slices and serve with the sauce.

Red Mullet & Coconut Loaf

This fish and coconut loaf is ideal to take along on picnics, because it can be served cold as well as hot.

NUTRITIONAL INFORMATION

Calories 138	Sugars 12g
Protein 11g	Fat 1g
Carbohydrate ...23g	Saturates 0g

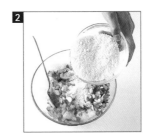

15 mins   1¼ hours

SERVES 4–6

I N G R E D I E N T S

225 g/8 oz red mullet fillets, skinned

tomatoes, deseeded and finely chopped

green peppers, finely chopped

onion, finely chopped

fresh red chilli, finely chopped

150 g/5½ oz breadcrumbs

600 ml/1 pint coconut liquid

salt and pepper

H O T   P E P P E R   S A U C E

125 ml/4 fl oz tomato ketchup

tsp West Indian hot pepper sauce

tsp hot mustard

T O   G A R N I S H

lemon twists

fresh chervil sprigs

1 Finely chop the fish and mix with the tomatoes, peppers, onion and chilli.

2 Stir in the breadcrumbs, coconut liquid and seasoning. If using fresh coconut, use a hammer and screwdriver or the tip of a sturdy knife to poke out the three 'eyes' in the top of the coconut and pour out the liquid.

3 Grease and base line a 500 g/1 lb 2 oz loaf tin and add the fish mixture.

4 Bake in a preheated oven, 200°C/ 400°F/ Gas Mark 6, for 1–1¼ hours until set.

5 To make the hot pepper sauce, mix together the tomato ketchup, hot pepper sauce and mustard until smooth and creamy.

6 To serve, cut the loaf into slices, garnish with lemon twists and chervil and serve hot or cold with the sauce.

COOK'S TIP

Be careful when preparing chillies because the juices can irritate the skin, especially the face. Wash your hands after handling them or wear clean rubber gloves to prepare them if preferred.

Migas

A wonderful brunch or late-night supper dish, this is made
by scrambling eggs with chillies, tomatoes and crisp tortilla chips.

NUTRITIONAL INFORMATION

Calories 441	Sugars 5g
Protein 22g	Fat 20g
Carbohydrate ...46g	Saturates 8g

 10 mins   10–12 mins

SERVES 4

INGREDIENTS

2 tbsp butter

6 garlic cloves, finely chopped

1 fresh green chilli, such as jalapeño or
serrano, deseeded and diced

1½ tsp ground cumin

6 ripe tomatoes, coarsely chopped

8 eggs, lightly beaten

8–10 corn tortillas, cut into strips and fried
until crisp, or an equal quantity of
tortilla chips

4 tbsp chopped fresh coriander

3–4 spring onions, thinly sliced

mild chilli powder, to garnish

VARIATION

Add browned minced beef or pork to
the softly scrambling egg mixture at
Step 3. A bunch of cooked, chopped,
spinach or chard can be stirred in
as well, to add fresh colour.

1 Melt half the butter in a pan. Add the
garlic and chilli and cook until
softened, but not browned. Add the cumin
and cook for 30 seconds, stirring
constantly, then add the tomatoes and
cook over a medium heat for a further
3–4 minutes, or until the tomato juices
have evaporated. Remove from the pan
and set aside.

2 Melt the remaining butter in a frying
pan over a low heat and pour in the
beaten eggs. Cook, stirring constantly,
until the eggs begin to set.

3 Add the chilli and tomato mixture,
stirring gently to mix into the eggs.

4 Carefully add the tortilla strips or
chips and continue cooking, stirring
once or twice, until the eggs are the
consistency you wish. The tortillas should
be pliable and chewy.

5 Transfer to a warmed serving platter
and surround with the chopped fresh
coriander and spring onions. Garnish with
a sprinkling of mild chilli powder and serve
immediately.

Eggs Oaxaca Style

Cooking an omelette, then cutting it into strips and simmering them in a spicy sauce makes an unusual dish for brunch or dinner.

NUTRITIONAL INFORMATION

Calories	260	Sugars	.........9g
Protein	........19g	Fat	..........16g
Carbohydrate	...10g	Saturates	.......4g

15 mins   15 mins

SERVES 4

INGREDIENTS

kg/2 lb 4 oz ripe tomatoes

bout 12 small button onions, halved

garlic cloves, unpeeled

fresh mild green chillies

nch of ground cumin

nch of dried oregano,

nch of sugar (optional)

–3 tsp vegetable oil

eggs, lightly beaten

–2 tbsp tomato purée

alt and pepper

–2 tbsp chopped fresh coriander,
  to garnish

1 Heat an ungreased, heavy-based frying pan, add the tomatoes and char ghtly, turning them once or twice. emove from the pan and set aside to cool.

2 Meanwhile lightly char the onions, garlic and chillies in the pan. Remove om the pan and set aside to cool slightly.

3 Cut the cooled tomatoes into pieces and place in a blender or food rocessor, with their charred skins.

4 Remove the stems and seeds from the chillies, then peel and chop. Remove

the skins from the garlic, then chop. Roughly chop the onions. Add the chillies, garlic and onions to the tomatoes.

5 Process to make a coarse purée, then add the cumin and oregano. Season with salt and pepper to taste and add sugar if necessary.

6 Heat the oil in a non-stick frying pan, add a ladleful of beaten eggs and cook to make a thin omelette. Continue to

make omelettes, stacking them on a plate as they are cooked. Slice the omelettes into noodle-like ribbons.

7 Bring the sauce to the boil, adjust the seasoning and add tomato purée to taste. Add the omelette strips, warm through and serve immediately, garnished with a sprinkling of fresh coriander.

Eggs with Refried Beans

In the Yucatan, this classic dish would be sandwiched between two crisp tortillas, but layering it all on top of one tortilla looks much more festive.

NUTRITIONAL INFORMATION

Calories	.661	Sugars	.13g
Protein	.35g	Fat	.29g
Carbohydrate	.66g	Saturates	.10g

  15 mins   25 mins

SERVES 4

INGREDIENTS

400 g/14 oz tomatoes, peeled and chopped

1 onion, chopped

1 garlic clove, finely chopped

½ fresh green chilli, such as jalapeño or serrano, deseeded and chopped

¼ tsp ground cumin

2 tbsp extra virgin olive oil

1 tbsp butter

1 plantain, peeled and diced

4 corn tortillas, warmed or fried crisply into a tostada

about 400 g/14 oz can refried beans, warmed with 2 tbsp of water

2 tbsp water

4 eggs

1 red pepper, grilled, peeled, deseeded and cut into strips

3–4 tbsp cooked green peas, cooled

4–6 tbsp diced cooked or smoked ham

50–75 g/2–3 oz crumbled feta cheese

3 spring onions, thinly sliced

salt and pepper

1 Put the tomatoes in a blender or food processor with the onion, garlic, chilli, cumin, salt and pepper and process to a purée.

2 Heat the oil in a heavy-based frying pan , then ladle in a little of the tomato mixture and cook until it reduces in volume and becomes almost paste-like. Continue adding and reducing the tomato mixture in this way. Keep warm.

3 Melt the butter in a heavy-based non-stick frying pan. Add the plantain and cook over a medium heat, stirring frequently, until browned. Remove the plantain and set aside. Spread the tortillas with the refried beans and keep warm in a low oven.

4 Add the water to the non-stick frying pan, break in an egg and cook until the white is set but the yolk is still soft. Remove from the pan and place on top of 1 tortilla. Cook the remaining eggs in the same way, adding them to the remaining tortillas.

5 To serve, spoon the warm sauce around the eggs on each tortilla. Sprinkle the diced plantain, pepper, peas, ham, feta cheese and spring onions over the top. Season with salt and pepper to taste and serve immediately.

Spicy Meat & Chipotle Hash

This speciality from the Puebla in Mexico makes divine soft tacos: simply serve with a stack of warm corn tortillas and let everyone roll their own.

NUTRITIONAL INFORMATION

Calories 210	Sugars 3g	
Protein 26g	Fat 10g	
Carbohydrate 4g	Saturates 4g	

10 mins

15–20 mins

SERVES 6

I N G R E D I E N T S

tbsp vegetable oil

onion, finely chopped

50 g/1 lb leftover cooked meat, cooled and cut into thin strips

tbsp mild chilli powder

ripe tomatoes, deseeded and diced

bout 225 ml/8 fl oz meat stock

–1 canned chipotle chilli, mashed, plus a little of the adobo sauce, or a dash of chipotle salsa

25 ml/4 fl oz soured cream

–6 tbsp chopped fresh coriander

–6 tbsp chopped radishes

–4 leaves crisp lettuce, shredded

1 Heat the oil in a frying pan , add the onion and cook over a low heat, tirring occasionally, for 5 minutes until oftened. Add the meat and sauté, stirring requently, for about 3 minutes, until ghtly browned.

2 Add the chilli powder, tomatoes and stock and cook, mashing the meat ently, until the tomatoes have isintegrated and reduced to a sauce.

3 Add the chipotle chilli or salsa and continue to cook and mash until the sauce and meat are nearly blended.

4 Serve the dish with a stack of warmed corn tortillas so that people can fill them with the meaty mixture to make tacos. Also serve soured cream, chopped fresh coriander, radishes and shredded lettuce for each person to add to the meat.

COOK'S TIP

Avocados add an interesting texture contrast to the spicy meat – serve with 2 sliced avocados, tossed with lime juice. Try serving on top of tostada, crisply fried tortillas, instead of wrapping taco-style.

Pad Thai Noodles

The combination of ingredients in this classic noodle dish varies, but it commonly contains a mixture of pork and prawns or other seafood.

NUTRITIONAL INFORMATION

Calories 477	Sugars 6g	
Protein 26g	Fat 14g	
Carbohydrate ...60g	Saturates 3g	

  10 mins   5 mins

SERVES 4

INGREDIENTS

250 g/9 oz rice stick noodles

3 tbsp groundnut oil

3 garlic cloves, finely chopped

115 g/4 oz pork fillet, chopped into
   5 mm/1/4 inch pieces

200 g/7 oz peeled, cooked prawns

1 tbsp sugar

3 tbsp Thai fish sauce

1 tbsp tomato ketchup

1 tbsp lime juice

2 eggs, beaten

115 g/4 oz beansprouts

TO GARNISH

1 tsp dried red chilli flakes

2 spring onions, thickly sliced

2 tbsp chopped fresh coriander

1 Soak the rice noodles in hot water for about 10 minutes or according to the packet instructions. Drain thoroughly and set aside.

2 Heat the groundnut oil in a large frying pan or wok, add the garlic and fry over a high heat for 30 seconds. Add the pork and stir-fry for 2–3 minutes until browned all over.

3 Stir in the prawns, then add the sugar, fish sauce, ketchup and lime juice, and continue stir-frying for a further 30 seconds.

4 Stir in the eggs and stir-fry until lightly set. Stir in the noodles, then add the beansprouts and stir-fry for a further 30 seconds to cook lightly.

5 Turn out on to a warm serving dish and scatter with chilli flakes, spring onions and coriander. Serve hot.

COOK'S TI
Drain the rice noodle
before adding them to th
pan, as excess moisture wi
spoil the texture of the dish

Noodles with Mushrooms

An alternative to classic dishes such as Pad Thai Noodles (see page 362), this quick and easy dish is very filling.

NUTRITIONAL INFORMATION

Calories	361	Sugars	.........3g
Protein	.........9g	Fat	.........12g
Carbohydrate	...53g	Saturates	.......2g

20 mins   8–10 mins

SERVES 4

INGREDIENTS

225 g/8 oz rice stick noodles

2 tbsp groundnut oil

1 garlic clove, finely chopped

2 cm/¾ inch piece fresh root ginger, finely chopped

4 shallots, thinly sliced

70 g/2½ oz shiitake mushrooms, sliced

100 g/3½ oz firm tofu, cut into 1.5 cm/ ⅝ inch dice

2 tbsp light soy sauce

1 tbsp rice wine

1 tbsp Thai fish sauce

1 tbsp smooth peanut butter

1 tsp chilli sauce

2 tbsp toasted peanuts, chopped

shredded fresh basil leaves, to serve

1 Soak the rice stick noodles in hot water for 15 minutes or according to the package directions. Drain well.

2 Heat the groundnut oil in a pan. Add the garlic, ginger and shallots and stir-fry for 1–2 minutes until softened and lightly browned.

3 Add the mushrooms and stir-fry over a medium heat for a further 2–3 minutes. Stir in the tofu and toss gently to brown lightly.

4 Mix together the soy sauce, rice wine, fish sauce, peanut butter and chilli sauce, then stir into the pan.

5 Stir in the rice noodles and toss to coat evenly in the sauce. Scatter with peanuts and shredded basil leaves and serve hot.

COOK'S TIP

For an easy store-cupboard dish, replace the shiitake mushrooms with a can of Chinese straw mushrooms. Alternatively, use dried shiitake mushrooms, soaked and drained before use.

Drunken Noodles

Perhaps this would be more correctly named 'drunkards' noodles', because it's a dish that is supposedly often eaten as a hangover cure.

NUTRITIONAL INFORMATION

Calories	278	Sugars	.........3g
Protein	........12g	Fat	...........7g
Carbohydrate	...40g	Saturates	.......1g

20 mins   8–10 mins

SERVES 4

INGREDIENTS

175 g/6 oz rice stick noodles

2 tbsp vegetable oil

1 garlic clove, crushed

2 small fresh green chillies, chopped

1 small onion, thinly sliced

150 g/5½ oz lean minced pork or chicken

1 small green pepper, deseeded and
   finely chopped

4 kaffir lime leaves, finely shredded

1 tbsp dark soy sauce

1 tbsp light soy sauce

½ tsp sugar

1 tomato, cut into thin wedges

2 tbsp fresh sweet basil leaves, finely
   shredded, to garnish

1 Soak the rice stick noodles in hot water for 15 minutes or according to the package directions. Drain well.

2 Heat the oil in a wok and stir-fry the garlic, chillies and onion for 1 minute.

3 Stir in the pork or chicken and stir-fry over a high heat for a further minute, then add the green pepper and continue stir-frying for a further 2 minutes.

4 Stir in the lime leaves, soy sauces and sugar. Add the noodles and tomato and toss well to heat thoroughly.

5 Sprinkle with the sliced basil leaves and serve hot.

COOK'S TIP

Fresh kaffir lime leaves freeze well, so if you buy more than you need, simply tie them in a tightly sealed plastic freezer bag and freeze for up to a month. They can be used straight from the freezer.

Rice Noodles with Spinach

This quick stir-fried noodle dish is simple to prepare, and makes a delicious light lunch in minutes.

NUTRITIONAL INFORMATION

Calories	159	Sugars	.........3g
Protein	.........8g	Fat	...........2g
Carbohydrate	...27g	Saturates	.......0g

🍳 20 mins   🕐 6–8 mins

SERVES 4

INGREDIENTS

115 g/4 oz thin rice stick noodles

2 tbsp dried shrimp (optional)

250 g/9 oz baby spinach

1 tbsp groundnut oil

2 garlic cloves, finely chopped

2 tsp Thai green curry paste

1 tsp sugar

1 tbsp light soy sauce

1 Soak the noodles in hot water for 15 minutes or according to the package directions, then drain well.

2 Put the dried shrimp in a bowl and add hot water to cover. Set aside to soak for 10 minutes, then drain well.

3 Wash the baby spinach thoroughly, drain well and pat dry. Remove any tough stalks.

4 Heat the oil in a large frying pan or wok and stir-fry the garlic for 1 minute. Stir in the curry paste and stir-fry for 30 seconds. Stir in the soaked shrimp and stir-fry for 30 seconds.

5 Add the spinach and stir-fry for 1–2 minutes until the leaves are just wilted.

6 Stir in the sugar and soy sauce, then add the noodles and toss thoroughly to mix evenly. Serve immediately.

COOK'S TIP

It is best to choose young spinach leaves for this dish, as they are beautifully tender and cook within a matter of seconds. If you can only get older spinach, however, shred the leaves before adding to the dish so they cook more quickly.

Stir-fried Rice with Egg

Many Thai rice dishes are made from leftover rice that has been cooked for an earlier meal. Any leftover vegetables or meat can be used too.

NUTRITIONAL INFORMATION

Calories 334   Sugars 49g
Protein ....7g   Fat 9g
Carbohydrate ...60g   Saturates 1g

5–10 mins   5 mins

SERVES 4

I N G R E D I E N T S

2 tbsp groundnut oil

1 egg, beaten with 1 tsp water

1 garlic clove, finely chopped

1 small onion, finely chopped

1 tbsp Thai red curry paste

250 g/9 oz long grain rice, cooked

55 g/2 oz cooked peas

1 tbsp Thai fish sauce

2 tbsp tomato ketchup

2 tbsp chopped fresh coriander

TO GARNISH

fresh red chillies

cucumber slices

1 To make chilli flowers for the garnish, hold the stem of each chilli with your fingertips and use a small sharp, pointed knife to cut a slit down the length from near the stem end to the tip. Turn the chilli about a quarter turn and make another cut. Repeat to make a total of 4 cuts, then scrape out the seeds. Cut each 'petal' again, in half or into quarters, to make 8–16 petals. Place the chilli in iced water.

2 Heat about 1 teaspoon of the oil in a wok. Pour in the egg mixture, swirling it to coat the pan evenly and make a thin layer. When set and golden, remove the egg from the pan and roll up. Set aside.

3 Add the remaining oil to the wok and stir-fry the garlic and onion for 1 minute. Add the curry paste, then stir in the rice and peas. Stir until heated through.

4 Stir in the fish sauce, ketchup and coriander. Remove the wok from the heat and pile the rice on to a warmed serving dish.

5 Slice the egg roll into spiral strips, without unrolling, and use to garnish the rice. Add the cucumber slices and chilli flowers. Serve hot.

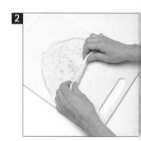

Crêpes with Curried Crab

Home-made crêpes are delicious – here, white crab meat is lightly flavoured with curry spices and tossed in a low-fat dressing.

NUTRITIONAL INFORMATION

Calories	279	Sugars	.........9g
Protein	........25g	Fat	..........7g
Carbohydrate	...31g	Saturates	......1g

40 mins   25 mins

SERVES 4

INGREDIENTS

115 g/4 oz buckwheat flour

1 large egg, beaten

300 ml/10 fl oz skimmed milk

125 g/4½ oz frozen spinach, thawed, well drained and chopped

2 tsp vegetable oil

FILLING

350 g/12 oz white crab meat

1 tsp mild curry powder

1 tbsp mango chutney

1 tbsp reduced-calorie mayonnaise

2 tbsp low-fat natural yogurt

2 tbsp chopped fresh coriander

TO SERVE

green salad

lemon wedges

1 Sift the flour into a bowl. Make a well in the centre of the flour and add the egg. Whisk in the milk, then blend in the spinach. Transfer to a jug and set aside for 30 minutes.

2 To make the filling, combine all the ingredients, except the coriander, in a bowl, cover and chill until required. Whisk the batter. Brush a small crêpe pan with a little oil, heat until hot and pour in enough batter to cover the base thinly. Cook for 1–2 minutes, flip over and cook for 1 minute until golden. Make 7 more crêpes, layering them on a plate with baking paper.

3 Stir the coriander into the crab mixture. Fold each crêpe into quarters. Open 1 fold and fill with the crab mixture. Serve warm, with a green salad and lemon wedges.

VARIATION

Try lean diced chicken in a light white sauce or peeled prawns instead of the crab.

Spicy Chickpea Snack

You can use dried chickpeas, soaked overnight, for this popular Indian snack, but the canned variety is just as flavoursome.

NUTRITIONAL INFORMATION

Calories 190   Sugars 4g
Protein ....9g   Fat 3g
Carbohydrate ...34g   Saturates 0.3g

5 mins   5 mins

SERVES 4

INGREDIENTS

2 medium potatoes

1 medium onion

400 g/14 oz can chickpeas, drained

2 tbsp tamarind paste

6 tbsp water

1 tsp chilli powder

2 tsp sugar

salt and pepper

TO GARNISH

1 tomato, sliced

2 fresh green chillies, chopped

fresh coriander leaves

1 Using a sharp knife, cut the potatoes into dice. Place them in a saucepan, add water just to cover and bring to the boil. Cover and simmer over a medium heat for 10 minutes until cooked through. Test by inserting the tip of a knife into the potatoes – they should feel soft and tender. Drain and set aside.

2 Using a sharp knife, finely chop the onion. Set aside until required. Put the chickpeas into a bowl.

3 Combine the tamarind paste and water. Add the chilli powder, sugar and 1 teaspoon salt and mix again. Pour the mixture over the chickpeas.

4 Add the onion and the diced potatoes to the chickpeas, and stir to mix. Season to taste with pepper.

5 Transfer to a serving bowl and garnish with tomatoes, chillies and coriander leaves.

COOK'S TIP

Chickpeas have a nutty flavour and slightly crunchy texture. Indian cooks also grind these to make a flour called gram or besan, which is used to make breads, thicken sauces, and to make batters for deep-fried dishes.

Potato & Mushroom Bake

Use any mixture of mushrooms for this creamy layered bake.
It can be served straight from the dish in which it is cooked.

NUTRITIONAL INFORMATION

Calories	304	Sugars 2g
Protein	.........4g	Fat 24g
Carbohydrate	...20g	Saturates 15g

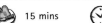

🕑 15 mins   ⏱ 1 hr

SERVES 4

INGREDIENTS

2 tbsp butter

500 g/1 lb 2 oz waxy potatoes, thinly sliced

150 g/5½ oz sliced mixed mushrooms

1 tbsp chopped fresh rosemary

4 tbsp chopped fresh chives

2 garlic cloves, crushed

150 ml/5 fl oz double cream

salt and pepper

snipped chives, to garnish

1 Grease a shallow round ovenproof dish with the butter.

2 Parboil the potatoes in a saucepan of boiling water for 10 minutes. Drain well. Layer a quarter of the potatoes in the base of the dish.

3 Arrange about a quarter of the mushrooms in a layer on top of the potatoes and sprinkle with a quarter each of the rosemary, chopped chives and garlic. Continue making layers in the same order, finishing with a layer of potatoes on top.

4 Pour the cream over the top of the potatoes. Season to taste with salt and pepper.

5 Cook in a preheated oven, 190°C/ 375°F/Gas Mark 5, for about 45 minutes or until the bake is golden brown and piping hot.

6 Garnish with snipped chives and serve immediately straight from the dish.

COOK'S TIP

For a special occasion, the bake may be made in a lined cake tin and then turned out to serve.

Cranberry Turkey Burgers

This recipe is bound to be popular with children and is very easy to prepare for their supper or tea.

NUTRITIONAL INFORMATION

Calories	209	Sugars	........15g
Protein	........22g	Fat	...........5g
Carbohydrate	...21g	Saturates	......1g

45 mins   25 mins

SERVES 4

INGREDIENTS

350 g/12 oz lean minced turkey

1 onion, finely chopped

1 tbsp chopped fresh sage

6 tbsp dry white breadcrumbs

4 tbsp cranberry sauce

1 egg white, lightly beaten

2 tsp sunflower oil

salt and pepper

TO SERVE

4 toasted Granary or wholemeal
   burger buns

½ lettuce, shredded

4 tomatoes, sliced

4 tsp cranberry sauce

COOK'S TIP

Look out for a variety of ready minced meats at your butchers or supermarket. If unavailable, you can mince your own by choosing lean cuts and processing them in a blender or food processor.

1 Combine the turkey, onion, sage, breadcrumbs and cranberry sauce and season to taste with salt and pepper, then bind with egg white.

2 Press into 4 x 10 cm/4 inch rounds, about 2 cm/¾ inch thick. Chill the burgers for 30 minutes.

3 Line a grill rack with baking parchment, making sure the ends are secured underneath the rack to ensure they don't catch fire. Place the burgers on top and brush lightly with oil. Put under a preheated moderate grill and cook for 10 minutes. Turn the burgers over, brush again with oil. Cook for a further 12–15 minutes until cooked through.

4 Fill the burger buns with lettuce, tomato and a burger and top with cranberry sauce.

Rice & Tuna Peppers

Grilled mixed sweet peppers are filled with tender tuna, sweetcorn, nutty brown and wild rice and grated, reduced-fat cheese.

NUTRITIONAL INFORMATION

Calories 332	Sugars 13g
Protein 27g	Fat 8g
Carbohydrate . . .42g	Saturates 4g

10 mins   50–60 mins

SERVES 4

I N G R E D I E N T S

50 g/2 oz wild rice

50 g/2 oz brown rice

4 assorted medium peppers

200 g/7 oz can tuna fish in brine, drained and flaked

325 g/11½ oz can sweetcorn kernels, drained

100 g/3½ oz reduced-fat mature Cheddar cheese, grated

1 bunch fresh basil leaves, shredded

2 tbsp dry white breadcrumbs

1 tbsp freshly grated Parmesan cheese

salt and pepper

fresh basil leaves, to garnish

crisp salad leaves, to serve

1 Place the wild rice and brown rice in different pans, cover with boiling water and bring back to the boil. Cook for about 40–50 minutes or according to the instructions on the packet. Drain the rice well.

2 Meanwhile, preheat the grill to medium. Halve the peppers, remove the seeds and stalks and arrange the peppers on the grill rack, cut side down. Cook for 5 minutes, turn over and cook for a further 4–5 minutes.

3 Transfer the cooked rice to a large bowl and add the flaked tuna and drained sweetcorn. Gently fold in the grated cheese. Stir the basil leaves into the rice mixture and season with salt and pepper to taste.

4 Divide the tuna and rice mixture into 8 equal portions. Pile each portion into each cooked pepper half. Mix together the breadcrumbs and Parmesan cheese and sprinkle over each pepper.

5 Place the peppers back under the grill again for 4–5 minutes until hot and golden brown.

6 Serve the peppers immediately, garnished with basil and accompanied with fresh, crisp salad leaves.

Cheese & Ham Savoury

Lean ham wrapped around crisp celery, topped with a light crust of cheese and spring onions, makes a delicious light lunch.

NUTRITIONAL INFORMATION

Calories	188	Sugars	.........5g
Protein	........15g	Fat	..........12g
Carbohydrate	....5g	Saturates	......7g

10 mins   10 mins

SERVES 4

I N G R E D I E N T S

4 celery sticks, with leaves

12 thin slices of lean ham

1 bunch of spring onions

175 g/6 oz low-fat soft cheese with garlic and herbs

6 tbsp low-fat natural yogurt

4 tbsp freshly grated Parmesan cheese

celery salt and pepper

T O   S E R V E

tomato salad

crusty bread

1 Wash the celery, remove the leaves and reserve for the garnish. Slice each celery stick into 3 equal portions.

2 Cut any visible fat off the ham and lay the slices on a chopping board. Place a piece of celery on each piece of ham and roll up. Place 3 ham and celery rolls in each of 4 small, heatproof dishes.

3 Trim the spring onions, then finely shred both the white and green parts. Sprinkle the spring onions over the ham and celery rolls and season with celery salt and pepper.

4 Combine the soft cheese and yogur and spoon the mixture over the har and celery rolls.

5 Preheat the grill to medium. Sprinkl each portion with 1 tablespoon grate Parmesan cheese and grill for 6–7 minute until hot and the cheese has formed crust. If the cheese starts to brown to quickly, lower the grill setting slightly.

6 Garnish with celery leaves and serv with a tomato salad and crusty bread

COOK'S TIP

Parmesan is useful in low-fat recipes because its intense flavour means you need to use only a small amount.

Soufflé Omelette

Sweet cherry tomatoes, mushrooms and peppery rocket leaves make a mouthwatering filling for these light, fluffy omelettes.

NUTRITIONAL INFORMATION

Calories	146	Sugars	.........2g
Protein	........10g	Fat	...........11g
Carbohydrate	....2g	Saturates	......2g

1¼ hours   45 mins

SERVES 4

INGREDIENTS

75 g/6 oz cherry tomatoes

225 g/8 oz mixed mushrooms, such as button, chestnut, shiitake and oyster

4 tbsp vegetable stock

small bunch of fresh thyme

4 eggs, separated

125 ml/4 fl oz water

4 egg whites

4 tsp olive oil

25 g/1 oz rocket leaves

salt and pepper

fresh thyme sprigs, to garnish

1 Halve the tomatoes and place them in a saucepan. Wipe the mushrooms with kitchen paper, trim if necessary and slice if large. Place the mushrooms in the pan with the tomatoes.

2 Add the stock and thyme, still tied together, to the pan. Bring to the boil, cover and simmer for 5–6 minutes until tender. Drain, remove the thyme and discard. Keep the mixture warm.

3 Meanwhile, separate the eggs and whisk the egg yolks with the water until frothy. In a clean, grease-free bowl, whisk the 8 egg whites until stiff and dry.

4 Spoon the egg yolk mixture into the egg whites and, using a metal spoon, fold together until well mixed. Take care not to knock out too much of the air.

5 For each omelette, brush a small omelette pan with 1 teaspoon of the oil and heat until hot. Pour in a quarter of the egg mixture and cook for 4–5 minutes until the mixture has set.

6 Finish cooking the omelette under a preheated medium grill for 2–3 minutes.

7 Transfer the omelette to a warm serving plate. Fill the omelette with a few rocket leaves, and a quarter of the mushroom and tomato mixture. Flip over the top of the omelette, garnish with sprigs of thyme and serve.

Potatoes with a Spicy Filling

Crisp, twice-baked potatoes are partnered with an unusual filling with the Middle Eastern flavours of chickpeas, cumin and coriander.

NUTRITIONAL INFORMATION

Calories 335	Sugars 7g	
Protein 15g	Fat 7g	
Carbohydrate ...57g	Saturates 1g	

 20 mins   1½ hrs

SERVES 4

I N G R E D I E N T S

4 large baking potatoes

1 tbsp vegetable oil, optional

430 g/15½ oz canned chickpeas, drained

1 tsp ground coriander

1 tsp ground cumin

4 tbsp chopped fresh coriander

150 ml/5 fl oz low-fat natural yogurt

salt and pepper

S A L A D

2 tomatoes

4 tbsp chopped fresh coriander

½ cucumber

½ red onion

1 Scrub the potatoes and pat them dry with absorbent kitchen paper. Prick them all over with a fork, brush with oil (if using) and season with salt and pepper.

2 Place the potatoes on a baking sheet and bake in a preheated oven, 200°C/400°F/Gas Mark 6, for 1–11/4 hours or until cooked through. Cool for 10 minutes.

3 Meanwhile, mash the chickpeas with a fork or potato masher. Stir in the ground coriander, cumin and half the fresh coriander. Cover and set aside.

4 Halve the cooked potatoes and scoop the flesh into a bowl, keeping the shells intact. Mash the flesh and gently mix into the chickpea mixture with the yogurt. Season to taste.

5 Fill the potato shells with the potato and chickpea mixture and place on a baking sheet. Return the potatoes to the oven and bake for 10–15 minutes until heated through.

6 Meanwhile, make the salad. Using a sharp knife, chop the tomatoes. Slice the cucumber and cut the red onion into thin slices. Toss all the ingredients together in a serving dish.

7 Serve the potatoes sprinkled with the remaining chopped coriander and the prepared salad.

COOK'S TIP

For an even lower fat version of this recipe, bake the potatoes without oiling them first.

Vegetable Curry

This vegetable curry is quick and easy to prepare and it tastes superb.
A colourful Indian salad and a mint raita make perfect accompaniments.

NUTRITIONAL INFORMATION

Calories ....473 Sugars 18g
Protein ....19g Fat 9g
Carbohydrate ...84g Saturates 1g

10 mins   50 mins

SERVES 4

INGREDIENTS

1 tbsp vegetable oil

2 garlic cloves, crushed

1 onion, chopped

3 celery sticks, sliced

1 apple, chopped

1 tbsp medium curry powder

1 tsp ground ginger

400 g/14 oz can chickpeas, rinsed
and drained

115 g/4 oz dwarf green beans, sliced

225 g/8 oz cauliflower, broken into florets

225 g/8 oz potatoes, cut into cubes

175 g/6 oz mushrooms, sliced

600 ml/1 pint vegetable stock

1 tbsp tomato purée

25 g/1 oz sultanas

175 g/6 oz basmati rice

1 tbsp garam masala

salad, to serve

MINT RAITA

200 ml/7 fl oz low-fat natural yogurt

55 g/2 oz fresh mint leaves, chopped

1 Heat the oil in a large saucepan. Add the garlic, onion, celery and apple and fry over a low heat, stirring occasionally, for 3–4 minutes. Add the curry powder and ginger and cook, stirring constantly, for 1 minute.

2 Add the chickpeas, green beans, cauliflower florets, potatoes, mushrooms, vegetable stock, tomato purée and sultanas and stir well to mix. Bring to the boil, then reduce the heat, cover and simmer for 35–40 minutes.

3 Meanwhile, make the mint raita. Combine the yogurt and mint in a small bowl. Cover with clingfilm and chill in the refrigerator until ready to serve.

4 Cook the rice in boiling, lightly salted water for 20 minutes or according to the instructions on the packet. Drain thoroughly.

5 Just before serving, stir the garam masala into the curry. Divide between 4 warmed serving plates and serve immediately with the rice, mint raita and salad.

Vermicelli with Clam Sauce

This is another cook-in-a-hurry recipe that transforms storecupboard ingredients into a dish with style.

NUTRITIONAL INFORMATION

Calories	392	Sugars	.........2g
Protein	........23g	Fat	..........15g
Carbohydrate	...37g	Saturates	......6g

 5 mins   🕐 20 mins

SERVES 4

INGREDIENTS

400 g/14 oz vermicelli, spaghetti, or other long pasta

2 tbsp butter

salt

fresh basil sprigs, to garnish

2 tbsp flaked Parmesan, to serve

SAUCE

1 tbsp olive oil

2 onions, chopped

2 garlic cloves, chopped

2 x 200 g/7 oz jars clams in brine

125 ml/4 fl oz white wine

4 tbsp chopped parsley

½ tsp dried oregano

pinch of grated nutmeg

pepper

1 Bring a large pan of lightly salted water to the boil. Add the pasta, bring back to the boil and cook for 8–10 minutes until tender, but still firm to the bite. Drain well, return to the pan and add the butter. Cover and shake. Set the pan aside and keep warm.

2 To make the clam sauce, heat the oil in a pan. Add the onion and cook over a low heat, stirring occasionally, for

5 minutes until softened. Stir in the garlic and cook for 1 further minute.

3 Strain the liquid from 1 jar of clams and pour it into the pan. Strain the liquid from the other jar of clams and discard. Reserve the clams.

4 Add the wine to the pan. Bring to simmering point, stirring constantly, and simmer for 3 minutes.

5 Add the clams and herbs to the pan and season to taste with pepper and nutmeg. Lower the heat and cook until the sauce is heated through.

6 Transfer the pasta to a warmed serving platter and pour the clam sauce over it.

7 Garnish with the basil and sprinkle on the Parmesan. Serve hot.

Mushroom Cannelloni

Thick pasta tubes are filled with a mixture of seasoned chopped mushrooms and baked in a rich, fragrant tomato sauce.

NUTRITIONAL INFORMATION

Calories	156	Sugar	.........8g
Protein	.........6g	Fats	...........1g
Carbohydrates	...21g	Saturates	.....0.2g

🧊 35 mins   🕐 1½ hrs

SERVES 4

I N G R E D I E N T S

350 g/12 oz chestnut mushrooms

1 onion, finely chopped

1 garlic clove, crushed

1 tbsp chopped fresh thyme

½ tsp ground nutmeg

4 tbsp dry white wine

55 g/2 oz fresh white breadcrumbs

12 dried 'quick-cook' cannelloni tubes

salt and pepper

Parmesan shavings, to garnish (optional)

T O M A T O   S A U C E

1 large red pepper

200 ml/7 fl oz dry white wine

450 ml/16 fl oz passata

2 tbsp tomato purée

2 bay leaves

1 tsp caster sugar

COOK'S TIP

Chestnut mushrooms, also known as champignons de Paris, are common cultivated mushrooms that may have brown or white caps.

1 Finely chop the mushrooms and place in a pan with the onion and garlic. Stir in the thyme, nutmeg and wine. Bring to the boil, cover and simmer for 10 minutes.

2 Stir in the breadcrumbs to bind the mixture together and season to taste with salt and pepper. Cool for 10 minutes.

3 To make the sauce, halve and deseed the pepper, place on the grill rack and cook for 8–10 minutes until charred. Set aside to cool for 10 minutes.

4 Once the pepper has cooled, peel off the charred skin. Chop the flesh and place in a food processor with the wine. Process until smooth, then scrape into a pan.

5 Mix the remaining sauce ingredients with the pepper and wine. Bring to the boil and simmer for 10 minutes. Remove and discard the bay leaves.

6 Cover the base of an ovenproof dish with a thin layer of the sauce. Fill the cannelloni with the mushroom mixture and place in the dish. Spoon over the remaining sauce, cover with foil and bake in a preheated oven, 200°C/400°F/Gas Mark 6, for 35–40 minutes. Garnish with Parmesan shavings, if using, and serve hot.

Vegetable Stir-fry

A range of delicious flavours are captured in this simple recipe, which is ideal if you are in a hurry.

NUTRITIONAL INFORMATION

Calories ....138 Sugars 5g
Protein ....3g Fat 12g
Carbohydrate ....5g Saturates 2g

 5 mins   25 mins

SERVES 4

I N G R E D I E N T S

3 tbsp vegetable oil

8 baby onions, halved

1 aubergine, cubed

225 g/8 oz courgettes, sliced

225 g/8 oz open-cap
   mushrooms, halved

2 cloves garlic, crushed

400 g/14 oz canned chopped tomatoes

2 tbsp sun-dried tomato paste

2 tbsp soy sauce

1 tsp sesame oil

1 tbsp Chinese rice wine or dry sherry

pepper

fresh basil leaves, to garnish

1 Heat the vegetable oil in a large preheated wok or frying pan.

2 Add the baby onions and aubergine to the wok or frying pan and stir-fry for 5 minutes, or until the vegetables are golden and just beginning to soften.

3 Add the courgettes, mushrooms, garlic, chopped tomatoes and sun-dried tomato paste to the wok and stir-fry for about 5 minutes. Reduce the heat and simmer for 10 minutes or until the vegetables are tender.

4 Add the soy sauce, sesame oil and rice wine or sherry to the wok, bring back to the boil and cook for 1 minute.

5 Season the vegetable stir-fry with freshly ground black pepper to taste and sprinkle with fresh basil leaves. Transfer to a warmed serving dish and serve immediately.

COOK'S TIP

Basil has a very strong flavour which is perfect with vegetables and Chinese flavourings. Instead of using basil simply as a garnish in this dish, try adding a handful of fresh basil leaves to the stir-fry in step 4.

Barbecue Mushrooms

Large mushrooms have more flavour than the smaller button mushrooms. Serve these mushrooms as part of a vegetarian barbecue.

NUTRITIONAL INFORMATION

Calories	148	Sugars	.........1g
Protein	........11g	Fat	..........7g
Carbohydrate	....11g	Saturates	......3g

10 mins   15 mins

SERVES 4

INGREDIENTS

12 open cap mushrooms

4 tsp olive oil

4 spring onions, chopped

100 g/3½ oz fresh brown breadcrumbs

1 tsp chopped fresh oregano

100 g/3½ oz low-fat mature
   Cheddar cheese

1 Remove the stalks from the mushrooms, reserving the caps. Chop the stalks finely.

2 Heat half the oil in a frying pan. Add the mushroom stalks and spring onions and cook over a low heat, stirring occasionally, for 5 minutes.

3 Transfer the mushroom stalks and spring onions to a large bowl with a draining spoon and add the breadcrumbs and oregano. Mix well.

4 Crumble the cheese into small pieces in a small bowl. Add the cheese to the breadcrumb mixture and mix well. Carefully spoon the stuffing mixture into the mushroom caps.

5 Drizzle the remaining oil over the stuffed mushrooms. Cook the mushrooms on an oiled rack over medium hot coals for 10 minutes or until cooked through. Alternatively, arrange on a baking sheet and bake in a preheated oven, 180°C/350°F/Gas Mark 4 for about 20 minutes or until cooked through.

6 Transfer the mushrooms to serving plates and serve hot.

VARIATION

For a change replace the cheese with finely-chopped chorizo sausage (remove the skin first), chopped hard-boiled eggs, chopped olives or chopped anchovy fillets. Mop up the juices with some crusty bread.

Lime Chicken Kebabs

These succulent chicken kebabs are coated in a sweet
lime dressing and are served with a lime and mango relish.

NUTRITIONAL INFORMATION

Calories ....199 Sugars 14g
Protein ....28g Fat 4g
Carbohydrate ...14g Saturates 1g

🧊 15 mins   🕐 10 mins

SERVES 4

I N G R E D I E N T S

4 lean skinless boneless chicken breasts,
   about 125 g/4½ oz each

3 tbsp lime marmalade

1 tsp white wine vinegar

½ tsp lime rind, finely grated

1 tbsp lime juice

salt and pepper

TO SERVE

lime wedges

boiled white rice, sprinkled with
   chilli powder

SALSA

1 small mango

1 small red onion

1 tbsp lime juice

1 tbsp chopped fresh coriander

COOK'S TIP

To prevent sticking, lightly oil
metal skewers or dip bamboo
skewers in water before threading
the chicken on to them.

1 Slice the chicken breasts into thin pieces and thread on to 8 skewers so that the meat forms an S-shape along each skewer.

2 Arrange the chicken kebabs on a grill rack. Combine the lime marmalade, vinegar, lime rind and juice. Season with salt and pepper. Brush the dressing over the chicken and cook under a preheated grill for 5 minutes. Turn the kebabs over, brush with the dressing again and grill for a further 4–5 minutes until cooked.

3 Meanwhile, prepare the salsa. Peel the mango and slice the flesh off the smooth, central stone. Dice the flesh into small pieces and place in a small bowl.

4 Peel and finely chop the onion and mix into the mango, with the lime juice and chopped coriander. Season to taste, cover and chill until required.

5 Serve the chicken kebabs with the salsa, accompanied with wedges of lime and boiled rice.

Prawn Pasta Bake

This dish is ideal for an easy family supper. You can use whatever pasta you like, but the tricolour varieties will give the most colourful results.

NUTRITIONAL INFORMATION

Calories	723	Sugars	.........9g
Protein	........56g	Fat	...........8g
Carbohydrate	...114g	Saturates	......2g

10 mins   50 mins

SERVES 4

INGREDIENTS

225 g/8 oz tricolour pasta shapes

1 tbsp vegetable oil

175 g/6 oz button mushrooms, sliced

1 bunch of spring onions, trimmed and chopped

400 g/14 oz canned tuna in brine, drained and flaked

175 g/6 oz peeled prawns, thawed if frozen

2 tbsp cornflour

425 ml/15 fl oz skimmed milk

4 medium tomatoes, thinly sliced

25 g/1 oz fresh breadcrumbs

25 g/1 oz reduced-fat Cheddar cheese, grated

salt and pepper

TO SERVE

wholemeal bread

fresh salad

1 Bring a large saucepan of lightly salted water to the boil. Add the pasta, bring back to the boil and cook for 8–10 minutes until tender, but still firm to the bite. Drain well.

2 Meanwhile, heat the oil in a large frying pan. Add the mushrooms and all but a handful of the spring onions and cook over a low heat, stirring occasionally, for 4–5 minutes until softened.

3 Place the cooked pasta in a bowl and stir in the mushroom mixture, tuna and prawns.

4 Blend the cornflour with a little milk to make a paste. Pour the remaining milk into a saucepan and stir in the paste. Heat, stirring, until the sauce begins to thicken. Season. Stir the sauce into the pasta mixture. Transfer to an ovenproof dish and place on a baking sheet.

5 Arrange the tomato slices over the pasta and sprinkle with the breadcrumbs and cheese. Bake in a preheated oven, 190°C/375°F/Gas Mark 5, for 25–30 minutes until golden. Serve sprinkled with the reserved spring onions and accompanied with bread and salad.

Italian Omelette

A baked omelette of substantial proportions with potatoes, onions, artichokes and sun-dried tomatoes.

NUTRITIONAL INFORMATION

Calories	481	Sugars	4g
Protein	22g	Fat	26g
Carbohydrate	42g	Saturates	10g

10 mins 45 mins

SERVES 4

INGREDIENTS

900 g/2 lb potatoes

1 tbsp vegetable oil

1 large onion, sliced

2 garlic cloves, chopped

6 sun-dried tomatoes in oil, drained and cut into strips

400g/14 oz can artichoke hearts, drained and halved

250 g/9 oz ricotta cheese

4 large eggs, beaten

2 tbsp milk

55 g/2 oz Parmesan cheese, grated

3 tbsp chopped fresh thyme

salt and pepper

1 Peel the potatoes and place them in a bowl of cold water (see Cook's Tip). Cut the potatoes into thin slices.

2 Bring a large pan of water to the boil and add the potato slices. Bring back to the boil, then simmer for 5–6 minutes or until just tender.

3 Heat the oil in a large, heavy-based frying pan . Add the onions and garlic and cook over a low heat, stirring occasionally, for about 3–4 minutes until softened, but not browned.

4 Add the sun-dried tomatoes and cook for a further 2 minutes.

5 Arrange a third of the potatoes in the bottom of a deep, ovenproof dish. Cover with a half the onion mixture, then half the artichokes, followed by half the ricotta. Repeat the layers in the same order, finishing with a layer of potato slices on top.

6 Combine the eggs, milk, half of the grated Parmesan and the thyme and season with salt and pepper to taste. Pour the mixture over the potatoes. Sprinkle the remaining Parmesan on top and bake in a preheated oven, 190°C/375°F/Gas Mark 5, for 20–25 minutes or until golden brown. Cut the omelette into slices and serve immediately.

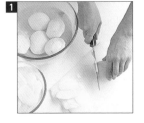  

COOK'S TIP

Placing the potatoes in a bowl of cold water will prevent them from turning brown while you are cutting the rest into slices.

Omelette in Tomato Sauce

These omelette strips are delicious smothered in a succulent and aromatic tomato and rosemary flavoured sauce.

NUTRITIONAL INFORMATION

Calories	198	Sugars	.........6g
Protein	........10g	Fat	..........15g
Carbohydrate	....6g	Saturates	.......8g

🍞 10 mins   🕐 35 mins

SERVES 4

I N G R E D I E N T S

tbsp butter

onion, finely chopped

garlic cloves, chopped

eggs, beaten

50 ml/5 fl oz milk

5 g/3 oz Gruyère cheese, diced

00g/14 oz can tomatoes, chopped

tbsp rosemary, stalks removed

50 ml/5 fl oz vegetable stock

reshly grated Parmesan cheese, for sprinkling

resh, crusty bread, to serve

1 Melt the butter in a large frying pan. Add the onion and garlic and cook over a low heat, stirring occasionally, for –5 minutes until softened.

2 Beat together the eggs and milk and add the mixture to the pan.

3 Using a spatula, raise the cooked edges of the omelette and tip any ncooked egg around the edge of the pan.

4 Sprinkle over the Gruyère. Cook for 5 minutes, turning once, until golden n both sides. Remove the omelette from he pan and roll up.

5 Add the tomatoes, rosemary and vegetable stock to the frying pan and bring to the boil, stirring constantly. Lower the heat and simmer for about 10 minutes until reduced and thickened.

6 Slice the omelette into strips and add to the tomato sauce. Cook for about 3–4 minutes or until piping hot.

7 Sprinkle the Parmesan cheese over the omelette strips and serve with fresh, crusty bread.

VARIATION

Try adding 100 g/3½ oz diced pancetta or unsmoked bacon in step 1 and cooking the meat with the onions.

Chicken Liver Crostini

Crostini are small pieces of toast with a savoury topping – in this case, chicken livers. This is a popular Italian antipasto dish.

NUTRITIONAL INFORMATION

Calories	250	Sugars	.........1g
Protein	........15g	Fat	...........9g
Carbohydrate	...28g	Saturates	.......2g

 10 mins   🕐 7–8 mins

SERVES 4

I N G R E D I E N T S

2 tbsp olive oil

1 garlic clove, finely chopped

225 g/8 oz fresh or thawed frozen chicken livers

2 tbsp white wine

2 tbsp lemon juice

4 fresh sage leaves, finely chopped or 1 tsp dried, crumbled sage

4 slices ciabatta or other Italian bread

salt and pepper

lemon wedges, to garnish

1 Heat the olive oil in a heavy-based frying pan and cook the garlic over a low heat, stirring constantly, for 1 minute. Remove the pan from the heat.

2 Rinse and roughly chop the chicken livers, using a sharp knife.

3 Return the pan to a medium heat. Add the chicken livers with the white wine and lemon juice. Cook, stirring frequently, for 3–4 minutes or until the juices from the chicken livers run clear. Stir in the sage and season to taste.

4 Toast the bread under a preheated grill for 2 minutes on both sides or until golden brown.

5 Spoon the hot chicken liver mixture on top of the toasted bread and serve garnished with wedges of lemon.

COOK'S TIP

Overcooked liver is dry and tasteless. Cook the chopped liver for only 3–4 minutes – it should be soft and tender.

Pasta with Smoked Salmon

This simple dish takes just moments to make, looks lovely, tastes fabulous and contains no saturated fat – what more could you possibly want?

NUTRITIONAL INFORMATION

Calories	222	Sugars	2g
Protein	11g	Fat	3g
Carbohydrate	42g	Saturates	0g

5 mins   10 mins

SERVES 4

INGREDIENTS

salt and pepper

225 g/8 oz dried fettuccine

1 tsp olive oil

1 garlic clove, finely chopped

55 g/2 oz smoked salmon, cut into thin strips

55 g/2 oz watercress leaves, plus extra to garnish

1 Bring a large saucepan of lightly salted water to the boil over a medium heat. Add the pasta, return to the boil and cook for 8–10 minutes, or until tender but still firm to the bite.

2 Meanwhile, heat the olive oil in a large non-stick frying pan. Add the chopped garlic and cook over a low heat, stirring constantly, for 30 seconds. Add the salmon strips and watercress, season to taste with pepper and cook for a further 30 seconds, or until the watercress has wilted.

3 Drain the cooked pasta and return to the saucepan. Mix the salmon and watercress mixture with the pasta. Toss the mixture thoroughly using 2 large forks. Divide between 4 large serving plates and garnish with extra watercress leaves. Serve immediately.

COOK'S TIP
You can often buy misshapen offcuts of smoked salmon for a fraction of the price of neat smoked salmon slices in some large supermarkets.

Smoked Ham Linguine

Served with freshly made Italian bread or tossed with pesto, this makes a mouthwatering light lunch.

NUTRITIONAL INFORMATION

Calories 537   Sugars 4g
Protein . . . . .22g   Fat 29g
Carbohydrate . . . .71g   Saturates 8g

 8–10 mins   20 mins

SERVES 4

INGREDIENTS

450 g/1 lb dried linguine

450 g/1 lb green broccoli florets

225 g/8 oz Italian smoked ham

salt and pepper

Italian bread, such as ciabatta or focaccia,
  to serve

Italian cheese sauce

1 tbsp butter

11/2 tsp plain flour

125 ml/4 fl oz milk

1 tbsp single cream

pinch of freshly grated nutmeg

25 g/1 oz grated Cheddar cheese

1 tbsp freshly grated Parmesan cheese

salt and pepper

COOK'S TIP

There are many types of Italian bread which would be suitable to serve with this dish. Ciabatta is made with olive oil and is available plain and with different additional ingredients, such as olives or sun-dried tomatoes.

1 First, make the Italian cheese sauce. Melt the butter in a pan, stir in the flour and cook for 1 minute. Remove from the heat and gradually whisk in the milk. Stir in the cream and nutmeg and season to taste with salt and pepper. Return to the heat, bring to the boil, stirring constantly, then simmer for 5 minutes. Remove from the heat and stir in the cheeses until melted and thoroughly blended. Set aside.

2 Bring a large pan of lightly salted water to the boil. Add the pasta and broccoli, bring back to the boil and cook for 8–10 minutes until the pasta is tender but still firm to the bite. Drain well.

3 Cut the Italian smoked ham into thin strips. Toss the linguine, broccoli and ham into the cheese sauce and gently warm through. Season with pepper and serve with Italian bread.

Spinach & Anchovy Pasta

This colourful light meal can be made with a variety of different pasta, including spaghetti and linguine.

NUTRITIONAL INFORMATION

Calories 619	Sugars 5g
Protein 21g	Fat 31g
Carbohydrate . . .67g	Saturates 3g

10 mins   25 mins

SERVES 4

I N G R E D I E N T S

900 g/2 lb fresh, young spinach leaves

400 g/14 oz dried fettuccine

5 tbsp olive oil

3 tbsp pine kernels

3 garlic cloves, crushed

8 canned anchovy fillets, drained
  and chopped

salt

1 Trim off any tough spinach stalks. Rinse the spinach leaves and place them in a large saucepan with only the water that is clinging to them after washing. Cover and cook over a high heat, shaking the pan from time, until the spinach has wilted, but retains its colour. Drain well, set aside and keep warm.

2 Bring a large pan of lightly salted water to the boil. Add the fettuccine, bring back to the boil and cook for 8–10 minutes until it is just tender, but still firm to the bite.

3 Meanwhile, heat 4 tablespoons of the olive oil in a pan. Add the pine kernels and fry until golden. Remove the pine kernels from the pan with a draining spoon and set aside until required.

4 Add the garlic to the pan and fry until golden. Add the anchovies and stir in the spinach. Cook, stirring constantly, for 2–3 minutes until heated through. Return the pine kernels to the pan.

5 Drain the fettuccine, toss in the remaining olive oil and transfer to a warm serving dish. Spoon the anchovy and spinach sauce over the fettuccine, toss lightly and serve immediately.

COOK'S TIP

If you are in a hurry, you can use frozen spinach. Thaw and drain it thoroughly, pressing out as much moisture as possible. Cut the leaves into strips and add to the dish with the anchovies in step 4.

Braised Fennel & Linguine

This aniseed-flavoured vegetable gives that little extra punch to this delicious creamy pasta dish.

NUTRITIONAL INFORMATION

Calories 650	Sugars 6g	
Protein 14g	Fat 39g	
Carbohydrate ...62g	Saturates 22g	

20 mins   50 mins

SERVES 4

INGREDIENTS

6 fennel bulbs

150 ml/5 fl oz vegetable stock

2 tbsp butter

6 slices rindless smoked bacon, diced

6 shallots, quartered

2½ tbsp plain flour

7 tbsp double cream

1 tbsp Madeira

450 g/1 lb dried linguine pasta

1 tbsp olive oil

salt and pepper

1 Trim the fennel bulbs, then peel off and reserve the outer layer of each. Cut the bulbs into quarters and put them in a large saucepan with the stock and the reserved outer layers. Bring to the boil, lower the heat and simmer for 5 minutes.

COOK'S TIP

Fennel will keep in the salad drawer of the refrigerator for 2–3 days, but it is best eaten as fresh as possible. Cut surfaces turn brown quickly, so do not prepare it too much in advance of cooking.

2 Using a draining spoon, transfer the fennel to a large dish. Discard the outer layers of the fennel bulbs. Bring the vegetable stock to the boil and reduce by half. Set aside.

3 Melt the butter in a frying pan. Add the bacon and shallots and fry over a medium heat, stirring frequently, for 4 minutes. Add the flour, reduced stock, cream and Madeira and cook, stirring constantly, for 3 minutes or until the

sauce is smooth. Season to taste with sa and pepper and pour over the fennel.

4 Bring a large saucepan of lightly salte water to the boil. Add the pasta and o bring back to the boil and cook for 8–1 minutes until tender, but still firm to the bit Drain and transfer to a deep ovenproof dish.

5 Add the fennel and sauce and braise i a preheated oven, 180°C/350°F/Ga Mark 4, for 20 minutes. Serve immediately

Baked Fennel Gratinati

Fennel is a common ingredient in Italian cooking. In this dish its distinctive flavour is offset by the smooth Béchamel Sauce.

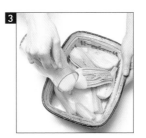

NUTRITIONAL INFORMATION

Calories ....426 Sugars 9g
Protein ....13g Fat 35g
Carbohydrate ...16g Saturates 19g

5–10 mins   45 mins

SERVES 4

INGREDIENTS

fennel bulbs

tbsp butter

50 ml/5 fl oz dry white wine

Béchamel Sauce (see page 6), enriched
with 2 egg yolks

5 g/1 oz fresh white breadcrumbs

tbsp freshly grated Parmesan cheese

salt and pepper

fennel fronds, to garnish

1 Remove any bruised or tough outer stalks of fennel and cut each bulb in half. Put into a pan of lightly salted boiling water and simmer for 20 minutes until tender, then drain.

2 Butter an ovenproof dish liberally and arrange the drained fennel in it.

3 Stir the wine into the Béchamel sauce and season with salt and pepper to taste. Pour over the fennel.

4 Sprinkle evenly with the breadcrumbs and then the Parmesan.

5 Bake in a preheated oven, 200°C/ 400°F/Gas Mark 6, for 20 minutes until the top is golden. Serve garnished with fennel fronds.

Rice & Peas

If you can get fresh peas – and willing helpers to shell them – do use them: you will need 1 kg/2 lb 4 oz. Add them to the pan with the stock.

NUTRITIONAL INFORMATION

Calories	409	Sugars	.........2g
Protein	........15g	Fat	..........23g
Carbohydrate	...38g	Saturates	......12g

🍲 10 mins   🕐 50 mins

SERVES 4

INGREDIENTS

1 tbsp olive oil

4 tbsp butter

55 g/2 oz pancetta or streaky bacon, chopped

1 small onion, chopped

1.4 litres/2½ pints hot chicken stock

200 g/7 oz risotto rice

3 tbsp chopped fresh parsley

225 g/8 oz fresh, frozen or canned petits pois

55 g/2 oz Parmesan cheese, grated

pepper

1 Heat the olive oil and half of the butter in a heavy-based pan. Add the pancetta or bacon and onion and cook over a low heat, stirring occasionally, for 5 minutes until the onion is softened and translucent, but not browned.

2 Add the stock and fresh peas, if using, to the pan and bring to the boil. Stir in the rice and season to taste with pepper. Bring to the boil, lower the heat and simmer, stirring occasionally, for about 20–30 minutes until the rice is tender.

3 Add the parsley and frozen or canned petits pois, if using, and cook for about 8 minutes until the peas are heated through. Stir in the remaining butter and the Parmesan.

4 Transfer to a warmed serving dish and serve immediately with freshly ground black pepper.

Filled Aubergines

Combined with tomatoes and melting mozzarella cheese, pasta makes a tasty filling for baked aubergine shells.

NUTRITIONAL INFORMATION

Calories . . . . . . .342 Sugars 6g
Protein . . . . .11g Fat 16g
Carbohydrate . . .40g Saturates 4g

🥘 25 mins   🕐 55 mins

SERVES 4

INGREDIENTS

225 g/8 oz dried penne or other short
  pasta shapes

4 tbsp olive oil, plus extra for brushing

2 aubergines

1 large onion, chopped

2 garlic cloves, crushed

400 g/14 oz canned chopped tomatoes

2 tsp dried oregano

55 g/2 oz mozzarella cheese, thinly sliced

25 g/1 oz Parmesan cheese, freshly grated

5 tbsp dry breadcrumbs

salt and pepper

salad leaves, to serve

1 Bring a large saucepan of lightly salted water to the boil. Add the pasta and tablespoon of the olive oil, bring back to the boil and cook for 8–10 minutes or until the pasta is just tender, but still firm to the bite. Drain, return to the pan, cover and keep warm.

2 Cut the aubergines in half lengthways and score around the inside with a sharp knife, being careful not to pierce the shells. Scoop out the flesh with a spoon. Brush the insides of the shells with olive oil. Chop the flesh and set aside.

3 Heat the remaining oil in a frying pan. Fry the onion over a low heat for 5 minutes, until softened. Add the garlic and fry for 1 minute. Add the chopped aubergine and fry, stirring frequently, for 5 minutes. Add the tomatoes and oregano and season to taste with salt and pepper. Bring to the boil and simmer for 10 minutes until thickened. Remove the pan from the heat and stir in the pasta.

4 Brush a baking sheet with oil and arrange the aubergine shells in a single layer. Divide half of the tomato and pasta mixture between them. Scatter over the slices of mozzarella, then pile the remaining tomato and pasta mixture on top. Mix the Parmesan cheese and breadcrumbs and sprinkle over the top, patting it lightly into the mixture.

5 Bake in a preheated oven, 200°C/ 400°C/Gas Mark 6, for about 25 minutes or until the topping is golden brown. Serve hot with a selection of mixed salad leaves.

Ciabatta Rolls

Sandwiches are always a welcome snack, but can be mundane.
These crisp rolls filled with roasted peppers and cheese are irresistible.

NUTRITIONAL INFORMATION

Calories	328	Sugars	.........6g
Protein	.........8g	Fat	..........19g
Carbohydrate	...34g	Saturates	.......9g

15 mins   10 mins

SERVES 4

INGREDIENTS

4 ciabatta rolls

2 tbsp olive oil

1 garlic clove, crushed

FILLING

1 red pepper

1 green pepper

1 yellow pepper

4 radishes, sliced

1 bunch of watercress

115 g/4 oz cream cheese

1 Slice the ciabatta rolls in half. Heat the olive oil and garlic in a saucepan. Pour the garlic and oil mixture over the cut surfaces of the rolls and set aside.

2 Halve and deseed the peppers and place, skin side up, on a grill rack. Cook under a preheated hot grill for 8–10 minutes until just beginning to char. Remove the peppers from the grill and place in a plastic bag. When cool enough to handle, peel and slice thinly.

3 Arrange the radish slices on 1 half of each roll with a few watercress leaves. Spoon the cream cheese on top. Pile the roasted peppers on top of the cream cheese and top with the other half of the roll. Serve immediately.

Pasta with Garlic & Broccoli

Broccoli coated in a garlic-flavoured cream sauce, served on herb tagliatelle. Try sprinkling with toasted pine kernels to add extra crunch.

NUTRITIONAL INFORMATION

Calories 538	Sugars 4g	
Protein 23g	Fat 29g	
Carbohydrate ...50g	Saturates 17g	

5 mins   5 mins

SERVES 4

INGREDIENTS

500 g/1 lb 2 oz broccoli

300 g/10½ oz garlic and herb
  cream cheese

4 tbsp milk

350 g/12 oz fresh herb tagliatelle

25 g/1 oz freshly grated
  Parmesan cheese

chopped fresh chives, to garnish

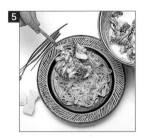

1 Cut the broccoli into even-size florets. Bring a pan of lightly salted water to the boil. Add the broccoli, bring back to the boil and cook for 3 minutes, then drain thoroughly.

2 Put the soft cheese into a pan and heat gently, stirring constantly, until melted. Add the milk and stir over a low heat until well combined.

3 Add the broccoli to the cheese mixture and stir to coat.

4 Meanwhile, bring a large pan of lightly salted water to the boil. Add the tagliatelle and bring back to the boil. Cook for 3–4 minutes until tender, but still firm to the bite.

5 Drain the tagliatelle thoroughly and divide among 4 warmed serving plates. Spoon the broccoli and cheese sauce on top. Sprinkle with grated Parmesan cheese, garnish with chopped chives and serve immediately.

COOK'S TIP

A herb flavoured pasta goes particularly well with the broccoli sauce, but failing this, a tagliatelle verde or 'paglia e fieno' (literally 'straw and hay' – thin green and yellow noodles) will fit the bill.

Mixed Mushroom Cakes

These cakes are packed with creamy potato and a variety of mushrooms and will be loved by vegetarians and meat-eaters alike.

NUTRITIONAL INFORMATION

Calories	298	Sugars	.......0.8g
Protein	.........5g	Fat	..........22g
Carbohydrate	...22g	Saturates	.......5g

  20 mins   25 mins

SERVES 4

I N G R E D I E N T S

500 g/1 lb 2 oz floury potatoes, diced

2 tbsp butter

175 g/6 oz mixed mushrooms, chopped

2 garlic cloves, crushed

1 small egg, beaten

1 tbsp chopped fresh chives, plus extra to garnish

flour, for dusting

vegetable oil, for frying

salt and pepper

salad, to serve

1 Cook the potatoes in a pan of lightly salted boiling water for 10 minutes or until cooked through.

2 Drain the potatoes well, mash with a potato masher or fork and set aside.

3 Meanwhile, melt the butter in a frying pan. Add the mushrooms and garlic and cook over a medium heat, stirring constantly, for 5 minutes. Drain well.

4 Stir the mushrooms and garlic into the potatoes, together with the beaten egg and chives.

5 Divide the mixture equally into 4 portions and shape them into round cakes. Toss them in the flour until the outsides of the cakes are completely coated, shaking off any excess.

6 Heat the oil in a frying pan. Add the mushroom cakes and fry over a medium heat for 10 minutes until they are golden brown, turning them over halfway through. Serve the cakes immediately, with a simple crisp salad.

COOK'S TIP

Prepare the cakes in advance, cover and set aside to chill in the refrigerator for up to 24 hours, if you wish.

Hash Browns

Hash Browns are a popular American recipe of fried potato squares, often served as brunch. This recipe includes extra vegetables.

NUTRITIONAL INFORMATION

Calories	339	Sugars	. . . . .9g
Protein	. . . . .10g	Fat	. . . . .21g
Carbohydrate	. . .29g	Saturates	. . . . . . .7g

  20 mins   45 mins

SERVES 4

I N G R E D I E N T S

500 g/1 lb 2 oz waxy potatoes

1 carrot, diced

1 celery stick, diced

55 g/2 oz button mushrooms, diced

1 onion, diced

2 garlic cloves, crushed

25 g/1 oz frozen peas, thawed

55 g/2 oz Parmesan cheese, freshly grated

1 tbsp vegetable oil

2 tbsp butter

salt and pepper

S A U C E

300 ml/10 fl oz passata

2 tbsp chopped fresh coriander

1 tbsp Worcestershire sauce

½ tsp chilli powder

1 tsp brown sugar

1 tsp American mustard

5 tbsp vegetable stock

1 Cook the potatoes in a saucepan of lightly salted boiling water for 10 minutes. Drain and set aside to cool. Meanwhile, cook the carrot in lightly salted boiling water for 5 minutes.

2 When the potatoes are cool enough to handle, grate them with a coarse grater.

3 Drain the carrot and add it to the grated potatoes, with the celery, mushrooms, onion, garlic, peas and cheese. Season to taste with salt and pepper.

4 Put all of the sauce ingredients in a small saucepan and bring to the boil. Reduce the heat to low and simmer for 15 minutes.

5 Divide the potato mixture into 8 portions of equal size and shape into flattened rectangles with your hands.

6 Heat the oil and butter in a frying pan and cook the hash browns in batches over a low heat for 4–5 minutes on each side, until crisp and golden brown.

7 Transfer the hash browns to a serving plate and serve immediately with the tomato sauce.

Spanish Potato Bake

In this variation of a traditional Spanish dish, huevos (eggs) are cooked on top of a spicy sausage, tomato and potato mixture.

NUTRITIONAL INFORMATION

Calories	443	Sugars	.........7g
Protein	........21g	Fat	..........25g
Carbohydrate	...36g	Saturates	......8g

5 mins 35 mins

SERVES 4

INGREDIENTS

675 g/1½ lb waxy potatoes, diced

3 tbsp olive oil

1 onion, halved and sliced

2 garlic cloves, crushed

400 g/14 oz canned plum
  tomatoes, chopped

85 g/3 oz chorizo sausage, sliced

1 green pepper, deseeded and cut
  into strips

½ tsp paprika

25 g/1 oz stoned black olives, halved

8 eggs

1 tbsp chopped fresh parsley

salt and pepper

crusty bread, to serve

1 Cook the diced potatoes in a saucepan of boiling water for 10 minutes or until softened. Drain and set aside.

2 Heat the olive oil in a large, heavy-based frying pan, add the onion and garlic and fry over a low heat, stirring occasionally, for 2–3 minutes until the onion has softened.

3 Add the tomatoes and cook over a low heat for about 10 minutes until the mixture has reduced slightly.

4 Stir the potatoes into the pan with the chorizo, green pepper, paprika and olives. Cook for 5 minutes, stirring constantly. Transfer the mixture to a shallow ovenproof dish.

5 Make 8 small hollows in the top of the mixture and break an egg into each hollow.

6 Cook in a preheated oven, 220°C/425°F/Gas Mark 7, for 5–6 minutes or until the eggs are just cooked. Sprinkle with parsley and serve with crusty bread.

VARIATION

Add a little extra spice to the dish by incorporating 1 teaspoon chilli powder in step 4, if desired.

Tomato & Sausage Pan-fry

This simple dish is delicious as a main meal. Choose good sausages flavoured with herbs or use flavoured sausages, such as mustard or leek.

NUTRITIONAL INFORMATION

Calories	458	Sugars	........11g
Protein	........21g	Fat	..........25g
Carbohydrate	...34g	Saturates	.......8g

5 mins

30 mins

SERVES 4

INGREDIENTS

600 g/1 lb 5 oz potatoes, sliced

1 tbsp vegetable oil

8 flavoured sausages

1 red onion, cut into 8 wedges

1 tbsp tomato purée

150 ml/5 fl oz red wine

150 ml/5 fl oz passata

2 large tomatoes, each cut into 8 wedges

175 g/6 oz broccoli florets, blanched

2 tbsp chopped fresh basil

salt and pepper

shredded fresh basil, to garnish

1 Cook the sliced potatoes in a saucepan of boiling water for 7 minutes. Drain thoroughly and set aside.

2 Meanwhile, heat the oil in a large, heavy-based frying pan. Add the sausages and cook over a medium-low heat for 5 minutes, turning them frequently to ensure that they are browned on all sides.

3 Add the onion pieces to the pan and cook, stirring occasionally, for a further 5 minutes.

4 Stir in the tomato purée, red wine and passata and mix well. Add the tomato wedges, broccoli florets and chopped basil and mix gently.

5 Add the parboiled potato slices to the pan. Cook the mixture for about 10 minutes or until the sausages are completely cooked through. Season to taste with salt and pepper.

6 Transfer to a warmed serving dish, garnish the pan-fry with fresh shredded basil and serve hot.

COOK'S TIP
Omit the passata from this recipe and use canned plum tomatoes or chopped tomatoes for convenience.

Chicken & Banana Cakes

Even plain potato cakes are a great favourite. In this recipe, the potatoes are combined with minced chicken and mashed banana.

NUTRITIONAL INFORMATION

Calories 439	Sugars 11g	
Protein 22g	Fat 23g	
Carbohydrate ...39g	Saturates 10g	

 5–10 mins ⏱ 25–30 mins

SERVES 4

I N G R E D I E N T S

450 g/1 lb floury potatoes, diced

225 g/8 oz minced chicken

1 large banana

2 tbsp plain flour

1 tsp lemon juice

1 onion, finely chopped

2 tbsp chopped fresh sage

2 tbsp butter

2 tbsp vegetable oil

150 ml/5 fl oz single cream

150 ml/5 fl oz chicken stock

salt and pepper

fresh sage leaves, to garnish

1 Cook the diced potatoes in a saucepan of boiling water for about 10 minutes until tender. Drain well and mash until smooth. Stir in the minced chicken.

2 Mash the banana and add it to the potato with the flour, lemon juice, onion and half of the chopped sage. Season to taste with salt and pepper and stir the mixture together.

3 Divide the mixture into 8 equal portions. With lightly floured hands, shape each portion into a round patty.

4 Heat the butter and oil in a frying pan, add the potato cakes and cook for 12–15 minutes or until cooked through, turning once. Remove from the pan and keep warm.

5 Stir the cream and stock into the pan with the remaining chopped sage. Cook over a low heat for 2–3 minutes.

6 Arrange the potato cakes on a warmed serving plate, garnish with fresh sage leaves and serve immediately with the cream and sage sauce.

COOK'S TIP

Do not boil the sauce once the cream has been added, as it will curdle. Cook it gently over a very low heat.

Penne & Butternut Squash

The creamy, nutty flavour of squash complements the 'al dente' texture of the pasta. This recipe has been adapted for the microwave oven.

NUTRITIONAL INFORMATION

Calories 499	Sugars 4g	
Protein 20g	Fat 26g	
Carbohydrate ...49g	Saturates 13g	

15 mins   30 mins

SERVES 4

I N G R E D I E N T S

2 tbsp olive oil

1 garlic clove, crushed

55 g/2 oz fresh white breadcrumbs

500 g/1 lb 2 oz peeled and deseeded butternut squash

3 tbsp water

500 g/1 lb 2 oz fresh penne, or other pasta shapes

1 tbsp butter

1 onion, sliced

115 g/4 oz ham, cut into strips

200 ml/7 fl oz single cream

55 g/2 oz Cheddar cheese, grated

2 tbsp chopped fresh parsley

salt and pepper

1 Combine the olive oil, garlic and breadcrumbs and spread out on a large plate. Cook on HIGH power for 4–5 minutes, stirring every minute, until crisp and beginning to brown. Remove from the microwave and set aside.

2 Dice the squash. Place in a large bowl with half of the water. Cover and cook on HIGH power for 8–9 minutes, stirring occasionally. Stand for 2 minutes.

3 Place the pasta in a large bowl, add a little salt and pour over boiling water to cover by 2.5 cm/1 inch. Cover and cook on HIGH power for 5 minutes, stirring once, until the pasta is just tender, but still firm to the bite. Stand, covered, for 1 minute before draining.

4 Place the butter and onion in a large bowl. Cover and cook on HIGH power for 3 minutes.

5 Coarsely mash the squash, using a fork. Add to the onion with the pasta, ham, cream, cheese, parsley and remaining water. Season generously and mix well.

Cover and cook on HIGH power for 4 minutes until heated through.

6 Serve the pasta sprinkled with the crisp garlic crumbs.

COOK'S TIP

If the squash weighs more than is needed for this recipe, blanch the excess for 3–4 minutes on HIGH power in a covered bowl with a little water. Drain, cool and place in a freezer bag. Store in the freezer for up to 3 months.

Pasta & Chilli Tomatoes

The pappardelle and vegetables are tossed in a delicious chilli and tomato sauce for a quick and economical meal.

NUTRITIONAL INFORMATION

Calories	353	Sugars	.........7g
Protein	........10g	Fat	..........24g
Carbohydrate	...26g	Saturates	.......4g

 15 mins   20 mins

SERVES 4

I N G R E D I E N T S

280 g/10 oz dried pappardelle

3 tbsp groundnut oil

2 garlic cloves, crushed

2 shallots, sliced

225 g/8 oz green beans, sliced

100 g/3½ oz cherry tomatoes, halved

1 tsp chilli flakes

4 tbsp crunchy peanut butter

150 ml/5 fl oz coconut milk

1 tbsp tomato purée

sliced spring onions, to garnish

1 Bring a large pan of lightly salted water to the boil. Add the pappardelle, bring back to the boil and cook for 8–10 minutes until tender, but still firm to the bite. Drain thoroughly and set aside.

2 Meanwhile, heat the groundnut oil in a large, heavy-based frying pan or preheated wok. Add the garlic and shallots and stir-fry for 1 minute.

3 Add the green beans and drained pasta to the frying pan or wok and stir-fry for 5 minutes. Add the cherry tomatoes and mix well.

4 Combine the chilli flakes, peanut butter, coconut milk and tomato purée. Pour the chilli mixture into the frying pan or wok, toss well to combine and heat through.

5 Transfer to warm serving dishes and garnish with spring onion slices. Serve immediately.

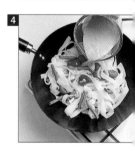

VARIATION

Add slices of chicken or beef to the recipe and stir-fry with the beans and pasta in step 3 for a more substantial main meal.

Filled Pitta Breads

Pitta breads are warmed over hot coals, then split and filled with a Greek salad tossed in a fragrant rosemary dressing.

NUTRITIONAL INFORMATION

Calories	456	Sugars 4g
Protein	........13g	Fat 25g
Carbohydrate	...49g	Saturates 7g

 15 mins   10 mins

SERVES 4

I N G R E D I E N T S

½ iceberg lettuce, roughly chopped

2 large tomatoes, cut into wedges

7.5 cm/3 inch piece of cucumber, cut into chunks

25 g/1 oz stoned black olives

115 g/4 oz feta cheese

4 pitta breads

D R E S S I N G

6 tbsp olive oil

3 tbsp red wine vinegar

1 tbsp crushed rosemary

½ tsp caster sugar

salt and pepper

1 To make the salad, combine the lettuce, tomatoes, cucumber and black olives.

2 Cut the feta cheese into chunks and add to the salad. Toss gently.

3 To make the dressing, whisk together the olive oil, red wine vinegar, rosemary and sugar. Season to taste with salt and pepper. Place in a small saucepan or heatproof bowl and heat very gently or place on the side of a barbecue to warm through gently.

4 Wrap the individual pitta breads tightly in foil and place on a hot barbecue for 2–3 minutes, turning once, to warm through.

5 Unwrap the breads and split them open. Fill with the Greek salad mixture and drizzle over the warm dressing. Serve immediately.

COOK'S TIP

Substitute different herbs for the rosemary – either oregano or basil would make a delicious alternative. Pack plenty of the salad into the pitta breads – they taste much better when they are full to bursting!

Thai-style Crab Sandwich

A hearty, open sandwich, topped with a classic flavour combination – crab with avocado and ginger. Perfect for a light summer lunch.

NUTRITIONAL INFORMATION

Calories	768	Sugars	.........3g
Protein	........26g	Fat	..........49g
Carbohydrate	...58g	Saturates	.......8g

 8 mins   0 mins

SERVES 2

INGREDIENTS

2 tbsp lime juice

2 cm/¾ inch piece fresh ginger root, grated

2 cm/¾ inch piece of lemon grass, finely chopped

5 tbsp mayonnaise

2 large slices crusty bread

1 ripe avocado

150 g/5½ oz cooked crab meat

pepper

fresh coriander sprigs, to garnish

1 Mix half the lime juice with the ginger and lemon grass. Add the mayonnaise and mix well.

2 Spread 1 tablespoon of mayonnaise smoothly over each slice of bread.

3 Halve the avocado and remove the stone. Peel and slice the flesh thinly, then arrange the slices on the bread. Sprinkle with lime juice.

4 Spoon the crab meat over the avocado, then add any remaining lime juice. Spoon over the remaining mayonnaise, season with freshly ground black pepper, top with a coriander sprig and serve immediately.

COOK'S TIP

To make lime-and-ginger mayonnaise, process 2 egg yolks, 1 tbsp lime juice and ½ tsp grated root ginger in a blender. With the motor running, gradually add 300ml/10 fl oz olive oil, drop by drop, until the mixture is thick and smooth. Season to taste with salt and pepper.

Stuffed Eggs

These savoury stuffed eggs make a good picnic dish or they can be popped into a lunchbox for an unusual treat.

NUTRITIONAL INFORMATION

Calories	337	Sugars	.........2g
Protein	........24g	Fat	..........28g
Carbohydrate	...22g	Saturates	.......5g

 15 mins   🕐 15 mins

SERVES 4

I N G R E D I E N T S

4 large eggs

100 g/3½ oz minced pork

170 g/6 oz can white crab meat, drained

1 garlic clove, crushed

1 tsp Thai fish sauce

½ tsp lemon grass, ground

1 tbsp chopped fresh coriander

1 tbsp desiccated coconut

100 g/3½ oz plain flour

about 150 ml/5 fl oz coconut milk

sunflower oil, for deep-frying

salt and pepper

green salad, to serve

cucumber flower, to garnish

1 Place the eggs in a pan of simmering water and bring to the boil, then simmer for 10 minutes. Drain the eggs, crack the shells and cool under cold running water. Peel off the shells.

2 Cut the eggs lengthways down the middle and scoop out the yolks. Place the yolks in a bowl with the pork, crab meat, garlic, fish sauce, lemon grass, coriander and coconut. Season with salt and pepper and mix the ingredients together thoroughly.

3 Divide the mixture into 8 equal portions, then fill each of the egg whites with the mixture, pressing together with your hands to form the shape of a whole egg.

4 Whisk together the flour and enough coconut milk to make a thick coating batter, then season with salt and pepper. Heat a 5 cm/2 inch depth of oil in a large pan to 190°C/375°F or until a cube of day-old bread browns in 30 seconds. Dip each egg into the coconut batter, then shake off the excess.

5 Fry the eggs, in 2 batches, for about 5 minutes, turning occasionally, until golden brown. Remove with a draining spoon and drain on kitchen paper. Serve warm or cold with a green salad garnished with cucumber flowers.

Thai-stuffed Omelette

Served with a colourful, crisp salad, this makes a tasty light lunch or supper dish and, on its own, could be served as a substantial starter.

NUTRITIONAL INFORMATION

Calories	250	Sugars	.........1g
Protein	........21g	Fat	..........18g
Carbohydrate	....2g	Saturates	.......4g

5–10 mins   25 mins

SERVES 4

INGREDIENTS

2 garlic cloves, chopped

4 black peppercorns

4 fresh coriander sprigs

2 tbsp vegetable oil

200 g/7 oz minced pork

2 spring onions, chopped

1 large, firm tomato, chopped

6 large eggs

1 tbsp Thai fish sauce

½ tsp ground turmeric

mixed salad leaves, to serve

1 Place the garlic, peppercorns and coriander in a mortar and crush with a pestle to a smooth paste.

2 Heat 1 tablespoon of the oil in a frying pan or wok over a medium heat. Add the paste and fry for 1–2 minutes until it just changes colour.

then pour a quarter of the egg mixture into the pan. As the mixture begins to set, stir lightly to ensure that all the liquid egg has set sufficiently.

3 Stir in the pork and stir-fry until it is lightly browned. Add the spring onions and tomato and stir-fry for a further minute, then remove the pan or wok from the heat.

5 Spoon a quarter of the pork mixture down the centre of the omelette, then fold the sides inwards, enclosing the filling. Make and fill 3 more omelettes with the remaining eggs and pork mixture.

COOK'S TIP

If you prefer, spread half the pork mixture evenly over one omelette, then place a second omelette on top, without folding. Cut into slim wedges to serve.

4 Heat the remaining oil in a small, heavy-based frying pan. Beat the eggs with the fish sauce and turmeric,

6 Slide the omelettes on to a warm serving plate and serve with the mixed salad leaves.

Sesame Noodles with Prawns

Delicately scented with sesame oil and seeds and fresh coriander, these noodles make an unusual lunch or supper dish.

NUTRITIONAL INFORMATION

Calories	430	Sugars	.........2g
Protein	........23g	Fat	..........15g
Carbohydrate	...56g	Saturates	.......3g

🍲 5 mins   🕐 10 mins

SERVES 4

I N G R E D I E N T S

1 garlic clove, chopped

1 spring onion, chopped

1 small fresh red chilli, deseeded and sliced

1 tbsp chopped fresh coriander

300 g/10½ oz fine egg noodles

2 tbsp vegetable oil

2 tsp sesame oil

1 tsp shrimp paste

225 g/8 oz raw prawns, peeled

2 tbsp lime juice

2 tbsp Thai fish sauce

1 tsp sesame seeds, toasted

1 Place the garlic, onion, chilli and coriander into a mortar and grind with a pestle to a smooth paste.

2 Drop the noodles into a pan of boiling water and bring back to the boil, then simmer for 4 minutes or according to the packet instructions.

3 Meanwhile, heat the vegetable and sesame oils in a pan and stir in the shrimp paste and ground coriander mixture. Stir over a medium heat for 1 minute.

4 Stir in the prawns and stir-fry for 2 minutes. Stir in the lime juice and fish sauce and cook for a further minute.

5 Drain the noodles and toss them into the wok. Sprinkle with the sesame seeds and serve immediately.

COOK'S TIP

The roots of coriander are widely used in Thai cooking, so if you can buy fresh coriander with the root attached, the whole plant can be used in this dish for maximum flavour. If not, just use the stems and leaves.

Hot & Sour Noodles

This simple, fast-food dish is sold from street food stalls in Thailand, with many and varied additions of meat and vegetables.

NUTRITIONAL INFORMATION

Calories .... .337	Sugars 1g	
Protein 10g	Fat .... .11g	
Carbohydrate ...53g	Saturates 1g	

5 mins   8 mins

SERVES 4

INGREDIENTS

250 g/9 oz dried medium egg noodles

1 tbsp sesame oil

1 tbsp chilli oil

1 garlic clove, crushed

2 spring onions, finely chopped

55 g/2 oz button mushrooms, sliced

40 g/1½ oz dried Chinese black
    mushrooms, soaked, drained and sliced

2 tbsp lime juice

3 tbsp light soy sauce

1 tsp sugar

shredded Chinese leaves, to serve

TO GARNISH

2 tbsp chopped fresh coriander

2 tbsp chopped, toasted peanuts

1 Cook the noodles in a large pan of boiling water for 3–4 minutes or according to the package instructions. Drain well, return to the pan, toss with the sesame oil and set aside.

2 Heat the chilli oil in a large frying pan or wok and quickly stir-fry the garlic, onions and button mushrooms for 2 minutes until just softened.

3 Add the black mushrooms, lime juice, soy sauce and sugar and continue stir-frying until boiling. Add the noodles and toss to mix.

4 Make a bed of shredded Chinese leaves on a serving platter and spoon the noodle mixture on top. Garnish with the fresh coriander and chopped peanuts and serve immediately.

COOK'S TIP

Thai chilli oil is very hot, so if you want a milder flavour, use vegetable oil for the initial cooking instead, then add a final drizzle of chilli oil just for seasoning.

Crispy Tofu with Chilli Sauce

Tempting golden cubes of fried tofu, with colourful fresh carrot and peppers, combine with a warm ginger sauce to make an unusual dish.

NUTRITIONAL INFORMATION

Calories 149	Sugars 9g
Protein 8g	Fat 9g
Carbohydrate . . .10g	Saturates 1g

 10 mins   5 mins

SERVES 4

I N G R E D I E N T S

300 g/10½ oz firm tofu

2 tbsp vegetable oil

1 garlic clove, sliced

1 carrot, cut into batons

½ green pepper, deseeded and cut into batons

1 fresh red bird-eye chilli, deseeded and finely chopped

2 tbsp soy sauce

1 tbsp lime juice

1 tbsp Thai fish sauce

1 tbsp soft light brown sugar

pickled garlic slices, to serve (optional)

1 Drain the tofu and pat dry with kitchen paper. Using a sharp knife, cut into 2 cm/¾ inch cubes.

2 Heat the oil in a wok. Add the garlic and stir-fry over a medium heat for 1 minute. Remove the garlic with a draining spoon and add the tofu, then fry quickly until well-browned, turning gently to brown on all sides.

3 Lift out the tofu with a draining spoon, drain well and keep hot. Stir the carrot and green pepper batons into the wok and stir-fry for 1 minute.

4 Spoon the carrot and peppers on to a warmed serving dish and pile the tofu on top.

5 Mix together the chilli, soy sauce, lime juice, fish sauce and sugar, stirring until the sugar is dissolved.

6 Spoon the sauce over the tofu and serve immediately topped with slices of pickled garlic, if you like.

COOK'S TIP

Make sure to buy firm fresh tofu for this dish – the softer 'silken' type is more like junket in texture and not firm enough to hold its shape well during frying. It is better for adding to soups.

Side Dishes

A clever choice of side dishes can turn an ordinary meal into a special occasion. Many of the recipes in this chapter, such as Thai Fragrant Coconut Rice and Vegetables with Vermouth, are quick and easy to prepare, yet will add a note of distinction to any meal.

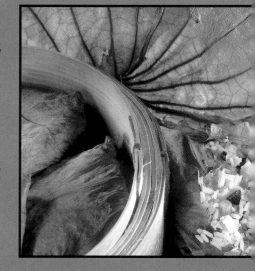

There can be few things more appetising than home-made bread and rolls. This chapter includes recipes from around the world – Herb Focaccia from Italy, Peshwari Naan from India and Irish Soda Bread.

Salsas, chutneys, dhals and raitas also feature to add that important finishing touch to family suppers and dinner parties alike.

Baked Fennel

Fennel is a very versatile vegetable, which is good cooked or used raw in salads. It is an especially popular ingredient in many Italian dishes.

NUTRITIONAL INFORMATION

Calories 111	Sugars 6g
Protein 7g	Fat 7g
Carbohydrate 7g	Saturates 3g

 10 mins   35 mins

SERVES 4

I N G R E D I E N T S

2 fennel bulbs

2 celery sticks, cut into 7.5 cm/
   3 inch pieces

6 sun-dried tomatoes, halved

200 ml/7 fl oz passata

2 tsp dried oregano

55 g/2 oz Parmesan cheese,
   freshly grated

1 Using a sharp knife, trim the fennel, discarding any tough outer leaves, and cut the bulb into quarters.

2 Bring a large pan of water to the boil, add the fennel and celery and cook for 8–10 minutes or until just tender. Remove with a draining spoon and drain.

3 Place the fennel pieces, celery and sun-dried tomatoes in a large ovenproof dish.

4 Mix the passata and oregano and pour the mixture over the fennel.

5 Sprinkle the surface evenly with the Parmesan cheese and bake in a preheated oven, 190°C/375°F/Gas Mark 5, for 20 minutes or until hot. Serve as a starter with fresh crusty bread or as a vegetable side dish.

Potatoes, Olives & Anchovies

This side dish makes a delicious accompaniment for grilled fish or for lamb chops. The fennel adds a subtle aniseed flavour.

NUTRITIONAL INFORMATION

Calories 202   Sugars 2g
Protein . . . . .7g   Fat 12g
Carbohydrate . . .19g   Saturates 1g

10 mins   30 mins

SERVES 4

INGREDIENTS

450 g/1 lb baby new potatoes, scrubbed

85 g/3 oz mixed olives

8 canned anchovy fillets, drained and chopped

2 tbsp olive oil

2 fennel bulbs, trimmed and sliced

2 fresh rosemary sprigs, stalks removed

salt

1 Bring a large pan of lightly salted water to the boil. Add the potatoes, bring back to the boil and simmer over a medium heat for 8–10 minutes or until tender. Remove the potatoes from the pan using a draining spoon and set aside to cool slightly.

2 Once the potatoes are cool enough to handle, cut them into wedges, using a sharp knife.

3 Stone the mixed olives with a cherry stoner or small, sharp knife and cut them in half.

4 Using a sharp knife, chop the anchovy fillets into thinner strips.

5 Heat the olive oil in a large, heavy-based frying pan. Add the potato wedges, sliced fennel and rosemary. Cook over a medium heat, gently stirring occasionally, for 7–8 minutes or until the potatoes are golden.

6 Stir in the olives and anchovies and cook for 1 minute or until completely warmed through.

7 Transfer the potato mixture to warmed individual serving plates and serve immediately.

COOK'S TIP
Fresh rosemary is a particular favourite with Italians, but you can experiment with your favourite herbs in this recipe, if you prefer.

Coconut Rice with Lentils

Rice and green lentils are cooked with coconut, lemon grass and curry leaves. This recipe will also serve two people as a main course.

NUTRITIONAL INFORMATION

Calories	511	Sugars	3g
Protein	12g	Fat	24g
Carbohydrate	67g	Saturates	15g

 5 mins   50 mins

SERVES 4

I N G R E D I E N T S

85 g/3 oz green lentils

250 g/9 oz long grain rice

2 tbsp vegetable oil

1 onion, sliced

2 garlic cloves, crushed

3 curry leaves

1 lemon grass stalk, chopped or grated rind of ½ lemon

1 fresh green chilli, deseeded and chopped

½ tsp cumin seeds

1½ tsp salt

85 g/3 oz creamed coconut

600 ml/1 pint hot water

2 tbsp chopped fresh coriander

T O   G A R N I S H

shredded radishes

shredded cucumber

1 Wash the lentils and place in a pan. Cover with cold water, bring to the boil and boil rapidly for 10 minutes.

2 Wash the rice thoroughly and drain well. Set aside until required.

3 Heat the vegetable oil in a large pan with a tight-fitting lid. Add the onion and cook over a medium heat, stirring occasionally, for 3–4 minutes. Stir in the garlic, curry leaves, lemon grass or lemon rind, chilli, cumin seeds and salt.

4 Drain the lentils and rinse them. Add to the onion and spices with the rice and mix well.

5 Combine the creamed coconut with the hot water and stir until dissolved. Stir the coconut liquid into the rice mixture and bring to the boil. Lower the heat, cover and simmer gently undisturbed, for 15 minutes.

6 Without removing the lid, remove the pan from the heat and set aside for 10 minutes to allow the rice and lentils to finish cooking in their own steam.

7 Stir in the coriander and remove and discard the curry leaves. Transfer to a warmed serving dish and serve garnished with the radishes and cucumber.

Vegetables in Coconut Milk

This is a deliciously crunchy way to prepare a mixture of raw vegetables and would be ideal as a buffet dish for a party.

NUTRITIONAL INFORMATION

Calories 201	Sugars 10g	
Protein 9g	Fat 13g	
Carbohydrate . . .13g	Saturates 3g	

🍠 5 mins   🕐 5 mins

SERVES 4

INGREDIENTS

1 fresh red chilli, deseeded and chopped

1 tsp coriander seeds

1 tsp cumin seeds

2 garlic cloves, crushed

uice of 1 lime

250 ml/9 fl oz coconut milk

115 g/4 oz beansprouts

115 g/4 oz white cabbage, shredded

115 g/4 oz mangetouts, trimmed

115 g/4 oz carrots, thinly sliced

115 g/4 oz cauliflower florets

3 tbsp peanut butter

grated or shaved coconut, to serve

1 Grind the chilli, coriander and cumin seeds, garlic and lime juice in a mortar with a pestle or in a food processor until a smooth paste.

2 Put the spice paste into a medium pan and heat gently for about 1 minute or until fragrant. Add the coconut milk and stir constantly until just about to boil.

3 Combine the beansprouts, shredded white cabbage, mangetouts, sliced carrots and cauliflower florets in a large mixing bowl.

4 Stir the peanut butter into the coconut mixture until well blended and then pour into the bowl, stirring to coat the vegetables. Serve garnished with grated or shaved coconut.

COOK'S TIP
If you prefer, the cauliflower, carrots and mangetouts may be blanched first for less bite.

Steamed Lotus Rice

The fragrance of the lotus leaves penetrates the rice, giving it a unique taste. Lotus leaves can be bought from specialist Chinese shops.

NUTRITIONAL INFORMATION

Calories 163	Sugars 0.1g
Protein 5g	Fat 6g
Carbohydrate ...2.1g	Saturates 1g

 35 mins   40 mins

SERVES 4

INGREDIENTS

2 lotus leaves

4 Chinese dried mushrooms

175 g/6 oz long grain rice

1 cinnamon stick

6 cardamom pods

4 cloves

1 tsp salt

2 eggs

1 tbsp vegetable oil

2 spring onions, chopped

1 tbsp soy sauce

2 tbsp sherry

1 tsp sugar

1 tsp sesame oil

1 Unfold the lotus leaves carefully and cut along the fold to divide each leaf in half. Lay on a large baking sheet and pour over enough hot water to cover. Soak for about 30 minutes until softened.

2 Meanwhile, place the mushrooms in a bowl, cover with warm water and set aside to soak for 20–25 minutes.

3 Bring a pan of water to the boil. Add the rice with the cinnamon stick, cardamom pods, cloves and salt, bring back to the boil and cook for 10 minutes – the rice should be partially cooked. Drain thoroughly and remove the cinnamon stick. Place the rice in a bowl.

4 Beat the eggs lightly. Heat the oil in a wok and cook the eggs quickly, stirring until set. Remove and set aside.

5 Drain the mushrooms, squeezing out the excess water. Remove the tough stems and chop the mushrooms. Stir int the rice with the cooked egg, sprin onions, soy sauce, sherry or rice win sugar and sesame oil.

6 Drain the lotus leaves and divide th rice into 4 portions. Place a portion i the centre of each leaf and fold up to for a parcel. Place in a steamer, cover an steam over simmering water fo 20 minutes. To serve, cut the tops of th lotus leaves open to expose the rice inside

Chinese Fried Rice

t is essential that the rice is both cold and dry, with
separate grains, in order to make this recipe properly.

NUTRITIONAL INFORMATION

Calories 475   Sugars 3g
Protein . . . . .16g   Fat 16g
Carbohydrate . . .72g   Saturates 3g

    5 mins   30 mins

SERVES 4

INGREDIENTS

00 ml/1¼ pints water

tsp salt

00 g/10½ oz long grain rice

eggs

tsp cold water

tbsp sunflower oil

spring onions, sliced diagonally

red, green or yellow pepper, seeded and
thinly sliced

–4 lean bacon rashers, rinded and cut
into strips

00 g/7 oz fresh beansprouts

15 g/1 oz frozen peas, thawed

tbsp soy sauce (optional)

alt and pepper

1 Pour the water into a wok with the
salt and bring to the boil. Rinse the
ce in a sieve under cold water until the
ater runs clear, drain well and add to the
oiling water. Stir well, then cover the wok
ghtly with the lid, and simmer gently for
2–13 minutes. (Don't remove the lid
uring cooking or the steam will escape
nd the rice will not be cooked.)

2 Remove the lid, stir the rice and
spread out on a large plate or baking
ay to cool and dry.

3 Beat each egg separately with salt
and pepper and 2 teaspoons of cold
water. Heat 1 tablespoon of the oil in the
wok, pour in the first egg, swirl it around
and cook, undisturbed, until set. Remove to
a board and cook the second egg. Cut the
omelettes into thin slices.

4 Add the remaining oil to the wok, add
the spring onions and pepper and stir-
fry for 1–2 minutes. Add the bacon and
continue to stir-fry for a further
1–2 minutes. Add the beansprouts and
peas and toss together thoroughly. Stir in
the soy sauce, if using.

5 Add the rice and seasoning and stir-
fry for about 1 minute, then add the
strips of omelette and continue to stir for
about 2 minutes or until the rice is piping
hot. Transfer to a warmed serving dish and
serve immediately.

Curried Rice with Tofu

Cooked rice is combined with marinated tofu, vegetables and peanuts to make this deliciously rich curry. Serve as part of a Thai meal.

NUTRITIONAL INFORMATION

Calories .... .598 Sugars 2g
Protein ....16g Fat 25
Carbohydrate ...81g Saturates 4g

15 mins 15 mins

SERVES 4

INGREDIENTS

1 tsp coriander seeds

1 tsp cumin seeds

1 tsp ground cinnamon

1 tsp cloves

1 star anise

1 tsp cardamom seeds

1 tsp white peppercorns

4 tbsp sunflower oil

6 shallots, roughly chopped

6 garlic cloves, roughly chopped

5 cm/2 inch piece of lemon grass, sliced

4 fresh red chillies, deseeded and chopped

grated rind of 1 lime

1 tsp salt

250 g/9 oz marinated tofu, cut into 2.5 cm/
    1 inch cubes

115 g/4 oz green beans, cut into 2.5cm/
    1 inch lengths

1 kg/2 lb 4 oz cooked rice

3 shallots, finely diced and deep-fried

1 spring onion, finely chopped

2 tbsp chopped roasted peanuts

1 tbsp lime juice

1 To make the curry paste, grind the coriander and cumin seeds, cinnamon, cloves, star anise, cardamom seeds and peppercorns in a mortar with a pestle or in a spice grinder or coffee grinder kept for the purpose.

2 Heat 1 tablespoon of the sunflower oil in a preheated wok until it is really hot. Add the chopped shallots, garlic and lemon grass and cook over a low heat for about 5 minutes until softened. Add the chillies and stir together with the dry spices. Stir in the lime rind and salt.

3 To make the curry, heat the remaining oil in a wok or large, heavy-based frying pan. Add the tofu and stir-fry gently over a high heat for 2 minutes to seal. Stir in the curry paste and beans. Add the rice and stir over a high heat for about 3 minutes.

4 Transfer to a warmed serving dish. Sprinkle with the deep-fried shallots, spring onion and peanuts. Squeeze over the lime juice and serve.

Toovar Dhal

Dried pulses and lentils can be cooked in similar ways, but the soaking and cooking times do vary, so check the pack for instructions.

NUTRITIONAL INFORMATION

Calories ....195 Sugars 4g
Protein ....11g Fat 5g
Carbohydrate ...28g Saturates 3g

10 mins   50 mins

SERVES 6

INGREDIENTS

tbsp vegetable ghee

large onion, finely chopped

garlic clove, crushed

tbsp grated fresh root ginger

tbsp cumin seeds, ground

tsp coriander seeds, ground

dried red chilli

5 cm/1 inch piece of cinnamon stick

tsp salt

tsp ground turmeric

25 g/8 oz split yellow peas, soaked in cold water for 1 hour and drained

00 g/14 oz can plum tomatoes

00 ml/½ pint water

tsp garam masala

1 Heat the ghee in a large saucepan, add the onion, garlic and ginger and y for 3–4 minutes until the onion has oftened slightly.

2 Add the cumin, coriander, chilli, cinnamon, salt and turmeric, then stir the split peas until well mixed.

3 Add the tomatoes, with their can juices, breaking up the tomatoes ightly with the back of a spoon.

4 Add the water and bring to the boil. Reduce the heat to very low and simmer, uncovered, stirring occasionally, for about 40 minutes until most of the liquid has been absorbed and the split peas are tender. Skim the surface occasionally with a slotted spoon to remove any scum.

5 Gradually stir in the garam masala, tasting after each addition, until it is to your taste. Serve hot.

COOK'S TIP
Use a non-stick saucepan if you have one, because the mixture is quite dense and does stick to the base of the pan occasionally. If the dhal is overstirred, the split peas will break up and the dish will not have much texture or bite.

Brindil Bhaji

This is one of the most delicious – and easiest – of the
Indian bhaji dishes and has a wonderful sweet spicy flavour.

NUTRITIONAL INFORMATION

Calories 117   Sugars 8g
Protein . . . . .3g   Fat 8g
Carbohydrate . . . .9g   Saturates 5g

 20 mins   🕐 20 mins

SERVES 4

INGREDIENTS

500 g/1 lb 2 oz aubergines, sliced

2 tbsp vegetable ghee

1 onion, thinly sliced

2 garlic cloves, sliced

2.5 cm/1 inch piece of fresh root
ginger, grated

½ tsp ground turmeric

1 dried red chilli

½ tsp salt

400 g/14 oz can tomatoes

1 tsp garam masala

fresh coriander sprigs, to garnish

VARIATION

Other vegetables can be used
instead of the aubergines.
Try courgettes, potatoes or peppers,
or any combination of these
vegetables, using the same sauce.

1 Cut the aubergine slices into finger-width strips.

2 Heat the vegetable ghee in a heavy-based pan. Add the onion and cook over a medium heat, stirring constantly, for 7–8 minutes, until very soft and just beginning to colour.

3 Add the garlic and aubergine strips, increase the heat and cook, stirring constantly, for 2 minutes. Stir in the ginger, turmeric, chilli, salt and tomatoes, with their can juices. Use the back of a wooden spoon to break up the tomatoes. Lower the heat and simmer, uncovered, for 15–20 minutes, until the aubergines are very soft.

4 Stir in the garam masala and simmer for a further 4–5 minutes.

5 Transfer the brindil bhaji to a warmed serving plate, garnish with fresh coriander sprigs and serve immediately.

Beans in Tomato Sauce

Nothing could be simpler, quicker or tastier than a delicious mix of beans cooked in a high-speed fresh tomato sauce.

NUTRITIONAL INFORMATION

Calories	221	Sugars	.....8g
Protein	.....12g	Fat	.....7g
Carbohydrate	...30g	Saturates	.....1g

 10 mins   15 mins

SERVES 4

INGREDIENTS

400g/14 oz can cannellini beans

400g/14 oz can borlotti beans

2 tbsp olive oil

1 celery stick, thinly sliced

2 garlic cloves, chopped

175 g/6 oz baby onions, halved

450 g/1 lb tomatoes

85 g/3 oz rocket

1   Drain both cans of beans and reserve 6 tablespoons of the liquid.

2   Heat the oil in a large pan. Add the celery, garlic and onions and sauté for 5 minutes or until the onions are golden.

3   Cut a cross in the base of each tomato and plunge them into boiling water for 30 seconds until the skins split. Remove them with a draining spoon and set aside until cool enough to handle. Peel off the skins and chop the flesh. Add the tomatoes and the reserved bean liquid to the pan and cook for 5 minutes.

4   Add the beans to the pan and cook for a further 3–4 minutes or until the beans are hot.

5   Stir in the rocket and allow to wilt slightly before serving.

COOK'S TIP

Another way to peel tomatoes is to cut a cross in the base, push it on to a fork and hold it over a gas flame, turning it slowly so that the skin heats evenly all over. The skin will start to bubble and split and should then slide off easily.

Chinese Omelette

This omelette contains chicken and prawns. It is cooked as a whole omelette and then sliced for serving as part of a Chinese meal.

NUTRITIONAL INFORMATION

Calories 309   Sugars 0g
Protein . . . . .34g   Fat 19g
Carbohydrate . . .0.2g   Saturates 5g

5 mins   5 mins

SERVES 4

I N G R E D I E N T S

8 eggs

225 g/8 oz cooked chicken, shredded

12 tiger prawns, peeled and deveined

2 tbsp chopped fresh chives

2 tsp light soy sauce

dash of chilli sauce

2 tbsp vegetable oil

1 Lightly beat the eggs in a large mixing bowl. Add the shredded chicken and tiger prawns, mixing well.

2 Stir in the chopped chives, light soy sauce and chilli sauce, mixing well to combine all the ingredients.

3 Heat the vegetable oil in a large heavy-based frying pan over a medium heat. Pour in the egg mixture, tilting the pan to coat the base evenly and completely.

4 Cook over a medium heat, gently stirring the omelette with a fork, until the surface is just set and the underside is a golden brown colour.

5 When the omelette is set, slide it out of the pan with the aid of a palette knife. Cut the Chinese omelette into squares or slices and serve immediately.

VARIATION

You could add extra flavour to the omelette by stirring in 3 tablespoons of finely chopped fresh coriander or 1 teaspoon of sesame seeds with the chives in step 2.

Caraway Cabbage

This makes a delicious vegetable accompaniment to all types of food: it can also be served as a vegetarian main dish.

NUTRITIONAL INFORMATION

Calories	223	Sugars	........17g
Protein	.........6g	Fat	..........14g
Carbohydrate	...18g	Saturates	.......1g

🜂 🜂

🥢 5 mins   🕐 10 mins

SERVES 4

I N G R E D I E N T S

500 g/1 lb 2 oz white cabbage

1 tbsp sunflower oil

4 spring onions, thinly sliced diagonally

6 tbsp raisins

55 g/2 oz walnut pieces or pecan nuts,
  roughly chopped

5 tbsp milk or vegetable stock

1 tbsp caraway seeds

1–2 tbsp chopped fresh mint

salt and pepper

fresh mint sprigs, to garnish

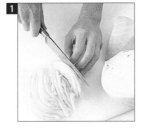

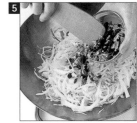

1 Remove any tough outer leaves from the cabbage and cut out the stem, then shred the leaves very finely, either by hand or using the fine slicing blade on a food processor.

2 Heat the sunflower oil in a wok, swirling it around until it is really hot.

3 Add the spring onions to the wok and stir-fry for 1–2 minutes.

4 Add the shredded cabbage and stir-fry for 3–4 minutes, keeping the cabbage moving all the time and stirring from the outside to the centre of the wok to prevent it from going brown.

5 Add the raisins, walnuts or pecans and milk or vegetable stock and cook, stirring constantly, for 3–4 minutes until the cabbage begins to soften slightly, but is still crisp.

6 Season to taste with salt and pepper, add the caraway seeds and 1 tablespoon of the chopped mint and cook for a further 1 minute. Transfer to a warm serving dish and serve sprinkled with the remaining chopped mint and garnished with sprigs of fresh mint.

VARIATION

Red cabbage may be cooked in the same way in the wok, but substitute 2 tablespoons red or white wine vinegar and 3 tablespoons water for the milk and add 1 tablespoon brown sugar. Add a finely chopped dessert apple if liked.

Ginger & Orange Broccoli

Thinly sliced broccoli florets are lightly stir-fried and served in a delightful ginger and orange sauce.

NUTRITIONAL INFORMATION

Calories	133	Sugars 6g
Protein	.........9g	Fat 7g
Carbohydrate	...10g	Saturates 1g

5 mins   10 mins

SERVES 4

INGREDIENTS

750 g/1 lb 10 oz broccoli

2 thin slices fresh root ginger

2 garlic cloves

1 orange

2 tsp cornflour

1 tbsp light soy sauce

½ tsp sugar

2 tbsp vegetable oil

1 Divide the broccoli into small florets. Peel the stems, using a vegetable peeler, and then cut the stems into thin slices, using a sharp knife.

2 Cut the ginger root into thin sticks and slice the garlic.

3 Peel 2 long strips of rind from the orange and cut into thin strips. Place the strips in a bowl, cover with cold water and set aside.

4 Squeeze the juice from the orange and mix with the cornflour, light soy sauce, sugar and 4 tablespoons water.

5 Heat the vegetable oil in a wok or large frying pan. Add the sliced broccoli stem and stir-fry for 2 minutes.

6 Add the ginger slices, garlic and broccoli florets and stir-fry for a further 3 minutes.

7 Stir the orange and soy sauce sauce mixture into the wok and cook stirring constantly, until the sauce has thickened and coated the broccoli.

8 Drain the reserved orange rind and stir into the wok. Transfer to a serving dish and serve immediately.

VARIATION

This dish could be made with cauliflower, if you prefer, or a mixture of cauliflower and broccoli.

Marinated Fennel

Fennel has a wonderful aniseed flavour which is ideal for grilling or barbecuing. This marinated recipe is really delicious.

NUTRITIONAL INFORMATION

Calories 117   Sugars 3g
Protein . . . . .1g   Fat 11g
Carbohydrate . . . .3g   Saturates 2g

1¼ hours   10 mins

SERVES 4

INGREDIENTS

2 fennel bulbs

1 red pepper, seeded and cut into large dice

1 lime, cut into 8 wedges

MARINADE

2 tbsp lime juice

4 tbsp olive oil

2 garlic cloves, crushed

1 tsp wholegrain mustard

1 tbsp chopped thyme

fennel fronds, to garnish

crisp salad, to serve

1 Cut off and reserve the fennel fronds for the garnish. Cut each of the bulbs into 8 pieces and place in a shallow dish. Add the pepper and mix well.

2 To make the marinade, combine the lime juice, olive oil, garlic, mustard and thyme. Pour the marinade over the fennel and pepper and toss to coat thoroughly. Cover with clingfilm and set aside to marinate for 1 hour.

3 Thread the fennel and pepper on to wooden skewers with the lime wedges. Cook the kebabs under a preheated medium grill, turning and

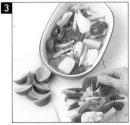

basting frequently with the marinade, for about 10 minutes. Alternatively, cook on a medium hot barbecue, turning and basting frequently, for about 10 minutes.

4 Transfer the kebabs to serving plates, garnish with fennel fronds and serve immediately with a crisp salad.

COOK'S TIP

Soak the skewers in cold water for 20 minutes before using to prevent them from burning during grilling. You could substitute 2 tablespoons orange juice for the lime juice and add 1 tbsp honey, if you prefer.

Ratatouille

A slow-cooked Provençal vegetable stew, this goes particularly well with roast lamb, but is also excellent with any grilled meat or poultry.

NUTRITIONAL INFORMATION

Calories	157	Sugars	........11g
Protein	.........4g	Fat	...........9g
Carbohydrate	...14g	Saturates	.......1g

40 mins   45 mins

SERVES 4–6

INGREDIENTS

1 large aubergine, about 300 g/10½ oz

5 tbsp olive oil

2 large onions, thinly sliced

2 large garlic cloves, crushed

4 courgettes, sliced

2 x 400 g/14 oz cans chopped tomatoes

1 tsp sugar

1 bouquet garni of 2 fresh thyme sprigs,
    2 large fresh parsley sprigs, 1 fresh basil
    sprig and 1 bay leaf, tied in a 7.5 cm/
    3 inch piece of celery

salt and pepper

fresh basil leaves, to garnish

1 Coarsely chop the aubergine, then place in a colander. Sprinkle with salt and set aside for 30 minutes to drain. Rinse well under cold running water to remove all traces of the salt and pat dry with kitchen paper.

2 Heat the olive oil in a large heavy-based flameproof casserole over a medium heat. Add the onions, lower the heat and cook, stirring occasionally, for 10 minutes until softened and light golden brown.

3 Add the garlic and continue to fry for 2 minutes until the onions are very tender and lightly browned.

4 Add the aubergine, courgettes, tomatoes, with their can juices, sugar and bouquet garni. Season with salt and pepper to taste. Bring to the boil, then lower the heat to very low, cover and simmer for 30 minutes.

5 Taste and adjust the seasoning if necessary. Remove and discard the bouquet garni. Garnish the vegetable stew with basil leaves and serve immediately.

COOK'S TIP

This is equally good served hot, at room temperature or chilled. To make a vegetarian meal, serve it over cooked couscous or with tabbouleh.

Sweet & Sour Courgettes

This versatile dish has a distinctly Middle Eastern flavour and, like many Mediterranean dishes, is well balanced and healthy.

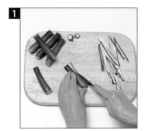
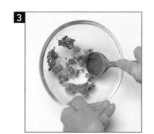

NUTRITIONAL INFORMATION

Calories	90	Sugars	.........5g
Protein	.........3g	Fat	...........4g
Carbohydrate	....5g	Saturates	.......1g

15 mins | 25–30 mins

SERVES 4–6

INGREDIENTS

00 g/1 lb 2 oz courgettes

tbsp olive oil

large garlic clove, finely chopped

tbsp white wine vinegar

tbsp water

–8 anchovy fillets, canned or salted

tbsp pine kernels

tbsp raisins

alt and pepper

esh flat leaf parsley sprigs, to garnish

1 Cut the courgettes into long, thin strips. Heat the olive oil in a large, eavy-based frying pan over a medium eat. Add the garlic and fry, stirring onstantly, for about 2 minutes.

2 Add the courgettes and cook, stirring frequently, until they just start to turn rown. Add the vinegar and water. Lower he heat and simmer, stirring frequently, r 10 minutes.

3 Meanwhile, drain the anchovies, if canned, or rinse if they are salted. oarsely chop, then use the back of a ooden spoon to mash them to a paste.

4 Stir the anchovies, pine kernels and raisins into the pan. Increase the heat

and stir until the courgettes are coated in a thin sauce and are tender. Taste and adjust the seasoning, remembering that the anchovies are very salty.

5 Either serve immediately or set aside to cool completely and then serve at room temperature. To serve, garnish with fresh parsley sprigs.

VARIATION

Replace the raisins with sultanas. Add a little grated lemon or orange rind for added zing.

Braised Fennel

So important in Mediterranean cooking, fennel is often braised and served as a vegetable accompaniment to meat, poultry or fish dishes.

NUTRITIONAL INFORMATION

Calories 149	Sugars 2g
Protein 6g	Fat 13g
Carbohydrate 2g	Saturates 7g

🥚 10 mins   🕐 45 mins

SERVES 4-6

INGREDIENTS

2 lemon slices

3 fennel bulbs

4½ tsp olive oil

3 tbsp butter

4 fresh thyme sprigs or ½ tbsp dried thyme

175 ml/6 fl oz chicken or vegetable stock

85 g/3 oz freshly grated Parmesan cheese

pepper

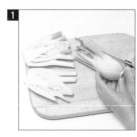  

COOK'S TIP

This is an ideal way to serve older fennel bulbs, but will not improve any that have been stored too long and dried out.

1 Bring a large pan of water to the boil and add the lemon slices. Trim the fennel bulbs and slice each of them lengthways. Add them to the pan, bring the water back to the boil and simmer the fennel for about 8 minutes until almost tender. Drain well.

2 Put the oil and butter in a flameproof casserole and melt over a medium heat. Swirl the melted mixture around so the bottom and sides of the casserole are well coated.

3 Add the fennel slices and stir until coated. Add the thyme and season with pepper to taste. Pour in the stock and sprinkle the cheese over the top.

4 Bake in a preheated oven, 200°C/400°F/Gas Mark 6 for 25–30 minutes until the fennel has absorbed the stock and is tender and the cheese has melted and become golden brown. Serve immediately.

Vegetables à la Grecque

'A la Grecque' is the French term for cooked vegetables left to cool in their highly flavoured cooking liquid and then served cold.

NUTRITIONAL INFORMATION

Calories	67	Sugars	.........4g
Protein	.........2g	Fat	..........4g
Carbohydrate	....6g	Saturates	.......1g

🧊 12¼ hrs   🕐 35–40 mins

SERVES 4–6

INGREDIENTS

250 g/9 oz small pickling onions

250 g/9 oz mushrooms

250 g/9 oz courgettes

450 ml/16 fl oz water

5 tbsp olive oil

2 tbsp lemon juice

2 strips lemon rind

2 large garlic cloves, thinly sliced

½ Spanish onion, finely chopped

1 bay leaf

15 black peppercorns, lightly crushed

10 coriander seeds, lightly crushed

pinch of dried oregano

finely chopped fresh flat leaf parsley or coriander, to garnish

focaccia, to serve

1 Put the small pickling onions in a heatproof bowl and pour over boiling water to cover. Set aside for 2 minutes, then drain. Peel and set aside.

2 Trim the mushroom stems. Cut the mushrooms into halves or quarters, if they are large, or leave whole if small. Trim the courgettes, cut off strips of the peel for a decorative finish, then cut into 5 mm/ ¼ inch slices. Set both the mushrooms and courgettes aside.

3 Put the water, olive oil, lemon juice and rind, garlic, Spanish onion, bay leaf, peppercorns, coriander seeds and oregano in a saucepan over a high heat and bring to the boil. Lower the heat and simmer for 15 minutes.

4 Add the small onions and continue to simmer for 5 minutes. Add the mushrooms and courgettes and simmer for a further 2 minutes. Using a draining spoon, transfer all the vegetables to a heatproof dish.

5 Return the liquid to the boil and boil until reduced to about 6 tablespoons. Pour the liquid over the vegetables and set aside to cool completely.

6 Cover with clingfilm and chill for at least 12 hours.

7 To serve, put the vegetables and cooking liquid in a serving dish and sprinkle the fresh herbs over them. Serve with chunks of focaccia.

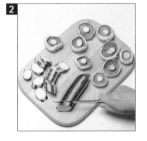  

Glazed Baby Onions

These onions are bathed in a rich, intensely flavoured glaze, making them a good accompaniment to any grilled or roasted meat.

NUTRITIONAL INFORMATION

Calories 81   Sugars 8g
Protein . . . . .1g   Fat 4g
Carbohydrate . . . .11g   Saturates 1g

10 mins   25 mins

SERVES 4–6

INGREDIENTS

500 g/1 lb 2 oz baby onions

2 tbsp olive oil

2 large garlic cloves, crushed

300 ml/10 fl oz vegetable or chicken stock

1 tbsp fresh thyme leaves

1 tbsp light brown sugar

2 tbsp red wine vinegar

about 1½ tsp balsamic vinegar

salt and pepper

fresh thyme sprigs, to garnish

1 Put the baby onions in a large heatproof bowl, pour over enough boiling water to cover and set aside for 2 minutes. Drain well.

2 Using a small knife and your fingers, peel off the skins, which should slip off easily.

3 Heat the olive oil in a large frying pan over a medium heat. Add the onions and cook, stirring constantly, for about 8 minutes until they are golden all over.

4 Add the garlic and cook, stirring, for 2 minutes. Add the stock, thyme leaves, sugar and wine vinegar, stirring until the sugar has dissolved.

5 Bring to the boil, then lower the heat and simmer gently for 10 minutes or until the onions are tender when you pierce them with the tip of a sharp knife and the cooking liquid is reduced to a syrupy glaze.

6 Stir in the balsamic vinegar. Season to taste with salt and pepper and add extra balsamic vinegar, if desired. Transfer to a serving dish and serve the onions either hot or cold, garnished with fresh thyme sprigs.

VARIATION

For extra texture, stir in 2 tablespoons toasted pine kernels just before serving. Do not add them earlier or they will become soft.

Spiced Lentils with Spinach

This dish is a good accompaniment to grilled lamb and veal dishes.
Serve with a tomato and onion salad for a vegetarian meal.

NUTRITIONAL INFORMATION

Calories	179	Sugars	.........3g
Protein	........11g	Fat	..........5g
Carbohydrate	...24g	Saturates	.......1g

 15 mins   35 mins

SERVES 4–6

INGREDIENTS

2 tbsp olive oil

1 large onion, finely chopped

1 large garlic clove, crushed

½ tbsp ground cumin

½ tsp ground ginger

250 g/9 oz Puy lentils

about 600 ml/1 pint vegetable or
    chicken stock

100 g/3½ oz baby spinach leaves

2 tbsp fresh mint leaves

1 tbsp fresh coriander leaves

1 tbsp fresh flat leaf parsley leaves

freshly squeezed lemon juice

salt and pepper

strips of lemon rind, to garnish

1 Heat the oil in a large frying pan over a medium heat. Add the onion and cook, stirring occasionally, for about 6 minutes. Stir in the garlic, cumin and ginger and cook, stirring occasionally, until the onion starts to brown.

2 Stir in the lentils. Pour in enough stock to cover the lentils by 2.5 cm/ 1 inch and bring to the boil. Lower the heat and simmer for 20–30 minutes until the lentils are tender.

3 Meanwhile, rinse the spinach leaves in several changes of cold water and shake dry. Finely chop the mint, coriander and parsley leaves.

4 If there isn't any stock left in the pan, add a little extra. Add the spinach and stir through until it just wilts. Stir in the mint, coriander and parsley. Adjust the seasoning, adding lemon juice and salt and pepper. Transfer to a serving bowl and serve, garnished with lemon rind.

COOK'S TIP

This recipe uses green lentils from Puy in France because they are good at keeping their shape even after long cooking. You can, however, also use orange or brown lentils but it is necessary to watch them while they cook or they will quickly turn to a mush.

Saucy Borlotti Beans

Fresh sage, a herb used frequently in Mediterranean cooking, adds a subtle flavour to these pink and white speckled beans.

NUTRITIONAL INFORMATION

Calories	84	Sugars	.........6g
Protein	.........4g	Fat	...........3g
Carbohydrate	...10g	Saturates	.......0g

20 mins   30 mins

SERVES 4–6

I N G R E D I E N T S

600 g/1 lb 5 oz fresh borlotti beans

4 large leaves fresh sage, torn

1 tbsp olive oil

1 large onion, thinly sliced

300 ml/10 fl oz good-quality bottled or home-made (see page 828) tomato sauce for pasta

salt and pepper

shredded fresh sage leaves, to garnish

 1 Shell the borlotti beans. Bring a saucepan of water to the boil, add the beans and torn sage leaves, bring back to the boil and simmer for about 12 minutes or until tender. Drain and set aside.

VARIATION

If fresh borlotti beans are unavailable, use 2 x 300 g/10 oz cans instead. Drain and rinse, then add with the sage and tomato sauce in Step 2.

2 Heat the olive oil in a large, heavy-based frying pan over a medium heat. Add the onion and cook, stirring occasionally, for about 5 minutes until softened and translucent, but not browned. Stir the tomato sauce into the pan with the cooked borlotti beans and the torn sage leaves.

3 Increase the heat and bring to the boil, stirring. Lower the heat, partially cover and simmer for about 10 minutes or until the the sauce has slightly reduced.

4 Adjust the seasoning, transfer to a serving bowl and serve hot, garnished with fresh sage leaves.

Flavoured Olives

You are sure to find Mediterranean stalls selling all kinds of flavoured olives. This nutritional analysis is based on a portion of 3 Provençal olives.

NUTRITIONAL INFORMATION

Calories	53	Sugars	.........0g
Protein	.........0g	Fat	...........6g
Carbohydrate	....0g	Saturates	.......1g

 10–15 mins   0 mins

MAKES 1 X 500 ML/18 FL OZ JAR

I N G R E D I E N T S

fresh herb sprigs, to serve

P R O V E N C A L   O L I V E S

3 dried red chillies

1 tsp black peppercorns

300 g/10½ oz black Niçoise olives in brine

2 lemon slices

1 tsp black mustard seeds

1 tbsp garlic-flavoured olive oil

fruity extra virgin olive oil

C A T A L A N   O L I V E S

½ grilled red or orange pepper

150 g/5½ oz black olives in brine

150 g/5½ oz pimento-stuffed olives in brine

1 tbsp capers in brine, rinsed

pinch of dried chilli flakes

4 tbsp chopped fresh coriander leaves

1 bay leaf

fruity extra virgin olive oil

G R E E K   O L I V E S

½ large lemon

300 g/10½ oz kalamata olives in brine

4 fresh thyme sprigs

1 shallot, very finely chopped

1 tbsp fennel seeds, lightly crushed

1 tsp dried dill

fruity extra virgin olive oil

1 To make the Provençal olives, place the dried red chillies and black peppercorns in a mortar and lightly crush. Drain and rinse the olives, then pat dry with kitchen paper. Put all the ingredients in a 500 ml/18 fl oz preserving jar, pouring in enough olive oil to cover.

2 Seal the jar and leave for at least 10 days before serving, shaking the jar daily.

3 To make the Catalan olives, finely chop the pepper. Drain and rinse both types of olives, then pat dry with kitchen paper. Put all the ingredients into a 500 ml/18 fl oz preserving jar, pouring in enough olive oil to cover. Seal and marinate as in Step 2.

4 To make the Greek olives, cut the lemon into 4 slices, then cut each slice into wedges. Drain and rinse the olives, then pat dry with kitchen paper.

5 Slice each olive lengthways on one side down to the stone. Put all the ingredients in a 500 ml/18 fl oz preserving jar, pouring in olive oil to cover. Seal and marinate as in Step 2.

6 To serve, spoon the olives into a bowl and garnish with fresh herbs.

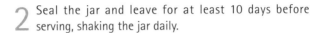

Greek Strained Yogurt

Smooth and creamy, this yogurt makes a refreshing start to hot days, spread on pitta bread for breakfast, or as a dip for an afternoon snack.

NUTRITIONAL INFORMATION*

Calories	32	Sugars	.........3g
Protein	.........2g	Fat	...........1g
Carbohydrate	....3g	Saturates	.......1g

 36½ hrs   0 mins

MAKES ABOUT 500 ML/18 FL OZ

INGREDIENTS

1 litre/1¾ pints natural yogurt

½ tsp salt

OPTIONAL TOPPINGS

fruity extra virgin olive oil

orange blossom or lavender honey

coriander seeds, crushed

paprika

very finely chopped fresh mint or coriander

finely grated lemon rind

1 Place a 125 x 75 cm/50 x 30 inch piece of muslin in a saucepan, cover with water and bring to the boil. Remove the pan from the heat and, using a wooden spoon, lift out the muslin. Wearing rubber gloves to protect your hands, wring the muslin dry.

2 Fold the muslin into a double layer and use it to line a colander or sieve set over a large bowl. Put the yogurt in a bowl and stir in the salt. Spoon the yogurt into the centre of the muslin.

3 Tie the muslin so it is suspended above the bowl. If your sink is deep enough, gather up the corners of the muslin and tie it to the tap. If not, lay a broom handle across 2 chairs and put the bowl between the chairs. Tie the muslin to the broom handle. Remove the colander or sieve and let the yogurt drain into the bowl for at least 12 hours.

4 Transfer the yogurt to a nylon sieve placed in a bowl. Cover lightly with clingfilm and refrigerate for 24 hours until soft and creamy. The yogurt will keep in the refrigerator for up to 5 days.

5 To serve, taste and add extra salt if needed. Spoon the yogurt into a bowl and sprinkle with the topping of your choice or a combination of toppings

* Nutritional information per 1 tablespoon of yogurt.

Spiced Pilau with Saffron

A Middle Eastern influence is evident in this fragrant pilau, studded with nuts, fruit and spices. Serve with roast lamb or a chicken dish.

NUTRITIONAL INFORMATION

Calories ....347 Sugars 9g
Protein ....5g Fat 11g
Carbohydrate ...60g Saturates 3g

  40 mins   30 mins

SERVES 4–6

I N G R E D I E N T S

pinch of saffron threads

450 ml/16 fl oz boiling water

1 tsp salt

2 tbsp butter

2 tbsp olive oil

1 large onion, very finely chopped

3 tbsp pine kernels

350 g/12 oz long grain rice

55 g/2 oz sultanas or raisins

6 green cardamom pods, lightly crushed

6 cloves

pepper

very finely chopped fresh coriander or flat
   leaf parsley, to garnish

1 Toast the saffron threads in dry frying pan over a medium heat stirring for 2 minutes or until they give off their aroma. Immediately tip them on to a plate.

2 Pour the boiling water into a measuring jug, stir in the saffron and 1 teaspoon salt and set aside for at least 30 minutes to infuse.

3 Melt the butter with the oil in a frying pan over a medium heat. Add the onion and cook, stirring occasionally, for about 5 minutes until softened.

4 Lower the heat, stir in the pine kernels and continue cooking for 2 minutes, stirring constantly, until they just start to turn golden. Take care that they do not burn.

5 Stir in the rice, ensuring that all the grains are coated with oil. Stir for 1 minute, then add the sultanas or raisins, cardamom pods and cloves. Pour in the saffron-flavoured water and bring to the boil. Lower the heat, cover and simmer gently for 15 minutes without removing the lid.

6 Remove the pan from the heat and set aside for 5 minutes without uncovering. Remove the lid and check that the rice is tender, all the liquid has been absorbed and the surface has small indentations all over.

7 Fluff up the rice with a fork. Taste and adjust the seasoning, if necessary, and stir the chopped herbs through. Serve the pilau immediately.

Spinach & Herb Orzo

Serve this quick and easy, vibrant green pasta dish with any grilled meat or seafood. Orzo is a kind of pasta shaped like long grains of barley.

NUTRITIONAL INFORMATION

Calories	304	Sugars	.........8g
Protein	........12g	Fat	...........6g
Carbohydrate	...54g	Saturates	.......1g

15–20 mins   10 mins

SERVES 4

INGREDIENTS

1 tsp salt

250 g/9 oz dried orzo

200 g/7 oz baby spinach leaves

150 g/5½ oz rocket

25 g/1 oz fresh flat leaf parsley leaves

25 g/1 oz fresh coriander leaves

4 spring onions

2 tbsp extra virgin olive oil

1 tbsp garlic-flavoured olive oil

pepper

TO SERVE

radicchio or other salad leaves

55 g/2 oz feta cheese, well drained and crumbled (optional)

lemon slices

1 Bring 2 pans of water to the boil, and put 12 ice cubes in a bowl of cold water. Add the salt and orzo to one of the pans, bring back to the boil and cook for 8–10 minutes until the pasta is tender, but still firm to the bite.

2 Meanwhile, remove the spinach stems if they are tough. Rinse the leaves in several changes of water to remove any grit. Coarsely chop the rocket, parsley, coriander and the green parts of the spring onions.

3 Add the spinach, rocket, parsley, coriander and spring onions to the second pan of boiling water and blanch for 15 seconds. Drain and transfer to the iced water to preserve the colour.

4 When the spinach, rocket, parsley, coriander and spring onions are cool, drain well and squeeze out all the excess water. Transfer to a small food processor and process. Add the olive oil and garlic-flavoured oil and process again until thoroughly blended.

5 Drain the orzo well and stir in the spinach mixture. Toss well and adjust the seasoning.

6 Line a serving platter with radicchio or other salad leaves and pile the orzo on top. Sprinkle with crumbled feta cheese, if using, and garnish with lemon slices. Serve hot or leave to cool to room temperature.

Thai Fragrant Coconut Rice

Basmati rice is cooked with creamed coconut, lemon grass, fresh ginger and spices to make a wonderfully aromatic, fluffy rice.

NUTRITIONAL INFORMATION

Calories 258   Sugars 0.4g
Protein . . . . .5g   Fat 6g
Carbohydrate . . .51g   Saturates 4g

 5 mins   🕐 20 mins

SERVES 4–6

I N G R E D I E N T S

2.5 cm/1 inch piece of fresh root
  ginger, sliced

2 cloves

1 piece of lemon grass, bruised
  and halved

2 tsp ground nutmeg

1 cinnamon stick

1 bay leaf

2 small thin strips lime rind

1 tsp salt

25 g/1 oz creamed coconut, chopped

600 ml/1 pint water

350 g/12 oz basmati rice

pepper

1 Place the ginger, cloves, lemon grass, nutmeg, cinnamon stick, bay leaf, lime rind, salt, creamed coconut and water in a large, heavy-based pan and bring to the boil over a low heat.

2 Add the rice, stir well, then cover and simmer over a very gentle heat for about 15 minutes or until all the liquid has been absorbed and the rice is tender but still has a bite to it.

3 Alternatively, bring the mixture to the boil, then cover tightly and turn off the heat. Leave for 20–25 minutes before removing the lid – the rice will be perfectly cooked.

4 Remove the pan from the heat, add pepper to taste, then fluff up the rice with a fork.

5 Remove the large pieces of spices and the lemon rind before serving.

COOK'S TIP

When using a whole stem of lemon grass, rather than chopped lemon grass, beat it well to bruise it so that the flavour is fully released. Grated lemon rind or a pared piece of lemon rind can be used instead.

Tomato Rice

Rice cooked with tomatoes and onions will add colour to your table, especially when garnished with green chillies and coriander.

NUTRITIONAL INFORMATION

Calories . . . . . . .866 Sugars 7g
Protein . . . . .15g Fat 46g
Carbohydrate . .106g Saturates 6g

 10 mins   35 mins

SERVES 4

INGREDIENTS

150 ml/5 fl oz vegetable oil

2 medium onions, sliced

1 tsp onion seeds

1 tsp finely chopped fresh root ginger

1 tsp crushed garlic

½ tsp ground turmeric

1 tsp chilli powder

1½ tsp salt

400 g/14 oz can tomatoes

500 g/1 lb 2 oz basmati rice

600 ml/1 pint water

TO GARNISH

3 fresh green chillies, finely chopped

fresh coriander leaves, chopped

3 hard-boiled eggs

COOK'S TIP

Onion seeds are always used whole in Indian cooking. They are often used in pickles and often sprinkled over the top of naan breads. Onion seeds don't have anything to do with the vegetable, but they look similar to the plant's seed, hence the name.

1 Heat the oil in a heavy-based pan. Add the onions and fry over a moderate heat, stirring frequently, for 5 minutes until golden brown.

2 Add the onion seeds, ginger, garlic, turmeric, chilli powder and salt, stirring to combine.

3 Reduce the heat, add the tomatoes and stir-fry for 10 minutes, breaking them up.

4 Add the rice to the tomato mixture, stirring gently to coat the rice completely. Stir in the water. Cover the pan and cook over a low heat until the water has been absorbed and the rice is tender, but still has some bite.

5 Transfer the tomato rice to a warmed serving dish. Garnish with the finely chopped green chillies, coriander leaves and hard-boiled eggs. Serve the tomato rice immediately.

Fidellos Tostados

The Sephardic Jews from Spain have been eating a very thin vermicelli-like pasta called fidellos for centuries.

NUTRITIONAL INFORMATION

Calories 327   Sugars 3g
Protein . . . . .9g   Fat 7
Carbohydrate . . .59g   Saturates 1g

5 mins   30 mins

SERVES 6

INGREDIENTS

350 g/12 oz vermicelli or angel hair pasta in coils, roughly broken

100 g/3½ oz long grain white rice

3 tbsp extra virgin olive oil

200 g/7 oz canned chopped tomatoes, drained

600 ml/1 pint chicken stock or water, plus extra if necessary

1 bay leaf

1–2 tsp chopped fresh oregano or 1 tsp dried oregano

½ tsp dried thyme leaves

salt and pepper

TO GARNISH

fresh oregano or thyme sprigs

chopped fresh oregano or thyme

1 Put the pasta and rice in a dry, large, heavy-based pan or flameproof casserole over a medium heat and cook for 5–7 minutes, stirring frequently, until light golden. (The pasta will break unevenly, but this does not matter.)

2 Stir in 2 tablespoons of the olive oil, with the chopped tomatoes, stock, bay leaf, oregano and thyme, then season with about 1 teaspoon of salt and pepper to taste.

3 Bring to the boil, reduce the heat to medium and simmer for about 8 minutes, stirring frequently, to help unwind and separate the pasta coils.

4 Reduce the heat to low, cover and cook for about 10 minutes until the rice and pasta are tender and all the liquid has been absorbed. If the rice and pasta are too firm, add about 125 ml/4 fl oz more stock or water and continue to cook, covered, for a further 5 minutes. Remove from the heat.

5 Using a fork, fluff the rice and pasta into a warmed, deep serving bowl and drizzle with the remaining oil. Sprinkle with the chopped oregano or thyme, garnish with fresh herb sprigs and serve immediately.

Spicy Potato-rice Pilaf

This spicy blend of potatoes, rice and peas can be served as part of an Indian meal, but is also rich enough to serve on its own.

NUTRITIONAL INFORMATION

Calories . . . . .217 Sugars 3g
Protein . . . . .6g Fat 4g
Carbohydrate . . .39g Saturates 0g

35 mins   30 mins

SERVES 4–6

I N G R E D I E N T S

200 g/7 oz basmati rice, soaked in cold water for 20 minutes

2 tbsp vegetable oil

½–¾ tsp cumin seeds

225 g/8 oz potatoes, cut into 1 cm/ ½ inch pieces

225 g/8 oz frozen peas, thawed

1 fresh green chilli, deseeded and thinly sliced (optional)

½ tsp salt

1 tsp garam masala

½ tsp ground turmeric

¼ tsp cayenne pepper

600 ml/1 pint water

2 tbsp chopped fresh coriander

1 red onion, finely chopped

natural yogurt, to serve

1 Rinse the soaked rice under cold running water until the water runs clear, drain and set aside.

2 Heat the oil in a large heavy-based saucepan over a medium heat. Add the cumin seeds and stir for about 10 seconds until the seeds pop and colour.

3 Add the potatoes, peas and green chilli, if using, and stir-fry for about 3 minutes until the potatoes are just beginning to soften.

4 Add the rice and cook, stirring frequently, until well coated and beginning to turn translucent.

5 Stir in the salt, garam masala, turmeric and cayenne pepper, then add the water. Bring to the boil, stirring once or twice, then reduce the heat, cover and simmer until most of the water is absorbed and the surface is filled with little steam-holes. Do not stir.

6 Reduce the heat to very low and, if possible, raise the pan about 2.5 cm/ 1 inch above the heat source by resting on a ring. Cover and steam for about 10 minutes longer. Remove from the heat, uncover and put a clean tea towel or kitchen paper over the rice. Re-cover and set aside for 5 minutes.

7 Gently fork the rice and potato mixture into a warmed serving bowl and sprinkle with the coriander and chopped red onion. Serve hot with the yogurt handed separately.

Coconut-scented Rice

Cooked slowly to produce a tender, creamy rice with lots of flavour, this makes an excellent accompaniment to grilled chicken, pork or even fish.

NUTRITIONAL INFORMATION

Calories	127	Sugars	.........2g
Protein	.........2g	Fat	...........1g
Carbohydrate	...29g	Saturates	.......0g

  5 mins   50 mins

SERVES 4–6

INGREDIENTS

350 ml/12 fl oz water

225 ml/8 fl oz coconut milk

1 tsp salt

200 g/7 oz long grain brown rice

2–3 strips of lemon rind

1 cinnamon stick

about 15 cloves

1 tbsp chopped fresh parsley

fresh coconut shavings (optional)

1 Bring the water to the boil in a heavy-based pan over medium heat and whisk in the coconut milk. Return the liquid to the boil, add the salt and sprinkle in the rice. Add the strips of lemon rind, the cinnamon stick and cloves.

2 Reduce the heat to low, cover and simmer gently for about 45 minutes until the rice is tender and the liquid is completely absorbed. Uncover and leave the rice over high heat for about 1 minute, to allow any steam to escape and the rice to dry out a little.

3 Remove and discard the cloves, then sprinkle with the chopped parsley and coconut, if using. Fluff up the grains and fork the rice into a warmed serving bowl and serve immediately.

VARIATION

For a more South-east Asian flavour, use 1 fresh red chilli, pierced in 2–3 places with a pin, a bruised lime leaf and a 7.5 cm/3 inch piece of lemon grass, lightly crushed, instead of the lemon rind and cloves.

Fragrant Orange Rice

This delicious rice, scented with star anise for a slightly exotic effect, is excellent served with Mediterranean and Middle Eastern meat stews.

NUTRITIONAL INFORMATION

Calories	177	Sugars	.........6g
Protein	.........3g	Fat	...........3g
Carbohydrate	...34g	Saturates	.......2g

10–25 mins   20–25 mins

SERVES 4–6

I N G R E D I E N T S

1–2 tbsp butter

3–4 shallots, finely chopped

200 g/7 oz basmati rice

2.5 cm/1 inch piece of fresh root ginger

1–2 fresh bay leaves, lightly bruised

2 star anise

1 small cinnamon stick

grated rind and juice of 1 orange

1 tbsp raisins, finely chopped

300 ml/10 fl oz chicken stock or water

salt and pepper

fresh coriander leaves, to garnish (optional)

1 Melt the butter in a heavy-based pan placed over a medium heat. Add the shallots and cook, stirring occasionally, for 2–3 minutes until translucent and beginning to soften.

2 Add the rice and cook, stirring frequently, for 3 minutes until the rice is well coated with the butter and is translucent. Using a large, heavy knife, lightly crush the piece of root ginger. Add to the pan with the bay leaves, star anise and cinnamon stick. Stir in the grated orange rind, orange juice and raisins and mix thoroughly.

3 Add the stock and bring to the boil. Season with salt and pepper to taste and reduce the heat. Cover and cook over a low heat for 15–18 minutes until the rice is tender and the liquid completely absorbed. Remove from the heat, uncover and place a clean tea towel over the rice. Re-cover and set aside for up to 20 minutes.

4 Fork the rice into a serving bowl and remove the bay leaves, star anise and cinnamon stick – or keep them in for decoration. Sprinkle the top with a few coriander leaves, if wished, and serve hot.

COOK'S TIP

Washing and soaking the rice removes any starch. Cover the rice with water and soak for about 20 minutes, stirring occasionally. Drain, then rinse under cold running water until the water runs clear. Drain and proceed with the recipe.

Lemon-scented Rice

The fresh clean flavours of this pilaf make it an ideal accompaniment for a wide variety of dishes from plain roasted meats to exotic curries.

NUTRITIONAL INFORMATION

Calories ....173 Sugars 0g
Protein ....3g Fat 4g
Carbohydrate ...33g Saturates 1g

🍲 10–15 mins ⏱ 30 mins

SERVES 6–8

INGREDIENTS

2 tbsp olive oil or butter

2–4 spring onions, finely chopped

3–4 tbsp chopped fresh mint

300 g/10½ oz long grain white rice

500 ml/18 fl oz chicken stock

1 lemon

salt and pepper

TO GARNISH

2–3 fresh mint sprigs

thin lemon slices

thin lime slices

1 Heat the oil or butter in a medium heavy-based saucepan over a medium heat. Add the spring onions and mint and cook, stirring constantly for about minute until brightly coloured and giving off their aroma.

2 Add the rice and cook, stirring frequently, for about 2 minutes until well coated with the oil or butter and just translucent. Add the chicken stock and bring to the boil, stirring once or twice. Season with salt and pepper to taste.

3 Pare 3–4 strips of lemon rind and add to the pan. Squeeze the juice from the lemon and stir into the rice and stock.

4 When the stock comes to the boil, reduce the heat to low and simmer gently, tightly covered, for about 20 minutes until the rice is tender and the stock absorbed. Remove the pan from the heat and set aside for 5–10 minutes.

5 Fork the rice into a warmed serving bowl, garnish with mint sprigs and slices of lemon and lime. Serve hot.

COOK'S TIP

This basic technique for pilaf rice can be used with other flavour combinations and herbs. The important thing is to fry the rice until well coated and add just enough water to be absorbed by the rice.

Stuffed Cabbage

Hailing from Eastern Europe, this recipe is a delicious way to stretch a small amount of meat.

NUTRITIONAL INFORMATION

Calories 424   Sugars 25g
Protein . . . . .29g   Fat 16g
Carbohydrate . . .42g   Saturates 5g

 20 mins   🕐 1 hr 50 mins

SERVES 6–8

INGREDIENTS

55 g/2 oz fresh white breadcrumbs

125 ml/4 fl oz milk

1 tbsp vegetable oil

1 onion, finely chopped

2 garlic cloves, finely chopped

450 g/1 lb minced beef

450 g/1 lb minced pork or veal

2 tbsp tomato ketchup

3 tbsp chopped fresh dill

1 tsp chopped fresh thyme leaves

100 g/3½ oz long grain white rice

salt and pepper

1 large cabbage, such as Savoy, leaves
   separated and blanched

TOMATO SAUCE

2 tbsp olive oil

2 large onions, thinly sliced

2 x 400 g/14 oz cans chopped tomatoes

450 ml/16 fl oz passata

50 ml/2 fl oz tomato ketchup

grated rind and juice of 1 large lemon

2 tbsp light brown sugar

85 g/3 oz raisins

1 Combine the breadcrumbs and the milk and set aside to soak. Heat the oil in a pan and cook the onion and garlic for about 2 minutes until soft.

2 Place the beef and pork or veal in a bowl. Mix in the ketchup, herbs, rice and seasoning. Add the breadcrumbs and cooked onion and garlic.

3 To make the tomato sauce, heat the oil and cook the onions for 3 minutes until soft. Stir in the tomatoes and the remaining ingredients and bring to the boil, then simmer for about 15 minutes, stirring occasionally. Set aside.

4 Spoon 1–2 tablespoons of the meat mixture on to a cabbage leaf above the stem end. Fold the stem end over the filling, then fold over the sides. Roll up to enclose. Repeat with the remaining leaves until the meat mixture is used up.

5 Spoon enough tomato sauce to cover the base of a large ovenproof dish. Arrange the filled cabbage rolls, seam side down, in the dish. Spoon the remaining sauce over the rolls to cover – add a little water if necessary. Cover tightly and bake in a preheated oven, 160°C/325°F/ Gas Mark 3, for about 1½ hours, basting once or twice.

6 Transfer the cabbage rolls to a warmed serving plate and keep warm. Heat the sauce to thicken, if necessary, then pour over the rolls and serve.

Iranian Steamed Crusty Rice

The trick is to achieve a light fragrant rice with a crunchy golden brown crust; it may take several attempts, but it's worth the effort!

NUTRITIONAL INFORMATION

Calories	330	Sugars	.........0g
Protein	.........5g	Fat	...........9g
Carbohydrate	...57g	Saturates	.......5g

5 mins 45 mins

SERVES 6

INGREDIENTS

425 g/15 oz basmati or long grain
  white rice

2 tbsp salt

4 tbsp butter or ghee

50 ml/2 fl oz water

1 Bring at least 2 litres/3½ pints of water to the boil. Add the salt. Gradually add the rice, then simmer for 7–10 minutes until almost tender, gently stirring occasionally. Drain and rinse under warm running water to remove any starch.

2 Heat the butter or ghee with the water in a large, heavy-based pan over a medium heat until the butter melts and the water is steaming. Remove half of this mixture and reserve. Spoon enough rice into the pan to cover the bottom, smoothing lightly and evenly.

3 Spoon the remaining rice into the pan. Cover the rice with a thin tea towel, then cover the pan tightly and reduce the heat to very low. Cook for 15 minutes.

4 Remove the covers and, with the handle of a wooden spoon, gently poke several holes into the rice to allow the steam to escape.

5 Pour the remaining butter and water mixture over the rice, re-cover as before and cook for 10–15 minutes. Uncover and transfer the pan to a chilled surface (see Cook's Tip). This helps to loosen the crust from the bottom.

6 Using a fork, fluff the loose rice into a serving bowl. Break up the crusty brown layer into pieces and arrange around the serving dish.

COOK'S TIP

To chill the work surface for cooling down the saucepan of hot rice, place 2 trays of ice-cubes on it ahead of time.

Courgettes & Tomatoes

Lightly cooked courgettes are mixed with ripe, juicy tomatoes and dressed with a chilli vinaigrette to create a perfect side salad.

NUTRITIONAL INFORMATION

Calories	.... .92	Sugars	.... .3g
Protein	....2g	Fat	.... .8g
Carbohydrate	.... .4g	Saturates	.... .1g

 30 mins   10 mins

SERVES 4–6

INGREDIENTS

1 large fresh mild green chilli, or a combination of 1 green pepper and ½–1 fresh green chilli

4 courgettes, sliced

2–3 garlic cloves, finely chopped

pinch of sugar

¼ tsp ground cumin

2 tbsp white wine vinegar

4 tbsp extra virgin olive oil

2–3 tbsp chopped fresh coriander

4 ripe tomatoes, diced or sliced

salt and pepper

1 Roast the mild chilli or the combination of the green pepper and chilli, in a heavy-based ungreased frying pan or under a preheated grill until the skin is charred. Place in a plastic bag, twist to seal well and set aside for 20 minutes.

2 Peel the skin from the chilli and pepper, if using, then remove the seeds and slice the flesh. Set aside.

3 Bring about 5 cm/2 inches water to the boil in the bottom of a steamer. Add the courgettes to the top part of the steamer, cover and steam for about 5 minutes until just tender.

4 Meanwhile, combine the garlic, sugar, cumin, vinegar, olive oil and coriander in a bowl. Stir in the chilli and pepper, if using, then season with salt and pepper to taste.

5 Arrange the courgettes and tomatoes in a serving bowl or on a platter and spoon over the chilli dressing. Toss gently, if wished, and serve.

VARIATION

Add 225 g/8oz cooked peeled prawns to the courgettes and tomatoes, then coat with the dressing as in Step 5.

Summer Squash Medley

Garlic butter and a hint of chilli flavour this summertime vegetable pot of squash and sweetcorn. Serve with almost any meaty main course.

NUTRITIONAL INFORMATION

Calories	140	Sugars 5g
Protein	.........4g	Fat 6g
Carbohydrate	...20g	Saturates 3g

10 mins   10 mins

SERVES 4–6

INGREDIENTS

corn cobs

small courgettes or other green summer squash, such as pattypan, cubed or sliced

small yellow summer squash, cubed or sliced

tbsp butter

garlic cloves, finely chopped

3–4 large, ripe tomatoes, diced

inch of mild chilli powder

inch of ground cumin

fresh green chilli, such as jalapeño, deseeded and chopped

inch of sugar

salt and pepper

1 Pour about 5 cm/2 inches water into the bottom of a steamer and bring to the boil. Add the corn cobs, courgettes or green squash and summer squash to the top part of the steamer, cover and steam for about 3 minutes until tender, depending on their maturity and freshness. Alternatively, blanch in boiling salted water for about 3 minutes, then drain. Set aside until they are cool enough to handle.

2 Using a large knife, slice the kernels off the corn cobs and set aside.

3 Melt the butter in a heavy-based frying pan. Add the garlic and cook for 1 minute to soften. Add the tomatoes, chilli powder, ground cumin, green chilli and sugar to taste. Season with salt and pepper to taste and cook over a low heat for a few minutes or until the flavours have mingled.

4 Add the corn kernels, courgettes and squash. Cook for 2 minutes, stirring, to warm through. Serve immediately.

VARIATION

Any leftovers will make a good base for a lovely summer soup. Simply thin with lots of stock and freshen up with chopped herbs.

Potatoes in Green Sauce

Earthy potatoes, served in a tangy spicy tomatillo sauce and topped with spring onions and soured cream, are delicious.

NUTRITIONAL INFORMATION

Calories 61	Sugars 1.4g	
Protein 2g	Fat 1.4g	
Carbohydrate . .10.6g	Saturates 0.2g	

 5 mins   🕐 25 mins

SERVES 5

INGREDIENTS

1 kg/2 lb 4 oz small waxy potatoes

1 onion, halved and unpeeled

8 garlic cloves, unpeeled

1 fresh green chilli

8 tomatillos, outer husks removed, or small tart tomatoes

225 ml/8 fl oz chicken, meat or vegetable stock, preferably homemade

1 tsp ground cumin

1 fresh thyme sprig or generous pinch of dried thyme

1 fresh oregano sprig or generous pinch of dried

2 tbsp vegetable or extra virgin olive oil

1 courgette, roughly chopped

1 bunch of fresh coriander, chopped

salt

1 Put the potatoes in a pan of lightly salted water. Bring to the boil and cook for about 15 minutes or until almost tender. Do not over-cook them. Drain and set aside.

2 Meanwhile lightly char the onion, garlic, chilli and tomatillos or tomatoes in a heavy-based, ungreased frying pan. Set aside, and when cool enough to handle, peel and chop the onion, garlic and chilli. Chop the tomatillos or tomatoes. Put in a blender or food processor with half the stock and process to form a purée. Add the cumin, thyme and oregano.

3 Heat the oil in the heavy-based frying pan. Add the purée and cook over a medium heat, stirring constantly, for 5 minutes to reduce slightly and concentrate the flavours.

4 Add the potatoes and courgette to the purée and pour in the remaining stock. Add about half of the chopped coriander and cook for a further 5 minutes or until the courgette is tender.

5 Transfer to a serving bowl and serve sprinkled with the remaining chopped coriander to garnish.

Two Classic Salsas

A Mexican meal is not complete without an accompanying salsa. These two salsas are ideal for seasoning any traditional dish.

NUTRITIONAL INFORMATION

Calories 21	Sugars 3g
Protein 1g	Fat 0g
Carbohydrate 4g	Saturates 0g

🧊 5 mins   🕐 0 mins

SERVES 4–6

INGREDIENTS

JALAPEÑO SALSA

onion, finely chopped

–3 garlic cloves, finely chopped

–6 tbsp coarsely chopped pickled
jalapeño chillies

ice of ½ lemon

bout ¼ tsp ground cumin

alt

SALSA CRUDA

–8 ripe tomatoes, finely chopped

bout 100 ml/3½ fl oz tomato juice

–4 garlic cloves, finely chopped

–1 bunch fresh coriander leaves,
coarsely chopped

inch of sugar

–4 fresh green chillies, such as jalapeño
or serrano, deseeded and finely chopped

–1 tsp ground cumin

–4 spring onions, finely chopped

alt

1 To make the jalapeño salsa, put the onion in a bowl with the garlic, lapeños, lemon juice and cumin. Season taste with salt and stir together. Cover ith clingfilm and chill in the refrigerator ntil required.

2 To make a chunky-textured salsa cruda, stir all the ingredients together in a bowl and season with salt to taste. Cover with clingfilm and chill in the refrigerator until required.

3 To make a smoother-textured salsa, process the ingredients in a blender or food processor. Scrape into a bowl, cover and chill as above.

COOK'S TIP
You can vary the amount of garlic, chillies and ground spices according to taste, but make sure the salsa has quite a 'kick', otherwise it will not be effective.

Hot Mexican Salsas

These salsas capture the inimitable tangy, spicy flavour of Mexico. Choose from a fresh minty fruit salsa, charred chilli salsa or a spicy 'green' salsa.

NUTRITIONAL INFORMATION

Calories	59	Sugars	.......12g
Protein	.........1g	Fat	...........0g
Carbohydrate	...12g	Saturates	.......0g

 10 mins   5 mins

SERVES 4–6

I N G R E D I E N T S

TROPICAL FRUIT SALSA

½–1 fresh green chilli

½–1 fresh red chilli

½ pineapple, peeled, cored and diced

1 mango, peeled, stoned and diced

½ red onion, chopped

1 tbsp sugar

juice of 1 lime

3 tbsp chopped fresh mint

salt

CHARRED CHILLI SALSA

2–3 fresh green chillies

1 green pepper

2 garlic cloves, finely chopped

juice of ½ lime

1 tsp salt

2–3 tbsp extra virgin olive oil

pinch each dried oregano and ground cumin

SALSA VERDE

450 g/1 lb oz canned tomatillos, drained

1–2 fresh green chillies

1 green pepper, deseeded and chopped

1 small onion, chopped

1 bunch fresh coriander, finely chopped

½ tsp ground cumin

salt

1 To make the tropical fruit salsa, deseed the green chilli and chop both chillies. Combine all the ingredients in a large bowl and season with salt to taste. Cover the bowl with clingfilm and chill in the refrigerator until required.

2 For the charred chilli salsa, char the chillies and green pepper in an ungreased frying pan. Cool, deseed, skin and chop. Combine the chillies and green pepper with the garlic, lime juice, salt and oil in a bowl. Top with oregano and cumin.

3 For the salsa verde, drain and chop the tomatillos. Deseed and finely chop the chillies and deseed and chop the green pepper. Combine all the ingredients in a bowl and season with salt to taste. If a smoother sauce is preferred, blend the ingredients in a food processor, then spoon into a bowl to serve.

Fresh Pineapple Salsa

This sweet fruity salsa is fresh and fragrant, a wonderful foil to spicy dishes and is perfect with food cooked on the barbecue.

NUTRITIONAL INFORMATION

Calories	37	Sugars 08
Protein	.........1g	Fat 0.5g
Carbohydrate	....8g	Saturates 0g

 15 mins 0 mins

SERVES 4

INGREDIENTS

ripe pineapple

ice of 1 lime or lemon

garlic clove, finely chopped

spring onion, thinly sliced

–1 fresh green or red chilli, deseeded and finely chopped

red pepper, deseeded and chopped

tbsp chopped fresh mint

tbsp chopped fresh coriander

inch of salt

inch of sugar

1 Using a long, sharp knife, cut off the top and bottom of the pineapple. Place the pineapple upright on a board, en slice off the skin, cutting downwards. any 'eyes' still remain, cut the out with small, pointed knife.

2 Cut the pineapple flesh into slices about 1 cm/½ inch thick, halve the ices and remove the cores. Dice the flesh.

Reserve any juice that accumulates as you cut the pineapple.

3 Place the pineapple and any juice in a bowl and stir in the lime juice, garlic, spring onion, chilli and red pepper. Stir in the chopped fresh mint and coriander. Add the salt and sugar and stir well to combine all the ingredients. Cover with clingfilm and chill until ready to serve.

COOK'S TIP

A fresh pineapple is ripe if it has a sweet aroma. The flesh will still be fairly firm to touch. Fresh-looking leaves are a sign of good condition.

Mexican Beans

A pot of beans, bubbling away on the stove, is the basic everyday food of Mexico – delicious and healthy!

NUTRITIONAL INFORMATION

Calories	282	Sugars	.........1g
Protein	........18g	Fat	...........1g
Carbohydrate	...50g	Saturates	.......0g

  8¼ hrs   2½ hrs

SERVES 4-6

I N G R E D I E N T S

500 g/1 lb 2 oz dried pinto or borlotti beans

fresh mint sprig

fresh thyme sprig

fresh flat leaf parsley sprig

1 onion, cut into chunks

salt

TO SERVE

warmed flour or corn tortillas

shreds of spring onion

1 Pick through the beans and remove any pieces of grit or stone. Put the beans in a bowl, cover with cold water and set aside to soak overnight. If you want to cut down on soaking time, bring the beans to the boil, boil for 5 minutes, then remove from the heat, cover and set aside for 2 hours.

2 Drain the beans, place in a pan and cover with fresh water. Add the mint, thyme and parsley sprigs. Bring to the boil, then reduce the heat to very low, cover and simmer gently for about 2 hours until the beans are tender. The best way to check that they are done is to sample a bean every so often after 1¾ hours cooking time.

3 Add the onion chunks and continu to cook until the onion and beans ar very tender.

4 To serve as a side dish, drain, seaso with salt and serve in a bowl line with warmed corn or flour tortillas garnished with spring onion shreds.

COOK'S TIP
If using the beans for refried beans, do not drain because the liquid is required for the recipe.

Rice with Lime

The tangy citrus taste of lime is marvellous with all sorts of rice dishes. You could add wild rice to this dish, if desired.

NUTRITIONAL INFORMATION

Calories ....227 Sugars 1g
Protein ....4g Fat 7g
Carbohydrate ...39g Saturates 1g

5 mins   15 mins

SERVES 4

INGREDIENTS

tbsp vegetable oil

small onion, finely chopped

garlic cloves, finely chopped

75 g/6 oz long grain rice

50 ml/16 fl oz chicken or vegetable stock

uice of 1 lime

tbsp chopped fresh coriander

1 Heat the oil in a heavy-based pan or flameproof casserole. Add the onion and garlic and cook gently, stirring occasionally, for 2 minutes.

2 Add the rice and cook for a further minute, stirring constantly. Pour in the stock, increase the heat and bring the rice to the boil. Reduce the heat to a very low simmer.

3 Cover and cook the rice for about 10 minutes or until it is just tender and the liquid is absorbed.

4 Sprinkle in the lime juice and fork the rice to fluff up and to mix the juice in. Sprinkle with the chopped coriander and serve immediately.

COOK'S TIP

Garnish the rice with sautéed plantains: slice a ripe peeled plantain on the diagonal, then fry in a heavy-based pan in a small amount of oil until browned in spots and are tender. Arrange in the bowl of rice.

Cumin Rice

Cumin seeds add a distinctive flavour to this colourful rice dish. Serve as a side dish for any roasted or barbecued meat.

NUTRITIONAL INFORMATION

Calories	258	Sugars	.........4g
Protein	.........5g	Fat	...........9g
Carbohydrate	...49g	Saturates	.......5g

🍚 20 mins   🕐 20 mins

SERVES 4

I N G R E D I E N T S

2 tbsp butter

1 tbsp vegetable oil

1 green pepper, deseeded and sliced

1 red pepper, deseeded and sliced

3 spring onions, thinly sliced

3–4 garlic cloves, finely chopped

175 g/6 oz long grain rice

1½ tsp cumin seeds

½ tsp dried oregano or marjoram, crushed

450 ml/16 fl oz chicken or vegetable stock

1 Heat the butter and oil in a heavy-based pan or flameproof casserole. Add the green and red peppers and cook, stirring occasionally, until softened.

2 Add the spring onions, garlic, rice and cumin seeds. Cook, stirring constantly, for about 5 minutes or until the rice turns slightly golden.

3 Add the oregano and stock to the pan or casserole, bring to the boil, then reduce the heat and simmer gently for 5–10 minutes until the rice tender.

4 Cover with a clean tea towel an remove from the heat. Set aside fo about 10 minutes. Fluff up the rice with fork and serve.

VARIATION

Fold through a portion or two of black beans, and serve as a side dish with hearty roasted meat or poultry.

Green Rice

A paste of roasted onions, garlic and chillies, puréed with lots of green coriander leaves, gives this rice a lovely fresh colour and stunning taste.

NUTRITIONAL INFORMATION

Calories ....386 Sugars 4g
Protein ....5g Fat 22g
Carbohydrate ...45g Saturates 2g

20 mins   20–25 mins

SERVES 4

INGREDIENTS

–2 onions, halved and unpeeled

–8 large garlic cloves, unpeeled

large mild chilli, or 1 green pepper and
  1 small green chilli

bunch of fresh coriander leaves, chopped

25 ml/8 fl oz chicken or vegetable stock

tbsp vegetable or olive oil

75 g/6 oz long grain rice

alt and pepper

resh coriander sprig, to garnish

1 Heat a heavy-based ungreased frying pan and cook the onion, garlic, chilli nd green pepper, if using, until lightly harred on all sides, including the cut ides of the onions. Cover and then set side to cool.

2 When the vegetables are cool enough to handle, remove the seeds and skins rom the chilli and green pepper, if using. hop the flesh.

3 Remove the skins from the onions and garlic and chop the flesh finely.

4 Place the chilli, green pepper, if using, onions and garlic in a food processor ith the coriander leaves and stock, then rocess to a smooth thin purée.

5 Heat the oil in a heavy-based pan and fry the rice until it is glistening and lightly browned in places, stirring to prevent it from burning. Add the vegetable purée, cover and cook over a low heat for 10–15 minutes until the rice is just tender.

6 Fluff up the rice with a fork, then cover and set for about 5 minutes. Adjust the seasoning, garnish with a sprig of coriander and serve.

COOK'S TIP
Leftover green rice is delicious mixed with minced beef and/or pork for savoury meatballs, or as a filling for peppers.

Rice with Black Beans

Any kind of bean cooking liquid is delicious for cooking rice – black beans are particularly good for their startling grey colour and earthy flavour.

NUTRITIONAL INFORMATION

Calories	252	Sugars	.........2g
Protein	.........5g	Fat	..........8g
Carbohydrate	...43g	Saturates	.......1g

15 mins   15 mins

SERVES 4

INGREDIENTS

1 onion, chopped

5 garlic cloves, chopped

225 ml/8 fl oz chicken or vegetable stock

2 tbsp vegetable oil

175 g/ 6 oz long grain rice

225 ml/8 fl oz liquid from cooking black beans (including some black beans, too)

½ tsp ground cumin

salt and pepper

TO GARNISH

3–5 spring onions, thinly sliced

2 tbsp chopped fresh coriander leaves

1 Put the onion in a blender or food processor with the garlic and stock and process to a chunky sauce.

2 Heat the oil in a heavy-based pan. Add the rice and cook over a low heat, stirring constantly, until it is golden. Add the onion mixture, with the cooking liquid from the black beans (and any beans, too). Add the cumin and season with salt and pepper to taste.

3 Cover the pan and cook over a low heat for about 10 minutes or until the rice is just tender. The rice should be a greyish colour and taste delicious.

4 Fluff up the rice with a fork, re-cover and set aside to rest for about 5 minutes. Serve sprinkled with thinly sliced spring onions and chopped coriander leaves.

VARIATION

Instead of black beans, use pinto beans or chickpeas. Proceed as above and serve with any savoury spicy sauce or as an accompaniment to roasted meat.

Lentils Simmered with Fruit

Although this might seem an unusual combination, when you taste this traditional Mexican dish you will discover just how delicious it is.

NUTRITIONAL INFORMATION

Calories	23	Sugars	........18g
Protein	........10g	Fat	..........7g
Carbohydrate	...36g	Saturates	.......1g

 5 mins   45 mins

SERVES 4

INGREDIENTS

125 g/4½ oz brown or green lentils

about 1 litre/1¾ pints water

2 tbsp vegetable oil

3 small to medium onions, chopped

4 garlic cloves, coarsely chopped

1 large tart apple, roughly chopped

about ¼ ripe pineapple, peeled and roughly chopped

2 tomatoes, deseeded and diced

1 almost ripe banana, cut into bite-size pieces

cayenne pepper

salt

fresh parsley sprig, to garnish

1 Put the lentils in a pan and add the water. Bring to the boil, then reduce the heat and simmer gently for about 40 minutes until the lentils are tender. Do not let them become mushy.

2 Meanwhile, heat the oil in a frying pan and fry the onions and garlic, over a low heat for 10 minutes until lightly browned. Add the apple and continue to cook until golden. Add the pineapple, heat through, stirring, then add the tomatoes. Cook over a medium heat until thickened, stirring occasionally.

3 Drain the lentils, reserving 125 ml/4 fl oz of the cooking liquid. Add the drained lentils to the sauce, stirring in the reserved liquid if necessary. Heat through for a minute to mingle the flavours.

4 Add the banana to the pan, then season to taste with cayenne pepper and salt. Garnish with the parsley sprig and serve immediately.

VARIATION
Instead of lentils, prepare the dish using cooked pinto or borlotti beans.

Balti Dhal

This dish uses chana dhal, a husked, split, black chickpea which is yellow on the inside and has a nutty taste.

NUTRITIONAL INFORMATION

Calories	132	Sugars	.........2g
Protein	.........6g	Fat	...........6g
Carbohydrate	...15g	Saturates	......1g

5 mins   1¼ hours

SERVES 4

INGREDIENTS

225 g/8 oz chana dhal or yellow split peas, washed

½ tsp ground turmeric

1 tsp ground coriander

1 tsp salt

4 curry leaves

2 tbsp oil

½ tsp asafoetida powder (optional)

1 tsp cumin seeds

2 onions, chopped

2 garlic cloves, crushed

1 cm/½ inch piece of fresh root ginger, grated

½ tsp garam masala

1. Put the chana dhal or yellow split peas in a large pan and pour in enough water to cover by 2.5 cm/1 inch. Bring to the boil and use a spoon to remove the scum that has formed.

2. Add the turmeric, ground coriander, salt and curry leaves. Lower the heat and simmer for 1 hour, until the chana dhal or yellow split peas are tender, but not mushy. Drain well.

3. Heat the oil in a karahi (Balti pan) or wok. Add the asafoetida, if using, and stir-fry for 30 seconds.

4. Add the cumin seeds and stir-fry until they start popping.

5. Add the onions and stir-fry for 5 minutes until golden brown.

6. Add the garlic, ginger, garam masala and chana dhal or yellow split peas and stir-fry for 2 minutes. Serve the Balti dhal immediately as a side dish with a curry meal or set aside to cool, then store in the refrigerator for later use.

COOK'S TIP

Dhal keeps well so it is a good idea to make a large amount and store it in the refrigerator or freezer in small portions. Reheat before serving.

Corn-on-the-Cob

Corn cobs are available nearly all the year round and can be barbecued with the husks on or off. Cook them as soon as possible after purchase.

NUTRITIONAL INFORMATION

Calories	79	Sugars	........2g
Protein	.........3g	Fat	..........2g
Carbohydrate	...14g	Saturates	.....0.2g

  25 mins   30–40 mins

SERVES 6

I N G R E D I E N T S

4–6 corn cobs

vegetable oil, for brushing

T O   S E R V E

butter (optional)

salt (optional)

1 Soak the cobs in lukewarm water for 20 minutes. Drain them thoroughly and pat dry with kitchen paper.

2 If the cobs have no husks, brush with oil and cook on a hot barbecue for 30 minutes, brushing occasionally with the oil and turning often.

3 If the cobs have husks, tear off all but the last 2 layers and brush with oil.

4 Cook on a hot barbecue for 40 minutes, brushing with oil once or twice and turning occasionally.

5 Serve the corn cobs hot, without the husks. If you like, add a knob of butter and season with salt to taste.

Aubergine Curry

This is a rich vegetable dish, ideal served with a tandoori chicken and naan bread. It is also delicious served as a vegetarian dish with rice.

NUTRITIONAL INFORMATION

Calories	73	Sugars	........6g
Protein	.........3g	Fat	...........4g
Carbohydrate	....6g	Saturates	......1g

15 mins   15 mins

SERVES 4

I N G R E D I E N T S

2 aubergines

225 ml/8 fl oz low-fat natural yogurt

2 cardamom pods

½ tsp ground turmeric

1 dried red chilli

½ tsp coriander seeds

½ tsp ground black pepper

1 tsp garam masala

1 clove

2 tbsp sunflower oil

1 onion, sliced lengthways

2 garlic cloves, crushed

1 tbsp grated fresh root ginger

6 ripe tomatoes, peeled, deseeded and quartered

fresh coriander, to garnish

1 Roast the aubergines over a naked flame or place under a preheated grill, turning frequently, for about 5 minutes until charred and black all over. Peel under cold running water. Cut off the stem ends and discard.

2 Put the peeled aubergines into a large bowl and mash lightly with a fork. Stir in the yogurt.

3 Grind the cardamom pods, turmeric, red chilli, coriander seeds, black pepper, garam masala and clove in a large mortar with a pestle or in a spice grinder.

4 Heat the oil in a wok or heavy-based frying pan over a moderate heat and cook the onion, garlic and ginger until softened. Add the tomatoes and ground spices, and stir well.

5 Add the aubergine mixture to the pan and stir well. Cook for 5 minutes over a low heat, stirring constantly, until all the flavours are combined and some of the liquid has evaporated.

6 Serve the aubergine immediately, garnished with coriander.

Casseroled Potatoes

This potato dish is cooked in the oven with leeks and wine.
It is very quick and simple to make and tastes superb.

NUTRITIONAL INFORMATION

Calories	187	Sugars	........2g
Protein	.........4g	Fat	..........3g
Carbohydrate	...31g	Saturates	......2g

🧈 10 mins   🕐 50 mins

SERVES 4

I N G R E D I E N T S

675 g/1½ lb waxy potatoes, cut into chunks

1 tbsp butter

2 leeks, sliced

150 ml/5 fl oz dry white wine

150 ml/5 fl oz vegetable stock

1 tbsp lemon juice

2 tbsp chopped mixed fresh herbs

salt and pepper

TO GARNISH

grated lemon rind

chopped mixed fresh herbs (optional)

1 Cook the potato chunks in a large saucepan of boiling water for 5 minutes. Drain thoroughly.

2 Meanwhile, melt the butter in a frying pan and cook the leeks for 5 minutes or until they have softened.

3 Spoon the partly cooked potatoes and leeks into an ovenproof dish.

4 Combine the white wine, vegetable stock, lemon juice and chopped mixed herbs in a jug. Season to taste with salt and pepper, then pour the mixture over the potatoes.

5 Cook in a preheated oven, 190°C/ 375°F/Gas Mark 5, for 35 minutes or until the potatoes are tender.

6 Garnish the potato casserole with lemon rind and fresh herbs, if using, and serve as an accompaniment to a casserole or roast meat.

COOK'S TIP

Cover the ovenproof dish halfway through cooking if the leeks start to brown on the top.

Vegetables with Vermouth

Serve these vegetables in their paper parcels to retain all the juices. The result is truly delicious.

NUTRITIONAL INFORMATION

Calories	62	Sugars	.........9g
Protein	.........2g	Fat	..........0.5g
Carbohydrate	...12g	Saturates	.....0.1g

  10 mins   20 mins

SERVES 4

INGREDIENTS

1 carrot, cut into batons

1 fennel bulb, sliced

100 g/3½ oz courgettes, sliced

1 red pepper, sliced

4 small onions, halved

125 ml/4 fl oz vermouth

4 tbsp lime juice

grated rind of 1 lime

pinch of paprika

4 fresh tarragon sprigs

salt and pepper

fresh tarragon sprigs, to garnish

1 Place all of the vegetables in a large bowl and mix well.

2 Cut 4 large squares of baking paper and place a quarter of the vegetables in the centre of each. Bring the sides of the paper up and pinch together to make an open parcel.

3 Mix together the vermouth, lime juice, lime rind and paprika and pour a quarter of the mixture into each parcel. Season with salt and pepper and add a tarragon sprig to each. Pinch the tops of the parcels together to seal.

4 Place the parcels in a steamer, cover and cook for 15–20 minutes or until the vegetables are tender. Garnish with tarragon sprigs and serve immediately.

COOK'S TIP

Vermouth is a fortified white wine flavoured with various herbs and spices. It is available in both sweet and dry forms.

Raitas

Raitas are easy to prepare, very versatile and have a cooling effect which will be appreciated if you are serving hot, spicy dishes.

NUTRITIONAL INFORMATION

Calories	33	Sugars	.........5g
Protein	.........3g	Fat	..........0.4g
Carbohydrate	....5g	Saturates	.....0.3g

 10 mins   🕐 5 mins

SERVES 4

I N G R E D I E N T S

MINT RAITA

200 ml/7 fl oz low-fat natural yogurt

50 ml/2 fl oz water

1 small onion, finely chopped

½ tsp mint sauce

½ tsp salt

3 fresh mint leaves, to garnish

CUCUMBER RAITA

225 g/8 oz cucumber

1 medium onion

½ tsp salt

½ tsp mint sauce

300 ml/10 fl oz low-fat natural yogurt

150 ml/5 fl oz water

fresh mint leaves, to garnish

AUBERGINE RAITA

1 medium aubergine

1 tsp salt

1 small onion, finely chopped

2 fresh green chillies, deseeded and finely chopped

200 ml/7 fl oz low-fat natural yogurt

3 tbsp water

1 To make the mint raita, place the yogurt in a bowl and whisk with a fork. Gradually whisk in the water. Add the onion, mint sauce and salt and blend together. Garnish with mint leaves.

2 To make the cucumber raita, peel and slice the cucumber. Chop the onion finely. Place the cucumber and onion in a large bowl, then add the salt and the mint sauce. Add the yogurt and the water, place the mixture in a blender and blend well. Serve garnished with mint leaves.

3 To make the aubergine raita, remove the top end of the aubergine and chop the rest into small pieces. Boil in a pan of water until softened, then drain and mash. Add the salt, onion and green chillies, mixing well. Whisk the yogurt with the water, add to the mixture and mix thoroughly.

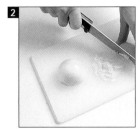

Sesame Seed Chutney

This chutney is delicious served with spiced rice dishes and also makes an unusual filling to spread in sandwiches.

NUTRITIONAL INFORMATION

Calories 120   Sugars 0g
Protein ....4g   Fat 12g
Carbohydrate ...0.2g   Saturates 2g

 10 mins   5 mins

SERVES 4

INGREDIENTS

8 tbsp sesame seeds

2 tbsp water

½ bunch of fresh coriander

3 fresh green chillies, chopped

1 tsp salt

2 tsp lemon juice

chopped fresh red chilli, to garnish

1 Place the sesame seeds in a large, heavy-based saucepan and dry roast them, stirring constantly. Set the sesame seeds aside to cool.

2 Once cooled, place the sesame seeds in a food processor or mortar and grind well to form a fine powder.

3 Add the water to the ground sesame seeds and mix thoroughly to form a smooth paste.

4 Finely chop the coriander. Add the chillies and coriander to the sesame seed paste and grind again.

5 Add the salt and lemon juice to the mixture and grind once again.

6 Remove the mixture from the food processor or mortar and transfer to a serving dish. Garnish with chopped red chilli and serve.

COOK'S TIP

Dry roasting brings out the flavour of spices and takes just a few minutes. You will be able to tell when the spices are ready because of the wonderful fragrance that develops. Stir the spices constantly to ensure that they do not burn.

Gram Flour Bread

This filling bread goes well with any vegetarian curry and lime pickle.
Store the gram flour in a cool, dark place in an airtight container.

NUTRITIONAL INFORMATION

Calories 112	Sugars 1g	
Protein 3g	Fat 2g	
Carbohydrate ...21g	Saturates 0g	

30 mins   15 mins

SERVES 4–6

INGREDIENTS

100 g/3½ oz wholemeal flour (ata or
  chapati flour), plus extra for dusting

85 g/3 oz gram flour

½ tsp salt

1 small onion

fresh coriander leaves, very
  finely chopped

2 fresh green chillies, deseeded and
  very finely chopped

150 ml/5 fl oz water

2 tsp ghee

1 Sift the wholemeal and gram flours together into a large mixing bowl. Add the salt to the flours and mix together thoroughly.

2 Chop the onion very finely. Blend the onion, coriander and chillies into the flour mixture.

3 Add the water and mix to form a soft dough. Cover the dough with a clean tea towel or clingfilm and set aside for about 15 minutes.

4 Turn out the dough and knead thoroughly for 5–7 minutes. Divide the dough into 8 equal portions.

5 Roll out the dough portions to rounds about 18 cm/7 inches in diameter on a lightly floured surface.

6 Place the dough portions individually in a frying pan and cook over a medium heat, turning three times and lightly greasing each side with the ghee each time. Transfer the gram flour bread to serving plates and serve hot.

COOK'S TIP

In Indian kitchens, gram flour is used to make breads, bhajis and batters and to thicken sauces and stabilise yogurt when it is added to hot dishes.

Spicy Cauliflower

This is a perfectly delicious way to serve cauliflower. It can be enjoyed as a salad or at a picnic, or as a side dish to a main meal.

NUTRITIONAL INFORMATION

Calories	68	Sugars	.........3g
Protein	.........5g	Fat	...........4g
Carbohydrate	....4g	Saturates	......1g

  5 mins   15 mins

SERVES 4

INGREDIENTS

500 g/1 lb 2 oz cauliflower, cut into florets

1 tbsp sunflower oil

1 garlic clove

½ tsp ground turmeric

1 tsp cumin seeds, ground

1 tsp coriander seeds, ground

1 tsp yellow mustard seeds

12 spring onions, thinly sliced

salt and pepper

1 Blanch the cauliflower in boiling water, drain and set aside. Cauliflower holds a lot of water, which tends to make it too soft, so turn the florets upside down at this stage and you will end up with a crisper result.

2 Heat the oil gently in a large, heavy frying pan or wok. Add the garlic clove, turmeric, ground cumin, ground coriander and mustard seeds. Stir well and cover the pan.

3 When you hear the mustard seeds popping, add the spring onions and stir well. Cook, stirring constantly, for 2 minutes until softened. Season to taste with salt and pepper.

4 Add the cauliflower and stir for 3–4 minutes until coated completely with the spices and thoroughly heated.

5 Remove and discard the garlic clove and serve the immediately.

COOK'S TIP

For a special occasion this dish looks great made with baby cauliflowers instead of florets. Peel off most of the outer leaves, leaving a few for decoration, and blanch the baby cauliflowers whole for 4 minutes and drain. Continue as in step 2.

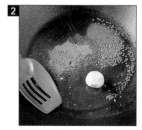

Trio of Potato Purées

These small moulds filled with layers of flavoured potato look very impressive. They are ideal with fish or roast meats.

NUTRITIONAL INFORMATION

Calories 170   Sugars 5g
Protein . . . . .7g   Fat 6g
Carbohydrate . . .24g   Saturates 3g

 15 mins   1¼ hrs

SERVES 4

INGREDIENTS

1 tbsp butter, plus extra for greasing

300 g/10½ oz floury potatoes, chopped

125 g/4½ oz swede, chopped

1 carrot, chopped

450 g/1 lb spinach

1 tbsp skimmed milk

2½ tbsp plain flour

1 egg

½ tsp ground cinnamon

1 tbsp orange juice

¼ tsp grated nutmeg

salt and pepper

carrot batons, to garnish

1 Lightly grease 4 x 150 ml/5 fl oz ramekins with a little butter.

2 Cook the potatoes in a saucepan of boiling water for 10 minutes. In separate pans cook the swede and carrot in boiling water for 10 minutes. Blanch the spinach in boiling water for 5 minutes. Drain the vegetables. Add the milk and butter to the potatoes and mash until smooth. Stir in the flour and egg.

3 Divide the potato mixture between 3 bowls. Spoon the swede into 1 bowl and mix well. Spoon the carrot into the second bowl and mix well. Spoon the spinach into the third bowl and mix well.

4 Add the cinnamon to the swede and potato mixture and season to taste. Stir the orange juice into the carrot and potato mixture. Stir the nutmeg into the spinach and potato mixture.

5 Spoon a layer of the swede and potato mixture into each of the ramekins and smooth the surface. Cover each with a layer of spinach and potato mixture, then top with the carrot and potato mixture. Cover the ramekins with kitchen foil and place in a roasting tin. Half-fill the tin with boiling water and cook in a preheated oven, 180°C/350°F/Gas Mark 4, for 40 minutes or until set.

6 Turn out on to warmed serving plates, garnish with the carrot batons and serve immediately.

Italian Potato Wedges

These oven-cooked potato wedges use classic pizza ingredients and are delicious served with plain meats, such as pork or lamb.

NUTRITIONAL INFORMATION

Calories 115   Sugars 4g

Protein . . . . .6g   Fat 5g

Carbohydrate . . .13g   Saturates 3g

 15 mins   35 mins

SERVES 4

INGREDIENTS

2 large waxy potatoes, unpeeled

4 large ripe tomatoes, peeled and deseeded

150 ml/5 fl oz vegetable stock

2 tbsp tomato purée

1 small yellow pepper, cut into strips

125 g/4½ oz button mushrooms, quartered

1 tbsp chopped fresh basil

55 g/2 oz cheese, grated

salt and pepper

1 Cut each of the potatoes into 8 equal wedges. Parboil the potatoes in a pan of boiling water for 15 minutes. Drain well and place in a shallow ovenproof dish.

2 Chop the tomatoes and add to the dish. Combine the vegetable stock and tomato purée, then pour the mixture over the potatoes and tomatoes.

3 Add the yellow pepper strips, mushrooms and basil. Season well with salt and pepper.

4 Sprinkle the grated cheese over the top and cook in a preheated oven, 190°C/375°F/Gas Mark 5, for about 15–20 minutes until the topping is golden brown. Serve at once.

Roasted Vegetables

Rosemary branches can be used as brushes for basting and as skewers.
Soak the rosemary skewers overnight to prevent them from charring.

NUTRITIONAL INFORMATION

Calories	16	Sugars 3g
Protein	.........1g	Fat 0.3g
Carbohydrate	....3g	Saturates 0g

  15 mins  15 mins

SERVES 6

I N G R E D I E N T S

1 small red cabbage

1 fennel bulb

1 orange pepper, cut into 4 cm/1½ inch dice

1 aubergine, halved and sliced into 1 cm/
½ inch pieces

2 courgettes, thickly sliced diagonally

olive oil, for brushing

6 rosemary twigs, about 15 cm/6 inches
long, soaked in cold water

salt and pepper

1 Put the red cabbage on its side on a chopping board and cut through the middle of its stem and heart. Divide each piece into 4, each time including a section of the stem in the slice to hold it together.

2 Prepare the fennel in the same way as the red cabbage.

3 Blanch the red cabbage and fennel in boiling water for 3 minutes, then drain well.

4 With a wooden skewer, carefully pierce a hole through the middle of each piece of vegetable.

5 Thread a piece of orange pepper, fennel, red cabbage, aubergine and courgette, on to each rosemary twig, gently pushing the rosemary through the skewer holes.

6 Brush liberally with olive oil and season with plenty of salt and pepper.

7 Cook over a hot barbecue or under a preheated grill for 8–10 minutes, turning occasionally. Serve immediately.

VARIATION
Fruit skewers are a deliciously quick and easy dessert. Thread pieces of banana, mango, peach, strawberry, apple and pear on to soaked wooden skewers and cook over the dying embers. Brush with sugar syrup towards the end of cooking.

Potato & Vegetable Curry

Meat is expensive in India and much of the population is vegetarian, so the cuisine is typified by tasty ways of cooking with vegetables.

NUTRITIONAL INFORMATION

Calories	301	Sugars	........10g
Protein	.........9g	Fat	..........12g
Carbohydrate	...41g	Saturates	.......1g

🍶 5 mins   🕐 45 mins

SERVES 4

INGREDIENTS

4 tbsp vegetable oil

675 g/1 lb 8 oz waxy potatoes, cut into large chunks

2 onions, quartered

3 garlic cloves, crushed

1 tsp garam masala

½ tsp ground turmeric

½ tsp ground cumin

½ tsp ground coriander

2 tsp grated fresh root ginger

1 fresh red chilli, chopped

225 g/8 oz cauliflower florets

4 tomatoes, peeled and quartered

75 g/2¾ oz frozen peas

2 tbsp chopped fresh coriander

300 ml/10 fl oz vegetable stock

shredded fresh coriander, to garnish

boiled rice or warm Indian bread, to serve

COOK'S TIP

Use a large heavy-based saucepan or frying pan for this recipe to ensure that the potatoes are cooked thoroughly.

1 Heat the vegetable oil in a large heavy-based saucepan or frying pan. Add the potato chunks, onions and garlic and fry over a low heat, stirring frequently, for 2–3 minutes.

2 Add the garam masala, turmeric, ground cumin, ground coriander, ginger and chilli to the pan, mixing the spices into the vegetables until they are well coated. Fry over a low heat, stirring constantly, for 1 minute.

3 Add the cauliflower florets, tomatoes, peas, chopped fresh coriander and vegetable stock to the curry mixture.

4 Cook the potato curry over a low heat for 30–40 minutes or until the potatoes are tender and completely cooked through.

5 Garnish the potato curry with fresh coriander and serve with plain boiled rice or warm Indian bread.

Cheese Crumble-topped Mash

Liven up mashed potato by topping it with a crumble mixture flavoured with herbs, mustard and onion, which turns crunchy on baking.

NUTRITIONAL INFORMATION

Calories . . . . .131 Sugars 1.4g
Protein . . . . .3.8g Fat 5.7g
Carbohydrate . .17.3g Saturates 3.4g

 10 mins   20-25 mins

SERVES 4

INGREDIENTS

900 g/2 lb floury potatoes, diced

2 tbsp butter

2 tbsp milk

55 g/2 oz mature cheese or blue
    cheese, grated

CRUMBLE TOPPING

3 tbsp butter

1 onion, cut into chunks

1 garlic clove, crushed

1 tbsp wholegrain mustard

175 g/ 6 oz fresh wholemeal breadcrumbs

2 tbsp chopped fresh parsley

salt and pepper

1 Cook the potatoes in a pan of lightly salted boiling water for 10 minutes or until cooked through.

2 Meanwhile, make the crumble topping. Melt the butter in a frying pan. Add the onion, garlic and wholegrain mustard and fry gently for 5 minutes, stirring constantly, until the onion chunks have softened.

3 Put the breadcrumbs and parsley in a mixing bowl and stir in the fried onion. Season to taste with salt and pepper.

4 Drain the potatoes thoroughly and place them in a mixing bowl. Add the butter and milk, then mash until smooth. Stir in the grated cheese while the potato is still hot.

5 Spoon the mashed potato into a shallow ovenproof dish and sprinkle with the crumble topping.

6 Cook in a preheated oven, 200°C/ 400°F/Gas Mark 6, for 10–15 minutes until the crumble topping is golden brown and crunchy. Serve immediately.

COOK'S TIP

For extra crunch, add freshly cooked vegetables, such as celery and peppers, to the mashed potato in step 4.

Cheese & Potato Plait

This bread has a delicious cheese and garlic flavour and is best eaten straight from the oven, as soon as it is the right temperature.

NUTRITIONAL INFORMATION

Calories	387	Sugars	.........1g
Protein	........13g	Fat	...........8g
Carbohydrate	...70g	Saturates	.......4g

2½ mins   55 mins

SERVES 8

INGREDIENTS

butter, for greasing

675 g/1½ lb strong white flour, plus extra for dusting

175 g/6 oz floury potatoes, diced

2 x 7 g sachets easy-blend dried yeast

450 ml/16 fl oz vegetable stock

2 garlic cloves, crushed

2 tbsp chopped fresh rosemary

115 g/4 oz grated Gruyère cheese

1 tbsp vegetable oil

1 tbsp salt

1 Lightly grease and flour a baking sheet. Cook the potatoes in a pan of boiling water for 10 minutes or until soft. Drain well and mash.

2 Transfer the mashed potatoes to a large mixing bowl, stir in the yeast, flour and stock and mix to form a smooth dough. Add the garlic, rosemary and 85 g/3 oz of the cheese and knead the dough for 5 minutes. Make a hollow in the dough, pour in the oil and knead the dough again.

3 Cover the dough and set it aside in a warm place for 1½ hours or until doubled in size.

4 Knead the dough again and divide it into 3 equal portions. Roll each portion into a sausage shape about 35 cm/14 inches long.

5 Press one end of each of the sausage shapes firmly together, then carefully plait the dough, without breaking it, and fold the remaining ends under, sealing them firmly.

6 Place the plait on the baking sheet, cover and set aside to rise for 30 minutes.

7 Sprinkle the remaining cheese over the top of the plait and cook in a preheated oven, 190°C/375°F/Gas Mark 5, for 40 minutes or until the base of the loaf sounds hollow when tapped. Serve while it is warm.

Mini Focaccia

This is a delicious Italian bread made with olive oil.
The topping of red onions and thyme is particularly flavoursome.

NUTRITIONAL INFORMATION

Calories	439	Sugars	.........3g
Protein	.........9g	Fat	.........15g
Carbohydrate	....71g	Saturates	.......2g

2¼ hrs   25 mins

SERVES 4

I N G R E D I E N T S

2 tbsp olive oil, plus extra for greasing

350 g/12 oz strong white flour

½ tsp salt

1 sachet easy-blend dried yeast

250 ml/9 fl oz lukewarm water

115 g/4 oz stoned green or black
     olives, halved

T O P P I N G

2 red onions, sliced

2 tbsp olive oil

1 tsp sea salt

1 tbsp thyme leaves

1 Lightly oil several baking sheets. Sift the flour and salt into a large mixing bowl, then stir in the yeast. Pour in the olive oil and lukewarm water and mix everything together to form a dough.

2 Turn the dough out on to a lightly floured surface and knead it for about 5 minutes. Alternatively, use an electric mixer with a dough hook.

3 Place the dough in a greased bowl, cover and set aside in a warm place for about 1–11/2 hours or until it has doubled in size. Knock back the dough by kneading it again for 1–2 minutes.

4 Knead half of the olives into the dough. Divide the dough into quarters and then shape the quarters into rounds. Place them on the baking sheets and push your fingers into the dough to create a dimpled effect.

5 To make the topping, sprinkle the red onions and remaining olives over the rounds. Drizzle over the oil and sprinkle with sea salt and thyme leaves. Cover and set aside to rise for 30 minutes.

6 Bake in a preheated oven, 190°C/ 375°F/Gas Mark 5, for 20–25 minutes or until the focaccia are golden.

7 Transfer to a wire rack to cool completely before serving.

VARIATION
Use this quantity of
dough to make 1 large
focaccia, if you prefer.

Mediterranean Bread

Many of the flavours of the Mediterranean are captured in this rustic loaf. It is a perfect accompaniment for pasta dishes, stews and casseroles.

NUTRITIONAL INFORMATION

Calories	222	Sugars	.........1g
Protein	.........5g	Fat	..........12g
Carbohydrate	...26g	Saturates	.......2g

2 HRS   40 mins

MAKES 1 LOAF

INGREDIENTS

400 g/14 oz plain flour, plus extra
  for dusting

1 sachet easy-blend dried yeast

1 tsp salt

1 tbsp coriander seeds, lightly crushed

2 tsp dried oregano

200 ml/7 fl oz lukewarm water

3 tbsp olive oil, plus extra for greasing

150 g/5½ oz sun-dried tomatoes in oil,
  drained, patted dry and chopped

85 g/3 oz feta cheese, drained, patted dry
  and cubed

115 g/4 oz black olives, patted dry, stoned
  and sliced

1 Combine the flour, yeast, salt, coriander seeds and oregano and make a well in the centre. Gradually add most of the water and the oil to make a dough. Gradually add the remaining water, if needed, drawing in all the flour.

2 Turn out on to a lightly floured surface and knead for 10 minutes, gradually kneading in the tomatoes, cheese and olives. Wash the bowl and lightly coat it with oil.

3 Shape the dough into a ball, put it in the bowl and turn the dough over.

Cover tightly and set aside the dough until it doubles in volume.

4 Turn the dough out on to a lightly floured surface. Knead lightly, then shape into a ball. Place on a lightly floured baking sheet. Cover and set aide to rise until it doubles in volume again.

5 Lightly sprinkle the top of the loaf with flour. Using a sharp knife, cut

3 shallow slashes in the top. Bake in a preheated oven, 230°C/450°F/Gas Mark 8 for 20 minutes. Lower the temperature to 200°C/400°F/Gas Mark 6 and bake for a further 20 minutes or until the loaf sounds hollow when you tap it on the bottom, transfer to a wire rack to cool completely. This loaf keeps well for up to 3 days in an airtight container.

Sesame Breadsticks

The irregular shape of these Greek-style breadsticks adds to their appeal. They are crisp and crunchy on the outside with a soft, chewy interior.

NUTRITIONAL INFORMATION

Calories 61	Sugars 0g
Protein 2g	Fat 2g
Carbohydrate . . .10g	Saturates 0g

1¾ hrs   10 mins

MAKES 32 STICKS

I N G R E D I E N T S

225 g/8 oz unbleached strong white flour, plus extra for dusting

225 g/8 oz strong wholemeal flour

1 sachet easy-blend dried yeast

2 tsp salt

½ tsp sugar

450 ml/16 fl oz lukewarm water

4 tbsp olive oil, plus extra for greasing

1 egg white, lightly beaten

sesame seeds, for sprinkling

1 Combine the flours, yeast, salt and sugar in a bowl and make a well in the centre. Gradually stir in most of the water and the olive oil to make a dough. Gradually add the remaining water, if necessary, drawing in all the flour.

2 Turn out on to a lightly floured surface and knead for about 10 minutes until smooth and elastic. Wash the bowl and lightly coat with olive oil.

3 Shape the dough into a ball, put it in the bowl and turn over so it is coated. Cover tightly with a tea towel or lightly oiled clingfilm and set aside in a warm place until the dough has doubled in volume. Meanwhile, line a baking sheet with baking paper.

4 Turn out the dough on to a lightly floured surface and knead lightly. Divide the dough into 2 equal pieces. Roll each piece into a 40 cm/16 inch rope and then cut each rope into 8 equal pieces. Cut each piece in half again to make a total of 32 pieces.

5 Cover the dough you are not working with a tea towel or clingfilm to prevent it from drying out. Roll each piece of dough into a thin 25 cm/10 inch rope on a very lightly floured surface. Carefully transfer the baking sheet.

6 Cover and set aside to rise for 10 minutes. Brush with the egg white, then sprinkle evenly and thickly with sesame seeds. Bake in a preheated oven, 230°C/450°F/ Gas Mark 8, for 10 minutes.

7 Brush again with egg white, and bake for a further 5 minutes or until golden brown and crisp. Transfer the breadsticks to wire racks to cool.

Olive Rolls

These country-style bread rolls depend on fruity olive oil and good-quality olives. You could use any of the Flavoured Olives (see page 431).

NUTRITIONAL INFORMATION

Calories 181   Sugars 1g
Protein . . . . .6g   Fat 3g
Carbohydrate . . .35g   Saturates 0.5g

1¾ hrs   30 mins

MAKES 16 ROLLS

I N G R E D I E N T S

115 g/4 oz olives in brine or
  oil, drained

750 g/1 lb 10 oz unbleached strong white
  flour, plus extra for dusting

1½ tsp salt

1 sachet easy-blend dried yeast

450 ml/16 fl oz lukewarm water

2 tbsp extra virgin olive oil, plus extra
  for brushing

4 tbsp finely chopped fresh oregano,
  parsley or thyme leaves or 1 tbsp dried
  mixed herbs

1 Stone the olives with an olive or cherry pitter and finely chop. Pat off the excess brine or oil with kitchen paper. Set aside.

2 Combine the flour, salt and yeast in a bowl and make a well in the centre. Gradually stir in most of the water and the olive oil to make a dough. Gradually add the remaining water, if necessary, drawing in all the flour.

3 Lightly knead in the chopped olives and herbs. Turn out the dough on to a lightly floured surface and knead for 10 minutes until smooth and elastic. Wash the bowl and lightly coat with oil.

4 Shape the dough into a ball, put it in the bowl and turn over so it is coated. Cover tightly with a tea towel or lightly oiled clingfilm and set aside to rise until it has doubled in volume. Dust a baking sheet with flour.

5 Turn out the dough on to a lightly floured surface and knead lightly. Roll the dough into 20 cm/8 inch ropes on a very lightly floured surface.

6 Cut the dough into 16 even piece Shape each piece into a ball and plac on the prepared baking sheet. Cover an set aside to rise for 15 minutes.

7 Lightly brush the top of each roll wit olive oil. Bake in a preheated ove 220°C/425°F/Gas Mark 7 for abou 25–30 minutes or until the rolls are golde brown. Transfer to a wire rack and se aside to cool completely.

Fougasse

This distinctive-looking bread, with its herringbone slits, is baked daily throughout Provence. It is best eaten on the day it is baked.

NUTRITIONAL INFORMATION

Calories 161	Sugars 1g	
Protein 5g	Fat 0g	
Carbohydrate . . . 36g	Saturates 0g	

1¾ hrs   25 mins

MAKES 2 LARGE LOAVES

INGREDIENTS

750 g/1 lb 10 oz unbleached strong white flour, plus extra for dusting

1 sachet easy-blend dried yeast

2 tsp salt

1 tsp sugar

450 ml/16 fl oz lukewarm water

olive oil, for greasing

1 Combine the flour, yeast, salt and sugar in a bowl and make a well in the centre. Gradually stir in most of the water to make a dough. Gradually add the remaining water, if necessary, drawing in all the flour.

2 Turn out on to a lightly floured surface and knead for 10 minutes until smooth and elastic. Wash the bowl and lightly coat with olive oil.

3 Shape the dough into a ball, put it in the bowl and turn the dough over. Cover the bowl tightly with a tea towel or lightly oiled clingfilm and set aside in a warm place to rise until the dough has doubled in volume.

4 Knock back the dough and turn out on to a lightly floured surface. Knead lightly, then cover with the upturned bowl and leave for 10 minutes.

5 Put a roasting tin of water in the bottom of the oven while it preheats to 230°C/450°F/Gas Mark 8. Lightly flour a baking sheet.

6 Divide the dough into 2 pieces and roll each one into a 30 cm/12 inch oval, 1 cm/½ inch thick. Using a sharp knife, cut 5 x 7.5 cm/3 inch slices on an angle in a herringbone pattern on each of the dough ovals. Cut all the way through the dough, using the tip of the knife to open the slits.

7 Spray the loaves with cold water. Bake for 20 minutes, turn upside down and continue baking for 5 minutes until the loaves sound hollow when tapped on the bottom. Transfer to wire racks to cool.

Herb Focaccia

Rich with olive oil, this bread is so delicious it would turn a simple salad or bowl of soup into a positive feast.

NUTRITIONAL INFORMATION

Calories 210	Sugars 1g
Protein 6g	Fat 5g
Carbohydrate 5g	Saturates 1g

2 hrs   15 mins

MAKES 1 LOAF

I N G R E D I E N T S

400 g/14 oz unbleached strong white flour, plus extra for dusting

1 sachet easy-blend dried yeast

1½ tsp salt

½ tsp sugar

300 ml/10 fl oz lukewarm water

3 tbsp extra virgin olive oil, plus extra for greasing

4 tbsp finely chopped fresh herbs

polenta or cornmeal, for sprinkling

coarse sea salt, for sprinkling

1 Combine the flour, yeast, salt and sugar in a bowl and make a well in the centre. Gradually stir in most of the water and 2 tablespoons of the olive oil to make a dough. Gradually add the remaining water, if necessary, drawing in all the flour.

2 Turn out on to a lightly floured surface and knead. Transfer to a bowl and lightly knead in the herbs for 10 minutes until soft but not sticky. Wash the bowl and lightly coat with olive oil.

3 Shape the dough into a ball, put it in the bowl and turn the dough over. Cover tightly with a tea towel or lightly greased clingfilm and set aside in a warm place to rise until the dough has doubled in volume. Meanwhile, sprinkle polenta over a baking sheet.

4 Turn the dough out on to a lightly floured surface and knead lightly. Cover with the upturned bowl and leave for 10 minutes.

5 Roll out and pat the dough into a 25 cm/10 inch circle, about 1 cm/½ inch thick and carefully transfer it to the prepared baking sheet. Cover with a tea towel and leave to rise again for 15 minutes.

6 Using a lightly oiled finger, poke indentations all over the surface of the loaf. Drizzle the remaining olive oil over and sprinkle lightly with sea salt. Bake in a preheated oven, 230°C/450°F/Gas Mark 8, for 15 minutes or until golden and the loaf sounds hollow when rapped on the bottom. Transfer to a wire rack to cool completely.

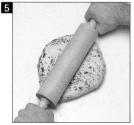

Yellow Split Pea Casserole

If ever there was a winter warmer, this is it – an intensely satisfying dish, ideal for serving with rice or fresh naan bread.

NUTRITIONAL INFORMATION

Calories	358	Sugars	........10g
Protein	........19g	Fat	..........12g
Carbohydrate	...45g	Saturates	......1g

 2¼ hrs   1½ hrs

SERVES 4

INGREDIENTS

2 tbsp ghee

1 tsp black mustard seeds

1 onion, finely chopped

2 garlic cloves, crushed

1 carrot, grated

2.5 cm/1 inch piece of fresh root ginger, grated

1 fresh green chilli, deseeded and finely chopped

1 tbsp tomato purée

250 g/9 oz yellow split peas, soaked in water for 2 hours and drained

400 g/14 oz can chopped tomatoes

500 ml/18 fl oz vegetable stock

225 g/8 oz pumpkin, diced

225 g/8 oz cauliflower, cut into florets

2 tbsp vegetable oil

1 large aubergine, diced

1 tbsp chopped fresh coriander

1 tsp garam masala

salt and pepper

1 Melt the ghee in a large pan over a medium heat. Add the mustard seeds and when they start to splutter, add the onion, garlic, carrot and ginger.

2 Cook, stirring occasionally, for about 5 minutes until the vegetables have softened. Add the green chilli and stir in the tomato purée. Stir in the split peas.

3 Add the tomatoes and stock and bring to the boil. Season to taste with salt and pepper.

4 Lower the heat and simmer gently, stirring occasionally, for 40 minutes. Add the pumpkin and cauliflower florets, cover and simmer for a further 30 minutes until the split peas are soft.

5 Meanwhile, heat the oil in a large, heavy-based frying pan over a high heat. Add the aubergine, and stir until sealed on all sides. Remove from the pan with a draining spoon and drain on kitchen paper.

6 Stir the aubergine into the split pea mixture with the coriander and garam masala. Check and adjust the seasoning if necessary. Transfer to a warmed serving dish and serve immediately.

Sauté of Summer Vegetables

The freshness of lightly cooked summer vegetables is enhanced by the aromatic flavour of a tarragon and white wine dressing.

NUTRITIONAL INFORMATION

Calories	217	Sugars	........8g
Protein	.........2g	Fat	..........18g
Carbohydrate	....9g	Saturates	.......9g

 10 mins 10–15 mins

SERVES 4

I N G R E D I E N T S

225 g/8 oz baby carrots, scrubbed

125 g/4½ oz runner beans

2 courgettes, trimmed

1 bunch of large spring onions

1 bunch of radishes

4 tbsp butter

2 tbsp light olive oil

2 tbsp white wine vinegar

4 tbsp dry white wine

1 tsp caster sugar

1 tbsp chopped fresh tarragon

salt and pepper

fresh tarragon sprigs, to garnish

1 Cut the carrots in half lengthways, slice the beans and courgettes, and halve the spring onions and radishes, so that all the vegetables are cut to even-size pieces.

2 Melt the butter in a large, heavy-based frying pan or wok. Add all the vegetables and fry them over a medium heat, stirring frequently, until they are tender, but still crisp and firm to the bite.

3 Meanwhile, pour the olive oil, vinegar, and white wine into a small saucepan and add the sugar. Place over a low heat,

stirring until the sugar has dissolved. Remove the pan from the heat and add the chopped tarragon.

4 When the vegetables are just cooked, pour over the 'dressing'. Stir through,

tossing the vegetables well to coat. Season to taste with salt and pepper and then transfer to a warmed serving dish. Garnish with sprigs of fresh tarragon and serve the sauté immediately.

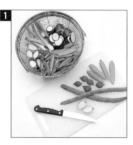

Seasonal Stir-fry

When selecting different fresh vegetables for this dish, bear in mind that there should always be a contrast in colour as well as texture.

NUTRITIONAL INFORMATION

Calories 108   Sugars 3g
Protein ....3g   Fat 9g
Carbohydrate ....4g   Saturates 1g

    10 mins   10 mins

SERVES 4

INGREDIENTS

medium red pepper, deseeded

15 g/4 oz courgettes

15 g/4 oz cauliflower

15 g/4 oz French beans

tbsp vegetable oil

few small slices of fresh root ginger

tsp salt

tsp sugar

–2 tbsp vegetable stock or
   water (optional)

tbsp light soy sauce

few drops of sesame oil (optional)

1 Using a sharp knife or Chinese cleaver, cut the red pepper into small squares. Thinly slice the courgettes. Trim the cauliflower and divide into small florets, discarding any thick stems. Make sure the vegetables are cut into roughly similar shapes and sizes to ensure that they cook evenly. Trim the French beans, then cut them in half.

2 Heat the vegetable oil in a preheated wok or large, heavy-based frying pan. Add the prepared vegetables with the ginger and stir-fry for about 2 minutes.

3 Add the salt and sugar to the wok or frying pan and continue to stir-fry for 1–2 minutes, adding a little vegetable stock or water if the mixture appears to be too dry. Do not add any liquid unless necessary.

4 Add the light soy sauce and sesame oil, if using, and stir well to coat the vegetables lightly.

5 Transfer the stir-fried vegetables to a warmed serving dish or bowl and serve immediately.

VARIATION

Almost any vegetables could be used in this dish, but make sure there is a good variety of colour, and always include several crisp vegetables such as carrots or mangetouts.

Sidekick Vegetables

Colourful vegetables are barbecued over hot coals to make this unusual hot salad, which is served with a spicy chilli sauce on the side.

NUTRITIONAL INFORMATION

Calories . . . . . . .224 Sugars 14g
Protein . . . . .4g Fat 15g
Carbohydrate . . .21g Saturates 2g

🍲 15 mins   🕐 30 mins

SERVES 4

INGREDIENTS

1 red pepper, deseeded

1 orange or yellow pepper, deseeded

2 courgettes

2 corn cobs

1 aubergine

olive oil, for brushing

chopped fresh thyme, rosemary and parsley

salt and pepper

lime or lemon wedges, to serve

DRESSING

2 tbsp olive oil

1 tbsp sesame oil

1 garlic clove, crushed

1 small onion, finely chopped

1 celery stick, finely chopped

1 small fresh green chilli, deseeded and chopped

4 tomatoes, chopped

5 cm/2 inch piece of cucumber, chopped

1 tbsp tomato purée

1 tbsp lime or lemon juice

1 To make the dressing, heat the olive and sesame oils together in a saucepan or frying pan. Add the garlic and onion, and cook over a low heat for about 3 minutes until softened.

2 Add the celery, chilli and tomatoes to the pan and cook, stirring frequently, for 5 minutes.

3 Stir in the cucumber, tomato purée and lime or lemon juice, and simmer over a low heat for 8–10 minutes until thick and pulpy. Season to taste with salt and pepper.

4 Cut the vegetables into thick slice and brush with a little olive oil.

5 Cook the vegetables over the ho coals of the barbecue for abou 5–8 minutes, sprinkling them with sal and pepper and fresh herbs as they cook and turning once.

6 Divide the vegetables between 4 serving plates and spoon some o the dressing on to the side. Serve immediately, sprinkled with a few more chopped herbs and accompanied by the lime or lemon wedges.

Spicy Peas & Spinach

This is quite a filling accompaniment and so should be served with a fairly light main course – it goes well with egg dishes.

NUTRITIONAL INFORMATION

Calories . . . . . . .340 Sugars 6g
Protein . . . . .21g Fat 14g
Carbohydrate . . .34g Saturates 2g

2¼ hrs   25 mins

SERVES 4

INGREDIENTS

25 g/8 oz green split peas

00 g/2 lb spinach

tbsp vegetable oil

onion, halved and sliced

tsp grated fresh root ginger

tsp ground cumin

tsp chilli powder

tsp ground coriander

garlic cloves, crushed

00 ml/½ pint vegetable stock

alt and pepper

esh coriander sprigs and lime wedges,
to garnish

1 Rinse the peas under cold running water. Transfer to a mixing bowl, over with cold water and set aside to oak for 2 hours. Drain well.

2 Place the spinach in a large saucepan with just the water clinging to its eaves after washing. Cook over a medium eat for 5 minutes until just wilted. Drain ell, squeeze out any excess moisture and oughly chop.

3 Heat the vegetable oil in a large saucepan and add the onion, ginger, umin, chilli powder, ground coriander and garlic. Cook over a low heat, stirring constantly, for 2–3 minutes.

4 Add the peas and spinach and stir in the stock. Cover and simmer for 10–15 minutes or until the peas are cooked and the liquid has been absorbed. Season with salt and pepper to taste. Transfer to a warmed serving dish, garnish with fresh coriander sprigs and lime wedges and serve immediately.

COOK'S TIP

Once the split peas have been added, stir occasionally to prevent them from sticking to the base of the pan.

Cauliflower & Spinach Curry

The contrast in colour in this recipe makes it very appealing to the eye, especially as the cauliflower is lightly coloured with yellow turmeric.

NUTRITIONAL INFORMATION

Calories ....228 Sugars 6g
Protein ....8g Fat 18g
Carbohydrate ....8g Saturates 2g

 10 mins   25 mins

SERVES 4

INGREDIENTS

1 medium cauliflower

6 tbsp vegetable oil

1 tsp mustard seeds

1 tsp ground cumin

1 tsp garam masala

1 tsp ground turmeric

2 garlic cloves, crushed

1 onion, halved and sliced

1 fresh green chilli, sliced

500 g/1 lb 2 oz spinach

5 tbsp vegetable stock

1 tbsp chopped fresh coriander

salt and pepper

fresh coriander sprigs, to garnish

1 Break the cauliflower into small florets.

2 Heat the oil in a deep flameproof casserole. Add the mustard seeds and cook until they begin to pop.

3 Stir in the remaining spices, the garlic, onion and chilli and cook, stirring constantly, for 2–3 minutes.

4 Add the cauliflower, spinach, stoc and chopped coriander and season t taste with salt and pepper. Cook over low heat for 15 minutes or until th cauliflower is tender. Uncover and boil fc 1 minute to thicken the juices.

5 Transfer the curry to a warme serving dish, garnish with coriande sprigs and serve.

COOK'S TIP

Mustard seeds are used throughout India and are particularly popular in southern Indian vegetarian cooking. They are fried in oil first to bring out their flavour before the other ingredients are added.

Baked Celery with Cream

This dish is sprinkled with breadcrumbs for a crunchy topping, underneath which is hidden a creamy celery and pecan mixture.

NUTRITIONAL INFORMATION

Calories 237   Sugars 5g
Protein ....7g   Fat 19g
Carbohydrate ....11g   Saturates 7g

15 mins   40 mins

SERVES 4

INGREDIENTS

head of celery

tsp ground cumin

tsp ground coriander

garlic clove, crushed

red onion, thinly sliced

5 g/2 oz pecan nut halves

50 ml/5 fl oz vegetable stock

50 ml/5 fl oz single cream

5 g/2 oz fresh wholemeal breadcrumbs

tbsp grated Parmesan cheese

alt and pepper

elery leaves, to garnish

1 Trim the celery and cut it into fine batons. Place the celery in an venproof dish with the cumin, ground oriander, garlic, red onion and pecan nut alves. Toss well to mix and to coat the egetables in the spices.

2 Combine the stock and cream in a jug, stirring well to mix. Pour the ream mixture over the vegetables. Season vith salt and pepper to taste.

3 Combine the breadcrumbs and cheese in a small bowl and sprinkle over the top to cover the vegetables.

4 Cook in a preheated oven, 200°C/ 400°F/Gas Mark 6, for 40 minutes or until the vegetables are tender and the topping is crispy. Garnish with celery leaves and serve immediately.

COOK'S TIP
Once grated, Parmesan cheese quickly loses its 'bite' so it is best to grate only the amount you need for the recipe. Wrap the rest tightly in foil and it will keep for several months in the refrigerator.

Bulgur Pilau

Bulgur wheat is very easy to use and, as well as being full of nutrients, it is a delicious alternative to rice, having a distinctive nutty flavour.

NUTRITIONAL INFORMATION

Calories 637	Sugars 25g
Protein 16g	Fat 26g
Carbohydrate ...90g	Saturates 11g

 15 mins   35–40 mins

SERVES 4

INGREDIENTS

6 tbsp butter or margarine

1 red onion, halved and sliced

2 garlic cloves, crushed

350 g/12 oz bulgur wheat

175 g/6 oz tomatoes, deseeded and chopped

55 g/2 oz baby corn cobs, halved lengthways

85 g/3 oz small broccoli florets

850 ml/1½ pints vegetable stock

2 tbsp clear honey

55 g/2 oz sultanas

53 g/2 oz pine kernels

½ tsp ground cinnamon

½ tsp ground cumin

salt and pepper

sliced spring onions, to garnish

1 Melt the butter or margarine in a large flameproof casserole over a medium heat. Add the onion and garlic and cook, stirring occasionally, for 2–3 minutes until softened, but not browned.

2 Add the bulgur wheat, tomatoes, corn cobs, broccoli florets and vegetable stock and bring to the boil. Reduce the heat, cover and simmer gently, stirring occasionally, for 15–20 minutes.

3 Stir in the honey, sultanas, pine kernels, ground cinnamon and cumin and season with salt and pepper to taste, mixing well. Remove the casserole from the heat, and set aside, covered, for 10 minutes.

4 Spoon the bulgur pilau into a warmed serving dish. Garnish with thinly sliced spring onions and serve the pilau immediately.

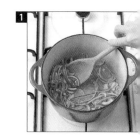
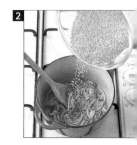

COOK'S TIP

The dish is left to stand for 10 minutes so that the bulgur can finish cooking and the flavours of the ingredients will mingle.

Soda Bread

This variation of traditional Irish soda bread is best eaten on the day it has been baked, when it is deliciously fresh.

NUTRITIONAL INFORMATION

Calories 203	Sugars 7g
Protein 8g	Fat 2g
Carbohydrate ...42g	Saturates 0g

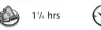

🧈 1¼ hrs   🕐 40 mins

SERVES 4

I N G R E D I E N T S

butter, for greasing

300 g/10½ oz plain white flour, plus extra for dusting

300 g/10½ oz plain wholemeal flour

2 tsp baking powder

1 tsp bicarbonate of soda

25 g/1 oz caster sugar

1 tsp salt

1 egg, beaten

425 ml/15 fl oz natural yogurt

1 Grease a baking sheet with butter and dust with flour.

2 Sift the flours, baking powder, bicarbonate of soda, sugar and salt into a large bowl and add any bran remaining in the sieve.

3 In a jug, beat together the egg and yogurt and pour the mixture into the dry ingredients. Mix everything together to make a soft and sticky dough.

4 On a lightly floured surface, knead the dough for a few minutes until it is smooth, then shape the dough into a round about 5 cm/2 inches deep.

5 Transfer the dough to the baking sheet. Mark a cross shape in the top of the loaf.

6 Bake in a preheated oven, 190°C/375°F/Gas Mark 5, for about 40 minutes or until the bread is golden brown all over.

7 Transfer the loaf to a wire rack and leave to cool completely. Cut into slices to serve.

VARIATION

For a fruity version of this soda bread, add 125g/4½ oz raisins to the dry ingredients in step 2.

Cheese & Chive Bread

This is a quick bread to make. It is full of a wonderful cheese flavour and, to enjoy it at its best, it should be eaten as fresh as possible.

NUTRITIONAL INFORMATION

Calories 190	Sugars 1g
Protein 7g	Fat 9g
Carbohydrate . . .22g	Saturates 5g

 25 mins   30 mins

SERVES 8

I N G R E D I E N T S

butter, for greasing

225 g/8 oz self-raising flour

1 tsp salt

1 tsp mustard powder

115 g/4 oz mature cheese, grated

2 tbsp chopped fresh chives

1 egg, beaten

2 tbsp butter, melted

150 ml/5 fl oz milk

1 Grease a 23 cm/9 inch square cake tin with a little butter and line the base with baking paper.

2 Sift the flour, salt and mustard powder into a large mixing bowl.

3 Reserve 3 tablespoons of the grated cheese for sprinkling over the top of the loaf before baking in the oven.

4 Stir the remaining grated cheese into the bowl, together with the chopped fresh chives. Mix well together.

5 Add the beaten egg, melted butter and milk to the dry ingredients and stir the mixture thoroughly to combine.

6 Pour the mixture into the prepared tin and spread evenly with a palette knife. Sprinkle over the reserved grated cheese.

7 Bake the loaf in a preheated oven 190°C/375°F/Gas Mark 5, for about 30 minutes.

8 Leave the bread to cool slightly in the tin. Turn out on to a wire rack to cool completely. Cut into triangles to serve.

COOK'S TIP

You can use any hard mature cheese of your choice – from Cheddar to pecorino – for this recipe.

Garlic Bread Rolls

This bread is not at all like the shop-bought, ready-made garlic bread. Instead it has a subtle flavour and a soft texture.

NUTRITIONAL INFORMATION

Calories	265	Sugars	.........3g
Protein	........10g	Fat	...........6g
Carbohydrate	...46g	Saturates	.......2g

🥖 🥖

 1¾ hrs   🕐 35 mins

SERVES 8

I N G R E D I E N T S

utter, for greasing

2 cloves garlic, peeled

50 ml/12 fl oz milk

50 g/1 lb strong white bread flour

tsp salt

sachet easy-blend dried yeast

tbsp dried mixed herbs

tbsp sunflower oil

egg, beaten

milk, for brushing

ock salt, for sprinkling

1 Lightly grease a baking sheet with a little butter.

2 Place the garlic cloves and milk in a saucepan, bring to the boil and immer gently for 15 minutes. Leave to ool slightly, then process in a blender or ood processor to purée the garlic.

3 Sift the flour and salt into a large mixing bowl and stir in the dried yeast nd mixed herbs.

4 Add the garlic-flavoured milk, sunflower oil and beaten egg to the ry ingredients and mix everything horoughly to form a dough.

5 Place the dough on a lightly floured work surface and knead lightly for a few minutes until smooth and soft.

6 Place the dough in a lightly greased bowl, cover and set aside to rise in a warm place for about 1 hour or until doubled in size.

7 Knock back the dough by kneading it for 2 minutes. Shape into 8 rolls and place on the baking sheet. Score the top of each roll with a knife, cover and set aside for 15 minutes.

8 Brush the rolls with milk and sprinkle rock salt over the top.

9 Bake in a preheated oven, 220°C/ 425°F/Gas Mark 7, for 15–20 minutes. Transfer the rolls to a wire rack and leave to cool before serving.

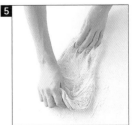

Sun-dried Tomato Rolls

These white rolls have the addition of finely chopped sun-dried tomatoes. The tomatoes are sold in jars and are available at most supermarkets.

NUTRITIONAL INFORMATION

Calories . . . . .214 Sugars 1g
Protein . . . . .5g Fat 12g
Carbohydrate . . .22g Saturates 7g

2¼ mins   15 mins

SERVES 4

I N G R E D I E N T S

butter, for greasing

225 g/8 oz strong white bread flour

½ tsp salt

1 sachet easy-blend dried yeast

100 g/3½ oz butter, melted and
  cooled slightly

3 tbsp milk, warmed

2 eggs, beaten

55 g/2 oz sun-dried tomatoes in oil, well
  drained and finely chopped

milk, for brushing

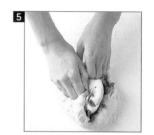

1 Lightly grease a baking sheet with a little butter.

2 Sift the flour and salt into a large mixing bowl. Stir in the yeast, then pour in the butter, milk and eggs. Mix together to form a dough.

3 Turn the dough on to a lightly floured surface and knead for about 5 minutes. Alternatively, use an electric mixer with a dough hook.

4 Place the dough in a greased bowl, cover and leave to rise in a warm place for 1–1½ hours or until the dough has doubled in size. Knock back the dough for 2–3 minutes.

5 Knead the sun-dried tomatoes into the dough, sprinkling the work surface with a little extra flour as the tomatoes are quite oily.

6 Divide the dough into 8 equal-size balls and place them on the prepared baking sheet. Cover and set aside to rise for about 30 minutes or until the rolls have doubled in size.

7 Brush the rolls with milk and bake in preheated oven, 230°C/450°F/Gas Mark 8, for 10–15 minutes or until the rolls are golden brown.

8 Transfer the rolls to a wire rack and leave to cool slightly before serving.

VARIATION

Add some finely chopped anchovies or olives to the dough in step 5 for extra flavour, if wished.

Garlic & Sage Bread

This freshly made herb bread is an ideal accompaniment to salads and soups and is dairy-free.

NUTRITIONAL INFORMATION

Calories . . . . .207 Sugars 3g
Protein . . . . .9g Fat 2g
Carbohydrate . . .42g Saturates 0g

1¼ hrs   30 mins

MAKES 6

I N G R E D I E N T S

oil, for greasing

250 g/9 oz strong brown bread flour

1 sachet easy-blend dried yeast

3 tbsp chopped fresh sage

2 tsp sea salt

3 garlic cloves, finely chopped

1 tsp clear honey

150 ml/5 fl oz lukewarm water

1 Grease a baking sheet. Sift the flour into a large mixing bowl and stir in the bran remaining in the sieve.

2 Stir in the easy-blend dried yeast, chopped sage and half of the sea salt. Reserve 1 teaspoon of the chopped garlic for sprinkling and stir the remainder into the bowl. Add the honey and lukewarm water and mix together to form a dough.

3 Turn the dough out on to a lightly floured surface and knead it for about 5 minutes until smooth and elastic (alternatively, use an electric mixer with a dough hook).

4 Place the dough in a greased bowl, cover with lightly oiled clingfilm and leave to rise in a warm place until doubled in size.

5 Knead the dough again for a few minutes. Roll it into a long sausage and then shape it into a ring. Place on the baking sheet. Cover and leave to rise for 30 minutes or until springy to the touch. Sprinkle with the remaining sea salt and garlic.

6 Bake the loaf in a preheated oven, 200°C/400°F/Gas Mark 6, for 25–30 minutes. Transfer to a wire rack to cool before serving.

COOK'S TIP

Roll the dough into a long sausage and then curve it into a circular shape. You can omit the sea salt for sprinkling, if you prefer.

Peshwari Naan

A tandoor oven throws out a ferocious heat; this bread is traditionally cooked on its side wall, where the heat is slightly less intense.

NUTRITIONAL INFORMATION

Calories 420   Sugars 13g
Protein . . . . .11g   Fat 9g
Carbohydrate . . .77g   Saturates 3g

 3¾ hrs   🕐 30 mins

SERVES 6

I N G R E D I E N T S

50 ml/2 fl oz lukewarm water

pinch of sugar

½ tsp easy-blend dried yeast

500 g/1 lb 2 oz strong bread flour, plus extra for dusting

½ tsp salt

50 ml/2 fl oz natural yogurt

2 tart eating apples, peeled, cored and diced

vegetable oil, for brushing

55 g/2 oz sultanas

55 g/2 oz flaked almonds

1 tbsp fresh coriander leaves

2 tbsp grated coconut

1 Combine the water and sugar in a bowl and sprinkle over the yeast. Set aside for 5–10 minutes, until the yeast has dissolved and the mixture is foamy.

2 Put the flour and salt into a bowl and make a well in the centre. Add the yeast mixture and yogurt. Draw in the flour until it is all absorbed. Mix thoroughly, adding enough lukewarm water to form a soft dough. Turn out on to a floured board and knead for 10 minutes until smooth. Put into an oiled bowl, cover and set aside for 3 hours in a warm place.

3 Meanwhile, line the grill pan with foil, shiny side up.

4 Put the apples into a saucepan with a little water. Bring to the boil, mash them down, reduce the heat and simmer for 20 minutes, mashing occasionally.

5 Divide the dough into 4 pieces and roll each piece out to a 20 cm/8 inch oval. Pull one end out into a teardrop shape, about 5 mm/¼ inch thick. Lay on a floured surface and prick the dough all over with a fork.

6 Brush both sides of the bread with vegetable oil. Place 1 oval under preheated grill at the highest setting. Cook for 3 minutes, turn the bread over, using tongs, and cook for a further 3 minutes. should have dark brown spots all over.

7 Spread a teaspoonful of the appl purée all over the bread, then sprinkl over a quarter of the sultanas, flake almonds, coriander leaves and the coconu Grill the remaining 3 ovals of dough an spread with the apple purée an flavourings in the same way.

Green Stir-fry

The basis of this recipe is pak choi, also known as bok choy or Chinese greens. If unavailable, use Swiss chard or Savoy cabbage instead.

NUTRITIONAL INFORMATION

Calories 107	Sugars 6g	
Protein 4g	Fat 8g	
Carbohydrate 6g	Saturates 1g	

 5 mins   🕐 10 mins

SERVES 4

I N G R E D I E N T S

2 tbsp groundnut oil

2 garlic cloves, crushed

½ tsp ground star anise

1 tsp salt

350 g/12 oz pak choi, shredded

225 g/8 oz baby spinach

25 g/1 oz mangetouts

1 celery stick, sliced

1 green pepper, deseeded and sliced

50 ml/2 fl oz vegetable stock

1 tsp sesame oil

1 Heat the groundnut oil in a preheated wok or large frying pan, swirling the it around the base until it is really hot.

2 Add the crushed garlic and stir-fry over a medium heat for about 30 seconds. Stir in the ground star anise, salt, shredded pak choi, spinach, mangetouts, celery and green pepper and stir-fry for 3–4 minutes.

3 Add the vegetable stock, lower the heat, cover the wok or frying pan and cook for 3–4 minutes. Remove the lid and stir in the sesame oil. Mix thoroughly to combine all the ingredients.

4 Transfer the green vegetable stir-fry to a warmed serving dish and serve immediately.

COOK'S TIP

Star anise is an important ingredient in Chinese cuisine. The attractive star-shaped pods are often used whole to add a decorative garnish to dishes. The flavour is similar to liquorice, but with spicy undertones and is quite strong.

Lemon Dhal

This dhal is eaten almost every day in most households in Hyderabad in India. Traditionally, it is cooked with tamarind, but lemon juice is easier.

NUTRITIONAL INFORMATION

Calories 386	Sugars 0.7g	
Protein 5g	Fat 35g	
Carbohydrate ...12g	Saturates 4g	

10 mins   30 mins

SERVES 4

INGREDIENTS

100 g/3½ oz masoor dhal

1 tsp finely chopped fresh root ginger

1 tsp crushed garlic

1 tsp chilli powder

½ tsp ground turmeric

425 ml/15 fl oz water

1 tsp salt

3 tbsp lemon juice

2 fresh green chillies

fresh coriander leaves

BAGHAAR

150 ml/5 fl oz vegetable oil

4 garlic cloves

6 dried red chillies

1 tsp white cumin seeds

1 Rinse the masoor dhal and place in a large saucepan. Add the ginger, garlic, chilli powder and turmeric. Stir in 300 ml/ 10 fl oz of the water and bring to the boil over a medium heat. Half cover the pan and simmer until the dhal is soft enough to be mashed.

2 Mash the dhal. Add the salt, lemon juice and the remaining water, stirring to mix thoroughly. It should be of a fairly smooth consistency.

3 Deseed the green chillies, if wished, and chop or slice. Add the chillies and coriander leaves to the dhal and set aside.

4 To make the baghaar, heat the oil in a heavy-based pan. Add the garlic, red chillies and white cumin seeds and fry for about 1 minute. Turn off the heat.

5 When the baghaar has cooled slightly, pour it over the dhal. If the dhal is too runny, set it, uncovered, over a medium heat for 3–5 minutes until it has thickened slightly.

6 Transfer the dhal to a warmed serving dish and serve hot.

Vegetable Samosas

Everyone will love these samosas as they are oven-baked rather than deep-fried. Serve with mango chutney as part of a light lunch.

NUTRITIONAL INFORMATION

Calories	139	Sugars	.........2g
Protein	.........4g	Fat	...........6g
Carbohydrate	...19g	Saturates	.......2g

 30 mins   35–40 mins

SERVES 4

INGREDIENTS

1 small potato, peeled and quartered

1 small carrot, halved

4 cauliflower florets

1 tsp sunflower or corn oil, plus extra for brushing

2 tsp lime juice

1 tbsp water

1 shallot, finely chopped

3 tbsp frozen peas

1 fresh green chilli, deseeded and finely chopped

½ tsp cumin seeds

½ tsp black cumin seeds

½ tsp ground turmeric

½ tsp ground coriander

beaten egg, to glaze

mango chutney, to serve

PASTRY

40 g/1½ oz malted flour

125 g/4½ oz plain flour, plus extra for dusting

40 g/1½ oz sunflower margarine

50–75 ml/2–2½ fl oz skimmed milk

1 Preheat the oven to 190°C/375°F/Gas Mark 5. Cook the potato, carrot and cauliflower in a small saucepan of boiling water for 10 minutes. Drain, leave to cool slightly, then chop. Put the oil, lime juice, water, shallot, peas, chilli and spices in a small pan, bring to the boil, then reduce the heat and simmer gently, stirring occasionally, for 3 minutes. Stir in the potato, carrot and cauliflower and transfer to a bowl to cool.

2 To make the pastry, sift the flours into a bowl, add the margarine and rub in with your fingertips until the mixture resembles breadcrumbs. Add just enough milk to make a firm dough. Turn out on to a lightly floured work surface and knead gently until smooth. Divide the dough into 4 equal pieces and roll each out into an 18 cm/7 inch round. Trim the edges and cut each round in half.

3 Brush a baking sheet with a little sunflower oil. Divide the vegetable mixture between the dough semi-circles, placing it on one half only and leaving a small border. Brush the edges with water, fold the dough over and seal, pressing the edges together. Brush with beaten egg, transfer to the baking sheet and bake in the oven for 20–25 minutes, or until golden brown. Serve hot or cold with mango chutney.

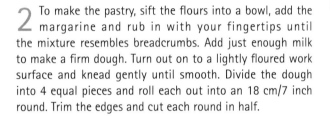

Kabli Chana Sag

Pulses such as chickpeas are widely used in India.
They need to be soaked overnight so prepare well in advance.

NUTRITIONAL INFORMATION

Calories 217	Sugars 5g	
Protein 12g	Fat 9g	
Carbohydrate . . .25g	Saturates 1g	

10 mins   1–2 hrs

SERVES 6

INGREDIENTS

225 g/8 oz chickpeas, soaked overnight
   and drained

5 cloves

2.5 cm/1 inch piece of cinnamon stick

2 garlic cloves

3 tbsp sunflower oil

1 small onion, sliced

3 tbsp lemon juice

1 tsp coriander seeds

2 tomatoes, peeled, deseeded and chopped

500 g/1 lb 2 oz spinach, rinsed and any
   tough stems removed

1 tbsp chopped fresh coriander

TO GARNISH

fresh coriander sprigs

lemon slices

1 Put the chickpeas into a saucepan with enough water to cover. Add the cloves, cinnamon and 1 whole unpeeled garlic clove that has been lightly crushed with the back of a knife to release the juices. Bring to the boil, reduce the heat and simmer for 1–2 hours or until the chickpeas are tender when tested with a skewer. Skim off any foam that comes to the surface.

2 Meanwhile, heat 1 tablespoon of the oil in a heavy-based pan. Crush the remaining garlic clove. Put it into the pan with the onion and cook over a moderate heat, stirring occasionally, for about 5 minutes.

3 Remove the cloves, cinnamon and garlic from the pan of chickpeas and discard. Drain the chickpeas. Place 85 g/ 3 oz of the chickpeas in a food processor with the onion and garlic, the lemon juice and 1 tablespoon of the oil and process until smooth. Alternatively, blend together with a fork in a bowl. Stir this purée into the remaining chickpeas.

4 Heat the remaining oil in a large frying pan, add the coriander seeds and stir for 1 minute until they give off their aroma. Add the tomatoes, stir and add the spinach. Cover and cook over a moderate heat for 1 minute. The spinach should be wilted, but not soggy. Stir in the chopped fresh coriander and remove the pan from the heat.

5 Transfer the chickpeas to a warmed serving dish and spoon over the spinach mixture. Garnish with the coriander sprigs and slices of lemon and serve immediately.

White Lentils

This dhal is dry when cooked, so give it a baghaar (seasoned oil dressing). It makes an excellent accompaniment to any meal of kormas.

NUTRITIONAL INFORMATION

Calories	129	Sugars	.........1g
Protein	.........6g	Fat	...........6g
Carbohydrate	...14g	Saturates	.......1g

 5 mins 45 mins

SERVES 4

INGREDIENTS

100 g/3½ oz urid dhal

1 tsp finely chopped fresh root ginger

600 ml/1 pint water

1 tsp salt

1 tsp pepper

fresh mint leaves, to garnish

chapatis, to serve

BAGHAAR

2 tbsp vegetable ghee

2 garlic cloves

2 fresh red chillies, finely chopped

1 Rinse the lentils thoroughly and put them in a large saucepan with the ginger. Add the water and bring to a boil. Cover and simmer over a medium heat for about 30 minutes. Check to see whether the lentils are cooked by rubbing them between your finger and thumb. If they are still a little hard in the middle, cook for a further 5–7 minutes. If necessary, remove the lid and cook until any remaining water has evaporated.

2 Add the salt and pepper to the lentils, mix well and set aside.

3 To make the baghaar, heat the ghee in a separate saucepan. Add the garlic and chopped red chillies and stir well to mix thoroughly.

4 Pour the garlic and chilli mixture over the lentils.

5 Transfer the white lentils to warmed individual serving dishes, garnish with mint leaves and serve hot with chapatis.

COOK'S TIP

Ghee was traditionally made from clarified butter, which can withstand higher temperatures than ordinary butter. Vegetable ghee has largely replaced it now because it is lower in saturated fats.

Split Peas with Vegetables

Here is a simple, yet nourishing and flavourful way of cooking yellow split peas. Vary the choice of vegetables and spices according to taste.

NUTRITIONAL INFORMATION

Calories	490	Sugars	........8g
Protein	.......21g	Fat	.........19g
Carbohydrate	...63g	Saturates	.......3g

  4¼ hrs   1 hr

SERVES 4

INGREDIENTS

225 g/8 oz dried yellow split peas

1.2 litres/2 pints water

½ tsp ground turmeric (optional)

500g/1 lb 2 oz new potatoes

5 tbsp vegetable oil

2 onions, coarsely chopped

175 g/6 oz button mushrooms

1 tsp ground coriander

1 tsp ground cumin

1 tsp chilli powder

1 tsp garam masala

425 ml/15 fl oz vegetable stock

½ cauliflower, broken into florets

85 g/3 oz frozen peas

175 g/6 oz cherry tomatoes, halved

salt and pepper

fresh mint sprigs, to garnish

VARIATION

Chana dhal (popular with vegetarians because of its high protein content) may be used instead of yellow split peas, if preferred. Chana dhal is similar to yellow split peas, although the grains are smaller and the flavour sweeter.

1 Place the split peas in a bowl, add the water and set aside to soak for at least 4 hours or overnight.

2 Place the peas and the soaking liquid in a large saucepan, stir in the turmeric, if using, and bring to the boil. Skim off any scum that rises to the surface, half-cover the pan and simmer gently for 20 minutes or until the peas are tender and almost dry. Remove the pan from the heat and set aside.

3 Meanwhile, cut the potatoes into 5 mm/¼ inch thick slices. Heat the oil in a flameproof casserole, add the onions, potatoes and mushrooms and cook over a low heat, stirring frequently, for 5 minute Stir in the spices and fry, stirring frequently, for 1 minute, then season with salt and pepper to taste and add the stoc and cauliflower florets.

4 Cover the pan and simmer, stirring occasionally, for 25 minutes or unt the potatoes are tender. Add the split pea (and any of the cooking liquid) and th frozen peas. Bring to the boil, cover an continue cooking for 5 minutes.

5 Stir in the halved cherry tomatoes an cook for 2 minutes. Taste and adjus the seasoning, if necessary. Serve hot garnished with mint sprigs.

Tarka Dhal

This is just one version of many dhals that are served throughout India; as many people are vegetarian, dhals form a staple part of the diet.

NUTRITIONAL INFORMATION

Calories 183   Sugars 4g
Protein ....8g   Fat 8g
Carbohydrate ...22g   Saturates 5g

10 mins   25 mins

SERVES 4

INGREDIENTS

2 tbsp ghee

2 shallots, sliced

1 tsp yellow mustard seeds

2 garlic cloves, crushed

8 fenugreek seeds

1 tsp grated fresh root ginger

½ tsp salt

125 g/4½ oz red lentils

1 tbsp tomato purée

600 ml/1 pint water

2 tomatoes, peeled and chopped

1 tbsp lemon juice

4 tbsp chopped fresh coriander

½ tsp garam masala

½ tsp chilli powder

1 Heat half of the ghee in a large saucepan and add the shallots. Cook for 2–3 minutes over a high heat, then add the mustard seeds. Cover the pan until the seeds begin to pop.

2 Immediately remove the lid from the pan and add the garlic, fenugreek, ginger and salt.

3 Stir once and add the lentils, tomato purée and water. Bring to the boil, then lower the heat and simmer gently for 10 minutes.

4 Stir in the tomatoes, lemon juice, and chopped coriander and simmer for 4–5 minutes until the lentils are tender.

5 Transfer to a serving dish. Heat the remaining ghee in a pan. Remove from the heat and stir in the garam masala and chilli powder. Pour over the tarka dhal and serve.

COOK'S TIP

The flavours in a dhal can be altered to suit your particular taste; for example, for extra heat, add more chilli powder or chillies, or add fennel seeds for a pleasant aniseed flavour.

Green Pumpkin Curry

The Indian pumpkin used in this curry is long and green and sold by weight. It can easily be bought from any Indian or Pakistani grocers.

NUTRITIONAL INFORMATION

Calories 347   Sugars 6g
Protein . . . . .2g   Fat 34g
Carbohydrate . . . .8g   Saturates 4g

 10 mins   30 mins

SERVES 4

I N G R E D I E N T S

150 ml/5 fl oz vegetable oil

2 medium onions, sliced

½ tsp white cumin seeds

500 g/1 lb 2 oz green pumpkin, cubed

1 tsp dried mango powder

1 tsp finely chopped fresh root ginger

1 tsp crushed garlic

1 tsp crushed dried red chilli

½ tsp salt

300 ml/10 fl oz water

chapatis or naan bread, to serve

1 Heat the vegetable oil in a large heavy-based frying pan. Add the onions and cumin seeds and fry over a medium heat, stirring occasionally, for about 5 minutes until the onions are light golden brown and the seeds are giving off their aroma.

2 Add the cubed pumpkin to the pan and stir-fry over a low heat for 3–5 minutes.

3 Combine the dried mango powder, ginger, garlic, chilli and salt. Add the spice mixture to the pan, stirring well to combine with the vegetables.

4 Add the water, cover and cook over a low heat, stirring occasionally, for 10–15 minutes.

5 Transfer to serving plates and serve with chapatis or naan bread.

COOK'S TIP

Cumin seeds are popular with Indian cooks because of their warm, pungent flavour and aroma. The seeds are sold whole or ground and are usually included as one of the flavourings in garam masala.

Okra Curry

This is a delicious dry bhujia (vegetarian curry) which should be served hot with chapatis. Okra is a tasty vegetable and needs few spices.

NUTRITIONAL INFORMATION

Calories 371   Sugars 8g
Protein . . . . .4g   Fat 35g
Carbohydrate . . .10g   Saturates 4g

 10 mins   30 mins

SERVES 4

INGREDIENTS

450 g/1 lb okra

150 ml/5 fl oz vegetable oil

2 medium onions, sliced

3 fresh green chillies, finely chopped

2 curry leaves

1 tsp salt

1 tomato, sliced

2 tbsp lemon juice

fresh coriander leaves

1 Rinse the okra and drain thoroughly. Using a sharp knife, chop off and discard the ends of the okra. Cut the okra into 2.5 cm/1 inch long pieces.

2 Heat the vegetable oil in a large, heavy-based frying pan. Add the onions, green chillies, curry leaves and salt and mix together. Stir-fry the vegetables over a low heat for 5 minutes.

3 Gradually add the okra, mixing in gently with a slotted spoon. Stir-fry the vegetable mixture over a medium heat for 12–15 minutes.

4 Add the sliced tomato to the pan and sprinkle over half the lemon juice. Taste and add more if required.

5 Sprinkle the coriander leaves into the pan, cover and simmer for a further 3–5 minutes.

6 Transfer the curry to warmed serving plates and serve hot.

COOK'S TIP
Okra has a remarkable glutinous quality which naturally thickens curries and casseroles.

Sweet Hot Carrots & Beans

Take care not to overcook the vegetables in this tasty dish – they are definitely at their best served tender-crisp.

NUTRITIONAL INFORMATION

Calories	268	Sugars	........16g
Protein	.........5g	Fat	..........19g
Carbohydrate	...19g	Saturates	.......3g

🥕 10 mins   🕐 15 mins

SERVES 4

INGREDIENTS

500 g/1 lb 2 oz young carrots

225 g/8 oz French beans

1 bunch spring onions

4 tbsp vegetable ghee or vegetable oil

1 tsp ground cumin

1 tsp ground coriander

3 cardamom pods, split and seeds removed

2 dried red chillies

2 garlic cloves, crushed

1–2 tsp clear honey

1 tsp lemon or lime juice

55 g/2 oz unsalted, toasted cashews

1 tbsp chopped fresh coriander or parsley

salt and pepper

TO GARNISH

slices of lime or lemon

fresh coriander sprigs

1 Cut the carrots lengthways into quarters and then in half crossways if very long. Trim the beans. Cut the spring onions into 5 cm/2 inch pieces.

2 Cook the carrots and beans in a saucepan of lightly salted boiling water for 5–6 minutes until tender-crisp. Drain well.

3 Heat the ghee or oil in a large frying pan, add the spring onions, carrots, beans, cumin, ground coriander, cardamom seeds and whole dried chillies. Cook over a low heat, stirring frequently, for 2 minutes.

4 Stir in the garlic, honey and lemon or lime juice and continue cooking, stirring occasionally, for a further 2 minutes. Season to taste with salt and pepper. Remove and discard the chillies.

5 Sprinkle the vegetables with the cashews and chopped coriander and mix together lightly. Serve immediately, garnished with lime or lemon slices and coriander sprigs.

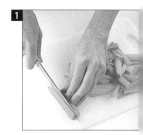

Long Beans with Tomatoes

Indian meals often need some green vegetables to complement the spicy dishes and to set off the richly flavoured sauces.

NUTRITIONAL INFORMATION

Calories 76   Sugars 3g
Protein . . . . .2g   Fat 6g
Carbohydrate . . . .4g   Saturates 3g

 15 mins   25 mins

SERVES 6

INGREDIENTS

500 g/1 lb 2 oz green beans, cut into
  5 cm/2 inch lengths

2 tbsp vegetable ghee

2.5 cm/1 inch piece of fresh root
  ginger, grated

1 garlic clove, crushed

1 tsp ground turmeric

½ tsp cayenne pepper

1 tsp ground coriander

4 tomatoes, peeled, seeded and diced

150 ml/5 fl oz vegetable stock

1 Blanch the beans briefly in boiling water, drain, refresh under cold running water and drain again.

2 Melt the ghee in a large saucepan over a moderate heat. Add the grated ginger and crushed garlic, stir and add the turmeric, cayenne and ground coriander. Stir over a low heat for about 1 minute until fragrant.

3 Add the diced tomatoes, tossing them until they are thoroughly coated in the spice mix.

4 Add the vegetable stock to the pan, bring to the boil and simmer over a medium-high heat, stirring occasionally, for about 10 minutes until the sauce has reduced and thickened.

5 Add the beans, reduce the heat to moderate and heat through, stirring constantly, for 5 minutes.

6 Transfer to a warmed serving dish and serve immediately.

COOK'S TIP

Ginger graters are an invaluable piece of equipment to have when cooking Indian food. These small, flat graters, made of either bamboo or china, can be held directly over the pan while you grate.

Spicy Corn

This dish is an ideal accompaniment to a wide range of Indian dishes and would also go well with a Western-style casserole.

NUTRITIONAL INFORMATION

Calories	162	Sugars	.........6g
Protein	.........2g	Fat	...........11g
Carbohydrate	...15g	Saturates	.......7g

 10 mins   10 mins

SERVES 4

INGREDIENTS

200 g/7 oz frozen or canned sweetcorn

1 tsp ground cumin

1 tsp crushed garlic

1 tsp ground coriander

1 tsp salt

2 fresh green chillies

1 medium onion, finely chopped

3 tbsp unsalted butter

4 red chillies, crushed

½ tsp lemon juice

1 tbsp fresh coriander leaves, plus extra to garnish

1 Thaw frozen sweetcorn, if using, or drain canned corn, and set aside.

2 Place the ground cumin, garlic, ground coriander, salt, 1 fresh green chilli and the onion in a mortar or a food processor and grind to form a smooth paste.

3 Heat the butter in a large frying pan. Add the onion and spice mixture to the pan and fry over a medium heat, stirring occasionally, for about 5–7 minutes.

4 Add the crushed red chillies to the mixture in the pan and stir to combine.

5 Add the sweetcorn to the pan and stir-fry for a further 2 minutes.

6 Add the remaining green chilli, lemon juice and the fresh coriander leaves to the pan, stirring to combine.

7 Transfer the spicy sweetcorn mixture to a warmed serving dish. Garnish with extra fresh coriander leaves and serve hot.

COOK'S TIP

Coriander is available ground or as seeds and is one of the essential ingredients in Indian cooking. Coriander seeds are often dry roasted before use to develop their flavour.

Fragrant Jasmine Rice

Jasmine rice has a delicate flavour and it can be served completely plain. This simple dish just has the light tang of lemon and soft scent of basil.

NUTRITIONAL INFORMATION

Calories	384	Sugars	.........0g
Protein	.........7g	Fat	...........4g
Carbohydrate	...86g	Saturates	.......1g

 15 mins   15 mins

SERVES 4

INGREDIENTS

400 g/14 oz jasmine rice

800 ml/28 fl oz water

rind of ½ lemon, finely grated

2 tbsp fresh sweet basil, chopped

1 Wash the rice in several changes of cold water until the water runs clear. Bring the water to the boil in a large pan, then add the rice.

2 Bring back to a rolling boil. Turn the heat to a low simmer, cover the pan and simmer for a further 12 minutes.

3 Remove the pan from the heat and set aside, covered, for 10 minutes. It is important to leave the pan tightly covered while the rice steams inside, so that the grains cook evenly and become fluffy and separate.

4 Fluff up the rice with a fork, then stir in the lemon rind. Serve sprinkled with basil leaves.

Coconut Rice with Pineapple

Cooking rice in coconut milk makes it very satisfying and nutritious, and this is often used as a base with meat, fish, vegetables or eggs.

NUTRITIONAL INFORMATION

Calories	278	Sugars	........11g
Protein	.........5g	Fat	...........7g
Carbohydrate	...54g	Saturates	.......5g

 5 mins 20 mins

SERVES 4

I N G R E D I E N T S

200 g/7 oz long grain rice

500 ml/18 fl oz coconut milk

2 lemon grass stalks

200 ml/7 fl oz water

2 fresh pineapple slices, peeled and diced

2 tbsp toasted coconut

chilli sauce, to serve

1 Wash the rice in several changes of cold water until the water runs clear. Place in a large pan with the coconut milk.

2 Place the lemon grass on a firm work surface and bruise it by hitting firmly with a rolling pin or meat mallet. Add the stalks to the pan.

3 Add the water and bring to the boil. Lower the heat, cover the pan tightly and simmer gently for 15 minutes. Remove the pan from the heat and fluff up the rice with a fork.

4 Remove and discard the lemon grass and stir in the pineapple. Sprinkle with toasted coconut and serve immediately with chilli sauce.

VARIATION

A sweet version of this dish can be made by simply omitting the lemon grass and stirring in palm sugar or caster sugar to taste during cooking. Serve as a dessert, with extra pineapple slices.

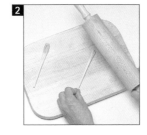

Chilli & Coconut Sambal

A sweet-sour sambal that goes well with grilled or barbecued fish. It can also be stirred into rice or noodles or curry dishes as extra flavouring.

NUTRITIONAL INFORMATION

Calories 118   Sugars 3g
Protein ....1g   Fat 11g
Carbohydrate ....3g   Saturates 10g

 10 mins   0 mins

SERVES 6–8

INGREDIENTS

1 small coconut

1 fresh pineapple slice, peeled and finely diced

1 small onion, finely chopped

2 small fresh green chillies, deseeded and chopped

5 cm/2 inch piece of lemon grass

½ tsp salt

1 tsp shrimp paste

1 tbsp lime juice

2 tbsp chopped fresh coriander

fresh coriander sprigs, to garnish

1 Puncture 2 of the coconut eyes with a screwdriver and pour the milk out from the shell. Crack the coconut shell, prise away the flesh and coarsely grate it into a bowl. Alternatively, grate the coconut using the grating blade in a food processor and then scrape into a bowl.

2 Mix the coconut with the pineapple, onion, chillies and lemon grass.

3 Blend together the salt, shrimp paste and lime juice, then stir into the coconut mixture.

4 Stir in the coriander. Spoon into a small dish to serve and garnish with fresh coriander sprigs.

VARIATION

To make a quicker version of this sambal, stir a teaspoon of Thai green curry paste into freshly grated coconut and add finely diced pineapple and lime juice to taste.

Vegetables in Peanut Sauce

This colourful mix of vegetables in a rich, spicy peanut sauce can be served either as a side dish or as a vegetarian main course.

NUTRITIONAL INFORMATION

Calories 249	Sugars 10g
Protein 10g	Fat 17g
Carbohydrate ...12g	Saturates 3g

10 mins

8–10 mins

SERVES 4

I N G R E D I E N T S

2 carrots

1 small cauliflower, trimmed

2 small heads pak choi

150 g/5½ oz French beans

2 tbsp vegetable oil

1 garlic clove, finely chopped

6 spring onions, sliced

1 tsp chilli paste

2 tbsp soy sauce

2 tbsp Chinese rice wine

4 tbsp smooth peanut butter

3 tbsp coconut milk

COOK'S TIP

It's important to cut the vegetables thinly into pieces of a similar size so that they cook quickly and evenly. Prepare all the vegetables before you start to cook.

1 Cut the carrots diagonally into thin slices. Cut the cauliflower into small florets, then slice the stalk thinly. Thickly slice the pak choi. Cut the beans into 3 cm/1¼ inch lengths.

2 Heat the oil in a large frying pan or wok. Add the garlic and spring onions and stir-fry over a medium heat for about 1 minute. Stir in the chilli paste and cook for a few seconds.

3 Add the carrots and cauliflower and stir-fry for 2–3 minutes.

4 Add the pak choi and beans and stir-fry for a further 2 minutes. Stir in the soy sauce and rice wine.

5 Mix the peanut butter with the coconut milk and stir into the pan, then cook, stirring constantly, for a further minute. Serve immediately.

Thai Red Bean Curry

The 'red' in the title refers not to the beans, but to the sauce, which has a warm, rusty red colour. This is a good way to serve fresh or frozen beans.

NUTRITIONAL INFORMATION

Calories 89	Sugars 4g	
Protein 2g	Fat 7g	
Carbohydrate 5g	Saturates 1g	

8 mins   10 mins

SERVES 4

INGREDIENTS

400 g/14 oz French beans

1 garlic clove, finely sliced

1 fresh red bird-eye chilli, deseeded and chopped

½ tsp paprika

1 piece of lemon grass stalk, finely chopped

2 tsp Thai fish sauce

125 ml/4 fl oz coconut milk

1 tbsp sunflower oil

2 spring onions, sliced

1 Cut the beans into 5 cm/2 inch pieces and cook in a small pan of boiling water for about 2 minutes. Drain well and set aside.

2 Place the garlic, chilli, paprika, lemon grass, fish sauce and coconut milk in a blender and process to a smooth paste. Alternatively, place in a mortar and pound to a smooth paste with a pestle.

3 Heat the oil in a heavy-based frying pan. Stir-fry the spring onions over a high heat for about 1 minute. Add the paste and bring the mixture to the boil.

4 Lower the heat and simmer gently for 3–4 minutes to reduce the liquid by about half. Add the beans and simmer for a further 1–2 minutes until tender and cooked through. Serve hot.

COOK'S TIP
Young runner beans can be used instead of French beans. Remove any strings from the beans, then cut at a diagonal angle into short lengths. Cook as in the recipe until tender.

Stir-fried Ginger Mushrooms

This quick vegetarian stir-fry is actually more like a rich curry,
with lots of warm spice and garlic, balanced with creamy coconut milk.

NUTRITIONAL INFORMATION

Calories ....174 Sugars 7g
Protein ....8g Fat 9g
Carbohydrate ...15g Saturates 1g

 10 mins   🕐 8 mins

SERVES 4

I N G R E D I E N T S

2 tbsp vegetable oil

3 garlic cloves, crushed

1 tbsp Thai red curry paste

½ tsp ground turmeric

425 g/14½ oz can Chinese straw
    mushrooms, drained and halved

2 cm/¾ inch piece of fresh root ginger,
    finely shredded

100 ml/3½ fl oz coconut milk

40 g/1½ oz dried Chinese black
    mushrooms, soaked, drained and sliced

1 tbsp lemon juice

1 tbsp light soy sauce

2 tsp sugar

½ tsp salt

8 cherry tomatoes, halved

200 g/7oz firm tofu, diced

fresh coriander leaves, to garnish

boiled fragrant rice, to serve

1 Heat the oil in a frying pan and stir-fry the garlic for about 1 minute. Stir in the curry paste and turmeric and cook for about a further 30 seconds.

2 Stir in the straw mushrooms and ginger and stir-fry for about 2 minutes. Stir in the coconut milk and bring to the boil.

3 Stir in the Chinese dried black mushrooms, lemon juice, soy sauce, sugar and salt and heat thoroughly. Add the tomatoes and tofu and toss gently to heat through.

4 Sprinkle the coriander leaves over the mixture and serve immediately with fragrant rice.

Potatoes in Creamed Coconut

A colourful way to serve potatoes that is quick and easy to make.
Serve it with spicy meat curries with a salad on the side.

NUTRITIONAL INFORMATION

Calories	93	Sugars	.......1.5g
Protein	........2.8g	Fat	..........4.8g
Carbohydrate	..10.3g	Saturates	.....4.0g

10 mins   15 mins

SERVES 4

INGREDIENTS

00 g/1 lb 5 oz potatoes

onion, thinly sliced

fresh red bird-eye chillies, finely chopped

tsp salt

tsp ground black pepper

5 g/3 oz creamed coconut

50 ml/12 fl oz vegetable or chicken stock

resh coriander or basil, chopped,
to garnish

1 Peel the potatoes thinly. Use a sharp knife to cut into 2 cm/¾ inch chunks.

2 Place the potatoes in a pan with the onion, chillies, salt, pepper and creamed coconut. Stir in the stock.

3 Bring to the boil, stirring, then lower the heat, cover the pan and simmer gently, stirring occasionally, until the potatoes are tender.

4 Adjust the seasoning to taste, then sprinkle with chopped coriander or basil. Serve immediately while hot.

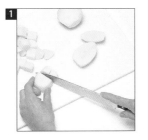  

COOK'S TIP

f the potatoes are
hin-skinned, or a new variety,
imply wash or scrub to remove any
irt and cook with the skins on. This
dds extra dietary fibre and nutrients
o the finished dish and cuts down on
he preparation time. Baby new
otatoes can be cooked whole.

Stir-fried Broccoli

Chinese oyster sauce has a sweet-salty flavour, ideal for adding a richly Oriental flavour to plain vegetables.

NUTRITIONAL INFORMATION

Calories 81   Sugars 2g
Protein . . . . .5g   Fat 4g
Carbohydrate . . . .6g   Saturates 1g

 5 mins   6–8 mins

SERVES 4

INGREDIENTS

400 g/14 oz broccoli

1 tbsp groundnut oil

2 shallots, finely chopped

1 garlic clove, finely chopped

1 tbsp Chinese rice wine or dry sherry

5 tbsp oyster sauce

¼ tsp ground black pepper

1 tsp chilli oil

1 Trim the broccoli and cut into small florets. Blanch in a saucepan of boiling water for about 30 seconds, then drain well.

2 Heat the oil in a large frying pan or wok and stir-fry the shallots and garlic for 1–2 minutes until golden brown.

3 Add the broccoli and stir-fry for 2 minutes. Add the wine and oyster sauce and stir for a further 1 minute.

4 Stir in the pepper and drizzle with little chilli oil just before serving. Serve the stir-fry hot.

COOK'S TIP

To make chilli oil, tuck fresh red or green chillies into a jar and top up with olive oil or a light vegetable oil. Cover with a lid and leave to infuse the flavour for at least 3 weeks before using.

Roasted Thai-spiced Peppers

A colourful side dish that also makes a good buffet party salad.
This is best made in advance to give time for the flavours to mingle.

NUTRITIONAL INFORMATION

Calories ....83 Sugars 17g
Protein ....2g Fat 1g
Carbohydrate ...17g Saturates 0g

1¼ hrs   5–10 mins

SERVES 4

INGREDIENTS

red peppers

yellow peppers

green peppers

fresh red bird-eye chillies, deseeded and finely chopped

lemon grass stalk, finely shredded

tbsp lime juice

tbsp palm sugar

tbsp Thai fish sauce

1 Roast the peppers under a hot grill, barbecue over hot coals or roast in a hot oven, turning them over occasionally, until the skins are blackened and charred. Set aside to cool slightly, then remove the skins. Cut each pepper in half and remove the core and seeds.

2 Thickly slice the peppers and transfer to a large mixing bowl.

3 Place the chillies, lemon grass, lime juice, sugar and fish sauce in a screw-top jar and shake vigorously until thoroughly mixed.

4 Pour the dressing over the peppers. Set aside to cool completely, cover with clingfilm and chill in the refrigerator for at least an hour before serving. Transfer to a serving dish to serve.

COOK'S TIP
The flavours will mingle best if the peppers are still slightly warm when you pour the dressing over. Prepare the dressing while the peppers are cooking, so it's ready to pour over when they are done.

Pak Choi with Crab Meat

Pak choi has a delicate, fresh flavour and crisp texture, which is best retained by quick cooking, making it an ideal choice for stir-frying.

NUTRITIONAL INFORMATION

Calories	101	Sugars	2g
Protein	9g	Fat	6g
Carbohydrate	3g	Saturates	1g

 5 mins   8 mins

SERVES 4

INGREDIENTS

2 heads pak choi, about 250 g/
  9 oz total weight

2 tbsp vegetable oil

1 garlic clove, thinly sliced

2 tbsp oyster sauce

100 g/3½ oz cherry tomatoes, halved

170 g/6 oz can white crab meat, drained

salt and pepper

1 Trim the pak choi and cut into 2.5 cm/1 inch thick slices.

2 Heat the oil in a large frying pan or wok and stir-fry the garlic over a high heat for 1 minute.

3 Add the pak choi and stir-fry for 2–3 minutes until the leaves wilt, but the stalks are still crisp.

4 Add the oyster sauce and tomatoes and stir-fry for a further minute.

5 Add the crab meat and season to tas with salt and pepper. Stir to he thoroughly and break up the distribution crab meat before serving.

VARIATION

If pak choi is not available, Chinese leaves make a good alternative for this dish.

Courgette Curry

This delicious curry is spiced with fenugreek seeds, which have a beautiful aroma and a distinctive taste.

NUTRITIONAL INFORMATION

Calories	188	Sugars	.........5g
Protein	.........3g	Fat	..........17g
Carbohydrate	....6g	Saturates	.......2g

20 mins | 15 mins

SERVES 4

INGREDIENTS

tbsp vegetable oil

medium onion, finely chopped

fresh green chillies, finely chopped

tsp finely chopped fresh root ginger

tsp crushed garlic

tsp chilli powder

00 g/1 lb 2 oz courgettes, thinly sliced

tomatoes, sliced

tbsp fresh coriander leaves, plus extra
to garnish

tsp fenugreek seeds

hapatis, to serve

1 Heat the oil in a large, heavy-based frying pan or wok. Add the onion, hillies, ginger, garlic and chilli powder nd stir-fry over a low heat for about 2–3 minutes until the onion is just eginning to soften.

2 Add the courgettes and the tomatoes and stir-fry over a medium heat for 5–7 minutes.

3 Add the coriander leaves and fenugreek seeds to the pan or wok and stir-fry over a medium heat for 5 minutes, until the vegetables are tender.

4 Remove the pan from the heat and transfer the courgette and fenugreek seed mixture to warmed serving dishes. Garnish with coriander leaves and serve hot with chapatis.

VARIATION

You could use coriander seeds instead of the fenugreek seeds, if you prefer.

Spinach & Chana Dhal

An attractive-looking dish, this makes a good accompaniment to almost any dish. For a contrast in colour and taste, serve with a tomato curry.

NUTRITIONAL INFORMATION

Calories 175   Sugars 1g
Protein ....6g   Fat 12g
Carbohydrate ...12g   Saturates 1g

 3 hrs 5 mins   45 mins

SERVES 6

INGREDIENTS

4 tbsp chana dhal

6 tbsp vegetable oil

1 tsp mixed onion and mustard seeds

4 dried red chillies

400–425 g/14–15 oz can spinach, drained

1 tsp finely chopped fresh root ginger

1 tsp ground coriander

1 tsp ground cumin

1 tsp salt

1 tsp chilli powder

2 tbsp lemon juice

1 fresh green chilli, deseeded and finely chopped, to garnish

1 Soak the chana dhal in a bowl of warm water for at least 3 hours, preferably overnight.

2 Place the dhal in a saucepan, cover with water and bring to the boil. Lower the heat and simmer gently for 30 minutes. Drain well.

3 Heat the oil in another saucepan. Add the mixed onion and mustard seeds and dried red chillies and fry, stirring constantly, until they turn a shade darker.

4 Add the drained spinach to the pan, mixing gently. Add the ginger, ground coriander, ground cumin, salt and chilli powder. Reduce the heat and gently stir-fry the mixture for 7-10 minutes.

5 Add the drained dhal to the pan and blend into the spinach mixture well, stirring gently so that it does not break up.

6 Transfer the mixture to a warmed serving dish. Sprinkle over the lemon juice and garnish with the chopped green chilli. Serve immediately.

COOK'S TIP

Very similar in appearance to moong dhal – the yellow split peas – chana dhal have slightly less shiny grains.

Pak Choi with Cashew Nuts

Plum sauce is readily available in jars and has a terrific, sweet flavour which superbly complements the vegetables.

NUTRITIONAL INFORMATION

Calories 241	Sugars 7g
Protein 7g	Fat 19g
Carbohydrate 11g	Saturates 4g

🍴 5 mins   🕐 15 mins

SERVES 4

I N G R E D I E N T S

2 red onions

175 g/6 oz red cabbage

2 tbsp groundnut oil

225 g/8 oz pak choi

2 tbsp plum sauce

100 g/3½ oz roasted cashew nuts

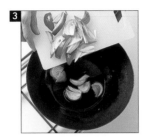

1 Using a sharp knife, cut the red onions into thin wedges and thinly shred the red cabbage.

2 Heat the groundnut oil in a large preheated wok or heavy-based frying pan until it is really hot.

3 Add the onion wedges to the wok or frying pan and stir-fry for about 5 minutes or until the onions are just beginning to brown.

4 Add the red cabbage to the wok and stir-fry for a further 2–3 minutes.

5 Add the pak choi leaves to the wok or frying pan and stir-fry for about 5 minutes or until the leaves have just wilted.

6 Drizzle the plum sauce over the vegetables, toss together until well combined and heat until the liquid is beginning to bubble.

7 Scatter the roasted cashew nuts over the stir-fry and transfer to warm serving bowls. Serve immediately.

VARIATION

Use unsalted peanuts instead of the cashew nuts, if you prefer.

Honey-fried Spinach

This stir-fry is the perfect accompaniment to tofu dishes and it is wonderfully quick and simple to make.

NUTRITIONAL INFORMATION

Calories 146	Sugars 9g
Protein 4g	Fat 9g
Carbohydrate ...10g	Saturates 2g

 5 mins 🕐 15 mins

SERVES 4

I N G R E D I E N T S

4 spring onions

3 tbsp groundnut oil

350 g/12 oz shiitake mushrooms, sliced

2 garlic cloves, crushed

350 g/12 oz baby leaf spinach

2 tbsp dry sherry

2 tbsp clear honey

1 Using a sharp knife, thickly slice the spring onions on the diagonal.

2 Heat the groundnut oil in a large preheated wok or frying pan with a heavy base.

3 Add the shiitake mushrooms to the wok or pan and stir-fry for about 5 minutes or until they have softened.

 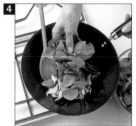 

4 Stir the crushed garlic into the wok or frying pan. Add the baby leaf spinach and stir-fry for a further 2–3 minutes or until the spinach leaves have just begun to wilt.

5 Mix together the dry sherry and clear honey in a small bowl until thoroughly combined. Drizzle the sherry and honey mixture over the spinach and heat through, stirring to coat the spinach leaves thoroughly in the mixture.

6 Transfer the stir-fry to warm serving dishes, scatter with the sliced spring onions and serve immediately.

COOK'S TIP

Single-flower honey has a better, more individual flavour than blended honey. Acacia honey is typically Chinese, but you could also try clover, lemon blossom, lime flower or orange blossom.

Broccoli & Black Bean Sauce

Broccoli works well with the black bean sauce and Chinese leaves in this recipe, while the almonds add extra crunch and flavour.

NUTRITIONAL INFORMATION

Calories	139	Sugars	.........3g
Protein	.........7g	Fat	..........10g
Carbohydrate	....5g	Saturates	.......1g

5 mins   15 mins

SERVES 4

INGREDIENTS

450 g/1 lb broccoli florets

2 tbsp sunflower oil

1 onion, sliced

2 garlic cloves, thinly sliced

25 g/1 oz flaked almonds

1 head Chinese leaves, shredded

4 tbsp black bean sauce

1 Bring a large saucepan of water to the boil. Add the broccoli florets to the pan and cook for 1 minute. Drain, rinse in cold water to prevent any further cooking and drain thoroughly again.

2 Meanwhile, heat the sunflower oil in a large preheated wok.

3 Add the onion and garlic slices to the wok and stir-fry until just beginning to brown.

4 Add the drained broccoli florets and the flaked almonds and stir-fry for a further 2–3 minutes.

5 Add the shredded Chinese leaves to the wok and stir-fry for a further 2 minutes.

6 Stir the black bean sauce into the vegetables, tossing to coat them thoroughly, and cook until the juices are just beginning to bubble.

7 Transfer the vegetables to warm serving bowls and serve immediately.

VARIATION

Use unsalted cashew nuts instead of the almonds, if preferred.

Poultry, Meat, Game and Fish

You don't have to make sacrifices to enjoy a healthy diet, but it does pay to be sensible. Ring the changes with occasional meat-free days, because red meat, in particular, is often quite high in fat. Poultry and game are both leaner and you can – and should – eat fish two or three times a week. Some countries

are renowned for their healthy diets and many of the mouthwatering dishes in this chapter have been inspired by their cuisines – sizzling Chinese stir-fries, flavourful Italian pasta sauces and succulent Mediterranean stews – while the range of fabulous fish and seafood dishes is virtually endless.

Oat-Crusted Chicken Pieces

A very low-fat chicken recipe with a refreshingly light, mustard-spiced sauce, which is ideal for a healthy lunchbox or a light meal with salad.

NUTRITIONAL INFORMATION

Calories	120	Sugars	.........3g
Protein	........15g	Fat	...........3g
Carbohydrate	....8g	Saturates	......1g

5 mins   40 mins

SERVES 4

INGREDIENTS

25 g/1 oz rolled oats

1 tbsp chopped fresh rosemary

4 skinless chicken quarters

1 egg white, lightly beaten

150 g/5½ oz natural low-fat fromage frais

2 tsp wholegrain mustard

salt and pepper

grated carrot salad, to serve

1 Combine the rolled oats, chopped fresh rosemary and salt and pepper.

2 Brush each piece of chicken evenly with a little egg white, then coat in the oat mixture.

3 Place the chicken pieces on a baking sheet and bake in a preheated oven, 200°C/400°F/Gas Mark 6, for about 40 minutes. Test to see if the chicken is cooked by inserted a skewer into the thickest part – the juices should run clear without a trace of pink.

4 Combine the fromage frais and mustard and season with salt and pepper to taste.

5 Serve the chicken, hot or cold, with the sauce and a grated carrot salad.

Chicken with Two Sauces

With its red and yellow pepper sauces, this quick and simple dish is colourful, healthy and perfect for an impromptu lunch or supper.

NUTRITIONAL INFORMATION

Calories 257   Sugars 7g
Protein ....29g   Fat 10g
Carbohydrate ....8g   Saturates 2g

10 mins   1½ hrs

SERVES 4

INGREDIENTS

2 tbsp olive oil

2 medium onions, finely chopped

2 garlic cloves, crushed

2 red peppers, chopped

pinch of cayenne pepper

2 tsp tomato purée

2 yellow peppers, chopped

pinch of dried basil

4 lean skinless, boneless chicken breasts

150 ml/5 fl oz dry white wine

150 ml/5 fl oz chicken stock

bouquet garni

salt and pepper

fresh herbs, to garnish

1 Heat 1 tablespoon of olive oil in each of 2 medium pans. Place half the chopped onions, 1 of the garlic cloves, the red peppers, cayenne pepper and tomato purée in 1 of the pans. Place the remaining onion and garlic, the yellow peppers and basil in the other pan.

2 Cover each pan and cook over a very low heat for 1 hour until the peppers are very soft. If either mixture becomes dry, add a little water. Transfer the contents of the first pan to a food processor and process, then sieve. Repeat with the contents of the other pan.

3 Return to the pans and season with salt and pepper. Gently reheat the sauces while the chicken is cooking.

4 Put the chicken breasts into a frying pan and add the wine and stock. Add the bouquet garni and bring the liquid to a simmer over a medium-low heat. Cook the chicken for about 20 minutes until tender and cooked through.

5 To serve, put a pool of each sauce on to 4 individual serving plates, slice the chicken breasts and arrange them on the plates. Garnish with fresh herbs and serve immediately.

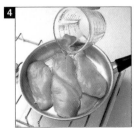

Golden Glazed Chicken

A glossy glaze with sweet and fruity flavours coats lean chicken breasts in this quick and tasty recipe.

NUTRITIONAL INFORMATION

Calories ....427 Sugars 11g
Protein ....39g Fat 12g
Carbohydrate ...42g Saturates 3g

5 mins   35 mins

SERVES 4

INGREDIENTS

6 skinless boneless chicken
  breast portions

1 tsp ground turmeric

1 tbsp wholegrain mustard

300 ml/10 fl oz orange juice

2 tbsp clear honey

2 tbsp sunflower oil

350 g/12 oz long grain rice

1 orange

3 tbsp chopped fresh mint

salt and pepper

fresh mint sprigs, to garnish

1 With a sharp knife, mark the surface of the chicken breasts in a diamond pattern and place in a single layer a shallow dish.

2 Combine the turmeric, mustard, orange juice and honey and pour the mixture over the chicken. Season with salt and pepper to taste. Chill until required.

3 Lift the chicken from the marinade and pat dry on kitchen paper. Reserve the marinade.

4 Heat the oil in a wide pan, add the chicken and sauté until golden, turning once. Drain off any excess oil. Pour the marinade into the pan, cover and simmer for 10–15 minutes until the chicken is tender.

5 Cook the rice in lightly salted boiling water for 15–20 minutes until tender, then drain well. Finely grate the orange rind and stir it into the rice with the mint.

6 Remove the peel and white pith from the orange and cut the flesh into segments.

7 Serve the chicken with the orange and mint rice, garnished with orange segments and mint sprigs.

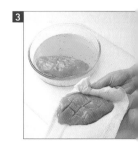

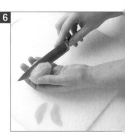

COOK'S TIP

To make a slightly sharper
sauce, use small grapefruit
instead of the oranges.

Spiced Chicken Casserole

Spices, herbs, fruit, nuts and vegetables are combined to make an appealing casserole with lots of flavour.

NUTRITIONAL INFORMATION

Calories	385	Sugars	........14g
Protein	........37g	Fat	..........15g
Carbohydrate	...19g	Saturates	.......2g

10 mins   2¼ hrs

SERVES 4

INGREDIENTS

3 tbsp olive oil

900 g/2 lb skinless, boneless
   chicken, sliced

10 shallots or pickling onions

3 carrots, chopped

55 g/2 oz chestnuts, sliced

55 g/2 oz flaked almonds, toasted

1 tsp freshly grated nutmeg

3 tsp ground cinnamon

300 ml/10 fl oz white wine

300 ml/10 fl oz chicken stock

175 ml/6 fl oz white wine vinegar

1 tbsp chopped fresh tarragon

1 tbsp chopped fresh flat leaf parsley

1 tbsp chopped fresh thyme

grated rind of 1 orange

1 tbsp dark muscovado sugar

125 g/4½ oz seedless black
   grapes, halved

sea salt and pepper

fresh herbs, to garnish

wild rice or puréed potato, to serve

1 Heat the olive oil in a large, heavy-based saucepan and add the chicken, shallots or pickling onions and carrots. Cook, stirring frequently, over a medium heat for about 6 minutes or until the chicken is browned.

2 Add the nuts, nutmeg, cinnamon, wine, stock, wine vinegar, herbs, orange rind and sugar and season to taste with salt and pepper. Simmer over a low heat for 2 hours until the meat is very tender. Stir the casserole occasionally.

3 Add the grapes just before serving and serve with wild rice or puréed potato. Garnish with herbs.

Chicken with Shallots

This recipe has an oriental flavour, which can be further enhanced with chopped spring onions, cinnamon and lemon grass.

NUTRITIONAL INFORMATION

Calories 277	Sugars 6g
Protein 28g	Fat 11g
Carbohydrate ...17g	Saturates 2g

15 mins   1 hr 50 mins

SERVES 4–8

INGREDIENTS

6 tbsp sesame oil

900 g/1¾ lb chicken meat

60 g/2 oz plain flour, seasoned

32 shallots, sliced

500 g/1 lb 2 oz wild mushrooms, roughly chopped

300 ml/10 fl oz chicken stock

2 tbsp Worcestershire sauce

1 tbsp honey

2 tbsp grated fresh root ginger

150 ml/5 fl oz yogurt

salt and pepper

flat-leaf parsley, to garnish

wild rice and white rice, to serve

COOK'S TIP

Mushrooms can be stored in the refrigerator for 24–36 hours. Keep them in paper bags because they 'sweat' in plastic. You do not need to peel mushrooms but wild mushrooms must be washed thoroughly.

1 Heat the oil in a large frying pan. Coat the chicken in the seasoned flour and cook for about 4 minutes, until browned all over. Transfer to a large deep casserole and keep warm until required.

2 Slowly fry the shallots and mushrooms in the juices.

3 Add the chicken stock, Worcestershire sauce, honey and fresh ginger, then season to taste with salt and pepper.

4 Pour the mixture over the chicken, and cover the casserole with a lid or cooking foil.

5 Cook in the centre of a preheated oven, 150°C/300°F/Gas Mark 2, for about 1½ hours, until the meat is very tender. Add the yogurt and cook for a further 10 minutes. Serve the casserole with a mixture of wild rice and white rice, and garnish with fresh parsley.

Spicy Tomato Chicken

These low-fat, spicy skewers are cooked in a matter of minutes – assemble them ahead of time and store in the refrigerator until needed.

NUTRITIONAL INFORMATION

Calories	195	Sugars	........11g
Protein	........28g	Fat	..........4g
Carbohydrate	...12g	Saturates	......1g

🧊 10 mins   🕐 10 mins

SERVES 4

I N G R E D I E N T S

500 g/1 lb 2 oz skinless, boneless
  chicken breasts

3 tbsp tomato purée

2 tbsp clear honey

2 tbsp Worcestershire sauce

1 tbsp chopped fresh rosemary

250 g/9 oz cherry tomatoes

fresh rosemary sprigs, to garnish

couscous or rice, to serve

1 Cut the chicken into 2.5 cm/1 inch chunks and place in a bowl.

2 Combine the tomato purée, honey, Worcestershire sauce and chopped rosemary in a small bowl. Add to the chicken, stirring to coat evenly.

3 Alternating the chicken pieces and cherry tomatoes, thread them on to

8 wooden skewers. (If the skewers have been soaked in water they will not char.)

4 Spoon over any remaining glaze. Cook under a preheated hot grill for about 8–10 minutes, turning occasionally, until the chicken is thoroughly cooked.

5 Serve on a bed of couscous or rice and garnish with sprigs of rosemary.

COOK'S TIP
Couscous is made from semolina that has been made into separate grains. It usually just needs moistening or steaming before serving.

Chicken with Bramble Sauce

This autumnal recipe can be made with freshly picked wild blackberries from the hedgerows if you're lucky enough to live near a good supply.

NUTRITIONAL INFORMATION

Calories 174   Sugars 5g
Protein ....27g   Fat 4g
Carbohydrate ....5g   Saturates 1g

🧊 1¼ hrs   🕐 20 mins

SERVES 4

INGREDIENTS

4 chicken breast portions or 8 thighs

4 tbsp dry white wine or cider

2 tbsp chopped fresh rosemary

pepper

fresh rosemary sprigs and blackberries,
 to garnish

SAUCE

200 g/7 oz blackberries

1 tbsp cider vinegar

2 tbsp redcurrant jelly

¼ tsp freshly grated nutmeg

1 Cut the chicken into 2.5 cm/1 inch pieces and place in a bowl. Sprinkle over the wine or cider and chopped rosemary and season to taste with pepper. Cover and set aside to marinate for at least an hour.

2 Drain the marinade from the chicken and thread the meat on to 8 metal or wooden skewers. Reserve the marinade for the sauce.

3 Cook under a preheated moderately hot grill for 8–10 minutes, turning occasionally, until golden.

4 To make the sauce, place the marinade in a pan with the blackberries and simmer gently until soft. Press though a sieve.

5 Return the blackberry purée to the pan, add the cider vinegar and redcurrant jelly and bring to the boil. Boil the sauce, uncovered, until it is reduced by about one-third.

6 Spoon a little bramble sauce on to each of 4 individual serving plates and place a chicken skewer on top. Sprinkle with nutmeg. Garnish each skewer with rosemary and blackberries. Serve immediately.

COOK'S TIP
If you use canned fruit,
omit the redcurrant jelly.

Thai Stir-fried Chicken

Coconut adds a creamy texture and delicious flavour to this Thai-style stir-fry, which is spiked with green chilli.

NUTRITIONAL INFORMATION

Calories 184	Sugars 6g	
Protein 24g	Fat 5g	
Carbohydrate 8g	Saturates 2g	

15 mins   10 mins

SERVES 4

INGREDIENTS

3 tbsp sesame oil

350 g/12 oz skinless, boneless chicken breast, thinly sliced

8 shallots, sliced

2 garlic cloves, finely chopped

2 tsp grated fresh root ginger

1 fresh green chilli, deseeded and finely chopped

1 red pepper, deseeded and thinly sliced

1 green pepper, deseeded and thinly sliced

3 courgettes, thinly sliced

2 tbsp ground almonds

1 tsp ground cinnamon

1 tbsp oyster sauce

20 g/¾ oz creamed coconut, grated

salt and pepper

1 Heat the sesame oil in a preheated wok or heavy-based frying pan. Add the chicken, season with salt and pepper to taste and stir fry over a medium heat for about 4 minutes.

2 Add the shallots, garlic, ginger and fresh green chilli and stir-fry for a further 2 minutes.

3 Add the red and green peppers and courgettes and stir-fry for about 1 minute.

4 Stir in the almonds, cinnamon, oyster sauce and creamed coconut and season to taste with salt and pepper. Stir-fry for 1 minute to heat through and then serve immediately.

COOK'S TIP

Creamed coconut is sold in blocks by supermarkets and oriental stores. It is a useful store-cupboard standby because it adds richness and depth of flavour.

Chicken & Noodle One-pot

Flavoursome chicken and vegetables are cooked with Chinese egg noodles in a coconut sauce. Serve in deep soup bowls.

NUTRITIONAL INFORMATION

Calories 256	Sugars 7g	
Protein 30g	Fat 8g	
Carbohydrate ...18g	Saturates 2g	

5 mins   20 mins

SERVES 4

I N G R E D I E N T S

1 tbsp sunflower oil

1 onion, sliced

1 garlic clove, crushed

2.5 cm/1 inch piece of fresh root
   ginger, grated

1 bunch of spring onions, sliced diagonally

500 g/1 lb 2 oz skinless chicken breast
   fillet, cut into bite-size pieces

2 tbsp mild curry paste

450 ml/16 fl oz coconut milk

300 ml/10 fl oz chicken stock

250 g/9 oz Chinese egg noodles

2 tsp lime juice

salt and pepper

fresh basil sprigs, to garnish

COOK'S TIP

If you enjoy hot flavours,
substitute the mild curry paste
in the above recipe with hot
curry paste (found in most
supermarkets) but reduce
the quantity to 1 tablespoon.

1 Heat the sunflower oil in a wok or large, heavy-based frying pan.

2 Add the onion, garlic, ginger and spring onions and stir-fry over a medium heat for 2 minutes until softened.

3 Add the chicken and curry paste and stir-fry for 4 minutes or until the vegetables and chicken are golden brown. Stir in the coconut milk, stock and salt and pepper to taste and mix well.

4 Bring to the boil, break the noodles into large pieces, if necessary, add to the wok or pan, cover and simmer, stirring occasionally, for about 6–8 minutes until the noodles are just tender.

5 Add the lime juice and adjust the seasoning if necessary.

6 Serve the chicken and noodle one-pot immediately in deep soup bowls, garnished with basil sprigs.

Chicken Pepperonata

All the sunshine colours and flavours of Italy are combined in this easy and economical dish.

NUTRITIONAL INFORMATION

Calories	328	Sugars	.........7g
Protein	........35g	Fat	..........15g
Carbohydrate	...13g	Saturates	.......4g

15 mins

40 mins

SERVES 4

INGREDIENTS

8 chicken thighs

2 tbsp wholemeal flour

2 tbsp olive oil

1 small onion, thinly sliced

1 garlic clove, crushed

1 large red pepper, deseeded and
 thinly sliced

1 large yellow pepper, deseeded and
 thinly sliced

1 large green pepper. deseeded and
 thinly sliced

400 g/14 oz can chopped tomatoes

1 tbsp chopped fresh oregano

salt and pepper

fresh oregano, to garnish

crusty wholemeal bread, to serve

1 Remove the skin from the chicken thighs and toss the meat in the flour.

2 Heat the oil in a wide frying pan and fry the chicken over a medium heat until sealed and lightly browned, then remove from the pan.

3 Add the onion to the pan, lower the heat and cook, stirring occasionally, for about 5 minutes until softened, but not browned. Add the garlic, pepper slices, tomatoes and oregano, then bring to the boil, stirring constantly.

4 Arrange the chicken on top of the vegetables, season to taste with salt and pepper, then cover the pan tightly and simmer for 20–25 minutes or until the chicken is completely cooked and tender.

5 Taste and adjust the seasoning, if necessary. Transfer the chicken to a plate. Spoon the vegetables on to a warmed serving platter and top with the chicken. Garnish with oregano and serve immediately with crusty wholemeal bread.

Gardener's Chicken

Any combination of small, young vegetables, such as courgettes, leeks and onions, can be roasted with this delicious stuffed chicken.

NUTRITIONAL INFORMATION

Calories	674	Sugars	........18g
Protein	........35g	Fat	..........40g
Carbohydrate	...45g	Saturates	......12g

🥔 10 mins 🕐 1¾ hrs

SERVES 4

INGREDIENTS

250 g/9 oz parsnips, chopped

2 small carrots, chopped

25 g/1 oz fresh breadcrumbs

¼ tsp freshly grated nutmeg

1 tbsp chopped fresh parsley

1.5 kg/3 lb chicken

1 bunch fresh parsley

½ onion

2 tbsp butter, softened

4 tbsp olive oil

500 g/1 lb 2 oz new potatoes, scrubbed

500 g/1 lb 2 oz baby carrots, trimmed

salt and pepper

1 To make the stuffing, put the parsnips and chopped carrots into a pan, half cover with water and bring to the boil. Lower the heat, cover and simmer until tender. Drain well, then process in a blender or food processor to a smooth purée. Transfer the purée to a bowl and set aside to cool.

2 Mix the breadcrumbs, nutmeg and parsley into the purée and season to taste with salt and pepper.

3 Put the stuffing into the neck end of the chicken and push a little under

the skin over the breast meat. Secure the flap of skin with a small metal skewer or cocktail stick.

4 Place the bunch of parsley and onion inside the cavity of the chicken, then place the chicken in a large roasting tin.

5 Spread the butter over the skin and season with salt and pepper, cover with foil and place in a preheated oven, 190°C/375°F/Gas Mark 5, for 30 minutes.

6 Meanwhile, heat the oil in a frying pan, and lightly brown the potatoes.

7 Transfer the potatoes to the roasting tin and add the baby carrots. Baste the chicken and continue to cook for a further hour, basting the chicken and vegetables after 30 minutes. Remove the foil for the last 20 minutes to allow the skin to crisp. Garnish the vegetables with chopped parsley and serve immediately.

Chicken & Almond Rissoles

Cooked potatoes and cooked chicken are combined to make tasty rissoles rolled in chopped almonds, then served with stir-fried vegetables.

NUTRITIONAL INFORMATION

Calories 161   Sugars 3g
Protein . . . . .12g   Fat 9g
Carbohydrate . . . .8g   Saturates 1g

35 mins   20 mins

SERVES 4

I N G R E D I E N T S

115 g/4 oz parboiled potatoes

1 carrot

115 g/4 oz cooked chicken

1 garlic clove, crushed

½ tsp dried tarragon or thyme

pinch of ground allspice or
   ground coriander

1 egg yolk or ½ egg, beaten

about 25 g/1 oz flaked almonds

salt and pepper

STIR-FRIED VEGETABLES

1 celery stick

2 spring onions, trimmed

1 tbsp groundnut oil

8 baby sweetcorn cobs

40 g/1½ oz mangetouts or sugar snap
   peas, trimmed

2 tsp balsamic vinegar

salt and pepper

2 Add the egg and bind the ingredients together. Divide the mixture in half and shape into 'sausages'. Chop the almonds and then evenly coat each rissole in the nuts. Place the rissoles in a greased ovenproof dish and cook in a preheated oven, 200°C/400°F/Gas Mark 6, for about 20 minutes until browned.

3 To prepare the stir-fried vegetables, cut the celery and spring onions on the diagonal into thin slices. Heat the oil in a frying pan and toss in the vegetables. Cook over a high heat for 1–2 minutes, then add the sweetcorn cobs and mangetouts or sugar snap peas and cook for 2–3 minutes. Finally, add the balsamic vinegar and season to taste with salt and pepper.

4 Place the rissoles on serving plates and add the stir-fried vegetables.

1 Grate the parboiled potatoes and raw carrots coarsely into a bowl. Finely chop or mince the chicken. Add to the vegetables with the garlic, herbs and spices and salt and pepper to taste.

Chicken & Corn Sauté

This quick and healthy dish is stir-fried, which means you need use only the minimum of oil for cooking.

NUTRITIONAL INFORMATION

Calories 280	Sugars 7g
Protein 31g	Fat 11g
Carbohydrate 9g	Saturates 2g

 5 mins   10 mins

SERVES 4

INGREDIENTS

4 skinless, boneless chicken breasts

250 g/9 oz baby corn cobs

250 g/9 oz mangetouts

2 tbsp sunflower oil

1 tbsp sherry vinegar

1 tbsp clear honey

1 tbsp light soy sauce

1 tbsp sunflower seeds

pepper

rice or Chinese egg noodles, to serve

1 Using a sharp knife, slice the chicken breasts into long, thin strips.

2 Cut the baby corn cobs in half lengthways and trim the mangetouts.

3 Heat the sunflower oil in a preheated wok or a wide frying pan.

4 Add the chicken and stir-fry over a fairly high heat for 1 minute.

5 Add the baby corn cobs and mangetouts and stir-fry over a moderate heat for 5–8 minutes, until evenly cooked. The vegetables should still be slightly crunchy.

6 Combine the sherry vinegar, honey and soy sauce in a small bowl.

7 Stir the vinegar mixture into the pan with the sunflower seeds.

8 Season to taste with pepper. Cook, stirring constantly, for 1 minute.

9 Serve the chicken and corn sauté hot with rice or Chinese egg noodles.

VARIATION

Rice vinegar or balsamic vinegar make good substitutes for the sherry vinegar.

Chicken Tikka

Traditionally, chicken tikka is cooked in a fiery-hot clay tandoori oven, but it works well on the barbecue, too.

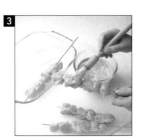

NUTRITIONAL INFORMATION

Calories	173	Sugars	.........6g
Protein	........28g	Fat	...........4g
Carbohydrate	....6g	Saturates	......2g

2¼ hrs   15 mins

SERVES 4

INGREDIENTS

4 skinless, boneless chicken breasts

½ tsp salt

4 tbsp lemon or lime juice

vegetable oil, for brushing

MARINADE

150 ml/5 fl oz low-fat natural yogurt

2 garlic cloves, crushed

2.5 cm/1 inch piece of fresh root
   ginger grated

1 tsp ground cumin

1 tsp chilli powder

½ tsp ground coriander

½ tsp ground turmeric

SAUCE

150 ml/5 fl oz low-fat natural yogurt

1 tsp mint sauce

1 Cut the chicken into 2.5 cm/1 inch cubes. Sprinkle with the salt and the citrus juice. Set aside for 10 minutes.

2 To make the marinade, combine all the ingredients in a small bowl until well mixed.

3 Thread the cubes of chicken on to skewers. Brush the marinade over the chicken. Cover and set aside to marinate in the refrigerator for at least 2 hours, preferably overnight. Cook the chicken skewers over hot coals, brushing with oil and turning frequently, for 15 minutes or until cooked through.

4 Meanwhile, combine the yogurt and mint sauce to make the sauce and serve with the chicken.

COOK'S TIP

Use the marinade to coat chicken portions, such as drumsticks, if you prefer. Cook over medium hot coals for 30–40 minutes, until the juices run clear when the chicken is pierced with a skewer.

Karahi Chicken

A karahi is an extremely versatile two-handled metal pan, similar to a wok. Food is always cooked over a high heat in a karahi.

NUTRITIONAL INFORMATION

Calories	270	Sugars	. . . . .1g
Protein	. . . . .41g	Fat	. . . . .11g
Carbohydrate	. . . .1g	Saturates	. . . . . .2g

  5 mins   20 mins

SERVES 4

I N G R E D I E N T S

2 tbsp ghee

3 garlic cloves, crushed

1 onion, finely chopped

2 tbsp garam masala

1 tsp coriander seeds, ground

½ tsp dried mint

1 bay leaf

750 g/1 lb 10 oz lean boneless chicken, diced

200 ml/7 fl oz chicken stock

1 tbsp chopped fresh coriander

salt

warm naan bread or chapatis, to serve

1 Heat the ghee in a karahi, wok or a large, heavy-based frying pan. Add the garlic and onion. Stir-fry for about 4 minutes until the onion is golden.

2 Stir in the garam masala, ground coriander, mint and bay leaf.

3 Add the diced chicken and cook over a high heat, stirring occasionally, for about 5 minutes. Add the stock, lower the heat and simmer for 10 minutes until the sauce has thickened and the chicken juices run clear when the meat is tested with a sharp knife.

4 Stir in the chopped fresh coriander and season with salt to taste, mix well and serve immediately with warm naan bread or chapatis.

COOK'S TIP
Always heat a karahi or wok before you add the oil to help maintain the high temperature.

Spicy Sesame Chicken

This is a quick and easy recipe for the grill or barbecue, perfect for lunch or to eat outdoors on a picnic.

NUTRITIONAL INFORMATION

Calories	110	Sugars	3g
Protein	15g	Fat	4g
Carbohydrate	3g	Saturates	1g

5 mins   15 mins

SERVES 4

INGREDIENTS

chicken quarters

150 ml/5 fl oz low-fat natural yogurt

finely grated rind and juice of 1 small lemon

2 tsp medium-hot curry paste

tbsp sesame seeds

TO SERVE

salad

naan bread

lemon wedges

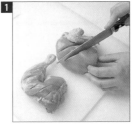

1 Remove the skin from the chicken and slash the flesh at intervals with a sharp knife.

2 Combine the yogurt, lemon rind, lemon juice and curry paste in a bowl.

3 Spread the mixture over the chicken and arrange on a foil-lined grill pan or baking sheet.

4 Place under a preheated and cook, turning once, for 12–15 minutes until golden brown and cooked. (Test by piercing the thickest part with a skewer; the juices should run clear.) Just before the end of the cooking time, sprinkle the chicken with the sesame seeds.

5 Serve with a salad, naan bread and lemon wedges.

VARIATION

Poppy seeds, fennel seeds or cumin seeds, or a mixture of all three, can also be used to sprinkle over the chicken.

Springtime Chicken Cobbler

Fresh spring vegetables are the basis of this colourful casserole, which is topped with hearty wholemeal dumplings.

NUTRITIONAL INFORMATION

Calories	560	Sugars	........10g
Protein	........39g	Fat	..........18g
Carbohydrate	...64g	Saturates	......4g

15 mins   1½ hours

SERVES 4

I N G R E D I E N T S

1 tbsp vegetable oil

8 skinless chicken drumsticks

1 small onion, sliced

350 g/12 oz baby carrots

2 baby turnips

125 g/4½ oz broad beans or peas

1 tsp cornflour

300ml/½ pint chicken stock

2 bay leaves

salt and pepper

C O B B L E R   T O P P I N G

250 g/9 oz plain wholemeal flour

2 tsp baking powder

2 tbsp soft sunflower margarine

2 tsp dry wholegrain mustard

55 g/2 oz low-fat mature Cheddar cheese, grated

skimmed milk, to mix, plus extra for brushing

sesame seeds, for sprinkling

1 Heat the oil in a large, heavy based pan and fry the chicken, turning occasionally, until golden brown. Drain well and place in a casserole. Add the onion to the pan and cook, stirring occasionally, for 2–3 minutes until softened.

2 Cut the carrots and turnips into equal-size pieces. Add to the casserole with the onions and beans or peas.

3 Blend the cornflour with a little of the stock, then stir in the rest and heat gently, stirring until boiling. Pour into the casserole and add the bay leaves. Season to taste with salt and pepper.

4 Cover tightly and bake in a preheated oven, 200°C/400°F/Gas Mark 6, for 50–60 minutes or until the chicken juices run clear when pierced with a skewer.

5 For the topping, sift the flour and baking powder. Mix in the margarine with a fork. Stir in the mustard, cheese and enough milk to mix to a fairly soft dough.

6 Roll out and cut 16 rounds with a 4 cm/1½ inch cutter. Uncover the casserole, arrange the scone rounds on top of the chicken, then brush with milk and sprinkle with sesame seeds. Return to the oven and bake for 20 minutes or until the topping is golden and firm.

Skewered Chicken Spirals

These unusual chicken kebabs have a wonderful Italian flavour, and the bacon helps keep them moist during cooking.

NUTRITIONAL INFORMATION

Calories 231   Sugars 1g
Protein . . . . .29g   Fat 13g
Carbohydrate . . . .1g   Saturates 5g

15 mins   10 mins

SERVES 4

INGREDIENTS

4 skinless, boneless chicken breasts

1 garlic clove, crushed

2 tbsp tomato purée

4 slices smoked back bacon

large handful of fresh basil leaves

vegetable oil for brushing

salt and pepper

green salad, to serve

1 Spread out a piece of chicken between two sheets of clingfilm and beat firmly with a rolling pin or meat mallet to flatten the chicken to an even thickness. Repeat with the remaining chicken breasts.

2 Combine the garlic and tomato purée and spread the mixture over the chicken. Lay a bacon slice over each, then sprinkle with the basil. Season with salt and pepper to taste.

3 Roll up each piece of chicken firmly, then cut into thick slices. Thread the slices on to 4 skewers, making sure the skewer holds the chicken in a spiral shape.

4 Brush lightly with oil and cook on a hot barbecue or under a preheated grill for about 10 minutes, turning once. Serve hot with a green salad.

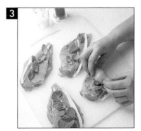

Chicken Tikka Kebabs

Chicken tikka is a low-fat Indian dish. Recipes vary, but you can try your own combination of spices to suit your personal taste.

NUTRITIONAL INFORMATION

Calories	191	Sugars	. . . . .8g
Protein	. . . . .30g	Fat	. . . . .4g
Carbohydrate	. . . .8g	Saturates	. . . . . .2g

2¼ hrs   15 mins

SERVES 4

I N G R E D I E N T S

4x 125 g/4½ oz boneless, skinless chicken breast portions

1 garlic clove, crushed

1 tsp grated fresh root ginger

1 fresh green chilli, deseeded and finely chopped

6 tbsp low-fat natural yogurt

1 tbsp tomato purée

1 tsp ground cumin

1 tsp ground coriander

1 tsp ground turmeric

1 large ripe mango

1 tbsp lime juice

salt and pepper

fresh coriander leaves, to garnish

TO SERVE

boiled white rice

lime wedges

mixed salad

warmed naan bread

1 Cut the chicken into 2.5 cm/1 inch cubes and place in a shallow dish.

2 Combine the garlic, ginger, chilli, yogurt, tomato purée, spices and seasoning. Spoon over the chicken, cover and chill for 2 hours.

3 Using a vegetable peeler, peel the skin from the mango. Slice down either side of the stone and cut the mango flesh into cubes. Toss in lime juice, cover and chill until required.

4 Thread the chicken and mango pieces alternately on to 8 skewers. Place the skewers on a grill rack and brush the chicken with the yogurt marinade and the lime juice left from the mango.

5 Place under a preheated moderate grill for 6–7 minutes. Turn over, brush again with the marinade and lime juice and cook for a further 6–7 minutes until the juices run clear when the chicken is pierced with a sharp knife.

6 Serve the kebabs immediately on a bed of rice on a warmed platter garnished with fresh coriander leaves and accompanied by lime wedges, salad and naan bread.

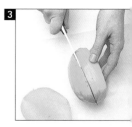

Sweet & Sour Drumsticks

Chicken drumsticks are marinated to impart a tangy, sweet-and-sour flavour and a shiny glaze before being cooked on a barbecue.

NUTRITIONAL INFORMATION

Calories 171	Sugars 9g
Protein 23g	Fat 5g
Carbohydrate ...10g	Saturates 1g

 1¼ hrs 20 mins

SERVES 4

INGREDIENTS

8 chicken drumsticks

4 tbsp red wine vinegar

2 tbsp tomato purée

2 tbsp soy sauce

2 tbsp clear honey

1 tbsp Worcestershire sauce

1 garlic clove

pinch of cayenne pepper

salt and pepper

crisp salad leaves, to serve

1 Skin the chicken drumsticks if desired and slash 2–3 times with a sharp knife. Put the chicken drumsticks into a non-metallic shallow dish, arranging them in a single layer.

2 Combine the vinegar, tomato purée. soy sauce, honey, Worcestershire sauce and garlic in a bowl. Season to taste with cayenne, salt and pepper. Pour the mixture over the chicken, turning to coat. Cover and set aside in the refrigerator to marinate for 1 hour.

3 Cook the drumsticks on a hot barbecue or under a preheated grill for about 20 minutes, brushing with the glaze several times during cooking until the chicken is well browned and the juices run clear when the thickest part is pierced with a skewer.

4 Transfer the drumsticks to a warmed serving dish and serve immediately with crisp salad leaves.

COOK'S TIP

For a tangy flavour, add the juice of 1 lime to the marinade. While the drumsticks are grilling, check regularly to ensure that they are not burning on the outside.

Orange Chicken Stir-fry

Chicken thighs are inexpensive, meaty and readily available. Although not so tender as breast portions, they are perfect for stir-frying.

NUTRITIONAL INFORMATION

Calories 267   Sugars 11g
Protein . . . . .23g   Fat 11g
Carbohydrate . . .15g   Saturates 2g

 10 mins   🕐 15 mins

SERVES 4

I N G R E D I E N T S

3 tbsp sunflower oil

350 g/12 oz skinless boneless chicken
   thighs, cut into thin strips

1 onion, sliced

1 garlic clove, crushed

1 red pepper, deseeded and sliced

85 g/3 oz mangetouts

4 tbsp light soy sauce

4 tbsp sherry

1 tbsp tomato purée

finely grated rind and juice of 1 orange

1 tsp cornflour

2 oranges

100 g/3½ oz beansprouts

cooked rice or noodles, to serve

1 Heat the oil in a large preheated wok. Add the chicken and stir-fry for 2–3 minutes or until sealed on all sides.

2 Add the onion, garlic, red pepper and mangetouts to the wok. Stir-fry for a further 5 minutes or until the vegetables are just tender and the chicken is completely cooked through.

3 Combine the soy sauce, sherry, tomato purée, orange rind and juice and the cornflour. Add to the wok and cook, stirring constantly, until the juices start to thicken.

4 Using a sharp knife, peel and segment the oranges. Add the segments to the wok with the beansprouts and heat through for a further 2 minutes.

5 Transfer the stir-fry to warmed serving plates and serve immediately with cooked rice or noodles.

COOK'S TIP

Beansprouts are sprouting mung beans and are a regular ingredient in Chinese cooking. They require very little cooking and may even be eaten raw, if wished.

Green Salsa Chicken Breasts

Chicken breast fillets bathed in a fragrant sauce make a delicate dish, perfect for dinner parties. Serve with rice to complete the meal.

NUTRITIONAL INFORMATION

Calories 349	Sugars 7g
Protein 34g	Fat 20g
Carbohydrate . . .10g	Saturates 12g

🍳 10 mins   🕐 20–25 mins

SERVES 4

INGREDIENTS

4 skinless chicken breast fillets

plain flour, for dusting

2–3 tbsp butter or a mixture butter and vegetable oil

450 g/1 lb mild green salsa or puréed tomatillos

225 ml/8 fl oz chicken stock

1–2 garlic cloves, finely chopped

3–5 tbsp chopped fresh coriander

½ fresh green chilli, deseeded and chopped

½ tsp ground cumin

salt and pepper

TO SERVE

225 ml/8 fl oz soured cream

several leaves cos lettuce, shredded

3–5 spring onions, thinly sliced

coarsely chopped fresh coriander

1 Sprinkle the chicken with salt and pepper,, then dredge in flour. Shake off the excess.

2 Melt the butter or heat the butter and oil mixture in a large, heavy-based frying pan. Add the chicken and cook over a medium-high heat, turning once, until the fillets are golden all over, but not quite cooked through – they will continue to cook slightly in the sauce. Remove from pan and set aside.

3 Place the salsa, stock, garlic, coriander, chilli and cumin in a pan and bring to the boil. Reduce the heat to a low simmer. Add the chicken breasts to the sauce, spooning the sauce over the chicken. Continue to cook until the chicken is cooked through and tender.

4 Remove the chicken from the pan and season with salt and pepper to taste. Serve immediately with the soured cream, shredded lettuce, sliced spring onions and chopped fresh coriander leaves.

Citrus-marinated Chicken

This is a great dish for a summer meal. The marinade gives the chicken an appetising flavour and helps keeps it succulent and moist.

NUTRITIONAL INFORMATION

Calories 315	Sugars 2g
Protein 42g	Fat 41g
Carbohydrate 4g	Saturates 6g

1¼ hrs   20–25 mins

SERVES 4

I N G R E D I E N T S

1 chicken, cut into 4 pieces

1 tbsp mild chilli powder

1 tbsp paprika

2 tsp ground cumin

juice and rind of 1 orange

juice of 3 limes

pinch of sugar

8–10 garlic cloves, finely chopped

1 bunch of fresh coriander,
    coarsely chopped

2–3 tbsp extra virgin olive oil

50 ml/2 fl oz beer, tequila, or pineapple
    juice (optional)

salt and pepper

fresh coriander sprigs, to garnish

T O   S E R V E

lime wedges

tomato, pepper and spring onion salad

1 Place the chicken pieces in a large non-metallic dish. Combine the chilli powder, paprika, cumin, orange juice and rind, lime juice, sugar, garlic, chopped coriander and olive oil in a bowl. Stir in the beer, tequila or pineapple juice, if using, and season to taste with salt and pepper.

2 Pour the marinade over the chicken, turn to coat well, then cover and set aside to marinate for at least an hour at room temperature. If possible, marinate in the refrigerator for 24 hours.

3 Remove the chicken from the marinade and pat dry with kitchen paper. Reserve the marinade.

4 Put the chicken on a grill pan and cook under a preheated grill for 20–25 minutes, turning once, until the chicken is cooked through. Alternatively, cook in a ridged griddled pan. Brush with the marinade occasionally. To test whether it is cooked, pierce a thick part with a skewer – the juices should run clear.

5 Transfer the chicken to warmed serving plates, garnish with coriander and serve immediately with lime wedges and a refreshing side salad.

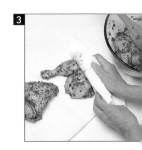

Poussins in Green Marinade

Flavoured with a green herb marinade, these elegant poussins are packed with lively Mexican flavours.

NUTRITIONAL INFORMATION

Calories	.614	Sugars	.6g
Protein	.44g	Fat	.49g
Carbohydrate	.8g	Saturates	.19g

3¼ hrs   15–20 mins

SERVES 4

INGREDIENTS

10 garlic cloves, chopped

juice of 1 lime

1 bunch of fresh coriander, finely chopped

½ fresh green chilli, deseeded and chopped

1 tsp ground cumin

4 poussins

350 g/12 oz crème fraîche

1 red pepper, roasted, peeled, deseeded and diced

¾–1 tsp marinade from chipotle canned in adobo or chipotle salsa

3–5 spring onions, thinly sliced

handful of toasted pumpkin seeds

salt and pepper

1 Combine 9 garlic cloves with the lime juice, about three-quarters of the fresh coriander, the green chilli and half the cumin in a bowl. Press the mixture on to the poussins and set to marinate for at least 3 hours in the refrigerator.

2 Place the poussins in a roasting tin and cook in a preheated oven, 200°C/ 400°F/ Gas Mark 5, for 15 minutes. Pierce the thigh of 1 poussin with a knife and if the juices run clear, it is cooked. If

necessary, return to the oven and continue to roast until cooked through.

3 Meanwhile, combine the crème fraîche with the red pepper, chipotle marinade or salsa and remaining garlic and cumin. Season with salt and pepper.

4 Serve each poussin with a spoonful of the pepper sauce and a sprinkling of the remaining coriander, the spring onions and pumpkin seeds. Serve immediately.

VARIATION

For barbecued lamb, skewer lamb chunks, such as shoulder or leg, on to metal or soaked bamboo skewers. Marinate in the green herbed marinade as in Step 1, then cook over the hot coals of a barbecue until the lamb is cooked to your liking.

Chicken with Purslane

Purslane has become fashionable, owing to its unique flavour and healthy dose of omega-3 fatty acids. It has always been popular in Mexico

NUTRITIONAL INFORMATION

Calories 414	Sugars 7g
Protein 43g	Fat 22g
Carbohydrate 11g	Saturates 5g

 1¾ hrs   50–60 mins

SERVES 4

INGREDIENTS

juice of 1 lime

6 garlic cloves, finely chopped

¼ tsp dried oregano

¼ tsp dried marjoram

¼ tsp dried thyme

½ tsp ground cumin

1 chicken, cut into 4 pieces

about 10 large dried mild chillies, such as pasilla, toasted

450 ml/16 fl oz boiling water

450 ml/16 fl oz chicken stock

3 tbsp extra virgin olive oil

700 g/1 lb 9 oz tomatoes, charred under the grill, peeled and deseeded

handful of corn tortilla chips, crushed

several large handfuls of fresh purslane, cut into bite-size lengths

½ lime

salt and pepper

lime wedges, to serve

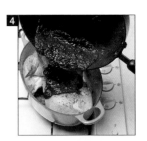

1 Combine the lime juice, half the garlic, the oregano, marjoram, thyme, cumin and salt to taste. Rub the mixture over the chicken and set aside to marinate for at least an hour at room temperature or overnight in the refrigerator.

2 Place the chillies in a pan and pour the boiling water over them. Cover and set aside for 30 minutes until softened. Remove the stems and seeds. Purée the chillies in a food processor or blender, adding just enough of the stock to make a smooth paste. Add the rest of the stock and mix well.

3 Heat 1 tablespoon of oil in a heavy-based frying pan. Add the chilli purée with the tomatoes and remaining garlic. Cook over a medium heat, stirring, until it has thickened and reduced by about half.

4 Remove the chicken from the marinade, reserving any marinade juices. Brown the chicken in the remaining oil, then place in flameproof casserole. Add any reserved juices and the reduced chilli sauce. Cover and simmer over a low heat for about 30 minutes until the chicken is tender and cooked through.

5 Stir the crushed tortillas into the sauce and cook for a few minutes, then add the purslane. Season with salt, pepper and a squeeze of lime. Heat through and serve with lime wedges.

Spanish Chicken with Garlic

The slow cooking takes all the harsh flavouring out of the garlic cloves and makes them meltingly tender in this simple dish.

NUTRITIONAL INFORMATION

Calories	496	Sugars	.........1g
Protein	........41g	Fat	..........22g
Carbohydrate	...15g	Saturates	.......5g

 15 mins   50 mins

SERVES 4

INGREDIENTS

2–3 tbsp plain flour

cayenne pepper

4 chicken quarters, patted dry

about 4 tbsp olive oil

20 large garlic cloves, each halved and green core removed

1 large bay leaf

450 ml/16 fl oz chicken stock

4 tbsp dry white wine

chopped fresh parsley, to garnish

salt and pepper

1 Put about 2 tablespoons of the flour in a bag and season to taste with cayenne, salt and pepper. Add a chicken piece and shake until it is lightly coated with the flour, shaking off the excess. Repeat with the remaining pieces, adding more flour and seasoning, if necessary.

2 Heat 3 tablespoons of the olive oil in a large frying pan. Add the garlic cloves and fry for about 2 minutes, stirring, to flavour the oil. Remove with a draining spoon and set aside.

3 Add the chicken pieces to the pan, skin side down, and fry for 5 minutes or until the skin is golden brown. Turn and

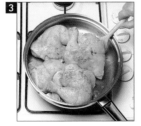

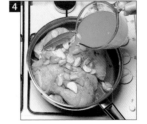

fry for a further 5 minutes, adding an extra 1–2 tablespoons of oil if necessary.

4 Return the garlic to the pan. Add the bay leaf, chicken stock and wine and bring to the boil. Lower the heat, cover and simmer for 25 minutes or until the chicken is tender and the garlic cloves are very soft.

5 Transfer the chicken to a serving platter and keep warm. Bring the cooking liquid to the boil and boil until reduced to about 250 ml/9 fl oz. Adjust the seasoning if necessary.

6 Spoon the sauce over the chicken pieces and sprinkle the garlic cloves around it. Garnish with parsley and serve.

Moroccan Chicken Couscous

'Couscous' is the name of both the small grains that are a staple of Moroccan kitchens and the fragrant stew traditionally served with them.

NUTRITIONAL INFORMATION

Calories	610	Sugars	24g
Protein	38g	Fat	13g
Carbohydrate	90g	Saturates	3g

 25 mins   1¼ hrs

SERVES 4–6

INGREDIENTS

3–4 tbsp olive oil

8 chicken pieces with bones, such as quarters, breasts and legs

2 large onions, chopped

2 large garlic cloves, crushed

2.5 cm/1 inch piece of fresh root ginger, finely chopped

150 g/5½ oz dried chickpeas, soaked overnight and drained

4 large carrots, cut into thick chunks

pinch of saffron threads, dissolved in 2 tbsp boiling water

finely grated rind of 2 lemons

2 red peppers, deseeded and sliced

2 large courgettes, cut into chunks

2 tomatoes, cored, deseeded and chopped

100 g/3½ oz dried apricots, chopped

½ tsp ground cumin

½ tsp ground coriander

½ tsp cayenne pepper

600 ml/1 pint water

1 tbsp butter

600 g/1 lb 5 oz instant couscous

salt and pepper

harissa, to serve (optional)

1 Heat 3 tablespoons of the oil in a large flameproof casserole. Pat the chicken pieces dry with kitchen paper, add to the oil, skin side down, and cook for 5 minutes until crisp and brown. Remove from the pan and set aside.

2 Add the onions to the pan, adding a little extra oil if necessary. Cook the onions for 5 minutes, then add the garlic and ginger and cook, stirring occasionally, for a further 2 minutes.

3 Return the chicken pieces to the casserole. Add the chickpeas, carrots, saffron and lemon rind. Pour in enough water to cover by 2.5 cm/1 inch and bring to the boil.

4 Lower the heat, cover and simmer for 45 minutes or until the chickpeas are tender. Add the peppers, courgettes, tomatoes, dried apricots, cumin, coriander and cayenne pepper and season with salt and pepper to taste. Re-cover and simmer for a further 15 minutes.

5 Meanwhile, bring the water to the boil. Stir in ½ teaspoon salt and the butter. Sprinkle in the couscous. Cover the pan tightly, remove from the heat and set aside for 10 minutes or until the grains are tender.

6 Fluff the couscous with a fork. Taste and adjust the seasoning of the stew if necessary. Spoon the couscous into individual bowls and serve the stew and a bowl of harissa, if using, separately.

Chicken Basquaise

Sweet peppers are typical of dishes from the Basque region in France. In this recipe, Bayonne ham, from the Pyrenees, adds a delicious flavour.

NUTRITIONAL INFORMATION

Calories 559	Sugars 8g
Protein 50g	Fat 21g
Carbohydrate ...44g	Saturates 6g

15 mins   1½ hrs

SERVES 4–5

INGREDIENTS

1.35 kg/3 lb chicken, cut into 8 pieces

flour, for dusting

3 tbsp olive oil

1 Spanish onion, thickly sliced

2 red or yellow peppers, deseeded and cut lengthways into thick strips

2 garlic cloves

150 g/5 oz spicy chorizo sausage, peeled and cut into 1 cm/½ inch pieces

1 tbsp tomato purée

200 g/7 oz long grain white rice

450 ml/16 fl oz chicken stock

1 tsp crushed dried chillies

½ tsp dried thyme

120 g/4 oz Bayonne or other air-dried ham, diced

12 dry-cured black olives

2 tbsp chopped fresh flat-leaf parsley

salt and pepper

1 Pat the chicken pieces dry with kitchen paper. Put 2 tablespoons flour in a plastic bag, season with salt and pepper and add the chicken pieces. Seal the bag and shake to coat the chicken.

2 Heat 2 tablespoons of the oil in a large flameproof casserole over a

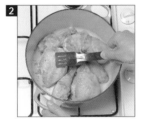

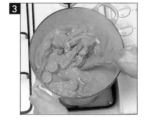

medium-high heat. Add the chicken and cook, turning frequently, for about 15 minutes until well browned all over. Transfer to a plate.

3 Heat the remaining oil in the casserole and add the onion and red peppers. Reduce the heat to medium and stir-fry until beginning to colour and soften. Add the garlic, chorizo and tomato purée and cook, stirring constantly, for about 3 minutes. Add the rice and cook, stirring to coat, for about 2 minutes until the rice is translucent.

4 Add the stock, crushed chillies and thyme, season to taste with salt and pepper and stir well. Bring to the boil. Return the chicken to the casserole, pressing it gently into the rice. Cover and cook over a very low heat for about 45 minutes until the chicken is cooked through and the rice is tender.

5 Gently stir the ham, black olives and half the parsley into the rice mixture. Re-cover and heat through for a further 5 minutes. Sprinkle with the remaining parsley and serve immediately.

Chicken with Mustard

The combination of chicken and a mustard and orange sauce is quite irresistible.

NUTRITIONAL INFORMATION

Calories	267	Sugars	........12g
Protein	........34g	Fat	...........8g
Carbohydrate	...16g	Saturates	.......2g

10 mins   20 mins

SERVES 4

I N G R E D I E N T S

1 tbsp sunflower or corn oil

4 skinless, boneless chicken breasts, about 140 g/5 oz each, all visible fat removed

salt and pepper

2 large oranges, peeled and cut into segments, juice reserved (see Cook's Tip)

2 tsp cornflour

150 ml/5 fl oz low-fat natural yogurt

1 tsp wholegrain mustard

fresh parsley sprigs, to garnish

1 Heat the oil in a large, heavy-based frying pan. Add the chicken breasts and cook over a medium–high heat for 5 minutes on each side, or until tender and the juices run clear when the meat is pierced with a skewer or the point of a knife. Season with a little salt and pepper, remove the chicken from the frying pan, cover with foil and keep warm.

2 Pour the orange juice into a small bowl and stir in the cornflour to make a smooth paste. Stir in the yogurt and mustard, then pour into the frying pan and bring to the boil over a low heat, stirring constantly.

3 Add the orange segments to the frying pan and season to taste with salt and pepper. Stir in any juices that have collected from the chicken. Spoon the sauce onto 4 large, warmed serving plates and top with the chicken. Garnish with parsley sprigs and serve immediately.

COOK'S TIP

Use a sharp knife to peel the oranges and make sure that you remove all the pith. Hold the oranges over a bowl to catch the juices and cut down between the membranes to separate into segments.

Ginger Chicken & Corn

Chicken wings and corn in a sticky ginger marinade are designed to be eaten with the fingers – there's no other way!

NUTRITIONAL INFORMATION

Calories	123	Sugars	.........3g
Protein	........14g	Fat	...........6g
Carbohydrate	....3g	Saturates	......1g

10 mins   20 mins

SERVES 4

INGREDIENTS

corn cobs

2 chicken wings

.5 cm/1 inch piece of fresh root ginger

tbsp lemon juice

tsp sunflower oil

tbsp golden caster sugar

baked potatoes or salad, to serve

1 Remove the husks and silks from the corn. Using a sharp knife, cut each cob into 6 slices.

2 Place the corn in a large bowl with the chicken wings.

3 Peel and grate the root ginger or chop very finely. Place in a bowl and add the lemon juice, sunflower oil and golden caster sugar. Mix together until thoroughly combined.

4 Toss the corn and chicken in the ginger mixture to coat evenly.

5 Thread the corn and chicken wings alternately on to metal or pre-soaked wooden skewers to make turning easier.

6 Cook under a preheated moderately hot grill or on a barbecue for about

15–20 minutes, basting with the gingery glaze and turning frequently until the corn is golden brown and tender and the chicken is cooked. Serve immediately with baked potatoes or salad.

COOK'S TIP
Cut off the wing tips before grilling because they burn very easily. Alternatively, you can cover them with small pieces of foil.

Thai-style Chicken Skewers

The chicken is marinated in an aromatic sauce before being cooked on the barbecue. Use bay leaves if kaffir lime leaves are unavailable.

NUTRITIONAL INFORMATION

Calories . . . . .218 Sugars 4g
Protein . . . . .28g Fat 10g
Carbohydrate . . . .5g Saturates 2g

2¼ hrs   20 mins

SERVES 4

INGREDIENTS

4 skinless boneless chicken breasts

1 onion, cut into wedges

1 large red pepper, deseeded

1 large yellow pepper deseeded

12 kaffir lime leaves

2 tbsp sunflower oil

2 tbsp lime juice

tomato halves, to serve

MARINADE

1 tbsp Thai red curry paste

150 ml/5 fl oz canned coconut milk

1 To make the marinade, place the red curry paste in a small pan over medium heat and cook for 1 minute. Add half of the coconut milk to the pan and bring the mixture to the boil. Boil for 2–3 minutes until the liquid has reduced by about two-thirds.

2 Remove the pan from the heat and stir in the remaining coconut milk. Set aside to cool.

3 Cut the chicken into 2.5 cm/1 inch pieces. Stir the chicken into the cold marinade, cover and chill in the refrigerator for at least 2 hours.

4 Cut the onion into wedges and cut the peppers into 2.5 cm/1 inch pieces.

5 Remove the chicken pieces from the marinade and thread them on to skewers, alternating the chicken with the vegetables and lime leaves.

6 Combine the oil and lime juice in a small bowl and brush the mixture over the kebabs. Barbecue the skewers over hot coals, turning and basting frequently. for 10–15 minutes until the chicken is cooked through. Barbecue the tomato halves for the last few minutes of the cooking time and serve with the chicken skewers.

COOK'S TIP

Cooking the marinade first intensifies the flavour. It is important to allow the marinade to cool before adding the chicken because bacteria may breed in the warm temperature.

Whisky Roast Chicken

An unusual change from a plain roast, with a distinctly warming Scottish flavour and a delicious oatmeal stuffing.

NUTRITIONAL INFORMATION

Calories 254	Sugars 6g	
Protein 27g	Fat 8g	
Carbohydrate 11g	Saturates 2g	

🍳 5 mins   🕐 1½ hours

SERVES 6

I N G R E D I E N T S

1 chicken, weighing 2 kg/4 lb 8 oz

vegetable oil, for brushing

1 tbsp heather honey

2 tbsp Scotch whisky

2 tbsp plain flour

300 ml/10 fl oz chicken stock

vegetables and sauté potatoes, to serve

S T U F F I N G

1 tbsp sunflower oil

1 medium onion, finely chopped

1 celery stick, thinly sliced

1 tsp dried thyme

4 tbsp rolled oats

4 tbsp chicken stock

salt and pepper

1 To make the stuffing, heat the oil in a pan and cook the onion and celery over a moderate heat, stirring occasionally, until softened and lightly browned.

2 Remove from the heat and stir in the thyme, oats and stock and season with salt and pepper to taste.

3 Stuff the neck end of the chicken with the mixture and tuck the neck flap under. Place in a roasting tin, brush lightly with oil, and roast in a preheated oven, 190°C/375°F/ Gas Mark 5, for about 1 hour.

4 Mix the honey with 1 tablespoon whisky and brush the mixture over the chicken. Return to the oven for a further 20 minutes or until the chicken is golden brown and the juices run clear when pierced through the thickest part with a skewer.

5 Lift the chicken on to a serving plate. Skim the fat from the juices, then stir in the flour. Stir over a moderate heat until the mixture bubbles, then gradually add the stock and remaining whisky to the pan.

6 Bring to the boil, stirring constantly, then simmer for 1 minute and serve the chicken with the sauce, vegetables and sauté potatoes.

Chicken & Lemon Skewers

A tangy lemon yogurt is served with these tasty lemon- and coriander-flavoured chicken skewers.

NUTRITIONAL INFORMATION

Calories 181	Sugars 6g	
Protein 30g	Fat 4g	
Carbohydrate 6g	Saturates 2g	

2¼ hours   15 mins

SERVES 4

INGREDIENTS

4 skinless boneless chicken breasts

1 tsp ground coriander

2 tsp lemon juice

300 m/10 fl oz low-fat natural yogurt

1 lemon

2 tbsp chopped, fresh coriander

vegetable oil, for brushing

salt and pepper

fresh coriander sprigs, to garnish

TO SERVE

lemon wedges

salad leaves

1 Cut the chicken into 2.5 cm/1 inch pieces and place them in a shallow, non-metallic dish.

2 Add the ground coriander, lemon juice and 4 tablespoons of the yogurt to the chicken and season to taste with salt and pepper. Mix together until thoroughly combined. Cover with clingfilm and set aside to marinate in the refrigerator for at least 2 hours, preferably overnight.

3 To make the lemon yogurt, put the remaining yogurt in a bowl. Peel and finely chop the lemon, discarding any pips and all traces of pith. Stir the lemon into the yogurt with the chopped fresh coriander. Cover with clingfilm and chill in the refrigerator until required.

4 Thread the chicken pieces on to metal or soaked bamboo skewers. Brush the barbecue rack with oil and cook the chicken over hot coals for about 15 minutes, brushing occasionally with the oil and turning frequently.

5 Transfer the chicken kebabs to warm serving plates and garnish with sprigs of fresh coriander. Serve with the lemon yogurt, lemon wedges and salad leaves.

Marmalade Chicken

Marmalade lovers will enjoy this festive recipe. You can use any favourite marmalade, such as lemon or grapefruit.

NUTRITIONAL INFORMATION

Calories 304   Sugars 20g
Protein ....29g   Fat 7g
Carbohydrate ...30g   Saturates 2g

🍥 🍥 🍥

🥄 10 mins   🕐 2 hours

SERVES 6

INGREDIENTS

1 chicken, weighing about 2.25 kg/5 lb

bay leaves

vegetable oil, for brushing

2 tbsp marmalade

STUFFING

1 tbsp sunflower oil

1 celery stick, finely chopped

1 small onion, finely chopped

125 g/4½ oz fresh wholemeal breadcrumbs

4 tbsp marmalade

2 tbsp chopped fresh parsley

1 egg, beaten

salt and pepper

SAUCE

2 tsp cornflour

2 tbsp orange juice

3 tbsp marmalade

150 ml/5 fl oz chicken stock

1 medium orange

2 tbsp brandy

1 Lift the neck flap of the chicken and remove the wishbone. Place a sprig of bay leaves inside the body cavity.

2 To make the stuffing, heat the oil in a pan and cook the celery and onion

until softened. Add the other ingredients. Season with salt and pepper to taste. Stuff the neck cavity of the chicken.

3 Place the chicken in a roasting tin and brush lightly with oil. Roast in a preheated oven, 190°C/375°F/Gas Mark 5, for about 1 hour 50 minutes or until the juices run clear when the chicken is pierced with a knife. Glaze the chicken with the marmalade.

4 For the sauce, blend the cornflour in a pan with the orange juice, then add the marmalade and stock. Heat gently, stirring constantly, until thickened. Remove from the heat.

5 Cut the segments from the orange, discarding all white pith and membrane, add to the sauce with the brandy and bring to the boil. Serve with the roast chicken.

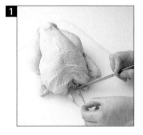

Garlic Chicken Cushions

Stuffed with creamy ricotta, spinach and garlic, then gently cooked in a rich tomato sauce, this chicken dish can be made ahead of time.

NUTRITIONAL INFORMATION

Calories	316	Sugars	.........6g
Protein	........40g	Fat	..........13g
Carbohydrate	....6g	Saturates	......5g

🧀 🧀 🧀

🧊 10 mins   🕐 40 mins

SERVES 4

INGREDIENTS

4 part-boned chicken breasts

115 g/4 oz frozen spinach, thawed

150 g/5½ oz low-fat ricotta cheese

2 garlic cloves, crushed

1 tbsp olive oil

1 onion, chopped

1 red pepper, deseeded and sliced

425 g/15 oz canned chopped tomatoes

6 tbsp wine or chicken stock

10 stuffed olives, sliced

salt and pepper

fresh flat leaf parsley sprigs, to garnish

pasta, to serve

1 Make a slit between the skin and meat on 1 side of each chicken breast. Lift the skin to form a pocket, being careful to leave the skin attached to the other side.

2 Put the spinach into a sieve and press out the water with a spoon. Mix with the ricotta, half the garlic and seasoning.

3 Carefully spoon the spinach mixture under the skin of each chicken breast, then secure the edge of the skin with cocktail sticks.

4 Heat the oil in a frying pan, add the onion and cook for a minute, stirring. Add the remaining garlic and the red pepper and cook for 2 minutes. Stir in the tomatoes, wine or stock, olives and seasoning. Set the sauce aside and chill the chicken if preparing in advance.

5 Bring the sauce to the boil, pour into an ovenproof dish and arrange the chicken breasts on top in a single layer.

6 Cook, uncovered in a preheated oven, 200°C/400°F/Gas Mark 6, for about 35 minutes until the chicken is golden and cooked through. Test by making a slit in 1 of the chicken breasts with a skewer to make sure the juices run clear.

7 Spoon a little of the sauce over the chicken breasts, then transfer to serving plates and garnish with parsley. Serve with pasta.

Rustic Chicken & Orange Pot

Low in fat and high in fibre, this colourful casserole makes a healthy, hearty and utterly delicious one-pot meal.

NUTRITIONAL INFORMATION

Calories	345	Sugars	.........6g
Protein	........29g	Fat	..........10g
Carbohydrate	...39g	Saturates	......2g

5 mins   1 hour

SERVES 4

I N G R E D I E N T S

8 skinless chicken drumsticks

2 tbsp wholemeal flour

1 tbsp olive oil

2 medium red onions

1 garlic clove, crushed

1 tsp fennel seeds

1 bay leaf

finely grated rind and juice of
  1 small orange

400 g/14 oz can chopped tomatoes

400 g/14 oz can cannellini or flageolet
  beans, drained

salt and black pepper

TOPPING

3 thick slices wholemeal bread,
  crusts removed

2 tsp olive oil

1 Toss the chicken in the flour to coat evenly. Heat the oil in a non-stick pan. Add the chicken and cook over a fairly high heat, turning frequently, until golden brown. Transfer to a large casserole.

2 Slice the red onions into thin wedges. Add to the pan and cook over a medium heat for a few minutes until lightly browned. Stir in the garlic, then add the onions and garlic to the casserole.

3 Add the fennel seeds, bay leaf, orange rind and juice, tomatoes and cannellini or flageolet beans and season to taste with salt and pepper.

4 Cover tightly and cook in a preheated oven, 190°C/375°F/Gas Mark 5, for 30–35 minutes until the chicken juices are clear and not pink when pierced through the thickest part with a skewer.

5 To make the topping, cut the bread into small dice and toss in the oil. Remove the lid from the casserole and sprinkle the bread cubes on top of the chicken. Bake for a further 15–20 minutes until the bread is golden and crisp.Serve immediately straight from the casserole.

Chicken & Beans

Pulses are a valuable source of nourishment. You could use any variety of pulses in this recipe, but adjust the cooking times accordingly.

NUTRITIONAL INFORMATION

Calories 291	Sugars 3g
Protein 33g	Fat 10g
Carbohydrate . . .18g	Saturates 2g

  12 hrs   1 hr

SERVES 4

I N G R E D I E N T S

225 g/8 oz dried black-eye beans, soaked overnight and drained

1 tsp salt

2 onions, chopped

2 garlic cloves, crushed

1 tsp ground turmeric

1 tsp ground cumin

1.25 kg/2 lb 12 oz chicken, jointed into 8 pieces

1 green pepper, deseeded and chopped

2 tbsp vegetable oil

2.5 cm/1 inch piece of fresh root ginger, grated

2 tsp coriander seeds

½ tsp fennel seeds

2 tsp garam masala

1 tbsp chopped fresh coriander, to garnish

COOK'S TIP

For convenience, you can use 425 g/15 oz canned black-eye beans instead of dried beans. Add them at step 2.

1 Put the dried black-eye beans into a Balti pan or wok with the salt, onions, garlic, turmeric and cumin. Cover the beans with water, bring to the boil and cook for 15 minutes.

2 Add the chicken and green pepper to the pan and bring to the boil. Lower the heat and simmer gently for 30 minutes until the beans are tender and the chicken juices run clear when the thickest parts of the pieces are pierce with a sharp knife or skewer.

3 Heat the oil in a Balti pan or wok an fry the ginger, coriander seeds an fennel seeds for 30 seconds.

4 Stir the spices into the chicken an add the garam masala. Simmer for further 5 minutes, garnish with choppe coriander and serve immediately.

Chicken & Spinach Lasagne

A delicious pasta bake with all the colours of the Italian flag – red tomatoes, green spinach and pasta, and white chicken and sauce.

NUTRITIONAL INFORMATION

Calories	358	Sugars	........12g
Protein	........42g	Fat	...........9g
Carbohydrate	...22g	Saturates	......4g

25 mins   50 mins

SERVES 4

INGREDIENTS

350 g/12 oz frozen chopped spinach, thawed and drained

½ tsp ground nutmeg

450 g/1 lb lean, cooked chicken, diced

4 sheets no pre-cook lasagne verde

1½ tbsp cornflour

425 ml/15 fl oz skimmed milk

4 tbsp freshly grated Parmesan cheese

salt and pepper

green salad, to serve

TOMATO SAUCE

400 g/14 oz can chopped tomatoes

1 medium onion, finely chopped

1 garlic clove, crushed

150 ml/5 fl oz white wine

3 tbsp tomato purée

1 tsp dried oregano

1 To make the tomato sauce, place the tomatoes in a pan and stir in the onion, garlic, wine, tomato purée and oregano. Bring to the boil and simmer for 20 minutes until thick. Season to taste with salt and pepper.

2 Drain the spinach again and pat dry on kitchen paper. Arrange the spinach in the base of an ovenproof dish. Sprinkle with nutmeg and season to taste.

3 Arrange the diced chicken over the spinach and spoon the tomato sauce over it. Arrange the sheets of lasagne over the tomato sauce.

4 Blend the cornflour with a little of the milk to make a paste. Pour the remaining milk into a pan and stir in the cornflour paste. Heat gently for 2–3 minutes, stirring constantly, until the sauce thickens. Season to taste with salt and pepper.

5 Spoon the sauce over the lasagne to cover it completely and transfer the dish to a baking sheet. Sprinkle the grated cheese over the sauce and bake in a preheated oven, 200°C/400°F/Gas Mark 6, for 25 minutes until golden-brown and bubbling. Serve immediately with a fresh green salad.

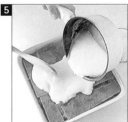

Chicken & Chilli Bean Pot

This aromatic chicken dish has a spicy Mexican kick. Chicken thighs have a wonderful flavour when cooked in this way.

NUTRITIONAL INFORMATION

Calories	.... .333	Sugars	........10g
Protein	........25g	Fat	..........13g
Carbohydrate	...32g	Saturates	......2g

10 mins   40 mins

SERVES 4

INGREDIENTS

2 tbsp plain flour

1 tsp chilli powder

8 chicken thighs or 4 chicken legs

3 tbsp vegetable oil

2 garlic cloves, crushed

1 large onion, chopped

1 green or red pepper, deseeded and chopped

300 ml/10 fl oz chicken stock

350 g/12 oz tomatoes, chopped

400 g/14 oz can red kidney beans, rinsed and drained

2 tbsp tomato purée

salt and pepper

1 Combine the flour and chilli powder in a shallow dish and add salt and pepper to taste. Rinse the chicken, but do not dry. Dip the chicken into the seasoned flour, turning to coat it on all sides.

2 Heat the oil in a large, deep frying pan or flameproof casserole and add the chicken. Cook over a high heat, turning the pieces frequently, for 3–4 minutes until browned all over.

3 Lift the chicken out of the pan or casserole with a draining spoon and drain on kitchen paper.

4 Add the garlic, onion and pepper to the pan and cook over a medium heat, stirring occasionally, for 2–3 minutes until softened.

5 Add the stock, tomatoes, kidney beans and tomato purée, stirring well. Bring to the boil, then return the chicken to the pan. Reduce the heat, cover and simmer for about 30 minutes until the chicken is tender. Taste and adjust the seasoning, if necessary, and serve.

COOK'S TIP
For extra intensity of flavour, use sun-dried tomato paste instead of ordinary tomato purée.

Sweet & Sour Chicken

This sweet-citrus chicken is delicious hot or cold. Sesame-flavoured noodles are the ideal accompaniment for the hot version.

NUTRITIONAL INFORMATION

Calories	248	Sugars	.........8g
Protein	........30g	Fat	...........8g
Carbohydrate	...16g	Saturates	......2g

5 mins   25 mins

SERVES 4

I N G R E D I E N T S

4 boneless chicken breasts, about
  125 g/4½ oz each

2 tbsp clear honey

1 tbsp dark soy sauce

1 tsp finely grated lemon rind

1 tbsp lemon juice

salt and pepper

TO GARNISH

1 tbsp chopped fresh chives

grated lemon rind

TO SERVE

225 g/8 oz rice noodles

2 tsp sesame oil

1 tbsp sesame seeds

1 tsp finely grated lemon rind

1 Skin and trim the chicken breasts to remove any excess fat, then wash and pat them dry with absorbent kitchen paper. Using a sharp knife, score the chicken breasts with a criss-cross pattern on both sides (making sure that you do not cut all the way through the meat).

2 Combine the honey, soy sauce, lemon rind and juice in a small bowl and season with black pepper.

3 Arrange the chicken breasts on the grill rack and brush with half the honey mixture. Cook under a preheated grill for 10 minutes, then turn over and brush with the remaining mixture. Cook for a further 8–10 minutes or until cooked through and tender. The juices should run clear when pierced with a skewer.

4 Meanwhile, prepare the noodles according to the instructions on the packet. Drain well and transfer to a warmed serving bowl. Add the sesame oil, sesame seeds and lemon rind and toss well to mix. Season to taste with salt and pepper and keep warm.

5 Drain the chicken and serve immediately with a small mound of noodles, garnished with chopped fresh chives and grated lemon rind.

Crispy Stuffed Chicken

An attractive main course of chicken breasts filled with mixed peppers and set on a delicious tomato sauce.

NUTRITIONAL INFORMATION

Calories . . . . . . .196 Sugars 4g
Protein . . . . .29g Fat 6g
Carbohydrate . . . .6g Saturates 2g

 20 mins   50 mins

SERVES 4

INGREDIENTS

4 boneless chicken breasts,
  150 g/5½ oz each, skinned

4 sprigs fresh tarragon

½ small orange pepper, deseeded and sliced

½ small green pepper, deseeded and sliced

15 g/1/2 oz wholemeal breadcrumbs

1 tbsp sesame seeds

4 tbsp lemon juice

1 small red pepper, halved and deseeded

200 g/7 oz canned chopped tomatoes

1 small red chilli, deseeded and chopped

¼ tsp celery salt

salt and pepper

fresh tarragon, to garnish

1 Make a slit in each of the chicken breasts with a small, sharp knife to create a pocket. Season inside each pocket with salt and pepper.

2 Place a sprig of tarragon and a few slices of orange pepper and green pepper in each pocket. Place the chicken breasts on a non-stick baking sheet and sprinkle the breadcrumbs and sesame seeds over them.

3 Spoon 1 tablespoon of lemon juice over each chicken breast and bake in a preheated oven, 190°C/375°F/Gas Mark 5, for 35–40 minutes until the chicken is tender and cooked through.

4 Meanwhile, preheat the grill to hot. Arrange the red pepper halves, skin side up, on the rack and cook for 5–6 minutes until the skin begins to char and blister. Set the grilled peppers aside to cool for about 10 minutes, then peel off the skins.

5 Put the red pepper in a blender, add the tomatoes, chilli and celery salt and process for a few seconds. Season to taste. Alternatively, finely chop the red pepper and press through a sieve with the tomatoes and chilli.

6 When the chicken is cooked, heat the sauce, spoon a little on to a warm plate and arrange a chicken breast in the centre. Garnish with tarragon and serve.

Chicken & Ham Lasagne

You can use your favourite mushrooms, such as chanterelles or oyster mushrooms, for this delicately flavoured dish.

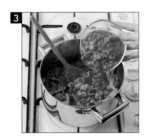

NUTRITIONAL INFORMATION

Calories	708	Sugars	........17g
Protein	........35g	Fat	..........35g
Carbohydrate	...57g	Saturates	......14g

🍲 40 mins   🕐 1¾ hrs

SERVES 4

INGREDIENTS

butter, for greasing

14 sheets pre-cooked lasagne

900 ml/1½ pints Béchamel Sauce
  (see page 6)

85 g/3 oz Parmesan cheese, freshly grated

CHICKEN AND WILD MUSHROOM SAUCE

2 tbsp olive oil

2 garlic cloves, crushed

1 large onion, finely chopped

225 g/8 oz wild mushrooms, sliced

300 g/10½ oz minced chicken

85 g/3 oz chicken livers, finely chopped

115 g/4 oz Parma ham, diced

150 ml/5 fl oz Marsala wine

280 g/10 oz canned chopped tomatoes

1 tbsp chopped fresh basil leaves

2 tbsp tomato purée

salt and pepper

1 To make the chicken and wild mushroom sauce, heat the olive oil in a large saucepan. Add the garlic, onion and mushrooms and cook, stirring frequently, for 6 minutes.

2 Add the minced chicken, chicken livers and Parma ham and cook over a low heat, stirring frequently, for about 12 minutes or until the meat has browned.

3 Stir the Marsala, tomatoes, basil and tomato purée into the mixture in the pan and cook for 4 minutes. Season with salt and pepper to taste, cover and simmer gently for 30 minutes. Uncover the pan, stir thoroughly and simmer for a further 15 minutes.

4 Lightly grease an ovenproof dish with butter. Arrange sheets of lasagne over the base of the dish, spoon over a layer of the chicken and wild mushroom sauce, then spoon over a layer of Béchamel sauce. Place another layer of lasagne on top and repeat the process twice, finishing with a layer of Béchamel sauce. Sprinkle over the grated cheese and bake in a preheated oven, 190°C/375°F/Gas Mark 5, for 35 minutes until golden brown and bubbling. Serve immediately.

Chicken Risotto Milanese

This famous dish is known throughout the world – it is perhaps the best known of all Italian risottos, although there are many variations.

NUTRITIONAL INFORMATION

Calories 857	Sugars 1g	
Protein 57g	Fat 38g	
Carbohydrate . . .72g	Saturates 21g	

 5 mins   55 mins

SERVES 4

I N G R E D I E N T S

125 g/4½ oz butter

900 g/2 lb skinless boneless chicken, thinly sliced

1 large onion, chopped

500 g/1 lb 2 oz arborio or carnaroli rice

600 ml/1 pint chicken stock

150 ml/5 fl oz white wine

1 tsp crumbled saffron

salt and pepper

55 g/2 oz grated Parmesan cheese, to serve

1 Heat 4 tablespoons of the butter in a deep frying pan and cook the chicken and onion until golden brown.

2 Add the rice, stir well and cook over a low heat for 15 minutes.

3 Heat the stock until boiling and gradually add to the rice. Add the white wine, saffron, salt and pepper to taste and mix well. Simmer gently for 20 minutes, stirring occasionally, and adding more stock if necessary.

4 Set aside for 2–3 minutes and just before serving, add a little more stock and simmer for 10 minutes. Serve the risotto, sprinkled with the grated Parmesan cheese and the remaining butter.

Chicken with Orange Sauce

The refreshing combination of chicken and orange sauce makes this a perfect dish for a warm summer evening.

NUTRITIONAL INFORMATION

Calories	797	Sugars	.......28g
Protein	........59g	Fat	..........25g
Carbohydrate	...77g	Saturates	.......6g

15 mins   25 mins

SERVES 4

I N G R E D I E N T S

tbsp rapeseed oil

tbsp olive oil

x 225 g/8 oz chicken suprêmes

50 ml/5 fl oz orange brandy

tbsp plain flour

50 ml/5 fl oz freshly squeezed
  orange juice

5 g/1 oz courgette, cut into thin batons

25 g/1 oz red pepper, cut into thin batons

5 g/1 oz leek, finely shredded

00 g/14 oz dried wholemeal spaghetti

large oranges, peeled and cut
  into segments

ind of 1 orange, cut into very fine strips

2 tbsp chopped fresh tarragon

50 ml/5 fl oz fromage frais or
  ricotta cheese

alt and pepper

resh tarragon leaves, to garnish

1 Heat the rapeseed oil and 1 tablespoon of the olive oil in a frying pan. Add the chicken and cook over a fairly high heat until golden brown. Add the orange brandy and cook for 3 minutes. Sprinkle in the flour and cook, stirring constantly, for 2 minutes.

2 Lower the heat and add the orange juice, courgette, red pepper and leek and season to taste. Simmer for 5 minutes until the sauce has thickened.

3 Meanwhile, bring a pan of lightly salted water to the boil. Add the spaghetti, bring back to the boil and cook for 10 minutes until tender but still firm to the bite. Drain the spaghetti, transfer to a warmed serving dish and drizzle over the remaining oil.

4 Add half of the orange segments, half of the orange rind, the tarragon and fromage frais or ricotta cheese to the sauce in the pan and cook for 3 minutes.

5 Place the chicken on top of the pasta, pour over a little sauce, garnish with orange segments, rind and tarragon. Serve immediately with any extra sauce.

Orecchiette with Chicken

Fiery dried chillies feature in a number of southern Italian pasta sauces, naturally partnered by tomatoes that flourish in the region.

NUTRITIONAL INFORMATION

Calories	390	Sugars	.........8g
Protein	........16g	Fat	...........9g
Carbohydrate	...62g	Saturates	.......1g

 25 mins   15 mins

SERVES 6

INGREDIENTS

800 g/1 lb 12 oz canned chopped tomatoes

4 dried red chillies

3 tbsp olive oil

1 onion, chopped

115 g/4 oz skinless, boneless chicken breast, cut into thin strips

350 g/12 oz mushrooms, sliced

3 garlic cloves, finely chopped

55 g/2 oz black olives

125 ml/4 fl oz dry white wine

450 g/1 lb dried orecchiette

2 tbsp chopped fresh flat-leaved parsley

salt and pepper

1 Place the tomatoes and their can juices in a large heavy-based saucepan with the chillies. Bring to the boil, then simmer gently for 20 minutes, or until reduced.

2 Meanwhile, heat 2 tablespoons of the olive oil in a heavy-based frying pan. Add the onion and cook over a low heat, stirring occasionally, for 5 minutes, or until softened. Add the chicken and cook, stirring frequently, for 8 minutes, or until golden brown. Add the mushrooms and garlic and cook, stirring frequently, for a further 5 minutes. Add the olives and wine and cook for 3–5 minutes, or until reduced.

3 While the chicken mixture is cooking, bring a heavy-based saucepan of lightly salted water to the boil. Add the pasta, return to the boil and cook for 8–10 minutes, or until tender but still firm to the bite. Rub the tomato and chilli mixture through a sieve into a bowl and reserve.

4 Drain the pasta well and transfer to a warmed serving dish. Stir the reserved tomato sauce into the chicken mixture with the parsley, season to taste with salt and pepper and spoon over the pasta. Toss lightly and serve.

COOK'S TIP

When rubbing the tomatoes through a sieve into a bowl, use the back of a wooden spoon to push them through. It is best to use a non-metallic sieve, as the metal may taint the flavour.

Potato, Leek & Chicken Pie

This pie has an attractive filo pastry case that has a 'ruffled' top made with strips of the pastry brushed with melted butter.

NUTRITIONAL INFORMATION

Calories 543	Sugars 7g
Protein 21g	Fat 27g
Carbohydrate ...56g	Saturates 16g

10 mins   1¼ hrs

SERVES 4

INGREDIENTS

225 g/8 oz waxy potatoes, cubed

5 tbsp butter

1 skinless chicken breast fillet, about
   175 g/6 oz, cubed

1 leek, sliced

150 g/5½ oz chestnut mushrooms, sliced

2½ tbsp plain flour

300 ml/10 fl oz milk

1 tbsp Dijon mustard

2 tbsp chopped fresh sage

225 g/8 oz filo pastry, thawed if frozen

3 tbsp butter, melted

salt and pepper

1 Cook the potato cubes in a saucepan of boiling water for 5 minutes. Drain and set aside.

2 Melt the butter in a frying pan and cook the chicken cubes for 5 minutes or until browned all over.

3 Add the leek and mushrooms and cook for 3 minutes, stirring. Stir in the flour and cook for 1 minute stirring constantly. Gradually stir in the milk and bring to the boil. Add the mustard, sage and potato cubes and simmer for 10 minutes.

4 Meanwhile, line a deep pie dish with half of the sheets of filo pastry. Spoon the sauce into the dish and cover with 1 sheet of pastry. Brush the pastry with butter and lay another sheet on top. Brush this sheet with butter.

5 Cut the remaining filo pastry into strips and fold them on to the top of the pie to create a ruffled effect. Brush the strips with the melted butter and cook in a preheated oven, 180°C/350°F/Gas Mark 4, for 45 minutes or until golden brown and crisp. Serve hot.

COOK'S TIP

If the top of the pie starts to brown too quickly, cover it with foil halfway through the cooking time to allow the pastry base to cook through without the top burning.

Potato Crisp Pie

This is a layered pie of potatoes, broccoli, tomatoes and chicken slices in a creamy sauce, topped with a crisp oat layer.

NUTRITIONAL INFORMATION

Calories	630	Sugars	........12g
Protein	........25g	Fat	.........40g
Carbohydrate	...38g	Saturates	......24g

 10 mins   55 mins

SERVES 4

I N G R E D I E N T S

600 g/1 lb 5 oz waxy potatoes, sliced

5 tbsp butter

1 skinless chicken breast fillet, about 175 g/6 oz

2 garlic cloves, crushed

4 spring onions, sliced

2½ tbsp plain flour

150 ml/5 fl oz dry white wine

150 ml/5 fl oz double cream

225 g/8 oz broccoli florets

4 large tomatoes, sliced

85 g/3 oz Gruyère cheese, sliced

225 ml/8 fl oz natural yogurt

4 tbsp rolled oats, toasted

1 Cook the potatoes in a saucepan of boiling water for 10 minutes. Drain and set aside.

2 Meanwhile, melt the butter in a large, heavy-based frying pan. Cut the chicken into strips and cook over a medium heat for 5 minutes, turning. Add the garlic and spring onions and cook for a further 2 minutes.

3 Stir in the flour and cook for 1 minute. Gradually stir in the wine and cream. Bring to the boil, stirring constantly, then reduce the heat until the sauce is simmering and cook for 5 minutes.

4 Meanwhile, blanch the broccoli in boiling water, drain and refresh in cold water.

5 Place half of the potatoes in the base of a pie dish and top with half of the tomatoes and half of the broccoli.

6 Spoon the chicken sauce on top and repeat the layers in the same order once more.

7 Arrange the Gruyère cheese on top and spoon over the yogurt. Sprinkle with the oats and cook in a preheated oven, 200°C/400°F/Gas Mark 6, for 25 minutes until the top is golden brown. Serve the pie immediately.

COOK'S TIP

Add chopped nuts, such as pine kernels, to the topping for extra crunch, if you prefer.

Chicken with Saffron Mash

The addition of fresh thyme, coriander and lemon juice complements the griddled chicken and saffron mash to perfection.

NUTRITIONAL INFORMATION

Calories	310	Sugars	........2g
Protein	........31g	Fat	..........10g
Carbohydrate	...25g	Saturates	.......2g

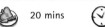

🧊 20 mins   🕐 25 mins

SERVES 4

I N G R E D I E N T S

550 g/1 lb 4 oz floury potatoes, cut into chunks

1 garlic clove, peeled

1 tsp saffron threads, crushed

1.2 litres/2 pints chicken or vegetable stock

4 skinless, boneless chicken breasts, trimmed of all visible fat

2 tbsp olive oil

1 tbsp lemon juice

1 tbsp chopped fresh thyme

1 tbsp chopped fresh coriander

1 tbsp coriander seeds, crushed

100 ml/3½ fl oz hot skimmed milk

salt and pepper

fresh thyme sprigs, to garnish

 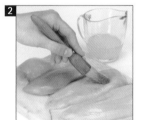 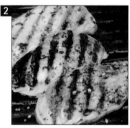

1 Put the potatoes, garlic and saffron in a large heavy-based saucepan, add the stock and bring to the boil. Cover and simmer for 20 minutes, or until tender.

2 Meanwhile, brush the chicken breasts all over with half the olive oil and all of the lemon juice. Sprinkle with the fresh thyme and coriander and crushed coriander seeds. Heat a griddle pan, add the chicken and cook over a medium–high heat for 5 minutes on each side, or until the juices run clear when the meat is pierced with a skewer or the point of a knife. Alternatively, cook the chicken breasts under a preheated grill for 5 minutes on each side.

3 Drain the potatoes and return the contents of the sieve to the saucepan. Add the remaining oil and the milk, season to taste with salt and pepper and mash until smooth. Divide the saffron mash between 4 large, warmed serving plates, top with a piece of chicken and garnish with a few sprigs of fresh thyme. Serve.

COOK'S TIP
Reserve the stock when you drain the potatoes. Reheat, stirring in 1 tablespoon of chopped fresh thyme and salt and pepper to taste, then serve as a soup.

Lemon Grass Chicken

An unusual recipe in which fresh lemon grass stalks are used as skewers, which impart their delicate lemony flavour to the chicken mixture.

NUTRITIONAL INFORMATION

Calories	140	Sugars	.........2g
Protein	........19g	Fat	...........7g
Carbohydrate	....2g	Saturates	.......1g

30 mins · 4–6 mins

SERVES 4

INGREDIENTS

2 long or 4 short lemon grass stalks

2 large boneless, skinless chicken breast portions, about 400 g/14 oz in total

1 small egg white

1 carrot, finely grated

1 small fresh red chilli, deseeded and chopped

2 tbsp chopped fresh garlic chives

2 tbsp chopped fresh coriander

1 tbsp sunflower oil

salt and pepper

fresh coriander and lime slices, to garnish

1 If the lemon grass stalks are long, cut them in half across the middle to make 4 short lengths. Cut each stalk in half lengthways, so you have 8 sticks.

2 Roughly chop the chicken pieces and place them in a food processor with the egg white. Process to a smooth paste, then add the carrot, chilli, chives, coriander and salt and pepper. Process for a few seconds to mix well.

3 Chill the mixture in the refrigerator for about 15 minutes. Divide the mixture into 8 equal portions and use your hands to shape the mixture around the lemon grass 'skewers'.

4 Brush the skewers with oil and grill under a preheated medium-hot grill for 4–6 minutes, turning them occasionally, until golden brown and thoroughly cooked. Alternatively, barbecue over medium-hot coals.

5 Serve hot, garnished with fresh coriander and slices of lime.

COOK'S TIP

If you can't find whole lemon grass stalks, use wooden or bamboo skewers instead, and add ½ teaspoon ground lemon grass to the mixture with the other flavourings.

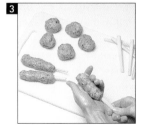
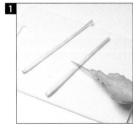

Chicken in Banana Leaves

Large leaves, such as banana, are often used in Thai cooking as a natural wrapping for all kinds of ingredients.

NUTRITIONAL INFORMATION

Calories	185	Sugars	.........0g
Protein	........18g	Fat	..........12g
Carbohydrate	...0.5g	Saturates	.......1g

  1¼ hrs 10–12 mins

SERVES 4–6

INGREDIENTS

garlic clove, chopped

tsp finely chopped fresh root ginger

tsp ground black pepper

fresh coriander sprigs

tbsp Thai fish sauce

tbsp whisky

boneless, skinless chicken breast portions

–3 banana leaves, cut into 7.5 cm/ 3 inch squares

unflower oil, for frying

weet chilli dipping sauce (see Cook's Tip), to serve

1 Place the garlic, ginger, pepper, coriander, Thai fish sauce and whisky in a mortar and grind to a smooth paste with a pestle.

2 Cut the chicken into 2.5 cm/1 inch chunks and toss in the paste to coat evenly. Cover and set aside in the refrigerator to marinate for about 1 hour.

3 Place a piece of chicken on a square of banana leaf and wrap it up like a parcel to enclose the chicken completely. Secure with wooden cocktail sticks or tie with a piece of bamboo string.

4 Heat a 3 mm/⅛ inch depth of oil in a heavy-based frying pan until hot.

5 Fry the parcels for 8–10 minutes, turning them over occasionally until golden brown and the chicken is thoroughly cooked. Serve immediately with a sweet chilli dipping sauce.

COOK'S TIP

To make a sweet chilli dip to serve with the chicken pieces, combine equal amounts of chilli sauce and tomato ketchup, then stir in a dash of rice wine to taste.

Roast Chicken with Ginger

This is a version of a sweet-and-sour chicken dish often sold by street traders in the East – they barbecue the chickens whole or cut in half.

NUTRITIONAL INFORMATION

Calories 260   Sugars 9g
Protein ....42g   Fat 5g
Carbohydrate ....11g   Saturates 2g

 8¼ hrs   1¼ hrs

SERVES 4

I N G R E D I E N T S

3 cm/1¼ inch piece fresh root ginger, finely chopped

2 garlic cloves, finely chopped

1 small onion, finely chopped

1 lemon grass stalk, finely chopped

½ tsp salt

1 tsp black peppercorns

1.5 kg/3 lb 5 oz chicken

1 tbsp coconut cream

2 tbsp lime juice

2 tbsp clear honey

1 tsp cornflour

2 tsp water

stir-fried vegetables, to serve

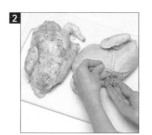

1 Put the ginger, garlic, onion, lemon grass, salt and peppercorns in a mortar and crush with a pestle to form a smooth paste.

2 Cut the chicken in half lengthways, using poultry shears or strong kitchen scissors. Spread the paste all over the chicken, both inside and out. Loosen the breast skin and gently spread the paste underneath. Transfer the chicken to a large plate, cover with clingfilm and set aside in the refrigerator to marinate overnight or at least for several hours.

3 Heat the coconut cream, lime juice and honey in a small pan, stirring until smooth. Brush a little of the mixture evenly over the chicken.

4 Place the chicken halves on a rack over a roasting tin half-filled with boiling water. Roast in a preheated oven, 180°C/350°F/Gas Mark 4, basting occasionally with the lime and honey mixture, for about 1 hour or until the

chicken is a rich golden brown and the juices run clear when the thickest part is pierced with a skewer.

5 Boil the water from the roasting tin to reduce it to about 100 ml/3½ fl oz. Blend the cornflour and water and stir into the reduced liquid. Heat gently to the boil, then stir until slightly thickened and clear. Serve the chicken with the sauce and stir-fried vegetables.

Chicken & Mango Stir-fry

A colourful, exotic mix of flavours that works surprisingly well, this dish is easy and quick to cook – ideal for a midweek family meal.

NUTRITIONAL INFORMATION

Calories 200   Sugars 5g
Protein . . . . .23g   Fat 6g
Carbohydrate . . . .7g   Saturates 1g

🧊 5 mins   🕐 12 mins

SERVES 4

INGREDIENTS

skinless, boneless chicken thighs

tsp grated fresh root ginger

garlic clove, crushed

small fresh red chilli, deseeded

large red pepper, deseeded

spring onions, thickly sliced diagonally

00 g/7 oz mangetouts

00 g/3½ oz baby corn cobs

large ripe mango

tbsp sunflower oil

tbsp light soy sauce

tbsp rice wine or sherry

tsp sesame oil

alt and pepper

nipped fresh chives, to garnish

1 Cut the chicken into long, thin strips and place in a bowl. Combine the inger, garlic and chilli, then stir the mixture into the chicken strips to coat hem evenly.

2 Slice the pepper thinly, cutting diagonally. Trim and diagonally slice he spring onions. Cut the mangetouts and orn cobs in half diagonally. Peel the mango, remove the stone and slice thinly.

3 Heat the sunflower oil in a large, preheated heavy-based frying pan or wok over a high heat. Add the chicken and stir-fry for 4–5 minutes until just turning golden brown. Add the pepper slices and stir-fry over a medium heat for 4–5 minutes until softened.

4 Add the spring onions, mangetouts and corn cobs and stir-fry for a further minute.

5 Combine the soy sauce, rice wine or sherry and sesame oil and stir the mixture into the wok. Add the mango slices and stir gently for 1 minute until heated through.

6 Season with salt and pepper to taste, garnish with snipped fresh chives and serve immediately.

Spicy Coriander Chicken

These simple marinated chicken portions are packed with powerful, zesty flavours, best accompanied by plain boiled rice and a cucumber salad.

NUTRITIONAL INFORMATION

Calories	171	Sugars	8g
Protein	31g	Fat	2g
Carbohydrate	9g	Saturates	0.5g

1¼ hrs   15–20 mins

SERVES 4

INGREDIENTS

4 skinless boneless chicken breast portions

2 garlic cloves, peeled

1 fresh green chilli, deseeded

2 cm/¾ inch piece of fresh root ginger,

4 tbsp chopped fresh coriander

rind of 1 lime, finely grated

3 tbsp lime juice

2 tbsp light soy sauce

1 tbsp caster sugar

175 ml/6 fl oz coconut milk

TO SERVE

plain boiled rice

cucumber and radish salad

1 Using a sharp knife, cut 3 deep slashes into the skinned side of each chicken breast portion. Place them in a single layer in a wide, non-metallic dish.

2 Put the garlic, chilli, ginger, coriander, lime rind and juice, soy sauce, caster sugar and coconut milk in a food processor and process to a smooth purée.

3 Spread the purée over both sides of the chicken portions, coating them evenly. Cover the dish with clingfilm and set aside to marinate in the refrigerator for about 1 hour.

4 Lift the chicken from the marinade, drain off the excess and place in a grill pan. Cook under a preheated grill for 12–15 minutes until thoroughly and evenly cooked.

5 Meanwhile, place the remaining marinade in a pan and bring to the boil. Lower the heat and simmer for several minutes to heat thoroughly. Remove the pan from the heat.

6 Place the chicken breast portions on warmed individual serving plates and pour over the sauce. Serve immediately accompanied with boiled rice and cucumber and radish salad.

Green Chicken Curry

Thai curries are traditionally very hot and designed to make a little go a long way – the thin, highly spiced juices are eaten with lots of rice.

NUTRITIONAL INFORMATION

Calories	193	Sugars	.........9g
Protein	........22g	Fat	..........8g
Carbohydrate	....9g	Saturates	.......1g

 10 mins   50 mins

SERVES 4

INGREDIENTS

6 boneless, skinless chicken thighs

400 ml/14 fl oz coconut milk

2 garlic cloves, crushed

2 tbsp Thai fish sauce

2 tbsp Thai green curry paste

12 baby aubergines

3 fresh green chillies, finely chopped

3 kaffir lime leaves, shredded

4 tbsp fresh coriander, chopped

boiled rice, to serve

1 Cut the chicken into bite-sized pieces. Pour the coconut milk into a large pan or wok and bring to the boil over a high heat.

2 Add the chicken, garlic and fish sauce to the pan or wok and bring back to the boil. Lower the heat and simmer gently for about 30 minutes or until the chicken is just tender.

3 Remove the chicken from the mixture with a draining spoon. Set aside and keep warm.

4 Stir the green curry paste into the pan until fully incorporated, then add the aubergines, chillies and lime leaves and simmer for 5 minutes.

5 Return the chicken to the pan or wok and bring to the boil. Season with salt and pepper to taste, then stir in the chopped coriander. Serve the curry immediately with boiled rice.

COOK'S TIP

Baby aubergines, or 'pea aubergines' as they are called in Thailand, are traditionally used in this curry, but they are not always easily available. If you can't find them in an Asian food shop, use chopped ordinary aubergine or substitute a few green peas.

Braised Garlic Chicken

The intense flavours of this dish are helped by the slow, gentle cooking. The meat should be almost falling off the bone.

NUTRITIONAL INFORMATION

Calories	282	Sugars	.........3g
Protein	........29g	Fat	..........16g
Carbohydrate	....5g	Saturates	.......3g

  15 mins   1 hr

SERVES 4

INGREDIENTS

4 garlic cloves, chopped

4 shallots, chopped

2 small fresh red chillies, deseeded and chopped

1 lemon grass stalk, finely chopped

1 tbsp chopped fresh coriander

1 tsp shrimp paste

½ tsp ground cinnamon

1 tbsp tamarind paste

2 tbsp vegetable oil

8 small chicken joints, such as drumsticks or thighs

300 ml/10 fl oz chicken stock

1 tbsp Thai fish sauce

1 tbsp smooth peanut butter

4 tbsp toasted peanuts, chopped

salt and pepper

stir-fried vegetables and boiled noodles, to serve

1 Place the garlic, shallots, chillies, lemon grass, coriander and shrimp paste in a mortar and grind with a pestle to an almost smooth paste. Stir in the cinnamon and tamarind paste.

2 Heat the oil in a wide frying pan or wok. Add the chicken joints, turning frequently, until they are golden brown on all sides. Remove them from the wok with a draining spoon and keep hot. Tip away any excess fat.

3 Add the garlic paste to the pan or wok and cook over a medium heat, stirring constantly, until lightly browned.

Stir in the stock and return the chicken to the pan.

4 Bring to the boil, then cover tightly, lower the heat and simmer, stirring occasionally, for 25–30 minutes until the chicken is tender and thoroughly cooked. Stir in the fish sauce and peanut butter and simmer the mixture gently for a further 10 minutes.

5 Season with salt and pepper to taste and sprinkle the toasted peanuts over the chicken. Serve immediately, with a colourful selection of stir-fry vegetables and boiled noodles.

Rice Noodles with Chicken

The great thing about stir-fries is you can cook with very little fat and still get lots of flavour, as in this light, healthy lunch dish.

NUTRITIONAL INFORMATION

Calories	329	Sugars	.........3g
Protein	........25g	Fat	...........4g
Carbohydrate	...46g	Saturates	.......1g

25 mins   10 mins

SERVES 4

I N G R E D I E N T S

00 g/7 oz rice stick noodles

tbsp sunflower oil

garlic clove, finely chopped

cm/¾ inch piece fresh root ginger, finely chopped

spring onions, chopped

fresh red bird-eye chilli, deseeded and sliced

00 g/10½ oz boneless, skinless chicken, finely chopped

chicken livers, finely chopped

celery stick, thinly sliced

carrot, cut into fine batons

00 g/10½ oz shredded Chinese leaves

tbsp lime juice

tbsp Thai fish sauce

tbsp soy sauce

tbsp shredded fresh mint

ices of pickled garlic

esh mint sprig, to garnish

1 Soak the rice noodles in hot water for 15 minutes or according to the package instructions. Drain well.

2 Heat the oil in a wok or large frying pan and stir-fry the garlic, ginger, spring onions and chilli for about 1 minute. Stir in the chicken and chicken livers, then stir-fry over a high heat for 2–3 minutes until beginning to brown.

3 Stir in the celery and carrot and stir-fry for 2 minutes to soften. Add the Chinese leaves, then stir in the lime juice, fish sauce and soy sauce.

4 Add the noodles and stir to heat thoroughly. Sprinkle with shredded mint and pickled garlic. Serve immediately, garnished with a mint sprig.

Sweet Maple Chicken

You can use any chicken portions for this recipe. Thighs are economical for large barbecue parties, but you could also use wings or drumsticks.

NUTRITIONAL INFORMATION

Calories ....122 Sugars 16g
Protein ....11g Fat 1g
Carbohydrate ...17g Saturates 1g

35 mins 20 mins

SERVES 6

INGREDIENTS

12 boneless chicken thighs

5 tbsp maple syrup

1 tbsp caster sugar

grated rind and juice of ½ orange

2 tbsp ketchup

2 tsp Worcestershire sauce

TO GARNISH

orange slices

fresh parsley sprigs

TO SERVE

Italian bread, such as focaccia

salad leaves

cherry tomatoes, quartered

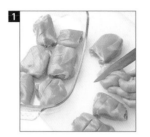

1 Using a long sharp knife, make 2–3 diagonal slashes in the flesh of the chicken to allow the flavours to permeate. Arrange the chicken thighs in a single layer in a shallow, non-metallic dish.

2 To make the marinade, combine the maple syrup, sugar, orange rind and juice, ketchup and Worcestershire sauce in a small bowl.

3 Pour the marinade over the chicken, turning the chicken well to coat thoroughly. Cover with clingfilm and chill in the refrigerator until required.

4 Remove the chicken from the marinade, reserving the marinade.

5 Transfer the chicken to the barbecue and cook over hot coals for 20 minutes, turning the chicken an basting with the marinade frequentl Alternatively, cook under a preheated gr for 20 minutes, turning and basting.

6 Transfer the chicken to warme serving plates and garnish with slice of orange and a sprig of parsley. Serv immediately with Italian bread, fresh sala leaves and cherry tomatoes.

Kebabs with Red Peppers

These chicken skewers are rather special and are well worth the extra effort needed to prepare them.

NUTRITIONAL INFORMATION

Calories	398	Sugars	........12g
Protein	........27g	Fat	..........22g
Carbohydrate	...25g	Saturates	.......4g

1½ hrs   20 mins

SERVES 4

INGREDIENTS

skinless boneless chicken breasts

tbsp olive oil

tbsp lemon juice

small onion, grated

tbsp fresh, chopped sage

tbsp sage and onion stuffing mix

tbsp boiling water

green peppers, deseeded

SAUCE

tbsp olive oil

red pepper, deseeded and finely chopped

small onion, finely chopped

inch of sugar

10 g/7½ oz can chopped tomatoes

1 Cut the chicken into even-sized pieces. Mix the oil, lemon juice, grated onion and sage and pour the mixture into a plastic bag. Add the chicken, seal the bag and shake to coat the chicken. Set aside in the refrigerator to marinate for at least 30 minutes, shaking the bag occasionally.

2 Place the stuffing mix in a heatproof bowl and add the boiling water, stir well until fully incorporated. Set aside until required.

3 Cut each green pepper into 6 strips, then blanch the strips in boiling water for 3–4 minutes until softened. Drain, refresh under cold running water, then drain well again.

4 Form about 1 teaspoon of the stuffing mixture into a ball and roll it up in a strip of green pepper. Repeat for the remaining stuffing mixture and pepper strips. Thread 3 pepper rolls on to each skewer alternately with pieces of chicken. Chill in the refrigerator.

5 To make the sauce, heat the oil in a small pan. Add the red pepper and onion and cook over a low heat, stirring occasionally, for 5 minutes. Stir in the sugar and tomatoes and simmer for about 5 minutes. Set aside and keep warm.

6 Barbecue the skewers on an oiled rack over hot coals, basting frequently with the remaining marinade, for about 15 minutes until the chicken is cooked. Serve with the red pepper sauce.

Maryland Chicken Kebabs

This is a barbecue variation of the traditional dish, Chicken Maryland. Serve with corn-on-the-cob (see page 457).

NUTRITIONAL INFORMATION

Calories	443	Sugars	........14g
Protein	........37g	Fat	..........26g
Carbohydrate	...16g	Saturates	.......6g

🍰 1¼–2¼ hrs   🕐 8–10 mins

SERVES 4

INGREDIENTS

8 skinless boneless chicken thighs

1 tbsp white wine vinegar

1 tbsp lemon juice

1 tbsp golden syrup or clear honey

6 tbsp olive oil

1 garlic clove, crushed

4 rashers rindless, smoked, streaky bacon

2 bananas

salt and pepper

TO SERVE

4 cooked corn-on-the-cob (see page 457)

mango chutney

1 Cut the chicken into bite-size pieces. Combine the vinegar, lemon juice, syrup or honey, oil, garlic and salt and pepper to taste in a large bowl. Add the chicken to the marinade and toss until the chicken is well coated. Cover and set aside to marinate for 1-2 hours.

2 Stretch the bacon rashers with the back of a knife and then cut each bacon rasher in half. Cut the bananas into 2.5 cm/1 inch lengths and brush them with lemon juice to prevent them from turning brown.

3 Wrap a piece of bacon around each piece of banana.

4 Remove the chicken from the marinade, reserving the marinade for basting. Thread the chicken pieces and the bacon and banana rolls alternately on to metal or bamboo skewers.

5 Barbecue the kebabs over hot coals for 8–10 minutes until the chicken is completely cooked through. Baste the kebabs with the marinade and turn the skewers frequently.

6 Serve with corn-on-the-cob and mango chutney.

VARIATION

For a quick Maryland-style dish, omit the marinating and cook the chicken thighs over hot coals for about 20 minutes, basting with the marinade. Barbecue the bananas in their skins beside the chicken. Serve the bananas split open with a teaspoon of mango chutney.

Sherried Liver Brochettes

Economical and flavoursome, these tasty chicken liver skewers make an ideal light lunch or a perfect addition to a summer brunch party.

NUTRITIONAL INFORMATION

Calories	767	Sugars	3g
Protein	31g	Fat	43g
Carbohydrate	51g	Saturates	8g

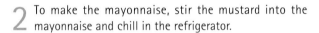

3½–4½ hrs   15 mins

SERVES 4

INGREDIENTS

400 g/14 oz chicken livers, trimmed and cleaned

3 slices rindless, streaky bacon

1 ciabatta loaf or small French stick

225 g/8 oz baby spinach

MARINADE

150 ml/5 fl oz dry sherry

4 tbsp olive oil

1 tsp wholegrain mustard

salt and pepper

MUSTARD MAYONNAISE

8 tbsp mayonnaise

1 tsp wholegrain mustard

1 Cut the chicken livers into 5 cm/2 inch pieces. To make the marinade, combine the sherry, oil, mustard and salt and pepper to taste in a shallow dish. Add the chicken livers to the marinade and toss until well coated. Set aside to marinate for 3–4 hours.

2 To make the mayonnaise, stir the mustard into the mayonnaise and chill in the refrigerator.

3 Stretch the bacon with the back of a knife and cut each slice in half. Remove the chicken livers from the marinade, reserving the marinade for basting. Wrap the bacon around half of the chicken liver pieces. Thread the bacon and chicken liver rolls and the plain chicken liver pieces alternately on to 6 pre-soaked wooden skewers.

4 Barbecue the skewers over hot coals for about 10–12 minutes, turning and basting with the reserved marinade frequently.

5 Meanwhile, cut the bread into 6 pieces and toast the cut sides on the barbecue until golden brown.

6 To serve, top the toasted bread with spinach leaves and place the brochettes on top. Spoon over the mustard mayonnaise and serve immediately.

Yellow Bean Chicken

Ready-made yellow bean sauce is available from large supermarkets and Chinese food stores. It is made from yellow soya beans and is quite salty.

NUTRITIONAL INFORMATION

Calories . . . . . . .234g   Sugars 1g
Protein . . . . .26g   Fat 12g
Carbohydrate . . . .6g   Saturates 2g

 25 mins   🕙 10 mins

SERVES 4

INGREDIENTS

450 g/1 lb skinless, boneless
   chicken breasts

1 egg white, beaten

1 tbsp cornflour

1 tbsp rice wine vinegar

1 tbsp light soy sauce

1 tsp caster sugar

3 tbsp vegetable oil

1 garlic clove, crushed

1 cm/½ inch piece of fresh root
   ginger, grated

1 green pepper, deseeded and diced

2 large mushrooms, sliced

3 tbsp yellow bean sauce

yellow or green pepper strips, to garnish

1 Trim any fat from the chicken and cut the meat into 2.5 cm/1 inch cubes.

2 Mix the egg white and cornflour in a shallow bowl. Add the chicken and turn in the mixture to coat. Set aside for 20 minutes.

3 Mix the rice wine vinegar, soy sauce and caster sugar in a bowl.

4 Remove the chicken from the egg white mixture.

5 Heat the oil in a preheated wok, add the chicken and stir-fry for 3–4 minutes until golden brown. Remove the chicken from the wok with a draining spoon, set aside and keep warm.

6 Add the garlic, ginger, pepper and mushrooms to the wok and stir-fry for 1–2 minutes.

7 Add the yellow bean sauce and cook for 1 minute. Stir in the vinegar mixture and return the chicken to the wok. Cook for 1–2 minutes and serve hot, garnished with pepper strips.

VARIATION

Black bean sauce would work equally well with this recipe. Although this would affect the appearance of the dish, because black bean sauce is much darker in colour, the flavours would be compatible.

Chicken Biryani

This biryani recipe may look rather complicated, but is not difficult to follow. You can substitute lamb, marinated overnight, for chicken.

NUTRITIONAL INFORMATION

Calories 382	Sugars 8g
Protein 42g	Fat 20g
Carbohydrate ...10g	Saturates 11g

🥄 3¼ mins   🕐 1½–1¾ hrs

SERVES 4

INGREDIENTS

1½ tsp fresh ginger root, finely chopped

1½ tsp fresh garlic, crushed

1 tbsp garam masala

1 tsp chilli powder

½ tsp ground turmeric

2 tsp salt

20 green/white cardamom seeds, crushed

300 ml/10 fl oz natural yogurt

1.5 kg/3 lb 5 oz chicken, skinned and cut into 8 pieces

150 ml/5 fl oz milk

saffron strands

6 tbsp ghee

2 medium onions, sliced

450 g/1 lb basmati rice

2 cinnamon sticks

4 black peppercorns

1 tsp black cumin seeds

4 fresh green chillies

fresh coriander leaves, finely chopped

4 tbsp lemon juice

1 Blend together the ginger, garlic, garam masala, chilli powder, turmeric, 1 tsp salt and cardamom seeds and mix with the yogurt and chicken pieces. Set aside to marinate for 3 hours.

2 Pour the milk into a pan and bring to the boil. Pour it over the saffron and set aside.

3 Heat the ghee in a pan and cook the onions until golden brown. Remove half of the onions and ghee from the pan and set aside.

4 Place the rice, cinnamon sticks, 4 peppercorns and the black cumin seeds in a pan of water. Bring the rice to the boil and remove from the heat when half-cooked. Drain and place in a bowl. Mix with the remaining salt.

5 Add the chicken mixture to the pan with the onions and ghee. Deseed the chillies, if wished, and finely chop. Add half each of the chillies, coriander, lemon juice and saffron. Add the rice and then the rest of the ingredients, including the fried onions and ghee. Cover tightly so no steam escapes. Cook on a low heat for 1 hour. Check that the meat is cooked through before serving. If the meat is not cooked, return to the heat and cook for a further 15 minutes. Mix thoroughly before serving hot.

Glazed Turkey Steaks

Prepare these steaks the day before they are needed and serve in toasted ciabatta bread, accompanied by crisp salad leaves.

NUTRITIONAL INFORMATION

Calories 219	Sugars 4g	
Protein 28g	Fat 10g	
Carbohydrate 4g	Saturates 1g	

  12 hrs   15 mins

SERVES 4

INGREDIENTS

100 g/3½ oz redcurrant jelly

2 tbsp lime juice

3 tbsp olive oil

2 tbsp dry white wine

¼ tsp ground ginger

pinch of grated nutmeg

4 turkey breast steaks

salt and pepper

TO SERVE

mixed salad leaves

vinaigrette dressing

1 ciabatta loaf

cherry tomatoes

1 Place the redcurrant jelly and lime juice in a pan and heat gently until the jelly melts. Add the oil, wine, ginger and nutmeg.

2 Place the turkey steaks in a shallow, non-metallic dish and season with salt and pepper. Pour over the marinade, turning the meat so that it is well coated. Cover and chill overnight.

3 Remove the turkey from the marinade, reserving the marinade for

basting, and barbecue on an oiled rack over hot coals for about 4 minutes on each side. Baste the turkey steaks frequently with the reserved marinade.

4 Meanwhile, toss the salad leaves in the vinaigrette dressing. Cut the ciabatta loaf in half lengthways and place, cut side down, at the side of the barbecue. Barbecue until golden. Place each steak on top of a salad leaf, sandwich between 2 pieces of bread and serve immediately with cherry tomatoes.

COOK'S TIP

Turkey and chicken escalopes are also ideal for cooking on the barbecue. Because they are thin, they cook through without burning on the outside. Leave them overnight in a marinade of your choice and cook, basting with a little lemon juice and oil.

Turkey with Cheese Pockets

Wrapping strips of bacon around the turkey helps to keep the cheese filling enclosed in the pocket – and adds extra flavour.

NUTRITIONAL INFORMATION

Calories 518	Sugars 0g
Protein 66g	Fat 28g
Carbohydrate 0g	Saturates 9g

15 mins   20 mins

SERVES 4

I N G R E D I E N T S

4 turkey breast portions, each about 225 g/8 oz

4 portions full-fat cheese (such as Bel Paese), 15 g/½ oz each

4 sage leaves or ½ tsp dried sage

8 rashers rindless streaky bacon

4 tbsp olive oil

2 tbsp lemon juice

salt and pepper

T O   S E R V E

garlic bread

salad leaves

cherry tomatoes

1 Carefully cut a pocket into the side of each turkey breast. Open out each breast a little and season inside with salt and pepper to taste.

2 Place a portion of cheese into each pocket, spreading it a little with a knife. Tuck a sage leaf into each pocket or sprinkle with a little dried sage.

3 Stretch the bacon out with the back of a knife. Wrap 2 pieces of bacon around each turkey breast, so that the pocket opening is completely covered.

4 Combine the oil and lemon juice in a small bowl.

5 Barbecue the turkey over medium hot coals for about 10 minutes on each side, basting with the oil and lemon mixture frequently.

6 Place the garlic bread at the side of the barbecue and toast lightly.

7 Transfer the turkey to warm serving plates. Serve with the toasted garlic bread, salad leaves and cherry tomatoes.

VARIATION

You can vary the cheese you use to stuff the turkey – try grated mozzarella or slices of Brie or Camembert. Also try placing 1 teaspoon of redcurrant jelly or cranberry sauce into each pocket instead of the sage.

Turkey & Sausage Kebabs

Serve these chilli-spiced and flavoursome kebabs with fresh bread, such as ciabatta, focaccia or a French stick.

NUTRITIONAL INFORMATION

Calories	238	Sugars	.........3g
Protein	........18g	Fat	..........17g
Carbohydrate	....3g	Saturates	.......5g

 1 hr   15 mins

SERVES 8

INGREDIENTS

350 g/12 oz turkey breast fillet

300 g/10½ oz chorizo sausage

1 eating apple

1 tbsp lemon juice

8 bay leaves

BASTE

6 tbsp olive oil

2 cloves garlic, crushed

1 fresh red chilli, deseeded and chopped

salt and pepper

1 To make the baste, place the oil, garlic and chilli in a small screw-top jar and season to taste with salt and pepper. Shake well to combine. Set aside for 1 hour for the garlic and chilli to flavour the oil.

COOK'S TIP

The flavoured oil used in this recipe can be used to baste any grilled meat, fish or vegetables. It will give plain foods a subtle chilli flavour and will keep in the refrigerator for about 2 weeks.

2 Cut the turkey into 2.5 cm/1 inch pieces. Cut the sausage into 2.5 cm/ 1 inch lengths. Cut the apple into chunks and remove the core. Toss the apple in lemon juice to prevent discoloration.

3 Thread the turkey and sausage pieces on to 8 metal or soaked bamboo skewers, alternating with the apple chunks and bay leaves.

4 Barbecue the kebabs over hot coal for about 15 minutes or until th turkey is cooked. Turn and baste th kebabs frequently with the flavoured oi Alternatively, cook under a preheated gril turning and basting frequently with the oi for 15 minutes.

5 Transfer the kebabs to warmed servin plates and serve immediately.

Turkey & Vegetable Loaf

This impressive-looking turkey loaf is flavoured with herbs and
a layer of juicy tomatoes and covered with courgette ribbons.

NUTRITIONAL INFORMATION

Calories	165	Sugars	.........1g
Protein	........36g	Fat	..........2g
Carbohydrate	....1g	Saturates	.....0.5g

🧊 10 mins 🕐 1¼ hrs

SERVES 4

INGREDIENTS

1 onion, finely chopped

1 garlic clove, crushed

900 g/2 lb lean minced turkey

1 tbsp chopped fresh parsley

1 tbsp chopped fresh chives

1 tbsp chopped fresh tarragon

1 egg white, lightly beaten

2 courgettes, 1 medium, 1 large

2 tomatoes

salt and pepper

tomato and herb sauce, to serve (optional)

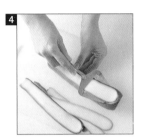

1 Line a non-stick loaf tin with baking paper. Place the onion, garlic and turkey in a bowl, add the herbs and season to taste with salt and pepper. Mix together with your hands, then add the egg white to bind.

2 Press half of the turkey mixture into the base of the tin. Trim and thinly slice the medium courgette and the tomatoes and arrange the slices over the meat. Top with the rest of the turkey mixture and press down firmly.

3 Cover with a layer of kitchen foil and place in a roasting tin. Pour in enough boiling water to come halfway up the sides of the loaf tin. Bake in a preheated oven, 190°C/375°F/Gas Mark 5, for 1–1¼ hours, removing the foil for the last 20 minutes of cooking. Test that the loaf is cooked by inserting a skewer into the centre – the juices should run clear. The loaf will also shrink away from the sides of the tin.

4 Meanwhile, trim the ends from the large courgette. Using a vegetable peeler or hand-held metal cheese slice, cut the courgette lengthways into thin slices. Bring a saucepan of water to the boil and blanch the courgette ribbons for 1–2 minutes until just tender. Drain and keep warm.

5 Remove the turkey loaf from the tin and transfer to a warm serving platter. Drape the courgette ribbons over the turkey loaf and serve with a tomato and herb sauce, if liked.

Beef Teriyaki

This Japanese-style teriyaki sauce complements barbecued beef, but it can also be used to accompany chicken or salmon.

NUTRITIONAL INFORMATION

Calories	184	Sugars	.........6g
Protein	........24g	Fat	...........5g
Carbohydrate	....8g	Saturates	......2g

   2¼ hrs 🕐 15 mins

SERVES 4

INGREDIENTS

450 g/1 lb extra thin lean beef steaks

8 spring onions, cut into short lengths

1 yellow pepper, deseeded and cut into chunks

green salad, to serve

SAUCE

1 tsp cornflour

2 tbsp dry sherry

2 tbsp white wine vinegar

3 tbsp soy sauce

1 tbsp dark muscovado sugar

1 garlic clove, crushed

½ tsp ground cinnamon

½ tsp ground ginger

1 Place the meat in a shallow, non-metallic dish. To make the sauce, combine the cornflour with the sherry to a smooth paste, then stir in the vinegar, soy sauce, sugar, garlic, cinnamon and ginger. Pour the sauce over the meat, turn to coat and set aside to marinate for at least 2 hours.

2 Remove the meat from the sauce, draining well. Pour the sauce into a small pan.

3 Cut the meat into thin strips and thread these, concertina-style, on to pre-soaked wooden skewers, alternating each strip of meat with pieces of spring onion and yellow pepper.

4 Gently heat the sauce until it is just simmering, stirring occasionally.

5 Barbecue the kebabs over hot coals for 5–8 minutes, turning and basting the beef and vegetables occasionally with the reserved teriyaki sauce.

6 Arrange the skewers on serving plates and pour the remaining sauce over the kebabs. Serve immediately with a green salad.

Sweet Lamb Fillet

Lamb fillet, enhanced by a sweet and spicy glaze, is cooked on
the barbecue in a kitchen foil parcel for deliciously moist results.

NUTRITIONAL INFORMATION

Calories 258	Sugars 13g	
Protein 24g	Fat 13g	
Carbohydrate ...13g	Saturates 5g	

🥄 5 mins   🕐 1 hr

SERVES 4

I N G R E D I E N T S

2 fillets of neck of lean lamb,
   each 225 g/8 oz

1 tbsp olive oil

½ onion, finely chopped

1 garlic clove, crushed

2.5 cm/1 inch piece of fresh root
   ginger, grated

5 tbsp apple juice

3 tbsp smooth apple sauce

1 tbsp light muscovado sugar

1 tbsp tomato ketchup

½ tsp mild mustard

salt and pepper

TO SERVE

green salad leaves,

croûtons

crusty bread

1 Place the lamb fillet on a large piece
of double thickness kitchen foil.
Season with salt and pepper to taste.

2 Heat the oil in a small pan and cook
the onion and garlic for 2–3 minutes
until softened but not browned. Stir in the
grated ginger and cook for 1 minute,
stirring occasionally. Stir in the apple juice,
apple sauce, sugar, ketchup and mustard

and bring to the boil. Boil rapidly for
about 10 minutes until reduced by half.
Stir the mixture occasionally so that it
does not burn and stick to the pan.

3 Brush half of the sauce over the lamb
fillets, then wrap up the lamb in the
kitchen foil to enclose it completely.
Barbecue the lamb parcels over hot coals
for about 25 minutes, turning the parcel
over occasionally.

4 Open out the kitchen foil and brush
the lamb with some of the remaining
sauce. Continue to barbecue for a further
15–20 minutes or until cooked through.

5 Place the lamb on a chopping board,
remove the foil and cut the meat into
thick slices. Transfer to serving plates and
spoon over the remaining sauce. Serve
with green salad leaves, croûtons and
fresh crusty bread.

Ginger Rice with Duck

For the best result, buy a 2.25 kg/5 lb duck, remove the breasts and use the carcass to make a flavourful stock.

NUTRITIONAL INFORMATION

Calories ....432 Sugars 4g
Protein ....27g Fat 16g
Carbohydrate ...48g Saturates 4g

 15 mins · 30 mins

SERVES 4–6

INGREDIENTS

2 duck breasts, cut diagonally into thin slices

2–3 tbsp Japanese soy sauce

1 tbsp mirin or medium sherry

2 tsp brown sugar

5 cm/2 inch piece of fresh root ginger, finely chopped or grated

4 tbsp groundnut oil

2 garlic cloves, crushed

300 g/10½ oz long grain white or brown rice

850 ml/1¾ pints chicken stock

115 g/4 oz cooked lean ham, thinly sliced

175 g/6 oz mangetouts, cut diagonally in half

40 g/1½ oz fresh beansprouts, rinsed

8 spring onions, thinly sliced diagonally

2–3 tbsp chopped fresh coriander

sweet or hot chilli sauce (optional)

1 Put the duck in a shallow bowl with a tablespoon of soy sauce, the mirin, half the brown sugar and one-third of the ginger. Stir to coat and set aside to marinate at room temperature.

2 Heat 2–3 tablespoons groundnut oil in a large heavy-based pan over a medium-high heat. Add the garlic and half the remaining ginger and stir-fry for about 1 minute until fragrant. Add the rice and cook, stirring, for about 3 minutes until translucent and beginning to colour.

3 Add 700 ml/1¼ pints stock and a teaspoon of soy sauce and bring to the boil. Reduce the heat to very low, cover and simmer for 20 minutes until the rice is tender and the liquid is absorbed. Do not uncover the pan, but remove from the heat and set aside.

4 Heat the remaining groundnut oil in a large wok. Drain the duck breast and gently stir-fry for about 3 minutes until just coloured. Add 1 tablespoon soy sauce and the remaining sugar and cook for 1 minute. Remove from the wok, set aside and keep warm.

5 Stir in the ham, mangetouts, beansprouts, spring onions, the remaining ginger and half the coriander. Add about 120 ml/4 fl oz of the stock and stir-fry for 1 minute or until the stock is almost reduced. Fork in the rice and toss together. Add a dash of chilli sauce.

6 To serve, turn into a serving dish, arrange the duck on top and sprinkle with the remaining coriander.

Duck with Lime & Kiwi Fruit

Tender breasts of duck served in thin slices, with a sweet but very tangy lime and wine sauce, full of pieces of kiwi fruit – sheer bliss.

NUTRITIONAL INFORMATION

Calories	264	Sugars	.........20g
Protein	.........20g	Fat	...........10g
Carbohydrate	...21g	Saturates	.......2g

1¼ hrs   15 mins

SERVES 4

I N G R E D I E N T S

4 boneless or part-boned duck breasts

grated rind and juice of 2 large limes

2 tbsp sunflower oil

4 spring onions, thinly sliced diagonally

125 g/4½ oz carrots, cut into thin batons

6 tbsp dry white wine

55 g/2 oz white sugar

2 kiwi fruit, peeled, halved and sliced

salt and pepper

fresh parsley sprigs and lime halves tied in knots (see Cook's Tip), to garnish

1 Trim any fat from the duck, then prick the skin all over with a fork and place in a shallow dish. Add half the grated lime and half the juice to the duck breasts, rubbing in thoroughly. Set aside in a cool place for at least 1 hour, turning the breasts at least once.

2 Drain the duck breasts, reserving the marinade. Heat 1 tbsp of oil in a wok. Add the duck and fry quickly to seal all over, then lower the heat and continue to cook for about 5 minutes, turning several times until just cooked through and well browned all over. Remove and keep warm.

3 Wipe the wok clean with kitchen paper and heat the remaining oil. Add the spring onions and carrots and stir-fry for 1 minute, then add the remaining lime marinade, wine and sugar. Bring to the boil and simmer for 2–3 minutes until slightly syrupy.

4 Add the duck breasts to the sauce, season to taste and add the kiwi fruit. Stir-fry for 1 minute or until really hot and both the duck and kiwi fruit are well coated in the sauce.

5 Cut each duck breast into slices, leaving a 'hinge' at one end, open out into a fan shape and arrange on plates.

Spoon the sauce over the duck, sprinkle with the remaining pieces of lime peel, garnish and serve immediately.

COOK'S TIP

To make the garnish, trim a piece off the base of each lime half so they stand upright. Pare off a thin strip of rind from the top of the lime halves, about 5 mm/¼ inch thick, but do not detach it. Tie the strip into a knot with the end bending over the cut surface of the lime.

Duck with Berry Sauce

Duck is a rich meat and is best accompanied by piquant fruit, as in this sophisticated dinner party dish.

NUTRITIONAL INFORMATION

Calories	293	Sugars	........10g
Protein	........28g	Fat	..........8g
Carbohydrate	...13g	Saturates	......2g

1¼ hrs   30 mins

SERVES 4

INGREDIENTS

450 g/1 lb boneless duck breasts

2 tbsp raspberry vinegar

2 tbsp brandy

1 tbsp clear honey

1 tsp sunflower oil, for brushing

salt and pepper

TO SERVE

2 kiwi fruit, peeled and thinly sliced

assorted vegetables

SAUCE

225 g/8 oz raspberries, thawed if frozen

300 ml/10 fl oz rosé wine

2 tsp cornflour blended with 4 tsp cold water

1 Skin and trim the duck breasts to remove any excess fat. Using a sharp knife, score the flesh in diagonal lines and pound it with a meat mallet or a covered rolling pin until it is 1.5 cm/¾ inch thick.

2 Place the duck breasts in a shallow dish. Combine the vinegar, brandy and honey in a small bowl and spoon it over the duck. Cover and chill in the refrigerator for about 1 hour.

3 Drain the duck breasts, reserving the marinade, and place on the grill rack.

Season and brush with a little oil. Cook for 10 minutes under a preheated grill, turn over, season to taste and brush with oil again. Cook for a further 8–10 minutes until the meat is cooked through.

4 Meanwhile, make the sauce. Reserve about 55 g/2 oz raspberries and place the rest in a pan. Add the reserved marinade and the wine. Bring to the boil and simmer for 5 minutes until slightly reduced. Strain the sauce through a sieve, pressing the raspberries with the back of a spoon. Return the liquid to the pan and add the cornflour paste. Heat through stirring, until thickened. Add the reserved raspberries and season to taste.

5 Thinly slice the duck breasts and alternate with slices of kiwi fruit. on warm serving plates. Spoon over the sauce and serve with a selection of vegetables.

Slices of Duckling with Pasta

A wonderful raspberry and honey sauce superbly counterbalances the richness of the duckling – served on a bed of linguine.

NUTRITIONAL INFORMATION

Calories	686	Sugars	........15g
Protein	........62g	Fat	..........20g
Carbohydrate	...70g	Saturates	.......7g

🍳 15 mins   🕐 25 mins

SERVES 4

I N G R E D I E N T S

4 x 275 g/9 oz boneless duckling breasts

2 tbsp butter

55 g/2 oz finely chopped carrots

4 tbsp finely chopped shallots

1 tbsp lemon juice

150 ml/5 fl oz meat stock

4 tbsp clear honey

115 g/4 oz fresh or thawed
   frozen raspberries

25 g/1 oz plain flour

1 tbsp Worcestershire sauce

400 g/14 oz dried linguine

salt and pepper

TO GARNISH

fresh raspberries

fresh flat leaf parsley sprigs

1 Trim and score the duck breasts with a sharp knife and season to taste with salt and pepper. Melt the butter in a frying pan, add the duck breasts and fry all over until lightly coloured.

2 Add the carrots, shallots, lemon juice and half the meat stock and simmer over a low heat for 1 minute. Stir in half of the honey and half of the raspberries.

Sprinkle over half of the flour and cook, stirring constantly for 3 minutes. Season with pepper to taste and add the Worcestershire sauce.

3 Stir in the remaining stock and cook for 1 minute. Stir in the remaining honey and remaining raspberries and sprinkle over the remaining flour. Cook for a further 3 minutes.

4 Remove the duck breasts from the pan, but leave the sauce to continue simmering over a very low heat.

5 Meanwhile, bring a large pan of lightly salted water to the boil. Add the linguine, bring back to the boil and cook for 8–10 minutes or until tender, but still firm to the bite. Drain and divide between 4 individual plates.

6 Slice the duck breast lengthways into 5 mm/¼ inch thick pieces. Pour a little sauce over the pasta and arrange the sliced duck in a fan shape on top of it. Garnish with raspberries and flat leaf parsley and serve immediately.

Duck with Chilli & Lime

Duck is excellent cooked with strong flavours, and when it is marinated and coated in this rich, dark, sticky glaze it's irresistible.

NUTRITIONAL INFORMATION

Calories 264	Sugars 1g
Protein 30g	Fat 11g
Carbohydrate . . .13g	Saturates 3g

3¼ hrs   10 mins

SERVES 4

INGREDIENTS

4 boneless duck breast portions

2 garlic cloves, crushed

4 tsp light brown sugar

3 tbsp lime juice

1 tbsp soy sauce

1 tsp chilli sauce

1 tsp vegetable oil

2 tbsp plum jam

125 ml/4 fl oz chicken stock

salt and pepper

1 Using a small, sharp knife, cut deep slashes in the skin of the duck to make a diamond pattern. Place the duck breasts in a wide, non-metallic dish.

2 Combine the garlic, sugar, lime juice, soy and chilli sauces, then spoon over the duck, turning well to coat them evenly. Cover the dish with clingfilm and set aside to marinate in the refrigerator for at least 3 hours or overnight.

3 Drain the duck, reserving the marinade. Heat a large, heavy-based pan until very hot and brush with the oil. Add the duck breast portions, skin side down, and cook for about 5 minutes or until the skin is browned and crisp. Carefully tip away the excess fat. Turn the duck breasts over.

4 Continue cooking on the other side for 2–3 minutes to brown. Add the reserved marinade, plum jam and stock and simmer for 2 minutes. Season to taste and with salt and pepper. Serve hot, with the juices spooned over.

COOK'S TIP

To reduce the overall fat content of this dish, remove the skin from the duck breast portions before cooking and reduce the cooking time slightly.

Curried Roasted Duck

In this recipe, the duck is 'roasted' under a hot grill until golden brown and crisp, so much of the fat drains off before adding it to the curry.

NUTRITIONAL INFORMATION

Calories . . . . .412 Sugars 18g
Protein . . . . .41g Fat 20g
Carbohydrate . . .19g Saturates 5g

40 mins   40 mins

SERVES 4

INGREDIENTS

1.6 kg/3 lb 8 oz duckling

2 tbsp groundnut oil

1 small pineapple

1 large onion, chopped

1 garlic clove, finely chopped

1 tsp finely chopped fresh root ginger

½ tsp ground coriander

1 tbsp Thai green curry paste

1 tsp soft light brown sugar

450 ml/16 fl oz coconut milk

1 tbsp chopped fresh coriander

salt and pepper

fresh red chilli strips, to garnish

boiled jasmine rice, to serve

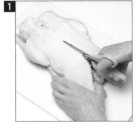 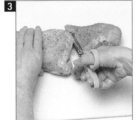 

1 Using a large knife or poultry shears, cut the duck in half lengthways, cutting through the line of the breastbone. Wipe inside and out with kitchen paper. Sprinkle with salt and pepper, prick the skin with a fork and brush with oil.

2 Place the duck, cut side down, on a grill pan and cook under a preheated hot grill for 25–30 minutes, turning occasionally, until golden brown. Tip away the fat in the pan at frequent intervals, as it may catch fire.

3 Set the duck aside to cool, then cut each half into 2 portions. Peel and core the pineapple and cut out the 'eyes'. Cut the flesh into dice.

4 Heat the remaining oil in a large pan. Add the onion and garlic and cook over a low heat, stirring occasionally, for 3–4 minutes until softened. Stir in the ginger, ground coriander, curry paste and brown sugar and stir-fry for 1 minute.

5 Stir in the coconut milk and bring to the boil. Add the duck pieces and the pineapple. Reduce the heat and simmer gently for 5 minutes. Sprinkle with coriander and serve on a bed of boiled jasmine rice, garnished with chilli strips.

Crispy Duck with Noodles

A robustly flavoured dish that makes a substantial main course.
Serve it with a refreshing cucumber salad or a light vegetable stir-fry.

NUTRITIONAL INFORMATION

Calories 433   Sugars 7g
Protein ....25g   Fat 18g
Carbohydrate ...59g   Saturates 2g

🍖 🍖

🍲 1¼ hrs   🕐 20 mins

SERVES 4

INGREDIENTS

3 duck breast portions, total weight about
  400 g/14 oz

2 garlic cloves, crushed

1½ tsp chilli paste

1 tbsp honey

3 tbsp dark soy sauce

½ tsp five-spice powder

250 g/9 oz rice stick noodles

1 tsp vegetable oil

1 tsp sesame oil

2 spring onions, sliced

100 g/3½ oz mangetouts

2 tbsp tamarind juice

sesame seeds, to garnish

1 Prick the duck breast skin all over with a fork and place in a deep dish.

2 Combine the garlic, chilli, honey, soy sauce and five-spice powder, then pour over the duck. Turn the breast portions over to coat them evenly, then cover and set aside to marinate in the refrigerator for at least 1 hour.

3 Meanwhile, soak the rice noodles in hot water for 15 minutes or according to the packet instructions. Drain well.

4 Drain the duck breast portions from the marinade and grill on a rack under high heat for about 10 minutes, turning them over occasionally, until they become a rich golden brown. Remove and slice thinly.

5 Heat the vegetable and sesame oils in a pan and stir-fry the spring onions and mangetouts for 2 minutes. Stir in the reserved marinade and the tamarind juice and bring to the boil.

6 Add the sliced duck and noodles and toss to heat thoroughly. Transfer to warmed serving plates and serve immediately, sprinkled with sesame seeds.

Citrus Duckling Skewers

The tartness of citrus fruit goes well with the rich meat of duckling.
Duckling makes a delightful change from chicken for the barbecue.

NUTRITIONAL INFORMATION

Calories 205	Sugars 5g	
Protein 24g	Fat 10g	
Carbohydrate 5g	Saturates 2g	

45 mins · 20 mins

SERVES 12

INGREDIENTS

3 skinless boneless duckling breasts

1 small red onion, cut into wedges

1 small aubergine, cut into cubes

lime and lemon wedges, to
    garnish (optional)

MARINADE

grated rind and juice of 1 lemon

grated rind and juice of 1 lime

grated rind and juice of 1 orange

1 garlic clove, crushed

1 tsp dried oregano

2 tbsp olive oil

dash of Tabasco sauce

1 Cut the duckling into bite-size pieces. Place in a non-metallic bowl with the prepared vegetables.

2 To make the marinade, place the lemon, lime and orange rinds and juices, garlic, oregano, oil and Tabasco sauce in a screw-top jar and shake until well combined. Pour the marinade over the duckling and vegetables and toss to coat. Set aside to marinate for 30 minutes.

3 Remove the duckling and vegetables from the marinade and thread them on to skewers, reserving the marinade.

4 Barbecue the skewers on an oiled rack over medium hot coals, turning and basting frequently with the reserved marinade, for 15-20 minutes until the meat is cooked through. Alternatively, cook under a preheated grill.

5 Serve the kebabs immediately, garnished with lime and lemon wedges for squeezing, if using.

COOK'S TIP

For more zing add 1 teaspoon of chilli sauce to the marinade. The meat can be marinated for several hours, but it is best to marinate the vegetables separately for only about 30 minutes.

Sesame Orange Duckling

Moist and flavourful, this dish is reminiscent of traditional duck à la orange but the flavour is even better.

NUTRITIONAL INFORMATION

Calories	.510	Sugars	.16g
Protein	.51g	Fat	.26g
Carbohydrate	.18g	Saturates	.7g

 2¼ hrs 40 mins

SERVES 4

I N G R E D I E N T S

4 tbsp soy sauce

2 tbsp fine-cut marmalade

2 tbsp orange juice

2 garlic cloves, crushed

1 cm/½ inch piece of fresh root ginger, grated

1 tbsp sherry vinegar

4 duckling portions

2 oranges, sliced

4 tbsp sesame seeds

T O   S E R V E

green salad leaves

fresh herbs

1 Combine the soy sauce, marmalade, orange juice, garlic, ginger and sherry vinegar in a small bowl.

2 Trim away any excess fat from the duckling portions.

3 Place the duckling portions in a shallow, non-metallic dish and pour over the orange mixture. Cover and set aside to marinate for at least 2 hours.

4 Divide most of the orange slices between 4 double-thickness pieces of kitchen foil, reserving some orange slices to serve. Place a duckling portion on top of the oranges and pour some of the marinade over each portion. Fold over the foil to enclose the duckling completely.

5 Barbecue over hot coals, turning occasionally, for about 40 minutes or until the meat is just cooked. Alternatively, cook under a preheated grill.

6 Remove the foil parcels from the heat and sprinkle the skin of the duckling with the sesame seeds. Place the duckling, skin side down, directly on the oiled rack over the hot coals and barbecue for a further 5 minutes until the skin is crisp. Alternatively, cook, skin side up, under the grill. Serve with the orange slices, salad leaves and fresh herbs.

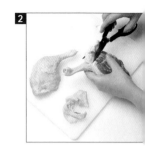

COOK'S TIP

Cooking the duckling in foil parcels keeps the meat moist and preserves the flavour of the marinade. If you prefer, omit the foil and cook them directly on the rack. Turn and baste frequently until cooked. Sprinkle with sesame seeds for the last few minutes of cooking.

Glazed Duckling

A salsa is a cross between a sauce and a relish. Salsas are easy to prepare and will liven up all kinds of simple grilled meats – like this one.

NUTRITIONAL INFORMATION

Calories	483	Sugars	........28g
Protein	.......48g	Fat	..........20g
Carbohydrate	...29g	Saturates	.......6g

 1¼ hrs   40–45 mins

SERVES 4

INGREDIENTS

2 tbsp Dijon mustard

1 tsp paprika

½ tsp ground ginger

½ tsp ground nutmeg

2 tbsp dark muscovado sugar

2 duckling halves

salad leaves, to serve

SALSA

225 g/8 oz can pineapple in natural juice

2 tbsp dark muscovado sugar

1 small red onion, finely chopped

1 fresh red chilli, deseeded and chopped

1 First, make the salsa. Drain the canned pineapple, reserving 2 tablespoons of the juice. Finely chop the pineapple flesh.

2 Place the pineapple, reserved juice, sugar, onion and chilli in a bowl and mix well. Cover with clingfilm and set aside for at least 1 hour for the flavours to develop fully.

3 Meanwhile, combine the mustard, paprika, ginger, nutmeg and sugar in a small bowl. Spoon the mixture on to the skin of the duckling halves and spread evenly over them.

4 Barbecue the duckling, skin side up, over hot coals for about 30 minutes. Turn the duckling over and barbecue for 10–15 minutes or until the duckling is cooked through.

5 Serve immediately with fresh salad leaves and the salsa.

VARIATION

Use canned apricots or peaches to make the salsa for a tasty alternative. The salsa is also delicious served with pork, lamb or chicken.

Duck with Mangoes

Use fresh mangoes in this recipe for a terrific flavour and colour.
If they are unavailable, use canned mangoes and rinse them before using.

NUTRITIONAL INFORMATION

Calories 235	Sugars 6g
Protein 23g	Fat 14g
Carbohydrate 6g	Saturates 2g

5 mins   35 mins

SERVES 4

INGREDIENTS

2 ripe mangoes

300 ml/10 fl oz chicken stock

2 garlic cloves, crushed

1 tsp grated fresh root ginger

2 large skinless duck breasts,
    225 g/8 oz each

3 tbsp vegetable oil

1 tsp wine vinegar

1 tsp light soy sauce

1 leek, sliced

chopped fresh parsley, to garnish

1 Peel the mangoes and cut the flesh from each side of the stones. Cut the flesh into strips.

2 Put half of the mango pieces and the chicken stock in a food processor and process until smooth. Alternatively, press half of the mangoes through a fine sieve and mix with the stock.

3 Rub the garlic and ginger over the duck breasts. Heat the oil in a preheated wok and cook the duck breasts, turning frequently, until sealed. Reserve the oil in the wok and remove the duck.

4 Place the duck breasts on a rack set over a roasting tin and cook in a preheated oven, 220°C/425°F/Gas Mark 7, for about 20 minutes, until the duck is cooked through.

5 Meanwhile, place the mango and stock mixture in a saucepan and add the wine vinegar and light soy sauce.

6 Bring the mixture to the boil and cook over a high heat, stirring constantly, until reduced by half.

7 Heat the oil reserved in the wok and stir-fry the sliced leek and remaining mango for 1 minute. Remove from the wok, transfer to a serving dish and keep warm until required.

8 Slice the cooked duck breasts and arrange the slices on top of the leek and mango mixture. Pour the sauce over the duck slices, garnish with chopped parsley and serve immediately.

Red Spiced Beef

A spicy stir-fry flavoured with paprika, chilli and tomato, with a crisp bite to it from the celery strips, makes a wonderful midweek supper.

NUTRITIONAL INFORMATION

Calories 431	Sugars 0g	
Protein 32g	Fat 28g	
Carbohydrate . . .14g	Saturates 10g	

40 mins   10 mins

SERVES 4

I N G R E D I E N T S

625 g/1 lb 6 oz sirloin or rump steak

2 tbsp paprika

2–3 tsp mild chilli powder

½ tsp salt

6 celery sticks

4 tomatoes, peeled, seeded and sliced

6 tbsp stock or water

2 tbsp tomato purée

2 tbsp clear honey

3 tbsp wine vinegar

1 tbsp Worcestershire sauce

2 tbsp sunflower oil

4 spring onions, thinly sliced diagonally

1–2 garlic cloves, crushed

celery leaves, to garnish (optional)

Chinese noodles, to serve

1 Using a sharp knife or meat cleaver, cut the steak across the grain into narrow strips about 1 cm/½ inch thick and place in a bowl.

2 Combine the paprika, chilli powder and salt, add to the beef and mix until the meat strips are evenly coated with the spices. Set the beef aside to marinate in a cool place for at least 30 minutes.

3 Cut the celery into 5 cm/2 inch lengths, then cut the lengths into strips about 5 mm/¼ inch thick.

4 Combine the stock, tomato purée, honey, vinegar and Worcestershire sauce and set aside.

5 Heat the oil in the wok until really hot. Add the spring onion, celery, tomatoes and garlic and stir-fry for about 1 minute until the vegetables are beginning to soften, then add the steak strips. Stir-fry over a high heat for 3–4 minutes until the meat is well sealed.

6 Add the sauce to the wok and continue to stir-fry briskly until thoroughly coated and sizzling.

7 Garnish with celery leaves, if liked and serve with noodles.

Beef & Orange Curry

A spicy blend of tender chunks of succulent beef
with the tang of orange and the warmth of Indian spices.

NUTRITIONAL INFORMATION

Calories 345   Sugars 24g
Protein . . . . .28g   Fat 13g
Carbohydrate . . .31g   Saturates 3g

 15 mins   1¼ hrs

SERVES 4

I N G R E D I E N T S

1 tbsp vegetable oil

225 g/8 oz shallots, halved

2 garlic cloves, crushed

450 g/1 lb lean rump or sirloin beef,
trimmed and cut into 2 cm/¾ inch cubes

3 tbsp curry paste

450 ml/16 fl oz Fresh Beef Stock
(see page 9)

4 medium oranges

2 tsp cornflour

salt and pepper

2 tbsp chopped fresh coriander, to garnish

boiled basmati rice, to serve

R A I T A

½ cucumber, finely diced

3 tbsp chopped fresh mint

150 ml/5 fl oz low-fat natural yogurt

1 Heat the oil in a large pan. Add the shallots, garlic and beef cubes and cook over a low heat, stirring occasionally,, for 5 minutes until the beef is evenly browned all over.

2 Blend together the curry paste and stock. Add the mixture to the beef and stir to mix thoroughly. Bring to the boil, cover and simmer for about 1 hour.

3 Grate the rind of 1 orange. Extract the juice from the orange and from 1 other. Peel the other 2 oranges, removing the pith. Slice between each segment and remove the flesh.

4 Blend the cornflour with the orange juice. At the end of the cooking time, stir the orange rind into the beef with the orange and cornflour mixture. Bring to the boil and simmer, stirring constantly, for

3–4 minutes until the sauce thickens. Season to taste with salt and pepper and stir in the orange segments.

5 To make the raita, mix the cucumber with the mint and stir in the yogurt. Season with salt and pepper to taste.

6 Serve the curry with rice and the cucumber raita, garnished with the chopped coriander.

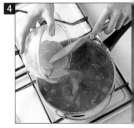

Meatballs with Relish

Minced beef labelled 'lean' may contain more fat than we would like.
Instead, buy a whole piece of lean beef, trim off the fat, and mince.

NUTRITIONAL INFORMATION

Calories 243	Sugars 5g	
Protein 30g	Fat 8g	
Carbohydrate ...14g	Saturates 3g	

🥖 🥖 🥖

🧊 15 mins   🕐 15–20 mins

SERVES 4

I N G R E D I E N T S

1 onion, finely chopped

2 garlic cloves, finely chopped

2 slices bread, crusts removed

500 g/1 lb 2 oz lean beef, minced

1 cooked baby beetroot, chopped

pinch of paprika

2 tsp finely chopped fresh thyme

1 egg

salt and pepper

fresh thyme sprigs, to garnish

TOMATO RELISH

150 ml/5 fl oz passata

2 tsp creamed horseradish

1 Preheat the oven to 230°C/450°F/ Gas Mark 8. To make the tomato relish, mix the passata and creamed horseradish together in a small bowl. Cover and set aside until required.

2 Put the chopped onion, garlic and 2 teaspoons of water in a small saucepan and simmer over a low heat for 5 minutes. Increase the heat, bring to the boil and cook until all the water has evaporated. Remove from the heat.

3 Meanwhile, tear the bread into pieces and place in a small bowl. Add enough cold water just to cover and leave to soak for 5 minutes. Squeeze the excess water from the bread and place in a bowl with the minced beef, onion and garlic mixture, beetroot, paprika, thyme and egg. Season to taste with salt and pepper and mix thoroughly.

4 Form the meatball mixture into 24 small balls between the palms of your hands. Thread 3 balls onto each of 8 skewers and place on a baking sheet. Bake the skewers in the preheated oven for 10 minutes, or until well browned. Transfer to a serving dish, garnish with a few sprigs of fresh thyme and serve with the tomato relish.

Lamb Biriyani

For an authentic finishing touch, garnish with crisply fried onion rings, toasted slivered almonds and chopped pistachio nuts.

NUTRITIONAL INFORMATION

Calories	668	Sugars	........16g
Protein	........41g	Fat	..........35g
Carbohydrate	...78g	Saturates	......15g

 3½ hrs   50 mins

SERVES 6–8

INGREDIENTS

900 g/2 lb boned lean leg or shoulder of lamb, cut into 2.5 cm/1 inch cubes

6 garlic cloves, finely chopped

4 cm/1½ inch piece of fresh root ginger, finely chopped

1 tbsp ground cinnamon

1 tbsp green cardamom pods, crushed

1 tsp whole cloves

2 tsp coriander seeds, crushed

2 tsp cumin seeds, crushed

½ tsp ground turmeric (optional)

2 fresh green chillies, chopped

grated rind and juice of 1 lime

1 bunch of fresh coriander, finely chopped

1 bunch of fresh mint, finely chopped

125 ml/4 fl oz natural yogurt

8 tbsp ghee, butter or vegetable oil

4 onions, 3 thinly sliced and 1 chopped

600 g/1 lb 5 oz basmati rice

2 cinnamon sticks, broken

½ nutmeg, freshly grated

3–4 tbsp raisins

1.2 litres/2 pints chicken stock

225 ml/8 fl oz hot milk

1 tsp saffron threads, lightly crushed

salt and pepper

1 Combine the lamb, garlic, spices, lime rind and juice and 2 tablespoons each of coriander and mint and yogurt. Set aside to marinate for 2–3 hours.

2 Heat half the fat in a large frying pan. Cook the sliced onions for 8 minutes until lightly browned. Add the meat and any juices. Season to taste. Stir in 225 ml/ 8 fl oz water and simmer for 18–20 minutes until the lamb is cooked.

3 Meanwhile, heat the remaining fat in a flameproof casserole. Add the chopped onion and cook for 2 minutes until soft. Add the rice and cook, stirring for 3–4 minutes until well coated. Add the cinnamon, nutmeg, raisins and stock. Bring to the boil, stirring once or twice, and season with salt and pepper. Simmer covered, over a low heat for 12 minutes until the liquid is reduced, but the rice is still a little firm.

4 Pour the hot milk over the saffron stand for 10 minutes. Remove the rice from the heat and stir in the saffron-milk. Fold in the lamb mixture. Cover and bake in a preheated oven, 350°C/180°F/ Gas Mark 4, until the rice is cooked.

Pork Stroganoff

Tender, lean pork, cooked in a tasty, rich tomato sauce is flavoured with the extra tang of natural yogurt.

NUTRITIONAL INFORMATION

Calories 223   Sugars 7g
Protein ....22g   Fat 10g
Carbohydrate ...12g   Saturates 3g

2¼ hrs   30 mins

SERVES 4

INGREDIENTS

350 g/12 oz lean pork fillet

tbsp vegetable oil

medium onion, chopped

garlic cloves, crushed

25 g/1 oz plain flour

tbsp tomato purée

425 ml/15 fl oz Fresh Chicken or Vegetable
  stock (see pages 8–9)

125 g/4½ oz button mushrooms, sliced

large green pepper, deseeded and diced

½ tsp ground nutmeg

tbsp low-fat natural yogurt,
  plus extra to serve

salt and pepper

white rice, freshly boiled, to serve

ground nutmeg, to garnish

1 Trim away any excess fat and silver skin from the pork, then cut the meat into slices 1 cm/½ inch thick.

2 Heat the oil in a large saucepan and gently fry the pork, onion and garlic for 4–5 minutes until they are lightly browned.

3 Stir in the flour and tomato purée, pour in the stock and stir to mix thoroughly.

4 Add the mushrooms, green pepper, seasoning and nutmeg. Bring to the boil, cover and simmer for 20 minutes until the pork is tender and cooked through.

5 Remove the saucepan from the heat and then stir in the yogurt.

6 Serve the pork and sauce on a bed of rice with an extra spoonful of yogurt, and garnish with a dusting of ground nutmeg.

COOK'S TIP

You can buy ready-made stock from leading supermarkets. Although more expensive, they are more nutritious than stock cubes, which are high in salt and artificial flavourings.

Caribbean Pork

Serve these tasty marinated pork chops with a coconut-flavoured savoury rice and accompanied with sweet potatoes.

NUTRITIONAL INFORMATION

Calories 740   Sugars 33g
Protein . . . . .39g   Fat 27g
Carbohydrate . . .78g   Saturates 12g

   2¼ hrs   20 mins

SERVES 4

I N G R E D I E N T S

4 pork loin chops

4 tbsp dark muscovado sugar

4 tbsp orange or pineapple juice

2 tbsp Jamaican rum

1 tbsp desiccated coconut

½ tsp ground cinnamon

mixed salad leaves, to serve

C O C O N U T   R I C E

225 g/8 oz basmati rice

450 ml/16 fl oz water

150 ml/5 fl oz coconut milk

4 tbsp raisins

4 tbsp roasted peanuts or cashew nuts

salt and pepper

2 tbsp desiccated coconut, toasted

VARIATION

These pork chops are delicious served with barbecued pineapple slices. Sprinkle the pineapple with dark muscovado sugar and cinnamon. Barbecue over hot coals for about 5 minutes, turning once, until piping hot.

1 Trim any excess fat from the pork and place it in a , non-metallic dish.

2 Combine the sugar, fruit juice, rum, coconut and cinnamon in a bowl, stirring until the sugar dissolves. Pour the mixture over the pork and set aside to marinate in the refrigerator for at least 2 hours or preferably overnight.

3 Remove the pork, reserving the marinade for basting. Barbecue over hot coals for 15–20 minutes, basting with the marinade.

4 Meanwhile, make the coconut rice Rinse the rice under cold water, plac it in a pan with the water and coconu milk and gradually bring to the boil. Sti cover and reduce the heat. Simmer gent for 12 minutes or until the rice is tende and the liquid has been absorbed. Fluff u with a fork.

5 Stir the raisins and nuts into the ric season with salt and pepper to tast and sprinkle with the coconut. Transfer th pork and rice to warm serving plates an serve with the mixed salad leaves.

Ham & Pineapple Kebabs

This traditional and much-loved combination of flavours always works well on the barbecue.

NUTRITIONAL INFORMATION

Calories	426	Sugars	........11g
Protein	........31g	Fat	..........29g
Carbohydrate	....11g	Saturates	......13g

🧊 15 mins   🕐 8 mins

SERVES 4

INGREDIENTS

450 g/1 lb thick ham steak

425 g/15 oz can pineapple pieces in natural juice

225 g/8 oz firm Brie, chilled

2 tbsp sunflower oil

1 garlic clove, crushed

1 tbsp lemon juice

½ tsp ground nutmeg

¼ tsp ground cloves

pepper

cooked rice, to serve

1 Cut the ham into even-size chunks. Place the chunks in a pan of boiling water and simmer for 5 minutes.

2 Drain the pineapple pieces and reserve 3 tablespoons of the juice. Cut the chilled cheese into large chunks.

3 To make the baste, combine the pineapple juice, oil, garlic, lemon juice, nutmeg, cloves and pepper to taste in a small screw-top jar and shake until well combined. Set aside until required.

4 Remove the ham from the pan with a draining spoon. Thread the ham on to skewers, alternating with the pineapple and cheese pieces.

5 Barbecue the kebabs over warm coals, turning and basting frequently with the oil and pineapple juice mixture, for 2–4 minutes on each side until the pineapple and ham are hot and the cheese is just beginning to melt. Do not overcook, otherwise the cheese will become runny and the kebabs will become a mess; allow enough time to reheat the ham and for the pineapple to warm through.

6 Serve the kebabs on a bed of cooked rice.

Saucy Sausages

Although there is much more to barbecues than sausages, they can make a welcome appearance from time to time.

NUTRITIONAL INFORMATION

Calories 369   Sugars 18g
Protein . . . . .15g   Fat 24g
Carbohydrate . . .25g   Saturates 7g

10 mins   35 mins

SERVES 4

INGREDIENTS

2 tbsp sunflower oil

1 large onion, chopped

2 garlic cloves, chopped

225 g/8 oz can chopped tomatoes

1 tbsp Worcestershire sauce

2 tbsp brown fruity sauce

2 tbsp light muscovado sugar

4 tbsp white wine vinegar

½ tsp mild chilli powder

¼ tsp mustard powder

dash of Tabasco sauce

450 g/1 lb sausages

salt and pepper

bread finger rolls, to serve

COOK'S TIP

Choose any well-flavoured sausages for this recipe. Lincolnshire sausages are a good choice as are Cumberland sausages. Venison sausages have a good, gamey flavour and taste wonderful cooked on the barbecue.

1 To make the sauce, heat the oil in a small pan and cook the onion and garlic for 4–5 minutes until softened and just beginning to brown.

2 Add the tomatoes, Worcestershire sauce, brown fruity sauce, sugar, wine vinegar, chilli powder, mustard powder, Tabasco sauce and salt and pepper to taste to the pan and bring to the boil.

3 Reduce the heat and simmer gently for 10–15 minutes until the sauce

begins to thicken slightly. Stir occasionall so that the sauce does not burn and stic to the bottom of the pan. Set aside an keep warm until required.

4 Barbecue the sausages over hot coal for 10–15 minutes, turning frequentl Do not prick them with a fork or the fa will run out and cause a fire.

5 Insert the sausages into the brea rolls and serve immediately with th barbecue sauce.

Pork & Sage Kebabs

The pork mince mixture is shaped into meatballs and threaded on to skewers. It has a slightly sweet flavour that is popular with children.

NUTRITIONAL INFORMATION

Calories	96	Sugars	.........0g
Protein	.........8g	Fat	...........7g
Carbohydrate	....2g	Saturates	.......2g

🧊 50 mins   🕐 8–10 mins

SERVES 12

INGREDIENTS

450 g/1 lb pork mince

25 g/1 oz fresh breadcrumbs

1 small onion, very finely chopped

1 tbsp chopped fresh sage

2 tbsp apple sauce

¼ tsp ground nutmeg

salt and pepper

BASTE

3 tbsp olive oil

1 tbsp lemon juice

TO SERVE

6 small pitta breads

mixed salad leaves

6 tbsp thick, natural yogurt

1 Place the minced pork in a mixing bowl with the breadcrumbs, onion, sage, apple sauce and nutmeg. Season with salt and pepper to taste. Mix until the ingredients are well combined.

2 Using your hands, shape the mixture into small balls about the size of large marbles. Place on a plate, cover with clingfilm and chill in the refrigerator for at least 30 minutes.

3 Meanwhile, soak 12 small wooden skewers in cold water for at least 30 minutes. Thread the pork meatballs on to the skewers. Cover with clingfilm and set aside in the refrigerator until you are ready to cook.

4 To make the baste, combine the olive oil and lemon juice in a small bowl, whisking with a fork until the mixture is well blended.

5 Barbecue the kebabs over hot coals for 8–10 minutes, turning and basting frequently with the lemon and oil mixture, until the meat is golden brown and cooked through.

6 Line the pitta breads with the salad leaves and spoon over some of the yogurt. Serve with the kebabs.

Pork Balls with Mint Sauce

Made with lean minced pork, the balls are first stir-fried, then braised in the wok with stock and pickled walnuts to give a tangy flavour.

NUTRITIONAL INFORMATION

Calories 318   Sugars 2g
Protein . . . . .30g   Fat 20g
Carbohydrate . . . .6g   Saturates 5g

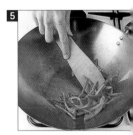

 5 mins   🕐 25 mins

SERVES 4

I N G R E D I E N T S

500 g/1 lb 2 oz lean minced pork

40 g/1½ oz fine fresh white breadcrumbs

½ tsp ground allspice

1 garlic clove, crushed

2 tbsp chopped fresh mint

1 egg, beaten

2 tbsp sunflower oil

1 red pepper, deseeded and thinly sliced

250 ml/9 fl oz chicken stock

4 pickled walnuts, sliced

salt and pepper

fresh mint, to garnish

rice or Chinese noodles, to serve

1 Combine the minced pork, breadcrumbs, allspice, garlic and half the chopped mint in a mixing bowl. Season to taste with salt and pepper, then bind together with the beaten egg.

2 Shape the meat mixture into 20 small balls with your hands, damping your hands if it is easier for shaping.

3 Heat the sunflower oil in a wok or heavy-based frying pan, swirling the oil around until really hot, then stir-fry the pork balls for about 4-5 minutes or until browned all over.

4 Remove the pork balls from the wok with a draining spoon as they are ready and drain thoroughly on absorbent kitchen paper.

5 Pour off all but 1 tablespoon of fat and oil from the wok or frying pan, then add the red pepper slices and stir-fry for 2-3 minutes or until they begin to soften, but not colour.

6 Add the chicken stock and bring to the boil. Season well with salt and pepper and return the pork balls to the wok, stirring well to coat in the sauce.

Simmer for 7-10 minutes, turning the pork balls from time to time.

7 Add the remaining chopped mint and the pickled walnuts to the wok and continue to simmer for 2-3 minutes, turning the pork balls regularly to coat them in the sauce.

8 Adjust the seasoning and serve the pork balls with rice or Chinese noodles or with a stir-fried vegetable dish, and garnished with sprigs of fresh mint.

Pork Fry with Vegetables

This is a very simple dish which lends itself to almost any combination of vegetables that you have to hand.

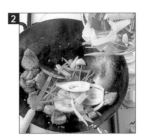

NUTRITIONAL INFORMATION

Calories	216	Sugars	.........3g
Protein	........19g	Fat	..........12g
Carbohydrate	....5g	Saturates	.......3g

5 mins   15 mins

SERVES 4

INGREDIENTS

350 g/12 oz lean pork fillet, thinly sliced

2 tbsp vegetable oil

2 garlic cloves, crushed

1 cm/½ inch piece of fresh root ginger, cut into slivers

1 carrot, cut into thin strips

1 red pepper, deseeded and diced

1 fennel bulb, sliced

25 g/1 oz water chestnuts, halved

85 g/3 oz beansprouts

2 tbsp Chinese rice wine

300 ml/ 10 fl oz pork or chicken stock

pinch of dark brown sugar

1 tsp cornflour

2 tsp water

1 Heat the oil in a preheated wok. Add the garlic, ginger and pork. Stir-fry for 1–2 minutes until the meat is sealed.

2 Add the carrot, pepper, fennel and water chestnuts and stir-fry for about 2–3 minutes.

3 Add the beansprouts and stir-fry for 1 minute. Remove the pork and vegetables, set aside and keep warm.

4 Add the Chinese rice wine, pork or chicken stock and sugar to the wok. Blend the cornflour to a smooth paste with the water and stir it into the sauce. Bring to the boil, stirring constantly until thickened and clear.

5 Return the meat and vegetables to the wok and cook for 1–2 minutes until heated through and coated with the sauce. Serve immediately.

VARIATION
Use dry sherry instead of the Chinese rice wine if you have difficulty obtaining it.

Stir-fried Pork with Pasta

This delicious dish, with its hint of Thai cuisine, will certainly get the taste buds tingling – and it's ready in next to no time.

NUTRITIONAL INFORMATION

Calories 751	Sugars 10g
Protein 37g	Fat 27g
Carbohydrate . . .96g	Saturates 8g

 10 mins   15 mins

SERVES 4

I N G R E D I E N T S

3 tbsp sesame oil

350 g/12 oz pork fillet, cut into thin strips

450 g/1 lb dried taglioni

8 shallots, sliced

2 garlic cloves, finely chopped

2.5 cm/1 inch piece of fresh root ginger, grated

1 fresh green chilli, finely chopped

1 red pepper, deseeded and thinly sliced

1 green pepper, deseeded and thinly sliced

3 courgettes, thinly sliced

2 tbsp ground almonds

1 tsp ground cinnamon

1 tbsp oyster sauce

55 g/2 oz creamed coconut, grated

salt and pepper

1   Heat the sesame oil in a preheated wok. Season the pork with salt and pepper to taste, add to the wok and stir-fry for 5 minutes.

2   Meanwhile, bring a large pan of lightly salted water to the boil. Add the taglioni, bring back to the boil and cook for about 10 minutes until just tender, but still firm to the bite. Drain, set the pasta aside and keep warm.

3   Add the shallots, garlic, ginger and chilli to the wok and stir-fry for 2 minutes. Add the peppers and courgette and stir-fry for 1 minute.

4   Finally, add the ground almonds, cinnamon, oyster sauce and creamed coconut to the wok and stir-fry for about 1 minute.

5   Transfer the taglioni to a warmed serving dish. Top with the stir-fry and serve immediately.

COOK'S TIP

Creamed coconut is available from Chinese and Asian food stores and some large supermarkets. It is sold in the form of compressed blocks and adds a concentrated coconut flavour to the dish.

Pork with Orange Sauce

In this recipe, the pork is garnished with gremolata, a popular Italian seasoning mixture with a citrus tang, for a refreshing summery flavour.

NUTRITIONAL INFORMATION

Calories	204	Sugars	.........1g
Protein	........26g	Fat	..........10g
Carbohydrate	....2g	Saturates	.......3g

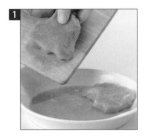

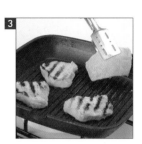

3¼ hrs   10 mins

SERVES 4

INGREDIENTS

4 tbsp freshly squeezed orange juice

4 tbsp red wine vinegar

2 garlic cloves, finely chopped

pepper

4 pork steaks, trimmed of all visible fat

olive oil, for brushing

GREMOLATA

3 tbsp finely chopped fresh parsley

grated rind of 1 lime

grated rind of ½ lemon

1 garlic clove, very finely chopped

1 Mix the orange juice, vinegar and garlic together in a shallow, non-metallic dish and season to taste with pepper. Add the pork, turning to coat. Cover and leave in the refrigerator to marinate for up to 3 hours.

2 Meanwhile, mix all the gremolata ingredients together in a small mixing bowl, cover with clingfilm and leave to chill in the refrigerator until required.

3 Heat a non-stick griddle pan and brush lightly with olive oil. Remove the pork from the marinade, reserving the marinade. Add the pork to the pan and cook over medium–high heat for 5 minutes on each side, or until the juices run clear when the meat is pierced with a skewer.

4 Meanwhile, pour the marinade into a small saucepan and simmer over a medium heat for 5 minutes, or until slightly thickened. Transfer the pork to a serving dish, pour the orange sauce over it and sprinkle with the gremolata. Serve immediately.

VARIATION

This dish would work equally well with chicken breast portions. Remove the skin from the cooked chicken before serving.

Potato, Sausage & Onion Pie

This is a delicious supper dish for all of the family. Use good-quality, preferably low-fat, herb sausages for a really tasty pie.

NUTRITIONAL INFORMATION

Calories ....399 Sugars 6g
Protein ....14g Fat 22g
Carbohydrate ...39g Saturates 11g

5–10 mins   40 mins

SERVES 4

I N G R E D I E N T S

2 large waxy potatoes, unpeeled and sliced

2 tbsp butter

4 thick pork and herb sausages

1 leek, sliced

2 garlic cloves, crushed

150 ml/5 fl oz vegetable stock

150 ml/5 fl oz dry cider or apple juice

2 tbsp chopped fresh sage

2 tbsp cornflour

4 tbsp water

85 g/3 oz mature cheese, grated

salt and pepper

1 Cook the sliced potatoes in a saucepan of boiling water for 10 minutes. Drain and set aside.

2 Meanwhile, melt the butter in a large, heavy-based frying pan and cook the sausages over a medium heat for about 8–10 minutes, turning them frequently so that they brown on all sides. Remove the sausages from the pan and cut them into thick slices.

3 Add the leek, garlic and sausage slices to the pan and cook for 2–3 minutes.

4 Add the vegetable stock, cider or apple juice and sage. Season with salt and pepper to taste.

5 Blend the cornflour with the water to a smooth paste. Stir it into the pan and bring to the boil, stirring constantly until the sauce is thick and clear. Spoon the mixture evenly into the base of a deep pie dish.

6 Arrange the potato slices on top of the sausage mixture to cover it completely. Season with salt and pepper to taste and sprinkle the grated cheese over the top.

7 Cook in a preheated oven, 190°C/375°F/Gas Mark 5, for 25–30 minutes or until the potatoes are cooked and the cheese is golden brown. Serve hot.

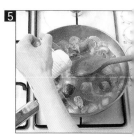

Nasi Goreng

A meal in itself, this mouthwatering fried rice dish is bursting with the exotic flavours of Indonesia. The perfect supper dish!

NUTRITIONAL INFORMATION

Calories	504	Sugars	.........8g
Protein	........49g	Fat	..........15g
Carbohydrate	...47g	Saturates	.......4g

🍚 15 mins   🕐 20 mins

SERVES 4

I N G R E D I E N T S

large onion, chopped

–3 garlic cloves

tsp shrimp paste

fresh red chillies, deseeded and chopped

bout 125 ml/4 fl oz vegetable oil

eggs, lightly beaten

50 g/1 lb beef rump steak, about 1 cm/
½ inch thick

carrots, cut into thin batons

75 g/6 oz Chinese long beans or green
beans, cut into 2.5 cm/1 inch pieces

small spring onions, cut into 1 cm/
½ inch pieces

50 g/9 oz raw shelled prawns

50 g/1 lb 10 oz cooked long grain white
rice, at room temperature

tbsp dark soy sauce

TO GARNISH

tbsp ready-fried onion flakes

0 cm/4 inch piece cucumber, deseeded
and cut into thin sticks

tbsp chopped fresh coriander

1 Put the onion, garlic, shrimp paste and chillies into a food processor and rocess until a paste forms. Add a little oil nd process until smooth. Set aside.

2 Heat 1–2 tablespoons oil in a large, non-stick frying pan. Pour in the egg to form a thin layer and cook for 1 minute until just set. Turn and cook for 5 seconds on the other side. Slide out and cut in half. Roll up each half, then slice into 5 mm/¼ inch wide strips. Set aside.

3 Heat 2 tablespoons oil in the same pan over a high heat and add the steak. Cook for 2 minutes on each side to brown and seal, but do not cook completely. Cool, then cut into thin strips and reserve.

4 Heat 2 tablespoons oil in a large wok over a medium-high heat. Add the reserved chilli paste and cook, stirring frequently, for about 3 minutes. Add 2 tablespoons oil, the carrots and long or green beans. Stir-fry for about 2 minutes. Add the spring onions, prawns and beef strips and stir-fry until the prawns have turned pink.

5 Stir in the rice, half the sliced omelette, 2 tablespoons soy sauce and 50 ml/2 fl oz water. Cover and steam for 1 minute. Spoon into a warmed serving dish, top with the remaining omelette and drizzle with the remaining soy sauce. Sprinkle with the onion flakes, cucumber and coriander and serve immediately.

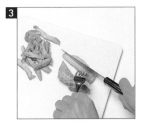  

Honey-glazed Duck

Chinese-style duck is incredibly easy to prepare, but makes an impressive and truly delicious main course for a dinner party.

NUTRITIONAL INFORMATION

Calories	230	Sugars	.........9g
Protein	........23g	Fat	...........9g
Carbohydrate	...14g	Saturates	.......3g

2¼ hrs   30 mins

SERVES 4

I N G R E D I E N T S

1 tsp dark soy sauce

2 tbsp clear honey

1 tsp garlic vinegar

2 garlic cloves, crushed

1 tsp ground star anise

2 tsp cornflour

2 tsp water

2 large boneless duck breasts, about 225g/8 oz each

TO GARNISH

celery leaves

cucumber wedges

snipped chives

1 Mix the soy sauce, honey, garlic vinegar, garlic and star anise. Blend the cornflour with the water to form a smooth paste and stir it into the mixture.

COOK'S TIP

If the duck begins to burn slightly while it is cooking in the oven, cover with foil. Check that the duck breasts are cooked through by inserting the point of a sharp knife into the thickest part of the flesh – the juices should run clear.

2 Place the duck breasts in a shallow ovenproof dish. Brush with the soy marinade, turning them to coat completely. Cover and set aside to marinate in the refrigerator for at least 2 hours, or overnight.

3 Remove the duck from the marinade and cook in a preheated oven, 220°C/425°F/Gas Mark 7, for 20–25 minutes, basting frequently with the glaze.

4 Remove the duck from the oven and transfer to a preheated grill Grill for about 3–4 minutes to caramelise the top without charring.

5 Remove the duck from the grill pan and cut it into thin slices. Arrange the duck slices on a warmed serving dish garnish with celery leaves, cucumber wedges and snipped chives and serve immediately.

Grilled Minced Lamb

This tasty dish with a hint of spice is a good way to perk up a dreary week, and it is quick enough to prepare after a busy day at work.

NUTRITIONAL INFORMATION

Calories 341   Sugars 5g
Protein . . . . .25g   Fat 24g
Carbohydrate . . . .8g   Saturates 6g

 10 mins   40 mins

SERVES 4

I N G R E D I E N T S

5 tbsp oil

2 onions, sliced

450 g/1 lb minced lamb

2 tbsp yogurt

1 tsp chilli powder

1 tsp finely chopped fresh root ginger

1 tsp fresh garlic, crushed

1 tsp salt

1½ tsp garam masala

½ tsp ground allspice

2 fresh green chillies

fresh coriander leaves

salad leaves, to serve

TO GARNISH

fresh coriander leaves, chopped

1 lemon, cut into wedges

1 Heat the oil in a pan. Add the sliced onions and cook over a low heat until golden brown.

2 Place the minced lamb in a large bowl. Add the yogurt, chilli powder, ginger, garlic, salt, garam masala and ground allspice and mix to combine. Add the lamb mixture to the fried onions and stir-fry for 10–15 minutes. Remove the mixture from the heat and set aside.

3 Meanwhile, place the chillies and half of the coriander leaves in a food processor and process. Alternatively, finely chop the chillies and coriander with a sharp knife. Set aside until required.

4 Put the minced lamb mixture in a food processor and process. Alternatively, place in a large bowl and mash with a fork. Mix the lamb mixture with the chillies and coriander and blend well.

5 Transfer the mixture to a shallow heatproof dish. Cook under a preheated medium-hot grill for 10–15 minutes, moving the mixture about with a fork. Watch it carefully to prevent it from burning.

6 Garnish with coriander leaves and lemon wedges and serve with salad leaves.

Minced Lamb with Peas

This version of a useful stand-by is livened up with chillies
and ginger and flavoured with garlic and coriander.

NUTRITIONAL INFORMATION

Calories	357	Sugars	.........3g
Protein	........25g	Fat	..........26g
Carbohydrate	....6g	Saturates	.......6g

 5 mins   🕐 25 mins

SERVES 4

I N G R E D I E N T S

6 tbsp oil

1 medium onion, sliced

3 fresh green chillies

1 bunch of fresh coriander

2 tomatoes, chopped

1 tsp salt

1 tsp finely chopped fresh root ginger

1 tsp fresh garlic, crushed

1 tsp chilli powder

450 g/1 lb lean minced lamb

100 g/3½ oz peas

1 Heat the oil in a medium-sized pan. Add the onion slices and cook, stirring constantly, until golden brown.

2 Add 2 of the green chillies, half of the fresh coriander leaves and the chopped tomatoes to the pan and reduce the heat to a gentle simmer.

3 Add the salt, ginger, garlic and chilli powder to the pan and stir thoroughly to combine.

4 Add the minced lamb to the pan and stir-fry the mixture for 7–10 minutes until the meat turns brown.

5 Stir in the peas and cook, stirring occasionally, for 3–4 minutes.

6 Transfer the lamb and pea mixture to warmed serving plates and garnish with the remaining chopped green chilli and the fresh coriander leaves.

COOK'S TIP

It is usually said that most of the heat of chillies is in the seeds. In fact, it is in the flesh surrounding the seeds. Deseeding the chilli removes most of this fiery flesh.

Lamb Tagine

This is a typical Moroccan mixture of meat, vegetables and apricots, flavoured with plenty of fresh herbs and spices.

NUTRITIONAL INFORMATION

Calories 267	Sugars 21g	
Protein 21g	Fat 11g	
Carbohydrate ...22g	Saturates 4g	

🧈 10 mins   🕐 1³/₄ hrs

SERVES 4

INGREDIENTS

1 tbsp sunflower or corn oil

1 onion, chopped

350 g/12 oz boneless lamb, trimmed of all visible fat and cut into 2.5-cm/1-inch cubes

1 garlic clove, finely chopped

600 ml/1 pint vegetable stock

grated rind and juice of 1 orange

1 tsp clear honey

1 cinnamon stick

1-cm/½-inch piece fresh root ginger, finely chopped

1 aubergine

4 tomatoes, peeled and chopped

115 g/4 oz no-soak dried apricots

2 tbsp chopped fresh coriander

salt and pepper

freshly cooked couscous, to serve

1 Heat the oil in a heavy-based frying pan or flameproof casserole. Add the onion and lamb and cook over a medium heat, stirring frequently, for 5 minutes, or until the meat is lightly browned all over. Add the garlic, vegetable stock, orange rind and juice, honey, cinnamon stick and ginger. Bring to the boil, then reduce the heat, cover and simmer for 45 minutes.

2 Using a sharp knife, halve the aubergine lengthways and slice thinly. Add to the frying pan with the chopped tomatoes and apricots. Cover the pan and cook for a further 45 minutes, or until the lamb is tender.

3 Stir in the coriander, season to taste with salt and pepper and serve immediately, straight from the frying pan, with the freshly cooked couscous.

COOK'S TIP

Large aubergines benefit from being sprinkled with salt and left to stand for 30 minutes to remove the bitter juices. Smaller aubergines can be used without salting.

Shish Kebabs

Barbecued lean lamb, vegetables and salad are tucked inside toasted pitta bread for an irresistible light meal.

NUTRITIONAL INFORMATION

Calories	296	Sugars	.........3g
Protein	........24g	Fat	..........21g
Carbohydrate	....4g	Saturates	.......6g

2½ hrs   8–10 mins

SERVES 4

INGREDIENTS

450 g/1 lb lean lamb

1 red onion, cut into wedges

1 green pepper, deseeded

MARINADE

1 onion

4 tbsp olive oil

grated rind and juice of ½ lemon

1 garlic clove, crushed

½ tsp dried oregano

½ tsp dried thyme

TO SERVE

4 pitta breads

crisp lettuce leaves, shredded

2 tomatoes, sliced

chilli sauce (optional)

1 Trim any fat from the lamb and cut into large, even-size chunks.

2 To make the marinade, grate the onion or chop it very finely in a food processor. Remove the juice by squeezing the onion between two plates set over a small bowl. Combine the onion juice with the remaining marinade ingredients in a non-metallic dish and add the meat. Toss the meat in the marinade to coat, cover with clingfilm and set aside to marinate in the refrigerator for at least 2 hours or overnight.

3 Divide the onion wedges in half. Cut the green pepper into chunks.

4 Remove the meat from the marinade, reserving the marinade for basting. Thread the meat on to skewers, alternating with the onion and pieces of green pepper. Barbecue for 8–10 minutes, turning and basting with the reserved marinade frequently.

5 Meanwhile, toast the pitta breads on the side of the barbecue until warmed through. To serve, split open the pitta breads and fill with a little shredded lettuce and the meat and vegetables. Top with tomatoes and chilli sauce, if using, and serve immediately.

VARIATION

These kebabs are delicious served with saffron-flavoured rice. For easy saffron rice, simply use saffron stock cubes when cooking the rice.

Pot Roasted Leg of Lamb

This dish from the Abruzzi region of Italy uses a slow cooking method. The meat absorbs the flavourings and becomes very tender.

NUTRITIONAL INFORMATION

Calories 734	Sugars 6g	
Protein 71g	Fat 42g	
Carbohydrate 7g	Saturates 15g	

35 mins   3 hrs

SERVES 4

INGREDIENTS

1.6 kg/3 lb 8 oz leg of lamb

3–4 fresh rosemary sprigs

115 g/4 oz streaky bacon rashers

4 tbsp olive oil

2–3 garlic cloves, crushed

2 onions, sliced

2 carrots, sliced

2 celery sticks, sliced

300 ml/10 fl oz dry white wine

1 tbsp tomato purée

300 ml/10 fl oz stock

350 g/12 oz tomatoes, peeled, quartered and deseeded

1 tbsp chopped fresh parsley

1 tbsp chopped fresh oregano or marjoram

salt and pepper

fresh rosemary sprigs, to garnish

1 Wipe the joint of lamb all over, trimming off any excess fat, then season with salt and pepper, rubbing well in. Lay the sprigs of rosemary over the lamb, cover evenly with the bacon rashers and tie in place with string.

2 Heat the oil in a frying pan and fry the lamb for about 10 minutes, turning several times. Remove from the pan.

3 Transfer the oil from the frying pan to a large flameproof casserole and cook the garlic and onion for 3–4 minutes until beginning to soften. Add the carrots and celery and cook for a few minutes longer.

4 Lay the lamb on top of the vegetables and press down to partly submerge. Pour the wine over the lamb, add the tomato purée and simmer for about 3–4 minutes. Add the stock, tomatoes and herbs and season to taste with salt and pepper. Bring back to the boil for a further 3–4 minutes.

5 Cover the casserole tightly and cook in a moderate oven, 180°C/350°F/Gas Mark 4, for 2–2½ hours until very tender.

6 Remove the lamb from the casserole and if preferred, take off the bacon and herbs along with the string. Keep warm. Strain the juices, skimming off any excess fat, and serve in a jug. The vegetables may be put around the joint or in a serving dish. Garnish with fresh sprigs of rosemary.

Veal Chops with Salsa Verde

This vibrant green Italian sauce adds a touch of Mediterranean flavour to any simply cooked meat or seafood.

NUTRITIONAL INFORMATION

Calories	.481	Sugars	.1g
Protein	.41g	Fat	.34g
Carbohydrate	.2g	Saturates	.5g

10 mins 5 mins

SERVES 4

INGREDIENTS

4 veal chops, such as loin chops, about 225 g/8 oz each and 2 cm/¾ inch thick

garlic-flavoured olive oil, for brushing

salt and pepper

fresh oregano or basil leaves, to garnish

SALSA VERDE

55 g/2 oz fresh flat leaf parsley leaves

3 canned anchovy fillets in oil, drained

1½ tsp capers in brine, rinsed and drained

1 shallot, finely chopped

1 garlic clove, halved, green core removed, and chopped

1 tbsp lemon juice

6 large fresh basil leaves or ¾ tsp freeze-dried basil

2 fresh oregano sprigs or ½ tsp dried oregano

125 ml/4 fl oz extra virgin olive oil

1 To make the salsa verde, put the parsley, anchovies, capers, shallot, garlic, lemon juice, basil and oregano in a blender or food processor and process until they are thoroughly chopped and blended.

2 With the motor running, add the oil through the top or feeder tube and process until thickened. Season with pepper to taste. Scrape to a bowl, cover with clingfilm and chill in the refrigerator.

3 Lightly brush the veal chops with olive oil and season to taste with salt and pepper. Place under a preheated grill and cook for about 3 minutes. Turn over, brush with more oil and grill for a further 2 minutes until cooked when tested with the tip of a knife.

4 Transfer the chops to warmed individual plates and spoon a little of the chilled salsa verde beside them. Garnish the chops with fresh oregano or basil and serve with the remaining salsa verde handed separately.

COOK'S TIP

The salsa verde will keep for up to 2 days in a covered container in the refrigerator. It is also fantastic served with grilled red mullet. Or use it to replace the pesto sauce in Mediterranean Monkfish (see page 748).

Citrus Osso Bucco

The orange and lemon rinds, together with fresh basil, give this traditional Italian dish a real southern flavour.

NUTRITIONAL INFORMATION

Calories	310	Sugars	.........4g
Protein	.......42g	Fat	...........6g
Carbohydrate	...16g	Saturates	.......2g

15 mins   1½ hrs

SERVES 6

INGREDIENTS

1–2 tbsp plain flour

6 meaty slices osso bucco

1 kg/2 lb 4 oz fresh tomatoes, peeled, deseeded and diced or 2 x 400 g/14 oz cans chopped tomatoes

1–2 tbsp olive oil

250 g/9 oz very finely chopped onions

250 g/9 oz finely diced carrots

225 ml/8 fl oz dry white wine

225 ml/8 fl oz veal stock

6 large basil leaves, torn

1 large garlic clove, very finely chopped

finely grated rind of 1 large lemon

finely grated rind of 1 orange

2 tbsp finely chopped fresh flat leaf parsley

salt and pepper

1 Put the flour in a plastic bag and season with salt and pepper. Add the osso bucco, a few pieces at a time, and shake until well coated. Remove and shake off the excess flour.

2 If using canned tomatoes, put them in a strainer and leave to drain.

3 Heat 1 tablespoon of the oil in a large flameproof casserole. Add the osso bucco and fry for 10 minutes on each slide until well browned. Remove from the pan.

4 Add 1–2 teaspoons more oil to the casserole if necessary. Add the onions and cook, stirring constantly, for about 5 minutes until soft. Stir in the carrots and cook until softened.

5 Add the tomatoes, wine, stock and basil and return the osso bucco to the pan. Bring to the boil, then lower the heat, cover and simmer for 1 hour. Check that the meat is tender with the tip of a knife. If not, continue cooking for 10 minutes and test again.

6 When the meat is tender, sprinkle with the garlic and lemon and orange rinds, re-cover and cook over a low heat for a further 10 minutes.

7 Taste and adjust the seasoning if necessary. Sprinkle with the parsley and serve immediately.

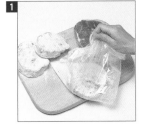

Basque Pork & Beans

Dried cannellini beans feature in many Italian, Spanish, French and Greek stews and casseroles, especially during the winter.

NUTRITIONAL INFORMATION

Calories	240	Sugars	.........6g
Protein	........30g	Fat	...........4g
Carbohydrate	...23g	Saturates	.......1g

15 mins   1½ hrs

SERVES 4–6

I N G R E D I E N T S

200 g/7 oz dried cannellini beans, soaked in cold water overnight

olive oil, for frying

600 g/1 lb 4 oz boneless leg of pork, cut into 5 cm/2 inch chunks

1 large onion, sliced

3 large garlic cloves, crushed

400 g/14 oz can chopped tomatoes

2 green peppers, deseeded and sliced

finely grated rind of 1 large orange

salt and pepper

finely chopped fresh parsley, to garnish

1 Drain the cannellini beans and put in a large pan with fresh water to cover. Bring to the boil and boil rapidly for 10 minutes. Lower the heat and simmer for 20 minutes. Drain and set aside.

VARIATIONS

Any leftover beans and peppers can be used as a pasta sauce. Add sliced and fried chorizo sausage for a spicier dish.

2 Add enough oil to cover the base of a frying pan in a very thin layer. Heat the oil over medium heat, add a few pieces of the pork and fry on all sides until brown. Remove from the pan and set aside. Repeat with the remaining pork.

3 Add 1 tablespoon oil to the frying pan, if necessary, then add the onion and cook for 3 minutes. Stir in the garlic and cook for a further 2 minutes. Return the pork to the pan.

4 Add the tomatoes and bring to the boil. Lower the heat, stir in the pepper slices, orange rind and the drained beans. Season with salt and pepper to taste.

5 Transfer the contents of the pan to a casserole. Cover the casserole and cook in a preheated oven, 180°C/350°F/Gas Mark 4, for 45 minutes until the beans and pork are tender. Sprinkle with chopped parsley and serve immediately straight from the casserole.

Country Pork with Onions

This rustic Mediterranean stew makes the most of inexpensive cuts that require slow cooking and robust flavouring.

NUTRITIONAL INFORMATION

Calories	335	Sugars	........10g
Protein	........35g	Fat	..........12g
Carbohydrate	...13g	Saturates	.......2g

🍖 15 mins   🕐 3¾–4¼ hrs

SERVES 4

INGREDIENTS

2 large pork hand and spring

2 large garlic cloves, sliced

3 tbsp olive oil

2 carrots, finely chopped

2 celery sticks, finely chopped

1 large onion, finely chopped

2 fresh thyme sprigs, broken into pieces

2 fresh rosemary sprigs, broken into pieces

1 large bay leaf

225 ml/8 fl oz dry white wine

225 ml/8 fl oz water

20 pickling onions

salt and pepper

roughly chopped fresh flat leaf parsley, to garnish

1 Using the tip of a sharp knife, make slits all over the pork and insert the garlic slices.

2 Heat 1 tablespoon of the oil in a flameproof casserole over a medium heat. Add the carrots, celery and onion and cook, stirring occasionally, for about 10 minutes until softened.

3 Place the pork on top of the vegetables. Sprinkle the thyme and rosemary over the meat. Add the bay leaf, wine and water and season with pepper.

4 Bring to the boil, then remove the casserole from the heat. Cover tightly and cook in a preheated oven, 160°C/325°F/Gas Mark 3, for 3½ hours or until the meat is very tender.

5 Meanwhile, put the onions in a bowl, pour over boiling water to cover and set aside for 1 minute. Drain, then slip off all the skins. Heat the remaining oil in a large, heavy-based frying pan. Add the onions, partially cover and cook over a low heat for 15 minutes, shaking the pan occasionally, until the onions are just starting to turn golden.

6 When the pork is tender, add the onions to the casserole and return to the oven for a further 15 minutes. Remove the pork and onions from the casserole and keep warm.

7 Using a large metal spoon, skim off as much fat as possible from the surface of the cooking liquid. Strain the cooking liquid into a bowl, pressing down lightly to extract the flavour; reserve the strained vegetables. Adjust the seasoning.

8 Cut the pork from the bones, if wished, then arrange on a serving platter with the onions and strained vegetables. Spoon the sauce over the meat and vegetables. Garnish with parsley.

Maltese Rabbit with Fennel

Rabbit is a popular ingredient in Malta. In some restaurants it features as the house speciality, rather than seafood as one might expect.

NUTRITIONAL INFORMATION

Calories	454	Sugars	.........3g
Protein	........36g	Fat	..........23g
Carbohydrate	...19g	Saturates	.......5g

15 mins   1¾ hrs

SERVES 4

I N G R E D I E N T S

5 tbsp olive oil

2 large fennel bulbs, sliced

2 carrots, diced

1 large garlic clove, crushed

1 tbsp fennel seeds

about 4 tbsp plain flour

2 wild rabbits, jointed

225 ml/8 fl oz dry white wine

225 ml/8 fl oz water

1 bouquet garni of 2 fresh flat leaf parsley sprigs, 1 fresh rosemary sprig and 1 bay leaf, tied in a 7.5 cm/3 inch piece of celery

salt and pepper

thick, crusty bread, to serve

TO GARNISH

finely chopped fresh flat leaf parsley or coriander

fresh rosemary sprigs

1 Heat 3 tablespoons of the olive oil in a large, flameproof casserole over a medium heat. Add the fennel and carrots and cook, stirring occasionally, for 5 minutes. Stir in the garlic and fennel seeds and cook for a further 2 minutes or until the fennel is tender. Remove the fennel and carrots from the casserole with a draining spoon and set aside.

2 Put the flour in a plastic bag and season with salt and pepper. Add 2 rabbit pieces and shake to lightly coat, then shake off any excess flour. Continue until all the pieces of rabbit are coated, adding more flour if necessary.

3 Add the remaining oil to the casserole. Fry the rabbit pieces for about 5 minutes on each side until golden brown, working in batches. Remove the rabbit from the casserole as it is cooked.

4 Pour in the wine and bring to the boil, stirring to scrape up all the sediment from the bottom. Return the rabbit pieces, fennel and carrots to the casserole and pour in the water. Add the bouquet garni and season with salt and pepper to taste.

5 Bring to the boil. Lower the heat, cover and simmer for about 1¼ hours until the rabbit is tender.

6 Discard the bouquet garni. Garnish with herbs and serve straight from the casserole with lots of bread to mop up the juices.

Azerbaijani Lamb Pilaf

This type of dish is popular in the Balkans, through Russia to the Middle East. The saffron and pomegranate juice give it an exotic air.

NUTRITIONAL INFORMATION

Calories	399	Sugars	. . . . .19g
Protein	. . . . .25g	Fat	. . . . .13g
Carbohydrate	. . .45g	Saturates	. . . . . . .4g

 10 mins   50 mins

SERVES 4–6

I N G R E D I E N T S

2–3 tbsp vegetable oil

650 g/1 lb 7 oz boneless lamb shoulder, cut into 2.5 cm/1 inch cubes

2 onions, coarsely chopped

1 tsp ground cumin

200 g/7 oz arborio, long grain or basmati rice

1 tbsp tomato purée

1 tsp saffron threads

100 ml/3½ fl oz pomegranate juice (see Cook's Tip)

850 ml/1½ pints lamb or chicken stock or water

115 g/4 oz dried apricots or prunes, ready soaked and halved

2 tbsp raisins

salt and pepper

TO SERVE

2 tbsp chopped fresh mint

2 tbsp chopped fresh watercress

1 Heat the oil in a large flameproof casserole or wide pan over a high heat. Add the lamb, in batches, and cook stirring and turning frequently, for about 7 minutes until lightly browned.

2 Add the onions, reduce the heat to medium-high and cook for about 2 minutes until beginning to soften. Add the cumin and rice and cook, stirring to coat, for about 2 minutes until the rice is translucent. Stir in the tomato purée and the saffron threads.

3 Add the pomegranate juice and stock and bring to the boil, stirring. Stir in the apricots or prunes and raisins. Reduce the heat to low, cover, and simmer for 20–25 minutes until the lamb and rice are tender and the liquid is absorbed.

4 To serve, season to taste, sprinkle the chopped mint and watercress over the pilaf and serve from the casserole.

COOK'S TIP

Pomegranate juice is available from Middle Eastern grocery stores. If you cannot find it, substitute unsweetened grape or apple juice.

Mumbar

This Middle Eastern dish is basically a long sausage coiled into a frying pan to simmer. The baharat, or spice mix, is a typical flavouring.

NUTRITIONAL INFORMATION

Calories 256   Sugars 3g
Protein ....25g   Fat 12g
Carbohydrate ...14g   Saturates 5g

25 mins   40 mins

SERVES 6–8

INGREDIENTS

100 g/3½ oz basmati rice

900 g/2 lb finely minced lamb

1 small onion, finely chopped

3–4 garlic cloves, crushed

1 bunch of fresh flat leaf parsley, finely chopped

1 bunch of fresh coriander finely chopped

2–3 tbsp tomato ketchup

1 tbsp vegetable oil

pared rind and juice of 1 lime

700 ml /1¼ pints hot lamb stock

salt and pepper

BAHARAT

2 tbsp black peppercorns

1 tbsp coriander seeds

2 tsp cloves

1½ tsp cumin seeds

1 tsp cardamom seeds

1 cinnamon stick, broken into small pieces

1 nutmeg

2 tbsp hot paprika

1 To make the baharat, grind the first 6 ingredients into a fine powder. Grate the whole nutmeg into the mix and stir in the paprika. Store in an airtight jar.

2 Bring a pan of salted water to the boil. Pour in the rice, return to the boil, then simmer until the rice is tender, but firm to the bite. Drain and rinse.

3 Place the lamb in a large bowl and break up with a fork. Add the onion, garlic, parsley, coriander, ketchup and 1 teaspoon of the baharat. Stir in the cooked rice and season to taste. Squeeze the mixture to make it paste-like.

4 Divide into 4–6 pieces and roll each into a sausage 2.5cm/1 inch thick. Brush a 23–25 cm/9–10 inch frying pan

with the oil. Starting in the centre of the pan, coil the sausage pieces, joining each piece, to form 1 long coiled sausage.

5 Press lightly to make an even layer then tuck the lime rind between the spaces of the coil. Add the lime juice, pour in the hot stock and cover with a heatproof plate to keep in place.

6 Bring to the boil, then simmer for about 10 minutes. Cover and cook for a further 15 minutes. Drain and slide the sausage on to a serving plate. Sprinkle with a little more of the baharat to serve.

Red Pork Curry

Thai food has become so popular in recent years that most ingredients can be found in your local supermarket.

NUTRITIONAL INFORMATION

Calories ....398 Sugars 12g
Protein ....38g Fat 9g
Carbohydrate ...47g Saturates 3g

 15 mins   45 mins

SERVES 4–6

I N G R E D I E N T S

900 g/2 lb boned pork shoulder, sliced

700 ml/1¼ pints coconut milk

2 fresh red chillies, deseeded and sliced

2 tbsp Thai fish sauce

2 tsp brown sugar

1 large red pepper, deseeded and sliced

6 kaffir lime leaves, shredded

½ bunch fresh mint leaves, shredded

½ bunch Thai basil leaves or Italian-style
   basil, shredded

cooked jasmine-scented or Thai fragrant
   rice, cooked and kept warm

R E D   C U R R Y   P A S T E

1 tbsp coriander seeds

2 tsp cumin seeds

2 tsp black or white peppercorns

1 tsp salt

5–8 dried hot red chillies

3–4 shallots, chopped

5–8 garlic cloves

5 cm/2 inch piece fresh galangal or root
   ginger root, coarsely chopped

2 tsp kaffir lime rind or 2 kaffir lime leaves

1 tbsp ground red chilli powder

1 tbsp shrimp paste

2 lemon grass stalks, thinly sliced

1 To make the red curry paste, grind the coriander seeds, cumin seeds, peppercorns and salt to a fine powder in a mortar with a pestle. Add the chillies, 1 at a time, according to taste, until ground.

2 Put the shallots, garlic, galangal or ginger, kaffir lime rind or leaves, chilli powder and shrimp paste in a food processor. Process for about 1 minute. Add the ground spices and process again. Adding water, a few drops at a time, continue to process until a thick paste forms. Scrape into a bowl and stir in the lemon grass.

3 Put about half the red curry paste in a large deep heavy-based frying pan with the pork. Cook over a medium heat, stirring gently, for 2–3 minutes until the pork is evenly coated and begins to brown.

4 Stir in the coconut milk and bring to the boil. Cook, stirring frequently, for about 10 minutes. Reduce the heat, stir in the chillies, Thai fish sauce and brown sugar and simmer for about 20 minutes. Add the red pepper and simmer for a further 10 minutes.

5 Chop the lime leaves and add to the curry with half the mint and basil. Transfer to a serving dish, sprinkle with the remaining mint and basil and serve with the rice.

Classic Beef Fajitas

Sizzling marinated strips of meat rolled up in soft flour tortillas with a tangy salsa are a real Mexican treat, perfect for relaxed entertaining.

NUTRITIONAL INFORMATION

Calories	623	Sugars	.........6g
Protein	........36g	Fat	..........23g
Carbohydrate	...72g	Saturates	.......7g

 45 mins   15–20 mins

SERVES 4–6

INGREDIENTS

700 g/1 lb 9 oz steak, cut into strips

6 garlic cloves, chopped

juice of 1 lime

pinch of mild chilli powder

pinch of paprika

pinch of ground cumin

1–2 tbsp extra virgin olive oil

12 flour tortillas

vegetable oil, for frying

1–2 avocados, stoned, peeled, sliced and tossed with lime juice

125 ml/4 fl oz soured cream

salt and pepper

PICO DE GALLO SALSA

8 ripe tomatoes, diced

3 spring onions, sliced

1–2 fresh green chillies, such as jalapeño or serrano, deseeded and chopped

3–4 tbsp chopped fresh coriander

5–8 radishes, diced

ground cumin

1 Combine the beef with half the garlic, half the lime juice, the chilli powder, paprika, cumin and olive oil. Add salt and pepper, mix well and marinate for at least 30 minutes at room temperature or up to overnight in the refrigerator.

2 To make the pico de gallo salsa, put the tomatoes in a bowl with the spring onions, green chilli, coriander and radishes. Season to taste with cumin, salt and pepper. Set aside.

3 Heat the tortillas in a lightly grease non-stick frying pan. Wrap in kitche foil, as you work, to keep them warm.

4 Stir-fry the meat in a little oil over high heat until browned and jus cooked through.

5 Serve the sizzling hot meat with th warm tortillas, the pico de gallo salsa avocado and soured cream for each perso to make his or her own rolled up fajitas.

Ropa Vieja

Fill warmed tortillas with this tender, browned beef and a selection of crisp vegetables to make wonderful tacos.

NUTRITIONAL INFORMATION

Calories ....495 Sugars 3g
Protein ....58g Fat 27g
Carbohydrate ....5g Saturates 10g

45 mins   2¼ hrs

SERVES 6

INGREDIENTS

1.5 kg/3 lb 5 oz flank steak or other stewing meat

beef stock

1 carrot, sliced

10 garlic cloves, sliced

2 tbsp vegetable oil

2 onions, thinly sliced

3–4 mild fresh green chillies, such as anaheim or poblano, deseeded and sliced

warmed flour tortillas, to serve

SALAD GARNISHES

3 ripe tomatoes, diced

8–10 radishes, diced

3–4 tbsp chopped fresh coriander

4–5 spring onions, chopped

1–2 limes, cut into wedges

2 Remove the pan from the heat and set the meat aside to cool in the liquid. When cool enough to handle, remove from the liquid and shred with your fingers and a fork.

3 Heat the oil in a large frying pan. Add the remaining garlic, onions and chillies and cook over a low heat, stirring occasionally, until lightly coloured. Remove from the pan and set aside.

4 Increase the heat. Add the meat to the pan and cook over a medium-high heat until browned and crisp. Transfer to a warmed serving dish. Top with the onion mixture and surround with the tomatoes, radishes, coriander, spring onions and lime wedges. Serve with warmed tortillas.

1 Put the meat in a large pan and cover with a mixture of stock and water. Add the carrot and half the garlic with salt and pepper to taste. Cover and bring to the boil, then reduce the heat to low. Skim the scum from the surface, then re-cover the pan and cook the meat gently for about 2 hours until very tender.

Michoacan Beef

This rich, smoky-flavoured Mexican stew is delicious; leftovers make a great filling for tacos, too!

NUTRITIONAL INFORMATION

Calories 315	Sugars 6g
Protein 41g	Fat 10g
Carbohydrate . . .16g	Saturates 3g

 10 mins   2 hrs

SERVES 4–6

INGREDIENTS

about 3 tbsp plain flour

1 kg/2 lb 4 oz stewing beef, cut into large bite-size pieces

2 tbsp vegetable oil

2 onions, chopped

5 garlic cloves, chopped

400 g/14 oz tomatoes, diced

1½ dried chipotle chillies, reconstituted, deseeded and cut into thin strips, or a few shakes of bottled chipotle salsa

1.5 litres/2¾ pints beef stock

350 g/12 oz green beans

pinch of sugar

salt and pepper

TO SERVE

simmered beans

cooked rice

COOK'S TIP

This is traditionally made with nopales, edible cacti, which give the dish a distinctive flavour. Look for them in specialist stores. For this recipe you need 350–400 g/12–14 oz canned or fresh nopales.

1 Place the flour in a large bowl and season with salt and pepper. Add the beef and toss to coat well. Remove from the bowl, shaking off the excess flour.

2 Heat the oil in a frying pan and brown the meat briefly over a high heat. Reduce the heat to medium, add the onions and garlic and cook for 2 minutes.

3 Add the tomatoes, chillies and stock, cover and simmer over a low heat for 1½ hours or until the meat is very tender, adding the green beans 15 minutes before the end of the cooking time. Skim off any fat that rises to the surface.

4 Transfer to individual bowls and serve with simmered beans and rice.

Spicy Pork with Prunes

Prunes add an earthy, wine flavour to this spicy stew.
Serve with tortillas or crusty bread to dip into the rich sauce.

NUTRITIONAL INFORMATION

Calories	352	Sugars	.........1g
Protein	........39g	Fat	..........12g
Carbohydrate	...24g	Saturates	.......2g

8¼ hrs   3–4 hrs

SERVES 4–6

INGREDIENTS

1.5 kg/3 lb 5 oz pork joint, such as leg
   or shoulder

juice of 2–3 limes

10 garlic cloves, chopped

3–4 tbsp mild chilli powder

4 tbsp vegetable oil

2 onions, chopped

500 ml/18 fl oz chicken stock

25 small tart tomatoes, roughly chopped

25 prunes, stoned

1–2 tsp sugar

pinch of ground cinnamon

pinch of ground allspice

pinch of ground cumin

salt

warmed corn tortillas, to serve

1 Combine the pork with the lime juice, garlic, chilli powder, 2 tablespoons of oil and salt. Set aside to marinate in the refrigerator overnight.

2 Remove the pork from the marinade. Wipe the pork dry with kitchen paper and reserve the marinade. Heat the remaining oil in a flameproof casserole and brown the pork evenly until just golden. Add the onions, the reserved marinade and stock. Cover and cook in a preheated oven, 180°C/350°F/Gas Mark 4, for about 2–3 hours until tender.

3 Spoon off fat from the surface of the cooking liquid and add the tomatoes. Continue to cook for about 20 minutes until the tomatoes are tender. Mash the tomatoes into a coarse purée. Add the prunes and sugar, then adjust the seasoning, adding cinnamon, allspice and cumin to taste, as well as extra chilli powder, if wished.

4 Increase the oven temperature to 200°C/400°F/Gas Mark 6 and return the meat and sauce to the oven for a further 20–30 minutes or until the meat has browned on top and the juices have thickened.

5 Remove the meat from the pan and set aside for a few minutes. Carefully carve it into thin slices and spoon the sauce over the top. Serve warm with corn tortillas.

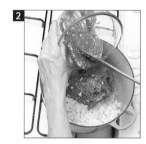

Red Mole of Pork & Chillies

Plantain and sesame seeds add a delicious hint of sweetness to this fragrant stew of pork and mild chillies.

NUTRITIONAL INFORMATION

Calories	432	Sugars	.........9g
Protein	........42g	Fat	..........21g
Carbohydrate	...20g	Saturates	.......4g

 15 mins 4 hrs

SERVES 6

INGREDIENTS

1.25 kg/2 lb 12 oz pork shoulder or lean belly, cut into bite-size pieces

1 onion, chopped

1 garlic bulb

2 bay leaves

1–2 stock cubes

6 dried ancho chillies

6 guajillo chillies

3–5 ripe large flavourful tomatoes

¼ tsp ground cloves

¼ tsp ground allspice

85 g/3 oz sesame seeds, toasted

1 large ripe plantain or banana, peeled and diced

3 tbsp vegetable oil

6–8 waxy potatoes, cut into chunks

3 tbsp yerba santa, or a combination of chopped fresh mint, oregano and coriander

1 cinnamon stick

salt and pepper

1 Place the pork in a large pan with the onion, garlic, bay leaves and salt and pepper. Fill with cold water to the top.

2 Bring to the boil, then reduce the heat to a slow simmer. Skim off the scum, then stir in the stock cubes. Cover and cook for about 3 hours until the meat is very tender.

3 Meanwhile, lightly roast the chillies in an ungreased heavy-based frying pan until they just change colour. Put them in a bowl and cover with boiling water. Cover and set aside for about 20–30 minutes until softened.

4 Roast the tomatoes in the frying pan, to brown the bases, then char the tops under a hot grill. Set aside to cool.

5 When the chillies are softened, remove the stems and seeds, then process them in a food processor or blender with enough liquid to make a paste. Add the roasted tomatoes, cloves and allspice, with two-thirds of the sesame seeds and the plantain. Purée until smooth.

6 Remove the meat from the pan and reserve. Skim the fat from the surface of the stock.

7 Heat the oil in a pan, add the tomato purée mixture and cook for about 10 minutes until thickened. Do not let it burn. Add the potatoes and the herbs with enough of the stock to keep the potatoes covered in sauce. Add the cinnamon stick.

8 Cover and cook until the potatoes are tender, then add the reserved meat and heat through. Serve in bowls, sprinkled with the reserved sesame seeds.

Chilli Verde

If tomatillos are not available, use fresh tomatoes and bottled green salsa instead, and add a good hit of lime juice at the end.

NUTRITIONAL INFORMATION

Calories ....433 Sugars 6g
Protein ....56g Fat 19g
Carbohydrate ....9g Saturates 4g

🔳 10 mins   🕐 1½ hrs

SERVES 4

INGREDIENTS

1 kg/2 lb 4 oz pork, cut into bite-
  size chunks

1 onion, chopped

2 bay leaves

1 garlic bulb, cut in half

1 stock cube

2 garlic cloves, chopped

450 g/1 lb oz fresh tomatillos, husks
  removed, cooked in a small amount of
  water until just tender, then chopped or
  450 g/1 lb canned tomatillos

2 large fresh mild green chillies, such as
  anaheim, or a combination of 1 green
  pepper and 2 jalapeño chillies, deseeded
  and chopped

3 tbsp vegetable oil

225 ml/8 fl oz pork or chicken stock

½ tsp mild chilli powder

½ tsp cumin

4–6 tbsp chopped fresh coriander,
  to garnish

TO SERVE

warmed flour tortillas

lime wedges

1 Place the pork in a large pan with the onion, bay leaves and garlic bulb. Add water to cover and bring to the boil. Skim off the scum from the surface and add the stock cube, stirring well to mix and dissolve. Reduce the heat to very low and simmer gently for about 1½ hours or until the meat is very tender.

2 Meanwhile, put the chopped garlic in a blender or food processor with the tomatillos and green chillies and pepper, if using. Process to a purée.

3 Heat the oil in a pan, add the tomatillo mixture and cook over a medium-high heat for about 10 minutes or until thickened. Add the stock, chilli powder and cumin.

4 When the meat is tender, remove from the pan and add to the sauce. Simmer gently to combine the flavours.

5 Garnish with the chopped coriander and serve with warmed tortillas and lime wedges.

Meatballs in a Spicy Sauce

Called 'albondigas' in Mexico, these tasty meatballs are set off brilliantly against the rich sauce and golden sweet potatoes.

NUTRITIONAL INFORMATION

Calories	540	Sugars	........29g
Protein	........31g	Fat	..........20g
Carbohydrate	...64g	Saturates	.......6g

 20 mins   20 mins

SERVES 4

INGREDIENTS

225 g/8 oz minced pork

225 g/8 oz minced beef or lamb

6 tbsp cooked rice or finely crushed tortilla chips

1 egg, lightly beaten

1½ onions, finely chopped

5 garlic cloves, finely chopped

½ tsp ground cumin

pinch of ground cinnamon

2 tbsp raisins

2 tbsp vegetable oil, plus extra for frying

1 tbsp molasses sugar

1–2 tbsp cider or wine vinegar

400 g/14 oz can tomatoes, drained and chopped

350 ml/12 fl oz beef stock

1–2 tbsp mild chilli or ancho chilli powder

1 tbsp paprika

1 tbsp chopped fresh coriander

1 tbsp chopped fresh parsley or mint

2 sweet potatoes, peeled and cut into small bite-size chunks

salt and pepper

grated cheese, to serve

1 Combine the meat with the rice or crushed tortilla chips, the egg, half the onion, half the garlic, the cumin, cinnamon and raisins.

2 Divide the mixture into even-size pieces and roll into balls. Fry the balls in a non-stick frying pan over a medium heat, adding a tiny amount of oil, if necessary, to help them brown. Remove the balls from the pan and set aside. Wipe the frying pan clean.

3 Place the molasses sugar in a blender or food processor with the vinegar, tomatoes, stock, chilli powder, paprika and remaining onion and garlic. Process together until blended, then stir in the chopped fresh herbs. Set aside.

4 Heat the oil in the cleaned frying pan add the sweet potatoes and cook until tender and golden brown. Pour in the blended sauce and add the meatballs to the pan. Cook for about 10 minutes until the meatballs are heated through and the flavours have completely combined. Season with salt and pepper to taste. Serve immediately accompanied with grated cheese.

Chilli con Carne

Probably the best-known Mexican dish and one that is a great favourite with all. The chilli content can be increased to suit your taste.

NUTRITIONAL INFORMATION

Calories	443	Sugars	........11g
Protein	........48g	Fat	..........15g
Carbohydrate	...30g	Saturates	......4g

 5 mins   🕐 2½ hrs

SERVES 4

INGREDIENTS

750 g/1 lb 10 oz lean braising or
   stewing steak

2 tbsp vegetable oil

1 large onion, sliced

2–4 garlic cloves, crushed

1 tbsp plain flour

425 ml//15 fl oz tomato juice

400 g/14 oz can tomatoes

1–2 tbsp sweet chilli sauce

1 tsp ground cumin

425 g/15 oz can red kidney beans, drained

½ teaspoon dried oregano

1–2 tbsp chopped fresh parsley

salt and pepper

chopped fresh herbs, to garnish

boiled rice and tortillas, to serve

1 Cut the beef into 2 cm/¾ inch cubes. Heat the oil in a flameproof casserole and fry the beef until well sealed. Remove from the casserole.

2 Add the onion and garlic to the casserole and cook until lightly browned. Stir in the flour and cook for 1–2 minutes. Stir in the tomato juice and tomatoes and bring to the boil. Replace the beef and add the chilli sauce, cumin and seasoning. Cover and place in a preheated oven, 160°C/325°F/Gas Mark 3, for 1½ hours or until almost tender.

3 Stir in the beans, oregano and parsley and adjust the seasoning to taste. Cover the casserole and return to the oven for 45 minutes. Serve sprinkled with herbs and with boiled rice and tortillas.

COOK'S TIP

Because chilli con carne requires quite a lengthy cooking time, it saves time and fuel to prepare double the quantity you need and freeze half of it to serve on another occasion. Thaw and use within 3–4 weeks.

Baked Ham with Sauce

A joint of gammon or collar bacon is first par-boiled then baked with a mustard topping. Serve hot or cold with this tangy Cumberland sauce.

NUTRITIONAL INFORMATION

Calories	414	Sugars	....4g
Protein	....70g	Fat	....13g
Carbohydrate	....4g	Saturates	....5g

 10 mins   5¾ hrs

SERVES 4–6

INGREDIENTS

2–3 kg/4–6 lb lean gammon or prime collar joint of bacon

2 bay leaves

1–2 onions, quartered

2 carrots, thickly sliced

6 cloves

GLAZE

1 tbsp redcurrant jelly

1 tbsp wholegrain mustard

CUMBERLAND SAUCE

1 orange

3 tbsp redcurrant jelly

2 tbsp lemon or lime juice

2 tbsp orange juice

2–4 tbsp port

1 tbsp wholegrain mustard

TO GARNISH

salad leaves

orange slices

1 Put the meat in a large pan. Add the bay leaves, onion, carrots and cloves and cover with cold water. Bring to the boil over a low heat, cover and simmer for half the cooking time. To calculate the cooking, time, allow 30 minutes per 500 g/1 lb 2 oz plus 30 minutes.

2 Drain the meat and remove the skin. Put the meat in a roasting tin and score the fat. To make the glaze, combine the ingredients and spread over the fat. Cook in a preheated oven, 180°C/350°F/ Gas Mark 4, for the remainder of the cooking time. Baste at least once.

3 To make the sauce, pare the rind from half the orange and cut into strips. Cook in boiling water for 3 minutes. Drain.

4 Place all the remaining sauce ingredients in a small pan and heat gently, stirring occasionally, until the redcurrant jelly dissolves. Add the orange rind strips and simmer gently for a further 3–4 minutes.

5 Slice the gammon or bacon and place on a warmed serving platter. Garnish with salad leaves and orange slices and serve with the Cumberland sauce.

Meatball Brochettes

Children will love these tasty meatballs on a skewer, which are economical and easy to make on the barbecue.

NUTRITIONAL INFORMATION

Calories	120	Sugars 2g
Protein	. . . . .17g	Fat 5g
Carbohydrate	. . . .2g	Saturates 2g

1 hr   10 mins

SERVES 4

INGREDIENTS

5 g/1 oz cracked wheat

50 g/12 oz lean minced beef

onion, very finely chopped (optional)

tbsp tomato ketchup

tbsp brown fruity sauce

tbsp chopped, fresh parsley

eaten egg, to bind

cherry tomatoes

button mushrooms

vegetable oil, to baste

bread finger rolls, to serve

1 Place the cracked wheat in a bowl and cover with boiling water. Set aside to soak for 20 minutes or until softened. Drain thoroughly and set aside to cool.

2 Place the soaked wheat, minced beef, onion, if using, ketchup, brown fruity sauce and chopped fresh parsley together in a mixing bowl and mix well until all the ingredients are well combined. Add a little beaten egg if necessary to bind the mixture together.

3 Using your hands, shape the meat mixture into 18 even-size balls. Set aside to chill in the refrigerator for 30 minutes.

4 Thread the meatballs on to 8 pre-soaked wooden skewers, alternating them with the cherry tomatoes and button mushrooms.

5 Brush the brochettes with a little oil and barbecue over hot coals, turning occasionally and brushing with a little more oil if the meat starts to dry out, for about 10 minutes until cooked through.

6 Transfer the brochettes to warm serving plates. Cut open the bread finger rolls and push the meat and vegetables off the skewer into the open rolls, using a fork.

Savoury Hotpot

This hearty lamb stew is full of vegetables and herbs, and is topped with a layer of crisp, golden potato slices – a satisfying family meal.

NUTRITIONAL INFORMATION

Calories 365	Sugars 5g
Protein 23g	Fat 11g
Carbohydrate ...48g	Saturates 4g

    15 mins   2 hrs

SERVES 4

INGREDIENTS

8 middle neck lean lamb chops, neck
   of lamb or any lean stewing lamb

1–2 garlic cloves, crushed

2 lamb's kidneys (optional)

1 large onion, thinly sliced

1 leek, sliced

2–3 carrots, sliced

1 tsp chopped fresh tarragon or sage, or
   ½ tsp dried tarragon or sage

1 kg/2 lb 4 oz potatoes, thinly sliced

300 ml/10 fl oz stock

2 tbsp margarine, melted, or
   1 tbsp vegetable oil

salt and pepper

chopped fresh parsley, to garnish

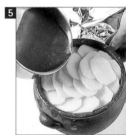

1 Trim any excess fat from the lamb, season well with salt and pepper and arrange in a large ovenproof casserole. Sprinkle with the garlic.

2 If using kidneys, remove the skin, halve and cut out the cores. Chop into small pieces and sprinkle them over the lamb.

3 Place the vegetables over the lamb, allowing the pieces to slip in between the meat, then sprinkle with the herbs.

4 Arrange the potato slices on top of the meat and vegetables, in an overlapping pattern.

5 Bring the stock to the boil, season with salt and pepper to taste, then pour over the casserole.

6 Brush the potatoes with the melted margarine or vegetable oil, cover with greased foil or a lid and cook in a preheated oven, 180°C/350°F/Gas Mark 4, for 1½ hours.

7 Remove the foil or lid from the casserole, increase the temperature to 220°C/425°F/Gas Mark 7 and return the casserole to the oven for about 30 minutes until the potatoes are browned.

8 Garnish the hotpot with the chopped fresh parsley and serve immediately.

Steak in a Wine Marinade

Fillet, sirloin, rump and entrecôte are all suitable cuts for this dish, although rump retains the most flavour.

NUTRITIONAL INFORMATION

Calories 356   Sugars 2g
Protein . . . . .41g   Fat 9g
Carbohydrate . . . .2g   Saturates 4g

🖐 🖐

3 hrs   🕐 15 mins

SERVES 4

I N G R E D I E N T S

4 rump steaks, about 250 g/9 oz each

600 ml/1 pint red wine

1 onion, quartered

2 tbsp Dijon mustard

2 garlic cloves, crushed

salt and pepper

4 large field mushrooms

olive oil for brushing

branch of fresh rosemary (optional)

1 Snip through the fat strip on the steaks in 3 places, so that the steak retains its shape when barbecued.

2 Combine the red wine, onion, mustard, garlic, salt and pepper. Lay the steaks in a shallow non-porous dish and pour over the marinade. Cover and chill in the refrigerator for 2–3 hours.

3 Remove the steaks from the refrigerator 30 minutes before you intend to cook them to let them come to room temperature. This is especially important if the steak is thick, so that it cooks more evenly and is not well done on the outside and raw in the middle.

4 Sear both sides of the steak – about 1 minute on each side – over a hot barbecue. If it is about 2.5 cm/1 inch thick, keep it over a hot barbecue and cook for about 4 minutes on each side. This will give a medium-rare steak – cook it more or less, to suit your taste. If the steak is a thicker cut, move it to a less hot part of the barbecue or further away from the coals. To test the readiness of the meat while cooking, simply press it with your finger – the more the meat yields, the less it is cooked.

5 Brush the mushrooms with the olive oil and cook them alongside the steak for 5 minutes, turning once. When you put the mushrooms on the barbecue, put the rosemary branch, if using, in the fire to flavour the meat slightly.

6 Remove the steak and set aside to rest for 1–2 minutes before serving. Slice the mushrooms and serve immediately with the meat.

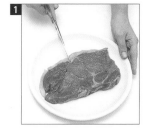

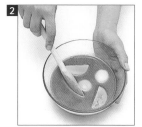

Beef & Potato Goulash

In this recipe, the potatoes are actually cooked in the goulash. For a change, you may prefer to substitute small, scrubbed new potatoes.

NUTRITIONAL INFORMATION

Calories ....477 Sugars 11g
Protein ....47g Fat 16g
Carbohydrate ...39g Saturates 5g

 15 mins   2¼ mins

SERVES 4

INGREDIENTS

2 tbsp vegetable oil

1 large onion, sliced

2 garlic cloves, crushed

750 g/1 lb 10 oz lean stewing steak

2 tbsp paprika

400 g/14 oz canned chopped tomatoes

2 tbsp tomato purée

1 large red pepper, deseeded and chopped

175 g/6 oz mushrooms, sliced

600 ml/1 pint beef stock

500 g/1 lb 2 oz potatoes, cut into large chunks

1 tbsp cornflour

salt and pepper

TO GARNISH

4 tbsp low-fat natural yogurt

paprika

chopped fresh parsley

1 Heat the oil in a large pan. Add the onion and garlic and cook over a medium heat, stirring occasionally, for 3–4 minutes until softened.

2 Cut the steak into chunks, add to the pan and cook over a high heat for about 3 minutes until browned all over.

3 Lower the heat to medium and stir in the paprika. Add the tomatoes, tomato purée, red pepper and mushrooms. Cook, stirring constantly, for 2 minutes.

4 Pour in the beef stock. Bring to the boil, stirring occasionally, then reduce the heat to low. Cover and simmer gently for about 1½ hours until the meat is cooked through and tender.

5 Add the potatoes, cover and cook fo a further 20–30 minutes until tender.

6 Blend the cornflour with a little wate and add to the pan, stirring unt thickened and blended. Cook for 1 minut then season with salt and pepper to taste Top with the yogurt, sprinkle over th paprika and chopped fresh parsley an serve immediately.

Ginger Beef with Chilli

Serve these fruity, hot and spicy steaks with noodles. Use a non-stick ridged frying pan to cook with a minimum of fat.

NUTRITIONAL INFORMATION

Calories 179	Sugars 8g	
Protein 21g	Fat 6g	
Carbohydrate 8g	Saturates 2g	

40 mins   10 mins

SERVES 4

INGREDIENTS

lean beef steaks, such as rump, sirloin or
fillet, 100 g/3½ oz each

tbsp ginger wine

.5 cm/1 inch piece of fresh root ginger,
finely chopped

garlic clove, crushed

tsp ground chilli

tsp vegetable oil

alt and pepper

resh red chilli strips, to garnish

TO SERVE

reshly cooked noodles

spring onions, shredded

RELISH

25 g/8 oz fresh pineapple

small red pepper

fresh red chilli

tbsp light soy sauce

piece of stem ginger in syrup, drained
and chopped

1 Trim any excess fat from the steaks if necessary. Using a meat mallet or covered rolling pin, pound the steaks until they are 1 cm/½ inch thick. Season on both sides with salt and pepper to taste and place in a shallow dish.

2 Combine the ginger wine, fresh root ginger, garlic and chilli and pour over the meat. Cover with clingfilm and chill for 30 minutes.

3 Meanwhile, make the relish. Peel and finely chop the pineapple and place it in a bowl. Halve, deseed and finely chop the pepper and chilli. Stir into the pineapple with the soy sauce and stem ginger. Cover with clingfilm and chill until required.

4 Brush a ridged grill pan with the oil and heat until very hot. Drain the beef and add to the pan, pressing down to seal. Lower the heat and cook for 5 minutes. Turn the steaks over and cook for a further 5 minutes.

5 Drain the steaks on kitchen paper and transfer to warmed serving plates. Garnish with chilli strips and serve with noodles, spring onions and the relish.

Lamb Couscous

Couscous is a dish that originated among the Berbers of North Africa.
When steamed, it is a delicious plump grain, ideal for serving with stews.

NUTRITIONAL INFORMATION

Calories ....537 Sugars 11g
Protein ....32g Fat 14g
Carbohydrate ...73g Saturates 4g

 15 mins   35 mins

SERVES 4

INGREDIENTS

2 medium red onions, sliced

juice of 1 lemon

1 large red pepper, deseeded and thickly sliced

1 large green pepper, deseeded and thickly sliced

1 large orange pepper, deseeded and thickly sliced

pinch of saffron strands

cinnamon stick, broken

1 tbsp clear honey

300 ml/10 fl oz vegetable stock

2 tsp olive oil

350 g/12 oz lean lamb fillet, trimmed and sliced

1 tsp harissa

200 g/7 oz can chopped tomatoes

425 g/15 oz can chickpeas, drained

350 g/12 oz precooked couscous

2 tsp ground cinnamon

salt and pepper

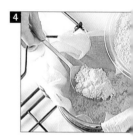

1 Toss the onions in the lemon juice and transfer to a pan. Stir in the peppers, saffron, cinnamon stick and honey. Pour in the stock, bring to the boil, cover and simmer for 5 minutes.

2 Meanwhile, heat the oil in a frying pan and gently fry the lamb for 3–4 minutes until browned all over.

3 Using a draining spoon, transfer the lamb to the pan with the onions and peppers. Season and stir in the harissa, tomatoes and chickpeas. Mix thoroughly, bring back to the boil and simmer, uncovered, for 20 minutes.

4 Soak the couscous, following th packet instructions. Bring a pan o water to the boil. Put the couscous in steamer or sieve lined with muslin ove the pan of boiling water. Cover and steam.

5 Transfer the couscous to a servin platter and dust with groun cinnamon. Discard the cinnamon stick an spoon the stew over the couscous.

Spicy Mexican Beans

These stewed beans form the basis of many Mexican recipes. Don't add salt until the beans are tender – it prevents them from softening.

NUTRITIONAL INFORMATION

Calories	234	Sugars	.........6g
Protein	........11g	Fat	..........13g
Carbohydrate	...20g	Saturates	......2g

 12 hrs   🕐 4 hrs

SERVES 4

I N G R E D I E N T S

225 g/8 oz pinto beans or cannellini beans
1 large onion, sliced
2 garlic cloves, crushed
1 litre /1¾ pints water
salt
chopped fresh coriander or parsley,
    to garnish

B E A N   S T E W

1 large onion, sliced
2 garlic cloves, crushed
3 rashers lean streaky bacon, diced
2 tbsp oil
400 g/14 oz can chopped tomatoes
1 tsp ground cumin
1 tbsp sweet chilli sauce

R E F R I E D   B E A N S

1 onion, chopped
2 garlic cloves, crushed
2 tbsp oil

1 Soak the beans in a bowl of cold water overnight. Drain the beans and put into a pan with the onion, garlic and water, bring to the boil, cover and simmer gently for 1½ hours. Stir well, add more boiling water, if necessary, and simmer, covered, for a further 1–1½ hours or until the beans are tender.

2 When the beans are tender, add salt to taste and continue to cook, uncovered, for about 15 minutes to allow most of the liquid to evaporate to form a thick sauce. Serve the basic beans hot sprinkled with chopped coriander or parsley. Alternatively, cool, then store in the refrigerator for up to 1 week.

3 To make a bean stew, fry the onion, garlic and bacon for 3–4 minutes in the oil, add the other ingredients and basic beans and bring to the boil. Cover and simmer for 30 minutes, then season.

4 To make refried beans, fry the onion and garlic in the oil until golden brown. Add a quarter of the basic beans with a little of their liquid and mash. Continue adding and mashing the beans, while simmering gently until thick. Adjust the seasoning and serve hot.

Sweet & Sour Venison Stir-fry

Venison is super-lean and low in fat, so it's the perfect choice for a healthy diet. Cooked quickly with crisp vegetables, it's ideal in a stir-fry.

NUTRITIONAL INFORMATION

Calories 219	Sugars 18g
Protein 23g	Fat 5g
Carbohydrate . . .20g	Saturates 1g

 15 mins   15 mins

SERVES 4

I N G R E D I E N T S

1 bunch of spring onions

1 red pepper

100 g/3½ oz mangetouts

100 g/3½ oz baby corn cobs

350 g/12 oz lean venison steak

1 tbsp vegetable oil

1 garlic clove, crushed

2.5 cm/1 inch piece fresh root ginger, finely chopped

3 tbsp light soy sauce, plus extra for serving

1 tbsp white wine vinegar

2 tbsp dry sherry

2 tsp clear honey

225 g/8 oz can pineapple pieces in natural juice, drained

25 g/1 oz beansprouts

freshly cooked rice, to serve

VARIATION

For a nutritious meal-in-one, cook 225 g/8 oz egg noodles in boiling water for 3–4 minutes. Drain and add to the pan in step 4, with the pineapple and beansprouts. Add an extra 2 tablespoons soy sauce with the pineapple and beansprouts.

1 Cut the spring onions into 2.5 cm/ 1 inch pieces. Halve and deseed the red pepper and cut it into 2.5 cm/1 inch pieces. Trim the mangetouts and baby corn cobs.

2 Trim any fat from the meat and cut it into thin strips. Heat the oil in a large frying pan or wok until hot and stir-fry the meat, garlic and ginger for 5 minutes.

3 Add the spring onions, red pepper, mangetouts and baby corn cobs, then stir in the soy sauce, vinegar, sherry and honey. Stir-fry for a further 5 minutes.

4 Carefully stir in the pineapple pieces and beansprouts and cook for a further 1–2 minutes to heat through. Serve with freshly cooked rice and extra soy sauce for dipping.

Lasagne Verde

The sauce in this delicious baked pasta dish can also be used as an alternative sauce for Spaghetti Bolognese.

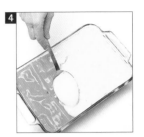

NUTRITIONAL INFORMATION

Calories	.619	Sugars	.7g
Protein	.29g	Fat	.45g
Carbohydrate	.21g	Saturates	.19g

 1¾ hrs   55 mins

SERVES 4

INGREDIENTS

1 quantity Pasticcio Sauce (see page 646)

1 tbsp olive oil

225 g/8 oz lasagne verde

butter, for greasing

Béchamel Sauce (see page 6)

55 g/2oz Parmesan cheese, freshly grated

salt

green salad, tomato salad or black olives, to serve

1 Make the Pasticcio Sauce as described on page 646, but cook for 10–12 minutes longer than the time given, in an uncovered pan, to allow the excess liquid to evaporate. It needs to be reduced to the consistency of a thick paste.

2 Have ready a large saucepan of boiling, salted water and add the olive oil. Drop the pasta sheets into the boiling water, a few at a time, and return the water to the boil before adding further pasta sheets. If you are using fresh lasagne, cook the sheets for a total of 8 minutes. If you are using dried or partly pre-cooked pasta, cook it according to the the packet instructions.

3 Remove the pasta sheets from the saucepan with a draining spoon. Spread them out in a single layer on clean, damp tea towels.

4 Grease a rectangular ovenproof dish, about 25–28 cm/10–11 inches long. To assemble the dish, spoon a little of the meat sauce into the prepared dish, cover with a layer of lasagne, then spoon over a little Béchamel Sauce and sprinkle with some of the cheese. Continue making layers in this way, covering the final layer of lasagne sheets with the remaining Béchamel Sauce.

5 Sprinkle on the remaining cheese and bake in a preheated oven, 190°C/375°F/Gas Mark 5, for 40 minutes or until the sauce is golden brown and bubbling. Serve with a green salad, a tomato salad, or a bowl of black olives.

Pasticcio

A recipe that has both Italian and Greek origins, this dish
may be served hot or cold, cut into thick, satisfying squares.

NUTRITIONAL INFORMATION

Calories	590	Sugars	.........8g
Protein	........34g	Fat	..........39g
Carbohydrate	...23g	Saturates	......16g

35 mins   1¼ hrs

SERVES 6

INGREDIENTS

225 g/8 oz fusilli, or other short
  pasta shapes

1 tbsp olive oil

4 tbsp double cream

salt

rosemary sprigs, to garnish

SAUCE

2 tbsp olive oil, plus extra for brushing

1 onion, thinly sliced

1 red pepper, deseeded and chopped

2 garlic cloves, chopped

625 g/1 lb 6 oz lean minced beef

400 g/14 oz canned chopped tomatoes

125 ml/4 fl oz dry white wine

2 tbsp chopped fresh parsley

50 g/1¾ oz canned anchovies, drained
  and chopped

salt and pepper

TOPPING

300 ml/10 fl oz natural yogurt

3 eggs

pinch of freshly grated nutmeg

55 g/2 oz Parmesan cheese,
  freshly grated

1 To make the sauce, heat the oil in a large frying pan and fry the onion and red pepper for 3 minutes. Stir in the garlic and cook for 1 minute. Add the beef and cook, stirring frequently, until browned.

2 Add the tomatoes and wine, stir well and bring to the boil. Simmer, uncovered, for 20 minutes or until the sauce is fairly thick. Stir in the parsley and anchovies and season to taste.

3 Bring a large pan of lightly salted water to the boil. Add the oil and pasta, bring back to the boil and cook for 8–10 minutes until tender, but still firm to the bite. Drain, then transfer to a bowl. Stir in the cream and set aside.

4 To make the topping, beat the yogurt with the eggs and nutmeg until well combined and season with salt and pepper to taste.

5 Brush a large, shallow ovenproof dish with oil. Spoon in half of the pasta mixture and cover with half of the meat sauce. Repeat these layers, then spread the topping evenly over the final layer. Sprinkle the grated Parmesan cheese evenly on top.

6 Bake in a preheated oven, 190°C/ 375°F/Gas Mark 5, for 25 minutes or until the topping is golden brown and bubbling. Garnish with sprigs of fresh rosemary and serve immediately.

Meatballs in Red Wine Sauce

A different twist is given to this traditional and ever-popular pasta dish with a rich, but subtle, sauce.

NUTRITIONAL INFORMATION

Calories 811   Sugars 7g
Protein . . . . .30g   Fat 43g
Carbohydrate . . .76g   Saturates 12g

45 mins   1½ hrs

SERVES 4

INGREDIENTS

150 ml/5 fl oz milk

150 g/5½ oz fresh white breadcrumbs

2 tbsp butter

9 tbsp olive oil

225 g/8 oz sliced oyster mushrooms

2½ tbsp wholemeal flour

200 ml/7 fl oz beef stock

150 ml/5 fl oz red wine

4 tomatoes, peeled and chopped

1 tbsp tomato purée

1 tsp brown sugar

1 tbsp finely chopped fresh basil

12 shallots, chopped

450 g/1 lb minced steak

1 tsp paprika

450 g/1 lb dried egg tagliatelle

salt and pepper

fresh basil sprigs, to garnish

1 Pour the milk into a bowl, add the breadcrumbs and set aside to soak for 30 minutes.

2 Heat half the butter and 4 tablespoons of the oil in a pan. Fry the mushrooms for 4 minutes, then stir in the flour and cook for 2 minutes. Add the stock and wine and simmer for 15 minutes. Add the tomatoes, tomato purée, sugar and basil. Season and simmer for 30 minutes.

3 Mix the shallots, steak and paprika with the breadcrumbs and season to taste. Shape the mixture into 14 meatballs.

4 Heat 4 tablespoons of the remaining oil and the rest of the butter in a large frying pan. Fry the meatballs, turning frequently, until brown all over. Transfer to a deep casserole, pour over the red wine and mushroom sauce, cover and bake in a preheated oven, 180°C/350°F/Gas Mark 4, for 30 minutes.

5 Bring a pan of lightly salted water to the boil. Add the pasta and the remaining oil, bring back to the boil and cook for 8–10 minutes or until tender, but still firm to the bite. Drain and transfer to a serving dish. Remove the casserole from the oven and cool for 3 minutes. Pour the meatballs and sauce on to the pasta, garnish and serve.

Polenta with Rabbit Stew

Polenta can be served fresh, as in this dish, or it can be cooled, then sliced and grilled or fried.

NUTRITIONAL INFORMATION

Calories	726	Sugars	........2g
Protein	........61g	Fat	..........25g
Carbohydrate	...55g	Saturates	.......6g

20 mins   1¾ minutes

SERVES 4

INGREDIENTS

butter, for greasing

300 g/10½ oz polenta or cornmeal

1 tbsp coarse sea salt

1.2 litres/2 pints water

4 tbsp olive oil

2 kg/4 lb 8 oz rabbit joints

3 garlic cloves, peeled

3 shallots, sliced

150 ml/5 fl oz red wine

1 carrot, sliced

1 celery stick, sliced

2 bay leaves

1 fresh rosemary sprig

3 tomatoes, peeled and diced

85 g/3 oz stoned black olives

salt and pepper

1 Grease a large ovenproof dish with a little butter. Mix the polenta, salt and water in a large pan, whisking well to prevent lumps from forming. Bring to the boil and boil for 10 minutes, stirring vigorously and constantly. Turn into the prepared dish and bake in a preheated oven, 190°C/375°F/Gas Mark 5, for 40 minutes.

2 Meanwhile, heat the oil in a large pan and add the rabbit pieces, garlic and shallots. Fry for 10 minutes until browned.

3 Stir in the wine and cook for a further 5 minutes.

4 Add the carrot, celery, bay leaves, rosemary, tomatoes, olives and 300 ml/10 fl oz water. Cover the pan and simmer for about 45 minutes or until the rabbit is tender. Season with salt and pepper to taste.

5 To serve, spoon or cut a portion of polenta and place on each serving plate. Top with a ladleful of rabbit stew. Serve immediately.

Potato Kibbeh

Kibbeh is a Middle Eastern dish, traditionally made with cracked wheat, lamb and spices. Serve with tahini, salad and warm Middle Eastern bread.

NUTRITIONAL INFORMATION

Calories	600	Sugars	.........4g
Protein	........20g	Fat	..........35g
Carbohydrate	...53g	Saturates	.......8g

40 mins   20 mins

SERVES 4

INGREDIENTS

175 g/6 oz bulgur wheat

350 g/12 oz floury potatoes, diced

2 small eggs

2 tbsp butter, melted

pinch of ground cumin

pinch of ground coriander

pinch of grated nutmeg

salt and pepper

vegetable oil, for deep-frying

STUFFING

175 g/6 oz minced lamb

1 small onion, chopped

1 tbsp pine kernels

25 g/1 oz dried apricots, chopped

pinch of grated nutmeg

pinch of ground cinnamon

1 tbsp chopped fresh coriander

2 tbsp lamb stock

1 Put the bulgur wheat in a bowl and pour in boiling water to cover. Set aside to soak for 30 minutes until the water has been absorbed and the bulgur wheat has swollen.

2 Meanwhile, cook the diced potatoes in a saucepan of boiling water for 10 minutes or until cooked through. Drain and mash until smooth.

3 Add the bulgur wheat to the mashed potatoes with the eggs, melted butter, cumin, coriander and nutmeg. Mix well and season with salt and pepper to taste.

4 To make the stuffing, dry-fry the lamb for 5 minutes, add the onion and cook for a further 2–3 minutes. Add the remaining stuffing ingredients and cook for 5 minutes until the lamb stock has been absorbed. Leave the mixture to cool

slightly, then divide into 8 portions. Roll each one into a ball.

5 Divide the potato mixture into 8 portions and flatten each into a round. Place a portion of stuffing in the centre of each round. Shape the coating around the stuffing to encase it.

6 Heat the oil in deep-fat fryer to 190°C/350°F or until a cube of bread browns in 30 seconds. Cook the kibbeh for 5–7 minutes until golden brown. Drain well and serve immediately.

Meatballs in Spicy Sauce

These meatballs are delicious served with plenty of warm crusty bread to 'mop up' the spicy sauce.

NUTRITIONAL INFORMATION

Calories ....95 Sugars 2.7g
Protein ....4.5g Fat 5.8g
Carbohydrate ...6.6g Saturates 2.3g

5 mins   1¼ hrs

SERVES 4

I N G R E D I E N T S

225 g/8 oz floury potatoes, diced

225 g/8 oz minced beef or lamb

1 onion, finely chopped

1 tbsp chopped fresh coriander

1 celery stick, finely chopped

2 garlic cloves, crushed

2 tbsp butter

1 tbsp vegetable oil

salt and pepper

chopped fresh coriander, to garnish

S A U C E

1 tbsp vegetable oil

1 onion, finely chopped

2 tsp soft brown sugar

400 g/14 oz canned chopped tomatoes

1 fresh green chilli, chopped

1 tsp paprika

150 ml/5 fl oz vegetable stock

2 tsp cornflour

1 Cook the diced potatoes in a saucepan of boiling water for 25 minutes until cooked through. Drain well and transfer to a large mixing bowl. Mash until smooth.

2 Add the minced beef or lamb, onion, coriander, celery and garlic and mix together well.

3 Bring the mixture together with your hands and roll it into 20 small balls.

4 To make the sauce, heat the oil in a pan and sauté the onion for 5 minutes. Add the remaining sauce ingredients and bring to the boil, stirring constantly. Lower the heat and simmer for 20 minutes.

5 Meanwhile, heat the butter and oil for the meatballs in a frying pan. Add the meatballs in batches and cook, turning frequently, for 10–15 minutes until browned. Keep warm while cooking the remainder. Serve the meatballs in a warm, shallow ovenproof dish with the sauce poured around them and garnished with the fresh coriander.

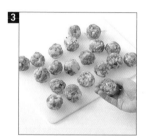

Potato, Beef & Peanut Pot

The spicy peanut sauce in this recipe will complement almost any meat; the dish is just as delicious made with chicken or pork.

NUTRITIONAL INFORMATION

Calories 559	Sugars 5g
Protein 35g	Fat 37g
Carbohydrate . . .24g	Saturates 13g

5 mins 1 hr

SERVES 4

INGREDIENTS

1 tbsp vegetable oil

5 tbsp butter

450 g/1 lb lean steak, cut into thin strips

1 onion, halved and sliced

2 garlic cloves, crushed

600 g/1 lb 5 oz waxy potatoes, cubed

1/2 tsp paprika

4 tbsp crunchy peanut butter

600 ml/1 pint beef stock

4 tbsp unsalted peanuts

2 tsp light soy sauce

55 g/2 oz sugar snap peas

1 red pepper, deseeded and cut into strips

fresh parsley sprigs, to garnish (optional)

1 Heat the oil and butter in a flameproof casserole.

2 Add the steak strips and fry them gently for about 3–4 minutes, stirring and turning the meat until it is sealed on all sides.

3 Add the onion and garlic and cook for a further 2 minutes, stirring constantly.

4 Add the potato cubes and cook for 3–4 minutes or until they begin to brown slightly.

5 Stir in the paprika and peanut butter, then gradually stir in in the beef stock. Bring the mixture to the boil, stirring frequently.

6 Finally, add the peanuts, soy sauce, sugar snap peas and red pepper.

7 Cover and cook over a low heat for 45 minutes or until the beef is cooked right through.

8 Garnish the dish with parsley sprigs, if desired, and serve immediately.

COOK'S TIP

Serve this dish with plain boiled rice or noodles, if you wish.

Potato & Meat Filo Parcels

These small parcels are perfect for special occasions. Crisp pastry encases a tasty potato and beef filling, cooked in red wine.

NUTRITIONAL INFORMATION

Calories 388	Sugars 5g	
Protein 15g	Fat 12g	
Carbohydrate ...53g	Saturates 5g	

 10 mins   35 mins

SERVES 4

I N G R E D I E N T S

225 g/8 oz waxy potatoes, finely diced

1 tbsp vegetable oil

115 g/4 oz minced beef

1 leek, sliced

1 small yellow pepper, deseeded and finely diced

115 g/4 oz button mushrooms, sliced

1 tbsp plain flour

1 tbsp tomato purée

6 tbsp red wine

6 tbsp beef stock

1 tbsp chopped fresh rosemary

225 g/8 oz filo pastry, thawed if frozen

2 tbsp butter, melted

salt and pepper

1 Cook the diced potatoes in a saucepan of boiling water for 5 minutes. Drain and set aside.

2 Meanwhile, heat the oil in a saucepan and fry the minced beef, leek, yellow pepper and mushrooms over a low heat for 5 minutes.

3 Stir in the flour and tomato purée and cook for 1 minute. Gradually add the red wine and beef stock, stirring to thicken. Add the chopped rosemary, season to taste with salt and pepper and set aside to cool slightly.

4 Lay 4 sheets of filo pastry on a work surface or board. Brush each sheet with butter and lay a second layer of filo on top. Trim the sheets to make four 20 cm/8 inch squares.

5 Brush the edges of the pastry with a little butter. Spoon a quarter of the beef mixture into the centre of each square. Bring up the corners and the sides of the squares to form a parcel, scrunching the edges together. Make sure that the parcels are well sealed by pressing the pastry together, otherwise the filling will leak.

6 Place the parcels on a baking sheet and brush with butter. Bake in a preheated oven, 180°C/350°F/Gas Mark 4, for 20 minutes. Serve hot.

Beef with Beansprouts

A quick and easy stir-fry for any day of the week, this simple beef recipe is a good one-pan main dish.

NUTRITIONAL INFORMATION

Calories 544	Sugars 8g	
Protein 39g	Fat 21g	
Carbohydrate ...55g	Saturates 5g	

🧊 5 mins   ⏱ 15 mins

SERVES 4

INGREDIENTS

1 bunch spring onions, thinly
   sliced lengthways

2 tbsp sunflower oil

1 garlic clove, crushed

1 tsp finely chopped fresh root ginger

500 g/1 lb 2 oz tender beef, cut into
   thin strips

1 large red pepper, deseeded and sliced

1 small fresh red chilli, deseeded
   and chopped

350 g/12 oz fresh beansprouts

1 small lemon grass stalk, finely chopped

2 tbsp smooth peanut butter

4 tbsp coconut milk

1 tbsp rice vinegar

1 tbsp soy sauce

1 tsp soft light brown sugar

250 g/9 oz medium egg noodles

salt and pepper

1 Set aside some of the sliced spring onions for the garnish. Heat the sunflower oil in a frying pan or wok over a high heat. Add the remaining spring onions, the garlic and ginger and stir-fry for 2–3 minutes until softened. Add the beef strips and stir-fry for 4–5 minutes until evenly browned.

2 Add the red pepper and stir-fry for a further 3–4 minutes. Add the chilli and beansprouts and stir-fry for 2 minutes. Combine the lemon grass, peanut butter, coconut milk, vinegar, soy sauce and sugar, then stir the mixture into the wok.

3 Meanwhile, cook the egg noodles in lightly salted boiling water for 4 minutes or according to the packet instructions. Drain and stir into the frying pan or wok, tossing to mix evenly.

4 Season with salt and pepper to taste. Sprinkle the reserved spring onion slices over the stir-fry and serve hot.

Beef Satay

Satay recipes vary throughout the East, but these little beef skewers are a classic version of the traditional dish.

NUTRITIONAL INFORMATION

Calories	489	Sugars 14g
Protein	. . . . .38g	Fat 31g
Carbohydrate	. . .17g	Saturates 8g

 2¼ hrs   15 mins

SERVES 4

INGREDIENTS

500 g/1 lb 2 oz beef fillet

2 garlic cloves, crushed

2 cm/¾ inch piece of fresh root ginger, finely grated

1 tbsp soft light brown sugar

1 tbsp dark soy sauce

1 tbsp lime juice

2 tsp sesame oil

1 tsp ground coriander

1 tsp ground turmeric

½ tsp chilli powder

chopped cucumber and red pepper, to serve

PEANUT SAUCE

300 ml/10 fl oz coconut milk

8 tbsp crunchy peanut butter

½ small onion, grated

2 tsp soft light brown sugar

½ tsp chilli powder

1 tbsp dark soy sauce

1 Cut the beef into 1 cm/½ inch cubes and place in a large bowl.

2 Add the garlic, ginger, sugar, soy sauce, lime juice, sesame oil, ground coriander, turmeric and chilli powder. Mix well to coat the pieces of meat evenly. Cover with clingfilm and set aside to marinate in the refrigerator for at least 2 hours, or overnight.

3 To make the peanut sauce, place all the ingredients in a heavy-based pan and stir over a medium heat until boiling. Remove from the heat and keep warm.

4 Thread the beef cubes on to bamboo skewers. Grill the skewers under a preheated grill for 3–5 minutes, turning often, until golden. Alternatively, barbecue over hot coals. It is important to cook the beef quickly, so make sure the grill or barbecue is very hot before you begin to cook. Serve skewers with the peanut sauce and garnish with chopped cucumber and red pepper pieces.

Beef with Lemon Grass

Colourful peppers help to complete this delicately flavoured stir-fry infused with lemon grass and ginger.

NUTRITIONAL INFORMATION

Calories	230	Sugars	........4g
Protein	........26g	Fat	..........12g
Carbohydrate	....6g	Saturates	.......3g

5 mins   8 mins

SERVES 4

INGREDIENTS

500 g/1 lb 2 oz lean beef fillet

2 tbsp vegetable oil

1 garlic clove, finely chopped

1 lemon grass stalk, finely shredded

2 tsp finely chopped fresh root ginger

1 red pepper, deseeded and thickly sliced

1 green pepper, deseeded and thickly sliced

1 onion, thickly sliced

2 tbsp lime juice

salt and pepper

boiled noodles or rice, to serve

1 If you have time, place the beef in the freezer for 30 minutes beforehand. This helps firm it up, which makes it easier to slice very thinly. Cut the beef into long, thin strips, cutting across the grain.

2 Heat the oil in a large frying pan or wok over a high heat. Add the garlic and stir-fry for 1 minute.

3 Add the beef and stir-fry for a further 2–3 minutes until lightly coloured. Stir in the lemon grass and ginger and remove the pan or wok from the heat.

4 Remove the beef from the pan or wok and set aside. Add the peppers and onion to the pan or wok and stir-fry over a high heat for 2–3 minutes until the onions are just turning golden brown and slightly softened.

5 Return the beef to the pan, stir in the lime juice and season to taste with salt and pepper. Serve immediately with noodles or rice.

COOK'S TIP

When preparing lemon grass, take care to remove the outer layers, which can be tough and fibrous. Use only the centre, tender part, which has the finest flavour.

Red-hot Beef with Cashews

Hot and spicy, these quick-cooked beef strips are very tempting.
Serve them with lots of plain rice and cucumber slices to offset the heat.

NUTRITIONAL INFORMATION

Calories 257	Sugars 1g	
Protein 32g	Fat 13g	
Carbohydrate 3g	Saturates 4g	

2¼–3¼ hrs   10 mins

SERVES 4

INGREDIENTS

500 g/1 lb 2 oz boneless, lean beef sirloin,
  thinly sliced

1 tsp vegetable oil

1 tsp sesame oil

4 tbsp unsalted cashew nuts

1 spring onion, thickly sliced diagonally

cucumber slices, to garnish

MARINADE

1 tbsp sesame seeds

1 garlic clove, chopped

1 tbsp finely chopped fresh ginger root

1 fresh red bird-eye chilli, chopped

2 tbsp dark soy sauce

1 tsp red curry paste

1 Cut the beef into 1 cm/½ inch wide strips. Place them in a large, non-metallic bowl.

2 To make the marinade, dry-fry the sesame seeds in a heavy-based pan over a medium heat for 2–3 minutes.

3 Place the seeds in a mortar with the garlic, ginger and chilli and grind to a smooth paste with a pestle. Add the soy sauce and curry paste and mix well.

4 Spoon the paste over the beef strips and toss well to coat the meat evenly. Cover and set aside to marinate in the refrigerator for 2–3 hours or overnight.

5 Heat a heavy-based frying pan or griddle until very hot and brush with vegetable oil. Add the beef strips and cook quickly, turning frequently, until lightly browned. Remove from the heat and spoon into a pile on a warmed serving dish.

6 Heat the sesame oil in a small pan and fry the cashew nuts until golden. Add the spring onions and stir-fry for 30 seconds. Sprinkle the mixture on to the beef and serve garnished with cucumber.

Hot Beef & Coconut Curry

The heat of the chillies in this red-hot curry is balanced and softened by the coconut milk, producing a creamy-textured and lavishly spiced dish.

NUTRITIONAL INFORMATION

Calories	230	Sugars	.........6g
Protein	........29g	Fat	..........10g
Carbohydrate	....8g	Saturates	.......3g

🥚 10 mins 🕐 45 mins

SERVES 4

INGREDIENTS

400 ml/14 fl oz coconut milk

2 tbsp Thai red curry paste

2 garlic cloves, crushed

500 g/1lb 2 oz braising steak

2 kaffir lime leaves, shredded

3 tbsp kaffir lime juice

2 tbsp Thai fish sauce

1 large fresh red chilli, deseeded and sliced

½ tsp ground turmeric

2 tbsp chopped fresh basil leaves

2 tbsp chopped fresh coriander leaves

salt and pepper

shredded coconut, to garnish

boiled rice, to serve

1 Place the coconut milk in a large pan and bring to the boil. Lower the heat and simmer gently over a low heat for about 10 minutes until the milk has thickened. Stir in the red curry paste and garlic and simmer for a further 5 minutes.

2 Cut the beef into 2 cm/¾ inch chunks, add to the pan and bring to the boil, stirring. Lower the heat and add the lime leaves, lime juice, fish sauce, chilli, turmeric and ½ teaspoon salt. Cover the pan and simmer gently for a further 20–25 minutes until the meat is tender and cooked through, adding a little water if the sauce looks too dry.

3 Stir in the basil and coriander and adjust the seasoning with salt and pepper to taste. Transfer to a warmed serving dish, sprinkle with coconut and serve with boiled rice.

COOK'S TIP

This recipe uses one of the larger, milder red chilli peppers – either fresno or Dutch – simply because they give more colour to the dish. If you prefer to use small Thai, or bird-eye, chillies, you'll still need only 1 as they are much hotter.

Beef Toppers

Beef burgers need never be dull when they are accompanied by one of these tasty toppings.

NUTRITIONAL INFORMATION

Calories ....537 Sugars 13g
Protein ....60g Fat 25g
Carbohydrate ...19g Saturates 8g

 1 hr   10–20 mins

SERVES 4

INGREDIENTS

700 g/1 lb 9 oz lean minced beef

1 onion, finely chopped

2 tbsp Worcestershire sauce

salt and pepper

sesame baps, toasted, to serve

SAVOURY MUSHROOMS

115 g/4 oz button mushrooms, sliced

1 tbsp soy sauce

1 tbsp Worcestershire sauce

GUACAMOLE

1 avocado

1 garlic clove

1 tbsp lemon juice

1 tbsp tomato relish

BARBECUE SAUCE

3 tbsp brown fruity sauce

3 tbsp tomato ketchup

1 tsp wholegrain mustard

1 tbsp clear honey

1 To make the savoury mushrooms, combine all the ingredients and set aside to marinate for at least 30 minutes.

2 To make the guacamole, peel, stone and mash the avocado. Combine it with the remaining ingredients, cover and chill in the refrigerator.

3 To make the barbecue sauce, combine all the ingredients, cover and chill.

4 To make the beefburgers, combine the minced beef, onion and Worcestershire sauce and season to taste with salt and pepper. Divide the mixture into 6 portions and pat each into a neat round, about 1 cm/½ inch thick. Cover and chill in the refrigerator for at least 30 minutes.

5 Barbecue over hot coals for 5–10 minutes on each side. Serve the burgers in the baps, with your chosen topping spooned on top.

Boozy Beef Steaks

A simple, whisky- or brandy-flavoured marinade
gives plain steaks a fabulous flavour for very little effort.

NUTRITIONAL INFORMATION

Calories 371	Sugars 5g	
Protein 48g	Fat 14g	
Carbohydrate 6g	Saturates 6g	

2¼ hrs   6–12 mins

SERVES 4

I N G R E D I E N T S

4 beef steaks

4 tbsp whisky or brandy

2 tbsp soy sauce

1 tbsp dark muscovado sugar

pepper

fresh parsley sprigs, to garnish

TO SERVE

slices of tomato

garlic bread

1 Make a few cuts in the edge of fat on each steak, using a sharp knife or kitchen scissors. This will prevent the meat from curling as it cooks.

2 Place the meat in a shallow, non-metallic dish.

3 Combine the whisky or brandy, soy sauce, sugar and pepper to taste in a small bowl, stirring until the sugar has dissolved. Pour the marinade over the steak, turning to coat. Cover with clingfilm and set aside to marinate in the refrigerator for at least 2 hours.

4 Drain the steak. Barbecue over hot coals, searing the meat over the hottest part of the barbecue for about 2 minutes on each side.

5 Move the steak to an area of the barbecue with slightly less intense heat (usually the sides) and cook for a further 4–10 minutes on each side, depending on how well done you like your steaks. Test the meat is cooked by inserting the tip of a knife into the meat – the juices will run from red when the meat is still rare, to clear as it becomes well cooked.

6 Meanwhile, lightly barbecue the slices of tomato for 1–2 minutes.

7 Transfer the meat and the tomatoes to warmed serving plates. Garnish each with a sprig of fresh parsley and serve immediately with garlic bread.

Surf & Turf Kebabs

This dish originated in Australia. The name refers to the prawns from the sea – the 'surf' - and the meat from the land – the 'turf'.

NUTRITIONAL INFORMATION

Calories	186	Sugars	.........0g
Protein	........20g	Fat	...........11g
Carbohydrate	....2g	Saturates	.......2g

🍖 35 mins   🕐 5–10 mins

SERVES 4

INGREDIENTS

450 g/1 lb rump or sirloin steak

18 raw prawns

MARINADE

5 tbsp oyster sauce

1 tbsp soy sauce

3 tbsp lemon juice

4 tbsp sunflower oil

1 Cut the steaks into 24 even-size pieces and place them in a non-metallic dish.

2 Peel and devein the prawns, leaving the tail attached.

3 To make the marinade, combine the oyster sauce, soy sauce, lemon juice and sunflower oil in a small bowl. Pour the mixture over the meat, turning to coat, and set aside to marinate for 15 minutes.

4 Add the prawns to the marinade, toss to coat, and marinate for 5 minutes.

5 Remove the steak cubes and prawns from the marinade, reserving the marinade for basting. Thread the meat on to metal or pre-soaked wooden skewers, alternating the steak with the prawns. (Pre-soaking wooden skewers helps to prevent them from burning.)

6 Barbecue the kebabs over hot coals for 5–10 minutes, basting with the reserved marinade and turning frequently.

7 Transfer the kebabs to warmed serving plates and serve immediately.

VARIATION

Other shellfish, such as lobster and crab, can be added to the skewers. These kebabs are also delicious marinated in and basted with a herb, garlic and oil marinade.

Beef with Wild Mushrooms

Choose fairly thick steaks for this dish – it will be easier to cut the pockets in the side of each one.

NUTRITIONAL INFORMATION

Calories 414	Sugars 0g	
Protein 49g	Fat 24g	
Carbohydrate 1g	Saturates 13g	

  10 mins   6–12 mins

SERVES 4

INGREDIENTS

4 fillet or sirloin steaks

2 tbsp butter

1–2 garlic cloves, crushed

150 g/5½ oz mixed wild mushrooms

2 tbsp chopped fresh parsley

TO SERVE

salad leaves

cherry tomatoes, halved

1 Place the steaks on a chopping board and using a sharp knife, cut a pocket in the side of each steak.

2 To make the stuffing, heat the butter in a frying pan, add the garlic and cook gently for about 1 minute.

3 Add the mushrooms to the pan and cook gently for 4–6 minutes until tender. Stir in the parsley.

4 Divide the mushroom mixture into 4 and insert a portion into the pocket of each steak. Seal the pocket closed with a cocktail stick. If preparing ahead, let the mixture cool before stuffing the steaks.

5 Barbecue the steaks over hot coals, searing the meat over the hottest part of the barbecue for about 2 minutes on each side. Move the steaks to an area with slightly less intense heat (usually the sides) and barbecue for a further 4–10 minutes on each side, depending on how well done you like your steaks.

6 Transfer the steaks to serving plates and remove the cocktail sticks. Serve with salad leaves and cherry tomatoes.

COOK'S TIP

Wild mushrooms, such as shiitake, oyster and chanterelle, are now readily available in supermarkets. Look for boxes of mixed wild mushrooms, which are usually cheaper than buying the different types individually.

Roasted Red Pork

This red-glazed, sweet and tender pork, of Chinese origin, is a colourful addition to many stir-fries, salads and soups.

NUTRITIONAL INFORMATION

Calories 276   Sugars 5g
Protein . . . . .34g   Fat 13g
Carbohydrate . . . .7g   Saturates 4g

8¼ hrs   1 hr

SERVES 4

INGREDIENTS

600 g/1 lb 5 oz pork fillet

red chilli flower, to garnish

Chinese leaves, shredded to serve

MARINADE

2 garlic cloves, crushed

1 tbsp grated fresh root ginger root

1 tbsp light soy sauce

1 tbsp Thai fish sauce

1 tbsp rice wine

1 tbsp hoisin sauce

1 tbsp sesame oil

1 tbsp palm sugar or soft brown sugar

½ tsp Chinese five-spice powder

a few drops red food colouring (optional)

1 Mix all the ingredients for the marinade together and spread the mixture over the pork, turning to coat evenly. Place in a large dish, cover and set aside in the refrigerator to marinate overnight.

2 Place a rack in a roasting tin, then half-fill the tin with boiling water. Lift the pork from the marinade and place on the rack. Reserve the marinade for later.

3 Roast in a preheated oven, 220°C/425°F/Gas Mark 7, for about 20 minutes. Baste with the reserved marinade, then lower the heat to 180°C/350°F/Gas Mark 4 and continue roasting for a further 35–40 minutes, basting occasionally with the marinade, until the pork is a rich reddish brown and thoroughly cooked.

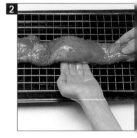

4 Transfer the pork to a chopping board and cut into even slices. Arrange the slices on a bed of shredded Chinese leaves on a serving platter, garnish with a red chilli flower and serve immediately.

COOK'S TIP

The pork may also be grilled. Cut the meat into slices or strips and coat in the marinade, then arrange on a foil-lined grill pan and grill under a high heat, turning occasionally and basting with marinade.

Pork with Soy & Sesame

Thai cooks are fond of adding sweet flavours to meat, as in this unusual pork dish, with soy and garlic to balance the sweetness of the honey.

NUTRITIONAL INFORMATION

Calories .... 322 Sugars 8g
Protein .... 35g Fat 14g
Carbohydrate ... 13g Saturates 14g

40 mins   35 mins

SERVES 4

I N G R E D I E N T S

2 pork fillets, about 275 g/9½ oz each

2 tbsp dark soy sauce

2 tbsp clear honey

2 garlic cloves, crushed

1 tbsp sesame seeds

1 onion, thinly sliced and pushed out into rings

1 tbsp seasoned plain flour

sunflower oil, for frying

crisp salad, to serve

1 Trim the pork fillets and place them in a wide non-metallic dish.

2 Combine the soy sauce, honey and garlic. Spread this mixture over the pork, turning the meat to coat it evenly. Set aside to marinate for 30 minutes.

3 Lift the pork fillets into a roasting tin or shallow ovenproof dish. Sprinkle evenly with sesame seeds.

4 Roast the pork in a preheated oven, 200°C/400°F/ Gas Mark 6, for about 20 minutes, spooning over any juices. Cover loosely with foil to prevent over-browning and roast for a further 10–15 minutes until the meat is thoroughly cooked.

5 Meanwhile, dip the onion rings in the flour and shake off the excess. Heat the oil and fry the onion rings until golden and crisp, turning occasionally.

6 Remove the pork from the oven and set aside for 5 minutes, then cut into slices. Serve the slices on a bed of crisp salad, garnished with fried onion rings.

COOK'S TIP

This pork is also excellent served cold, and it's a good choice for picnics, especially served with a spicy sambal or chilli relish.

Spicy Fried Minced Pork

A warmly spiced dish, this is ideal for a quick family meal. Just cook fine egg noodles for an accompaniment while the meat sizzles.

NUTRITIONAL INFORMATION

Calories	278	Sugars	.........4g
Protein	........28g	Fat	16
Carbohydrate	....7g	Saturates	.......4g

 5 mins   15 mins

SERVES 4

I N G R E D I E N T S

2 garlic cloves

3 shallots

2 tbsp sunflower oil

2 tsp finely chopped fresh root ginger

500 g/1 lb 2 oz lean minced pork

2 tbsp Thai fish sauce

1 tbsp dark soy sauce

1 tbsp red curry paste

4 dried kaffir lime leaves, crumbled

4 plum tomatoes, chopped

3 tbsp chopped fresh coriander

salt and pepper

boiled fine egg noodles, to serve

T O   G A R N I S H

fresh coriander sprigs

COOK'S TIP

Dried kaffir lime leaves are a useful store-cupboard ingredient as they can be crumbled easily straight into quick dishes such as this. If you prefer to use fresh kaffir lime leaves, shred them finely and add to the dish.

1 Peel and finely chop the garlic and shallots. Heat the oil in a wok over a medium heat. Add the garlic, shallots and ginger and stir-fry for about 2 minutes. Stir in the pork and continue stir-frying until golden brown.

2 Stir in the fish sauce, soy sauce, curry paste and lime leaves and stir-fry for a further 1–2 minutes over a high heat.

3 Add the chopped tomatoes and cook stirring occasionally, for a furthe 5–6 minutes.

4 Stir in the chopped coriander and season to taste with salt and peppe Serve hot, spooned on to boiled fine eg noodles, garnished with coriander sprigs.

Thai-spiced Sausages

These mildly spiced little sausages are a good choice for a buffet meal.
They can be made a day in advance, and are equally good hot or cold.

NUTRITIONAL INFORMATION

Calories	206	Sugars	.........0g
Protein	........22g	Fat	...........11g
Carbohydrate	....4g	Saturates	.......2g

15 mins   8–10 mins

SERVES 4

INGREDIENTS

400 g/14 oz lean minced pork

4 tbsp cooked rice

1 garlic clove, crushed

1 tsp Thai red curry paste

1 tsp ground black pepper

1 tsp ground coriander

½ tsp salt

3 tbsp lime juice

2 tbsp chopped fresh coriander

3 tbsp groundnut oil

coconut sambal or soy sauce, to serve

1 Place the pork, rice, garlic, curry paste, pepper, ground coriander, salt, lime juice and chopped coriander in a bowl and knead together with your hands to mix evenly.

2 Use your hands to shape the mixture into 12 small sausage shapes. If you can buy sausage casings, fill the casings and twist at intervals.

3 Heat the oil in a large frying pan over a medium heat. Add the sausages, in batches if necessary, and fry for 8–10 minutes, turning them over occasionally, until they are evenly golden brown. Serve hot with a coconut sambal or soy sauce.

COOK'S TIP

These sausages can also be served as an appetiser – shape the mixture into slightly smaller shapes to make about 16 bite-size sausages. Serve them with a soy dip.

Thai-style Burgers

If your family likes to eat burgers, try these – they have a much more interesting flavour than conventional hamburgers!

NUTRITIONAL INFORMATION

Calories	358	Sugars	.........1g
Protein	........23g	Fat	..........29g
Carbohydrate	....2g	Saturates	.......5g

 15 mins 6–8 mins

SERVES 4

INGREDIENTS

1 small lemon grass stalk

1 small fresh red chilli, deseeded

2 garlic cloves, peeled

2 spring onions

200 g/7 oz closed-cup mushrooms

400 g/14 oz minced pork

1 tbsp Thai fish sauce

3 tbsp chopped fresh coriander

sunflower oil, for frying

2 tbsp mayonnaise

1 tbsp lime juice

salt and pepper

TO SERVE

4 sesame hamburger buns

shredded Chinese leaves

1 Place the lemon grass, chilli, garlic and spring onions in a food processor and process to a smooth paste. Add the mushrooms and process until very finely chopped.

2 Add the minced pork, fish sauce and coriander. Season to taste with salt and pepper, then divide the mixture into 4 equal portions and shape with lightly floured hands into flat burger shapes.

3 Heat the oil in a heavy-based frying pan over a medium heat. Add the burgers and fry for 6–8 minutes until well cooked or as you like them.

4 Meanwhile, mix the mayonnaise with the lime juice. Split the hamburger buns and spread the lime-flavoured mayonnaise on the cut surfaces. Add a few shredded Chinese leaves, top with a burger and sandwich together. Serve immediately, while still hot.

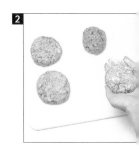

COOK'S TIP

You can add a spoonful of your favourite relish to each burger, or alternatively, add a few pieces of crisp pickled vegetables for a change of texture.

Red Lamb Curry

This curry uses the typically red-hot chilli flavour of Thai red curry paste, made with dried red chillies, to give it a warm, russet-red colour.

NUTRITIONAL INFORMATION

Calories	363	Sugars	........11g
Protein	........29g	Fat	..........19g
Carbohydrate	...21g	Saturates	.......6g

5 mins

35–40 mins

SERVES 4

I N G R E D I E N T S

00 g/1 lb 2 oz boneless lean
  leg of lamb

tbsp vegetable oil

large onion, sliced

garlic cloves, crushed

tbsp red curry paste

50 ml/5 fl oz coconut milk

tbsp soft light brown sugar

large red pepper, deseeded and
  thickly sliced

25 ml/4 fl oz lamb or beef stock

tbsp Thai fish sauce

tbsp lime juice

25 g/8 oz can water chestnuts, drained

tbsp fresh coriander, chopped

tbsp fresh basil, chopped

alt and pepper

oiled jasmine rice, to serve

esh basil leaves, to garnish

1 Trim the meat and cut it into 3 cm/1¼ inch cubes. Heat the oil in a arge frying pan or wok over a high heat nd stir-fry the onion and garlic for –3 minutes to soften. Add the meat and tir-fry until lightly browned.

2 Stir in the curry paste and cook for a few seconds, then add the coconut milk and sugar and bring to the boil. Reduce the heat and simmer for 15 minutes, stirring occasionally.

3 Stir in the red pepper, stock, fish sauce and lime juice, cover and continue simmering for a further 15 minutes or until the meat is tender.

4 Add the water chestnuts, coriander and basil, adjust the seasoning to taste. Serve with jasmine rice garnished with fresh basil leaves.

COOK'S TIP

This curry can also be made with other lean red meats. Try replacing the lamb with trimmed duck breasts or pieces of lean braising beef.

Red Wine Lamb Skewers

Use the best quality red wine you can afford. Instead of using fresh herbs, you can add a bouquet garni to the marinade.

NUTRITIONAL INFORMATION

Calories 353   Sugars 5g
Protein . . . . .24g   Fat 21g
Carbohydrate . . . .7g   Saturates 6g

 2½ hrs   8–10 mins

SERVES 4

INGREDIENTS

450 g/1 lb lean lamb

12 button onions or shallots

12 button mushrooms

MARINADE

150 ml/5 fl oz red wine

4 tbsp olive oil

2 tbsp brandy (optional)

1 onion, sliced

1 bay leaf

fresh thyme sprig

2 fresh parsley sprigs

TO SERVE

salad leaves

cherry tomatoes

1 Carefully trim away any excess fat from the lamb. Cut the lamb into large pieces.

2 To make the marinade, combine the wine, oil, brandy, onion, bay leaf and thyme and parsley sprigs in a non-metallic dish.

3 Add the meat and toss to coat. Cover the dish with clingfilm and set aside to marinate in the refrigerator for at least 2 hours or preferably overnight.

4 Bring a pan of water to a rolling boil, drop in the unpeeled button onions and blanch them for 3 minutes. Drain and refresh under cold water, and then drain again. Trim the onions and remove their skins.

5 Remove the meat from the marinade, reserving the liquid for basting. Thread the meat on to skewers, alternating with the button onions and mushrooms.

6 Barbecue the kebabs over hot coals for 8–10 minutes, turning and basting the meat and vegetables with the reserved marinade a few times.

7 Transfer the kebabs to warmed serving plates and serve with fresh salad leaves and cherry tomatoes.

VARIATION

This recipe also works well with beef. Bacon rolls can also be added to the skewers, if you like.

Lamb & Black Bean Burritos

Stir-fried marinated lamb strips are paired with earthy black beans in these tasty filled tortillas.

NUTRITIONAL INFORMATION

Calories	.551	Sugars	.4g
Protein	.45g	Fat	.19g
Carbohydrate	.52g	Saturates	.7g

4¼ hrs   15–20 mins

SERVES 4

INGREDIENTS

600 g/1 lb 5 oz lean lamb

2 garlic cloves, finely chopped

Juice of ½ lime

½ tsp mild chilli powder

½ tsp ground cumin

pinch of dried oregano

1–2 tbsp extra virgin olive oil

400 g/14 oz cooked or canned black beans, seasoned with cumin, salt and pepper

4 large flour tortillas

2–3 tbsp chopped fresh coriander

salsa of your choice

salt and pepper

1 Slice the lamb into thin strips, then combine with the garlic, lime juice, chilli powder, cumin, oregano and olive oil. Season with salt and pepper. Set aside to marinate in the refrigerator for 4 hours.

2 Warm the black beans with a little water in a pan.

3 Heat the tortillas in an ungreased non-stick frying pan, sprinkling them with a few drops of water as they heat; wrap the tortillas in a clean tea towel as you work to keep them warm.

Alternatively, heat through in a stack in the pan, alternating the top and bottom tortillas so that they warm evenly.

4 Stir-fry the lamb in a heavy-based non-stick frying pan over high heat until browned on all sides. Remove from the heat.

5 Spoon some of the beans and browned meat into a tortilla, sprinkle with coriander, then top with salsa and roll up. Repeat with the remaining tortillas and serve immediately.

VARIATION
Add a spoonful or two of cooked rice to each burrito.

Carnitas

In this classic Mexican dish, pieces of pork are first simmered to make them meltingly tender, then browned until irresistibly crisp.

NUTRITIONAL INFORMATION

Calories	236	Sugars	.........1g
Protein	........36g	Fat	..........9g
Carbohydrate	....3g	Saturates	.......3g

  45 mins 2½ hrs

SERVES 4–6

INGREDIENTS

1 kg/2 lb 4 oz pork, such as lean belly

1 onion, chopped

1 garlic bulb, cut in half

½ tsp ground cumin

2 meat stock cubes

2 bay leaves

vegetable oil, for frying

salt and pepper

fresh chilli strips, to garnish

TO SERVE

cooked rice

refried beans (see page 643)

salsa of your choice

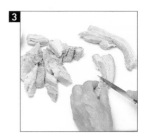

1 Place the pork in a heavy-based pan with the onion, garlic, cumin, stock cubes and bay leaves. Add just enough water to cover. Bring to the boil, then reduce the heat to very low. Skim off the foam and scum that forms on the surface of the liquid.

2 Simmer very gently for about 2 hours or until the meat is cooked through and tender. Remove the pan from the heat and set the meat aside to cool in the cooking liquid.

3 Remove the meat from the pan with a draining spoon. Cut off any rind (roast separately to make crackling). Cut the meat into bite-size pieces and sprinkle with salt and pepper to taste. Reserve 300 ml/10 fl oz of the cooking liquid.

4 Brown the meat in a heavy-based frying pan for about 15 minutes to cook out the fat. Add the reserved cooking liquid and reduce. Cover and cook the meat for a further 15 minutes, turning the meat occasionally.

5 Transfer the meat to a serving dish, garnish with chilli strips and serve with rice, refried beans and salsa.

Simmered Medley

A big pot of 'cocido' is warming on a cold day, great for a family meal.
Serve with a selection of several salsas and a stack of corn tortillas.

NUTRITIONAL INFORMATION

Calories ....555 Sugars 17g
Protein ....47g Fat 33g
Carbohydrate ...19g Saturates 12g

🔥 10 mins 🕐 2¼ hrs

SERVES 6–8

I N G R E D I E N T S

900 g/2 lb boneless pork

2 bay leaves

1 onion, chopped

3 garlic cloves, finely chopped

2 tbsp chopped fresh coriander

1 carrot, thinly sliced

2 celery sticks, diced

2 chicken stock cubes

½ chicken, cut into portions

4–5 ripe tomatoes, diced

½ tsp mild chilli powder

grated rind of ¼ orange

¼ tsp ground cumin

juice of 3 oranges

1 courgette, cut into bite-size pieces

¼ cabbage, thinly sliced and blanched

1 apple, cut into bite-size pieces

about 10 prunes, stoned

¼ tsp ground cinnamon

pinch of ground ginger

2 hard chorizo sausages, about 350 g/12 oz
  in total, cut into bite-size pieces

salt and pepper

rice, tortillas and salsa, to serve

1 Combine the pork, bay leaves, onion, garlic, coriander, carrot and celery in a large pan and fill with cold water. Bring to the boil, skim off the scum on the surface. Reduce the heat and simmer gently for 1 hour.

2 Add the stock cubes to the pan, with the chicken, tomatoes, chilli powder, orange rind and cumin. Cook for a further 45 minutes or until the chicken is tender. Spoon off the fat that forms on the top.

3 Add the orange juice, courgette, cabbage, apple, prunes, cinnamon, ginger and chorizo. Simmer for a further 20 minutes or until the courgette is soft and tender and the chorizo is completely cooked through.

4 Season the stew with salt and pepper to taste. Serve immediately with rice, tortillas and salsa.

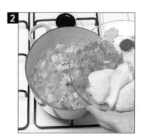

Traditional Provençal Daube

It isn't sunny all year round in the Mediterranean. In the winter, when the fierce winds blow, warming hearty stews are welcome.

NUTRITIONAL INFORMATION

Calories 312	Sugars 4g
Protein 21g	Fat 12g
Carbohydrate . . .20g	Saturates 3g

4½ hrs   3½–4 hrs

SERVES 4–6

INGREDIENTS

700 g/1 lb 9 oz boneless lean stewing beef, such as leg, cut into 5 cm/2 inch pieces

400 ml/14 fl oz full-bodied dry red wine

2 tbsp olive oil

4 large garlic cloves, crushed

4 shallots, thinly sliced

250 g/9 oz unsmoked lardons

5–6 tbsp plain flour

250 g/9 oz large chestnut mushrooms, sliced

400 g/14 oz can chopped tomatoes

1 large bouquet garni of 1 bay leaf, 2 dried thyme sprigs and 2 fresh parsley sprigs, tied in a 7.5 cm/3 inch piece of celery

5 cm/2 inch strip of dried orange rind (optional)

450 ml/16 fl oz oz beef stock

50 g/1¾ oz can anchovy fillets in oil

2 tbsp capers in brine, drained and rinsed

2 tbsp red wine vinegar

2 tbsp finely chopped fresh parsley

salt and pepper

1 Place the stewing beef in a non-metallic bowl with the wine, olive oil, half the garlic and the shallots. Cover and set aside to marinate for at least 4 hours, stirring occasionally.

2 Meanwhile, place the lardons in a pan of water, bring to the boil and simmer for 10 minutes. Drain.

3 Place 4 tablespoons of the flour in a bowl and stir in about 2 tablespoons water to make a thick paste. Cover with clingfilm and set aside.

4 Strain the marinated beef, reserving the marinade. Pat the beef dry and toss in seasoned flour.

5 Arrange a layer of lardons, mushrooms and tomatoes in a large flameproof casserole, then add a layer of beef.

Continue layering until all the ingredient are used, tucking in the bouquet garni and orange rind, if using.

6 Pour in the beef stock and reserved marinade. Spread the flour paste around the rim of the casserole. Press on the lid to make a tight seal (make more paste if necessary).

7 Cook in a preheated oven, 160°C 325°F/Gas Mark 3, for 2½ hours Meanwhile, drain the anchovies, then mash with the capers and remaining garlic in a mortar with a pestle.

8 Remove the casserole, break the seal and stir in the mashed anchovies vinegar and parsley. Re-cover and continue cooking for 1–1½ hours until the meat is tender. Taste and adjust the seasoning and serve immediately.

Vitello Tonnato

This classic dish of cold, thinly sliced veal with a creamy
tuna sauce makes the most luxurious hot-weather meal.

NUTRITIONAL INFORMATION

Calories 205	Sugars 0g
Protein 3g	Fat 8g
Carbohydrate 0g	Saturates 2g

🧊 10 hrs   🕐 1¼–1½ hrs

SERVES 6–8

INGREDIENTS

boned and rolled piece of veal leg, about
900 g/2 lb boned weight

live oil

alt and pepper

TUNA MAYONNAISE

50 g/5½ oz can tuna in olive oil

large eggs

bout 3 tbsp lemon juice

live oil

TO GARNISH

black olives, stoned and halved

tbsp capers in brine, rinsed and drained

nely chopped fresh flat leaf parsley

mon wedges

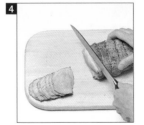

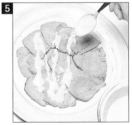

1 Rub the veal all over with oil and
pepper and place in a roasting tin .
over the meat with a piece of foil if there
n't any fat on it, then roast in a
reheated oven, 230°C/450°F/ Gas Mark 8,
r 10 minutes. Lower the temperature to
80°C/350°F/Gas Mark 4 and continue
asting for 1 hour for medium or
¼ hours for well-done. Set the veal aside
cool completely, reserving any juices in
e roasting tin.

2 Drain the tuna, reserving the oil.
Blend the eggs in a food processor
with 1 teaspoon of the lemon juice and a
pinch of salt. Add olive oil to the tuna oil
to make up to 300 ml/10 fl oz.

3 With the motor running, add the oil
to the eggs, drop by drop, until a thin
mayonnaise forms. Add the tuna and
process until smooth. Blend in lemon juice
to taste. Adjust the seasoning.

4 Slice the meat very thinly. Add any
juices to the reserved roasting juices.
Gradually pour the veal juices into the
tuna mayonnaise, whisking to a thin,
pouring consistency.

5 Layer the veal slices with the sauce
on a platter, ending with a layer of
sauce. Cover and chill overnight. Garnish
with olives, capers and of parsley. Arrange
lemon wedges around the edge and serve.

Lamb Skewers on Rosemary

Wild rosemary scents the air all over the Mediterranean – here, branches of the herb are used as skewers for succulent lamb cubes.

NUTRITIONAL INFORMATION

Calories	286	Sugars	.........5g
Protein	........27g	Fat	..........16g
Carbohydrate	....7g	Saturates	.......6g

4 hrs   10–12 mins

MAKES 4

INGREDIENTS

500 g/1 lb 2 oz boneless leg of lamb

4 long, thick branches of fresh rosemary

1 or 2 red peppers, depending on the size

12 large garlic cloves, peeled

olive oil

Spiced Pilau with Saffron (see page 433), to serve

MARINADE

2 tbsp olive oil

2 tbsp dry white wine

½ tsp ground cumin

1 fresh oregano sprig, chopped

1 At least 4 hours before cooking, cut the lamb into 5 cm/2 inch cubes. Combine all the marinade ingredients in a bowl. Add the lamb cubes, stir to coat and set aside to marinate for at least 4 hours.

2 An hour before cooking, put the rosemary in a bowl of cold water and set aside to soak.

3 Slice the tops off the peppers. Cut the peppers in half, then quarters and remove the seeds. Cut the quarters into 5 cm/2 inch pieces.

4 Bring a small pan of water to the boil, add the red pepper pieces and garlic cloves and blanch for 1 minute. Drain and refresh under cold running water and drain well again. Pat dry with kitchen paper and set aside.

5 Remove the rosemary branches from the water and pat dry with kitchen paper. To make the skewers, remove the rosemary needles from about the first 4 cm/1¾ inches of the branches so you have a 'handle' to turn them over with while grilling.

6 Thread alternate pieces of lamb, garli and red pepper pieces on to th 4 rosemary skewers: the meat should b tender enough to push the sprig through i but, if not, use a metal skewer to poke hole in the centre of each cube.

7 Lightly oil the grill rack. Place th skewers on the rack about 12.5 cm 5 inches under a preheated hot grill an cook for 10–12 minutes, brushing with an leftover marinade or with olive oil an turning, until the meat is cooked. Serv with the pilau.

Cypriot Lamb with Orzo

This recipe, which uses an inexpensive cut of lamb, fits the bill when you are catering for a crowd as it requires little attention while cooking.

NUTRITIONAL INFORMATION

Calories	447	Sugars	.........5g
Protein	........44g	Fat	..........15g
Carbohydrate	...36g	Saturates	.......7g

30 mins   3¾–4¼ hrs

SERVES 6

INGREDIENTS

large garlic cloves

shoulder of lamb

x 400 g/14 oz cans chopped tomatoes

fresh thyme sprigs

fresh parsley sprigs

bay leaf

25 ml/4 fl oz water

50 g/9 oz orzo pasta

salt and pepper

fresh thyme sprigs, to garnish

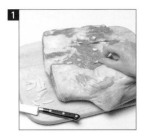

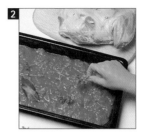

1 Cut the garlic cloves in half and remove the green cores, then thinly slice. Using the tip of a sharp knife, make slits all over the lamb shoulder, then insert the garlic slices into the slits.

2 Tip the tomatoes and their juices into a roasting tin large enough to hold the lamb shoulder. Add the thyme, parsley and bay leaf. Place the lamb on top, skin side up, and cover the tin tightly with a sheet of foil, shiny side down. Scrunch the foil all around the edge so that none of the juices can escape during cooking.

3 Place the tin in a preheated oven, 160°C/325°F/Gas Mark 3, and cook for 3½–4 hours until the lamb is cooked through and tender and the tomatoes are reduced to a thick sauce.

4 Remove the lamb from the roasting tin and set aside. Using a large metal spoon, skim off as much fat from the surface of the tomato sauce as possible.

5 Add the water and orzo to the tomatoes, stirring so the grains are submerged. Add a little extra water if the sauce seems too thick. Season to taste with salt and pepper. Return the lamb to the roasting tin.

6 Re-cover the roasting tin and return to the oven for 15 minutes or until the orzo is tender. Remove and discard the bay leaf. Set the lamb aside to rest for about 10 minutes, then slice and serve with the orzo in tomato sauce, garnished with fresh thyme sprigs.

Beef in Beer

Beef and beer is a traditional combination in all brewing countries.
Use a strong dark beer or stout to create the fullest flavour.

NUTRITIONAL INFORMATION

Calories	224	Sugars	5g
Protein	27g	Fat	9g
Carbohydrate	6g	Saturates	3g

15 mins   2–2½ hrs

SERVES 4

INGREDIENTS

few sprigs of fresh parsley

1 tbsp sunflower or corn oil

500 g/1 lb 2 oz lean stewing steak,
   trimmed of all visible fat and cut into
   2.5 cm/1 inch cubes

1 onion, chopped

200 g/7 oz chestnut mushrooms, cut in half

4 tsp dark muscovado sugar

350 ml/12 fl oz beef stock

300 ml/10 fl oz dark beer or stout

salt and pepper

2 Add the onion to the frying pan and cook over a low heat, stirring occasionally, for 3 minutes. Add the mushrooms and sugar and cook, stirring occasionally, for 10 minutes. Transfer to the casserole with a slotted spoon.

3 Add the beef stock, dark beer and reserved parsley to the casserole and season to taste with salt and pepper. Bring to the boil, cover and simmer over a very low heat for 1½–2 hours, or until tender. Serve hot.

1 Using a sharp knife, chop the fresh parsley finely and set aside until required. Heat the sunflower oil in a large, heavy-based frying pan. Add the stewing steak and cook, stirring frequently, for 10 minutes, or until browned all over. Using a slotted spoon, transfer the meat to a large flameproof casserole dish.

Beef in Black Bean Sauce

Because the cooking time when stir-frying is so brief, the vegetables retain most of their nutrients – and their flavour and texture too.

NUTRITIONAL INFORMATION

Calories	190	Sugars	.........3g
Protein	........16g	Fat	..........9g
Carbohydrate	...12g	Saturates	.......2g

🥘 6¼ hrs 🕐 15 mins

SERVES 4

INGREDIENTS

225 g/8 oz lean rump steak

1 tbsp peanut or corn oil

225 g/8 oz broccoli, cut into florets

115 g/4 oz baby corn cobs, cut in
  half diagonally

3 tbsp water

4 spring onions, sliced diagonally

225 g/8 oz canned water chestnuts,
  drained, rinsed and sliced

MARINADE

1 tbsp fermented black beans, soaked in
  cold water for 5–10 minutes

2 tbsp dark soy sauce

2 tbsp Chinese rice vinegar

1 tbsp peanut or corn oil

1 tsp brown sugar

1 garlic clove, thinly sliced

1 tbsp finely chopped fresh root ginger

1 Trim the steak of all visible fat and thinly slice. Put the steak in a shallow, non-metallic dish. To make the marinade, mash the black beans in a bowl with a fork. Stir in the remaining ingredients until thoroughly blended. Pour the marinade over the steak, turning to coat thoroughly. Cover with clingfilm and leave in the refrigerator to marinate for up to 6 hours.

2 Heat the peanut oil in a preheated wok or large frying pan. Drain the steak and reserve the marinade. Stir-fry the steak over a medium–high heat for 3 minutes, then transfer to a plate. Add the broccoli and baby corn cobs to the wok and stir in the water. Cover and steam over a low heat for 5 minutes, or until the vegetables are tender.

3 Add the spring onions and water chestnuts to the wok. Stir-fry for 2 minutes. Return the steak to the wok and pour in the reserved marinade. Cook, stirring, until heated through, then serve.

COOK'S TIP

Fermented black beans are available in cans or bags from Chinese food shops. They should be soaked in cold water before use to remove any excess salt.

Spaghetti & Shellfish

Frozen shelled prawns from the freezer can become the star ingredient in this colourful and tasty dish.

NUTRITIONAL INFORMATION

Calories	.510	Sugars	.38g
Protein	.33g	Fat	.24g
Carbohydrate	.44g	Saturates	.11g

35 mins | 30 mins

SERVES 4

INGREDIENTS

225 g/8 oz dried short-cut spaghetti, or long spaghetti broken into 15 cm/ 6 inch lengths

1 tbsp olive oil

300 ml/10 fl oz chicken stock

1 tsp lemon juice

1 small cauliflower, cut into florets

2 carrots, thinly sliced

115 g/4 oz mangetouts

4 tbsp butter

1 onion, sliced

225 g/8 oz courgettes, thinly sliced

1 garlic clove, chopped

350 g/12 oz frozen shelled prawns, thawed

2 tbsp chopped fresh parsley

25 g/1 oz Parmesan, grated

½ tsp paprika

salt and pepper

4 unshelled prawns, to garnish (optional)

1 Bring a large pan of lightly salted water to the boil. Add the pasta, bring back to the boil and cook for 8–10 minutes until tender, but still firm to the bite. Drain, then return to the pan and stir in the oil. Keep warm.

2 Bring the stock and lemon juice to the boil. Add the cauliflower and carrots and cook for 3–4 minutes until barely tender. Remove with a draining spoon and set aside. Add the mangetouts and cook for 1–2 minutes until they begin to soften. Remove with a draining spoon and add to the other vegetables. Reserve the stock for future use.

3 Melt half of the butter in a frying pan over a medium heat and cook the onion and courgettes for about 3 minutes. Add the garlic and prawns and cook for a further 2–3 minutes until thoroughly heated through.

4 Stir in the reserved vegetables and heat through. Season to taste with salt and pepper, then stir in the remaining butter.

5 Transfer the spaghetti to a warmed serving dish. Pour on the sauce and sprinkle with parsley. Toss well, using 2 forks, until thoroughly coated. Sprinkle on the grated cheese and paprika, and garnish with unshelled prawns, if using. Serve immediately.

Charred Tuna Steaks

Tuna has a firm flesh, which is ideal for barbecuing, but it can be a little dry unless it is marinated first.

NUTRITIONAL INFORMATION

Calories	153	Sugars	.........1g
Protein	........29g	Fat	..........3g
Carbohydrate	....1g	Saturates	......1g

🍤 2 hrs   🕐 15 mins

SERVES 4

INGREDIENTS

4 tuna steaks

3 tbsp light soy sauce

1 tbsp Worcestershire sauce

1 tsp wholegrain mustard

1 tsp caster sugar

1 tbsp sunflower oil

green salad, to serve

TO GARNISH

flat leaf parsley

lemon wedges

1 Place the tuna steaks in a single layer a shallow dish.

2 Combine the light soy sauce, Worcestershire sauce, mustard, sugar and oil in a small bowl. Pour the marinade over the tuna steaks. Gently turn the tuna steaks to coat well.

3 Cover with clingfilm and set aside in the refrigerator to marinate for at least 30 minutes and up to 2 hours.

4 Remove the tuna steaks from the marinade, reserving the marinade for basting. Barbecue over hot coals for 10–15 minutes, turning once and basting frequently with the reserved marinade.

5 Transfer the tuna steaks to warmed serving plates. Garnish with flat leaf parsley and lemon wedges and serve immediately with a fresh green salad.

COOK'S TIP

If a marinade contains soy sauce, the marinating time should be limited, usually to 2 hours. If it is allowed to marinate for too long, the fish will dry out and become tough.

Baked Sea Bass

Sea bass is often paired with subtle oriental flavours.
For a special occasion, you may like to bone the fish.

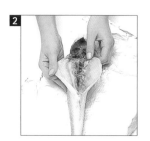

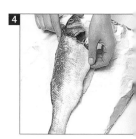

NUTRITIONAL INFORMATION

Calories	140	Sugars	.......0.1g
Protein	........29g	Fat	...........1g
Carbohydrate	...0.1g	Saturates	.....0.2g

10 mins   15 mins

SERVES 4–6

INGREDIENTS

2 sea bass, about 1 kg/2 lb 4 oz each, cleaned and scaled

2 spring onions, green part only, cut into strips

5 cm/2 inch piece of fresh root ginger, cut into strips

2 garlic cloves, unpeeled, lightly crushed

2 tbsp mirin or dry sherry

salt and pepper

TO SERVE

pickled sushi ginger (optional)

soy sauce

1 For each fish lay out a double thickness of foil and oil the top piece well or lay a piece of baking paper over the foil.

COOK'S TIP

Fresh sea bass is just as delicious when cooked very simply. Stuff the fish with garlic and chopped herbs, brush with olive oil and bake in the oven.

2 Place the fish in the middle of the foil and expose the cavities. Divide the spring onion and ginger between each cavity. Put a garlic clove in each cavity.

3 Pour the mirin or dry sherry over both fish and season them to taste with salt and pepper.

4 Close the cavities and lay each fish on its side. Bring over the foil and fold

the edges together to seal securely. Fold each end neatly.

5 Cook over a medium barbecue for 15 minutes, turning once.

6 To serve, remove the foil and cut each fish into two or three pieces. Serve them with the pickled sushi ginger, if using, accompanied by soy sauce according to taste.

Italian Fish Stew

This robust stew is full of Mediterranean flavours. If you do not want to prepare the fish yourself, ask your local fishmonger to do it for you.

NUTRITIONAL INFORMATION

Calories ....236 Sugars 4g
Protein ....20g Fat 7g
Carbohydrate ...25g Saturates 1g

5–10 mins   25 mins

SERVES 4

INGREDIENTS

2 tbsp olive oil

2 red onions, finely chopped

1 garlic clove, crushed

2 courgettes, sliced

400 g/14 oz can chopped tomatoes

850 ml/1½ pints fish or vegetable stock

85 g/3 oz dried pasta shapes

350 g/12 oz firm white fish, such as cod, haddock or hake

1 tbsp chopped fresh basil or oregano or 1 tsp dried oregano

1 tsp grated lemon rind

1 tbsp cornflour

1 tbsp water

salt and pepper

fresh basil or oregano sprigs, to garnish

1 Heat the oil in a large pan. Add the onions and garlic and cook over a low heat, stirring occasionally, for about 5 minutes until softened. Add the courgettes and cook, stirring frequently, for 2–3 minutes.

2 Add the tomatoes and stock to the pan and bring to the boil. Add the pasta, bring back to the boil, reduce the heat and cover. Simmer for 5 minutes.

3 Skin and bone the fish, then cut it into chunks. Add to the pan with the basil or oregano and lemon rind and simmer gently for 5 minutes until the fish is opaque and flakes easily (take care not to overcook it) and the pasta is tender, but still firm to the bite.

4 Blend the cornflour with the water to a smooth paste and stir into the stew. Cook gently for 2 minutes, stirring constantly, until thickened. Season with salt and pepper to taste.

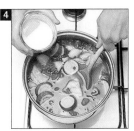

5 Ladle the stew into 4 warmed soup bowls. Garnish with basil or oregano sprigs and serve immediately.

Prawn Bhuna

This is a fiery recipe with subtle undertones. As the flavour of the prawns should be noticeable, the spices should not take over this dish.

NUTRITIONAL INFORMATION

Calories	141	Sugars	.......0.4g
Protein	........19g	Fat	...........7g
Carbohydrate	....1g	Saturates	......1g

 15 mins   🕐 20 mins

SERVES 4–6

I N G R E D I E N T S

2 dried red chillies, deseeded if liked

3 fresh green chillies, finely chopped

1 tsp ground turmeric

½ tsp pepper

1 tsp paprika

3 garlic cloves, crushed

2 tsp white wine vinegar

½ tsp salt

500 g/1 lb 2 oz uncooked peeled king prawns

3 tbsp oil

1 onion, very finely chopped

175 ml/6 fl oz water

2 tbsp lemon juice

2 tsp garam masala

fresh coriander, to garnish

1 Combine the chillies, spices, garlic, vinegar and salt in a non-metallic bowl. Stir in the prawns and set aside for 10 minutes.

2 Heat the oil in a large frying pan or wok, add the onion and cook, stirring occasionally, for 3–4 minutes until soft.

3 Add the prawns and the spice mixture to the pan and stir-fry over a high heat for 2 minutes. Reduce the heat, add the water and boil for 10 minutes, stirring occasionally, until the water has evaporated and the curry is fragrant.

4 Stir in the lemon juice and garam masala then transfer the mixture to a warm serving dish and garnish with fresh coriander sprigs. Serve immediately.

COOK'S TIP

Garam masala should be used sparingly and is generally added to foods towards the end of their cooking time. It is also used sprinkled over cooked meats, vegetables and pulses as a garnish.

Seafood in Red Curry Sauce

For something very quick and simple that sets your tastebuds alight, try this inspired dish of prawns in a wonderfully spicy sauce.

NUTRITIONAL INFORMATION

Calories	175	Sugars	.........3g
Protein	........29g	Fat	...........5g
Carbohydrate	....3g	Saturates	......1g

10 mins   10 mins

SERVES 4

INGREDIENTS

tbsp vegetable oil

spring onions, sliced

lemon grass stalk

cm/½ inch piece of fresh root ginger

50 ml/9 fl oz coconut milk

tbsp Thai red curry paste

tbsp Thai fish sauce

00 g/1 lb 2 oz raw king prawns

tbsp chopped fresh coriander

resh chillies, to garnish

1 Heat the vegetable oil in a wok or large frying pan. Add the spring onions and cook gently for about minutes until softened.

2 Bruise the stalk of lemon grass using a meat mallet or rolling pin. Peel and finely grate the fresh root ginger.

3 Add the lemon grass and ginger to the wok or frying pan with the coconut milk, Thai red curry paste and Thai fish sauce. Heat gently until the coconut milk is almost boiling.

4 Peel the prawns, leaving the tails intact. Remove the black vein along the back of each prawn.

5 Add the prawns to the wok or frying pan with the chopped coriander and cook gently for 5 minutes.

6 Transfer the prawns with the sauce to a warm serving bowl, garnish with fresh chillies and serve immediately.

VARIATION

Try this recipe using Thai green curry sauce instead of red. Both varieties are obtainable from many supermarkets – look for them in the oriental foods section.

Baked Crab with Ginger

In Chinese restaurants, only live crabs are used, but ready-cooked ones can be used at home quite successfully.

NUTRITIONAL INFORMATION

Calories 261   Sugars 0.5g
Protein . . . . .18g   Fat 17g
Carbohydrate . . . .5g   Saturates 2g

🍲 35 mins   🕐 10 mins

SERVES 4

I N G R E D I E N T S

1 large or 2 medium crabs, weighing about
  750 g/1 lb 10 oz in total

2 tbsp Chinese rice wine or dry sherry

1 egg, lightly beaten

1 tbsp cornflour

3–4 tbsp vegetable oil

1 tbsp finely chopped fresh root ginger

3–4 spring onions, cut into short lengths

2 tbsp light soy sauce

1 tsp sugar

about 5 tbsp Chinese Stock (see page 8)
  or water

½ tsp sesame oil

fresh coriander leaves, to garnish

COOK'S TIP

Crabs are almost always sold ready-cooked. The crab should feel heavy for its size, and when it is shaken, there should be no sound of water inside. A good medium-sized crab should yield about 500 g/1 lb 2 oz meat, enough for 3-4 people.

1 Cut the crab in half from the underbelly. Break off the claws and crack them with the back of a cleaver or a large kitchen knife.

2 Discard the legs and crack the shell, breaking it into several pieces. Discard the feathery gills from both sides of the body and the stomach sac. Place the crab meat in a bowl.

3 Combine the wine or sherry, egg and cornflour. Pour the mixture over the crab meat and set aside to marinate for 10–15 minutes.

4 Heat the vegetable oil in a preheated wok. Stir-fry the crab meat with the chopped ginger and spring onions for 2–3 minutes.

5 Add the soy sauce, sugar and stock or water, blend well and bring to the boil. Cover and cook for 3–4 minutes, then remove the lid, sprinkle with sesame oil and serve, garnished with coriander leaves.

Herrings with Hot Pesto

Oily fish, such as herrings and mackerel, form a vital part of the healthy diet, because they are rich in essential omega 3 fatty acids.

NUTRITIONAL INFORMATION

Calories	382	Sugars	.........2g
Protein	........28g	Fat	..........29g
Carbohydrate	....3g	Saturates	.......5g

 10 mins   10 mins

SERVES 4

INGREDIENTS

4 herrings or small mackerel, cleaned
  and gutted

2 tbsp olive oil

225 g/8 oz tomatoes, peeled, deseeded
  and chopped

8 canned anchovy fillets in oil, drained
  and chopped

about 30 fresh basil leaves

55 g/2 oz pine nuts

2 garlic cloves, crushed

1 Cook the herrings or mackerel under a preheated grill for about 8–10 minutes on each side or until the skin is slightly charred on both sides.

2 Meanwhile, heat 1 tablespoon of the olive oil in a large pan. Add the tomatoes and anchovies and cook over a medium heat for 5 minutes.

3 To make the pesto sauce, place the basil, pine nuts, garlic and remaining oil into a food processor and process to form a smooth paste. Alternatively, pound the ingredients by hand in a mortar with a pestle.

4 Add the pesto mixture to the pan of tomato and anchovy and stir to heat through.

5 Spoon some of the pesto sauce on to warmed individual serving plates. Place the fish on top and pour the rest of the pesto sauce over the fish. Serve immediately.

Fish with Black Bean Sauce

Steaming is one of the preferred methods of cooking whole fish in China because it maintains both the flavour and the texture.

NUTRITIONAL INFORMATION

Calories	292	Sugars	.........3g
Protein	........44g	Fat	..........7g
Carbohydrate	....6g	Saturates	.....0.4g

10 mins   10 mins

SERVES 4

INGREDIENTS

900 g/2 lb whole snapper, cleaned and scaled

3 garlic cloves, crushed

2 tbsp black bean sauce

1 tsp cornflour

2 tsp sesame oil

2 tbsp light soy sauce

2 tsp caster sugar

2 tbsp dry sherry

1 small leek, shredded

1 small red pepper, deseeded and cut into thin strips

shredded leek and lemon wedges, to garnish

boiled rice or noodles, to serve

1 Rinse the fish inside and out with cold running water and pat dry with kitchen paper.

2 Make 2–3 diagonal slashes in the flesh on each side of the fish, using a sharp knife. Rub the garlic into the fish.

3 Combine the black bean sauce, cornflour, sesame oil, light soy sauce, sugar and dry sherry.

4 Place the fish in a shallow heatproof dish and pour the sauce mixture over the top. Sprinkle the shredded leek and pepper strips on top of the sauce.

5 Place the dish in the top of a steamer, cover and steam for 10 minutes or until the fish is cooked through.

6 Transfer the fish to a serving dish, garnish with shredded leek and lemon wedges and serve immediately with boiled rice or noodles.

COOK'S TIP

Insert the point of a sharp knife into the fish to test if it is cooked. The fish is cooked through if the knife goes into the flesh easily.

Fragrant Tuna Steaks

Fresh tuna steaks are very meaty – they have a firm texture,
yet the flesh is succulent. Tuna is rich in valuable omega 3 oils.

NUTRITIONAL INFORMATION

Calories	239	Sugars	.......0.1g
Protein	........42g	Fat	..........8g
Carbohydrate	...0.5g	Saturates	......2g

15 mins　　　15 mins

SERVES 4

INGREDIENTS

4 tuna steaks, 175 g/6 oz each

½ tsp finely grated lime rind

1 garlic clove, crushed

2 tsp olive oil

1 tsp ground cumin

1 tsp ground coriander

1 tbsp lime juice

pepper

fresh coriander, to garnish

TO SERVE

avocado relish (see Cook's Tip)

tomato wedges

lime wedges

1 Trim the skin from the tuna steaks, rinse and pat dry on absorbent kitchen paper.

2 In a small bowl, combine the grated lime rind, garlic, olive oil, cumin, ground coriander and pepper, to taste, to make a paste.

3 Spread the paste thinly on both sides of the tuna. Heat a non-stick, ridged frying pan until hot and press the tuna steaks into the pan to seal them. Lower the heat and cook for 5 minutes. Turn the fish over and cook for a further

4–5 minutes until the fish is cooked through. Drain on kitchen paper and transfer to a warmed serving plate.

4 Sprinkle the lime juice and chopped coriander over the fish. Serve immediately with avocado relish, and tomato and lime wedges.

COOK'S TIP

For the avocado relish, peel, stone and chop a small ripe avocado. Mix in 1 tablespoon lime juice, 1 tablespoon chopped fresh coriander, 1 finely chopped small red onion and some chopped mango or tomato. Season to taste.

Salmon with Pineapple

Presentation plays a major part in Chinese cooking and this dish demonstrates this perfectly with the wonderful combination of colours.

NUTRITIONAL INFORMATION

Calories	347	Sugars	........12g
Protein	........24g	Fat	..........20g
Carbohydrate	...16g	Saturates	.......3g

 10 mins   15 mins

SERVES 4

I N G R E D I E N T S

100 g/3½ oz baby corn cobs

2 tbsp sunflower oil

1 red onion, sliced

1 orange pepper, deseeded and sliced

1 green pepper, deseeded and sliced

450 g/1 lb salmon fillet, skinned

1 tbsp paprika

225 g/8 oz canned cubed pineapple in natural juice, drained

100 g/3½ oz beansprouts

2 tbsp tomato ketchup

2 tbsp soy sauce

2 tbsp medium sherry

1 tsp cornflour

1 Cut each baby corn cob in half. Heat the oil in a large preheated wok. Add the onion, peppers and baby corn cobs to the wok and stir-fry for 5 minutes.

2 Rinse the salmon fillet under cold running water and pat dry with kitchen paper.

3 Cut the salmon flesh into thin strips and place in a large bowl. Sprinkle with the paprika and toss well to coat.

4 Add the salmon to the wok together with the pineapple and stir-fry for a further 2–3 minutes or until the fish is tender.

5 Add the beansprouts to the wok and toss well.

6 Mix together the tomato ketchup, soy sauce, sherry and cornflour. Add to the wok and cook until the juices start to thicken. Transfer to warm serving plates and serve immediately.

VARIATION

You can use trout fillets instead of the salmon as an alternative, if you prefer.

Gingered Monkfish

This dish is a real treat and is perfect for special occasions. Monkfish has a tender flavour which is ideal with asparagus, chilli and ginger.

NUTRITIONAL INFORMATION

Calories	133	Sugars	.........0g
Protein	........21g	Fat	..........5g
Carbohydrate	....1g	Saturates	.......1g

5 mins   10 mins

SERVES 4

INGREDIENTS

450 g/1 lb monkfish

1 tbsp grated fresh root ginger

2 tbsp sweet chilli sauce

1 tbsp corn oil

100 g/3½ oz fine asparagus

3 spring onions, sliced

1 tsp sesame oil

1   Remove any membrane from the monkfish. Using a sharp knife, slice the monkfish into thin flat rounds. Set aside until required.

2   Mix together the grated root ginger and the sweet chilli sauce in a small bowl until thoroughly blended. Brush the ginger and chilli sauce mixture over the monkfish pieces, using a pastry brush.

COOK'S TIP

Monkfish is quite expensive, but it is well worth using, as it has a wonderful flavour and texture. At a push, you could use cubes of chunky cod fillet instead.

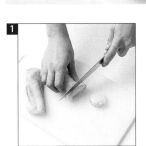

3   Heat the corn oil in a large preheated wok or heavy-based frying pan.

4   Add the monkfish pieces, asparagus and chopped spring onions to the wok or frying pan and cook over a medium heat for about 5 minutes, constantly stirring very gently so the fish pieces do not break up.

5   Remove the wok or frying pan from the heat, drizzle the sesame oil over the stir-fry and toss gently to combine.

6   Transfer the stir-fried gingered monkfish to warm serving plates and serve immediately.

Goan Fish Curry

Goan cuisine is famous for seafood and vindaloo dishes, which tend to be very hot. This recipe is a mild curry, but very flavourful.

NUTRITIONAL INFORMATION

Calories 302	Sugars 7g
Protein 31g	Fat 17g
Carbohydrate 8g	Saturates 7g

 30 mins   12 mins

SERVES 4

INGREDIENTS

750 g/1 lb 10 oz monkfish fillet, cut into chunks

1 tbsp cider vinegar

1 tsp salt

1 tsp ground turmeric

3 tbsp vegetable oil

2 garlic cloves, crushed

1 small onion, finely chopped

2 tsp ground coriander

1 tsp cayenne pepper

2 tsp paprika

2 tbsp tamarind pulp plus 2 tbsp boiling water (see method)

85 g/3 oz creamed coconut, cut into pieces

300 ml/ 10 fl oz warm water

plain boiled rice, to serve

1 Put the fish on a plate and drizzle the vinegar over it. Combine half the salt and half the turmeric and sprinkle evenly over the fish. Cover and set aside for 20 minutes.

2 Heat the oil in a heavy-based frying pan and add the garlic. Brown slightly, then add the onion and cook, stirring occasionally, for 3–4 minutes until soft, but not browned. Add the ground coriander and stir for 1 minute.

3 Mix the remaining turmeric, cayenne and paprika with about 2 tablespoons water to make a paste. Add to the pan and cook over a low heat for 1–2 minutes.

4 Stir the tamarind pulp and boiling water. When thickened and the pulp has come away from the seeds, rub through a sieve. Discard the seeds.

5 Add the coconut, warm water and tamarind paste to the pan and stir until the coconut has dissolved. Add the fish and any juices on the plate and simmer gently for 4–5 minutes until the sauce has thickened and the fish is just tender. Serve on a bed of plain boiled rice.

Thai Green Fish Curry

This pale green curry paste can be used as the basis for all sorts of Thai dishes. It is also delicious with chicken and beef.

NUTRITIONAL INFORMATION

Calories 217	Sugars 3g
Protein 12g	Fat 17g
Carbohydrate 5g	Saturates 10g

 15 mins   15 mins

SERVES 4

INGREDIENTS

2 tbsp vegetable oil

1 garlic clove, chopped

1 small aubergine, diced

125 ml/4 fl oz coconut cream

2 tbsp Thai fish sauce

1 tsp sugar

225 g/8 oz firm white fish, cut into pieces, such as cod, haddock, halibut

125 ml/4 fl oz fish stock

2 kaffir lime leaves, finely shredded

about 15 leaves Thai basil, if available, or ordinary basil

plain boiled rice or noodles, to serve

GREEN CURRY PASTE

5 fresh green chillies, deseeded and chopped

2 tsp chopped lemon grass

1 large shallot, chopped

2 garlic cloves, chopped

1 tsp grated fresh root ginger or galangal

2 fresh coriander roots, chopped

½ tsp ground coriander

¼ tsp ground cumin

1 kaffir lime leaf, finely chopped

1 tsp shrimp paste (optional)

½ tsp salt

1 Make the curry paste. Put all the ingredients into a blender or spice grinder and blend to a smooth paste, adding a little water if necessary. Alternatively, pound together all the ingredients, using a mortar and pestle, until smooth. Set aside.

2 Heat the oil in a frying pan or wok until almost smoking. Add the garlic and fry until golden. Add the curry paste and stir-fry for a few seconds before adding the aubergine. Stir-fry for about 4–5 minutes until softened.

3 Add the coconut cream. Bring to the boil and stir until the cream thickens and curdles slightly. Add the fish sauce and sugar and stir into the mixture.

4 Add the fish pieces and stock. Simmer, stirring occasionally, for 3–4 minutes until the fish is just tender. Add the lime leaves and basil, and then cook for a further minute.

5 Transfer the curry to a warmed serving dish and serve with plain boiled rice or noodles.

Cod with Cheese & Tomato

Fish and cheese have a natural affinity. Here, fish is oven-baked, topped with cheese and grilled – far less fattening than a creamy cheese sauce.

NUTRITIONAL INFORMATION

Calories	159	Sugars	.........6g
Protein	........19g	Fat	...........7g
Carbohydrate	....6g	Saturates	.......4g

 40 mins   25 mins

SERVES 4

I N G R E D I E N T S

4 cod or other firm white fish fillets,
   about 175 g/6 oz each

grated rind and juice of 1 orange

8 canned anchovy fillets, drained and
   patted dry

175 g/6 oz haloumi cheese

4 beef tomato slices

fresh parsley sprigs, to garnish

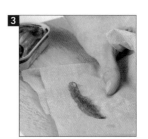

1 Place the fish in a large, shallow, non-metallic flameproof dish. Sprinkle with the orange rind and pour the juice over it. Cover with clingfilm and leave to marinate in the refrigerator for 30 minutes.

2 Preheat the oven to 180°C/350°F/ Gas Mark 4. Remove the clingfilm and re-cover the dish with foil. Bake in the preheated oven for 15–20 minutes, or until the flesh flakes easily.

3 Preheat the grill to medium. Drain the anchovy fillets on kitchen paper and arrange 2 fillets on each piece of cod.

Place under a preheated grill for 1 minute. Cut the haloumi cheese into 4 slices and place 1 slice on top of each cod fillet. Top with the tomato slices and return to the grill for a further 1–2 minutes, or until the cheese has charred slightly and the tomato is beginning to soften. Transfer to a serving plate, garnish with a few sprigs of fresh parsley and serve immediately.

COOK'S TIP

Citrus juices will begin to 'cure' fish after 1 hour, so make sure that you don't leave the fish to marinate for too long.

Haddock Baked in Yogurt

This is a very simple, convenient, but flavoursome dish, using mainly storecupboard ingredients – apart from the fresh fish.

NUTRITIONAL INFORMATION

Calories	448	Sugars	........16g
Protein	........47g	Fat	..........21g
Carbohydrate	...20g	Saturates	.......8g

20 mins   40 mins

SERVES 4

INGREDIENTS

2 large onions, thinly sliced

900 g/2 lb haddock fillet

425 ml/15 fl oz natural yogurt

2 tbsp lemon juice

1 tsp sugar

2 tsp ground cumin

2 tsp ground coriander

pinch of garam masala

pinch of cayenne pepper

1 tsp grated fresh ginger root

3 tbsp vegetable oil

55 g/2 oz cold unsalted butter, diced

salt and pepper

1 Line the base of a large ovenproof dish or casserole with the onion slices. Cut the fish widthways into strips about 5 cm/2 inches wide and lay the strips in a single layer over the onions.

2 In a bowl, combine the yogurt, lemon juice, sugar, cumin, coriander, garam masala, cayenne, ginger and oil and season to taste with salt and pepper. Pour this sauce over the fish, tipping the dish to make sure it runs under the fish as well. Cover tightly with kitchen foil or a lid.

3 Bake in a preheated oven, 190°C/375°F/Gas Mark 5 for 30 minutes or until the fish is just tender.

4 Carefully pour the sauce off the fish into a pan. Bring to the boil over a low heat and simmer to reduce to about 350 ml/12 fl oz. Remove from the heat.

5 Add the cubes of butter to the sauce and whisk until melted and fully incorporated. Pour the sauce over the fish and serve immediately.

COOK'S TIP

When you pour the sauce off the fish it will look thin and separated, but reducing and stirring in the butter will help to amalgamate it.

Cod Italienne

Not strictly authentic, but this dish uses the typical Italian ingredients of tomatoes, capers, olives and basil to make a delicious supper dish.

NUTRITIONAL INFORMATION

Calories	387	Sugars	.........8g
Protein	........44g	Fat	..........16g
Carbohydrate	...10g	Saturates	.......6g

 15 mins   1½ hrs

SERVES 4

I N G R E D I E N T S

2 tbsp olive oil

1 onion, finely chopped

2 garlic cloves, finely chopped

2 tsp chopped fresh thyme

150 ml/5 fl oz red wine

2 x 400 g/14 oz cans chopped tomatoes

pinch of sugar

55 g/2 oz stoned black olives, roughly chopped

55 g/2 oz stoned green olives, roughly chopped

2 tbsp capers, drained, rinsed and roughly chopped

2 tbsp chopped fresh basil

4 cod steaks, each weighing about 175 g/6 oz

150 g/5½ oz buffalo Mozzarella, drained and sliced

salt and pepper

buttered noodles, to serve

1 Heat the olive oil in a large pan. Add the onion and cook over a low heat, stirring occasionally, for 5 minutes until softened, but not coloured.

2 Add the garlic and thyme and cook, stirring, constantly, a further minute.

3 Add the red wine and increase the heat. Simmer until reduced and syrupy. Add the tomatoes and sugar and bring to the boil. Cover and simmer gently for 30 minutes. Uncover and simmer for a further 20 minutes until thick. Stir in the olives, capers and basil. Season to taste with salt and pepper.

4 Arrange the cod steaks in a shallow ovenproof dish and spoon the tomato sauce over the top. Bake in a preheated oven, 190°C/ 375°F/Gas Mark 5, for 20–25 minutes, until the fish is just tender.

5 Remove the dish from the oven and arrange the mozzarella slices on top of the fish.

6 Return to the oven for a further 5–10 minutes until the cheese has melted. Serve with buttered noodles.

Cod Curry

Using curry paste in this recipe makes it quick
and easy to prepare. It makes an ideal family supper.

NUTRITIONAL INFORMATION

Calories	310	Sugars	.........4g
Protein	........42g	Fat	..........8g
Carbohydrate	...19g	Saturates	.......1g

🍞 🍞

🧊 10 mins   🕐 25 mins

SERVES 4

I N G R E D I E N T S

1 tbsp vegetable oil

1 small onion, chopped

2 garlic cloves, chopped

2.5 cm/1 inch piece of fresh ginger root,
  roughly chopped

2 large ripe tomatoes, peeled and
  roughly chopped

150 ml/5 fl oz fish stock

1 tbsp medium curry paste

1 tsp ground coriander

400 g/14 oz can chickpeas, drained
  and rinsed

750 g/1 lb 10 oz cod fillet, cut into
  large chunks

4 tbsp chopped fresh coriander

4 tbsp thick yogurt

salt and pepper

steamed basmati rice, to serve

1 Heat the oil in a large pan and add the onion, garlic and ginger. Cook over a low heat for 4–5 minutes until softened. Remove from the heat. Put the onion mixture into a food processor or blender with the tomatoes and fish stock and process until smooth.

2 Return to the pan with the curry paste, ground coriander and chickpeas. Mix together well, then simmer gently for 15 minutes until thickened.

3 Add the pieces of fish and return to a simmer. Cook for 5 minutes until the fish is just tender. Remove from the heat and set aside for 2–3 minutes.

4 Stir in the coriander and yogurt. Season and serve with basmati rice.

VARIATIONS
Instead of cod, make
this curry using raw prawns
and omit chickpeas.

Home-salted Cod

After a period of unpopularity, salt cod is now becoming fashionable. You will need to begin preparing this dish two days ahead.

NUTRITIONAL INFORMATION

Calories 283   Sugars 0g
Protein ....39g   Fat 7g
Carbohydrate ....7g   Saturates 1g

 50 hrs   2¼ hrs

SERVES 6

INGREDIENTS

55 g/2 oz sea salt

1.5 kg/3 lb 5oz fresh boneless cod fillet, from the head end, skin on

225 g/8 oz dried chickpeas, soaked overnight

1 fresh red chilli

4 garlic cloves

2 bay leaves

1 tbsp olive oil

300 ml10 fl oz chicken stock

pepper

extra virgin olive oil, to drizzle

GREMOLATA

3 tbsp chopped fresh parsley

2 garlic cloves, finely chopped

finely grated rind of 1 lemon

1 Sprinkle the salt over both sides of the cod. Place in a shallow dish, cover and chill for 48 hours. Rinse the fish under cold running water, then set aside to soak in cold water for 2 hours.

2 Drain the chickpeas, rinse and drain again. Put into a large pan. Add double their volume of water and bring to the boil over a low heat. Remove any scum that rises to the surface. Split the chilli lengthways and add to the chickpeas with the garlic cloves and bay leaves. Cover and simmer for 1½–2 hours until very tender, skimming occasionally.

3 Drain the cod and pat dry with kitchen paper. Brush with the olive oil and season with black pepper. Cook under a preheated grill or on a hot ridged grill pan for 3–4 minutes on each side until tender. Meanwhile, add the chicken stock to the chickpeas and bring back to the boil. Remove from the heat and keep warm.

4 For the gremolata, combine the parsley, garlic and grated lemon rind.

5 To serve, ladle the chickpeas and their cooking liquid into 6 warmed soup bowls. Top with the grilled cod and sprinkle over the gremolata. Drizzle generously with olive oil and serve immediately.

Cotriade

This is a rich French stew of fish and vegetables, flavoured with saffron and herbs. The fish and vegetables, and the soup, are served separately.

NUTRITIONAL INFORMATION

Calories 81   Sugars 0.9g
Protein . . . . .7.4g   Fat 3.9g
Carbohydrate . . .3.8g   Saturates 1.1g

🍞 🍞 🍞

🕐 15 mins   🕐 40 mins

SERVES 4

I N G R E D I E N T S

large pinch of saffron

600 ml/1 pint hot fish stock

1 tbsp olive oil

2 tbsp butter

1 onion, sliced

2 garlic cloves, chopped

1 leek, sliced

1 small fennel bulb, thinly sliced

450 g/1 lb potatoes, cut into chunks

150 ml/5 fl oz dry white wine

1 tbsp fresh thyme leaves

2 bay leaves

4 ripe tomatoes, peeled and chopped

2 lb mixed fish fillets, such as haddock,
    hake, mackerel, red or grey mullet,
    roughly chopped

2 tbsp chopped fresh parsley

salt and pepper

crusty bread, to serve

1 Using a mortar and pestle, crush the saffron and add it to the fish stock. Stir the mixture and set aside to infuse for at least 10 minutes.

2 Heat the oil and butter together in a large, heavy-based saucepan. Add the onion and cook over a low heat, stirring occasionally, for 4–5 minutes until softened. Add the garlic, leek, fennel and potatoes. Cover and cook for a further 10–15 minutes until the vegetables are softened.

3 Add the white wine and simmer rapidly for 3–4 minutes until reduced by about half. Add the thyme, bay leaves and tomatoes and stir well. Add the saffron-infused fish stock. Bring to the boil, cover and simmer over a low heat for about 15 minutes until all the vegetables are tender.

4 Add the fish, return to the boil and simmer for a further 3–4 minutes until all the fish is tender. Add the parsley and season to taste. Using a draining spoon, remove the fish and vegetables to a warmed serving dish. Serve the soup with plenty of crusty bread.

VARIATION
Once the fish and vegetables have been cooked, you could process the soup in a food processor or blender and pass it through a sieve to give a smooth fish soup.

Squid Stew

This is a rich and flavourful stew of slowly cooked squid, in a sauce of tomatoes and red wine. The squid becomes very tender.

NUTRITIONAL INFORMATION

Calories 284	Sugars 5g	
Protein 31g	Fat 12g	
Carbohydrate 9g	Saturates 2g	

20 mins

2¼ hrs

SERVES 4

INGREDIENTS

750 g/1 lb 10 oz squid

3 tbsp olive oil

1 onion, chopped

3 garlic cloves, finely chopped

1 tsp fresh thyme leaves

400 g/14 oz can chopped tomatoes

150 ml/5 fl oz red wine

300 ml/10 fl oz water

1 tbsp chopped fresh parsley

salt and pepper

1 To prepare whole squid, hold the body firmly and grasp the tentacles just inside the body. Pull firmly to remove the innards. Find the transparent 'quill' and remove. Grasp the wings on the outside of the body and pull to remove the outer skin.

VARIATIONS

This recipe can be used as the basis for a more substantial fish stew. Before adding the parsley, add extra seafood such as scallops, pieces of fish fillet and large prawns. Cook for a further 2 minutes.

Trim the tentacles just below the beak and reserve. Wash the body and tentacles under cold running water. Slice the body into rings. Drain well on kitchen paper.

2 Heat the oil in a large, flameproof casserole. Add the prepared squid and cook over a medium heat, stirring occasionally, until lightly browned.

3 Reduce the heat and add the onion, garlic and thyme. Cook for a further 5 minutes until softened.

4 Stir in the tomatoes, red wine and water. Bring to the boil and cook in a preheated oven, 140°C/275°F/Gas Mark 1 for 2 hours. Stir in the parsley and season to taste. Serve immediately.

Spanish Fish Stew

This is an impressive-looking Catalan dish using two classic Spanish cooking methods – the *sofrito* and the *picada*.

NUTRITIONAL INFORMATION

Calories	346	Sugars	.........4g
Protein	........37g	Fat	..........13g
Carbohydrate	....11g	Saturates	.......2g

30 mins   1 hr

SERVES 6

INGREDIENTS

5 tbsp olive oil

2 large onions, finely chopped

2 tomatoes, peeled, deseeded and diced

2 slices white bread, crusts removed

4 almonds, toasted

3 garlic cloves, roughly chopped

350 g/12 oz cooked lobster

200 g/7 oz cleaned squid

200 g/7 oz monkfish fillet

200 g/7 oz cod fillet, skinned

1 tbsp plain flour

6 large raw prawns

6 langoustines

18 live mussels, scrubbed, beards removed

8 large live clams, scrubbed

1 tbsp chopped fresh parsley

125 ml/4 fl oz brandy

salt and pepper

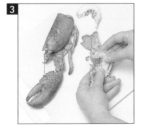

1 Heat 3 tablespoons of the oil and cook the onions gently for 10–15 minutes until lightly golden. Add the tomatoes and cook until they have disintegrated.

2 Heat 1 tablespoon of the remaining oil and fry the slices of bread until crisp. Break into pieces and put into a mortar with the almonds and 2 garlic cloves. Pound to a fine paste. Alternatively, process in a food processor.

3 Split the lobster lengthways. Remove and discard the intestinal vein, the stomach sac and the spongy gills. Crack the claws and remove the meat. Take out the flesh from the tail and chop into large chunks. Slice the squid into rings.

4 Season the monkfish, cod and lobster and dust with flour. Heat a little of the remaining oil and separately brown the monkfish, cod, lobster, squid, prawns and langoustines. Arrange them in a flameproof casserole as they brown.

5 Add the mussels and clams and the remaining garlic and parsley. Set the pan over a low heat. Pour over the brandy and ignite. When the flames have died down, add the tomato mixture and just enough water to cover. Bring to the boil and simmer for 3–4 minutes until the mussels and clams have opened. Stir in the bread mixture and season. Simmer for a further 5 minutes and serve.

Moroccan Fish Tagine

A tagine is a Moroccan cooking vessel consisting of an earthenware dish with a domed lid that has a steam hole in the top.

NUTRITIONAL INFORMATION

Calories 188	Sugars 5g	
Protein 17g	Fat 11g	
Carbohydrate 7g	Saturates 1g	

🧊 10 mins 🕐 1¼ hrs

SERVES 4

INGREDIENTS

2 tbsp olive oil

1 large onion, finely chopped

pinch of saffron strands

½ tsp ground cinnamon

1 tsp ground coriander

½ tsp ground cumin

½ tsp ground turmeric

200 g/7 oz can chopped tomatoes

300 ml/10 fl oz fish stock

4 small red mullet cleaned, boned and heads and tails removed

55 g/2 oz stoned green olives

1 tbsp chopped preserved lemon

3 tbsp fresh chopped fresh coriander

salt and pepper

couscous, to serve

1 Heat the olive oil in a large pan or flameproof casserole. Add the onion and cook gently, stirring occasionally, for 10 minutes without colouring until softened. Add the saffron, cinnamon, ground coriander, cumin and turmeric and cook for a further 30 seconds, stirring.

2 Add the chopped tomatoes and fish stock and stir well. Bring to the boil, cover and simmer for 15 minutes. Uncover and simmer for a further 20–35 minute until thickened.

3 Cut each red mullet in half, then add the pieces to the pan, pushing them into the sauce. Simmer gently for a further 5–6 minutes until the fish is just cooked.

4 Carefully stir in the olives, preserved lemon and the chopped coriander. Season to taste and serve with couscous.

COOK'S TIP

For preserved lemons, take enough lemons to fill a preserving jar. Quarter them lengthways without cutting all the way through. Pack them with 55 g/2 oz sea salt per lemon. Add the juice of 1 more lemon and top up with water to cover. Leave for 1 month.

Stewed Sardines

This is an unusual stew of sardines cooked with baby onions, tomatoes, olives, raisins, Marsala and pine kernels.

NUTRITIONAL INFORMATION

Calories	412	Sugars	14g
Protein	26g	Fat	27g
Carbohydrate	15g	Saturates	5g

1¼ hrs   50 mins

SERVES 4

INGREDIENTS

55 g/2 oz raisins

3 tbsp Marsala

4 tbsp olive oil

225 g/8 oz baby onions, halved if large

2 garlic cloves, chopped

1 tbsp chopped fresh sage

4 large tomatoes, peeled and chopped

150 ml/5 fl oz fish or vegetable stock

2 tbsp balsamic vinegar

450 g/1 lb fresh sardines, cleaned

25 g/1 oz stoned black olives

25 g/1 oz pine kernels, toasted

2 tbsp chopped fresh parsley

1 Put the raisins in a small bowl and pour over the Marsala. Set aside to soak for about 1 hour until the raisins are plump. Strain, reserving both the Marsala and the raisins.

2 Heat the olive oil in a large pan and fry the onions over a low heat for 15 minutes until they are golden and tender. Add the garlic and sage and cook for a further minute.

3 Add the chopped tomatoes, cook for a further 2–3 minutes, then add the stock, balsamic vinegar and reserved Marsala. Bring to the boil, cover and simmer for 25 minutes.

4 Add the sardines to the stew and simmer gently for 2–3 minutes before adding the raisins, olives and pine kernels. Simmer for a final 2–3 minutes until the sardines are cooked. Add the parsley and serve immediately.

VARIATIONS

Substitute Home-salted Cod (see page 696) or smoked cod for the sardines.

Red Prawn Curry

Like all Thai curries, this one has as its base a paste of chillies and spices and a sauce of coconut milk.

NUTRITIONAL INFORMATION

Calories	149	Sugars	.........4g
Protein	........15g	Fat	...........7g
Carbohydrate	....6g	Saturates	.......1g

🧅 15 mins   🕐 10 mins

SERVES 4

INGREDIENTS

2 tbsp vegetable oil

1 garlic clove, finely chopped

1 tbsp red curry paste (see below)

200 ml/7 fl oz coconut milk

2 tbsp Thai fish sauce

1 tsp sugar

12 large raw prawns, deveined

2 kaffir lime leaves, finely shredded

1 small fresh red chilli, deseeded and thinly sliced

10 leaves Thai basil, if available, or ordinary basil

RED CURRY PASTE:

3 dried long red chillies

½ tsp ground coriander

¼ tsp ground cumin

½ tsp ground black pepper

2 garlic cloves, chopped

2 lemon grass stalks, chopped

1 kaffir lime leaf, finely chopped

1 tsp grated fresh root ginger or galangal

1 tsp shrimp paste (optional)

½ tsp salt

1 Make the red curry paste. Put all the ingredients in a blender or spice grinder and blend to a smooth paste, adding a little water if necessary. Alternatively, pound the ingredients together using a mortar and pestle until smooth. Set aside.

2 Heat the oil in a wok or frying pan until almost smoking. Add the chopped garlic and fry until golden. Add 1 tablespoon of the curry paste and cook, stirring constantly, for a further minute. Add half the coconut milk, the fish sauce and the sugar. Stir well until the mixture has thickened slightly.

3 Add the prawns and simmer for 3–4 minutes until they turn colour. Add the remaining coconut milk, the lime leaves and fresh red chilli. Cook for a further 2–3 minutes until the prawns are just tender.

4 Add the basil leaves and stir until wilted. transfer to a warmed serving dish and serve immediately.

Curried Prawns

The best way to approach this recipe is to prepare everything beforehand, including measuring out the spices. The cooking time is then very quick.

NUTRITIONAL INFORMATION

Calories 272   Sugars 5g
Protein .... 29g   Fat 15g
Carbohydrate .... 5g   Saturates 2g

  40 mins   🕐 15 mins

SERVES 4

INGREDIENTS

350 g/12 oz small courgettes

1 tsp salt

450 g/1 lb cooked tiger prawns

5 tbsp vegetable oil

4 garlic cloves, finely chopped

5 tbsp chopped fresh coriander

1 fresh green chilli, deseeded and
   finely chopped

½ tsp ground turmeric

1½ tsp ground cumin

pinch of cayenne pepper

200 g/7 oz can chopped tomatoes

1 tsp grated fresh root ginger

1 tbsp lemon juice

lime wedges, to garnish

steamed basmati rice, to serve

1 Cut the courgettes into batons. Put into a colander, sprinkle with a little of the salt and set aside for 30 minutes. Rinse, drain and pat dry. Spread the prawns on kitchen paper to drain.

2 Heat the oil in a wok or frying pan over a high heat. Add the garlic. As soon as the garlic begins to brown, add the courgettes, coriander, chilli, turmeric, cumin, cayenne, tomatoes, ginger, lemon juice and remaining salt. Stir well and bring to the boil.

3 Cover and simmer over a low heat for about 5 minutes. Uncover and add the prawns.

4 Increase the heat to high and simmer for about 5 minutes until the liquid is reduced to a thick sauce. Serve with basmati rice, garnished with lime wedges.

VARIATION

If you can't find cooked tiger prawns for this recipe, use cooked peeled prawns instead but these release quite a lot of liquid, so you may need to increase the final simmering time to thicken the sauce.

Grilled Red Mullet

Try to get small red mullet for this dish. If you can only get larger fish, serve one for each person and increase the cooking time accordingly.

NUTRITIONAL INFORMATION

Calories	 111	Sugars	.... 0.8g
Protein	.... 10.2g	Fat	.... 5.4g
Carbohydrate	... 5.9g	Saturates	..... 0.7g

10 mins   20 mins

SERVES 4

INGREDIENTS

1 lemon, thinly sliced

2 garlic cloves, crushed

4 fresh flat leaf parsley sprigs

4 fresh thyme sprigs

8 fresh sage leaves

2 large shallots, sliced

8 small red mullet, cleaned

8 slices Parma ham

salt and pepper

SAUTÉ POTATOES AND SHALLOTS

4 tbsp olive oil

900 g/2 lb potatoes, diced

8 whole garlic cloves, unpeeled

12 small whole shallots

FOR THE DRESSING

4 tbsp olive oil

1 tbsp lemon juice

1 tbsp chopped fresh flat-leaf parsley

1 tbsp chopped fresh chives

salt and pepper

1 For the sauté potatoes and shallots, heat the olive oil in a large frying pan and add the potatoes, garlic cloves and shallots. Cook gently, stirring frequently, for 12–15 minutes until they are golden, crisp and tender.

2 Meanwhile, divide the lemon slices, halved if necessary, garlic, parsley, thyme, sage and shallots between the cavities of the fish. Season well. Wrap a slice of Parma ham around each fish. Secure with a cocktail stick.

3 Arrange the fish on a grill pan and cook under a preheated hot grill for 5–6 minutes on each side until tender.

4 To make the dressing, combine the olive oil and the lemon juice with the chopped flat-leaf parsley and chives and stir together well. Season with salt and pepper to taste.

5 Divide the potatoes and shallots among 4 serving plates and top each with the fish. Drizzle the dressing over them and serve immediately.

Poached Rainbow Trout

This colourful, flavoursome dish is served cold and therefore makes a lovely summer lunch or *al fresco* supper dish.

NUTRITIONAL INFORMATION

Calories	99	Sugars	.......1.1g
Protein	........5.7g	Fat	..........6.3g
Carbohydrate	...3.7g	Saturates	.......1g

 25 mins 1 hr

SERVES 4

INGREDIENTS

.3 kg/3 lb rainbow trout fillets

700 g/1 lb 9 oz new potatoes

3 spring onions, finely chopped

1 egg, hard-boiled and chopped

COURT-BOUILLON

850 ml/1½ pints cold water

850 ml/1½ pints dry white wine

3 tbsp white wine vinegar

2 large carrots, roughly chopped

1 onion, roughly chopped

2 celery sticks, roughly chopped

2 leeks, roughly chopped

2 garlic cloves, roughly chopped

2 fresh bay leaves

4 fresh parsley sprigs

4 fresh thyme sprigs

6 black peppercorns

1 tsp salt

WATERCRESS MAYONNAISE

1 egg yolk

1 tsp Dijon mustard

1 tsp white wine vinegar

2 oz watercress leaves, chopped

225 ml/8 fl oz light olive oil

salt and pepper

1 First make the court-bouillon. Place all the ingredients in a large saucepan and bring to the boil over a low heat. Cover and simmer for about 30 minutes. Strain the liquid through a fine sieve into a clean pan. Bring to the boil again and simmer rapidly, uncovered, for 15–20 minutes until the court-bouillon is reduced to 600 ml/1 pint.

2 Place the trout in a large frying pan. Add the court-bouillon and bring to the boil over a low heat. Remove from the heat and set the fish aside in the poaching liquid to cool.

3 Meanwhile, make the watercress mayonnaise. Put the egg yolk, mustard, wine vinegar, watercress and salt and pepper to taste into a food processor or blender and process for 30 seconds until foaming. Begin adding the olive oil, drop by drop, until the mixture begins to thicken. Continue adding the oil in a slow steady stream until it is all incorporated. Add a little hot water if the mixture seems too thick. Season to taste and set aside.

4 Cook the potatoes in plenty of lightly salted boiling water for about 12–15 minutes until soft and tender. Drain well and refresh them under cold running water. Set the potatoes aside until cold.

5 When the potatoes are cold, cut them in half, if they are very large, and toss thoroughly with the watercress mayonnaise, finely chopped spring onions and hard-boiled egg.

6 Carefully lift the fish from the poaching liquid and drain on kitchen paper. Carefully pull the skin away from each of the trout fillets and serve immediately with the potato salad.

Baked Lemon Sole

A simple mixture of herbs, lemon juice and garlic is delicious, but will not overwhelm the delicate flavour of the fish.

NUTRITIONAL INFORMATION

Calories	197	Sugars	.........0g
Protein	........30g	Fat	...........8g
Carbohydrate	....0g	Saturates	.......1g

 15 mins | 5 mins

SERVES 4

I N G R E D I E N T S

2 garlic cloves

4 lemon sole fillets, about 175 g/6 oz each

1 shallot, finely chopped

2 fresh lemon thyme sprigs, plus extra
   to garnish

2 fresh lemon balm sprigs, plus extra
   to garnish

salt and pepper

grated rind and juice of 1 lemon

2 tbsp extra virgin olive oil

1 Preheat the oven to 180°C/350°F/ Gas Mark 4. Using a sharp knife, thinly slice the garlic and set aside.

2 Arrange the sole fillets in a single layer in the base of a large ovenproof dish and sprinkle with the shallot. Place the reserved garlic slices and fresh herb sprigs on top of the fillets and season to taste with salt and pepper. Mix the lemon juice and olive oil together in a small jug and pour it over the fish.

3 Bake in the preheated oven for 15 minutes, or until the fish flakes easily when tested with a fork. Sprinkle with lemon rind, garnish with the extra fresh herbs and serve immediately.

COOK'S TIP

Lemon sole is not related to Dover sole and is less expensive, but still has a fine flavour and delicate flesh. It is available from most large supermarkets.

Barbecued Monkfish

Monkfish cooks very well on a barbecue because it is a firm-fleshed fish. Make sure that you remove the membrane before cooking.

NUTRITIONAL INFORMATION

Calories 219	Sugars 0g	
Protein 28g	Fat 12g	
Carbohydrate 1g	Saturates 2g	

2¼ hrs   5–6 mins

SERVES 4

INGREDIENTS

 tbsp olive oil

grated rind of 1 lime

 tsp Thai fish sauce

 garlic cloves, crushed

 tsp grated fresh root ginger

 tbsp chopped fresh basil

700 g/1 lb 9 oz monkfish fillet, cut into chunks

 limes, each cut into 6 wedges

salt and pepper

1 Combine the olive oil, lime rind, fish sauce, garlic, grated ginger and basil in a non-metallic bowl. Season to taste with salt and pepper and set aside.

2 Wash the fish chunks and pat dry with kitchen paper. Add them to the marinade and mix well to coat. Cover and set aside in the refrigerator to marinate for 2 hours, stirring occasionally.

3 If you are using bamboo skewers, soak them in cold water for 30 minutes to prevent them from charring.

4 Lift the monkfish pieces from the marinade with a draining spoon and thread them on to the skewers, alternating with the lime wedges.

5 Transfer the skewers, either to a hot barbecue or to a preheated ridged grill pan. Cook for 5–6 minutes, turning regularly, until the fish is tender. Serve the skewers immediately.

VARIATION
You could use any type of white fleshed fish for this recipe but sprinkle the pieces with salt and leave for 2 hours to firm the flesh, before rinsing, drying and then adding to the marinade.

Swordfish Steaks

Swordfish has a firm, meaty texture, but has a tendency to dry out during cooking unless well marinated first.

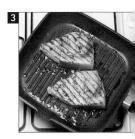

NUTRITIONAL INFORMATION

Calories	548	Sugars	.........0g
Protein	........28g	Fat	..........48g
Carbohydrate	....1g	Saturates	.......7g

 2¼ hrs   4–6 mins

SERVES 4

INGREDIENTS

4 x swordfish steaks, about 150 g/
   5½ oz each

4 tbsp olive oil

1 garlic clove, crushed

1 tsp lemon rind

lemon wedges, to garnish

SALSA VERDE

25 /1 oz flat leaf parsley leaves

15 g/½ oz mixed fresh herbs, such as basil,
   mint, chives

1 garlic clove, chopped

1 tbsp capers, drained and rinsed

1 tbsp green peppercorns in brine, drained

4 anchovies in oil, drained and
   roughly chopped

1 tsp Dijon mustard

125 ml/4 fl oz extra virgin olive oil

salt and pepper

VARIATIONS
Any firm fleshed-fish will
do this recipe. Try tuna or
even shark instead.

1 Wash the dry the swordfish steaks and place in a non-metallic dish. Combine the olive oil, garlic and lemon rind. Pour over the swordfish steaks and set aside to marinate for 2 hours.

2 For the salsa verde, put all the ingredients into a food processor or blender. Process to a smooth paste, adding a little warm water if necessary. Season to taste with salt and pepper and set aside.

3 Remove the swordfish steaks from the marinade. Cook on a barbecue or in a preheated ridged grill pan for 2–3 minutes each side until tender. Serve immediately with the salsa verde and garnished with lemon wedges.

Swordfish or Tuna Fajitas

Fajitas are usually made with chicken or lamb, but using a firm fish, such as swordfish or tuna, works very well too.

NUTRITIONAL INFORMATION

Calories	766	Sugars	........12g
Protein	........52g	Fat	..........36g
Carbohydrate	...63g	Saturates	......10g

1¼–2¼ hrs   7 mins

SERVES 4

INGREDIENTS

3 tbsp olive oil

2 tsp chilli powder

1 tsp ground cumin

pinch of cayenne pepper

1 garlic clove, crushed

900 g/2 lb swordfish or tuna

1 red pepper, deseeded and thinly sliced

1 yellow pepper, deseeded and thinly sliced

2 courgettes, cut into batons

1 large onion, thinly sliced

12 soft flour tortillas

1 tbsp lemon juice

3 tbsp chopped fresh coriander

salt and pepper

150 ml/5 fl oz soured cream, to serve

GUACAMOLE

1 large avocado, peeled and stoned

1 tomato, peeled, deseeded and diced

1 garlic clove, crushed

dash of Tabasco sauce

2 tbsp lemon juice

salt and pepper

1 Combine the olive oil, chilli powder, cumin, cayenne and garlic. Cut the swordfish or tuna into large chunks and mix with the marinade. Set aside for 1–2 hours.

2 Heat a large frying pan until hot. Add the fish and its marinade to the pan and cook, stirring occasionally, for 2 minutes until the fish begins to brown.

3 Add the red pepper, yellow pepper, courgettes and onion and continue cooking for a further 5 minutes until the vegetables have softened but are still firm.

4 Meanwhile, warm the tortillas in a low oven or microwave according to the packet instructions.

5 To make the guacamole, mash the avocado flesh with a fork until fairly smooth, stir in the tomato, garlic, Tabasco and lemon juice. Season to taste with salt and pepper.

6 Add the lemon juice, coriander and seasoning to the fish and vegetable mix. Spoon some of the mixture down the warmed tortilla. Top with guacamole and a spoonful of soured cream and roll up.

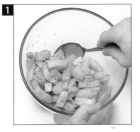

Smoked Fish Pie

What cookbook would be complete without a fish pie? This is
a classic version with smoked fish, prawns and vegetables.

NUTRITIONAL INFORMATION

Calories	562	Sugars	.........9g
Protein	........42g	Fat	..........29g
Carbohydrate	...35g	Saturates	......16g

    10 mins   1½ hrs

SERVES 4

INGREDIENTS

2 tbsp olive oil

1 onion, finely chopped

1 leek, thinly sliced

1 carrot, diced

1 celery stick, diced

115 g/4 oz button mushrooms, halved

grated rind of 1 lemon

350 g/12 oz skinless smoked cod or
    haddock fillets, cubed

350 g/12 oz skinless white fish fillets, such
    as haddock, hake or monkfish, cubed

8 oz peeled cooked prawns

2 tbsp chopped fresh parsley

1 tbsp chopped fresh dill

SAUCE

4 tbsp butter

4 tbsp plain flour

1 tsp mustard powder

600 ml/1 pint milk

85 g/3 oz Gruyère cheese, grated

TOPPING

675 g/1½ lb potatoes, unpeeled

4 tbsp butter, melted

4 tbsp Gruyère cheese, grated

salt and pepper

1 For the sauce, melt the butter in a large saucepan, add the flour and mustard powder. Stir until smooth and cook over a very low heat for 2 minutes without colouring. Gradually whisk in the milk until smooth. Simmer gently for 2 minutes, then stir in the grated cheese until melted and smooth. Remove the pan from the heat and put a piece of clingfilm over the surface of the sauce to prevent a skin from forming. Set aside.

2 Meanwhile, for the topping, cook the whole potatoes in plenty of lightly salted boiling water for about 15 minutes until tender. Drain well and set aside until cool enough to handle.

3 Heat the olive oil in a clean pan and add the onion. Fry over a low heat, stirring occasionally, for 5 minutes until softened. Add the sliced leek, the diced carrot and celery and the mushrooms and cook for a further 10 minutes, stirring occasionally, until all the vegetables have softened. Stir in the grated lemon rind and cook briefly.

4 Add the softened vegetables with the fish, prawns, parsley and dill to the sauce. Season to taste and transfer to a greased 1.75 litre/3 pint casserole.

5 Peel the cooled potatoes and grate them coarsely. Mix with the melted butter. Cover the fish and vegetable mixture with the grated potato and sprinkle with the grated Gruyère cheese.

6 Cover loosely with foil and bake in a preheated oven at 200°C/400°F/Gas Mark 6, for 30 minutes. Remove the foil and bake for an additional 30 minutes until the topping is tender and golden and the filling is bubbling. Serve immediately with your favourite selection of vegetables.

Hake Steaks with Chermoula

The cooking time may seem long and indeed you could decrease it slightly if you prefer, but in Morocco they like their fish well cooked!

NUTRITIONAL INFORMATION

Calories	 590	Sugars 1g
Protein	.... 42g	Fat 46g
Carbohydrate	.... 2g	Saturates 7g

🍲 1¼ hrs   🕐 35–40 mins

SERVES 4

INGREDIENTS

4 hake steaks, about 225 g/8 oz each

115 g/4 oz stoned green olives

freshly cooked vegetables, to serve

MARINADE

6 tbsp finely chopped fresh coriander

6 tbsp finely chopped fresh parsley

6 garlic cloves, crushed

1 tbsp ground cumin

1 tsp ground coriander

1 tbsp paprika

pinch of cayenne pepper

150 ml/5 fl oz fresh lemon juice

300 ml/10 fl oz olive oil

1 For the marinade, combine the fresh coriander, parsley, garlic, cumin, ground coriander, paprika, cayenne, lemon juice and olive oil in a bowl.

2 Wash the hake steaks and pat dry with kitchen paper. Place them in an ovenproof dish. Pour the marinade over the fish and set aside for at least 1 hour and preferably overnight.

3 Before cooking, sprinkle the olives over the fish. Cover the dish with foil.

4 Cook in a preheated oven, 160°C/ 325°F/Gas Mark 3 for 35–40 minutes until the fish is tender. Serve immediately with freshly cooked vegetables.

VARIATION
Remove the fish from the marinade and dust with seasoned flour. Fry in oil or clarified butter until golden. Warm the marinade, but do not boil, and serve as a sauce with lemon slices.

Stuffed Mackerel

This is an easier variation of a Middle Eastern recipe for stuffed mackerel which involves removing the mackerel flesh, while leaving the skin intact.

NUTRITIONAL INFORMATION

Calories 488	Sugars 12g	
Protein 34g	Fat 34g	
Carbohydrate ...12g	Saturates 6g	

10 mins   20 mins

SERVES 4

I N G R E D I E N T S

4 large mackerel, cleaned

1 tbsp olive oil

1 small onion, thinly sliced

1 tsp ground cinnamon

½ tsp ground ginger

2 tbsp raisins

2 tbsp pine kernels, toasted

8 vine leaves in brine, drained

salt and pepper

VARIATION

This stuffing works equally well with many other fish, including sea bass and red mullet.

1 Wash the fish, pat dry with kitchen paper and set aside. Heat the oil in a small frying pan and add the onion. Cook gently for 5 minutes until softened. Add the cinnamon and ginger and cook for 30 seconds, then add the raisins and pine kernels. Season to taste. Remove from the heat and allow to cool.

2 Stuff each fish with a quarter of the stuffing mixture. Wrap each fish in 2 vine leaves, securing with cocktail sticks.

3 Cook on a preheated barbecue or ridged grill pan for 5 minutes on each side until the vine leaves have scorched and the fish is tender. Serve immediately.

Tuna Fishcakes

These fishcakes make a satisfying and quick midweek supper. The tomato sauce is flavoured with a tempting combination of lemon, garlic and basil.

NUTRITIONAL INFORMATION

Calories	638	Sugars	.........5g
Protein	........35g	Fat	..........40g
Carbohydrate	...38g	Saturates	.......5g

5 mins   1¼ hrs

SERVES 4

I N G R E D I E N T S

225 g/8 oz potatoes, cubed

1 tbsp olive oil

1 large shallot, finely chopped

1 garlic clove, finely chopped

1 tsp fresh thyme leaves

400 g/14 oz canned tuna in olive
   oil, drained

grated rind of ½ lemon

1 tbsp chopped fresh parsley

2–3 tbsp plain flour

1 egg, lightly beaten

115 g/4 oz fresh breadcrumbs

vegetable oil, for frying

salt and pepper

QUICK TOMATO SAUCE

2 tbsp olive oil

400 g/14 oz canned chopped tomatoes

1 garlic clove, crushed

½ tsp sugar

grated rind of ½ lemon

1 tbsp chopped fresh basil

salt and pepper

1 For the tuna fishcakes, cook the potatoes in plenty of boiling salted water for 12–15 minutes until tender. Mash, leaving a few lumps, and set aside.

2 Heat the oil in a small frying pan and cook the shallot gently for 5 minutes until softened. Add the garlic and thyme leaves and cook for an additional minute. Allow to cool slightly, then add to the potatoes with the tuna, lemon rind, parsley and seasoning. Mix together well but leave some texture.

3 Form the mixture into 6–8 cakes. Dip the cakes first in the flour, then the egg and finally, the breadcrumbs to coat. Chill for 30 minutes.

4 For the tomato sauce, put the olive oil, tomatoes, garlic, sugar, lemon rind, and basil into a saucepan, season to taste with salt and pepper and bring to the boil. Cover and simmer for 30 minutes. Uncover and simmer for 15 minutes until thickened.

5 Heat enough oil in a frying pan to cover the base generously. Fry the fishcakes in batches for 3–4 minutes each side until golden and crisp. Drain on kitchen paper while you fry the remaining fishcakes. Serve hot with the tomato sauce.

Salmon Frittata

A frittata is an Italian slow-cooked omelette, similar to the Spanish tortilla. Here it is filled with salmon, herbs and vegetables.

NUTRITIONAL INFORMATION

Calories 300	Sugars 5g
Protein 22g	Fat 21g
Carbohydrate 7g	Saturates 8g

  15 mins 1 hr

SERVES 6

INGREDIENTS

250 g/9 oz skinless, boneless salmon

3 fresh thyme sprigs

fresh parsley sprig

5 black peppercorns

½ small onion, sliced

½ celery stick, sliced

½ carrot, chopped

175 g/6 oz asparagus spears, chopped

85 g/3 oz baby carrots, halved

4 tbsp butter

1 large onion, thinly sliced

1 garlic clove, finely chopped

115 g/4 oz peas, fresh or frozen

8 eggs, lightly beaten

2 tbsp chopped fresh parsley

1 tbsp chopped fresh dill

salt and pepper

lemon wedges, to garnish

TO SERVE

crème fraîche

salad

crusty bread

1 Place the salmon in a pan with 1 thyme sprig, the parsley sprig, peppercorns, onion, celery and carrot. Add water and bring to the boil. Remove the pan from the heat and set aside for 5 minutes. Lift out the fish, flake the flesh and set aside. Discard the poaching liquid.

2 Blanch the asparagus in boiling water for 2 minutes. Drain and refresh under cold water. Blanch the carrots for 4 minutes. Drain and refresh under cold water. Drain again and pat dry. Set aside.

3 Heat half the butter in a large frying pan and add the onion. Cook gently for 8–10 minutes until softened, but not coloured. Add the garlic and remaining thyme and cook for a further minute. Add the asparagus, carrots and peas and heat through. Remove from the heat.

4 Add the vegetables to the eggs with the chopped parsley, dill, salmon and seasoning and stir briefly. Heat the remaining butter in the pan and return the mixture to the pan. Cover and cook over a low heat for 10 minutes.

5 Cook under a preheated medium grill for a further 5 minutes until set and golden. Serve hot or cold in wedges topped with a spoon of crème fraîche, salad and crusty bread. Garnish with lemon wedges.

Mixed Seafood Brochettes

If your fishmonger sells turbot steaks, you will probably need one large skinned and boned steak for this dish.

NUTRITIONAL INFORMATION

Calories	455	Sugars	.........0g
Protein	........32g	Fat	..........20g
Carbohydrate	...39g	Saturates	.......9g

2¼ hrs   20 mins

SERVES 4

INGREDIENTS

225 g/8 oz skinless turbot fillet

225 g/8 oz skinless salmon fillet

8 scallops

8 large tiger prawns or langoustines

16 fresh bay leaves

1 lemon, sliced

4 tbsp olive oil

grated rind 1 lemon

4 tbsp chopped fresh mixed herbs, such as thyme, parsley, chives, basil

pepper

LEMON BUTTER RICE

175 g/6 oz long grain rice

grated rind and juice 1 lemon

4 tbsp butter

salt and pepper

TO GARNISH

lemon wedges

fresh dill sprigs

1 Chop the turbot and salmon into 8 pieces each. Thread on to 8 skewers, with the scallops and tiger prawns or langoustines, alternating with the bay leaves and lemon slices. Put the skewers into a non-metallic dish in a single layer if possible.

2 Combine the olive oil, lemon rind, herbs and pepper. Pour this mixture over the fish. Cover and set aside to marinate for 2 hours, turning once or twice.

3 For the lemon butter rice, bring a large pan of lightly salted water to the boil and add the rice and lemon rind. Return to the boil, then lower the heat and simmer for 7–8 minutes until the rice is tender. Drain thoroughly and immediately stir in the lemon juice and butter. Season with salt and pepper to taste.

4 Meanwhile, lift the fish brochettes from their marinade and cook on a hot barbecue or under a preheated hot grill for 8–10 minutes, turning frequently, until cooked through. Serve with lemon butter rice and garnish with lemon wedges and dill.

Chargrilled Scallops

Marinated scallops, chargrilled and served with couscous
studded with colourful vegetables and herbs – simply wonderful.

NUTRITIONAL INFORMATION

Calories	401	Sugars	.........3g
Protein	........20g	Fat	..........21g
Carbohydrate	...34g	Saturates	.......3g

2½ hrs   8 mins

SERVES 4

I N G R E D I E N T S

16 king scallops

3 tbsp olive oil

grated rind of 1 lime

2 tbsp chopped fresh basil

2 tbsp chopped fresh chives

1 garlic clove, finely chopped

pepper

J E W E L L E D   C O U S C O U S

225 g/ 8 oz couscous

½ red pepper, deseeded and halved

½ yellow pepper, deseeded and halved

4 tbsp extra virgin olive oil

115 g/4 oz cucumber, chopped into 1 cm/
  ½ inch pieces

3 spring onions, finely chopped

1 tbsp lime juice

2 tbsp shredded fresh basil

salt and pepper

T O   G A R N I S H

fresh basil leaves

lime wedges

1 Put the scallops into a non-metallic dish. Combine the olive oil, lime rind, basil, chives, garlic and pepper. Pour over the scallops and cover. Set aside to marinate for 2 hours.

2 Cook the couscous according to the packet instructions, omitting any butter recommended.

3 Brush the pepper halves with a little oil and place under a preheated hot grill for 5–6 minutes, turning once, until the skins are charred and the flesh is tender. Put in a plastic bag and set aside until cool enough to handle. Peel off the skins and chop the flesh into 1 cm/ ½ inch pieces. Add to the couscous with the remaining olive oil, cucumber, spring onions, lime juice and seasoning.

4 Lift the scallops from the marinade with a draining spoon and thread on to 4 skewers. Cook on a hot barbecue or preheated ridged grill pan for 1 minute on each side until charred and firm but not quite cooked through. Remove from the heat and set aside to rest for 2 minutes.

5 Stir the shredded basil into the couscous and divide it among individual serving plates. Put a skewer on each, garnish with basil leaves and lime wedges. Serve immediately.

Seafood Lasagne

You can use any fish and any sauce you like in this recipe:
try smoked finnan haddock and whisky sauce, or cod with cheese sauce.

NUTRITIONAL INFORMATION

Calories	790	Sugars	........23g
Protein	........55g	Fat	..........32g
Carbohydrate	...74g	Saturates	......19g

30 mins   45 mins

SERVES 4

INGREDIENTS

450 g/1 lb finnan haddock fillet, skin
   removed and flesh flaked

115 g/ 4 oz prawns

115 g/4 oz sole fillet, skin removed and
   flesh sliced

juice of 1 lemon

4 tbsp butter

3 leeks, very thinly sliced

6 tbsp plain flour

about 600 ml/1 pint milk

2 tbsp clear honey

200g/7 oz mozzarella cheese, grated

450g/1 lb pre-cooked lasagne

55 g/2 oz Parmesan cheese, freshly grated

pepper

1 Put the haddock fillet, prawns and sole fillet into a large bowl and season with pepper and lemon juice to taste. Set aside while you make the sauce.

2 Melt the butter in a large saucepan. Add the leeks and cook over a low heat, stirring occasionally, for 8 minutes until softened. Add the flour and cook, stirring constantly, for 1 minute. Gradually stir in enough milk to make a thick, creamy sauce.

3 Blend in the honey and mozzarella cheese and cook for a further 3 minutes. Turn off the heat and mix in the fish and prawns.

4 Make alternate layers of fish sauce and lasagne in an ovenproof dish, finishing with a layer of fish sauce on top. Generously sprinkle over the grated Parmesan cheese and bake in a preheated oven,180°C/350°F/Gas Mark 4, for 30 minutes. Serve immediately.

VARIATION
For a cider sauce, substitute 1 finely chopped shallot for the leeks, 300 ml/10 fl oz cider and 300 ml/10 fl oz double cream for the milk and 1 teaspoon mustard for the honey. For a Tuscan sauce, substitute 1 chopped fennel bulb for the leeks; omit the honey.

Spaghetti al Vongole

This is a very full-flavoured and elegant looking dish, especially if you can find small clams which often have richly coloured shells.

NUTRITIONAL INFORMATION

Calories 471	Sugars 9g	
Protein 24g	Fat 8g	
Carbohydrate . . .75g	Saturates 1g	

🦪 🦪

🧂 10 mins   🕙 1 hr

SERVES 4

INGREDIENTS

900 g/2 lb live clams, scrubbed

2 tbsp olive oil

1 large onion, finely chopped

2 garlic cloves, finely chopped

1 tsp fresh thyme leaves

150 ml/5 fl oz white wine

400 g/14 oz can chopped tomatoes

350 g/12 oz dried spaghetti

1 tbsp chopped fresh parsley

salt and pepper

1 Put the clams into a large pan with just the water clinging to their shells. Cook, covered, over a high heat, shaking the pan occasionally, for 3–4 minutes until all the clams have opened. Remove from the heat and strain, reserving the cooking liquid. Discard any clams that remain closed. Set aside.

COOK'S TIP

If you are able to get only very large clams, reserve a few in their shells to garnish and shell the rest.

2 Heat the oil in a pan and add the onion. Cook for 10 minutes over a low heat until softened, but not coloured. Add the garlic and thyme and cook for a further 30 seconds.

3 Increase the heat and add the white wine. Simmer rapidly until reduced and syrupy. Add the tomatoes and reserved clam liquid. Cover and simmer for 15 minutes. Uncover and simmer for a further 15 minutes until thickened. Season to taste with salt and pepper.

4 Meanwhile, bring a large pan of lightly salted water to the boil. Add the pasta, bring back to the boil and cook for 8–10 minutes until tender, but still firm to the bite. Drain the pasta well and return to the pan.

5 Add the clams to the tomato sauce and heat through for 2–3 minutes. Add the parsley and stir well. Add the tomato sauce to the pasta and toss together until the pasta is well coated in sauce. Serve immediately.

Squid Ink Pasta

This is a dramatic looking dish, with its jet-black pasta
and rich sauce of squid. Definitely one for special occasions.

NUTRITIONAL INFORMATION

Calories . . . . .418 Sugars 2g
Protein . . . . .22g Fat 12g
Carbohydrate . . .56g Saturates 2g

🧊 1½ hrs 🕐 30 mins

SERVES 6

INGREDIENTS

450 g/1 lb squid with their ink

300 g/10½ oz strong white bread flour

100 g/3½ oz fine semolina

2 eggs

SAUCE

4 tbsp olive oil

2 garlic cloves, finely chopped

1 tsp paprika

3 plum tomatoes, peeled, deseeded
   and diced

150 ml/5 fl oz white wine

1 tbsp chopped fresh parsley

salt and pepper

1 To prepare the squid, grasp the head
   and tentacles and pull to remove the
innards. The silvery ink sac lies at the
furthest point from the tentacles – be
careful to keep it intact. Cut the ink sac
away from the innards. Cut the tentacles
just below the beak and discard the
remaining innards. Remove the 'quill' from
the body and remove the wings and skin.
Wash the body and tentacles well.

2 Slice the body widthways into rings
   and set aside with the tentacles. Slit
open the ink sac and dilute with water to
make 50 ml/2 fl oz. Set aside.

3 To make the pasta, sift together the
   flour and semolina. Make a well in the
centre and add the eggs. Using a wooden
spoon, draw the flour and eggs together.
Gradually add the squid ink – you may not
need it all. Mix to a firm dough. Add a
little more water if it seems too stiff and a
little more flour if it seems too wet.
Alternatively, put all the ingredients in the
bowl of a mixer fitted with a kneading
hook and mix together. Knead the dough
for 10 minutes until smooth and elastic.
The dough should have the feel of soft
leather and be neither sticky nor should it
break easily. Wrap in clingfilm and set
aside for 30 minutes.

4 Using a pasta machine, thinly roll out
   the dough and cut into thin ribbons.
Alternatively, roll out by hand on a lightly
floured surface and cut into ribbons with a
sharp knife or pasta wheel. Hang to dry.

5 Meanwhile, make the sauce, heat the
   oil in a pan and add the garlic and
paprika. Fry over a medium heat for
30 seconds. Add the squid and cook,
stirring constantly, for 4–5 minutes until
lightly browned and firm. Add the
tomatoes and cook for 3–4 minutes until
collapsed. Add the white wine and simmer
gently for 15 minutes. Stir in the parsley
and season to taste with salt and pepper.

6 Meanwhile, bring a large pan of
   lightly salted water to the boil. Add
the pasta, bring back to the boil and cook
for 2–3 minutes until tender, but still firm
to the bite. Drain, turn into a serving bowl,
toss with the sauce and serve immediately.

Fideua

Fideua is a pasta dish which can be found south of Valencia, in western Spain. It is very like a paella but is made with very fine pasta.

NUTRITIONAL INFORMATION

Calories	373	Sugars	.........4g
Protein	........23g	Fat	..........8g
Carbohydrate	...52g	Saturates	.......1g

 10 mins   20 mins

SERVES 6

INGREDIENTS

3 tbsp olive oil

1 large onion, chopped

2 garlic cloves, finely chopped

pinch of saffron, crushed

½ tsp paprika

3 tomatoes, peeled, deseeded and chopped

350 g/12 oz egg vermicelli, broken roughly into 5 cm/2 inch lengths

150 ml/5 fl oz white wine

300 ml/10 fl oz fish stock

12 large raw prawns

18 live mussels, scrubbed and bearded

350 g/12 oz cleaned squid, cut into rings

18 large clams, scrubbed

2 tbsp chopped fresh parsley

salt and pepper

lemon wedges, to serve

1 Heat the oil in a large frying pan or paella pan. Add the onion and cook over a low heat for 5 minutes until softened. Add the garlic and cook for a further 30 seconds. Add the saffron and paprika and stir well. Add the tomatoes and cook for a further 2–3 minutes until they have collapsed.

2 Add the vermicelli and stir well. Add the wine and boil rapidly until it has been absorbed.

3 Add the fish stock, prawns, mussels, squid and clams. Stir and return to a low simmer for 10 minutes until the prawns and squid are cooked through and the mussels and clams have opened. Discard any that remain shut. The stock should be almost completely absorbed.

4 Add the parsley and season to taste with salt and pepper. Serve immediately in warmed bowls, garnished with lemon wedges.

VARIATION

Use whatever combination of seafood you prefer. Try langoustines, prawns and monkfish.

Thai Noodles

This classic Thai noodle dish is flavoured with the ubiquitous Thai fish sauce, roasted peanuts and prawns.

NUTRITIONAL INFORMATION

Calories	344	Sugars	.........2g
Protein	........21g	Fat	..........17g
Carbohydrate	...27g	Saturates	.......2g

10 mins   5 mins

SERVES 4

INGREDIENTS

350 g/12 oz cooked, peeled tiger prawns

115 g/4 oz flat rice noodles or
   rice vermicelli

4 tbsp vegetable oil

2 garlic cloves, finely chopped

1 egg

2 tbsp lemon juice

4½ tsp Thai fish sauce

½ tsp sugar

2 tbsp chopped, roasted peanuts

½ tsp cayenne pepper

2 spring onions, cut into 2.5 cm/
   1 inch pieces

55 g/2 oz fresh beansprouts

1 tbsp chopped fresh coriander

lemon wedges, to serve

1 Drain the tiger prawns on kitchen paper to remove excess moisture. Set aside. Cook the rice noodles according to the packet instructions. Drain well and set aside until required.

2 Heat the oil in a wok or large, heavy-based frying pan and add the garlic. Cook, stirring constantly, until just golden. Add the egg and stir quickly to break it up. Cook for a few seconds.

3 Add the prawns and noodles, scraping down the sides of the wok or pan to ensure they mix with the egg and garlic.

4 Add the lemon juice, fish sauce, sugar, half the peanuts, the cayenne, spring onions and half the beansprouts stirring quickly all the time. Cook over a high heat for a further 2 minutes until everything is heated through.

5 Turn on to a warmed serving plate. Top with the remaining peanuts and beansprouts and sprinkle with the coriander. Serve with lemon wedges.

VARIATION

This is a basic dish to which lots of different cooked seafood could be added. Cooked squid rings, mussels and langoustines would all work just as well.

Kedgeree

Originally, an Indian dish of rice and lentils, kedgeree has come to be a dish of rice, spices and smoked fish served with hard-boiled eggs.

NUTRITIONAL INFORMATION

Calories	457	Sugars	.........3g
Protein	........33g	Fat	..........18g
Carbohydrate	...40g	Saturates	.......6g

15 mins   35 mins

SERVES 4

INGREDIENTS

450 g/1 lb smoked haddock fillet

2 tbsp olive oil

1 large onion, chopped

2 garlic cloves, finely chopped

½ tsp ground turmeric

½ tsp ground cumin

1 tsp ground coriander

175 g/6 oz basmati rice

4 medium eggs

2 tbsp butter

1 tbsp chopped fresh parsley

TO SERVE

lemon wedges

mango chutney

1 Pour boiling water over the haddock fillet and set aside for 10 minutes. Lift the fish from the water, discard the skin and bones and flake the flesh. Reserve the water.

2 Heat the oil in a large pan and add the onion. Cook for 10 minutes over a medium heat until starting to brown. Add the garlic and cook for a further 30 seconds. Add the turmeric, cumin and coriander and stir-fry for 30 seconds until the spices smell fragrant. Stir in the rice.

3 Measure 350 ml/12 fl oz of the haddock poaching water and add to the pan. Stir well and bring to the boil. Cover and cook over a very low heat for about 12–15 minutes until the rice is tender and the stock has been completely absorbed.

4 Meanwhile, bring a small pan of water to the boil and add the eggs. When the water has returned to the boil cook the eggs for 8 minutes. Immediately drain the eggs and refresh under cold water to stop them from further cooking. Set aside.

5 Add the reserved fish pieces, the butter and parsley to the rice. Turn on to a large serving dish. Shell and quarter the eggs and arrange on top of the rice. Serve with lemon wedges and mango chutney.

Jambalaya

Jambalaya is a dish of Cajun origin. There are as many versions of this dish as there are people who cook it. Here is a straightforward one.

NUTRITIONAL INFORMATION

Calories	283	Sugars	.........8g
Protein	........30g	Fat	.........14g
Carbohydrate	...12g	Saturates	.......3g

🧊 10 mins   🕐 45 mins

SERVES 4

INGREDIENTS

2 tbsp vegetable oil

2 onions, roughly chopped

1 green pepper, deseeded and
  roughly chopped

2 celery sticks, roughly chopped

3 garlic cloves, finely chopped

2 tsp paprika

300 g/10½ oz skinless, boneless chicken
  breasts, chopped

100 g/3½ oz kabanos sausages, chopped

3 tomatoes, peeled and chopped

450 g/1 lb long grain rice

850 ml/1½ pint hot chicken or fish stock

1 tsp dried oregano

2 bay leaves

12 large prawn tails

4 spring onions, finely chopped

2 tbsp chopped fresh parsley

salt and pepper

salad, to serve

1 Heat the vegetable oil in a large frying pan and add the onions, pepper, celery and garlic. Cook over a low heat, stirring occasionally, for about 8–10 minutes until all the vegetables have softened. Add the paprika and cook for a further 30 seconds. Add the chicken and sausages and cook for 8–10 minutes until lightly browned. Add the tomatoes and cook for 2–3 minutes until collapsed.

2 Add the rice to the pan and stir well. Pour in the hot stock and stir in the oregano and bay leaves. Cover and simmer for 10 minutes over a very low heat.

3 Add the prawns and stir well. Cover again and cook for a further 6–8 minutes until the rice is tender and the prawns are cooked through.

4 Stir in the spring onions and parsley and season to taste. Serve with salad.

COOK'S TIP

Jambalaya is a versatile dish which has some basic ingredients – onions, green peppers, celery, rice and seasonings – to which you can add whatever you have to hand.

Lobster Risotto

This is a special occasion dish, just for two. However, you could easily double the recipe for a dinner party if necessary.

NUTRITIONAL INFORMATION

Calories	487	Sugars	.........8g
Protein	........10g	Fat	..........10g
Carbohydrate	...86g	Saturates	.......2g

   15 mins   35 mins

SERVES 2

INGREDIENTS

1 cooked lobster, about 400–450 g/
  14 oz–1 lb

4 tbsp butter

1 tbsp olive oil

1 onion, finely chopped

1 garlic clove, finely chopped

1 tsp fresh thyme leaves

175 g/6 oz arborio rice

600 ml/1 pint simmering fish stock

150 ml/5 fl oz sparkling wine

1 tsp green or pink peppercorns in brine,
  drained and roughly chopped

1 tbsp chopped fresh parsley

1 To prepare the lobster, remove the claws by twisting. Crack the claws using the back of a large knife and set aside. Split the body lengthways. Remove and discard the intestinal vein, the stomach sac and the spongy gills. Remove the meat from the tail and roughly chop. Set aside with the claws.

2 Heat half the butter and the oil in a large frying pan. Add the onion and cook gently for 4–5 minutes until softened. Add the garlic and cook for a further 30 seconds. Add the thyme and rice. Cook, stirring for 1–2 minutes until the rice is well coated and translucent.

3 Increase the heat under the pan to medium and begin adding the stock, a ladleful at a time, stirring well between additions. Continue for 2–25 minutes until all the stock has been absorbed.

4 Add the lobster meat and claws. Stir in the wine, increasing the heat. When the wine is absorbed, remove the pan from the heat and stir in the peppercorns, remaining butter and parsley. Set aside for 1 minute then serve immediately.

VARIATION

For a slightly cheaper version substitute 450 g/1 lb prawns for the lobster.

Prawn & Asparagus Risotto

An unusual and striking dish with fresh prawns and asparagus is very simple to prepare and ideal for impromptu supper parties.

NUTRITIONAL INFORMATION

Calories 566	Sugars 4g	
Protein 30g	Fat 14g	
Carbohydrate ...86g	Saturates 2g	

🌶 🌶 🌶

🍲 10 mins   🕐 40 mins

SERVES 4

INGREDIENTS

1.2 litres/2 pints vegetable stock

375 g/12 oz asparagus, cut into 5 cm/
   2 inch lengths

2 tbsp olive oil

1 onion, finely chopped

1 garlic clove, finely chopped

375 g/12 oz arborio rice

450 g/1 lb raw tiger prawns, peeled
   and deveined

2 tbsp olive paste or tapenade

2 tbsp chopped fresh basil

salt and pepper

Parmesan cheese shavings, to garnish

1 Bring the vegetable stock to the boil in a large pan. Add the asparagus and cook for 3 minutes until just tender. Strain, reserving the stock, and refresh the asparagus under cold running water. Drain and set aside.

2 Heat the oil in a large, heavy-based frying pan. Add the onion and cook over a low heat, stirring occasionally, for 5 minutes until softened. Add the garlic and cook for a further 30 seconds. Add the rice and cook, stirring constantly for about 1–2 minutes until coated with the oil and slightly translucent.

3 Keep the stock on a low heat. Increase the heat under the frying pan to medium and begin adding the stock, a ladleful at a time, stirring well between additions. Continue until almost all the stock has been absorbed. This should take 20–25 minutes.

4 Add the prawns and asparagus with the last ladleful of stock and cook fora further 5 minutes until the prawns and rice are tender and the stock has been absorbed. Remove from the heat.

5 Stir in the olive paste, basil and seasoning and set aside for 1 minute. Serve immediately, garnished with Parmesan shavings.

Spicy Monkfish Rice

A Thai-influenced dish of rice, cooked in coconut milk, with spicy grilled monkfish and fresh peas – what could be better?

NUTRITIONAL INFORMATION

Calories	440	Sugars	.........8g
Protein	........22g	Fat	..........14g
Carbohydrate	...60g	Saturates	.......2g

 30 mins   30 mins

SERVES 4

INGREDIENTS

1 fresh hot red chilli, deseeded and chopped

1 tsp crushed chilli flakes

2 garlic cloves, chopped

pinch of saffron

3 tbsp roughly chopped fresh mint leaves

4 tbsp olive oil

2 tbsp lemon juice

375 g/12 oz monkfish fillet, cut into bite-size pieces

1 onion, finely chopped

225 g/8 oz long grain rice

400g/14 oz can chopped tomatoes

200 ml/7 fl oz coconut milk

115 g/4 oz peas

salt and pepper

2 tbsp chopped fresh coriander, to garnish

1 Process the chilli, chill flakes, garlic, saffron, mint, olive oil and lemon juice in a food processor or blender until combined, but not smooth.

2 Put the monkfish into a non-metallic dish and pour over the spice paste, turning to coat. Cover and set aside for 20 minutes to marinate.

3 Heat a large pan until very hot. Using a draining spoon, lift the monkfish from the marinade and add, in batches, to the hot pan. Cook for 3–4 minutes until browned and firm. Remove with a draining spoon and set aside.

4 Add the onion and remaining marinade to the pan and cook for 5 minutes until softened and lightly browned. Add the rice and stir until well coated. Add the tomatoes and coconut milk. Bring to the boil, cover and simmer very gently for 15 minutes. Stir in the peas, season and arrange the fish over the top. Cover with foil and continue to cook over a very low heat for 5 minutes. Serve garnished with the chopped coriander.

Herring & Potato Pie

The combination of herrings, apples and potatoes is popular throughout northern Europe. In salads, one often sees the addition of beetroots.

NUTRITIONAL INFORMATION

Calories	574	Sugars	........10g
Protein	........17g	Fat	..........36g
Carbohydrate	...48g	Saturates	.....19g

🕑 20 mins   🕐 1 hr

SERVES 4

INGREDIENTS

tbsp Dijon mustard

15 g/4 oz butter, softened

50 g/1 lb herrings, filleted

50 g/1 lb 10 oz potatoes

large onion, sliced

cooking apples, thinly sliced

tsp chopped fresh sage

00 ml/1 pint hot fish stock

5 g/2 oz ciabatta, crusts removed and made into breadcrumbs

alt and pepper

esh parsley sprigs, to garnish

1 Mix the mustard with 2 tablespoons of the butter until smooth. Spread this mixture over the cut sides of the herring fillets. Season and roll up the fillets. Set aside. Generously grease a 2.25 litre/4 pint pie dish with some of the remaining butter.

2 Thinly slice the potatoes, using a mandoline if possible. Blanch for 3 minutes in plenty of lightly salted boiling water until just tender. Drain well, refresh under cold water and then pat dry.

3 Heat 2 tablespoons of the remaining butter in a frying pan and add the sliced onion. Cook gently for 8–10 minutes until soft but not coloured. Remove from the heat and set aside.

4 Put half the potato slices into the base of the pie dish with some seasoning, then add half the apple and half the onion. Put the herring fillets on top of the onion and sprinkle with the sage. Repeat the layers in reverse order, ending with potato. Season well and add enough hot stock to come halfway up the sides of the dish.

5 Melt the remaining butter and stir in the breadcrumbs until well combined. Sprinkle the breadcrumbs over the pie. Bake in a preheated oven, 190°C/375°F/Gas Mark 5, for 40–50 minutes until the breadcrumbs are golden and the herrings are cooked through. Serve garnished with parsley.

VARIATION

herrings are unavailable,
ubstitute mackerel or sardines.

Pizza Marinara

Traditionally, a pizza topped with mixed seafood would have no cheese but in this case it helps to protect the fish from overcooking.

NUTRITIONAL INFORMATION

Calories . . . . . . .638 Sugars 5g
Protein . . . . .55g Fat 26g
Carbohydrate . . .50g Saturates 11g

 15 mins 25 mins

SERVES 4

INGREDIENTS

½ quantity Basic Pizza Dough (see page 838)

1 quantity Basic Tomato Sauce (see page 7)

handful of fresh basil leaves

MIXED SEAFOOD

16 live mussels, scrubbed and bearded

16 large live clams, scrubbed

1 tbsp olive oil

12 raw tiger prawns

225 g/8 oz cleaned squid, cut into rings

2 x 150 g/5½ oz mozzarella cheese, drained and sliced

olive oil, for drizzling

salt and pepper

1 To prepare the seafood, put the mussels and clams in a pan with only the water clinging to their shells. Cover and cook over a high heat, shaking occasionally, for 3–4 minutes until the shells have opened. Discard any that remain closed.

2 Strain the shellfish, discarding the cooking liquid. Set aside to cool. When cool enough to handle, remove the mussels and clams from their shells and set aside.

3 Heat the oil in a frying pan and add the prawns and squid. Cook for 2–3 minutes until the prawns have turned pink and the squid has become firm.

4 Preheat the oven to 230°C/450°F/Ga Mark 8 with baking sheets on the to and middle shelves. Divide the pizza doug and in half and shape into 25 cm/10 inc in rounds. Put on to floured baking sheets

5 Spread half the tomato sauce on eac pizza and add the mussels, clam tiger prawns and squid. Season to tast with salt and pepper and top with th sliced mozzarella. Drizzle with olive oil ar place the baking sheets on top of th preheated baking sheets.

6 Cook for 12–15 minutes, swappin halfway through the cooking tim until golden. Serve immediately, sprinkle with the basil.

Sole Meunière

Sole has a delicate and subtle flavour, so it is best cooked very simply, rather than being smothered in a rich sauce.

NUTRITIONAL INFORMATION

Calories 363	Sugars 3g	
Protein 36g	Fat 14g	
Carbohydrate ...25g	Saturates 5g	

5 mins   12 mins

SERVES 4

INGREDIENTS

225 ml/8 fl oz milk

115 g/4 oz plain flour

salt and pepper

700 g/1 lb 9 oz Dover sole fillets

25 g/1 oz butter

1–2 tbsp sunflower oil

2 tbsp chopped fresh parsley

lemon wedges, to garnish

1 Pour the milk into a large, shallow dish. Place the flour on a large, flat plate and season to taste with salt and pepper.

2 Dip the sole in the milk and then in the flour, turning to coat. Shake off any excess.

3 Melt the butter with the sunflower oil in a large, heavy-based frying pan. Add the fish fillets, in batches, and cook over a low heat for 2–3 minutes on each side, or until lightly browned. Keep each batch warm while you cook the remaining fish, then sprinkle with the parsley and serve immediately, garnished with the lemon wedges.

John Dory en Papillote

The beauty of this dish is that the fish cooks with a selection of vegetables so you need cook only some boiled new potatoes to serve with it.

NUTRITIONAL INFORMATION

Calories	368	Sugars	.........2g
Protein	........49g	Fat	..........18g
Carbohydrate	....3g	Saturates	.......3g

   10 mins   15 mins

SERVES 4

INGREDIENTS

2 John Dory, filleted

115 g/4 oz stoned black olives

12 cherry tomatoes, halved

115 g/4 oz green beans

handful of fresh basil leaves

4 fresh lemon slices

4 tsp olive oil

salt and pepper

fresh basil leaves, to garnish

boiled new potatoes, to serve

1 Wash and dry the fish fillets and set aside. Cut 4 large rectangles of baking paper measuring about 45 x 30 cm/18 x 12 inches. Fold in half to give a 23 x 30 cm/9 x 12 inch rectangle. Cut this into a large heart shape and open out.

2 Lay 1 John Dory fillet on 1 half of the paper heart. Top with a quarter of the olives, tomatoes, green beans, basil and 1 lemon slice. Drizzle over 1 teaspoon of olive oil and season to taste with salt and pepper.

3 Fold over the other half of the paper and fold the edges of the paper together to enclose. Repeat to make 4 parcels.

4 Place the parcels on a baking sheet and cook in a preheated oven, 200°C/400°F/Gas Mark 6, for about 15 minutes or until the fish is tender.

5 Transfer each parcel to a serving plate, unopened, allowing your guests to open their parcels and enjoy the wonderful aroma. Suggest that they garnish their portions with fresh basil and serve with a generous helping of boiled new potatoes.

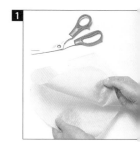

VARIATIONS

Try spreading the fish with a little olive paste, some chopped sun-dried tomatoes, a little goat's cheese and fresh basil.

Sea Bass with Artichokes

Baby artichokes are slowly cooked with olive oil, garlic, thyme and lemon to create a soft blend of flavours that harmonise very well with the fish.

NUTRITIONAL INFORMATION

Calories	400	Sugars	.........3g
Protein	........28g	Fat	..........30g
Carbohydrate	....7g	Saturates	.......5g

🧊 20 mins   🕐 35 mins

SERVES 6

INGREDIENTS

.75 kg/4 lb baby artichokes

½ tbsp fresh lemon juice, plus the cut halves of the lemon

50 ml/5 fl oz olive oil, plus extra for brushing

0 garlic cloves, thinly sliced

tbsp fresh thyme, plus extra, to garnish

x 115 g/4 oz sea bass fillets

tbsp olive oil

alt and pepper

rusty bread, to serve

1 Peel away the tough outer leaves of each artichoke until the heart is revealed. Slice off the pointed top at about halfway between the point and the top of the stem. Cut off the stem and pare off what is left of the dark green leaves surrounding the bottom of the artichoke.

2 Submerge the prepared artichokes in water containing the cut halves of the lemon to prevent them from browning. When all the artichokes have been prepared, turn them, choke side down, and slice thinly.

3 Warm the olive oil in a large pan and add the sliced artichokes, garlic, thyme, lemon juice and seasoning. Cover and cook the artichokes over a low heat for 20–30 minutes, without colouring, until tender.

4 Meanwhile, brush the sea bass fillets with olive oil and season well. Cook on a preheated ridged grill pan or barbecue for 3–4 minutes on each side until just tender.

5 Divide the stewed artichokes between serving plates and top each with a sea bass fillet. Garnish with chopped thyme and serve with lots of crusty bread.

VARIATIONS
Artichokes cooked this way also suit cod, halibut or salmon.

Sea Bass with Ratatouille

Sea bass is surely the king of round fish. Here it is cooked very simply and served with a highly flavoured sauce of ratatouille and a basil dressing.

NUTRITIONAL INFORMATION

Calories ....373 Sugars 9g
Protein ....42g Fat 18g
Carbohydrate ...10g Saturates 3g

🍲 45 mins   🕐 1 hr

SERVES 4

INGREDIENTS

2 large sea bass, filleted

olive oil, for brushing

salt and pepper

RATATOUILLE

1 large aubergine

2 medium courgettes

1 tbsp sea salt

4 tbsp olive oil

1 medium onion, roughly chopped

2 garlic cloves, crushed

½ red pepper, deseeded and
  roughly chopped

½ green pepper, deseeded and
  roughly chopped

2 large tomatoes, peeled and chopped

1 tbsp chopped fresh basil

DRESSING

5 tbsp roughly chopped fresh basil

2 garlic cloves, roughly chopped

4 tbsp olive oil

1 tbsp lemon juice

salt and pepper

1 To make the ratatouille, roughly chop the aubergine and courgettes. Put them in a colander with the salt and set aside to drain for 30 minutes. Rinse thoroughly and pat dry on kitchen paper. Set aside.

2 Heat the oil in a large pan and add the onion and garlic. Cook over a low heat, stirring occasionally, for 10 minutes until softened. Add the peppers, aubergine and courgettes. Season to taste and stir well. Cover and simmer very gently for 30 minutes until all the vegetables have softened. Add the tomatoes and cook for a further 15 minutes.

3 Meanwhile make the dressing. Put the basil, garlic, and half the olive oil into a food processor and process unt finely chopped. Add the remaining olive o lemon juice and seasoning.

4 Season the sea bass fillets and brus with a little oil. Preheat a frying pa until very hot and add the fish, skin sid down. Cook for 2–3 minutes until the ski is browned and crispy. Turn the fish an cook for a further 2–3 minutes until jus cooked through.

5 To serve, stir the basil into th ratatouille then divide betwee 4 serving plates. Top with the fresh frie fish and spoon around the dressing.

 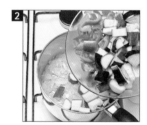 

Whole Sea Bass with Ginger

This is a lovely oriental-inspired dish of sea bass, delicately flavoured with spring onions, ginger and soy sauce.

NUTRITIONAL INFORMATION

Calories	185	Sugars	.........1g
Protein	........31g	Fat	...........6g
Carbohydrate	....2g	Saturates	.......1g

🧊 10 mins ⏱ 15 mins

SERVES 4

INGREDIENTS

00 g/1 lb 12 oz whole sea bass, cleaned and scaled

tbsp light soy sauce

spring onions, cut into long, fine shreds

tbsp finely shredded fresh root ginger

tbsp fresh coriander leaves

tsp sunflower oil

tsp sesame oil

tbsp hot fish stock

me wedges, to garnish

teamed rice, to serve

1 Wash the fish and pat dry with kitchen paper. Brush all over with tablespoons of the soy sauce. Sprinkle alf the spring onions and all the ginger ver a steaming tray or large plate and put he fish on top.

2 Half fill a large pan with water and fit a steamer on top. Bring the water to he boil. Put the steaming plate with the ea bass into the steamer and cover with a ight-fitting lid. Keeping the water boiling, team the fish for 10–12 minutes until ender and cooked through.

3 Carefully remove the plate and lift the fish on to a serving platter, leaving behind the spring onions and ginger. Scatter over the remaining spring onions and coriander leaves.

4 Put the sunflower oil into a small pan and heat until almost smoking. Add the sesame oil and immediately pour the hot oils over the fish and spring onions.

Mix the remaining soy sauce with the fish stock and pour this over the fish. Serve immediately with steamed rice and garnished with lime wedges.

Cold Poached Cod Steaks

Poached cod has a very delicate flavour. Here it is teamed with a piquant relish of finely diced, colourful vegetables, both served cold.

NUTRITIONAL INFORMATION

Calories	395	Sugars	.........4g
Protein	.........3g	Fat	..........27g
Carbohydrate	....5g	Saturates	.......4g

2¼ hrs   20 mins

SERVES 4

I N G R E D I E N T S

1 small carrot, thinly sliced

1 small onion, thinly sliced

1 celery stick, thinly sliced

3 fresh parsley sprigs

3 fresh thyme sprigs

1 garlic clove, sliced

1.75 litres/3 pints water

1 tsp salt

4 x 175 g/6 oz cod steaks

PICKLED VEGETABLE RELISH

1 small carrot, finely diced

¼ red pepper, deseeded and finely diced

½ small red onion, finely diced

1 garlic clove, finely chopped

3 tbsp finely diced cornichon pickles

4 tbsp chopped stoned green olives

1 tbsp capers, drained and rinsed

2 salted anchovies, soaked in several changes of water for 15 minutes, chopped

1 tbsp red wine vinegar

100 ml/3½ fl oz olive oil

2 tbsp chopped fresh parsley

salt and pepper

salad leaves, to serve

1 Put the carrot, onion, celery, parsley, thyme, garlic, water and salt into a large pan. Bring to the boil and simmer gently for 10 minutes. Add the fish and poach for 5–7 minutes until just firm in the centre. Remove the fish with a draining spoon and set aside to cool. Chill in the refrigerator for 2 hours.

2 Meanwhile, make the pickled vegetable relish. In a non-metallic bowl, combine the carrot, red pepper, re onion, garlic, cornichons, olives, caper anchovies, vinegar, olive oil and parsle Season to taste, adding a little mor vinegar or olive oil to taste. Cover and chi in the refrigerator for 1 hour.

3 To serve, place a cold cod steak o each of 4 serving plates. Spoon th relish over the top. Serve immediately wit dressed salad leaves.

Cuttlefish in their own Ink

This is a dramatic-looking dish owing to the inclusion of the cuttlefish ink. Although typically Spanish, it is teamed with polenta here.

NUTRITIONAL INFORMATION

Calories . . . . .430 Sugars 2g
Protein . . . . .24g Fat 14g
Carbohydrate . . .44g Saturates 2g

🍲 15 mins   🕐 45 mins

SERVES 4

INGREDIENTS

50 g/1 lb small cuttlefish or squid, with their ink

tbsp olive oil

small onion, finely chopped

garlic cloves, finely chopped

tsp paprika

75 g/6 oz ripe tomatoes, peeled, deseeded and chopped

50 ml/5 fl oz red wine

50 ml/5 fl oz fish stock

25 g/8 oz instant polenta

tbsp chopped fresh flat leaf parsley

alt and pepper

1 Cut off the cuttlefish tentacles in front of the eyes and remove the beak from the centre of the tentacles. Cut the head from the body and discard. Cut open the body section along the dark coloured back. Remove the cuttle bone and the entrails, reserving the ink sac. Skin the body. Chop the flesh roughly and set aside. Split open the ink sac and dilute the ink in a little water. Set aside.

2 Heat the oil in a large pan and add the onion. Cook gently for 8–10 minutes until softened and golden. Add the garlic and cook for a further 30 seconds. Add the cuttlefish and cook for a further 5 minutes until starting to brown. Add the paprika and stir for 30 seconds before adding the tomatoes. Cook for 2–3 minutes until collapsed.

3 Add the red wine, fish stock and diluted ink and stir well. Bring to the boil and simmer gently, uncovered, for 25 minutes until the cuttlefish is tender and the sauce has thickened. Season to taste with salt and pepper.

4 Meanwhile, cook the polenta according to the packet instructions. When cooked, remove from the heat and stir in the parsley and seasoning.

5 Divide the polenta between serving plates and top with the cuttlefish and its sauce.

Noisettes of Salmon

This is an interesting and elegant way of presenting ordinary salmon steaks. It will taste even better if you can obtain wild salmon.

NUTRITIONAL INFORMATION

Calories	.381	Sugars	.3g
Protein	.36g	Fat	.26g
Carbohydrate	.3g	Saturates	.4g

20 mins   25 mins

SERVES 4

I N G R E D I E N T S

4 salmon steaks

4 tbsp butter, softened

1 garlic clove, crushed

2 tsp mustard seeds

2 tbsp chopped fresh thyme

1 tbsp chopped fresh parsley

2 tbsp vegetable oil

4 tomatoes, peeled, deseeded and chopped

salt and pepper

TO SERVE

new potatoes

green vegetables or salad

1 Carefully remove the central bone from the salmon steaks and cut the steaks in half. Curl each piece around to form a medallion and tie with string.

VARIATION

You can make cod steaks into noisettes in the same way. Cook them with butter flavoured with fresh chives and basil.

Blend together the butter, garlic, mustard seeds, thyme and parsley and season to taste with salt and pepper. Set aside.

2 Heat the oil in a ridged pan or frying pan and brown the salmon noisettes on both sides, in batches if necessary. Drain thoroughly on kitchen paper and set aside to cool.

3 Cut 4 pieces of baking paper into 30 cm/12 inch squares. Place 2 salmon noisettes on top of each square and to with a little of the flavoured butter ar tomato. Draw up the edges of the pape and fold together to enclose the fish. Pla on a baking sheet.

4 Cook the parcels in a preheated ove 200°C/400°F/Gas Mark 6, for abo 10–15 minutes or until the salmon cooked through. Serve immediately wi new potatoes and a green vegetable your choice.

Cajun Spiced Fish

Cajun cooking is marked with a practical approach that makes the most of the locally available ingredients in the countryside around New Orleans.

NUTRITIONAL INFORMATION

Calories	215	Sugars	.........2g
Protein	........33g	Fat	...........8g
Carbohydrate	....2g	Saturates	.......2g

5 mins   10 mins

SERVES 4

INGREDIENTS

1 tbsp lime juice

2 tbsp low-fat natural yogurt

4 swordfish steaks, about 175 g/6 oz each

sunflower or corn oil, for brushing

lemon wedges, to serve

SPICE MIX

1 tsp paprika

1 tsp cayenne pepper

1 tsp ground cumin

1 tsp mustard powder

1 tsp dried oregano

1 First make the spice mix by blending all the ingredients in a bowl. Mix the lime juice and yogurt in a separate bowl.

2 Pat the fish steaks dry with kitchen paper, then brush both sides with the yogurt mixture. Use your hands to coat both sides of the fish with the spice mix, rubbing it well into the flesh.

3 Brush a griddle pan with a little sunflower oil. Add the fish steaks and cook for 5 minutes over a medium heat, then turn over and cook for a further 4 minutes, or until the flesh flakes easily when tested with a fork. Serve straight from the pan with lemon wedges.

Stuffed Monkfish Tail

A very impressive-looking dish which is very simple to prepare.
Although monkfish is quite expensive, there is very little wastage.

NUTRITIONAL INFORMATION

Calories 154   Sugars 0g
Protein ....24g   Fat 6g
Carbohydrate ....0g   Saturates 1g

 30 mins   🕐 25 mins

SERVES 6

I N G R E D I E N T S

750 g/1 lb 10 oz monkfish tail, skinned
   and trimmed

6 slices Parma ham

4 tbsp chopped fresh mixed herbs, such
   as parsley, chives, basil, sage

1 tsp finely grated lemon rind

2 tbsp olive oil

salt and pepper

T O   S E R V E

stir-fried vegetables

new potatoes

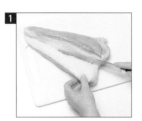
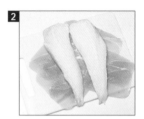
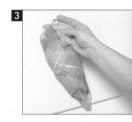

1 Using a sharp knife, carefully cut down each side of the central bone of the monkfish to leave 2 fillets. Wash the fillets and pat dry with kitchen paper.

COOK'S TIP

It is possible to remove the central bone from a monkfish tail without separating the 2 fillets completely. This makes it easier to stuff, but takes some practice.

2 Lay the Parma ham slices widthways on a clean work surface so that they overlap slightly. Lay the fish fillets lengthways on top of the ham so that the 2 cut sides face each other.

3 Combine the herbs and lemon rind. Season well. Pack this mixture on to the cut surface of 1 monkfish fillet. Press the 2 fillets together and wrap tightly with the Parma ham slices. Secure with string or cocktail sticks.

4 Heat the olive oil in a large ovenproof frying pan and place the fish in the pan, seam side down first, and brown the wrapped monkfish tail all over.

5 Cook in a preheated oven, 200°C/ 400°F/Gas Mark 6, for 25 minutes until golden and the fish is tender. Remove from the oven and set aside to rest for 10 minutes before slicing thickly. Serve with shredded stir-fried vegetables and new potatoes.

Spinach Roulade

Although something of a dinner party cliché,
a roulade is still an attractive and very appetising dish.

NUTRITIONAL INFORMATION

Calories	331	Sugars	.........5g
Protein	........27g	Fat	..........21g
Carbohydrate	...10g	Saturates	.......9g

  25 mins | 40 mins

SERVES 4

INGREDIENTS

olive oil, for brushing

225 g/8 oz frozen spinach, thawed and
 well drained

2 tbsp butter

4 tbsp plain flour

200 ml/7 fl oz milk

4 eggs, separated

1 tbsp chopped fresh tarragon

½ tsp freshly grated nutmeg

salt and pepper

FILLING

375 g/12 oz skinless smoked cod fillet

125 g/4 oz ricotta cheese

25 g/1 oz Parmesan cheese, grated

4 spring onions, finely chopped

2 tbsp freshly chopped chives

55 g/2 oz sun-dried tomatoes in olive oil,
 drained and finely chopped

1 Brush a 33 x 23 cm/13 x 9 inch Swiss
 roll tin with olive oil and line with
baking paper. Squeeze the spinach to
remove as much liquid as possible. Chop
finely and set aside.

2 Melt the butter in a pan, add the flour
 and cook for 30 seconds, stirring
constantly. Gradually add the milk until
smooth, stirring constantly. Bring
gradually to the boil and simmer, stirring
constantly, for 2 minutes. Remove from
the heat and set aside to cool slightly.

3 Stir in the spinach, egg yolks,
 tarragon, nutmeg and seasoning.
Whisk the egg whites until they hold stiff
peaks. Fold a large spoonful into the
spinach mixture to slacken it, then fold in
the remaining egg whites, carefully but
thoroughly to avoid losing any volume.
Pour the mixture into the prepared tin and
smooth the surface.

4 Cook in a preheated oven, 200°C/
 400°F/Gas Mark 6, for 15 minutes
until risen and golden and firm in the
centre. Turn out immediately on to a clean
tea towel, peel off the baking paper and
roll up from a short end.

5 For the filling, cover the cod fillet
 with boiling water and set aside for
10 minutes until just tender. Remove the
fish and flake the flesh carefully, removing
any bones. Combine with the ricotta,
Parmesan, spring onions, chives and sun-
dried tomatoes and season to taste.

6 Unroll the roulade and spread with
 the cod mixture, leaving a 2.5 cm/
1 inch border all around. Tightly re-roll the
roulade and return to the oven, seam side
down, for 20 minutes. Remove from the
oven, transfer to a serving plate and serve.

Seafood Rice

This satisfying rice casserole, bursting with Mediterranean flavours, can be made with any combination of seafood you choose.

NUTRITIONAL INFORMATION

Calories	.571	Sugars	.18g
Protein	.25g	Fat	.16g
Carbohydrate	.81g	Saturates	.3g

 15 mins 1 hr

SERVES 4–6

INGREDIENTS

4 tbsp olive oil

16 large raw peeled prawns

225 g/8 oz cleaned squid, sliced

2 green peppers, deseeded and cut
   lengthways into 1 cm/½ inch strips

1 large onion, finely chopped

4 garlic cloves, finely chopped

2 bay leaves

1 tsp saffron threads

½ tsp dried crushed chillies

400 g/14 oz arborio or Valencia rice

225 ml/8 fl oz dry white wine

850 ml/1½ pints fish, chicken or
   vegetable stock

12–16 littleneck clams, well scrubbed

12–16 large mussels, well scrubbed

salt and pepper

2 tbsp chopped fresh flat leaf parsley

RED PEPPER SAUCE

2–3 tbsp olive oil

2 onions, finely chopped

4–6 garlic cloves, finely chopped

4–6 Italian roasted red peppers in olive oil

400 g/14 oz can chopped tomatoes

1–1½ tsp hot paprika

salt

1 To make the red pepper sauce, heat the oil in a pan. Add the onions and cook for 6–8 minutes until golden. Stir in the garlic and cook for a minute. Add the remaining ingredients and simmer gently, stirring occasionally, for about 10 minutes. Process in a food processor to a smooth sauce, Set aside and keep warm.

2 Heat half the oil in a wide pan over a high heat. Add the prawns and stir-fry for 2 minutes until pink. Transfer to a plate. Add the squid and stir-fry for about 2 minutes until just firm. Set aside with the prawns.

3 Heat the remaining oil in the pan, add the green peppers and onion and stir-fry for about 6 minutes until just tender.

Stir in the garlic, bay leaves, saffron and chillies and cook for 30 seconds. Add the rice and cook, stirring constantly, until thoroughly coated.

4 Add the wine and stir until absorbed. Add the stock and season to taste with salt and pepper. Bring to the boil and cover. Simmer gently for about 20 minutes until the rice is just tender and the liquid is almost absorbed.

5 Add the clams and mussels. Re-cover and cook for about 10 minutes until the shells open. Discard any that remain closed. Stir in the prawns and squid. Re-cover and heat through. Sprinkle with the chopped parsley and serve immediately with the sauce.

Crab Risotto

A different way to make the most of crab, this rich-tasting and colourful risotto is full of interesting flavours.

NUTRITIONAL INFORMATION

Calories	447	Sugars	........11g
Protein	........22g	Fat	..........13g
Carbohydrate	...62g	Saturates	.......2g

15 mins   50 mins

SERVES 4–6

INGREDIENTS

2–3 large red peppers

3 tbsp olive oil

1 onion, finely chopped

1 small fennel bulb, finely chopped

2 celery sticks, finely chopped

¼–½ tsp cayenne pepper

350 g/12 oz arborio or carnaroli rice

800 g/1 lb 12 oz can Italian peeled plum
    tomatoes, drained and chopped

50 ml/2 fl oz dry white vermouth (optional)

1.5 litres/2¾ pints fish or chicken
    stock, simmering

450 g/1 lb fresh cooked crab meat

50 ml/2 fl oz lemon juice

2–4 tbsp chopped fresh parsley or chervil

salt and pepper

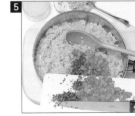

1 Grill the peppers until the skins are charred. Transfer to a plastic bag and twist to seal. When cool enough to handle, peel off the charred skins, working over a bowl to catch the juices. Remove the cores and seeds. Chop the flesh and set aside, reserving the juices.

2 Heat the olive oil in a large heavy-based pan. Add the onion, fennel and celery and cook over a low heat, stirring occasionally, for 2–3 minutes until the vegetables are softened. Add the cayenne and rice and cook, stirring frequently, for about 2 minutes until the rice is translucent and well coated.

3 Stir in the chopped tomatoes and vermouth, if using. The liquid will bubble and steam rapidly. When the liquid is almost absorbed, add a ladleful (about 225 ml/8 fl oz) of the simmering stock. Cook, stirring constantly, until the liquid is completely absorbed.

4 Continue adding the stock, about half a ladleful at a time, allowing each addition to be absorbed before adding the next. This should take 20–25 minutes. The risotto should have a creamy consistency and the rice should be tender, but still firm to the bite.

5 Stir in the red peppers and reserved juices, the crab meat, lemon juice and parsley or chervil and heat. Season with salt and pepper to taste. Serve the risotto immediately.

Risotto with Clams

This simple recipe is an excellent way of using the tiny Venus clams when they are in season. The tomatoes add a splash of colour.

NUTRITIONAL INFORMATION

Calories ....463 Sugars 4g
Protein ....25g Fat 12g
Carbohydrate ...65g Saturates 2g

 15 mins   40 mins

SERVES 6

INGREDIENTS

50 ml/2 fl oz olive oil

1 large onion, finely chopped

2 kg/4 lb 8 oz tiny clams, such as Venus, well scrubbed

125 ml/4 fl oz dry white wine

1 litre/1¾ pints fish stock

600 ml/1 pint water

3 garlic cloves, finely chopped

½ tsp crushed dried chilli

400 g/14 oz arborio or carnaroli rice

3 ripe plum tomatoes, peeled and coarsely chopped

3 tbsp lemon juice

2 tbsp chopped fresh chervil or parsley

salt and pepper

1 Heat 1–2 tablespoons of the oil in a large heavy-based pan over a medium-high heat. Add the onion and stir-fry for about 1 minute. Add the clams and wine and cover tightly. Cook for 2–3 minutes, shaking the pan frequently, until the clams begin to open. Remove from the heat and discard any clams that do not open.

2 When cool enough to handle, remove the clams from their shells. Rinse in the cooking liquid. Cover the clams and set aside. Strain the cooking liquid through a coffee filter or a sieve lined with kitchen paper and reserve.

3 Bring the fish stock and water to the boil in a pan, then reduce the heat and keep at a gentle simmer.

4 Heat the remaining olive oil in a large, heavy-based pan over a medium heat. Add the garlic and chilli and cook gently for 1 minute. Add the rice and cook, stirring frequently, for about 2 minutes until translucent and well coated with oil.

5 Add a ladleful (about 225 ml/8 fl oz/) of the simmering stock mixture; it will bubble and steam rapidly. Cook, stirring constantly, until the liquid is completely absorbed.

6 Continue adding the stock, about half a ladleful at a time, allowing each addition to be absorbed before adding the next – never allow the rice to cook 'dry'. This should take 20–25 minutes. The risotto should have a creamy consistency and the rice should be tender, but still firm to the bite.

7 Stir in the tomatoes, reserved clams and their cooking liquid, the lemon juice and chervil. Heat through gently. Season to taste with salt and pepper and serve immediately.

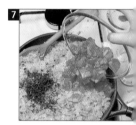

Rich Lobster Risotto

Although lobster is expensive, this dish is worth it.
Keeping it simple allows the lobster flavour to come through.

NUTRITIONAL INFORMATION

Calories 688	Sugars 3g	
Protein 32g	Fat 31g	
Carbohydrate ...69g	Saturates 16g	

10 mins   25 mins

SERVES 4

INGREDIENTS

tbsp vegetable oil

tbsp unsalted butter

shallots, finely chopped

300 g/10½ oz arborio or carnaroli rice

½ tsp cayenne pepper

85 ml/3 fl oz dry white vermouth

1.5 litres/2¾ pints shellfish, fish or chicken
stock, simmering

225 g/8 oz cherry tomatoes, quartered
and deseeded

2–3 tbsp double or whipping cream

450 g/1 lb cooked lobster meat, cut into
coarse chunks

2 tbsp chopped fresh chervil or dill

salt and white pepper

1 Heat the oil and half the butter in a large heavy-based pan over a medium heat. Add the shallots and cook, stirring occasionally, for about 2 minutes until just beginning to soften. Add the rice and cayenne and cook, stirring frequently, for about 2 minutes until the rice is translucent and well coated with the oil and butter.

2 Pour in the vermouth; it will bubble and steam rapidly and evaporate almost immediately. Add a ladleful (about 225 ml/8 fl oz) of the simmering stock and cook, stirring constantly, until the stock is completely absorbed.

3 Continue adding the stock, about half a ladleful at a time, allowing each addition to be completely absorbed before adding the next – never allow the rice to cook 'dry'. This process should take about 20–25 minutes. The risotto should have a creamy consistency and the rice should be tender, but still firm to the bite.

4 Stir in the tomatoes and cream and cook for about 2 minutes.

5 Add the cooked lobster meat with the remaining butter and chervil and cook long enough to just heat the lobster meat gently. Serve immediately.

Pickled Tuna

When Mediterranean fishermen bring in a bountiful catch, some of the fish is traditionally preserved so that it can be enjoyed a few days later.

NUTRITIONAL INFORMATION

Calories	714	Sugars	........10g
Protein	........55g	Fat	..........48g
Carbohydrate	...13g	Saturates	.......8g

25¾ hrs   25 mins

SERVES 4

INGREDIENTS

4 large tuna steaks, each about 225 g/8 oz and 2 cm/¾ inch thick

225 ml/8 fl oz olive oil

2 large red onions, thinly sliced

2 carrots, thinly sliced

2 large bay leaves, torn

1 garlic clove, very finely chopped

225 ml/8 fl oz white wine vinegar or sherry vinegar

½ tsp dried chilli flakes, crushed

1 tbsp coriander seeds, lightly crushed

salt and pepper

finely chopped fresh parsley, to garnish

1 Rinse the tuna and pat dry with kitchen paper. Heat 4 tablespoons of the oil in a large frying pan, preferably non-stick.

2 Add the tuna steaks to the pan and fry for 2 minutes over a medium–high heat. Turn the steaks and continue to cook for 2 minutes until browned and medium cooked, or 4 minutes for well done. Remove the tuna from the pan and drain well on kitchen paper. Set aside to cool.

3 Heat the remaining oil in the pan. Add the onions and cook for

8 minutes until soft, but not brown. Stir in the carrots, bay leaves, garlic, vinegar and dried chillies and season with salt and pepper to taste. Cook for a further 10 minutes or until the carrots are tender. Stir in the coriander seeds 1 minute before the end of the cooking time.

4 When the tuna is cool, remove any skin and bones from. Break each of the steaks into 4 or 5 large chunks.

5 Put the fish pieces in a non-metallic bowl and pour the hot onion mixture over. Very gently mix together, taking care not to break up the fish pieces.

6 Set aside until completely cool, then cover with clingfilm and chill in the refrigerator for at least 24 hours: the fish will stay fresh in the refrigerator for up to 5 days. To serve, sprinkle with parsley and serve at room temperature.

Seafood Stew

Similar to Bouillabaisse, this meal-in-a-pot should contain the best of the day's catch – even if it's from a supermarket.

NUTRITIONAL INFORMATION

Calories 226   Sugars 4g
Protein ....31g   Fat 9g
Carbohydrate ....6g   Saturates 1g

45 mins   30 mins

SERVES 4–6

INGREDIENTS

225 g/8 oz clams

700 g/1 lb 9 oz mixed fish, such as sea bass, skate, red snapper, rock fish and any Mediterranean fish you can find

12–18 tiger prawns

about 3 tbsp olive oil

1 large onion, finely chopped

2 garlic cloves, very finely chopped

2 tomatoes, halved, deseeded and chopped

700 ml/1¼ pints Fresh Fish Stock (see page 8), or good-quality, ready-made chilled fish stock

1 tbsp tomato purée

1 tsp fresh thyme leaves

pinch of saffron threads

pinch of sugar

salt and pepper

finely chopped fresh parsley, to garnish

1 Soak the clams in a bowl of lightly salted water for 30 minutes. Rinse them under cold, running water and lightly scrub to remove any sand from the shells. Discard any broken clams or open clams that do not shut when firmly tapped with the back of a knife, as these will be unsafe to eat.

2 Prepare the fish as necessary, removing any skin and bones, then cut into bite-size chunks.

3 To prepare the prawns, break off the heads. Peel off the shells, leaving the tails intact, if wished. Using a small knife, make a slit along the back of each and remove the thin black vein. Set all the seafood aside.

4 Heat the oil in a large pan. Add the onion and cook for 5 minutes, stirring. Add the garlic and cook for about another 2 minutes until the onion is soft, but not brown.

5 Add the tomatoes, stock, tomato purée, thyme leaves, saffron threads and sugar, then bring to the boil, stirring to dissolve the tomato purée. Lower the heat, cover and simmer for 15 minutes. Season to taste with salt and pepper.

6 Add the seafood and simmer until the clams open and the fish flakes easily. Discard any clams that do not open. Garnish and serve immediately.

Prawn Skewers

Prawns of all sizes are popular fare in the Mediterranean, where they are often cooked very simply by grilling – the key is not to overcook.

NUTRITIONAL INFORMATION

Calories	203	Sugars	.........4g
Protein	........81g	Fat	..........17g
Carbohydrate	....4g	Saturates	.......3g

 45 mins   2–3½ mins

MAKES 8 SKEWERS

I N G R E D I E N T S

32 large tiger prawns

olive oil, for brushing

skordalia (see page 129) or aïoli (see page 128), to serve

MARINADE

125 ml/4 fl oz extra virgin olive oil

2 tbsp lemon juice

1 tsp finely chopped fresh red chilli

1 tsp balsamic vinegar

pepper

TOMATO SALSA

2 large tomatoes, peeled, deseeded and chopped

4 spring onions, white parts only, very finely chopped

1 red pepper, peeled, deseeded and chopped

1 orange or yellow pepper, peeled, deseeded and chopped

1 tbsp extra virgin olive oil

2 tsp balsamic vinegar

4 fresh basil sprigs

salt and pepper

1 To make the marinade, place all the ingredients in a non-metallic bowl and whisk together until thoroughly combined. Set aside.

2 To prepare the prawns, break off the heads. Peel off the shells, leaving the tails intact. Using a small knife, make a slit along the back and remove the thin black vein. Add the prawns to the marinade and stir until well coated. Cover and chill for 15 minutes.

3 Make the salsa. Put all the ingredients, except the basil, in a non-metallic bowl and toss together. Season to taste with salt and pepper. Cover and chill until required.

4 Thread 4 prawns on to a metal skewer bending each in half. Repeat with 7 more skewers. Brush with marinade.

5 Brush a grill rack with oil. Place the skewers on the rack, then cook under a preheated hot grill, about 7.5 cm/ 3 inches from the heat; for 1 minute. Turn the skewers over, brush again and cook for a further 1–1½ minutes until the prawns turn pink and opaque.

6 Tear the basil leaves and toss with the salsa. Arrange each skewer on a plate with some salsa and garnish with parsley. Serve with skordalia or aïoli for dipping.

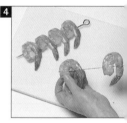

Swordfish à la Maltese

The firm texture of swordfish means it is often simply grilled, but it also lends itself to this delicate technique of cooking in a paper parcel.

NUTRITIONAL INFORMATION

Calories	303	Sugars	........10g
Protein	........34g	Fat	.........13g
Carbohydrate	...13g	Saturates	.......3g

15 mins

30 mins

SERVES 4

INGREDIENTS

1 tbsp fennel seeds

2 tbsp extra virgin olive oil, plus extra for brushing and drizzling

2 large onions, thinly sliced

1 small garlic clove, crushed

4 swordfish steaks, about 175 g/6 oz each

1 large lemon, halved

2 large tomatoes, finely chopped

4 fresh thyme sprigs

salt and pepper

1 Place the fennel seeds in a dry frying pan over a medium-high heat and toast, stirring constantly, until they give off their aroma. Watch carefully, as they can easily burn. Immediately tip the seeds out of the pan on to a plate. Set aside.

2 Heat 2 tablespoons of the olive oil in the pan. Add the onions and cook over a low heat, stirring occasionally, for 5 minutes. Add the garlic and continue to cook until the onions are very soft and tender, but not brown. Remove the pan from the heat.

3 Cut out 4 x 30 cm/12 inch circles of baking paper. Very lightly brush the centre of each paper circle with olive oil. Divide the onions equally between the

paper circles, flattening them out to about the size of the fish steaks.

4 Top the onions in each parcel with a swordfish steak. Squeeze lemon juice over the fish steaks and drizzle with a little olive oil. Sprinkle the tomatoes and fennel seeds over the top, add a fresh thyme sprig to each swordfish steak and season with salt and pepper to taste.

5 Fold the edges of the paper together, scrunching them tightly so no cooking juices escape. Place on a baking sheet and cook in a preheated oven, 200°C/400°F/ Gas Mark 6, for 20 minutes.

6 To test if the fish is cooked, open 1 parcel and pierce the flesh with a knife – it should flake easily. Serve straight from the paper parcels.

Mediterranean Monkfish

Some of the best seafood dishes are the simplest and this recipe proves the point. This is a delicious dish to serve in the summer.

NUTRITIONAL INFORMATION

Calories	401	Sugars	5g
Protein	39g	Fat	25g
Carbohydrate	6g	Saturates	7g

15 mins   16–18 mins

SERVES 4

INGREDIENTS

600 g/1 lb 4 oz cherry tomatoes, a mixture of yellow and red, if available

2 monkfish fillets, about 350 g/12 oz each

8 tbsp pesto sauce

salt and pepper

fresh basil sprigs, to garnish

new potatoes, to serve

1 Cut the tomatoes in half and scatter, cut sides up, on the base of an ovenproof serving dish. Set aside.

2 Using your fingers, rub off the thin grey membrane that covers monkfish.

3 If the skin has not been removed, place the fish skin side down on the work surface. Loosen enough skin at one end of the fillet so you can grip it. Work from the front to the back. Insert the knife, almost flat, and using a gentle sawing action, remove the skin. Rinse the fillets well and pat dry with kitchen paper.

4 Place the fillets on top of the tomatoes, tucking the thin end under, if necessary, (see Cook's Tip). Spread 4 tablespoons of the pesto sauce over each fillet and season with pepper.

5 Cover the dish tightly with foil, shiny side down. Place in a preheated oven, 230°C/450°F/Gas Mark 8, and roast for 16–18 minutes until the fish is cooked through, the flesh flakes easily and the tomatoes are collapsing into a thick sauce.

6 Adjust the seasoning, if necessary. Garnish with basil sprigs and serve immediately with new potatoes.

COOK'S TIP

Monkfish fillets are often cut from the tail, which means one end is much thinner than the rest and prone to over-cooking. If you can't get fillets that are the same thickness, fold the thin end under to ensure even cooking.

Wrapped Red Mullet

Fresh thyme, which grows wild throughout the region, flavours this rustic Mediterranean dish. Serve with boiled new potatoes.

NUTRITIONAL INFORMATION

Calories ....329 Sugars 8g
Protein ....37g Fat 16g
Carbohydrate ....9g Saturates 5g

20 mins   35 mins

SERVES 4

INGREDIENTS

3 tbsp olive oil, plus extra for rubbing

2 large red peppers, deseeded and thinly sliced

2 large fennel bulbs, thinly sliced

1 large garlic clove, crushed

8 fresh thyme sprigs, plus extra to garnish

20–24 vine leaves in brine

1 lemon

4 red mullet, about 225 g/8 oz each, scaled and gutted

salt and pepper

1 Heat the oil in a large frying pan over a medium–low heat. Add the peppers, fennel, garlic and 4 sprigs of thyme and stir together. Cook, stirring occasionally, for about 20 minutes until the vegetables are cooked thoroughly and are very soft, but not browned.

2 Meanwhile, rinse the vine leaves under cold, running water and pat dry with kitchen paper. Slice 4 thin slices off the lemon, then cut each slice in half. Finely grate the rind of ½ the lemon.

3 Stuff the mullet cavities with the lemon slices and remaining thyme

sprigs. Rub a little olive oil on each fish and sprinkle with the lemon rind. Season with salt and pepper to taste.

4 Depending on the size of the mullet, wrap 5 or 6 vine leaves around each fish to enclose completely. Put the wrapped mullet on top of the fennel and peppers. Cover the pan and cook over a medium–low heat for 12–15 minutes until

the mullet are cooked through and the flesh flakes easily when tested with the tip of a knife.

5 Transfer the cooked fish to warmed individual plates and spoon the fennel and peppers beside them. Garnish with thyme sprigs and serve immediately.

 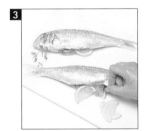 

Mussels Marinara

The Spanish, French and Italians all serve variations of this simple mussel recipe, which is universally popular.

NUTRITIONAL INFORMATION

Calories	278	Sugars	.........6g
Protein	........18g	Fat	..........14g
Carbohydrate	...10g	Saturates	.......2g

  40 mins   20 mins

SERVES 4

INGREDIENTS

2 kg/4 lb 8 oz live mussels

4 tbsp olive oil

4–6 large garlic cloves, halved

2 x 400 g /14 oz cans chopped tomatoes

300 ml/10 fl oz dry white wine

2 tbsp finely chopped fresh flat leaf parsley, plus extra to garnish

1 tbsp finely chopped fresh oregano

salt and pepper

French bread, to serve

1 Soak the mussels in a bowl of lightly salted water for 30 minutes. Rinse them under cold, running water and lightly scrub to remove any sand from the shells. Using a small sharp knife, remove the 'beards' from the shells.

2 Discard any broken mussels or open mussels that do not shut when firmly tapped with the back of a knife. This indicates they are dead and could cause food poisoning if eaten. Rinse the mussels again, then set aside in a colander.

3 Heat the olive oil in a large pan or pot over a medium-high heat. Add the garlic and cook, stirring, for about 3 minutes. Using a draining spoon, remove the garlic from the pan.

4 Add the tomatoes and their juice, the wine, parsley and oregano and bring to the boil, stirring. Lower the heat, cover and simmer for 5 minutes to allow the flavours to blend.

5 Add the mussels, cover the pan and simmer for 5–8 minutes, shaking the pan regularly, until the mussels open. Using a draining spoon, transfer the mussels to serving bowls, discarding any that remain closed.

6 Season the sauce with salt and pepper to taste. Ladle the sauce over the mussels, sprinkle with extra chopped parsley and serve immediately with plenty of fresh French bread to mop up the delicious juices.

Yucatecan Fish

Annatto seeds are rock-hard little red seeds with a lemony flavour that need to be soaked overnight before you can grind them.

NUTRITIONAL INFORMATION

Calories 179	Sugars 1g
Protein 24g	Fat 8g
Carbohydrate 1g	Saturates 2g

 3½ hrs   🕐 15 mins

SERVES 8

INGREDIENTS

4 tbsp annatto seeds, soaked in
    water overnight

3 garlic cloves, finely chopped

1 tbsp mild chilli powder

1 tbsp paprika

1 tsp ground cumin

½ tsp dried oregano

2 tbsp beer or tequila

juice of 1 lime and l orange or 3 tbsp
    pineapple juice

2 tbsp olive oil

2 tbsp chopped fresh coriander

¼ tsp ground cinnamon

¼ tsp ground cloves

1 kg/2 lb 4 oz swordfish steaks

banana leaves, for wrapping (optional)

fresh coriander leaves, to garnish

orange wedges, to serve

2 Smear the annatto paste on to the swordfish steaks, cover and set aside to marinate in the refrigerator for at least 3 hours or overnight.

3 Wrap the fish steaks in banana leaves, tying with string to make parcels. Bring water to the boil in a steamer, then add a batch of fish parcels to the top part of the steamer and cook for about 15 minutes or until the fish is cooked through and flakes easily.

4 Alternatively, cook the fish without wrapping in the banana leaves. To cook on the barbecue, place in a hinged basket or on a rack and cook over the hot coals for 5–6 minutes on each side until cooked through. Or cook the fish under a preheated grill for 5–6 minutes on each side until cooked through.

5 Garnish with coriander and serve immediately with orange wedges for squeezing over the fish.

1 Drain the annatto seeds, then crush them to a paste with a pestle in a mortar. Work in the garlic, chilli powder, paprika, cumin, oregano, beer or tequila, fruit juice, olive oil, fresh coriander, cinnamon and cloves.

Prawns in Green Sauce

The sweet briny flesh of prawns is wonderful paired with the smoky scent of chipotle chillies.

NUTRITIONAL INFORMATION

Calories	225	Sugars	........13g
Protein	........24g	Fat	...........8g
Carbohydrate	...17g	Saturates	.......1g

 10 mins   15–20 mins

SERVES 4

INGREDIENTS

2 tbsp vegetable oil

3 onions, chopped

5 garlic cloves, chopped

5–7 ripe tomatoes, diced

175–225 g/6–8 oz green beans, cut into 5 cm/2 inch pieces and blanched for 1 minute

¼ tsp ground cumin

pinch of ground allspice

pinch of ground cinnamon

½–1 canned chipotle chilli in adobo marinade, with some of the marinade

450 ml/16 fl oz fish stock or water mixed with a fish stock cube

450 g/1 lb raw prawns, peeled

fresh coriander sprigs

1 lime, cut into wedges

1 Heat the oil in a large pan. Add the onions and garlic and cook over a low heat, stirring occasionally, for about 5–10 minutes until softened. Add the tomatoes and cook for 2 minutes.

2 Add the green beans, cumin, allspice, cinnamon, chipotle chilli and marinade and fish stock. Bring to the boil, then reduce the heat and simmer for a few minutes to combine the flavours.

3 Add the prawns and cook, stirring gently, for 1–2 minutes only, then remove the pan from the heat and set the prawns aside to steep in the hot liquid to finish cooking. They are cooked when they have turned a bright pink colour.

4 Serve the prawns immediately, garnished with the fresh coriander and accompanied by the lime wedges.

VARIATION

If you can find them, use bottled nopales (edible cacti), cut into strips, to add an exotic touch to the dish.

Barbecued Clams

Cook with Mexican flair by serving up clams from the barbecue, topped with a spicy sweetcorn salsa.

NUTRITIONAL INFORMATION

Calories 189   Sugars 9g
Protein ....23g   Fat 2g
Carbohydrate ...21g   Saturates 1g

35 mins   10 mins

SERVES 4

INGREDIENTS

2 kg/4 lb 8 oz live clams

5 ripe tomatoes

2 garlic cloves, finely chopped

225 g/8 oz can sweetcorn, drained

3 tbsp finely chopped fresh coriander

3 spring onions, thinly sliced

¼ tsp ground cumin

juice of ½ lime

½–1 fresh green chilli, deseeded and finely chopped

salt

lime wedges, to serve

1 Place the clams in a large bowl. Cover with cold water and add a handful of salt. Set aside to soak for 30 minutes.

2 Meanwhile, peel the tomatoes. Place them in a heatproof bowl, pour boiling water over to cover and stand for 30 seconds. Drain and plunge into cold water. The skins will then slide off easily. Cut the tomatoes in half, deseed, then chop the flesh.

3 To make the salsa, combine the tomatoes, chopped garlic, sweetcorn, coriander, spring onions, cumin, lime juice and chilli in a bowl. Season with salt to taste. Cover and set aside.

4 Drain the clams, discarding any that are open. Place the clams on the hot coals of a barbecue, allowing about 5 minutes per side. They will pop open when they are ready. Discard any that remain closed.

5 Transfer to a plate. Top with the salsa and serve with lime wedges for squeezing over the clams.

VARIATION
Mussels can be used in place of the clams very successfully.

Chilli-marinated Prawns

Avocado salsa is delicious spooned on to anything spicy from the grill or barbecue, especially seafood.

NUTRITIONAL INFORMATION

Calories 321	Sugars 2g	
Protein 31g	Fat 21g	
Carbohydrate 4g	Saturates 4g	

15 mins

3–5 mins

SERVES 4

INGREDIENTS

650 g/1 lb 7 oz large prawns, shelled

½ tsp ground cumin

½ tsp mild chilli powder

½ tsp paprika

2 tbsp orange juice

grated rind of 1 orange

2 tbsp extra virgin olive oil

2 tbsp chopped fresh coriander, plus extra to garnish

2 ripe avocados

½ onion, finely chopped

¼ fresh green or red chilli, deseeded and chopped

juice of ½ lime

salt and pepper

VARIATION

For luscious sandwiches, toast crusty rolls, cut in half and buttered, over the hot coals and fill them with the cooked prawns and avocado sauce.

1 Combine the prawns with the cumin, chilli powder, paprika, orange juice and rind, olive oil and half the coriander. Season to taste with salt and pepper.

2 Thread the prawns on to metal skewers, or bamboo skewers soaked in cold water for 30 minutes.

3 Cut the avocados in half around the stone. Twist apart, then remove the stone with a knife. Carefully peel off the

skin, then dice the flesh. Immediately combine the avocados with the remaining coriander, onion, chilli and lime juice. Season with salt and pepper and set aside.

4 Place the prawns on a hot barbecue and cook for only a few minutes on each side.

5 Serve the prawns, garnished with coriander and accompanied by the avocado sauce.

Simmered Squid

This flavourful squid dish from Vera Cruz in Mexico would be good with warmed flour tortillas, for do-it-yourself tacos.

NUTRITIONAL INFORMATION

Calories 307	Sugars 6g	
Protein 36g	Fat 14g	
Carbohydrate . . .10g	Saturates 2g	

10 mins   20 mins

SERVES 4

I N G R E D I E N T S

tbsp extra virgin olive oil

00 g/2 lb cleaned squid, cut into rings
and tentacles

onion, chopped

garlic cloves, chopped

00 g/14 oz can chopped tomatoes

–1 fresh mild green chilli, deseeded
and chopped

tbsp finely chopped fresh parsley

tsp chopped fresh thyme

tsp chopped fresh oregano

tsp chopped fresh marjoram

inch of ground cinnamon

inch of ground allspice

inch of sugar

5–20 pimiento-stuffed green olives, sliced

tbsp capers

alt and pepper

tbsp chopped fresh coriander, to garnish

1 Heat the oil in a pan and lightly fry the squid until it turns opaque. Season with salt and pepper and remove from the pan with a draining spoon.

2 Add the onion and garlic to the remaining oil in the pan and cook until softened. Stir in the tomatoes, chilli, herbs, cinnamon, allspice, sugar and olives. Cover and cook over a medium-low heat for 5–10 minutes until the mixture thickens slightly. Uncover the pan and cook for a further 5 minutes to concentrate the flavours and reduce the liquid.

3 Stir in the reserved squid and any of the juices that have gathered. Add the capers and heat through.

4 Adjust the seasoning if necessary, then serve immediately, garnished with fresh coriander.

Pan-fried Scallops Mexicana

Scallops, with their sweet flesh, are delicious with the piquant flavours of Mexico. They are best prepared simply, served with lime.

NUTRITIONAL INFORMATION

Calories	182	Sugars	.........0g
Protein	........22g	Fat	...........9g
Carbohydrate	....4g	Saturates	.......4g

5 mins   10 mins

SERVES 4–8

I N G R E D I E N T S

2 tbsp butter

2 tbsp extra virgin olive oil

650 g/1 lb 7 oz scallops, shelled

4–5 spring onions, thinly sliced

3–4 garlic cloves, finely chopped

½ fresh green chilli, deseeded and finely chopped

2 tbsp finely chopped fresh coriander

juice of ½ lime

salt and pepper

lime wedges, to serve

VARIATION

Mix leftover scallops with a little aïoli or mayonnaise mixed with garlic and a little olive oil. Serve with roasted peppers on a bed of greens, with a handful of salty black olives.

1 Heat half the butter and olive oil in a heavy-based frying pan until the butter foams.

2 Add the scallops and cook quickly until just turning opaque; do not overcook. Remove from the pan with a draining spoon and keep warm.

3 Add the remaining butter and oil to the pan, then toss in the spring onions and garlic and cook over a medium heat until the spring onions are wilted Return the scallops to the pan.

4 Remove the pan from the heat an add the chopped chilli and coriande Squeeze in the lime juice. Season with sa and pepper to taste and stir to mix well.

5 Serve immediately with lime wedge for squeezing over the scallops.

Spicy Grilled Salmon

The woody smoked flavours of the chipotle chilli are delicious brushed on to salmon for grilling.

NUTRITIONAL INFORMATION

Calories	419	Sugars	2g
Protein	41g	Fat	28g
Carbohydrate	2g	Saturates	5g

1¼ hrs   6–8 mins

SERVES 4

INGREDIENTS

salmon steaks, about 175–225 g/
6–8 oz each

lime slices, to garnish

MARINADE

4 garlic cloves

2 tbsp extra virgin olive oil

pinch of ground allspice

pinch of ground cinnamon

juice of 2 limes

1–2 tsp marinade from canned chipotle
chillies or bottled chipotle chilli salsa

¼ tsp ground cumin

pinch of sugar

salt and pepper

TO SERVE

tomato wedges

3 spring onions finely chopped

shredded lettuce

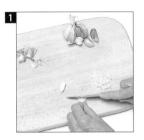

1 To make the marinade, finely chop the garlic and place in a bowl with the olive oil, allspice, cinnamon, lime juice, chipotle marinade, cumin and sugar. Add salt and pepper and stir.

2 Coat the salmon with the marinade, then place in a non-metallic dish. Marinate for at least 1 hour.

3 Transfer the salmon to a grill pan and cook under a preheated grill for 3–4 minutes on each side. Alternatively, cook the salmon over hot coals on a barbecue until cooked through.

4 To serve, mix the tomato wedges with the spring onions. Place the salmon on individual serving plates and arrange the tomato salad and shredded lettuce beside it. Garnish with lime slices and serve immediately.

VARIATION
The marinade also goes well with fresh tuna steaks.

Fish Baked with Lime

Tangy and simple to prepare, this is excellent served with rice and beans for an easy lunch – serve with a glass of chilled beer.

NUTRITIONAL INFORMATION

Calories 302	Sugars 4g
Protein 47g	Fat 10g
Carbohydrate 5g	Saturates 1g

10–15 mins   15–20 mins

SERVES 4

I N G R E D I E N T S

1 kg/2 lb 4 oz white fish fillets, such as bass, plaice or cod

1 lime, halved

3 tbsp extra virgin olive oil

1 large onion, finely chopped

3 garlic cloves, finely chopped

2–3 pickled jalapeño chillies (jalapeños en escabeche), chopped

6–8 tbsp chopped fresh coriander

salt and pepper

lemon and lime wedges, to serve

1 Place the fish fillets in a bowl and sprinkle with salt and pepper. Squeeze the juice from the lime over the fish.

2 Heat the olive oil in a frying pan. Add the onion and garlic and cook for about 2 minutes, stirring frequently, until softened. Remove from the heat.

3 Place a third of the onion mixture and a little of the chillies and coriander in the bottom of a shallow ovenproof dish or roasting tin. Arrange the fish on top. Top with the remaining onion mixture, chillies and coriander.

4 Bake in a preheated oven, 180°C/ 350°F/Gas Mark 4, for 15–20 minutes or until the fish has become slightly opaque and firm to the touch. Serve immediately, with lemon and lime wedges for squeezing over the fish.

VARIATION

Add sliced flavourful fresh tomatoes, or canned chopped tomatoes, to the onion mixture at the end of Step 2.

Mackerel with Lime

The secret of this dish lies in the simple, fresh flavours which perfectly complement the richness of the barbecued fish.

NUTRITIONAL INFORMATION

Calories	302	Sugars	.........0g
Protein	........21g	Fat	..........24g
Carbohydrate	....0g	Saturates	......4g

10 mins · 10 mins

SERVES 4

I N G R E D I E N T S

4 small mackerel

¼ tsp ground coriander

¼ tsp ground cumin

4 fresh coriander sprigs

3 tbsp chopped, fresh coriander

1 fresh red chilli, deseeded and chopped

grated rind and juice of 1 lime

2 tbsp sunflower oil

salt and pepper

1 lime, sliced, to garnish

chilli flowers (optional), to garnish

salad leaves, to serve

1 To make the chilli flower, if using, cut the tip of small chillies lengthways into thin strips, leaving the chillies intact at the stem end. Remove the seeds and place the chillies in iced water.

2 Clean and gut the mackerel, if this has not been done by the fishmonger, removing the heads if preferred. Rinse and pat dry. Sprinkle the fish with the ground spices and salt and pepper to taste. Sprinkle 1 teaspoon of chopped coriander inside the cavity of each fish.

3 Combine the chopped coriander, chilli, lime rind and juice and the oil in a small bowl. Brush the mixture liberally over the fish.

4 Place the fish in a hinged rack. Barbecue over hot coals for 3–4 minutes on each side, turning once. Brush frequently with the remaining basting mixture. Transfer to plates and garnish with chilli flowers, if using, and lime slices, and serve with salad leaves.

COOK'S TIP

This recipe is suitable for other oily fish, such as trout, herring or sardines.

Fish & Yogurt Quenelles

These quenelles, made from a thick purée of fish and yogurt, can be prepared well in advance and stored in the refrigerator before poaching.

NUTRITIONAL INFORMATION

Calories ....228 Sugars 7g
Protein ....39g Fat 2g
Carbohydrate ...14g Saturates 1g

45 mins   15 mins

SERVES 4

INGREDIENTS

750 g/1 lb 10 oz white fish fillets, such as cod, coley or whiting, skinned

2 small egg whites

½ tsp ground coriander

1 tsp ground mace

150 ml/5 fl oz low-fat natural yogurt

1 small onion, sliced

salt and pepper

mixture of boiled basmati rice and wild rice, to serve

SAUCE

1 bunch of watercress, trimmed

300 ml/10 fl oz chicken stock

2 tbsp cornflour

150 ml/5 fl oz low-fat natural yogurt

2 tbsp low-fat crème fraîche

1 Cut the fish into pieces and process it in a food processor for 30 seconds. Add the egg whites and process for a further 30 seconds to a stiff paste. Add the coriander, mace, seasoning and the yogurt and process until smooth. Cover and chill for at least 30 minutes.

2 Spoon the mixture into a piping bag, and pipe into sausage shapes about 10 cm/4 inches long. Alternatively, take rounded dessert spoons of the mixture and shape into ovals using 2 spoons.

3 Bring about 5 cm/2 inches of water to the boil in a frying pan and add the onion. Lower the quenelles into the water, using a fish slice or spoon. Cover the pan, and poach for 8 minutes, turning once. Remove with a draining spoon and drain.

4 Chop the watercress, reserving a few sprigs for garnish. Process the remainder with the stock, then pour into a small pan. Stir the cornflour into the yogurt and pour the mixture into the pan. Bring to the boil, stirring.

5 Stir in the crème fraîche, season and remove from the heat. Garnish with the watercress sprigs. Serve immediately.

Fish & Rice with Dark Rum

Based on a traditional Cuban recipe, this dish is similar to Spanish paella, but it has the added kick of dark rum.

NUTRITIONAL INFORMATION

Calories	.547	Sugars	.9g
Protein	.27g	Fat	.4g
Carbohydrate	.85g	Saturates	.1g

2¼ hrs   35 mins

SERVES 4

INGREDIENTS

450 g/1 lb firm white fish fillets (such as cod or monkfish), skinned and cut into 2.5 cm/1 inch cubes

2 tsp ground cumin

2 tsp dried oregano

2 tbsp lime juice

150 ml/5 fl oz dark rum

1 tbsp dark muscovado sugar

3 garlic cloves, finely chopped

1 large onion, chopped

1 medium red pepper, deseeded and sliced into rings

1 medium green pepper, deseeded and sliced into rings

1 medium yellow pepper, deseeded and sliced into rings

1.2 litres/2 pints fish stock

350 g/12 oz long grain rice

salt and pepper

crusty bread, to serve

TO GARNISH

fresh oregano leaves

lime wedges

1 Place the cubes of fish in a bowl and add the cumin, oregano, lime juice, rum and sugar. Season to taste with salt and pepper. Mix thoroughly, cover with clingfilm and set aside to chill for 2 hours.

2 Meanwhile, place the garlic, onion and peppers in a large pan. Pour in the stock and stir in the rice. Bring to the boil, lower the heat cover and simmer for 15 minutes.

3 Gently stir in the fish and the marinade juices. Bring back to the boil and simmer, uncovered, stirring occasionally but taking care not to break up the fish, for about 10 minutes until the fish is cooked through and the rice is tender.

4 Season to taste with salt and pepper and transfer to a warmed serving plate. Garnish with fresh oregano and lime wedges and serve with crusty bread.

Smoked Haddock Casserole

This quick, easy and inexpensive dish would be ideal for a midweek family supper, because it is both nourishing and filling.

NUTRITIONAL INFORMATION

Calories	525	Sugars	.........8g
Protein	........41g	Fat	..........18g
Carbohydrate	...53g	Saturates	......10g

 20 mins   45 mins

SERVES 4

INGREDIENTS

2 tbsp butter, plus extra for greasing

450 g/1 lb smoked haddock fillets, cut into 4 slices

600 ml/1 pint milk

2½ tbsp plain flour

pinch of freshly grated nutmeg

3 tbsp double cream

1 tbsp chopped fresh parsley

2 eggs, hard-boiled and mashed to a pulp

450 g/1 lb dried fusilli pasta

1 tbsp lemon juice

salt and pepper

boiled new potatoes and beetroot, to serve

1 Thoroughly grease a casserole with butter. Put the haddock in the casserole and pour in the milk. Bake in a preheated oven, 200°C/400°F/Gas Mark 6, for about 15 minutes.

2 Carefully pour the cooking liquid into a jug without breaking up the fish. Set the fish aside in the casserole.

3 Melt the butter in a saucepan and stir in the flour. Gradually whisk in the reserved cooking liquid. Season to taste with salt, pepper and nutmeg. Stir in the cream, parsley and mashed hard-boiled egg and cook, stirring constantly, for 2 minutes.

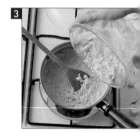

4 Meanwhile, bring a large saucepan of lightly salted water to the boil. Add the fusilli and lemon juice, bring back to the boil and cook for 8–10 minutes until tender, but still firm to the bite.

5 Drain the pasta and spoon and tip it over the fish. Top with the egg sauce and return the casserole to the oven for 10 minutes.

6 Serve the casserole immediately with boiled new potatoes and beetroot.

VARIATION

You can use any type of dried pasta for this casserole. Try penne, conchiglie or rigatoni.

A Seafood Medley

You can use almost any kind of sea fish in this recipe.
Red sea bream is an especially good choice.

NUTRITIONAL INFORMATION

Calories	699	Sugars	.........4g
Protein	........56g	Fat	..........35g
Carbohydrate	...35g	Saturates	......20g

🐚 🐚 🐚

20 mins | 30 mins

SERVES 4

INGREDIENTS

2 raw tiger prawns

2 raw shrimp

450 g/1 lb fillet of sea bream

4 tbsp butter

2 scallops, shelled

125 g/4½ oz freshwater prawns

juice and finely grated rind of 1 lemon

pinch of saffron powder or threads

1 litre/1¾ pints vegetable stock

150 ml/5 fl oz rose petal vinegar

450 g/1 lb dried farfalle

150 ml/5 fl oz white wine

1 tbsp pink peppercorns

115 g/4 oz baby carrots

150 ml/5 fl oz double cream or
fromage frais

salt and pepper

 Peel and devein the prawns and peel
the shrimp. Thinly slice the sea bream.
Melt the butter in a frying pan, add the sea
bream, scallops, prawns and shrimp and
cook for 1–2 minutes.

2 Season with pepper to taste. Add the
lemon juice and grated rind. Very
carefully add a pinch of saffron powder or
a few strands of saffron to the cooking
juices (not to the seafood).

3 Remove the seafood from the pan, set
aside and keep warm.

4 Return the pan to the heat and add
the stock. Bring to the boil and then
reduce by one-third. Add the rose petal
vinegar and cook for approximately
4 minutes until reduced.

5 Bring a pan of lightly salted water to
the boil. Add the pasta, bring back to
the boil and cook for 8–10 minutes until
tender, but still firm to the bite. Drain the
pasta, transfer to a serving plate and top
with the seafood.

6 Add the wine, peppercorns, and
carrots to the pan and reduce the
sauce for 6 minutes. Add the cream or
fromage frais and simmer for 2 minutes.

7 Pour the sauce over the seafood and
pasta and serve immediately.

Potato-topped Cod

This simple dish has a spicy breadcrumb topping over layers of cod and potatoes. It is cooked in the oven until crisp and golden.

NUTRITIONAL INFORMATION

Calories	118	Sugars	.........1g
Protein	........9.8g	Fat	.........4.4g
Carbohydrate	..10.5g	Saturates	.....2.6g

 5–10 mins   35 mins

SERVES 4

INGREDIENTS

5 tbsp butter

900 g/2 lb waxy potatoes, sliced

1 large onion, finely chopped

1 tsp wholegrain mustard

1 tsp garam masala

pinch of chilli powder

1 tbsp chopped fresh dill

85 g/3 oz fresh breadcrumbs

700g /1 lb 9 oz cod fillets

4 tbsp grated Gruyère cheese

salt and pepper

fresh dill sprigs, to garnish

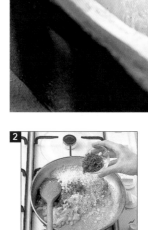

1 Melt half of the butter in a frying pan. Add the potatoes and fry for 5 minutes, turning until they are browned all over. Remove the potatoes from the pan with a draining spoon.

2 Add the remaining butter to the frying pan and stir in the onion, mustard, garam masala, chilli powder, dill and breadcrumbs. Cook for 1–2 minutes, stirring and mixing well.

3 Layer half of the potatoes in the base of an ovenproof dish and place the cod fillets on top. Cover the cod fillets with the rest of the potato slices. Season to taste with salt and pepper.

4 Spoon the spicy mixture from the frying pan over the potatoes and sprinkle with the grated cheese.

5 Cook in a preheated oven, 200°C/ 400°F/Gas Mark 6, for 20–25 minutes or until the topping is golden and crisp and the fish is cooked through. Remove from the oven, garnish with fresh dill sprigs and serve immediately.

COOK'S TIP

This dish is ideal served with baked vegetables, which can be cooked in the oven at the same time.

Smoked Fish & Potato Pâté

This smoked fish pâté is given a tart fruity flavour by the gooseberries, which complement the fish perfectly.

NUTRITIONAL INFORMATION

Calories 418   Sugars 4g
Protein . . . . .18g   Fat 25g
Carbohydrate . . .32g   Saturates 6g

 20 mins   10 mins

SERVES 4

I N G R E D I E N T S

650 g/1 lb 7 oz floury potatoes, diced

300 g/10½ oz smoked mackerel, skinned and flaked

75 g/2¾ oz cooked gooseberries

1 tsp lemon juice

1 tbsp low-fat crème fraîche

1 tbsp capers

1 gherkin, chopped

1 tbsp chopped dill pickle

1 tbsp chopped fresh dill

salt and pepper

lemon wedges, to garnish

toast or warm crusty bread, to serve

1 Cook the diced potatoes in a saucepan of boiling water for 10 minutes until tender, then drain well.

2 Place the cooked potatoes in a food processor or blender.

3 Add the skinned and flaked smoked mackerel and process for 30 seconds until fairly smooth. Alternatively, place the ingredients in a bowl and then mash them with a fork.

4 Add the cooked gooseberries, lemon juice and crème fraîche to the fish and potato mixture. Blend for a further 10 seconds or mash well.

5 Stir in the capers, gherkin, dill pickle, and fresh dill. Season well with salt and pepper.

6 Turn the fish pâté into a serving dish, garnish with lemon wedges and serve with slices of toast or warm crusty bread cut into chunks or slices.

COOK'S TIP

Use stewed, canned or bottled cooked gooseberries for convenience and to save time, or when fresh gooseberries are out of season.

Layered Fish & Potato Pie

This is a really delicious and filling dish. Layers of potato slices and mixed fish are cooked in a creamy sauce and topped with grated cheese.

NUTRITIONAL INFORMATION

Calories 116	Sugars 1.9g
Protein 6.2g	Fat 6.1g
Carbohydrate ...9.7g	Saturates 3.8g

 10 mins   🕐 55 mins

SERVES 4

I N G R E D I E N T S

900 g/2 lb waxy potatoes, sliced

5 tbsp butter

1 red onion, halved and sliced

5 tbsp plain flour

450 ml/16 fl oz milk

150 ml/5 fl oz double cream

225 g/8 oz smoked haddock fillet, cubed

225 g/8 oz cod fillet, cubed

1 red pepper, deseeded and diced

115 g/4 oz broccoli florets

55 g/2 oz Parmesan cheese, freshly grated

salt and pepper

1 Cook the sliced potatoes in a saucepan of boiling water for 10 minutes. Drain and set aside.

2 Meanwhile, melt the butter in a saucepan, add the onion and fry gently for 3–4 minutes.

3 Add the flour and cook for 1 minute. Blend in the milk and cream and bring to the boil, stirring until the sauce has thickened.

4 Arrange half of the potato slices in the base of a shallow ovenproof dish.

5 Add the fish, red pepper and broccoli to the sauce and cook over a low heat for 10 minutes. Season with salt and pepper, then spoon the mixture over the potatoes in the dish.

6 Arrange the remaining potato slices in a layer over the fish mixture and then sprinkle the grated Parmesan cheese over the top.

7 Cook in a preheated oven, 180°C/ 350°F/Gas Mark 4, for 30 minutes or until the potatoes are cooked and the topping is golden.

COOK'S TIP
Choose your favourite combination of fish, adding salmon or various shellfish for special occasions.

Thai Steamed Mussels

Thai cooks are fond of basil, and frequently sprinkle it over salads and soups. The familiar sweet basil is suitable for this dish.

NUTRITIONAL INFORMATION

Calories	252	Sugars	.........2g
Protein	........22g	Fat	..........14g
Carbohydrate	....8g	Saturates	.......8g

 15 mins   5 mins

SERVES 2

INGREDIENTS

kg/2 lb 4 oz fresh mussels in shells

2 shallots, finely chopped

lemon grass stalk, thinly sliced

garlic clove, finely chopped

3 tbsp Chinese rice wine or sherry

2 tbsp lime juice

tbsp Thai fish sauce

2 tbsp butter

4 tbsp chopped fresh basil

salt and pepper

fresh basil leaves, to garnish

crusty bread, to serve

1 Scrub the mussels, removing any beards. Rinse in and drain. Discard any that do not close when tapped or that have damaged shells.

2 Place the shallots, lemon grass, garlic, rice wine, lime juice and fish sauce in a large pan and place over a high heat.

3 Add the mussels, cover and steam for about 2–3 minutes, shaking the pan occasionally during cooking until the mussel shells open.

4 Discard any mussels which have not opened, then stir in the chopped basil and season with salt and pepper.

5 Lift out the mussels with a draining spoon and divide between 2 deep bowls. Quickly whisk the butter into the pan juices until incorporated, then pour the juices over the mussels.

6 Garnish each bowl with fresh basil leaves and serve with plenty of crusty bread to mop up the juices.

COOK'S TIP

If you prefer to serve this dish as a starter, this amount will be enough for four portions. Fresh clams in shells are also very good when cooked by this method.

Sweet & Sour Seafood

This unusual seafood dish with a sweet lime dressing can be doubled up for a buffet-style main dish and is a good dish to prepare for a crowd.

NUTRITIONAL INFORMATION

Calories	97	Sugars	.........5g
Protein	........13g	Fat	...........2g
Carbohydrate	....8g	Saturates	.......0g

 20 mins   🕙 10 mins

SERVES 4

INGREDIENTS

18 live mussels

6 large scallops

200 g/7 oz baby squid, cleaned

2 shallots, finely chopped

6 raw tiger prawns, peeled and deveined

¼ cucumber

1 carrot, peeled

¼ head Chinese leaves, shredded

DRESSING

4 tbsp lime juice

2 garlic cloves, finely chopped

2 tbsp Thai fish sauce

1 tsp sesame oil

1 tbsp soft light brown sugar

2 tbsp chopped fresh mint

¼ tsp ground black pepper

salt

1 Scrub the mussels and remove any 'beards'. Discard any damaged mussels or open ones that do not close when firmly tapped. Steam them in just the water which clings to them for 1–2 minutes until opened. Lift out with a draining spoon, reserving the liquid in the pan. Discard any mussels that have not opened.

2 Separate the corals from the scallops and cut the whites in half horizontally. Cut the tentacles from the squid and slice the body cavities into rings.

3 Add the shallots to the liquid in the pan and simmer over a high heat until the liquid is reduced to about 3 tablespoons. Add the scallops, squid and tiger prawns and stir for 2–3 minutes until cooked. Remove and spoon the mixture into a wide bowl.

4 Cut the cucumber and carrot in half lengthways, then slice thinly on a diagonal angle to make long, pointed slices. Toss with the Chinese leaves.

5 To make the dressing, place all the ingredients in a screw-top jar and shake well until evenly combined. Season with salt to taste.

6 Toss the vegetables and seafood together. Spoon the dressing over the vegetables and seafood and serve immediately.

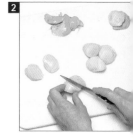

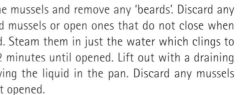

Steamed Yellow Fish Fillets

Thailand has an abundance of fresh fish, which is an important part of the local diet. Steaming is popular and suits many different types of fish.

NUTRITIONAL INFORMATION

Calories	165	Sugars	.........1g
Protein	........23g	Fat	...........2g
Carbohydrate	...13g	Saturates	.......1g

 15 mins   12–15 mins

SERVES 4

INGREDIENTS

500 g/1 lb 2 oz firm fish fillets, such as red snapper, sole or monkfish

1 dried red bird-eye chilli

1 small onion, chopped

3 garlic cloves, chopped

2 fresh coriander sprigs

1 tsp coriander seeds

½ tsp turmeric

½ tsp ground black pepper

1 tbsp Thai fish sauce

2 tbsp coconut milk

1 small egg, beaten

2 tbsp rice flour

fresh red and green chilli strips, to garnish

soy sauce, to serve

1 Remove any skin from the fish and cut the fillets diagonally into long 2 cm/¾ inch wide strips.

2 Place the dried chilli, onion, garlic, coriander and coriander seeds in a mortar and grind with a pestle to a smooth paste.

3 Add the turmeric, pepper, fish sauce, coconut milk and beaten egg, stirring well to mix.

4 Dip the fish strips into the paste mixture, then into the rice flour to coat lightly.

5 Bring the water in the bottom of a steamer to the boil, then arrange the fish strips in the top of the steamer. Cover and steam for about 12–15 minutes until the fish is just firm.

6 Transfer to a serving plate, garnish with chillies and serve with soy sauce.

COOK'S TIP

If you don't have a steamer, improvise by placing a large metal colander over a large pan of boiling water and cover with an upturned plate to enclose the fish as it steams.

Thai Baked Fish

Almost any whole fish can be cooked by this method, but snapper, sea bass or John Dory are particularly good with the Thai flavours.

NUTRITIONAL INFORMATION

Calories	267	Sugars	.........9g
Protein	........38g	Fat	..........8g
Carbohydrate	....11g	Saturates	.......2g

 15 mins 35 mins

SERVES 4

INGREDIENTS

handful of fresh sweet basil leaves

750 g/1 lb 10 oz whole red snapper, sea bass or John Dory, cleaned

2 tbsp groundnut oil

2 tbsp Thai fish sauce

2 garlic cloves, crushed

1 tsp finely grated fresh galangal or root ginger, finely grated

2 large fresh red chillies, sliced diagonally

1 yellow pepper, deseeded and diced

1 tbsp palm sugar

1 tbsp rice vinegar

2 tbsp water or fish stock

2 tomatoes, deseeded and sliced into thin wedges

COOK'S TIP

Large red chillies are less hot than the tiny red bird-eye chillies, so you can use them more freely in cooked dishes such as this for a mild heat. Remove the seeds if you prefer.

1 Reserve a few fresh basil leaves for garnish and tuck the rest inside the body cavity of the fish.

2 Heat 1 tablespoon oil in a wide frying pan and fry the fish quickly to brown, turning once. Place the fish on a large piece of foil in a roasting tin and spoon over the fish sauce. Wrap the foil over the fish loosely and bake in a preheated oven, 190°C/375°F/Gas Mark 5, for about 25–30 minutes until just cooked through.

3 Meanwhile, heat the remaining oil and fry the garlic, galangal and chillies for 30 seconds. Add the pepper and stir-fry for a further 2–3 minutes until softened, but not browned.

4 Stir in the sugar, rice vinegar and water, then add the tomatoes and bring to the boil over a low heat. Remove the pan from the heat.

5 Remove the fish from the oven and transfer to a warmed serving plate. Add the fish juices to the pan, stir in then spoon the sauce over the fish and sprinkle with the reserved basil leaves. Serve immediately.

Curry Crust Cod

An easy, economical main dish that transforms a plain piece
of fish into an exotic meal – try it with other white fish, too.

NUTRITIONAL INFORMATION

Calories	223	Sugars	.........1g
Protein	........31g	Fat	..........4g
Carbohydrate	...16g	Saturates	.......0g

15 mins   35–40 mins

SERVES 4

INGREDIENTS

tsp sesame oil

cod fillets, about 150 g/5½ oz each

5 g/3 oz fresh white breadcrumbs

tbsp blanched almonds, chopped

tsp Thai green curry paste

nd of ½ lime, finely grated

alt and pepper

me slices and rind and mixed green
  leaves, to garnish

oiled new potatoes, to serve

1 Brush the sesame oil over the base of
a wide, shallow ovenproof dish or
asting tin, then place the pieces of cod
a single layer.

2 Combine the fresh breadcrumbs
chopped, almonds, curry paste and
rated lime rind, stirring well to blend
horoughly and evenly. Season to taste
ith salt and pepper.

3 Spoon the crumb mixture over the
fish, pressing down lightly. Bake in a
preheated oven, 200°C/400°F/ Gas Mark 6,
for 35–40 minutes until the fish is cooked
through and the curry crumb topping is
golden brown.

4 Serve hot, garnished with lime slices,
lime rind and mixed green leaves and
accompanied with boiled new potatoes.

COOK'S TIP
To test whether the
fish is cooked through, use a
fork to pierce it in the thickest
part – if the flesh is white all the
way through and flakes apart
easily, it is cooked sufficiently.

Fried Fish with Soy & Ginger

This impressive dish is worth cooking for a special dinner, as it really is a talking point. Buy a very fresh whole fish on the day you plan to cook it.

NUTRITIONAL INFORMATION

Calories ....290 Sugars 7g
Protein ....27g Fat 11g
Carbohydrate ...23g Saturates 1g

🥩 20 mins   🕐 20 mins

SERVES 4–6

I N G R E D I E N T S

6 dried Chinese mushrooms

3 tbsp rice vinegar

2 tbsp soft light brown sugar

3 tbsp dark soy sauce

7.5 cm/3 inch piece of fresh root ginger, finely chopped

4 spring onions, sliced diagonally

2 tsp cornflour

2 tbsp lime juice

1 sea bass, about 1 kg/2 lb 4 oz, cleaned

4 tbsp plain flour

sunflower oil, for deep-frying

salt and pepper

shredded Chinese leaves and radish slices, to serve

1 radish, sliced but left whole, to garnish

1 Soak the dried mushrooms in hot water for about 10 minutes, then drain well, reserving 100 ml/3½ fl oz of the liquid. Cut the mushrooms into thin slices.

2 Combine the reserved mushroom liquid with the rice vinegar, sugar and soy sauce. Place in a pan with the mushrooms and bring to the boil. Reduce the heat and simmer for 3–4 minutes.

3 Add the ginger and spring onions and simmer for 1 minute. Blend the cornflour and lime juice to a smooth paste, stir into the pan and cook, stirring constantly, for 1–2 minutes until the sauce thickens and clears. Set the sauce aside while you cook the fish.

4 Season the fish inside and out with salt and pepper, then dust lightly with flour, shaking off the excess.

5 Heat a 2.5 cm/1 inch depth of oil in a wide pan to 190°C/375°F or until a cube of bread browns in 30 seconds.

Carefully lower the fish into the oil and f it on one side for approximately 3– minutes until golden. Use two meta spatulas or fish slices to turn the fis carefully and then fry it on the other si for a further 3–4 minutes until it golden brown.

6 Lift the fish out of the pan, drainir off the excess oil, and place on serving plate. Heat the sauce until boilin then spoon it over the fish. Serv immediately, surrounded by shredde Chinese leaves with sliced radishes ar garnished with the sliced whole radish.

Sweet & Sour Tuna

Tuna is a firm, meaty-textured fish that is abundant in the seas around Thailand. You can also use shark or mackerel in this piquant dish.

NUTRITIONAL INFORMATION

Calories 303	Sugars 12g	
Protein 31g	Fat 12g	
Carbohydrate ...20g	Saturates 3g	

🍧 10 mins 🕐 15 mins

SERVES 4

INGREDIENTS

4 fresh tuna steaks, about 500 g/1 lb 2 oz total weight

¼ tsp ground black pepper

2 tbsp groundnut oil

1 onion, diced

1 small red pepper, deseeded and cut into thin batons

1 garlic clove, crushed

½ cucumber, deseeded and cut into thin batons

2 pineapple slices, diced

1 tsp finely chopped fresh root ginger

1 tbsp soft light brown sugar

1 tbsp cornflour

1½ tbsp lime juice

1 tbsp Thai fish sauce

250 ml/9 fl oz fish stock

lime and cucumber slices, to garnish

1 Sprinkle the tuna steaks with pepper on both sides. Heat a heavy frying pan or griddle and brush with a little of the oil. Cook the tuna steaks for about 8 minutes, turning them over once.

2 Heat the remaining oil in another pan and gently cook the onion, pepper and garlic for 3–4 minutes to soften.

3 Turn off the heat and stir in the cucumber batons, pineapple slices, chopped ginger and sugar.

4 Blend the cornflour with the lime juice and fish sauce, then stir into the stock and add to the pan. Stir over a medium heat until boiling, then cook for 1–2 minutes until thickened and clear.

5 Spoon the sauce over the tuna and serve immediately garnished with lime slices and cucumber.

COOK'S TIP

Tuna can be served quite lightly cooked, and can be dry if it is overcooked.

Thai-spiced Salmon

Marinated in delicate Thai spices and quickly pan-fried to perfection, these salmon fillets are ideal for a special dinner.

NUTRITIONAL INFORMATION

Calories	329	Sugars	.........0g
Protein	........30g	Fat	..........23g
Carbohydrate	....0g	Saturates	.......4g

 40 mins   4–5 mins

SERVES 4

INGREDIENTS

2.5 cm/1 in piece of fresh root ginger, grated

1 tsp coriander seeds, crushed

¼ tsp chilli powder

1 tbsp lime juice

1 tsp sesame oil

4 salmon fillets with skin, about 150 g/ 5½ oz each

2 tbsp vegetable oil

boiled rice and stir-fried vegetables, to serve

1 Combine the grated ginger, crushed coriander, chilli powder, lime juice and sesame oil.

2 Place the salmon in a wide, non-metallic dish or on a plate and spoon the mixture over the flesh side of the fillets, spreading it to coat each piece of salmon evenly.

3 Cover the dish with clingfilm and chill the salmon in the refrigerator for 30 minutes.

4 Heat a wide, heavy-based frying pan or griddle pan with the oil over a high heat. Place the salmon on the hot pan or griddle, skin side down.

5 Cook the salmon for 4–5 minutes without turning, until the salmon is crusty underneath and the flesh flakes easily. Serve immediately with boiled rice and stir-fried vegetables.

COOK'S TIP

It's important to use a heavy-based pan or solid griddle for this recipe, so the fish cooks evenly throughout without sticking. If the fish is very thick, you may prefer to turn it over carefully to cook on the other side for 2–3 minutes.

Salmon with Red Curry

If you can't find any banana leaves to wrap the fish, use foil or baking paper, which work equally well.

NUTRITIONAL INFORMATION

Calories . . . . .351 Sugars 6g
Protein . . . . .36g Fat 20g
Carbohydrate . . . .6g Saturates 3g

10 mins   15–20 mins

SERVES 4

INGREDIENTS

salmon steaks, about 175 g/6 oz each

banana leaves, halved

garlic clove, crushed

tsp grated fresh root ginger

tbsp Thai red curry paste

tsp soft light brown sugar

tbsp Thai fish sauce

tbsp lime juice

TO GARNISH

me wedges

nely chopped fresh red chilli

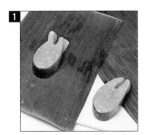  

1 Place a salmon steak on the centre of each half banana leaf.

2 Combine the garlic, ginger, curry paste, sugar and fish sauce. Spread his mixture evenly over the surface of each steak and sprinkle with lime juice.

3 Wrap the banana leaves around the fish, tucking in the sides as you go to

make a neat, compact bundle. Alternatively, use baking paper or foil.

4 Place the parcels seam side down on a baking sheet and bake in a preheated oven, 220°C/425°F/Gas Mark 7, for 15–20 minutes until the fish is cooked and the banana leaves are beginning to brown serve garnished with lime wedges and chopped chilli.

COOK'S TIP

Fresh banana leaves are often sold in packs containing several leaves, but if you buy more than you need, they will store in the refrigerator for about a week.

Spicy Thai Seafood Stew

The fish in this fragrant, curry-like stew can be varied according to taste or availability, but do choose ones that stay firm when cooked.

NUTRITIONAL INFORMATION

Calories	267	Sugars	.........7g
Protein	........42g	Fat	...........7g
Carbohydrate	....9g	Saturates	.......1g

5 mins   10 mins

SERVES 4

I N G R E D I E N T S

200 g/7 oz prepared squid

500 g/1 lb 2 oz firm white fish fillet, preferably monkfish or halibut

1 tbsp sunflower oil

4 shallots, finely chopped

2 garlic cloves, finely chopped

2 tbsp green Thai curry paste

2 small lemon grass stalks, finely chopped

1 tsp shrimp paste

500 ml/18 fl oz coconut milk

200 g/7 oz raw tiger prawns, peeled and deveined

12 live clams, scrubbed

8 fresh basil leaves, finely shredded, plus extra to garnish

boiled rice, to serve

COOK'S TIP

If you prefer, fresh mussels in shells can be used instead of clams – add them in Step 4 and follow the recipe.

1 Cut the squid body cavities into thick rings and cut the fish fillet into bite-size chunks.

2 Heat the oil in a large frying pan or wok and stir-fry the shallots, garlic and curry paste for 1–2 minutes. Add the lemon grass and shrimp paste, stir in the coconut milk and bring to the boil.

3 Reduce the heat to low. When the liquid is simmering gently, add the white fish chunks, squid rings and prawns to the pan. Stir and then simmer fo 2 minutes.

4 Add the clams and simmer for further minute until the clams ope Discard any clams that do not open.

5 Scatter the shredded basil leaves ove the stew and serve immediatel garnished with whole basil leaves an spooned over boiled rice.

Squid with Black Bean Sauce

Squid really is wonderful if cooked quickly, as in this recipe, and contrary to popular belief, it is not tough and rubbery unless it is overcooked.

NUTRITIONAL INFORMATION

Calories	180	Sugars	.........2g
Protein	........19g	Fat	...........7g
Carbohydrate	...10g	Saturates	.......1g

5 mins   20 mins

SERVES 4

INGREDIENTS

450 g/1 lb squid rings

2 tbsp plain flour

½ tsp salt

1 green pepper

2 tbsp groundnut oil

1 red onion, sliced

160 g/5¾ oz jar black bean sauce

1 Rinse the squid rings under cold running water and pat thoroughly dry with kitchen paper.

2 Place the plain flour and salt in a bowl and mix together. Add the squid rings and toss until they are evenly coated. Shake off any excess.

3 Using a sharp knife, deseed the green pepper. Slice the flesh into thin strips.

4 Heat the groundnut oil in a large preheated wok or heavy-based frying pan, swirling the oil around the base of the wok until it is really hot.

5 Add the pepper strips and red onion to the wok or frying pan and stir-fry for about 2 minutes or until the vegetables are just beginning to soften.

6 Add the squid rings to the wok or frying pan and cook for a further

5 minutes or until the squid is cooked through and tender. Be careful not to overcook the squid.

7 Add the black bean sauce to the wok and heat through until the cooking juices are just bubbling. Transfer the squid stir-fry to warm serving bowls and serve immediately.

COOK'S TIP
Serve this recipe with fried rice or noodles tossed in soy sauce, if you wish.

Spicy Lime Scallops

Really fresh scallops have a delicate flavour and texture, needing only minimal cooking, as in this simple stir-fry.

NUTRITIONAL INFORMATION

Calories	145	Sugars	.........1g
Protein	........17g	Fat	...........7g
Carbohydrate	....4g	Saturates	.......3g

 10 mins   8 mins

SERVES 4

INGREDIENTS

16 large scallops

1 tbsp butter

1 tbsp vegetable oil

1 tsp crushed garlic

1 tsp grated fresh root ginger

1 bunch of spring onions, thinly sliced

finely grated rind of 1 kaffir lime

1 small fresh red chilli, deseeded and very finely chopped

3 tbsp kaffir lime juice

lime wedges and boiled rice, to serve

1 Trim the scallops, then wash and pat dry. Separate the corals from the white parts, then horizontally slice each white part in half, making 2 rounds.

2 Heat the butter and oil in a frying pan or wok. Add the garlic and ginger and stir-fry for 1 minute without browning. Add the spring onions and stir-fry for a further minute.

3 Add the scallops and stir-fry over a high heat for 4–5 minutes. Stir in the lime rind, chilli and lime juice and cook for a further minute.

4 Serve the scallops hot, with the juice spooned over them, accompanied by lime wedges and boiled rice.

COOK'S TIP

If fresh scallops are not available, frozen ones can be used, but make sure they are thoroughly thawed before you cook them.

Prawn Skewers with Chilli

Whole tiger prawns cook very quickly on a barbecue or under a grill, so they're ideal for summertime cooking, indoors or outside.

NUTRITIONAL INFORMATION

Calories	106	Sugars	.........8g
Protein	........11g	Fat	..........3g
Carbohydrate	....8g	Saturates	.......1g

2¼ hrs   10 mins

SERVES 4

INGREDIENTS

1 garlic clove, chopped

1 fresh red bird-eye chilli, deseeded and chopped

1 tbsp tamarind paste

1 tbsp sesame oil

1 tbsp dark soy sauce

2 tbsp lime juice

1 tbsp soft light brown sugar

16 large whole raw tiger prawns

crusty bread, lime wedges and salad leaves, to serve

1 Put the garlic, chilli, tamarind, sesame oil, soy sauce, lime juice and sugar in a small pan. Stir over a low heat until the sugar is dissolved, then remove from the heat and set aside to cool completely.

2 Wash and dry the prawns and place in a single layer in a wide, non-metallic dish. Spoon the marinade over the prawns and turn them over to coat evenly. Cover the dish with clingfilm and set aside in the refrigerator to marinate for at least 2 hours, or preferably overnight.

3 Meanwhile, soak 4 bamboo or wooden skewers in water for about 30 minutes. Drain and thread 4 prawns on to each skewer.

4 Grill the skewers under a preheated hot grill for 5–6 minutes, turning them over once, until they turn pink and begin to brown. Alternatively, barbecue over hot coals.

5 Thread a wedge of lime on to the end of each skewer and serve with crusty bread and salad leaves.

Rice with Seafood

This soup-like main course rice dish is packed with a tempting array of fresh seafood and is typically Thai in flavour.

NUTRITIONAL INFORMATION

Calories	370	Sugars	. . . . .0g
Protein	. . . . .27g	Fat	. . . . .8g
Carbohydrate	. . .52g	Saturates	. . . . . . .1g

5–10 mins   20 mins

SERVES 4

INGREDIENTS

12 live mussels, scrubbed and bearded

2 litres/3½ pints fish stock

2 tbsp vegetable oil

1 garlic clove, crushed

1 tsp grated fresh root ginger

1 fresh red bird-eye chilli, chopped

2 spring onions, chopped

225 g/8 oz long grain rice

2 small squid, cleaned and sliced

100 g/3½ oz firm white fish fillet, such as halibut or monkfish, cut into chunks

100 g/3½ oz raw prawns, peeled

2 tbsp Thai fish sauce

3 tbsp chopped fresh coriander

1 Discard any mussels with damaged shells or open ones that do not close when firmly tapped with a knife. Pour 4 tablespoons of the stock into a large pan. Add the mussels, cover and cook over a medium heat, shaking the pan until the mussels open. Remove from the heat and discard any which do not open.

2 Heat the oil in a large frying pan or wok and fry the garlic, ginger, chilli and spring onions for 30 seconds. Add the remaining stock and bring to the boil.

3 Stir in the rice, then add the squid, fish chunks and prawns. Lower the heat and simmer gently for 15 minutes or until the rice is cooked. Add the fish sauce and mussels.

4 Ladle into wide bowls and sprinkle with coriander before serving.

COOK'S TIP

You could use leftover cooked rice for this dish. Just simmer the seafood gently until cooked, then stir in the rice at the end.

Blackened Fish

The word 'blackened' refers to the spicy, Cajun marinade that is used to coat the fish and that chars slightly as it cooks.

NUTRITIONAL INFORMATION

Calories 331	Sugars 0g	
Protein 37g	Fat 20g	
Carbohydrate 0g	Saturates 8g	

 10 mins   20 mins

SERVES 4

INGREDIENTS

4 white fish steaks, such as cod, conger eel, shark or catfish

1 tbsp paprika

1 tsp dried thyme

1 tsp cayenne pepper

1 tsp freshly ground black pepper

½ tsp freshly ground white pepper

½ tsp salt

¼ tsp ground allspice

2 tbsp unsalted butter

3 tbsp sunflower oil

1 Rinse the fish steaks and pat them dry with absorbent kitchen paper.

2 Combine the paprika, thyme, cayenne, black pepper, white pepper, salt and allspice in a shallow dish.

3 Place the butter and oil in a small pan and heat, stirring occasionally, until the butter melts.

4 Brush the butter mixture liberally all over the fish steaks, on both sides.

5 Dip the fish into the spice mixture until well coated on both sides.

6 Barbecue the fish over hot coals for approximately 10 minutes on each side, turning once. Continue to baste the fish with the remaining butter mixture during the cooking time. Alternatively, cook the fish under a preheated grill, brushing frequently with the butter mixture, until cooked through and tender. Serve immediately.

VARIATION

A whole fish - red mullet, for example - rather than steaks is also delicious cooked this way. The spicy seasoning can also be used to coat chicken portions, if you prefer.

Chargrilled Bream

Bream have quite tough scales, which need to be removed before cooking. Ask the fishmonger to do this for you.

NUTRITIONAL INFORMATION

Calories	397	Sugars	.........1g
Protein	........35g	Fat	..........28g
Carbohydrate	....1g	Saturates	.......3g

15 mins   20–30 mins

SERVES 2

I N G R E D I E N T S

2 small sea bream, scaled, gutted, trimmed and cleaned

2 lemon slices

2 bay leaves

salt and pepper

B A S T E

4 tbsp olive oil

2 tbsp lemon juice

½ tsp chopped fresh oregano

½ tsp chopped fresh thyme

T O   G A R N I S H

fresh bay leaves

fresh thyme sprig

lemon wedges

COOK'S TIP

The flavour will be enhanced if you use good fresh ingredients in the sauce. Dried herbs can be used, but remember that the flavour is much more intense, so use only half the quantity of the fresh herbs listed here.

1 Using a sharp knife, cut 2–3 deep slashes into the bodies of both fish in order to help them fully absorb the flavour of the basting sauce.

2 Place a slice of lemon and a bay leaf inside the cavity of each fish. Season inside the cavity with salt and pepper.

3 In a small bowl, combine the ingredients for the baste using a fork. Alternatively, place the basting ingredients in a small screw-top jar and shake vigorously to combine.

4 Brush some of the baste liberally over the fish and place them on a rack over hot coals. Barbecue for 20-30 minutes, turning and basting frequently. Alternatively, cook under a preheated grill, basting frequently.

5 Transfer the fish to a serving plate, garnish with fresh bay leaves, thyme and lemon wedges and serve.

Salmon Brochettes

These tasty kebabs have a lovely summery flavour, perfect for the barbecue. Serve on bread croûtes with fresh tomato sauce.

NUTRITIONAL INFORMATION

Calories 535   Sugars 7g
Protein . . . . .26g   Fat 42g
Carbohydrate . . .14g   Saturates 7g

35 mins   15 mins

SERVES 4

I N G R E D I E N T S

450 g/1 lb salmon, skinned and cut into
   large chunks

1 tbsp cornflour

½ tsp salt

½ tsp pepper

1 small egg white, beaten

1 red pepper, deseeded and cut into chunks

1 green pepper, deseeded and cut
   into chunks

4 tbsp olive oil

ciabatta bread, to serve

T O M A T O   S A U C E

4 tomatoes, deseeded and quartered

¼ cucumber, peeled, deseeded
   and chopped

8 fresh basil leaves

6 tbsp olive oil

2 tbsp lemon juice

salt and pepper

1 Place the salmon in a shallow dish and sprinkle over the cornflour and season to taste with salt and pepper. Add the beaten egg white and toss well to coat. Set aside to chill for 15 minutes.

2 Thread the pieces of salmon on to 4 skewers, alternating the fish pieces with the chunks of red and green peppers. Set the skewers aside while you make the tomato sauce.

3 To make the sauce, place all of the ingredients in a food processor and chop coarsely. Alternatively, chop the tomatoes, cucumber and basil leaves by hand and mix with the oil and lemon juice. Season to taste with salt and pepper. Cover and chill in the refrigerator until required.

4 Barbecue the salmon brochettes over hot coals for 10 minutes, brushing frequently with olive oil to prevent them from drying during cooking. Alternatively, cook under a preheated grill.

5 Slice the ciabatta bread at an angle to produce 4 long slices. Lightly toast on the barbecue or under the grill.

6 Spread the tomato sauce over each slice of bread and top with a salmon brochette. Serve immediately.

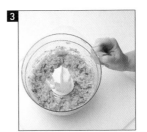

VARIATION

Serve the salmon brochettes on toasted French sticks, if preferred.

Nutty Stuffed Trout

Stuff the trout just before cooking. If you prefer, the fish can be cooked in foil parcels on the barbecue or in a moderate oven.

NUTRITIONAL INFORMATION

Calories 356   Sugars 2g
Protein . . . . .40g   Fat 17g
Carbohydrate . . . .11g   Saturates 3g

 10 mins   25 mins

SERVES 4

I N G R E D I E N T S

4 medium trout, cleaned

2 tbsp sunflower oil

1 small onion, finely chopped

55 g/2 oz toasted mixed nuts, chopped

grated rind of 1 orange

2 tbsp orange juice

85 g/3 oz fresh wholemeal breadcrumbs

1 egg, beaten

oil for brushing

salt and pepper

orange slices, to garnish

orange and watercress salad, to serve

1 Season the trout inside and out with salt and pepper.

COOK'S TIP

For the dressing, combine 2 tablespoons orange juice, 1 tablespoon white wine vinegar, 3 tablespoons olive oil, ½ teaspoon wholegrain mustard and salt and pepper to taste. Pour the dressing over the salad just before serving.

2 To make the stuffing, heat the oil in a small pan and add the chopped onion. Cook over a low heat for approximately 5 minutes until softened. Remove the pan from the heat and then stir in the chopped mixed nuts, grated orange rind, orange juice and wholemeal breadcrumbs. Add just enough of the beaten egg to bind the mixture together.

3 Divide the stuffing into 4 equal portions and spoon them into the cavity of each fish.

4 Brush the fish liberally with oil and barbecue over medium hot coals for 10 minutes on each side, turning once. When the fish is cooked the flesh will be white and firm and the skin will be beginning to crispen.

5 Transfer the fish to individual serving plates and garnish with orange slices.

6 Serve the fish with an orange and watercress salad and an orange and mustard dressing (see Cook's Tip, left).

Bacon & Scallop Skewers

Wrapping bacon around the scallops helps to protect the delicate flesh from the intense heat and allows them to cook without becoming tough.

NUTRITIONAL INFORMATION

Calories	.271	Sugars	.6g
Protein	.17g	Fat	.20g
Carbohydrate	.7g	Saturates	.5g

2½ hrs   5 mins

SERVES 4

INGREDIENTS

grated rind and juice of ½ lemon

4 tbsp sunflower oil

½ tsp dried dill

12 scallops

1 red pepper

1 green pepper

1 yellow pepper

6 rashers smoked streaky bacon

1 Combine the lemon rind and juice, oil and dill in a non-metallic dish. Add the scallops and mix thoroughly to coat in the marinade. Set aside to marinate for 1–2 hours.

2 Cut the red, green and yellow peppers in half and deseed them. Cut the pepper halves into 2.5 cm/1 inch pieces and then set aside until required.

3 Carefully remove the rind from the bacon. Stretch the rashers with the back of a knife, then cut each one in half.

4 Remove the scallops from the reserved marinade, reserving any excess marinade. Wrap a piece of bacon around each scallop.

5 Thread the scallops on to skewers, alternating with the pepper pieces.

6 Barbecue the bacon and scallop skewers over hot coals for about 5 minutes, basting frequently with the lemon and oil marinade.

7 Transfer to warmed serving plates and serve immediately.

VARIATION
Peel 4–8 raw prawns and add them to the marinade with the scallops. Thread them on to the skewers alternating with the scallops and peppers.

Herb & Garlic Prawns

Prawns cook very rapidly – and if overcooked, develop an unpleasant texture. However, there is no virtue in undercooking them.

NUTRITIONAL INFORMATION

Calories	150	Sugars	.........0g
Protein	........16g	Fat	...........9g
Carbohydrate	....1g	Saturates	.......5g

 50 mins   12 mins

SERVES 4

INGREDIENTS

350 g/12 oz raw prawns, peeled
  and deveined

2 tbsp chopped fresh parsley

4 tbsp lemon juice

2 tbsp olive oil

5 tbsp butter

2 garlic cloves, chopped

salt and pepper

1 Place the prawns in a shallow, non-metallic dish with the parsley and lemon juice and season with salt and pepper to taste. Cover and set aside to marinate in the herb mixture for at least 30 minutes.

2 Heat the oil and butter in a small pan with the garlic until the butter melts. Stir to mix thoroughly.

3 Remove the prawns from the marinade with a draining spoon and add them to the pan containing the garlic butter. Stir until well coated, then thread the prawns on to skewers.

4 Barbecue the kebabs over hot coals for 5–10 minutes, turning the skewers occasionally, until the prawns turn pink and are cooked through. Brush the prawns with the remaining garlic butter during the cooking time. Alternatively, cook under a preheated grill, turning and brushing frequently with the garlic butter.

5 Transfer the herb and garlic prawn kebabs to warmed serving plates. Drizzle over any of the remaining garlic butter and serve immediately.

VARIATION

If raw prawns are unavailable, use cooked prawns, but reduce the cooking time. Small cooked prawns can also be cooked in a kitchen foil parcel instead of on the skewers.

Steamed Stuffed Snapper

Red mullet may be used instead of the snapper, although they are a little more difficult to stuff because of their size. Use one mullet per person.

NUTRITIONAL INFORMATION

Calories 406	Sugar 4g
Protein 68g	Fat 9g
Carbohydrate 9g	Saturates 0g

🥗 20 mins ⏲ 10 mins

SERVES 4

INGREDIENTS

1.4 kg/3 lb whole snapper, cleaned
   and scaled

175 g/6 oz spinach

orange slices and shredded spring onion,
   to garnish

STUFFING

55 g/2 oz cooked long grain rice

1 tsp grated fresh root ginger

2 spring onions, finely chopped

2 tsp light soy sauce

1 tsp sesame oil

½ tsp ground star anise

1 orange, segmented and chopped

1 Rinse the fish inside and out under cold running water and pat dry with kitchen paper.

2 Blanch the spinach for 40 seconds, rinse in cold water and drain well, pressing out as much moisture as possible.

3 Arrange the spinach on a heatproof plate and place the fish on top.

4 To make the stuffing, combine the cooked rice, grated ginger, spring onions, soy sauce, sesame oil, star anise and orange in a bowl.

5 Spoon the stuffing into the body cavity of the fish, pressing it in well with a spoon.

6 Cover the plate and cook in a steamer for 10 minutes or until the fish is cooked through.

7 Garnish the fish with orange slices and spring onion and serve.

COOK'S TIP

The name 'snapper' covers a family of tropical and subtropical fish that vary in colour. They may be red, orange, pink, grey or blue-green. Some are striped or spotted and they range in size from about 15 cm/6 inches to 90 cm/3 ft.

Braised Fish Fillets

Almost any white fish, such as lemon sole or plaice, can be used to make this delicious dish with a Chinese flavour.

NUTRITIONAL INFORMATION

Calories ....107 Sugars 2g
Protein ....17g Fat 2g
Carbohydrate ....6g Saturates 0.3g

  35 mins   10 mins

SERVES 4

INGREDIENTS

3–4 small Chinese dried mushrooms

300–350 g/10½–12 oz fish fillets

1 tsp salt

½ egg white, lightly beaten

1 tsp cornflour

600 ml/1 pint vegetable oil

1 tsp finely chopped fresh root ginger

2 spring onions, finely chopped

1 garlic clove, finely chopped

½ small green pepper, deseeded
    and diced

½ small carrot, thinly sliced

55 g/2 oz canned sliced bamboo shoots,
    drained and rinsed

½ tsp sugar

1 tbsp light soy sauce

1 tsp rice wine or dry sherry

1 tbsp chilli bean sauce

2–3 tbsp vegetable stock or water

a few drops of sesame oil

1 Soak the dried mushrooms in a bowl of warm water for 30 minutes. Drain thoroughly on kitchen paper, reserving the soaking water for stock or soup. Squeeze the mushrooms to extract all of the moisture, cut off and discard any hard stems and slice the caps thinly.

2 Cut the fish into bite-size pieces, then place in a shallow dish and mix with a pinch of salt, the egg white and cornflour, turning the fish to coat well.

3 Heat the oil in a preheated wok. Add the fish pieces to the wok and deep-fry for about 1 minute. Remove the fish pieces with a draining spoon and leave to drain on kitchen paper.

4 Carefully pour off the excess oil, leaving about 1 tablespoon in the wok. Add the ginger, spring onions and garlic and cook over a medium heat for a few seconds to flavour the oil, then add the green pepper, carrots and bamboo shoots and stir-fry for about 1 minute.

5 Add the sugar, soy sauce, wine, chilli bean sauce, stock or water and the remaining salt and bring to the boil. Add the fish pieces, stirring to coat with the sauce, and braise for 1 minute. Sprinkle with sesame oil and serve.

Bengali-style Fish

Fresh fish is eaten a great deal in Bengal and this dish is made with mustard oil, which gives the fish a good flavour.

NUTRITIONAL INFORMATION

Calories 356   Sugars 4g
Protein . . . . .32g   Fat 23g
Carbohydrate . . . .5g   Saturates 3g

15 mins   25–35 mins

SERVES 4

INGREDIENTS

1 tsp ground turmeric

1 tsp salt

1 kg/2 lb 4 oz cod fillet, skinned and cut into pieces

6 tbsp corn oil

4 fresh green chillies

1 tsp finely chopped fresh root ginger

1 tsp crushed garlic

2 medium onions, finely chopped

2 tomatoes, finely chopped

6 tbsp mustard oil

450 ml/16 fl oz water

chopped fresh coriander leaves, to garnish

1 Combine the turmeric and salt in a small bowl. Spoon the mixture over the fish pieces.

2 Heat the oil in a frying pan. Add the fish and cook over a low heat until pale golden yellow. Remove the fish with a draining spoon and set aside.

3 Place the fresh chillies, ginger, garlic, onions, tomatoes and mustard oil in a mortar and grind with a pestle to a fine paste. Alternatively, process the ingredients in a food processor.

4 Transfer the spice paste to a heavy-based pan and dry-fry over a low heat, stirring occasionally, until golden brown and aromatic.

5 Remove the pan from the heat and gently place the fish pieces into the paste, without breaking them up. Return the pan to the heat, add the water and cook over a medium heat, stirring occasionally, for 15–20 minutes or until the fish is tender and cooked through.

6 Serve immediately, garnished with chopped coriander.

Vegetables

Whether you are a vegetarian or a meat-eater, vegetable dishes are the perfect choice for a healthy diet. Most vegetables are naturally low in fats, high in fibre and packed with essential vitamins and minerals – and they are full of flavour, too. With this chapter you are spoilt for choice with a huge

range of dishes that takes full advantage of the breath-taking versatility of vegetables. Some are just perfect filled with a tasty stuffing, while others make wonderful pasta sauces and succulent curries. Vegetable kebabs are a real treat on the barbecue and don't overlook the delights of crêpes and omelettes.

Vegetable Chilli

This is a hearty and flavourful soup that is good on its own or spooned over cooked rice or baked potatoes for a more substantial meal.

NUTRITIONAL INFORMATION

Calories 213	Sugars 11g	
Protein 12g	Fat 10g	
Carbohydrate ...21g	Saturates 5g	

10 mins   1¼ hrs

SERVES 5–6

INGREDIENTS

1 medium aubergine, peeled if wished, cut into 2.5 cm/1 inch slices

1 tbsp olive oil, plus extra for brushing

1 large red or yellow onion, finely chopped

2 red or yellow peppers, deseeded and finely chopped

3–4 garlic cloves, finely chopped or crushed

2 x 400 g/14 oz cans chopped tomatoes

1 tbsp mild chilli powder

½ tsp ground cumin

½ tsp dried oregano

2 small courgettes, quartered lengthways and sliced

400 g/14 oz can kidney beans, drained and rinsed

450 ml/16 fl oz water

1 tbsp tomato purée

6 spring onions, finely chopped

115 g/4 oz grated Cheddar cheese

salt and pepper

1 Brush the aubergine slices on 1 side with olive oil. Heat half the oil in a large, heavy-based frying pan over a medium-high heat. Add the aubergine slices, oiled side up, and cook for 5–6 minutes until browned on 1 side. Turn the slices over, cook on the other side until browned and transfer to a plate. Cut into bite-size pieces.

2 Heat the remaining oil in a large saucepan over a medium heat. Add the onion and peppers and cook, stirring occasionally, for 3–4 minutes until the onion is just softened, but not browned. Add the garlic and continue cooking for 2–3 minutes or until the onion us just beginning to colour.

3 Add the tomatoes, chilli powder, cumin and oregano. Season to taste with salt and pepper. Bring just to the boil, reduce the heat, cover and simmer gently for 15 minutes.

4 Add the sliced courgettes, aubergine pieces and kidney beans. Stir in the water and the tomato purée. Bring back to the boil, then cover the pan and continue simmering for about 45 minutes or until the vegetables are tender. Taste and then adjust the seasoning if necessary. If you prefer a hotter dish, stir in a little more chilli powder.

5 Ladle into warmed bowls and top with spring onions and cheese.

Stuffed Red Peppers

Stuffed peppers are a well known and popular dish, but this is a new version adapted for the barbecue.

NUTRITIONAL INFORMATION

Calories 144   Sugars 4g
Protein ....1g   Fat 12g
Carbohydrate ....9g   Saturates 2g

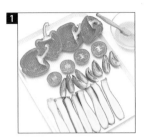

40 mins   10 mins

SERVES 4

INGREDIENTS

2 red peppers, halved lengthways and deseeded

2 tomatoes, halved

2 courgettes, thinly sliced lengthways

1 red onion, cut into 8 sections, each section held together by the root

4 tbsp olive oil

2 tbsp fresh thyme leaves

55 g/2 oz mixed basmati and wild rice, cooked

salt and pepper

1 Put the red peppers, tomatoes, courgettes and onion sections on to a baking sheet.

2 Brush the vegetables with olive oil and sprinkle with the thyme leaves.

3 Cook the pepper, onion and courgette over a medium barbecue for about 6 minutes, turning once.

4 When the peppers are cooked and tender, put a spoonful of the cooked rice into each of the halves.

5 Add the tomato halves to the barbecue and cook for 2–3 minutes only. Serve all the vegetables hot, seasoned with plenty of salt and pepper.

COOK'S TIP
When char-grilled, red, orange and yellow peppers all take on a remarkable sweet quality.

Pasta & Bean Casserole

A satisfying winter dish, this is a slow-cooked, one-pot meal.
The haricot beans need to be soaked overnight, so prepare well in advance.

NUTRITIONAL INFORMATION

Calories	323	Sugars	.........5g
Protein	........13g	Fat	..........12g
Carbohydrate	...41g	Saturates	.......2g

25 mins | 3½ mins

SERVES 4

INGREDIENTS

225 g/8 oz dried haricot beans,
  soaked overnight and drained

225 g/8 oz dried penne, or other
  short pasta shapes

6 tbsp olive oil

850 ml/1½ pints vegetable stock

2 large onions, sliced

2 garlic cloves, chopped

2 bay leaves

1 tsp dried oregano

1 tsp dried thyme

5 tbsp red wine

2 tbsp tomato purée

2 celery sticks, sliced

1 fennel bulb, sliced

115 g/4 oz mushrooms, sliced

225 g/8 oz tomatoes, sliced

1 tsp dark muscovado sugar

55 g/2 oz dry white breadcrumbs

salt and pepper

TO SERVE

salad leaves

crusty bread

1 Put the beans in a large pan, add water to cover and bring to the boil. Boil the beans rapidly for 20 minutes, then drain them and set aside.

2 Cook the pasta for only 3 minutes in a large pan of boiling salted water, adding 1 tablespoon of the oil. Drain in a colander and set aside.

3 Put the beans in a large flameproof casserole, pour in the vegetable stock and stir in the remaining olive oil, the onions, garlic, bay leaves, herbs, wine and tomato purée.

4 Bring to the boil, cover the casserole and cook in a preheated oven, 180°C/350°F/Gas Mark 4, for 2 hours.

5 Remove the casserole from the oven and add the reserved pasta, the celery, fennel, mushrooms and tomatoes and season to taste with salt and pepper.

6 Stir in the sugar and sprinkle the breadcrumbs on top. Cover the casserole again, return to the oven and continue cooking for 1 hour. Serve straight from the casserole with salad leaves and crusty bread.

Artichoke & Olive Spaghetti

The tasty flavours and delightful textures of artichoke hearts and black olives make a winning combination.

NUTRITIONAL INFORMATION

Calories	393	Sugars	........11g
Protein	........14g	Fat	...........11g
Carbohydrate	...63g	Saturates	.......2g

20 mins   35 mins

SERVES 4

INGREDIENTS

2 tbsp olive oil

1 large red onion, chopped

2 garlic cloves, crushed

1 tbsp lemon juice

4 baby aubergines, quartered

600 ml/1 pint passata

2 tsp caster sugar

2 tbsp tomato purée

400 g/14 oz can artichoke hearts, drained and halved

115 g/4 oz stoned black olives

350 g/12 oz wholewheat dried spaghetti

salt and pepper

fresh basil sprigs, to garnish

olive bread, to serve

1 Heat 1 tablespoon of the oil in a large, heavy-based frying pan. Add the onion, garlic, lemon juice and aubergines and cook over a low heat, stirring occasionally, for 4–5 minutes or until lightly browned.

2 Pour in the passata, season with salt and pepper to taste and stir in the sugar and tomato purée. Bring to the boil, reduce the heat and simmer gently for 20 minutes.

3 Gently stir in the artichoke hearts and olives and cook for 5 minutes.

4 Meanwhile, bring a large pan of lightly salted water to the boil. Add the pasta, bring back to the boil and cook for 8–10 minutes or until tender, but still firm to the bite. Drain, toss in the remaining oil and season to taste.

5 Transfer the spaghetti to a warmed serving bowl and top with the vegetable sauce. Garnish with basil sprigs and serve with olive bread.

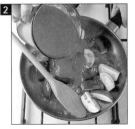

Oriental-style Millet Pilau

Millet makes an interesting alternative to rice, which is the more traditional ingredient for a pilau. Serve with a crisp oriental salad.

NUTRITIONAL INFORMATION

Calories	660	Sugars	........28g
Protein	........15g	Fat	..........27g
Carbohydrate	...94g	Saturates	.......5g

🍓 20 mins   ⏱ 30 mins

SERVES 4

INGREDIENTS

300 g/10½ oz millet grains

1 tbsp vegetable oil

1 bunch of spring onions, white and green parts, chopped

1 garlic clove, crushed

1 tsp grated fresh root ginger

1 orange pepper, seeded and diced

600 ml/1 pint water

1 orange

115 g/4 oz chopped stoned dates

2 tsp sesame oil

115 g/4 oz roasted cashew nuts

2 tbsp pumpkin seeds

salt and pepper

oriental salad vegetables, to serve

1 Place the millet in a large pan and toast over a medium heat, shaking the pan occasionally, for 4–5 minutes, until the grains begin to crack and pop.

2 Heat the oil in another pan. Add the spring onions, garlic, ginger and pepper and cook over a medium heat, stirring frequently, for 2–3 minutes until just softened, but not browned. Add the millet and pour in the water.

3 Using a vegetable peeler, pare the rind from the orange and add the rind to the pan. Squeeze the juice from the orange into the pan. Season to taste with salt and pepper.

4 Bring to the boil, reduce the heat, cover and cook gently for 20 minutes until all the liquid has been absorbed.

Remove the pan from the heat, stir in the dates and sesame oil and set aside to stand for 10 minutes.

5 Remove and discard the orange rind and stir in the cashew nuts. Pile into a warmed serving dish, sprinkle with pumpkin seeds and serve immediately with oriental salad vegetables.

Aubergine Bake

This dish combines layers of aubergine, tomato sauce, mozzarella and Parmesan cheese to create a very tasty starter or light lunch.

NUTRITIONAL INFORMATION

Calories	232	Sugars	.........8g
Protein	........10g	Fat	..........18g
Carbohydrate	....8g	Saturates	.......6g

5 mins   45 mins

SERVES 4

I N G R E D I E N T S

3–4 tbsp olive oil

2 garlic cloves, crushed

2 large aubergines

100 g/3½ oz mozzarella cheese,
   thinly sliced

200 ml/7 fl oz passata

55 g/2 oz Parmesan cheese, freshly grated

1 Heat 2 tablespoons of the olive oil in a large, heavy-based frying pan. Add the garlic and cook, stirring constantly, for 30 seconds.

2 Slice the aubergines lengthways. Add the slices to the pan and cook in the oil for 3–4 minutes on each side or until tender. (You will probably have to cook them in batches, so add the remaining oil as necessary.)

3 Remove the aubergines with a draining spoon and drain on absorbent kitchen paper.

4 Place a layer of aubergine slices in a shallow ovenproof dish. Cover with a layer of mozzarella and then pour over a third of the passata. Continue layering in the same order, finishing with a layer of passata on top.

5 Generously sprinkle the grated Parmesan cheese over the top and bake in a preheated oven, 200°C/400°F/Gas Mark 6, for 25–30 minutes.

6 Transfer to serving plates and set aside to cool, then serve warm or chilled.

Chargrilled Vegetables

This medley of peppers, courgettes, aubergine and red onion can be served on its own or as an unusual side dish.

NUTRITIONAL INFORMATION

Calories ....66 Sugars 7g
Protein ....2g Fat 3g
Carbohydrate ....7g Saturates 0.5g

15 mins   15 mins

SERVES 4

INGREDIENTS

1 large red pepper

1 large green pepper

1 large orange pepper

1 large courgette

4 baby aubergines

2 medium red onions

2 tbsp lemon juice

1 tbsp olive oil

1 garlic clove, crushed

1 tbsp chopped fresh rosemary or 1 tsp dried rosemary

salt and pepper

TO SERVE

cracked wheat, cooked

tomato and olive relish

1 Halve and deseed the peppers and cut into even-size pieces, about 2.5 cm/ 1 inch wide.

2 Trim the courgettes, cut in half lengthways and slice into 2.5 cm/ 1 inch pieces. Place the peppers and courgettes in a large bowl.

3 Trim the aubergines and quarter them lengthways. Peel the onions, then cut each of them into 8 even-size wedges. Add the aubergines and onions to the peppers and courgettes.

4 In a small bowl, whisk the lemon juice with the olive oil, garlic and rosemary Season to taste with salt and pepper. Pour the mixture over the vegetables and stir to coat evenly.

5 Thread the vegetables on to 8 metal or pre-soaked wooden skewers.

Arrange the kebabs on the grill rack and cook under a preheated grill, turning frequently, for about 10–12 minutes until the vegetables are lightly charred and just softened. Alternatively, cook on a barbecue over hot coals, turning frequently, for about 8–10 minutes until softened and beginning to char.

6 Drain the kebabs and serve immediately on a bed of cracked wheat with a tomato and olive relish.

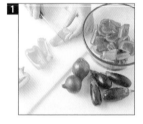  

Spaghetti with Ricotta

This light pasta dish has a delicate flavour ideally suited for a summer lunch.

NUTRITIONAL INFORMATION

Calories	701	Sugars	........12g
Protein	.......17g	Fat	.........40g
Carbohydrate	...73g	Saturates	......15g

5 mins   25 mins

SERVES 4

INGREDIENTS

350 g/12 oz dried spaghetti

5 tbsp butter

2 tbsp chopped fresh flat leaf parsley

115 g/4 oz freshly ground almonds

115 g/4 oz ricotta cheese

inch of freshly grated nutmeg

inch of ground cinnamon

150 ml/5 fl oz crème fraîche

2 tbsp olive oil

125 ml/4 fl oz hot chicken stock

1 tbsp pine kernels

salt and pepper

fresh flat leaf parsley sprigs, to garnish

1 Bring a pan of lightly salted water to the boil. Add the spaghetti, bring back to the boil and cook for 8–10 minutes until tender, but still firm to the bite.

2 Drain the pasta, return to the pan and toss with the butter and chopped parsley. Set aside and keep warm.

3 To make the sauce, combine the ground almonds, ricotta cheese, nutmeg, cinnamon and crème fraîche in a small pan and stir over a low heat to a thick paste. Gradually stir in the oil. When the oil has been fully incorporated, gradually stir in the hot chicken stock, until smooth. Season to taste with pepper.

4 Transfer the spaghetti to a warm serving dish, pour the sauce over it and toss together well (see Cook's Tip). Sprinkle over the pine kernels, garnish with the sprigs of flat leaf parsley and serve immediately.

COOK'S TIP

Use 2 large forks to toss spaghetti or other long pasta, so that it is thoroughly coated with the sauce. Special spaghetti forks are available from some cookware departments and kitchen shops.

Lemon Spaghetti

Steaming vegetables helps to preserve their nutritional content and allows them to retain their bright, natural colours and crunchy texture.

NUTRITIONAL INFORMATION

Calories	133	Sugars	.........8g
Protein	.........8g	Fat	...........1g
Carbohydrate	...25g	Saturates	.....0.2g

10 mins   25 mins

SERVES 4

INGREDIENTS

225 g/8 oz celeriac

2 medium carrots

2 medium leeks

1 small red pepper

1 small yellow pepper

2 garlic cloves

1 tsp celery seeds

1 tbsp lemon juice

300 g/10½ oz spaghetti

salt

chopped celery leaves, to garnish

LEMON DRESSING

1 tsp finely grated lemon rind

1 tbsp lemon juice

4 tbsp low-fat natural fromage frais

salt and pepper

2 tbsp snipped fresh chives

1 Peel the celeriac and carrots, cut into thin batons and place in a bowl. Trim and slice the leeks, rinse under cold running water to flush out any trapped dirt, then shred finely. Halve, deseed and slice the peppers. Peel and thinly slice the garlic.

2 Add all of the vegetables to the bowl with the celeriac and the carrots. Toss the vegetables with the celery seeds and lemon juice.

3 Bring a large pan of lightly salted water to the boil. Add the pasta, bring back to the boil and cook for 8–10 minutes until tender, but still firm to the bite. Drain and keep warm.

4 Meanwhile, bring another large pan of water to the boil, put the vegetables in a steamer and place over the boiling water. Cover and steam for 6–7 minutes or until tender.

5 Meanwhile, mix the ingredients for the lemon dressing together.

6 Transfer the spaghetti and vegetables to a warmed serving bowl and mix with the dressing. Garnish with chopped celery leaves and serve.

Mixed Bean Pan-fry

Fresh green beans have a wonderful flavour that is hard to beat.
If you cannot find fresh beans, use thawed, frozen beans instead.

NUTRITIONAL INFORMATION

Calories	179	Sugars	.........4g
Protein	........10g	Fat	...........11g
Carbohydrate	...10g	Saturates	.......1g

10 mins | 15 mins

SERVES 4

INGREDIENTS

350 g/12 oz mixed green beans, such as
French and broad beans, podded

2 tbsp vegetable oil

2 garlic cloves, crushed

1 red onion, halved and sliced

225 g/8 oz firm marinated tofu, diced

1 tbsp lemon juice

½ tsp ground turmeric

1 tsp ground mixed spice

150 ml/5 fl oz vegetable stock

2 tsp sesame seeds

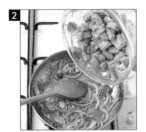
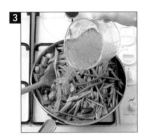

1 Trim and chop the French beans and set aside until required.

2 Heat the oil in a medium frying pan. Add the garlic and onion and cook over a low heat, stirring frequently, for 2 minutes. Add the tofu and cook, stirring gently occasionally, for a further 2–3 minutes, until just beginning to turn golden brown.

3 Add the French beans and broad beans. Stir in the lemon juice, turmeric, ground mixed spice and vegetable stock and bring to the boil over a medium heat.

4 Reduce the heat and simmer for about 5–7 minutes or until the beans are tender. Sprinkle with sesame seeds and serve immediately.

VARIATION
Use smoked tofu instead of marinated tofu for an alternative and quite distinctive flavour.

Penne & Vegetables

The sweet cherry tomatoes in this recipe add colour and flavour and are complemented by the black olives and mixed peppers.

NUTRITIONAL INFORMATION

Calories 380	Sugars 6g
Protein 8g	Fat 16g
Carbohydrate ...48g	Saturates 7g

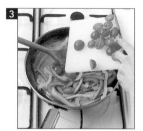

 10 mins 25 mins

SERVES 4

INGREDIENTS

225 g/8 oz dried penne

2 tbsp olive oil

2 tbsp butter

2 garlic cloves, crushed

1 green pepper, deseeded and thinly sliced

1 yellow pepper, deseeded and thinly sliced

16 cherry tomatoes, halved

1 tbsp chopped oregano

125 ml/4 fl oz dry white wine

2 tbsp quartered, stoned black olives

75 g/2¾ oz rocket

salt and pepper

fresh oregano sprigs, to garnish

1 Bring a large pan of lightly salted water to the boil. Add the pasta, bring back to the boil and cook for 8–10 minutes until tender, but still firm to the bite. Drain thoroughly.

2 Heat the oil and butter in a pan until the butter melts. Sauté the garlic for 30 seconds. Add the peppers and cook, stirring occasionally, for 3–4 minutes.

3 Stir in the cherry tomatoes, oregano, wine and olives and cook for 3–4 minutes. Season with salt and pepper and stir in the rocket until just wilted.

4 Transfer the pasta to a serving dish, spoon over the sauce and garnish.

VARIATION

If rocket is unavailable, spinach makes a good substitute. Follow the same cooking instructions as for rocket.

Tofu & Vegetable Stir-fry

This is a quick dish to prepare, making it the perfect choice for a midweek supper dish, after a busy day at work!

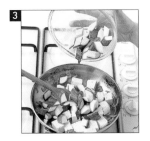

NUTRITIONAL INFORMATION

Calories 124   Sugars 2g
Protein . . . . .6g   Fat 6g
Carbohydrate . . . .11g   Saturates 1g

5 mins   25 mins

SERVES 4

INGREDIENTS

175 g/6 oz potatoes, cubed

1 tbsp vegetable oil

1 red onion, sliced

225 g/8 oz firm tofu, diced

2 courgettes, diced

8 canned artichoke hearts, halved

150 ml/5 fl oz passata

1 tbsp sweet chilli sauce

1 tbsp soy sauce

1 tsp caster sugar

2 tbsp chopped fresh basil

salt and pepper

1 Cook the potatoes in a saucepan of lightly salted boiling water for 10 minutes. Drain thoroughly and set aside until required.

2 Heat the vegetable oil in a wok or large frying pan and stir-fry the red onion for 2 minutes until it has softened.

3 Stir in the tofu and courgettes and stir-fry for 3–4 minutes until they begin to brown slightly.

4 Add the cooked potatoes to the wok or frying pan, stirring gently to mix.

5 Stir in the artichoke hearts, passata, sweet chilli sauce, soy sauce, sugar and basil.

6 Season to taste with salt and pepper and cook for a further 5 minutes, stirring constantly.

7 Transfer the tofu and vegetable stir-fry to serving dishes and serve immediately.

COOK'S TIP
Canned artichoke hearts should be drained thoroughly and rinsed before use because they often have salt added.

Roasted Vegetable Pilaf

Red rice has an aromatic, nutty flavour which complements the robust flavours of the roasted root vegetables.

NUTRITIONAL INFORMATION

Calories	773	Sugars	........30g
Protein	........11g	Fat	..........42g
Carbohydrate	...94g	Saturates	.......9g

15 mins   1¼ hrs

SERVES 4–6

INGREDIENTS

125 ml/4 fl oz olive oil

grated rind and juice of 1 orange

2 tbsp balsamic vinegar

2 tsp coriander seeds, lightly crushed

1 bay leaf

½ tsp crushed dried chillies

8–10 small raw beetroots, trimmed, scrubbed and halved

250 g/9 oz shallots or baby onions

6–8 baby parsnips

4–6 baby carrots

1 tsp chopped fresh rosemary leaves

400 g/14 oz red rice

850 ml/1½ pints hot chicken stock

1 red onion

1 small carrot, cut into thin batons

1 leek, cut into 1 cm/½ inch rounds

85 g/3 oz pine kernels, lightly roasted

1 tsp light brown sugar

1–2 tbsp chopped fresh coriander

150 g/5½ oz dried cranberries or raisins, soaked in boiling water for 15 minutes

salt and pepper

TO SERVE

225 ml/8 fl oz soured cream

2 tbsp chopped roasted walnuts

1. Put 4 tablespoons of the olive oil in a large bowl and whisk in the orange rind and juice, vinegar, coriander seeds, bay leaf and crushed chillies. Add the beetroots, shallots, parsnips and baby carrots and stir to coat.

2. Turn into a roasting tin (and roast in a preheated oven, 200°C/400°F/Gas Mark 6, turning occasionally, for 45–55 minutes until tender. Remove from the oven, sprinkle with the rosemary and salt and pepper and keep warm.

3. Put the rice in a large pan with the hot stock. Place over a medium-high heat and bring to the boil. Reduce the heat to low, cover and simmer for about 40 minutes until the rice is tender and the stock absorbed. Remove from the heat, but do not uncover.

4. Heat the remaining oil in a large pan. Add the onion and carrot batons and cook for 8–10 minutes until tender. Add the leek, pine kernels, sugar and coriander and cook for 2–3 minutes until the vegetables are lightly caramelized. Drain the dried fruit and stir into the vegetable mixture with the rice. Season with salt and pepper.

5. Arrange the roasted vegetables and rice on a serving platter and top with the soured cream. Sprinkle with the chopped walnuts and serve.

Risotto Primavera

This is a nice way to use those first green vegetables which signal the spring (*la primavera* in Italian). Feel free to add other vegetables.

NUTRITIONAL INFORMATION

Calories 381	Sugars 3g	
Protein 13g	Fat 19g	
Carbohydrate . . .43g	Saturates 8g	

15 mins   40 mins

SERVES 6–8

I N G R E D I E N T S

25 g/8 oz fresh thin asparagus spears

tbsp olive oil

75 g/6 oz young green beans, cut into
2.5 cm/1 inch pieces

75 g/6 oz young courgettes, quartered and
cut into 2.5 cm/1 inch lengths

25 g/8 oz fresh shelled peas

onion, finely chopped

–2 garlic cloves, finely chopped

50 g/12 oz arborio or carnaroli rice

.5 litres/2¾ pints chicken stock,
simmering, plus extra 2 tbsp

spring onions, cut into 2.5 cm/
1 inch lengths

tbsp unsalted butter

15 g/4 oz freshly grated Parmesan cheese

tbsp chopped fresh chives

tbsp shredded fresh basil

alt and pepper

pring onions, to garnish (optional)

1. Trim the woody ends of the asparagus and cut off the tips. Cut the stems to 2.5 cm/1 inch pieces and set aside with the tips.

2. Heat 2 tablespoons of the olive oil in a large frying pan over a high heat until very hot. Add the asparagus, beans, courgettes and peas and stir-fry for 3–4 minutes until they are bright green and just beginning to soften. Set aside.

3. Heat the remaining olive oil in a large heavy-based pan over a medium heat. Add the onion and cook for about 1 minute until it begins to soften. Stir in the garlic and cook for 30 seconds. Add the rice and cook, stirring frequently, for 2 minutes until translucent and coated with oil.

4. Add a ladleful (about 225 ml/ 8 fl oz) of the hot stock; the stock will bubble rapidly. Cook, stirring constantly, until the stock is absorbed.

5. Continue adding the stock, about half a ladleful at a time, allowing each addition to be absorbed before adding the next – never allow the rice to cook 'dry'. This should take 20–25 minutes. The risotto should have a creamy consistency and the rice should be tender, but still firm to the bite.

6. Stir in the stir-fried vegetables and spring onions with a little more stock. Cook for 2 minutes, stirring frequently, then season with salt and pepper. Stir in the butter, Parmesan, chives and basil.

7. Remove the pan from the heat, cover and set aside for about 1 minute. Transfer the risotto to a warmed serving dish, garnish with spring onions, if wished, and serve immediately.

Courgette & Basil Risotto

An easy way of livening up a simple risotto is to use a flavoured olive oil – here a basil-flavoured oil heightens the taste of the dish.

NUTRITIONAL INFORMATION

Calories	460	Sugars	.........5g
Protein	........13g	Fat	..........18g
Carbohydrate	...64g	Saturates	.......7g

5–10 mins   35 mins

SERVES 4–6

INGREDIENTS

4 tbsp basil-flavoured extra virgin olive oil, plus extra for drizzling

4 courgettes, diced

1 yellow pepper, deseeded and diced

2 garlic cloves, finely chopped

1 large onion, finely chopped

400 g/14 oz arborio or carnaroli rice

4 tbsp dry white vermouth

1.5 litres/2¾ pints chicken or vegetable stock, simmering

2 tbsp unsalted butter, at room temperature

large handful of fresh basil leaves, torn, plus a few leaves to garnish

85 g/3 oz freshly grated Parmesan cheese

1 Heat half the oil in a large frying pan over high heat. When very hot, but not smoking, add the courgettes and yellow pepper and stir-fry for 3 minutes until lightly golden. Stir in the garlic and cook for about 30 seconds longer. Transfer to a plate and set aside.

2 Heat the remaining oil in a large heavy-based pan over a medium heat. Add the onion and cook, stirring occasionally, for about 2 minutes until softened. Add the rice and cook, stirring frequently, for about 2 minutes until the rice is translucent and well coated with the olive oil.

3 Pour in the vermouth; it will bubble and steam rapidly and evaporate almost immediately. Add a ladleful (about 225 ml/8 fl oz) of the simmering stock and cook, stirring constantly until the stock is completely absorbed.

4 Continue adding the stock, about half a ladleful at a time, allowing each addition to be absorbed before adding the next. This should take 20–25 minutes. The risotto should have a creamy consistenc[] and the rice should be tender, but still fir[] to the bite.

5 Stir in the courgette mixture with an[] juices, the butter, basil and grate[] Parmesan. Drizzle with a little oil an[] garnish with basil. Serve hot.

Risotto Verde

Baby spinach and fresh herbs are the basis of this colourful, refreshing and summery risotto.

NUTRITIONAL INFORMATION

Calories	374	Sugars	.........5g
Protein	........10g	Fat	..........9g
Carbohydrate	...55g	Saturates	......2g

5 mins   45 mins

SERVES 4

INGREDIENTS

1.7 litres/3 pints vegetable stock

2 tbsp olive oil

2 garlic cloves, crushed

2 leeks, shredded

225 g/8 oz arborio rice

300 ml/10 fl oz dry white wine

4 tbsp chopped fresh mixed herbs

225 g/8 oz baby spinach

3 tbsp low-fat natural yogurt

salt and pepper

shredded leek, to garnish

1 Pour the stock into a large pan and bring to the boil. Reduce the heat to simmer.

2 Meanwhile, heat the oil in a separate pan and cook the garlic and leeks, stirring occasionally, for 2–3 minutes until softened, but not browned.

3 Stir in the rice and cook stirring constantly, until translucent and well coated with oil.

4 Pour in half of the wine and a little of the hot stock; it will bubble and steam rapidly. Cook over a gentle heat until all of the liquid has been absorbed.

5 Add the remaining stock and wine and cook over a low heat for 25 minutes or until the rice is creamy.

6 Stir in the chopped mixed herbs and baby spinach, season to taste with salt and pepper and cook for a further 2 minutes. Stir in the natural yogurt, garnish with the shredded leek and serve the risotto immediately.

COOK'S TIP

Do not hurry the process of cooking the risotto as the rice must absorb the liquid slowly in order for it to reach the correct consistency.

Potatoes with Goat's Cheese

This makes a luscious side dish to serve with meat or a satisfying vegetarian main course. Goat's cheese is a traditional food of Mexico.

NUTRITIONAL INFORMATION

Calories	725	Sugars	.........4g
Protein	........30g	Fat	..........43g
Carbohydrate	...56g	Saturates	.....28g

2 mins   35 mins

SERVES 4

I N G R E D I E N T S

1.25 kg/2 lb 12 oz baking potatoes, peeled and cut into chunks

pinch of salt

pinch of sugar

200 ml/7 fl oz crème fraîche

125 ml/4 fl oz vegetable or chicken stock

3 garlic cloves, finely chopped

a few shakes of bottled chipotle salsa, or 1 dried chipotle, reconstituted, deseeded and thinly sliced

225 g/8 oz goat's cheese, sliced

175 g/6 oz mozzarella or Cheddar cheese, grated

55 g/2 oz Parmesan or pecorino cheese, grated

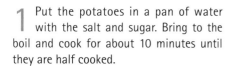   

1 Put the potatoes in a pan of water with the salt and sugar. Bring to the boil and cook for about 10 minutes until they are half cooked.

2 Combine the crème fraîche with the stock, garlic and chipotle salsa.

3 Arrange half the potatoes in a casserole. Pour half the crème fraîche sauce over the potatoes and cover with the goat's cheese. Top with the remaining potatoes and the sauce.

4 Sprinkle with the grated mozzarella or Cheddar cheese, then with the grated Parmesan or pecorino.

5 Bake in a preheated oven, 180°C/350°F/Gas Mark 4, for about 25 minutes, until the potatoes are tender and the cheese topping is lightly golden and has become crisp in places. Serve immediately straight from the casserole.

Vegetable Tostadas

Top a crisp tostada – fried tortilla – with spicy
vegetables and you have a vegetarian feast!

NUTRITIONAL INFORMATION

Calories	541	Sugars	. . . . .10g
Protein	. . . . .25g	Fat	. . . . .20g
Carbohydrate	. . .69g	Saturates	. . . . . . .9g

10 mins   20 mins

SERVES 4

INGREDIENTS

4 corn tortillas

vegetable oil, for frying

2–3 tbsp extra virgin olive oil or
vegetable oil

2 potatoes, diced

1 carrot, diced

3 garlic cloves, finely chopped

1 red pepper, deseeded and diced

1 tsp mild chilli powder

1 tsp paprika

½ tsp ground cumin

3–4 ripe tomatoes, diced

115 g/4 oz green beans, blanched and cut
into bite-size lengths

pinch of dried oregano

400 g/14 oz cooked black beans, drained

225 g/8 oz crumbled feta cheese

3–4 leaves cos lettuce, shredded

3–4 spring onions, thinly sliced

1 To make the tostadas, fry the tortillas in a small
amount of oil in a non-stick pan until crisp.

2 Heat the olive oil in a frying pan, add the potatoes and
carrot and cook until softened. Add the garlic, red
pepper, chilli powder, paprika and cumin. Cook for
2–3 minutes until the peppers have softened.

3 Add the tomatoes, green beans and oregano. Cook for
8–10 minutes until the vegetables are tender and form
a sauce-like mixture. The mixture should not be too dry;
add a little water if necessary, to keep it moist.

4 Heat the black beans in a pan with a tiny quantity
of water and keep warm. Reheat the tostadas under
the grill.

5 Layer the beans over the hot tostadas, then sprinkle
with the cheese and top with a few spoonfuls of the
hot vegetables in sauce. Serve immediately, each tostada
sprinkled with the lettuce and spring onions.

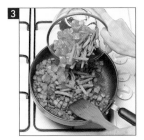

Black Bean Chilli

Black beans are fragrant and flavourful; enjoy this bean stew Mexican style with soft tortillas, or Californian style with crisp tortilla chips.

NUTRITIONAL INFORMATION

Calories	428	Sugars	........11g
Protein	........31g	Fat	..........10g
Carbohydrate	...53g	Saturates	.......2g

 8¼ hrs 2¾ hrs

SERVES 4

INGREDIENTS

400 g/14 oz dried black beans

2 tbsp olive oil

1 onion, chopped

5 garlic cloves, coarsely chopped

2 slices bacon, diced (optional)

½–1 tsp ground cumin

½–1 tsp mild chilli powder

1 red pepper, deseeded and diced

1 carrot, diced

400 g/14 oz fresh tomatoes, diced, or chopped canned tomatoes

1 bunch of fresh coriander, coarsely chopped

salt and pepper

1 Soak the beans overnight in cold water to cover, then drain. Put in a pan, cover with water and bring to the boil. Boil for 10 minutes, then reduce the heat and simmer for about 1½ hours until tender. Drain well, reserving 225 ml/8 fl oz of the cooking liquid.

2 Heat the oil in a frying pan. Add the onion and garlic and cook over a low heat, stirring occasionally, for 2 minutes. Stir in the bacon, if using, and cook, stirring occasionally, until the bacon is cooked and the onion is softened. but not browned.

3 Stir in the cumin and chilli powder and continue to cook, stirring constantly, for a few seconds. Add the red pepper, carrot and tomatoes. Cook over a medium heat for about 5 minutes.

4 Add half the coriander and the beans and their reserved liquid. Season to taste with salt and pepper. Simmer for 30–45 minutes or until the stew is very flavourful and thickened.

5 Stir in the remaining coriander, taste and adjust the seasoning, if necessary and serve immediately.

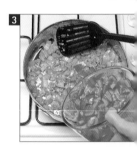

COOK'S TIP

You can use canned beans, if wished: drain and use 225 ml/8 fl oz water for the liquid added in Step 4.

Dolmas

Start a Greek meal with these vegetarian stuffed vine leaves. You will need a large frying pan with a lid to hold all the stuffed vine leaves.

NUTRITIONAL INFORMATION

Calories	82	Sugars	.........2g
Protein	.........1g	Fat	...........7g
Carbohydrate	....5g	Saturates	.......1g

1¼ hrs   45 mins

MAKES 25–30

INGREDIENTS

225 g/8 oz vine leaves preserved in brine, about 40 in total

150 ml/5 fl oz olive oil

4 tbsp lemon juice

300 ml/10 fl oz water

lemon wedges, to serve

FILLING

115 g/4 oz long-grain rice, not basmati

350 ml/12 fl oz water

55 g/2 oz currants

55 g/2 oz pine kernels, chopped

2 spring onions, very finely chopped

1 tbsp very finely chopped fresh coriander

1 tbsp very finely chopped fresh parsley

1 tbsp very finely chopped fresh dill

finely grated rind of ½ lemon

salt and pepper

1 Rinse the vine leaves under cold running water and place them in a heatproof bowl. Pour over enough boiling water to cover and set aside to soak for 5 minutes. Drain well.

2 Meanwhile, place the rice and water in a pan with a pinch of salt and bring to the boil. Lower the heat, cover and simmer for 10–12 minutes or until all the liquid is completely absorbed. Drain and set aside to cool.

3 Stir the currants, pine kernels, spring onions, coriander, parsley, dill and lemon rind into the cooled rice. Season to taste with salt and pepper.

4 Line the bottom of a large frying pan with 3 or 4 of the thickest vine leaves or with any that are torn.

5 Put a vine leaf on the work surface, vein side upwards, with the pointed end facing away from you. Put a small, compact roll of the rice stuffing at the base of the leaf. Fold up the bottom end of the leaf.

6 Fold in each side to overlap in the centre. Roll up the leaf around the filling. Squeeze lightly in your hand. Continue this process with the remaining leaves and stuffing mixture.

7 Place the leaf rolls in a single layer in the pan, seam side down. Combine the olive oil, lemon juice and water and pour into the pan.

8 Fit a heatproof plate over the rolls and cover the pan. Simmer for 30 minutes. Remove from the heat and set the stuffed vine leaves aside to cool in the liquid. Serve chilled with lemon wedges.

Spinach & Herb Frittata

If you find the prospect of turning over a Spanish tortilla daunting, try this Italian version of a flat omelette, that finishes cooking under a grill.

NUTRITIONAL INFORMATION

Calories	145	Sugars	.........0g
Protein	.........8g	Fat	..........12g
Carbohydrate	....1g	Saturates	......13g

  15 mins   12 mins

SERVES 6–8

INGREDIENTS

4 tbsp olive oil

6 spring onions, sliced

250 g/9 oz young spinach leaves, any coarse stems removed, rinsed

6 large eggs

3 tbsp finely chopped mixed fresh herbs, such as flat leaf parsley, thyme and coriander

2 tbsp freshly grated Parmesan cheese, plus extra for garnishing

salt and pepper

fresh parsley sprigs, to garnish

1 Heat a 25 cm/10 inch frying pan, preferably non-stick with a flameproof handle, over a medium heat. Add the oil and heat. Add the spring onions and cook for about 2 minutes.

2 Add the spinach and cook until it just wilts.

3 Beat the eggs in a large bowl and season to taste with salt and pepper. Using a draining spoon, transfer the spinach and onions to the bowl of eggs and stir in the herbs. Pour the excess oil left in the frying pan into a heatproof jug, then scrape off the crusty bits from the base of the pan.

4 Reheat the pan. Add 2 tablespoons of the reserved oil. Pour in the egg mixture, smoothing it into an even layer. Cook, shaking the pan occasionally, for 6 minutes or until the base is set when you lift up the side with a spatula.

5 Sprinkle the top of the frittata with the Parmesan. Place the pan under a preheated grill and cook for about 3 minutes or until the excess liquid is set and the cheese is golden.

6 Remove the pan from the heat and slide the frittata on to a serving plate. Set aside for at least 5 minutes before cutting and garnishing with extra Parmesan and parsley. Serve hot, warm or at room temperature.

Lentil & Mushroom Pie

This makes a great dish for a dinner party main course, as it is rich in texture, tasty and filling, and the topping looks hugely appetizing.

NUTRITIONAL INFORMATION

Calories	439	Sugars	.........2g
Protein	........18g	Fat	..........9g
Carbohydrate	...75g	Saturates	.......4g

🧈 1 hr 10 mins ⏱ 1½ hrs

SERVES 6

INGREDIENTS

175 g/6 oz Puy or green lentils

2 bay leaves

6 shallots, sliced

1.2 litres/2 pints vegetable stock

salt and pepper

55 g/2 oz butter

225 g/8 oz long-grain rice

8 sheets filo pastry, thawed if frozen

2 tbsp chopped fresh parsley

2 tsp chopped fresh fennel or savory

4 eggs, 1 beaten and 3 hard-boiled and sliced

225 g/8 oz field mushrooms

1 Preheat the oven to 190°C/375°F/Gas Mark 5. Put the lentils, bay leaves and half the shallots into a large, heavy-based saucepan. Add half the stock, bring to the boil and simmer for 25 minutes, or until the lentils are tender. Remove from the heat, season to taste with salt and pepper and leave to cool completely.

2 Melt half the butter in a heavy-based saucepan, then add the remaining shallots and cook, stirring occasionally, for 5 minutes, or until softened.

3 Stir in the rice and cook, stirring constantly, for 1 minute, then add the remaining stock. Season to taste with salt and pepper and bring to the boil. Reduce the heat, then cover and simmer for 15 minutes. Remove the saucepan from the heat and leave to cool completely.

4 Melt the remaining butter over a low heat, then brush an ovenproof dish with a little of it. Arrange the filo sheets in the dish with the sides overhanging (these will make the pie lid), brushing each sheet with melted butter. Add the parsley and fennel to the rice mixture, then beat in the beaten egg.

5 Make layers of rice, hard-boiled egg, lentils and mushrooms in the dish, seasoning each layer. Bring up the filo sheets and scrunch into folds on top of the pie. Brush with melted butter and chill for 15 minutes.

6 Bake in the oven for 45 minutes. Leave to stand for 10 minutes before serving.

Pizza Biancas

Simple, fresh flavours are the highlight of this thin pizza.
For the best results, use buffalo mozzarella imported from Italy.

NUTRITIONAL INFORMATION

Calories	1191	Sugars	.........5g
Protein	........60g	Fat	..........40g
Carbohydrate	..158g	Saturates	......21g

  1½ hrs 15 mins

MAKES TWO 23 CM/9 INCH PIZZAS

INGREDIENTS

400 g/14 oz plain flour, plus extra
  for dusting

1 sachet easy-blend dried yeast

1 tsp salt

1 tbsp extra virgin olive oil, plus extra
  for greasing

TOPPING

2 courgettes

300 g/10½ oz buffalo mozzarella

1½–2 tbsp finely chopped fresh rosemary,
  or ½ tbsp dried rosemary

1 To make the crust, heat 225 ml/8 fl oz water in the microwave on High for 1 minute or until it reads 52°C/125°F on an instant-read thermometer. Alternatively, heat the water in a pan over a low heat until lukewarm.

2 Stir the flour, yeast and salt together and make a well in the centre. Stir in most of the water with the olive oil to make a dough. Add the remaining water, if necessary, to form a soft dough.

3 Turn out on to a lightly floured surface and knead for about 10 minutes until smooth but still soft. Wash the bowl and lightly coat with olive oil. Shape the dough into a ball, put in the bowl and turn the dough over so it is coated. Cover and set aside until doubled in size.

4 Turn the dough out on to a lightly floured surface. Quickly knead a few times, then cover with the upturned bowl and set aside for 10 minutes.

5 Meanwhile, using a vegetable peeler, cut long, thin strips of courgettes. Drain and dice the mozzarella.

6 Divide the dough in half and shape each half into a ball. Cover 1 ball and roll out the other into a 23 cm/9 inch round. Place the round on a lightly floured baking sheet.

7 Scatter half the mozzarella over the base. Add half the courgette strips and sprinkle with half the rosemary. Repeat with the remaining dough and topping ingredients.

8 Bake in a preheated oven, 220°C/ 425°F/Gas Mark 7, for 15 minutes or until crispy. Serve immediately.

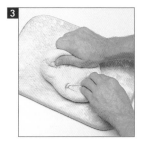

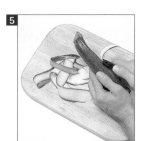

Baked Aubergine Gratin

Serve plenty of crusty French bread with this dish because it soaks up the delicious juices.

NUTRITIONAL INFORMATION

Calories	261	Sugars	.........5g
Protein	........20g	Fat	..........18g
Carbohydrate	....6g	Saturates	......10g

45 mins

40 mins

SERVES 4–6

INGREDIENTS

1 large aubergine, about 800 g/1 lb 12 oz

300 g/10½ oz mozzarella cheese

85 g/3 oz Parmesan cheese

olive oil

about 250 ml/9 fl oz Tomato Sauce (see page 7), or good-quality bottled tomato sauce for pasta

salt and pepper

1 Top and tail the aubergine and, using a sharp knife, cut it into 5 mm/¼ inch slices crossways. Arrange the slices on a large plate, sprinkle with salt and set aside for 30 minutes to drain.

2 Meanwhile, drain and grate the mozzarella cheese and finely grate the Parmesan cheese. Set aside.

3 Rinse the aubergine slices thoroughly under cold running water and pat dry with kitchen paper. Lightly brush a baking sheet with olive oil and arrange the aubergine slices in a single layer. Brush the tops with olive oil.

4 Roast in a preheated oven, 200°C/ 400°F/Gas Mark 6, for 5 minutes. Using tongs, turn the slices over, then brush with a little more olive oil and bake for a further 5 minutes or until the

aubergine is cooked through and tender. Do not turn off the oven.

5 Spread about 1 tablespoon olive oil over the bottom of a gratin dish or other ovenproof serving dish. Add a layer of aubergine slices, about a quarter of the tomato sauce and top with a quarter of the mozzarella. Season to taste with salt and pepper.

6 Continue layering until all the ingredients are used, ending with a layer of sauce. Sprinkle the Parmesan over the top. Bake for 30 minutes until bubbling. Set aside for about 5 minutes before serving.

Chinese Vegetable Pancakes

Chinese pancakes are made with hardly any fat – they are simply flattened white flour dough.

NUTRITIONAL INFORMATION

Calories	312	Sugars	.........5g
Protein	........13g	Fat	..........19g
Carbohydrate	...25g	Saturates	......7g

 5 mins   🕙 10 mins

SERVES 4

INGREDIENTS

1 tbsp vegetable oil

1 garlic clove, crushed

2.5 cm/1 inch piece of fresh root ginger, grated

1 bunch of spring onions, trimmed and shredded lengthways

100 g/3½ oz mangetouts, shredded

225 g/8 oz tofu, drained and cut into 1 cm/ ½ inch pieces

2 tbsp dark soy sauce, plus extra to serve

2 tbsp hoisin sauce, plus extra to serve

55 g/2 oz canned bamboo shoots, drained

55 g/2 oz canned water chestnuts, drained and sliced

100 g/3½ oz beansprouts

1 small fresh red chilli, deseeded and thinly sliced

1 small bunch of fresh chives

12 soft Chinese pancakes

TO SERVE

shredded Chinese leaves

1 cucumber, sliced

strips of fresh red chilli

1 Heat the oil in a non-stick wok or a large frying pan and stir-fry the garlic and ginger for 1 minute.

2 Add the spring onions, mangetouts, tofu, soy and hoisin sauces. Stir-fry for 2 minutes.

3 Add the bamboo shoots, water chestnuts, beansprouts and chilli to the pan. Stir-fry gently for 2 minutes until the vegetables are just tender.

4 Snip the chives into 2.5 cm/1 inch lengths and stir into the mixture.

5 Heat the pancakes according to the packet instructions and keep warm.

6 Divide the vegetables and tofu equally between the pancakes. Roll up and serve with Chinese leaves, cucumber, chilli strips, and soy and hoisin sauces for dipping.

Mixed Vegetable Balti

Any combination of vegetables or pulses can be used in this recipe. It would make a good dish for an informal vegetarian supper party.

NUTRITIONAL INFORMATION

Calories	207	Sugars	.........6g
Protein	.........8g	Fat	...........9g
Carbohydrate	...24g	Saturates	......1g

10 mins   1 hr

SERVES 4

INGREDIENTS

225 g/8 oz split yellow peas

3 tbsp vegetable oil

1 tsp onion seeds

2 onions, sliced

115 g/4 oz courgettes, sliced

115 g/4 oz potatoes, cut into 1 cm/
   ½ inch cubes

115 g/4 oz carrots, sliced

1 small aubergine, sliced

225 g/8 oz tomatoes, chopped

300 ml/10 fl oz water

3 garlic cloves, chopped

1 tsp ground cumin

1 tsp ground coriander

1 tsp salt

2 fresh green chillies, sliced

½ tsp garam masala

2 tbsp chopped fresh coriander

3 Add the onions and stir-fry over a medium heat until golden brown.

4 Add the courgettes, potatoes, carrots and aubergine to the pan. Stir-fry the vegetables for about 2 minutes.

5 Stir in the tomatoes, water, garlic, cumin, ground coriander, salt, chillies, garam masala and reserved split peas.

6 Bring to the boil, then lower the heat and simmer for 15 minutes until all the vegetables are tender.

7 Stir the fresh coriander into the vegetables. Transfer to a warmed serving dish and serve immediately.

1 Put the split peas into a pan and cover with lightly salted water. Bring to the boil and simmer for 30 minutes. Drain the peas and keep warm.

2 Heat the oil in a karahi or wok, add the onion seeds and fry until they start popping.

Tofu Skewers

Although tofu is rather bland on its own, it develops a fabulous flavour when it is marinated in garlic and herbs.

NUTRITIONAL INFORMATION

Calories	149	Sugars	.........5g
Protein	........13g	Fat	..........9g
Carbohydrate	....5g	Saturates	......1g

40 mins   15 mins

SERVES 4

INGREDIENTS

350 g/12 oz tofu

1 red pepper

1 yellow pepper

2 courgettes

8 button mushrooms

lemon slices, to garnish

MARINADE

grated rind and juice of ½ lemon

1 garlic clove, crushed

½ tsp chopped fresh rosemary

½ tsp chopped fresh thyme

1 tbsp walnut oil

1 To make the marinade, combine the lemon rind and juice, garlic, rosemary, thyme and oil in a shallow dish.

2 Drain the tofu, pat it dry on kitchen paper and cut it into squares with a sharp knife. Add to the marinade and toss to coat. Cover and set aside to marinate for 20–30 minutes.

3 Meanwhile, deseed and cut the peppers into 2.5 cm/1 inch pieces. Blanch in boiling water for 4 minutes, refresh in cold water and drain.

4 Using a canelle knife or potato peeler, remove strips of peel from the courgettes. Cut the courgette into 2.5 cm/ 1 inch chunks.

5 Remove the tofu from the marinade, reserving the liquid. Thread it on to 8 skewers, alternating with the peppers, courgette and button mushrooms.

6 Barbecue the skewers over medium hot coals for about 6 minutes, turning and basting with the reserved marinade. Alternatively, cook under a preheated grill. Transfer the skewers to warmed individual serving plates, garnish with slices of lemon and serve.

Potato & Tomato Calzone

These pizza dough Italian pasties are best served hot with a salad for a delicious lunch or supper dish.

NUTRITIONAL INFORMATION

Calories . . . . . . .524 Sugars 8g
Protein . . . . .17g Fat 8g
Carbohydrate . .103g Saturates 2g

1½ hrs   35 mins

SERVES 4

I N G R E D I E N T S

DOUGH

450 g/1 lb white bread flour

1 tsp easy blend dried yeast

300 ml/10 fl oz vegetable stock

1 tbsp clear honey

1 tsp caraway seeds

skimmed milk, for glazing

vegetable oil, for greasing

FILLING

1 tbsp vegetable oil

225 g/8 oz waxy potatoes, diced

1 onion, halved and sliced

2 garlic cloves, crushed

40 g/1½ oz sun-dried tomatoes, chopped

2 tbsp chopped fresh basil

2 tbsp tomato purée

2 celery sticks, sliced

50 g/1¾ oz mozzarella cheese, grated

1 To make the dough, sift the flour into a large mixing bowl and stir in the yeast. Make a well in the centre of the mixture. Stir in the vegetable stock, honey and caraway seeds and bring the mixture together to form a dough.

2 Turn the dough out on to a lightly floured surface and knead for 8 minutes until smooth. Place the dough in a lightly oiled mixing bowl, cover and leave to rise in a warm place for 1 hour or until it has doubled in size.

3 Meanwhile, make the filling. Heat the oil in a frying pan and add all the remaining ingredients except for the cheese. Cook for about 5 minutes, stirring.

4 Divide the risen dough into 4 pieces. On a lightly floured surface, roll them out to form four 18 cm/ 7 inch circles. Spoon equal amounts of the filling on to one half of each circle. Sprinkle the cheese over the filling. Brush the edge of the dough with milk and fold the dough over to form 4 semi-circles, pressing to seal the edges.

5 Place on a non-stick baking tray and brush with milk. Cook in a preheated oven, 220°C/425°F/Gas Mark 7, for 30 minutes until golden and risen.

Coconut Vegetable Curry

A mildly spiced but richly flavoured Indian-style dish full of different textures and flavours. Serve with naan bread to soak up the tasty sauce.

NUTRITIONAL INFORMATION

Calories	159	Sugars	.........8g
Protein	.........8g	Fat	...........6g
Carbohydrate	...19g	Saturates	......1g

1¾ hrs   35 mins

SERVES 4

INGREDIENTS

1 large aubergine, cut into 2.5 cm/
   1 inch cubes

2 tbsp vegetable oil

2 garlic cloves, crushed

1 fresh green chilli, deseeded and
   finely chopped

1 tsp grated fresh root ginger

1 onion, finely chopped

2 tsp garam masala

8 cardamom pods

1 tsp ground turmeric

1 tbsp tomato purée

700 ml/1¼ pints Fresh Vegetable Stock (see
   page 8)

1 tbsp lemon juice

225 g/8 oz potatoes, diced

250 g/9 oz small cauliflower florets

225 g/8 oz okra, trimmed

225 g/8 oz frozen peas

150 ml/5 fl oz coconut milk

salt and pepper

flaked coconut, to garnish

naan bread, to serve

1 Layer the aubergine in a bowl, sprinkling with salt as you go. Set aside for 30 minutes. Rinse well under running water. Drain and dry. Set aside.

2 Heat the oil in a large pan and gently cook the garlic, chilli, ginger, onion and spices for 4–5 minutes.

3 Stir in the tomato purée, stock, lemon juice, potatoes and cauliflower and mix well. Bring to the boil, cover and simmer for 15 minutes.

4 Stir in the aubergine, okra, peas and coconut milk and season with salt and pepper to taste. Continue to simmer, uncovered, for a further 10 minutes until tender. Discard the cardamom pods. Pile the curry on to a warmed serving platter, garnish with flaked coconut and serve with naan bread.

Stuffed Vegetables

You can fill your favourite vegetables with this nutty-tasting combination of cracked wheat, tomatoes and cucumber.

NUTRITIONAL INFORMATION

Calories	194	Sugars	.........7g
Protein	.........5g	Fat	...........4g
Carbohydrate	...36g	Saturates	.....0.5g

40 mins   25 mins

SERVES 4

INGREDIENTS

4 large beef tomatoes

4 medium courgettes

2 orange peppers

salt and pepper

FILLING

225 g/8 oz cracked wheat

¼ cucumber

1 medium red onion

2 tbsp lemon juice

2 tbsp chopped fresh coriander

2 tbsp chopped fresh mint

1 tbsp olive oil

2 tsp cumin seeds

TO SERVE

warm pitta bread

low-fat hummus

1 Cut off the tops of the tomatoes and reserve. Using a teaspoon, scoop out the tomato pulp, chop and place in a bowl. Season the tomato shells, then turn them upside down on kitchen paper.

2 Trim the courgettes and cut a V-shaped groove lengthways down each one. Finely chop the cut-out courgette flesh and add to the tomato pulp. Season the courgettes shells and set aside. Halve the peppers. Leaving the stalks intact, cut out the seeds and discard. Season the pepper shells and set aside.

3 To make the filling, soak the cracked wheat according to the instructions on the packet. Finely chop the cucumber and add to the reserved tomato pulp and courgette mixture. Finely chop the red onion, and add to the vegetable mixture with the lemon juice, herbs, olive oil, and cumin and mix together well. Season to taste with salt and pepper.

4 When the wheat has soaked, mix with the vegetables and stuff into the tomato, courgette and pepper shells. Place the tops on the tomatoes, transfer to a roasting tin and bake in a preheated oven, 220°C/400°F/Gas Mark 6, for about 20–25 minutes until cooked through. Drain and serve with pitta bread and hummus.

Curried Vegetable Kebabs

Warmed Indian bread is served with barbecued vegetable kebabs, which are brushed with a curry-spiced yogurt baste.

NUTRITIONAL INFORMATION

Calories ......396 Sugars 11g
Protein ....13g Fat 13g
Carbohydrate ...60g Saturates 0.3g

25 mins 20 mins

SERVES 4

INGREDIENTS

YOGURT BASTE

150 ml/5 fl oz low-fat natural yogurt

1 tbsp chopped fresh mint or 1 tsp dried mint

1 tsp ground cumin

1 tsp ground coriander

½ tsp chilli powder

pinch of ground turmeric

pinch of ground ginger

salt and pepper

KEBABS

8 small new potatoes

1 small aubergine

1 courgette, cut into chunks

8 chestnut or closed-cup mushrooms

8 small tomatoes

fresh mint sprigs, to garnish

warm naan bread, to serve

1 To make the spiced yogurt baste, combine the yogurt and the spices. Season to taste with salt and pepper. Cover and chill.

2 Boil the potatoes until just tender. Meanwhile, chop the aubergine into chunks and sprinkle them liberally with salt. Set aside for 10–15 minutes to extract the bitter juices. Rinse and drain them well. Drain the potatoes.

3 Thread the vegetables on to 4 metal or wooden skewers, alternating the different types. If using wooden skewers, soak in warm water for 10 minutes.

4 Place the skewers in a shallow dish and evenly coat with the yogurt baste. Cover with clingfilm and chill until required. Wrap the naan bread in foil and place towards one side of the barbecue to warm through.

5 Cook the kebabs over the barbecue, basting with any remaining spiced yogurt, until they just begin to char slightly. Serve the kebabs immediately with the warmed naan bread, garnished with sprigs of fresh mint.

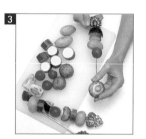

Aubergine Gratin

Similar to a simple moussaka, this recipe is made up of layers of tomatoes, aubergine and potatoes.

NUTRITIONAL INFORMATION

Calories 409   Sugars 17g
Protein . . . . .28g   Fat 14g
Carbohydrate . . .45g   Saturates 3g

15 mins   1¼ hrs

SERVES 4

I N G R E D I E N T S

450 g/1 lb waxy potatoes, sliced

1 tbsp vegetable oil

1 onion, chopped

2 garlic cloves, crushed

450 g/1 lb tofu, diced

2 tbsp tomato purée

2 tbsp plain flour

300 ml/10 fl oz vegetable stock

2 large tomatoes, sliced

1 aubergine, sliced

2 tbsp chopped fresh thyme

500 ml/18 fl oz low-fat natural yogurt

2 eggs, beaten

salt and pepper

1 Cook the sliced potatoes in a pan of boiling water for 10 minutes until just tender but not breaking up. Drain and set aside.

2 Heat the oil in a heavy-based pan and cook the onion and garlic, stirring occasionally, for 2–3 minutes.

3 Add the diced tofu, tomato purée and flour and cook, stirring constantly, for 1 minute. Gradually stir in the vegetable stock and bring to the boil, stirring constantly. Reduce the heat and simmer for 10 minutes.

4 Arrange a layer of the potato slices in the base of a deep ovenproof dish. Spoon the tofu mixture on top.

5 Layer the tomatoes, then the aubergine and then the remaining potato slices on top of the tofu mixture, so that it is completely covered.

6 Combine the yogurt and beaten eggs in a bowl and season to taste with salt and pepper. Spoon the yogurt topping over the sliced potatoes.

7 Cook the gratin in a preheated oven, 190°C/375°F/Gas Mark 5, for 35–45 minutes or until the topping is browned. Serve hot.

Vegetable Curry

This colourful and interesting mixture of vegetables, cooked in a spicy sauce, is excellent served with rice and naan bread.

NUTRITIONAL INFORMATION

Calories	.421	Sugars	.20g
Protein	.12g	Fat	.24g
Carbohydrate	.42g	Saturates	.3g

 10 mins   45 mins

SERVES 4

INGREDIENTS

225 g/8 oz turnips or swede

1 aubergine

350 g/12 oz new potatoes

225 g/8 oz cauliflower

225 g/8 oz button mushrooms

1 large onion

3 carrots

6 tbsp vegetable ghee or vegetable oil

2 garlic cloves, crushed

4 tsp finely chopped fresh root ginger

1–2 fresh green chillies, deseeded and chopped

1 tbsp paprika

2 tsp ground coriander

1 tbsp mild or medium curry powder or paste

450 ml/16 fl oz vegetable stock

400 g/14 oz canned chopped tomatoes

1 green pepper, deseeded and sliced

1 tbsp cornflour

150 ml/5 fl oz coconut milk

2–3 tbsp ground almonds

salt

fresh coriander sprigs, to garnish

1 Cut the turnips or swede, aubergine and potatoes into 1 cm/1/2 inch cubes. Divide the cauliflower into small florets. Leave the mushrooms whole or slice them thickly if preferred. Slice the onion and carrots.

2 Heat the ghee or oil in a large pan. Add the onion, turnip or swede, potato and cauliflower and cook over a low heat, stirring frequently, for 3 minutes.

3 Add the garlic, ginger, chillies, paprika, ground coriander and curry powder or paste and cook, stirring, for 1 minute.

4 Add the stock, tomatoes, aubergine and mushrooms and season with salt. Cover and simmer, stirring occasionally, for about 30 minutes or until tender. Add the green pepper and carrots, cover and cook for a further 5 minutes.

5 Blend the cornflour with the coconut milk to a smooth paste and stir into the mixture. Add the ground almonds and simmer, stirring constantly, for 2 minutes. Taste and adjust the seasoning if necessary. Transfer to serving plates and serve hot, garnished with coriander sprigs.

Pesto Pasta

Italian pesto is usually laden with fat. This version has just as much flavour, but is much healthier.

NUTRITIONAL INFORMATION

Calories	283	Sugars	.........5g
Protein	........14g	Fat	...........3g
Carbohydrate	...37g	Saturates	......1g

1 hr 🕐 30 mins

SERVES 4

INGREDIENTS

25 g/8 oz chestnut mushrooms, sliced

150 ml/5 fl oz fresh vegetable stock

175 g/6 oz asparagus, trimmed and cut into
  5 cm/2 inch lengths

300 g/10½ oz green and white tagliatelle

400 g/14 oz canned artichoke hearts,
  drained and halved

grissini, to serve

PESTO

2 large garlic cloves, crushed

15 g/½ oz fresh basil leaves

6 tbsp low-fat natural fromage frais

2 tbsp freshly grated Parmesan cheese

salt and pepper

TO GARNISH

shredded fresh basil leaves

Parmesan shavings

1 Place the mushrooms in a pan with the stock. Bring to the boil, cover and simmer for 3–4 minutes until just tender. Drain and set aside, reserving the cooking liquid to use in soups if wished.

2 Bring a small pan of water to the boil and cook the asparagus for 3–4 minutes until just tender. Drain and set aside until required.

3 Bring a large pan of lightly salted water to the boil. Add the pasta, bring back to the boil and cook until tender, but still firm to the bite: 8–10 minutes for dried pasta or 2–3 minutes for fresh tagliatelle. Drain, return to the pan and keep warm.

4 Meanwhile, make the pesto. Place all of the ingredients in a blender or food processor and process for a few seconds until smooth. Alternatively, finely chop the basil and mix all the ingredients together.

5 Add the mushrooms, asparagus and artichoke hearts to the pasta and cook, stirring, over a low heat for 2–3 minutes., Remove from the heat and mix with the pesto.

6 Transfer to a warm bowl. Garnish with basil and Parmesan and serve.

Mixed Bean Stir-fry

Any type of canned beans can be used, such as butter beans or black-eyed beans, but rinse them under cold water and drain well before use.

NUTRITIONAL INFORMATION

Calories	326	Sugars	........16g
Protein	........18g	Fat	...........7g
Carbohydrate	...51g	Saturates	......1g

10 mins   10 mins

SERVES 4

INGREDIENTS

400 g/14 oz can red kidney beans

400 g/14 oz can cannellini beans

6 spring onions

200 g/7 oz can pineapple rings or pieces in natural juice, chopped

2 tbsp pineapple juice

3-4 pieces of stem ginger

2 tbsp ginger syrup from the jar

thinly pared rind of ½ lime or lemon, cut into julienne strips

2 tbsp lime or lemon juice

2 tbsp soy sauce

1 tsp cornflour

1 tbsp sesame oil

115 g/4 oz French beans, cut into 4 cm/ 1½ inch lengths

225 g/8 oz can bamboo shoots

salt and pepper

1 Drain all the beans, rinse under cold water and drain again very thoroughly.

2 Cut 4 spring onions into narrow diagonal slices. Thinly slice the remainder and reserve for garnish.

3 Combine the pineapple and juice, ginger and syrup, lime rind and juice, soy sauce and cornflour in a bowl.

4 Heat the oil in the wok, swirling it around until really hot. Add the diagonally sliced spring onions and stir-fry for about a minute, then add the French beans. Drain and thinly slice the bamboo shoots, add to the pan and continue to stir-fry for 2 minutes.

5 Add the pineapple and ginger mixture and bring just to the boil. Add the canned beans and stir until very hot – for about a minute.

6 Season to taste with salt and pepper, sprinkle with the reserved chopped spring onions and serve.

COOK'S TIP

Beans are an important source of protein for vegetarians. Combine them with rice or other cereals for a really healthy balance.

Biryani with Onions

An assortment of vegetables cooked with tender rice, flavoured and coloured with bright yellow turmeric and other warming Indian spices.

NUTRITIONAL INFORMATION

Calories 223	Sugars 18g
Protein 8g	Fat 4g
Carbohydrate . . .42g	Saturates 1g

🍲 1¼ hrs   🕒 25 mins

SERVES 4

I N G R E D I E N T S

175 g/6 oz basmati rice, rinsed

55 g/2 oz red lentils, rinsed

1 bay leaf

6 cardamom pods, split

1 tsp ground turmeric

6 cloves

1 tsp cumin seeds

1 cinnamon stick, broken

1 onion, chopped

225 g/8 oz cauliflower, broken into
    small florets

1 large carrot, diced

100 g/3½ oz frozen peas

55 g/2 oz sultanas

600 ml/1 pint Fresh Vegetable Stock (see
    page 8)

salt and pepper

naan bread, to serve

C A R A M E L I Z E D   O N I O N S

2 tsp vegetable oil

1 medium red onion, shredded

1 medium onion, shredded

2 tsp caster sugar

 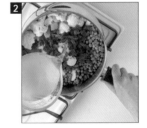 

1 Place the rice, lentils, bay leaf, spices, onion, cauliflower, carrot, peas and sultanas in a large pan. Season with salt and pepper to taste and mix well.

2 Pour in the stock, bring to the boil, cover and simmer for 15 minutes, stirring occasionally, until the rice is tender. Remove from the heat and set aside, covered, for 10 minutes to allow the stock to be absorbed. Remove and discard the bay leaf, cardamom pods, cloves and cinnamon stick.

3 Heat the oil in a frying pan and add the onions. Fry them over a medium heat for about 3–4 minutes until they are just softened. Add the caster sugar, increase the heat and then cook, stirring constantly, for a further 2–3 minutes until the onions are golden.

4 Gently combine the rice and vegetables and transfer to warm serving plates. Spoon over the caramelized onions and serve immediately with plain, warmed naan bread.

Gnocchi with Tomato Sauce

Freshly made potato gnocchi are delicious, especially when they are topped with a fragrant tomato sauce.

NUTRITIONAL INFORMATION

Calories	.216	Sugars	.5g
Protein	.5g	Fat	.6g
Carbohydrate	.39g	Saturates	.1g

30 mins   45 mins

SERVES 4

INGREDIENTS

350 g/12 oz floury potatoes, halved

85 g/3 oz self-raising flour, plus extra for dusting

2 tsp dried oregano

2 tbsp vegetable oil

1 large onion, chopped

2 garlic cloves, chopped

400 g/14 oz canned chopped tomatoes

½ vegetable stock cube dissolved in 100 ml/3½ fl oz boiling water

2 tbsp fresh basil, shredded, plus whole leaves to garnish

salt and pepper

Parmesan cheese, freshly grated, to serve

1 Bring a large saucepan of water to the boil. Add the potatoes and cook for 12–15 minutes or until tender. Drain and set aside to cool.

2 Peel and then mash the potatoes with the salt and pepper, sifted flour and oregano. Mix together with your hands to form a dough.

3 Heat the oil in a pan. Add the onions and garlic and cook for 3–4 minutes. Add the tomatoes and stock and cook, uncovered, for 10 minutes. Season with salt and pepper to taste.

4 Roll the potato dough into a sausage about 2.5 cm/1 inch in diameter. Cut the sausage into 2.5 cm/1 inch lengths. Flour your hands, then press a fork into each piece to create a series of ridges on one side and the indent of your index finger on the other.

5 Bring a large saucepan of water to the boil, add the gnocchi in batches and cook for 2–3 minutes. They should rise to the surface when cooked. Remove from the pan with a draining spoon, drain well and keep warm while you cook the remaining batches.

6 Stir the basil into the tomato sauce and pour over the gnocchi. Garnish with basil leaves and season with pepper to taste. Sprinkle with grated Parmesan and serve immediately.

VARIATION

The gnocchi can also be served with a pesto sauce made from fresh basil leaves, pine kernels, garlic, olive oil and pecorino or Parmesan cheese

Green Easter Pie

This traditional Easter risotto pie is from the Piedmont region in northern Italy. Serve it warm or chilled in slices.

NUTRITIONAL INFORMATION

Calories	392	Sugars	.........3g
Protein	........17g	Fat	..........17g
Carbohydrate	...41g	Saturates	.......5g

🔺 25 mins   🕐 50 mins

SERVES 4

I N G R E D I E N T S

butter, for greasing

85 g/3 oz rocket leaves

2 tbsp olive oil

1 onion, chopped

2 garlic cloves, chopped

200 g/7 oz arborio rice

700 ml/1¼ pints hot chicken or
  vegetable stock

125 ml/4 fl oz white wine

55 g/2 oz Parmesan cheese,
  freshly grated

115 g/4 oz frozen peas, thawed

2 tomatoes, diced

4 eggs, beaten

3 tbsp fresh marjoram, chopped

55 g/2 oz fresh breadcrumbs

salt and pepper

4. Add the rice to the frying pan, mix well to combine, then begin adding the stock a ladleful at a time. Wait until each ladleful of stock has been absorbed before adding the next.

5. Continue to cook the mixture, adding the wine, until the rice is tender. This will take at least 15 minutes. Remove the pan from the heat.

6. Stir in the Parmesan cheese, peas, rocket leaves, tomatoes, eggs and 2 tablespoons of the marjoram. Season to taste with salt and pepper.

7. Spoon the risotto into the prepared tin and level the surface by pressing down with the back of a wooden spoon.

8. Top with the breadcrumbs and the remaining marjoram.

9. Bake in a preheated oven, 180°C/350°F/Gas Mark 4, for 30 minutes or until set. Cut into slices and serve.

1. Lightly grease a 23 cm/9 inch deep cake tin and line the base.

2. Using a sharp knife, roughly chop the rocket leaves.

3. Heat the oil in a frying pan and fry the onion and garlic over a low heat for 4–5 minutes or until softened.

Pasta Omelette

This is a superb way of using up any leftover
pasta, such as penne, macaroni or conchiglie.

NUTRITIONAL INFORMATION

Calories	460	Sugars	.........3g
Protein	........16g	Fat	..........34g
Carbohydrate	...23g	Saturates	.......6g

10 mins   15–20 mins

SERVES 2

INGREDIENTS

4 tbsp olive oil

1 small onion, chopped

1 fennel bulb, thinly sliced

115 g/4 oz potato, diced

1 garlic clove, chopped

4 eggs

1 tbsp chopped fresh flat leaf parsley

pinch of chilli powder

100 g/3½ oz cooked short pasta

2 tbsp stuffed green olives, halved

salt and pepper

fresh marjoram sprigs, to garnish

tomato salad, to serve

1 Heat half of the oil in a heavy-based
frying pan over a low heat. Add the
onion, fennel and potato and cook, stirring
occasionally, for 8-10 minutes, until the
potato is just tender.

2 Stir in the garlic and cook for
1 minute. Remove the pan from the
heat, transfer the vegetables to a plate
and set aside.

3 Beat the eggs until they are frothy.
Stir in the parsley and season with
salt, pepper and a pinch of chilli powder.

4 Heat 1 tbsp of the remaining oil in a
clean frying pan. Add half of the egg
mixture to the pan, then add the cooked
vegetables, pasta and half of the olives.
Pour in the remaining egg mixture and
cook until the sides begin to set.

5 Lift up the edges of the omelette with
a palette knife to allow the uncooked
egg to spread underneath. Cook, shaking
the pan occasionally, until the underside is
a light golden brown colour.

6 Slide the omelette out of the pan or
to a plate. Wipe the pan with kitchen
paper and heat the remaining oil. Inver
the omelette into the pan and cook unti
the other side is a golden brown colour.

7 Slide the omelette on to a warmed
serving dish and garnish with th
remaining olives and the marjoram. Cu
into wedges and serve with a tomato salad.

Three Cheese Bake

Serve this dish while the cheese is still hot and melted, because cooked cheese turns very rubbery if it is allowed to cool down.

NUTRITIONAL INFORMATION

Calories	710	Sugars	.........6g
Protein	........34g	Fat	..........30g
Carbohydrate	...80g	Saturates	......16g

🧀 5 mins 🕐 1 hr

SERVES 4

INGREDIENTS

butter, for greasing

400 g/14 oz dried penne pasta

2 eggs, beaten

350 g/12 oz ricotta cheese

4 fresh basil sprigs

115 g/4 oz mozzarella or halloumi
cheese, grated

70 g/2½ oz Parmesan cheese,
freshly grated

salt and pepper

fresh basil leaves, to garnish (optional)

selection of cooked vegetables, to serve

1 Lightly grease a large ovenproof dish with butter.

2 Bring a pan of lightly salted water to the boil. Add the pasta, bring back to the boil and cook for 8–10 minutes until just tender, but still firm to the bite. Drain the pasta, set aside and keep warm.

3 Beat the eggs into the ricotta cheese and season to taste.

4 Spoon half of the pasta into the base of the prepared dish and cover with half of the basil leaves.

5 Spoon over half of the ricotta cheese mixture. Sprinkle over the mozzarella or halloumi cheese and top with the remaining basil leaves. Cover with the remaining pasta and then spoon over the remaining ricotta cheese mixture. Lightly sprinkle the freshly grated Parmesan cheese over the top.

6 Bake in a preheated oven, 190°C/ 375°F/Gas Mark 5, for 30–40 minutes until golden brown and the cheese topping is hot and bubbling. Garnish with fresh basil leaves and serve immediately with a selection of cooked vegetables.

Traditional Cannelloni

You can buy ready made dried pasta tubes. However, if using fresh pasta (see page 6), you must cut out squares and roll them yourself.

NUTRITIONAL INFORMATION

Calories 342	Sugars 6g
Protein 15g	Fat 15g
Carbohydrate ...38g	Saturates 8g

 50 mins   30 mins

SERVES 4

INGREDIENTS

20 tubes dried cannelloni (about 200 g/ 7 oz) or 20 square sheets of fresh pasta (about 350 g/12 oz)

250 g/9 oz ricotta cheese

150 g/5½ oz frozen spinach, thawed

½ small red pepper, deseeded and diced

2 spring onions, chopped

butter, for greasing

150 ml/5 fl oz hot vegetable or stock

1 quantity Tomato Sauce (see page 7), made with 2 tbsp chopped fresh basil instead of parsley

25 g/1 oz Parmesan or pecorino cheese, freshly grated

salt and pepper

1 If necessary, pre-cook dried cannelloni. Bring a large pan of water to the boil, add the pasta, bring back to the boil and cook for 3–4 minutes. Cook in batches if this is easier.

2 Combine the ricotta, spinach, pepper, and spring onions in a bowl and season to taste with salt and pepper.

3 Lightly grease an ovenproof dish, large enough to contain all of the pasta tubes in a single layer, with a little butter. Spoon the ricotta mixture into the pasta tubes and place them into the prepared dish. If you are using fresh sheets of pasta, spread the ricotta mixture along one side of each fresh pasta square and roll up to form a tube.

4 Combine the stock and tomato Sauce and pour it over the pasta tubes.

5 Sprinkle the Parmesan or pecorino cheese over the cannelloni and bake in a preheated oven, 190°C/375°F/Gas Mark 5, for 20–25 minutes or until the pasta is cooked through and the topping is golden and bugling. Serve immediately.

VARIATION

If you would prefer a creamier version, omit the stock and the Tomato Sauce and replace with Béchamel Sauce (see page 6).

Paglia e Fieno

The name of this traditional dish – 'straw and hay' –
refers to the colours of the pasta when mixed together.

NUTRITIONAL INFORMATION

Calories	699	Sugars	.........7g
Protein	........26g	Fat	..........39g
Carbohydrate	...65g	Saturates	......23g

10 mins   10 mins

SERVES 4

INGREDIENTS

4 tbsp butter

450 g/1 lb fresh peas, shelled

200 ml/7 fl oz double cream

450 g/1 lb mixed fresh green and white
  spaghetti or tagliatelle

55 g/2 oz freshly grated Parmesan cheese,
  plus extra to serve

pinch of freshly grated nutmeg

salt and pepper

1 Melt the butter in a large pan. Add
the peas and cook, over a low heat,
for 2–3 minutes.

2 Using a measuring jug, pour 150 ml/
5 fl oz of the cream into the pan,
bring to the boil and then simmer for
1–1½ minutes or until slightly thickened.
Remove the pan from the heat.

3 Meanwhile, bring a large pan of
lightly salted water to the boil. Add
the spaghetti or tagliatelle, bring back to
the boil and cook for 2–3 minutes or until
just tender, but still firm to the bite.
Remove the pan from the heat, drain the
pasta thoroughly and return to the pan.

4 Add the peas and cream sauce to the
pasta. Return the pan to the heat and
add the remaining cream and the

Parmesan cheese and season to taste with
salt, pepper and grated nutmeg.

5 Using 2 forks, gently toss the pasta to
coat with the peas and cream sauce,
while heating through.

6 Transfer the pasta to a warmed
serving dish and serve immediately,
with extra Parmesan cheese.

VARIATION
Cook 140 g/5 oz sliced
button or oyster mushrooms in 4
tablespoons butter over a low
heat for 4–5 minutes. Stir into the
peas and cream sauce just before
adding to the pasta in step 4.

Green Tagliatelle with Garlic

A rich pasta dish for garlic lovers everywhere. It is quick and easy to prepare and full of flavour.

NUTRITIONAL INFORMATION

Calories	474	Sugars	.........3g
Protein	........16g	Fat	..........24g
Carbohydrate	...52g	Saturates	.......9g

 20 mins   15 mins

SERVES 4

INGREDIENTS

2 tbsp walnut oil

1 bunch of spring onions, sliced

2 garlic cloves, thinly sliced

225 g/8 oz sliced mushrooms

450 g/1 lb fresh green and white tagliatelle

225 g/8 oz frozen spinach, thawed and drained

115 g/4 oz full-fat soft cheese with garlic and herbs

4 tbsp single cream

55 g/2 oz chopped, unsalted pistachio nuts

2 tbsp shredded fresh basil

salt and pepper

Italian bread, to serve

fresh basil sprigs, to garnish

1 Heat the walnut oil in a large frying pan. Add the spring onions and garlic and cook for 1 minute until just softened.

2 Add the mushrooms to the pan, stir well, cover and cook over a low heat for about 5 minutes until just softened, but not browned.

3 Meanwhile, bring a large pan of lightly salted water to the boil. Add the tagliatelle, bring back to the boil and cook for 3–5 minutes or until tender, but still firm to the bite. Drain the tagliatelle thoroughly and return to the pan.

4 Add the spinach to the frying pan and heat through for 1–2 minutes. Add the cheese to the pan and heat until slightly melted. Stir in the cream and cook, without allowing the mixture to come to the boil, until warmed through.

5 Pour the sauce over the pasta, season to taste with salt and pepper and mix well. Heat through gently, stirring constantly, for 2–3 minutes.

6 Transfer the pasta to a warmed serving dish and sprinkle with the pistachios and shredded basil. Garnish with the fresh basil sprigs and serve immediately with focaccia, ciabatta or other Italian bread of your choice.

Patriotic Pasta

The ingredients of this dish have the same
bright colours as the Italian flag – hence its name.

NUTRITIONAL INFORMATION

Calories	325	Sugars	.........5g
Protein	.........8g	Fat	..........13g
Carbohydrate	...48g	Saturates	.......2g

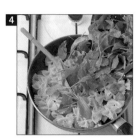

  5 mins   15 mins

SERVES 4

I N G R E D I E N T S

450 g/1 lb dried farfalle

3 tbsp olive oil

450 g/1 lb cherry tomatoes

85 g/3 oz rocket

salt and pepper

pecorino cheese, to garnish

1 Bring a large pan of lightly salted
water to the boil. Add the farfalle,
bring back to the boil and cook for
8–10 minutes or until tender, but still firm
to the bite. Drain the farfalle thoroughly
and return to the pan.

2 Cut the cherry tomatoes in half and
trim the rocket.

3 Heat the olive oil in a large, heavy-
based pan. Add the tomatoes to the
pan and cook for 1 minute.

4 Add the farfalle and the rocket to the
pan and stir gently over a low heat
until thoroughly mixed and warmed
through, but don't overcook – the rocket
should just have wilted. Season to taste
with salt and pepper.

5 Meanwhile, using a vegetable peeler,
shave thin slices of pecorino cheese.

6 Transfer the farfalle and vegetables to
a warmed serving dish. Garnish with
the pecorino cheese shavings and serve
the pasta immediately.

COOK'S TIP

Pecorino cheese is a hard
sheep's-milk cheese which
resembles Parmesan and is often
used for grating over a variety of
dishes. It has a sharp flavour and is
used only in small quantities.

Pasta & Vegetable Sauce

The different shapes and textures of the vegetables make a mouthwatering presentation in this light and summery dish.

NUTRITIONAL INFORMATION

Calories 389   Sugars 4g
Protein . . . . .16g   Fat 20g
Carbohydrate . . .38g   Saturates 11g

 10 mins   🕐 30 mins

SERVES 4

INGREDIENTS

225 g/8 oz dried gemelli or other
   pasta shapes

1 broccoli head, cut into florets

2 courgettes, sliced

225 g/8 oz asparagus spears

115 g/4 oz mangetouts

115 g/4 oz frozen peas

2 tbsp butter

3 tbsp vegetable stock

4 tbsp double cream

freshly grated nutmeg

2 tbsp chopped fresh parsley

2 tbsp freshly grated Parmesan cheese

salt and pepper

1 Bring a large pan of lightly salted water to the boil. Add the pasta, bring back to the boil and cook for 8–10 minutes or until tender, but still firm to the bite. Drain the pasta, return to the pan, cover and keep warm.

2 Steam the broccoli, courgettes, asparagus spears and mangetouts over a pan of boiling salted water until they are just beginning to soften. Remove from the heat and refresh in cold water. Drain and set aside.

3 Bring a small pan of lightly salted water to the boil. Add the frozen peas and cook for 3 minutes. Drain the peas, refresh in cold water and then drain again. Set aside with the other vegetables.

4 Put the butter and vegetable stock in a pan over a medium heat. Add all of the vegetables, reserving a few of the asparagus spears, and toss carefully with a wooden spoon until they have heated through, taking care not to break them up.

5 Stir in the cream and heat through without bringing to the boil. Season to taste with salt, pepper and nutmeg.

6 Transfer the pasta to a warmed serving dish and stir in the chopped parsley. Spoon over the vegetable sauce and sprinkle over the Parmesan cheese. Arrange the reserved asparagus spears in a pattern on top and serve.

Mushroom & Cheese Risotto

Make this creamy risotto with Italian arborio rice and freshly grated Parmesan cheese for the best results.

NUTRITIONAL INFORMATION

Calories	358	Sugars	.........3g
Protein	........11g	Fat	..........14g
Carbohydrate	...50g	Saturates	.......5g

 20 mins   40 mins

SERVES 4

INGREDIENTS

2 tbsp olive or vegetable oil

225 g/8 oz arborio rice

2 garlic cloves, crushed

1 onion, chopped

2 celery sticks, chopped

1 red or green pepper, deseeded
   and chopped

225 g/8 oz mushrooms, sliced

1 tbsp chopped fresh oregano or 1 tsp
   dried oregano

1 litre/1¾ pints vegetable stock

55 g /2 oz sun-dried tomatoes in olive oil,
   drained and chopped (optional)

55 g/2 oz finely grated Parmesan cheese

salt and pepper

TO GARNISH

fresh flat leaf parsley sprigs

fresh bay leaves

1 Heat the oil in a wok or large frying pan. Add the rice and cook, stirring constantly, for 5 minutes.

2 Add the garlic, onion, celery and pepper and cook, stirring constantly, for 5 minutes. Add the mushrooms and cook for 3–4 minutes.

3 Stir in the oregano and stock. Heat until just boiling, then reduce the heat, cover and simmer for 20 minutes or until the rice is tender and creamy.

4 Add the sun-dried tomatoes, if using, and season to taste with salt and pepper. Stir in half of the grated Parmesan cheese. Top with the remaining cheese, garnish with flat leaf parsley and bay leaves and serve.

Bread Dough Base

Traditionally, pizza bases are made from bread dough; this recipe will give you a base similar to an Italian pizza.

NUTRITIONAL INFORMATION

Calories	182	Sugars	.........2g
Protein	.........5g	Fat	...........3g
Carbohydrate	...36g	Saturates	.....0.5g

1½ hrs   0 mins

SERVES 4

I N G R E D I E N T S

15 g/½ oz fresh yeast or 1 tsp dried or easy-blend yeast

6 tbsp lukewarm water

½ tsp sugar

1 tbsp olive oil

175 g/6 oz plain flour, plus extra for dusting

1 tsp salt

1 Combine the fresh yeast with the water and sugar in a bowl. If using dried yeast, sprinkle it over the surface of the water and whisk in until dissolved.

2 Set aside in a warm place for 10–15 minutes until frothy on the surface. Stir in the olive oil.

3 Sift the flour and salt into a large bowl. If using easy-blend yeast, stir it in. Make a well in the centre and pour in the yeast liquid, or water and oil (without the sugar for easy-blend yeast).

4 Using either floured hands or a wooden spoon, mix together to form a dough. Turn out on to a floured work surface and knead for about 5 minutes or until smooth and elastic.

5 Place the dough in a large greased plastic bag and set aside in a warm place for about 1 hour or until doubled in size. Airing cupboards are often the best places for this process, as the temperature remains constant.

6 Turn out on to a lightly floured work surface and 'knock back' by punching the dough. This releases any air bubbles which would make the pizza uneven. Knead 4 or 5 times. The dough is now ready to use.

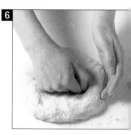

Giardiniera Pizza

As the name implies, this colourful pizza should be topped with fresh vegetables from the garden, especially in the summer months.

🍳 15 mins 🕐 20 mins

SERVES 4

INGREDIENTS

6 spinach leaves

Bread Dough Base (see page 838) or
1 x 25 cm/10 inch pizza base

Basic Tomato Sauce (see page 7)

1 tomato, sliced

1 celery stick, thinly sliced

½ green pepper, deseeded and thinly sliced

1 baby courgette, sliced

25 g/1 oz asparagus tips

25 g/1 oz sweetcorn, thawed if frozen

4 tbsp peas, thawed if frozen

4 spring onions, trimmed and chopped

1 tbsp chopped fresh mixed herbs

55 g/2 oz mozzarella cheese, grated

2 tbsp freshly grated Parmesan cheese

1 artichoke heart

olive oil, for drizzling

salt and pepper

surface. Place the round on a large greased baking sheet or pizza pan and push up the edge a little. Spread with the tomato sauce.

3 Arrange the spinach leaves on the sauce, followed by the tomato slices. Top with the remaining vegetables and the fresh mixed herbs.

4 Combine the cheeses and sprinkle over the pizza. Place the artichoke heart in the centre. Drizzle the pizza with a little olive oil and season to taste.

5 Bake in a preheated oven, 200°C/400°F/Gas Mark 6, for 18–20 minutes or until the edges are crisp and golden brown. Serve immediately.

1 Remove any tough stalks from the spinach and wash the leaves in cold water. Pat dry with kitchen paper.

2 Roll out or press the pizza base, using a rolling pin or your hands, into a 25 cm/10 inch circle on a lightly floured work

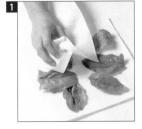  

Mushroom & Walnut Pizza

Wild mushrooms make a delicious pizza topping when mixed with walnuts and Roquefort cheese.

NUTRITIONAL INFORMATION

Calories	499	Sugars	.........9g
Protein	........13g	Fat	..........32g
Carbohydrate	...42g	Saturates	......11g

 10 mins   25 mins

SERVES 4

INGREDIENTS

Bread Dough Base (see page 838) or
  1 x 25 cm/10 inch pizza base

Basic Tomato Sauce (see page 7)

115 g/4 oz soft cheese

1 tbsp chopped fresh mixed herbs, such as
  parsley, oregano and basil

225 g/8 oz wild mushrooms, such as oyster,
  shiitake or ceps, or 115 g/4 oz each wild
  and button mushrooms

2 tbsp olive oil, plus extra for drizzling

¼ tsp fennel seeds

4 tbsp roughly chopped walnuts

40 g/1½ oz blue cheese

salt and pepper

fresh flat leaf parsley sprig, to garnish

1 Roll out or press the pizza base, using a rolling pin or your hands, into a 25 cm/10 inch circle on a lightly floured work surface. Place on a large greased baking sheet or pizza pan and push up the edge a little with your fingers to form a rim.

2 Carefully spread the tomato sauce almost to the edge of the pizza base. Dot with the soft cheese and chopped fresh herbs.

3 Wipe and slice the mushrooms. Heat the oil in a large frying pan or wok and stir-fry the mushrooms and fennel seeds for 2–3 minutes. Spread over the pizza with the walnuts.

4 Crumble the blue cheese over the pizza, drizzle with a little olive oil and season with salt and pepper to taste.

5 Bake in a preheated oven, 200°C/400°F/Gas Mark 6, for 18–20 minutes or until the edge is crisp and golden. Serve immediately, garnished with a sprig of flat leaf parsley.

Florentine Pizza

A pizza adaptation of Eggs Florentine – sliced hard-boiled eggs on freshly cooked spinach, with a crunchy almond topping.

NUTRITIONAL INFORMATION

Calories	474	Sugars	.........7g
Protein	........19g	Fat	..........26g
Carbohydrate	...43g	Saturates	.....7.5g

20 mins   20 mins

SERVES 4

INGREDIENTS

Bread Dough Base (see page 838) or
   1 x 25 cm/10 inch pizza base

3 tbsp olive oil, plus extra for drizzling

2 tbsp freshly grated Parmesan cheese

Basic Tomato Sauce (see page 7)

175 g/6 oz spinach

1 small red onion, thinly sliced

¼ tsp freshly grated nutmeg

2 hard-boiled eggs

15 g/½ oz fresh white breadcrumbs

55 g/2 oz Jarlsberg, Cheddar or Gruyère
   cheese, grated

2 tbsp flaked almonds

salt and pepper

1 Roll out or press the dough, using a rolling pin or your hands, into a 25 cm/10 inch circle on a lightly floured work surface. Brush with the olive oil and sprinkle with the Parmesan. Place on a large greased baking sheet or pizza pan and push up the edge slightly. Spread the tomato sauce almost to the edge.

2 Remove the stalks from the spinach and wash the leaves thoroughly in plenty of cold water. Drain well and pat off the excess water with kitchen paper.

3 Heat the remaining oil and cook the onion for 5 minutes until softened. Add the spinach and cook until just wilted. Drain off any excess liquid. Arrange on the pizza and sprinkle over the nutmeg.

4 Shell and slice the eggs. Arrange the slices of egg on top of the spinach.

5 Combine the breadcrumbs, cheese and almonds and sprinkle over. Drizzle with a little olive oil and season to taste.

6 Bake in a preheated oven, 200°C/ 400°F/Gas Mark 6, for 18–20 minutes, or until the edge is crisp and golden. Serve the pizza immediately.

Pepper & Red Onion Pizza

The vibrant colours of the peppers and onion make this a delightful pizza. Served cut into fingers, it is ideal for a party or buffet.

NUTRITIONAL INFORMATION

Calories	380	Sugars	19g
Protein	7g	Fat	17g
Carbohydrate	53g	Saturates	2g

 25 mins   25 mins

SERVES 8

INGREDIENTS

Bread Dough Base (see page 838)

2 tbsp olive oil, plus extra for drizzling

½ red pepper deseeded and thinly sliced

½ green pepper, deseeded and thinly sliced

½ yellow pepper, deseeded and thinly sliced

1 small red onion, thinly sliced

1 garlic clove, crushed

Basic Tomato Sauce (see page 7)

3 tbsp raisins

4 tbsp pine kernels

1 tbsp chopped fresh thyme

salt and pepper

1 Roll out or press the dough, using a rolling pin or your hands, on a lightly floured work surface to fit a 30 x 18 cm/ 12 x 7 inch greased Swiss roll tin. Place the dough in the tin and push up the edges slightly.

2 Cover with clingfilm and set the dough aside in a warm place for about 10 minutes to rise slightly.

3 Heat the oil in a large frying pan. Add the peppers, onion and garlic and cook gently for 5 minutes until they have softened. Set aside to cool.

4 Spread the tomato sauce over the base of the pizza almost to the edge.

5 Sprinkle over the raisins and top with the cooled pepper mixture. Add the pine kernels and thyme. Drizzle with a little olive oil and season to taste with salt and pepper.

6 Bake in a preheated oven, 200°C/ 400°F/Gas Mark 6, for 18–20 minutes, or until the edges are crisp and golden. Cut into fingers and serve immediately.

Mediterranean Crêpes

A rich tomato and herb filling makes these delicious crêpes completely irresistible. Serve with a crisp, leafy salad.

NUTRITIONAL INFORMATION

Calories 376	Sugars 12g	
Protein 11g	Fat 22g	
Carbohydrate ...36g	Saturates 7g	

25 mins 1¼ hrs

SERVES 4

INGREDIENTS

115 g/4 oz plain flour

salt

1 egg, lightly beaten

300 ml/10 fl oz milk

4 tsp sunflower oil, plus extra for brushing

FILLING

2 tbsp olive oil

1 onion, chopped

2 garlic cloves, finely chopped

1 small aubergine, diced

1 red pepper, deseeded and diced

4 tomatoes, peeled and diced

1 tbsp sun-dried tomato purée

1 tbsp chopped fresh parsley

2 tsp chopped fresh thyme

salt and pepper

TOPPING

25 g/1 oz butter, melted

3 tbsp freshly grated Parmesan cheese

1 Preheat the oven to 190°C/375°F/Gas Mark 5. Sift the flour with a pinch of salt into a bowl. Using a wooden spoon, beat in the egg and half the milk. Continue beating until the mixture is smooth and lump free. Stir in the remaining milk and 1 tsp of the oil. Transfer to a jug.

2 Brush a crêpe pan with the remaining oil and heat well. Stir the batter and add a little to the pan, then quickly tilt and rotate the crêpe pan to cover the base with a thin layer. Cook for 1 minute, or until the underside is golden. Flip over with a palette knife and cook the second side for 30 seconds, until golden. Slide the crêpe out on to a plate. Cook the remaining batter in the same way to make 12 crêpes, stacking them on the plate interleaved with greaseproof paper. Keep warm.

3 To make the filling, heat the oil in a heavy-based frying pan. Add the onion and cook, stirring occasionally, for 5 minutes, or until softened. Add the garlic, aubergine and red pepper and cook, stirring occasionally, for 10 minutes. Stir in the tomatoes, tomato purée, parsley and thyme. Season to taste, cover and simmer for 15 minutes. Lightly brush an ovenproof dish with oil. Divide the filling between the crêpes, roll up and place in the dish, seam-side down. Brush with melted butter, sprinkle with the cheese and bake in the preheated oven for 15 minutes. Serve immediately.

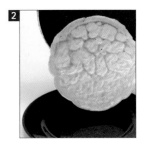

Vermicelli & Vegetable Flan

Lightly cooked vermicelli is pressed into a flan ring and baked with a creamy mushroom filling to make an attractive, as well as tasty dish.

NUTRITIONAL INFORMATION

Calories 528	Sugars 6g	
Protein 15g	Fat 32g	
Carbohydrate ...47g	Saturates 17g	

  15 mins   1 hr

SERVES 4

INGREDIENTS

6 tbsp butter, plus extra for greasing

225 g/8 oz dried vermicelli or spaghetti

1 tbsp olive oil

1 onion, chopped

140 g/5 oz button mushrooms

1 green pepper, cored, deseeded and sliced into thin rings

150 ml/5 fl oz milk

3 eggs, lightly beaten

2 tbsp double cream

1 tsp dried oregano

freshly grated nutmeg

3 tbsp freshly grated Parmesan cheese

salt and pepper

tomato and basil salad, to serve (optional)

1 Generously grease a 20 cm/8 inch loose-bottomed flan tin with a little butter.

2 Bring a large pan of lightly salted water to the boil. Add the vermicelli and olive oil, bring back to the boil and cook for 8–10 minutes until tender, but still firm to the bite. Drain, return to the pan, add 2 tablespoons of the butter and shake the pan to coat the pasta.

3 Press the pasta on to the base and around the sides of the flan tin to make a flan case.

4 Melt the remaining butter in a frying pan over a medium heat. Add the onion and fry over a low heat, stirring occasionally, until it is softened.

5 Add the mushrooms and pepper rings to the frying pan and cook, stirring, for 2–3 minutes. Spoon the onion, mushroom and pepper mixture into the flan case and press it evenly into the base.

6 Beat together the milk, eggs and cream, stir in the oregano and season to taste with nutmeg and pepper. Carefully pour this mixture over the vegetables and then sprinkle with the Parmesan cheese.

7 Bake the flan in a preheated oven, 180°C/350°F/Gas Mark 4, for about 40–45 minutes or until the filling has set.

8 Carefully slide the flan out of the tin and serve warm with a tomato and basil salad, if wished.

Feta & Spinach Omelette

This quick chunky omelette has pieces of potato cooked into the egg mixture and is then filled with feta cheese and spinach.

NUTRITIONAL INFORMATION

Calories	564	Sugars	.........6g
Protein	........30g	Fat	..........39g
Carbohydrate	...25g	Saturates	......19g

 20 mins    25–30 mins

SERVES 4

INGREDIENTS

6 tbsp butter

1.3 kg/3 lb waxy potatoes, diced

3 garlic cloves, crushed

1 tsp paprika

2 tomatoes, peeled, deseeded and diced

12 eggs

pepper

FILLING

225 g/8 oz baby spinach

1 tsp fennel seeds

125 g/4½ oz feta cheese, diced (drained weight)

4 tbsp natural yogurt

1 Heat 1 tablespoon of the butter in a frying pan and cook the potatoes over a low heat, stirring, for 7–10 minutes until golden. Transfer to a bowl.

2 Add the garlic, paprika and tomatoes to the pan and cook for a further 2 minutes.

3 Whisk the eggs together and season with pepper. Pour the eggs into the potatoes and mix well.

4 Cook the spinach in boiling water for 1 minute until just wilted. Drain and refresh under cold running water. Pat dry with kitchen paper. Stir in the fennel seeds, feta cheese and yogurt.

5 Heat a quarter of the remaining butter in a 15 cm/6 inch omelette pan. Ladle a quarter of the egg and potato mixture into the pan. Cook, turning once, for 2 minutes, until set.

6 Transfer the omelette to a serving plate. Spoon a quarter of the spinach mixture on to half of the omelette, then fold the omelette in half over the filling. Repeat to make 4 omelettes.

VARIATION

Use any other cheese, such as blue cheese, instead of the feta, and blanched broccoli in place of the baby spinach, if you prefer.

Creamy Stuffed Mushrooms

These oven-baked mushrooms are covered with a creamy potato and mushroom filling topped with melted cheese.

NUTRITIONAL INFORMATION

Calories 214	Sugars 1g	
Protein 5g	Fat 17g	
Carbohydrate 11g	Saturates 11g	

 40 mins   40 mins

SERVES 4

INGREDIENTS

25 g/1 oz dried ceps

225 g/8 oz floury potatoes, diced

2 tbsp butter, melted

4 tbsp double cream

2 tbsp chopped fresh chives

8 large open-capped mushrooms

4 tbsp grated Emmenthal cheese

150 ml/5 fl oz vegetable stock

salt and pepper

fresh chives, to garnish

1 Place the dried ceps in a small bowl. Add sufficient boiling water to cover and set aside to soak for 20 minutes.

2 Meanwhile, cook the potatoes in a medium saucepan of lightly salted boiling water for 10 minutes until cooked through and tender. Drain well and mash until smooth.

3 Drain the soaked ceps and then chop them finely. Mix them into the mashed potato.

4 Thoroughly blend the butter, cream and chives together and pour the mixture into the ceps and potato mixture, mixing well. Season to taste with salt and pepper.

5 Remove the stalks from the open-capped mushrooms. Chop the stalks and stir them into the potato mixture. Spoon the mixture into the open-capped mushrooms and sprinkle the grated cheese over the top.

6 Arrange the filled mushrooms in a shallow ovenproof dish and pour in the vegetable stock.

7 Cover the dish and cook in a preheated oven, 220°C/425°F/Gas Mark 7, for 20 minutes. Remove the lid and cook for 5 minutes until golden.

8 Garnish the mushrooms with fresh chives and serve at once.

VARIATION

Use fresh mushrooms instead of the dried ceps, if preferred, and stir a mixture of chopped nuts into the mushroom stuffing mixture for extra crunch.

Potato-filled Naan Breads

This is a filling Indian sandwich. Spicy potatoes fill the naan breads, which are served with a cool cucumber raita and lime pickle.

NUTRITIONAL INFORMATION

Calories 244	Sugars 7g
Protein 8g	Fat 8g
Carbohydrate . . .37g	Saturates 1g

10 mins

25 mins

SERVES 4

INGREDIENTS

225 g/8 oz waxy potatoes, scrubbed and diced

1 tbsp vegetable oil

1 onion, chopped

2 garlic cloves, crushed

1 tsp ground cumin

1 tsp ground coriander

½ tsp chilli powder

1 tbsp tomato purée

3 tbsp vegetable stock

85 g/3 oz baby spinach, shredded

4 small or 2 large naan breads

lime pickle, to serve

RAITA

150 ml/5 fl oz low-fat natural yogurt

4 tbsp diced cucumber

1 tbsp chopped fresh mint

1 Cook the diced potatoes in a saucepan of boiling water for 10 minutes. Drain thoroughly.

2 Heat the vegetable oil in a separate saucepan and cook the onion and garlic over a low heat, stirring frequently, for 3 minutes. Add the spices and cook for a further 2 minutes.

3 Stir in the potatoes, tomato purée, vegetable stock and spinach. Cook for 5 minutes until the potatoes are tender.

4 Warm the naan breads in a preheated oven, 150°C/300°F/Gas Mark 2, for about 2 minutes.

5 To make the raita, mix the yogurt, cucumber and mint together in a small bowl.

6 Remove the naan breads from the oven. Using a sharp knife, cut a pocket in the side of each bread. Spoon the spicy potato mixture into each pocket.

7 Serve the filled naan breads immediately, accompanied by the raita and lime pickle.

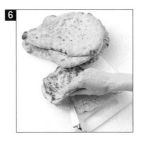

COOK'S TIP

To give the raita a much stronger flavour, make it in advance and chill in the refrigerator until ready to serve.

Potato-topped Vegetables

This is a very colourful and nutritious dish, packed full of crunchy vegetables in a tasty white wine sauce.

NUTRITIONAL INFORMATION

Calories	413	Sugars	........11g
Protein	........19g	Fat	..........18g
Carbohydrate	...41g	Saturates	......11g

  20 mins 1¼ hrs

SERVES 4

INGREDIENTS

1 carrot, diced

175 g/6 oz cauliflower florets

175 g/6 oz broccoli florets

1 fennel bulb, sliced

85 g/3 oz green beans, halved

2 tbsp butter

2½ tbsp plain flour

150 ml/5 fl oz vegetable stock

150 ml/5 fl oz dry white wine

150 ml/5 fl oz milk

175 g/6 oz chestnut mushrooms, quartered

2 tbsp chopped fresh sage

TOPPING

900 g/2 lb floury potatoes, diced

2 tbsp butter

4 tbsp natural yogurt

70 g/2½ oz Parmesan cheese, freshly grated

1 tsp fennel seeds

salt and pepper

1 Cook the carrot, cauliflower, broccoli, fennel and beans in a large saucepan of boiling water for 10 minutes until just tender. Drain the vegetables thoroughly and set aside.

2 Melt the butter in a saucepan. Stir in the flour and cook for 1 minute. Remove from the heat and stir in the stock, wine and milk. Return to the heat and bring to the boil, stirring until thickened. Stir in the reserved vegetables, mushrooms and sage.

3 Meanwhile, make the topping. Cook the potatoes in boiling water for 10–15 minutes. Drain and mash with the butter, yogurt and half the cheese. Stir in the fennel seeds. Season to taste.

4 Spoon the vegetable mixture into a 1 litre/1¾ pint pie dish. Spoon the potato over the top and sprinkle with the remaining cheese. Cook in a preheated oven, 190°C/375°F/Gas Mark 5, for 30–35 minutes or until golden. Serve hot.

Three Cheese Soufflé

This soufflé is very simple to make, yet it has a delicious flavour and melts in the mouth. Choose three alternative cheeses, if preferred.

NUTRITIONAL INFORMATION

Calories 447	Sugars 1g	
Protein 22g	Fat 23g	
Carbohydrate ...41g	Saturates 11g	

  10 mins   55 mins

SERVES 4

I N G R E D I E N T S

2 tbsp butter

2 tsp plain flour

900 g/2 lb floury potatoes

8 eggs, separated

4 tbsp grated Gruyère cheese

4 tbsp crumbled blue cheese

4 tbsp grated mature Cheddar

salt and pepper

1 Butter a 2.25 litre/4 pint soufflé dish and dust with the flour. Set aside.

2 Cook the potatoes in a saucepan of boiling water until tender. Mash until very smooth and then transfer to a mixing bowl to cool.

3 Beat the egg yolks into the potato and stir in the Gruyère cheese, blue cheese and Cheddar, mixing well. Season to taste with salt and pepper.

4 Whisk the egg whites until standing in peaks, then gently fold them into the potato mixture with a metal spoon until fully incorporated.

5 Spoon the potato mixture into the prepared soufflé dish.

6 Cook in a preheated oven, 220°C/ 425°F/Gas Mark 7, for 35–40 minutes until risen and set. Serve immediately.

COOK'S TIP

Insert a fine skewer into the centre of the soufflé; it should come out clean when the soufflé is fully cooked through.

Nutty Harvest Loaf

This attractive and nutritious loaf is also utterly delicious. Served with a fresh tomato sauce, it can be eaten hot or cold with salad.

NUTRITIONAL INFORMATION

Calories . . . . . . .554 Sugars 12g
Protein . . . . .16g Fat 37g
Carbohydrate . . .43g Saturates 16g

20 mins   1½ hrs

SERVES 4

I N G R E D I E N T S

2 tbsp butter, plus extra
   for greasing

450 g/1 lb floury potatoes, diced

1 onion, chopped

2 garlic cloves, crushed

115 g/4 oz unsalted peanuts

85 g/3 oz fresh white breadcrumbs

1 egg, beaten

2 tbsp chopped fresh coriander

150 ml/5 fl oz vegetable stock

85 g/3 oz sliced mushrooms

55 g/2 oz sun-dried tomatoes in oil
   drained and sliced

salt and pepper

S A U C E

150 ml/5 fl oz crème fraîche

2 tsp tomato purée

2 tsp clear honey

2 tbsp chopped fresh coriander

1 Grease a 450 g/1 lb loaf tin. Cook the potatoes in a saucepan of boiling water for 10 minutes until cooked through. Drain well, mash and set aside.

2 Melt half of the butter in a frying pan. Add the onion and garlic and fry gently for 2–3 minutes until soft. Finely chop the nuts or process them in a food processor for 30 seconds with the breadcrumbs.

3 Mix the chopped nuts and breadcrumbs into the potatoes with the egg, coriander and vegetable stock. Stir in the onion and garlic and mix well.

4 Melt the remaining butter in the frying pan, add the sliced mushrooms and cook for 2–3 minutes.

5 Press half of the potato mixture into the base of the loaf tin. Spoon the mushrooms on top and sprinkle with the sun-dried tomatoes. Spoon the remaining potato mixture on top and smooth the surface. Cover with foil and bake in a preheated oven, 190°C/375°F/Gas Mark 5, for 1 hour or until firm to the touch.

6 Meanwhile, mix the sauce ingredients together. Cut the nutty harvest loaf into slices and serve with the sauce.

Vegetable Cake

This is a savoury version of a cheesecake with a layer of fried potatoes as a delicious base. Use frozen mixed vegetables for the topping, if you like.

NUTRITIONAL INFORMATION

Calories	502	Sugars	.........8g
Protein	........16g	Fat	..........31g
Carbohydrate	...41g	Saturates	......14g

🍲 20 mins   🕐 45 mins

SERVES 4

INGREDIENTS

BASE

2 tbsp vegetable oil, plus extra for brushing

1.25 kg/2 lb 12 oz waxy potatoes, thinly sliced

TOPPING

1 tbsp vegetable oil

1 leek, chopped

1 courgette, grated

1 red pepper, deseeded and diced

1 green pepper, deseeded and diced

1 carrot, grated

2 tsp chopped parsley

225 g/8 oz full-fat soft cheese

4 tbsp grated mature cheese

2 eggs, beaten

salt and pepper

shredded cooked leek, to garnish

salad, to serve

1 Brush a 20 cm/8 inch springform cake tin with oil.

2 To make the base, heat the oil in a frying pan. Cook the potato slices until softened and browned. Drain on kitchen paper and place in the base of the tin.

3 To make the topping, heat the oil in a separate frying pan. Add the leek and fry over a low heat, stirring frequently, for 3–4 minutes until softened.

4 Add the courgette, peppers, carrot and parsley to the pan and cook over a low heat for 5–7 minutes or until the vegetables have softened.

5 Meanwhile, beat the cheeses and eggs together in a bowl. Stir in the vegetables and season to taste with salt and pepper. Spoon the mixture evenly over the potato base.

6 Cook in a preheated oven, 190°C/375°F/Gas Mark 5, for 20–25 minutes until the cake is set.

7 Remove the vegetable cake from the tin, transfer to a warm serving plate, garnish with shredded leek and serve with a crisp salad.

Pan Potato Cake

This tasty meal is made with sliced potatoes, tofu and vegetables cooked in the pan from which it is served.

NUTRITIONAL INFORMATION

Calories	452	Sugars	.........6g
Protein	........17g	Fat	..........28g
Carbohydrate	...35g	Saturates	......13g

 15 mins   30 mins

SERVES 4

INGREDIENTS

675 g/1 lb 8 oz waxy potatoes,
    unpeeled and sliced

1 carrot, diced

225 g/8 oz small broccoli florets

5 tbsp butter

2 tbsp vegetable oil

1 red onion, quartered

2 garlic cloves, crushed

175 g/6 oz firm tofu, diced

2 tbsp chopped fresh sage

85 g/3 oz mature cheese, grated

1 Cook the sliced potatoes in a large saucepan of boiling water for 10 minutes. Drain thoroughly.

2 Meanwhile, cook the carrot and broccoli florets in a separate pan of boiling water for 5 minutes. Remove with a draining spoon.

3 Heat the butter and oil in a 23 cm/ 9 inch frying pan. Add the onion and garlic and fry over a low heat for 2–3 minutes. Add half of the potato slices, covering the base of the pan.

4 Cover the potato slices with the carrot, broccoli and tofu. Sprinkle with half of the sage and cover with the remaining potato slices. Sprinkle the grated cheese over the top.

5 Cook over a moderate heat for 8–10 minutes. Then place the pan under a preheated medium grill for about 2–3 minutes, or until the cheese melts and browns.

6 Garnish with the remaining chopped sage and serve immediately, straight from the pan.

COOK'S TIP

Make sure that the mixture fills the whole width of your frying pan to enable the layers to remain intact.

Layered Vegetable Bake

Simplicity itself, this tasty bake makes a superb meal in itself or can be served as an accompaniment, in which case it will serve 8 people.

NUTRITIONAL INFORMATION

Calories 174	Sugars 4g	
Protein 5g	Fat 4g	
Carbohydrate 33g	Saturates 1g	

10 mins   1½ hrs

SERVES 4

INGREDIENTS

1 tbsp olive oil, for brushing

675 g/1½ lb potatoes

2 leeks

2 beef tomatoes

8 fresh basil leaves

1 garlic clove, finely chopped

300 ml/10 fl oz vegetable stock

salt and pepper

1 Preheat the oven to 180°C/350°F/Gas Mark 4. Brush an ovenproof dish with a little of the olive oil. Prepare all the vegetables. Peel and slice the potatoes, trim and slice the leeks and slice the tomatoes. Place a layer of potato slices in the base of the dish, sprinkle with half the basil leaves and cover with a layer of leeks. Top with a layer of tomato. Repeat these layers until all the vegetables are used up, ending with a layer of potatoes.

2 Stir the finely chopped garlic into the vegetable stock and season to taste with salt and pepper. Pour the stock over the layers of vegetables and brush the top of the potatoes with the remaining olive oil.

3 Bake in the preheated oven for 1½ hours, or until the vegetables are tender and the topping is golden brown. Serve immediately.

VARIATION
You could add 2 thinly sliced courgettes to the layers of leeks for an even more substantial supper dish.

Layered Pies

These individual pies of layered potato, aubergine and courgettes baked in a tomato sauce can be made in advance, so are good for entertaining.

NUTRITIONAL INFORMATION

Calories	427	Sugars	.........8g
Protein	........22g	Fat	..........21g
Carbohydrate	...41g	Saturates	.......8g

 40 mins   1 hr 20 mins

SERVES 4

INGREDIENTS

3 large waxy potatoes, thinly sliced

1 small aubergine, thinly sliced

1 courgette, sliced

3 tbsp vegetable oil

1 onion, diced

1 green pepper, deseeded and diced

1 tsp cumin seeds

2 tbsp chopped fresh basil

200 g/7 oz can chopped tomatoes

175 g/6 oz mozzarella cheese, sliced

225 g/8 oz tofu, sliced

55 g/2 oz fresh white breadcrumbs

2 tbsp grated Parmesan cheese

salt and pepper

basil leaves, to garnish

1 Cook the sliced potatoes in a pan of boiling water for 5 minutes. Drain and set aside.

2 Put the aubergine slices on a plate, sprinkle with salt and leave for 20 minutes. Meanwhile, blanch the courgette in a pan of boiling water for 2-3 minutes. Drain and set aside.

3 Meanwhile, heat 2 tbsp of the oil in a frying pan. Add the onion and cook over a low heat, stirring occasionally, for 2–3 minutes until softened. Add the green pepper, cumin seeds, basil and canned tomatoes. Season to taste with salt and pepper and simmer for 30 minutes.

4 Rinse the aubergine slices thoroughly under cold running water and pat dry with kitchen paper. Heat the remaining oil in a large frying pan. Add the aubergine slices and cook over a medium heat for 3–5 minutes, turning to brown both sides. Drain and set aside.

5 Arrange half of the potato slices in the base of 4 small loose-based flan tins. Cover with half of the courgette slices, half of the aubergine slices and half of the mozzarella slices. Lay the tofu on top and spoon over the tomato sauce. Repeat the layers of vegetables and cheese in the same order.

6 Mix the breadcrumbs and Parmesan together and sprinkle over the top. Cook in a preheated oven, 190°C/375°F/Gas Mark 5, for 25–30 minutes or until golden. Garnish with fresh basil leaves and serve the pies immediately.

Vegetable-stuffed Paratas

This bread can be quite rich and is usually made for special occasions. It can be eaten on its own or with a vegetable curry.

NUTRITIONAL INFORMATION

Calories	391	Sugars	.........2g
Protein	.........6g	Fat	..........24g
Carbohydrate	...40g	Saturates	.....2.5g

25 mins   30–35 mins

SERVES 4

I N G R E D I E N T S

D O U G H

225 g/8 oz wholemeal flour (ata or chapati flour)

½ tsp salt

200 ml/7 fl oz water

100 g/3½ oz vegetable ghee

2 tbsp ghee, for frying

F I L L I N G

675 g/1½ lb potatoes

½ tsp turmeric

1 tsp garam masala

1 tsp finely chopped fresh root ginger

1 tbsp fresh coriander leaves

3 green chillies, finely chopped

1 tsp salt

1 To make the paratas, mix the flour, salt, water and ghee in a bowl to form a dough.

2 Divide the dough into 6–8 equal portions. Roll each portion out on to a floured work surface. Brush the middle of the dough portions with ½ teaspoon of ghee. Fold the dough portions in half, roll into a pipe-like shape, flatten with the palms of your hands, then roll around a finger to form a coil. Roll out again, using flour to dust when necessary, to form a round about 18 cm/7 inches in diameter.

3 Place the potatoes in a saucepan of boiling water and cook until soft enough to be mashed.

4 Blend the turmeric, garam masala, ginger, coriander leaves, chillies and salt together in a bowl.

5 Add the spice mixture to the mashed potato and mix well. Spread about 1 tablespoon of the spicy potato mixture on each dough portion and cover with another rolled-out piece of dough. Seal the edges well.

6 Heat 2 teaspoons of ghee in a heavy-based frying pan. Place the paratas gently in the pan, in batches, and fry, turning and moving them about gently with a flat spoon, until golden.

7 Remove the paratas from the frying pan and serve immediately.

Spinach Frittata

This Italian dish may be made with many flavourings. Spinach is used as the main ingredient in this recipe for colour and flavour.

NUTRITIONAL INFORMATION

Calories 307	Sugars 4g
Protein 15g	Fat 25g
Carbohydrate 6g	Saturates 8g

  20 mins   20 mins

SERVES 4

INGREDIENTS

450 g/1 lb spinach

2 tsp water

4 eggs, beaten

2 tbsp single cream

2 garlic cloves, crushed

55 g/2 oz canned sweetcorn, drained

1 celery stick, chopped

1 fresh red chilli, chopped

2 tomatoes, deseeded and diced

2 tbsp olive oil

2 tbsp butter

4 tbsp pecan nut halves

2 tbsp grated pecorino cheese

25 g/1 oz Fontina cheese, cubed

a pinch of paprika

COOK'S TIP

Be careful not to burn the underside of the frittata during the initial cooking stage – this is why it is important to use a heavy-based frying pan. Add a little extra oil to the pan when you turn the frittata over, if required.

1 Cook the spinach in 2 teaspoons of water in a covered pan for 5 minutes. Drain thoroughly and pat dry on absorbent kitchen paper.

2 Beat the eggs in a bowl and stir in the spinach, single cream, garlic, sweetcorn, celery, chilli and tomatoes until the ingredients are well mixed.

3 Heat the oil and butter in a 20 cm/ 8 inch heavy-based frying pan over a medium heat.

4 Spoon the egg mixture into the frying pan and sprinkle with the pecan nut halves, pecorino and Fontina cheeses and paprika. Cook, without stirring, over a medium heat for 5–7 minutes or until the underside of the frittata is brown.

5 Put a large plate over the pan and invert to turn out the frittata. Slide it back into the frying pan and cook the other side for a further 2–3 minutes. Serve the frittata straight from the frying pan or transfer to a serving plate.

Italian Vegetable Tart

A rich tomato pastry base topped with a mouthwatering selection of vegetables and cheese makes a tart that's tasty as well as attractive.

NUTRITIONAL INFORMATION

Calories	438	Sugars	.........8g
Protein	.........9g	Fat	..........28g
Carbohydrate	...40g	Saturates	......15g

1¾ hrs 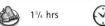 40 mins

SERVES 4

INGREDIENTS

1 aubergine, sliced

2 tbsp salt

4 tbsp olive oil

1 garlic clove, crushed

1 large yellow pepper, deseeded and sliced

300 ml/10 fl oz Basic Tomato Sauce (see page 7)

115 g/4 oz sun-dried tomatoes in oil, drained and halved if necessary

175 g/6 oz Mozzarella, drained and thinly sliced

PASTRY

225 g/8 oz plain flour, plus extra for dusting

pinch of celery salt

115 g/4 oz butter or margarine, plus extra for greasing

2 tbsp tomato purée

2–3 tbsp milk

1 To make the pastry, sift the flour and celery salt into a bowl and rub in the butter or margarine until the mixture resembles fine breadcrumbs.

2 Combine the tomato purée and milk and stir into the mixture to form a firm dough. Knead gently on a lightly floured surface until smooth. Wrap and chill for 30 minutes.

3 Grease a 28 cm/11 inch loose-based flan tin. Roll out the pastry on a lightly floured surface and use to line the tin. Trim and prick all over with a fork. Chill for 30 minutes.

4 Meanwhile, layer the aubergine in a dish, sprinkling with the salt. Set aside for 30 minutes.

5 Bake the pastry case in a preheated oven, 200°C/400°F/Gas Mark 6, for 20–25 minutes until cooked and lightly golden. Set aside. Increase the oven temperature to 230°C/450°F/Gas Mark 8.

6 Rinse the aubergine thoroughly under cold running water and pat dry with kitchen paper. Heat 3 tablespoons of the oil in a heavy-based frying pan and fry the garlic, aubergine and pepper for 5–6 minutes until just softened. Drain on kitchen paper.

7 Spread the pastry case with the tomato sauce and arrange the cooked vegetables, sun-dried tomatoes and mozzarella on top. Brush with the remaining olive oil and bake for 5 minutes until the cheese is just melting. Remove from the oven and serve immediately.

Vegetables & Tofu

This is a simple, clean-tasting dish of green vegetables, tofu and pasta, lightly tossed in olive oil.

NUTRITIONAL INFORMATION

Calories 400	Sugars 5g
Protein 19g	Fat 17g
Carbohydrate ...46g	Saturates 5g

25 mins   20 mins

SERVES 4

INGREDIENTS

225 g/8 oz asparagus

115 g/4 oz mangetouts

225 g/8 oz French beans

1 leek

225 g/8 oz shelled small broad beans

300 g/10½ oz dried fusilli

2 tbsp olive oil

2 tbsp butter or margarine

1 garlic clove, crushed

225 g/8 oz tofu, cut into 2.5 cm/ 1 inch cubes

55 g/2 oz stoned green olives in brine, drained

salt and pepper

freshly grated Parmesan cheese, to serve

1 Cut the asparagus into 5 cm/2 inch lengths. Thinly slice the mangetouts diagonally and slice the French beans into 2.5 cm/1 inch pieces. Thinly slice the leek.

2 Bring a large pan of water to the boil and add the asparagus, green beans and broad beans. Bring back to the boil and cook for 4 minutes. Drain well, rinse in cold water and drain again. Set aside.

3 Bring a large pan of lightly salted water to the boil. Add the pasta, bring back to the boil and cook for 8–10 minutes until tender, but still firm to the bite. Drain well. Toss in 1 tablespoon of the oil and season to taste.

4 Meanwhile, heat the remaining oil and the butter or margarine in a wok or large frying pan and gently cook the leek, garlic and tofu for 1–2 minutes until the vegetables have just softened.

5 Stir in the mangetouts and cook for 1 further minute.

6 Add the blanched vegetables and olives to the pan and heat through for 1 minute. Carefully stir in the pasta and adjust the seasoning if necessary. Cook for 1 minute and pile into a warmed serving dish. Serve immediately sprinkled with Parmesan.

Nutty Rice Burgers

Serve these burgers in toasted sesame seed baps. If you wish, add a slice of cheese to top the burger at the end of cooking.

NUTRITIONAL INFORMATION

Calories 517	Sugars 5g	
Protein 16g	Fat 26g	
Carbohydrate . . .59g	Saturates 6g	

🍲 1¼ hrs   🕐 30 mins

SERVES 4

INGREDIENTS

1 tbsp sunflower oil

1 small onion, finely chopped

100 g/3½ oz finely chopped mushrooms

350 g/12 oz cooked brown rice

100 g/3½ oz breadcrumbs

85 g/3 oz chopped walnuts

1 egg

2 tbsp brown fruity sauce

dash of Tabasco sauce

salt and pepper

vegetable oil

6 individual cheese slices (optional)

TO SERVE

onion slices

tomato slices

6 sesame seed baps

1 Heat the oil in a large pan and cook the onions for 3–4 minutes until they just begin to soften. Add the mushrooms and cook for a further 2 minutes.

2 Remove the pan from the heat. Transfer to a bowl and stir in the cooked rice, breadcrumbs, walnuts, egg, and sauces to taste into the vegetables. Season to taste with salt and pepper and mix well.

3 Shape the mixture into 6 burgers, pressing the mixture together with your fingers. Set aside to chill in the refrigerator for at least 30 minutes.

4 Barbecue the burgers on an oiled rack over medium coals for 5–6 minutes on each side, turning once and frequently basting with oil. Alternatively, cook under a preheated grill.

5 If liked, top the burgers with a slice of cheese 2 minutes before the end of the cooking time. Barbecue or grill the onion and tomato slices for 3–4 minutes until they are just beginning to colour.

6 Toast the sesame seed baps at the side of the barbecue. Serve the burgers in the baps, together with the barbecued onions and tomatoes.

Vegetable Crêpes

Crêpes are ideal for filling with your favourite ingredients.
In this recipe they are packed with a deliciously spicy vegetable filling.

NUTRITIONAL INFORMATION

Calories	509	Sugars	........10g
Protein	........17g	Fat	.........34g
Carbohydrate	...36g	Saturates	.......9g

 15 mins   🕐 45 mins

SERVES 4

INGREDIENTS

CREPES

100 g/3½ oz plain flour

pinch of salt

1 egg, lightly beaten

300 ml/10 fl oz milk

vegetable oil, for frying

FILLING

2 tbsp vegetable oil

1 leek, shredded

½ tsp chilli powder

½ tsp ground cumin

55 g/2 oz mangetouts

100 g/3½ oz button mushrooms,

1 red pepper, deseeded and sliced

4 tbsp cashew nuts, chopped

SAUCE

2 tbsp margarine

3 tbsp plain flour

150 ml/5 fl oz vegetable stock

150 ml/5 fl oz milk

1 tsp Dijon mustard

85 g/3 oz Cheddar cheese, grated

2 tbsp chopped fresh coriander

1 For the crêpes, sift the flour and salt into a bowl. Beat in the egg and milk to make a batter.

2 For the filling, heat the oil and cook the leek for 2–3 minutes. Add the remaining ingredients and cook, stirring constantly, for 5 minutes.

3 For the sauce, melt the margarine and add the flour. Cook, stirring, for 1 minute. Remove from the heat, stir in the stock and milk and return to the heat. Bring to the boil, stirring until thickened.

Stir in the mustard, half the cheese and the coriander and cook for 1 minute.

4 Heat 1 tbsp of oil in a small frying pan. Pour off the oil and add about 2½ tablespoons of the batter. Tilt to cover the base. Cook for 2 minutes, turn and cook the other side for 1 minute. Repeat with the remaining batter. Spoon a little of the filling along the centre of each crêpe and roll up. Place in a flameproof dish and pour the sauce on top. Top with cheese and heat under a hot grill for 3–5 minutes or until the cheese melts.

Aubergine Rolls

Thin slices of aubergine are fried in olive oil and garlic, and then topped with pesto sauce and finely grated mozzarella cheese.

NUTRITIONAL INFORMATION

Calories	278	Sugars	.........2g
Protein	.........4g	Fat	..........28g
Carbohydrate	....2g	Saturates	.......7g

15-20 mins   20 mins

SERVES 4

INGREDIENTS

aubergines, thinly sliced lengthways

tbsp olive oil, plus extra
for brushing

garlic clove, crushed

tbsp pesto

175 g/6 oz mozzarella cheese, grated

basil leaves, torn into pieces

salt and pepper

fresh basil leaves, to garnish

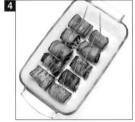

1 Place the aubergine slices in slices in a colander or on a plate and sprinkle liberally with salt. Set aside for 10–15 minutes to extract the bitter juices. Turn the slices over and repeat. Rinse thoroughly under cold running water and drain on kitchen paper.

2 Heat the olive oil in a large frying pan and add the garlic. Add the aubergine slices, a few at a time, and fry lightly on both sides over a medium heat. Drain them on kitchen paper.

3 Spread the pesto on 1 side of the aubergine slices. Top with the grated mozzarella and sprinkle with the torn basil leaves. Season to taste with salt and pepper. Roll up the slices and secure with wooden cocktail sticks.

4 Lightly brush an ovenproof dish with a little olive oil and arrange the aubergine rolls in it.. Place in a preheated oven, 180°C/350°F/Gas Mark 4, and bake for 8–10 minutes.

5 Transfer the aubergine rolls to a warmed serving plate. Scatter with fresh basil leaves and serve immediately.

COOK'S TIP

Most aubergines produced commercially these days do not have bitter juices that must be removed before cooking. Nevertheless, salting is a good idea if the aubergines are to be fried, because it prevents them from absorbing too much oil.

Mushroom Tarts

Different varieties of mushrooms are becoming more widely available in supermarkets, so use this recipe to make the most of them.

NUTRITIONAL INFORMATION

Calories	494	Sugars	.........2g
Protein	.........9g	Fat	..........35g
Carbohydrate	...38g	Saturates	......18g

15 mins   20 mins

SERVES 4

INGREDIENTS

500 g/1 lb 2 oz filo pastry, thawed if frozen

115 g/4 oz butter, melted

1 tbsp hazelnut oil

4 tbsp pine kernels

350 g/12 oz mixed mushrooms, such as button, chestnut, oyster and shiitake

2 tsp chopped fresh parsley

225 g/8 oz soft goat's cheese

salt and pepper

fresh parsley sprigs to garnish

lettuce, tomatoes, cucumber and spring onions, to serve

1 Cut the sheets of filo pastry into pieces about 10 cm/4 inches square and use them to line 4 individual tart tins, brushing each layer of pastry with melted butter. Line the tins with foil or baking paper and baking beans. Bake in a preheated oven, 200°C/ 400°F/Gas Mark 6, for about 6–8 minutes or until light golden brown.

2 Remove the tarts from the oven and carefully take out the foil or baking paper and baking beans. Reduce the oven temperature to 180°C/350°F/Gas Mark 4.

3 Put any remaining butter into a large pan with the hazelnut oil and fry the pine kernels until golden brown. Remove from the pan drain on kitchen paper.

4 Add the mushrooms to the pan and cook gently, stirring frequently, for about 4–5 minutes. Add the parsley and season to taste with salt and pepper.

5 Spoon one-quarter of the goat's cheese into the base of each tart.

Divide the mushrooms equally between them and sprinkle pine nuts over the top.

6 Return the tarts to the oven for about 5 minutes to heat through and then serve them, garnished with sprigs of parsley. Serve with lettuce, tomatoes, cucumber and spring onions.

Almond & Sesame Roast

Toasted almonds are combined with sesame seeds, rice and vegetables in this tasty roast. Serve it with a delicious onion and mushroom sauce.

NUTRITIONAL INFORMATION

Calories	.612	Sugars	.7g
Protein	.22g	Fat	.46g
Carbohydrate	.29g	Saturates	.13g

🥄 30-40 mins 🕐 35 mins

SERVES 4

INGREDIENTS

2 tbsp sesame or olive oil

1 small onion, finely chopped

55 g/2 oz risotto rice

300 ml/10 fl oz vegetable stock

1 large carrot, grated

1 large leek, finely chopped

2 tsp sesame seeds, toasted

85 g/3 oz chopped almonds, toasted

55 g/2 oz ground almonds

85 g/3 oz grated mature Cheddar cheese

2 eggs, beaten

1 tsp dried mixed herbs

butter, for greasing

salt and pepper

fresh flat leaf parsley sprigs, to garnish

fresh vegetables, to serve

SAUCE

1 tbsp butter

1 small onion, finely chopped

125 g/4 oz finely chopped mushrooms

1 tbsp plain flour

300 ml/10 fl oz vegetable stock

1 Heat the oil in a large frying pan and cook the onion gently for 2–3 minutes. Add the rice and cook gently for 5–6 minutes, stirring frequently.

2 Add the stock, bring to the boil, lower the heat and simmer for 15 minutes or until the rice is tender. Add a little extra water if necessary. Remove from the heat and transfer to a large mixing bowl.

3 Add the carrot, leek, sesame seeds, almonds, cheese, beaten eggs and herbs. Mix well and season with salt and pepper to taste. Transfer the mixture to a greased 500 g/1 lb 2 oz loaf tin,smoothing the surface. Bake in a preheated oven, 180°C/ 350°F/Gas Mark 4, for 1 hour until set and firm. Leave in the tin for 10 minutes.

4 To make the sauce, melt the butter in a small pan and cook the onion until dark golden brown. Add the mushrooms and cook for 2 minutes. Stir in the flour, cook gently for 1 minute, then gradually add the stock. Bring to the boil, stirring constantly, until thickened and blended. Season to taste with salt and pepper.

5 Turn out the nut roast, slice and serve, garnished with parsley sprigs, with fresh vegetables, accompanied by the onion and mushroom sauce.

Nut & Vegetable Stir-fry

In this colourful stir-fry, vegetables are cooked in a wonderfully aromatic sauce which combines peanuts, chilli, coconut, coriander and turmeric.

NUTRITIONAL INFORMATION

Calories 446   Sugars 17g
Protein ....14g   Fat 25g
Carbohydrate ...42g   Saturates 5g

 10 mins   15 mins

SERVES 4

INGREDIENTS

115 g/4 oz unsalted roasted peanuts

2 tsp hot chilli sauce

175 ml/6 fl oz coconut milk

2 tbsp soy sauce

1 tbsp ground coriander

pinch of ground turmeric

1 tbsp dark muscovado sugar

3 tbsp sesame oil

3-4 shallots, thinly sliced

1 garlic clove, thinly sliced

1–2 fresh red chillies, deseeded and finely chopped

1 large carrot, cut into fine strips

1 yellow pepper, deseeded and sliced

1 red pepper, deseeded and sliced

1 courgette, cut into fine strips

115 g/4 oz sugar-snap peas, trimmed

7.5 cm/3 inch piece of cucumber, cut into strips

250 g/9 oz oyster mushrooms,

250 g/9 oz canned chestnuts, drained

2 tsp grated fresh root ginger

finely grated rind and juice of 1 lime

1 tbsp chopped fresh coriander

salt and pepper

lime slices, to garnish

1 To make the peanut sauce, grind the peanuts in a blender or chop very finely. Put into a small pan with the hot chilli sauce, coconut milk, soy sauce, ground coriander, ground turmeric and dark muscovado sugar. Set over a low heat and simmer gently for 3–4 minutes. Keep warm and set aside until required.

2 Heat the sesame oil in a wok or large, heavy-based frying pan. Add the shallots, garlic and chillies and stir-fry over a medium heat for 2 minutes.

3 Add the carrot, peppers, courgette and sugar-snap peas to the wok or pan and stir-fry for 2 more minutes.

4 Add the cucumber, mushrooms chestnuts, ginger, lime rind and juice and fresh coriander and stir-fry briskly fo about 5 minutes or until the vegetables are crisp, yet still crunchy. Season to taste with salt and pepper.

5 Divide the stir-fry between 4 warmed serving plates and garnish with slices of lime. Transfer the peanut sauce to a serving bowl and serve immediately with the vegetables.

Creamy Baked Fennel

Fennel tastes fabulous in this creamy sauce, flavoured with caraway seeds. A crunchy breadcrumb topping gives an interesting texture.

NUTRITIONAL INFORMATION

Calories 292	Sugars 5g	
Protein 10g	Fat 23g	
Carbohydrate ...12g	Saturates 14g	

🔔 10 mins   ⏲ 45 mins

SERVES 4

I N G R E D I E N T S

2 tbsp lemon juice

2 fennel bulbs, thinly sliced

4 tbsp butter, plus extra for greasing

115 g/4 oz low-fat soft cheese

150 m/5 fl oz single cream

150 m/5 fl oz milk

1 egg, lightly beaten

2 tsp caraway seeds

55 g/2 oz fresh white breadcrumbs

salt and pepper

fresh parsley sprigs, to garnish

1 Bring a pan of water to the boil and add the lemon juice and fennel. Cook for 2–3 minutes to blanch, drain well and place in a greased ovenproof dish.

2 Beat the soft cheese in a bowl until smooth. Add the cream, milk and beaten egg, and beat until combined. Season to taste with salt and pepper and pour the mixture over the fennel.

3 Melt 1 tablespoon of the butter in a small frying pan and fry the caraway seeds over a low heat, stirring constantly, for 1–2 minutes until they release their aroma. Sprinkle them over the fennel.

4 Melt the remaining butter in a frying pan. Add the breadcrumbs and fry over a low heat, stirring frequently, until lightly browned. Sprinkle them evenly over the top of the fennel.

5 Place in a preheated oven, 180°C/350°F/Gas Mark 4, and bake for 25–30 minutes or until the fennel is tender. Serve immediately, garnished with sprigs of parsley.

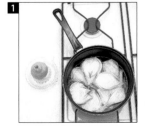

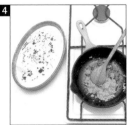

Feta Cheese Patties

Grated carrots, courgettes and feta cheese are combined with cumin seeds, poppy seeds, curry powder and chopped fresh parsley.

NUTRITIONAL INFORMATION

Calories 217	Sugars 6g
Protein 6g	Fat 16g
Carbohydrate . . .12g	Saturates 7g

15 mins   20 mins

SERVES 4

INGREDIENTS

2 large carrots

1 large courgette

1 small onion

55 g/2 oz feta cheese

4 tbsp plain flour

¼ tsp cumin seeds

½ tsp poppy seeds

1 tsp medium curry powder

1 tbsp chopped fresh parsley

1 egg, beaten

2 tbsp butter

2 tbsp vegetable oil

salt and pepper

fresh herb sprigs, to garnish

1 Grate the carrots, courgette, onion and feta cheese coarsely, either by hand or process in a food processor.

2 Combine the flour, cumin seeds, poppy seeds, curry powder and parsley in a large bowl. Season to taste with salt and pepper.

3 Add the carrot mixture to the seasoned flour, tossing well to combine. Stir in the beaten egg.

4 Heat the butter and oil in a large, heavy-based frying pan. Place heaped tablespoonfuls of the carrot mixture in the pan, flattening them slightly with the back of the spoon. Cook over a low heat for about 2 minutes on each side until crisp and golden brown. Drain on kitchen paper and keep warm. Cook more patties in the same way until all the mixture is used.

5 Serve immediately, garnished with sprigs of fresh herbs.

Filled Jacket Potatoes

Cook these potatoes conventionally, wrap them in foil and keep them warm at the edge of the barbecue, ready to fill with inspired mixtures.

NUTRITIONAL INFORMATION

Calories 564	Sugars 14g	
Protein 21g	Fat 29g	
Carbohydrate . . .58g	Saturates 18g	

 15 mins   1 hr 5 mins

SERVES 4

INGREDIENTS

4 large or 8 medium baked potatoes

paprika or chilli powder, or chopped fresh
  herbs, to garnish

MEXICAN RELISH

225 g/8 oz can sweetcorn, drained

½ red pepper, deseeded and chopped

5 cm/2 inch piece of cucumber,
  finely chopped

½ tsp chilli powder

salt and pepper

CHEESE & CHIVES

115 g/4 oz full-fat soft cheese

115 g/4 oz natural fromage frais

115 g/4 oz blue cheese, cut into cubes

1 celery stick, finely chopped

2 tsp snipped fresh chives

celery salt and pepper

SPICY MUSHROOMS

2 tbsp butter or margarine

225 g/8 oz button mushrooms

150 ml/5 fl oz natural yogurt

1 tbsp tomato purée

2 tsp mild curry powder

salt and pepper

1 Scrub the potatoes and prick them with a fork. Bake in a preheated oven, 200°C/400°F/Gas Mark 6, for about 1 hour, until just tender.

2 To make the Mexican relish, put half the sweetcorn into a bowl. Process the remainder in a blender or food processor for 10–15 seconds. Alternatively, chop and mash roughly by hand. Add the puréed corn to the corn kernels with the pepper, cucumber and chilli powder. Season to taste with salt and pepper.

3 To make the cheese & chives filling, combine the soft cheese and fromage frais until smooth. Add the blue cheese, celery and chives. Season to taste with celery salt and pepper.

4 To make the spicy mushrooms, melt the butter or margarine in a small frying pan. Add the mushrooms and cook gently for 3–4 minutes. Remove from the heat and stir in the yogurt, tomato purée and curry powder. Season to taste with salt and pepper.

5 Wrap the cooked potatoes in foil and keep warm at the edge of the barbecue. Serve the fillings sprinkled with paprika or chilli powder or herbs.

Cheeseburgers in Buns

Soya mince and seasonings combine to make these tasty vegetarian burgers, which are topped with cheese.

NUTRITIONAL INFORMATION

Calories	.551	Sugars	.4g
Protein	.29g	Fat	.24g
Carbohydrate	.57g	Saturates	.5g

1¼ hrs   10 mins

SERVES 4

INGREDIENTS

150 g/5½ oz dehydrated soya mince

300 ml10 fl oz vegetable stock

1 small onion, finely chopped

125 g/4½ oz plain flour

1 egg, beaten

1 tbsp chopped fresh herbs

1 tbsp mushroom ketchup or soy sauce

2 tbsp vegetable oil

4 burger buns

4 cheese slices

salt and pepper

BARBECUE SAUCE

2 tbsp tomato ketchup

3 tbsp sweet chutney

1 tbsp Worcestershire sauce

2 tsp Dijon mustard

1 tbsp white wine vinegar

2 tbsp fruity brown sauce

TO GARNISH

dill pickle

tomato slices

TO SERVE

lettuce, cucumber and spring onion salad

1 Put the soya mince into a large bowl. Pour in the vegetable stock and set aside to soak for about 15 minutes until it has been absorbed.

2 Meanwhile, make the barbecue sauce. combine the tomato ketchup, chutney, Worcestershire sauce and mustard. Stir in the vinegar and fruity brown sauce, then cover and chill until required.

3 Add the onion, flour, beaten egg and chopped herbs to the soya mince and mix thoroughly. Stir in the mushroom ketchup or soy sauce and season to taste with salt and pepper, stirring to mix again.

4 Form the mixture into 8 burgers. Cover and chill until ready to cook.

5 Brush the burgers with oil and barbecue over hot coals, turning once. Allow about 5 minutes on each side. Alternatively, cook under a preheated grill.

6 Split the buns and top with a burger. Lay a cheese slice on top and garnish with barbecue sauce, dill pickle and tomato slices. Serve with a salad made with lettuce, spring onions and sliced cucumber.

Marinated Brochettes

These tofu and mushroom brochettes are marinated in a lemon, garlic and herb mixture so that they soak up a delicious flavour.

NUTRITIONAL INFORMATION

Calories ....192 Sugars 0.5g
Protein ....11g Fat 16g
Carbohydrate ....1g Saturates 2g

2¼ hrs   6 mins

SERVES 4

INGREDIENTS

1 lemon

1 garlic clove, crushed

4 tbsp olive oil

4 tbsp white wine vinegar

1 tbsp chopped fresh herbs, such as rosemary, parsley and thyme

300 g/10½ oz smoked tofu

350 g/12 oz mushrooms

salt and pepper

fresh herbs, to garnish

TO SERVE

mixed salad leaves

cherry tomatoes, halved

1 Finely grate the rind from the lemon and squeeze out the juice.

2 Add the garlic, olive oil, vinegar and chopped herbs and mix well. Season to taste with salt and pepper.

3 Slice the tofu into large chunks with a sharp knife. Thread the pieces on to metal or wooden skewers, alternating them with the mushrooms.

4 Place the brochettes in a shallow, non-metallic dish and pour over the marinade. Cover with clingfilm and chill in

the refrigerator for 1–2 hours, turning the brochettes in the marinade occasionally.

5 Remove the brochettes from the dish, reserving the marinade. Cook on a medium hot barbecue, brushing them frequently with the marinade and turning often, for 6 minutes until cooked through and golden brown. Alternatively, cook under a preheated grill, turning frequently and brushing with the reserved marinade.

6 Transfer to warmed serving plates, garnish with fresh herbs and serve immediately with mixed salad leaves and cherry tomatoes.

Vine Leaf Parcels

A wonderful combination of soft cheese, chopped dates,
ground almonds and lightly fried nuts is encased in vine leaves.

NUTRITIONAL INFORMATION

Calories 459   Sugars 8g
Protein ....12g   Fat 42g
Carbohydrate ....9g   Saturates 20g

25 mins   15 mins

SERVES 4

INGREDIENTS

300 g/10½ oz full-fat soft cheese

55 g/2 oz ground almonds

2 tbsp chopped stoned dates

2 tbsp butter

4 tbsp flaked almonds

12–16 vine leaves

salt and pepper

barbecued baby corn, to serve

TO GARNISH

fresh rosemary sprigs

tomato wedges

1 Beat the soft cheese in a large bowl until smooth. Add the ground almonds and chopped dates and mix together thoroughly. Season to taste with salt and pepper.

2 Melt the butter in a small frying pan. Add the flaked almonds and fry over a very low heat, stirring constantly, for 2–3 minutes, until golden brown. Remove from the heat and set aside to cool for a few minutes.

3 Mix the fried almonds into the soft cheese mixture, stirring well to combine thoroughly.

4 Soak the vine leaves in water, if specified on the packet. Drain them, lay them out on a work surface and spoon an equal amount of the soft cheese mixture on to each. Fold over the leaves to enclose the filling.

5 Wrap the vine leaf parcels in foil, 1 or 2 per foil package. Place over the barbecue to heat through for about 8–10 minutes, turning once. Serve with barbecued baby corn and garnish with sprigs of rosemary and tomato wedges.

Turkish Kebabs

A spicy chickpea sauce is served with colourful, barbecued vegetable kebabs – perfect for a late Sunday lunch on a warm summer's day.

NUTRITIONAL INFORMATION

Calories 303   Sugars 13g
Protein ....13g   Fat 15g
Carbohydrate ...30g   Saturates 2g

15 mins   15 mins

SERVES 4

INGREDIENTS

SAUCE

4 tbsp olive oil

3 garlic cloves, crushed

1 small onion, finely chopped

425 g/15 oz can chickpeas, rinsed
   and drained

300 ml/10 fl oz natural yogurt

1 tsp ground cumin

½ tsp chilli powder

lemon juice

salt and pepper

KEBABS

1 aubergine

1 red pepper, seeded

1 green pepper, seeded

4 plum tomatoes

1 lemon, cut into wedges

8 small bay leaves

olive oil, for brushing

---

1 To make the sauce, heat the olive oil in a small frying pan. Add the garlic and onion and cook over a medium heat, stirring occasionally, for about 5 minutes, until the onion is softened and has turned golden brown.

2 Put the chickpeas and yogurt into a blender or food processor and add the cumin, chilli powder and onion mixture. Process for about 15 seconds until smooth. Alternatively, mash the chickpeas with a potato masher and stir in the yogurt, ground cumin, chilli powder and onion mixture.

3 Scrape the puréed mixture into a bowl and season to taste with lemon juice, salt and pepper. Cover with clingfilm and chill in the refrigerator until ready to serve.

4 To prepare the kebabs, cut the vegetables into large chunks and thread them on to 4 skewers, placing a bay leaf and lemon wedge at both ends of each kebab.

5 Brush the kebabs with olive oil and cook them on the barbecue, turning frequently, for 5–8 minutes. Alternatively, cook under a preheated grill. Heat the chickpea sauce and serve with the kebabs.

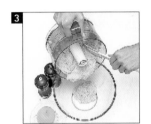

Barbecued Bean Pot

Cook this tasty vegetable and Quorn casserole conventionally, then keep it piping hot over the barbecue.

NUTRITIONAL INFORMATION

Calories 381	Sugars 17g	
Protein 21g	Fat 19g	
Carbohydrate . . .34g	Saturates 3g	

 10 mins   1 hr

SERVES 4

INGREDIENTS

4 tbsp butter or margarine

1 large onion, chopped

2 garlic cloves, crushed

2 carrots, sliced

2 celery sticks, sliced

1 tbsp paprika

2 tsp ground cumin

400 g/14 oz can chopped tomatoes

425 g/15 oz can mixed beans, rinsed and drained

150 ml/5 fl oz vegetable stock

1 tbsp muscovado sugar or black treacle

350 g/12 oz Quorn or soya cubes

salt and pepper

crusty French bread, to serve

1 Melt the butter or margarine in a large flameproof casserole and cook the onion and garlic over a medium heat, stirring occasionally, for about 5 minutes, until golden brown.

2 Add the carrots and celery and cook, stirring occasionally, for a further 2 minutes, then stir in the paprika and ground cumin.

3 Add the tomatoes and beans. Pour in the stock and add the sugar or treacle. Bring to the boil, then reduce the heat and simmer, uncovered, stirring occasionally, for 30 minutes.

4 Add the Quorn or soya cubes to the casserole, cover and cook, stirring occasionally, for a further 20 minutes.

5 Season to taste with salt and pepper, then transfer the casserole to the barbecue, setting it to one side to keep hot.

6 Ladle on to plates and serve with crusty French bread.

VARIATION

If you prefer, cook the casserole in a preheated oven, 190°C/375°F/Gas Mark 5 from step 3, but keep the dish covered. Instead of mixed beans you could use just one type of canned beans.

Stuffed Mushrooms

Use large open-cap mushrooms for this recipe for their flavour and suitability for filling.

NUTRITIONAL INFORMATION

Calories	273	Sugars	.........5g
Protein	........13g	Fat	..........18g
Carbohydrate	...15g	Saturates	.......5g

15 mins   25 mins

SERVES 4

INGREDIENTS

8 open-cap mushrooms

1 tbsp olive oil

1 small leek, chopped

1 celery stick, chopped

100 g/3½ oz firm tofu, diced

1 courgette, chopped

1 carrot, chopped

100 g/3½ oz wholemeal breadcrumbs

2 tbsp chopped fresh basil

1 tbsp tomato purée

2 tbsp pine kernels

85 g/3 oz grated Cheddar cheese

150 ml/5 fl oz vegetable stock

salt and pepper

salad, to serve

1 Remove the stalks from the mushrooms and chop finely. Reserve the caps.

2 Heat the olive oil in a large, heavy-based frying pan over a medium heat. Add the chopped mushroom stalks, leek, celery, tofu, courgette and carrot and cook, stirring constantly, for 3–4 minutes.

3 Stir in the breadcrumbs, chopped basil, tomato purée and pine kernels. Season with salt and pepper to taste and mix thoroughly.

4 Spoon the mixture into the mushroom caps and top with the grated cheese.

5 Place the mushrooms in a shallow ovenproof dish and pour the vegetable stock around them.

6 Cook in a preheated oven, 220°C/425°F/Gas Mark 7, for 20 minutes or until cooked through and the cheese has melted. Remove the mushrooms from the dish and serve immediately with a salad.

Vegetable Burgers & Chips

These spicy vegetable burgers are delicious, especially in a warm bun or roll and served with light oven chips.

NUTRITIONAL INFORMATION

Calories 461	Sugars 4g	
Protein 18g	Fat 17g	
Carbohydrate . . .64g	Saturates 2g	

45 mins   1 hr

SERVES 4

INGREDIENTS

VEGETABLE BURGERS

100 g/3½ oz spinach

2 tbsp olive oil

1 leek, chopped

2 garlic cloves, crushed

100 g/3½ oz mushrooms, chopped

300 g/10½ oz firm tofu, chopped

1 tsp chilli powder

1 tsp curry powder

1 tbsp chopped fresh coriander

75 g/2¾ oz fresh wholemeal breadcrumbs

TO SERVE

burger bap or roll

salad leaves

CHIPS

2 large potatoes

2 tbsp plain flour

1 tsp chilli powder

2 tbsp olive oil

1 To make the burgers, cook the spinach in a little boiling water for 2 minutes. Drain thoroughly and pat dry with kitchen paper.

2 Heat 1 tablespoon of the oil in a frying pan and sauté the leek and garlic for 2–3 minutes. Add the remaining ingredients, except the breadcrumbs, and cook for 5–7 minutes until the vegetables have softened. Toss in the spinach and cook for 1 minute.

3 Transfer the mixture to a food processor and process for 30 seconds until almost smooth. Transfer to a bowl, stir in the breadcrumbs, mixing well, and set aside until cool enough to handle. Using floured hands, form the mixture into 4 equal-size burgers. Chill for 30 minutes.

4 To make the chips, cut the potatoes into thin wedges and cook in a pan of boiling water for 10 minutes. Drain and toss in the flour and chilli powder. Lay the chips on a baking sheet and sprinkle with the oil. Cook in a preheated oven, 200°C/400°F/Gas Mark 6, for 30 minutes or until golden.

5 Meanwhile, heat the remaining oil in a frying pan and cook the burgers for 8–10 minutes, turning once. Place in a bap, add some salad leaves and serve with the chips.

Garlic Mushroom Pizza

This pizza dough is flavoured with garlic and herbs and topped with mixed mushrooms and melting cheese for a really delicious pizza.

NUTRITIONAL INFORMATION

Calories	541	Sugars	.........5g
Protein	.......16g	Fat	..........15g
Carbohydrate	...91g	Saturates	.......6g

🧊 45 mins   🕐 30 mins

SERVES 4

I N G R E D I E N T S

D O U G H

450 g/1 lb strong white flour, plus extra for dusting

2 tsp easy-blend dried yeast

2 garlic cloves, crushed

2 tbsp chopped fresh thyme

2 tbsp olive oil, plus extra for brushing

300 ml/10 fl oz lukewarm water

T O P P I N G

2 tbsp butter or margarine

350 g/12 oz mixed mushrooms, sliced

2 garlic cloves, crushed

2 tbsp chopped fresh parsley, plus extra to garnish

2 tbsp tomato purée

6 tbsp passata

85 g/3 oz mozzarella cheese, grated

salt and pepper

1 Put the flour, yeast, garlic and thyme in a bowl. Make a well in the centre and gradually stir in the oil and water. Bring together to form a soft dough.

2 Turn the dough on to a floured surface and knead for 5 minutes or until smooth. Roll into a 35 cm/14 inch round. Brush a baking sheet with a little oil and place the dough base on it. Set aside in a warm place for 20 minutes or until the dough puffs up.

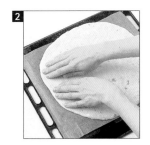

3 Meanwhile, make the topping. Melt the margarine or butter in a frying pan and cook the mushrooms, garlic and parsley over a low heat for 5 minutes.

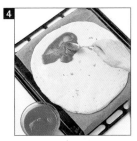

4 Combine the tomato purée and passata and spoon on to the pizza base, leaving a 1 cm/½ inch edge of dough. Spoon the mushroom mixture on top. Season to taste with salt and pepper and sprinkle the cheese on top.

5 Cook the pizza in a preheated oven, 190°C/375°F/Gas Mark 5, for 20–25 minutes or until the base is crisp and the cheese has melted. Garnish with chopped parsley and serve immediately.

Cress & Cheese Tartlets

These tasty and attractive individual tartlets are great served hot at lunchtime or cool for picnic food.

NUTRITIONAL INFORMATION

Calories	.410	Sugars	.4g
Protein	.15g	Fat	.29g
Carbohydrate	.24g	Saturates	.19g

20 mins   25 mins

SERVES 4

INGREDIENTS

100 g/3½ oz plain flour, plus extra for dusting

pinch of salt

6 tbsp butter or margarine

2–3 tbsp cold water

2 bunches of watercress

2 garlic cloves, crushed

1 shallot, chopped

150 g/5½ oz grated Cheddar cheese

4 tbsp natural yogurt

½ tsp paprika

1 Sift the flour into a mixing bowl and add the salt. Rub 2 tbsp of the butter or margarine into the flour until the mixture resembles breadcrumbs. Stir in enough of the cold water to make a smooth dough.

VARIATION

Use spinach instead of the watercress, making sure it is well drained before mixing with the remaining filling ingredients.

2 Roll the dough out on a lightly floured surface and use to line 4 x 10 cm/4 inch tartlet tins. Prick the bases with a fork and set aside to chill in the refrigerator.

3 Heat the remaining butter or margarine in a frying pan. Discard the stems from the watercress. Add the leaves to the pan with the garlic and shallot and cook for 1–2 minutes until wilted.

4 Remove the pan from the heat and stir in the grated Cheddar cheese, yogurt and paprika.

5 Spoon the mixture into the pastry cases and cook in a preheated oven, 180°C/350°F/Gas Mark 4, for 20 minutes or until the filling is just firm. Turn out the tartlets and serve immediately, if serving hot, or place on a wire rack to cool, if serving cold.

Stuffed Vegetable Snacks

In this recipe, aubergines are filled with a spicy bulgur wheat and vegetable stuffing for a delicious light meal.

NUTRITIONAL INFORMATION

Calories	360	Sugars	. . . . .17g
Protein	. . . . .9g	Fat	. . . . .16g
Carbohydrate	. . .50g	Saturates	. . . . . . .2g

40 mins   30 mins

SERVES 4

I N G R E D I E N T S

4 medium aubergines

175 g/6 oz bulgur wheat

300 ml/10 fl oz boiling water

3 tbsp olive oil

2 garlic cloves, crushed

2 tbsp pine kernels

½ tsp ground turmeric

1 tsp chilli powder

2 celery sticks, chopped

4 spring onions, chopped

1 carrot, grated

55 g/2 oz button mushrooms, chopped

2 tbsp raisins

2 tbsp chopped fresh coriander

salt

green salad, to serve

1 Cut the aubergines in half lengthways and scoop out the flesh with a teaspoon without piercing the 'shells'. Chop the flesh and set aside. Rub the insides of the aubergines with a little salt and set aside for 20 minutes.

2 Meanwhile, put the bulgur wheat in a large bowl and pour the boiling water over it. Set aside for about 20 minutes or until the bulgur wheat has completely absorbed the water.

3 Heat the oil in a heavy-based frying pan. Add the garlic, pine kernels, turmeric, chilli powder, celery, spring onions, carrot, mushrooms and raisins and cook over a low heat, stirring occasionally, for 2–3 minutes.

4 Stir in the reserved aubergine flesh and cook for a further 2–3 minutes. Add the chopped coriander, mixing well.

5 Remove the pan from the heat and stir in the bulgur wheat. Rinse the aubergine shells under cold water and pat dry with kitchen paper.

6 Spoon the bulgur filling into the aubergines and place in a roasting tin. Pour in a little boiling water and cook in a preheated oven, 180°C/350°F/Gas Mark 4, for about 15–20 minutes until piping hot. Remove from the oven, transfer to a warmed serving plate and serve hot with a green salad.

Lentil Croquettes

These mildly spiced croquettes are an ideal light lunch served with a crisp salad and a tahini dip.

NUTRITIONAL INFORMATION

Calories	409	Sugars	.........5g
Protein	........19g	Fat	..........17g
Carbohydrate	...48g	Saturates	.......2g

 1¼ hrs  1 hr

SERVES 4

INGREDIENTS

225 g/8 oz split red lentils

1 green pepper, deseeded and finely chopped

1 red onion, finely chopped

2 garlic cloves, crushed

1 tsp garam masala

½ tsp chilli powder

1 tsp ground cumin

2 tsp lemon juice

2 tbsp chopped unsalted peanuts

600 ml/1 pint water

1 egg, beaten

3 tbsp plain flour

1 tsp ground turmeric

1 tsp chilli powder

4 tbsp vegetable oil

salt and pepper

salad leaves and herbs, to serve

1 Put the lentils in a large pan with the pepper, onion, garlic, garam masala, chilli powder, ground cumin, lemon juice and peanuts. Add the water and bring to the boil. Reduce the heat and simmer gently, stirring occasionally, for about 30 minutes or until all the liquid has been absorbed.

2 Remove the mixture from the heat and set aside to cool slightly. Beat in the egg and season to taste with salt and pepper. Set aside to cool completely.

3 With floured hands, form the mixture into 8 rectangles or ovals.

4 Combine the flour, turmeric and chilli powder on a small plate. Roll the croquettes in the spiced flour mixture to coat thoroughly.

5 Heat the oil in a large frying pan. Add the croquettes, in batches, and fry, turning once, for about 10 minutes until crisp on both sides. Transfer to warmed serving plates and serve the croquettes immediately with crisp salad leaves and fresh herbs.

Brown Rice Gratin

This dish is extremely versatile and could be made with any vegetables that you have to hand and basmati rice instead of brown.

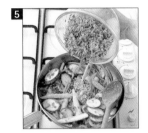

NUTRITIONAL INFORMATION

Calories 321   Sugars 6g
Protein . . . . .10g   Fat 18g
Carbohydrate . . .32g   Saturates 9g

15 mins   1 hr

SERVES 4

I N G R E D I E N T S

100 g/3½ oz brown rice

2 tbsp butter or margarine, plus extra
    for greasing

1 red onion, chopped

2 garlic cloves, crushed

1 carrot, cut into thin batons

1 courgette, sliced

85 g/3 oz baby corn cobs,
    halved lengthways

2 tbsp sunflower seeds

3 tbsp chopped fresh mixed herbs

100 g/3½ oz grated mozzarella cheese

2 tbsp wholemeal breadcrumbs

salt and pepper

1 Cook the rice in a pan of lightly salted boiling water for 20 minutes until tender. Drain well.

2 Lightly grease an 850 ml/1½ pint ovenproof dish with butter.

3 Melt the butter in a frying pan. Cook the onion over a low heat, stirring constantly, for 2 minutes or until soft.

4 Add the garlic, carrot, courgette and baby corn cobs and cook, stirring constantly, for a further 5 minutes until the vegetables are softened.

5 Combine the drained rice with the sunflower seeds and mixed herbs and stir into the pan. Stir in half of the mozzarella cheese and season with salt and pepper to taste.

6 Spoon the mixture into the prepared dish and top with the breadcrumbs and remaining cheese. Cook in a preheated oven, 180°C/350°F/Gas Mark 4, for about 25–30 minutes or until the cheese has begun to turn golden. Serve immediately.

Green Lentil Pan-fry

The green lentils used in this recipe require soaking, but are worth it for the flavour. If time is short, use red split lentils that don't need soaking.

NUTRITIONAL INFORMATION

Calories	490	Sugars	........12g
Protein	........26g	Fat	..........18g
Carbohydrates	...61g	Saturates	.......8g

30 mins   45 mins

SERVES 4

I N G R E D I E N T S

150 g/5½ oz green lentils

4 tbsp butter or vegetarian margarine

2 garlic cloves, crushed

2 tbsp olive oil

1 tbsp cider vinegar

1 red onion, cut into 8 pieces

55 g/2 oz baby corn cobs, halved lengthways

1 yellow pepper, deseeded and cut into strips

1 red pepper, deseeded and cut into strips

55 g/2 oz green beans, halved

125 ml/4 fl oz vegetable stock

2 tbsp clear honey

salt and pepper

crusty bread, to serve

1 Soak the lentils in a large saucepan of cold water for 25 minutes. Bring to the boil, reduce the heat and simmer for 20 minutes. Drain thoroughly.

2 Add 1 tablespoon of the butter or vegetarian margarine, 1 garlic clove, 1 tablespoon of oil and the vinegar to the lentils and mix well.

3 Melt the remaining butter or margarine and oil in a frying pan and stir-fry the remaining garlic, the onion, corn cobs, peppers and green beans for 3–4 minutes.

4 Add the vegetable stock and bring to the boil. Simmer for about 10 minutes or until the liquid has evaporated.

5 Add the honey and season to taste. Stir in the lentil mixture and cook for 1 minute. Spoon on to warmed serving plates and serve with crusty bread.

VARIATION

This pan-fry is very versatile – you can use a mixture of your favourite vegetables, if you prefer. Try courgettes, carrots or mangetouts.

Cashew Nut Paella

Paella traditionally contains chicken and fish, but this recipe is packed with vegetables and nuts for a truly delicious and simple vegetarian dish.

NUTRITIONAL INFORMATION

Calories 406	Sugars 8g	
Protein 10g	Fat 22g	
Carbohydrate ...44g	Saturates 6g	

 15 mins   🕐 35 mins

SERVES 4

INGREDIENTS

2 tbsp olive oil

1 tbsp butter

1 red onion, chopped

150 g/5½ oz arborio rice

1 tsp ground turmeric

1 tsp ground cumin

½ tsp chilli powder

3 garlic cloves, crushed

1 fresh green chilli, deseeded and sliced

1 green pepper, deseeded and diced

1 red pepper, deseeded and diced

85 g/3 oz baby corn cobs,
   halved lengthways

2 tbsp stoned black olives

1 large tomato, deseeded and diced

450 ml/16 fl oz vegetable stock

85 g/3 oz unsalted cashew nuts

55 g/2 oz frozen peas

2 tbsp chopped fresh parsley

pinch of cayenne pepper

salt and pepper

fresh herbs, to garnish

1 Heat the olive oil and butter in a large frying pan or paella pan until the butter has melted.

2 Add the onion and cook over a medium heat, stirring constantly, for 2–3 minutes until softened.

3 Stir in the rice, turmeric, cumin, chilli powder, garlic, sliced chilli, green and red peppers, corn cobs, olives and tomato and cook over a medium heat, stirring occasionally, for 1–2 minutes.

4 Pour in the stock and bring the mixture to the boil. Reduce the heat and cook gently, stirring constantly, for 20 minutes.

5 Add the cashew nuts and peas and cook, stirring occasionally, for a further 5 minutes. Season to taste with salt and pepper and sprinkle with fresh chopped parsley and a pinch of cayenne pepper. Transfer to warm serving plates, garnish with fresh herbs and serve immediately.

Lentil & Rice Casserole

This is a really hearty dish, perfect for cold days when a filling hot dish is just what you need to keep the winter out.

NUTRITIONAL INFORMATION

Calories	.312	Sugars	.9g
Protein	.20g	Fat	.2g
Carbohydrate	.51g	Saturates	.0.4g

 15 mins   40 mins

SERVES 4

INGREDIENTS

225 g/8 oz split red lentils

55 g/2 oz long grain rice

1.2 litres/2 pints vegetable stock

1 leek, cut into chunks

3 garlic cloves, crushed

400 g/14 oz can chopped tomatoes

1 tsp ground cumin

1 tsp chilli powder

1 tsp garam masala

1 red pepper, deseeded and sliced

100 g/3½ oz small broccoli florets

8 baby corn cobs, halved lengthways

55 g/2 oz French beans, halved

1 tbsp shredded fresh basil

salt and pepper

fresh basil sprigs, to garnish

VARIATION

You can vary the rice in this recipe – use brown or wild rice, if you prefer.

 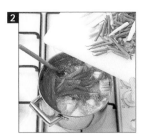 

1 Place the lentils, rice and vegetable stock in a large flameproof casserole and cook over a low heat, stirring occasionally, for 20 minutes.

2 Add the leek, garlic, tomatoes and their can juice, ground cumin, chilli powder, garam masala, sliced pepper, broccoli, corn cobs and French beans to the pan.

3 Bring the mixture to the boil, reduce the heat, cover and simmer for a further 10–15 minutes or until the vegetables are tender.

4 Add the shredded basil and season with salt and pepper to taste.

5 Garnish with fresh basil sprigs and serve immediately.

Vegetable Chop Suey

Make sure that the vegetables are all cut into pieces of a similar size in this recipe, so that they cook within the same amount of time.

NUTRITIONAL INFORMATION

Calories . . . . . . .155 Sugars 6g
Protein . . . . .4g Fat 12g
Carbohydrate . . . .9g Saturates 2g

5 mins   5 mins

SERVES 4

INGREDIENTS

1 yellow pepper, deseeded

1 red pepper, deseeded

1 carrot

1 courgette

1 fennel bulb

1 onion

55 g/2 oz mangetouts

2 tbsp peanut oil

3 garlic cloves, crushed

1 tsp grated fresh root ginger

115 g/4 oz beansprouts

2 tsp light brown sugar

2 tbsp light soy sauce

125 ml/4 fl oz vegetable stock

1 Cut the peppers, carrot, courgette and fennel into thin slices. Cut the onion into quarters and then cut each quarter in half. Slice the mangetouts diagonally to create the maximum surface area.

2 Heat the oil in a preheated wok, add the garlic and ginger and stir-fry for 30 seconds. Add the onion and stir-fry for a further 30 seconds.

3 Add the peppers, carrot, courgette, fennel and mangetouts to the wok and stir-fry for 2 minutes.

4 Add the beansprouts to the wok and stir in the sugar, soy sauce and stock. Reduce the heat to low and simmer for 1–2 minutes until the vegetables are tender and coated in the sauce.

5 Transfer the vegetables and sauce to a serving dish and serve immediately.

VARIATION

Use any combination of colourful vegetables that you have to hand to make this versatile dish.

Cauliflower & Broccoli Flan

This really is a tasty flan, the pastry case for which may be made in advance and frozen until required.

NUTRITIONAL INFORMATION

Calories	252	Sugars	.........3g
Protein	.........7g	Fat	..........16g
Carbohydrate	...22g	Saturates	.......5g

 15 mins   50 mins

SERVES 4

INGREDIENTS

PASTRY

175 g/6 oz plain flour, plus extra for dusting

pinch of salt

½ tsp paprika

1 tsp dried thyme

6 tbsp margarine

3 tbsp water

FILLING

100 g/3½ oz cauliflower florets

100 g/3½ oz broccoli florets

1 onion, cut into 8 wedges

2 tbsp butter or margarine

1 tbsp plain flour

6 tbsp vegetable stock

125 ml/4 fl oz milk

85 g/3 oz grated Cheddar cheese

salt and pepper

paprika, to garnish

1 To make the pastry, sift the flour and salt into a bowl. Add the paprika and thyme and rub in the margarine. Stir in the water and bind to form a dough.

2 Roll out the pastry on a floured surface and use to line an 18 cm/ 7 inch loose-based flan tin. Prick the base with a fork and line with baking paper. Fill with baking beans and bake in a preheated oven, 190°C/375°F/ Gas Mark 5, for 15 minutes. Remove the paper and beans and return the pastry case to the oven for 5 minutes.

3 To make the filling, cook the vegetables in a pan of lightly salted boiling water for 10–12 minutes until tender. Drain and reserve.

4 Melt the butter in a pan. Add the flour and cook, stirring constantly, for 1 minute. Remove from the heat, stir in the stock and milk and return to the heat. Bring to the boil, stirring constantly, and add 55 g/2 oz of the cheese. Season to taste with salt and pepper.

5 Spoon the cauliflower, broccoli and onion into the pastry case. Pour over the sauce and sprinkle with the remaining grated cheese. Return the flan to the oven for 10 minutes until the cheese is golden and bubbling. Garnish with paprika and serve immediately.

Macaroni Cheese & Tomato

This is a really simple, family dish which is inexpensive and easy to prepare and cook. Serve with a salad or fresh green vegetables.

NUTRITIONAL INFORMATION

Calories	592	Sugars	.........6g
Protein	........28g	Fat	..........29g
Carbohydrate	...57g	Saturates	......17g

15 mins   35-40 mins

SERVES 4

INGREDIENTS

225 g/8 oz dried elbow macaroni

175 g/6 oz grated Cheddar cheese

100 g/3½ oz grated Parmesan cheese

1 tbsp butter or margarine, plus extra for greasing

4 tbsp fresh white breadcrumbs

1 tbsp chopped fresh basil

TOMATO SAUCE

1 tbsp olive oil

1 shallot, finely chopped

2 garlic cloves, crushed

500 g/1 lb 2 oz canned chopped tomatoes

1 tbsp chopped fresh basil

salt and pepper

3 Combine the grated Cheddar and Parmesan in a bowl. Grease a deep, ovenproof dish. Spoon one-third of the tomato sauce into the base of the dish, cover with one-third of the macaroni and then top with one-third of the mixed cheeses. Season to taste with salt and pepper. Repeat these layers twice, ending with a layer of grated cheese.

4 Combine the breadcrumbs and basil and sprinkle evenly over the top. Dot the topping with the butter or margarine and cook in a preheated oven, 190°C/375°F/Gas Mark 5, for 25 minutes or until the the topping is golden brown and bubbling. Serve immediately.

1 To make the tomato sauce, heat the oil in a heavy-based pan. Add the shallots and garlic and cook, stirring constantly, for 1 minute. Add the tomatoes and basil and season with salt and pepper to taste. Cook over a medium heat, stirring constantly, for 10 minutes.

2 Meanwhile, bring a large pan of lightly salted water to the boil. Add the macaroni, bring back to the boil and cook for 8 minutes or until tender, but still firm to the bite. Drain well.

Winter Vegetable Casserole

This hearty supper dish is best served with plenty of warm crusty bread to mop up the delicious juices.

NUTRITIONAL INFORMATION

Calories 211   Sugars 6g
Protein . . . . .11g   Fat 6g
Carbohydrate . . .26g   Saturates 0.8g

 10 mins   40 mins

SERVES 4

INGREDIENTS

1 tbsp olive oil

1 red onion, halved and sliced

3 garlic cloves, crushed

225 g/8 oz spinach

1 fennel bulb, cut into 8 wedges

1 red pepper, deseeded and diced

1 tbsp plain flour

450 ml/16 fl oz vegetable stock

6 tbsp dry white wine

400 g/14 oz can chickpeas, drained

1 bay leaf

1 tsp ground coriander

½ tsp paprika

salt and pepper

fennel fronds, to garnish

COOK'S TIP

Use other canned pulses or mixed beans instead of the chickpeas, if you prefer.

1 Heat the olive oil in a large flameproof casserole. Add the onion and garlic and cook over a low heat, stirring frequently, for 1 minute. Add the spinach and cook, stirring occasionally, for 4 minutes or until wilted.

2 Add the fennel and red pepper and cook, stirring, for 2 minutes.

3 Stir in the flour and cook, stirring constantly, for 1 minute.

4 Add the stock, wine, chickpeas, bay leaf, ground coriander and paprika, cover and simmer for 30 minutes. Season to taste with salt and pepper, garnish with fennel fronds and serve immediately straight from the casserole.

Sweet & Sour Tofu

Sweet-and-sour sauce was one of the first Chinese sauces introduced to Western diets, and remains one of the most popular.

NUTRITIONAL INFORMATION

Calories	205	Sugars	........12g
Protein	........11g	Fat	...........11g
Carbohydrate	...17g	Saturates	.......1g

5 mins | 10 mins

SERVES 4

I N G R E D I E N T S

2 celery sticks

1 carrot

1 green pepper, deseeded

85 g/3 oz mangetouts

2 tbsp vegetable oil

2 garlic cloves, crushed

8 baby corn cobs

115 g/4 oz beansprouts

450 g/1 lb firm tofu, cubed

rice or noodles, to serve

S A U C E

2 tbsp light brown sugar

2 tbsp wine vinegar

225 ml/8 fl oz vegetable stock

1 tsp tomato purée

1 tbsp cornflour

1 Using a sharp knife, thinly slice the celery, cut the carrot into thin strips, dice the pepper and cut the mangetouts in half diagonally.

2 Heat the vegetable oil in a preheated wok until it is almost smoking. Reduce the heat slightly, add the crushed garlic, celery, carrot, pepper, mangetouts and baby corn cobs and stir-fry for 3–4 minutes.

3 Add the beansprouts and tofu to the wok and cook for 2 minutes, stirring frequently.

4 To make the sauce, combine the sugar, wine vinegar, stock, tomato purée and cornflour, stirring well to mix. Stir into the wok, bring to the boil and cook, stirring constantly, until the sauce thickens and clears. Continue to cook for 1 minute. Serve with rice or noodles.

COOK'S TIP

Be careful not to break up the tofu cubes when stirring.

Potato & Lemon Casserole

This is based on a Moroccan dish in which potatoes are spiced with coriander and cumin and cooked in a lemon sauce.

NUTRITIONAL INFORMATION

Calories 338	Sugars 8g	
Protein 5g	Fat 23g	
Carbohydrate . . .29g	Saturates 2g	

15 mins   35 mins

SERVES 4

INGREDIENTS

100 ml/3½ fl oz olive oil

2 red onions, cut into 8 wedges

3 garlic cloves, crushed

2 tsp ground cumin

2 tsp ground coriander

pinch of cayenne pepper

1 carrot, thickly sliced

2 small turnips, quartered

1 courgette, sliced

500 g/1 lb 2 oz potatoes, thickly sliced

juice and rind of 2 large lemons

300 ml/10 fl oz vegetable stock

2 tbsp chopped fresh coriander

salt and pepper

1 Heat the olive oil in a flameproof casserole. Add the onion and sauté over a medium heat, stirring frequently, for 3 minutes.

2 Add the garlic and cook for 30 seconds. Stir in the cumin, ground coriander and cayenne and cook, stirring constantly, for 1 minute.

3 Add the carrot, turnips, courgette and potatoes and stir to coat in the oil.

4 Add the lemon juice and rind and the vegetable stock. Season to taste with salt and pepper. Cover and cook over a medium heat, stirring occasionally, for 20–30 minutes until tender.

5 Remove the lid, sprinkle in the chopped fresh coriander and stir well. Serve immediately.

COOK'S TIP

Check the vegetables while they are cooking, because they may begin to stick to the pan. Add a little more boiling water or stock if necessary.

Vegetable Cannelloni

This dish is made with prepared cannelloni tubes, but may also be made by rolling ready-bought lasagne sheets.

NUTRITIONAL INFORMATION

Calories	594	Sugars	........12g
Protein	........13g	Fat	.........38g
Carbohydrate	...52g	Saturates	.......7g

🕐 10 mins ⏱ 45 mins

SERVES 4

INGREDIENTS

1 aubergine

125 ml/4 fl oz olive oil

225 g/8 oz spinach

2 garlic cloves, crushed

1 tsp ground cumin

85 g/3 oz mushrooms, chopped

12 cannelloni tubes

salt and pepper

TOMATO SAUCE

1 tbsp olive oil

1 onion, chopped

2 garlic cloves, crushed

2 x 400 g/14 oz cans chopped tomatoes

1 tsp caster sugar

2 tbsp chopped fresh basil

55 g/2 oz sliced mozzarella

1 Cut the aubergine into small dice. Heat the oil in a frying pan. Add the aubergine and cook over a moderate heat, stirring frequently, for 2–3 minutes.

2 Add the spinach, garlic, cumin and mushrooms and reduce the heat. Season to taste with salt and pepper and cook, stirring constantly, for 2–3 minutes. Spoon the mixture into the cannelloni tubes and place in an ovenproof dish in a single layer.

3 To make the sauce, heat the olive oil in a pan and cook the onion and garlic for 1 minute. Add the tomatoes, sugar and basil and bring to the boil. Reduce the heat and simmer gently for about 5 minutes. Spoon the sauce over the cannelloni tubes.

4 Arrange the sliced mozzarella on top of the sauce and cook in a preheated oven, 190°C/375°F/Gas Mark 5, for about 30 minutes or until the cheese is bubbling and golden brown. Serve immediately.

Cauliflower Bake

The red of the tomatoes is a great contrast to the cauliflower and herbs, making this dish appealing to both the eye and the palate.

NUTRITIONAL INFORMATION

Calories 305   Sugars 9g
Protein ....15g   Fat 14g
Carbohydrate ...31g   Saturates 6g

 10 mins   40 mins

SERVES 4

INGREDIENTS

500 g/1 lb 2 oz cauliflower, broken
    into florets

600 g/1 lb 5 oz potatoes, cubed

100 g/3½ oz cherry tomatoes

SAUCE

2 tbsp butter or margarine

1 leek, sliced

1 garlic clove, crushed

3 tbsp plain flour

300 ml/10 fl oz milk

85 g/3 oz mixed cheese, such as Cheddar,
    Parmesan and Gruyère, grated

½ tsp paprika

2 tbsp chopped fresh flat leaf parsley

salt and pepper

chopped fresh parsley, to garnish

1 Cook the cauliflower in a saucepan of boiling water for 10 minutes. Drain well and reserve. Meanwhile, cook the potatoes in a pan of boiling water for 10 minutes, drain and reserve.

2 To make the sauce, melt the butter or margarine in a saucepan and sauté the leek and garlic for 1 minute. Stir in the flour and cook, stirring constantly, for 1 minute. Remove the pan from the heat and gradually stir in the milk, 55 g/ 2 oz of the cheese, the paprika and parsley. Return the pan to the heat and

bring to the boil, stirring constantly. Season with salt and pepper to taste.

3 Spoon the cauliflower into a deep ovenproof dish. Add the cherry tomatoes and top with the potatoes. Pour the sauce over the potatoes and sprinkle on the remaining cheese.

4 Cook in a preheated oven, 180˚C/ 350˚F/Gas Mark 4, for 20 minutes or until the vegetables are cooked through and the cheese is golden brown and bubbling. Garnish and serve immediately.

VARIATION

This dish could be made with broccoli instead of the cauliflower as an alternative.

Artichoke & Cheese Tart

Artichoke hearts are delicious to eat and are delicate in flavour and appearance. They are ideal for cooking in a cheese-flavoured pastry case.

NUTRITIONAL INFORMATION

Calories 276   Sugars 3g
Protein . . . . .10g   Fat 19g
Carbohydrate . . .18g   Saturates 10g

15 mins   30 mins

SERVES 8

INGREDIENTS

175 g/6 oz plain wholemeal flour, plus extra for dusting

2 garlic cloves, crushed

6 tbsp butter or margarine

3 tbsp water

salt and pepper

FILLING

2 tbsp olive oil

1 red onion, halved and sliced

10 canned or fresh artichoke hearts

100 g/3½ oz grated Cheddar cheese

55 g/2 oz crumbled Gorgonzola cheese

2 eggs, beaten

1 tbsp chopped fresh rosemary

150 ml/5 fl oz milk

1 To make the pastry, sift the flour into a mixing bowl, add a pinch of salt and the garlic. Rub in the butter or margarine with the fingertips until the mixture resembles breadcrumbs. Stir in the water and bring the mixture together to form a dough.

2 Roll out the pastry on a lightly floured surface to fit a 20 cm/8 inch flan tin. Prick the pastry with a fork.

3 Heat the oil in a frying pan. Add the onion and cook over a medium heat, stirring occasionally, for 3 minutes. Add the artichoke hearts and cook, stirring frequently, for a further 2 minutes.

4 Combine the Cheddar, Gorgonzola, beaten eggs, rosemary and milk in a large bowl. Remove the artichoke and onion mixture from the pan with a draining spoon and transfer to the cheese mixture, stirring gently. Season to taste with salt and pepper.

5 Spoon the artichoke and cheese mixture into the pastry case and cook in a preheated oven, 200°C/400°F/Gas Mark 6, for 25 minutes or until cooked and set. Serve the flan hot or cold.

Summertime Tagliatelle

This is a really fresh-tasting dish, made with courgettes and cream, which is ideal with a crisp white wine and some crusty bread.

NUTRITIONAL INFORMATION

Calories	502	Sugars	.........5g
Protein	........16g	Fat	..........30g
Carbohydrate	...44g	Saturates	.......9g

10 mins   20 mins

SERVES 4

INGREDIENTS

650 g/1 lb 7 oz courgettes

6 tbsp olive oil

3 garlic cloves, crushed

3 tbsp chopped fresh basil

2 fresh red chillies, deseeded and sliced

juice of 1 large lemon

5 tbsp single cream

4 tbsp grated Parmesan cheese

225 g/8 oz dried tagliatelle

salt and pepper

crusty bread, to serve

1 Using a swivel vegetable peeler, slice the courgettes into thin ribbons.

2 Heat the oil in a frying pan and cook the garlic for 30 seconds.

3 Add the courgette ribbons and cook over a low heat, stirring constantly, for 5–7 minutes. Stir in the basil, chillies, lemon juice, cream and Parmesan cheese and season with salt and pepper to taste. Keep warm over a very low heat.

4 Meanwhile, bring a large pan of lightly salted water to the boil. Add the pasta, bring back to the boil and cook for 8–10 minutes until tender, but still firm to the bite. Drain thoroughly and put the pasta in a warm serving bowl.

5 Pile the courgette mixture on top of the pasta. Serve hot with crusty bread.

COOK'S TIP

Lime juice could be used instead of the lemon. As limes are usually smaller, squeeze the juice from 2 fruits.

Spinach & Nut Pasta

Use any pasta shapes that you have for this recipe – fusilli were used here. Multi-coloured pasta is visually the most attractive to use.

NUTRITIONAL INFORMATION

Calories	603	Sugars	.........5g
Protein	........12g	Fat	..........41g
Carbohydrate	...46g	Saturates	.......6g

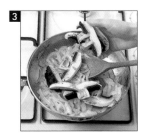

5 mins   15 mins

SERVES 4

I N G R E D I E N T S

225 g/8 oz dried pasta shapes

125 ml/4 fl oz olive oil

2 garlic cloves, crushed

1 onion, quartered and sliced

3 large flat mushrooms, sliced

225 g/8 oz spinach

2 tbsp pine kernels

5 tbsp dry white wine

salt and pepper

Parmesan shavings, to garnish

1 Bring a large pan of lightly salted water to the boil. Add the pasta, bring back to the boil and cook for 8–10 minutes until tender, but still firm to the bite. Drain well.

2 Meanwhile, heat the oil in a large pan. Add the garlic and onion and cook over a low heat, stirring occasionally, for 1 minute.

3 Add the sliced mushrooms to the pan and cook over a medium heat, stirring occasionally, for 2 minutes.

4 Lower the heat, add the spinach and cook, stirring occasionally, for about 4–5 minutes or until the spinach has just wilted.

5 Stir in the pine kernels and wine, season to taste with salt and pepper and cook for 1 minute.

6 Transfer the pasta to a warm serving bowl and toss the sauce into it, mixing well. Garnish with shavings of Parmesan cheese and serve immediately.

COOK'S TIP

Grate a little nutmeg over the dish for extra flavour, as this spice has a particular affinity with spinach.

Cantonese Garden Vegetables

This dish tastes as fresh as it looks. Try to get hold of baby vegetables because they look and taste so much better in this dish.

NUTRITIONAL INFORMATION

Calories 130	Sugars 8g
Protein 6g	Fat 8g
Carbohydrate 8g	Saturates 1g

 5 mins   10 mins

SERVES 4

INGREDIENTS

2 tbsp groundnut oil

1 tsp Chinese five-spice powder

85 g/3 oz baby carrots, halved

2 celery sticks, sliced

2 baby leeks, sliced

55 g/2 oz mangetouts

4 baby courgettes, halved lengthways

8 baby corn cobs

225 g/8 oz firm marinated tofu, cubed

4 tbsp fresh orange juice

1 tbsp clear honey

cooked rice or noodles, to serve

TO GARNISH

celery leaves

orange rind

VARIATION

Lemon juice would be just as delicious as the orange juice in this recipe, but use 3 tablespoons instead of 4 tablespoons.

1 Heat the groundnut oil in a preheated wok or large, heavy-based frying pan until almost smoking.

2 Add the Chinese five-spice powder, carrots, celery, leeks, mangetouts, courgettes and corn cobs and stir-fry for 3–4 minutes.

3 Add the tofu to the wok or frying pan and cook for a further 2 minutes, constantly stirring gently so the tofu does not break up into smaller pieces.

4 Stir the fresh orange juice and clear honey into the wok or frying pan, then reduce the heat and cook for a further 1–2 minutes.

5 Transfer the stir-fry to a serving dish, garnish with celery leaves and orange rind and serve with rice or noodles.

Pear & Walnut Pasta

This is quite an unusual combination of ingredients in a savoury dish, but is absolutely wonderful tossed into a fine pasta, such as spaghetti.

NUTRITIONAL INFORMATION

Calories	508	Sugars	.........9g
Protein	........15g	Fat	..........27g
Carbohydrate	...50g	Saturates	......11g

10 mins　　20 mins

SERVES 4

I N G R E D I E N T S

225 g/8 oz dried spaghetti

2 small ripe pears, peeled and sliced

150 ml/10 fl oz vegetable stock

5 tbsp dry white wine

2 tbsp butter

1 tbsp olive oil

1 red onion, quartered and sliced

1 garlic clove, crushed

55 g/2 oz walnut halves

2 tbsp chopped fresh oregano

1 tbsp lemon juice

85 g/3 oz dolcelatte cheese

salt and pepper

fresh oregano sprigs, to garnish

1 Bring a large pan of lightly salted water to the boil. Add the pasta, bring back to the boil and cook for 8–10 minutes until tender, but still firm to the bite. Drain thoroughly and keep warm until required.

2 Meanwhile, place the pears in a pan and pour in the stock and wine. Poach the pears over a low heat for about 10 minutes until tender. Remove the pears with a draining spoon and reserve the cooking liquid. Set the pears aside.

3 Heat the butter and oil in a pan until the butter melts. Add the onion and garlic and cook over a low heat, stirring frequently, for 2–3 minutes.

4 Stir in the walnut halves, chopped oregano and lemon juice. Stir in the reserved pears with 4 tablespoons of the poaching liquid.

5 Crumble the dolcelatte cheese into the pan and cook over a low heat, stirring occasionally, for 1–2 minutes or until the cheese is just beginning to melt. Season with salt and pepper to taste.

6 Add the pasta and toss in the sauce, using 2 forks. Transfer to a serving dish, garnish with oregano and serve.

Vegetable Galette

This is a simply scrumptious dish of aubergines and courgettes layered with a quick tomato sauce and melted cheese.

NUTRITIONAL INFORMATION

Calories 412   Sugars 12g
Protein . . . . .13g   Fat 34g
Carbohydrate . . .13g   Saturates 11g

🥗 40 mins   🕐 1¼ hrs

SERVES 4

INGREDIENTS

2 large aubergines, sliced

4 courgettes, sliced

2 x 400 g/14 oz cans chopped
    tomatoes, drained

2 tbsp tomato purée

2 garlic cloves, crushed

4 tbsp olive oil

1 tsp caster sugar

2 tbsp chopped fresh basil

olive oil, for frying

225 g/8 oz mozzarella cheese, sliced

salt and pepper

fresh basil leaves, to garnish

 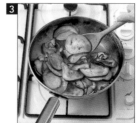 

1 Put the aubergine slices in a colander and sprinkle generously with salt. Set aside for 30 minutes, then rinse well under cold running water and drain. Thinly slice the courgettes.

2 Meanwhile, put the tomatoes, tomato purée, garlic, olive oil, sugar and chopped basil into a pan and simmer for 20 minutes or until reduced by half. Season to taste with salt and pepper.

3 Heat 2 tablespoons of olive oil in a large frying pan and cook the

aubergine slices for 2–3 minutes until just beginning to brown. Remove from the pan.

4 Add a further 2 tablespoons of oil to the pan and cook the courgette slices until browned.

5 Lay half of the aubergine slices in the base of an ovenproof dish. Cover with

half of the tomato sauce and then add a layer of courgettes. Top with half of the mozzarella slices.

6 Repeat the layers and bake in a preheated oven, 180°C/ 350°F/Gas Mark 4, for 45–50 minutes or until the vegetables are tender. Garnish with basil leaves and serve immediately.

Spinach Pancakes

Serve these pancakes as a light lunch or supper dish,
with a tomato and basil salad for a dramatic colour contrast.

NUTRITIONAL INFORMATION

Calories 663	Sugars 9g	
Protein 32g	Fat 48g	
Carbohydrate ...28g	Saturates 18g	

25 mins   25 mins

SERVES 4

INGREDIENTS

90 g/3 oz wholemeal flour

1 egg

150 ml/5 fl oz natural yogurt

3 tbsp water

1 tbsp vegetable oil, plus extra for brushing

200 g/7 oz frozen leaf spinach, thawed
and puréed

pinch of grated nutmeg

salt and pepper

TO GARNISH

lemon wedges

fresh coriander sprigs

FILLING

1 tbsp vegetable oil

3 spring onions, thinly sliced

225 g/8 oz ricotta cheese

4 tbsp natural yogurt

85 g/3 oz grated Gruyère cheese

1 egg, lightly beaten

115 g/4 oz unsalted cashew nuts

2 tbsp chopped fresh parsley

pinch of cayenne pepper

1 Sift the flour and salt into a bowl and tip in any bran in the strainer. Whisk the egg with the yogurt, water and oil. Gradually pour it on to the flour, beating constantly. Stir in the spinach and season with pepper and nutmeg to taste.

2 To make the filling, heat the oil in a pan and fry the spring onions until translucent. Remove with a draining spoon and drain on kitchen paper. Beat the ricotta with the yogurt and half the Gruyère. Beat in the egg and stir in the cashew nuts and parsley. Season with salt and cayenne to taste.

3 Lightly brush a small, heavy frying pan with oil and heat. Pour in 3–4 tablespoons of the pancake batter and tilt the pan so that it covers the base.

Cook for about 3 minutes until bubbles appear in the centre. Turn and cook the other side for about 2 minutes until lightly browned. Slide the pancake on to a warmed plate, cover with foil and keep warm while you cook the remainder. The batter should make 8–12 pancakes.

4 Spread a little filling over each pancake and fold in half and then half again, envelope style. Spoon the remaining filling into the opening.

5 Grease a shallow, ovenproof dish and arrange the pancakes in a single layer. Sprinkle on the remaining cheese and cook in a preheated oven, 180°C/350°F/Gas Mark 4, for about 15 minutes. Serve hot, garnished with lemon wedges and coriander sprigs.

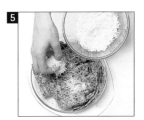

Red Curry with Cashews

This is a wonderfully quick dish to prepare. If you don't have time to prepare the curry paste, it can be bought ready-made.

NUTRITIONAL INFORMATION

Calories 274	Sugars 5g
Protein 10g	Fat 10g
Carbohydrate ...38g	Saturates 3g

25 mins   15 mins

SERVES 4

INGREDIENTS

250 ml/9 fl oz coconut milk

1 kaffir lime leaf

¼ tsp light soy sauce

4 baby corn cobs, halved lengthways

115 g/4 oz broccoli florets

115 g/4½ oz French beans, cut into 5 cm/
  2 inch pieces

4 tbsp cashew nuts

15 fresh basil leaves

1 tbsp chopped fresh coriander

1 tbsp chopped roasted peanuts, to garnish

RED CURRY PASTE

7 fresh red chillies, halved, deseeded
  and blanched

2 tsp cumin seeds

2 tsp coriander seeds

2.5 cm/1 inch piece of galangal, chopped

½ lemon grass stalk, chopped

1 tsp salt

grated rind of 1 lime

4 garlic cloves, chopped

3 shallots, chopped

2 kaffir lime leaves, shredded

1 tbsp vegetable oil

1 To make the curry paste, grind all the ingredients in a large mortar with a pestle or in a grinder. Alternatively, process briefly in a food processor. (The quantity of red curry paste is more than required for this recipe. Store for up to 3 weeks in a sealed jar in the refrigerator.)

2 Put a wok or large, heavy-based frying pan over a high heat, add 3 tablespoons of the red curry paste and stir until it gives off its aroma. Reduce the heat to medium.

3 Add the coconut milk, kaffir lime leaf, light soy sauce, baby corn cobs, broccoli florets, French beans and cashew nuts. Bring to the boil and simmer for about 10 minutes until the vegetables are cooked, but still firm and crunchy.

4 Remove and discard the lime leaf and stir in the basil leaves and coriander. Transfer to a warmed serving dish, garnish with peanuts and serve immediately.

Feta & Potato Cakes

Served with a salad these tasty vegetable patties make
a satisfying light lunch, and they are very easy to prepare.

NUTRITIONAL INFORMATION

Calories	269	Sugars	.........1g
Protein	.........9g	Fat	..........16g
Carbohydrate	...24g	Saturates	.......1g

1 hr 20 mins   35 mins

SERVES 4

INGREDIENTS

500 g/1 lb 2 oz floury potatoes, unpeeled

salt and pepper

4 spring onions, chopped

115 g/4 oz feta cheese, crumbled

2 tsp chopped fresh thyme

1 egg, beaten

1 tbsp lemon juice

plain flour, for dusting

3 tbsp sunflower or corn oil

fresh chives, to garnish

1 Cook the potatoes in lightly salted boiling water for about 25 minutes, or until tender. Drain and peel. Place the potatoes in a bowl and mash well with a potato masher or fork.

2 Add the spring onions, feta, thyme, egg and lemon juice and season to taste with salt and pepper. Mix thoroughly. Cover the bowl with clingfilm and chill in the refrigerator for 1 hour.

3 Take small handfuls of the potato mixture and roll between the palms of your hands into balls about the size of a walnut. Flatten each one slightly and dust all over with flour.

4 Heat the sunflower oil in a frying pan over a high heat and cook the potato cakes, in batches if necessary, until golden brown on both sides. Drain on kitchen paper and serve, garnished with chives.

COOK'S TIP

You can substitute other smooth cheeses such as goat's cheese for the feta, if you have some in the refrigerator that needs using up.

Winter Vegetable Cobbler

Seasonal fresh vegetables are casseroled with lentils, then topped with a ring of fresh cheese scones to make this tasty cobbler.

NUTRITIONAL INFORMATION

Calories	734	Sugars	........22g
Protein	........27g	Fat	..........30g
Carbohydrate	...96g	Saturates	......16g

 20 mins 40 mins

SERVES 4

INGREDIENTS

1 tbsp olive oil

1 garlic clove, crushed

8 small onions, halved

2 celery sticks, sliced

225 g/8 oz swede, chopped

2 carrots, sliced

½ small cauliflower, broken into florets

225 g/8 oz mushrooms, sliced

400 g/14 oz can chopped tomatoes

55 g/2 oz red lentils

2 tbsp cornflour

3–4 tbsp water

300 ml/10 fl oz vegetable stock

2 tsp Tabasco sauce

2 tsp chopped fresh oregano

fresh oregano sprigs, to garnish

COBBLER TOPPING

225 g/8 oz self-raising flour

4 tbsp butter

115 g/4 oz grated mature Cheddar cheese

2 tsp chopped fresh oregano

1 egg, lightly beaten

150 ml/5 fl oz milk

salt

1 Heat the oil and cook the garlic and onions for 5 minutes. Add the celery, swede, carrots and cauliflower and cook for 2–3 minutes. Add the mushrooms, tomatoes and lentils. Mix the cornflour and water and stir into the pan with the stock, Tabasco and oregano.

2 Transfer to an ovenproof dish, cover and bake in a preheated oven, 180°C/350°F/Gas Mark 4, for 20 minutes.

3 To make the topping, sift the flour with a pinch of salt into a bowl. Rub in the butter, then stir in most of the cheese and the chopped herbs. Beat the egg with the milk and add enough to the dry ingredients to make a soft dough. Knead lightly, roll out to 1 cm/½ inch thick and cut into 5 cm/2 inch rounds.

4 Remove the dish from the oven and increase the temperature to 200°C/400°F/Gas Mark 6. Arrange the scones around the edge of the dish, brush with the remaining egg and milk and sprinkle with the reserved cheese. Cook for a further 10–12 minutes. Garnish and serve

Spinach Pancake Layer

Nutty-tasting buckwheat pancakes are combined with a cheese and spinach mixture and baked with a crispy topping.

NUTRITIONAL INFORMATION

Calories 467	Sugars 10g
Protein 29g	Fat 26g
Carbohydrate . . .31g	Saturates 7g

45 mins

1 hr 5 mins

SERVES 4

I N G R E D I E N T S

115 g/4 oz buckwheat flour

1 egg, beaten

1 tbsp walnut oil

300 ml/10 fl oz milk

2 tsp vegetable oil

FILLING

1 kg/2 lb 4 oz young spinach leaves

2 tbsp water

2 tsp walnut oil

1 bunch of spring onions, white and green parts, chopped

1 egg, beaten

1 egg yolk

225 g/8 oz cottage cheese

½ tsp grated nutmeg

4 tbsp grated mature Cheddar cheese

1 tbsp walnut pieces

salt and pepper

1 Sift the flour into a bowl and add any husks that remain in the sieve.

2 Make a well in the centre and add the egg and walnut oil. Gradually whisk in the milk to make a smooth batter. Set aside for 30 minutes.

3 To make the filling, wash the spinach and pack into a pan with just the water clinging to its leaves. Cover tightly and cook on a high heat for 5–6 minutes until soft.

4 Drain well and set aside to cool. Heat the walnut oil and cook the spring onions for 2–3 minutes until just soft. Drain on kitchen paper and set aside.

5 Whisk the batter. Brush a small crêpe pan with oil, heat until hot and pour in enough batter just to cover the base. Cook for 1–2 minutes until set, flip over and cook for 1 minute until golden on the underside. Turn on to a warmed plate.

Repeat to make 8–10 pancakes, layering them with baking paper.

6 Chop the spinach and pat dry with kitchen paper. Combine with the spring onions, beaten egg, egg yolk, cottage cheese and nutmeg and season to taste with salt and pepper.

7 Layer the pancakes and spinach mixture on a baking sheet lined with baking paper, finishing with a pancake. Sprinkle with Cheddar cheese and bake in a preheated oven, 190°C/ 375°F/Gas Mark 5, for 20–25 minutes until firm and golden. Sprinkle with the walnuts and serve immediately.

Indian-style Omelette

Omelettes are very versatile: they go with almost anything and you can also serve them at any time of the day.

NUTRITIONAL INFORMATION

Calories . . . . . . .132 Sugars 1g
Protein . . . . .7g Fat 11g
Carbohydrate . . . .2g Saturates 2g

 10 mins   20 mins

SERVES 4

I N G R E D I E N T S

1 small onion, very finely chopped

2 fresh green chillies, deseeded and
finely chopped

2 tbsp finely chopped fresh
coriander leaves

4 eggs

1 tsp salt

2 tbsp vegetable oil

fresh basil sprigs, to garnish

toasted bread or crisp green salad, to serve

1 Place the onion, chillies and coriander in a large mixing
bowl and mix together.

2 Whisk the eggs in a separate bowl. Stir the onion
mixture into the eggs. Add the salt and whisk again.

3 Heat 1 tablespoon of the oil in a large, heavy-based
frying pan over a medium heat. Place a ladleful of the
omelette batter in the pan. Cook the omelette, turning once
and pressing down with a flat spoon to make sure that the
egg is cooked right through, until the omelette is just firm
and golden brown.

4 Repeat the same process with the remaining batter. Set
the omelettes aside, as you make them and keep warm
while you make the remaining batches.

5 Serve the omelettes hot garnished with fresh basil
sprigs and accompanied by toasted bread. Alternatively,
simply serve the omelettes with a crisp green salad for a
light lunch.

COOK'S TIP

Whether intensively farmed
or free-range, eggs are susceptible
to bacteria. Never use cracked
or dirty eggs and store them in
the refrigerator, for up to 2 weeks,
pointed end downwards. Bring
them to room temperature
about 30 minutes before using.

Rice with Fruit & Nuts

Here is a tasty and filling rice dish that is nice and spicy and includes fruits for a refreshing flavour and toasted nuts for a crunchy texture.

NUTRITIONAL INFORMATION

Calories	423	Sugars	........19g
Protein	........10g	Fat	..........17g
Carbohydrate	...62g	Saturates	.......2g

20 mins   1 hr

SERVES 6

INGREDIENTS

4 tbsp vegetable ghee or vegetable oil

1 large onion, chopped

2 garlic cloves, crushed

2.5 cm/1 inch piece of fresh root ginger, chopped

1 tsp chilli powder

1 tsp cumin seeds

1 tbsp mild or medium curry powder or paste

300 g/10½ oz brown rice

850 ml/1½ pints boiling vegetable stock

400 g/14 oz can chopped tomatoes

175 g/6 oz ready-to-eat dried apricots or peaches, cut into slivers

1 red pepper, deseeded and diced

85 g/3 oz frozen peas

1–2 small, slightly green bananas

55–85 g/2–3 oz toasted nuts, such as almonds, cashews and hazelnuts or pine kernels

salt and pepper

fresh coriander sprigs, to garnish

1 Heat the ghee or oil in a large pan. Add the onion and cook over a low heat for 3 minutes. Stir in the garlic, ginger, spices and rice and cook gently, stirring constantly, for 2 minutes, until the rice is coated in the spiced oil.

2 Pour in the boiling stock, add the chopped tomatoes and season with salt and pepper to taste. Bring to the boil, then reduce the heat, cover and simmer gently for 40 minutes or until the rice is almost cooked and most of the liquid has been absorbed.

3 Add the slivered apricots or peaches, diced red pepper and peas. Cover and continue cooking for 10 minutes. Remove from the heat and set aside for 5 minutes without uncovering.

4 Peel and slice the bananas. Uncover the rice mixture and fork through to mix the ingredients and fluff up the rice. Add the toasted nuts and sliced bananas and toss together lightly. Transfer to a warmed serving platter and then garnish with the fresh coriander sprigs. Serve immediately.

Savoury Flan

This tasty flan combines a delicious filling of lentils
and red peppers in a crisp wholemeal pastry case.

NUTRITIONAL INFORMATION

Calories	287	Sugars	.........5g
Protein	........10g	Fat	...........5g
Carbohydrate	...35g	Saturates	.......3g

 45 mins   50 mins

SERVES 8

INGREDIENTS

PASTRY

225 g/8 oz plain wholemeal flour

7 tbsp margarine, cut into small pieces

4 tbsp water

FILLING

175 g/6 oz red lentils, rinsed

300 ml/10 fl oz vegetable stock

1 tbsp margarine

1 onion, chopped

2 red peppers, deseeded and diced

1 tsp yeast extract

1 tbsp tomato purée

3 tbsp chopped fresh parsley

pepper

1 To make the pastry, place the flour in a mixing bowl and rub in the margarine. Stir in the water and bring together to form a dough. Wrap and chill in the refrigerator for 30 minutes.

2 Meanwhile, make the filling. Put the lentils in a pan with the stock, bring to the boil and simmer for 10 minutes until tender. Mash to a purée.

3 Melt the margarine in a small pan and cook the onion and red peppers, stirring frequently, until just soft. Stir in the lentil purée, yeast extract, tomato purée and parsley. Season with pepper.

4 On a lightly floured surface, roll out the dough and line a 24 cm/9½ inch loose-based quiche tin. Prick the base with a fork and spoon the lentil mixture into the pastry case.

5 Bake in a preheated oven, 200°C/ 400°F/Gas Mark 6, for 30 minutes, until the filling is firm.

VARIATION

Add sweetcorn to the flan in step 3 for a colourful and tasty change.

Spiced Spinach & Lentils

This interesting combination of lentils and spiced vegetables is delicious served with parathas, chapatis or naan bread and yogurt.

NUTRITIONAL INFORMATION

Calories	362	Sugars	.........9g
Protein	........20g	Fat	..........13g
Carbohydrate	...44g	Saturates	.......2g

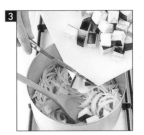

 15 mins   🕐 30 mins

SERVES 4

I N G R E D I E N T S

225 g/8 oz split red lentils

700 ml/1¼ pints water

1 onion

1 aubergine

1 red pepper, deseeded

2 courgettes

115 g/4 oz mushrooms

225g/8 oz leaf spinach

4 tbsp vegetable ghee or vegetable oil

1 fresh green chilli, deseeded and chopped

1 tsp ground cumin

1 tsp ground coriander

2.5 cm/1 inch piece of fresh root ginger, chopped

150 ml/5 fl oz vegetable stock

salt

fresh coriander sprigs, to garnish

1 Place the lentils in a pan with the water. Cover and simmer for 15 minutes until soft, but still whole.

2 Meanwhile, quarter and slice the onion. Cut the aubergine and red pepper into 1 cm/½ inch pieces. Cut the courgettes into 1 cm/½ inch thick slices. Slice the mushrooms. Discard any coarse spinach stalks and wash the leaves well.

3 Heat the ghee or oil in a large pan, add the onion and red pepper and cook gently for 3 minutes, stirring frequently. Stir in the aubergine, mushrooms, chilli, spices and ginger and cook gently for 1 minute. Add the spinach and stock and season with salt to taste. Stir until the spinach leaves wilt. Cover and simmer for about 10 minutes or until the vegetables are just tender.

4 Make a border of the lentils on a warm serving plate and spoon the vegetable mixture into the centre. (The lentils may be stirred into the vegetable mixture, instead of being used as a border, if wished.) Garnish with coriander sprigs and serve immediately.

COOK'S TIP

Wash the spinach thoroughly in several changes of cold water as it can be gritty. Drain well and shake off excess water from the leaves before adding it to the pan.

Fried Rice with Spicy Beans

This rice is really colourful and crunchy with the addition of sweetcorn and red kidney beans.

NUTRITIONAL INFORMATION

Calories	363	Sugars	.........3g
Protein	........10g	Fat	...........11g
Carbohydrate	...61g	Saturates	.......2g

 10 mins 🕐 25 mins

SERVES 4

INGREDIENTS

3 tbsp sunflower oil

1 onion, finely chopped

225 g/8 oz long grain rice

1 green pepper, deseeded and diced

1 tsp chilli powder

600 ml/1 pint boiling water

100 g/3½ oz canned sweetcorn

225 g/8 oz canned red kidney beans, drained and rinsed

2 tbsp chopped fresh coriander, plus extra for garnish (optional)

1 Heat the sunflower oil in a large preheated wok.

2 Add the onion and stir-fry over a medium heat for about 2 minutes or until softened.

COOK'S TIP

For perfect fried rice, the raw rice should ideally be soaked in a bowl of water for a short time before cooking to remove excess starch. Short grain Oriental rice can be substituted for the long grain rice.

3 Lower the heat, add the rice, green pepper and chilli powder and stir-fry for 1 minute.

4 Pour in the boiling water. Bring back to the boil, then reduce the heat and simmer for 15 minutes.

5 Stir in the sweetcorn, kidney beans and coriander and heat through, stirring occasionally.

6 Transfer to a warmed serving bowl and serve hot, sprinkled with extra coriander, if wished.

Brazil Nut & Mushroom Pie

The button mushrooms give this wholesome vegan pie a wonderful aromatic flavour. The pie can be frozen uncooked and baked from frozen.

NUTRITIONAL INFORMATION

Calories 530   Sugars 4g
Protein . . . . .12g   Fat 38g
Carbohydrate . . .38g   Saturates 8g

1 hr   50 mins

SERVES 6

INGREDIENTS

PASTRY

225 g/8 oz plain wholemeal flour

100 g/3½ oz margarine, cut into small pieces

4 tbsp water

soya milk, to glaze

FILLING

2 tbsp margarine

1 onion, chopped

1 garlic clove, finely chopped

115 g/4 oz button mushrooms, sliced

1 tbsp plain flour

150 ml/5 fl oz vegetable stock

175 g/6 oz Brazil nuts

1 tbsp tomato purée

85 g/3 oz fresh wholemeal breadcrumbs

2 tbsp chopped fresh parsley

½ tsp pepper

1 To make the pastry, place the flour in a mixing bowl and rub in the margarine with your fingertips until the mixture resembles fine breadcrumbs. Stir in the water and bring together to form a smooth dough. Knead lightly, then wrap and chill in the refrigerator for 30 minutes.

2 To make the filling, melt half of the margarine in a pan. Add the onion, garlic and mushrooms and cook over a medium heat, stirring occasionally, for 5 minutes, until softened.

3 Add the flour and cook for 1 minute, stirring constantly. Gradually add the stock, stirring until the sauce is smooth and beginning to thicken.

4 Chop the Brazil nuts. Stir the tomato purée, nuts, breadcrumbs, parsley and pepper into the pan. Remove from the heat and set aside to cool slightly.

5 On a lightly floured surface, roll out two-thirds of the pastry and use to line a 20 cm/8 inch loose-based flan tin or pie dish. Spread the filling in the pastry case. Brush the edges of the pastry with soya milk. Roll out the remaining pastry to fit the top of the pie. Seal the edges, make a slit in the top of the pastry and brush with soya milk to glaze.

6 Bake in a preheated oven, 200°C/ 400°F/Gas Mark 6, for 30–40 minutes, until golden brown. Serve immediately.

Vegetarian Sausages

The delicious cheese flavour will make these sausages a hit with vegetarians who need not feel left out when it comes to a barbecue.

NUTRITIONAL INFORMATION

Calories	213	Sugars	.........4g
Protein	.........8g	Fat	..........12g
Carbohydrate	...19g	Saturates	.......4g

 50 mins 25 mins

MAKES 8

I N G R E D I E N T S

1 tbsp sunflower oil

1 small onion, finely chopped

55 g/2 oz finely chopped mushrooms

½ red pepper, deseeded and finely chopped

400 g/14 oz can cannellini beans, rinsed and drained

100 g/3½ oz fresh breadcrumbs

100 g/3½ oz grated Cheddar cheese

1 tsp dried mixed herbs

1 egg yolk

seasoned plain flour

vegetable oil, to baste

TO SERVE

bread rolls

slices of fried onion

1 Heat the oil in a pan. Add the onion, mushrooms and red pepper and cook over a low heat, stirring frequently, for 5 minutes or until softened.

2 Mash the cannellini beans in a large mixing bowl with a potato masher. Add the onion, mushroom and pepper mixture, the breadcrumbs, grated Cheddar, herbs and egg yolk and mix together well.

3 Press the mixture together with your fingers and shape into 8 sausages.

Roll each sausage in the seasoned flour to coat evenly. Set aside to chill in the refrigerator for at least 30 minutes.

4 Barbecue the sausages on a sheet of oiled foil set over medium coals for 15–20 minutes, turning and basting

frequently with oil, until golden. Alternatively, cook under a preheated grill, basting frequently with the oil.

5 Split a bread roll down the middle and insert a layer of fried onions. Place the sausage in the roll and serve immediately.

Paprika Potatoes

Baked potatoes are an easy and welcome snack on a cold day, and here they are given a new twist with an interesting, colourful, creamy filling.

NUTRITIONAL INFORMATION

Calories	177	Sugars	.........4g
Protein	.........6g	Fat	...........1g
Carbohydrate	...38g	Saturates	.......0g

15 mins   1 hr 10 mins

SERVES 4

I N G R E D I E N T S

4 baking potatoes

125 ml/4 fl oz vegetable stock

1 onion, finely chopped

1 garlic clove, finely chopped

125 ml/4 fl oz natural yogurt

2 tsp paprika

salt and pepper

1 Preheat the oven to 200°C/400°F/Gas Mark 6. Prick the potatoes with a fork and bake for 1 hour, or until tender. Just before the potatoes are ready, pour the stock into a saucepan and add the onion and garlic. Bring to the boil and simmer for 5 minutes.

2 Remove the potatoes from the oven and cut a lengthways slice from the top of each. Do not switch off the oven. Carefully scoop out the flesh with a teaspoon, leaving the shells. Stir the flesh into the onion mixture, add half the yogurt and 1½ teaspoons of the paprika, season and stir. Push through a sieve with the back of a wooden spoon.

3 Spoon the potato mixture into the potato shells and return to the oven for 10 minutes, or until heated through. Top the potatoes with the remaining yogurt, sprinkle over the remaining paprika and serve immediately.

COOK'S TIP

If you like to eat the nutritious skin of baked potatoes, to keep it crisp rub the potatoes with a little olive oil before putting them in the oven.

Thai-spiced Mushrooms

An unusual dish that makes a good vegetarian main course. Serve the mushrooms with a colourful fresh salad.

NUTRITIONAL INFORMATION

Calories 147	Sugars 2g
Protein 6g	Fat 12g
Carbohydrate 4g	Saturates 1g

 10 mins   10 mins

SERVES 4

I N G R E D I E N T S

8 large, flat mushrooms

3 tbsp sunflower oil

2 tbsp light soy sauce

1 garlic clove, crushed

2 cm/¾ inch piece of fresh galangal or root ginger, grated

1 tbsp Thai green curry paste

8 baby corn cobs, sliced

3 spring onions, chopped

115 g/4 oz beansprouts

100 g/3½ oz firm tofu, diced

2 tsp sesame seeds, toasted

TO SERVE

chopped cucumber

sliced red pepper

1 Remove the stalks from the mushrooms and set aside. Place the caps on a baking sheet. Mix 2 tablespoons of the sunflower oil with 1 tablespoon of the light soy sauce and brush all over the mushroom caps.

2 Cook the mushroom caps under a preheated broiler until golden and tender, turning them over once.

3 Meanwhile, chop the mushroom stalks finely. Heat the remaining oil in a heavy-based frying pan or wok and stir-fry the stalks with the garlic and galangal or ginger for 1 minute.

4 Stir in the curry paste, baby corn and spring onions and stir-fry for 1 minute. Add the beansprouts and stir for a further minute.

5 Add the tofu and remaining soy sauce, then toss lightly to heat through. Spoon the mixture into the mushroom caps.

6 Sprinkle with the sesame seeds. Serve immediately with chopped cucumber and sliced red pepper.

COOK'S TIP

Galangal and ginger can be frozen for several weeks, either peeled and finely chopped ready to add to dishes, or in whole pieces. Thaw the piece or grate finely from frozen.

Oriental Vegetables

Serve this colourful mixture with a pile of golden, crispy noodles as a vegetarian main course or on its own to accompany meat dishes.

NUTRITIONAL INFORMATION

Calories 148	Sugars 7g	
Protein 8g	Fat 7g	
Carbohydrate ...14g	Saturates 1g	

 2 mins   8 mins

SERVES 4

INGREDIENTS

1 aubergine

salt

2 tbsp vegetable oil

3 garlic cloves, crushed

4 spring onions, chopped

1 small red pepper, deseeded and
    thinly sliced

4 baby corn cobs, halved lengthways

80 g/3 oz mangetouts

200 g/7 oz Chinese mustard greens,
    coarsely shredded

425 g/14½ oz canned Chinese straw
    mushrooms, drained

115 g/4 oz beansprouts

2 tbsp rice wine

2 tbsp yellow bean sauce

2 tbsp dark soy sauce

1 tsp chilli sauce

1 tsp sugar

125 ml/4 fl oz chicken or vegetable stock

1 tsp cornflour

2 tsp water

1 Trim the aubergine and cut into 5 cm/2 inch long matchsticks. Place in a colander, sprinkle with salt and set aside to drain for 30 minutes. Rinse in cold water and dry with kitchen paper.

2 Heat the oil in a frying pan or wok and stir-fry the garlic, spring onions and pepper over a high heat for 1 minute. Stir in the aubergine pieces and stir-fry for a further minute or until softened.

3 Stir in the baby corn cobs and mangetouts and stir-fry for about 1 minute. Add the mustard greens, mushrooms and beansprouts and stir-fry for 30 seconds.

4 Mix together the rice wine, yellow bean sauce, soy sauce, chilli sauce and sugar and add to the pan with the stock. Bring to the boil, stirring constantly.

5 Blend the cornflour with the water to form a smooth paste. Stir quickly into the pan or wok and cook for a further minute. Serve immediately.

Spiced Cashew Nut Curry

This unusual vegetarian dish is best served as a side dish with other curries and with rice to soak up the wonderfully rich, spiced juices.

NUTRITIONAL INFORMATION

Calories . . . . . . .455 Sugars 6g
Protein . . . . .13g Fat 39g
Carbohydrate . . .16g Saturates 11g

 8¼ hrs   25 mins

SERVES 4

INGREDIENTS

250 g/9 oz unsalted cashew nuts

1 tsp coriander seeds

1 tsp cumin seeds

2 cardamom pods, crushed

1 tbsp sunflower oil

1 onion, thinly sliced

1 garlic clove, crushed

1 small fresh green chilli, deseeded
  and chopped

1 cinnamon stick

½ tsp ground turmeric

4 tbsp coconut cream

300 ml/10 fl oz hot vegetable stock

3 kaffir lime leaves, finely shredded

salt and pepper

boiled jasmine rice, to serve

1 Soak the cashew nuts in cold water overnight. Drain thoroughly. Crush the coriander seeds, cumin seeds and cardamom pods with a pestle and mortar.

2 Heat the oil and stir-fry the onion and garlic for 2–3 minutes to soften, but not brown. Add the chilli, crushed spices, cinnamon stick and turmeric and stir-fry for a further minute.

3 Add the coconut cream and the hot stock to the pan. Bring to the boil, then add the cashew nuts and lime leaves.

4 Cover the pan, lower the heat and simmer for about 20 minutes. Serve hot, accompanied by jasmine rice.

COOK'S TIP

All spices give the best flavour when freshly crushed, but if you prefer, you can use ground spices instead of crushing them yourself in a mortar with a pestle.

Yellow Curry

Potatoes are not highly regarded in Thai cookery because rice is the traditional staple. This dish is a tasty exception.

NUTRITIONAL INFORMATION

Calories 160   Sugars 4g
Protein . . . . .3g   Fat 10g
Carbohydrate . . .15g   Saturates 1g

5 mins   15 mins

SERVES 4

INGREDIENTS

2 garlic cloves, finely chopped

3 cm/1¼ inch piece of galangal, finely chopped

1 lemon grass stalk, finely chopped

1 tsp coriander seeds

3 tbsp vegetable oil

2 tsp Thai red curry paste

½ tsp ground turmeric

200 ml/7 fl oz coconut milk

250 g/9 oz potatoes, cubed

100 ml/3½ fl oz vegetable stock

200 g/7 oz young spinach leaves

1 small onion, thinly sliced into rings

1 Place the garlic, galangal, lemon grass and coriander seeds in a mortar and pound continuously with a pestle until a smooth paste forms.

2 Heat 2 tablespoons of the oil in a frying pan or wok. Stir in the garlic paste and stir-fry for 30 seconds. Stir in the curry paste and turmeric, then add the coconut milk and bring the mixture to the boil.

3 Add the potatoes and stock. Return to the boil, then lower the heat and simmer, uncovered, for 10–12 minutes until the potatoes are almost tender.

4 Stir in the spinach and simmer until the leaves are wilted.

5 Fry the onion in the remaining oil until crisp and golden brown. Place on top of the curry just before serving.

COOK'S TIP

Choose a firm, waxy potato for this dish, one that will keep its shape during cooking, in preference to a floury variety that will break up easily once cooked.

Sweet Potato Cakes

Enticing little tasty mouthfuls of sweet potato, served hot
and sizzling from the pan with a delicious fresh tomato sauce.

NUTRITIONAL INFORMATION

Calories 349   Sugars 9g
Protein . . . . .4g   Fat 24g
Carbohydrate . . .32g   Saturates 3g

15 mins   15 mins

SERVES 4

I N G R E D I E N T S

500 g/1 lb 2 oz sweet potatoes

2 garlic cloves, crushed

1 small fresh green chilli, chopped

2 fresh coriander sprigs, chopped

1 tbsp dark soy sauce

plain flour, for shaping

vegetable oil, for frying

sesame seeds, for sprinkling

S O Y - T O M A T O   S A U C E

2 tsp vegetable oil

1 garlic clove, finely chopped

1½ tsp finely chopped fresh root ginger

3 tomatoes, peeled and chopped

2 tbsp dark soy sauce

1 tbsp lime juice

2 tbsp chopped fresh coriander

1 To make the soy-tomato sauce, heat the oil in a wok and stir-fry the garlic and ginger for about 1 minute. Add the tomatoes and stir-fry for a further 2 minutes. Remove from the heat and stir in the soy sauce, lime juice and chopped coriander. Set aside and keep warm.

2 Peel the sweet potatoes and grate finely (you can do this quickly with a food processor). Place the garlic, chilli and coriander in a mortar and crush to a smooth paste with a pestle. Stir in the soy sauce and mix with the sweet potatoes.

3 Divide the mixture into 12 equal portions. Dip into flour and pat into a flat, round patty shape.

4 Heat a shallow layer of oil in a wide frying pan. Fry the sweet potato patties in batches over a high heat until golden, turning once.

5 Drain on kitchen paper and sprinkle with sesame seeds. Serve hot, with a spoonful of the soy-tomato sauce.

COOK'S TIP

Although deeper in colour than light soy sauce, dark soy sauce is not so strongly flavoured and is sweeter.

Thai-style Omelette

In Thailand, egg dishes such as this one are eaten as part
of a main course or as a snack, depending on the time of day.

NUTRITIONAL INFORMATION

Calories	304	Sugars	.........7g
Protein	........11g	Fat	..........24g
Carbohydrate	....11g	Saturates	.......4g

10 mins   10 mins

SERVES 4

INGREDIENTS

3 tbsp vegetable oil

1 garlic clove, finely chopped

1 small onion, finely chopped

1 small aubergine, diced

½ small green pepper, deseeded
  and chopped

1 tomato, diced

1 large dried Chinese black mushroom,
  soaked, drained and sliced

1 tbsp light soy sauce

½ tsp sugar

¼ tsp ground black pepper

2 large eggs

salad leaves, tomato wedges and cucumber
  slices, to garnish

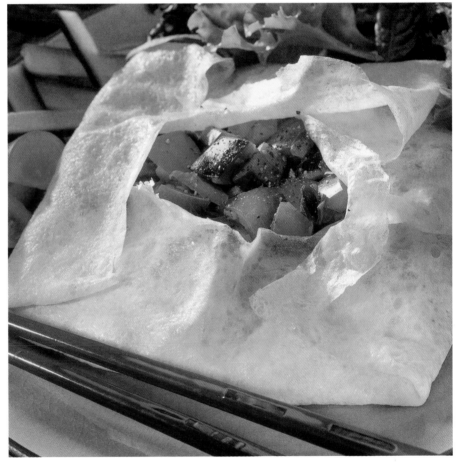

1 Heat half the oil in a pan and cook
the garlic over a high heat for
30 seconds. Add the onion and aubergine
and stir-fry until golden.

2 Add the green pepper and stir-fry for
a further minute. Stir in the tomato,
mushroom, soy sauce, sugar and pepper.
Remove from the pan and keep hot.

3 Beat the eggs lightly. Heat the
remaining oil, swirling to coat the
pan. Pour in the eggs and swirl to set
around the pan. When the egg is set,
spoon the filling into the centre. Fold in
the sides of the omelette to make a neat,
square parcel.

4 Slide the omelette carefully on to a
warmed dish and then garnish it with
a selection of salad leaves and some
tomato wedges and cucumber slices. Serve
the omelette hot.

COOK'S TIP

If you heat the pan thoroughly
before adding the oil, and heat the
oil before adding the ingredients,
you should not have a problem with
ingredients sticking to the pan.

Desserts

For many people, a meal seems incomplete without a dessert, yet it can be difficult to find recipes that do not involve masses of sugar, lashings of cream and mountains of chocolate. People with a sweet tooth, but a sensible eye on a healthy diet need look no further than this chapter. Fruit is an obvious ingredient, but there are many more possibilities – and much more exciting choices – than simple fruit salads. Rice puddings have come a long way from the nursery, especially when given a professional Oriental touch, and this chapter also includes many other traditional and family favourites – with a healthy twist.

Green Fruit Salad

This delightfully refreshing fruit salad is the perfect finale for a Chinese meal. It has a lovely light syrup made with fresh mint and honey.

NUTRITIONAL INFORMATION

Calories	157	Sugars	.......34g
Protein	.........1g	Fat	..........0.2g
Carbohydrate	...34g	Saturates	.......0g

30 mins   15 mins

SERVES 4

INGREDIENTS

1 small Charentais or honeydew melon

2 green apples

2 kiwi fruit

115 g/4 oz seedless white grapes

fresh mint sprigs, to decorate

SYRUP

1 orange

150 ml/5 fl oz white wine

150 ml/5 fl oz water

4 tbsp clear honey

fresh mint sprigs

1 To make the syrup, pare the rind from the orange using a potato peeler.

2 Put the orange rind in a pan with the white wine, water and clear honey. Bring to the boil, then simmer gently for 10 minutes.

3 Remove the syrup from the heat. Add the mint sprigs and set aside to cool.

4 To prepare the fruit, first slice the melon in half and scoop out the seeds. Use a melon baller or a teaspoon to make melon balls.

5 Core and chop the apples. Peel and slice the kiwi fruit.

6 Strain the cooled syrup into a serving bowl, removing and reserving the orange rind and discarding the mint sprigs.

7 Add the apple, grapes, kiwi fruit and melon to the serving bowl. Stir through gently to mix.

8 Serve the fruit salad, decorated with sprigs of fresh mint and some of the reserved orange rind.

COOK'S TIP

Single-flower honey has a better, more individual flavour than blended honey. Acacia honey is typically Chinese, but you could also try clove, lemon blossom, lime flower or orange blossom.

Orange & Grapefruit Salad

Sliced citrus fruits with a delicious almond and honey dressing make an unusual and refreshing dessert.

NUTRITIONAL INFORMATION

Calories 217	Sugars 33g
Protein 4g	Fat 9g
Carbohydrate . . .33g	Saturates 1g

2¼ hrs   3 mins

SERVES 4

I N G R E D I E N T S

2 grapefruit, ruby or plain

4 oranges

pared rind and juice of 1 lime

4 tbsp clear honey

2 tbsp warm water

1 fresh mint sprig, roughly chopped

55 g/2 oz chopped walnuts

1 Using a sharp knife, slice the top and bottom from the grapefruits, then slice away the rest of the skin and pith.

2 Cut between each segment of the grapefruit and remove the fleshy part only, discarding the membranes.

3 Using a sharp knife, slice the top and bottom from the oranges, then slice away the rest of the skin and pith.

4 Cut between each segment of the oranges to remove the fleshy part, discarding the membranes. Add the orange segments to the grapefruit.

5 Place the lime rind, 2 tablespoons of lime juice, the honey and the warm water in a small bowl. Whisk with a fork to mix the dressing.

6 Pour the dressing over the segmented fruit, add the chopped mint and mix well. Set aside to chill in the refrigerator for 2 hours for the flavours to mingle.

7 Place the chopped walnuts on a baking sheet. Toast lightly under a preheated medium grill for 2–3 minutes or until browned.

8 Sprinkle the toasted walnuts over the fruit and serve.

Citrus Meringue Crush

This is an excellent way to use up left-over meringue shells and is very simple to prepare. Serve with a spoonful of tangy fruit sauce.

NUTRITIONAL INFORMATION

Calories	165	Sugars	........32g
Protein	.........5g	Fat	...........1g
Carbohydrate	...37g	Saturates	.....0.4g

🍰 2 hrs   🕐 10 mins

SERVES 4

INGREDIENTS

8 ready-made meringue nests

300 ml/10 fl oz low-fat natural yogurt

½ tsp finely grated orange rind

½ tsp finely grated lemon rind

½ tsp finely grated lime rind

2 tbsp orange liqueur or unsweetened orange juice

TO DECORATE

sliced kumquat

grated lime rind

SAUCE

55 g/2 oz kumquats

8 tbsp unsweetened orange juice

2 tbsp lemon juice

2 tbsp lime juice

2 tbsp water

2–3 tsp caster sugar

1 tsp cornflour mixed with 1 tbsp water

1 Place the meringues in a plastic bag and using a rolling pin, crush into small pieces. Place in a mixing bowl. Stir in the yogurt, grated citrus rinds and the liqueur or juice. Spoon the mixture into 4 mini-basins and freeze for 1½–2 hours until firm.

2 Thinly slice the kumquats and place them in a small pan with the fruit juices and water. Bring gently to the boil and then simmer over a low heat for 3–4 minutes until the kumquats soften.

3 Sweeten with sugar to taste, stir in the cornflour mixture and cook, stirring, until thickened. Pour into a small bowl, cover the surface with clingfilm and set aside to cool – the film will help prevent a skin from forming. Chill in the refrigerator until required.

4 To serve, dip the meringue basins in hot water for 5 seconds or until they loosen and turn on to serving plates. Spoon over a little sauce, decorate with slices of kumquat and lime rind and serve.

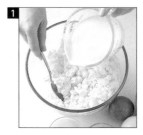

Fruit & Fibre Layers

A good, hearty dessert, guaranteed to fill you up.
Use your own favourite dried fruits in the compote.

NUTRITIONAL INFORMATION

Calories 348	Sugars 61g
Protein 10g	Fat 2g
Carbohydrate ...77g	Saturates 1g

2 hrs   15 mins

SERVES 4

I N G R E D I E N T S

115 g/4 oz no-need-to-soak dried apricots

115 g/4 oz no-need-to-soak prunes

115 g/4 oz no-need-to-soak dried peaches

55g /2 oz dried apple

25 g/1 oz dried cherries

450 ml/16 fl oz unsweetened apple juice

6 cardamom pods

6 cloves

1 cinnamon stick, broken

300 ml/10 fl oz low-fat natural yogurt

115 g/4 oz crunchy oat cereal

apricot slices, to decorate

1 Place the apricots, prunes, peaches, apples and cherries in a pan and pour in the apple juice. Add the cardamom pods, cloves and cinnamon stick, bring to the boil and simmer for 10–15 minutes until the fruits are plump and tender.

2 Remove the pan from the heat and set aside to cool completely, then transfer the mixture to a bowl and chill in the refrigerator for 1 hour. Remove and discard the spices from the fruits.

3 Spoon the compote into 4 dessert glasses, layering it alternately with yogurt and oat cereal, finishing with the oat cereal on top.

4 Decorate each dessert with slices of apricot and serve at once.

COOK'S TIP

Check the ingredients labels of dried fruit because several types have added sugar or are rolled in sugar and this will affect the sweetness – and nutritional value – of the dish that you use them in.

Apples in Red Wine

This simple combination of apples and raspberries cooked in red wine is a colourful and tempting dessert.

NUTRITIONAL INFORMATION

Calories	221	Sugars	........39g
Protein	.........2g	Fat	...........4g
Carbohydrate	...39g	Saturates	......1g

 5 mins   20 mins

SERVES 4

INGREDIENTS

4 eating apples

2 tbsp lemon juice

40 g/1½ oz low-fat spread

55 g/2 oz light muscovado sugar

1 small orange

1 cinnamon stick, broken

150 ml/5 fl oz red wine

225 g/8 oz raspberries, hulled and thawed if frozen

fresh mint sprigs, to decorate

1 Peel and core the apples, then cut them into thick wedges. Place the apples in a bowl and toss thoroughly in the lemon juice to prevent the fruit from turning brown.

2 In a frying pan, gently melt the low-fat spread over a low heat, add the sugar and stir to form a paste.

3 Stir the apple wedges into the pan and cook, stirring, for 2 minutes until well coated in the sugar paste.

4 Using a vegetable peeler, pare off a few strips of orange rind. Add the orange rind to the pan with the cinnamon pieces. Squeeze the juice from the orange and pour into the pan with the red wine. Bring to the boil, then simmer for 10 minutes, stirring constantly.

5 Add the raspberries and cook for 5 minutes until the apples are tender.

6 Discard the orange rind and cinnamon pieces. Transfer the apple and raspberry mixture to a serving plate with the wine sauce. Decorate with a sprig of fresh mint and serve hot.

VARIATION

For other fruity combinations, cook the apples with blackberries, blackcurrants or redcurrants. You may need to add more sugar if you use currants as they are not so sweet as raspberries.

Baked Pears with Cinnamon

This simple, healthy recipe is easy to prepare and cook but is deliciously warming. For a treat, serve hot on a pool of low-fat custard.

NUTRITIONAL INFORMATION

Calories 207   Sugars 35g
Protein . . . . .3g   Fat 6g
Carbohydrate . . .37g   Saturates 2g

 10 mins   25 mins

SERVES 4

INGREDIENTS

4 ripe pears

2 tbsp lemon juice

4 tbsp light muscovado sugar

1 tsp ground cinnamon

55 g/2 oz low-fat spread

finely shredded lemon rind, to decorate

low-fat custard, to serve

1 Core and peel the pears, then slice them in half lengthways and brush them all over with the lemon juice to prevent them from discoloring. Place the pears, cored side down, in a small non-stick roasting tin.

2 Place the sugar, cinnamon and low-fat spread in a small saucepan and heat gently, stirring constantly, until the sugar has dissolved. Keep the heat very low to stop too much water evaporating from the low-fat spread as it gets hot. Spoon the mixture over the pears.

3 Bake the pears in a preheated oven, 200°C/400°F/Gas Mark 6, for 20–25 minutes or until they are tender and golden, occasionally spooning the sugar mixture over the fruit during the cooking time.

4 To serve, heat the low-fat custard in a small saucepan over a low heat or in a bowl in the microwave until it is piping hot and spoon a little over the surface of each of 4 warm dessert plates. Then arrange 2 pear halves on each plate.

5 Decorate the pears with a little finely shredded lemon rind and serve immediately.

VARIATION

For alternative flavours, replace the cinnamon with ground ginger and serve the pears sprinkled with chopped stem ginger in syrup. Alternatively, use ground allspice and spoon over some warmed dark rum to serve.

Creamy Fruit Parfait

On the tiny Greek island of Kythera, this luscious combination of summer fruits and yogurt is served at tavernas as well as in homes.

NUTRITIONAL INFORMATION

Calories	.261	Sugars	.17g
Protein	.10g	Fat	.18g
Carbohydrate	.17g	Saturates	.7g

 15 mins 0 mins

SERVES 4–6

I N G R E D I E N T S

225 g/8 oz cherries

2 large peaches

2 large apricots

700 ml/1¼ pints Greek Strained Yogurt (see page 432), or natural thick yogurt

55 g/2 oz walnut halves

2 tbsp flower-scented honey

fresh redcurrants or berries, to decorate (optional)

1 To prepare the fruit, use a cherry or olive stoner to remove the cherry stones. Cut each cherry in half. Cut the peaches and apricots in half lengthways and remove the stones, then finely chop the flesh of all the fruit.

2 Place the finely chopped cherries, peaches and apricots in a bowl and gently stir together.

3 Spoon one-third of the yogurt into an attractive glass serving bowl. Top with half the fruit mixture.

4 Repeat with another layer of yogurt and fruit and, finally, top with the remaining yogurt.

5 Place the walnuts in a small food processor and pulse until chopped, but not finely ground. Sprinkle the walnuts over the top layer of the yogurt.

6 Drizzle the honey over the nuts and yogurt. Cover the bowl with clingfilm and chill in the refrigerator for at least 1 hour. Decorate the bowl with a small bunch of redcurrants, if using, just before serving.

 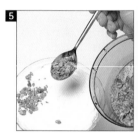 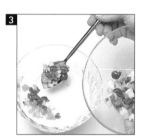

VARIATIONS

Vary the fruit to whatever is best in the market. Berries, figs, seedless grapes and melons are also delicious in this simple family-style dessert.

Almond Rice Custard

This traditional Turkish dessert is simply an almond milk thickened with ground rice. Serve with the traditional decoration of strawberries.

NUTRITIONAL INFORMATION

Calories 220   Sugars 20g
Protein ....9g   Fat 10g
Carbohydrate ...24g   Saturates 2g

50 mins   30 mins

SERVES 6

INGREDIENTS

5 g/3 oz whole blanched almonds

litre/1¾ pints milk

25 g/1 oz rice flour

pinch of salt

5 g/2 oz sugar

½ tsp almond essence or 1 tbsp almond-
    flavour liqueur

oasted flaked almonds, to decorate

TO SERVE (OPTIONAL)

50 g/12 oz fresh strawberries, sliced,
    sprinkled with 2 tbsp sugar and chilled

1 Put the almonds in a food processor and process until a thick paste forms. Bring 225 ml/8 fl oz of the milk to the boil. Gradually pour into the almond paste, with the machine running, until the mixture is smooth. Set aside for about 10 minutes.

2 Combine the rice flour, salt and sugar in a large bowl, then stir in about 4–5 tablespoons of the milk to form a smooth paste.

3 Bring the remaining milk to the boil in a heavy-based pan. Pour the hot milk into the rice flour paste and stir constantly, then return the mixture to the pan and bring to the boil. Reduce the heat and simmer for about 10 minutes until smooth and thickened. Remove from the heat.

4 Strain the almond milk through a very fine sieve into the simmering rice custard, pressing through the almonds with the back of a spoon. Return to the heat and simmer for a further 7–10 minutes or until the mixture becomes thick.

5 Remove from the heat and stir in the almond essence. Cool slightly, stirring, then pour into individual bowls. Sprinkle with the almonds and serve with the strawberries, if wished. Chill to serve later, if preferred.

Black Rice Pudding

This sticky black rice is like congée, the traditional rice porridge eaten all over South-East Asia for breakfast or as a base for other dishes.

NUTRITIONAL INFORMATION

Calories	300	Sugars	.......33g
Protein	.........4g	Fat	..........5g
Carbohydrate	...62g	Saturates	.......4g

 25 mins   30 mins

SERVES 6–8

INGREDIENTS

300 g/10½ oz black glutinous rice

850 ml/1½ pints boiling water

1 vanilla pod, split, black seeds removed and reserved

225 g/8 oz light brown sugar

55 g/2 oz packet coconut powder

400 ml/14 fl oz can thick coconut milk

2 ripe mangoes

6 passion fruit

TO DECORATE

shredded fresh coconut (optional)

fresh mint leaves

1 Put the rice in a large heavy-based pan and pour in the boiling water. Add the vanilla pod and seeds to the pan. Return to the boil, stirring once or twice. Reduce the heat to low and simmer, covered, for about 25 minutes until the rice is tender and the liquid almost absorbed; do not uncover during cooking.

2 Remove from the heat and stir in the sugar, coconut powder and half the coconut milk. Stir until the sugar is dissolved. Cover and set aside for 10 minutes. If the rice becomes too thick, add a little more of the coconut milk or a little milk or water.

3 Cut each mango lengthways along each side of the large stone to remove the flesh. Peel the mangoes, thinly slice and arrange on a serving plate.

4 Cut the passion fruit crossways in half and scoop out the pulp and juice. Spoon them over the mango slices.

5 Spoon the warm pudding into wide shallow bowls and decorate with shredded coconut and mint leaves. Drizzle some of the remaining coconut milk around the edges, if wished. Serve with the mango salad.

Orange-scented Rice

This delicious creamy pudding is flavoured with fresh oranges, orange-flavoured liqueur and two kinds of ginger.

NUTRITIONAL INFORMATION

Calories 412   Sugars 64g
Protein . . . . .7g   Fat 6g
Carbohydrate . . .82g   Saturates 4g

2 hrs   45 mins

SERVES 6

INGREDIENTS

140 g/5 oz round grain rice

225 ml/8 fl oz freshly squeezed
    orange juice

pinch of salt

500 ml/18 fl oz milk

1 vanilla pod, split

5 cm/2 inch piece of fresh root ginger,
    gently bruised

200 g/7 oz sugar

50 ml/2 fl oz double cream

4 tbsp orange-flavoured liqueur

2 tbsp butter

4–6 seedless oranges

2 pieces of stem ginger, sliced thinly, plus
    2 tbsp ginger syrup from the jar

ground ginger, for dusting

1 Put the rice in a pan with the orange juice and salt. Bring to the boil, skimming off any foam. Reduce the heat and simmer for about 10 minutes, stirring occasionally, until the juice is absorbed.

2 Gradually stir in the milk, add the vanilla pod and root ginger and simmer for 30 minutes, stirring frequently, until the milk is absorbed and the rice is very tender. Remove from the heat. Remove the vanilla pod and ginger root.

3 Stir in half the sugar, half the cream, the orange liqueur and butter until the sugar is dissolved and the butter is melted. Set aside to cool, then stir in the remaining cream and pour into a bowl. Cover and set aside at room temperature.

4 Pare the rind from the oranges and reserve. Working over a bowl to catch the juices, remove the pith from all the oranges. Cut out the segments and drop into the bowl. Stir in the stem ginger and syrup. Chill in the refrigerator.

5 Cut the pared orange rind into thin strips and blanch for 1 minute. Drain and rinse. Bring 225 ml/8 fl oz water to the boil with the remaining sugar. Add the rind strips and simmer gently until the syrup is reduced by half. Set aside to cool.

6 Serve the rice with the chilled oranges and top with the caramelized orange rind strips.

Lebanese Almond Rice

This delicate rice cream is flavoured with almonds and rosewater.
If pomegranates are in season, decorate with the gorgeous pink seeds.

NUTRITIONAL INFORMATION

Calories	199	Sugars	........17g
Protein	.........7g	Fat	...........9g
Carbohydrate	...23g	Saturates	.......2g

🍧 2½ hrs   🕐 10 mins

SERVES 6

I N G R E D I E N T S

40 g/1½ oz rice flour

pinch of salt

700 ml/1¼ pints milk

55 g/2 oz caster sugar

85 g/3 oz ground almonds

1 tbsp rosewater

T O   D E C O R A T E

2 tbsp chopped pistachios or toasted
 flaked almonds

pomegranate seeds (optional)

washed rose petals (optional)

1 Put the rice flour in a bowl, stir in the salt and make a well in the centre.

2 Pour in about 50 ml/2 fl oz of the milk and whisk thoroughly to form a smooth paste.

3 Bring the remaining milk to the boil in a heavy-based pan. Whisk in the rice flour paste and the sugar and cook, stirring constantly, until the mixture thickens and bubbles. Reduce the heat and simmer gently for 5 minutes.

4 Whisk in the ground almonds until the pudding is smooth and thickened, then remove from the heat to cool slightly. Stir in the rosewater and cool completely, stirring occasionally.

5 Divide the mixture between 6 glasses or pour into a serving bowl. Chill for at least 2 hours before serving.

6 To serve, sprinkle with the pistachios or almonds, pomegranate seeds and rose petals, if wished.

COOK'S TIP

For a smoother texture, this can be made without the ground almonds. Stir 2 tablespoons of cornflour into the ground rice and use a little more of the milk to make the paste. Proceed as directed, omitting the ground almonds.

Mini Orange Rice Cakes

These mini rice cakes, fragrant with orange or sometimes lemon rind, are found in many of the bakeries and coffee shops in Florence.

NUTRITIONAL INFORMATION

Calories 97	Sugars 9g
Protein 3g	Fat 3g
Carbohydrate ...15g	Saturates 2g

🍰 1½ hrs   🕐 20 mins

MAKES ABOUT 16

 N G R E D I E N T S

700 ml/1¼ pints milk

pinch of salt

1 vanilla pod, split, seeds removed
   and reserved

100 g/3½ oz arborio rice

100 g/3½ oz sugar

2 tbsp butter

grated rind of 2 oranges

2 eggs, separated

2 tbsp orange-flavoured liqueur or rum

1 tbsp freshly squeezed orange juice

icing sugar, for dusting

1 orange, chopped, to decorate

1 Bring the milk to the boil in a large pan over a medium-high heat. Add the salt and vanilla pod and seeds and sprinkle in the rice. Return to the boil, stirring once or twice. Reduce the heat and simmer, stirring frequently, for about 10 minutes.

2 Add the sugar and butter and simmer for about 10 minutes, stirring frequently, until thick and creamy. Pour into a bowl and stir in the orange rind. Remove the vanilla pod. Cool to room temperature, stirring occasionally.

3 Beat the egg yolks with the liqueur and orange juice, then beat into the cooled rice mixture.

4 Beat the egg whites until they hold their peaks almost stiff, but not too dry. Stir a spoonful into the rice mixture to lighten it, then gently fold in the remaining whites.

5 Spoon the mixture into 50 ml/2 fl oz muffin pan cups, lined with paper liners, filling to the brim. Bake in a preheated oven, 190°C/375°F/Gas Mark 5, for about 20 minutes until golden and cooked through. Place on a wire rack to cool for 2 minutes, then remove the liners. Set aside to cool completely.

6 Decorate with chopped orange and dust with icing sugar before serving.

Italian Lemon Rice Cake

This lemony cake should have a crisp crust with a soft moist centre. Soaking the currants in rum brings out their fruitiness.

NUTRITIONAL INFORMATION

Calories 283	Sugars 24g
Protein 7g	Fat 10g
Carbohydrate ...41g	Saturates 6g

1¼ hrs   1¼ hrs

SERVES 8–10

INGREDIENTS

1 litre/1¾ pints milk

pinch of salt

200 g/7 oz arborio or pudding rice

1 vanilla pod, split

55 g/2 oz currants

50 ml/2 fl oz rum or water

2 tsp melted butter, for greasing

cornmeal or polenta, for dusting

140 g/5 oz sugar

grated rind of 1 large lemon

4 tbsp butter, diced

3 eggs

2–3 tbsp lemon juice (optional)

icing sugar

TO SERVE

175 g/6 oz mascarpone cheese

2 tbsp rum

2 tbsp whipping cream

1 Bring the milk to the boil. Sprinkle in the salt and rice and bring back to the boil. Add the vanilla pod and seeds. Lower the heat and simmer, stirring occasionally for 30 minutes.

2 Meanwhile, bring the currants and rum to the boil, then set aside.

3 Brush the base and side of a 25 cm/10 inch loose-based cake tin with butter. Dust with 2–3 tablespoons of cornmeal and shake out any excess.

4 Remove the rice from the heat and remove the vanilla pod. Stir in all but 1 tablespoon of sugar, with the lemon rind and butter, until the sugar is dissolved. Place in iced water to cool. Stir in the soaked currants and remaining rum.

5 Using an electric mixer, beat the eggs for about 2 minutes until light and foamy. Gradually beat in about half the rice mixture, then stir in the rest. If using, stir in the lemon juice.

6 Pour into the prepared tin and smooth the top. Sprinkle with the reserved sugar and bake in a preheated oven, 160°C/325°F/Gas Mark 3 for about 40 minutes until risen and golden and slightly firm. Cool in the tin on a wire rack.

7 Remove the sides of the tin and dust the top with icing sugar. Transfer the cake to a serving plate. Whisk the mascarpone with the rum and cream and serve with the cake.

Spicy Carrot-rice Loaf

Rice flour gives this delicious loaf a tender crumb while
the cooked rice adds a chewy texture. Use any kind of cooked rice.

NUTRITIONAL INFORMATION

Calories 330	Sugars 27g	
Protein 5g	Fat 12g	
Carbohydrate . . .53g	Saturates 7g	

🥘 1½ hrs   🕐 1–1¼ hrs

SERVES 8–10

I N G R E D I E N T S

115 g/4 oz butter, melted and cooled, plus extra for greasing

225 g/8 oz plain flour, plus extra for dusting

85 g/3 oz rice flour

2 tsp baking powder

½ tsp bicarbonate of soda

½ tsp salt

1 tsp ground cinnamon

½ tsp freshly ground nutmeg

½ tsp ground ginger

55 g/2 oz cooked arborio or long grain white rice

55 g/2 oz chopped pecan nuts

85 g/3 oz sultanas or raisins

3 eggs

200 g/7 oz sugar

115 g/4 oz light brown sugar

2 carrots, grated

icing sugar, for dusting

1 Lightly grease a 23 x 12.5 cm/ 9 x 5 inch loaf tin. Line with non-stick baking paper and grease with a little butter. Dust lightly with flour.

2 Sift the flour, rice flour, baking powder, bicarbonate of soda, salt and spices into a bowl. Add the rice, nuts and sultanas or raisins and toss well to coat. Make a well in the centre of the dry ingredients and set aside.

3 Using an electric mixer, beat the eggs for about 2 minutes until light and foaming. Add the sugars and continue beating for a further 2 minutes. Beat in the melted butter, then stir in the grated carrots until blended.

4 Pour the egg and carrot mixture into the well and, using a fork, stir until a soft batter forms. Do not over mix; the batter should be slightly lumpy.

5 Pour into the prepared tin and smooth the top. Bake in a preheated oven, 180°C/350°F/Gas Mark 4, for about 1–1¼ hours until risen and golden. Cover the loaf with foil if it colours too quickly.

6 Cool the loaf in the tin on a wire rack for about 10 minutes. Carefully turn out and set aside to cool completely. Dust with a little icing sugar and cut into thin slices to serve.

Aztec Oranges

Simplicity itself, this refreshing orange dessert is hard to beat
and is the perfect follow-up to a hearty, spiced main course dish.

NUTRITIONAL INFORMATION

Calories 98	Sugars 20g
Protein 2g	Fat 0g
Carbohydrate ...20g	Saturates 0g

 45 mins   🕐 0 mins

SERVES 4–6

I N G R E D I E N T S

6 oranges

1 lime

2 tbsp tequila

2 tbsp orange-flavoured liqueur

dark soft brown sugar, to taste

fine lime rind strips, to decorate (see
Cook's Tip)

1 Using a sharp knife, cut a slice off the
top and bottom of the oranges, then
remove the peel and pith, cutting
downwards and taking care to retain the
shape of the oranges.

2 Holding the oranges on their side, cut
them horizontally into slices.

3 Place the oranges in a bowl. Cut the
lime in half and squeeze over the
oranges. Sprinkle with the tequila and
liqueur, then sprinkle over sugar to taste.

4 Cover with clingfilm and chill in the
refrigerator until ready to serve, then
transfer to a serving dish and garnish with
lime strips.

COOK'S TIP

To make the decoration, finely
pare the rind from a lime using
a vegetable peeler, then cut into
thin strips. Blanch in boiling water
for 2 minutes. Drain and rinse
under cold running water. Drain
again and pat dry with kitchen paper.

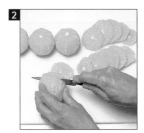

Pineapple Compote

For a more elaborate dish, accompany the pineapple with a scoop of good-quality pineapple sorbet.

NUTRITIONAL INFORMATION

Calories	87	Sugars	........19g
Protein	.........1g	Fat	...........0g
Carbohydrate	...19g	Saturates	.......0g

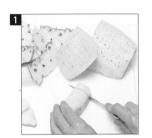

45 mins   0 mins

SERVES 4–6

INGREDIENTS

1 ripe pineapple

sugar

juice of 1 lemon

2–3 tbsp tequila or a few drops of vanilla essence

several fresh mint sprigs, leaves removed and cut into thin strips

fresh mint sprig, to decorate

1 Using a sharp knife, cut off the top and bottom of the pineapple. Place upright on a board, then slice off the skin, cutting downwards. Cut in half, remove the core, then cut the flesh into slices. Cut the fruit into chunks.

2 Put the pineapple in a bowl and sprinkle with the sugar, lemon juice, tequila or vanilla essence.

3 Toss the pineapple to coat well, then chill until ready to serve.

4 To serve, arrange on a serving plate and sprinkle with the mint strips. Decorate the dish with a mint sprig.

COOK'S TIP

Make sure you slice off the 'eyes' when removing the skin from the pineapple.

Oranges & Strawberries

Ideal as a summery dessert, this dish can also be served as a fresh fruit dish with brunch. The oranges enhance the delicate flavour of the berries.

NUTRITIONAL INFORMATION

Calories	84	Sugars	.......20g
Protein	.........2g	Fat	...........0g
Carbohydrate	...20g	Saturates	.......0g

 45 mins   🕐 0 mins

SERVES 4

INGREDIENTS

3 sweet oranges

225 g/8 oz strawberries

grated rind and juice of 1 lime

1–2 tbsp caster sugar

fresh mint sprig, to decorate

1 Using a sharp knife, cut a slice off the top and bottom of the oranges, then remove the peel and all the pith, cutting downwards and taking care to retain the shape of the oranges.

2 Using a small sharp knife, cut down between the membranes of the oranges to remove the segments. Discard the membranes.

3 Hull the strawberries, pulling the leaves off with a pinching action. Cut into slices, along the length of the strawberries.

4 Put the oranges and strawberries in a bowl, then sprinkle with the lime rind, lime juice and sugar. Chill in the refrigerator until ready to serve.

5 To serve, transfer to a serving bowl and decorate the dish with a mint sprig.

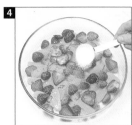

VARIATION

An optional hint of orange-flavoured liqueur is delicious on this – reduce or omit the sugar. You can replace the oranges with mangoes, and the strawberries with blackberries, for a dramatically coloured dessert.

Icy Fruit Blizzard

Keep a store of prepared fruit in the freezer, then whirl it up into this refreshing dessert, which is as light and healthy as it is satisfying.

NUTRITIONAL INFORMATION

Calories ....178 Sugars 43g

Protein ....2g Fat 1g

Carbohydrate ...43g Saturates 0g

2¼ hrs   0 mins

SERVES 4

INGREDIENTS

1 pineapple

1 large piece of deseeded watermelon, peeled and cut into small pieces

225 g/8 oz strawberries or other berries, hulled and whole or sliced

1 mango, peach or nectarine, peeled and sliced

1 banana, peeled and sliced

orange juice

caster sugar

1 Cover 2 non-stick baking sheets or ordinary baking sheets with a sheet of clingfilm. Arrange the fruit on top and freeze for at least 2 hours or until firm and icy.

2 Place 1 type of fruit in a food processor and process until it is broken up into small pieces.

3 Add a little orange juice and sugar, to taste, and continue to process until it forms a granular mixture. Repeat with the remaining fruit. Arrange in chilled bowls and serve immediately.

Cottage Cheese Hearts

These look very attractive when they are made in the French coeur à la crème china moulds, but small ramekins could be used instead.

NUTRITIONAL INFORMATION

Calories 114	Sugars 19g
Protein 9g	Fat 1g
Carbohydrate . . .19g	Saturates 0.4g

🍓 1¼ hrs   🕐 0 mins

SERVES 4

INGREDIENTS

150 g/5½ oz low-fat cottage cheese

150 ml/5 fl oz low-fat natural fromage frais

1 medium egg white

2 tbsp caster sugar

1–2 tsp vanilla essence

rose-scented geranium leaves, to decorate (optional)

SAUCE

225 g/8 oz strawberries

4 tbsp unsweetened orange juice

2–3 tsp icing sugar

1 Line 4 heart-shaped moulds with clean muslin. Place a sieve over a mixing bowl and using the back of a metal spoon, press through the cottage cheese. Mix in the fromage frais.

2 Whisk the egg white until stiff. Fold into the cheese mixture with the caster sugar and vanilla essence.

3 Spoon the cheese mixture into the moulds and smooth the tops. Place on a wire rack over a tray and set aside to chill in the refrigerator for 1 hour until firm and drained.

4 Meanwhile, make the sauce. Wash the strawberries under cold running water. Reserving a few strawberries for decoration, hull and chop the remainder.

5 Place the strawberries in a blender or food processor with the orange juice and process until smooth. Alternatively, push the strawberries through a sieve to purée them, then add the icing sugar to taste and mix well. Scrape into a bowl, cover and set aside to chill in the refrigerator until required.

6 Remove the cheese hearts from the moulds and transfer to serving plates.

7 Remove the muslin, decorate with strawberries and geranium leaves, if using, and serve with the sauce.

Carrot & Ginger Cake

This melt-in-the-mouth version of a favourite cake has a fraction of the fat of the traditional cake.

NUTRITIONAL INFORMATION

Calories	249	Sugars	........28g
Protein	.........7g	Fat	...........6g
Carbohydrate	...46g	Saturates	......1g

🌀 🌀 🌀

🍰 15 mins   ⏱ 1¼ hrs

SERVES 10

INGREDIENTS

butter, for greasing

225 g/8 oz plain flour

1 tsp baking powder

1 tsp bicarbonate of soda

2 tsp ground ginger

½ tsp salt

175 g/6 oz light muscovado sugar

225 g/8 oz carrots, grated

2 pieces chopped stem ginger

25 g/1 oz grated fresh root ginger

60 g/2 oz seedless raisins

2 medium eggs, beaten

3 tbsp corn oil

juice of 1 orange

FROSTING

225 g/8 oz low-fat soft cheese

4 tbsp icing sugar

1 tsp vanilla essence

TO DECORATE

grated carrot

finely chopped stem ginger

ground ginger

1 Preheat the oven to 180°C/350°F/Gas Mark 4. Grease and line a 20.5 cm/ 8 inch round cake tin with baking paper.

2 Sift the flour, baking powder, bicarbonate of soda, ground ginger and salt into a bowl. Stir in the sugar, carrots, stem ginger, fresh root ginger and raisins. Beat together the eggs, oil and orange juice, then pour into the bowl. Mix the ingredients together well.

3 Spoon the mixture into the tin and bake in the oven for 1–1¼ hours until firm to the touch or until a fine skewer inserted into the centre of the cake comes out clean.

4 To make the frosting, place the soft cheese in a bowl and beat to soften. Sift in the icing sugar and add the vanilla essence. Mix well.

5 Remove the cake from the tin and smooth the frosting over the top. Decorate the cake and serve.

Chocolate Cheese Pots

These super-light desserts are just the thing if you have a craving for chocolate. Serve on their own or with a selection of fruits.

NUTRITIONAL INFORMATION

Calories 117   Sugars 17g
Protein . . . . .9g   Fat 1g
Carbohydrate . . .18g   Saturates 1g

 40 mins   0 mins

SERVES 4

INGREDIENTS

300 ml/10 fl oz low-fat natural
fromage frais

150 ml/5 fl oz low-fat natural yogurt

2 tbsp icing sugar

4 tsp low-fat drinking chocolate powder

4 tsp cocoa powder

1 tsp vanilla essence

2 tbsp dark rum, optional

2 egg whites

4 chocolate cake decorations

TO SERVE

pieces of kiwi fruit, orange and banana

strawberries and raspberries

1 Combine the fromage frais and low-fat yogurt in a bowl. Sift in the icing sugar, drinking chocolate and cocoa powder and mix well. Add the vanilla essence and rum, if using.

2 In a clean bowl, whisk the egg whites until stiff. Using a metal spoon, gently fold the egg whites into the chocolate mixture.

3 Spoon the fromage frais and chocolate mixture into 4 small china dessert pots and set aside in the refrigerator to chill for about 30 minutes.

4 Decorate each chocolate cheese pot with a chocolate cake decoration and serve with an assortment of fresh fruit, such as kiwi fruit, orange, banana, strawberries and raspberries.

COOK'S TIP

This mixture would make an excellent filling for a cheesecake. Make the base out of crushed amaretti biscuits and egg white, and set the filling with 2 tablespoons powdered gelatine dissolved in 2 tablespoons of boiling water.

Strawberry Meringues

The combination of aromatic strawberries and rose water with crisp caramelized sugar meringues makes this a truly irresistible dessert.

NUTRITIONAL INFORMATION

Calories	145	Sugars	........35g
Protein	.........3g	Fat	..........0.3g
Carbohydrate	...35g	Saturates	.....0.1g

1 hr   3½ hrs

SERVES 4

I N G R E D I E N T S

3 egg whites

pinch of salt

175 g/6 oz light muscovado sugar, crushed

225 g/8 oz strawberries, hulled

2 tsp rose water

150 ml/5 fl oz low-fat natural fromage frais

extra strawberries, to serve (optional)

TO DECORATE

rose-scented geranium leaves

rose petals

1 In a large grease-free bowl, whisk the egg whites with the salt until very stiff and dry. Gradually whisk in the sugar, a spoonful at a time, until the mixture is stiff again.

2 Line a baking sheet with baking paper and drop 12 spoonfuls of the meringue mixture on to it. Bake in a preheated oven, 120°C/250°F/Gas Mark ½, for 3–3½ hours until completely dried out and crisp. Set aside to cool.

3 Reserve 55 g/2 oz of the strawberries. Place the remaining strawberries in a blender or food processor and blend for a few seconds until smooth.

4 Alternatively, mash the strawberries with a fork and press through a sieve to form a purée paste. Stir in the rose water. Chill until required.

5 To serve, slice the reserved strawberries lengthways. Sandwich the meringues together with fromage frais and sliced strawberries.

6 Spoon the strawberry rose purée paste on to 6 serving plates and top with a meringue.

7 Decorate with rose petals and rose-scented geranium leaves, and serve with extra strawberries, if using.

Pears with Maple Cream

These spicy cinnamon pears are accompanied by a delicious melt-in-the-mouth maple and ricotta cream – you won't believe it's low in fat!

NUTRITIONAL INFORMATION

Calories	190	Sugars	28g
Protein	6g	Fat	7g
Carbohydrate	28g	Saturates	4g

10 mins   25 mins

SERVES 4

INGREDIENTS

1 lemon

4 firm pears

300 ml/10 fl oz dry cider or unsweetened apple juice

1 cinnamon stick, broken in half

fresh mint leaves to decorate

MAPLE RICOTTA CREAM

115 g/4 oz low-fat ricotta cheese

115 g/4 oz low-fat natural fromage frais

½ tsp ground cinnamon

½ tsp grated lemon rind

1 tbsp maple syrup

lemon rind, to decorate

1 Using a vegetable peeler, remove the rind from the lemon and place in a non-stick frying pan. Squeeze the lemon and pour into a shallow bowl.

2 Peel the pears, then halve and core them. Toss them in the lemon juice to prevent discoloration. Place in the frying pan and pour over the remaining lemon juice.

3 Add the cider or apple juice and cinnamon stick halves. Gently bring to the boil, lower the heat so the liquid just simmers and cook the pears for 10 minutes. Remove the pears using a slotted spoon. Reserve the cooking liquid. Place the pears in a warmed heatproof serving dish, cover with foil and put in a warming drawer or low oven.

4 Return the pan to the heat, bring to the boil, then simmer for 8–10 minutes until reduced by half. Spoon over the pears.

5 To make the maple ricotta cream, combine all the ingredients. Decorate the cream with lemon rind and the pears with mint leaves and serve together.

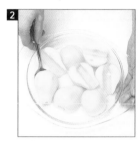

COOK'S TIP

Comice or Conference pears are suitable for this recipe. Pears ripen quickly and can bruise easily. It's best to buy them just before you plan to cook them.

Chocolate & Pineapple Cake

Decorated with thick yogurt and canned pineapple, this is a low-fat cake, but it is by no means lacking in flavour.

NUTRITIONAL INFORMATION

Calories	199	Sugars	........19g
Protein	.........5g	Fat	...........9g
Carbohydrate	...28g	Saturates	......3g

10 mins   25 mins

SERVES 9

I N G R E D I E N T S

150 g/5½ oz low-fat spread, plus extra
   for greasing

125 g/4½ oz caster sugar

100 g/3½ oz self-raising flour, sifted

3 tbsp cocoa powder, sifted

1½ tsp baking powder

2 eggs

225g/8 oz can pineapple pieces in
   natural juice

125 ml/4 fl oz low-fat thick natural yogurt

about 1 tbsp icing sugar

grated chocolate, to decorate

1 Lightly grease a 20 cm/8 inch square cake tin with a little low-fat spread.

2 Place the low-fat spread, caster sugar, flour, cocoa powder, baking powder and eggs in a large mixing bowl. Beat with a wooden spoon or electric hand whisk until smooth.

3 Pour the cake mixture into the prepared tin and level the surface. Bake in a preheated oven, 190°C/325°F/ Gas Mark 5, for 20–25 minutes or until springy to the touch. Set aside to cool slightly in the tin before transferring to a wire rack to cool completely.

4 Drain the pineapple, chop the pineapple pieces and drain again. Reserve a little pineapple for decoration, then stir the remainder into the yogurt and sweeten to taste with icing sugar.

5 Spread the pineapple and yogurt mixture over the cake and decorate with the reserved pineapple pieces. Sprinkle with the grated chocolate.

Summer Fruit Salad

A mixture of soft summer fruits in an orange-flavoured syrup with a dash of port. Serve with low-fat fromage frais.

NUTRITIONAL INFORMATION

Calories	110	Sugars	.......26g
Protein	.........1g	Fat	..........0.1g
Carbohydrate	...26g	Saturates	......0g

 5 mins   10 mins

SERVES 6

I N G R E D I E N T S

85 g/3 oz caster sugar

5 tbsp water

grated rind and juice of 1 small orange

250 g/9 oz redcurrants, stripped from their stalks

2 tsp arrowroot

2 tbsp port

115 g/4 oz blackberries

115 g/4 oz blueberries

115 g/4 oz strawberries

225 g/8 oz raspberries

low-fat fromage frais, to serve

1 Put the sugar, water and grated orange rind into a heavy-based pan and heat gently, stirring until the sugar has dissolved.

COOK'S TIP

Although this salad is really best made with fresh fruits in season, you can achieve an acceptable result with frozen equivalents, with perhaps the exception of strawberries. You can buy frozen fruits of the forest, which would be ideal, in most supermarkets.

2 Add the redcurrants and orange juice, bring to the boil and simmer gently for 2–3 minutes.

3 Strain the fruit, reserving the syrup, and put into a bowl.

4 Blend the arrowroot with a little water. Return the syrup to the pan, add the arrowroot and bring to the boil, stirring constantly until thickened.

5 Add the port and mix together well. Then pour the syrup over the redcurrants in the bowl.

6 Add the blackberries, blueberries, strawberries and raspberries. Mix the fruit together and set aside to cool until required. Serve in individual glass dishes with low-fat fromage frais.

Fruity Muffins

The perfect choice for people on a low-fat diet,
these little cakes contain no butter, just a little corn oil.

NUTRITIONAL INFORMATION

Calories 162	Sugars 11g
Protein 4g	Fat 4g
Carbohydrate ...28g	Saturates 1g

 10 mins   30 mins

MAKES 10

I N G R E D I E N T S

225 g/8 oz self-raising wholemeal flour

2 tsp baking powder

25 g/1 oz light muscovado sugar

100 g/3½ oz no-need-to-soak dried
   apricots, finely chopped

1 medium banana, mashed with 1 tbsp
   orange juice

1 tsp finely grated orange rind

300 ml/10 fl oz skimmed milk

1 egg, beaten

3 tbsp corn oil

2 tbsp rolled oats

fruit spread, honey or maple syrup,
   to serve

1 Place 10 paper muffin cases in a deep patty tin. Sift the flour and baking powder into a mixing bowl, adding any husks that remain in the sieve. Stir in the sugar and chopped apricots.

2 Make a well in the centre and add the banana, orange rind, milk, beaten egg and oil. Mix together well to form a thick batter. Divide the batter evenly among the 10 paper cases.

3 Sprinkle with a few rolled oats and bake in a preheated oven, 200°C/ 400°F/Gas Mark 6, for 25–30 minutes until well risen and firm to the touch or until a skewer inserted into the centre comes out clean.

4 Transfer the muffins to a wire rack to cool slightly. Serve the muffins while still warm with a little fruit spread, honey or maple syrup.

VARIATION

If you like dried figs, they make a deliciously crunchy alternative to the apricots; they also go very well with the flavour of orange. Other no-need-to-soak dried fruits, chopped finely, can be used as well.

Almond Trifles

Amaretti biscuits made with ground almonds have a high fat content.
Use biscuits made from apricot kernels for a lower fat content.

NUTRITIONAL INFORMATION

Calories 241	Sugars 23g
Protein 9g	Fat 6g
Carbohydrate . . .35g	Saturates 2g

 1¼ hrs   0 mins

SERVES 4

INGREDIENTS

8 amaretti biscuits

4 tbsp brandy or Amaretto liqueur

225 g/8 oz raspberries

300 ml/10 fl oz low-fat custard

300 ml/10 fl oz low-fat natural
     fromage frais

1 tsp almond essence

15 g/½ oz flaked almonds, toasted

1 tsp cocoa powder

1 Place the biscuits in a mixing bowl
and using the end of a rolling pin,
carefully crush them into small pieces.

2 Divide the crushed biscuits among
4 serving glasses. Sprinkle over the
brandy or liqueur and set aside for about
30 minutes to soften.

3 Top the layer of biscuits with a layer
of raspberries, reserving a few for
decoration, and spoon over enough
custard just to cover.

4 Combine the fromage frais with the
almond essence and spoon the
mixture over the custard, smoothing the
surface. Chill in the refrigerator for about
30 minutes.

5 Before serving, sprinkle with toasted
almonds and dust with cocoa powder.

6 Decorate the trifles with the reserved
raspberries and serve immediately.

VARIATION

Try this trifle with assorted summer
fruits. If they are a frozen mix, use
them frozen and allow them to thaw
so that the juices soak into the
biscuit base – it will taste delicious.

Spun Sugar Pears

Whole pears are poached in a Madeira syrup in the microwave, then served with a delicate spun sugar surround.

NUTRITIONAL INFORMATION

Calories	166	Sugars	........41g
Protein	........0.3g	Fat	...........0g
Carbohydrate	...41g	Saturates	......0g

20 mins | 35 mins

SERVES 4

INGREDIENTS

150 ml/5 fl oz water

150 ml/5 fl oz sweet Madeira wine

115 g/4 oz caster sugar

2 tbsp lime juice

4 ripe pears, peeled, stalks left on

fresh mint sprigs, to decorate

SPUN SUGAR

115 g/4 oz caster sugar

3 tbsp water

1 Combine the water, Madeira, sugar and lime juice in a large bowl. Cover and cook on HIGH power for 3 minutes. Stir well until the sugar dissolves.

2 Peel the pears and cut a thin slice from the base of each, so that they stand upright.

3 Add the pears to the bowl, spooning the wine syrup over them. Cover and cook on HIGH power for about 10 minutes, turning the pears over every few minutes, until they are tender. The cooking time may vary slightly depending on the ripeness of the pears. Set aside to cool, covered, in the syrup.

4 Remove the cooled pears from the syrup and set aside on serving plates. Cook the syrup, uncovered, on HIGH power for about 15 minutes until reduced by half and thickened slightly. Set aside for 5 minutes. Spoon the syrup over the pears.

5 To make the spun sugar, combine the sugar and water in a bowl. Cook, uncovered, on HIGH power for

1½ minutes. Stir until the sugar has dissolved completely. Continue to cook on HIGH power for about 5–6 minutes more until the sugar has caramelized.

6 Wait for the caramel bubbles to subside and set aside for 2 minutes. Dip a teaspoon in the caramel and spin sugar around each pear in a circular motion. Serve decorated with mint.

Rich Fruit Cake

Serve this moist, fruit-laden cake for a special occasion.
It would also make an excellent Christmas cake.

NUTRITIONAL INFORMATION

Calories 772	Sugars 137g	
Protein 14g	Fat 5g	
Carbohydrate ..179g	Saturates 1g	

 35 mins   1¾ hrs

SERVES 4

INGREDIENTS

butter or margarine, for greasing

175 g/6 oz unsweetened stoned dates

115 g/4 oz no-need-to-soak dried prunes

200 ml/7 fl oz unsweetened orange juice

2 tbsp treacle

1 tsp finely grated lemon rind

1 tsp finely grated orange rind

225 g/8 oz self-raising wholemeal flour

1 tsp mixed spice

115 g/4 oz seedless raisins

115 g/4 oz golden sultanas

115 g/4 oz currants

115 g/4 oz dried cranberries

3 large eggs, separated

TO DECORATE

1 tbsp apricot jam, softened

icing sugar, to dust

175 g/6 oz sugarpaste

strips of orange rind

strips of lemon rind

1 Grease and line a deep 20 cm/8 inch round cake tin. Chop the dates and prunes and place in a pan. Pour over the orange juice and simmer for 10 minutes. Remove the pan from the heat and beat the fruit mixture until puréed. Add the treacle and lemon and orange rinds. Set aside to cool.

2 Sift the flour and spice into a bowl, adding any husks that remain in the sieve. Add the dried fruits. When the date and prune mixture is cool, whisk in the egg yolks. In a clean bowl, whisk the egg whites until stiff. Spoon the fruit mixture into the dry ingredients and mix together.

3 Gently fold in the egg whites. Transfer to the prepared tin and bake in a preheated oven, 170°C/325°F/ Gas Mark 3, for 1½ hours. Set aside to cool.

4 Remove the cake from the tin and brush the top with jam. Dust the work surface with icing sugar and roll out the sugarpaste thinly. Lay the sugarpaste over the top of the cake and trim the edges. Decorate with orange and lemon rind.

Summer Fruit Clafoutis

Serve this mouthwatering French-style fruit-in-batter
pudding hot or cold with low-fat fromage frais or yogurt.

NUTRITIONAL INFORMATION

Calories 228	Sugars 26g	
Protein 9g	Fat 2g	
Carbohydrate ...42g	Saturates 1g	

  1¾ hrs   50 mins

SERVES 4

I N G R E D I E N T S

500 g/1 lb 2 oz prepared fresh assorted soft
fruits, such as blackberries, raspberries,
strawberries, blueberries, cherries,
gooseberries, redcurrants, blackcurrants

4 tbsp soft fruit liqueur such as crème de
cassis, kirsch or framboise

4 tbsp skimmed milk powder

115 g/4 oz plain flour

pinch of salt

55 g/2 oz caster sugar

2 eggs, beaten

300 ml/10 fl oz skimmed milk

1 tsp vanilla essence

2 tsp caster sugar, for dusting

TO SERVE

assorted soft fruits

low-fat yogurt or natural fromage frais

1 Place the assorted fruits in a mixing bowl and spoon
over the fruit liqueur. Cover and chill for 1 hour for the
fruit to macerate.

2 In a large bowl, combine the skimmed milk powder,
flour, salt and sugar. Make a well in the centre and
gradually whisk in the eggs, milk and vanilla essence, using
a balloon whisk, until smooth. Transfer to a jug and set
aside for 30 minutes.

3 Line the base of a 23 cm/9 inch round ovenproof dish
with baking paper and spoon in the fruits and juices.

4 Whisk the batter again and pour it over the fruits,
stand the dish on a baking sheet and bake in a
preheated oven, 200°C/400°F/Gas Mark 6, for 50 minutes
until firm, risen and golden brown.

5 Dust with caster sugar. Serve immediately with extra
fruits, low-fat natural yogurt or fromage frais.

Tofu Cake

This cake has a rich creamy texture just like cheesecake, but contains no dairy produce. With crushed biscuits it is easy to make a 'pastry' case.

NUTRITIONAL INFORMATION

Calories . . . . . . .282 Sugars 17g
Protein . . . . .9g Fat 15g
Carbohydrate . . .29g Saturates 4g

10 mins   45 mins

SERVES 4

INGREDIENTS

55 g/2 oz margarine, melted, plus extra for greasing

115 g/4 oz low-fat digestive biscuits, crushed

55 g/2 oz stoned dates, chopped

4 tbsp lemon juice

rind of 1 lemon

3 tbsp water

350 g/12 oz firm tofu

150 ml/5 fl oz apple juice

1 banana, mashed

1 tsp vanilla essence

1 mango, peeled and chopped

1 Lightly grease an 18 cm/7 inch round loose-bottomed cake tin.

2 Mix together the digestive biscuit crumbs and melted margarine in a bowl. Press the mixture into the base of the prepared tin.

3 Put the chopped dates, lemon juice, lemon rind and water into a pan and bring to the boil.

4 Simmer for 5 minutes until the dates are soft, then mash them roughly.

5 Place the mixture in a blender or food processor with the tofu, apple juice, mashed banana and vanilla essence and process to a thick, smooth purée. Pour the tofu purée into the prepared biscuit crumb base and smooth the surface.

6 Bake in a preheated oven, 180°C/350°F/Gas Mark 4, for 30–40 minutes until lightly golden. Set aside to cool in the tin, then chill before serving.

7 Place the chopped mango in a blender and process until smooth. Scrape into a bowl. Serve it as a sauce with the chilled cheesecake.

Fruit Loaf with Apple Spread

This sweet, fruity loaf is ideal served for tea or as a healthy snack.
The fruit spread can be made quickly while the cake is in the oven.

NUTRITIONAL INFORMATION

Calories	733	Sugars	. . . . . . .110g
Protein	. . . . .12g	Fat	. . . . .5g
Carbohydrate	. . .171g	Saturates	. . . . . .1g

1¹/₄ hrs   2 hrs

SERVES 4

I N G R E D I E N T S

175 g/6 oz rolled oats

100 g/3½ oz light muscovado sugar

1 tsp ground cinnamon

115 g/4 oz sultanas

175 g/6 oz seedless raisins

2 tbsp malt extract

300 ml/10 fl oz unsweetened apple juice

175 g/6 oz self-raising wholemeal flour

1½ tsp baking powder

strawberries and apple wedges, to serve

F R U I T   S P R E A D

225 g/8 oz strawberries, washed and hulled

2 eating apples, cored, chopped and mixed
   with 1 tbsp lemon juice to prevent them
   from browning

300 ml/10 fl oz unsweetened apple juice

1 Grease and line a 900 g/2 lb loaf tin
   and set aside. Place the oats, sugar,
cinnamon, sultanas, raisins and malt
extract in a mixing bowl. Pour in the apple
juice, stir well and set aside to soak for
30 minutes.

2 Sift in the flour and baking powder,
   adding any husks that remain in the
sieve, and fold in using a metal spoon.

Spoon the mixture into the prepared tin
and bake in a preheated oven, 180°C/
350°F/Gas Mark 4, for 1½ hours until firm
or until a skewer inserted into the centre
comes out clean.

3 Remove the tin from the oven and
   place on a wire rack to cool for about
10 minutes, then turn the loaf out on to
the rack and set aside to cool completely.

4 Meanwhile, make the fruit spread.
   Place the strawberries and apples in a
pan and pour in the apple juice. Bring to
the boil, cover and simmer for 30 minutes.
Beat the sauce well and spoon into a
clean, warmed jar. Set aside to cool, then
seal and label.

5 Serve the loaf with the fruit spread
   and strawberries and apple wedges.

Warm Currants in Cassis

Crème de cassis is a blackcurrant-based liqueur which comes from France and is an excellent flavouring for fruit dishes.

NUTRITIONAL INFORMATION

Calories	202	Sugars	........35g
Protein	.........2g	Fat	..........6g
Carbohydrate	...35g	Saturates	......4g

 10 mins   10 mins

SERVES 4

INGREDIENTS

350 g/12 oz blackcurrants

225 g/8 oz redcurrants

4 tbsp caster sugar

grated rind and juice of 1 orange

2 tsp arrowroot

2 tbsp crème de cassis

whipped cream or low-fat fromage frais, to serve

1 Using a fork, strip the blackcurrants and redcurrants from their stalks and put in a pan.

2 Add the caster sugar and orange rind and juice and heat gently, stirring, until the sugar has dissolved. Bring to the boil and simmer gently for 5 minutes.

3 Strain the currants and place in a bowl, then return the juice to the pan.

4 Blend the arrowroot with a little water and mix into the juice in the pan. Boil the mixture until thickened.

5 Set aside to cool slightly, then stir in the cassis.

6 Serve in individual dishes with whipped cream or fromage frais.

Winter Puddings

An interesting alternative to the familiar and ever-popular summer pudding that uses dried fruits and a tasty malt loaf.

NUTRITIONAL INFORMATION

Calories 447	Sugars 68g	
Protein 9g	Fat 11g	
Carbohydrate ...80g	Saturates 5g	

12 hrs   15 mins

SERVES 4

I N G R E D I E N T S

325 g/11½ oz fruit malt loaf

150 g/5½ oz no-need-to-soak dried
    apricots, coarsely chopped

85 g/3 oz dried apple, coarsely chopped

425 ml/15 fl oz orange juice

1 tsp grated orange rind, plus extra
    to decorate

2 tbsp orange liqueur

low-fat crème fraîche or low-fat natural
    fromage frais, to serve

1 Cut the malt loaf into 5 mm/½ inch thick slices.

2 Place the apricots, apple and orange juice in a pan. Bring to the boil, then simmer for 10 minutes. Remove the fruit using a draining spoon and reserve the liquid. Place the fruit in a dish and set aside to cool. Stir in the orange rind and orange liqueur.

3 Line 4 x 175 ml/6 fl oz pudding basins or ramekin dishes with baking paper.

4 Cut 4 circles from the malt loaf slices to fit the tops of the moulds and cut the remaining slices to line them.

5 Soak the malt loaf slices in the reserved fruit syrup, then arrange around the base and sides of the moulds. Trim away any crusts which overhang the edges. Fill the centres with the chopped fruit, pressing down well, and place the malt loaf circles on top.

6 Cover with baking paper and weigh each basin down with a 225g/ 8 oz

weight or a food can. Chill in the refrigerator overnight.

7 Remove the weight and baking paper. Carefully turn the puddings out on to 4 serving plates. Remove the lining paper.

8 Decorate with orange rind and serve the winter puddings with crème fraîche or fromage frais.

Red Fruits with Frothy Sauce

A colourful combination of soft fruits, served with a marshmallow sauce, is an ideal dessert when summer fruits are in season.

NUTRITIONAL INFORMATION

Calories	219	Sugars	55g
Protein	2g	Fat	0.3g
Carbohydrate	55g	Saturates	0g

🧊 1¼ hrs   🕐 20 mins

SERVES 4

INGREDIENTS

225 g/8 oz redcurrants, trimmed, thawed if frozen

225 g/8 oz cranberries

85 g/3 oz light muscovado sugar

200 ml/7 fl oz unsweetened apple juice

1 cinnamon stick, broken

300 g/10½ oz small strawberries, hulled and halved

SAUCE

225 g/8 oz raspberries, thawed if frozen

2 tbsp fruit cordial

100 g/3½ oz marshmallows

1 Place the redcurrants, cranberries and sugar in a pan. Pour in the apple juice and add the cinnamon stick. Bring the mixture to the boil and simmer gently for 10 minutes until the fruit is soft.

2 Stir the strawberries into the fruit mixture and mix well. Transfer the mixture to a bowl, cover with clingfilm and set aside to chill in the refrigerator for about 1 hour. Remove and discard the cinnamon stick.

3 Just before serving, make the sauce. Place the raspberries and fruit cordial in a small pan, bring to the boil and simmer for 2–3 minutes until the fruit is just beginning to soften. Stir the marshmallows into the raspberry mixture and heat through, stirring, until the marshmallows begin to melt.

4 Transfer the fruit salad to serving bowls. Spoon over the raspberry and marshmallow sauce and serve.

COOK'S TIP

This sauce is delicious poured over low-fat ice cream. For an extra-colourful sauce, replace the raspberries with an assortment of summer berries.

Fruity Potato Cake

Sweet potatoes mix beautifully with fruit and brown sugar in this unusual cake. Add a few drops of rum or brandy if you like.

NUTRITIONAL INFORMATION

Calories	275	Sugars	........44g
Protein	.........6g	Fat	...........5g
Carbohydrate	...55g	Saturates	......2g

15 mins   1½ hrs

SERVES 6

I N G R E D I E N T S

1 tbsp butter, melted, plus extra
    for greasing

675 g/1½ lb sweet potatoes, diced

115 g/4 oz demerara sugar

3 eggs

3 tbsp skimmed milk

1 tbsp lemon juice

grated rind of 1 lemon

1 tsp caraway seeds

115 g/4 oz dried fruits, such as apple,
    pear or mango, chopped

2 tsp baking powder

1 Lightly grease an 18 cm/7 inch square cake tin.

2 Bring a large pan of water to the boil. Add the sweet potatoes, bring back to the boil and cook for 10 minutes or until soft. Drain and mash until smooth.

3 Transfer the mashed sweet potatoes to a mixing bowl while still hot and add the butter and sugar, mixing thoroughly to dissolve.

4 Beat in the eggs, skimmed milk, lemon juice and rind, caraway seeds and chopped dried fruit. Add the baking powder and mix well.

5 Pour the mixture into the prepared cake tin and smooth the top. Cook in a preheated oven, 160°C/ 325°F/Gas Mark 3, for 1–11/4 hours or until cooked

through and a skewer inserted into the centre comes out clean.

6 Remove the cake from the tin and transfer to a wire rack to cool. Cut into thick slices to serve or wrap in clingfilm and store in the freezer. (To serve, thaw and warm through.)

Paper-thin Fruit Pies

The extra-crisp pastry cases, filled with slices of fruit and glazed with apricot jam, are best served hot with low-fat custard.

NUTRITIONAL INFORMATION

Calories	158	Sugars	........12g
Protein	.........2g	Fat	..........10g
Carbohydrate	...14g	Saturates	......2g

 20 mins 15 mins

SERVES 4

I N G R E D I E N T S

1 medium eating apple

1 medium ripe pear

2 tbsp lemon juice

55 g/2 oz low-fat spread

4 rectangular sheets of filo pastry, thawed if frozen

2 tbsp low-sugar apricot jam

1 tbsp unsweetened orange juice

1 tbsp finely chopped pistachio nuts, shelled

2 tsp icing sugar, for dusting

low-fat custard, to serve

1 Core and thinly slice the apple and pear and immediately toss them in the lemon juice to prevent them from turning brown. Gently melt the low-fat spread in a pan over a low heat.

2 Cut the sheets of pastry into 4 and cover with a clean, damp tea towel. Brush 4 non-stick Yorkshire pudding tins, measuring 10 cm/4 inch in diameter, with a little of the low-fat spread.

3 Working on each pie separately, brush 4 sheets of pastry with low-fat spread. Press a small sheet of pastry into the base of 1 tin. Arrange the other sheets of pastry on top at slightly different angles. Repeat with the other sheets of pastry to make another 3 pies.

4 Arrange the apple and pear slices alternately in the centre of each pastry case and lightly crimp the edges of the pastry of each pie.

5 Mix the jam and orange juice together until smooth and brush over the fruit. Bake in a preheated oven, 200°C/400°F/Gas Mark 6, for 12–15 minutes. Sprinkle with the pistachio nuts, dust lightly with icing sugar and serve hot with low-fat custard.

VARIATION

Other combinations of fruit are equally delicious. Try peach and apricot, raspberry and apple, or pineapple and mango.

Lace Crêpes with Fruit

These super-light crêpes melt in the mouth. They are filled with a gingered fruit salad of melon, grapes and lychees.

NUTRITIONAL INFORMATION

Calories 176	Sugars 22g
Protein 3g	Fat 2g
Carbohydrate ...36g	Saturates 0.2g

🍦 10 mins   🕐 5 mins

SERVES 4

INGREDIENTS

3 egg whites

4 tbsp cornflour

3 tbsp cold water

1 tsp vegetable oil

FRUIT FILLING

350 g/12 oz fresh lychees

¼ Galia melon

175 g/6 oz seedless green grapes

1 cm/½ inch piece of fresh root ginger

2 pieces of stem ginger in syrup

2 tbsp ginger wine or dry sherry.

1 To make the fruit filling, peel the lychees and remove the stones. Place the lychees in a bowl. Scoop out the seeds from the melon and remove the skin. Cut the melon flesh into small pieces and place in the bowl.

2 Wash and dry the grapes, remove the stalks and add to the bowl. Peel the ginger and cut into thin shreds or grate finely. Drain the stem ginger pieces, reserving the syrup, and chop the ginger pieces finely.

3 Stir the root and stem ginger into the bowl with the ginger wine or sherry and the stem ginger syrup. Cover with clingfilm and set aside.

4 Meanwhile, prepare the crêpes. In a small jug, combine the egg whites, cornflour and cold water, stirring until very smooth.

5 Brush a small non-stick crêpe pan with oil and heat until hot. Drizzle the surface of the pan with a quarter of the cornflour mixture to give a lacy effect. Cook for a few seconds until set, then carefully lift out and transfer to absorbent kitchen paper to drain. Set aside and keep warm. Repeat with the remaining mixture to make 4 crêpes in total.

6 To serve, place a crêpe on each of 4 serving plates and top with the fruit filling. Fold over the crêpes and serve hot.

Crispy-topped Fruit Bake

The sugar cubes give a lovely crunchy texture to this easy-to-make blackberry and apple dessert.

NUTRITIONAL INFORMATION

Calories 227   Sugars 30g
Protein ....5g   Fat 1g
Carbohydrate ...53g   Saturates 0.2g

    15 mins   1 hr

SERVES 10

INGREDIENTS

butter or margarine, for greasing

350 g/12 oz cooking apples

3 tbsp lemon juice

300 g/10½ oz self-raising wholemeal flour

½ tsp baking powder

1 tsp ground cinnamon, plus extra
   for dusting

175 g/6 oz prepared blackberries, thawed
   if frozen, plus extra to decorate

175 g/6 oz light muscovado sugar

1 medium egg, beaten

200 ml/7 fl oz low-fat natural fromage frais

55 g/2 oz white or brown sugar cubes,
   lightly crushed

sliced eating apple, to decorate

1 Grease and line a 900 g/2 lb loaf tin with a little butter or margarine. Core, peel and finely dice the apples. Place them in a pan with the lemon juice, bring to the boil, cover and simmer for about 10 minutes until soft and pulpy. Beat well and set aside to cool.

2 Sift the flour, baking powder and cinnamon into a bowl, adding any husks that remain in the sieve. Stir in 115 g/4 oz blackberries and the sugar.

3 Make a well in the centre of the ingredients and add the egg, fromage frais and cooled apple purée. Mix well to incorporate thoroughly. Spoon the mixture into the prepared loaf tin and smooth over the top.

4 Sprinkle with the remaining blackberries, pressing them down into the cake mixture, and top with the crushed sugar cubes. Bake in a preheated oven, 190°C/375°F/Gas Mark 5, for 40–45 minutes. Remove from the oven and set aside in the tin to cool.

5 Remove the cake from the tin and peel away the lining paper. Serve dusted with cinnamon and decorated with extra blackberries and apple slices.

VARIATION

Try replacing the blackberries with blueberries. Use the canned or frozen variety if fresh blueberries are unavailable.

Italian Bread Pudding

This deliciously rich pudding is cooked with cream and apples and is delicately flavoured with orange.

NUTRITIONAL INFORMATION

Calories ....387 Sugars 31g
Protein ....8g Fat 20g
Carbohydrate ...45g Saturates 12g

 45 mins   🕐 25 mins

SERVES 4

I N G R E D I E N T S

1 tbsp butter

2 small eating apples, peeled, cored and
  sliced into rings

85 g/3 oz granulated sugar

2 tbsp white wine

4 thick slices of bread (about 115 g/4 oz)
  crusts removed (day-old baguette
  is ideal)

300 ml/10 fl oz single cream

2 eggs, beaten

pared rind of 1 orange, cut into matchsticks

1 Lightly grease a 1.2 litre/2 pint deep ovenproof dish with the butter.

2 Arrange the apple rings in the bottom of the dish. Sprinkle half of the sugar over the apples.

3 Pour the wine over the apples. Add the bread slices, pushing them down with your hands to flatten them slightly.

4 Mix the cream with the eggs, the remaining sugar and the orange rind and pour the mixture over the bread. Leave to soak for 30 minutes.

5 Bake the pudding in a preheated oven, 180°C/350°F/Gas Mark 4, for about 25 minutes until golden and set. Remove the pudding from the oven, leave to cool slightly and serve warm.

Cream Custards

Individual pan-cooked cream custards are flavoured with nutmeg and topped with caramelized orange strips.

NUTRITIONAL INFORMATION

Calories	406	Sugars	........38g
Protein	.........8g	Fat	..........26g
Carbohydrate	...38g	Saturates	......15g

 2¼ hrs   25 mins

SERVES 4

INGREDIENTS

450 ml/16 fl oz single cream

100 g/3¾ oz caster sugar

1 orange

2 tsp grated nutmeg

3 large eggs, beaten

1 tbsp clear honey

1 tsp ground cinnamon

1 Place the cream and sugar in a large non-stick pan and heat gently, stirring, until the sugar caramelizes.

2 Finely grate half of the orange rind and stir it into the pan with the nutmeg.

3 Add the eggs and cook over a low heat for 10–15 minutes, stirring constantly until thickened.

4 Strain the custard through a fine sieve into 4 shallow serving dishes. Set aside to chill in the refrigerator for 2 hours.

5 Meanwhile, pare the remaining orange rind with a vegetable peeler and cut it into thin batons.

6 Place the honey and cinnamon in a pan with 2 tablespoons of water and heat gently. Add the orange rind and cook for 2–3 minutes, stirring constantly, until the mixture has caramelized.

7 Pour the mixture into a bowl and separate out the orange strips. Set aside to cool until set.

8 Once the custards have set, decorate them with the caramelized orange rind and serve.

COOK'S TIP

The cream custards will keep for 1–2 days in the refrigerator. Decorate with the caramelized orange rind just before serving.

German Noodle Pudding

This rich and satisfying pudding is a traditional Jewish recipe that will quickly become popular with all the family.

NUTRITIONAL INFORMATION

Calories 719	Sugars 28g
Protein 20g	Fat 45g
Carbohydrate . . .62g	Saturates 25g

10 mins   45 mins

SERVES 4

I N G R E D I E N T S

4 tbsp butter, plus extra for greasing

175 g/6 oz ribbon egg noodles

115 g/4 oz cream cheese

225 g/8 oz cottage cheese

85 g/3 oz caster sugar

2 eggs, lightly beaten

125 ml/4 fl oz soured cream

1 tsp vanilla essence

pinch of ground cinnamon

1 tsp grated lemon rind

25 g/1 oz flaked almonds

25 g/1 oz dry white breadcrumbs

icing sugar, for dusting

1 Lightly grease an oval ovenproof dish with a little butter. Bring a large pan of water to the boil. Add the noodles, bring back to the boil and cook over a medium heat for 10 minutes, until tender, but still firm to the bite. Drain and set aside.

2 Beat the cream cheese with the cottage cheese and caster sugar in a mixing bowl until the mixture is smooth. Add the beaten eggs, a little at a time, beating thoroughly after each addition.

3 Stir in the soured cream, vanilla essence, cinnamon and lemon rind and fold in the noodles. Transfer the mixture to the prepared dish and smooth the surface.

4 Melt the butter in a small frying pan over a low heat. Add the almonds and fry, stirring constantly, for about 1–1½ minutes, until they are lightly coloured. Remove the frying pan from the heat and stir the breadcrumbs into the almonds.

5 Sprinkle the almond and breadcrumb mixture evenly over the pudding and bake in a preheated oven, 180°C/350°F/Gas Mark 4, for 35–40 minutes until just set. Dust the top with a little sifted icing sugar and serve immediately.

VARIATION

Although not authentic, you could add 3 tablespoons of raisins with the lemon rind in step 3, if liked.

Peaches & Mascarpone

If you prepare these in advance, all you have to do is pop the peaches on the barbecue when you are ready to serve them.

NUTRITIONAL INFORMATION

Calories	301	Sugars	........24g
Protein	.........6g	Fat	..........20g
Carbohydrate	...24g	Saturates	.......9g

 10 mins   10 mins

SERVES 4

INGREDIENTS

4 peaches

175 g/6 oz mascarpone cheese

40 g/1½ oz pecan or walnuts, chopped

1 tsp sunflower oil

4 tbsp maple syrup

1 Cut the peaches in half and remove the stones. If you are preparing this recipe in advance, press the peach halves together again and wrap them in clingfilm until required.

2 Combine the mascarpone and pecans or walnuts in a small bowl. Set aside to chill in the refrigerator until required.

3 To serve, brush the peaches with a little oil and place on a rack set over medium hot coals. Barbecue them for 5–10 minutes, turning once, until hot.

4 Transfer the peaches to a serving dish and top with the mascarpone cheese mixture.

5 Drizzle the maple syrup over the peaches and mascarpone filling and serve immediately.

VARIATION

You can use nectarines instead of peaches for this recipe. Remember to choose ripe but firm fruit which won't go soft and mushy when it is barbecued. Prepare the nectarines in the same way as the peaches and barbecue for 5–10 minutes.

Orange & Almond Cake

This light and tangy citrus cake from Sicily is better eaten as a dessert than as a cake. It is especially good served at the end of a large meal.

NUTRITIONAL INFORMATION

Calories 399	Sugars 20g	
Protein 8g	Fat 31g	
Carbohydrate . . .23g	Saturates 13g	

30 mins 40 mins

SERVES 8

INGREDIENTS

4 eggs, separated

115 g/4 oz caster sugar, plus 2 tsp for the cream

finely grated rind and juice of 2 oranges

finely grated rind and juice of 1 lemon

115 g/4 oz ground almonds

4 tbsp self-raising flour

200 ml/7 fl oz whipping cream

1 tsp ground cinnamon

4 tbsp flaked almonds, toasted

icing sugar, for dusting

1 Grease and line the base of an 18 cm/ 7 inch round deep cake tin.

2 Blend the egg yolks with the sugar until the mixture is thick and creamy. Whisk half of the orange rind and all of the lemon rind into the egg yolks.

3 Combine the orange and lemon juice with the ground almonds and stir into the egg yolks. Fold in the flour. Whisk the egg whites until stiff and gently fold in.

4 Pour the mixture into the tin and smooth the surface. Bake in a preheated oven, 180°C/350°F/Gas Mark 4, for 35–40 minutes or until golden and springy to the touch. Set aside to cool in the tin for 10 minutes and then turn out on to a rack to cool completely.

5 Whip the cream to form soft peaks. Stir in the remaining orange rind, cinnamon and sugar.

6 Cover the cake with the almonds, dust with icing sugar and serve with the cream.

VARIATION

To serve with a syrup, boil the juice and finely grated rind of 2 oranges, 85 g/3 oz caster sugar and 2 tablespoons water for 5–6 minutes. Stir in 1 tablespoon orange liqueur just before serving.

Raspberry Shortcake

For this lovely summery dessert, two crisp rounds of shortbread are sandwiched together with fresh raspberries and lightly whipped cream.

NUTRITIONAL INFORMATION

Calories	496	Sugars	........14g
Protein	.........4g	Fat	..........41g
Carbohydrate	...30g	Saturates	......26g

 40 mins   🕐 15 mins

SERVES 8

INGREDIENTS

100 g/3½ oz butter, cut into cubes, plus extra for greasing

175 g/6 oz self-raising flour

85 g/3 oz caster sugar

1 egg yolk

1 tbsp rose water

600 ml/1 pint whipping cream, lightly whipped

225 g/8 oz raspberries, plus a few extra for decoration

TO DECORATE

icing sugar

mint leaves

1 Lightly grease 2 baking sheets with a little butter.

2 To make the shortcake, sift the self-raising flour into a bowl. Add the butter and rub it into the flour with your fingertips until the mixture resembles fine breadcrumbs.

3 Stir the sugar, egg yolk and rose water into the mixture and bring together with your fingers to form a soft dough. Divide the dough in half.

4 Roll out each piece of dough to a 20 cm/8 inch round on a lightly floured surface. Carefully lift each one with the rolling pin on to the prepared baking sheets. Gently crimp the edges of the dough with your finger.

5 Bake in a preheated oven, 190°C/ 375°F/Gas Mark 5, for 15 minutes until lightly golden. Transfer the shortcakes to a wire rack and leave to cool completely.

6 Mix the whipped cream with the raspberries and spoon the mixture on top of one of the shortcakes, spreading it out evenly. Top with the other shortcake round, dust with a little icing sugar and decorate with the extra raspberries and mint leaves.

COOK'S TIP

The shortcake can be made a few days in advance and stored in an airtight container until required.

Sweet Potato Bread

This is a great-tasting loaf, coloured light orange by the sweet potato. Added sweetness from the honey is offset by the tangy orange rind.

NUTRITIONAL INFORMATION

Calories ....267 Sugars 7g
Protein ....4g Fat 9g
Carbohydrate ...45g Saturates 4g

1½ hrs   1¼ hrs

SERVES 8

I N G R E D I E N T S

5 tbsp butter, plus extra for greasing

225 g/8 oz sweet potatoes, diced

150 ml/5 fl oz lukewarm water

2 tbsp clear honey

2 tbsp vegetable oil

3 tbsp orange juice

75 g/2¾ oz semolina

225 g/8 oz strong white flour

1 x 7 g sachet easy blend dried yeast

1 tsp ground cinnamon

grated rind of 1 orange

1 Lightly grease a 675 g/1½ lb loaf tin. Cook the sweet potatoes in a saucepan of boiling water for about 10 minutes or until soft. Drain well and mash until smooth.

2 Meanwhile, mix the water, honey, oil, and orange juice together in a large mixing bowl.

3 Add the mashed sweet potatoes, semolina, three-quarters of the flour, the yeast, ground cinnamon and grated orange rind and mix thoroughly to form a dough. Set aside for about 10 minutes.

4 Dice the butter and knead it into the dough with the remaining flour. Knead for about 5 minutes until smooth.

5 Place the dough in the prepared loaf tin. Cover and set aside in a warm place for 1 hour or until doubled in size.

6 Cook the loaf in a preheated oven, 190°C/375°F/Gas Mark 5, for 45–60 minutes, or until the base sounds hollow when tapped. Serve the bread warm, cut into slices.

Potato Muffins

Using potatoes in sweet dishes may seem an odd idea, but, in fact, they add a lightness and lift to all kinds of baked goods.

NUTRITIONAL INFORMATION

Calories	100	Sugars	11g
Protein	3g	Fat	2g
Carbohydrate	19g	Saturates	1g

 10 mins   30 mins

MAKES 12

INGREDIENTS

butter, for greasing

85 g/3 oz self-raising flour, plus extra for dusting

175 g/6 oz floury potatoes, diced

2 tbsp soft light brown sugar

1 tsp baking powder

115 g/4 oz raisins

4 eggs, separated

1 Lightly grease and flour 12 muffin tins. Cook the diced potatoes in a saucepan of boiling water for 10 minutes or until tender. Drain thoroughly and mash until smooth.

2 Transfer the mashed potatoes to a mixing bowl and add the flour, sugar, baking powder, raisins and egg yolks. Stir well to mix thoroughly.

3 In a clean bowl, whisk the egg whites until they are standing in peaks. Using a metal spoon, gently fold them into the potato mixture until fully incorporated.

4 Divide the mixture among the prepared tins.

5 Cook in a preheated oven, 200°C/ 400°F/Gas Mark 6, for 10 minutes. Reduce the oven temperature to 160°C/ 325°F/Gas Mark 3 and cook the muffins for 7–10 minutes or until risen.

6 Remove the muffins from the tins and serve warm.

COOK'S TIP

Instead of spreading the muffins with plain butter, serve them with cinnamon butter made by blending 5 tablespoons butter with a large pinch of ground cinnamon.

Fruit & Nut Loaf

This loaf is like a fruit bread which may be served warm or cold, perhaps spread with a little margarine or butter or topped with jam.

NUTRITIONAL INFORMATION

Calories	531	Sugars	.......53g
Protein	........12g	Fat	.........14g
Carbohydrate	...96g	Saturates	......2g

🕐 1 hr   🕐 40 mins

SERVES 4

INGREDIENTS

225 g/8 oz white bread flour, plus extra for dusting

½ tsp salt

1 tbsp margarine, plus extra for greasing

2 tbsp soft light brown sugar

100 g/3½ oz sultanas

55 g/2 oz no-need to soak dried apricots, chopped

55 g/2 oz chopped hazelnuts

2 tsp easy-blend dried yeast

6 tbsp orange juice

6 tbsp low-fat natural yogurt

2 tbsp sieved apricot jam

1 Sift the flour and salt into a bowl. Rub in the margarine and stir in the sugar, sultanas, apricots, nuts and yeast.

2 Warm the orange juice in a pan but do not allow it to boil.

3 Stir the warm orange juice into the flour mixture with the natural yogurt and then bring the mixture together to form a dough.

4 Knead the dough on a lightly floured surface for 5 minutes until smooth and elastic. Shape into a round and place on a lightly greased baking sheet. Cover with a clean tea towel and set aside to rise in a warm place until doubled in size.

5 Cook the loaf in a preheated oven, 220°C/425°F/Gas Mark 7, for about 35–40 minutes until cooked through. Transfer to a cooling rack and brush the cake with the apricot jam. Let the cake cool before serving.

COOK'S TIP

To test whether yeast bread or cake is done, tap the loaf from underneath. If it sounds hollow, the bread or cake is ready.

Tropical Fruit Fool

Fruit fools are always popular, and this light, tangy version will be no exception. You can use your favourite fruits in this recipe.

NUTRITIONAL INFORMATION

Calories	149	Sugars	........25g
Protein	.........6g	Fat	..........0.4g
Carbohydrate	...32g	Saturates	.....0.2g

 35 mins   🕐 0 mins

SERVES 4

INGREDIENTS

1 medium ripe mango

2 kiwi fruit

1 medium banana

2 tbsp lime juice

½ tsp finely grated lime rind, plus extra to decorate

2 egg whites

425 g/15 oz can low-fat custard

½ tsp vanilla essence

2 passion fruit

1 Peel the mango, then slice either side of the smooth, flat central stone. Roughly chop the flesh and process the fruit in a food processor or blender until smooth. Alternatively, mash with a fork.

2 Peel the kiwi fruit, chop the flesh into small pieces and place in a bowl. Peel and chop the banana and add to the bowl. Toss all of the fruit in the lime juice and rind and mix well.

3 In a grease-free bowl, whisk the egg whites until stiff and then gently fold in the custard and vanilla essence until thoroughly mixed.

4 In 4 tall glasses, alternately layer the chopped fruit, mango purée and custard mixture, finishing with the custard on top. Set aside to chill in the refrigerator for 20 minutes.

5 Halve the passion fruits, scoop out the seeds and spoon the passion fruit over the fruit fools. Decorate each serving with the extra lime rind and serve.

VARIATION

Other tropical fruits to try include paw-paw purée, with chopped pineapple and dates or pomegranate seeds to decorate.

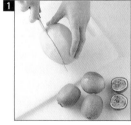

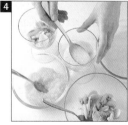

Mixed Fruit Brûlées

Traditionally a rich mixture made with cream, this fruit-based version is just as tempting using low-fat smetana and fromage frais as a topping.

NUTRITIONAL INFORMATION

Calories 165	Sugars 21g
Protein 5g	Fat 7g
Carbohydrate ...21g	Saturates 5g

 5 mins   5 mins

SERVES 4

INGREDIENTS

450 g/1 lb prepared assorted summer fruits, such as strawberries, raspberries, blackcurrants, redcurrants and cherries, thawed if frozen

150 ml/5 fl oz smetana

150 ml/5 fl oz low-fat natural fromage frais

1 tsp vanilla essence

4 tbsp demerara sugar

1 Divide the prepared strawberries, raspberries, blackcurrants, redcurrants and cherries evenly among 4 small heatproof ramekin dishes.

2 Combine the smetana, fromage frais and vanilla essence.

3 Spoon the mixture over the fruit, to cover it completely.

4 Top each serving with 1 tablespoon demerara sugar and place the desserts under a preheated grill for 2–3 minutes until the sugar melts and begins to caramelise. Set aside for a couple of minutes before serving.

COOK'S TIP

Look out for half-fat creams, in single and double varieties. They are good substitutes for occasional use. Alternatively, in this recipe, double the quantity of fromage frais for a lower-fat version.

Orchard Fruits Bristol

An elegant fruit salad of poached pears and apples, oranges and strawberries in a wine and caramel syrup topped with crumbled caramel.

NUTRITIONAL INFORMATION

Calories	395	Sugars	........94g
Protein	.........3g	Fat	..........0.5g
Carbohydrate	...94g	Saturates	......0g

🍓 30 mins   🕐 20 mins

SERVES 4

INGREDIENTS

4 oranges

175 g/6 oz granulated sugar

4 tbsp water

150 ml/5 fl oz white wine

4 firm pears

4 eating apples

115 g/4 oz strawberries

1 Pare the rind thinly from 1 orange and cut into narrow strips. Cook in the minimum of boiling water for 3–4 minutes until tender. Drain and reserve the cooking liquid. Squeeze the juice from this and 1 other orange.

2 Lay a sheet of non-stick baking paper on a baking sheet or board.

3 Heat the sugar gently in a pan until it melts, then continue without stirring until it turns a pale golden brown. Pour half the caramel quickly on to the parchment and set aside to set.

4 Add the water and squeezed orange juice immediately to the caramel left in the pan with 150 ml/5 fl oz of the reserved cooking liquid. Heat until it melts, then add the wine and remove the pan from the heat.

5 Peel, core and slice the pears and apples thickly (you can leave the apple skins on, if you prefer) and add to the caramel syrup. Bring gently to the boil and simmer for 3–4 minutes until just beginning to soften – they should still be firm in the centre. Transfer the pears and apples to a bowl.

6 Cut away the peel and pith from the remaining oranges and either ease out the segments or cut into slices, discarding any pips. Add to the other fruits. Hull the strawberries and halve, quarter or slice thickly, depending on the size, and add to the other fruits.

7 Add the orange strands to the syrup and bring back to the boil for 1 minute, then pour over the fruits. Set aside until cold, then break up the caramel and sprinkle over the fruit. Cover and chill until ready to serve.

COOK'S TIP

The caramel will begin to melt when added to the fruit, so do this as near to serving as possible.

Giggle Cake

It's a mystery how this cake got its name –
perhaps it's because it's easy to make and fun to eat.

NUTRITIONAL INFORMATION

Calories	493	Sugars	........66g
Protein	.........6g	Fat	..........15g
Carbohydrate	...90g	Saturates	.......3g

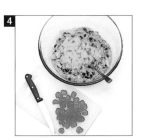

25 mins   1¼ hrs

SERVES 8

INGREDIENTS

350 g/12 oz mixed dried fruit

125 g/4½ oz butter or margarine, plus extra
for greasing

175 g/6 oz soft brown sugar

225 g/8 oz self-raising flour

pinch of salt

2 eggs, beaten

225 g/8 oz can chopped pineapple, drained

125 g/4½ oz glacé cherries, halved

1 Put the mixed dried fruit into a large bowl and cover with boiling water. Set aside to soak for 10–15 minutes, then drain well.

2 Put the butter or margarine and sugar into a large pan and heat gently until melted. Add the drained mixed dried fruit and cook over a low heat, stirring frequently, for 4–5 minutes. Remove from the heat and transfer to a mixing bowl. Set aside to cool.

3 Sift together the flour and salt into the dried fruit mixture and stir well. Add the eggs, mixing until the ingredients are thoroughly incorporated.

4 Add the pineapples and cherries to the cake mixture and stir to combine.

Transfer to a greased and lined 1 kg/2 lb loaf tin and level the surface.

5 Bake in a preheated oven, 180°C/ 350°F/Gas Mark 4, for about 1 hour. Test the cake with a fine skewer; if it comes out clean, the cake is cooked. If not, return to the oven for a few more minutes. Transfer to a wire rack to cool completely before serving.

VARIATION

If you wish, add 1 teaspoon ground mixed spice to the cake mixture, sifting it in with the flour. Bake the cake in an 18 cm/7 inch round cake tin if you don't have a loaf tin of the right size. Remember to grease and line it first.

Eve's Pudding

This is a popular family favourite pudding with soft apples on the bottom and a light buttery sponge on top.

NUTRITIONAL INFORMATION

Calories 365	Sugars 40g	
Protein 5g	Fat 14g	
Carbohydrate ...58g	Saturates 7g	

15 mins   45 mins

SERVES 4

INGREDIENTS

6 tbsp butter, plus extra for greasing

450 g/1 lb cooking apples, peeled, cored and sliced

85 g/3 oz granulated sugar

1 tbsp lemon juice

55 g/2 oz sultanas

85 g/3 oz caster sugar

1 egg, beaten

150 g/5½ oz self-raising flour

3 tbsp milk

25 g/1 oz flaked almonds

custard or double cream, to serve

COOK'S TIP

To increase the almond flavour of this pudding, add 25 g/1 oz ground almonds with the flour in step 4.

1 Grease an 900 ml/1½ pint ovenproof dish with butter.

2 Mix the apples with the granulated sugar, lemon juice and sultanas. Spoon the mixture into the prepared dish.

3 In a bowl, cream the butter and caster sugar together until pale. Add the beaten egg, a little at a time.

4 Carefully fold in the self-raising flour and stir in the milk to give a soft, dropping consistency.

5 Spread the mixture over the apples and sprinkle with the flaked almonds.

6 Bake in a preheated oven, 180°C/ 350°F/Gas Mark 4, for 40–45 minutes until the sponge is golden brown.

7 Serve the pudding piping hot, accompanied by homemade custard or double cream.

Plum Cobbler

This is a popular dessert which can be adapted to suit almost all types of fruit if plums are not available.

NUTRITIONAL INFORMATION

Calories	430	Sugars	........46g
Protein	.........7g	Fat	..........12g
Carbohydrate	...79g	Saturates	.......7g

10 mins   40 mins

SERVES 6

I N G R E D I E N T S

butter, for greasing

1 kg/2 lb 4 oz plums, stoned and sliced

100 g/3 ½ oz caster sugar

1 tbsp lemon juice

250 g/9 oz plain flour

2 tsp baking powder

85 g/3 oz granulated sugar

1 egg, beaten

150 ml/5 fl oz buttermilk

85 g/3 oz butter, melted and cooled

double cream, to serve

1 Lightly grease a 2 litre/3 ½ pint ovenproof dish with butter.

2 In a large bowl, mix together the plums, caster sugar, lemon juice and 25 g/1 oz of the plain flour.

3 Spoon the coated plums into the bottom of the prepared ovenproof dish, spreading them out evenly.

4 Sift the remaining flour, together with the baking powder into a large bowl and add the granulated sugar. Stir well to combine.

5 Add the beaten egg, buttermilk and cooled melted butter. Mix everything gently together to form a soft dough.

6 Place spoonfuls of the dough on top of the fruit mixture until it is almost completely covered.

7 Bake the cobbler in a preheated oven, 190°C/375°F/Gas Mark 5, for about 35–40 minutes until the topping is golden brown and the plums are bubbling.

8 Serve the pudding piping hot, with double cream.

COOK'S TIP

If you cannot find buttermilk, try using soured cream.

Banana & Cranberry Loaf

The addition of chopped nuts, mixed peel, fresh orange juice and dried cranberries makes this a rich, moist tea bread.

NUTRITIONAL INFORMATION

Calories 388	Sugars 40g
Protein 5g	Fat 17g
Carbohydrate . . .57g	Saturates 2g

 45 mins   1 hr

SERVES 8

INGREDIENTS

butter, for greasing

175 g/6 oz self-raising flour

½ tsp baking powder

150 g/5½ oz soft brown sugar

2 bananas, mashed

55 g/2 oz chopped mixed peel

25 g/1 oz chopped mixed nuts

55 g/2 oz dried cranberries

5–6 tbsp orange juice

2 eggs, beaten

150 ml/5 fl oz sunflower oil

85 g/3 oz icing sugar, sifted

grated rind of 1 orange

1 Grease a 900 g/2 lb loaf tin and line the base with baking paper.

2 Sift the flour and baking powder into a mixing bowl. Stir in the brown sugar, bananas, chopped mixed peel, nuts and dried cranberries.

3 Stir the orange juice, eggs and sunflower oil together until well combined. Add the mixture to the dry ingredients and mix until thoroughly blended. Spoon the mixture into the prepared loaf tin and use a palette knife to smooth the top.

4 Bake in a preheated oven, 180°C/ 350°F/Gas Mark 4, for about 1 hour until firm to the touch or until a fine skewer inserted into the centre of the loaf comes out clean.

5 Turn out the loaf and leave it to cool on a wire rack.

6 Mix the icing sugar with a little water and drizzle the icing over the loaf. Sprinkle the orange rind over the top. Leave the icing to set before serving the loaf in slices.

COOK'S TIP

This tea bread will keep for a couple of days. Wrap it carefully and store in a cool, dry place.

Tropical Fruit Bread

The flavours in this bread will bring a touch of sunshine to your dining room, whatever the time of year.

NUTRITIONAL INFORMATION

Calories . . . . . . .228 Sugars 10g
Protein . . . . .6g Fat 7g
Carbohydrate . . .37g Saturates 5g

1¼ hrs   30 mins

SERVES 4

INGREDIENTS

2 tbsp butter, cut into small pieces, plus extra for greasing

350 g/12 oz strong white bread flour

55 g/2 oz bran

½ tsp salt

½ tsp ground ginger

1 sachet easy-blend dried yeast

25 g/1 oz soft brown sugar

250 ml/9 fl oz lukewarm water

85 g/3 oz glacé pineapple, finely chopped

25 g/1 oz dried mango, finely chopped

55 g/2 oz desiccated coconut, toasted

1 egg, lightly beaten

2 tbsp coconut shreds

1 Grease a baking sheet. Sift the flour into a large mixing bowl. Stir in the bran, salt, ginger, dried yeast and sugar. Rub in the butter with your fingers, then add the water and mix to form a dough.

2 On a lightly floured surface, knead the dough for 5–8 minutes until smooth. Alternatively, use an electric mixer with a dough hook. Place the dough in a greased bowl, cover and leave to rise in a warm place for 30 minutes, until doubled in size.

3 Knead the pineapple, mango and desiccated coconut into the dough. Shape into a round and place on the baking sheet. Score the top with the back of a knife. Cover and leave for a further 30 minutes in a warm place.

4 Brush the loaf with the beaten egg and sprinkle with the coconut shreds. Bake in a preheated oven, 220°C/425°F/ Gas Mark 7, for about 30 minutes or until golden brown.

5 Leave the bread to cool on a wire rack before serving.

COOK'S TIP

To test the bread after the second rising, gently poke the dough with your finger –it should spring back if it has risen enough.

Olive Oil, Fruit & Nut Cake

It is worth using a good quality olive oil for this cake because this will determine its flavour. The cake will keep well in an airtight container.

NUTRITIONAL INFORMATION

Calories 309	Sugars 17g
Protein 4g	Fat 17g
Carbohydrate ...38g	Saturates 3g

 10 mins   45 mins

SERVES 8

INGREDIENTS

butter, for greasing

225 g/8 oz self-raising flour

55 g/2 oz caster sugar

125 ml/4 fl oz milk

4 tbsp orange juice

150 ml/5 fl oz olive oil

100 g/3½ oz mixed dried fruit

25 g/1 oz pine kernels

1 Grease an 18 cm/7 inch cake tin and line with baking paper.

2 Sift the flour into a mixing bowl and stir in the caster sugar.

3 Make a well in the centre of the dry ingredients and pour in the milk and orange juice. Stir the mixture with a wooden spoon, gradually beating in the flour and sugar.

4 Pour in the olive oil, stirring well so that all of the ingredients are thoroughly mixed.

5 Stir the mixed dried fruit and pine kernels into the mixture and spoon into the prepared tin. Smooth the top with a palette knife.

6 Bake in a preheated oven, 180°C/ 350°F/Gas Mark 4, for about 45 minutes, until the cake is golden and firm to the touch.

7 Leave the cake to cool in the tin for a few minutes before transferring to a wire rack to cool completely.

8 Serve the cake warm or cold and cut into slices.

COOK'S TIP

Pine kernels are best known as the flavouring ingredient in the classic Italian pesto, but here they give a delicate, slightly resinous flavour to this cake.

Crunchy Fruit Cake

Polenta adds texture to this fruit cake, as well as a golden yellow colour. It also acts as a flour, binding the ingredients together.

NUTRITIONAL INFORMATION

Calories	328	Sugars	........33g
Protein	........59g	Fat	..........15g
Carbohydrate	...47g	Saturates	.......7g

5–10 mins   1 hr

MAKES 1 LOAF

INGREDIENTS

100 g/3½ oz butter, softened, plus extra for greasing

100g/3½ oz caster sugar

2 eggs, beaten

50 g/1¾ oz self-raising flour, sifted

1 tsp baking powder

100 g/3½ oz polenta

225 g/8 oz mixed dried fruit

25 g/1 oz pine kernels

grated rind of 1 lemon

4 tbsp lemon juice

2 tbsp milk

1 Grease an 18 cm/7 inch cake tin with a little butter and line the base with baking paper.

2 In a bowl, whisk together the butter and sugar until light and fluffy.

3 Whisk in the beaten eggs, a little at a time, whisking thoroughly after each addition.

4 Gently fold the flour, baking powder and polenta into the mixture until totally incorporated.

5 Stir in the mixed dried fruit, pine kernels, grated lemon rind, lemon juice and milk.

6 Spoon the mixture into the prepared tin and level the surface.

7 Bake in a preheated oven, 180°C/350°F/Gas Mark 4, for about 1 hour or until a fine skewer inserted into the centre of the cake comes out clean.

8 Leave the cake to cool in the tin before turning out.

VARIATION

To give a crumblier light fruit cake, omit the polenta and use 150 g/5½ oz self-raising flour instead.

Apple Cake with Cider

This can be warmed through and served with cream for a dessert or eaten as a cake at tea time or with a morning cup of coffee.

NUTRITIONAL INFORMATION

Calories 263	Sugars 22g
Protein 4g	Fat 9g
Carbohydrate . . .43g	Saturates 5g

1 hr 5 mins   40 mins

SERVES 8

INGREDIENTS

85 g/3 oz butter, cut into small pieces, plus extra for greasing

225 g/8 oz self-raising flour

1 tsp baking powder

85 g/3 oz caster sugar

55 g/2 oz dried apple, chopped

85 g/3 oz raisins

150 ml/5 fl oz sweet cider

1 egg, beaten

175 g/6 oz raspberries

1 Grease a 20 cm/8 inch cake tin and line with baking paper.

2 Sift the flour and baking powder into a mixing bowl and rub in the butter with your fingertips until the mixture resembles fine breadcrumbs.

3 Stir in the caster sugar, chopped dried apple and raisins.

4 Pour in the sweet cider and egg and mix together until thoroughly blended. Stir in the raspberries very gently so they do not break up.

5 Pour the mixture into the prepared cake tin.

6 Bake in a preheated oven, 190°C/ 375°F/Gas Mark 5, for about 40 minutes until risen and lightly golden.

7 Leave the cake to cool in the tin, then turn out on to a wire rack. Leave until completely cold before serving.

VARIATION

If you don't want to use cider or you are making the cake for children, replace it with clear apple juice.

Oat & Raisin Biscuits

These oaty, fruity biscuits couldn't be easier to make and are delicious served with a creamy rum and raisin ice cream.

NUTRITIONAL INFORMATION

Calories	227	Sugars	.......22g
Protein	.........4g	Fat	...........7g
Carbohydrate	...39g	Saturates	.......3g

50 mins   15 mins

SERVES 4

INGREDIENTS

4 tbsp butter, plus extra for greasing

125 g/4½ oz caster sugar

1 egg, beaten

50 g/1¾ plain flour

½ tsp salt

½ tsp baking powder

175 g/6 oz rolled oats

125 g/4½ oz raisins

2 tbsp sesame seeds

1 Lightly grease 2 baking sheets with a little butter.

2 In a large mixing bowl, cream together the butter and sugar until light and fluffy.

3 Gradually add the beaten egg, beating well after each addition, until thoroughly combined.

4 Sift the flour, salt and baking powder into the creamed mixture. Mix gently to combine. Add the rolled oats, raisins and sesame seeds and mix together until thoroughly combined.

5 Place spoonfuls of the mixture, spaced well apart on the prepared baking sheets to allow room to expand during cooking, and flatten them slightly with the back of a spoon.

6 Bake the biscuits in a preheated oven, 180°C/350°F/Gas Mark 4, for 15 minutes.

7 Leave the biscuits to cool slightly on the baking sheets.

8 Carefully transfer the biscuits to a wire rack and leave to cool completely before serving.

COOK'S TIP
To enjoy these biscuits at their best, store them in an airtight container.

Chocolate Mousse

This is a light and fluffy mousse with a subtle hint of orange. It is wickedly delicious served with a fresh fruit sauce.

NUTRITIONAL INFORMATION

Calories 164	Sugars 24g	
Protein 5g	Fat 5g	
Carbohydrate ...25g	Saturates 3g	

2¼ hrs   5 mins

SERVES 8

INGREDIENTS

100 g/3½ oz plain chocolate, melted

300 ml/10 fl oz natural yogurt

150 ml/5 fl oz Quark

4 tbsp caster sugar

1 tbsp orange juice

1 tbsp brandy

1½ tsp gelatine, or gelozone
   (vegetarian gelatine)

9 tbsp cold water

2 large egg whites

TO DECORATE

roughly grated dark and white chocolate

orange rind

1 Put the melted chocolate, yogurt, Quark, sugar, orange juice and brandy in a food processor or blender and process for 30 seconds. Transfer the mixture to a large bowl.

2 Sprinkle the gelatine or gelozone over the water and stir until dissolved.

3 In a pan, bring the gelatine or gelozone and water to the boil for 2 minutes. Cool slightly, then stir into the chocolate mixture.

4 Whisk the egg whites until stiff peaks form and fold into the chocolate mixture using a metal spoon.

5 Line a 500 g/1 lb 2 oz loaf tin with clingfilm. Spoon the mousse into the tin. Chill in the refrigerator for 2 hours until set. Turn the mousse out on to a serving plate, decorate with grated chocolate and orange rind and serve.

COOK'S TIP

For a quick fruit sauce, process a can of mandarin segments in natural juice in a food processor and press through a strainer. Stir in 1 tablespoon clear honey and serve with the mousse.

Berry Cheesecake

Use a mixture of berries, such as blueberries, blackberries, raspberries and strawberries, for a really fruity cheesecake.

NUTRITIONAL INFORMATION

Calories 478	Sugars 28g	
Protein 10g	Fat 32g	
Carbohydrate ...40g	Saturates 15g	

2¼ hrs   5 mins

SERVES 8

INGREDIENTS

BASE

6 tbsp margarine

175 g/6 oz oatmeal biscuits

55 g/2 oz desiccated coconut

TOPPING

1½ tsp gelatine

9 tbsp cold water

125 ml/4 fl oz evaporated milk

1 egg

6 tbsp light brown sugar

450 g/1 lb soft cream cheese

350 g/12 oz mixed berries

2 tbsp clear honey

1 Melt the margarine in a pan. Put the biscuits into a food processor and process until crushed or crush finely with a rolling pin. Stir the crumbs into the margarine with the coconut.

2 Press the mixture evenly into a base-lined 20 cm/8 inch springform tin) and set aside to chill in the refrigerator.

3 To make the topping, sprinkle the gelatine over the water and stir to dissolve. Bring to the boil and boil for 2 minutes. Set aside to cool slightly.

4 Beat the milk with the egg, sugar and cream cheese until smooth. Stir in 55 g/2 oz of the berries. Add the gelatine in a thin stream, stirring constantly.

5 Spoon the mixture on to the biscuit base and return to the refrigerator to chill for 2 hours or until set.

6 Remove the cheesecake from the tin and transfer to a serving plate. Arrange the remaining berries on top of the cheesecake and drizzle the honey over the top. Serve.

Steamed Coffee Sponge

This sponge pudding is very light and is delicious served with a coffee or chocolate sauce.

NUTRITIONAL INFORMATION

Calories ....343 Sugars 21g
Protein ....9g Fat 12g
Carbohydrate ...54g Saturates 4g

 10 mins   1–1¼ hrs

SERVES 4

INGREDIENTS

2 tbsp margarine

2 tbsp soft brown sugar

2 eggs

5½ tbsp plain flour

¾ tsp baking powder

6 tbsp milk

1 tsp coffee essence

SAUCE

300 ml/10 fl oz milk

1 tbsp soft brown sugar

1 tsp cocoa powder

2 tbsp cornflour

1 Lightly grease a 600 ml/1 pint pudding basin. Cream the margarine and sugar until light and fluffy, then beat in the eggs.

2 Gradually stir in the flour and baking powder, then stir in the milk and coffee essence to make a smooth batter.

3 Spoon the mixture into the pudding basin and cover with a pleated piece of baking paper and then a pleated piece of foil, securing around the bowl with tightly tied string.

4 Place in a steamer or large pan half full of boiling water. Cover and steam for 1–1¼ hours or until cooked through.

5 To make the sauce, put the milk, sugar and cocoa powder in a pan and heat until the sugar dissolves. Blend the cornflour with 4 tablespoons of cold water to a paste and stir into the pan. Bring the

sauce to the boil, stirring until thickened. Cook over a gentle heat for 1 minute.

6 Turn the pudding out on to a warmed serving plate and spoon the sauce over the top. Serve immediately.

Fruit Brûlée

This is a cheat's brûlée, in that yogurt is used to cover a base of fruit, before being sprinkled with sugar and grilled.

NUTRITIONAL INFORMATION

Calories 311   Sugars 48g
Protein . . . . .7g   Fat 11g
Carbohydrate . . .48g   Saturates 7g

1¼ hrs   15 mins

SERVES 4

I N G R E D I E N T S

4 plums, stoned and sliced

2 cooking apples, peeled and sliced

1 tsp ground ginger

600 ml/1 pint Greek-style yogurt

2 tbsp icing sugar, sifted

1 tsp almond essence

85 g/3 oz demerara sugar

1 Put the plums and apples in a pan with 2 tablespoons of water and cook for 7–10 minutes, until tender, but not mushy. Set aside to cool, then stir in the ground ginger.

2 Using a draining spoon, spoon the mixture into the base of a shallow, heatproof serving dish.

3 Combine the yogurt, icing sugar and almond essence and spoon on to the fruit to cover.

4 Sprinkle the demerara sugar over the top of the yogurt and cook under a hot grill for 3–4 minutes or until the sugar has melted and formed a crust.

5 Set aside to chill in the refrigerator for 1 hour before serving.

Pear Cake

This is a really moist cake, deliciously flavoured with chopped pears and cinnamon and drizzled with honey.

NUTRITIONAL INFORMATION

Calories	.119	Sugars	.16g
Protein	.2g	Fat	.0.3g
Carbohydrate	.29g	Saturates	.0g

 1 hr   🕐 1½ hrs

SERVES 12

INGREDIENTS

margarine, for greasing

4 pears, peeled and cored

2 tbsp water

200 g/7 oz plain flour

2 tsp baking powder

100 g/3½ oz soft light brown sugar

4 tbsp milk

2 tbsp clear honey, plus extra for drizzling

2 tsp ground cinnamon

2 egg whites

1 Grease and line the base of a 20 cm/ 8 inch cake tin.

2 Put 1 pear in a food processor with the water and process until almost smooth. Transfer to a mixing bowl.

3 Sift in the flour and baking powder. Beat in the sugar, milk, honey and cinnamon and mix well.

4 Chop all but 1 of the remaining pears and add to the mixture.

5 Whisk the egg whites until peaks form and gently fold into the mixture until fully blended.

6 Slice the remaining pear and arrange it in a fan pattern on the base of the prepared tin.

7 Spoon the cake mixture into the tin and cook in a preheated oven, 150°C/ 300°F/Gas Mark 2, for 1¼ –1½ hours or until cooked through.

8 Remove the cake from the oven and set aside to cool in the tin for 10 minutes. Turn the cake out on to a wire cooling rack and drizzle with honey. Set aside to cool completely, then cut into slices to serve.

COOK'S TIP

To test if the cake is cooked through, insert a skewer into the centre – if it comes out clean, the cake is cooked. If not, return the cake to the oven and test at frequent intervals.

Mixed Fruit Crumble

In this crumble, tropical fruits are flavoured with ginger and coconut, for something a little different and very tasty.

10 mins   50 mins

SERVES 4

INGREDIENTS

2 mangoes, sliced

1 papaya, seeded and sliced

225 g/8 oz fresh pineapple, cubed

1½ tsp ground ginger

100 g/3½ oz margarine

100 g/3½ oz light brown sugar

175 g/6 oz plain flour

55 g/2 oz desiccated coconut, plus extra to decorate

1 Place the fruit in a pan with ½ teaspoon of the ground ginger, 2 tablespoons of the margarine and 4 tablespoons of the sugar. Cook over a low heat for 10 minutes until the fruit softens. Spoon the fruit into the base of a shallow ovenproof dish.

2 Combine the flour and remaining ginger. Rub in the remaining margarine until the mixture resembles fine breadcrumbs. Stir in the remaining sugar and the coconut and spoon over the fruit to cover completely.

3 Cook the crumble in a preheated oven, 180°C/350°F/Gas Mark 4, for about 40 minutes or until the top is crisp. Decorate with a sprinkling of desiccated coconut and serve.

Banana & Mango Tart

Bananas and mangoes are a great combination of colours and flavours, especially when topped with toasted coconut chips.

NUTRITIONAL INFORMATION

Calories	235	Sugars	........17g
Protein	.........4g	Fat	..........10g
Carbohydrate	...35g	Saturates	.......5g

1¼ hrs   5 mins

SERVES 8

INGREDIENTS

20 cm/8 inch ready-made pastry case

FILLING

2 small ripe bananas

1 mango, sliced

3½ tbsp cornflour

6 tbsp demerara sugar

300 ml/10 fl oz soya milk

150 ml/5 fl oz coconut milk

1 tsp vanilla essence

toasted coconut chips, to decorate

1 Slice the bananas and arrange half in the pastry case with half of the mango pieces.

2 Put the cornflour and sugar in a pan and mix together. Gradually, whisk in the soya milk and coconut milks until combined. Simmer over a low heat, whisking constantly, for 2–3 minutes until the mixture thickens.

3 Stir in the vanilla essence, then spoon the mixture over the fruit.

4 Top with the remaining fruit and toasted coconut chips. Chill in the refrigerator for 1 hour before serving.

COOK'S TIP

Coconut chips are available in some supermarkets and most health food shops. It is worth using them as they look much more attractive and are not so sweet as desiccated coconut.

Chocolate Cheesecake

This cheesecake takes a little time to prepare and cook but is well worth the effort. It is quite rich and is good served with a little fresh fruit.

NUTRITIONAL INFORMATION

Calories	471	Sugars	........20g
Protein	........10g	Fat	..........33g
Carbohydrate	...28g	Saturates	.......5g

1¼ hrs   1–1¼ hrs

SERVES 12

INGREDIENTS

100 g/3½ oz plain flour

100 g/3½ oz ground almonds

200 g/7 oz muscovado sugar

150 g/5½ oz margarine

675 g/1 lb 8 oz firm tofu

175 ml/6 fl oz vegetable oil

125 ml/4 fl oz orange juice

175 ml/6 fl oz brandy

6 tbsp cocoa powder, plus extra
  to decorate

2 tsp almond essence

TO DECORATE

icing sugar

Cape gooseberries

1 Put the flour, ground almonds and 1 tablespoon of the sugar in a bowl and mix well. Rub the margarine into the mixture to form a dough.

2 Lightly grease and line the base of a 23 cm/9 inch springform tin. Press the dough into the base of the tin to cover, pushing the dough right up to the edge of the tin.

3 Roughly chop the tofu and put in a food processor with the vegetable oil, orange juice, brandy, cocoa powder, almond essence and remaining sugar and process until smooth and creamy. Pour over the base in the tin and cook in a preheated oven, 160°C/325°F/Gas Mark 3, for about 1–1¼ hours or until set.

4 Leave to cool in the tin for 5 minutes, then remove from the tin and chill in the refrigerator. Dust with icing sugar and cocoa powder. Decorate with Cape gooseberries and serve.

COOK'S TIP

Cape gooseberries make an attractive decoration for many desserts. Peel open the papery husks to expose the bright orange fruits.

Date & Apricot Tart

There is no need to add any extra sugar to this filling because the dried fruit is naturally sweet.

NUTRITIONAL INFORMATION

Calories	359	Sugars	........34g
Protein	.........7g	Fat	..........15g
Carbohydrate	...53g	Saturates	.......2g

45 mins   50 mins

SERVES 8

INGREDIENTS

225 g/8 oz plain wholemeal flour, plus extra for dusting

55 g/2 oz mixed nuts, ground

100 g/3½ oz margarine, cut into small pieces

4 tbsp water

225 g/8 oz dried apricots, chopped

225 g/8 oz chopped stoned dates

425 ml/15 fl oz apple juice

1 tsp ground cinnamon

grated rind of 1 lemon

custard, to serve (optional)

1 Place the flour and ground nuts in a mixing bowl and rub in the margarine with your fingertips until the mixture resembles breadcrumbs. Stir in the water and bring together to form a dough. Wrap the dough in clingfilm and chill in the refrigerator for 30 minutes.

2 Meanwhile, place the apricots and dates in a pan, with the apple juice, cinnamon and lemon rind. Bring to the boil, cover and simmer over a low heat for about 15 minutes until the fruit softens. Mash to a purée.

3 Reserve a small ball of pastry for making lattice strips. On a lightly

floured surface, roll out the rest of the dough to form a round and use to line a 23 cm/9 inch loose-based quiche tin.

4 Spread the fruit filling evenly over the base of the pastry case. Roll out the reserved pastry and cut into strips 1 cm/ ½ inch wide. Cut the strips to fit the tart and twist them across the top of the fruit to form a decorative lattice pattern. Moisten the edges of the strips with a little water and seal them firmly around the rim of the tart.

5 Bake in a preheated oven, 200°/ 400°F/Gas Mark 6, for 25–30 minutes until golden brown. Cut into slices and serve immediately with custard, if using.

Fruity Queen of Puddings

A scrumptious version of a classic British pudding, made here with fresh bananas and apricot jam.

NUTRITIONAL INFORMATION

Calories	406	Sugars	........60g
Protein	........13g	Fat	...........7g
Carbohydrate	...77g	Saturates	.......3g

30 mins   1 hr

SERVES 4

I N G R E D I E N T S

115 g/4 oz fresh white breadcrumbs

600 ml/1 pint milk

3 eggs

½ tsp vanilla essence

4 tbsp caster sugar

2 bananas

1 tbsp lemon juice

3 tbsp apricot jam

1 Sprinkle the breadcrumbs into a 1 litre/1¾ pint ovenproof dish. Heat the milk until lukewarm, then pour it over the breadcrumbs.

2 Separate 2 of the eggs and beat the yolks with the remaining whole egg. Add to the dish with the vanilla essence and half the sugar, stirring well to mix. Set aside for 10 minutes.

3 Bake in a preheated oven, 180°C/350°F/Gas Mark 4, for 40 minutes until set. Remove the dish from the oven.

4 Slice the bananas and sprinkle with the lemon juice. Spoon the apricot jam on to the pudding and spread out to cover the surface. Arrange the banana slices on top of the apricot jam.

5 Whisk the egg whites until stiff, then add the remaining sugar. Continue whisking until the meringue is very stiff and glossy.

6 Pile the meringue on top of the pudding, return to the oven and cook for a further 10–15 minutes until the meringue is just set and golden brown. Serve immediately.

COOK'S TIP
The meringue will have a soft, marshmallow-like texture, unlike a hard meringue which is cooked slowly for 2–3 hours, until dry. Always use a grease-free bowl and whisk for beating egg-whites.

Rice & Banana Brûlée

Take a can of rice pudding, flavour it with orange rind, stem ginger, raisins and sliced bananas and top with a brown sugar glaze.

NUTRITIONAL INFORMATION

Calories 509   Sugars 98g
Protein . . . . .9g   Fat 6g
Carbohydrate . . .112g   Saturates 4g

🝆 50 mins   🕙 2–3 mins

SERVES 2

INGREDIENTS

400 g/14 oz can creamed rice pudding

grated rind of ½ orange

2 pieces of stem ginger, finely chopped

2 tsp ginger syrup from the jar

40 g/1½ oz raisins

1–2 bananas

1–2 tsp lemon juice

4–5 tbsp demerara sugar

1 Empty the can of rice pudding into a bowl and stir in the grated orange rind, ginger, ginger syrup and raisins.

2 Cut the bananas diagonally into slices, toss in the lemon juice to prevent them from discolouring, drain and divide between 2 individual flameproof dishes.

3 Spoon the rice mixture in an even layer over the bananas so that the dishes are almost full.

4 Sprinkle an even layer of sugar over the rice in each dish.

5 Place the dishes under a preheated moderate grill and heat until the sugar melts, taking care the sugar does not burn.

6 Set aside to cool until the caramel sets, then chill in the refrigerator until ready to serve. Tap the caramel with the back of a spoon to break it.

COOK'S TIP

Canned rice pudding is very versatile and is delicious heated with orange segments and grated apples added. Try it served cold with grated chocolate and mixed chopped nuts stirred through it.

Berry Yogurt Ice

This refreshing ice makes a wonderful summer dessert after a filling meal, as it is light and cooling without the richness – or fat – of ice cream.

NUTRITIONAL INFORMATION

Calories	118	Sugars	6g
Protein	6g	Fat	6g
Carbohydrate	6g	Saturates	3g

  4¼ hrs   5 mins

SERVES 4

INGREDIENTS

125 g/4½ oz raspberries

125 g/4½ oz blackberries

125 g/4½ oz strawberries

1 large egg

175 ml/6 fl oz Greek yogurt

125 ml/4 fl oz red wine

2¼ tsp powdered gelatine

fresh berries, to decorate

1 Put the raspberries, blackberries and strawberries in a blender or food processor and process until a smooth purée forms. Rub the purée through a sieve into a bowl to remove the seeds.

2 Break the egg and separate the yolk and white into separate bowls. Stir the egg yolk and yogurt into the berry purée and set the egg white aside.

3 Pour the wine into a heatproof bowl and sprinkle the gelatine on the surface. Leave to stand for 5 minutes to soften, then set the bowl over a saucepan of simmering water until the gelatine has dissolved. Pour the mixture into the berry purée in a steady stream, whisking constantly. Transfer the mixture to a freezerproof container and freeze for 2 hours, or until slushy.

4 Whisk the egg white in a spotlessly clean, greasefree bowl until very stiff. Remove the berry mixture from the freezer and fold in the egg white. Return to the freezer and freeze for 2 hours, or until firm. To serve, scoop the berry yogurt ice into glass dishes and decorate with fresh berries of your choice.

COOK'S TIP

Vegetarians can use a vegetarian gelatine, which is available in health food shops, to make this ice. Follow the instructions on the packet and proceed as in main recipe.

Lime Cheesecakes

These cheesecakes are flavoured with lime and mint, and set on a base of crushed digestive biscuits mixed with chocolate.

NUTRITIONAL INFORMATION

Calories 696   Sugars 44g
Protein . . . . .18g   Fat 40g
Carbohydrate . . .70g   Saturates 22g

3 hrs   5 mins

SERVES 2

INGREDIENTS

BASE

2 tbsp butter, plus extra for greasing

25 g/1 oz dark chocolate

90 g/3 oz crushed digestive biscuits

FILLING

finely grated rind of 1 lime

85 g/3 oz curd cheese

85 g/3 oz low-fat soft cheese

1 fresh mint sprig, very finely
   chopped (optional)

1 tsp gelatine

1 tbsp lime juice

1 egg yolk

3 tbsp caster sugar

TO DECORATE

whipped cream

kiwi fruit slices

fresh mint sprigs

1 Grease 2 fluted, loose-based 11 cm/4½ inch flan tins thoroughly. To make the base, melt the butter and chocolate in a heatproof bowl over a pan of gently simmering water or melt in a microwave set on HIGH power for about 1 minute. Stir until smooth.

2 Stir the crushed biscuits evenly through the melted chocolate and then press into the bases of the flan tins, levelling the surface. Chill until set.

3 To make the filling, put the grated lime rind and cheeses into a bowl and beat until smooth and evenly blended, then beat in the mint, if using.

4 Dissolve the gelatine in the lime juice in a heatproof bowl over a pan of simmering water or in a microwave oven set on HIGH power for about 30 seconds.

5 Beat the egg yolk and sugar together until creamy and fold into the cheese mixture, followed by the dissolved gelatine. Pour over the base and chill until set.

6 To serve, remove the cheesecakes carefully from the flan tins. Decorate with whipped cream, slices of kiwi fruit and mint sprigs.

Baked Semolina Pudding

Succulent plums simmered in orange juice and mixed spice complement this rich and creamy semolina pudding perfectly.

NUTRITIONAL INFORMATION

Calories	304	Sugars	........32g
Protein	.........9g	Fat	..........12g
Carbohydrate	...43g	Saturates	.......4g

 5 mins   🕐 45 mins

SERVES 4

INGREDIENTS

2 tbsp butter or margarine

600 ml/1 pint milk

finely pared rind and juice of 1 orange

55 g/2 oz semolina

pinch of grated nutmeg

2 tbsp caster sugar

1 egg, beaten

TO SERVE

knob of butter

grated nutmeg

SPICED PLUMS

225 g/8 oz plums, halved and stoned

150 ml/5 fl oz orange juice

2 tbsp caster sugar

½ tsp ground mixed spice

1 Grease a 1 litre/1¾ pint ovenproof dish with a little of the butter or margarine. Put the milk, the remaining butter or margarine and the orange rind in a pan. Sprinkle in the semolina and bring to the boil over a low heat, stirring constantly. Simmer gently for 2–3 minutes. Remove the pan from the heat.

2 Add the nutmeg, orange juice and sugar, stirring well. Add the egg and stir to mix.

3 Transfer the mixture to the prepared dish and bake in a preheated oven, 190°C/375°F/Gas Mark 5, for about 30 minutes until lightly browned.

4 To make the spiced plums, put the plums, orange juice, sugar and spice into a pan and simmer gently for about 10 minutes until the plums are tender.

Remove the pan from the heat and set aside to cool slightly.

5 Top the semolina pudding with a knob of butter and a sprinkling of grated nutmeg and serve with the spiced plums.

Fruity Pancake Bundles

This unusual pancake is filled with a sweet cream flavoured with ginger, nuts and apricots and served with a raspberry and orange sauce.

NUTRITIONAL INFORMATION

Calories	610	Sugars	........60g
Protein	........19g	Fat	..........20g
Carbohydrate	...94g	Saturates	.......5g

  15 mins   35 mins

SERVES 2

INGREDIENTS

BATTER

55 g/2 oz plain flour

pinch of salt

¼ tsp ground cinnamon

1 egg

135 ml/4½ fl oz milk

white vegetable fat, for frying

FILLING

1½ tsp plain flour, sifted

1½ tsp cornflour

1 tbsp caster sugar

1 egg

150 ml/5 fl oz milk

4 tbsp chopped nuts

40 g/1½ oz ready-to-eat dried apricots, chopped

1 piece of stem or crystallised ginger, finely chopped

SAUCE

3 tbsp raspberry preserve

4½ tsp orange juice

finely grated rind of ¼ orange

1 To make the batter, sift the flour, salt and cinnamon into a bowl and make a well in the centre. Add the egg and milk and gradually beat in until smooth.

2 Melt a little fat in a medium frying pan. Pour in half the batter. Cook for 2 minutes until golden, then turn and cook the other side for about 1 minute until browned. Set aside and make a second pancake.

3 For the filling, beat the flour with the cornflour, sugar and egg. Gently heat the milk in a pan, then beat 2 tablespoons of it into the flour mixture. Transfer to the pan and cook gently, stirring constantly until thick. Remove from the heat, cover with baking paper to prevent a skin from forming and set aside to cool.

4 Beat the nuts, apricots and ginger into the cooled mixture and put a heaped tablespoonful in the centre of each pancake. Gather and squeeze the edges together to make a bundle. Place in an ovenproof dish and bake in a preheated oven, 180°C/350°F/Gas Mark 4, for 15–20 minutes until hot but not too brown.

5 To make the sauce, melt the preserve gently with the orange juice, then strain. Return to a clean pan with the orange rind and heat through. Serve with the pancakes.

Carrot Dessert

This makes an impressive dinner-party dessert. It is best served warm with cream and can be made well in advance because it freezes well.

NUTRITIONAL INFORMATION

Calories ....509 Sugars 54g
Protein ....8g Fat 30g
Carbohydrate ...55g Saturates 19g

 10 mins   1 hr

SERVES 6

INGREDIENTS

1.5 kg/3 lb 5 oz carrots

10 tbsp ghee

600 ml/1 pint milk

175 ml/6 fl oz evaporated milk

10 whole cardamoms, peeled and crushed

8–10 tbsp sugar

TO DECORATE

4 tbsp chopped pistachio nuts

2 leaves varq (silver leaf), optional

1 Grate the carrots. Heat the ghee in a large, heavy-based pan over a medium heat. Add the grated carrots and stir-fry for about 15–20 minutes or until the moisture from the carrots has evaporated and the carrots have darkened in colour.

2 Add the milk, evaporated milk, cardamoms and sugar stir-fry for a further 30–35 minutes until the mixture is a rich brownish-red colour.

3 Transfer the carrot mixture to a large shallow dish. Decorate with the pistachio nuts and varq, if using, and serve immediately.

COOK'S TIP

Pure ghee is best for this dessert, because it will taste better. However, if you are trying to limit your fat intake, you can use vegetable ghee instead.

Pancakes with Apples

The sharpness of the apples contrasts with the sweetness of the butterscotch sauce in this mouthwatering pancake recipe.

NUTRITIONAL INFORMATION

Calories	543	Sugars	........55g
Protein	.........8g	Fat	.........24g
Carbohydrate	...78g	Saturates	......14g

15 mins   45 mins

SERVES 4

INGREDIENTS

125 g/4½ oz plain flour

pinch of salt

1 tsp finely grated lemon rind

1 egg

300 ml/10 fl oz milk

1–2 tbsp vegetable oil, plus extra for greasing

pared lemon rind, to garnish

FILLING

225 g/8 oz cooking apples, peeled, cored and sliced

2 tbsp sultanas

SAUCE

85 g/3 oz butter

3 tbsp golden syrup

85 g/3 oz light muscovado sugar

1 tbsp rum or brandy (optional)

1 tbsp lemon juice

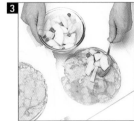

1 Sift the flour and salt into a bowl. Add the lemon rind, egg and milk and whisk to make a smooth batter.

2 Heat a little oil in a heavy-based frying pan. Make 8 thin pancakes, using extra oil as required. Stack the cooked pancakes, layering them with kitchen paper.

3 To make the filling, cook the apples with the sultanas in a little water until soft. Divide the mixture evenly between the pancakes and roll up or fold into triangles. Brush an ovenproof dish with a little oil and arrange the pancakes in it. Bake in a preheated oven, 160°C/ 325°F/ Gas Mark 3, for 15 minutes until warmed through.

4 To make the sauce, melt the butter, syrup and sugar together in a pan, stirring well. Add the rum or brandy, if using, and the lemon juice. Do not allow the mixture to boil.

5 Serve the pancakes on warm plates, with a little sauce poured over and garnished with lemon rind.

Sweet Potato Dessert

This unusual milky dessert is very easy to make and is equally delicious whether it is eaten hot or cold.

NUTRITIONAL INFORMATION

Calories 234	Sugars 23g
Protein 5g	Fat 3g
Carbohydrate ...51g	Saturates 1g

 15 mins   🕐 20 mins

SERVES 4

INGREDIENTS

1 kg/2 lb 4 oz sweet potatoes

850 ml/1½ pints milk

175 g/6 oz sugar

chopped almonds, to decorate

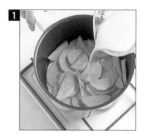

1 Using a sharp knife, peel the sweet potatoes. Rinse them and then cut them into slices. Place in a large pan. Cover with 600 ml/1 pint of the milk and cook over a low heat until the sweet potato is soft enough to be mashed.

2 Remove the sweet potatoes from the heat and mash thoroughly until completely smooth. Add the sugar and the remaining milk and stir gently until completely blended together.

3 Return the pan to the heat and simmer the mixture until it starts to thicken (it should reach the consistency of a creamy soup).

4 Transfer to a serving dish. Decorate with almonds and serve immediately.

COOK'S TIP

Sweet potatoes are longer than ordinary potatoes and have a pinkish or yellowish skin with yellow or white flesh. As their name suggests, they taste slightly sweet.

Spiced Fruit Garland

There is nothing like the delicious smell of yeast cooking for creating a warm atmosphere. It must be something to do with the anticipation.

NUTRITIONAL INFORMATION

Calories 327	Sugars 28g
Protein 6g	Fat 11g
Carbohydrate . . .55g	Saturates 5g

 1½ hrs   30 mins

SERVES 12

I N G R E D I E N T S

400 g/14 oz strong white flour, plus extra
   for dusting

½ tsp salt

4 tbsp butter

4 tbsp caster sugar

1 sachet easy-blend dried yeast

175 ml/6 fl oz lukewarm milk

1 egg, beaten

vegetable oil, for brushing

F I L L I N G

150 g/5½ oz mixed dried fruit

25 g/1 oz glacé cherries, chopped

55 g/2 oz ground almonds

4 tbsp light muscovado sugar

1 tsp ground cinnamon

½ tsp ground nutmeg

2 tbsp butter, melted

T O   D E C O R A T E

55 g/2 oz icing sugar

glacé cherries

chopped nuts

angelica

1 Sift the flour and salt into a large bowl. Rub in the butter and stir in the sugar and yeast. Make a well in the centre and add the milk and egg. Draw in the flour gradually, mixing well to make a smooth dough.

2 Knead the dough on a lightly floured surface for about 8–10 minutes. Place in a lightly oiled bowl, cover and set aside in a warm place to rise until doubled in size.

3 Knead lightly for 1 minute and then roll out into a 40 x 23 cm/16 x 9 inch rectangle. Combine all the filling ingredients and spread over the rectangle, leaving a 2 cm/¾ in border around the edge. From the long edge, roll the rectangle into a cylinder, pressing the edge to seal it. Form the roll into a circle, sealing the ends together.

4 Lift the ring on to a greased baking sheet and cut it into 12 slices, without cutting right through. Twist each slice so that a cut surface lies uppermost. Set aside in a warm place for 30–40 minutes to rise.

5 Bake in a preheated oven, 200°C/400°F/Gas Mark 6, for 25–30 minutes. Cool on a wire rack. Mix the icing sugar with a little water to make a thin glacé icing and drizzle over. Arrange the cherries on top and sprinkle with the chopped nuts and angelica.

Ground Almonds in Milk

Traditionally served at breakfast in India, this almond-based dish is said to sharpen the mind. However, it can be served as a delicious dessert.

NUTRITIONAL INFORMATION

Calories 314   Sugars 18g
Protein . . . . .8g   Fat 21g
Carbohydrate . . .23g   Saturates 3g

   5 mins   10 mins

SERVES 4

INGREDIENTS

2 tbsp vegetable or pure ghee

4 tbsp plain flour

100 g/3½ oz ground almonds

300 ml/10 fl oz milk

55 g/2 oz sugar

fresh mint leaves, to decorate

1 Place the ghee in a small, heavy-based pan and melt over a gentle heat, stirring constantly so that it doesn't burn.

2 Reduce the heat and add the flour, constantly stirring vigorously to remove any lumps. Stir in the almonds.

3 Gradually stir in the milk and sugar. Bring to the boil, stirring constantly. Continue cooking, stirring constantly, for 3–5 minutes or until the mixture is smooth and reaches the consistency of a creamy soup.

4 Transfer to a serving dish, decorate with fresh mint leaves and serve hot.

Apricot Slices

These vegan slices are ideal for children's lunches.
They are full of flavour and made with healthy ingredients.

NUTRITIONAL INFORMATION

Calories	198	Sugars 13g
Protein	. . . . .4g	Fat 9g
Carbohydrate	. . .25g	Saturates 2g

50 mins   1 hr

makes 12

INGREDIENTS

PASTRY

100 g/3½ oz margarine, cut into
  small pieces, plus extra for greasing

225 g/8 oz wholemeal flour

55 g/2 oz finely ground mixed nuts

4 tbsp water

soya milk, to glaze

FILLING

225 g/8 oz dried apricots

grated rind of 1 orange

300 ml/10 fl oz apple juice

1 tsp ground cinnamon

55 g/2 oz raisins

1 Lightly grease a 23 cm/9 inch square cake tin. To make the pastry, place the flour and nuts in a mixing bowl and rub in the margarine with your fingers until the mixture resembles breadcrumbs. Stir in the water and bring together to form a dough. Wrap and set aside to chill in the refrigerator for 30 minutes.

2 To make the filling, place the apricots, orange rind and apple juice in a pan and bring to the boil. Simmer for 30 minutes until the apricots are mushy. Cool slightly, then process in a food processor or blender to a purée. Alternatively, press the mixture through a fine strainer. Stir in the cinnamon and raisins.

3 Divide the pastry in half, roll out 1 half and use to line the base of the tin. Spread the apricot purée over the top and brush the edges of the pastry with water. Roll out the rest of the dough to fit over the top of the apricot purée. Press down and seal the edges.

4 Prick the top of the pastry with a fork and brush with soya milk. Bake in a preheated oven, 200°C/400°F/Gas Mark 6, for 20–25 minutes until the pastry is golden. Set aside to cool slightly before cutting into 12 bars. Serve either warm or cold.

COOK'S TIP

These slices will keep in an
airtight container for 3–4 days.

Mangoes in Syrup

A simple, fresh-tasting fruit dessert to round off a rich meal perfectly. Serve the mango lightly chilled.

NUTRITIONAL INFORMATION

Calories 117   Sugars 30g
Protein . . . . .1g   Fat 0g
Carbohydrate . . .30g   Saturates 0g

1 hr   5 mins

SERVES 4

I N G R E D I E N T S

2 large, ripe mangoes

1 lime

1 lemon grass stalk, chopped

3 tbsp caster sugar

1 Peel the mangoes, then cut away the flesh from either side of the the large stones. Slice the flesh into long, thin slices and arrange them in a large, chilled serving dish.

2 Remove a few shreds of the rind from the lime and reserve for decoration, then cut the lime in half and squeeze out the juice.

3 Place the lime juice in a small pan with the lemon grass and sugar. Heat gently, without boiling, until the sugar is completely dissolved. Remove from the heat and set aside to cool completely.

4 Strain the cooled syrup into a jug and pour evenly over the mango slices. Sprinkle with the lime rind strips, cover and chill before serving.

COOK'S TIP
To serve this dessert on a hot day, particularly if it is to stand for a while, place the dish on a bed of crushed ice to keep the fruit and syrup chilled.

Rose Ice

A delicately perfumed sweet granita ice, which is coarser than many ice creams. This looks very pretty on a glass dish scattered with rose petals.

NUTRITIONAL INFORMATION

Calories	76	Sugars	.........9g
Protein	.........2g	Fat	...........4g
Carbohydrate	....9g	Saturates	.......3g

 3 hrs   10 mins

SERVES 4

I N G R E D I E N T S

400 ml/14 fl oz water

2 tbsp coconut cream

4 tbsp sweetened condensed milk

2 tsp rosewater

a few drops pink food colouring (optional)

pink rose petals, to decorate

1 Place the water in a small pan and add the coconut cream. Heat the mixture gently without boiling, stirring.

2 Remove from the heat and allow to cool. Stir in the condensed milk, rosewater and food colouring, if using.

3 Pour into a freezer container and freeze for 1–1½ hours until slushy.

4 Remove from the freezer and break up the ice crystals with a fork. Return to the freezer and freeze until firm.

5 Spoon the ice roughly into a pile on a serving dish and scatter with rose petals to serve.

COOK'S TIP

To prevent the ice from thawing too quickly at the table, nestle the base of the serving dish in another dish filled with crushed ice.

Mango & Lime Sorbet

A refreshing sorbet is the perfect way to round off a spicy Thai meal, and mangoes make a deliciously smooth-textured, velvety sorbet.

NUTRITIONAL INFORMATION

Calories	158	Sugars	........34g
Protein	.........1g	Fat	...........3g
Carbohydrate	...34g	Saturates	.......2g

4 hrs   4 mins

SERVES 4

INGREDIENTS

6 tbsp caster sugar

100 ml/3½ fl oz water

rind of 3 limes, finely grated

2 tbsp coconut cream

2 large, ripe mangoes

135 ml/4½ fl oz lime juice

curls of fresh coconut, toasted, to decorate

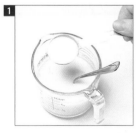  

1 Place the sugar, water and lime rind in a small pan and heat gently, stirring constantly, until the sugar dissolves. Boil rapidly for 2 minutes to reduce slightly, then remove from the heat and strain into a bowl or jug. Stir in the coconut cream and set aside to cool.

2 Halve the mangoes, remove the stones and peel thinly. Chop the flesh roughly and place in a food processor with the lime juice. Process to a smooth purée and transfer to a small bowl.

3 Pour the cooled syrup into the mango purée, mixing evenly. Tip into a freezer container and freeze for 1 hour, or until slushy in texture. (Alternatively, use an electric ice-cream maker.)

4 Remove the container from the freezer and beat with an electric mixer to break up the ice crystals.

Refreeze for a further hour, then remove from the freezer and beat the contents again until smooth.

5 Cover the container, return to the freezer and freeze until firm. To serve, remove from the freezer and leave at room temperature for about 15 minutes to soften slightly before scooping. Sprinkle with toasted coconut to serve.

COOK'S TIP

If you prefer, canned mangoes in syrup can be used to make the sorbet. Omit the sugar and water, and infuse the lime rind in the canned syrup instead.

Lychee & Ginger Sorbet

A refreshing palate-cleanser after a rich meal, this sorbet couldn't be easier to make, and can be served with a fruit salad.

NUTRITIONAL INFORMATION

Calories 159	Sugars 40g
Protein 2g	Fat 0g
Carbohydrate ...40g	Saturates 0g

🍧 4 hrs   🕐 0 mins

SERVES 4

INGREDIENTS

2 x 400 g/14 oz cans lychees in syrup

rind of 1 lime, finely grated

2 tbsp lime juice

3 tbsp stem ginger syrup

2 egg whites

TO DECORATE

starfruit slices

slivers of stem ginger

1 Drain the lychees, reserving the syrup. Place the fruits in a blender or food processor with the lime rind, juice and stem ginger syrup and process until completely smooth. Transfer to a mixing bowl.

2 Mix the purée thoroughly with the reserved syrup, then pour into a freezerproof container and freeze for about 1–1½ hours until slushy in texture. (Alternatively, use an ice-cream maker.)

3 Remove from the freezer and whisk to break up the ice crystals. Whisk the egg whites in a clean, dry bowl until stiff, then quickly and lightly fold them into the iced lychee mixture.

4 Return to the freezer and freeze until firm. Remove from the freezer 15 minutes before serving to soften slightly. Serve the sorbet in scoops, with slices of starfruit and ginger to decorate.

COOK'S TIP

It is not recommended that raw egg whites are served to very young children, pregnant women, the elderly or anyone weakened by chronic illness. The egg whites may be left out of this recipe, but you will need to whisk the sorbet a second time.

Pineapple with Lime

Thai pineapples are sweet and fragrant, and this local
fruit appears regularly as a dessert, usually served very simply.

NUTRITIONAL INFORMATION

Calories	93	Sugars	........23g
Protein	.........1g	Fat	..........0g
Carbohydrate	...23g	Saturates	.......0g

 40 mins   ⏱ 1 min

SERVES 4

INGREDIENTS

1 pineapple

2 cardamom pods

4 tbsp water

1 strip of lime rind, thinly pared

1 tbsp soft light brown sugar

3 tbsp lime juice

fresh mint sprigs and whipped cream,
to decorate

1 Using a sharp knife, cut the top and base from the pineapple, then cut away the peel and remove all the 'eyes' from the flesh. Cut into quarters and remove the core. Slice the pineapple flesh lengthways.

2 Crush the cardamom pods in a mortar with a pestle and place in a small pan with the lime rind and water. Heat gently until the mixture is boiling, then simmer for 30 seconds.

3 Remove the pan from the heat and stir in the sugar until it has dissolved, then cover and set aside to infuse for 5 minutes.

4 Add the lime juice, stir well to mix, then strain the syrup over the pineapple. Chill for 30 minutes.

5 Arrange the pineapple on a serving dish, spoon the syrup over it and serve decorated with fresh mint sprigs and whipped cream.

COOK'S TIP

To remove the 'eyes' from pineapple, cut off the peel, then use a small sharp knife to cut a V-shaped channel down the pineapple, cutting diagonally through the lines of brown 'eyes' in the flesh, to make spiralling cuts around the fruit.

Mung Bean Custards

Mung beans give this sweet custard an unusual texture, and it's a real treat served with a generous spoonful of crème fraîche.

NUTRITIONAL INFORMATION

Calories	163	Sugars	........19g
Protein	.........8g	Fat	...........3g
Carbohydrate	...29g	Saturates	.......1g

  40 mins   50–60 mins

SERVES 6

INGREDIENTS

115 g/4 oz dried mung beans

2 eggs, beaten

175 ml/6 fl oz coconut milk

100 g/3½ oz caster sugar

1 tbsp ground rice

1 tsp ground cinnamon

butter, for greasing

TO DECORATE

ground cinnamon

crème fraîche or whipped cream

finely grated lime rind

sliced starfruit

pomegranate seeds

1 Place the beans in a pan with enough water to cover. Bring to the boil, then lower the heat and simmer for about 30–40 minutes until the beans are very tender. Drain well.

2 Mash the beans, then press through a sieve to make a smooth purée. Place the bean purée, eggs, coconut milk, sugar, rice flour and cinnamon in a large bowl and beat well until mixed.

3 Grease and base-line 4 x 150 ml/ 5 fl oz pudding-shaped moulds or ramekin dishes and pour in the mixture. Place on a baking sheet and bake in a preheated oven, 180°C/350°F/Gas Mark 4, for 20–25 minutes or until just set.

4 Cool the custards, run a knife around the edges to loosen and turn out on to a serving plate. Sprinkle with cinnamon. Top with crème fraîche or whipped cream and sprinkle with lime rind. Serve with starfruit and pomegranate seeds.

COOK'S TIP

To save time, use canned mung beans. Omit Step 1, drain the beans thoroughly and continue with step 2.

Bananas in Coconut Milk

An unusual dessert which is equally good served hot or cold.
This is a classic Thai combination of fruits and vegetables.

NUTRITIONAL INFORMATION

Calories ....157 Sugars 36g
Protein ....2g Fat 1g
Carbohydrate ...38g Saturates 0g

 10 mins   3–5 mins

SERVES 4

INGREDIENTS

4 large bananas

350 ml/12 fl oz coconut milk

2 tbsp caster sugar

pinch of salt

½ tsp orange-flower water

1 tbsp shredded fresh mint

2 tbsp mung beans, cooked

fresh mint sprigs, to decorate

1 Peel the bananas and cut them into short chunks. Place in a large, heavy-based pan with the coconut milk, caster sugar and salt. Heat gently until boiling, then simmer for 1 minute. Remove the pan from the heat.

2 Sprinkle the orange-flower water over, stir in the mint and spoon into a serving dish.

3 Place the mung beans in a heavy-based frying pan and cook over a high heat until turning crisp and golden, shaking the pan occasionally. Remove, cool slightly and crush lightly in a mortar with a pestle.

4 Sprinkle the toasted beans over the bananas and serve warm or cold, decorated with fresh mint sprigs.

COOK'S TIP

If you prefer, the mung beans could be replaced with flaked, toasted almonds or hazelnuts.

Thai Rice Pudding

This Thai-style version of rice pudding is mildly spiced and creamy, with a rich custard topping. It's excellent served warm or cold.

NUTRITIONAL INFORMATION

Calories 351	Sugars 16g	
Protein 7g	Fat 21g	
Carbohydrate . . .37g	Saturates 16g	

 10 mins   1–1¼ hrs

SERVES 4

INGREDIENTS

100 g/3½ oz short grain rice

2 tbsp palm sugar

1 cardamom pod, split

300 ml/10 fl oz coconut milk

150 ml/5 fl oz water

3 eggs

200 ml/7 fl oz coconut cream

1½ tbsp caster sugar

sweetened coconut flakes, to decorate

fresh fruit, to serve

1 Place the rice and palm sugar in a pan. Crush the seeds from the cardamom pod in a mortar with a pestle and add to the pan. Stir in the coconut milk and water.

2 Bring to the boil, stirring to dissolve the sugar. Lower the heat and simmer, uncovered, stirring occasionally, for about 20 minutes until the rice is tender and most of the liquid is absorbed.

3 Spoon the rice into 4 individual ovenproof dishes and spread evenly. Place the dishes in a wide roasting tin with water to come about halfway up the sides.

4 Beat the eggs with the coconut cream and caster sugar and spoon over the rice. Cover with foil and bake in a preheated oven, 180°C/ 350°F/Gas Mark 4, for about 45–50 minutes until the custard sets.

5 Serve the rice puddings warm or cold, with fresh fruit and decorated with coconut flakes.

COOK'S TIP

Cardamom is quite a powerful spice, so if you find it too strong, it can be left out altogether or replaced with a little ground cinnamon.

Balinese Banana Pancakes

These little stacks of rich banana pancakes, drizzled with fragrant lime juice, are quite irresistible at any time of day.

NUTRITIONAL INFORMATION

Calories	225	Sugars	........11g
Protein	.........9g	Fat	...........7g
Carbohydrate	...34g	Saturates	.......2g

🍤 1¼ hrs   🕐 20 mins

SERVES 6

I N G R E D I E N T S

175 g/6 oz plain flour

pinch of salt

4 eggs, beaten

2 large, ripe bananas, peeled and mashed

300 ml/10 fl oz coconut milk

vegetable oil, for frying

TO DECORATE

sliced banana

6 tbsp lime juice

icing sugar

coconut cream

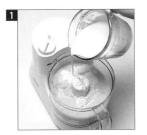

1 Place the flour, salt, eggs, bananas and coconut milk in a blender or food processor and process to a smooth batter. Alternatively, if you don't have a food processor, sift the flour and salt into a bowl and make a well in the centre, then add the remaining ingredients and beat well until smooth.

2 Chill the batter for 1 hour. Remove from the refrigerator and beat briefly again. Heat a small amount of oil in a small frying pan until very hot.

3 Drop tablespoonfuls of batter into the pan. Cook until the pancakes are golden underneath.

4 Turn over and cook the other side until golden brown. Cook in batches until all the batter is used up, making about 36 pancakes. Remove and drain on kitchen paper.

5 Serve the pancakes in a stack, decorated with sliced bananas, sprinkled with lime juice and icing sugar and topped with coconut cream.

COOK'S TIP

These little pancakes are best eaten hot and freshly cooked, so keep them hot in a low oven while the others are cooking.

Coconut Pancakes

These pretty, lacy-thin pancakes are sold by Thai street vendors, often coloured a delicate pale pink or tinted green.

NUTRITIONAL INFORMATION

Calories	218	Sugars	8g
Protein	6g	Fat	7g
Carbohydrate	31g	Saturates	2g

10 mins   20 mins

SERVES 4

INGREDIENTS

115 g/4 oz rice flour

3 tbsp caster sugar

pinch of salt

2 eggs

600 ml/1 pint coconut milk

4 tbsp desiccated coconut

vegetable oil, for frying

2 tbsp palm sugar, to decorate

fresh mango or banana, to serve

1 Place the rice flour, sugar and salt in a bowl and add the eggs and coconut milk, whisking until a smooth batter forms. Alternatively, place all the ingredients in a blender and process to a smooth batter. Beat in half the coconut.

2 Heat a small amount of oil in a wide, heavy-based frying pan. Pour in a little batter, swirling the pan to cover the surface thinly and evenly. Cook until pale golden underneath.

3 Turn or toss the pancake and cook the other side until light golden brown.

4 Turn out the pancakes and keep hot while using the remaining batter to make a total of 8 pancakes.

5 Serve the pancakes folded or loosely rolled, with slices of mango or banana and sprinkled with palm sugar and the remaining coconut, toasted.

COOK'S TIP

Rice flour gives the pancakes a light, smooth texture, but if it's not available, use ordinary plain flour instead.

Barbecued Baked Apples

When they are wrapped in kitchen foil, apples bake to perfection on the barbecue and make a delightful finale to any meal.

NUTRITIONAL INFORMATION

Calories . . . . . . .294 Sugars 30g
Protein . . . . .3g Fat 18g
Carbohydrate . . .31g Saturates 7g

 15 mins   🕐 25–30 mins

SERVES 4

I N G R E D I E N T S

4 medium cooking apples

4 tbsp chopped walnuts

4 tbsp ground almonds

25 g/1 oz light muscovado sugar

25 g/1 oz cherries, chopped

25 g/1 oz stem ginger, chopped

1 tbsp amaretto (optional)

2 tbsp butter

single cream or natural yogurt, to serve

1 Core the apples and using a knife, score each around the middle to prevent the skins from splitting during barbecuing.

2 To make the filling, combine the walnuts, almonds, sugar, cherries, ginger and amaretto liqueur, if using, in a small bowl.

3 Spoon the filling mixture into each apple, pushing it down into the hollowed-out core. Mound a little of the filling mixture on top of each apple.

4 Place each apple on a large square of double thickness kitchen foil and generously dot all over with the butter. Wrap up the foil so that the apple is completely enclosed.

5 Barbecue the foil parcels over hot coals for 25–30 minutes or until the apples are tender.

6 Transfer the apples to warm, individual serving plates. Serve immediately with lashings of single cream or thick natural yogurt.

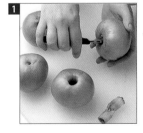  

COOK'S TIP

If the coals are dying down, place the kitchen foil parcels directly on them, raking them up around the apples. Barbecue for 25–30 minutes and serve with the cream or yogurt.

Baked Bananas

The orange-flavoured cream can be prepared in advance but do not make up the banana parcels until just before you need to cook them.

NUTRITIONAL INFORMATION

Calories 380	Sugars 40g	
Protein 2g	Fat 18g	
Carbohydrate ...43g	Saturates 11g	

 30 mins 10 mins

SERVES 4

INGREDIENTS

4 bananas

2 passion fruit

4 tbsp orange juice

4 tbsp orange-flavoured liqueur

ORANGE-FLAVOURED CREAM

150 ml/5 fl oz double cream

3 tbsp icing sugar

2 tbsp orange-flavoured liqueur

1 To make the orange-flavoured cream, pour the double cream into a mixing bowl and sprinkle over the icing sugar. Whisk the mixture until it is standing in soft peaks. Carefully fold in the orange-flavoured liqueur and chill in the refrigerator until required.

2 Peel the bananas and place each one on a sheet of kitchen foil.

VARIATION

Leave the bananas in their skins for a really quick dessert. Split the banana skins and pop in 1–2 squares of chocolate. Wrap the bananas in kitchen foil and bake for 10 minutes or until the chocolate has just melted.

3 Cut the passion fruit in half and squeeze the juice of each half over each banana. Spoon over the orange juice and liqueur.

4 Fold the kitchen foil over the top of the bananas so that they are completely enclosed.

5 Place the parcels on a baking sheet and bake the bananas in a preheated

oven, 180°C/350°F/Gas Mark 4, for about 10 minutes or until they are just tender (test by inserting a cocktail stick).

6 Transfer the foil parcels to warm, individual serving plates. Open out the foil parcels at the table and then serve immediately with the chilled orange-flavoured cream.

Piña Colada Pineapple

The flavours of pineapple and coconut blend as well together on the barbecue as they do in the well-known cocktail.

NUTRITIONAL INFORMATION

Calories 231   Sugars 22g
Protein . . . . .1g   Fat 15g
Carbohydrate . . .22g   Saturates 11g

15 mins   25 mins

SERVES 4

INGREDIENTS

1 small pineapple

2 tbsp unsalted butter

25 g/1 oz light muscovado sugar

55 g/2 oz fresh coconut, grated

2 tbsp coconut-flavoured liqueur or rum

1 Using a very sharp knife, cut the pineapple into quarters and then remove the tough core from the centre, leaving the leaves attached.

2 Carefully cut the pineapple flesh away from the skin. Remove any 'eyes' with small sharp knife. Make horizontal cuts across the flesh of the pineapple quarters.

3 Place the butter in a pan and heat gently until melted, stirring constantly. Brush the melted butter over the pineapple and sprinkle with the sugar.

4 Cover the pineapple leaves with kitchen foil in order to prevent them from burning and transfer the pineapple quarters to a rack set over hot coals.

5 Barbecue the pineapple for about 10 minutes.

6 Sprinkle the coconut over the pineapple and barbecue, cut side up, for a further 5–10 minutes or until the pineapple is piping hot.

7 Transfer the pineapple to serving plates and remove the foil from the leaves. Spoon a little coconut-flavoured liqueur or rum over the pineapple and serve immediately.

COOK'S TIP
Fresh coconut has the best flavour for this dish. If you prefer, however, you can use desiccated coconut.

Exotic Fruit Pancakes

These pancakes are filled with an exotic array of tropical fruits.
Decorate lavishly with tropical flowers or mint sprigs.

NUTRITIONAL INFORMATION

Calories	382	Sugars	........24g
Protein	.........7g	Fat	..........17g
Carbohydrate	...53g	Saturates	.......3g

 40 mins   35 mins

SERVES 4

I N G R E D I E N T S

B A T T E R

125 g/4½ oz plain flour

pinch of salt

1 egg

1 egg yolk

300 ml/10 fl oz coconut milk

4 tsp vegetable oil, plus extra for frying

F I L L I N G

1 banana

1 papaya

juice of 1 lime

2 passion fruit

1 mango, peeled, stoned and sliced

4 lychees, stoned and halved

1–2 tbsp clear honey

flowers or fresh mint sprigs, to decorate

1 Sift the flour and salt into a bowl. Make a well in the centre and add the egg, egg yolk and a little of the coconut milk. Gradually draw the flour into the egg mixture, beating well and gradually adding the remaining coconut milk to make a smooth batter. Stir in the oil. Cover and chill for 30 minutes.

2 Peel and slice the banana and place in a bowl. Peel and slice the papaya, discarding the seeds. Add to the banana with the lime juice and mix well. Cut the passion fruit in half and scoop out the flesh and seeds into the fruit bowl. Stir in the mango, lychees and honey.

3 Heat a little oil in a 15 cm/6 inch frying pan. Pour in just enough of the pancake batter to cover the base of the pan and tilt so that it spreads thinly and evenly. Cook until the pancake is just set and the underside is lightly browned, turn and briefly cook the other side. Remove from the pan and keep warm. Repeat with the remaining batter to make a total of 8 pancakes.

4 To serve, place a little of the prepared fruit filling along the centre of each pancake and then roll it into a cone shape. Lay seam side down on warmed serving plates, decorate with flowers or mint sprigs and serve.

Sticky Sesame Bananas

These tasty morsels are a real treat. Pieces of banana are dipped in caramel and then sprinkled with a few sesame seeds.

NUTRITIONAL INFORMATION

Calories . . . . .215 Sugars 38g
Protein . . . . .6g Fat 3g
Carbohydrate . . .41g Saturates 1g

 10 mins   20 mins

SERVES 4

INGREDIENTS

4 ripe medium bananas

3 tbsp lemon juice

115 g/4 oz caster sugar

4 tbsp cold water

2 tbsp sesame seeds

150 ml/5 fl oz low-fat natural fromage frais

1 tbsp icing sugar

1 tsp vanilla essence

TO DECORATE

shredded lemon rind

shredded lime rind

1 Peel the bananas and cut into 5 cm/ 2 inch pieces. Place the banana pieces in a bowl, spoon over the lemon juice and stir well to coat – this will help prevent the bananas from discolouring.

2 Place the sugar and water in a small pan and heat gently, stirring constantly, until the sugar dissolves. Bring to the boil and cook for 5–6 minutes until the mixture turns golden brown.

3 Meanwhile, drain the bananas and blot with kitchen paper to dry. Line a baking sheet or board with baking paper and arrange the bananas, well spaced apart, on top.

4 When the caramel is ready, drizzle it over the bananas, working quickly because the caramel sets almost instantly. Sprinkle the sesame seeds over the caramelised bananas and set aside to cool for 10 minutes.

5 Mix the fromage frais with the icing sugar and vanilla essence.

6 Peel the bananas away from the paper and arrange on serving plates.

7 Serve the fromage frais as a dip, decorated with the shredded lemon and lime rind.

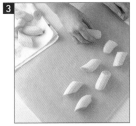

Balsamic Strawberries

Generations of Italian cooks have known that the unlikely combination of freshly ground black pepper and ripe, juicy strawberries is fantastic.

NUTRITIONAL INFORMATION

Calories	132	Sugars	.........5g
Protein	.........1g	Fat	..........12g
Carbohydrate	....5g	Saturates	.......7g

4¼ hrs   0 mins

SERVES 4–6

I N G R E D I E N T S

450 g/1 lb fresh strawberries

2–3 tbsp balsamic vinegar

fresh mint leaves, torn, plus extra to decorate (optional)

115–175 g/4–6 oz mascarpone cheese

pepper

1 Wipe the strawberries with a damp cloth, rather than rinsing them, so they do not become soggy. Using a paring knife, cut off the green stalks at the top and then use the tip of the knife to remove the core.

2 Cut each strawberry in half lengthways or into quarters if large. Transfer to a bowl.

COOK'S TIP

This is most enjoyable when it is made with the best-quality balsamic vinegar, one that has aged slowly and has turned thick and syrupy. Unfortunately, the genuine mixture is always expensive. Less expensive versions are artificially sweetened and coloured with caramel.

3 Add the balsamic vinegar, allowing ½ tablespoon per person. Add several twists of ground black pepper, then gently stir together. Cover with clingfilm and chill for up to 4 hours.

4 Just before serving, stir in torn mint leaves to taste. Spoon the mascarpone into bowls and spoon the berries on top. Decorate with a few mint leaves, if wished. Sprinkle with extra pepper to taste.

Figs with Orange Cream

Luscious, sweet fresh figs are served with a delicate sauce, flavoured with a hint of orange.

NUTRITIONAL INFORMATION

Calories	20	Sugars	........13g
Protein	.........3g	Fat	..........18g
Carbohydrate	...14g	Saturates	.......9g

🍧 24 hrs   🕐 3–5 mins

SERVES 4

INGREDIENTS

8 large fresh figs

4 large fresh fig leaves, if available, rinsed and dried

CREME FRAICHE (OPTIONAL)

2 tbsp buttermilk

300 ml/10 fl oz double cream

ORANGE-BLOSSOM CREAM

125 ml/4 fl oz crème fraîche, homemade or bought

about 4 tbsp orange-blossom water

1 tsp orange-blossom honey

finely grated rind of ½ orange

2 tbsp flaked almonds, to decorate (optional)

 1 If you are making the crème fraîche, begin at least a day ahead. Put the buttermilk in a preserving jar or a jar with a screw top. Add the cream, close securely and shake to blend. Set aside at room room temperature for 6–8 hours until set, then chill for at least 8 hours and up to 4 days. It will develop a slight tangy flavour. Lightly beat before using.

2 To toast the almonds for the decoration, place in a dry frying pan over a medium heat and stir until lightly browned. Take care that they do not burn. Immediately tip the almonds out of the pan. Set aside.

3 To make the orange-blossom cream, put the crème fraîche in a small bowl and stir in the orange-blossom water with the orange-blossom honey and orange rind. Taste and add a little extra orange-blossom water if necessary.

4 To serve, cut the stems off the figs, but do not peel them. Stand the figs upright with the pointed end upwards. Cut each into quarters without cutting all the way through, so you can open them out into attractive 'flowers'.

5 If you are using fig leaves, place one in the centre of each serving plate. Arrange 2 figs on top of each leaf, and spoon a small amount of the orange-flavoured cream alongside them. Sprinkle the cream with the toasted flaked almonds if desired, just before serving.

Poached Peaches

Soaking the peaches overnight is an old Turkish tip to prevent the fruit from becoming too soft and falling apart while they are being poached.

NUTRITIONAL INFORMATION

Calories 372	Sugars 34g
Protein 3g	Fat 20g
Carbohydrate ...34g	Saturates 12g

  24 hrs   🕐 10 mins

SERVES 4–6

INGREDIENTS

8–12 ripe peaches

1 large lime

450 ml/16 fl oz fruity, dry white wine

1 tbsp black peppercorns, lightly crushed

7.5 cm/3 inch cinnamon stick, halved

finely pared rind of 1 unwaxed lemon

100 g/3½ oz caster sugar

fresh mint sprigs, to decorate

AMARETTO-MASCARPONE CREAM

2 tbsp Amaretto liqueur

250 g/9 oz mascarpone cheese

1 Fill a large bowl with iced water. Bring a large pan of water to the boil. Add the peaches and cook for 1 minute. Using a draining spoon, immediately transfer the peaches to the iced water to stop the cooking process.

2 Squeeze the juice from the lime into a bowl of water. Peel the peaches, then quarter each and remove the stone. Drop the fruit into the lime water as it is prepared. Cover and chill in the refrigerator for 24 hours.

3 Meanwhile, make the amaretto-mascarpone cream. Stir the amaretto into the mascarpone until thoroughly incorporated, cover and chill.

4 Place the wine, peppercorns, cinnamon, lemon rind and sugar in a pan over a medium-high heat and stir until the sugar dissolves.

5 Boil the syrup for 2 minutes. Reduce to a simmer. Remove the peaches from the refrigerator, add them to the syrup and poach for 2 minutes or until tender – they should not be falling apart.

6 Using a draining spoon, transfer the peaches to a bowl. Bring the syrup to a boil and continue boiling until thickened and reduced to about 125 ml/4 fl oz. Pour the syrup into a heatproof bowl and set aside to cool. When cool, pour over the peaches. Cover and chill until required. To serve, decorate with mint.

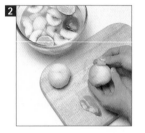

Lemon & Nut Rice Pudding

Rice is transformed into a creamy, family-style dessert. At the height of summer, serve well chilled with a mixture of summer berries.

NUTRITIONAL INFORMATION

Calories	332	Sugars	........22g
Protein	........11g	Fat	..........10g
Carbohydrate	...52g	Saturates	.......3g

 1½ hrs   🕐 25 mins

SERVES 4

I N G R E D I E N T S

1 tsp cornflour

850 ml/1½ pints milk, plus an extra 2 tbsp

125 g/4½ oz short grain rice

about 2 tbsp sugar or 1 tbsp clear honey

finely grated rind of 1 large lemon

freshly squeezed lemon juice

55 g/2 oz shelled pistachio nuts

1 Place the cornflour in a small bowl and stir in 2 tablespoons of the milk, stirring until there are no lumps. Rinse a pan with cold water.

2 Place the remaining milk and the cornflour mixture in the pan over a medium–high heat and heat, stirring occasionally, until small bubbles form all around the edge. Do not boil.

3 Stir in the rice, lower the heat and continue stirring for 20 minutes or until all but about 2 tablespoons of the excess liquid has evaporated and the rice grains are tender.

4 Remove from the heat and pour into a heatproof bowl. Stir in sugar to taste. Stir in the lemon rind, then stir in lemon juice to taste. Set the bowl aside to cool completely.

5 Tightly cover the top of the cool rice with a sheet of clingfilm and chill in the refrigerator for at least 1 hour – the colder the rice is, the better it tastes with fresh fruit.

6 Meanwhile, finely chop the pistachio nuts. To serve, spoon the rice pudding into individual bowls and sprinkle with the chopped nuts.

COOK'S TIP

It is important to rinse the pan in Step 1 to prevent the milk scorching on the sides or base.

Orange & Bitters Sorbet

Made from a distinctive Italian drink and freshly squeezed orange juice, this smooth, pale-pink sorbet is a cooling dessert with a refreshing tang.

NUTRITIONAL INFORMATION

Calories	212	Sugars	....52g
Protein	....2g	Fat	....0g
Carbohydrate	...52g	Saturates	....0g

 3 hrs   3–5 mins

SERVES 4–6

INGREDIENTS

3–4 large oranges

225 g/8 oz caster sugar

600 ml/1 pint water

3 tbsp red Italian bitters, such as Campari

2 large egg whites

TO DECORATE

fresh mint leaves

candied citrus peel (optional)

1 Working over a bowl to catch any juice, pare the rind from 3 of the oranges, without removing the bitter white pith. If some of the pith does come off with the rind, use the knife to scrape it off.

2 Put the sugar and water in a pan and stir over a low heat until dissolved. Increase the heat and boil for 2 minutes, without stirring. Using a wet pastry brush, brush any crystals down the side of the pan, if necessary.

3 Remove the pan from the heat and pour into a heatproof non-metallic bowl. Add the orange rind and set aside to infuse while the mixture cools to room temperature.

4 Roll the pared oranges back and forth on the work surface, pressing down firmly. Cut them in half and squeeze 125 ml/4½ fl oz juice. If you need more juice, squeeze the extra orange.

5 When the syrup is cool, stir in the orange juice and bitters. Strain into a container, cover and chill for at least 30 minutes.

6 Put the mixture in an ice-cream maker and churn for about 15 minutes. Alternatively, follow the instructions on page 1001. Whisk the egg

follow the instructions on page 1001.

whites in a clean, grease-free bowl until stiff peaks form.

7 Add the egg whites to the ice-cream maker and continue churning for 5 minutes or according to the manufacturer's instructions. Transfer to a shallow, freezerproof container, cover and freeze for up to 2 months.

8 About 15 minutes before serving, place the ice cream in the refrigerator to soften. Scoop into bowls and serve decorated with mint leaves and candied citrus peel, if wished.

Lemon Granita

Soft and granular, this iced dessert has a sharp, zingy flavour, which is refreshing and ideal for rounding off any rich meal.

NUTRITIONAL INFORMATION

Calories . . . . .78 Sugars 20g
Protein . . . . .1g Fat 0g
Carbohydrate . . .20g Saturates 0g

4 hrs   5 mins

SERVES 4–6

INGREDIENTS

4 large unwaxed lemons

100 g/3½ oz caster sugar

700 ml/1¼ pints water

fresh mint sprigs, to decorate (optional)

1 Pare 6 strips of rind from 1 of the lemons, then finely grate the remaining rind from the remaining lemons, being very careful not to remove any bitter white pith.

2 Roll the lemons back and forth on the work surface, pressing down firmly. Cut each in half and squeeze 125 ml/4 fl oz juice. Add the grated rind to the juice. Set aside.

3 Put the pared strips of lemon rind, sugar and water in a pan and stir over a low heat to dissolve the sugar. Increase the heat and boil for 4 minutes, without stirring. Use a wet pastry brush to brush down any spatters on the side of the pan. Remove from the heat, pour into a non-metallic bowl and set aside to cool.

4 Remove the strips of rind from the syrup. Stir in the grated rind and juice. Transfer to a shallow metal container, cover and freeze for up to 3 months.

5 Chill serving bowls 30 minutes before serving. To serve, invert the container on to a chopping board. Rinse a cloth in very hot water, wring it out, then rub on the bottom of the container for 15 seconds. Give the container a shake and the mixture should fall out.

6 Break up the granita with a knife and transfer to a food processor. Process until it becomes granular. Serve in the chilled bowls (or in scooped-out lemons). Decorate with mint sprigs, if wished.

VARIATION
Lemon-scented herbs add a unique and unexpected flavour. Add 4 small lemon balm sprigs or 2 lemon thyme sprigs to the syrup in Step 3. Remove and discard with the pared rind in Step 4. Or stir ½ tablespoon finely chopped lemon thyme into the mixture in Step 4.

Espresso Granita

Enjoy this crunchy granita as a cooling mid-morning
snack or as a light dessert at the end of an al fresco supper.

NUTRITIONAL INFORMATION

Calories	133	Sugars	........35g
Protein	.........0g	Fat	...........0g
Carbohydrate	...35g	Saturates	.......0g

 4 hrs   5 mins

SERVES 4–6

INGREDIENTS

200 g/7 oz caster sugar

600 ml/1 pint water

½ tsp vanilla essence

600 ml/1 pint very strong espresso
   coffee, chilled

fresh mint, to garnish

1 Put the sugar in a pan with the water
and stir over a low heat to dissolve
the sugar. Increase the heat and boil for 4
minutes, without stirring. Use a wet pastry
brush to brush down any spatters on the
side of the pan.

2 Remove the pan from the heat and
pour the syrup into a heat-proof non-
metallic bowl. Sit the bowl in the kitchen
sink filled with iced water to speed up the
cooling process. Stir in the vanilla and
coffee and leave until completely cool.

3 Transfer to a shallow metal container,
cover and freeze for up to 3 months.

4 Thirty minutes before serving, place
individual serving bowls in the
refrigerator to chill.

5 To serve, invert the container on to a
chopping board. Rinse a cloth in very
hot water, wring it out then rub on the
bottom of the container for 15 seconds.
Give the container a sharp shake and the
mixture should fall out.

6 Break up the granita with a knife and
transfer to a food processor. Process
until it becomes grainy and crunchy. Serve
in the chilled bowls, decorated with mint.

COOK'S TIP

A very dark, fruit-flavoured
espresso is the only choice for
this Italian speciality. Otherwise the
flavour will be marred by the freezing.

Ricotta-lemon Cheesecake

Italian bakers pride themselves on their baked ricotta cheesecakes, studded with fruit soaked in spirits.

NUTRITIONAL INFORMATION

Calories 188   Sugars 21g
Protein . . . . .6g   Fat 8g
Carbohydrate . . .23g   Saturates 4g

3¾ hrs   30–40 mins

SERVES 6–8

I N G R E D I E N T S

55 g/2 oz sultanas

3 tbsp Marsala or grappa

butter, for greasing

2 tbsp semolina, plus extra for dusting

350 g/12 oz ricotta cheese, drained

3 large egg yolks, beaten

100 g/3½ oz caster sugar

3 tbsp lemon juice

2 tbsp candied orange peel, finely chopped

finely grated rind of 2 large lemons

T O   D E C O R A T E

icing sugar

fresh mint sprigs

redcurrants or berries (optional)

3 Using a wooden spoon, press the ricotta cheese though a nylon sieve into a bowl. Beat in the egg yolks, sugar, semolina and lemon juice and continue beating until blended.

4 Fold in the sultanas, orange peel and lemon rind. Pour into the prepared tin and smooth the surface.

5 Bake the cheesecake in the centre of a preheated oven, 180°C/350°F/Gas Mark 4 for 30–40 minutes until firm when you press the top and coming away slightly from the side of the tin.

6 Turn off the oven and open the door. Leave the cheesecake to cool in the turned-off oven for 2–3 hours. To serve, remove from the pan and transfer to a plate. Sift over a layer of icing sugar from at least 30 cm/12 inches above the cheesecake to dust the top and sides lightly. Decorate with mint and redcurrants, if wished.

1 Soak the sultanas in the Marsala or grappa in a small bowl for about 30 minutes or until the liquid has been absorbed and the fruit is swollen.

2 Meanwhile, cut out a circle of baking paper to fit the base of a loose-based 20 cm/8 inch round cake tin that is about 5 cm/2 inches deep. Grease the side and base of the tin and line the base. Lightly dust with semolina and tip out the excess.

index